American Casebook Series
Hornbook Series and Basic Legal Texts
Nutshell Series

of

WEST PUBLISHING COMPANY
P.O. Box 64526
St. Paul, Minnesota 55164–0526

ACCOUNTING

Faris' Accounting and Law in a Nutshell, 377 pages, 1984 (Text)

Fiflis, Kripke and Foster's Teaching Materials on Accounting for Business Lawyers, 3rd Ed., 838 pages, 1984 (Casebook)

Siegel and Siegel's Accounting and Financial Disclosure: A Guide to Basic Concepts, 259 pages, 1983 (Text)

ADMINISTRATIVE LAW

Davis' Cases, Text and Problems on Administrative Law, 6th Ed., 683 pages, 1977 (Casebook)

Davis' Basic Text on Administrative Law, 3rd Ed., 617 pages, 1972 (Text)

Davis' Police Discretion, 176 pages, 1975 (Text)

Gellhorn and Boyer's Administrative Law and Process in a Nutshell, 2nd Ed., 445 pages, 1981 (Text)

Mashaw and Merrill's Cases and Materials on Administrative Law-The American Public Law System, 2nd Ed., 975 pages, 1985 (Casebook)

Robinson, Gellhorn and Bruff's The Administrative Process, 2nd Ed., 959 pages, 1980, with 1983 Supplement (Casebook)

ADMIRALTY

Healy and Sharpe's Cases and Materials on Admiralty, 875 pages, 1974 (Casebook)

Maraist's Admiralty in a Nutshell, 390 pages, 1983 (Text)

Sohn and Gustafson's Law of the Sea in a Nutshell, 264 pages, 1984 (Text)

AGENCY—PARTNERSHIP

Fessler's Alternatives to Incorporation for Persons in Quest of Profit, 258 pages, 1980 (Casebook)

AGENCY—PARTNERSHIP—Continued

Henn's Cases and Materials on Agency, Partnership and Other Unincorporated Business Enterprises, 2nd Ed., 733 pages, 1985 (Casebook)

Reuschlein and Gregory's Hornbook on the Law of Agency and Partnership, 625 pages, 1979, with 1981 pocket part (Text)

Seavey, Reuschlein and Hall's Cases on Agency and Partnership, 599 pages, 1962 (Casebook)

Selected Corporation and Partnership Statutes and Forms, approximately 555 pages, 1985

Steffen and Kerr's Cases and Materials on Agency-Partnership, 4th Ed., 859 pages, 1980 (Casebook)

Steffen's Agency-Partnership in a Nutshell, 364 pages, 1977 (Text)

AGRICULTURAL LAW

Meyer, Pedersen, Thorson and Davidson's Agricultural Law: Cases and Materials, 931 pages, 1985 (Casebook)

AMERICAN INDIAN LAW

Canby's American Indian Law in a Nutshell, 288 pages, 1981 (Text)

Getches, Rosenfelt and Wilkinson's Cases on Federal Indian Law, 660 pages, 1979, with 1983 Supplement (Casebook)

ANTITRUST LAW

Gellhorn's Antitrust Law and Economics in a Nutshell, 2nd Ed., 425 pages, 1981 (Text)

Gifford and Raskind's Cases and Materials on Antitrust, 694 pages, 1983 with 1985 Supplement (Casebook)

Hovenkamp's Economics and Federal Antitrust Law, Student Ed., 414 pages, 1985 (Text)

List current as of April, 1985

ANTITRUST LAW—Continued

Oppenheim, Weston and McCarthy's Cases and Comments on Federal Antitrust Laws, 4th Ed., 1168 pages, 1981 with 1985 Supplement (Casebook)

Posner and Easterbrook's Cases and Economic Notes on Antitrust, 2nd Ed., 1077 pages, 1981, with 1984–85 Supplement (Casebook)

Sullivan's Hornbook of the Law of Antitrust, 886 pages, 1977 (Text)

See also Regulated Industries, Trade Regulation

ART LAW

DuBoff's Art Law in a Nutshell, 335 pages, 1984 (Text)

BANKING LAW

Lovett's Banking and Financial Institutions in a Nutshell, 409 pages, 1984 (Text)

Symons and White's Teaching Materials on Banking Law, 2nd Ed., 993 pages, 1984 (Casebook)

BUSINESS PLANNING

Epstein and Scheinfeld's Teaching Materials on Business Reorganization Under the Bankruptcy Code, 216 pages, 1980 (Casebook)

Painter's Problems and Materials in Business Planning, 2nd Ed., 1008 pages, 1984 (Casebook)

Selected Securities and Business Planning Statutes, Rules and Forms, 470 pages, 1985

CIVIL PROCEDURE

Casad's Res Judicata in a Nutshell, 310 pages, 1976 (text)

Cound, Friedenthal, Miller and Sexton's Cases and Materials on Civil Procedure, 4th Ed., approximately 1147 pages, 1985 with 1985 Supplement (Casebook)

Ehrenzweig, Louisell and Hazard's Jurisdiction in a Nutshell, 4th Ed., 232 pages, 1980 (Text)

Federal Rules of Civil-Appellate-Criminal Procedure—West Law School Edition, approximately 500 pages, 1985

Friedenthal, Kane and Miller's Hornbook on Civil Procedure, Student Edition, approximately 870 pages, 1985 (Text)

Hodges, Jones and Elliott's Cases and Materials on Texas Trial and Appellate Procedure, 2nd Ed., 745 pages, 1974 (Casebook)

Hodges, Jones and Elliott's Cases and Materials on the Judicial Process Prior to Trial in Texas, 2nd Ed., 871 pages, 1977 (Casebook)

Kane's Civil Procedure in a Nutshell, 271 pages, 1979 (Text)

CIVIL PROCEDURE—Continued

Karlen's Procedure Before Trial in a Nutshell, 258 pages, 1972 (Text)

Karlen, Meisenholder, Stevens and Vestal's Cases on Civil Procedure, 923 pages, 1975 (Casebook)

Koffler and Reppy's Hornbook on Common Law Pleading, 663 pages, 1969 (Text)

Marcus and Sherman's Complex Litigation—Cases and Materials on Advanced Civil Procedure, approximately 900 pages, 1985 (Casebook)

Park's Computer-Aided Exercises on Civil Procedure, 2nd Ed., 167 pages, 1983 (Coursebook)

Siegel's Hornbook on New York Practice, 1011 pages, 1978 with 1985 Pocket Part (Text)

See also Federal Jurisdiction and Procedure

CIVIL RIGHTS

Abernathy's Cases and Materials on Civil Rights, 660 pages, 1980 (Casebook)

Cohen's Cases on the Law of Deprivation of Liberty: A Study in Social Control, 755 pages, 1980 (Casebook)

Lockhart, Kamisar and Choper's Cases on Constitutional Rights and Liberties, 5th Ed., 1298 pages plus Appendix, 1981, with 1985 Supplement (Casebook)—reprint from Lockhart, et al. Cases on Constitutional Law, 5th Ed., 1980

Vieira's Civil Rights in a Nutshell, 279 pages, 1978 (Text)

COMMERCIAL LAW

Bailey's Secured Transactions in a Nutshell, 2nd Ed., 391 pages, 1981 (Text)

Epstein and Martin's Basic Uniform Commercial Code Teaching Materials, 2nd Ed., 667 pages, 1983 (Casebook)

Henson's Hornbook on Secured Transactions Under the U.C.C., 2nd Ed., 504 pages, 1979 with 1979 P.P. (Text)

Murray's Commercial Law, Problems and Materials, 366 pages, 1975 (Coursebook)

Nordstrom and Clovis' Problems and Materials on Commercial Paper, 458 pages, 1972 (Casebook)

Nordstrom and Lattin's Problems and Materials on Sales and Secured Transactions, 809 pages, 1968 (Casebook)

Nordstrom, Murray and Clovis' Problems and Materials on Sales, 515 pages, 1982 (Casebook)

Selected Commercial Statutes, 1389 pages, 1985

Speidel, Summers and White's Teaching Materials on Commercial and Consumer Law, 3rd Ed., 1490 pages, 1981 (Casebook)

Stockton's Sales in a Nutshell, 2nd Ed., 370 pages, 1981 (Text)

LAW SCHOOL PUBLICATIONS—Continued

COMMERCIAL LAW—Continued

Stone's Uniform Commercial Code in a Nutshell, 2nd Ed., 516 pages, 1984 (Text)

Uniform Commercial Code, Official Text with Comments, 994 pages, 1978

UCC Article 9, Reprint from 1962 Code, 128 pages, 1976

UCC Article 9, 1972 Amendments, 304 pages, 1978

Weber and Speidel's Commercial Paper in a Nutshell, 3rd Ed., 404 pages, 1982 (Text)

White and Summers' Hornbook on the Uniform Commercial Code, 2nd Ed., 1250 pages, 1980 (Text)

COMMUNITY PROPERTY

Mennell's Community Property in a Nutshell, 447 pages, 1982 (Text)

Verrall and Bird's Cases and Materials on California Community Property, 4th Ed., 549 pages, 1983 (Casebook)

COMPARATIVE LAW

Barton, Gibbs, Li and Merryman's Law in Radically Different Cultures, 960 pages, 1983 (Casebook)

Glendon, Gordon and Osakive's Comparative Legal Traditions: Text, Materials and Cases on the Civil Law, Common Law, and Socialist Law Traditions, approximately 1190 pages, 1985 (Casebook)

Glendon, Gordon, and Osakwe's Comparative Legal Traditions in a Nutshell, 402 pages, 1982 (Text)

Langbein's Comparative Criminal Procedure: Germany, 172 pages, 1977 (Casebook)

COMPUTERS AND LAW

Mason's An Introduction to the Use of Computers in Law, 223 pages, 1984 (Text)

CONFLICT OF LAWS

Cramton, Currie and Kay's Cases-Comments-Questions on Conflict of Laws, 3rd Ed., 1026 pages, 1981 (Casebook)

Scoles and Hay's Hornbook on Conflict of Laws, Student Ed., 1085 pages, 1982 (Text)

Scoles and Weintraub's Cases and Materials on Conflict of Laws, 2nd Ed., 966 pages, 1972, with 1978 Supplement (Casebook)

Siegel's Conflicts in a Nutshell, 469 pages, 1982 (Text)

CONSTITUTIONAL LAW

Engdahl's Constitutional Power in a Nutshell: Federal and State, 411 pages, 1974 (Text)

Lockhart, Kamisar and Choper's Cases-Comments-Questions on Constitutional Law, 5th Ed., 1705 pages plus Appendix, 1980, with 1985 Supplement (Casebook)

CONSTITUTIONAL LAW—Continued

Lockhart, Kamisar and Choper's Cases-Comments-Questions on the American Constitution, 5th Ed., 1185 pages plus Appendix, 1981, with 1985 Supplement (Casebook)—reprint from Lockhart, et al. Cases on Constitutional Law, 5th Ed., 1980

Manning's The Law of Church-State Relations in a Nutshell, 305 pages, 1981 (Text)

Miller's Presidential Power in a Nutshell, 328 pages, 1977 (Text)

Nowak, Rotunda and Young's Hornbook on Constitutional Law, 2nd Ed., Student Ed., 1172 pages, 1983 (Text)

Rotunda's Modern Constitutional Law: Cases and Notes, 2nd Ed., approximately 1055 pages, 1985, with 1985 Supplement (Casebook)

Williams' Constitutional Analysis in a Nutshell, 388 pages, 1979 (Text)

See also Civil Rights

CONSUMER LAW

Epstein and Nickles' Consumer Law in a Nutshell, 2nd Ed., 418 pages, 1981 (Text)

McCall's Consumer Protection, Cases, Notes and Materials, 594 pages, 1977, with 1977 Statutory Supplement (Casebook)

Selected Commercial Statutes, 1389 pages, 1985

Spanogle and Rohner's Cases and Materials on Consumer Law, 693 pages, 1979, with 1982 Supplement (Casebook)

See also Commercial Law

CONTRACTS

Calamari & Perillo's Cases and Problems on Contracts, 1061 pages, 1978 (Casebook)

Calamari and Perillo's Hornbook on Contracts, 2nd Ed., 878 pages, 1977 (Text)

Corbin's Text on Contracts, One Volume Student Edition, 1224 pages, 1952 (Text)

Fessler and Loiseaux's Cases and Materials on Contracts, 837 pages, 1982 (Casebook)

Freedman's Cases and Materials on Contracts, 658 pages, 1973 (Casebook)

Friedman's Contract Remedies in a Nutshell, 323 pages, 1981 (Text)

Fuller and Eisenberg's Cases on Basic Contract Law, 4th Ed., 1203 pages, 1981 (Casebook)

Hamilton, Rau and Weintraub's Cases and Materials on Contracts, 830 pages, 1984 (Casebook)

Jackson and Bollinger's Cases on Contract Law in Modern Society, 2nd Ed., 1329 pages, 1980 (Casebook)

Keyes' Government Contracts in a Nutshell, 423 pages, 1979 (Text)

LAW SCHOOL PUBLICATIONS—Continued

CONTRACTS—Continued

Reitz's Cases on Contracts as Basic Commercial Law, 763 pages, 1975 (Casebook)

Schaber and Rohwer's Contracts in a Nutshell, 2nd Ed., 425 pages, 1984 (Text)

COPYRIGHT

See Patent and Copyright Law

CORPORATIONS

Hamilton's Cases on Corporations—Including Partnerships and Limited Partnerships, 2nd Ed., 1108 pages, 1981, with 1981 Statutory Supplement and 1985 Supplement (Casebook)

Hamilton's Law of Corporations in a Nutshell, 379 pages, 1980 (Text)

Henn's Cases on Corporations, 1279 pages, 1974, with 1980 Supplement (Casebook)

Henn and Alexander's Hornbook on Corporations, 3rd Ed., Student Ed., 1371 pages, 1983 (Text)

Jennings and Buxbaum's Cases and Materials on Corporations, 5th Ed., 1180 pages, 1979 (Casebook)

Selected Corporation and Partnership Statutes, Regulations and Forms, 555 pages, 1985

Solomon, Stevenson and Schwartz' Materials and Problems on Corporations: Law and Policy, 1172 pages, 1982 with 1984 Supplement (Casebook)

CORPORATE FINANCE

Hamilton's Cases and Materials on Corporate Finance, 895 pages, 1984 (Casebook)

CORRECTIONS

Krantz's Cases and Materials on the Law of Corrections and Prisoners' Rights, 2nd Ed., 735 pages, 1981, with 1982 Supplement (Casebook)

Krantz's Law of Corrections and Prisoners' Rights in a Nutshell, 2nd Ed., 384 pages, 1983 (Text)

Popper's Post-Conviction Remedies in a Nutshell, 360 pages, 1978 (Text)

Robbins' Cases and Materials on Post Conviction Remedies, 506 pages, 1982 (Casebook)

Rubin's Law of Criminal Corrections, 2nd Ed., 873 pages, 1973, with 1978 Supplement (Text)

CREDITOR'S RIGHTS

Bankruptcy Code, Rules and Forms, Law School and C.L.E. Ed., 602 pages, 1984

Epstein's Debtor-Creditor Law in a Nutshell, 2nd Ed., 324 pages, 1980 (Text)

Epstein and Landers' Debtors and Creditors: Cases and Materials, 2nd Ed., 689 pages, 1982 (Casebook)

CREDITOR'S RIGHTS—Continued

Epstein and Sheinfeld's Teaching Materials on Business Reorganization Under the Bankruptcy Code, 216 pages, 1980 (Casebook)

LoPucki's Player's Manual for the Debtor-Creditor Game, 123 pages, 1985 (Coursebook)

Riesenfeld's Cases and Materials on Creditors' Remedies and Debtors' Protection, 3rd Ed., 810 pages, 1979 with 1979 Statutory Supplement and 1981 Case Supplement (Casebook)

White's Bankruptcy and Creditor's Rights: Cases and Materials, 812 pages, 1985 (Casebook)

CRIMINAL LAW AND CRIMINAL PROCEDURE

Cohen and Gobert's Problems in Criminal Law, 297 pages, 1976 (Problem book)

Davis' Police Discretion, 176 pages, 1975 (Text)

Dix and Sharlot's Cases and Materials on Criminal Law, 2nd Ed., 771 pages, 1979 (Casebook)

Federal Rules of Civil-Appellate-Criminal Procedure—West Law School Edition, approximately 500 pages, 1985

Grano's Problems in Criminal Procedure, 2nd Ed., 176 pages, 1981 (Problem book)

Israel and LaFave's Criminal Procedure in a Nutshell, 3rd Ed., 438 pages, 1980 (Text)

Johnson's Cases, Materials and Text on Substantive Criminal Law in its Procedural Context, 3rd Ed., approximately 750 pages, 1985 (Casebook)

Kamisar, LaFave and Israel's Cases, Comments and Questions on Modern Criminal Procedure, 5th ed., 1635 pages plus Appendix, 1980 with 1985 Supplement (Casebook)

Kamisar, LaFave and Israel's Cases, Comments and Questions on Basic Criminal Procedure, 5th Ed., 869 pages, 1980 with 1985 Supplement (Casebook)—reprint from Kamisar, et al. Modern Criminal Procedure, 5th ed., 1980

LaFave's Modern Criminal Law: Cases, Comments and Questions, 789 pages, 1978 (Casebook)

LaFave and Israel's Hornbook on Criminal Procedure, Student Ed., 1142 pages, 1985 (Text)

LaFave and Scott's Hornbook on Criminal Law, 763 pages, 1972 (Text)

Langbein's Comparative Criminal Procedure: Germany, 172 pages, 1977 (Casebook)

Loewy's Criminal Law in a Nutshell, 302 pages, 1975 (Text)

LAW SCHOOL PUBLICATIONS—Continued

CRIMINAL LAW AND CRIMINAL PROCEDURE—Continued

Saltzburg's American Criminal Procedure, Cases and Commentary, 2nd Ed., 1193 pages, 1985 with 1985 Supplement (Casebook)

Uviller's The Processes of Criminal Justice: Investigation and Adjudication, 2nd Ed., 1384 pages, 1979 with 1979 Statutory Supplement and 1983 Update (Casebook)

Uviller's The Processes of Criminal Justice: Adjudication, 2nd Ed., 730 pages, 1979. Soft-cover reprint from Uviller's The Processes of Criminal Justice: Investigation and Adjudication, 2nd Ed. (Casebook)

Uviller's The Processes of Criminal Justice: Investigation, 2nd Ed., 655 pages, 1979. Soft-cover reprint from Uviller's The Processes of Criminal Justice: Investigation and Adjudication, 2nd Ed. (Casebook)

Vorenberg's Cases on Criminal Law and Procedure, 2nd Ed., 1088 pages, 1981 with 1985 Supplement (Casebook)

See also Corrections, Juvenile Justice

DECEDENTS ESTATES

See Trusts and Estates

DOMESTIC RELATIONS

Clark's Cases and Problems on Domestic Relations, 3rd Ed., 1153 pages, 1980 (Casebook)

Clark's Hornbook on Domestic Relations, 754 pages, 1968 (Text)

Krause's Cases and Materials on Family Law, 2nd Ed., 1221 pages, 1983 (Casebook)

Krause's Family Law in a Nutshell, 400 pages, 1977 (Text)

Krauskopf's Cases on Property Division at Marriage Dissolution, 250 pages, 1984 (Casebook)

ECONOMICS, LAW AND

Goetz' Cases and Materials on Law and Economics, 547 pages, 1984 (Casebook)

Manne's The Economics of Legal Relationships—Readings in the Theory of Property Rights, 660 pages, 1975 (Text)

See also Antitrust, Regulated Industries

EDUCATION LAW

Alexander and Alexander's The Law of Schools, Students and Teachers in a Nutshell, 409 pages, 1984 (Text)

Morris' The Constitution and American Education, 2nd Ed., 992 pages, 1980 (Casebook)

EMPLOYMENT DISCRIMINATION

Player's Cases and Materials on Employment Discrimination Law, 2nd Ed., 782 pages, 1984 (Casebook)

Player's Federal Law of Employment Discrimination in a Nutshell, 2nd Ed., 402 pages, 1981 (Text)

See also Women and the Law

ENERGY LAW

Rodgers' Cases and Materials on Energy and Natural Resources Law, 2nd Ed., 877 pages, 1983 (Casebook)

Selected Environmental Law Statutes, 786 pages, 1985

Tomain's Energy Law in a Nutshell, 338 pages, 1981 (Text)

See also Natural Resources Law, Environmental Law, Oil and Gas, Water Law

ENVIRONMENTAL LAW

Bonine and McGarity's Cases and Materials on the Law of Environment and Pollution, 1076 pages, 1984 (Casebook)

Findley and Farber's Cases and Materials on Environmental Law, 2nd Ed., approximately 800 pages, 1985 (Casebook)

Findley and Farber's Environmental Law in a Nutshell, 343 pages, 1983 (Text)

Rodgers' Hornbook on Environmental Law, 956 pages, 1977 with 1984 pocket part (Text)

Selected Environmental Law Statutes, 786 pages, 1985

See also Energy Law, Natural Resources Law, Water Law

EQUITY

See Remedies

ESTATES

See Trusts and Estates

ESTATE PLANNING

Kurtz' Cases, Materials and Problems on Family Estate Planning, 853 pages, 1983 (Casebook)

Lynn's Introduction to Estate Planning, in a Nutshell, 3rd Ed., 370 pages, 1983 (Text)

See also Taxation

EVIDENCE

Broun and Meisenholder's Problems in Evidence, 2nd Ed., 304 pages, 1981 (Problem book)

Cleary and Strong's Cases, Materials and Problems on Evidence, 3rd Ed., 1143 pages, 1981 (Casebook)

Federal Rules of Evidence for United States Courts and Magistrates, 337 pages, 1984

Graham's Federal Rules of Evidence in a Nutshell, 429 pages, 1981 (Text)

LAW SCHOOL PUBLICATIONS—Continued

EVIDENCE—Continued

Kimball's Programmed Materials on Problems in Evidence, 380 pages, 1978 (Problem book)

Lempert and Saltzburg's A Modern Approach to Evidence: Text, Problems, Transcripts and Cases, 2nd Ed., 1296 pages, 1983 (Casebook)

Lilly's Introduction to the Law of Evidence, 486 pages, 1978 (Text)

McCormick, Elliott and Sutton's Cases and Materials on Evidence, 5th Ed., 1212 pages, 1981 (Casebook)

McCormick's Hornbook on Evidence, 3rd Ed., Student Ed., 1155 pages, 1984 (Text)

Rothstein's Evidence, State and Federal Rules in a Nutshell, 2nd Ed., 514 pages, 1981 (Text)

Saltzburg's Evidence Supplement: Rules, Statutes, Commentary, 245 pages, 1980 (Casebook Supplement)

FEDERAL JURISDICTION AND PROCEDURE

Currie's Cases and Materials on Federal Courts, 3rd Ed., 1042 pages, 1982 (Casebook)

Currie's Federal Jurisdiction in a Nutshell, 2nd Ed., 258 pages, 1981 (Text)

Federal Rules of Civil-Appellate-Criminal Procedure—West Law School Edition, approximately 500 pages, 1985

Forrester and Moye's Cases and Materials on Federal Jurisdiction and Procedure, 3rd Ed., 917 pages, 1977 with 1981 Supplement (Casebook)

Redish's Cases, Comments and Questions on Federal Courts, 878 pages, 1985 (Casebook)

Vetri and Merrill's Federal Courts, Problems and Materials, 2nd Ed., 232 pages, 1984 (Problem Book)

Wright's Hornbook on Federal Courts, 4th Ed., Student Ed., 870 pages, 1983 (Text)

FUTURE INTERESTS

See Trusts and Estates

IMMIGRATION LAW

Aleinikoff and Martin's Immigration Process and Policy, approximately 950 pages, 1985 (Casebook)

Weissbrodt's Immigration Law and Procedure in a Nutshell, 345 pages, 1984 (Text)

INDIAN LAW

See American Indian Law

INSURANCE

Dobbyn's Insurance Law in a Nutshell, 281 pages, 1981 (Text)

Keeton's Cases on Basic Insurance Law, 2nd Ed., 1086 pages, 1977

INSURANCE—Continued

Keeton's Basic Text on Insurance Law, 712 pages, 1971 (Text)

Keeton's Case Supplement to Keeton's Basic Text on Insurance Law, 334 pages, 1978 (Casebook)

Keeton's Programmed Problems in Insurance Law, 243 pages, 1972 (Text Supplement)

York and Whelan's Cases, Materials and Problems on Insurance Law, 715 pages, 1982, with 1985 Supplement (Casebook)

INTERNATIONAL LAW

Henkin, Pugh, Schachter and Smit's Cases and Materials on International Law, 2nd Ed., 1152 pages, 1980, with Documents Supplement (Casebook)

Jackson's Legal Problems of International Economic Relations, 1097 pages, 1977, with Documents Supplement (Casebook)

Kirgis' International Organizations in Their Legal Setting, 1016 pages, 1977, with 1981 Supplement (Casebook)

Weston, Falk and D'Amato's International Law and World Order—A Problem Oriented Coursebook, 1195 pages, 1980, with Documents Supplement (Casebook)

Wilson's International Business Transactions in a Nutshell, 2nd Ed., 476 pages, 1984 (Text)

INTERVIEWING AND COUNSELING

Binder and Price's Interviewing and Counseling, 232 pages, 1977 (Text)

Shaffer's Interviewing and Counseling in a Nutshell, 353 pages, 1976 (Text)

INTRODUCTION TO LAW

Dobbyn's So You Want to go to Law School, Revised First Edition, 206 pages, 1976 (Text)

Hegland's Introduction to the Study and Practice of Law in a Nutshell, 418 pages, 1983 (Text)

Kinyon's Introduction to Law Study and Law Examinations in a Nutshell, 389 pages, 1971 (Text)

See also Legal Method and Legal System

JUDICIAL ADMINISTRATION

Carrington, Meador and Rosenberg's Justice on Appeal, 263 pages, 1976 (Casebook)

Nelson's Cases and Materials on Judicial Administration and the Administration of Justice, 1032 pages, 1974 (Casebook)

JURISPRUDENCE

Christie's Text and Readings on Jurisprudence—The Philosophy of Law, 1056 pages, 1973 (Casebook)

LAW SCHOOL PUBLICATIONS—Continued

JUVENILE JUSTICE

Fox's Cases and Materials on Modern Juvenile Justice, 2nd Ed., 960 pages, 1981 (Casebook)

Fox's Juvenile Courts in a Nutshell, 3rd Ed., 291 pages, 1984 (Text)

LABOR LAW

Gorman's Basic Text on Labor Law—Unionization and Collective Bargaining, 914 pages, 1976 (Text)

Leslie's Labor Law in a Nutshell, 403 pages, 1979 (Text)

Nolan's Labor Arbitration Law and Practice in a Nutshell, 358 pages, 1979 (Text)

Oberer, Hanslowe and Andersen's Cases and Materials on Labor Law—Collective Bargaining in a Free Society, 2nd Ed., 1168 pages, 1979, with 1979 Statutory Supplement and 1982 Case Supplement (Casebook)

See also Employment Discrimination, Social Legislation

LAND FINANCE

See Real Estate Transactions

LAND USE

Hagman's Cases on Public Planning and Control of Urban and Land Development, 2nd Ed., 1301 pages, 1980 (Casebook)

Hagman's Hornbook on Urban Planning and Land Development Control Law, 706 pages, 1971 (Text)

Wright and Gitelman's Cases and Materials on Land Use, 3rd Ed., 1300 pages, 1982 (Casebook)

Wright and Wright's Land Use in a Nutshell, 2nd Ed., approximately 350 pages (Text)

LEGAL HISTORY

Presser and Zainaldin's Cases on Law and American History, 855 pages, 1980 (Casebook)

See also Legal Method and Legal System

LEGAL METHOD AND LEGAL SYSTEM

Aldisert's Readings, Materials and Cases in the Judicial Process, 948 pages, 1976 (Casebook)

Berch and Berch's Introduction to Legal Method and Process, 550 pages, 1985 (Casebook)

Bodenheimer, Oakley and Love's Readings and Cases on an Introduction to the Anglo-American Legal System, 161 pages, 1980 (Casebook)

Davies and Lawry's Institutions and Methods of the Law—Introductory Teaching Materials, 547 pages, 1982 (Casebook)

Dvorkin, Himmelstein and Lesnick's Becoming a Lawyer: A Humanistic Perspective on Legal Education and Professionalism, 211 pages, 1981 (Text)

LEGAL METHOD AND LEGAL SYSTEM—Continued

Fryer and Orentlicher's Cases and Materials on Legal Method and Legal System, 1043 pages, 1967 (Casebook)

Greenberg's Judicial Process and Social Change, 666 pages, 1977 (Coursebook)

Kelso and Kelso's Studying Law: An Introduction, 587 pages, 1984 (Coursebook)

Kempin's Historical Introduction to Anglo-American Law in a Nutshell, 2nd Ed., 280 pages, 1973 (Text)

Kimball's Historical Introduction to the Legal System, 610 pages, 1966 (Casebook)

Murphy's Cases and Materials on Introduction to Law—Legal Process and Procedure, 772 pages, 1977 (Casebook)

Reynolds' Judicial Process in a Nutshell, 292 pages, 1980 (Text)

See also Legal Research and Writing

LEGAL PROFESSION

Aronson, Devine and Fisch's Problems, Cases and Materials on Professional Responsibility, 745 pages, 1985 (Casebook)

Aronson and Weckstein's Professional Responsibility in a Nutshell, 399 pages, 1980 (Text)

Mellinkoff's The Conscience of a Lawyer, 304 pages, 1973 (Text)

Mellinkoff's Lawyers and the System of Justice, 983 pages, 1976 (Casebook)

Pirsig and Kirwin's Cases and Materials on Professional Responsibility, 4th Ed., 603 pages, 1984 (Casebook)

Schwartz and Wydick's Problems in Legal Ethics, 285 pages, 1983 (Casebook)

Selected Statutes, Rules and Standards on the Legal Profession, 276 pages, Revised 1984

Smith's Preventing Legal Malpractice, 142 pages, 1981 (Text)

Wolfram's Hornbook on Professional Responsibility, Student Edition, approximately 950 pages (Text)

LEGAL RESEARCH AND WRITING

Cohen's Legal Research in a Nutshell, 4th Ed., 450 pages, 1985 (Text)

Cohen and Berring's How to Find the Law, 8th Ed., 790 pages, 1983. Problem book by Foster and Kelly available (Casebook)

Cohen and Berring's Finding the Law, 8th Ed., Abridged Ed., 556 pages, 1984 (Casebook)

Dickerson's Materials on Legal Drafting, 425 pages, 1981 (Casebook)

Felsenfeld and Siegel's Writing Contracts in Plain English, 290 pages, 1981 (Text)

Gopen's Writing From a Legal Perspective, 225 pages, 1981 (Text)

Mellinkoff's Legal Writing—Sense and Nonsense, 242 pages, 1982 (Text)

LAW SCHOOL PUBLICATIONS—Continued

LEGAL RESEARCH AND WRITING—Continued

Rombauer's Legal Problem Solving—Analysis, Research and Writing, 4th Ed., 424 pages, 1983 (Coursebook)

Squires and Rombauer's Legal Writing in a Nutshell, 294 pages, 1982 (Text)

Statsky's Legal Research, Writing and Analysis, 2nd Ed., 167 pages, 1982 (Coursebook)

Statsky's Legislative Analysis: How to Use Statutes and Regulations, 2nd Ed., 217 pages, 1984 (Text)

Statsky and Wernet's Case Analysis and Fundamentals of Legal Writing, 2nd Ed., 441 pages, 1984 (Text)

Teply's Programmed Materials on Legal Research and Citation, 334 pages, 1982. Student Library Exercises available (Coursebook)

Weihofen's Legal Writing Style, 2nd Ed., 332 pages, 1980 (Text)

LEGISLATION

Davies' Legislative Law and Process in a Nutshell, 279 pages, 1975 (Text)

Nutting and Dickerson's Cases and Materials on Legislation, 5th Ed., 744 pages, 1978 (Casebook)

Statsky's Legislative Analysis: How to Use Statutes and Regulations, 2nd Ed., 217 pages, 1984 (Text)

LOCAL GOVERNMENT

McCarthy's Local Government Law in a Nutshell, 2nd Ed., 404 pages, 1983 (Text)

Michelman and Sandalow's Cases-Comments-Questions on Government in Urban Areas, 1216 pages, 1970, with 1972 Supplement (Casebook)

Reynolds' Hornbook on Local Government Law, 860 pages, 1982 (Text)

Valente's Cases and Materials on Local Government Law, 2nd Ed., 980 pages, 1980 with 1982 Supplement (Casebook)

MASS COMMUNICATION LAW

Gillmor and Barron's Cases and Comment on Mass Communication Law, 4th Ed., 1076 pages, 1984 (Casebook)

Ginsburg's Regulation of Broadcasting: Law and Policy Towards Radio, Television and Cable Communications, 741 pages, 1979, with 1983 Supplement (Casebook)

Zuckman and Gayne's Mass Communications Law in a Nutshell, 2nd Ed., 473 pages, 1983 (Text)

MEDICINE, LAW AND

King's The Law of Medical Malpractice in a Nutshell, 340 pages, 1977 (Text)

Shapiro and Spece's Problems, Cases and Materials on Bioethics and Law, 892 pages, 1981 (Casebook)

MEDICINE, LAW AND—Continued

Sharpe, Fiscina and Head's Cases on Law and Medicine, 882 pages, 1978 (Casebook)

MILITARY LAW

Shanor and Terrell's Military Law in a Nutshell, 378 pages, 1980 (Text)

MORTGAGES

See Real Estate Transactions

NATURAL RESOURCES LAW

Laito's Cases and Materials on Natural Resources Law, approximately 930 pages, 1985 (Casebook)

See also Energy Law, Environmental Law, Oil and Gas, Water Law

NEGOTIATION

Edwards and White's Problems, Readings and Materials on the Lawyer as a Negotiator, 484 pages, 1977 (Casebook)

Williams' Legal Negotiation and Settlement, 207 pages, 1983 (Coursebook)

OFFICE PRACTICE

Hegland's Trial and Practice Skills in a Nutshell, 346 pages, 1978 (Text)

Strong and Clark's Law Office Management, 424 pages, 1974 (Casebook)

See also Computers and Law, Interviewing and Counseling, Negotiation

OIL AND GAS

Hemingway's Hornbook on Oil and Gas, 2nd Ed., Student Ed., 543 pages, 1983 (Text)

Huie, Woodward and Smith's Cases and Materials on Oil and Gas, 2nd Ed., 955 pages, 1972 (Casebook)

Lowe's Oil and Gas Law in a Nutshell, 443 pages, 1983 (Text)

See also Energy and Natural Resources Law

PARTNERSHIP

See Agency—Partnership

PATENT AND COPYRIGHT LAW

Choate and Francis' Cases and Materials on Patent Law, 2nd Ed., 1110 pages, 1981 (Casebook)

Miller and Davis' Intellectual Property—Patents, Trademarks and Copyright in a Nutshell, 428 pages, 1983 (Text)

Nimmer's Cases on Copyright and Other Aspects of Entertainment Litigation, 3rd Ed., approximately 1000 pages, 1985 (Casebook)

POVERTY LAW

Brudno's Poverty, Inequality, and the Law: Cases-Commentary-Analysis, 934 pages, 1976 (Casebook)

POVERTY LAW—Continued

LaFrance, Schroeder, Bennett and Boyd's Hornbook on Law of the Poor, 558 pages, 1973 (Text)

See also Social Legislation

PRODUCTS LIABILITY

Noel and Phillips' Cases on Products Liability, 2nd Ed., 821 pages, 1982 (Casebook)

Noel and Phillips' Products Liability in a Nutshell, 2nd Ed., 341 pages, 1981 (Text)

PROPERTY

Aigler, Smith and Tefft's Cases on Property, 2 volumes, 1339 pages, 1960 (Casebook)

Bernhardt's Real Property in a Nutshell, 2nd Ed., 448 pages, 1981 (Text)

Boyer's Survey of the Law of Property, 766 pages, 1981 (Text)

Browder, Cunningham and Smith's Cases on Basic Property Law, 4th Ed., 1431 pages, 1984 (Casebook)

Bruce, Ely and Bostick's Cases and Materials on Modern Property Law, 1004 pages, 1984 (Casebook)

Burby's Hornbook on Real Property, 3rd Ed., 490 pages, 1965 (Text)

Burke's Personal Property in a Nutshell, 322 pages, 1983 (Text)

Chused's A Modern Approach to Property: Cases-Notes-Materials, 1069 pages, 1978 with 1980 Supplement (Casebook)

Cohen's Materials for a Basic Course in Property, 526 pages, 1978 (Casebook)

Cunningham, Stoebuck and Whitman's Hornbook on the Law of Property, Student Ed., 916 pages, 1984 (Text)

Donahue, Kauper and Martin's Cases on Property, 2nd Ed., 1362 pages, 1983 (Casebook)

Hill's Landlord and Tenant Law in a Nutshell, 319 pages, 1979 (Text)

Moynihan's Introduction to Real Property, 254 pages, 1962 (Text)

Uniform Land Transactions Act, Uniform Simplification of Land Transfers Act, Uniform Condominium Act, 1977 Official Text with Comments, 462 pages, 1978

See also Real Estate Transactions, Land Use

PSYCHIATRY, LAW AND

Reisner's Law and the Mental Health System, Civil and Criminal Aspects, 696 pages, 1985 (Casebooks)

REAL ESTATE TRANSACTIONS

Bruce's Real Estate Finance in a Nutshell, 2nd Ed., 262 pages, 1985 (Text)

Maxwell, Riesenfeld, Hetland and Warren's Cases on California Security Transactions in Land, 3rd Ed., 728 pages, 1984 (Casebook)

REAL ESTATE TRANSACTIONS—Continued

Nelson and Whitman's Cases on Real Estate Transfer, Finance and Development, 2nd Ed., 1114 pages, 1981, with 1983 Supplement (Casebook)

Nelson and Whitman's Hornbook on Real Estate Finance Law, 2nd Ed., Standard Ed., approximately 900 pages, 1985 (Text)

Osborne's Cases and Materials on Secured Transactions, 559 pages, 1967 (Casebook)

REGULATED INDUSTRIES

Gellhorn and Pierce's Regulated Industries in a Nutshell, 394 pages, 1982 (Text)

Morgan, Harrison and Verkuil's Cases and Materials on Economic Regulation of Business, 2nd Ed., 670 pages, 1985 (Casebook)

Pozen's Financial Institutions: Cases, Materials and Problems on Investment Management, 844 pages, 1978 (Casebook)

See also Mass Communication Law, Banking Law

REMEDIES

Dobbs' Hornbook on Remedies, 1067 pages, 1973 (Text)

Dobbs' Problems in Remedies, 137 pages, 1974 (Problem book)

Dobbyn's Injunctions in a Nutshell, 264 pages, 1974 (Text)

Friedman's Contract Remedies in a Nutshell, 323 pages, 1981 (Text)

Leavell, Love and Nelson's Cases and Materials on Equitable Remedies and Restitution, 3rd Ed., 704 pages, 1980 (Casebook)

McCormick's Hornbook on Damages, 811 pages, 1935 (Text)

O'Connell's Remedies in a Nutshell, 2nd Ed., 325 pages, 1985 (Text)

York, Bauman and Rendleman's Cases and Materials on Remedies, 4th Ed., approximately 1025 pages, 1985 (Casebook)

REVIEW MATERIALS

Ballantine's Problems

Black Letter Series

Smith's Review Series

West's Review Covering Multistate Subjects

SECURITIES REGULATION

Hazen's Hornbook on The Law of Securities Regulation, Student Ed., 739 pages, 1985 (Text)

Ratner's Securities Regulation: Materials for a Basic Course, 2nd Ed., 1050 pages, 1980 with 1982 Supplement (Casebook)

Ratner's Securities Regulation in a Nutshell, 2nd Ed., 322 pages, 1982 (Text)

LAW SCHOOL PUBLICATIONS—Continued

SECURITIES REGULATION—Continued

Selected Securities and Business Planning Statutes, Rules and Forms, 470 pages, 1985

SOCIAL LEGISLATION

Hood and Hardy's Workers' Compensation and Employee Protection Laws in a Nutshell, 274 pages, 1984 (Text)

LaFrance's Welfare Law: Structure and Entitlement in a Nutshell, 455 pages, 1979 (Text)

Malone, Plant and Little's Cases on Workers' Compensation and Employment Rights, 2nd Ed., 951 pages, 1980 (Casebook)

See also Poverty Law

TAXATION

Dodge's Cases and Materials on Federal Income Taxation, approximately 825 pages, 1985 (Casebook)

Dodge's Federal Taxation of Estates, Trusts and Gifts: Principles and Planning, 771 pages, 1981 with 1982 Supplement (Casebook)

Garbis and Struntz' Cases and Materials on Tax Procedure and Tax Fraud, 829 pages, 1982 with 1984 Supplement (Casebook)

Gunn's Cases and Materials on Federal Income Taxation of Individuals, 785 pages, 1981 with 1985 Supplement (Casebook)

Hellerstein and Hellerstein's Cases on State and Local Taxation, 4th Ed., 1041 pages, 1978 with 1982 Supplement (Casebook)

Kahn and Gann's Corporate Taxation and Taxation of Partnerships and Partners, 2nd Ed., 1204 pages, 1985 (Casebook)

Kragen and McNulty's Cases and Materials on Federal Income Taxation: Individuals, Corporations, Partnerships, 4th Ed., approximately 1200 pages, 1985 (Casebook)

McNulty's Federal Estate and Gift Taxation in a Nutshell, 3rd Ed., 509 pages, 1983 (Text)

McNulty's Federal Income Taxation of Individuals in a Nutshell, 3rd Ed., 487 pages, 1983 (Text)

Posin's Hornbook on Federal Income Taxation of Individuals, Student Ed., 491 pages, 1983 with 1985 pocket part (Text)

Rice and Solomon's Problems and Materials in Federal Income Taxation, 3rd Ed., 670 pages, 1979 (Casebook)

Rose and Raskind's Advanced Federal Income Taxation: Corporate Transactions—Cases, Materials and Problems, 955 pages, 1978 (Casebook)

Selected Federal Taxation Statutes and Regulations, approximately 1300 pages, 1985

Sobeloff and Weidenbruch's Federal Income Taxation of Corporations and Stockholders in a Nutshell, 362 pages, 1981 (Text)

TORTS

Christie's Cases and Materials on the Law of Torts, 1264 pages, 1983 (Casebook)

Dobbs' Torts and Compensation—Personal Accountability and Social Responsibility for Injury, 955 pages, 1985 (Casebook)

Green, Pedrick, Rahl, Thode, Hawkins, Smith and Treece's Cases and Materials on Torts, 2nd Ed., 1360 pages, 1977 (Casebook)

Green, Pedrick, Rahl, Thode, Hawkins, Smith, and Treece's Advanced Torts: Injuries to Business, Political and Family Interests, 2nd Ed., 544 pages, 1977 (Casebook)—reprint from Green, et al. Cases and Materials on Torts, 2nd Ed., 1977

Keeton, Keeton, Sargentich and Steiner's Cases and Materials on Torts, and Accident Law, 1360 pages, 1983 (Casebook)

Kionka's Torts in a Nutshell: Injuries to Persons and Property, 434 pages, 1977 (Text)

Malone's Torts in a Nutshell: Injuries to Family, Social and Trade Relations, 358 pages, 1979 (Text)

Prosser and Keeton's Hornbook on Torts, 5th Ed., Student Ed., 1286 pages, 1984 (Text)

Shapo's Cases on Tort and Compensation Law, 1244 pages, 1976 (Casebook)

See also Products Liability

TRADE REGULATION

McManis' Unfair Trade Practices in a Nutshell, 444 pages, 1982 (Text)

Oppenheim, Weston, Maggs and Schechter's Cases and Materials on Unfair Trade Practices and Consumer Protection, 4th Ed., 1038 pages, 1983 (Casebook)

See also Antitrust, Regulated Industries

TRIAL AND APPELLATE ADVOCACY

Appellate Advocacy, Handbook of, 249 pages, 1980 (Text)

Bergman's Trial Advocacy in a Nutshell, 402 pages, 1979 (Text)

Binder and Bergman's Fact Investigation: From Hypothesis to Proof, 354 pages, 1984 (Coursebook)

Goldberg's The First Trial (Where Do I Sit?, What Do I Say?) in a Nutshell, 396 pages, 1982 (Text)

Haydock, Herr and Stempel's, Fundamentals of Pre-Trial Litigation, 768 pages, 1985 (Casebook)

Hegland's Trial and Practice Skills in a Nutshell, 346 pages, 1978 (Text)

Hornstein's Appellate Advocacy in a Nutshell, 325 pages, 1984 (Text)

Jeans' Handbook on Trial Advocacy, Student Ed., 473 pages, 1975 (Text)

McElhaney's Effective Litigation, 457 pages, 1974 (Casebook)

LAW SCHOOL PUBLICATIONS—Continued

TRIAL AND APPELLATE ADVOCACY— Continued

Nolan's Cases and Materials on Trial Practice, 518 pages, 1981 (Casebook)

Parnell and Shellhaas' Cases, Exercises and Problems for Trial Advocacy, 171 pages, 1982 (Coursebook)

Sonsteng, Haydock and Boyd's The Trialbook: A Total System for Preparation and Presentation of a Case, Student Ed., 404 pages, 1984 (Coursebook)

TRUSTS AND ESTATES

Atkinson's Hornbook on Wills, 2nd Ed., 975 pages, 1953 (Text)

Averill's Uniform Probate Code in a Nutshell, 425 pages, 1978 (Text)

Bogert's Hornbook on Trusts, 5th Ed., 726 pages, 1973 (Text)

Clark, Lusky and Murphy's Cases and Materials on Gratuitous Transfers, 3rd Ed., approximately 1200 pages, 1985 (Casebook)

Gulliver's Cases and Materials on Future Interests, 624 pages, 1959 (Casebook)

Gulliver's Introduction to the Law of Future Interests, 87 pages, 1959 (Casebook)— reprint from Gulliver's Cases and Materials on Future Interests, 1959

McGovern's Cases and Materials on Wills, Trusts and Future Interests: An Introduction to Estate Planning, 750 pages, 1983 (Casebook)

Mennell's Cases and Materials on California Decedent's Estates, 566 pages, 1973 (Casebook)

Mennell's Wills and Trusts in a Nutshell, 392 pages, 1979 (Text)

TRUSTS AND ESTATES—Continued

Powell's The Law of Future Interests in California, 91 pages, 1980 (Text)

Simes' Hornbook on Future Interests, 2nd Ed., 355 pages, 1966 (Text)

Turrentine's Cases and Text on Wills and Administration, 2nd Ed., 483 pages, 1962 (Casebook)

Uniform Probate Code, 5th Ed., Official Text With Comments, 384 pages, 1977

Waggoner's Future Interests in a Nutshell, 361 pages, 1981 (Text)

WATER LAW

Getches' Water Law in a Nutshell, 439 pages, 1984 (Text)

Trelease's Cases and Materials on Water Law, 3rd Ed., 833 pages, 1979, with 1984 Supplement (Casebook)

See also Energy Law, Natural Resources Law, Environmental Law

WILLS

See Trusts and Estates

WOMEN AND THE LAW

Kay's Text, Cases and Materials on Sex-Based Discrimination, 2nd Ed., 1045 pages, 1981, with 1983 Supplement (Casebook)

Thomas' Sex Discrimination in a Nutshell, 399 pages, 1982 (Text)

See also Employment Discrimination

WORKERS' COMPENSATION

See Social Legislation

CASES AND MATERIALS ON
GRATUITOUS TRANSFERS
WILLS, INTESTATE SUCCESSION, TRUSTS, GIFTS, FUTURE INTERESTS AND ESTATE AND GIFT TAXATION

Third Edition

By

Elias Clark

Lafayette S. Foster Professor of Law, Yale University

Louis Lusky

Betts Professor of Law, Columbia University

Arthur W. Murphy

Joseph Solomon Professor of Law, Columbia University

AMERICAN CASEBOOK SERIES

WEST PUBLISHING CO.
ST. PAUL, MINN., 1985

Library of Congress Cataloging in Publication Data

Clark, Elias.
  Gratuitous transfers, wills, intestate succession,
trusts, gifts, and future interests.

  (American casebook series)
  Rev. ed. of: Cases and materials on gratuitous
transfers. 2nd ed. 1977.
  Includes index.
  1. Inheritance and succession—United States—Cases.
2. Gifts—United States—Cases. 3. Future interests—
United States—Cases. I. Lusky, Louis. II. Murphy,
Arthur W. III. Clark, Elias. Cases and materials on
gratuitous transfers. IV. Title. V. Series.

KF753.A7C3 1985   346.7305'2   85–10571
ISBN 0–314–91766–7   347.30652

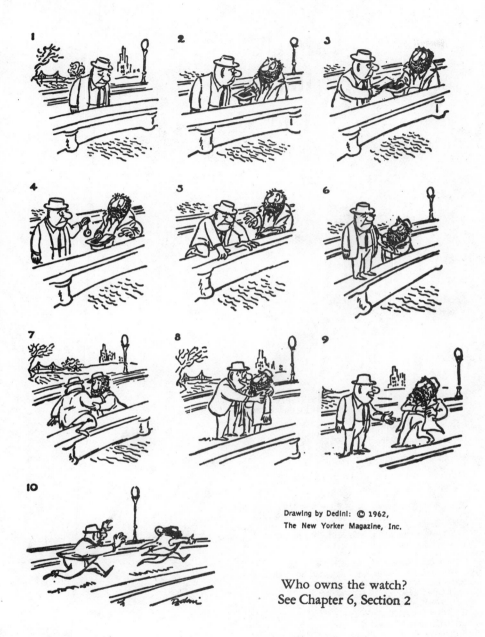

Drawing by Dedini: © 1962,
The New Yorker Magazine, Inc.

Who owns the watch?
See Chapter 6, Section 2

*

Preface to the Third Edition

We have set out in the preface to the first edition the origins and objectives of this book. Because we believe they are still valid, we have retained the basic organization of materials used in the earlier editions—though, to be sure, the presentation of the estate and gift tax materials has been substantially rewritten.

To those who think of the estates field as static, developments over the last decade must be astonishing. This edition explores a number of developments that have brought substantial changes to the law: the publication and adoption of the Uniform Probate Code, in whole or in part, in a significant number of states, the enactment in 1976 and 1981 of extensive revisions to the federal estate and gift taxes, the application of constitutional principles to the inheritance rights of illegitimate children and to statutes prescribing different benefits for males and females, and the introduction of the sharing principle into statutes defining the rights of husbands and wives in marital property.

In the text and notes the decedent is usually identified as the husband and the surviving spouse as the wife. We know, of course, that in a given case the wife, as the co-head of the family, may be the transferor and the husband a beneficiary. We have, however, continued the traditional identification because it coincides with the statistical fact that the odds are greatly in favor of the wife's surviving her husband. We have also refrained from using the words "testatrix," "executrix" and "administratrix." The need throughout is only to identify the office, the sex of the occupant of that office being of no relevance.

Our senior colleague, Ashbel G. Gulliver, died on July 3, 1974. The contributions made by Professor Gulliver to this volume are described in the first preface. Because of illness at the time, Professor Gulliver did not actively participate in the final stages of preparation of the first edition, but he did review most of the manuscript and express his willingness to be listed as the senior editor. Because he did not have an opportunity to participate in the preparation of the second and third editions of this volume, we do not feel at liberty to attach his name to work the existence of which he was unaware. We do, however, wish to acknowledge that many of his splendid contributions remain intact. Particularly noteworthy in this regard are the historical introductions and a number of the long notes following cases in the Future Interests chapter.

We are grateful to the authors and publishers who have consented to our use of quotations from their copyrighted works. In addition, we wish to express our gratitude to the many students who served as research and editorial assistants in the preparation of the several editions of this book, to colleagues from other schools for their helpful suggestions, and to

Cathy J. Briganti for her invaluable assistance in preparing the manuscript for publication.

ELIAS CLARK
LOUIS LUSKY
ARTHUR W. MURPHY

June 1, 1985

Preface to the First Edition

Every casebook is constructed primarily to meet the teaching needs of its editors, and this one is no exception. Our criteria for inclusion and exclusion of materials may be of interest to other teachers who will be considering the book for their own use.

The book has two main objectives. It is designed, first, to equip the general practitioner for practice in the estates field—more specifically, for planning, drafting and administration in an estate of medium size which does not involve major tax problems. The second purpose is to provide the broad base of general information from which the prospective specialist may proceed to more detailed study.

After an introductory chapter, six chapters (Two through Seven) on the forms of transfer set out the law of intestate succession; protection of the family; wills, including the formalities of execution, capacity, undue influence and fraud, and revocation; gifts; and trusts. The trusts chapter covers methods of creation and termination and considers the special problems of charitable, constructive, resulting, insurance, spendthrift and discretionary trusts. Although we touch only lightly upon certain types of inter vivos property arrangements, such as community property and joint tenancies, the coverage of inter vivos transfers is believed to be sufficient for appreciation of the interrelationship between inter vivos and testamentary giving. We have included in these chapters a substantial amount of note and text material to expedite consideration of essential but relatively uncomplicated points.

The final three chapters are designed to be introductory rather than definitive. Our purpose is to give the student a respectable background in fiduciary administration, future interests and transfer taxation, without preempting the subject matter from more detailed exploration in advanced courses.

Chapter Eight on fiduciary administration explains the procedures for probating a will, appointing a fiduciary, and processing the claims of creditors. It also suggests the major outlines of fiduciary responsibility, with particular reference to management of trust funds. It touches upon the significant doctrines but makes no attempt to illustrate how they operate in all the areas of possible application. The inclusion of a section on jurisdiction and choice of law reflects the belief that these problems are of central importance in some estates, and the fear that they are either ignored in the traditional conflicts course or are analyzed without sufficient awareness of the complex problems facing the fiduciary and his lawyer.

Future interests presents a problem. On the one hand, there is not enough time in a comprehensive course for full coverage of this intricate, history-burdened subject—coverage that would provide the student with equipment for complex litigation and title work. A full separate course would be needed for that. On the other hand, familiarity with certain aspects of future interests is necessary for the general practitioner who is called upon for planning and drafting work, which is the work that most lawyers do in the trusts and estates field.

Chapter Nine therefore adopts what is believed to be a novel approach. After an opening section on classification and terminology, which consists mainly of textual notes, there is a section that covers the basic features of the Rule against Perpetuities. Then follows a section entitled "Common Pitfalls," which contains a series of cases illustrating the traps into which the unsophisticated draftsman may blunder: Fertile Octogenarian, Unborn Widow, and so on. Section Four guards against the danger of the student's thinking that an instrument drafted (by someone else) without regard for the high standards of draftsmanship recommended by the earlier sections will *necessarily* fail. The various salvage rules that courts and legislatures have developed to prevent the parties from suffering too much from the carelessness of lawyers—such as severed shares and alternative contingencies, and the recent "wait and see" statutes—are considered. Finally, there is a section on powers of appointment which covers both perpetuities and nonperpetuities aspects of such powers.

The principle on which the future interests materials have been selected is relevance to drafting and planning. For that reason, little attention is paid to construction and to the ancient beginnings. And substantial economy of space and time has been achieved by dealing with a number of subjects (such as class gifts) in the context of the perpetuities materials, rather than under separate headings.

Approximately 75 pages of tax material are included (Chapter Ten), in the belief that any learning in this field is incomplete without an appreciation that all substantial gratuitous transfers of property have tax consequences. The difficult question is what to try to cover. Here, as with future interests, we have been guided by the needs of the generalist rather than the expert. Accordingly, the materials attempt to give an overview of the structure and interrelationship of the estate and gift taxes, plus some more intensive exposure to specific subjects which we think are most important to the general practitioner. These include the taxability of lifetime transfers, as "in contemplation of death" or because of the retention of "strings" over the property by the transferor; powers of appointment; the marital deduction; and split gift provisions. The chapter includes a brief summary of the pertinent principles of income taxation of trusts and estates.

A final note on our perspective seems appropriate because it has had an influence on the selection and organization of materials. The opening chapter asks the student to consider the role of wealth transmission in contemporary society and to develop tentative theories as to the proper forms of legal control. Thereafter, as the student studies separate strands of doctrine, he is urged to consider the functional justification for each doctrine, the role of the doctrine in shaping the overall institution of wealth transmission, and the methods whereby its contributions might be improved. And yet, despite the persistent emphasis on the present policy justification for the doctrine, it is our belief that an appreciation of its origin will enhance the student's understanding and heighten his interest. Historical antecedents are therefore described, mostly in text and note material, wherever they aid appraisal of the present law.

The book is believed to have considerable flexibility as a teaching tool. For example, it is to be used at Columbia for a comprehensive course that will cover the whole book, and at Yale for two courses—one of which will cover the first seven chapters and another the two chapters on administration of estates and future interests. It is not hard to devise other possible ways of dividing the subject matter to fit the curricula of particular schools.

This book has been many years in various stages of gestation. It began as mimeographed teaching materials, prepared by Professor Gulliver in 1932, to be used in new courses at the Yale Law School which he was then pioneering. These courses represented one of the earliest developments in the consolidation of what had been up to that time separate courses in Wills and Trusts. During the following decade, the materials were revised by Professor Gulliver with the aid of students and research assistants, of whom Mrs. Catherine J. Tilson made the most extensive, imaginative and discriminating contributions. At the end of that period, the courses were taken over by Professor Henry A. Fenn, who made further revisions before leaving the Yale faculty to become Dean of the College of Law of the University of Florida. Much remains in the final manuscript from these early developments; particularly noteworthy in this regard are the historical surveys.

In 1965 Professor Clark, who was then responsible for the teaching of the estates materials at Yale, joined with Professors Lusky and Murphy, his counterparts at Columbia, in a collaboration to publish a book that could be used at both schools. Then followed a year and a half of revision, updating of all cases and notes, and addition of new materials to effect a broader coverage (particularly in the wills and trusts chapters). Two new chapters, one on taxation and the other on future interests, were added. A large proportion of the materials on future interests is taken verbatim from Gulliver, Cases and Materials on the Law of Future Interests (1959). During this last stage, Professor Gulliver has been kept apprised of developments but has not participated directly in the final preparation of the manuscript for publication and should not be held accountable for errors contained therein.

We are grateful to the authors and publishers who have consented to our use of quotations from their copyrighted works. In addition, we also express our appreciation to the succession of students and research assistants who have made many contributions to the development of these materials over the years. * * *

> ASHBEL GREEN GULLIVER
> ELIAS CLARK
> LOUIS LUSKY
> ARTHUR W. MURPHY

June 1, 1967   *

Acknowledgments

The editors wish to acknowledge permission to reproduce from the following copyrighted material:

Scott, Control of Property By the Dead, 65 University of Pennsylvania Law Review 632 (1917), reprinted with permission of the University of Pennsylvania Law Review.

Leach, Perpetuities in Perspective, 65 Harvard Law Review 728 (1952), copyright © 1952 by the Harvard Law Review Association, reprinted with permission of the Harvard Law Review Association.

Excerpts from Chapter One, "The Family and Inheritance Study in Perspective," in THE FAMILY AND INHERITANCE by Marvin B. Sussman, Judith N. Cates, David T. Smith, with the collaboration of Lodoska K. Clausen, © 1970 Russell Sage Foundation.

Table of Consanguinity and Chart of Relationships from California Estate Administration (1960), reprinted with permission of the copyright owners, the Regents of the University of California.

Westfall, Estate Planning, p. 43 (2d Ed. 1982), reprinted with permission of the publisher, Foundation Press.

Plumez, Adoption: Where Have All the Babies Gone?, N.Y. Times Magazine p. 34, April 13, 1980, reprinted with permission of the New York Times Company.

Bruch, Management Powers and Duties Under California's Property Laws: Recommendations for Reform, 34 Hastings L.J. 229, 233–234 (1982), reprinted with permission of the author.

American Law of Property (1952), Little, Brown and Company, excerpts from volumes 1, 2 and 3, reprinted with permission of Little, Brown and Company.

Rheinstein and Glendon, The Law of Decedents' Estates, pp. 89–92, copyright 1971, Foundation Press, reprinted with permission of the publisher.

Macdonald, Fraud on the Widow's Share, 21–24 (1960) reprinted with permission of Michigan Legal Publications, University of Michigan Law School.

Plager, The Spouse's Nonbarrable Share: A Solution in Search of a Problem, 33 U. of Chi.L.Rev. 681 (1966), reprinted with permission of the author and the University of Chicago Law Review.

Wedgwood, The Economics of Inheritance, 189–192 (1929), reprinted with permission of the publishers, Routledge and Kegan Paul, Ltd.

Katz, The Silent World of Doctor and Patient, pp. 142–143 (1984), reprinted with permission of The Free Press, a Division of Macmillan, Inc.

Gulliver and Tilson, Classification of Gratuitous Transfers, 51 Yale Law Journal 1 (1941), reprinted with permission of the Yale Law Journal.

Langbein, Substantial Compliance With The Wills Act, 88 Harv.L.Rev. 489 (1975), reprinted with permission of the author and the Harvard Law Review Association.

Powell, How Far Should Freedom of Disposition Go?, The Second Mortimer H. Hess Lecture delivered October 8, 1970 by Richard R. Powell, 26 Record of the Association of the Bar of the City of New York 8 (Jan. 1971), reprinted with permission of the Association of the Bar of the City of New York.

Alford, Collecting a Decedent's Assets Without Ancillary Administration, 18 Southwestern Law Journal 329 (1964), reprinted with permission of the Southwestern Law Journal.

Wellman, Recent Developments in the Struggle for Probate Reform, 79 Mich.L.Rev. 501, 504–506, 510 (1981), reprinted with permission of the author and the Michigan Law Review Association.

Niles, A Contemporary View of Liability for Breach of Trust, reprinted from Trusts & Estates, January 1975, p. 12; February 1975, p. 82. Copyright Communication Channels, Inc., 461 Eighth Avenue, New York, N.Y. 10001, 1975.

Langbein and Posner, Market Funds and Trust Investment Law, 1976 A.B.F.Res.J. 1, reprinted with permission of the American Bar Foundation Research Journal.

Langbein and Posner, Social Investing and the Law of Trusts, 79 Mich.L.Rev. 72, 83–84 (1980), reprinted with permission of Professor Langbein and the Michigan Law Review Association.

Robinson, Trust Allocation Doctrine and Corporate Stock: The Law Must Respond to Economics, 50 Texas L.Rev. 747, 762–63 (1972), reprinted with permission of the Fred B. Rothman & Co. and the Texas Law Review.

Powell on Real Property, by Richard R. Powell, Supplement Annotations by Patrick J. Rohan, Vol. 2, ¶ 274, copyright 1976, Matthew Bender, reprinted with permission of the publisher.

Simes and Smith, The Law of Future Interests, § 1117, copyright 1956, West Publishing Company, reprinted with permission of the publisher.

Leach, Perpetuities: The Nutshell Revisited, 78 Harvard Law Review 986 (1965), copyright © 1965 by the Harvard Law Review Association, reprinted with permission of the Harvard Law Review Association.

Leach, Perpetuities in a Nutshell, originally appearing in 51 Harvard Law Review 638 (1938), copyright © 1938 by the Harvard Law Review Association, revised and reprinted as revised in Leach, Cases and Text on the Law of Wills, Second Edition, 1960 Revision, published by Little, Brown and Company, copyright © 1960 by W. Barton Leach, reprinted with permission of the Harvard Law Review Association and Professor W. Barton Leach.

Lowndes, Kramer and McCord, Federal Estate and Gift Taxes, §§ 9.14, 9.22, 28.2, copyright 1974, West Publishing Company, reprinted with permission of the publisher.

Bittker, The Church and Spiegel Cases: Section 811(c) Gets a New Lease on Life, 58 Yale Law Journal 825 (1949), reprinted with permission of the Yale Law Journal.

Bittker, Federal Taxation of Income, Estates and Gifts, Vol. 3, ¶ 82.1.2 (Warren, Gorham, and Lamont 1981), reprinted with the permission of the author.

Warren and Surrey, Federal Estate and Gift Taxation (1961 Edition), pp. 759–763, reprinted with permission of The Foundation Press, Inc.

Death Tax Clauses in Wills and Trusts: Discussion and Sample Clauses, 19 Real Property, Probate and Trust Journal 495, 500–505 (1984), reprinted with permission of the publisher.

Bittker, Stone & Klein, Federal Income Taxation, pp. 738–740 (6th Ed., Little, Brown and Company 1984), reprinted with permission of Professor Bittker.

American Law Institute, Restatement of the Law of Trusts, Second; Restatement of the Law of Property; Restatement of the Law of Conflict of Laws, Second; reprinted with permission of The American Law Institute.

Drawing by Dedini from the June 2, 1962 issue of the New Yorker, reprinted with permission of the New Yorker Magazine, Inc.

*

Summary of Contents

Table of Contents

*

Table of Cases

The names of principal cases in italics. All others roman.

*

Table of Statutes, Model and Uni-Form Laws, and American Law Institute Restatements

---

TREASURY REGULATIONS

AMERICAN LAW INSTITUTE RESTATE-MENTS

CONFLICT OF LAWS, SECOND

PROPERTY

TRUSTS, SECOND

*

Table of Abbreviations Used in Referring to Texts

Am.L.Prop.: American Law of Property (1952), written by various authors and edited by Casner.

Bl.Com.: Blackstone, Commentaries on the Law of England (1765–69).

Gray: Gray, Rule against Perpetuities (4th ed., 1942).

Holds.: Holdsworth, History of English Law (1922–1938).

Kales: Kales, Estates, Future Interests and Illegal Conditions and Restraints in Illinois (2d ed., 1920).

Kent Com.: Kent, Commentaries on American Law (1840).

Mait.Eq.: Maitland, Equity (1909).

Plucknett: Plucknett, Concise History of the Common Law (5th ed., 1956).

P. & M.: Pollock and Maitland, History of English Law (2d ed., 1923).

Powell: Powell, Real Property (1976).

Simes (hb): Simes, Future Interests, Hornbook Series (2d ed., 1966).

Simes and Smith: Simes and Smith, Law of Future Interests (2d ed., 1956).

Tiffany: Tiffany, The Law of Real Property (2d ed., 1920).

*

CASES AND MATERIALS ON
GRATUITOUS TRANSFERS

WILLS, INTESTATE SUCCESSION, TRUSTS, GIFTS, FUTURE INTERESTS AND ESTATE AND GIFT TAXATION

*

Chapter One

THE POLICY DETERMINANTS

These materials are designed to introduce the area of law which deals with the gratuitous transfer of wealth by will, gift, trust and intestate succession. The estates field is bread and butter to the lawyer. Planning, drafting, and administering estates and trusts is a major activity of individual practitioners and requires a separate department in law firms of substantial size. Even the specialist whose professional interests are far removed from the field may be compelled at the request of a friend or client or in considering his or her own affairs to turn his or her attention to these matters. Estates lawyers look at problems from the point of view of the individual property owner whom they represent. Their objective, in general terms, is to insure that their client's intent is carried out with a minimum of problems and a minimum of tax burdens. They know that contact with the law is direct, frequent and unavoidable. Estate, inheritance, gift and income taxes are an ever-present consideration, and failure to satisfy the formalities of transfer or ambiguities in the documents of transfer may produce rival claimants to the property. But judicial intervention is not limited to matters in controversy. Rather, it is the traditional procedure in this country to administer estates and testamentary trusts, including those which are not controverted, under court supervision. Thus it is that in addition to the large body of substantive law in the field there is a separate set of procedural rules regulating the administration process.

With few exceptions, of which death taxes are the most notable, this accumulation of substantive and procedural rules rests on one basic premise: In a capitalistic economy based on the institution of private property owners have the widest possible latitude in disposing of their property in accordance with their own wishes whether they be wise or foolish. The statutes and cases in the field have as their purpose the discovery of the true intent of the property owner, not to thwart it, but to give it effect.

The fact that the law and those who practice it seem only concerned with the individual property owner must not obscure society's stake in the wealth transmission process. No systematic attempt has been made to estimate the dollar magnitude of the continuous flow of wealth by gratuitous transfers or to evaluate its impact on the structure of American life. Each year approximately 2 million persons die in the United States.

Most of these deaths bring about a transfer of property whether it is a few articles of personal property, a small insurance policy, a pension, a claim to current wages and social security, or millions of dollars and a controlling interest in an important corporation. The cumulative value of these death transfers plus the value of inter vivos gifts and of transfers caused by the shift in interest or termination of trusts has not been accurately established. We do have a few isolated statistics. By the end of 1982, the total life insurance outstanding amounted to $4,477 billion with $48 billion from life policies and annuities being paid out to beneficiaries during the year. The estate tax returns filed in 1983 listed a total in gross estates of $50.39 billion ($11.5 billion in corporate stock, $12 billion in real estate, $5.9 billion in cash, $4 billion in bonds, $1.9 billion in life insurance, and $3.2 billion in notes and mortgages represented the largest categories of holdings) against which were subtracted $24.3 billion in deductions. A total of $5.2 billion in estate taxes was collected from 35,148 estates. The significance of these figures can best be appreciated by emphasizing that the estates of only about 5 percent of the people who died in the taxable period, admittedly the wealthiest, filed estate tax returns, with only about 1.76 percent actually paying any tax. It is a reasonable projection from those statistics to speculate that the total wealth passing at death each year must be well in excess of $100 billion.

The economics of the process are not the only basis on which to judge its impact on society. Wealth is an important factor in determining the stability of the family. The opportunities for power, position and enlightenment which accrue to the beneficiaries of a large estate are obvious. In the less well-endowed family failure to anticipate and provide for the death of the head of the family may mean the collapse of a small business, the termination of the children's education or the necessity to turn to government sources for support. Wealth may be used to insure a secure and united family. Contrariwise it may, if persons of like class, say children or grandchildren, are treated unequally, ignite the nastiest fights known to the law. Expectations of inheritance or fears of disinheritance frequently control the behavior of members of the family and their relationships to each other. Love, hate, jealousy, avarice—the whole range of human emotions—are involved.

Inevitably the ethical, economic, sociological and psychological aspects of the process have brought challenges to the principle of unlimited property owners' control. Although frequently more speculative than scientific, considerable literature has evolved during the last several centuries on the subject. The critics of the process cannot easily be dismissed as misguided radicals or worse; they include such defenders of capitalism as Andrew Carnegie and Theodore Roosevelt. It is not to be suggested that these critics advocate that restrictions be placed on all gratuitous transfers. Most of them agree that a person should be permitted relatively unrestricted enjoyment of wealth which he or she has earned and that such enjoyment should include the power of giving it away during life. The criticism is directed at the proposition that a person should also be permitted to direct how the wealth is to be distributed after his or her death and that the recipients of his or her bounty should have unlimited enjoyment of it even though they did not contribute to its accumulation.   As might be expected, there is wide variation in the proposed solutions to the problem.   Some, as in the case of Carnegie and Roosevelt, make their criticism of inheritance (inheritance as used in this context is not limited to distribution by the laws of intestate succession but includes all death transfers by intestacy, will, insurance, or survivorship of a joint tenant) to support an argument for a mild death tax levied at rates graduated in accordance with the size of the estate.   Others go much further and advocate the abolition of inheritance with some exceptions for spouses, minor children and invalids who are dependent upon the decedent for support.   An obvious question, usually left unanswered, is how much is to be excepted.

Vagueness as to proposed alternatives is one weakness in the literature on the subject.   At least two others, generally admitted by the authors, should be noted.   First, no one has researched, statistically or otherwise, such questions as whether persons require the incentive of unlimited inheritance rights to spur them to the utmost in productive effort during their lives, or whether the average beneficiary has the competence to use inherited wealth for the best interests of the community; as a consequence, conclusions as to these and many other questions can only be based on conjecture.   Second, there is a tendency to leave obscure the standards and policies against which the principle of unlimited inheritance is being tested.   Illustrative of both of these weaknesses are the following generalizations summarizing some of the recurring arguments made for and against inheritance.

In criticism:

1. A basic democratic ideal is to secure, as nearly as may be, equality of opportunity.   Inheritance violates this ideal; it causes and aggravates inequality by perpetuating a hereditary aristrocracy based on such fortuities as death, survival and the fortunate choice of parents.   The recipients of inherited wealth have not earned it, nor does it bear any relationship to their productive abilities or performance.

2. Property should serve the living.   The dead cannot wisely dictate the best uses of such property, particularly when they attempt to do so for long periods of time.

3. Inheritance permits large amounts of wealth and power to be thrust on persons who are wholly unprepared or incompetent to use it wisely or for the best interests of the community.

4. Receipt of large amounts of wealth causes indolence and therefore deprives the community of the productive energies of the recipient.

In defense:

1. Inheritance is an incentive for the accumulation of wealth and therefore an incentive for the utmost in productive effort during life.

2. Hereditary wealth is an important source of investment capital and as such is absolutely necessary to the continued expansion of our economy.

3. Inheritance permits continued support of dependents.

4. Hereditary wealth is an important source of support for cultural and charitable institutions to the benefit of the entire community.

5. Any unfairness of inheritance is mitigated by the fact that many of the traditional recipients (spouse and children) did at least indirectly contribute to the amassing of the wealth.

6. Abolition of inheritance would mean public ownership of all wealth—an unsatisfactory and drastic solution to the problem of inequality.

SECTION ONE.   FREEDOM OF TESTATION AND PUBLIC POLICY

NUNNEMACHER v. STATE

Supreme Court of Wisconsin, 1906.
129 Wis. 190, 108 N.W. 627.

WINSLOW, J.   This is an action commenced in this court under the provisions of section 3200, Rev.St.1898, to recover from the state the amount of an inheritance tax paid under protest pursuant to an order of the county court of Waukesha county.   The complaint is based upon the ground that chapter 44, p. 65, of the Laws of 1903, under which the tax was levied and paid, is unconstitutional.   The Attorney General interposed a general demurrer to the complaint, and thus the question of the constitutionality of the law is squarely presented.

* * *

The constitutionality of this law, and of any similar law, is now attacked upon the following general grounds: First, that the right to take property by inheritance or by will is a natural right protected by the Constitution, which cannot be wholly taken away or substantially impaired by the Legislature; * * *.

With the first of these propositions we agree.   We are fully aware that the contrary proposition has been stated by the great majority of the courts of this country, including the Supreme Court of the United States. The unanimity with which it is stated is perhaps only equaled by the paucity of reasoning by which it is supported.   In its simplest form it is thus stated: "The right to take property by devise or descent is the creature of the law and not a natural right."   Magoun v. Bank, 170 U.S. 283, 18 S.Ct. 594, 42 L.Ed. 1037.   In Eyre v. Jacob, 14 Grat. (Va.) 422, 73 Am.Dec. 367, it is stated more sweepingly thus: "It [the Legislature] may tomorrow, if it pleases, absolutely repeal the statute of wills, and that of descents and distributions, and declare that, upon the death of a party, his property shall be applied to the payment of his debts and the residue appropriated to public uses."

* * *

That there are inherent rights existing in the people prior to the making of any of our Constitutions is a fact recognized and declared by the Declaration of Independence, and by substantially every state Constitution. Our own Constitution says in its very first article: "All men are born equally free and independent and have certain inherent rights; among these are life, liberty and the pursuit of happiness; to secure these rights governments are instituted among men deriving their just powers from the consent of the governed." Notice the language, "to secure these (inherent) rights governments are instituted;" not to manufacture new rights or to confer them on its citizens, but to conserve and secure to its citizens the exercise of pre-existing rights. It is true that the inherent rights here referred to are not defined but are included under the very general terms of "life, liberty and the pursuit of happiness." It is relatively easy to define "life and liberty," but it is apparent that the term "pursuit of happiness" is a very comprehensive expression which covers a broad field. Unquestionably this expression covers the idea of the acquisition of private property; not that the possession of property is the supreme good, but that there is planted in the breast of every person the desire to possess something useful or something pleasing which will serve to render life enjoyable, which shall be his very own, and which he may dispose of as he chooses, or leave to his children or his dependents at his decease. To deny that there is such universal desire, or to deny that the fulfillment of this desire contributes in a large degree to the attainment of human happiness is to deny a fact as patent as the shining of the sun at noonday. And so we find that, however far we penetrate into the history of the remote past, this idea of the acquisition and undisturbed possession of private property has been the controlling idea of the race, the supposed goal of earthly happiness. From this idea has sprung every industry, to preserve it governments have been formed, and its development has been coincident with the development of civilization. And so we also find that, from the very earliest times, men have been acquiring property, protecting it by their own strong arm if necessary, and leaving it for the enjoyment of their descendants; and we find also that the right of the descendants, or some of them, to succeed to the ownership has been recognized from the dawn of human history. The birthright of the first-born existed long before Esau sold his right to the wily Jacob, and the Mosaic law fairly bristles with provisions recognizing the right of inheritance as then long existing, and regulating its details. The most ancient known codes recognize it as a right already existing and Justice Brown was clearly right when he said, in U.S. v. Perkins, 163 U.S. 625, 16 S.Ct. 1073, 41 L.Ed. 287: "The general consent of the most enlightened nations has from the earliest historical period recognized a natural right in children to inherit the property of their parents."

The existence of the right to dispose of property by will in the earliest times is not so easy of proof. Nevertheless it seems there can be no doubt of the fact. The biblical writings show the exercise of the right from the times of Abraham and Mr. Schouler in his work on Wills (2d Ed.) § 13, says that history "confirms the opinion that the practice of allowing the owner of property to direct its destination after his death, or at least of imposing general rules of inheritance, is coeval with civilization itself, and so close, in fact, upon the origin of property and property rights as not to be essentially separated in point of antiquity." The laws of Solon allowed the willing of personal property in Athens, and the laws of the Twelve Tables in Rome. In England the right of testamentary disposition of personal and real property, or at least a part of it, was recognized from the very earliest times, but lands could not be willed after the Norman invasion and the establishment of feudal tenures until St. 32 Henry VIII, c. 1, §§ 1–5. Cassoday on Wills, § 31 et seq.; 30 A. & E. Enc.Law, p. 549. So clear does it seem to us from the historical point of view that the right to take property by inheritance or will has existed in some form among civilized nations from the time when the memory of man runneth not to the contrary, and so conclusive seems the argument that these rights are a part of the inherent rights which governments, under our conception, are established to conserve, that we feel entirely justified in rejecting the dictum so frequently asserted by such a vast array of courts that these rights are purely statutory and may be wholly taken away by the Legislature. It is true that these rights are subject to reasonable regulation by the Legislature, lines of descent may be prescribed, the persons who can take as heirs or devisees may be limited, collateral relatives may doubtless be included or cut off, the manner of the execution of wills may be prescribed, and there may be much room for legislative action in determining how much property shall be exempted entirely from the power to will so that dependents may not be entirely cut off. These are all matters within the field of regulation. The fact that these powers exist and have been universally exercised affords no ground for claiming that the Legislature may abolish both inheritances and wills, turn every fee-simple title into a mere estate for life, and thus, in effect, confiscate the property of the people once every generation.

* * *

[The Court concluded that the inheritance tax under challenge was a reasonable exercise of the State's right to regulate and tax transfers of property. The statute was therefore held constitutional, and the demurrer to the complaint was sustained.]

* * *

BLACKSTONE, COMMENTARIES, Vol. 2, pp. 9–12 (21st ed., 1844):

The most universal and effectual way of abandoning property, is by the death of the occupant: when, both the actual possession and intention of keeping possession ceasing, the property which is founded upon such possession and intention ought also to cease of course. For, naturally speaking, the instant a man ceases to be, he ceases to have any dominion: else if he had a right to dispose of his acquisitions one moment beyond his life, he would also have a right to direct their disposal for a million of ages after him: which would be highly absurd and inconvenient. All property must therefore cease upon death, considering men as absolute individuals, and unconnected with civil society: for, then, by the principles before established, the next immediate occupant would acquire a right in all that the deceased possessed.   *   *   *

The right of inheritance, or descent to the children and relations of the deceased, seems to have been allowed much earlier than the right of devising by testament. We are apt to conceive at first view that it has nature on its side; yet we often mistake for nature what we find established by long and inveterate custom. It is certainly a wise and effectual, but clearly a political, establishment; since the permanent right of property, vested in the ancestor himself, was no *natural,* but merely a *civil* right.   *   *   * [I]t is probable that [the right of inheritance arose] *   *   * from a plainer and more simple principle. A man's children or nearest relations are usually about him on his death-bed, and are the earliest witnesses of his decease. They become therefore generally the next immediate occupants, till at length, in process of time, this frequent usage ripened into general law. And therefore also in the earliest ages, on failure of children, a man's servants born under his roof were allowed to be his heirs; being immediately on the spot when he died. For, we find the old patriach Abraham expressly declaring, that "since God had given him no seed, his steward Eliezer, one born in his house, was his heir." Genesis xv, 3.   *   *   *

Wills therefore, and testaments, rights of inheritance and successions, are all of them creatures of the civil or municipal laws, and accordingly are in all respects regulated by them; every distinct country having different ceremonies and requisites to make a testament completely valid: neither does any thing vary more than the right of inheritance under different national establishments.

Notes

1. A comprehensive discussion of the historical and philosophical background to the law of wills appears in McMurray, Liberty of Testation, 14 Ill. L.Rev. 96 (1919). The author concludes that the will is by no means a universal institution, that it was unknown to the early law of Greece, India, Egypt, Babylon and Israel, and that the modern conception of the will was developed in the Roman law and came to us through the influence of the church.

2. For a general discussion of freedom of testation and other matters germane to this Chapter, see the essays collected in Death, Taxes and Family Property (Halbach, ed. 1977).

BIRD v. PLUNKETT

Supreme Court of Errors of Connecticut, 1953.
139 Conn. 491, 95 A.2d 71, 36 A.L.R.2d 127.

BROWN, Chief Justice. The plaintiff brought this action for a declaratory judgment to determine whether the defendant Plunkett, who had been convicted of manslaughter in causing the death of his wife, is entitled to take title and the full beneficial interest in her entire estate pursuant to the provisions of her will or whether the full title or, if not, the beneficial interest under a constructive trust passes to the plaintiff and the defendant Curtis as the heirs at law and next of kin of the testatrix. The material facts alleged in the complaint as amended may be thus summarized: On November 1, 1949, in Stamford, the defendant Plunkett shot and killed his wife, Esther Bird Plunkett. Upon an indictment charging him with murder in the second degree of his wife, Plunkett was convicted of manslaughter on March 15, 1950. Article second of her will, executed October 30, 1942, provided: "I give, devise and bequeath to my beloved husband, James Garret Plunkett, if he be living at the time of my death, my entire estate, both real and personal * * * for his own use and benefit forever." The will was duly admitted to probate on November 21, 1949. The plaintiff Bird and the defendant Curtis, hereinafter referred to as the plaintiffs, are the next of kin and heirs at law of the testatrix. The executor threatens to distribute the entire estate to Plunkett.

The defendant Plunkett demurred to the amended complaint on the ground that it alleged that he "was charged with the crime of murder in the second degree in the killing of his late wife and that he was convicted of the crime of manslaughter and under Section 7062 of the General Statutes, Revision of 1949, it appears that only a person finally adjudged guilty of murder in the first or second degree is barred to inheritance from or participation under the will of the person killed." Section 7062 is entitled "Person guilty of murder not to inherit from victim." Its pertinent provisions are: "No person finally adjudged guilty, either as the principal or accessory, of murder in the first or second degree shall be entitled to inherit or take any part of the real or personal estate of the person killed, whether under the provisions of any act relating to intestate succession, or as devisee or legatee, or otherwise under the will of such person * * *. With respect to inheritance from or participation under the will of the person killed, the person so finally adjudged guilty of murder in the first or second degree shall be considered to have predeceased the person killed." The question for decision is whether the demurrer was properly sustained on the ground that conviction of manslaughter did not bar the defendant Plunkett from taking under his late wife's will, because § 7062 bars only those finally adjudged guilty of murder in the first or second degree. This is a question of first impression in Connecticut. While there is a conflict of authority in the decisions of other jurisdictions, there is an unusual abundance of cases in which the issue has been ruled upon.

In determining the proper interpretation of § 7062, we must keep the provisions of three other statutes clearly in mind. Section 7309 relates to succession by a surviving spouse to property of the other who dies intestate. Section 6951, entitled "Wills, how made and executed", prescribes what is essential to the making of a valid will in Connecticut. Section 6956 provides: "If, after the making of a will, the testator shall marry or a child shall be born to [him] or a minor child shall be legally adopted by him, and no provision [was made in his] will for such contingency, [it] shall operate as a revocation of such will. No will or codicil shall be revoked in any other manner except by burning, cancelling, tearing or obliterating it by the testator or by some person in his presence by his direction, or by a later will or codicil." The express terms of the first statute leave no room for doubt that under it, if it controlled and if Plunkett's wife when killed by him had left no will, he would inherit her entire estate as intestate, since the complaint shows that there was neither a parent nor a child surviving. From the express terms of the statute as to the making of wills and the statute concerning their revocation, with the explicit and positive provisions in the latter as to what alone can accomplish revocation, it is equally clear that, if these statutes controlled, Plunkett under his wife's will would derive title to her entire estate. Section 7062 by its express terms applies as to both testate and intestate property and so clearly provides that one finally convicted of first or second degree murder of his victim, from whom he claims to take, is barred, whether or not there is a will. In this case, the question is reduced to whether § 7062 can be construed to preclude Plunkett, as a killer, from taking, notwithstanding he has not been convicted of murder as expressly required by the statute.

The gist of the plaintiffs' argument, as we understand it, involves these propositions: The decisions of the courts do not create the common law but, when rendered, are only declaratory of the law that already exists. In the absence of a statute excluding the common-law authority of the courts, no person can take a devise or a legacy under the will of a testator whom he has feloniously killed, or, if he takes the legal title, he is subject to a constructive trust in favor of the heirs at law or next of kin. Section 7062 does not affect the common-law authority of the court to declare invalid or void a devise or a legacy in the will of a testator feloniously killed by the devisee or the legatee or to impose a constructive trust upon the devisee or the legatee. The statute has only the specific and limited application of permitting, in cases to which it applies, the introduction of the judgment of guilty of murder in the first or second degree to prove, in a civil action, the commission of the act charged—evidence which otherwise would be inadmissible. Page v. Phelps, 108 Conn. 572, 588, 143 A. 890.

Proceeding upon this thesis and, so, assuming that § 7062, instead of constituting an effective declaration as to the only killer who is precluded from receiving property by the death of his victim, the plaintiffs treat the statute as procedural merely, leaving unaffected an undeclared common-law power, which it is claimed exists in the court, to apply the ancient maxim that no one shall be allowed to profit by his own wrong and so to rule that no felonious killer can succeed to the property of his victim. It is upon the claimed power of the court to give effect to this maxim in the instant case, regardless of the positive provisions of the three statutes recited above, that the plaintiffs rely to preclude the right of the defendant Plunkett to take. As authority for this contention they rely upon principles enunciated in Riggs v. Palmer, 115 N.Y. 506, 22 N.E. 188, 5 L.R.A. 340, and subsequent decisions which have adopted a similar view.

In that case there was no statute similar to § 7062. The sole question was whether the testator's grandson, who had murdered the testator, could take as a beneficiary under his will. The majority opinion stated,

115 N.Y. at page 509, 22 N.E. at page 189, that, while the purpose of the statutes concerning wills was "to enable testators to dispose of their estates to the objects of their bounty at death, and to carry into effect their final wishes legally expressed", and it "was the intention of the lawmakers that the donees in a will should have the property given to them", it "never could have been their intention that a donee who murdered the testator to make the will operative should have any benefit under it." The court then stated, 115 N.Y. at page 511, 22 N.E. at page 190, this as the ground of accomplishing the result: "Such an intention is inconceivable. We need not, therefore, be much troubled by the general language contained in the laws. Besides, all laws, as well as all contracts, may be controlled in their operation and effect by general, fundamental maxims of the common law. No one shall be permitted to profit by his own fraud, or to take advantage of his own wrong, or to found any claim upon his own iniquity, or to acquire property by his own crime. These maxims are dictated by public policy, have their foundation in universal law administered in all civilized countries, and have nowhere been superseded by statutes." The majority concluded that the crime of the grandson deprived him of any interest in his grandfather's estate.

In accord with the holding in the Riggs case, a minority of courts have held that one who has feloniously killed his benefactor cannot inherit from him notwithstanding there is no express statute similar to § 7062. In re Estate of Wilkins, 192 Wis. 111, 119, 211 N.W. 652, 51 A.L.R. 1106, and note, 1113; Price v. Hitaffer, 164 Md. 505, 514, 165 A. 470; De Zotell v. Mutual Life Ins. Co., 60 S.D. 532, 538, 547, 245 N.W. 58; Slocum v. Metropolitan Life Ins. Co., 245 Mass. 565, 570, 139 N.E. 816, 27 A.L.R. 1517; Perry v. Strawbridge, 209 Mo. 621, 632, 108 S.W. 641, 16 L.R.A., N.S., 244; In the Estate of Hall, [1914] P. 1. In these decisions, as in the Riggs case, the courts have based their denial of the killer's right to take on a "reasonable interpretation" of the descent statutes and have read into them the common-law maxim and the civil-law rule that benefits of statutes in derogation of the common law will not be enforced where to do so would be against public policy.

Two of the judges in the Riggs case filed a strong dissenting opinion. In it they pointed out, 115 N.Y. at page 515 et seq., 22 N.E. at page 191, that the question could not "be affected by considerations of an equitable nature," that the court was "bound by the rigid rules of law, which have been established by the legislature, and within the limits of which the determination of this question is confined", and that a will could not be altered or revoked after the testator's death "through an appeal to the courts, when the legislature has by its enactments prescribed exactly when and how wills may be made, altered, and revoked, and * * * when they have been fully complied with, has left no room for the exercise of an equitable jurisdiction by courts over such matters. * * * [A] valid will must continue as a will always, unless revoked in the manner provided by the statutes. Mere intention to revoke a will does not have the effect of revocation." The dissent further points out, 115 N.Y. at page 519, 22 N.E. at page 192, that intention, " 'however well authenticated, or however defeated, is not sufficient' ", and that public policy does not demand that the killer's succession to the testator's property "should be avoided because of his criminal act, when the laws are silent. Public policy does not demand it; for the demands of public policy are satisfied by the proper execution of the laws and the punishment of the crime." Other courts have severely criticized the majority opinion in the Riggs case and the rule of the English courts. Among such authorities are: Deem v. Millikin, 6 Ohio Cir.Ct.R. 357, 359, affirmed, 53 Ohio St. 668, 44 N.E. 1134; Shellenberger v. Ransom, 41 Neb. 631, 641, 59 N.W. 935, 25 L.R.A. 564; Wall v. Pfanschmidt, 265 Ill. 180, 183, 193, 106 N.E. 785, L.R.A.1915C, 328; Box v. Lanier, 112 Tenn. 393, 407, 79 S.W. 1042, 64 L.R.A. 458. The state of the authorities is thus well summarized: "There seems to be no escape on principle from the conclusion that at common law, and under the statutes and constitutions of the various states of the Union, courts are not warranted in disregarding the course of descent and distribution, or the conclusiveness of duly executed wills, to divert the succession from the murderers of ancestors or testators, and the authorities now strongly preponderate in this direction." 1 Woerner, American Law of Administration (3d Ed.), p. 188; note, 51 A.L.R. 1096.

As an alternative or supplemental claim, the plaintiffs urge that if the defendant Plunkett is not precluded from succeeding to the legal title under the principle of the Riggs case, he should be held to take the title as constructive trustee ex maleficio for the benefit of the plaintiffs. Several years after the Riggs case was decided, this theory was recognized by the New York court in Ellerson v. Westcott, 148 N.Y. 149, 154, 42 N.E. 540, as affording a method of equitable relief under such circumstances. The principle has been adopted in some other cases. Van Alstyne v. Tuffy, 103 Misc. 455, 458, 169 N.Y.S. 173; Whitney v. Lott, 134 N.J.Eq. 586, 591, 36 A.2d 888; Bryant v. Bryant, 193 N.C. 372, 379, 137 S.E. 188, 51 A.L.R. 1100; Garner v. Phillips, 229 N.C. 160, 162, 47 S.E.2d 845. It has been rejected, however. Welsh v. James, 408 Ill. 18, 21, 95 N.E.2d 872. The latter case reaches the result in accord with the weight of authority discussed above, because the vice in the legal remedy is not cured by resort to equity. The net effect is the same and would still result in a disregard of the statutes of descent or devise and in adding a punishment for crime not provided by the legislature and partaking of attainder and forfeiture. Furthermore, in so far as the instant case is concerned, the lack of any allegation of intent on the part of Plunkett to kill for the purpose of obtaining his wife's property is sufficient to differentiate the case from Dowd v. Tucker, 41 Conn. 197, and Buckingham v. Clark, 61 Conn. 204, 23 A. 1085, cited by the plaintiffs in support of a claimed constructive trust. In each of those cases, the bequest had been obtained by an express representation that it would be applied for the benefit of the person claiming the constructive trust. The maxim that one should not be permitted to profit by his own wrong of itself is insufficient upon the facts to entitle the plaintiffs to equitable relief. See Davis v. Margolis, 108 Conn. 645, 649, 144 A. 665; Restatement, Restitution § 187, comment e. The supplemental claim of the plaintiffs for relief on the ground of a constructive trust is unavailing, since they cannot prevail under the doctrine of the Riggs case.

As stated above, there was no statute similar to § 7062 involved in the decision of the Riggs case. These further cases, of many which could be cited, in addition to those mentioned in the second paragraph above, support the majority view that, in the absence of such a statute, a killer is not precluded from taking: Hagan v. Cone, 21 Ga.App. 416, 417, 94 S.E. 602; In re Carpenter's Estate, 170 Pa. 203, 208, 32 A. 637, 29 L.R.A. 145; Crumley v. Hall, 202 Ga. 588, 43 S.E.2d 646; Welsh v. James, 408 Ill. 18, 21, 95 N.E.2d 872; Owens v. Owens, 100 N.C. 240, 241, 6 S.E. 794; Gollnik v. Mengel, 112 Minn. 349, 351, 128 N.W. 292; Eversole v. Eversole, 169 Ky. 793, 795, 185 S.W. 487, L.R.A.1916E, 593; see also Cleaveland, Hewitt & Clark, Probate Law & Practice, p. 807; 1 Woerner, American Law of Administration (3d Ed.) § 64a. These authorities make clear that judicial tribunals have no concern with the policy of legislation and that they cannot engraft upon the provisions of the statutes of descent and distribution an exception to bar one who feloniously kills his bene-factor from succeeding to the latter's property. A number of cases which accord in result with those adopting the doctrine of the Riggs case are concerned with contract rights as distinguished from statutory rights and when properly analyzed may be harmonized with decisions supporting the majority view. This is well illustrated by a comparison of two Ohio cases. In Filmore v. Metropolitan Life Ins. Co., 82 Ohio St. 208, 92 N.E. 26, 28 L.R.A.,N.S., 675, a husband who was the beneficiary under a policy insuring his wife's life and who had been convicted of killing her was denied recovery. In Deem v. Millikin, 6 Ohio Cir.Ct.R. 357, 359, af-firmed, 53 Ohio St. 668, 44 N.E. 1134, it was held that a murderer was not barred from inheriting from his victim. Thus, the killer was barred by his felonious act in the former but not in the latter. The same holds true of two Pennsylvania cases, Green v. Metropolitan Life Ins. Co., 23 Pa.Dist. & Co.R. 574, and In re Carpenter's Estate, 170 Pa. 203, 32 A. 637, 29 L.R.A. 145. See note, 70 A.L.R. 1539, 1541. See also Murchison v. Murchison, Tex.Civ.App., 203 S.W. 423, where a wife who had killed her husband and was denied recovery as the beneficiary under a policy of insurance on his life was, as his sole heir, awarded the proceeds of the policy after they had been paid into his estate. In life insurance cases the usual equitable principles and the law pertaining to fraud are applied to contract rights. These principles are not, however, applied in cases involving succession to property by inheritance or devise. The distinc-tion lies in the fact that in the former cases the result may be reached without violating the statutes of descent.

The plaintiffs seek to distinguish the majority rule as one relating to intestate but not to testate estates. The suggestion is made that this is so since laws governing intestacy are purely statutory, while the rules controlling wills are subject to judicial control. This hardly constitutes a sound basis for distinction, for, as was pointed out earlier in this opinion, descent of the decedent's property in this case would be fully dependent upon the statutory provisions mentioned, whether it was testate or intestate. As Dean Ames has stated in discussing the Riggs case, "In the case of the devise, if the legal title did not pass to the devisee, it must be because the testator's will was revoked by the crime of his grandson. But when the legislature has enacted that no will shall be revoked except in certain specified modes, by what right can the court declare a will revoked by some other mode? In the case of inheritance, surely, the court cannot lawfully say that the title does not descend, when the statute, the supreme law, says that it shall descend." Ames, Lectures on Legal History, p. 312.

After full consideration of the reasons advanced by counsel and those contained in the many authorities which have been cited, it is our conclusion that, at the time when § 7062 was originally adopted as § 1316i of the 1947 Supplement to the General Statutes, the right of a surviving husband who had killed his wife to succeed to the latter's property was dependent solely upon the application of the provisions of either the statutes as to wills or the statutes as to succession, as the case might be, unaffected by any such rule of the common law as is claimed by the plaintiffs. The effect of the adoption of § 7062 is the remaining question. The conclusion just stated leaves little force to the plaintiffs' principal argument in support of the construction of § 7062 for which they contend. It limits the question of interpretation simply to a determination of the effect to be accorded this section as an amendment of the statutes concerning wills and succession referred to above. As so viewed, its wording is so clear and free from ambiguity as to leave little room for doubt as to its meaning. In so far as applicable to the facts of the instant case, it simply states that "[n]o person finally adjudged guilty * * * of murder in the first or second degree shall be entitled to inherit or take any part" of the property "of the person killed," either by virtue of any succession statute or under the will of such person. When § 7062 is read in connection with the other statutes to which reference has been made, the plaintiffs' suggestion that one convicted of "manslaughter" of the testatrix and not "murder" is by its terms barred from taking under her will is without merit.

The language of § 7062 is so plain that we merely mention certain factors which confirm the fact that it means just what it says. Similar statutes have been enacted in a large number of states, apparently because of a general opinion that otherwise inheritance under statute or devise could not be barred to one guilty of killing his benefactor. These statutes have been strictly construed as penal statutes and the prohibition held to extend no further than the crimes named and the estates delineated. We mention but a few of the many cases so holding. In Estate of Kirby, 162 Cal. 91, 92, 121 P. 370, 39 L.R.A.,N.S., 1088; In re Tarlo's Estate, 315 Pa. 321, 324, 172 A. 139; Harrison v. Moncravie, 8 Cir., 264 F. 776, 784; Blanks v. Jiggetts, 192 Va. 337, 342, 64 S.E.2d 809, 24 A.L.R.2d 1114; Hogg v. Whitham, 120 Kan. 341, 342, 242 P. 1021; In re Estate of Emerson, 191 Iowa 900, 901, 906, 183 N.W. 327; Wenker v. Landon, 161 Or. 265, 271, 88 P.2d 971; Smith v. Greenburg, 121 Colo. 417, 422, 218 P.2d 514; Strickland v. Wysowatcky, Colo., 250 P.2d 199.

Only three decisions have been brought to our attention where, under such a statute, the plaintiffs' interpretation is sustained: Garner v. Phillips, 229 N.C. 160, 162, 47 S.E.2d 845; Smith v. Todd, 155 S.C. 323, 336, 152 S.E. 506, 70 A.L.R. 1529; Metropolitan Life Ins. Co. v. Hill, 115 W.Va. 515, 518, 177 S.E. 188. The last two of these are life insurance cases.

A final cogent fact indicative that the legislature's intent in adopting § 7062 was not to exclude other than "convicted murderers" from taking appears from a colloquy in the house of representatives. When the bill was proposed for passage, a member asked whether under it, if one feloniously killed his benefactor and committed suicide before he was convicted of the crime, his estate could inherit. The chairman of the committee presenting the bill stated in reply: "Mr. Speaker, it would seem to me that is clearly set forth in the bill. The slayer must first have been found guilty. That particular point is covered. Under this bill the intent is to cover a situation where the felonious slayer has been found guilty. The provisions of the law would not become operative until the person's guilt had been established. The situation which the gentleman from Old Lyme has mentioned would not come under the provisions of this bill." Conn.H.Proc., 1947 Sess., H.B. 64 (May 26, 1947). We take judicial notice of this transcript of the legislative proceedings. See General Hospital Society v. New Haven County, 127 Conn. 53, 59, 14 A.2d 746; Institute of Living v. Town and City of Hartford, 133 Conn. 258, 265, 50 A.2d 822. The chairman's statement was in the nature of a supplemental report to the legislature and, like a committee report, may properly be considered as an aid to the determination of the legislative intent. 2 Sutherland, Statutory Construction (3d Ed.), p. 502; Connnecticut Rural Roads Improvement Ass'n v. Hurley, 124 Conn. 20, 26, 197 A. 90. Section 7062 does not preclude a felonious killer of his benefactor, who is his wife, from succeeding to her property, whether by will or under the succession statute, unless he has been convicted of either first or second degree murder.

Inasmuch as all the facts alleged in the complaint as amended stood admitted upon the demurrer, the case presented a pure question of law for determination. Since the prayers for relief, predicated upon these facts, sought not only a declaratory judgment but also affirmative and coercive relief, the demurrer was properly addressed to the complaint on the ground stated. Hill v. Wright, 128 Conn. 12, 16, 20 A.2d 388.

There is no error.

JENNINGS and INGLIS, JJ., concur.

O'SULLIVAN, Associate Justice (concurring). Since the General Assembly has now determined our public policy respecting inheritance by unlawful homicide, I can concur in the result reached by my colleagues. Such inheritance is prohibited, under the limitations set by legislative enactment, only when the homicide amounts to murder and only when the would-be inheritor has been convicted of that crime. General Statutes § 7062. I disagree, however, with that part of the opinion which holds that, prior to the passage of the statute in 1947, Sup.1947, § 1316i, the common law of Connecticut permitted a murderer to take from his victim by will or descent. A majority of my brethren take the position that, in spite of its repulsiveness, inheritance by murder was legally justified before 1947 because, they say, its prevention would have required the court to nullify the statute of wills and the statute of descent and distribution. This reasoning, it seems to me, is faulty. Equity offers a method which will result in nullifying neither statute. Under that method, both statutes are permitted to operate. By resort to equity, however, the property passing to the murderer would be impressed with a constructive trust for the benefit of those who, in case of testacy, would have been entitled to the property on the death of the testator if the devise or bequest to the murderer had been revoked, or for the benefit of those who, in case of intestacy, would have been the heirs or next of kin of the intestate if the murderer had predeceased him. Restatement, Restitution § 187; Colton v. Wade, Del.Ch., 80 A.2d 923, 925; Vesey v. Vesey, Minn., 54 N.W.2d 385, 388; Whitney v. Lott, 134 N.J.Eq. 586, 590, 36 A.2d 888; Riggs v. Palmer, 115 N.Y. 506, 511, 22 N.E. 188, 5 L.R.A. 340; Bryant v. Bryant, 193 N.C. 372, 377, 137 S.E. 188, 51 A.L.R. 1100; Ames, Lectures on Legal History, p. 310; 3 Bogert, Trusts, § 478, p. 50; 4 Pomeroy, Equity Jurisprudence (5th Ed.) § 1054d; 3 Scott, Trusts, § 492; note, 51 A.L.R. 1096, 1098. I refuse to concede that equity would permit a person to profit from such an atrocious act as murder.

BALDWIN, J., concurs.

Notes

1. By a series of amendments enacted between 1965 and 1983, Section 45–279 of the Connecticut General Statutes (the successor statute to Section 7062 which is discussed in the principal case) was changed to read:

(a) A person finally adjudged guilty, either as the principal or accessory, of murder, shall not inherit or receive any part of the estate of the deceased, whether under the provisions of any act relating to intestate succession, or as devisee or legatee, or otherwise under the will of the deceased, or receive any property as beneficiary or survivor of the deceased; and such person shall not inherit or receive any part of the estate of any other person when such homicide terminated an intermediate estate, or hastened the time of enjoyment. With respect to inheritance under the will of the deceased, or rights to property as beneficiary of the deceased, the person whose participation in the estate of another or whose right to property as such beneficiary is so prevented under the provisions of this section shall be considered to have predeceased the person killed. With respect to property owned in joint tenancy with rights of survivorship with the deceased, the final adjudication as guilty, either as principal or accessory, of murder, shall be a severance of the joint tenancy, and shall convert the joint tenancy into a tenancy in common as to the person so adjudged and the deceased but not as to any remaining joint tenant or tenants, such severance being effective as of the time such adjudication of guilty becomes final. When such jointly owned property is real property, a certified copy of the final adjudication as guilty shall be recorded by the fiduciary of the deceased's estate, or may be recorded by any other interested party in the land records of the town where such real property is situated.

(b) In all other cases where a defendant has been convicted of killing another person, the right of such defendant to inherit or take any part of such estate of the person killed or to inherit or take any estate as to which such homicide terminated an intermediate estate, or hastened the time of enjoyment, or to take any property as beneficiary or survivor of the deceased shall be determined by the common law, including equity. *ie one shall not benef from own wrongdoing*

[Subsection (c) makes the statute applicable to a beneficiary of a life insurance policy or annuity and states that a conviction under certain designated statutes shall be conclusive for the purposes of this subsection.]

The estate in Bird v. Plunkett was substantial (reported to be in the neighborhood of $300,000) and the crime serious. The judge who presided at the criminal trial was quoted as follows: "The trial was without any evidence of circumstances which would mitigate or extenuate the shooting * * *." Clark, Crime Does Not Pay—Except Perhaps for Homicide, 27 Conn.B.J. 170, 171 (1953). Because the issue of the felonious slayer inheriting from his victim had not arisen again in Connecticut by 1967, it appears that the addition of subsection (b) in that year represented a delayed reaction to the analysis and holding in Bird v. Plunkett. Does the cryptic paragraph (b) guarantee that a case presenting the same facts would be decided differently today?

2. Practically all jurisdictions now have statutes that bar a slayer from taking property from the victim because of the death. Some of the statutes require that the slayer be convicted of murder (or, as variously described in the statutes, "of intentionally causing the death," "of willfully causing or procuring the death," or "of an unlawful killing"). A husband who killed his wife but who committed suicide before any criminal action was taken against him was allowed to inherit his wife's estate by intestacy, United Trust Co. v. Pyke, 199 Kan. 1, 427 P.2d 67 (1967); Tarlo's Estate, 315 Pa. 321, 172 A. 139 (1934) (the law of Pennsylvania has since been changed to no longer require an adjudication of guilt). A man, whom the jury found guilty of murdering his wife and son, died of bone cancer before the penalty phase of his trial began, rendering his conviction unofficial because he was not sentenced. At issue was the question whether his or his wife's heirs were entitled to inherit nearly one million in insurance money. A hearing was scheduled for January 15, 1985, in the Los Angeles County Superior Court on a request by the district attorney's office for a posthumous sentence of the deceased slayer in order to settle the inheritance issue. The lawyer for the slayer's heirs observed that "Mr. Morgan [the husband-slayer] is no longer here, and any time a person is sentenced, that party must be in court". N.Y. Times, Dec. 26, 1984, p. 11, col. 6. A conviction in one state has been held not to be a bar in another state. Harrison v. Moncravie, 264 F. 776 (8th Cir. 1920), appeal dismissed 255 U.S. 562, 41 S.Ct. 374, 65 L.Ed. 787 (1921).

 The Uniform Probate Code Section 2–803(a) and (e) bars "[A] surviving spouse, heir or devisee who feloniously and intentionally kills the decedent." "A final judgment of conviction of felonious and intentional killing is conclusive * * *," but, if there is no such conviction, the civil court may find the facts on the basis of a preponderance of evidence. For a similar procedure see Cal. Prob. Code § 258. It has been held that principles of double jeopardy, res judicata, and collateral estoppel do not bar a civil proceeding to determine a daughter's entitlement to inherit under her mother's will, following the daughter's acquittal in a criminal trial on charges of murdering her mother. Matter of Estate of Congdon, 309 N.W.2d 261 (Minn.1981) (court cited differences in parties and degrees of burden of proof between the two actions). The civil proceedings may deal with issues of guilt and proximate cause traditionally reserved for the criminal process. See e.g., Matter of Estate of Eliasen, 105 Idaho 234, 668 P.2d 110 (1983) (widow's gunshot wound of her husband interrupted his chemotherapy treatments for stomach cancer and was a substantial factor and proximate cause of his death, thereby barring her from inheriting from him); Estate of Sargent v. Benton State Bank, 279 Ark. 402, 652 S.W.2d 10 (1983) (evidence insufficient to demonstrate that son's involvement with his brother and mother in the murder of his father made him an accomplice). A conviction in the criminal proceeding does not always render the guilty party ineligible to inherit from his victim. See e.g., In re Estate of Klein, 474 Pa. 416, 378 A.2d 1182 (1977) (accident, caused by husband's drunken driving that resulted in his wife's death for which he was convicted of involuntary manslaughter, did not constitute a "willful" slaying under the statute); Matter of Estate of Safran, 102 Wis.2d 79, 306 N.W.2d 27, 25 A.L.R.4th 766 (1981) (conviction, on a plea of no contest, of causing his mother's death by "reckless conduct" did not automatically disqualify son from inheriting; matter remanded to see whether killing was unlawful and intentional). Should the fact that the slayer was under a disability and could not be convicted in a criminal action preclude a holding in the civil proceeding that the slayer is barred from inheriting? Compare Matter of Estates of Josephsons, 297 N.W.2d 444 (N.D.1980) (13-year old son-slayer barred from inheriting from parents whom he had shot) with Estates of Ladd, 91 Cal.App.3d 219, 153 Cal.Rptr. 888 (1979) (mother acquitted on charge of murdering two sons by reason of insanity entitled to inherit from them because she did not "unlawfully and intentionally" cause their deaths) and In re Vadlamudi Estate, 183 N.J.Super. 342, 443 A.2d 1113 (1982) (same principle recognized; case remanded for findings as to slayer's sanity).

The debate as to whether the common law barred the slayer without statutory authorization continues to arise in situations where the statute is not applicable. To the effect that if the statute does not bar the slayer the common law maxim cannot be invoked to impose a constructive trust on him, see Wadsworth v. Siek, 254 N.E.2d 738 (Prob.Ct. Cuyahoga County, Ohio, 1970); for the opposite view, see Hill v. Lewis, 21 Md.App. 121, 318 A.2d 850 (1974) (husband not, however, barred because the killing was not proved); Metropolitan Life Insurance Company v. Wenckus, 244 A.2d 424 (Maine, 1968) (widow who pleaded guilty to voluntary manslaughter barred from taking husband's life insurance; the court indicated the same rule would apply to his estate). In a recent New York case, Estate of Janice L. Jordan Grant, N.Y.L.J., April 12, 1984, p. 12, col. 6 (Surr.Ct. Bronx County), the surrogate held that a husband convicted of manslaughter in the second degree (recklessly causing the death of another) in the death of his wife, could not take an intestate share in her estate or receive the proceeds of an insurance policy on her life of which he was the designated beneficiary. The Surrogate relied on Riggs v. Palmer, cited in the main case, and a 1984 statute (admittedly not controlling) providing for forfeiture of the proceeds of certain crimes (N.Y. CPLR Art. 13–A) as expressing a public policy supportive of a denial of the husband's rights even though the crime of which he was convicted was not an "intentional killing."

3. It was argued on behalf of the plaintiff Bird that the limited purpose of the statute was to permit the introduction of the judgment of guilty in a civil action. A Minnesota case examines in depth the common law rule that a criminal judgment is not admissible as evidence in a civil action and holds that it is not applicable to exclude evidence of a conviction of murder in a case where husband is claiming $1,055,000 of insurance on the life of his wife whom he has been convicted of slaying. Travelers Insurance Company v. Thompson, 281 Minn. 547, 163 N.W.2d 289 (1968).

4. On the problem generally, see Maki and Kaplan, Elmer's Case Revisited: The Problem of the Murdering Heir, 41 Ohio St.L.J. 905 (1980); McGovern, Homicide and Succession to Property, 68 Mich.L.Rev. 65 (1969); Wade, Acquisition of Property by Wilfully Killing Another, A Statutory Solution, 49 Harv.L.Rev. 715 (1936); Annot., Homicide as Precluding Taking under Will or by Intestacy, 25 A.L.R.4th 787.

Litigation began in 1954, which was not finally concluded until 1968, involving the famous will of Stephen Girard who, at his death in 1831, left a major share of his substantial fortune to the City of Philadelphia as trustee to establish a school for "poor, male, white orphan children" between the ages of 6 and 10. By 1954 the school, known as Girard College, had prospered with an enrollment of over 1,000 students and an endowment of almost one hundred million dollars. The endowment and financial administration of the school were managed by the City Treasurer's office while the responsibility for educational policy was vested in a self-perpetuating Board of Directors of City Trusts. In 1954 two Negro boys, who were qualified in every way except race, applied for and were denied admission. This action was upheld by the Pennsylvania courts on the ground that "the beneficiaries of the charity of Stephen Girard are not being determined by the State of Pennsylvania, nor by the City of Philadelphia, nor by this Court, but solely by Girard himself in the exercise of his undoubted right to dispose of his property by will * * *." In re Girard's Estate, 386 Pa. 548, 550, 551, 127 A.2d 287, 288 (1956). The Supreme Court of the United States, summarily and without hearing oral argument, upset this ruling and held that the City Board was engaged in state action proscribed by the Fourteenth Amendment. Pennsylvania v. Board of Directors of City Trusts, 353 U.S. 230, 77 S.Ct. 806, 1 L.Ed.2d 792 (1957), rehearing denied 353 U.S. 989, 77 S.Ct. 1281, 1 L.Ed.2d 1146. The decision was a per curiam opinion citing only Brown v. Board of Education, 347 U.S. 483, 74 S.Ct. 686, 98 L.Ed. 873, 38 A.L.R.2d 1180 (1954). On remand the Pennsylvania courts, true to their earlier promises, removed the City Board as trustee, replacing it with a "private" board made up of thirteen citizens, a number of whom were reported to have been members of the former board. The decisions did not make clear what agency was then responsible for investing and managing the endowment funds. In re Girard College Trusteeship, 391 Pa. 434, 138 A.2d 844 (1958). The U.S. Supreme Court denied the petition for certiorari, 357 U.S. 570, 78 S.Ct. 1383, 2 L.Ed.2d 1546 (1958), rehearing denied 358 U.S. 858, 79 S.Ct. 14, 3 L.Ed.2d 92. See generally, Clark,

Charitable Trusts, the Fourteenth Amendment and the Will of Stephen Girard, 66 Yale L.J. 979 (1957).

In 1968 the Third Circuit Court of Appeals upheld a District Court order that Girard College be desegregated, holding that there existed a "close, indispensable relationship between the College, the City of Philadelphia and the Commonwealth of Pennsylvania * * *" and that the judicial substitution of private trustees in place of the City Board was impermissible state action. The majority opinion stated "that the decision [of the Supreme Court] in Evans v. Newton governs the issue before us." Commonwealth of Pennsylvania v. Brown, 392 F.2d 120 (C.A.3d, 1968), certiorari denied 391 U.S. 921, 88 S.Ct. 1811, 20 L.Ed.2d 657 (1968).

The several holdings in the Girard College case influenced the claims made by litigants in other cases involving charitable trusts which contained discriminatory limitations and shaped the responses made by the courts to those claims. That influence is apparent throughout the Evans v. Newton litigation. The Georgia courts, for instance, had relied almost exclusively on the Supreme Court's 1958 denial of certiorari as justification for permitting the transfer of the park to private trustees. Evans v. Newton, 220 Ga. 280, 138 S.E.2d 573 (1964), reversed 382 U.S. 296, 86 S.Ct. 486, 15 L.Ed.2d 373 (1966). Evans v. Abney, infra, presents an issue which was not raised in the Girard College litigation. The outcome demonstrates that a testator's control over his property remains substantial long after his death.

EVANS v. ABNEY

Supreme Court of the United States, 1970.
396 U.S. 435, 90 S.Ct. 628, 24 L.Ed.2d 634.

Mr. Justice BLACK delivered the opinion of the Court.

Once again this Court must consider the constitutional implications of the 1911 will of United States Senator A. O. Bacon of Georgia which conveyed property in trust to Senator Bacon's home city of Macon for the creation of a public park for the exclusive use of the white people of that city. As a result of our earlier decision in this case which held that the park, Baconsfield, could not continue to be operated on a racially discriminatory basis, Evans v. Newton, 382 U.S. 296, 86 S.Ct. 486, 15 L.Ed.2d 373 (1966), the Supreme Court of Georgia ruled that Senator Bacon's intention to provide a park for whites only had become impossible to fulfill and that accordingly the trust had failed and the parkland and other trust property had reverted by operation of Georgia law to the heirs of the Senator. 224 Ga. 826, 165 S.E.2d 160 (1968). Petitioners, the same Negro citizens of Macon who have sought in the courts to integrate the park, contend that this termination of the trust violates their rights to equal protection and due process under the Fourteenth Amendment. We granted certiorari because of the importance of the questions involved. 394 U.S. 1012, 89 S.Ct. 1628, 23 L.Ed.2d 38 (1969). For the reasons to be stated, we are of the opinion that the judgment of the Supreme Court of Georgia should be, and it is, affirmed.

The early background of this litigation was summarized by Mr. Justice Douglas in his opinion for the Court in Evans v. Newton, 382 U.S., at 297–298, 86 S.Ct. at 487–488:

In 1911 United States Senator Augustus O. Bacon executed a will that devised to the Mayor and Council of the City of Macon, Georgia, a tract of land which, after the death of the Senator's wife and daughters, was to be used as 'a park and pleasure ground' for white people only, the Senator stating in the will that while he had only the kindest feeling for the Negroes he was of the opinion that 'in their social relations the two races (white and negro) should be forever separate.' The will provided that the park should be under the control of a Board of Managers of seven persons, all of whom were to be white. The city kept the park segregated for some years but in time let Negroes use it, taking the position that the park was a public facility which it could not constitutionally manage and maintain on a segregated basis.

Thereupon, individual members of the Board of Managers of the park brought this suit in a state court against the City of Macon and the trustees of certain residuary beneficiaries of Senator Bacon's estate, asking that the city be removed as trustee and that the court appoint new trustees, to whom title to the park would be transferred. The city answered, alleging it could not legally enforce racial segregation in the park. The other defendants admitted the allegation and requested that the city be removed as trustee.

Several Negro citizens of Macon intervened, alleging that the racial limitation was contrary to the laws and public policy of the United States, and asking that the court refuse to appoint private trustees. Thereafter the city resigned as trustee and amended its answer accordingly. Moreover, other heirs of Senator Bacon intervened and they and the defendants other than the city asked for reversion of the trust property to the Bacon estate in the event that the prayer of the petition were denied.

The Georgia court accepted the resignation of the city as trustee and appointed three individuals as new trustees, finding it unnecessary to pass on the other claims of the heirs. On appeal by the Negro intervenors, the Supreme Court of Georgia affirmed, holding that Senator Bacon had the right to give and bequeath his property to a limited class, that charitable trusts are subject to supervision of a court of equity, and that the power to appoint new trustees so that the purpose of the trust would not fail was clear. 220 Ga. 280, 138 S.E.2d 573.

The Court in Evans v. Newton, supra, went on to reverse the judgment of the Georgia Supreme Court and to hold that the public character of Baconsfield "requires that it be treated as a public institution subject to the command of the Fourteenth Amendment, regardless of who now has title under state law." 382 U.S., at 302, 86 S.Ct., at 490. Thereafter, the Georgia Supreme Court interpreted this Court's reversal of its decision as requiring that Baconsfield be henceforth operated on a nondiscriminatory basis. "Under these circumstances," the state high court held, "we are of the opinion that the sole purpose for which the trust was created has become impossible of accomplishment and has been terminated." Evans v. Newton, 221 Ga. 870, 871, 148 S.E.2d 329, 330 (1966). Without further elaboration of this holding, the case was remanded to the Georgia trial court to consider the motion of Guyton G. Abney and others, successor trustees of Senator Bacon's estate, for a ruling that the trust had become unenforceable and that accordingly the trust property had reverted to the Bacon estate and to certain named heirs of the Senator. The motion was opposed by petitioners and by the Attorney General of Georgia, both of whom argued that the trust should be saved by applying the *cy pres* doctrine to amend the terms of the will by striking the racial restrictions and opening Baconsfield to all the citizens of Macon without regard to race or color. The trial court, however, refused to appy *cy pres*. It held that the doctrine was inapplicable because the park's segregated, whites-only character was an essential and inseparable part of the testator's plan. Since the "sole purpose" of the trust was thus in irreconcilable conflict with the constitutional mandate expressed in our opinion in Evans v. Newton, the trial court ruled that the Baconsfield trust had failed and that the trust property had by operation of law reverted to the heirs of Senator Bacon. On appeal, the Supreme Court of Georgia affirmed.

We are of the opinion that in ruling as they did the Georgia courts did no more than apply well-settled general principles of Georgia law to determine the meaning and effect of a Georgia will. At the time Senator Bacon made his will Georgia cities and towns were, and they still are, authorized to accept devises of property for the establishment and preservation of "parks and pleasure grounds" and to hold the property thus received in charitable trust for the exclusive benefit of the class of persons named by the testator. Ga.Code Ann., c. 69–5 (1967); Ga.Code Ann. §§ 108–203, 108–207 (1959). These provisions of the Georgia Code explicitly authorized the testator to include, if he should choose, racial restrictions such as those found in Senator Bacon's will. The city accepted the trust with these restrictions in it. When this Court in Evans v. Newton, supra, held that the continued operation of Baconsfield as a segregated park was unconstitutional, the particular purpose of the Baconsfield trust as stated in the will failed under Georgia law. The question then properly before the Georgia Supreme Court was whether as a matter of state law the doctrine of *cy pres* should be applied to prevent the trust itself from failing. Petitioners urged that the *cy pres* doctrine allowed the Georgia courts to strike the racially restrictive clauses in Bacon's will so that the terms of the trust could be fulfilled without violating the Constitution.

The Georgia *cy pres* statutes upon which petitioners relied provide:

"When a valid charitable bequest is incapable for some reason of execution in the exact manner provided by the testator, donor, or founder, a court of equity will carry it into effect in such a way as will as nearly as possible effectuate his intention." Ga.Code Ann. § 108–202 (1959).

"A devise or bequest to a charitable use will be sustained and carried out in this State; and in all cases where there is a general intention manifested by the testator to effect a certain purpose, and the particular mode in which he directs it to be done shall fail from any cause, a court of chancery may, by approximation, effectuate the purpose in a manner most similar to that indicated by the testator." Ga.Code Ann. § 113–815 (1959).

The Georgia courts have held that the fundamental purpose of these *cy pres* provisions is to allow the court to carry out the general charitable intent of the testator where this intent might otherwise be thwarted by the impossibility of the particular plan or scheme provided by the testator. Moss v. Youngblood, 187 Ga. 188, 200 S.E. 689 (1938). But this underlying logic of the *cy pres* doctrine implies that there is a certain class of cases in which the doctrine cannot be applied. Professor Scott in his treatise on trusts states this limitation on the doctrine of *cy pres* which is common to many States as follows:

> "It is not true that a charitable trust never fails where it is impossible to carry out the particular purpose of the testator. In some cases * * * it appears that the accomplishment of the particular purpose and only that purpose was desired by the testator and that he had no more general charitable intent and that he would presumably have preferred to have the whole trust fail if the particular purpose is impossible of accomplishment. In such a case the cy pres doctrine is not applicable." 4 A. Scott, The Law of Trusts § 399, p. 3085 (3d ed. 1967).

In this case, Senator Bacon provided an unusual amount of information in his will from which the Georgia courts could determine the limits of his charitable purpose. Immediately after specifying that the park should be for "the sole, perpetual and unending, use, benefit and enjoyment of the white women, white girls, white boys and white children of the City of Macon," the Senator stated that "the said property under no circumstances * * * (is) to be * * * at any time for any reason devoted to any other purpose or use excepting so far as herein specifically authorized." And the Senator continued:

> "I take occasion to say that in limiting the use and enjoyment of this property perpetually to white people, I am not influenced by any unkindness of feeling or want of consideration for the Negroes, or colored people. On the contrary I have for them the kindest feeling, and for many of them esteem and regard, while for some of them I have sincere personal affection.

> "I am, however, without hesitation in the opinion that in their social relations the two races * * * should be forever separate and that they should not have pleasure or recreation grounds to be used or enjoyed, together and in common."

The Georgia courts, construing Senator Bacon's will as a whole, Yerbey v. Chandler, 194 Ga. 263, 21 S.E.2d 636 (1942), concluded from this and other language in the will that the Senator's charitable intent was not "general" but extended only to the establishment of a segregated park for the benefit of white people. The Georgia trial court found that "Senator Bacon could not have used language more clearly indicating his intent that the benefits of Baconsfield should be extended to white persons only, or more clearly indicating that this limitation was an essential and indispensable part of his plan for Baconsfield." App. 519. Since racial separation was found to be an inseparable part of the testator's intent, the Georgia courts held that the State's *cy pres* doctrine could not be used to alter the will to permit racial integration. See Ford v. Thomas, 111 Ga. 493, 36 S.E. 841 (1900); Adams v. Bass, 18 Ga. 130 (1855). The Baconsfield trust was therefore held to have failed, and, under Georgia law, "[w]here a trust is expressly created, but [its] uses * * * fail from any cause, a resulting trust is implied for the benefit of the grantor, or testator, or his heirs." Ga.Code Ann. § 108–106(4) (1959).[1] The Georgia courts concluded, in effect, that Senator Bacon would have rather had the whole trust fail than have Baconsfield integrated.

When a city park is destroyed because the Constitution requires it to be integrated, there is reason for everyone to be disheartened. We agree with petitioners that in such a case it is not enough to find that the state court's result was reached through the application of established principles of state law. No state law or act can prevail in the face of contrary federal law, and the federal courts must search out the fact and truth of any proceeding or transaction to determine if the Constitution has been violated. Presbyterian Church in United States v. Hull Church, 393 U.S. 440, 89 S.Ct. 601, 21 L.Ed.2d 658 (1969); New York Times Co. v. Sullivan, 376 U.S. 254, 84 S.Ct. 710, 11 L.Ed.2d 686 (1964). Here, however, the action of the Georgia Supreme Court declaring the Baconsfield trust terminated presents no violation of constitutionally protected rights, and any harshness that may have resulted from the state court's decision can be attributed solely to its intention to effectuate as nearly as possible the explicit terms of Senator Bacon's will.

Petitioners first argue that the action of the Georgia court violates the United States Constitution in that it imposes a drastic "penalty," the "forfeiture" of the park, merely because of the city's compliance with the constitutional mandate expressed by this Court in Evans v. Newton. Of course, Evans v. Newton did not speak to the problem of whether Ba-

---

1. Although Senator Bacon's will did not contain an express provision granting a reverter to any party should the trust fail, § 108–106(4) of the Georgia Code quoted in the text makes such an omission irrelevant under state law. At one point in the Senator's will he did grant "all remainders and reversions" to the city of Macon, but the Supreme Court of Georgia showed in its opinion that this language did not relate in any way to what should happen upon a failure of the trust but was relevant only to the initial vesting of the property in the city. The Georgia court said:

"Senator Bacon devised a life estate in the trust property to his wife and two daughters, and the language pointed out by the intervenors appears in the following provision of the will: 'When my wife, Virginia Lamar Bacon and my two daughters, Mary Louise Bacon Sparks and Augusta Lamar Bacon Curry, shall all have departed this life, and immediately upon the death of the last survivor of them, it is my will that all right, title and interest in and to said property hereinbefore described and bounded, both legal and equitable, including all remainders and reversions and every estate in the same of whatsoever kind, shall thereupon vest in and belong to the Mayor and Council of the City of Macon, and to their successors forever, in trust etc.' This language concerned remainders and reversions prior to the vesting of the legal title in the City of Macon, as trustee, and not to remainders and reversions occurring because of a failure of the trust, which Senator Bacon apparently did not contemplate, and for which he made no provision." 224 Ga. 826, 831, 165 S.E.2d 160, 165.

[Editors' Note: Throughout the book, editors' footnotes to opinions and other quoted materials are identified as such. All others are from the original material. Footnotes to opinions and other quoted materials are numbered consecutively from the beginning of each chapter. Editors' footnotes are indicated by asterisks.]

consfield should or could continue to operate as a park; it held only that its continued operation as a park had to be without racial discrimination. But petitioners now want to extend that holding to forbid the Georgia courts from closing Baconsfield on the ground that such a closing would penalize the city and its citizens for complying with the Constitution. We think, however, that the will of Senator Bacon and Georgia law provide all the justification necessary for imposing such a "penalty." The construction of wills is essentially a state-law question, Lyeth v. Hoey, 305 U.S. 188, 59 S.Ct. 155, 83 L.Ed. 119 (1938), and in this case the Georgia Supreme Court, as we read its opinion, interpreted Senator Bacon's will as embodying a preference for termination of the park rather than its integration. Given this, the Georgia court had no alternative under its relevant trust laws, which are long standing and neutral with regard to race, but to end the Baconsfield trust and return the property to the Senator's heirs.

A second argument for petitioners stresses the similarities between this case and the case in which a city holds an absolute fee simple title to a public park and then closes that park of its own accord solely to avoid the effect of a prior court order directing that the park be integrated as the Fourteenth Amendment commands. Yet, assuming *arguendo* that the closing of the park would in those circumstances violate the Equal Protection Clause, that case would be clearly distinguishable from the case at bar because there it is the State and not a private party which is injecting the racially discriminatory motivation. In the case at bar there is not the slightest indication that any of the Georgia judges involved were motivated by racial animus or discriminatory intent of any sort in construing and enforcing Senator Bacon's will. Nor is there any indication that Senator Bacon in drawing up his will was persuaded or induced to include racial restrictions by the fact that such restrictions were permitted by the Georgia trust statutes. *Supra,* at 630–631. On the contrary, the language of the Senator's will shows that the racial restrictions were solely the product of the testator's own full-blown social philosophy. Similarly, the situation presented in this case is also easily distinguishable from that presented in Shelley v. Kraemer, 334 U.S. 1, 68 S.Ct. 836, 92 L.Ed. 1161 (1948), where we held unconstitutional state judicial action which had affirmatively enforced a private scheme of discrimination against Negroes. Here the effect of the Georgia decision eliminated all discrimination against Negroes in the park by eliminating the park itself, and the termination of the park was a loss shared equally by the white and Negro citizens of Macon since both races would have enjoyed a constitutional right of equal access to the park's facilities had it continued.

Petitioners also contend that since Senator Bacon did not expressly provide for a reverter in the event that the racial restrictions of the trust failed, no one can know with absolute certainty that the Senator would have preferred termination of the park rather than its integration, and the decision of the Georgia court therefore involved a matter of choice. It might be difficult to argue with these assertions if they stood alone, but then petitioners conclude: "Its [the court's] choice, the anti-Negro choice, violates the Fourteenth Amendment, whether it be called a 'guess,' an item in 'social philosophy,' or anything else at all." We do not understand petitioners to be contending here that the Georgia judges were motivated either consciously or unconsciously by a desire to discriminate against Negroes. In any case, there is, as noted above, absolutely nothing before this Court to support a finding of such motivation. What remains of petitioners' argument is the idea that the Georgia courts had a constitutional obligation in this case to resolve any doubt about the testator's intent in favor of preserving the trust. Thus stated, we see no merit in the argument. The only choice the Georgia courts either had or exercised in this regard was their judicial judgment in construing Bacon's will to determine his intent, and the Constitution imposes no requirement upon the Georgia courts to approach Bacon's will any differently than they would approach any will creating any charitable trust of any kind. Surely the Fourteenth Amendment is not violated where, as here, a state court operating in its judicial capacity fairly applies its normal principles of construction to determine the testator's true intent in establishing a charitable trust and then reaches a conclusion with regard to that intent which, because of the operation of neutral and non-discriminatory state trust laws, effectively denies everyone, whites as well as Negroes, the benefits of the trust.

Another argument made by petitioners is that the decision of the Georgia courts holding that the Baconsfield trust had "failed" must rest logically on the unspoken premise that the presence or proximity of Negroes in Baconsfield would destroy the desirability of the park for whites. This argument reflects a rather fundamental misunderstanding of Georgia law. The Baconsfield trust "failed" under that law not because of any belief on the part of any living person that whites and Negroes might not enjoy being together but, rather, because Senator Bacon who died many years ago intended that the park remain forever for the exclusive use of white people.

Petitioners also advance a number of considerations of public policy in opposition to the conclusion which we have reached. In particular, they regret, as we do, the loss of the Baconsfield trust to the City of Macon, and they are concerned lest we set a precedent under which other charitable trusts will be terminated. It bears repeating that our holding today reaffirms the traditional role of the States in determining whether or not to apply their *cy pres* doctrines to particular trusts. Nothing we have said here prevents a state court from applying its *cy pres* rule in a case where the Georgia court, for example, might not apply its rule. More fundamentally, however, the loss of charitable trusts such as Baconsfield is part of the price we pay for permitting deceased persons to exercise a continuing control over assets owned by them at death. This aspect of freedom of testation, like most things, has its advantages and disadvantages. The responsibility of this Court, however, is to construe and enforce the Constitution and laws of the land as they are and not to legislate social policy on the basis of our own personal inclinations.

In their lengthy and learned briefs, the petitioners and the Solicitor General as *amicus curiae* have advanced several arguments which we have not here discussed. We have carefully examined each of these arguments, however, and find all to be without merit.

The judgment is Affirmed.

Mr. Justice MARSHALL took no part in the consideration or decision of this case.

Mr. Justice DOUGLAS, dissenting.

Bacon's will did not leave any remainder or reversion in "Baconsfield" to his heirs. He left "all remainders and reversions and every estate in the same of whatsoever kind" to the City of Macon. He further provided that the property "under no circumstances, or by any authority whatsoever" should "be sold or alienated or disposed of, or at any time for any reason" be "devoted to any other purpose or use excepting so far as herein specifically authorized."

Giving the property to the heirs, rather than reserving it for some municipal use, does therefore as much violence to Bacon's purpose as would a conversion of an "all-white" park into an "all-Negro park."

* * *

Moreover, putting the property in the hands of the heirs will not necessarily achieve the racial segregation that Bacon desired. We deal with city real estate. If a theatre is erected, Negroes cannot be excluded. If a restaurant is opened, Negroes must be served. If office or housing structures are erected, Negro tenants must be eligible. If a church is erected, mixed marriage ceremonies may be performed. If a court undertook to attach a racial-use condition to the property once it became "private," that would be an unconstitutional covenant or condition.

Bacon's basic desire can be realized only by the repeal of the Fourteenth Amendment. So the fact is that in the vicissitudes of time there is no constitutional way to assure that this property will not serve the needs of Negroes.

The Georgia decision, which we today approve, can only be a gesture toward a state-sanctioned segregated way of life, now *passé*. It therefore should fail as the imposition of a penalty for obedience to a principle of national supremacy.

Mr. Justice BRENNAN, dissenting.

* * *

No record could present a clearer case of the closing of a public facility for the sole reason that the public authority that owns and maintains it cannot keep it segregated. This is not a case where the reasons or motives for a particular action are arguably unclear, cf. Palmer v. Thompson, 419 F.2d 1222 (C.A.5th Cir. 1969) (en banc), nor is it one where a discriminatory purpose is one among other reasons, cf. Johnson v. Branch, 364 F.2d 177 (C.A.4th Cir. 1966), nor one where a discriminatory purpose can be found only by inference, cf. Gomillion v. Lightfoot, 364 U.S. 339, 81 S.Ct. 125, 5 L.Ed.2d 110 (1960). The reasoning of the Georgia Supreme Court is simply that Senator Bacon intended Baconsfield to be a segregated public park, and because it cannot be operated as a segregated public park any longer, Watson v. Memphis, 373 U.S. 526, 83 S.Ct. 1314, 10 L.Ed.2d 529 (1963); see Mayor & City Council of Baltimore v. Dawson, 350 U.S. 877, 76 S.Ct. 133, 100 L.Ed. 7 (1955), the park must be closed down and Baconsfield must revert to Senator Bacon's heirs. This Court agrees that this "city park is [being] destroyed because the Constitution require[s] it to be integrated * * *." No one has put forward any other reason why the park is reverting from the City of Macon to the heirs of Senator Bacon. It is therefore quite plain that but for the constitutional prohibition on the operation of segregated public parks, the City of Macon would continue to own and maintain Baconsfield.

I have no doubt that a public park may constitutionally be closed down because it is too expensive to run or has become superfluous, or for some other reason, strong or weak, or for no reason at all. But under the Equal Protection Clause a State may not close down a public facility solely to avoid its duty to desegregate that facility. In Griffin v. County School Board, 377 U.S. 218, 231, 84 S.Ct. 1226, 1233, 12 L.Ed.2d 256 (1964), we said, "Whatever nonracial grounds might support a State's allowing a county to abandon public schools, the object must be a constitutional one, and grounds of race and opposition to desegregation do not qualify as constitutional." In this context what is true of public schools is true of public parks. When it is as starkly clear as it is in this case that a public facility would remain open but for the constitutional command that it be operated on a nonsegregated basis, the closing of that facility conveys an unambiguous message of community involvement in racial discrimination. Its closing for the sole and unmistakable purpose of avoiding desegregation, like its operation as a segregated park, "generates [in Negroes] a feeling of inferiority as to their status in the community that may affect their hearts and minds in a way unlikely ever to be undone." Brown v. Board of Education, 347 U.S. 483, 494, 74 S.Ct. 686, 691, 98 L.Ed. 873 (1954). It is no answer that continuing operation as a segregated facility is a constant reminder of a public policy that stigmatizes one race, whereas its closing occurs once and is over. That difference does not provide a constitutional distinction: state involvement in discrimination is unconstitutional, however short-lived.

The Court, however affirms the judgment of the Georgia Supreme Court on the ground that the closing of Baconsfield did not involve state action. The Court concedes that the closing of the park by the city "solely to avoid the affect of a prior court order directing that the park be integrated" would be unconstitutional. However, the Court finds that in this case it is not the State or city but "a private party which is injecting the racially discriminatory motivation," ante, at [24]. The exculpation of the State and city from responsibility for the closing of the park is simply indefensible on this record. This discriminatory closing is permeated with state action: at the time Senator Bacon wrote his will Georgia statutes expressly authorized and supported the precise kind of discrimination provided for by him; in accepting title to the park, public officials of the City of Macon entered into an arrangement vesting in private persons the power to enforce a reversion if the city should ever incur a constitutional obligation to desegregate the park; it is a *public* park that is being closed for a discriminatory reason after having been operated for nearly half a century as a segregated *public* facility; and it is a state court that is enforcing the racial restriction that keeps apparently willing parties of different races from coming together in the park. That is state action in overwhelming abundance. I need emphasize only three elements of the state action present here.

First, there is state action whenever a State enters into an arrangement that creates a private right to compel or enforce the reversion of a public facility. Whether the right is a possibility of reverter, a right of entry, an executory interest, or a contractual right, it can be created only with the consent of a public body or official, for example the official action involved in Macon's acceptance of the gift of Baconsfield. The State's involvement in the creation of such a right is also involvement in its enforcement; the State's assent to the creation of the right necessarily contemplates that the State will enforce the right if called upon to do so. Where, as in this case, the State's enforcement role conflicts with its obligation to comply with the constitutional command against racial segregation the attempted enforcement must be declared repugnant to the Fourteenth Amendment.

Moreover, a State cannot divest itself by contract of the power to perform essential governmental functions. E.g., Contributors to Pennsylvania Hospital v. City of Philadelphia, 245 U.S. 20, 38 S.Ct. 35, 62 L.Ed. 124 (1917); Stone v. Mississippi, 101 U.S. 814, 25 L.Ed. 1079 (1880). Thus a State cannot bind itself not to operate a public park in accordance with the Equal Protection Clause, upon pain of forfeiture of the park. The decision whether or not a public facility shall be operated in compliance with the Constitution is an essentially *governmental* decision. An arrangement that purports to prevent a State from complying with the Constitution cannot be carried out, Evans v. Newton, supra; see Commonwealth of Pennsylvania v. Board of Directors, 353 U.S. 230, 77 S.Ct. 806, 1 L.Ed.2d 792 (1957). Nor can it be enforced by a reversion; a racial restriction is simply invalid when intended to bind a public body and cannot be given any effect whatever, cf. Commonwealth of Pennsylvania v. Brown, 392 F.2d 120 (C.A.3d Cir. 1968).

Initially the City of Macon was willing to comply with its constitutional obligation to desegregate Baconsfield. For a time the city allowed Negroes to use the park, "taking the position that the park was a public facility which it could not constitutionally manage and maintain on a segregated basis." Evans v. Newton, *supra,* 382 U.S. at 297, 86 S.Ct. at 487. But the Mayor and Council reneged on their constitutional duty when the present litigation began, and instead of keeping Baconsfield desegregated they sought to sever the city's connection with it by resigning as trustees and telling Superintendent James to stop maintaining the park. The resolution of the Mayor and Council upon their resignation as trustees makes it very clear that the probability of a reversion had induced them to abandon desegregation. Private interests of the sort asserted by the respondents here cannot constitutionally be allowed to control the conduct of public affairs in that manner.

A finding of discriminatory state action is required here on a second ground. Shelley v. Kraemer, 334 U.S. 1, 68 S.Ct. 836, 92 L.Ed. 1161 (1948), stands at least for the proposition that where parties of different races are willing to deal with one another a state court cannot keep them from doing so by enforcing a privately devised racial restriction. See also Sweet Briar Institute v. Button, 280 F.Supp. 312 (D.C.W.D.Va.1967) (state attorney general enjoined from enforcing privately devised racial restriction). Nothing in the record suggests that after our decision in Evans v. Newton, supra, the city of Macon retracted its previous willingness to manage Baconsfield on a nonsegregated basis, or that the white beneficiaries of Senator Bacon's generosity were unwilling to share it with Negroes, rather than have the park revert to his heirs. Indeed, although it may be that the city would have preferred to keep the park segregated, the record suggests that, given the impossibility of that goal, the city wanted to keep the park open. The resolution by which the Mayor and Council resigned as trustees prior to the decision in Evans v. Newton, supra, reflected, not opposition to the admission of Negroes into the park, but a fear that if Negroes were admitted the park would be lost to the city. The Mayor and Council did not participate in this litigation after the decision in Evans v. Newton. However, the Attorney General of Georgia was made a party after remand from this Court, and, acting "as parens patriae in all legal matters pertaining to the administration and disposition of charitable trusts in the State of Georgia in which the rights of beneficiaries are involved," he opposed a reversion to the heirs and argued that Baconsfield should be maintained "as a park for all the citizens of the State of Georgia." Thus, so far as the record shows, this is a case of a state court's enforcement of a racial restriction to prevent willing parties from dealing with one another. The decision of the Georgia courts thus, under Shelley v. Kraemer, constitutes state action denying equal protection.

Finally, a finding of discriminatory state action is required on a third ground. In Reitman v. Mulkey, 387 U.S. 369, 87 S.Ct. 1627, 18 L.Ed.2d 830 (1967), this Court announced the basic principle that a State acts in violation of the Equal Protection Clause when it singles out racial discrimination for particular encouragement, and thereby gives it a special preferred status in the law, even though the State does not itself impose or compel segregation. This approach to the analysis of state action was foreshadowed in Mr. Justice White's separate opinion in Evans v. Newton, supra. There Mr. Justice White comprehensively reviewed the law of trusts as that law stood in Georgia in 1905, prior to the enactment of §§ 69–504 and 69–505 of the Georgia Code. He concluded that prior to the enactment of those statutes "it would have been extremely doubtful" whether Georgia law authorized "a trust for park purposes when a portion of the public was to be excluded from the park." 382 U.S., at 310, 86 S.Ct., at 494. Sections 69–504 and 69–505 removed this doubt by expressly permitting dedication of land to the public for use as a park open to one race only. Thereby Georgia undertook to facilitate racial restrictions as distinguished from all other kinds of restriction on access to a public park. *Reitman* compels the conclusion that in doing so Georgia violated the Equal Protection Clause.

In 1911, only six years after the enactment of §§ 69–504 and 69–505, Senator Bacon, a lawyer, wrote his will. When he wrote the provision creating Baconsfield as a public park open only to the white race, he was not merely expressing his own testamentary intent, but was taking advantage of the special power Georgia had conferred by §§ 69–504 and 69–505 on testators seeking to establish racially segregated public parks. As Mr. Justice White concluded in Evans v. Newton, " 'the State through its regulations has become involved to such a significant extent' in bringing about the discriminatory provision in Senator Bacon's trust that the racial restriction 'must be held to reflect   *   *   *   state policy and therefore to violate the Fourteenth Amendment.' " 382 U.S., at 311, 86 S.Ct., at 495. This state-encouraged testamentary provision is the sole basis for the Georgia courts' holding that Baconsfield must revert to Senator Bacon's heirs. The Court's finding that it is not the State of Georgia but "a private party which is injecting the racially discriminatory motivation" inexcusably disregards the State's role in enacting the statute without which Senator Bacon could not have written the discriminatory provision.

This, then, is not a case of private discrimination. It is rather discrimination in which the State of Georgia is "significantly involved," and enforcement of the reverter is therefore unconstitutional. Cf. Burton v. Wilmington Parking Authority, 365 U.S. 715, 81 S.Ct. 856, 6 L.Ed.2d 45 (1961); Robinson v. Florida, 378 U.S. 153, 84 S.Ct. 1693, 12 L.Ed.2d 771 (1964).

I would reverse the judgment of the Supreme Court of Georgia.

Notes

1. In Bob Jones University v. United States, 461 U.S. 574, 103 S.Ct. 2017, 76 L.Ed.2d 157 (1983), the Supreme Court upheld the denial of tax exemption to a university and a private school, both of which had racially discriminatory admissions policies which they claimed to be based on religious grounds. The case attracted great public attention because of the Reagan administration's refusal to support the Internal Revenue Service ruling. (See The Supreme Court, 1982 Term, 97 Harv.L.Rev. 1, 262 (note 15)). While the decision establishes that the IRS position was authorized by statute, and the constitutionality of the statute as so interpreted, it sheds little light on the status of other discriminatory practices, or, indeed, the constitutionality of a tax statute authorizing exemptions for racially discriminatory institutions.

2. One question left open after the Bob Jones University case is whether federal and state tax exemptions accorded charitable trusts and foundations and the administrative relationship which exists between such charities and the tax authorities constitute sufficient governmental involvement to require the trusts and foundations to satisfy constitutional obligations of non-discrimination. The Second Circuit Court of Appeals, sitting en banc, divided on the question with the majority holding that a sifting of the facts and weighing of the circumstances

might well lead to a conclusion that the defendant foundations are "substantially dependent upon their exempt status, that the regulatory scheme is both detailed and intrusive, that the scheme carries connotations of government approval * * *, and that they serve some public function * * *" and that as a consequence a finding of "state action" would be appropriate. Jackson v. Statler Foundation, 496 F.2d 623 (2 Cir. 1974). Judge Friendly argued in dissent at pages 639–40:

> The interest in preserving an area of untrammeled choice for private philanthropy is very great. Even among philanthropic institutions, the activities of charitable family foundations, receiving no government benefit other than tax exemption, should be the last to be swept, under a "sifting of facts and exercise of judgment," within the concept of state action. There are hundreds of thousands of foundations ranging from the giants to the pigmies. While most foundations, particularly large ones, give mainly to institutions serving all races and creeds, although hardly in the completely nondiscriminatory way required of public institutions, I see nothing offensive, either constitutionally or morally, in a foundation's choosing to give preferentially or even exclusively to Jesuit seminaries, to Yeshivas, to black colleges or to the NAACP. Indeed, I find it something of a misnomer to apply the pejorative term "racial discrimination" to a *failure* to make a charitable gift.

> * * * Donors are not going to be willing to spend their time and money, or to have directors and staffs of foundations spend theirs, in defending actions like this one. If the federal courts take over the supervision of philanthropy, there will ultimately be no philanthropy to supervise.

The majority opinion relies on McGlotten v. Connally, 338 F.Supp. 448 (D.D.C.1972), as authority for the proposition that tax benefits constitute federal subsidies and make the recipient subject to constitutional obligations and federal civil rights legislation. In that case a three-judge district court held that a fraternal order which excludes nonwhites from membership is not entitled to tax exemptions nor are gifts to it for charitable purposes deductible by the donors. An article warned:

> If full sway is given to the *McGlotten* theory that tax allowances are equivalent to direct grants of public funds and hence impose constitutional obligations on the recipient, no one will be immune. As we have pointed out, the Internal Revenue Code is a pudding with plums for everyone. Bittker and Kaufman, Taxes and Civil Rights: "Constitutionalizing" the Internal Revenue Code, 82 Yale L.J. 51, 86 (1972).

3. A number of the opinions, in both the Girard College and Evans v. Newton cases, expressed concern that the application of the equal protection clause to charitable trusts would destroy a wide variety of beneficial enterprises. In particular, a threat to trusts in support of religious activities was envisioned. Mr. Justice Bell, concurring in the Pennsylvania Supreme Court decision in In re Girard's Estate, 386 Pa. 548, 613, 127 A.2d 287, 318 (1956), warned of dire consequences:

> If the present contention of the City is correct, its effect will be catastrophic on testamentary church and charitable bequests, as well as on the law of Wills in Pennsylvania. The constitutional prohibition against discrimination—the Fourteenth Amendment—is not confined to color; *it prohibits the States* from making any discrimination because of race, creed or

color. It follows logically and necessarily that if an individual cannot constitutionally leave his money to an orphanage or to a private home and college for poor white male orphans, he cannot constitutionally leave his money to a Catholic, or Episcopal, or Baptist, or Methodist, or Lutheran or Presbyterian Church; or to a Synagogue for Orthodox Jews; or to a named Catholic Church or to a named Catholic priest for Masses for the repose of his soul, or for other religious or charitable purposes. That would shock the people of Pennsylvania and the people of the United States more than a terrible earthquake or a large atomic bomb.

A Missouri testator died in 1965 at the age of 98 leaving approximately $8,500,000 to the McWilliams Memorial Hospital Trust with the directions that the income was to be used annually by the trustees for the "maintenance and support of Protestant Christian Hospitals * * * contributing to the maintenance, support and care of sick and infirm patients in said Hospitals, born of white parents in the United States of America * * *." The Missouri Supreme Court held that this description of the beneficiaries was unambiguous and that because no state action was involved the trust was not invalidated by the Fourteenth Amendment. First National Bank of Kansas City v. Danforth, 523 S.W.2d 808 (1975), certiorari denied 421 U.S. 992, 95 S.Ct. 1999, 2424, 44 L.Ed.2d 483 (1975).

4. In Sweet Briar Institute v. Button, 280 F.Supp. 312 (W.D.Va.1967) a three-judge district court enjoined the state attorney general from enforcing a provision in the will of the founder of the college restricting enrollment to "white girls and young women." The statutory rule that the attorney general is the proper party to supervise charitable trusts provides the basis for the argument that state action is essential before any restriction imposed by a testator is enforcible. (The attorney general's role in the process is examined in Chapter Seven, Section 7, p. 578.) If the trustees desegregate in defiance of the testator's express command, the attorney general must decide whether to initiate an enforcement proceeding. If he seeks a judicial order requiring compliance, the discrimination becomes the direct result of intervention by the judiciary at the instigation of an officer of the executive. If he does nothing, the testamentary restriction is not enforceable and is practically a nullity. Under this theory all charitable trusts and foundations would be subject to the Fourteenth Amendment and a new and far-reaching control would be introduced into the process. Clark, Charitable Trusts, the Fourteenth Amendment and the Will of Stephen Girard, 66 Yale L.J. 979 (1957). Cf. Friendly, The Dartmouth College Case and the Public-Private Penumbra, 12 Tex.Q. (2d Supp.) 141, 171 (1969).

is this considered "not state action" ?

The courts have steadfastly refused to expand the concept of state action to include the supervision of a charitable trust by the court or attorney general. As recently stated by the New York Court of Appeals in holding that the equal protection clause did not prohibit the enforcement of private charitable trusts providing scholarship aid for male students only: "A court's application of its equitable power to permit the continued administration of the trusts invoked in these appeals falls outside the ambit of the Fourteenth Amendment." Matter of Estate of Wilson, 59 N.Y.2d 461, 479, 465 N.Y.S.2d 900, 909, 452 N.E.2d 1228 (1983) (reprinted infra, p. 567). Lockwood v. Killian, 172 Conn. 496, 375 A.2d 998 (1977) involved a testamentary charitable trust to grant college scholarships to beneficiaries chosen by a special selection committee created for that purpose, from among "needy, deserving boys from the graduating classes of the preceding month of June from the high schools of the County of Hartford and State of Connecticut, whose high school marks for their individual and respective entire high school course shall have been at least an average of seventy (70) points or better, who are members of the Caucasian race and who have severally, specifically professed themselves to be of the Protestant Congregational Faith." Members of the selection committee requested instructions from the court because there was an insufficient number of applicants for the scholarships. The trial court applied cy pres and removed the racial and gender restrictions. On an appeal by the Attorney General from the refusal of the trial court to strike the religious qualification as unlawful, the Supreme Court of Connecticut upheld the restriction as a private discrimination not involving state action notwithstanding the "necessary participation" of the Attorney General in a cy pres proceeding brought by the selection committee. This position was reaffirmed, following a remand for further proceedings. 179 Conn. 62, 425 A.2d 909 (1979). Justice Bogdanski argued in dissent:

> In the instant case this court has acted to remove two of the three discriminatory restrictions in order to permit the trust to continue to function and to retain its status as a charitable trust. By retaining the religious restriction present in this trust, this court has clearly involved the state in sanctioning and enforcing private discrimination. The failure of this court to remove this religious restriction is thus clearly offensive to the fourteenth amendment of the United States constitution and to article first, § 20 of the constitution of this state.

> * * *

> The attorney general is required by § 3–125 of the General Statutes to "represent the public interest in the protection of any gifts, legacies or devises intended for public or charitable purposes." To my mind, the attorney general's role in this case is, of itself, sufficient to constitute state action. Of greater significance, however, is the current involvement of the judiciary. "That the action of state courts and judicial officers in their official capacities is to be regarded as action of the State within the meaning of the Fourteenth Amendment, is a proposition which has long been established by decisions of this Court." Shelley v. Kraemer, 334 U.S. 1, 14, 68 S.Ct. 836, 92 L.Ed. 1161. The judicial act of the highest court in the state, in authoritatively construing and enforcing its laws, is the act of the state. * * * 179 Conn. at pp. 73–75, 425 A.2d at pp. 914–915.

For a summary of the position that the role of the probate and other courts in supervising the administration of estates and trusts is _ministerial and not governmental_ with the courts "merely acting in a nonsignificant neutral capacity which does not constitute state action," see Mayers v. Ridley, 151 U.S.App.D.C. 45, 73, 465 F.2d 630, 658 (C.A.D.C.1972) (Judge Tamm dissenting). It was unsuccessfully argued two decades ago that the Board of Directors of City Trusts was only acting in a ministerial capacity when it enforced the restrictions in Girard's will.

See generally, Lusky, National Policy and the Dead Hand—The Race-Conscious Trust, 28 Record of Ass'n of Bar of City of N.Y. 265 (1973), 112 Trusts & Estates 554 (1973); Adams, Racial and Religious Discrimination in Charitable Trusts: A Current Analysis of Constitutional and Trust Law Solutions, 25 Clev.St.L.J. 1 (1976).

race, creed or color?

5. Religious eligibility standards for individual bequests or benefits under private trusts (i.e., stipulations that the beneficiary must marry, raise children, etc. within a specified religion as a condition to receiving benefits) have been held not to be subject to the equal protection clause of the Fourteenth Amendment. Gordon v. Gordon, 332 Mass. 197, 208, 124 N.E.2d 228, 235 (1955), certiorari denied 349 U.S. 947, 75 S.Ct. 875, 99 L.Ed. 1273 (1955); United States National Bank v. Snodgrass, 202 Or. 530, 275 P.2d 860, 50 A.L.R.2d 725 (1954).

6. It is the clear message in the above cases that the court is neutral and involved in the administration process only mechanically as the agency to carry out the testator's intent. Does it follow from this proposition that the court is powerless to intervene when it determines that the testator's intent is in furtherance of a purpose that violates public policy? Consider the following facts taken from the N.Y. Times, March 5, 1982, p. B3, cols. 4, 5 and 6.

Fred L. Sparks died at age 65 on February 18, 1981. His will left 10% of his $300,000 estate to the Palestine Liberation Organization. Among other beneficiaries who received percentages of the estate were the Overseas Press Club, the Maryknoll Fathers, the New York Public Library, and the late Viscount Robin Maugham, a nephew of the author W. Somerset Maugham.

There was no suggestion that Mr. Sparks lacked testamentary capacity or was subject to undue influence. He was a native New Yorker, the son of Bennett E. Siegelstein, a lawyer who once served in the N.Y. State Assembly and founded the Menorah Home and Hospital for the Aged in Brooklyn. He was a newspaper writer, working many years for the Chicago Daily News before returning to New York in 1953 to join the staff of the World Telegram and Sun. He won a Pulitzer Prize in 1951 for his reporting on postwar Europe. Friends said that he was deeply moved by his experiences while covering the plight of Palestinian refugees following the Israeli war of independence in 1948.

Attorneys for the American Jewish Congress and the Anti-Defamation League of B'nai B'rith challenged the bequest because the P.L.O. is a "terrorist organization," engaged in "a campaign of terror to eradicate the State of Israel". "The American system of justice and the Surrogate's Court should not be used to funnel money to an organization engaged in violent crime." They claimed further that to uphold this bequest would legitimize similar gifts to the Irish Republican Army, Basque separatists, and the F.A.L.N., the Puerto Rican terrorist group.

Mr. Zehdi Labib Terzi, the P.L.O.'s permanent observer to the United Nations, argued in defense of the bequest. "This is a violation of Mr. Sparks' rights to dispose of his funds according to his wishes. If this man were alive, who could prevent him from giving whatever he wants to whomever he wants."

The New York Civil Liberties Union agreed with this later position and filed an amicus brief in defense of the bequest. The thrust of the Union's position was summarized in a statement by Dorothy Samuels, executive director of the Union: "We have grave misgivings about the process being established by the Manhattan Surrogate of allowing an intrusive and ill-defined inquiry into a political organization under the broad rubric of 'public policy'". The National Lawyers Guild also filed an appearance in favor of the bequest.

The issue never came to trial. A compromise was concluded between the executor of the estate, the New York attorney general, the P.L.O., and the executor of the estate of Viscount Maugham under which the $30,000 was turned over to the International Committee of the Red Cross to be used "solely for the betterment of the living conditions of the Palestinian people. The use shall be limited to providing aid to civilian hospital facilities in the form of medicine, medical care, foods and new housing." The four outside organizations were recognized as having amicus standing but were not signatories to the agreement. N.Y. Times, Feb. 7, 1984, p. B3, cols. 4, 5 and 6.

7. At one time eleven states had statutes which conditioned the ability of a non-resident alien to take property in intestacy or under a will upon the existence of a reciprocal right of United States citizens to take property in the alien's country. Ten other states had statutes requiring payment into court of property to which a non-resident alien was entitled under a will, or intestacy, when it appeared that the alien would not have the "benefit use or control" of the property. The constitutionality of those "iron curtain" statutes, so-called because they were most frequently applied to aliens in countries in eastern Europe was upheld in Clark v. Allen, 331 U.S. 503, 67 S.Ct. 1431, 91 L.Ed. 1633 (1947). In Zschernig v. Miller, 389 U.S. 429, 88 S.Ct. 664, 19 L.Ed.2d 683 (1968) the Supreme Court refused to overrule Clark v. Allen but struck down the Oregon iron curtain statute "as applied" as an intrusion into the federal domain. On the effect of the ambiguous opinion in Zschernig see Note, The Demise of the "Iron Curtain" Statute, 18 Vill.L.Rev. 49 (1972). See also Berman, Soviet Heirs in American Courts, 62 Colum.L.Rev. 257 (1962).

SECTION TWO. LIMITATIONS ON THE SIZE OF ESTATES AND THE DURATION OF OWNER CONTROL

The preceding cases put to challenge any notion of an absolute right of testation. Each involves an inquiry into the extent to which the inheritance process must give way to an overriding social policy. The several decisions reveal basic and recurring attitudes toward the competing claims made on behalf of the intent of the property owner, the welfare of the beneficiaries, and the interests of society. They have a further significance in illustrating the sources out of which priorities among these competing claims are established. Historically the states have always had primary jurisdiction over decedents' estates. Bird v. Plunkett raises interesting questions as to the limits of competence of both the courts and the legislatures in the exercise of that jurisdiction, while Evans v. Abney illustrates the ever-present possibility of conflict between local and national policy.

The discussions of these points illustrate a number of fundamental principles which run throughout the law of estates, but, because the factual problems involved are of infrequent occurrence, the cases do not involve general curbs on inheritance of the type demanded by critics of the process. The critics have, however, had a measure of success, and there are today three types of limitations which are applied generally to estates and trusts: first, the state and federal taxing power effects a reduction in the size of estates available for distribution; second, the Rule against Perpetuities which has evolved over three centuries of court decision (plus a number of statutes) is designed to place an outer limit on the duration of time that testators can control the uses of their property; and third, state statutes by direct prohibition, suggestion, and mild bribery seek to channel dispositive patterns to favor the spouse and to a lesser extent the children and charities.

In a few estates these limitations may have dramatic consequences, but these are the extraordinary cases, either where the estate is unusually large or where the decedent has attempted an unnatural disposition. The vast bulk of estates remain relatively untouched by these restraints; for them the law operates only to give effect to the decedent's wishes. It seems likely that in the near future the concept of a married couple sharing marital property (i.e., husband and wife each owning half of the property acquired during the marriage) will be more widely incorporated into the law, but, in a sense, this development will only make official an understanding about property already held by the great majority of testators. No other changes appear to be in the offing. Despite the theorizing about the inequities of inheritance, there has never been significant popular demand in this country for its abolition. The transfer of large concentrations of wealth from generation to generation is subject to some restriction by federal and state death taxes, but beyond this few are willing to go.

A. TAX LIMITATIONS WHICH AFFECT THE SIZE AND ENJOYMENT OF ESTATES AND GIFTS

State inheritance taxes were first enacted during the nineteenth century, but it was not until this century, particularly with the advent of the federal estate tax in 1916, that the various transfer taxes, both state and federal, were developed as important limitations on concentrations of inherited wealth. The federal estate and gift taxes are given more detailed treatment in Chapter Ten, p. 887, infra. But in an introduction to the wealth transmission process some note should be taken of the important role they play in shaping that process.

1. *Federal Income Tax.* This tax enters into the field in two obvious ways: first, it makes the accumulation of large fortunes more difficult, and, second, it taxes to the beneficiary the income earned from inherited wealth and makes his enjoyment of it less complete than his benefactor may have anticipated. But the influence of the income tax on estates is infinitely more subtle and pervasive than this. Indeed, avoidance of the tax affects all human activity taken with respect to property—kinds of property to be given away, sold, or retained; form of business ownership; the timing and forms of lifetime gifts; the extent of charitable giving—to mention but a few of the important types of decisions that are shaped by tax considerations.

2. *State Death Taxes.* All states with the exception of Nevada impose some kind of death tax. Up until quite recently the most common form of death tax was the inheritance tax. An inheritance tax is to be distinguished from an estate tax in that the former is levied on the privilege of receiving property from the dead, while the latter is on the privilege of transmitting property at death. It has been summarized in this

way: " * * * the distinction is between a tax [an estate tax] graduated according to the size of the decedent's entire estate and one [an inheritance tax] that is graduated for each beneficiary according to the size of his share and his relationship to the decedent." Bittker and Clark, Federal Estate and Gift Taxation, Introduction p. xxxii (5th ed. 1984). A number of states continue to use an inheritance tax (see e.g., Conn. Gen. Stat. Ann. §§ 12–340 through 12–390). Others have adopted an estate tax. Some of this latter group (see e.g., N.Y. Tax Law § 951 through § 963) have modelled their estate taxes on the federal statute by defining the state-taxed "gross estate" in the same manner as the federal "gross estate" and carrying over the federal deductions, including the unlimited marital deduction. This system has the advantage of allowing the state tax collector to "hitchhike" on the federal audit.

These state taxes touch many more estates than does the federal estate tax because the permissible exemptions are very much lower. But in terms of overall impact on large individual estates their impact is more limited because the rates do not graduate sharply. In addition, a percentage credit is allowed against the federal estate tax for state death duties with the result that the federal government is paying at least part of the state death tax. Sixteen states, including such a populous one as California (Cal. Rev. & Tax. §§ 13301, 13302), have repealed (or in a few states never enacted) their estate or inheritance taxes and now rely exclusively on what is known as a "sponge" or "pick-up" tax designed to collect only the amount covered by the federal credit.

3. *Federal Estate and Gift Taxes.* The federal taxes are particularly noteworthy in this context for two reasons: they cause the most immediate and drastic depletion of large estates, and they were originally justified almost exclusively in social policy terms as a means of cutting down on the transfer of excessive concentrations of wealth from generation to generation. The estate and gift taxes are not important sources of government revenue. Of the total revenue collected by the United States these taxes average about one per cent— infinitesimal in comparison with the income tax and meager in comparison with such taxes as those imposed on alcohol and tobacco. Nor, can these taxes be justified as devices to combat fluctuations in the business cycle. As pointed out by Professors Bittker and Clark: "[I]t is hard to escape the conclusion that today's gift and estate taxes rest squarely on equalitarian foundations, to which these other theories are little more than decorative buttresses." Bittker and Clark, Federal Estate and Gift Taxation, Introduction, p. xxvi (5th ed. 1984).

Another authority puts it this way: "Justification for the federal estate tax must be sought in its social significance. It is aimed directly at the destruction of large accumulations of property. * * * [T]he federal estate tax is part of a deliberate plan to redistribute both the capital and income of the nation." Lowndes, Tax Avoidance and the Federal Estate Tax, 7 Law & Cont. Problems 328 (1940).

The estate tax is imposed on the transfer at death of the net estate of every citizen or resident of the United States (as well as some nonresident aliens). The net estate is equal to the gross estate less certain allowable deductions including funeral and administration expenses and debts of the decedent. The gross estate includes all the property owned at death such as cash, land and securities, along with other less obvious interests in property over which the decedent had some control and also the value of certain inter vivos transfers made by him or her which are treated as substitutes for testamentary transfers. It is possible for the gross estate to exceed by far the wealth which the decedent had title to immediately before death.

The federal gift tax was a later development, having been finally enacted in 1932 (six years after the repeal of the 1924 gift tax), in order to curb the use of inter vivos transfers to avoid both the estate and income taxes. It is imposed on all transfers over which the donor has surrendered all control and for which the donor has not received in return "adequate and full" consideration. However, gifts up to $10,000 per donee in any year may be made without gift tax consequences.

In recent years, beginning in 1976, major changes in gift and estate taxes have been enacted. Prior to the Tax Reform Act of 1976, estate and gift taxes were imposed at separate rates (the latter 75% of the former). In addition, the gift tax provided for a "lifetime exemption" of $30,000 (i.e., no tax was payable on the first $30,000 of gifts made by a taxpayer) and the estate tax had a separate $60,000 exemption (i.e., no tax was payable on the first $60,000 of property owned at death or otherwise includible in the estate). As more fully explained in Chapter Ten below, there is now a single "unified" rate for all transfers during life and at death, and a single "credit" instead of the two separate exemptions. When fully effective in 1987, the credit will be equal to an exemption of $600,000, i.e. no tax is payable on the first $600,000 of property transferred by gift or at death. Moreover, since 1981, there is no tax payable on transfers by gift or at death between spouses.

Another major change effected in 1976 was the enactment of a "generation skipping transfer tax." Prior to 1976, for example, a mother might leave her large estate, typically in trust, with the provision that her son was to receive the income for life, remainder over at the son's death to the son's children. A tax was imposed at the grantor's death and again at the grandchildren's deaths, assuming that they still owned the property at that time. No tax was imposed at the son's death even though the son had substantial enjoyment of the property during his life. Under current law the "transfer" from the son to the next generation is the occasion for a tax levied on the corpus of the trust.

The overall impact of these taxes on hereditary wealth and the gift-making process has been the subject of a variety of opinions. The family of the multi-millionaire decedent who took no steps while alive to minimize the effect of taxes on his or her estate is likely to be shocked at the size of the tax bite. On the other hand, even without resort to the most sophisticated estate planning devices, it has been possible to reduce taxes sharply. And, while the 1976 amendments have eliminated many of the pre-existing advantages of lifetime gifts over transfers at death, and have subjected most of the straightforward types of generation skipping transfers to tax, there is considerable skepticism that the new provisions will be a serious obstacle to sophisticated methods of tax avoidance. See, e.g., Cooper, A Voluntary Tax? New Perspectives on Sophisticated Tax Avoidance, 77 Colum.L.Rev. 161 (1977). For a concise discussion of the estate and gift tax and proposals for reform, see Introduction to Bittker & Clark, Federal Estate and Gift Taxation (5th ed. 1984). At the least, it may be concluded that while the estate and gift taxes have been a prime factor in shaping the ways people dispose of their wealth, they have not depleted large family estates as substantially nor had such a large effect on the economy as was widely predicted at one time.

Whatever the long term effect of unification and the generation skipping transfer tax may turn out to be, the immediate effect of the recent amendments, particularly the sharp increase in the size of estates escaping tax and the exemption from tax of transfers between spouses introduced by the Economic Recovery Tax Act of 1981, will be to substantially reduce the number of estates subject to tax. One estimate prepared for Congress was that only 0.3% of decedents dying in 1981 had taxable estates over $600,000. Even allowing for inflation, it seems likely that when the exemption is fully phased in as of 1987 less than 1% of the estates of decedents will be subject to tax. And even for those estates which are taxed, the maximum rate of tax will be 50% (as of 1988), compared to a maximum rate of 77% in 1975 and earlier years.

B. LIMITATIONS ON THE DURATION OF OWNER CONTROL

Not infrequently persons believe that they are sufficiently clairvoyant to dictate with wisdom and fairness how their property should be used and by whom for an indefinite period after their deaths. The principle of unlimited inheritance would seem to give such persons the right to do so. But property is for the use of the living, and no dead person can foresee the best uses to which it should be put. The law, through centuries of struggle, has evolved the Rule against Perpetuities to cope with this dilemma. But as a solution to the problem the Rule leaves much to be desired.

Roughly speaking, the Rule permits a property owner to tie up his or her property for a period not to exceed twenty-one years after the death of persons living at the time of his or her death. Out of this simple idea developed an incredible tangle of conflicting interpretations, opinions and exceptions. No attempt at clarification will be made here. The purpose of these materials is to introduce the Rule, to locate it in the overall process as an important policy limitation, and to suggest the extent to which it is doing its job. Detailed discussion is reserved for Chapter Nine, Section Three, at p. 744.

SCOTT, CONTROL OF PROPERTY BY THE DEAD, 65 U. of Pa.L.Rev. 527, 632, 639–640 (1917) (footnotes omitted):

One very definite limit set by public policy to the power of the testator to control property after his death is the time limit. This policy finds its chief expression in the Rule against Perpetuities, of which the classic

The Rule :

formulation is that of Professor Gray: "No interest is good unless it must vest, if at all, not later than twenty-one years after some life in being at the creation of the interest." This rule is intended to prevent a testator from designating the persons who shall enjoy his bounty unto the third and fourth generation of those who come after him. It relates only to the time of vesting of interests and not to the time of their enjoyment, nor to their duration nor to their assignability. It applies to equitable estates as well as to legal estates and to powers of appointment as well as to estates. It is perhaps the most sweeping and the most important limitation on the power to control property after death. But it is questionable whether the period is not too long. The fact that any, and any number of, lives may be selected, makes the possible period more than a century, if the testator is careful to choose a sufficient number of lives of sufficiently youthful persons.

LYNN, THE RULE AGAINST PERPETUITIES AS AN INSTRUMENT OF COMMUNITY POLICY: APPLICATION OF THE RULE TO GIFTS FOR THE CARE OF DEPENDENTS AND SUCCESSORS (a graduate thesis available in the Yale Law Library) 75–77 (1952):

Whatever the community policies at stake in a wealth-transmission problem, initiative for the enforcement of these policies is left largely to disappointed private individuals. If a person dies without a will, the state intervenes quickly and positively on behalf of his spouse and other dependents and successors. But the magic formula of drawing a will supplants community action, and the resistance to a will is left, not to the community, but to the private parties who will profit most by the successful resistance. Curiously enough, will contests can be "settled" out of court, so that an otherwise invalid disposition may never be challenged, and thus evade the sanctions imposed on other testamentary dispositions where the acumen of opposing counsel is not sufficiently high to effectuate a settlement. The whole area of transmission of wealth by will may, therefore, be removed from the community's superintendence merely by agreement of the parties. The tax-collector will receive his due, but the policies and interests of the community may easily be circumvented by the act of agreement—an evasion not open to industrial or business combinations.

The enforcement of the policies may be initiated by a great variety of persons for an equally diverse group of reasons. In most cases, the person who sets the otherwise-dormant community machinery in motion is a dissatisfied member of the testator's family group who attempts to share in a division of the testator's estate not provided for in the will. He may seek to do this by obtaining a "construction" of the will by the court, or by challenging the validity of certain provisions under the Rule against Perpetuities. Where the testator or donor has imposed certain behavior or dispositive limitations, the cestui of a testamentary trust or the vendee of realty may seek to challenge the circumscription by invoking the Rule. The notoriously cautious corporate fiduciary may not desire to proceed with the distribution of an estate without ascertaining that the legality of such distribution cannot later be challenged. Less frequently, the tax-collector may initiate proceedings to prevent the hurdling of a generation or two of taxes.

The existing confusion in cases involving the Rule against Perpetuities revolves around a series of judicial failures: (1) The syntactical statement of the Rule has made precise application to a given set of facts precarious; (2) the courts have failed to distinguish the variables in a future interests problem with any clarity, and have treated the language, the reference to time or person or event, the type of problem, and the relevant policies as a conglomerate of ingredients without assay, thus resulting in a totally befogged approach; (3) the relevant policies have never been explicitly stated or analyzed, so that the formulation of Lord Nottingham in 1685 remains as clear a statement as that of any judge of today; (4) the enforcement of the policies has been left almost entirely to private parties, with resulting haphazardness in the administration of the Rule.

LEACH, PERPETUITIES IN PERSPECTIVE: ENDING THE RULE'S REIGN OF TERROR, 65 Harv.L.Rev. 721, 725–727 (1952) (footnotes omitted):

The Rule persists in personifying itself to me as an elderly female clothed in the dress of a bygone period who obtrudes her personality into current affairs with bursts of indecorous energy. Time was when she stood at the center of family activity, necessary to the family welfare. A new generation with new problems has arisen; yet she persists in treating ancient issues as present realities and in applying her own familiar solutions. Asserting an authority derived from an earlier day, she insists that a stockade be built around the house to protect it from Indians even though the Indians are memories, the stockade is highly uneconomical, friendly neighbors are rebuffed, and the policeman and fireman are impeded in performing their protective functions.

A case can be made for this personification. When in 1680 Lord Nottingham heard argument on the Duke of Norfolk's Case and summoned as advisors the chiefs of the three common-law courts, the public welfare was threatened by the desires of the great families to parcel out the soil of England among them and impose upon it the dead-hand control of perpetual family settlements. Two centuries earlier the courts had nullified the Statute De Donis by permitting disentailment, and these judges did not now propose to allow the innovations of the Statute of Uses to create new "perpetuities." The threat was real. A firmly restrictive rule was called for. The Duke of Norfolk's Case is notable as validating one limitation upon which Nottingham disagreed with all three of his common-law brethren; it is not so often remembered that the four judges were unanimous in striking out another whole series of executory interests.

The family-dynasty mentality flourished in the eighteenth century and reached a fine fruition in the will of Peter Thellusson who, if unable himself to join the company of the great families, schemed to balloon his relatively small fortune into an empire of British soil for his unborn descendants. Parliament promptly countered the threat of dynastic accumulations by the "Thellusson Act". A dozen or so state legislatures have also passed statutes prohibiting certain types of accumulations although it is an open question whether the need for such legislation in this country has ever existed.

The Stately Homes of England reified the ambitions of the great English families in the nineteenth and early twentieth centuries. At that time the Rule against Perpetuities still served a useful purpose in countering the urge to family aggrandizement. But the taxation following two world wars has put an end to the era of the Stately Homes. One by one they have passed to the National Trust, or have been converted into girls' schools or nursing homes, or opened to the public as museums with the family living in a few rooms in one wing hoping to stave off the day of surrender by collecting shillings from tourists.

The situation in this country is similar in kind though it differs in degree. The Newport palaces and the Fifth Avenue mansions have been turned over to the wreckers, and none replace them. These things are symbols, but important ones. In part they symbolize a conviction that "family" has lost importance; but mostly they highlight the fact that large properties for family uses simply have no place in mid-century economics.

Graduated estate and income taxes have largely eliminated any threat to the public welfare from family dynasties built either on great landed estates or on great capital wealth. If there were at this present date no Rule against Perpetuities it seems unlikely that there would be a clamor for such a rule either in the legislatures or in the courts. It does no harm to continue the Rule as a restraint on the whims of an occasional refugee from the nineteenth century, but we should make sure that it is limited to that cautionary function and does not disrupt the prudent dispositions of reasonable men.

The old lady of our allegory must learn to sit by the fire and confine her activity to a few words of wise advice from time to time; she must forego this skittish activity that has caused such trouble and damage in the household.

* * *

C. PROTECTION OF THE FAMILY

SUSSMAN, CATES AND SMITH, THE FAMILY AND INHERITANCE
4–7 (with deletions) (1970).

Edmund Burke once said, "The power of perpetuating our property in families is one of the most valuable and interesting circumstances belonging to it, and that which tends the most to the perpetuation of society itself." [2]   The likelihood of perpetuating property within family systems is potentially diminished by the presence of testamentary freedom, which allows the testator to will property away from the family in favor of outsiders. The exercise of this freedom without considering the context in which it occurs appears to be in sharp contradiction with the major intent of inheritance: to provide continuity to family systems and to maintain the social structure. Yet testamentary freedom is an accommodation mechanism in American society. It functions to meet multiple demands: those of continuity; a multilineal descent system; values that espouse freedom, democracy, and rationality; and a complex and highly differentiated modern industrial society.

*   *   *

Succession law reveals an uneasy compromise among the interests of the individual, the family, and the community. Because man cannot live alone and determine for himself exactly what he wants to do in a given situation, such a compromise puts controls over the exercise of testamentary freedom. To understand the resulting limitations, it is necessary to consider a series of related questions: What kinds of property are not subject to testation? Is it likely that the needs of the community will be considered before the needs of the family? How much property is subject to the will of the testator? Namely, what kinds of property does he have control over that are judged not vital to the survival of the community or the family? Lastly, can the testator include or exclude any person he desires?

Assets garnered through forced savings—for example, some company and union insurance and benefit programs and programs sponsored by the government under social security legislation—are not available to be freely distributed by the testator. These valuable rights in job-related death or survivorship benefits specify recipients; and in almost all instances, these assets are allocated to surviving spouses and children. There is a marked increase in such benefit programs in modern societies, whereby the decedent's successors are predetermined by statutes, and the implementation of the transfer of such assets is done automatically and impersonally by a bureaucratic public or quasi-public agency.

The testator of a small estate is effectively restricted in his freedom to distribute because the estate can be consumed entirely in payment of debts or by the exemption, year's allowance, and other provisions awarded to the widow, widower, or children. Limited assets induce forced succession even though the testator might have had other things in mind.

The more wealthy testator can to some degree choose his successors and distribute his estate in a manner in keeping with his desires; he has the greatest opportunity to express testamentary freedom. But even in this instance, state and federal estate taxes prevent him from freely

---

2. Edmund Burke, *Reflections on the French Revolution and Other Essays* (New York: E. P. Dutton & Co., Inc., 1910), p. 49.

disposing of all his assets.   The progressive tax on estates forces the testator to leave an increasingly larger proportion of his estate to the public.   All he can do is to determine the manner in which he serves the public, either through progressively increasing estate taxes (depending upon the size of his estate) or through tax-free gifts to charity.   *   *   *

*   *   *

The current societal posture toward testamentary freedom is predicated on values which assure that caring for one's own kin and orderly social relationships among family members are highly desirable.   Testamentary freedom is highly correlated with the condition of sufficient assets.   A person has to have equity in order to be able to dispense it. Individuals who are well-to-do usually have sufficient assets to take care of the natural objects of their bounty and also to give to others.   Frequently, their spouses and children are not in great need of their beneficence.   In many instances, wives will have legacies from their own side of the family, and children may in part have been taken care of by grandparents.   Well-to-do individuals are in the best position to meet their familial responsibilities and to a large degree fulfill community expectations, based on an assessment of the financial and status needs of their potential descendants.   If spouses and children are amply provided for from other sources, such as legacies and trusts, or are potential inheritors from grandparents and members of their own familial line and will thus be enabled to maintain sufficiently their position and status within the community, then testators have an alternative for distribution of their assets and are more likely to exercise testamentary freedom.   The allocations that they would make to institutions and nonrelated individuals would meet with no disapproval because they would have fulfilled community expectations of taking care of their next of kin.

For most individuals, will making is related to the desire to exercise testamentary freedom under conditions that warrant its use.   It is possible to say that the making of a will is tantamount to testamentary freedom.   In an ideological sense, it is.   In practice, however, will makers conform, by and large, to cultural prescriptions of familial responsibility over generational time.   The will provides a mechanism for exercising preferred choices if conditions and circumstances are appropriate.

The materials in Chapters Two and Three are designed to illustrate how the law of estates, either directly or indirectly, is geared to the preservation of family security and stability.   Generalization being difficult, discussion of the subject matter is reserved for those chapters.

SECTION THREE.   THE ELUSIVE DISTINCTION BETWEEN LIFE AND DEATH TRANSFERS

A core problem running throughout the law of gratuitous transfers involves the time when a transfer becomes effective.   If the transfer occurs at the death of the transferor it is described as "testamentary," a conclusionary word which means that the transfer is only valid if it conforms to the requirements of the Statute of Wills.　If, on the other hand, the transfer is effective during life its validity is established by a different set of abstract criteria.　The issue comes up frequently because a number of flexible devices, of which the trust is the prime example, allow property owners to give away their property in a technical sense while retaining during their lives many of the beneficial incidents of that property.　Persons may want the satisfaction of seeing their children enjoy their inheritance before their deaths with the further hope of avoiding onerous burdens such as death taxes and probate costs which attend death transfers.　At the same time (unlike King Lear) they may have nagging doubts as to the capacity of their children to manage the property wisely, plus fears that they may suffer reverses which will require that they recall the property to their own use.　If they reconcile these apparently inconsistent aims by creating an inter vivos trust for their children over which they retain substantial control for their lives the question may arise whether the trust becomes effective at the time they transfer the property to the trustee or only at the time of their deaths when they can no longer control it.

The two cases which follow introduce the problem in terms of the basic property question of whether the transfer is valid or invalid.　How can they be reconciled?　Why should there be a penalty for trying to avoid the Statute of Wills?　What function does this statute perform that its integrity must be so closely guarded?　If a transfer is invalidated as testamentary the property will devolve, except where there is a valid will, by intestacy.　Is there a reason for preferring this statutory distribution to one designed by the property owner?

The issue transcends in importance the initial question of who among competing gratuitous transferees is to receive the property.　Community policy imposes claims against an estate at death for taxes and in behalf of a surviving spouse.　It is therefore of significance to determine what property is included in the estate at death.　Then too the property owner who is determined to disinherit his or her spouse or to avoid taxes will seek to find a way to rid him or herself of the burdens of ownership without leaving him or herself impoverished.　It is in this sense that any further discussion of policy limitations on the inheritance process must await some understanding of the dichotomy between life and death transfers. As we shall see, the dividing line is defined in highly abstract, conceptual terms.　Furthermore, solutions are not uniform;　a transfer may be effective for one purpose but ineffective for another.　So elusive is the concept that there is not even agreement as to a single definition of a completed gift for the purposes of the federal income, estate, and gift taxes.

BUTLER v. SHERWOOD

Supreme Court of New York, Appellate Division, Third Department, 1921.
196 App.Div. 603, 188 N.Y.S. 242.
Affirmed mem. 233 N.Y. 655, 135 N.E. 957 (1922).

WOODWARD, J.　Ella F. Sherwood, being about to undergo an operation for a cancer, made and executed an instrument in writing, in form a quitclaim deed, of all her real estate and personal property, to her husband. This instrument bears date of January 25, 1916. The plaintiff is the brother and only heir at law of Ella F. Sherwood, and brings this action to set aside the said instrument, on the ground that it was procured by undue influence, and that there was never any transfer of the property under the instrument. Upon the trial of the action there does not appear to have been any serious contention of conduct amounting to fraud, and there is little room for doubt that Ella F. Sherwood intended to place her property where it would be vested in her husband, this defendant, upon her death. If she has failed in this purpose, it is because she has sought to accomplish an entirely legal result by an illegal method—because she has attempted to accomplish by an instrument in the form of a deed that which could be accomplished only by a will. The learned court at Special Term has found that the instrument relied upon by the defendant was of a testamentary character, and did not comply with the statutory requirements of a will, and that it was therefore void. 114 Misc.Rep. 483, 186 N.Y.Supp. 712. See Decedent Estate Law (Consol.Laws, c.13) § 21. The defendant appeals.

The instrument in question provides that it is between Ella Francis Sherwood and Edward H. Sherwood, and that—

> "the said party of the first part, in consideration of the sum of one dollar, love and affection, and other good and valuable considerations," does hereby "remise, release and forever quitclaim unto the said party of the second part, his heirs and assigns forever," all of the real estate of the said Ella F. Sherwood, wherever situate, "to have and to hold the same unto the party of the second part, his heirs, executors, administrators and assigns forever," and "for the same considerations, I do hereby sell, assign, transfer, convey and set over unto the party of the second part, all personal property, bills, notes, deposits in bank, certificates of stock, and all choses in action, evidences of indebtedness due me, and all my personal property of whatever name or kind the same may be and wheresoever situate, to have and to hold the same unto the party of the second part, his executors, administrators and assigns forever."

If the instrument had ended here, and had been executed and delivered, it would, of course, have operated to divest Ella F. Sherwood of her property and to have vested it in Edward H. Sherwood. But this would not have accomplished the purpose which Ella F. Sherwood had in mind; she wanted to hold the ownership and possession of her property until her death, and then to vest it in her husband. She had, however, been through a will contest in connection with the estate of a former husband, and, as she told her friends, she had no faith in wills; she wanted to fix her property where it would be disposed of without a contest, and, of course, invited one. She provided that—

> "this conveyance and transfer are made upon the condition that the party of the second part, my husband, survive me, and the same is intended to vest and take effect only upon my decease and until said time the same shall be subject to revocation upon the part of the party of the first part."

This instrument was delivered to the defendant, but what did it convey? It could not be determined at any time prior to her death whether

her husband survived her, and unless he survived her there was clearly no intention of conveying to him. Moreover, she provided that the conveyance and transfer "are intended to vest and take effect only upon my decease"; so that there was no time prior to her death when the instrument could have any effect, and when that event took place the law determined the disposition to be made of her estate, in the absence of a valid will. There was no moment from the time of making the instrument down to the very instant of dissolution when any rights could vest under the intent or language of this deed, and beyond this it was provided that, "until said time, the same shall be subject to revocation upon the part of the party of the first part"; so that the supposed grantor was in full control of the property during all of her life subsequent to the making of the deed, with the right reserved to revoke the instrument itself. No right whatever passed to the defendant under the terms of the deed; it was not to take effect until the decease of the party of the first part, and then only upon the condition that the defendant survived her. This is not the case of a deed executed and delivered to a third party, with instructions not to record or deliver the same until the death of the grantor. Such a deed, absolute in form and to take effect immediately, divests the grantor of his interest in the property, making its enjoyment to depend upon the date of his death; but here the instrument is, by its terms, to take effect only upon the decease of the grantor, and at a time when the law operates to prevent a transfer otherwise than by a last will and testament.

It is impossible to sustain this transaction as an executed gift of the personal property, for that was subject to the same conditions and limitations as the real estate.

"It is an elementary rule," say the court in Young v. Young, 80 N.Y. 422, 435 (36 Am.Rep. 634), "that such a gift cannot be made to take effect in possession in futuro. Such a transaction amounts only to a promise to make a gift, which is nudum pactum. Pitts v. Mangum, 2 Bailey (S.C.) 588. There must be a delivery of possession with a view to pass a present right of property. 'Any gift of chattels which expressly reserves the use of the property to the donor for a certain period, or (as commonly appears in the cases which the court have had occasion to pass upon) as long as the donor shall live, is ineffectual.' Schouler on Pers. Prop. vol. 2, p. 118, and cases cited; Vass v. Hicks, 3 Murphy (N.C.) 494. This rule has been applied, even where the gift was made by a written instrument or deed purporting to transfer the title, but containing the reservation."

In the case here under consideration the instrument itself is limited to take effect upon the death of the donor if the donee shall survive her, and there is no pretense that any of the personal property itself was ever delivered to the defendant. Delivery by the donor, either actual or constructive, operating to divest the donor of possession of and dominion over the thing, is a constant and essential factor in every transaction which takes effect as a completed gift. Instruments may be ever so formally executed by the donor, purporting to transfer title to the donee, or there may be the most explicit declaration of intention to give, or of an actual present gift, yet, unless there is a delivery, the intention is defeated.

Beaver v. Beaver, 117 N.Y. 421, 429, 22 N.E. 940, 6 L.R.A. 403, 15 Am.St.Rep. 531.

While there is a recital of a consideration of $1, and every legal mode of acquisition of real property except by descent is denominated in law a purchase, and the person who thus acquires it is a purchaser, there is no doubt that the transaction here under consideration possesses all of the essential qualities of a gift, as distinguished from a valuable consideration supporting a bargain and sale (Ten Eyck v. Witbeck, 135 N.Y. 40, 44, 45, 31 N.E. 994, 31 Am.St.Rep. 809, and authorities there cited; Real Property Law [Consol. Laws, c. 50] § 246); and as this gift was not to take effect until the death of the grantor, upon the survival of the named grantee, and even the instrument itself might be revoked, it must be clear that Ella F. Sherwood undertook to accomplish by a deed what the law requires to be done by will, and, of course, she has failed. The judgment appealed from should be affirmed.

Judgment affirmed, without costs. All concur.

Notes

1. Under the intestate laws of New York in force at this time the husband was entitled to $2,000 and one-half of the surplus of personal property, and the brother would get all the real property and the balance of the personal property. The husband's rights in the wife's real property under the estate of curtesy as it then existed in New York only became effective if a child was born of the marriage.

2. Early in the century, as property owners became increasingly aware of the onerous burdens that attached to death transfers, they resorted to more sophisticated property transmission devices which allowed them to rid themselves of technical title while retaining many of the incidents of beneficial ownership. The inter vivos deed proved adaptable for that purpose. Most of the cases which examined the validity of those deeds demonstrated an abundance of flexibility in finding doctrinal grounds for sustaining the transfers as valid. See, e.g., Tennant v. John Tennant Memorial Home, 167 Cal. 570, 140 P. 242 (1914) (deed reserving to grantor life estate, power of revocation and power to sell and appropriate proceeds held valid on theory deed passed to grantee a present vested remainder subject to be divested by the exercise of the reserved powers); Mays v. Burleson, 180 Ala. 396, 61 So. 75 (1913) (accord on similar though not identical provisions, court arguing that reservation of power to revoke indicated that instrument was not intended to be testamentary, since the reservation of such a power would be superfluous in a will, which is automatically revocable); Montgomery v. Reeves, 167 Ga. 623, 146 S.E. 311 (1929) (provision that "this deed is made with the condition attached that same is not to take effect until after the death of the maker, he reserving to himself the right to control same and the rents and profits thereof as long as he lives" held not to invalidate deed, which was construed as passing immediate title, with enjoyment postponed until the death of the grantor, although the lower court said: "I think this paper is a will, as plain as it can be; it is not to take effect until after the death of the grantor"); Pelt v. Dockery, 176 Ark. 418, 3 S.W.2d 62 (1928) (provision inserted by grantor reading: "It being understood and agreed that this deed is to take effect and be in force after my death, and that the title to said land is to remain in me so long as I may live" held not to

invalidate deed, the court stating that the intent to give was obvious, that the other provisions were in the form of a deed, and that "when we consider the whole instrument and keep in mind the fact that it was not only executed and delivered but recorded, ·and that there was no power of revocation, and the further fact that we should give the instrument such a construction as will uphold it if possible, it seems to us that the instrument must be construed as a deed"); Thomas v. Williams, 105 Minn. 88, 117 N.W. 155 (1908) (deed conveying to grantee "in case he survives" grantor held valid as conveying "a present contingent right in the land in the nature of a contingent fee," the right vesting on delivery of the deed, although the enjoyment of the right was postponed until the happening of the contingency). The modern cases continue to use the same doctrinal justifications to uphold the transfers. Witherspoon v. Witherspoon, 402 S.W.2d 699 (Ky.1966); Westerfeld v. Huckaby, 474 S.W.2d 189 (Tex.1972); Black v. Poole, 230 Ga. 129, 196 S.E.2d 20 (1973). Occasionally the owner retains too much control, and a court will balk. Gardner v. Thames, 223 Ga. 378, 154 S.E.2d 926 (1967); Wheeler v. Rines, 375 S.W.2d 48 (Mo.1964).

See in general Gulliver & Tilson, Classification of Gratuitous Transfers, 51 Yale L.J. 1 (1941); Ritchie, What Is a Will?, 49 Va.L.Rev. 759 (1963); Browder, Giving or Leaving—What Is a Will?, 75 Mich.L.Rev. 845 (1977); Annot., 31 A.L.R.2d 532.

FARKAS v. WILLIAMS
Supreme Court of Illinois, 1955.
5 Ill.2d 417, 125 N.E.2d 600.

HERSHEY, Justice. This is an appeal from a decision of the Appellate Court, First District, which affirmed a decree of the circuit court of Cook County finding that certain declarations of trust executed by Albert B. Farkas and naming Richard J. Williams as beneficiary were invalid and that Regina Farkas and Victor Farkas, as coadministrators of the estate of said Albert B. Farkas, were the owners of the property referred to in said trust instruments, being certain shares of capital stock of Investors Mutual, Inc.

Said coadministrators, herein referred to as plaintiffs, filed a complaint in the circuit court of Cook County for a declaratory decree and other relief against said Richard J. Williams and Investors Mutual, Inc., herein referred to as defendants. The plaintiffs asked the court to declare their legal rights, as coadministrators, in four stock certificates issued by Investors Mutual Inc. in the name of "Albert B. Farkas, as trustee for Richard J. Williams" and which were issued pursuant to written declarations of trust. The decree of the circuit court found that said declarations were testamentary in character, and not having been executed with the formalities of a will, were invalid, and directed that the stock be awarded to the plaintiffs as an asset of the estate of said Albert B. Farkas. Upon appeal to the Appellate Court, the decree was affirmed. See 3 Ill.App.2d 248, 121 N.E.2d 344. We allowed defendants' petition for leave to appeal.

Albert B. Farkas died intestate at the age of sixty-seven years, a resident of Chicago, leaving as his only heirs-at-law brothers, sisters, a nephew and a niece. Although retired at the time of his death, he had for many years practiced veterinary medicine and operated a veterinarian establishment in Chicago. During a considerable portion of that time, he employed the defendant Williams, who was not related to him.

On four occasions (December 8, 1948; February 7, 1949; February 14, 1950; and March 1, 1950) Farkas purchased stock of Investors Mutual, Inc. At the time of each purchase he executed a written application to Investors Mutual, Inc., instructing them to issue the stock in his name "as trustee for Richard J. Williams." Investors Mutual, Inc., by its agent, accepted each of these applications in writing by signature on the face of the application. Coincident with the execution of these applications, Farkas signed separate declarations of trust, all of which were identical except as to dates. The terms of said trust instruments are as follows:

"Declaration of Trust—Revocable. I, the undersigned, having purchased or declared my intention to purchase certain shares of capital stock of Investors Mutual, Inc. (the Company), and having directed that the certificate for said stock be issued in my name as trustee for Richard J. Williams as beneficiary, whose address is 1704 W. North Ave. Chicago, Ill., under this Declaration of Trust Do Hereby Declare that the terms and conditions upon which I shall hold said stock in trust and any additional stock resulting from reinvestments of cash dividends upon such original or additional shares are as follows:

"(1) During my lifetime all cash dividends are to be paid to me individually for my own personal account and use; provided, however, that any such additional stock purchased under an authorized reinvestment of cash dividends shall become a part of and subject to this trust.

"(2) Upon my death the title to any stock subject hereto and the right to any subsequent payments or distributions shall be vested absolutely in the beneficiary. The record date for the payment of dividends, rather than the date of declaration of the dividend, shall, with reference to my death, determine whether any particular dividend shall be payable to my estate or to the beneficiary.

"(3) During my lifetime I reserve the right, as trustee, to vote, sell, redeem, exchange or otherwise deal in or with the stock subject hereto, but upon any sale or redemption of said stock or any part thereof, the trust hereby declared shall terminate as to the stock sold or redeemed, and I shall be entitled to retain the proceeds of sale or redemption for my own personal account and use.

"(4) I reserve the right at any time to change the beneficiary or revoke this trust, but it is understood that no change of beneficiary and no revocation of this trust except by death of the beneficiary, shall be effective as to the Company for any purpose unless and until written notice thereof in such form as the Company shall prescribe is delivered to the Company at Minneapolis, Minnesota. The decease of the beneficiary before my death shall operate as a revocation of this trust.

"(5) In the event this trust shall be revoked or otherwise terminated, said stock and all rights and privileges thereunder shall belong to and be exercised by me in my individual capacity.

"(6) The Company shall not be liable for the validity or existence of any trust created by me, and any payment or other consideration made or given by the Company to me as trustee or otherwise, in connection with said stock or any cash dividends thereon, or in the event of my death prior to revocation, to the beneficiary, shall to the extent of such payment fully release and discharge the Company from liability with respect to said stock or any cash dividends thereon."

The applications and declarations of trust were delivered to Investors Mutual, Inc., and held by the company until Farkas' death. The stock certificates were issued in the name of Farkas as "trustee for Richard J. Williams" and were discovered in a safety-deposit box of Farkas after his death, along with other securities, some of which were in the name of Williams alone.

The sole question presented on this appeal is whether the instruments entitled "Declaration of Trust—Revocable" and executed by Farkas created valid *inter vivos* trusts of the stock of Investors Mutual, Inc. The plaintiffs contend that said stock is free and clear from any trust or beneficial interest in the defendant Williams, for the reason that said purported trust instruments were attempted testamentary dispositions and invalid for want of compliance with the statute on wills. The defendants, on the other hand, insist that said instruments created valid *inter vivos* trusts and were not testamentary in character.

It is conceded that the instruments were not executed in such a way as to satisfy the requirements of the statute on wills; hence, our inquiry is limited to whether said trust instruments created valid *inter vivos* trusts effective to give the purported beneficiary, Williams, title to the stock in question after the death of the settlor-trustee, Farkas. To make this determination we must consider: ① whether upon execution of the so-called trust instruments defendant Williams acquired an interest in the subject matter of the trusts, the stock of defendant Investors Mutual, Inc., ② whether Farkas, as settlor-trustee, retained such control over the subject matter of the trusts as to render said trust instruments attempted testamentary dispositions.

First, upon execution of these trust instruments did defendant Williams presently acquire an interest in the subject matter of the intended trusts?

If no interest passed to Williams before the death of Farkas, the intended trusts are testamentary and hence invalid for failure to comply with the statute on wills. Oswald v. Caldwell, 225 Ill. 224, 80 N.E. 131; Troup v. Hunter, 300 Ill. 110, 133 N.E. 56; Restatement of the Law of Trusts, section 56.

But considering the terms of these instruments we believe Farkas did intend to presently give Williams an interest in the property referred to. For it may be said, at the very least, that upon his executing one of these instruments, he showed an intention to presently part with some of the incidents of ownership in the stock. Immediately after the execution of each of these instruments, he could not deal with the stock therein referred to the same as if he owned the property absolutely, but

only in accordance with the terms of the instrument.   He purported to
set himself up as trustee of the stock for the benefit of Williams, and the
stock was registered in his name as trustee for Williams.   Thus assuming
to act as trustee, he is held to have intended to take on those obligations
which are expressly set out in the instrument, as well as those fiduciary
obligations implied by law.   In addition, he manifested an intention to
bind himself to having this property pass upon his death to Williams,
unless he changed the beneficiary or revoked the trust, and then such
change of beneficiary or revocation was not to be effective as to Investors
Mutual, Inc., unless and until written notice thereof in such form as the
company prescribed was delivered to them at Minneapolis, Minnesota.
An absolute owner can dispose of his property, either in his lifetime or
by will, in any way he sees fit without notifying or securing approval
from anyone and without being held to the duties of a fiduciary in so
doing.

It seems to follow that what incidents of ownership Farkas intended
to relinquish, in a sense he intended Williams to acquire.   That is, Williams was to be the beneficiary to whom Farkas was to be obligated, and
unless Farkas revoked the instrument in the manner therein set out or
the instrument was otherwise terminated in a manner therein provided
for, upon Farkas's death Williams was to become absolute owner of the
trust property.   It is difficult to name this interest of Williams, nor is
there any reason for so doing so long as it passed to him immediately
upon the creation of the trust.   As stated in 4 Powell, The Law of Real
Property, at page 87: "Interests of beneficiaries of private express trusts
run the gamut from valuable substantialities to evanescent hopes.   Such
a beneficiary may have any one of an almost infinite variety of the possible aggregates of rights, privileges, powers and immunities."

An additional problem is presented here, however, for it is to be noted
that the trust instruments provide: "The decease of the beneficiary before
my death shall operate as a revocation of this trust."   The plaintiffs argue
that the presence of this provision removes the only possible distinction
which might have been drawn between these instruments and a will.
Being thus conditioned on his surviving, it is argued that the "interest"
of Williams until the death of Farkas was a mere expectancy.   Conversely, they assert, the interest of Farkas in the securities until his death
was precisely the same as that of a testator who bequeaths securities by
his will, since he had all the rights accruing to an absolute owner.

Admittedly, had this provision been absent the interest of Williams
would have been greater, since he would then have had an inheritable
interest in the lifetime of Farkas.   But to say his interest would have
been greater is not to say that he here did not have a beneficial interest,
properly so-called, during the lifetime of Farkas.   The provision purports
to set up but another "contingency" which would serve to terminate the
trust.   The disposition is not testamentary and the intended trust is valid,
even though the interest of the beneficiary is contingent upon the existence of a certain state of facts at the time of the settlor's death.   Restatement of the Law of Trusts, section 56, comment f.   In an example

contained in the previous reference, the authors of the Restatement have referred to the interest of a beneficiary under a trust who must survive the settlor (and where the settlor receives the income for life) as a contingent equitable interest in remainder.

This question of whether any interest passed immediately is also involved in the next problem considered, namely, the quantum of power retained by a settlor which will cause an intended *inter vivos* trust to fail as an attempted testamentary disposition. Therefore, much of what is said in the next part of the opinion, as well as the authorities cited, will pertain to this interest question.

Second, did Farkas retain such control over the subject matter of the trust as to render said trust instruments attempted testamentary dispositions?

In each of these trust instruments, Farkas reserved to himself as settlor the following powers: (1) the right to receive during his lifetime all cash dividends; (2) the right at any time to change the beneficiary or revoke the trust; (3) upon sale or redemption of any portion of the trust property, the right to retain the proceeds therefrom for his own use.

Additionally, Farkas reserved the right to act as sole trustee, and in such capacity, he was accorded the right to vote, sell, redeem, exchange or otherwise deal in the stock which formed the subject matter of the trust.

We shall consider first those enumerated powers which Farkas reserved to himself as settlor.

It is well established that the retention by the settlor of the power to revoke, even when coupled with the reservation of a life interest in the trust property, does not render the trust inoperative for want of execution as a will. Kelly v. Parker, 181 Ill. 49, 54 N.E. 615; Bear v. Millikin Trust Co., 336 Ill. 366, 168 N.E. 349, 73 A.L.R. 173; Gurnett v. Mutual Life Ins. Co., 356 Ill. 612, 191 N.E. 250; Bergmann v. Foreman State Trust & Savings Bank, 273 Ill.App. 408, 32 A.L.R.2d 1279–1282.

Only when it is thought that there are additional reservations present of such a substantial nature as to amount to the retention of full ownership is a court likely to invalidate an *inter vivos* trust by reason of its not being executed as a will. (See Restatement of the Law of Trusts, section 57.) In 1 Scott, The Law of Trusts, section 57.1, the author says at pages 336–337: "It is immaterial whether the settlor reserves simply a power to revoke the whole trust at one time or whether he reserves also a power to revoke the trust as to any part of the property from time to time. It is immaterial whether the power to revoke includes a power to revoke by will as well as a power to revoke by a transaction *inter vivos*. It is immaterial that the settlor reserves not only a power to revoke the trust but in addition a power to alter or modify its terms."

However, it is not every so-called additional reservation of power that will be deemed sufficient to invalidate a trust of this nature. In 32 A.L.R.2d 1270, it is stated at pages 1276–1277: "The later cases, as do the earlier ones, justify the general conclusion that many and extensive rights and power [sic] may be reserved by a settlor, in addition to a life interest and power of revocation, without defeating the trust. The instrument is likely to be upheld notwithstanding it includes additionally the reservation of power to amend the trust in whole or in part, or extensive powers over investments, management, or administration, or power to appoint or remove trustees or to appoint interests in remainder, or the right to act as trustee or as one of the trustees, or to enjoy limited rights in the principal, or to withdraw part or all of the principal, or to possess, use, or enjoy the trust property, or to sell or mortgage the property or any of it and appropriate the proceeds."

We conclude therefore, in accordance with the great weight of authority, said powers which Farkas reserved to himself as settlor were not such as to render the intended trusts invalid as attempted testamentary dispositions.

A more difficult problem is posed, however, by the fact that Farkas is also trustee, and as such, is empowered to vote, sell, redeem, exchange and otherwise deal in and with the subject matter of the trusts.

That a settlor may create a trust of personal property whereby he names himself as trustee and acts as such for the beneficiary is clear. Restatement of the Law of Trusts, section 17.

Moreover, the later cases indicate that the mere fact that the settlor in addition to making himself sole trustee also reserves a life interest and a power of revocation does not render the trust invalid as testamentary in character. 32 A.L.R.2d 1286. In 1 Scott, The Law of Trusts, it is stated at pages 353–354: "The owner of property may create a trust not only by transferring the property to another person as trustee, but also by declaring himself trustee. Such a declaration of trust, although gratuitous, is valid.   * * *   Suppose, however, that the settlor reserves not only a beneficial life interest but also a power of revocation. It would seem that such a trust is not necessarily testamentary. The declaration of trust immediately creates an equitable interest in the beneficiaries, although the enjoyment of the interest is postponed until the death of the settlor, and although the interest may be divested by the exercise of the power of revocation. The disposition is not essentially different from that which is made where the settlor transfers the property to another person as trustee. It is true that where the settlor declares himself trustee he controls the administration of the trust. As has been stated, if the settlor transfers property upon trust and reserves not only a power of revocation but also power to control the administration of the trust, the trust is testamentary. There is this difference, however: the power of control which the settlor has as trustee is not an irresponsible power and can be exercised only in accordance with the terms of the trust." See also Restatement of the Law of Trusts, section 57, comment b.

In the instant case the plaintiffs contend that Farkas, as settlor-trustee, retained complete control and dominion over the securities for his own benefit during his lifetime. It is argued that he had the power to deal with the property as he liked so long as he lived and owed no enforceable duties of any kind to Williams as beneficiary.

* * *

That the retention of the power by Farkas as trustee to sell or redeem the stock and keep the proceeds for his own use should not render these trust instruments testamentary in character becomes more evident upon analyzing the real import and significance of the powers to revoke and to amend the trust, the reservation of which the courts uniformly hold does not invalidate an *inter vivos* trust.

It is obvious that a settlor with the power to revoke and to amend the trust at any time is, for all practical purpose, in a position to exert considerable control over the trustee regarding the administration of the trust. For anything believed to be inimicable to his best interests can be thwarted or prevented by simply revoking the trust or amending it in such a way as to conform to his wishes. Indeed, it seems that many of those powers which from time to time have been viewed as "additional powers" are already, in a sense, virtually contained within the overriding power of revocation or the power to amend the trust. Consider, for example, the following: (1) the power to consume the principal; (2) the power to sell or mortgage the trust property and appropriate the proceeds; (3) the power to appoint or remove trustees; (4) the power to supervise and direct investments; and (5) the power to otherwise direct and supervise the trustee in the administration of the trust. Actually, any of the above powers could readily be assumed by a settlor with the reserved power of revocation through the simple expedient of revoking the trust, and then, as absolute owner of the subject matter, doing with the property as he chooses. Even though no actual termination of the trust is effectuated, however, it could hardly be questioned but that the mere existence of this power in the settlor is sufficient to enable his influence to be felt in a practical way in the administration of the trust. In the Garrett case, the court quoted as follows from Van Cott v. Prentice, 104 N.Y. 45, 10 N.E. 257: " 'That language [providing that the trustee should hold the property subject to the grantor's control and direction] only repeats, in another form, the effect of the reserved power of revocation. The existence of that inevitably leaves in the settlor an absolute control, since at any moment he may end the trust and resume possession of the fund as his own. * * * Its continued existence was to be absolutely subject to the direction and control of Prentice (settlor),—a result always inevitable where a power of revocation is reserved.' " In 1 Bogert, Trusts and Trustees, section 104, the author states at pages 484–485: "Often the grantor-settlor holds back for himself the power to manage the property directly and indirectly. He provides that he himself shall have power to sell, lease, mortgage, pay taxes, make investments, and perform other acts of trust administration, or that he shall have authority to direct the trustees how they shall perform these duties. These reservations have not generally been deemed to show that the grantor remains during his life the master of the property to such an extent as to make his gift to the *cestuis* testamentary. So long as the trust continues, the *cestuis* have equitable interests, no matter who acts for them in protecting those interests, whether it be trustee or settlor. If the exercise of these powers by the settlor involves the total or partial destruction of the trust, as where the settlor has power to sell the *res* and keep the proceeds, the power seems to be treated as practically that of revocation of the trust. It leaves an equitable interest in the *cestuis* till revocation. It shows a vested interest, subject to divestment, and not the lack of any interest at all."

In the case at bar, the power of Farkas to vote, sell, redeem, exchange or otherwise deal in the stock was reserved to him as trustee, and it was only upon sale or redemption that he was entitled to keep the proceeds for his own use. Thus, the control reserved is not as great as in those cases where said power is reserved to the owner as settlor. For as trustee he must so conduct himself in accordance with standards applicable to trustees generally. It is not a valid objection to this to say that Williams would never question Farkas' conduct, inasmuch as Farkas could then revoke the trust and destroy what interest Williams has. Such a possibility exists in any case where the settlor has the power of revocation. Still, Williams has rights the same as any beneficiary, although it may not be feasible for him to exercise them. Moreover, it is entirely possible that he might in certain situations have a right to hold Farkas' estate liable for breaches of trust committed by Farkas during his lifetime. In this regard, consider what would happen if, without having revoked the trust, Farkas as trustee had given the stock away without receiving any consideration therefor, had pledged the stock improperly for his own personal debt and allowed it to be lost by foreclosure or had exchanged the stock for another security or other worthless property in such manner as to constitute gross impropriety and gross negligence. In such instances, it would seem in accordance with the terms of these instruments that Williams would have had an enforceable claim against Farkas' estate for whatever damage had been suffered. Contrast this with the rights of a legatee or devisee under a will. The testator could waste the property or do anything with it he wished during his lifetime without incurring any liability to those designated by the will to inherit the property. In any event, if Farkas as settlor could reserve the power to sell or otherwise deal with the property and retain the proceeds, which the cases indicate he could, then it necessarily follows that he should have the right to sell or otherwise deal with the property as trustee and retain the proceeds from a sale or redemption without having the instruments rendered invalid as testamentary dispositions.

Another factor often considered in determining whether an *inter vivos* trust is an attempted testamentary disposition is the formality of the transaction. Restatement of the Law of Trusts, section 57, comment g; Stouse v. First National Bank, Ky., 245 S.W.2d 914, 32 A.L.R.2d 1261; United Building and Loan Association v. Garrett, D.C., 64 F.Supp. 460; In re Sheasley's Trust, 366 Pa. 316, 77 A.2d 448. Historically, the purpose behind the enactment of the statute on wills was the prevention of fraud. The requirement as to witnesses was deemed necessary because a will is ordinarily an expression of the secret wish of the testator, signed out of the presence of all concerned. The possibility of forgery and fraud are ever present in such situations. Here, Farkas executed four separate applications for stock of Investors Mutual, Inc., in which he directed that the stock be issued in his name as trustee for Williams, and he executed four separate declarations of trust in which he declared he was holding said stock in trust for Williams. The stock certificates in question were issued in his name as trustee for Williams. He thus manifested his intention in a solemn and formal manner.

For the reasons stated, we conclude that these trust declarations executed by Farkas constituted valid *inter vivos* trusts and were not attempted testamentary dispositions. It must be conceded that they have, in the words of Mr. Justice Holmes in Bromley v. Mitchell, 155 Mass. 509, 30 N.E. 83, a "testamentary look." Moreover, it must be admitted that the line should be drawn somewhere, but after a study of this case we do not believe that point has here been reached.

The judgment of the Appellate Court affirming the decree of the circuit court of Cook County is reversed, and the cause is remanded to the circuit court of Cook County, with directions to enter a decree in favor of the defendants.

Reversed and remanded, with directions.

Notes

1. It is highly unlikely that any court today would dissent from the judgment of the Illinois court that the trusts created by Mr. Farkas were valid. As observed in 1 Scott on Trusts 485 (3d ed. 1967): "The trend of the modern authorities is to uphold an inter vivos trust no matter how extensive may be the powers reserved by the settlor."

One commentator has written critically of the analytical process by which the transfer must be classified as a present gift in order to be sustained. He asks: "Why insist on finding a present interest that is lacking?" Langbein, The Nonprobate Revolution and the Future of the Law of Succession, 97 Harv.L.Rev. 1108, 1129 (1984). He points out that such will substitutes as revocable trusts, joint accounts, life insurance and pensions are in universal use today and account for much of the wealth that is gratuitously transferred and that their acceptance does not contravene the policies traditionally put forward to justify probate and administration. He concludes that rather than pretending that will substitutes are lifetime transfers we should recognize them as "wills" that need not comply with the Statute of Wills and apply the same rules of construction to "probate" wills as we do to "nonprobate" wills. In this regard, UPC § 6–201 states that a provision in an insurance policy, employment contract, conveyance, trust agreement, pension plan and the like directing payment or transfer at death "is deemed to be non-testamentary."

2. Every jurisdiction has a number of cases dealing with the question of inter vivos trusts being testamentary. A representative sampling includes: National Shawmut Bank v. Joy, 315 Mass. 457, 53 N.E.2d 113 (1944); Cramer v. Hartford-Connecticut Trust Co., 110 Conn. 22, 147 A. 139, 73 A.L.R. 201 (1929); Wilson v. Fulton Nat. Bank of Atlanta, 188 Ga. 691, 4 S.E.2d 660 (1939); Bolles v. Toledo Trust Co., 144 Ohio 195, 58 N.E.2d 381, 157 A.L.R. 1164 (1944); In re Shapley's Deed of Trust, 353 Pa. 499, 46 A.2d 227, 164 A.L.R. 877 (1946); Leggroan v. Zion Savings Bank, 120 Utah 93, 232 P.2d 746 (1951); In re Gould's

Trust, 34 Misc.2d 58, 227 N.Y.S.2d 128 (1962);   Coleman v. First National Bank of Nevada, 506 P.2d 86 (Nev.1973).

3. A third party beneficiary contract is not rendered invalid as testamentary by the fact that the performance date is established by the death of one of the parties. In re Estate of Verbeek, 2 Wash.App. 144, 467 P.2d 178 (1970) (real estate contract in favor of son and daughter-in-law); In re Estate of Hillowitz, 22 N.Y.2d 107, 291 N.Y.S.2d 325, 238 N.E.2d 723 (1968) (a partnership agreement in favor of the surviving partner); In re Estate of Gross, 35 A.D.2d 830, 317 N.Y.S.2d 45 (1970) (stockholders' agreement in favor of surviving wife); Gordon v. Portland Trust Bank, 201 Or. 648, 271 P.2d 653, 53 A.L.R.2d 1106 (1954) (life insurance payable to a trust or other designated beneficiary).

4. Modern property owners are using a variety of will substitutes to implement their estate plans. It is frequently suggested that the volume of wealth passing in this manner far exceeds the value of wealth being disposed of by wills or intestate succession statutes. See e.g., Langbein, supra. Such devices as trusts, joint accounts, and insurance are discussed in later chapters. The facts in the Farkas case introduce one common pattern. A person, the husband for example, creates a revocable inter vivos trust, naming himself and a bank or other person, such as an adult child, as trustees, funding it with securities and/or life insurance on his own life, and directing that the income from the trust be paid to him for life, then to his wife for life, with the remainder going over at their deaths outright or in further trust to their children and grandchildren. He will then execute a simple will directing that the probate estate be added to the trust corpus at his death (pourover wills are discussed infra, p. 322–323). His wife may execute a similar trust or join as co-grantor of his trust. [Because they have the power of revocation over the trust, they cannot expect it to afford them any tax advantages.] The non-tax reasons for creating such a trust are listed in Westfall, Estate Planning, 43 (2d ed. 1982):

(1) To avoid making the trust provisions a matter of public record in the local probate court, as would be necessary if it were created by the grantor's will;

(2) To anticipate and provide for the grantor's incapacity by transferring property while he is competent to act to a trustee whose powers will not be revoked by the grantor's subsequent incompetency;

(3) To avoid interruption and delays in the management of the trust assets at the time of the grantor's death;

(4) To choose as the governing state law for the trust, that of a state other than the grantor's domicile at his death;

(5) To avoid creation of a "court" trust. [Eds. Note. A trust created by will may be subject to the continuing jurisdiction of the court and the trustee thus required to file periodic accounts.]

Chapter Two

INTESTATE SUCCESSION

SECTION ONE. INTRODUCTION

Intestate succession is the method of transfer prescribed by legislatures for property of which a deceased owner has made no effective inter vivos or testamentary disposition. It may take effect even if the deceased owner has left a validly executed will, since it will cover any property not effectually transferred by that will. It may be adopted deliberately as a satisfactory disposition, or to avoid the trouble and expense of a will. It may take effect inadvertently due to ignorance of the law, procrastination in making a will until the opportunity is gone through death or loss of capacity, or errors in the drafting or execution of the instruments of transfer which render them ineffective.

Some legal devolution of property left undisposed of by its former owner at his or her death is obviously desirable to prescribe and enforce an orderly and equitable distribution. The alternative would be a chaotic situation in which mere priority of seizure might control. Assuming the desirability of some system, the problem of selecting the recipients of the property remains.

One issue involves the extent to which the state, as distinguished from individuals, should participate in the property. A person's attitude on this question will necessarily be largely colored by his or her social, economic and political philosophy. Increasing the share of the state in the estates of decedents, whether testate or intestate, would obviously be one means of achieving a redistribution of wealth. The American system of succession, however, is primarily based on the concept of private property and the resultant postulate that individual succession is desirable. The two legal methods by which the state may share are escheat and taxation. Escheat is a rare event, since it has two prerequisites which seldom coincide: first, failure of the deceased to make any disposition of the property; and, second, absence of any intestate successors. The latter contingency hardly ever occurs, since it is usually not difficult to find claimants to an estate of any value, and at least one of them is apt to be genuine. And, if the deceased had no known relatives, he or she might well have left his or her property by will to friends or to charity. Taxation, on the other hand, is a vital and omnipresent factor affecting testamentary and inter vivos transfers as well as intestate succession.

Tax problems and the impact of death and gift taxes on estates are examined in Chapter Ten p. 887.

Assuming the desirability of individual succession, the next problem is to determine the identity of the successors. The Anglo-American system, like those of other countries, gives the intestate property to the family of the deceased owner. There is little judicial discussion of possible justifications of this method of distribution. It has been accepted as proper, and the courts do not feel it necessary to spend time and effort elaborating on the rationale of such simple and non-controversial results as are usually involved in intestacy cases. The following theoretical rationalizations may be suggested:

1. Since the law of this field is predicated upon the individualistic system of private property and its corollary that owners of property have the power to determine their successors in ownership, the intestate scheme should seek to reach a result that would probably be intended by persons in the position of the deceased intestate. In other words, their supposed desires are still paramount although they have not expressed them in a will, and the intestate scheme should therefore approximate the disposition that they would have preferred if they had exercised the testamentary power. It is to be postulated that they would want their nearest relatives to take, as those most likely to have had close social and economic connections with them. Close social associations may be assumed to connote mutual affection as a general rule (although some of the most acrimonious disputes no doubt arise among close relatives). Close economic connections may justify receiving property by intestacy in two ways: first, as in the case of inheritance between spouses or by parents from their children, as giving some return to those who are likely to have assisted in building up the estate; second, as in the case of inheritance by one spouse from the other or by a child from a parent, as continuing the support of those who are likely to have been supported by the intestate during his or her lifetime, and as perhaps preventing them from becoming public charges. These factors may be brought within an intent formula by saying that intestates would prefer to benefit those for whom they felt affection, or would like to have some return made to one who had contributed to the estate, or would be anxious to continue inter vivos support.

The objection to any such theory is, of course, its highly speculative character. Even in the case of a will, where only one individual is involved, where actual statements of intention exist in the will, and where surrounding circumstances may be considered, ascertainment of the supposed intent of the testator is frequently guesswork, the judge being required to follow the fictional process of manufacturing an intent for the testator about a question to which the testator never gave any thought. But a scheme of intestate succession involves the formulation of rules applicable equally to thousands of different individuals, without the benefit of any statements of intent and without consideration of the widely varying social and economic relationships that exist between relatives in different families. Efforts to rationalize intestate succession in terms of the probable intent of the intestate are likely to produce nothing much better than a blind guess.

2. Intestate succession is a necessary administrative device. Any scheme that does not seem obviously unfair is probably satisfactory for this purpose, provided that it is as clear and definite as possible (so that property owners may know whether a different disposition would be preferable) and is rapid and efficient in operation (so that delays in distribution and undue expenditure of time by the courts may be avoided). The objective of achieving a just distribution is much less important than it would be if intestacy were inevitable; the initiative and judgment of the individual owner may justifiably be relied on to avoid the operation of intestate succession by inter vivos or testamentary transfers better suited to meet the exigencies of particular situations. Distribution to relatives is, on the whole, easy to administer through specific statutory designations or simple calculations of degrees of relationship; difficulties arising out of factual proof of consanguinity or some such special relationship as adoption are only occasional. Any more flexible and discretionary arrangement framed to meet the equities of particular cases would be far more difficult and time-consuming and would reduce the expeditious facility of the present system.

Admittedly, distribution among the family will not lead to the most equitable result in every case, especially if the property goes to those outside the immediate family circle. Families are tending to become less unified and relatives less closely associated because of such modern developments as the greater frequency of divorce; the shift from rural to urban life, substituting the small home or apartment for the larger and more permanent family homestead; and the enormous increase in the ease and rapidity of transportation and communication, resulting in a much greater geographical spread of business organizations and a more migratory population. A close friend might well be preferred, in terms of either fairness or the probable intent of the deceased, to a fifth cousin in Australia whom the intestate has never seen. But proof of the vague and subjective relationship of friendship would be difficult and time-consuming, and a court might hold its judicial determination impossible. And single instances of injustice, actual or imaginary, should not be over-dramatized. For every case of succession by an unknown or remote relative, there are probably hundreds where the property is received by the husband, wife, or children. The widespread adoption and consistent retention of distribution among the family indicates that it corresponds with present and past mores in this and other civilizations; and its appropriateness can be supported in terms of an intent formula by the fact that relatives are customarily the chief beneficiaries in wills.

Assuming the propriety of basing intestate succession on the family relationship, the final problem is to determine which members of the family shall take the property in the particular case. The underlying theory is that the nearest relatives of the intestate will succeed to the exclusion of his more remote relatives, although, as will appear in connection with the cases infra, this generalization requires qualification.

It has been argued that the family, for this purpose, should be limited to those close relationships which connote social and economic connections with the deceased, in order to increase the financial resources of the state and to eliminate what the Germans have described as the "laughing heir," whose joy at receiving an unexpected windfall is unmitigated by grief at the untimely demise of a relative whom he has never seen. The categories of blood relatives are, however, so broadly defined in the statutes of this country that the instances in which the estate passes to the state by escheat because there is no one eligible to claim it are rare. But see Note 2, infra, at p. 72.

In the law of intestate succession the distinction between lineal and collateral relatives is important. Lineals are relatives one of whom is descended in a direct line from the other; persons' lineal descendants are their children, grandchildren, great-grandchildren, etc.; their lineal ascendants or ancestors are their parents, grandparents, great-grandparents, etc. Collaterals are relatives who are lineally descended from a common ancestor but not one from the other; persons' collateral relatives include their brothers and sisters, uncles and aunts, nephews and nieces, cousins, etc. In computing degrees of consanguinity among lineals, each generation counts as a degree; thus, a person is related to his or her parents and children in the first degree, to grandparents and grandchildren in the second degree, etc.

In computing degrees of consanguinity among collaterals the first step is to determine the common ancestor of the intestate and the claimant. Under the method used in this country and England and known historically as the civil law method of computation, the degree of relationship between collaterals equals the sum of the lineal relationships of both to the common ancestor; thus a sister of the deceased is related to him in the second degree, their father or mother being the common ancestor; his niece in the third degree, the father or mother of the deceased being the common ancestor. Another method, known as the canon law rule, counted only the line of the more remote from the common ancestor between the claimant and the decedent. This method was employed by the ecclesiastical courts in England in determining the validity of marriages between relatives and is of very little significance in establishing inheritance rights today.

The preference of relatives closer in degree represents the adoption of the "gradual" system, followed at common law for the distribution of personal property. Real property, on the other hand, descended at common law in accordance with the "parentelic" system. Under the parentelic system (some vestiges of which remain today), descendants of a nearer ancestor of the decedent are preferred over descendants of a more remote ancestor, without regard to the degree of their relationship to the decedent. Thus a grandniece of the decedent (who is four degrees removed from him) will take ahead of an aunt of the decedent (three degrees removed) because she is descended from—is "within the parentela of"—the decedent's parents, while the aunt is within the more remote parentela of the decedent's grandparents.

The principle of representation, when applicable, permits children or more remote lineal descendants of a predeceased relative of the intestate to stand in their predeceased ancestor's shoes for the purpose of inheritance. If the latter, for example, was related in the second degree to the intestate and if his or her descendants are permitted to take by representation, they are also considered as related in the second degree to the intestate for this purpose, even though they may individually be relatives of the fourth or fifth degree. Those who take by representation are said to take per stirpes (by the stocks or roots); those who take in their own right and not by representation are said to take per capita.

In considering the statutes and cases on intestate succession the following charts may be helpful. They are reproduced from "California Estate Administration" (California Continuing Education of the Bar, 1960) with permission of the Regents of the University of California, holder of the copyright, and of Hon. Otho G. Lord, former Commissioner of the Superior Court, Los Angeles County, California, the author of the charts. To Commissioner Lord, and to Felix Stumpf, administrator of the Department of Continuing Education of the Bar, special appreciation is expressed.

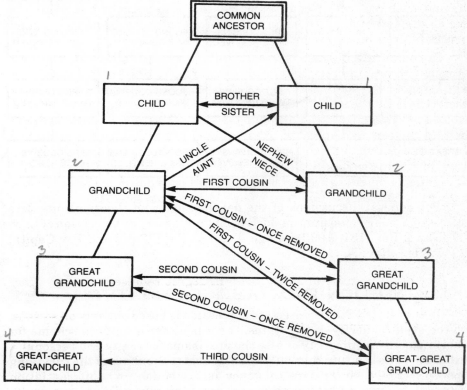

CHART OF RELATIONSHIPS
Through a Common Ancestor

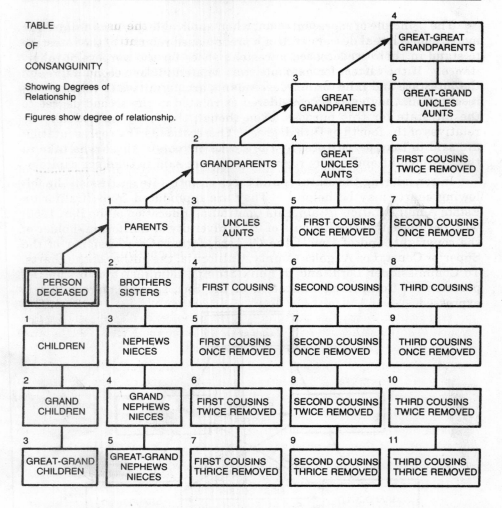

TABLE

OF

CONSANGUINITY

Showing Degrees of
Relationship

Figures show degree of relationship.

For general discussions of the development and theory of intestate succession, see Symposium on Succession to Property by Operation of Law, 20 Iowa L.Rev. 181 (1935); Page, Descent Per Stirpes and Per Capita, 1946 Wis.L.Rev. 3.

SECTION TWO. AMERICAN STATUTES

In the United States, intestate succession is based entirely on statute. In the great majority of the states, there is either a uniform scheme for real and personal property or else the provisions for realty and personalty differ only slightly and then only with respect to the share of the surviving spouse. The clear modern tendency is to abolish any differentiation between the two, as having at the present time solely a historical justification. The statutes typically describe intestate successors in two ways: first, by enumerating certain close relatives who, in their own right or by right of representation, have a priority to the exclusion of persons more remotely related; and, second, after all close relatives have been named, by identifying more remote heirs through the use of a general term like "next of kin." In the latter case, those entitled to take are determined by computing degrees. The following provisions of New York law and the Uniform Probate Code are representative of modern legislation throughout the country. The statutes of individual states should be consulted as to specific details.

New York Estates, Powers and Trusts Law

§ 4–1.1 Descent and Distribution of a Decedent's Estate

The property of a decedent not disposed of by will, after payment of administration and funeral expenses, debts and taxes, shall be distributed as follows:

(a) If a decedent is survived by:

(1) A spouse and children or their issue, money or personal property not exceeding in value four thousand dollars and one-third of the residue to the spouse, and the balance thereof to their children or to their issue per stirpes.

(2) A spouse and only one child, or a spouse and only the issue of one deceased child, money or personal property not exceeding in value four thousand dollars and one-half of the residue to the spouse, and the balance thereof to the child or to his issue per stirpes.

(3) A spouse and both parents, and no issue, twenty-five thousand dollars and one-half of the residue to the spouse, and the balance thereof to the parents. If there is no surviving spouse, the whole to the parents.

(4) A spouse and one parent, and no issue, twenty-five thousand dollars and one-half of the residue to the spouse, and the balance thereof to the parent. If there is no surviving spouse, the whole to the parent.

(5) A spouse, and no issue or parent, the whole to the spouse.

(6) Issue, and no spouse, the whole to the issue per stirpes.

(7) Brothers or sisters or their issue, and no spouse, issue or parent, the whole to the brothers or sisters or to their issue per stirpes.

(8) Grandparents only, the whole to the grandparents. If there are no grandparents, the whole to the issue of the grandparents in the nearest degree of kinship to the decedent per capita.

(9) Great-grandparents only, the whole to the great-grandparents. If there are no great-grandparents, the whole to the issue of great-grandparents in the nearest degree of kinship to the decedent per capita. Provided that in the case of a decedent who is survived by great-grandparents only, or the issue of great-grandparents only, such great-grandparents or the issue of such great-grandparents shall not be entitled to inherit from the decedent unless the decedent was at the time of his death an infant or an adjudged incompetent. Provided, further, that this subparagraph nine shall be applicable only to the estates of persons dying on or after its effective date.

(b) If the distributees of the decedent are in equal degree of kinship to him, their shares are equal.

Consanguinity = kinship

(c) There is no distribution per stirpes except in the case of the decedent's issue, brothers or sisters and the issue of brothers or sisters.

(d) For all purposes of this section, decedent's relatives of the half blood shall be treated as if they were relatives of the whole blood.

(e) Distributees of the decedent, conceived before his death but born alive thereafter, take as if they were born in his lifetime.

(f) The right of an adopted child to take a distributive share and the right of succession to the estate of an adopted child continue as provided in the domestic relations law.

(g) A distributive share passing to a surviving spouse under this section is in lieu of any right of dower to which such spouse may be entitled.

Uniform Probate Code

Section 2–101.   [Intestate Estate]

Any part of the estate of a decedent not effectively disposed of by his will passes to his heirs as prescribed in the following sections of this Code.

Section 2–102.   [Share of the Spouse]

The intestate share of the surviving spouse is:

(1) if there is no surviving issue or parent of the decedent, the entire intestate estate;

(2) if there is no surviving issue but the decedent is survived by a parent or parents, the first [$50,000], plus one-half of the balance of the intestate estate;

(3) if there are surviving issue all of whom are issue of the surviving spouse also, the first [$50,000], plus one-half of the balance of the intestate estate;

(4) if there are surviving issue one or more of whom are not issue of the surviving spouse, one-half of the intestate estate.

Section 2–103.   [Share of Heirs Other Than Surviving Spouse]

The part of the intestate estate not passing to the surviving spouse under Section 2–102, or the entire intestate estate if there is no surviving spouse, passes as follows:

(1) to the issue of the decedent; if they are all of the same degree of kinship to the decedent they take equally, but if of unequal degree, then those of more remote degree take by representation;

(2) if there is no surviving issue, to his parent or parents equally;

(3) if there is no surviving issue or parent, to the issue of the parents or either of them by representation;

(4) if there is no surviving issue, parent or issue of a parent, but the decedent is survived by one or more grandparents or issue of grandparents, half of the estate passes to the paternal grandparents if both survive, or to the surviving paternal grandparent, or to the issue of the paternal

grandparents if both are deceased, the issue taking equally if they are all of the same degree of kinship to the decedent, but if of unequal degree those of more remote degree take by representation; and the other half passes to the maternal relatives in the same manner; but if there be no surviving grandparent or issue of grandparent on either the paternal or the maternal side, the entire estate passes to the relatives on the other side in the same manner as the half.

Section 2–104.   [Requirement That Heir Survive Decedent For 120 Hours]

Any person who fails to survive the decedent by 120 hours is deemed to have predeceased the decedent for purposes of homestead allowance, exempt property and intestate succession, and the decedent's heirs are determined accordingly.   If the time of death of the decedent or of the person who would otherwise be an heir, or the times of death of both, cannot be determined, and it cannot be established that the person who would otherwise be an heir has survived the decedent by 120 hours, it is deemed that the person failed to survive for the required period.   This section is not to be applied where its application would result in a taking of intestate estate by the state under Section 2–105.

Section 2–105.   [No Taker]

If there is no taker under the provisions of this Article, the intestate estate passes to the [state].

Section 2–106.   [Representation]

If representation is called for by this Code, the estate is divided into as many shares as there are surviving heirs in the nearest degree of kinship and deceased persons in the same degree who left issue who survive the decedent, each surviving heir in the nearest degree receiving one share and the share of each deceased person in the same degree being divided among his issue in the same manner.

SECTION THREE.   COMPUTATION OF DEGREES— DISTRIBUTION AMONG COLLATERALS MORE REMOTE THAN BROTHERS AND SISTERS

IN RE WENDEL'S WILL
Surrogate's Court of New York, New York County, 1932.
143 Misc. 480, 257 N.Y.S. 87.

FOLEY, S.   This is a proceeding for the probate of the purported last will and testament of the decedent, Miss Wendel.   The supplemental citation directed to numerous alleged heirs and next of kin, who were specifically named therein, was recently returnable before me.   Service was also directed by publication generally to all those claiming to be heirs and next of kin of the decedent.   Over sixteen hundred claimants through their attorneys or personally have appeared and contend that they are within the class of legal distributees.   Application has also been made by the proponents of the will to procure the filing of a bill of particulars by these various claimants. The proponents seek to obtain a verified statement of the degree of relationship claimed and the particulars of the ancestry of the claimants and of their collateral relationship to Miss Wendel. Upon the return of the order to show cause for the bill of particulars and the return of the supplemental citation, the scope of the immediate application was widened by the various attorneys representing the opposing parties. They seek the advice and direction of the court as to a method of simplifying the issues, of expediting the disposal of certain preliminary questions which have been raised, and of reaching an ultimate determination of the validity or invalidity of the propounded will. Over one hundred and sixty attorneys or firms of attorneys have appeared in the proceeding.

The Surrogate stated upon the hearing that respect for justice and for our system of probate practice required that an orderly and expeditious mode of procedure, consistent with the rights of all the parties, should be established. The Surrogate also stressed the necessity for the co-operation of all the attorneys who have appeared, in order that undue delay, burdensome expense, or other injustice should be avoided. The proceeding is only extraordinary in the number of claimants who have appeared. The magnitude of the estate is relatively unimportant, for in other large estates similar difficulties have not arisen.

1. In accordance with the suggestion of the attorneys and the pronounced policy of the Surrogate, the order of procedure for the trial and the disposal of the successive issues, preliminary and final, will be as follows:

(A) The jurisdiction of the Surrogate's Court of New York County over the probate proceeding will be first brought on and determined. That question involves an adjudication as to whether Miss Wendel died a legal resident of New York county or Westchester county. If it be found that this court has no jurisdiction, the entire proceeding will be remitted to Westchester County for further action there.

(B) If jurisdiction be found in this court, there will be taken up next the trial of the relationship of the claimants to the decedent. Those claiming to be of the nearest degree will be tried first. When the standing of one person of the nearest degree is established, the status of only those claiming to be within that degree will be heard.

(C) Every other person beyond that degree has no legal interest in this estate and all appearances for such distantly related persons will be stricken out on motion.

(D) If Rosa Dew Stansbury is proven to be of the nearest degree the validity of the waiver executed by her and filed in this proceeding will be next tried.

(E) Finally, if there are any persons found to be next of kin and heirs at law of Miss Wendel, and legally entitled to contest the will, the trial of their objections to the validity of the will shall be brought on and determined.

2. The application for a bill of particulars is granted. The mere assertion of a claim of relationship to the decedent does not entitle a person to appear and contest the will. The fact that a claimant bears the name "Wendel," without any supporting proof of relationship, is worthless. The legal standing of a claimant as one of the next of kin and heirs at law of the maker of the alleged will must first be established before a contest will be permitted. Matter of Cook's Will, 244 N.Y. 63, 154 N.E. 823, 55 A.L.R. 806. Furthermore, only those within the nearest degree of kinship are entitled to contest the will. It appears to be conceded in the present proceeding that Miss Wendell left no descendants, no brothers or sisters, or nephews or nieces. The claimants rely upon their contention that they are first cousins or of a more remote collateral relationship.

The attention of counsel is called to the fact that our recent revision of the inheritance laws made by chapter 229 of the Laws of 1929 fundamentally changed the classes of persons entitled to inherit the property of a person dying without a will, or the classes of persons entitled to contest a will. Reports of the Commission to Investigate Defects in the Laws of Estates, Legislative Document No. 69 of 1930. The rules for the inheritance of property of every nature, real and personal, were made uniform. The inheritance of property was concentrated, instead of being scattered to the more distant relations. The former antiquated method of computing the degree of consanguinity and the canons of descent formerly relating to real property were abolished, Decedent Estate Law, § 81, as added by Laws 1929, c. 229, § 6, as amended by Laws 1930, c. 174, § 2. In their place there was substituted the modern method of computing degrees, and the rules of inheritance applicable formerly to personal property. The material provisions of section 81, Decedent Estate Law, read as follows: "All existing modes, rules and canons of descent are hereby abolished. The determination of the degrees of consanguinity of distributees of real and personal property shall be uniform, and shall be in accordance with the rules as applied immediately before the taking effect of this section to the determination of the next of kin of an intestate leaving personal property. All distinctions between the persons who take as heirs at law or next of kin are abolished and the descent of real property and the distribution of personal property shall be governed by this article except as otherwise specifically provided by law. * * *" Further statutory rules may be found in article 3 of the Decedent Estate Law and particularly section 83 thereof (added by Laws 1929, c. 229, § 6, as amended).

An important change was made as to the inheritance of real estate in the abolition of the former rule which permitted representation in collateral lines to the remotest degree. Representation is now permitted only as far as brothers and sisters and their descendants. Beyond brothers and sisters and their descendants, only persons within the nearest degree of relationship to the decedent are entitled to inherit intestate real or personal property. In other words, where there is a group of first cousins, as the nearest relatives, they alone are entitled to inherit. In such case if there are children or grandchildren of deceased first cousins, they are not entitled to inherit. The same rule applies to the ascertainment of the class of next of kin or heirs where there are second cousins or third cousins or more distant classes of relatives. When persons of the nearest degree of relationship establish that standing, those more remote are excluded.

These changes in the Decedent Estate Law took effect on September 1, 1930. Miss Wendel died thereafter on the 13th day of March, 1931. The new statutes, therefore, regulate and affect the property left by her and the determination of her heirs and next of kin.

For the benefit of the attorneys who have appeared in this proceeding, the statutory method of computing the degree of relationship to Miss Wendel may be shown by example. The statutory rule of computation requires the exclusion of the decedent and the counting of each person in the chain of ascent to and including the common ancestor, and then the counting downward of each subsequent descendant from the common ancestor to the claimant. Jessup-Redfield, Surrogate's Courts (8th Ed.) p. 2482, and the Appendix entitled "Descent and Distribution" by Surrogate Feely, p. 2779 et seq. Thus, Rosa Dew Stansbury is alleged in the petition to be the sole next of kin of Miss Wendel. The method of computing the degree of her relationship, starting from the decedent and excluding her from the count, is as follows:

CHART OF RELATIONSHIPS

Through a Common Ancestor

Tobias E. Stansbury—Third Degree
(Great Grandfather of decedent)
Common Ancestor

↑	↑
Henrietta Stansbury Dew,	Carville S. Stansbury
Second Degree	Fourth Degree
(Grandmother of decedent)	(Granduncle of decedent)
↑	↓
Mary Ann Dew Wendel	Rosa Dew Stansbury
First Degree	Fifth Degree
(Mother of decedent)	(Alleged next of kin of decedent)
↑	
Ella V. von E. Wendel	
(Decedent)	

There are certain claimants who contend they are first cousins. They would be of the fourth degree. If such status be ultimately established by them, Rosa Dew Stansbury, and every person claiming to be within the fifth degree, and those of every other more remote degree, are not proper parties to this proceeding. Similarly, if next of kin of the fifth degree establish their status, all persons beyond that degree must be eliminated and their appearances stricken out. Similar procedure must be adopted as to each widened circle of kinship beyond the established status of the nearest group of legal next of kin. In order to simplify the issues, the Surrogate has provided in the order of procedure set forth above that the claims of those persons contending that they are of the nearest degree to Miss Wendel should be tried first.

3. A suggestion has been made for the convenience of counsel that the proponents file genealogical charts of the ancestors and collaterals of Miss Wendel to a reasonable degree. That suggestion will be adopted by the Surrogate. It would appear that such procedure will assist attorneys in identifying the relationship of their clients, and the probability or improbability of their being next of kin of the decedent. Such charts, with the available dates of birth, death, and marriage of the ancestors of Miss Wendel to a reasonable degree, and of her collaterals to a reasonable degree, are directed to be filed by the proponents with the probate clerk of this court on or before April 25, 1932. These instructions and reasonable inquiry by the attorneys for the various claimants should disclose to them the possibility of a near relationship of their clients to the decedent. Where such relationship to Miss Wendel is revealed as too remote, or where no relationship at all is disclosed, it will be the duty of the attorney, as an officer of the court, to inform his client of the fact and the law, and promptly to withdraw, by written notice, his appearance in the proceeding.

4. The bill of particulars by the various claimants will be directed to be served upon the proponents' attorneys and filed in this court on or before May 21, 1932. The most important item of such bill is a definite statement of the numerical degree of the relationship of the specific claimant to Miss Wendel, with the further information as to the specific names in the chain from the decedent to the claimant, of the ancestors and descendants from the common ancestor.

The proposed form of the bill of particulars submitted by the proponents is approved as modified by the Surrogate. For the convenience of the attorneys for the various claimants and the Surrogate, the proponents are directed to print and supply copies of such form of a bill of particulars. The expense thereof may be charged out of the estate.

* * *

Notes

1. The Wendel estate ultimately produced over 2,000 claimants, the most dramatic of whom was one Thomas Patrick Morris, who claimed to be the nephew of Miss Wendel on the theory that he was the child of a secret marriage of her brother, John Gottlieb Wendel; his claim proved spurious, however, and he was convicted of conspiracy to defraud. The will contest was finally dropped after payment of a substantial sum to the nearest proved relatives.

Another aside on this case appeared in Time Magazine during the summer of 1950:

> Russia—Canine Canard. In his rich, full dog's life, Tobey, a small white French poodle, achieved fame of a sort. The last of a succession of Tobeys owned by rich, eccentric Miss Ella Virginia von Echtzel Wendel, he slept on a little bed in Miss Wendel's own bedroom in her house on Man-

hattan's Fifth Avenue, and ate delicate meals of sliced liver on a tiny table. When Miss Wendel died in 1931, aged 78, Tobey was looked after by two servants. Newsmen dubbed Tobey "the richest dog in the world." But, while Miss Wendel left an estate of $40 million, her will made no mention of Tobey. Two years later, the executors of the estate decided that Tobey, having reached a sickly and snappish nine years, should end his life painlessly at the veterinarian's.

Last week the late, long-forgotten Tobey achieved new fame. Moscow Radio Commentator Berko told listeners about "the little dog Tobey who lives in a very beautiful, richly decorated house, built by the best architects in the country. * * * His mistress, a mad American woman, left it $75 million * * * The dog sleeps on a golden bed. It is attended by a staff of 45 servants and six lawyers." Moral for Moscow: "While the millionaire dog lives in a beautiful private house, the children of the workers, dressed in tatters, roam the streets begging for a piece of bread. Like stray dogs, they sleep in the open * * * searching for food in the rubbish."

Miss Wendel's story continues to excite interest. Laporte, John M. Harlan Saves the Ella Wendel Estate, 59 A.B.A.J. 868 (1973).

2. The typical intestate succession statute specifies that if no one survives within certain enumerated classes of close relatives then the estate descends to remote heirs who are identified through the use of a general term such as "next of kin." Conn.Gen.Stat. § 45–276 is representative as it states that if no spouse, children or their representatives, parent, brother or sister or their representatives survive, "then the residue of the estate shall be distributed equally to the next of kin in equal degree, * * * and no representatives to be admitted among collaterals after the representatives of brothers and sisters * * *. In ascertaining the next of kin in all cases, the rule of the civil law shall be used." Under this expansive formula any blood relative, however remote, may succeed to the estate unless excluded by nearer relatives. The Surrogate in the Wendel case applies the civil law method of computing degrees of relationship which is the standard approach in this country for ascertaining "next of kin." Under the so-called canon law rule Rosa would be related to the decedent in the third degree (the longest line from the common ancestor, Tobias, is Ella's and includes herself, Mary and Henrietta). This method of computation is obsolete today.

An increasing number of statutes, of which the New York and Uniform Probate Code sections, set out supra, at pp. 65–67, are representative, impose limits, terminating the right to inherit after the descendants of decedent's grandparents. This limitation is designed to foreclose succession by the "laughing heir." In 1971 paragraph (a)(9), supra, was added to the New York statute, extending the right to inherit to great grandparents or their issue in the nearest degree if the decedent at the time of death was under eighteen or an adjudged incompetent. If a person dies without a will or a relative who qualifies to take under the intestate succession statute, the estate goes to the state by escheat. The number of estates which escheat, though still representing only a minute percentage of the overall number of estates being administered and distributed, will increase. Several New York cases, decided after the enactment of the revised statute, have concluded that the property goes to the state. In re Estate of Schaefer, 76 Misc.2d 488, 351 N.Y.S.2d 312 (1973); In re Willingham's Estate,

51 Misc.2d 516, 273 N.Y.S.2d 562 (1966). See also from another jurisdiction, State v. Witherspoon, 293 N.C. 321, 237 S.E.2d 822 (1977) (persons in the sixth degree of relationship to decedent not entitled to take; statute cuts off inheritance at the fifth degree).

3. As the principal case indicates, the laws of intestate succession have applications other than the distribution of estates in the absence of a will. They create a status which allows a person to contest the will and requires that he be among the group of interested persons to whom notice of the probate proceeding be directed. Kerin v. Goldfarb, 160 Conn. 463, 280 A.2d 143 (1971) (cousins have no standing to appeal a probate decree which holds that the aunt, being related in a closer degree, takes the estate to their exclusion). The theory of the will contest in the Wendel case was that testatrix lacked the mental capacity to make a will. Under the present New York statute, who would have standing to make this claim in the Wendel case?

4. Miss Wendel apparently left only one will. If she had executed two wills, both of them covering all her property, one in 1915 and the other in 1925, and if the 1915 will were effective unless revoked by the 1925 will, who would be entitled to contest the 1925 will?

A will may be revoked by destruction or mutilation, as well as by a later will either expressly revoking it or containing provisions inconsistent with it. In this hypothetical case it is assumed that the 1915 will was not physically destroyed or mutilated. See Stephens v. Brady, 209 Gal 428, 73 S.E.2d 182 (1952). See generally, Annot., Standing of Legatee or Devisee Under Alleged Prior or Subsequent Will to Oppose Probate or Contest Will, 39 A.L.R.3d 321. On revocation, see Chapter Five, Section Four, p. 324.

5. As indicated in the principal case and in the statutes of New York and Connecticut, supra, representation is not allowed after the issue of brothers and sisters. This arbitrary cutoff is justified as a matter of administrative convenience, it being too complicated to apply to the many people who might be that distantly related to the decedent, as well as by the conviction that these people are not real objects of the decedent's bounty. Most states cut off representation at this point, but not all. See UPC § 2–103(4), supra, pp. 66–67, which permits representation to the issue of grandparents. For an application of this provision, see In re Estate of Snigler, 205 Neb. 24, 285 N.W.2d 836 (1979).

6. If a decedent dies leaving as his or her only surviving relatives a first cousin (related through the grandparents) and a great aunt (related through the great grandparents) both are in the fourth degree to the decedent and presumably each takes half the estate. A number of states, however, have retained the parentelic principle and hold that the cousin, because her common ancestor is a closer relation to the decedent than is the great aunt's, will take all to the exclusion of the great aunt. For an example of such a statute, see West's Ann. Cal. Probate Code § 226.

7. It is customary to speak of the "common ancestor." This is legal shorthand since, except in the half-blood relationship (infra), there are two common ancestors (i.e., mother and father, grandmother and grandfather, etc). In a jurisdiction which determines "next of kin" by degrees of relationship it makes no difference whether the remote collateral is related through the mother or father of the decedent. His or her standing to take depends only on the degree of relationship being closer than or as close as the other claimants'. A number

of jurisdictions attempt to recognize equality of responsibility to the family of the father and the mother. UPC § 2–103(4), supra, is representative.

Under such a statute decedent's mother's cousin (related to decedent in the fifth degree) could take one half decedent's estate while the other half is divided up among decedent's father's brothers and sisters (aunts and uncles of decedent, who are related in the third degree). A distribution which divides the estate between the two families even though the recipients are not related to the decedent in equal degrees was ordered in State v. Tullar, 11 Ariz.App. 112, 462 P.2d 409 (1969) and Golden v. York, 407 S.W.2d 293 (Tex.App.1966); contra, Matter of Estate of Gregory, 616 P.2d 186 (Colo.App.1980) (relatives of maternal grandparents take to the exclusion of relatives of paternal great-grandparents). If there are no surviving relatives on one side of the family the entire estate goes to the relatives on the other side. State v. Estate of Loomis, 553 S.W.2d 166 (Tex.App.1977) (entire estate awarded to descendants of maternal grandparents; half did not escheat to the state). The Texas statute saved a share of the multi-million dollar Howard Hughes estate (estimates of the magnitude of the estate range from $160 million to $2 billion) for the three granddaughters of Hughes's paternal uncle; their share would have otherwise been added to the estate going to 16 relatives on the maternal side. Reed v. Cameron, unpublished opinion, Texas Court of Appeals, First Judicial District, Aug. 1, 1983.

8. The administrative procedures set up by Surrogate Foley in this case have served as prototypes. See, In re Powers' Estate, 194 Misc. 979, 91 N.Y. S.2d 802 (1949). As to the type of evidence admissible to prove relationships, see In re Morris' Will, 277 App.Div. 211, 98 N.Y.S.2d 997 (1950). Fortunately cases of this kind are extremely rare. Perhaps the most sensational of all was concluded in Philadelphia in 1953. On November 16, 1930 Henrietta E. Garrett died intestate leaving an estate in excess of $17,000,000, a fortune originally accumulated from the sale of snuff. During the next twenty years some 26,000 persons claimed the estate as next of kin; some 2,000 hearings took place; over 1,100 witnesses were heard; and the record finally totaled 390 volumes covering over 115,000 pages. In 1950 a special Master filed a 900-page report which decreed distribution to three first cousins of Mrs. Garrett; his report was affirmed by the Orphans' Court in 1952 and the Supreme Court of Pennsylvania in 1953 (total time elapsed to settle the estate came to 23 years). In re Garrett's Estate, 372 Pa. 438, 94 A.2d 357 (1953).

SECTION FOUR. REPRESENTATION— DISTRIBUTION AMONG LINEALS AND THE FIRST COLLATERAL LINE

IN RE MARTIN'S ESTATE
Supreme Court of Vermont, 1923.
96 Vt. 455, 120 A. 862.

POWERS, J. Jennie E. Martin, late of Calais, died intestate, leaving as next of kin three grandchildren: Alice E. Martin, Bourke Martin, and Ned Martin. Alice E. is the daughter of Earle Martin; the others are the sons of Charles Martin. The probate court, by the decree appealed from, distributed the estate of Jennie E. by dividing it into three equal parts, and giving one of these parts to each of the grandchildren. The appellant, the guardian of Alice E., claims that the distribution should have been per stirpes, and not per capita. The case comes here by direct appeal under G.L. 3451.

The right to succeed to the property of an ancestor is not a natural right (Gaines v. Strong's Estate, 40 Vt. 354), but a "gift of the law" (Succession of Lacosst, 142 La. 673, 77 South. 497; Jones v. Jones, 234 U.S. 615, 34 Sup.Ct. 937, 58 L.Ed. 1500). Hence the rights of these grandchildren in the estate of the intestate are just what the statute of descent gives them. All agree that the whole question depends upon a proper construction of Canon I, of G.L. 3416, which reads as follows:

"In equal shares to the children of said deceased person or the legal representatives of deceased children."

The appellant insists that these grandchildren, being "representatives of deceased children," take by representation; and if this is so, it will be difficult to avoid her conclusion that they take per stirpes; for their rights would be determined by those of the persons they represent. In common with many, if not all, the American states, we get our law of descent largely from the English statute of distributions (22, 23 Charles II), Hatch v. Hatch, 21 Vt. 450; 2 Kent, * 426, under which it became settled at a very early day that the doctrine of representation applied only when the claimants were related to the intestate in unequal degrees; and that when they were equally related to him, they took directly and per capita—not by representation and per stirpes. For, it was said, the latter method would not then be necessary to prevent the exclusion of those in a remoter degree of relationship, and therefore would be contrary to the spirit and policy of the statute, which aimed at a just and equal distribution. 2 Kent, *425; 2 Will.Exrs. 1605; 2 Blacks. 517; Bacon's Abridg.Exrs. 1, 3; Walsh v. Walsh, Pre.Ch. 514, a case which the Lord Chancellor said in Davers v. Dewes, 3 P.Will. 50, was decided upon great deliberation, and that it was "fit that matter should now (1730) be at rest."

So when we adopted the English statute, this was the settled English interpretation of it; and it must be taken that we adopted the construction with the statute. Adams v. Field, 21 Vt. 256; Warner v. Warner's Est., 37 Vt. 356; Bosquet v. Howe Scale Co. (Vt.) 120 Atl. 171. This rule has been approved by high authority in this country. "The rule of representation," says Chief Justice Shaw in Knapp v. Windsor, 6 Cush. (Mass.) 156, "applies only from necessity, or where there are lineal heirs in different degrees, as children and the children of a deceased child. * * *" Equally direct and positive is the approval of the doctrine in Nichols v. Shepard, 63 N.H. 391, and Preston v. Cole, 64 N.H. 459, 13 Atl. 788. It follows, as is quite generally held in this country, that those who take as a class take equally. Hillhouse v. Chester, 3 Day (Conn.) 166, 213, 3 Am.Dec. 265; Snow v. Snow, 111 Mass. 389; Brown v. Baraboo, 90 Wis. 151, 62 N.W. 921, 30 L.R.A. 320. Or, to state it as above, those equally related to an intestate participate equally in his estate. 4 Kent, *375; note to In re Ingram, 12 Am.St.Rep. 112. So manifestly just is this rule that in the construction of a doubtful statute it should be given preference.   Lipman's Appeal, 30 Pa. 180, 72 Am.Dec. 692.

Such equality of benefit is the unmistakable spirit of our statute of descent.   It runs all through it.   Thus, children, under Canon I, share equally;   father and mother, under Canon III, share equally;   brothers and sisters, under Canon IV, share equally;   and next of kin, under Canon V, share equally.   In harmony with these provisions, then, we hold that it was the intention of the Legislature that grandchildren, who alone survive the ancestor, should take equally.   In other words, that they should take as heirs, and not by representation.   In such cases, the effect is the same as if the statute read "in equal shares to the descendants of such deceased person"—the clause providing for representation applying only when inequality of relationship exists.

Judgment affirmed.   Let the result be certified to the probate court.

GODWIN v. MARVEL

Orphans' Court of Delaware, Kent County, 1953.
99 A.2d 354.

James H. Satterfield died intestate in 1950, owning a house and lot in Frederica.   He left to survive him no widow, no father or mother, and no brothers or sisters.   There were five brothers and sisters who predeceased him, all leaving children or issue of deceased children to survive them.   Altogether there were eleven nephews and nieces, some of whom predeceased the intestate leaving issue.   The petition filed in this case avers that the proceeds of the real estate should be divided equally among the living nephews and nieces and the issue of those who died before the intestate or, in other words, that the primary number of shares is eleven. The appearing respondents contend that the division should be per stirpes or, in other words, that the number of primary shares is five.

The pertinent statute is 12 Del.C. § 502, which gives the rules of descent of real estate.   It provides for descent first to children and issue of deceased children;   if there be none, then to father and mother or the survivor of them.   Paragraph (3) reads in part as follows:

"If there be no father or mother, then in equal shares to his brothers and sisters, and the lawful issue of any deceased brother or sister, by right of representation.   *   *   *."

Paragraph (4) provides if there be no brother or sister or issue of such, then the descent is to the next of kin in equal degree, and the lawful issue of such next of kin, by right of representation.

CAREY, Judge.   This case presents the problem of whether our intestate statute requires a per capita division among nephews and nieces, or a per stirpes division based upon the number of brothers and sisters of the intestate, where none of those brothers and sisters survive.

This question was answered, as to personal property, by Chancellor Ridgely in Richard Baning's Will, Orph.Ct., 3 Del.Cas. 49 in the year 1822.   The statute under which his decision was rendered is found in 1

Del.Laws 284, being Chapter CXIX, 24 Geo. II. The Chancellor there pointed out a material difference between our statute and the English Statute of Distribution (22 & 23 Car. II, c. 10). He showed that, under the English statute, distribution among nephews and nieces was per capita because that act made no specific mention of brothers or sisters or their issue. It gave the surplus to the children or their representatives and, if there were none, "equally to every of the next of kindred who are in equal degree, and those who legally represent them". The Chancellor next showed that under our Act then in force, if there were no children or issue of such, the residue was distributed equally among the brothers and sisters or their representatives, and only gave the residue to the next of kindred in the absence of brothers and sisters, or issue thereof. He directed a per stirpes division.

The statute upon which the Baning case was based contained exactly the same language for the distribution of personal property as for the descent of real estate, and although the decision dealt with personal property, it applied with equal force to real estate. It accordingly becomes important to ascertain whether the present law of Delaware is or is not substantially the same as it stood in 1822.

In examining the legislative history of our Act, it is interesting to notice the provisions of Chapter 6, 12 Williams [sic] III, adopted in 1700, and published in 1 Del.Laws, Appendix Page 26. Like the English statute of descents, this Act, if there were no children or issue thereof, gave both the personal and real estate to the next of kindred in equal degree and those who legally represent them. There seems to have been little change in this scheme until the Act of 24 Geo. II, c. 119, when for the first time it was expressly provided that, if there be no children or legal representatives thereof, the estate should be distributed equally among the brothers and sisters or their legal representatives. If there were none, then it passed to the next of kindred in equal degree or those who legally represent them. As indicated above, it was this statute which was in effect when the Baning case was decided.

In the year 1827 a new statute was adopted, being found in 7 Del.Laws 316. It applied only to real estate and gave it, if there were no children or issue of them, "to every the brothers and sisters * * * and the lawful issue of any such brothers and sisters who shall have died before the deceased of the intestate". It also contained this provision: "The issue of children, brothers, sisters, or other kin, who shall have died before the decease of the intestate, shall in all cases take according to stocks by right of representation, that is to say; the same share which such children, brothers, sisters or other kin if living would have taken: and this rule shall hold although the descent shall be entirely to issue of deceased children, brothers, sisters or other kin". Two years later in 1829, a statute was adopted which altered the manner of distribution of personal property. 7 Del.Laws 217, 227. It designated the same order of descent in similar language as did the Act of 1827 but, in contrast to the proviso found in the latter act, contained this paragraph: "Distribution among children, brothers, sisters, or other kin in equal degree shall be in equal portions; but issue of children, brothers or other kin who shall have died before the intestate, shall take according to stocks by right of representation; and this rule shall hold although the distribution be entirely among such issue". It will be noticed that the statute of distribution, enacted only two years after the statute of descent, contained an express direction that distribution among children, brothers or other kin in equal degrees shall be in equal portions; and this statement still appears in our present law of distribution. 12 Del.C. § 513. It was not included in the Act of 1827, however, nor is it found in our present law of descents. 12 Del.C. § 501.

The Act of 1827 was changed in a number of minor respects in the Revised Code of 1852, Chapter 85. The language there used was "in equal shares to his brothers and sisters, and the lawful issue of any deceased brother or sister, by right of representation. * * *." The words, "inheritance * * * by right of representation" are defined as taking place when the issue of a deceased heir takes the same share, or right in the estate of another person, which their parent would have taken, if living. It then says "such representation shall hold although the descent shall be entirely to issue of deceased children, brothers, sisters, or other kin."

The language of the Revised Code of 1852 is substantially the same as is found in the present Code. Its meaning is, in my opinion, the same as the act of Geo. II as interpreted by Chancellor Ridgely, in so far as the present case is concerned. Whether this is true with respect to personal property in the light of the change made in 1829 need not now be considered.

The petitioners have relied upon In re Cavender's Estate, 14 Del.Ch. 465, 130 A. 746, which was followed by In re Estate of White, 27 Del.Ch. 438, 37 A.2d 167. Both of those cases dealt with the fourth, rather than the third, paragraph of the rules of descent, which applies when there are no brothers or sisters or issue of them, and which in such case gives the realty to the next of kin in equal degree, and the lawful issue of them, by right of representation. It is true that the Cavender opinion quotes with approval language from both Blackstone and Kent which would cast doubt upon the correctness of the Baning holding were it not for the difference in the old English Statute and the Delaware law, but the Court quoted those eminent authorities only for the purpose of assisting in determining the proper interpretation of Paragraph (4), and the Court clearly had no intention of passing upon the meaning of Paragraph (3). The effect of the two cases is this: under (4), descent is directly to the next of kin in equal degree in equal shares, and representation takes place only when there are issue of deceased next of kin of that degree; under (3) descent is to the brothers and sisters, and the issue of any who are deceased take by representation even though no brother or sister survives the intestate.

My conclusion is that the proper method of dividing the proceeds from the sale of the real estate in this case is the method suggested by the respondents, to wit: a per stirpes division based upon the number of brothers and sisters. The decree of distribution will be based upon this conclusion.

Notes

1. The terms "per capita" and "per stirpes" are used so indiscriminately in the cases and statutes that they more frequently confuse than clarify the issue. Per stirpes means to take by the stocks or as the representative of an ancestor who is of a closer relationship to but who has predeceased the decedent. Per capita means to take in one's own right. The confusion sets in because a per capita distribution at one generation level is held not to preclude persons more remotely related from taking by representation of a deceased person who would have been on that generation level had he been alive. In this latter situation both per capita and per stirpes principles are being applied. The typical question presented in the cases involves the identification of the generation level at which the initial division into shares is to be made. A strict per stirpes distribution makes the division at the first level of relationship to the decedent whether anyone is alive on that level or not. Under this approach in the Martin case, the property would be divided into halves representing the respective shares of the two deceased sons, Earle and Charles. The other method of distribution makes the initial division into shares at the first generation level where some person is alive and treats all persons on that level equally. In the Martin case, the first generation level of living persons is that of Alice, Bourke and Ned and the property is therefore divided into thirds. This method of distribution is properly classified as per capita when the statute specifically identifies the persons at this level as takers (e.g. "and then in equal shares to the grandchildren and the representatives of any deceased grandchildren") and does not refer to them as representatives of deceased children. It should be noted that if any grandchild has predeceased the decedent leaving issue that issue may take by representation the share of their ancestor.

Many decisions agree with the reasoning set out in the Martin case and divide the property equally at the first generation level on which some one has survived the decedent. See e.g. Washburn v. Scurlock, 5 Ohio App.3d 125, 449 N.E.2d 797 (1982); Hockman v. Lowe, 624 S.W.2d 719 (Tex.App.1981); Brice v. Seebeck, 595 P.2d 441 (Okl.1979); In re Estate of Brown, 158 Mont. 413, 492 P.2d 914 (1972); In re Le Roux's Estate, 55 Wash.2d 889, 350 P.2d 1001 (1960).

A number of jurisdictions apply a strict per stirpes distribution in the manner of Godwin v. Marvel. In In re Tierney's Estate, 216 A.2d 683 (Del.Ch.1965) the Godwin rule was made applicable to personal property. See e.g. In re Frear's Estate, 180 Cal.App.2d 829, 4 Cal.Rptr. 801 (1960) (reviews the California authority construing the statute, "in equal shares to his brothers and sisters and to the descendants of deceased brothers and sisters by right of representation," as requiring a per stirpes distribution); In re Davol's Estate, 100 So.2d 188 (Fla.1958) (Florida statute specifically calls for per stirpes distribution); see also, Housley v. Laster, 176 Tenn. 174, 140 S.W.2d 146 (1940); Swenson v. Lewison, 135 Minn. 145, 160 N.W. 253 (1916); Cook v. Catlin, 25 Conn. 387 (1856).

See generally, Annot., Descent and Distribution to Nieces and Nephews as Per Stirpes or Per Capita, 19 A.L.R.2d 191; Page, Descent Per Stirpes and Per Capita, 1946 Wis.L.Rev. 3 (analyzing, tracing the history and criticizing the confusing and indiscriminate use of the terms).

2. Decedent died intestate leaving no lineal ascendants or descendants, but leaving descendants of two deceased brothers, A and B. A had two children, C and D. C survived the intestate. D predeceased the intestate, leaving two children, E and F, surviving the intestate. B had three children, G, H, and I, all of whom survived the intestate. Assuming that all descendants of brothers are permitted to take by representation, how would the estate be distributed under the methods of distribution outlined above?

If G had also predeceased the intestate leaving three surviving children, J, K, and L, how would E, F, J, K, and L share in the estate? In re Poindexter's Estate, 221 N.C. 246, 20 S.E.2d 49, 140 A.L.R. 1138 (1942); Maud v. Catherwood, 67 Cal.App.2d 636, 155 P.2d 111 (1945); Note, 25 N.Y.U.L.Rev. 863, 869 (1950).

In terms of the decedent's probable intent what might be said for each method of distribution? Is it significant that when testators specify in wills how future generations are to take they almost invariably direct a per stirpes distribution?

3. Decedent died intestate, leaving as his closest surviving relatives his maternal grandmother and a paternal aunt (i.e. his father's sister). The aunt claimed that decedent's estate should be divided two-thirds to her and one third to the grandmother. Her theory rested on the premise that her deceased father and mother (decedent's paternal grandparents) were each entitled to a third of the estate and that she was entitled to their shares by representation. The court awarded the estate, half to the maternal grandmother and half to the paternal aunt, noting that to give the latter a "double share would produce an unacceptable result, considering among other factors her greater degree of removal from the decedent." Wood v. Wood, 160 N.J.Super 597, 390 A.2d 703 (1978). As the court noted, this issue could not arise today because New Jersey has adopted the Uniform Probate Code provision discussed in Note 7, p. 73–74, supra.

4. A person who is entitled to property by representation is held, by the weight of authority, to take the property directly from the decedent and not from the ancestor whom he is representing. This means that the property is not subject to claims against the ancestor's estate. Sam died survived by the children of a predeceased brother, Daniel. Daniel owed Sam approximately $5,000. The share passes to the children of Daniel by intestacy without being charged with Daniel's debt even though the children are taking per stirpes as representatives of Daniel. In re Berk's Estate, 196 Cal.App.2d 278, 16 Cal. Rptr. 492 (1961); the authorities are reviewed in Annots., 1 A.L.R. 1037; 75 A.L.R. 888; and 164 A.L.R. 747. UPC § 2–111 states: "A debt owed to the decedent is not charged against the intestate share of any person except the debtor. If the debtor fails to survive the decedent, the debt is not taken into account in computing the intestate share of the debtor's issue."

5. Except for adopted children and the intestate's spouse, succession is based entirely on blood relationship. Thus a daughter- or son-in-law does not participate in the estate as an heir of parents-in-law when his or her spouse has previously died. In re Vigil's Estate, 38 N.M. 383, 34 P.2d 667, 93 A.L.R. 1506 (1934); Schultz v. Schultz, 183 Iowa 920, 167 N.W. 674 (1918); Dunaway v. McEachern, 37 So.2d 767 (Miss.1948). Nor does an unadopted step-child participate in the estate of his step-father or -mother. In re Estate of McLaughlin, 11 Wash.App. 320, 523 P.2d 437 (1974); In re Wall's Will, 216 N.C.

805, 5 S.E.2d 837 (1939); but see Ohio Revised Code § 2105.06(I) which says, "If there are no next of kin, to stepchildren or their lineal descendants, per stirpes"; Kest v. Lewis, 169 Ohio St. 317, 159 N.E.2d 449 (1959). Stepchildren and daughters- and sons-in-law may be accorded the favored position of children under other state statutes such as inheritance tax laws. Needless to say, the widow of intestate's deceased brother is not a representative of the brother entitled to take the brother's share. In re Meyer's Will, 56 N.J.Super. 167, 152 A.2d 160 (1959).

6. The extent to which the statutory intestate distribution conforms to the probable intent of the property owner has been the subject of several inquiries through the analysis of representative wills. In a substantial majority of estates the preferred plan is to leave everything to the spouse, omitting the children. This preference is not due to any want of affection for the children but rather is the result of trust in the living spouse to take care of the children and provide for them at his or her death. If no spouse survives, the estate regularly descends to the children or their issue. If no spouse or issue survive, no discernible patterns of disposition emerge. Sussman, Cates, Smith, The Family and Inheritance, Ch. 5, pages 83–120 (1970). Other samplings tend to confirm these findings. Browder, Recent Patterns of Testate Succession in the United States and England, 67 Mich.L.Rev. 1303 (1969); Dunham, the Method, Process and Frequency of Wealth Transmission at Death, 30 Chi.L.Rev. 241 (1963); Powell and Looker, Decedents' Estates—Illumination from Probate and Tax Records, 30 Col.L.Rev. 919 (1930); Ward and Beuscher, The Inheritance Process in Wisconsin, 1950 Wis.L.Rev. 393. The same dispositive patterns emerge in community property states. Price, The Transmission of Wealth at Death in a Community Property Jurisdiction, 50 Wash.L.Rev. 277 (1975). For a study using sociobiological techniques to discern the probate intent of persons who die intestate, see Beckstrom, Sociobiology and Intestate Wealth Transfers, 72 N.W. U.L.Rev. 216 (1981).

Up until a decade or two ago the typical intestate statute gave one-third to the spouse and two-thirds to the issue and, in the event no issue survived, required the spouse to share with the decedent's parents or brothers and sisters. Recent reforms in many states have substantially augmented the spouse's share and made it exclusive if no issue survives. The promulgation of the Uniform Probate Code has inspired a number of comprehensive analyses of intestate statutes. Curry, Intestate Succession and Wills: A Comparative Analysis of Article II of the Uniform Probate Code and the Law of Ohio, 34 Ohio St.L.J. 114 (1973); O'Connell and Effland, Intestate Succession and Wills: A Comparative Analysis of the Law of Arizona and the Uniform Probate Code, 14 Ariz.L.Rev. 205 (1972).

7. The focus here has been exclusively on the situation where there is no will. Actually these principles have a much greater impact on the wealth transmission process in terms of number of cases and size of the estates involved in situations where there is a will. The problem arises where there is a direction to distribute ultimate remainders to "my descendants" or "my brother's heirs, issue, relations," etc. It is not much of a trick under the Rule against Perpetuities to construct a trust which will endure for 100 years by which time a person can have accumulated a large number of descendants. See City of Wheeling v. Zane, 154 W.Va. 34, 173 S.E.2d 158 (1970) (determining the heirs of the grantor of an 1821 deed who died in 1831); Osgood v. Vivada, 94 N.H.

222, 50 A.2d 227 (1946) (construction of an 1862 will). The problem with these dispositions is to find the intent of the testators. Because they usually had given no thought whatsoever to the family pattern as it actually turned out, their intent may well be open to a number of plausible interpretations. In making a decision the only specific guidelines available may be the definitions which have evolved under the law of intestate succession. The New York statute, EPTL § 2–1.1 and § 1–2.5, defines "heirs," "heirs at law" and "next of kin," unless a contrary intent is shown, as being the distributees set out in the intestate succession statutes. The recent statutes which cut off the right of inheritance at the issue of grandparents may create unintended results. A testator who directs that the remainder of a trust is to go to heirs or next of kin is not likely to have intended the State of New York to be included within that class as a possible beneficiary. The statutes which make this result possible are discussed in Note 2, supra, at p. 72–73.

Some wills specify per stirpes or per capita and are still ambiguous, as in the bequest to named beneficiaries, "in equal shares, per stirpes and not per capita." Do the beneficiaries take equally or do they take by representation through their parents? Matter of Will of Griffin, 411 So.2d 766 (Miss.1982) (named beneficiaries take equally; per stirpes direction only applicable to determine substituted legatees if a designated beneficiary dies before will becomes effective); for a similar interpretation of language setting out a legacy to a class of children, "to be divided among them per stirpes, share and share alike", see Hartford National Bank and Trust Co. v. Thrall, 184 Conn. 497, 440 A.2d 200 (1981).

Consider the confusion that results from language such as "to each of my heirs share and share alike" or "in equal shares to my issue." A person dies leaving 100 living children, grandchildren and greatgrandchildren. Do they each get ¹⁄₁₀₀ of the estate or do living parents cut off their children of more remote degree? See, for instance, Warren v. First New Haven Nat. Bank, 150 Conn. 120, 186 A.2d 794 (1962) (changing the ancient rule in Connecticut and holding that remote issue could not compete with their living parents for a share). Other problems arising out of the term "heirs" will be dealt with in Chapter Nine, at p. 802.

SECTION FIVE. SOURCE OF PROPERTY AS A REFERENCE—THE HALF-BLOOD AND OTHERS

IN RE ESTATE OF ROBBS

Supreme Court of Oklahoma, 1972.
504 P.2d 1228.

WILLIAMS, Justice. This appeal presents a question of statutory interpretation in a factual setting never considered by this Court before. It involves the general scheme of descent and distribution found in our statutes of intestate succession.

The question is whether the exception following the word "unless" in our half blood statute, 84 O.S.1971, § 222, is applicable only when the half blood kindred and whole blood kindred are related to decedent in the same degree, or whether it operates to disinherit nearer half blood kindred *not* of the blood of the ancestor in favor of more remote whole blood kindred of the decedent who *are* of the blood of the ancestor.

§ 222 provides as follows:

"Kindred of the half-blood inherit equally with those of the whole blood *in the same degree,* unless the inheritance come to the intestate by descent, devise or gift of some one of his ancestors, in which case all those who are not of the blood of such ancestors must be excluded from such inheritance." (Emphasis added).

The decedent in this case was Lucinda Robbs. She died unmarried and without issue, father, mother, or full brothers or sisters. Her surviving kindred are a maternal half brother and the children of some maternal half brothers and maternal half sisters, on the one hand, and some paternal cousins on the other. The contest is between these two sets of rival claimants. A substantial portion of her estate, and the only portion involved in this appeal, consisted of real estate devised to her by a paternal uncle. It is agreed that an uncle is within the broad definition accorded the word "ancestors" in our half blood statute.

The county court decreed that the paternal ancestral estate descended to the half blood maternal kindred of decedent (her kindred of the 2nd and 3rd degrees; see 84 O.S.1971, § 221); the district court decreed that it descended to the paternal cousins (decedent's kindred of the 4th degree).

It is said that the rule of the common law excluding the half blood from an inheritance has never met with favor in the United States, and that *even in the absence of a statute such as our § 222,* "the half blood is usually held to take equally with the whole blood, such rule being based either on the intent of the legislature as gathered from the other sections of the statutes of descent, or on the theory that the common-law rule was founded on the feudal law and is not applicable to our institutions". 141 A.L.R. 977. This is the case in Oklahoma. In 1924, in Thompson v. Smith, 102 Okl. 150, 227 P. 77, this Court said:

"* * * where the statute refers to brothers and sisters of the decedent, the same is held to include one-half brothers and one-half sisters in determining the right to inherit. * * * Therefore it is plain that, instead of [§ 222] being an enabling statute, it must be construed to be a qualification of the general rule in the preceding section [now 84 O.S.1971, § 213]."

Many of the other states of this country have half blood statutes that are identical, or almost identical, with our § 222. Under the varying constructions of these statutes, two divergent lines of authority have emerged on the question of whether the statutes operate to disinherit the decedent's nearer kindred of the half blood not of the blood of the ancestor in favor of decedent's more remote kindred of the whole blood who are of the blood of the ancestor. See annotation at 141 A.L.R. 977.

* * *

For convenience we will refer to the conflicting conclusions reached as the California rule and the Arkansas rule. In *Thompson,* this Court quite specifically rejected the California rule and adopted the Arkansas rule, holding with regard to § 222 that "said section qualifies the general rule as to inheritance by those of the half blood found in [84 O.S.1971, § 213 Second] and the half blood is excluded from an inheritance that came to the deceased by descent, devise or gift of some one of his ancestors, and that the rule in Kelly v. McGuire, 15 Ark. [555] 586, be followed." In *Kelly,* the Arkansas Court had held, in 1854, that under the Arkansas version of the half blood statute, "where the inheritance is in any one line, if [sic] there goes in succession   *   *   *   precisely as if the other line was extinct, and precisely as the inheritance of a bastard would take a course in his mother's line, he having no father's line at all." Under this construction of the half blood statute, decedent's half blood kindred not of the blood of the ancestor were totally disinherited in favor of decedent's kindred of the whole blood who were of the blood of the ancestor, regardless of whether they were related to decedent "in the same degree."

The California rule which was examined and rejected by this Court in *Thompson* was apparently first stated by the California court in In re Smith's Estate, 131 Cal. 433, 63 P. 729. In that case, in 1901, the court held in effect that the California half blood statute, identical with our § 222, was applicable only in situations where the half blood kindred and whole blood kindred were related to decedent "in the same degree", in which case the half blood kindred not of the blood of the ancestor would be excluded from inheriting the ancestral property. Under that construction, the half blood statute would not operate to disinherit nearer half blood kindred in favor of whole blood kindred in a more remote degree. For a more recent exposition of the California rule, see In re Ryan's Estate, 21 Cal. 498, 133 P.2d 626.

In view of the unequivocal language of this Court in *Thompson,* which was later reaffirmed in In re Long's Estate, 180 Okl. 28, 67 P.2d 41, 110 A.L.R. 1002, it must be said that in the case now before us the trial court and the Court of Appeals respectively were justified in rendering and affirming judgment in favor of decedent's more remote kindred of the whole blood (the paternal cousins) and in excluding the nearer kindred of the half blood.

Nevertheless, upon careful consideration, and for the reasons set out below, we have concluded that this Court erred in *Thompson* in rejecting the California rule and adopting the Arkansas rule.

1. Perhaps the principal reason for rejecting the rule set out in In re Smith's Estate, 131 Cal. 433, 63 P. 729, was stated by this Court as follows in *Thompson:*

> "In the case of In re Smith's Estate, supra, the conclusion reached was upon the theory that such statutes as [§ 222] are regarded as enabling laws conferring upon kindred of the one-half blood a right of inheritance not theretofore enjoyed equally with those of the whole blood."

This was not correct. This Court obviously overlooked the following language in In re Smith: "Hence the provision [the California half blood statute] has no application as between kindred in different degrees, but the relative claims of these [the half blood kindred] are determined exclusively by the provisions of section 1386 of the Civil Code, where the term 'brothers and sisters,' and other terms denoting kindred of various degrees, are used in their proper sense, and 'according to the approved usage of the language'   *   *   *   *mand *must be held to include those of the half as well as of the whole blood"* (emphasis added).   To the same effect, see Lynch v. Lynch, 132 Cal. 214, 64 P. 284, decided two months after *Smith,* in which the California court said   " * * *   where the term 'brothers' or 'sisters' is used without limitation it includes half-brothers and half-sisters."   Thus, the general rule in California as in Oklahoma is that kindred of the half blood inherit under the general statutes of descent, and the respective half blood statutes cannot be said to confer a right of inheritance "not theretofore enjoyed."

2. In *Thompson,* this Court said that our half blood statute   " *   *   * is also identical in material parts to section 2533 of Mansfield's Digest of the Laws of Arkansas."   Again, this is not correct.   That section, the Arkansas half blood statute, now codified without change as Ark.Stats. 1947, § 61–112, is as follows:

> "Relations of the half-blood shall inherit equally with those of the whole blood in the same degree; *and the descendants of such relatives shall inherit in the same manner as the descendants of the whole blood,* unless the inheritance come to the intestate by descent, devise, or gift, of some one of his ancestors, in which case all those who are not of the blood of such ancestor shall be excluded from such inheritance."   (Emphasis added).

Of course the portion emphasized above is not found in our § 222. Considering the grammatical construction of the Arkansas half blood statute only, the exception following the word "unless" applies only to *descendants* of the half blood relations, and not the half blood relations themselves (although it has not been so construed by the Arkansas courts). It may be noted in passing that the difficult problems confronting Arkansas courts in the construction of Arkansas statutes of descent are compounded by the next section (§ 61–113) which provides, among other things, that in all cases not covered by the statutes, descent shall be "according to the course of the common law".   This section has no counterpart in Oklahoma statutes.

Since (1) the California rule stated in *Smith* was based upon a statute identical with our § 222, which cannot be distinguished upon the basis that the California half blood statute is an enabling law and ours is not as this Court mistakenly indicated in *Thompson;* and (2) since the Arkansas statute construed in *Kelly* was not, as this Court also indicated in *Thompson,* "identical in material parts" with our § 222; and (3) since this Court's decisions construing our half blood statute were perhaps unduly influenced by the Indian allotments question which was usually presented in the same cases (there being more reason to preserve the Indian allotment in the Indian blood line); we are forced to the conclusion that our holding in *Thompson* rejecting the California rule and adopting the Arkansas rule was erroneous.

We therefore hold that our half blood statute, 84 O.S.1971, § 222, is applicable only when the surviving half blood kindred and whole blood kindred are related to decedent in the same degree, and that it does not operate to disinherit nearer half blood kindred not of the blood of the ancestor in favor of more remote whole blood kindred who are of the blood of the ancestor.

This Court has discussed or considered § 222 in sixteen cases (one was a dissenting opinion separately published). See Shepard's Oklahoma Citations. Because of the differing factual situations, no useful purpose would be served by discussing them in detail here. We note that of all of the sixteen cases, only in *Thompson,* would the result have been different under the rule we adopt today. (There the surviving half brother would not have been excluded). Not even in *Thompson* can it be said that a more remote relative of the whole blood was favored over a nearer half blood relative of the decedent, because in that case the prevailing heir, under 84 O.S.1971, § 213 Second, was the surviving husband of decedent. He inherited because of the provisions of § 213 Second, and not because he was of the blood of the ancestor and the excluded half brother was not.

In this connection it may be noted that in the last case in which this Court considered § 222, DeRoin v. Whitetail, Okl., 312 P.2d 967, the half brother who was excluded by the trial court's judgment did not appeal, and the precise question here involved was not presented in that case.

The opinion of the Court of Appeals is vacated; the judgment of the District Court of Muskogee County is reversed and the cause is remanded to the trial court with directions to enter judgment in accordance with the views herein expressed.

BERRY, C. J., and IRWIN, LAVENDER, BARNES and SIMMS, JJ., concur.

DAVISON, V. C. J., and JACKSON and HODGES, JJ., dissent.

JACKSON, Justice (dissenting). The difficulty I have in interpreting 84 O.S.1971, § 222, stems from its arrangement and substance. It is a one-sentence section and deals with two kinds of kindred and two different sources of an estate. In addition, as sometimes occurs, we find ourselves interpreting former decisions of this court as distinguished from interpreting the statute. Section 222, with numerals added, provides as follows:

(1) "Kindred of the half-blood inherit equally with those of the whole blood in the same degree, (2) unless the inheritance come to the intestate by descent, devise or gift of some one of his ancestors, in which case all those who are not of the blood of such ancestors must be excluded from such inheritance."

That part of the sentence identified as number (2) constitutes an exception to provision number (1) so that if we make a new sentence out of provision number (2) it would provide substantially as follows:

"*If* the inheritance come to the intestate by descent, devise or gift of some one of his ancestors, all those who are not of the blood of such ancestors must be excluded from such inheritance."

In the instant case Lucinda Robbs died intestate leaving an estate consisting of personal and real property. The real estate was devised to her by her paternal uncle, William Wallace Robbs. Thus under the exception, identified here as number (2), Lucinda Robbs' real estate which was devised to her by her paternal uncle, William Wallace Robbs, will descend exclusively to Lucinda's heirs who are of the blood of her paternal uncle, William Wallace Robbs.   Lucinda's personal property, which I assume was acquired by her own industry, would descend as provided in the first part of Section 222.   That is, "Kindred of the half-blood inherit equally with those of the whole blood in the same degree."   This can only mean that her nearest of kin will inherit the property acquired by her own industry whether of half-blood or whole-blood, pursuant to the provisions of 84 O.S.1971, § 213.

I believe the conclusion I have reached is in harmony with earlier decisions of this court as expressed in Thompson v. Smith, 102 Okl. 150, 227 P. 77, and in In re Long's Estate, 180 Okl. 28, 67 P.2d 41.

Former decisions of this court and the history of Section 222 are thoroughly discussed by Albert R. Matthews (now of Muskogee, Oklahoma) in 13 Oklahoma Law Review 440–445.   He appears to be of the view * * * that the doctrine of ancestral property should be abolished by the Legislature.   I agree that the problem should be reviewed by our Legislature.

I would deny certiorari and thus affirm the judgment of the trial court and the decision of the Court of Appeals.

I am authorized to say that DAVISON, V. C. J., and HODGES, J., concur in the views herein expressed.

Notes

1. A history of the Oklahoma Statute is set out and the result of the principal case anticipated in Note, 13 Okl.L.Rev. 440 (1960).

2. The three basic approaches to the status of the half blood in the intestate scheme are as follows:

(a) Half bloods share equally with whole bloods without qualification. See e.g. N.Y. EPTL 4–1.1(d), supra, p. 66; see also, UPC § 2–107.

(b) Half bloods share equally with whole bloods with the qualification as to source of title.   See Oklahoma statute set out in the principal case.

(c) Half bloods can only participate if there are no whole bloods. See e.g, Conn.Gen.Stat.Ann. § 45–276; under a statute of this kind, the children of decedent's whole-blood brothers take the entire estate to the exclusion of his half-blood sister.   Jones v. Stubbs, 434 So.2d 1362 (Miss. 1983).

What justification can be made for each of these approaches?

3. Despite the modern tendency to make no distinction between real and personal property as to intestate distribution some jurisdictions have limited the definition of ancestral estate to the identical real property which came to the intestate from the ancestor.   Thus half bloods may share equally with whole bloods as to ancestral personal property and as to non-identical real property. Authority for this distinction can be traced back to early English law.   A 1943 California case, however, gives it a more modern justification, pointing out that the discrimination against half bloods is "illogical" and "is being looked on with increasing disfavor in the states where it still exists".   In re Ryan's Estate, 21 C.2d 498, 133 P.2d 626 (1943), noted 31 Cal.L.Rev. 334 (1943).

4. There is no requirement under the statute that the whole blood relative of a deceased be of the same blood as the ancestor. For the anomalous results which may follow see De Roin v. Whitetail, 312 P.2d 967 (Okl.1957). The courts have rejected strained definitions when claimants have attempted to manipulate half blood statutes to their advantage. The whole blood sister of decedent was not allowed to take to the exclusion of a half-blood nephew, because the decedent's three previous husbands were not her "ancestors." In re Long's Estate, 180 Okl. 28, 67 P.2d 41, 110 A.L.R. 1002 (1936). An unadopted step-daughter failed to persuade the appellate court that she was entitled to inherit from her stepfather on the theory that by his marriage to her mother she was related to him in the half blood. Humphrey v. Tolson, 128 U.S.App.D.C. 18, 384 F.2d 987 (D.C.Cir. 1966).

5. Source of title to the property is used as a reference point in other types of distribution statutes. See, for example, West's Ann.Cal.Prob.Code § 229 (if the decedent leaves no living spouse or issue, the portion of the decedent's estate attributable to a predeceased spouse goes to the predeceased spouse's family); In re Hanson's Estate, 179 Cal.App.2d 32, 3 Cal.Rptr. 482 (1960) (following the widow's death intestate, community property received from husband who had predeceased her returned to husband's sister; widow's next of kin not entitled to share). Several states have statutes saving an infant's estate to the parent's family from which the title was derived. Kentucky Rev.Stat. 391.020(2) is representative. A number of statutes establish the same rule for the intestate distribution of an adopted child's estate, see for example, Ill.—S.H.A. ch. 110½, ¶¶ 2–4(b).

√ SECTION SIX.   HEIRSHIP BY CONTRACT AND DECREE—THE ADOPTED CHILD

While adoption is recognized by the civil law and is found in many societies, ancient and modern, primitive and civilized, it did not exist as such in England until 1926. 16 and 17 Geo. 5, c. 29. It therefore has no common law basis and is entirely dependent on statutes in the United States, and it only became general in this country in the latter half of the 19th century. The history of adoption is described in Huard, The Law of Adoption: Ancient and Modern, 9 Vand.L.Rev. 743 (1956); Brosnan, The Law of Adoption, 22 Colum.L.Rev. 332 (1922).

From the outset, statutes in this country gave adopted children the right to take by intestacy from their adoptive parents, but on the other ramifications of the effect of adoption on inheritance, in particular the extent to which adopted children retained rights to inherit from their natural parents and kin, the statutes were, up until quite recently, incomplete and diverse. This condition was probably due to intestate succession's being considered a subsidiary issue in the drafting of statutes enacted primarily for the humanitarian objective of providing for the welfare of children. Today, a large majority of the states have enacted statutes which transplant the child into the adoptive family as if born in that family and sever all the child's ties, including reciprocal rights of inheritance by intestacy, with his or her natural parents and family. This legislation has clarified the child's status and thus contributed to the expeditious administration of intestate estates. As the material that follows demonstrates, not all the problems have been removed.

IN RE ESTATES OF DONNELLY

Supreme Court of Washington, 1972.
81 Wash.2d 430, 502 P.2d 1163, 60 A.L.R.3d 620.

NEILL, Associate Justice. May an adopted child inherit from her natural grandparents? Both the trial court and the Court of Appeals (5 Wash.App. 158, 486 P.2d 1158 (1971)), answered "yes." We granted review (79 Wash.2d 1010 (1971)), and disagree. In speaking of heirs and inheritance, we refer to the devolution of property by law in intestacy and not by testamentary or other voluntary disposition.

John J. and Lily Donnelly, husband and wife, had two children, a daughter, Kathleen M., now Kathleen M. Kelly, and a son, John J., Jr. The son had one child, Jean Louise Donnelly, born October 28, 1945. Jean Louise's father, John J. Donnelly, Jr., died on July 9, 1946, less than a year after her birth. Her mother, Faith Louise Donnelly, married Richard Roger Hansen on April 22, 1948. By a decree entered August 11, 1948, Jean Louise was adopted by her step-father with the written consent of her natural mother. She lived with her mother and adoptive father as their child and kept the name Hansen until her marriage to Donald J. Iverson. Thus she is a party to this action as Jean Louise Iverson.

Lily Donnelly, the grandmother, died October 7, 1964, leaving a will in which she named but left nothing to her two children. All of her property she left to her husband, John J. Donnelly, Sr., Jean Louise Iverson's grandfather.

John J. Donnelly, Sr., the grandfather, died September 15, 1970, leaving a will dated October 16, 1932, in which he left his entire estate to his wife, Lily, who had predeceased him. He, too, named but left nothing to his two children, and made no provision for disposition of his property in event his wife predeceased him. His daughter, Kathleen M. Kelly, as administratrix with wills annexed of the estates of her parents, brought this petition to determine heirship and for a declaration that Jean Louise Iverson, the granddaughter, take nothing and that she, Kathleen M. Kelly, the daughter, be adjudged the sole heir of her mother and father, Lily and John J. Donnelly, Sr., to the exclusion of Jean Louise Iverson, her niece and their granddaughter.

The trial court decided that each was an heir. It concluded that Jean Louise Iverson, daughter of John J. Donnelly, Jr., and granddaughter of his father, John J. Donnelly, Sr., should inherit one-half of the latter's estate and that Kathleen M. Kelly, daughter of John J. Donnelly, Sr., should inherit the other half of the estate.

Kathleen M. Kelly, the daughter of decedent, appealed to the Court of Appeals which affirmed, and now to this court.

* * *

Thus, a statutory right to inherit one-half of the grandfather's estate is vested in Jean Louise Iverson, the granddaughter, unless that right is divested by operation of RCW 11.04.085, which declares that an adopted child is not to be considered an heir of his natural parents:

> A lawfully adopted child shall not be considered an "heir" of his natural parents for purposes of this title.

When the question of the right of an adopted child to inherit from his natural parents came before us, the intent of the legislature was clear from the literal language of the statute. We held that RCW 11.04.085 prevents an adopted child from taking a share of the natural parent's estate by intestate succession. In re Estate of Wiltermood, 78 Wash.2d 238, 242–243, 472 P.2d 536 (1970). However, reference to the literal language of RCW 11.04.085 does not answer the instant question, *i.e.,* whether, by declaring that an adopted child shall not take from his natural parent, the legislature also intended to remove the adopted child's capacity to represent the natural parent and thereby take from the natural grandparent.

* * *

The legislature has addressed itself to the inheritance rights of adopted children in both the probate and domestic relations titles of RCW (RCW Titles 11 and 26.) For example, RCW 26.32.140 also directly affects the inheritance rights of an adopted child:

> By a decree of adoption the natural parents shall be divested of all legal rights and obligations in respect to the child, and *the child* shall be free from all legal obligations of obedience and maintenance in respect to them, and *shall be* to all intents and purposes, and for all legal incidents, *the child, legal heir, and lawful issue of his or her adopter or adopters, entitled to all rights and privileges, including the right of inheritance* and the right to take under testamentary disposition, and subject to all the obligations of a child of the adopter or adopters begotten in lawful wedlock.

(Italics ours.)

* * *

It is clear that: (1) the adopted child cannot take from his natural parent because he is no longer an "heir" (RCW 11.04.085); and, (2) the adopted child enjoys complete inheritance rights from the adoptive parent, as if he were the natural child of the adoptive parent (RCW 26.32.140). Both statutes are in harmony with the fundamental spirit of our adoption laws—i.e., that for all purposes the adopted child shall be treated as a "child of the adopter * * * begotten in lawful wedlock."

* * *

The question at bench should, therefore, be decided in the context of the broad legislative objective of giving the adopted child a "fresh start" by treating him as the natural child of the adoptive parent, and severing all ties with the past. We believe it clearly follows that the legislature intended to remove an adopted child from his natural bloodline for purposes of intestate succession.

The trial court and Court of Appeals, however, held that although an adopted child may not take *from* a natural parent dying intestate, the same child may take *through* the natural parent, by representation, if the natural parent dies before the natural grandparent. Little supportive reasoning is offered for this inconsistent result. In reaching its conclusion, the Court of Appeals reasoned that consanguineal ties are so fundamental that an explicit expression of legislative intent is required to deprive an adopted child of the bounty which would normally be his by reason of the "intuitive impulses" generated by the blood relationship. In re Estates of Donnelly, 5 Wash.App. 158, 164, 486 P.2d 1158 (1971). The Court of Appeals reasoned that had the legislature desired to remove an adopted child from its natural bloodline, it could have used the word "kin" in place of the word "parents" in RCW 11.04.085. Thus, since RCW 11.04.085 does not specify that an adopted child may not take from an intestate natural grandparent, this capacity is not lost.

* * *

Obviously, the legislature did *not* consider consanguinity to be of controlling importance where the blood relationship must be presumed to be strongest—the natural parent. Moreover, RCW 26.32.140 provides that an adopter and his kin shall inherit from an adopted child to the exclusion of the child's natural parents or kin. Thus if respondent here had predeceased her natural grandfather, he would not have been permitted to inherit from his natural grandchild, any "intuitive impulses" of kinship notwithstanding. And, if consanguinity had *in fact* moved the grandparent to provide for respondent here, he could easily have done so by will.

The legislative policy of providing a "clean slate" to the adopted child permeates our scheme of adoption. The natural grandparents are not entitled to notice of any hearing on the matter of adoption. RCW 26.32.080. RCW 26.32.150 provides that, unless otherwise requested by the adopted, all records of the adoption proceeding shall be sealed and not open to inspection. Pursuant to RCW 26.32.120, a decree for adoption shall provide: (1) for the issuance of a certificate of birth for the adopted child, containing such information as the court may deem proper; and (2) that the records of the registrar shall be secret. RCW 70.58.210 declares that the new birth certificate shall bear the new name of the child and the names of the adoptive parents of the child, but shall make no reference to the adoption of the child. Thus, the natural grandparents have no assurance that they will know the new name or residence of the adopted child. Indeed, in the usual "out of family" adoption situation the administrator of a deceased natural grandparent's estate will be unable to locate—much less to identify—the post-adoption grandchild.

The consistent theme of the relevant legislation is that the new family of the adopted child is to be treated as his natural family. The only conclusion consistent with the spirit of our overlapping adoption and inheritance statutes is that RCW 11.04.085 was intended to transfer all rights of inheritance out of the natural family upon adoption and place them entirely within the adopted family.

Respondent suggests it is most probable that the legislature never considered the problem of inheritance by adopted persons from their remote natural kin when it passed RCW 11.04.085. Thus, respondent contends that the word "parents" should be strictly construed. We disagree.

* * *

The broad legislative purpose underlying our statutes relating to adopted children is consistent only with the inference that RCW 11.04.085 was intended to remove respondent, an adopted child, from her natural bloodline for inheritance purposes. If the adopted child cannot take from her natural father, she should not represent him and take from his father.

The chain of inheritance was broken by respondent's adoption. Reversed.

HAMILTON, C. J., and STAFFORD, WRIGHT and UTTER, JJ., concur.

HALE, Associate Justice (dissenting).

I dissent. This court asks whether an adoptive child may inherit from her natural grandparents. Both the trial court and the Court of Appeals, 5 Wash.App. 158, 486 P.2d 1158 (1971) answered yes, and I agree. I would, therefore, adopt the opinion of the Court of Appeals verbatim as declaring the law of the state in this case.

But there are other reasons, I think, why the granddaughter is entitled to an inheritance and why the statute, RCW 11.04.085, declaring that an adopted child shall not be *considered* an heir of his natural parents, does not operate to disinherit the granddaughter from her grandfather's estate. As the Court of Appeals so clearly delineated, the statute applies to a parent and child; it does not, except by the most strained analysis and construction, apply to grandparent and grandchild—particularly where the adoption arose from the marriage of the grandchild's widowed natural mother. The grandchild's adoption by her widowed mother's second husband should not be held to affect the lineal relationship between granddaughter and grandfather.

One should note the absence of the simple declarative in RCW 11.04.085. The statute does not say that the adopted child shall not inherit, but instead employs the less categorical terminology that an adopted child shall not be *considered* an "heir of his natural parents" for the purpose of the title. In reaching the result obtained, the court has had to follow what appears to me to be a labyrinthine maze of statutory interpretation, which I find both unnecessary and inapplicable. If the legislature had intended that the grandchild be disinherited, it could readily have said so. This would, of course, have raised the constitutional question of whether the legislature can lawfully provide that some grandchildren may inherit from their grandparents and greatgrandparents and other grandchildren in the same degrees of propinquity shall not, and whether there exists sufficient basis under the constitution to sustain the creation of two distinct classes of grandchildren under the descent and distribution statutes.

If the circumstances of this case are changed slightly, the flaw in the court's opinion becomes apparent. Had the plaintiff granddaughter, Jean

Louise Iverson, in this case been the sole surviving descendant of her grandfather, John J. Donnelly, Sr., then under the court's opinion, all of the estate of her grandfather, John J. Donnelly, Sr., would escheat to the state. Such a forfeiture of estate, I think, was neither intended by the legislature nor reasonably contemplated by the language it employed in RCW 11.04.085.

One can readily agree with the court's proposition that the legislature has designed the adoption and inheritance code so as to make an adopted child the full equal in law with a natural child and, so far as the law can do so, to establish a relationship between adopted parents and adopted children identical to that of natural parents and children. To that end it expressly enacted that the *natural parents* are divested of all legal rights and obligations; that the adopted child becomes "to all legal intents and purposes and for all legal incidents" the child, legal heir and lawful issue of her adopters, RCW 26.32.140, and that all adoption papers shall be sealed, and remain unopened except upon order of the superior court for good cause shown, and, if so opened, to be sealed again as before. RCW 26.32.150.

But nothing in the Court of Appeals opinion militates against the integrity and totality of an adoption. To the contrary, that opinion augments this legislatively declared public policy of upholding and preserving the adoption, where this court's opinion will operate against it. Here, the grandfather's son died; his widowed daughter-in-law eventually remarried, and she consented that her new husband adopt her daughter. The new family relationship created by the marriage and adoption presented none of the circumstances of an adoption designed in law to cut off all familial and legal relationships with the adopted child's natural mother nor her grandparents either. The grandchild continued to live with her natural mother and adoptive father presumably with the full knowledge of her grandfather, whose lineal descendant she remained. None of the factors upon which the legislature legislated to seal the records of adoption against the grandfather existed here, and, although the adoption statute makes this granddaughter no less an adopted daughter of her mother's husband, it ought not to be read to make her less a granddaughter of her natural grandfather either. The statute which the court now says disinherits the granddaughter cannot, as the court now says, serve to give the natural granddaughter a "fresh start" (Op. p. 7) or a "clean slate" in the relationship created by the adoption. One is hard put to find where a statute which operates to cut off the plaintiff grandchild from her grandfather's estate gives her a fresh start or a clean slate. The statute could not, and thus did not, sever all ties with the past. While it might have severed whatever legal ties existed between her and her dead father, whose heir she had *already* been, the adoption could not be reasonably said to do the *same* with respect to her natural grandfather.

* * *

Thus, as earlier observed, I would affirm the Court of Appeals and thereby affirm the trial court.

FINLEY, HUNTER, and ROSELLINI, JJ., concur.

Notes

1. At one time, the prevailing view was that an adopted child was entitled to inherit from his or her natural parents.   Comment, The Adopted Child's Inheritance from Intestate Natural Parents, 55 Ia.L.Rev. 739 (1970); Note, Property Rights as Affected by Adoption, 25 Brook.L.Rev. 231, 242–247 (1959). The modern trend favors statutes that expressly prohibit adopted children from inheriting the estates of their intestate natural parents, and a majority of states have enacted such legislation.   UPC § 2–109 is representative.   What is the justification for the modern trend in terms of the probable intent of the parties? Administrative convenience?   Welfare of the child?   See generally Binavince, Adoption and the Law of Descent and Distribution: A Comparative Study and a Proposal for Model Legislation, 51 Corn.L.Q. 152 (1966).   A few states continue to permit an adopted child some rights of inheritance in the intestate estate of his or her natural parents or family.   See e.g., In re Estate of Cregar, 30 Ill.App.3d 798, 333 N.E.2d 540 (1975) (niece and nephew may inherit from natural aunt who died intestate without closer relatives); Alack v. Phelps, 230 So.2d 789 (Miss.1970) (children adopted by grandparents may participate in action for wrongful death of natural father).   A child has no vested rights under the intestate statute as it existed at the time of adoption and therefore cannot participate in the distribution of his or her natural parent's estate when the statute has been amended to bar that right before the parent has died.   See e.g., In re Estate of Wiltermood, 78 Wn.2d 238, 472 P.2d 536 (1970), cited in the principal case.

2. Most of the statutes which disallow the right to inherit from the natural parents make an exception for the natural parent whose new spouse adopts his or her stepchild.   Some of the statutes go a step further in this situation and, contrary to the holding in the principal case, preserve the inheritance rights with and through both natural parents. See e.g., UPC § 2–109.   On the basis of an Ohio statute of this kind, it was held that a child whose stepfather had adopted her could inherit through her natural father from the estate of the latter's mother.   First National Bank of East Liverpool v. Collar, 27 Ohio Misc. 88, 272 N.E.2d 916 (1971).   In the absence of a controlling statute, other authority supports the *Donnelly* analysis.   Matter of Estate of Holt, 95 N.M. 412, 622 P.2d 1032 (1981).   Under facts similar to those of the principal case, the paternal grandparents have been denied visitation privileges with a child who has been adopted by his stepfather.   Wilson v. Wallace, 274 Ark. 48, 622 S.W.2d 164 (1981); Browning v. Tarwater, 215 Kan. 501, 524 P.2d 1135 (1974).   Visitation rights have been upheld when authorized by a court as being in the best interests of the child.   People ex rel. Sibley, etc. v. Sheppard, 54 N.Y.2d 320, 445 N.Y.S.2d 420, 429 N.E.2d 1049 (1981) (authorization not an unconstitutional invasion of adoptive parents' rights); see also Johnson v. Fallon, 129 Cal.App.3d 71, 181 Cal.Rptr. 414 (1982) (although statute allowing visitation rights under the facts of the *Donnelly* case inapplicable to the particular situation, court still may find such rights to be in the best interests of the child).

3. If the jurisdiction allows the child to inherit from both sets of parents, there is usually a statutory direction that the child's intestate estate (in absence of a spouse and/or issue) goes to the adoptive parents rather than the natural parents, except that a number of statutes reserve to the natural family property which came to the child from that family.   See e.g., Ill.—S.H.A. ch. 110½, ¶ 2–4(b).   It has been held, however, in the absence of either adoptive or natural

parents that the natural kin are entitled to the adopted child's intestate estate to the exclusion of relatives by adoption.   Matter of Estate of Edwards, 273 N.W.2d 118 (S.D.1978) (natural half sister inherits in preference to niece of adoptive mother, although intestate's property came from adoptive family);   Black v. Washam, 57 Tenn.App. 601, 421 S.W.2d 647 (1967) (adopted child's estate escheats rather than going to collateral heirs of adoptive parents).   Results of this kind are becoming less likely as more and more states are legislating a complete integration of the child into the adoptive family, as if a natural child of that family, and decreeing that the child henceforward is to be considered a "stranger" to the natural family for inheritance purposes.   See e.g., In re Estate of Neil, 187 Neb. 364, 191 N.W.2d 448 (1971) (21 nieces and nephews of adoptive mother entitled to inherit).   The courts regularly extend inheritance rights to the adopted child's lineal line.   Thus the children of an adopted child take by intestacy from their adoptive grandparents.   In re Miner's Estate, 359 Mich. 579, 103 N.W.2d 498 (1960);   Annot., Right of Children of Adopted Child to Inherit from Adopting Parent, 94 A.L.R.2d 1200.   Generally today an adopted child is entitled to inherit from the collateral kin of the adoptive parents.   There is an occasional dissent on the grounds that the intestate, for example an aunt or uncle of an adoptive parent, is a "stranger to the adoption."   Before enacting the Uniform Probate Code, Utah law did not authorize the child to inherit from collateral relatives of the adoptive parents.   In re Estate of Smith, 7 Utah 2d 405, 326 P.2d 400 (1965).   The case for treating the child as if he or she was born in the adoptive family is made in the dissent at pages 401–405 (footnotes omitted):

The ground most frequently advanced as to why an adopted child should inherit only from his adoptive parents and not through them to other adoptive relatives is that the adoption proceeding is one of contract with the adopting parents and that only they are bound.   This appears to me to be a very superficial view of the matter.   By way of analogy, the marriage contract is only between the two spouses and in simple terms, yet it creates a comprehensive relationship, not only between the immediate parties, but for everyone else, particularly the members of both families involved, and the family to be.   Likewise the adoption contract creates a personal relationship between the immediate parties, that is, the same relationship as the natural relationship of parent and child, and it has its effect upon others.

It is patent that the view that the effect of the adoption proceeding is limited to the parties to the contract is entirely too restricted.   If such were the case, an adopted child would not even have any family relationship to brothers and sisters in the family[;]   only one minor facet of such a limitation would be the failure to inherit from each other.   A plainly incongruous result and squarely inconsistent with the mandate of the adoption statutes as hereinafter pointed out.

An adjunct of the restricted contract basis for opposing inheritance in the family by the adopted child is that the adoptive parents can agree to take for themselves an heir, but they cannot thus take one for their kindred and "impose" him upon the family.   The supposition that one would adopt a child and take on the serious and onerous responsibilities of parenthood with any such ulterior motive as "imposing an heir" on his own parents or other relatives is so unrealistic as to be ludicrous.   There is no more danger of this than that one would go about having natural children for such purpose.   The fact that heirs can be, and are, voluntarily brought into being by the biological process has not given rise to any claim it is being done, or overdone, for the sole purpose of imposing heirs on relatives.   Yet if statistics are to be credited, families are acquired more readily that way and a good deal more often than by adoption.   The manner in which one acquires his family is his business and to be done in the way he best can manage.   If for reasons sufficient unto himself, he acquires his child or family by adoption, I submit that there can be found no sound reason in law, morals or logic why he or his children should be discriminated against by being refused full acceptance into the family for all purposes including inheritance.

The further fact is that the relatives are not defenseless against any such "imposition"; but by the easy expedient of making a will can remove any such burden, the same as they can as to other heirs.   It is no answer to say that a grandparent who loves and desires his adopted grandchild to inherit can so provide by will.   Every aspect of such argument applies with equal force to natural children.   Both can be either included or excluded from inheritance by will.   But the natural child has the advantage that he inherits unless expressly excluded, whereas the adopted child has no more right than a stranger, because anyone can be included by will.   The fact is that for various reasons many people just don't get around to making wills.   This results in the exclusion of the adopted child as a member of the family insofar as that particular aspect of family unity is concerned. He is a member of the family, yet he is not, and the realization of this fact by him and other members of the family leaves an area of rejection which is, in many instances, more important psychologically than is concern over material values.

The matter of blood relationship is also given as a "reason" for not allowing the adopted child to inherit.   An appraisal of the contention reveals that it is of no such importance as to be controlling.   Instances of babies being exchanged at birth a la "Puddinhead Wilson"; and babies or children being taken into families where ties of love and affection have grown, attest that the matter of accident of birth becomes completely submerged and is quite unimportant in comparison to the other ties that develop between human beings.   They corroborate the thesis of the social scientists that the essence of the family relationship is sociological rather than merely physiological.   People who think otherwise are sometimes surprised to realize that the most persuasive proof of such fact exists in every well ordered family, including their own.   The husband and wife are not related to each other by blood, as they are to their own brothers and sisters, and other relatives.   Yet through their common interests and companionship the bond of love and affection is usually such that few would admit it inferior to that with their "blood" relatives.   Most everyone has in his family tree some examples which make this point abundantly clear.

4. If the right to inherit from the natural parents is continued, the child has opportunities to take in several different capacities.   Two specific situations have arisen:

(a) Intestate had two children, A and B.   B survived the intestate, but A predeceased him leaving two children, X and Y, surviving.   After the death of A, the intestate adopted his granddaughter, X, as his adopted daughter. How much of intestate's estate is X entitled to claim? A few decisions would permit X to take in two capacities. In re Benner's Estate, 109 Utah 172, 166 P.2d 257 (1946) (under U.P.C. § 2–109, now in force in Utah, X would be able to inherit only as an adopted child); In re Estate of Cregar, 30 Ill.App.3d 798, 333 N.E.2d 540 (1975) (niece and nephew entitled to take in two capacities from estate of deceased aunt). Following the *Cregar* case, the Illinois statute was amended to state that an adopted child, who is related by blood to the adopting parent, may only inherit in the capacity of an adopted child or descendant of an adopted child. Ill.— S.H.A ch. 110½, ¶ 2.4(d). If the statute has been amended so the child can no longer inherit from the natural parents, he or she is entitled to take in only the adopted capacity. Cox v. Cox, 262 S.C. 8, 202 S.E.2d 6 (1974); Crego v. Monfiletto, 104 N.J.Super. 416, 250 A.2d 161 (1969).

(b) Child X is adopted by Mr. and Mrs. Smith. Mrs. Smith dies and Mr. Smith agrees to the adoption of X by Mr. and Mrs. Jones. Mr. Smith then dies intestate leaving brothers and sisters surviving. X argues that when he was adopted by Mr. and Mrs. Smith he was decreed by statute to have the same status as a natural child of the Smiths and that he is therefore entitled to Mr. Smith's estate as the sole surviving lineal descendant. The cases are fairly evenly divided on whether X is entitled to inherit, following a second adoption, from the first adoptive parents. The cases are collected and described in In re Leichtenberg's Estate, 7 Ill.2d 545, 131 N.E.2d 487 (1956). Statutory amendments abolishing the right to inherit from natural parents have the affect of also abolishing claims against the intestate estates of the first adoptive parents. In re Estate of Luckey, 206 Neb. 53, 291 N.W.2d 235 (1980); Matter of Estate of Adolphson, 403 Mich. 590, 271 N.W.2d 511 (1978).

5. Modern adoption procedures sever the child's connection with the natural parents or parent in order to foster the development of the psychological parent-child relationship between the child and the adoptive parents. Typically, an adoption proceeding must be held in a closed court, the original birth certificate is replaced by a second one, reciting the new name of the child and the names of the adoptive parents, and all records of the proceeding are confidential. Annot., Records of Concluded Adoption Proceedings, 83 A.L.R.3d 800, 802–803. As stated in an explanatory note on the confidentiality of the records, Uniform Adoption Act § 16, which is representative, is designed "to negate the impact of any right to know law" by securing all records of adoption from inspection except by court order. 9 ULA 49. The case to the effect that the dominant policy in these proceedings must be the "best interests of the child" is made in Goldstein, Freud, and Solnit, Beyond the Best Interests of the Child (1979).

It is recommended practice to inform the child that he or she is adopted. Id. page 23. Some adopted children want more information. They do not accept the conventional wisdom that makes them the children of the adoptive family and are insisting on their right to know their full biological heritage. One advocate of amended laws to give adopted children access to records attacks the statutes that sever the relationship to natural parents as neither wise nor just and provides studies of the anguish incurred by adoptees seeking their identities and of the special psychological dislocations suffered by adopted children. Lifton, Lost and Found, (1979). These petitions for information have had a degree of success in the courts. See Annot., supra. A number of states have passed legislation setting out in detail procedures for the disclosure of information from adoption records, including who may petition, what information may be disclosed at what stages of the child's life, and what safeguards must be followed to protect the interests of the child, the adoptive parents, and the natural parents.   See e.g. Conn.Gen.Stat.Ann. § 45–68(a)–(n).   See generally, The Adult Adoptee's Constitutional Right to Know His Origins, 48 So. Cal.L.Rev. 1196 (1975); Sealed Adoption Records and the Constitutional Right of Privacy of the Natural Parent, 34 Rut.L.Rev. 451 (1982); Adoption: Sealed Adoption Record Law—Constitutional Violation or a Need for Judicial Reform?, 35 Okl.L.Rev. 575 (1982).

6. Inheritance from the adoptive parents presupposes a valid legal adoption.   There is, however, ample authority that a contract for adoption may give rise to a recovery even though a legal adoption has not occurred, where there has been sufficient reliance on the contract to justify a specific performance remedy.   Note, Equitable Adoption: They Took Him into Their Home and Called Him Fred, 58 Va.L.Rev. 727 (1972); Comment, Equitable Adoption: A Necessary Doctrine?, 35 So.Cal.L.Rev. 491 (1962).   Among recent cases the contract was equitably enforced in In re Prewitt, 17 Ariz.App. 396, 498 P.2d 470 (1972); Monahan v. Monahan, 14 Ill.2d 449, 153 N.E.2d 1 (1958), and denied in Wilks v. Langley, 248 Ark. 227, 451 S.W.2d 209 (1970).   An equitable adoption may qualify a person as an heir but not make her a "legally adopted child" within the meaning of the inheritance tax statute which grants preferential treatment to children and formally adopted children.   Goldberg v. Robertson, 615 S.W.2d 59 (Mo.1981).   Out-of-state or -country adoptions may present difficult conflict of laws problems.   See, for instance, In re Dreer's Estate, 404 Pa. 368, 173 A.2d 102 (1961).

7. A cognate situation involves the status of the adopted child under a will. The problems are more frequently litigated and involve a much greater volume of wealth.   A's will sets up a trust, income to his nephew B for life, remainder over at B's death to B's "children," "issue," "descendants" or "heirs."   Do such words include B's adopted daughter?   Questions of this kind turn on A's intent, not on an application of the local intestate succession statutes, although such statutes are generally cited as expressing the local policy and as therefore having some bearing on A's intent.   Many states have enacted statutes which stipulate that unless the instrument expresses a contrary intention persons described as "issue, lawful issue, children, descendants, heirs, heirs at law, next of kin, distributees (or by any term of like import)" include adopted children.   See e.g., N.Y.—McKinney's EPTL § 2–1.3.

In the absence of a statute, an important index of intent has traditionally been whether the testator knew and appeared to approve of the adoption before executing his or her will and whether the testator considered the adopted child a stranger or a member of the family.   But see Elliott v. Hiddleson, 303 N.W.2d 140 (Ia.1981) (court discarded the "stranger to adoption" rule and declared adopted child a "lineal heir" under adoptive grandfather's will; cases from other jurisdictions reviewed).   If the intent remains ambiguous, the words themselves may assume significance.   For instance, the word "child" would seem to include "adopted child", while "issue" usually connotes a blood relationship.   But see Bankers Trust Co. v. Brotherton, 31 N.Y.2d 322, 338 N.Y.S.2d 895, 291 N.E.2d 137 (1972) (instrument that predated statute construed so that "issue" included adopted children).   The same issue may arise in the will of a member of the natural parents' family. Compare Crumpton v. Mitchell, 303 N.C. 657, 281 S.E.2d 1 (1981) (children taken out of the family by adoption not entitled to take as "issue" under natural grandparents' deed) with Matter of Estate of Daigle, 642 P.2d 527 (Colo.App.1982) ("children" in natural father's will included two children who had been adopted by first wife's second husband).

See generally, Adopted Children as Members of a Class, Second Report of N.Y. Temporary Commission on Estates, Appendix F, 221 (1963); Oler, Construction of Private Instruments Where Adopted Children Are Concerned, 43 Mich.L.Rev. 705, 901 (1945) (an extensive study of the whole subject); Rights of Adopted Children to Take Under a Will as "Children" or "Lawful Issue," When Adopted After Testator's Death, 31 S.Cal.L.Rev. 441 (1958); Annot., Adopted Child—Rights Under Will, 86 A.L.R.2d 1.

A will provided that the corpus of a testamentary trust should go at the death of testatrix' son to the son's heirs and that if son should die without heirs then it was to go to certain charities. The son adopted his own wife and thus made her his heir under the mother's will. It was held that the adoption was not void as against public policy or as vitiating the common law unity of husband and wife or as permitting an incestuous relationship. Bedinger v. Graybill's Executor, 302 S.W.2d 594 (Ky.1957); see also Ex parte Libertini, 244 Md. 542, 224 A.2d 443 (1966) (lower court committed error in declaring adoption of 35-year old woman by an unmarried 56-year old woman invalid as a "perversion of the entire adoptive process"); but cf. Pennington v. Citizens Fidelity Bank & Trust Co., 390 S.W.2d 671 (Ky.1965) (adoption by 71-year old wife of her 74-year old husband did not make him her "child" under the will of wife's mother); Schaefer v. Merchants' National Bank of Cedar Rapids, 160 N.W.2d 318 (Iowa 1968) (adopted adult not a "direct heir" under the will). See generally, Annot., Adoption of Adult, 21 A.L.R.3d 1012, 1034–44.

8. The demand for children to adopt far exceeds the supply. Plumez, Adoption: Where Have All the Babies Gone?, N.Y. Times Magazine p. 34, April 13, 1980. The author points up the problem with the following statistics:

* * * For a variety of reasons, the vast majority of pregnant teenagers who reject abortion and marriage are now rejecting adoption, also. It is estimated that 93 percent who bear illegitimate children plan to raise them alone. So while the illegitimate rate has soared (14 percent of all births are now illegitimate), the adoption rate has plummeted, and the social consequences are enormous. The total number of adoptions in America peaked in 1970 at 175,000. By 1977 the number was down to 104,000. Only about 25,000 of those cases involved infants adopted by unrelated couples. The majority of adoptions now involve adults adopting children of relatives, including step-parent adoptions. More and more older children and foster children are also being adopted.

But demand for adoptable babies remains strong. Although many infertility problems are now correctable, between 5 percent and 10 percent of all married couples in this country remain involuntarily infertile, and, according to one study, one in four tries to adopt.

If the dysfunction making conception impossible is the husband's, a childless couple may resort to artificial insemination of the wife (the introduction of the semen of a donor, who is almost always unknown to the couple, into the reproductive tract of the wife by means of a syringe) to produce a child who is, to the couple's joy, the biological child of at least one of them. It is estimated that this process accounts for 20,000 babies a year.   The arrangements may be made by the family doctor or the couple may seek the services of one of a number of frozen-sperm banks (said to be 17 in 1980) in the country, which altogether offer for sale over 100,000 sperm samples, some of which have been in storage for up to five years.   Donor selection is based on a form filled out by the couple, indicating desired characteristics such as height, weight, hair color, race, and religion.   If the husband is not completely infertile, some of his sperm may be added to that of the donor, raising the possibility, considered remote in most cases, that the husband is the biological father.   Fleming, New Frontiers in Conception, N.Y. Times Magazine p. 14, July 20, 1980.

There is a female analogue to artificial insemination that is available to the childless couple when the wife is unable to conceive or carry a baby to term. The process, known as in vitro fertilization, involves fertilization of the female's ovum by the male's sperm outside the body of the female, followed by a transfer of the fertilized egg to the uterus of the biological mother or a surrogate mother. The egg may be that of the wife or a donor and the sperm that of the husband. For a description of the process and of the ethical problems raised by it, see Note, In Vitro Fertilization: Hope for Childless Couples Breeds Legal Exposure for Physicians, 17 U. of Rich.L.Rev. 311 (1983).

If as a result of one of these new reproductive technologies the child is the biological child of the husband and wife, no legal problems, other than perhaps evidentiary ones, arise.   As one commentator has, however, observed, it is theoretically possible for six persons to have a basis for claiming parenthood of a child conceived by in vitro fertilization.   Comment, New Reproductive Technologies: The Legal Problem and a Solution, 49 Tenn.L.Rev. 303, 305 (1982) (" * * * it is now technically possible to obtain a human ovum from a female and human sperm from a male (the genetic mother and father), fertilize the ovum *in vitro*, implant the resultant embryo in the uterus of a second female (the gestational mother, who may also be married to a second male—the gestational father) where the embryo is brought to full term, and upon delivery of the infant transfer custody of the new born to a third party (the nurtural father or mother).").   For a comprehensive review of the variety of relationships that may be involved and of the complex legal issues that may result, see Wadlington, Artificial Conception: The Challenge for Family Law, 69 Va.L.Rev. 465, 488–496 (1983).

As yet, there are no cases involving the inheritance rights of and from the child.   There are cases holding that the husband, who actively participates in making the arrangements and consents to his wife's artificial insemination, is the legal father of the child.   People v. Sorenson, 68 Cal.App.2d 280, 66 Cal. Rptr. 7, 437 P.2d 495 (1968) (husband liable for non-support); In re Adoption of Anonymous, 74 Misc.2d 99, 345 N.Y.S.2d 430 (1973) (husband's consent required to the adoption of the child by a new family).   Approximately half the states have enacted statutes that recognize artificial insemination and make the child the legitimate child of the mother and the consenting husband.   49 Tenn.L.Rev., supra, p. 306, fn. 15; for representative statutes, see N.Y.— McKinney's Dom.Rel.Law § 73 and Conn.Gen.Stat.Ann. § 45–69(f)–(n).   Many of these statutes specifically state that the child may inherit from the mother and consenting father as if he or she were their natural child and that no rights exist between the child and the biological father.   These statutes only speak about a married woman and her consenting husband, leaving unresolved the status of the single parent who desires to have a child by artificial insemination. See Kern and Ridolfi, The Fourteenth Amendment's Protection of a Woman's Right to be a Single Parent Through Artificial Insemination by Donor, 7 Women's Rights L.Rptr. 251 (1982).

In vitro fertilization of humans is of relatively recent origin and is described as "a highly sophisticated procedure that must be performed by a physician with special skills, training, and facilities." Wadlington, supra, p. 487. The numbers of babies born in this fashion are infinitesimal in comparison with the numbers produced by artifical insemination and, the numbers are never likely to become comparable. There are as yet no state or federal statutes relating to in vitro fertilization. To the extent that the procedure requires the couple to enter into an agreement with a surrogate mother to carry their fertilized egg during gestation, the arrangement may be vulnerable to challenge under the statutes which make unenforceable contracts for the adoption of children in return for compensation. Authority exists in at least two states, Kentucky and Michigan, that contracts involving surrogate parenthood are illegal. See Wadlington, supra, p. 501–503; Note, In Defense of Surrogate Parenting: A Critical Analysis of the Recent Kentucky Experience, 69 Ky.L.J. 877 (1981) (critique of Kentucky attorney general's opinion that such contracts are illegal, with a suggestion that the equal protection clause of the fourteenth amendment is violated when an infertile woman is denied the right to obtain a child by implantation of her egg in a surrogate mother, while an infertile male and his wife are free to use artificial insemination). It should be noted further that approximately half the states have statutes that bar fetal research, some of which are arguably broad enough to prohibit in vitro fertilization.

In addition to the articles cited above, see generally on the various legal and ethical aspects of the subject, Comment, Artificial Human Reproduction: Legal Problems Presented by the Test Tube Baby, 28 Emory L.J. 1045 (1979); Artificial Insemination and the Law, 1982 Brigham Young U.L.Rev. 935. Coleman, Surrogate Motherhood: Analysis of the Problems and Suggestions for Solutions, 50 Tenn.L.Rev. 71 (1982).

SECTION SEVEN. ILLEGITIMACY

The common law of inheritance treated illegimate children with extreme severity—an attitude said to be partly the product of a desire to discourage illicit sexual intercourse. Bastards were filius nullius, the children of no one; they were isolated from their forbears; their sole relatives were their own issue. They therefore could not inherit from any lineal ancestors or collateral relatives; nor could the ancestors or relatives inherit from them. They were prohibited from inheriting land from their own issue by the rule forbidding inheritance by lineal ascendants until the statutory abolition of that rule in 1833; their lineal descendants, however, could inherit from them. Children who were born while their parents were lawfully married were legitimate, even if conceived before marriage; but children born out of lawful wedlock could not be legitimated except by an Act of Parliament. The common law refused to adopt the doctrine of the civil and the canon law that children born before the marriage of their parents were legitimated by that marriage. These doctrines prevailed in England until the Legitimacy Act of 1926, which recognized legitimation by subsequent marriage except in the case of adulterous birth, and authorized, under certain circumstances, reciprocal inheritance between illegitimate children and their mothers. 16 and 17 Geo. V, c. 60 §§ 1, 9 (1926), 2 Comp.Stats. of Eng. 25.   See 2 Halsbury's Laws of England (2d Ed. 1931) 557; 1 Bl.Com. 459; 2 Bl.Com. 247–49, 505.

Any assumption that these common law rules of inheritance could have a real effect in preventing unsanctioned sexual acts seems quite naive, and the unfairness of visiting the sins of the progenitors upon their innocent issue is apparent.   The American statutes from the outset reflected a less rigorous climate of morality and amelioriated in some measure the common law status of illegitimate children.   Discrimination against illegitimates, however, has not been eliminated from the statutes. It is the general rule today that reciprocal rights of inheritance exist between illegitimate children and their mothers and their mothers' kin. Up until a decade ago, most of the statutes stated that illegitimate children, unless they had been legitimated by the subsequent marriage of the father and mother, were not entitled to inherit from their fathers, nor their fathers from them.   This difference in the treatment of illegitimates from legitimates has traditionally been justified in terms of the difficulties of proving the identity of the father.   In three cases, Labine v. Vincent, Trimble v. Gordon, and Lalli v. Lalli, infra, these restrictive statutes were challenged in the Supreme Court as being overbroad and violative of the equal protection clause of the Fourteenth Amendment when applied in cases where there was no doubt as to the identity of the father.   The majority opinion in Trimble went a long way toward establishing a constitutional basis for an illegitimate child to inherit from the father as if he or she were legitimate when the father's identity was not in dispute.   As noted in Justice Blackmun's concurring opinion, Lalli represents a retreat from the advanced position taken in Trimble and does restore to the states wide latitude in enacting statutes requiring that the child's status as an heir be determined in an authoritative manner before the father's death.   Nonetheless, this trilogy of cases has had an impact, causing states to reexamine their statutes and to enact new legislation that enlarges the possibilities of inheritance between illegitimate children and their fathers.   The statutes are diverse, and those of individual states must be consulted.

LALLI v. LALLI

Supreme Court of the United States, 1978.
439 U.S. 259, 99 S.Ct. 518, 58 L.Ed.2d 503.

Mr. Justice POWELL announced the judgment of the Court and delivered an opinion, in which THE CHIEF JUSTICE and Mr. Justice STEWART join.

This case presents a challenge to the constitutionality of § 4–1.2 of New York's Estates, Powers, and Trusts Law, which requires illegitimate children who would inherit from their fathers by intestate succession to provide a particular form of proof of paternity. Legitimate children are not subject to the same requirement.

I

Appellant Robert Lalli claims to be the illegitimate son of Mario Lalli who died intestate on January 7, 1973, in the State of New York. Appellant's mother, who died in 1968, never was married to Mario. After Mario's widow, Rosamond Lalli, was appointed administratrix of her husband's estate, appellant petitioned the Surrogate's Court for Westchester County for a compulsory accounting, claiming that he and his sister Maureen Lalli were entitled to inherit from Mario as his children. Rosamond Lalli opposed the petition. She argued that even if Robert and Maureen were Mario's children, they were not lawful distributees of the estate because they had failed to comply with § 4–1.2,[1] which provides in part:

"An illegitimate child is the legitimate child of his father so that he and his issue inherit from his father if a court of competent jurisdiction has, during the lifetime of the father, made an order of filiation declaring paternity in a proceeding instituted during the pregnancy of the mother or within two years from the birth of the child."

Appellant conceded that he had not obtained an order of filiation during his putative father's lifetime. He contended, however, that § 4–1.2, by imposing this requirement, discriminated against him on the basis of his illegitimate birth in violation of the Equal Protection Clause of the Fourteenth Amendment. Appellant tendered certain evidence of his relationship with Mario Lalli, including a notarized document in which Lalli, in consenting to appellant's marriage, referred to him as "my son," and several affidavits by persons who stated that Lalli had acknowledged openly and often that Robert and Maureen were his children.

The Surrogate's Court noted that § 4–1.2 had previously, and unsucessfully been attacked under the Equal Protection Clause. After reviewing recent decisions of this Court concerning discrimination against illegitimate children, particularly Labine v. Vincent, 401 U.S. 532, 91 S.Ct. 1017, 28 L.Ed.2d 288 (1971), and three New York decisions affirming the constitutionality of the statute, In re Belton, 70 Misc.2d 814, 335

---

1. Section 4–1.2 in its entirety provides:

"(a) For the purposes of this article:

"(1) An illegitimate child is the legitimate child of his mother so that he and his issue inherit from his mother and from his maternal kindred.

[Paragraph (2) is set out in the opinion.]

"(3) The existence of an agreement obligating the father to support the illegitimate child does not qualify such child or his issue to inherit from the father in the absence of an order of filiation made as prescribed by subparagraph (2).

"(4) A motion for relief from an order of filiation may be made only by the father, and such motion must be made within one year from the entry of such order.

"(b) If an illegitimate child dies, his surviving spouse, issue, mother, maternal kindred and father inherit and are entitled to letters of administration as if the decedent were legitimate, provided that the father may inherit or obtain such letters only if an order of filiation has been made in accordance with the provisions of subparagraph (2)." N.Y. Est., Powers & Trusts Law § 4–1.2 (McKinney 1967).

N.Y.S.2d 177 (Surr.Ct.1972); In re Hendrix, 68 Misc.2d 439, 444, 326 N.Y.S.2d 646, 652 (Surr.Ct.1971); In re Crawford, 64 Misc.2d 758, 762–763, 315 N.Y.S.2d 890, 895 (Surr.Ct.1970), the court ruled that appellant was properly excluded as a distributee of Lalli's estate and therefore lacked status to petition for a compulsory accounting.

On direct appeal the New York Court of Appeals affirmed. In re Lalli, 38 N.Y.2d 77, 378 N.Y.S.2d 351, 340 N.E.2d 721 (1975). It understood *Labine* to require the State to show no more than that "there is a rational basis for the means chosen by the Legislature for the accomplishment of a permissible State objective." 38 N.Y.2d, at 81, 378 N.Y.S.2d, at 354, 340 N.E.2d, at 723. After discussing the problems of proof peculiar to establishing paternity, as opposed to maternity, the court concluded that the State was constitutionally entitled to require a judicial decree during the father's lifetime as the exclusive form of proof of paternity.

Appellant appealed the Court of Appeals' decision to this Court. While that case was pending here, we decided Trimble v. Gordon, 430 U.S. 762, 97 S.Ct. 1459, 52 L.Ed.2d 31 (1977). Because the issues in these two cases were similar in some respects, we vacated and remanded to permit further consideration in light of *Trimble*. Lalli v. Lalli, 431 U.S. 911, 97 S.Ct. 2164, 53 L.Ed.2d 220 (1977).

On remand, the New York Court of Appeals, with two judges dissenting, adhered to its former disposition. In re Lalli, 43 N.Y.2d 65, 400 N.Y.S.2d 761, 371 N.E.2d 481 (1977). It acknowledged that *Trimble* contemplated a standard of judicial review demanding more than "a mere finding of some remote rational relationship between the statute and a legitimate State purpose." 43 N.Y.2d. at 67, 400 N.Y.S.2d, at 762, 371 N.E.2d, at 482, though less than strictest scrutiny. Finding § 4–1.2 to be "significantly and determinatively different" from the statute overturned in *Trimble,* the court ruled that the New York law was sufficiently related to the State's interest in " 'the orderly settlement of estates and the dependability of titles to property passing under intestacy laws,' " 43 N.Y.2d, at 67, 400 N.Y.S.2d, at 763–764, 69–70, 371 N.E.2d, at 482–483, quoting *Trimble,* supra, 430 U.S., at 771, 97 S.Ct., at 1465 to meet the requirements of equal protection.

Appellant again sought review here, and we noted probable jurisdiction. 435 U.S. 921, 98 S.Ct. 1482, 55 L.Ed.2d 514 (1978). We now affirm.

II

We begin our analysis with *Trimble*. At issue in that case was the constitutionality of an Illinois statute providing that a child born out of wedlock could inherit from his intestate father only if the father had "acknowledged" the child and the child had been legitimated by the intermarriage of the parents. The appellant in *Trimble* was a child born out of wedlock whose father had neither acknowledged her nor married her mother. He had, however, been found to be her father in a judicial decree ordering him to contribute to her support. When the father died intestate, the child was excluded as a distributee because the statutory requirements for inheritance had not been met.

We concluded that the Illinois statute discriminated against illegitimate children in a manner prohibited by the Equal Protection Clause. Although, as decided in Mathews v. Lucas, 427 U.S. 495, 506, 96 S.Ct. 2755, 2762, 49 L.Ed.2d 651 (1976), and reaffirmed in *Trimble,* supra, 430 U.S., at 767, 97 S.Ct., at 1464, classifications based on illegitimacy are not subject to "strict scrutiny," they nevertheless are invalid under the Fourteenth Amendment if they are not substantially related to permissible state interests. Upon examination, we found that the Illinois law failed that test.

Two state interests were proposed which the statute was said to foster: the encouragement of legitimate family relationships and the maintenance of an accurate and efficient method of disposing of an intestate decedent's property. Granting that the State was appropriately concerned with the integrity of the family unit, we viewed the statute as bearing "only the most attenuated relationship to the asserted goal." *Trimble,* supra, at 768, 97 S.Ct., at 1464. We again rejected the argument that "persons will shun illicit relations because the offspring may not one day reap the benefits" that would accrue to them were they legitimate. Weber v. Aetna Casualty & Surety Co., 406 U.S. 164, 173, 92 S.Ct. 1400, 1405, 31 L.Ed.2d 768 (1972). The statute therefore was not defensible as an incentive to enter legitimate family relationships.

Illinois' interest in safeguarding the orderly disposition of property at death was more relevant to the statutory classification. We recognized that devising "an appropriate legal framework" in the furtherance of that interest "is a matter particularly within the competence of the individual States." *Trimble,* supra, 430 U.S., at 771, 97 S.Ct., at 1465. An important aspect of that framework is a response to the often difficult problem of proving the paternity of illegitimate children and the related danger of spurious claims against intestate estates. See infra, at 525–526. These difficulties, we said, "might justify a more demanding standard for illegitimate children claiming under their fathers' estates than that required either for illegitimate children claiming under their mothers' estates or for legitimate children generally." *Trimble,* supra, at 770, 97 S.Ct., at 1465.

The Illinois statute, however, was constitutionally flawed because, by insisting upon not only an acknowledgment by the father, but also the marriage of the parents, it excluded "at least some significant categories of illegitimate children of intestate men [whose] inheritance rights can be recognized without jeopardizing the orderly settlement of estates or the dependability of titles to property passing under intestacy laws." Id., at 771, 97 S.Ct., at 1465. We concluded that the Equal Protection Clause required that a statute placing exceptional burdens on illegitimate children in the furtherance of proper state objectives must be more " 'carefully tuned to alternative considerations,' " id., at 772, 97 S.Ct., at 1466, quoting Mathews v. Lucas, supra, 427 U.S., at 513, 96 S.Ct., at 2766, than was true of the broad disqualification in the Illinois law.

III

The New York statute, enacted in 1965, was intended to soften the rigors of previous law which permitted illegitimate children to inherit only from their mothers. See infra, at 525. By lifting the absolute bar to paternal inheritance, § 4–1.2 tended to achieve its desired effect. As in *Trimble,* however, the question before us is whether the remaining statutory obstacles to inheritance by illegitimate children can be squared with the Equal Protection Clause.

A

At the outset we observe that § 4–1.2 is different in important respects from the statutory provision overturned in *Trimble.* The Illinois statute required, in addition to the father's acknowledgment of paternity, the legitimation of the child through the intermarriage of the parents as an absolute precondition to inheritance. This combination of requirements eliminated "the possibility of a middle ground between the extremes of complete exclusion and case-by-case determination of paternity." *Trimble,* 430 U.S., at 770–771, 97 S.Ct., at 1465. As illustrated by the facts in *Trimble,* even a judicial declaration of paternity was insufficient to permit inheritance.

Under § 4–1.2, by contrast, the marital status of the parents is irrelevant. The single requirement at issue here is an evidentiary one— that the paternity of the father be declared in a judicial proceeding sometime before his death.[2] The child need not have been legitimated in order to inherit from his father. Had the appellant in *Trimble* been governed by § 4–1.2, she would have been a distributee of her father's estate. See In re Lalli, 43 N.Y.2d, at 68 n. 2, 400 N.Y.S.2d at 762 n. 2, 371 N.E.2d, at 482 n. 2.

A related difference between the two provisions pertains to the state interests said to be served by them. The Illinois law was defended, in part, as a means of encouraging legitimate family relationships. No such justification has been offered in support of § 4–1.2. The Court of Appeals disclaimed that the purpose of the statute, "even in small part, was to discourage illegitimacy, to mold human conduct or to set societal norms." In re Lalli, supra, 43 N.Y.2d, at 70, 400 N.Y.S.2d, at 764, 371

---

2. Section 4–1.2 requires not only that the order of filiation be made during the lifetime of the father, but that the proceeding in which it is sought be commenced "during the pregnancy of the mother or within two years from the birth of the child." The New York Court of Appeals declined to rule on the constitutionality of the two-year limitation in both of its opinions in this case because appellant concededly had never commenced a paternity proceeding at all. Thus, if the rule that paternity be judicially declared during his father's lifetime were upheld, appellant would lose for failure to comply with that requirement alone. If, on the other hand, appellant prevailed in his argument that his inheritance could not be conditioned on the existence of an order of filiation, the two-year limitation would become irrelevant since the paternity proceeding itself would be unnecessary. See In re Lalli, 43 N.Y.2d 65, 68 n. 1, 400 N.Y.S.2d 761, 762 n. 1, 371 N.E.2d 481, 482 n. 1 (1977); In re Lalli, 38 N.Y.2d 77, 80 n., 378 N.Y.S.2d 351, 353 n., 340 N.E.2d 721, 723 n. (1975). As the New York Court of Appeals has not passed upon the constitutionality of the two-year limitation, that question is not before us. Our decision today therefore sustains § 4–1.2 under the Equal Protection Clause only with respect to its requirement that a judicial order of filiation be issued during the lifetime of the father of an illegitimate child.

N.E.2d, at 483. The absence in § 4–1.2 of any requirement that the parents intermarry or otherwise legitimate a child born out of wedlock and our review of the legislative history of the statute, infra, at 525–526, confirm this view.

Our inquiry, therefore, is focused narrowly. We are asked to decide whether the discrete procedural demands that § 4–1.2 places on illegitimate children bear an evident and substantial relation to the particular state interests this statute is designed to serve.

B

The primary state goal underlying the challenged aspects of § 4–1.2 is to provide for the just and orderly disposition of property at death. We long have recognized that this is an area with which the States have an interest of considerable magnitude. *Trimble,* supra, 430 U.S., at 771; Weber v. Aetna Casualty & Surety Co., 406 U.S., at 170, 92 S.Ct., at 1404; Labine v. Vincent, 401 U.S., at 538, 91 S.Ct., at 1021; see also Lyeth v. Hoey, 305 U.S. 188, 193, 59 S.Ct. 155, 158, 83 L.Ed. 119 (1938); Mager v. Grima, 8 How. 490, 493, 12 L.Ed. 1168 (1850).

This interest is directly implicated in paternal inheritance by illegitimate children because of the peculiar problems of proof that are involved. Establishing maternity is seldom difficult. As one New York Surrogate's Court has observed: "[T]he birth of the child is a recorded or registered event usually taking place in the presence of others. In most cases the child remains with the mother and for a time is necessarily reared by her. That the child is the child of a particular woman is rarely difficult to prove." In re Ortiz, 60 Misc.2d 756, 761, 303 N.Y.S.2d 806, 812 (1969). Proof of paternity, by contrast, frequently is difficult when the father is not part of a formal family unit. "The putative father often goes his way unconscious of the birth of a child. Even if conscious, he is very often totally unconcerned because of the absence of any ties to the mother. Indeed the mother may not know *who* is responsible for her pregnancy." Ibid. (emphasis in original); accord, In re Flemm, 85 Misc.2d 855, 861, 381 N.Y.S.2d 573, 576–577 (Surr. Ct. 1975); In re Hendrix, 68 Misc.2d, at 443, 326 N.Y.S.2d, at 650; *Trimble,* supra, 430 U.S., at 770, 772, 97 S.Ct., at 1465, 1466.

Thus, a number of problems arise that counsel against treating illegitimate children identically to all other heirs of an intestate father. These were the subject of a comprehensive study by the Temporary State Commission on the Modernization, Revision and Simplification of the Law of Estates. This group, known as the Bennett Commission, consisted of individuals experienced in the practical problems of estate administration. In re Flemm, supra, 85 Misc.2d, at 858, 381 N.Y.S.2d, at 575. The Commission issued its report and recommendations to the legislature in 1965. See Fourth Report of the Temporary State Commission on the Modernization, Revision and Simplification of the Law of Estates, Legis. Doc.No. 19 (1965) (hereinafter Commission Report). The statute now codified as § 4–1.2 was included.

Although the overarching purpose of the proposed statute was "to alleviate the plight of the illegitimate child," Commission Report 37, the

Bennett Commission considered it necessary to impose the strictures of § 4–1.2 in order to mitigate serious difficulties in the administration of the estates of both testate and intestate decedents. The Commission's perception of some of these difficulties was described by Surrogate Sobel, a member of "the busiest [surrogate's] court in the State measured by the number of intestate estates which traffic daily through this court," In re Flemm, supra, at 857, 381 N.Y.S.2d, at 574, and a participant in some of the Commission's deliberations:

> "An illegitimate, if made an unconditional distributee in intestacy, must be served with process in the estate of his parent or if he is a distributee in the estate of the kindred of a parent. * * * And, in probating the will of his parent (though not named a beneficiary) or in probating the will of any person who makes a class disposition to 'issue' of such parent, the illegitimate must be served with process. * * * How does one cite and serve an illegitimate of whose existence neither family nor personal representative may be aware? And of greatest concern, how achieve finality of decree in *any* estate when there always exists the possibility however remote of a secret illegitimate lurking in the buried past of a parent or an ancestor of a class of beneficiaries? Finality in decree is essential in the Surrogate's Courts since title to real property passes under such decree. Our procedural statutes and the Due Process Clause mandate notice and opportunity to be heard to all necessary parties. Given the right to intestate succession, *all* illegitimates must be served with process. This would be no real problem with respect to those few estates where there are 'known' illegitimates. But it presents an almost insuperable burden as regards 'unknown' illegitimates. The point made in the [Bennett] commission discussions was that instead of affecting only a few estates, procedural problems would be created for many—some members suggested a majority—of estates." 85 Misc.2d, at 859, 381 N.Y.S.2d, at 575–576.

Cf. In re Leventritt, 92 Misc.2d 598, 601–602, 400 N.Y.S.2d 298, 300–301 (Surr.Ct.1977).

Even where an individual claiming to be the illegitimate child of a deceased man makes himself known, the difficulties facing an estate are likely to persist. Because of the particular problems of proof, spurious claims may be difficult to expose. The Bennett Commission therefore sought to protect "innocent adults and those rightfully interested in their estates from fraudulent claims of heirship and harassing litigation instituted by those seeking to establish themselves as illegitimate heirs." Commission Report 265.

C

As the State's interests are substantial, we now consider the means adopted by New York to further these interests. In order to avoid the problems described above, the Commission recommended a requirement designed to ensure the accurate resolution of claims of paternity and to minimize the potential for disruption of estate administration. Accuracy is enhanced by placing paternity disputes in a judicial forum during the lifetime of the father. As the New York Court of Appeals observed in its first opinion in this case, the "availability [of the putative father] should be a substantial factor contributing to the reliability of the fact-finding process." In re Lalli, 38 N.Y.2d, at 82, 378 N.Y.S.2d, at 355, 340 N.E.2d, at 724. In addition, requiring that the order be issued during the father's lifetime permits a man to defend his reputation against "unjust accusations in paternity claims," which was a secondary purpose of § 4–1.2. Commission Report 266.

The administration of an estate will be facilitated, and the possibility of delay and uncertainty minimized, where the entitlement of an illegitimate child to notice and participation is a matter of judicial record before the administration commences. Fraudulent assertions of paternity will be much less likely to succeed, or even to arise, where the proof is put before a court of law at a time when the putative father is available to respond, rather than first brought to light when the distribution of the assets of an estate is in the offing.[3]

Appellant contends that § 4–1.2, like the statute at issue in *Trimble,* excludes "significant categories of illegitimate children" who could be allowed to inherit "without jeopardizing the orderly settlement" of their intestate fathers' estates. *Trimble,* 430 U.S., at 771, 97 S.Ct., at 1465. He urges that those in his position—"known" illegitimate children who, despite the absence of an order of filiation obtained during their fathers' lifetimes, can present convincing proof of paternity—cannot rationally be denied inheritance as they pose none of the risks § 4–1.2 was intended to minimize.[4]

We do not question that there will be some illegitimate children who would be able to establish their relationship to their deceased fathers without serious disruption of the administration of estates and that, as applied to such individuals, § 4–1.2 appears to operate unfairly. But few statutory classifications are entirely free from the criticism that they sometimes produce inequitable results. Our inquiry under the Equal Protection Clause does not focus on the abstract "fairness" of a state law, but on whether the statute's relation to the state interests it is intended to promote is so tenuous that it lacks the rationality contemplated by the Fourteenth Amendment.

---

3. In affirming the judgment below, we do not, of course, restrict a State's freedom to require proof of paternity by means other than a judicial decree. Thus, a State may prescribe any *formal* method of proof, whether it be similar to that provided by § 4–1.2 or some other regularized procedure that would assure the authenticity of the acknowledgment. As we noted in *Trimble,* 430 U.S., at 772 n. 14, 97 S.Ct., at 1466 n. 14, such a procedure would be sufficient to satisfy the State's interests. See also n. [6], infra.

4. Appellant claims that in addition to discriminating between illegitimate and legitimate children, § 4–1.2, in conjunction with N.Y. Dom.Rel.Law § 24 (McKinney 1977), impermissibly discriminates between classes of illegitimate children. Section 24 provides that a child conceived out of wedlock is nevertheless legitimate if, before or after his birth, his parents marry, even if the marriage is void, illegal, or judicially annulled. Appellant argues that by classifying as "legitimate" children born out of wedlock whose parents later marry, New York has, with respect to these children, substituted marriage for § 4–1.2's requirement of proof of paternity. Thus, these "illegitimate" children escape the rigors of the rule unlike their unfortunate counterparts whose parents never marry.

Under § 24, one claiming to be the legitimate child of a deceased man would have to prove not only his paternity but also his maternity and the fact of the marriage of his parents. These additional evidentiary requirements make it reasonable to accept less exacting proof of paternity and to treat such children as legitimate for inheritance purposes.

The Illinois statute in *Trimble* was constitutionally unacceptable because it effected a total statutory disinheritance of children born out of wedlock who were not legitimated by the subsequent marriage of their parents. The reach of the statute was far in excess of its justifiable purposes. Section 4–1.2 does not share this defect. Inheritance is barred only where there has been a failure to secure evidence of paternity during the father's lifetime in the manner prescribed by the State. This is not a requirement that inevitably disqualifies an unnecessarily large number of children born out of wedlock.

The New York courts have interpreted § 4–1.2 liberally and in such a way as to enhance its utility to both father and child without sacrificing its strength as a procedural prophylactic. For example, a father of illegitimate children who is willing to acknowledge paternity can waive his defenses in a paternity proceeding, e.g., In re Thomas, 87 Misc.2d 1033, 387 N.Y.S.2d 216 (Surr.Ct.1976), or even institute such a proceeding himself.[5] N.Y. Family Court Act § 522 (McKinney Supp. 1978); In re Flemm, 85 Misc.2d, at 863, 381 N.Y.S.2d, at 578. In addition, the courts have excused "technical" failures by illegitimate children to comply with the statute in order to prevent unnecessary injustice. E.g., In re Niles, 53 A.D.2d 983, 385 N.Y.S.2d 876 (1976), appeal denied, 40 N.Y.2d 809, 392 N.Y.S.2d 1027, 360 N.E.2d 1109 (1977) (filiation order may be signed *nunc pro tunc* to relate back to period prior to father's death when court's factual finding of paternity had been made); In re Kennedy, 89 Misc.2d 551, 554, 392 N.Y.S.2d 365, 367 (Surr.Ct.1977) (judicial support order treated as "tantamount to an order of filiation," even though paternity was not specifically declared therein).

As the history of § 4–1.2 clearly illustrates, the New York Legislature desired to "grant to illegitimates *in so far as practicable* rights of inheritance on a par with those enjoyed by legitimate children," Commission Report 265 (emphasis added), while protecting the important state interests we have described. Section 4–1.2 represents a carefully considered legislative judgment as to how this balance best could be achieved.

Even if, as Mr. Justice BRENNAN believes, § 4–1.2 could have been written somewhat more equitably, it is not the function of a court "to hypothesize independently on the desirability or feasibility of any possible alternative[s]" to the statutory scheme formulated by New York. Mathews v. Lucas, 427 U.S., at 515, 96 S.Ct., at 2767. "These matters of practical judgment and empirical calculation are for [the State]. * * * In the end, the precise accuracy of [the State's] calculations is not a matter of specialized judicial competence; and we have no basis to question their

---

5. In addition to making intestate succession possible, of course, a father is always free to provide for his illegitimate child by will. See In re Flemm, 85 Misc.2d 855, 864, 381 N.Y.S.2d 573, 579 (Surr.Ct.1975).

detail beyond the evident consistency and substantiality." Id., at 515–516, 96 S.Ct. at 2767.[6]

We conclude that the requirement imposed by § 4–1.2 on illegitimate children who would inherit from their fathers is substantially related to the important state interests the statute is intended to promote. We therefore find no violation of the Equal Protection Clause.

The judgment of the New York Court of Appeals is affirmed.

For the reasons stated in his dissent in Trimble v. Gordon, 430 U.S. 762, 777, 97 S.Ct. 1459, 1468, 52 L.Ed.2d 31 (1977), Mr. Justice REHN-QUIST concurs in the judgment of affirmance.

Mr. Justice STEWART, concurring.

It seems to me that Mr. Justice POWELL's opinion convincingly demonstrates the significant differences between the New York law at issue here and the Illinois law at issue in Trimble v. Gordon, 430 U.S. 762, 97 S.Ct. 1459, 52 L.Ed.2d 31. Therefore, I cannot agree with the view expressed in Mr. Justice BLACKMUN's opinion concurring in the judgment that Trimble v. Gordon is now "a derelict," or with the implication that in deciding the two cases the way it has this Court has failed to give authoritative guidance to the courts and legislatures of the several States.

---

6. The dissent of Mr. Justice Brennan would reduce the opinion in Trimble v. Gordon, supra, to a simplistic holding that the Constitution *requires* a State, in a case of this kind, to recognize as sufficient any "formal acknowledgment of paternity." This reading of *Trimble* is based on a single phrase lifted from a footnote. 430 U.S., at 772 n. 14, 97 S.Ct., at 1466. It ignores both the broad rationale of the Court's opinion and the context in which the note and the phrase relied upon appear. The principle that the footnote elaborates is that the States are free to recognize the problems arising from different forms of proof and to select those forms "carefully tailored to eliminate imprecise and unduly burdensome methods of establishing paternity." Ibid. The New York Legislature, with the benefit of the Bennett Commission's study, exercised this judgment when it considered and rejected the possibility of accepting evidence of paternity less formal than a judicial order. Commission Report 266–267.

The "formal acknowledgment" contemplated by *Trimble* is such as would minimize post-death litigation, i.e., a regularly prescribed, legally recognized method of acknowledging paternity. See n. [3], supra. It is thus plain that footnote 14 in *Trimble* does not sustain the dissenting opinion. Indeed, the document relied upon by the dissent is not an acknowledgment of paternity at all. It is a simple "Certificate of Consent" that apparently was required at the time by New York for the marriage of a minor. It consists of one sentence:

"THIS IS TO CERTIFY that I, who have hereto subscribed may name, do hereby consent that Robert Lalli who is my son and who is under the age of 21 years, shall be united in marriage to Janice Bivins by any minister of the gospel or other person authorized by law to solemnize marriages." App. A–14.

Mario Lalli's signature to this document was acknowledged by a notary public, but the certificate contains no oath or affirmation as to the truth of its contents. The notary did no more than confirm the identity of Lalli. Because the certificate was executed for the purpose of giving consent to marry, not of proving biological paternity, the meaning of the words "my son" is ambiguous. One can readily imagine that had Robert Lalli's half-brother, who was not Mario's son but who took the surname Lalli and lived as a member of his household, sought permission to marry, Mario might also have referred to him as "my son" on a consent certificate.

The important state interests of safeguarding the accurate and orderly disposition of property at death, emphasized in *Trimble* and reiterated in our opinion today, could be frustrated easily if there were a constitutional rule that any notarized but unsworn statement identifying an individual as a "child" must be accepted as adequate proof of paternity regardless of the context in which the statement was made.

Mr. Justice BLACKMUN, concurring in the judgment.

I agree with the result the Court has reached and concur in its judgment. I also agree with much that has been said in the plurality opinion. My point of departure, of course, is at the plurality's valiant struggle to distinguish, rather than overrule, Trimble v. Gordon, 430 U.S. 762, 97 S.Ct. 1459, 52 L.Ed.2d 31 (1977), decided just the Term before last, and involving a small probate estate (an automobile worth approximately $2,500) and a sad and appealing fact situation. Four Members of the Court, like the Supreme Court of Illinois, found the case "constitutionally indistinguishable from Labine v. Vincent, 401 U.S. 532, 91 S.Ct. 1017, 28 L.Ed.2d 288 (1971)," and were in dissent. Id., at 776, 777, 97 S.Ct., at 1468.

It seems to me that the Court today gratifyingly reverts to the principles set forth in Labine v. Vincent. What Mr. Justice Black said for the Court in *Labine* applies with equal force to the present case and, as four of us thought, to the Illinois situation with which *Trimble* was concerned.

I would overrule *Trimble,* but the Court refrains from doing so on the theory that the result in *Trimble* is justified because of the peculiarities of the Illinois Probate Act there under consideration. This, of course, is an explanation, but, for me, it is an unconvincing one. I therefore must regard *Trimble* as a derelict, explainable only because of the overtones of its appealing facts, and offering little precedent for constitutional analysis of State intestate succession laws. If *Trimble* is not a derelict, the corresponding statutes of other States will be of questionable validity until this Court passes on them, one by one, as being on the *Trimble* side of the line or the *Labine-Lalli* side.

Mr. Justice BRENNAN, with whom Mr. Justice WHITE, Mr. Justice MARSHALL, and Mr. Justice STEVENS join, dissenting.

Trimble v. Gordon, 430 U.S. 762, 97 S.Ct. 1459, 52 L.Ed.2d 31 (1977), declares that the state interest in the accurate and efficient determination of paternity can be adequately served by requiring the illegitimate child to offer into evidence a "formal acknowledgment of paternity." Id., at 772 n. 14, 97 S.Ct., at 1466. The New York statute is inconsistent with this command. Under the New York scheme, an illegitimate child may inherit intestate only if there has been a judicial finding of paternity during the lifetime of the father.

The present case illustrates the injustice of the departure from *Trimble* worked by today's decision sustaining the New York rule. All interested parties concede that Robert Lalli is the son of Mario Lalli. Mario Lalli supported Robert during his son's youth. Mario Lalli formally acknowledged Robert Lalli as his son. See In re Lalli, 38 N.Y.2d 77, 79, 378 N.Y.S.2d 351, 352, 340 N.E.2d 721, 722 (1975). Yet, for want of a judicial order of filiation entered during Mario's lifetime, Robert Lalli is denied his intestate share of his father's estate.

There is no reason to suppose that the injustice of the present case is aberrant. Indeed it is difficult to imagine an instance in which an illegitimate child, acknowledged and voluntarily supported by his father, would ever inherit intestate under the New York scheme. Social welfare agencies, busy as they are with errant fathers, are unlikely to bring paternity proceedings against fathers who support their children. Similarly, children who are acknowledged and supported by their fathers are unlikely to bring paternity proceedings against them. First, they are unlikely to see the need for such adversary proceedings. Second, even if aware of the rule requiring judicial filiation orders, they are likely to fear provoking disharmony by suing their fathers. For the same reasons, mothers of such illegitimates are unlikely to bring proceedings against the fathers. Finally, fathers who do not even bother to make out wills (and thus die intestate) are unlikely to take the time to bring formal filiation proceedings. Thus, as a practical matter, by requiring judicial filiation orders entered during the lifetime of the fathers, the New York statute makes it virtually impossible for acknowledged and freely supported illegitimate children to inherit intestate.

Two interests are said to justify this discrimination against illegitimates. First, it is argued, reliance upon mere formal public acknowledgments of paternity would open the door to fraudulent claims of paternity. I cannot accept this argument. I adhere to the view that when "a father has formally acknowledged his child * * * there is no possible difficulty of proof, and no opportunity for fraud or error. This purported interest [in avoiding fraud] * * * can offer no justification for distinguishing between a formally acknowledged illegitimate child and a legitimate one." Labine v. Vincent, 401 U.S. 532, 552, 91 S.Ct. 1017, 1028, 28 L.Ed.2d 288 (1971) (BRENNAN, J., dissenting).

But even if my confidence in the accuracy of formal public acknowledgments of paternity were unfounded, New York has available less drastic means of screening out fraudulent claims of paternity. In addition to requiring formal acknowledgments of paternity, New York might require illegitimates to prove paternity by an elevated standard of proof, e.g., clear and convincing evidence, or even beyond a reasonable doubt: Certainly here, where there is no factual dispute as to the relationship between Robert and Mario Lalli, there is no justification for denying Robert Lalli his intestate share.

Second, it is argued, the New York statute protects estates from belated claims by unknown illegitimates. I find this justification even more tenuous than the first. Publication notice and a short limitations period in which claims against the estate could be filed could serve the asserted state interest as well as, if not better than, the present scheme. In any event, the fear that unknown illegitimates might assert belated claims hardly justifies cutting off the rights of known illegitimates such as Robert Lalli. I am still of the view that the state interest in the speedy and efficient determination of paternity "is completely served by public acknowledgment of parentage and simply does not apply to the case of acknowledged illegitimate children." Id., at 558 n. 30, 91 S.Ct., at 1030 n. 30 (BRENNAN, J., dissenting).

I see no reason to retreat from our decision in Trimble v. Gordon. The New York statute on review here, like the Illinois statute in *Trimble,* excludes "forms of proof which do not compromise the State['s] interests." Trimble v. Gordon, supra, at 772 n. 14, 97 S.Ct., at 1466 n. 14. The statute thus discriminates against illegitimates through means not substantially related to the legitimate interests that the statute purports to promote. I would invalidate the statute.

Notes

1. N.Y.—McKinney's EPTL 4–1.2 has subsequently been amended to substitute the words "born out of wedlock" for "illegitimate", to grant on the child's death rights to inherit and to obtain letters of administration to the father and paternal kin if the child's paternity has been established, and to provide the following methods of establishing paternity:

(2) A child born out of wedlock is the legitimate child of his father so that he and his issue inherit from his father and his paternal kindred if:

(A) a court of competent jurisdiction has, during the lifetime of the father, made an order of filiation declaring paternity or;

(B) the father of the child has signed an instrument acknowledging paternity, provided that

(i) such instrument is acknowledged or executed or proved in the form required to entitle a deed to be recorded in the presence of one or more witnesses and acknowledged by such witness or witnesses, in either case, before a notary public or other officer authorized to take proof of deeds and

(ii) such instrument is filed within sixty days from the making thereof with the putative father registry established by the state department of social services * * *

(iii) the department of social services shall, within seven days of the filing of the instrument, send written notice by registered mail to the mother and other legal guardian of such child, notifying them that an acknowledgment of paternity instrument acknowledged or executed by such father has been duly filed or;

(C) paternity has been established by clear and convincing evidence and the father of the child has openly and notoriously acknowledged the child as his own.

2. The holdings in Lalli and Trimble taken together create an uncertain standard against which the states must measure their statutes. Legitimation by the subsequent marriage of the mother and father is now widely recognized. It appears that the states must also make available a procedure whereby paternity may be established during the father's lifetime. The extent to which access to this procedure may be limited by a statute of limitations (the New York statute in Lalli required that the proceeding be initiated within two years after the birth of the child) was left unresolved. In Mills v. Habluetzel, 456 U.S. 91, 102 S.Ct. 1549, 71 L.Ed.2d 770 (1982), the Supreme Court held that a Texas statute, at issue in a non-support case, prescribing a one-year statute of limitation for a paternity suit, violated the equal protection clause of the Fourteenth Amendment. The opinion stated (p. 99):

* * * Such restrictions will survive equal protection scrutiny to the extent they are related to a legitimate state interest. See Lalli v. Lalli

* * *. The State's interest in avoiding the litigation of stale or fraudulent claims will justify those periods of limitation that are sufficiently long to present a real threat of loss or diminution of evidence, or an increased vulnerability to fraudulent claims.

Prior to the issuance of the Court's decision, Texas had changed the limitation period for paternity suits from one to four years. Five justices joined in a concurring opinion written by Justice O'Connor, who had not been a member of the Court at the time of the Trimble and Lalli cases, stating that the Court's ruling was not to be interpreted as an approval of the four-year statute. On the basis of the Mills decision, the Eleventh Circuit Court of Appeals declared the Alabama intestacy statute unconstitutional when applied to a situation where the father went into a coma from an accident four months before the child's birth and died four months after the birth. Handley, by and through Herron v. Schweiker, 697 F.2d 999, 1001 (11th Cir. 1983). The Court pointed out that the child did not have a "meaningful opportunity to be legitimated through a paternity proceeding, which, under Alabama law [see also the New York law at issue in the Lalli case. Eds.], must be maintained during the father's lifetime".

What additional opportunities the state gives the child to prove paternity depends on how it balances the claims of the child to equal treatment against the policy holding that the expeditious administration of decedents' estates requires that a person's status as an heir be established by the time of decedent's death. In this connection, the state constitution may impose more exacting standards than those required under the Lalli ruling. See Lowell v. Kowalski, 380 Mass. 663, 405 N.E.2d 135 (1980) (judicial adjudication as sole means of determining paternity not sufficient under Massachusetts equal rights amendment when father had acknowledged paternity on numerous occasions both orally and in writing). A number of states recognize acknowledgment by the father as an appropriate proof of paternity; some require that the acknowledgment be notarized and filed with the court clerk. See e.g. Herndon v. Robinson, 57 N.C.App. 318, 291 S.E.2d 305 (1982) (such a provision held constitutional). A few states permit a child to prove paternity before or after the father's death by "clear and convincing evidence". See e.g. Ill.—S.H.A. ch. 110½ ¶ 2–2(h) (this provision was adopted after the previous Illinois statute was held unconstitutional in Trimble v. Gordon); under Puerto Rican law biological paternity may be shown by a "preponderence of evidence on whatever type of proof is presented". Mendoza v. Secretary of Health and Human Services, 655 F.2d 10, 13 (1st Cir. 1981). UPC § 2–109 states that parentage may be established under the Uniform Parentage Act (9A ULA 626) or in states that have not adopted the Act as follows:

* * * a person born out of wedlock is a child of the mother. That person is also a child of the father, if:

(i) the natural parents participated in a marriage ceremony before or after the birth of the child, even though the attempted marriage is void; or

(ii) the paternity is established by an adjudication before the death of the father or is established thereafter by clear and convincing proof, but the paternity established under this subparagraph is ineffective to qualify the father or his kindred to inherit from or through the child unless the father has openly treated the child as his, and has not refused to support the child.

3. An illegitimate child died intestate without leaving a spouse, issue, or maternal kin.   Were the children of the putative father's brother entitled to inherit as the only heirs or did the property go to the City of Fredericksburg under the Virginia escheat statute?   The court denied the putative cousins' argument that the then Virginia statute (since replaced by one similar to UPC § 2–109), allowing the maternal but not the paternal kin to inherit was unconstitutional.   Trimble and Lalli were distinguished because no disability was being visited upon an innocent illegitimate child and because the father had never acknowledged or supported the child.   King v. Commonwealth of Virginia, 221 Va. 251, 269 S.E.2d 793 (1980) (estate escheated).

Is a grandchild, born out of wedlock, entitled to share in the income of a trust as a "grandchild" under the will of her father's mother?   The court held the canon of construction that, absent an expression of contrary intent, a person born out of wedlock shall be considered the child of the mother and not of the father was constitutionally flawed.   On the facts, the illegitimate grandchild was entitled to a share of the trust income.   Estate of Dulles, 494 Pa. 180, 431 A.2d 208 (1981).

SECTION EIGHT.   OTHER QUALIFICATIONS ON THE RIGHT TO INHERIT

A.   EXISTENCE AT DEATH OF INTESTATE

The transfer of title by intestate succession does not take place until the death of the intestate and a dead person cannot receive title.   It is therefore axiomatic that no rights under intestate succession can be claimed by or on behalf of a relative who predeceased the intestate.   A claim by living persons under the doctrine of representation is a different matter, since representation is merely a method of attempting to secure a proper distribution among the living, and is not predicated upon the vesting of any interest in the predeceased relatives themselves.   If the deceased and the alleged intestate successor die in a common disaster such as an automobile, train or plane accident, shipwreck, fire, flood, or earthquake, obvious difficulties of proof of survivorship arise.   See Chapman, The Presumption of Survivorship, 62 U.Pa.L.Rev. 585 (1914); 57 Am.L.Rev. 911 (interesting factual account of problem arising out of sinking of Lusitania).   Most states have enacted some version of the Uniform Simultaneous Death Act, 8 ULA 605–627 (1972), which establishes for all types of transfer (will, intestacy, trust, joint tenancy, insurance, etc.), unless the document specifically sets out a different distribution, the principle that when "there is no sufficient evidence that the persons have died otherwise than simultaneously, the property of each person shall be disposed of as if he had survived * * *."   See Annot., Simultaneous Death Act, 39 A.L.R.3d 1332.   In a number of statutes a fixed time is established which the beneficiary must survive in order to take.   Uniform Probate Code Section 2–104 (120 hours); Ohio Rev.Code Ann. § 2105.21 (30 days).

The case of an heir born after the death of the intestate was covered at common law, as far as succession to realty was concerned, by what has been referred to as the doctrine of shifting descent. Under this rule, a relative born at any time after the death of the intestate, whether conceived or not at the time of the latter's death, would be entitled to share. Thus, if the nearest intestate successor at the death of the intestate was his sister, and the parents (who could not inherit realty at common law) also survived, the sister's intestate share was liable at any time to be divested partially by the birth of other sisters (who would share equally with her as coparceners), or entirely by the birth of a brother (who would take everything under primogeniture and the preference for males). This doctrine reflected the mores of the time, when land remained in the same family from generation to generation. Because its detrimental effect on the marketability of titles makes it inappropriate for the modern era of commerce in realty, it has become obsolete in this country. Bates v. Brown, 72 U.S. (5 Wall.) 710, 18 L.Ed. 535 (1866); for an illustration of the doctrine being applied see Throop v. Williams, 5 Conn. 98 (1823) (sisters born four years after the death of the intestate allowed to share).

However, notwithstanding the repudiation of this doctrine as such, the birth of a relative after the death of the intestate does not usually bar him or her from inheritance in this country if he or she was conceived before the intestate's death. The latter proviso greatly curtails the time during which the title may remain uncertain, and this rule follows the principle prevailing generally in property law that a child en ventre sa mere, if subsequently born alive, is considered as in being for purposes beneficial to it. This was the rule adopted in England for intestate succession to personalty. Burnet v. Mann, 1 Ves.Sr. 157, 27 Eng.Reprint, 953 (1748). In some states, however, this doctrine is restricted to children or to descendants of the intestate, and collaterals must actually be born at the intestate's death in order to inherit. For a discussion of the legal and medical problems involved, see Matter of Wells, 129 Misc. 447, 221 N.Y.S. 714 (1927) (280 days presumed period of gestation).

The techniques for freezing sperm in sperm banks are sufficiently developed to permit conception of a child long after the death of the father. A number of commentators have discussed situations in which posthumous conception might take place. Leach, Perpetuities in the Atomic Age: The Sperm Bank and the Fertile Decedent, 48 A.B.A.J. 942 (1962) (replenishing mankind after an atomic holocaust); Thies, A Look to the Future: Property Rights and the Posthumously Conceived Child, 110 T. & E. 922 (1971) (widow wants a child following the premature death of her husband); Wadlington, Artificial Conception: The Challenge for Family Law, 69 Va.L.Rev. 465, 500 (1983).

Mario and Elsa Rios went to the Queen Victoria Medical Center in Melbourne Australia in 1981 to try to have a child of their own. Three ova from Elsa were fertilized. One was implanted in Elsa, but she later had a miscarriage. The other two were frozen for possible future use. In 1983, Mario and Elsa were killed in an airplane crash in Chile, each leaving an intestate estate of approximately a million dollars. The clinic subsequently made it known that the eggs had been fertilized by the sperm of a donor. Mario left an adult son by a previous marriage surviving; Elsa had no children. N.Y. Times, June 21, 1984, p. 16, cols. 1–2. Are the frozen ova in being and entitled to take as intestate successors? What are the obligations of the administrators of the estates and the clinic?

These possibilities are only the beginning. In the not too distant future reproduction may be accomplished without sperm. In lower forms of animal and plant life scientists have achieved asexual reproduction by cloning ("cell tissue from an adult organism is developed into a separate, but genetically identical, organism"), nuclear transplantation ("removal of the haploid nucleus from an unfertilized ovum and the implantation of a diploid nucleus"), and parthenogenesis ("use of physical and chemical stimuli in place of male genetic materials"). Kindregan, State Power Over Human Fertility and Individual Liberty, 23 Hastings L.J. 1401, 1416–1419 (1972). When these techniques are perfected, the means will be available for the genetic engineers to shape the composition of the population. If the suggestion seems absurd, it is to be admitted that no one can predict the future impact on society of over-population, starvation and exhaustion of natural resources. Among the legal problems which would follow from the state's imposing eugenic controls, the capacity of the child to inherit will not command a high priority.

B. UNWORTHY HEIRS

In general, conduct toward the decedent which might, in accordance with conventional community standards, seem ethically reprehensible does not bar an heir from sharing in the decedent's estate either by intestate succession or will. See generally Atkinson on Wills, 147–158 (1953). Certain types of misconduct have been made grounds for disqualification by statute in a number of jurisdictions. 1. *Breach of obligation to a child*. Under § 4–1.4 of the N.Y.—McKinney's EPTL a parent may not share in the estate of a child if he or she has neglected, abandoned, or refused to furnish support for that child. 2. *Violation of the marital obligations*. The Statute of Westminster II, 1285, 13 Edw. 1, c. 34, barred a woman from dower if she abandoned her husband and lived in adultery with another. In a few jurisdictions this limitation has been applied as a part of the common law; but the more modern authority adopts the view that, in the absence of a statute, adultery does not work a forfeiture. Annot., Adultery on Part of Surviving Spouse as Affecting Marital Rights in Deceased Spouse's Estate, 13 A.L.R.3d 486. Sec. 5–1.2 of the N.Y.—McKinney's EPTL does not mention adultery but does bar either spouse who either has obtained a divorce (or legal separation) whether or not that divorce is recognized as valid under New York law; has abandoned the deceased spouse; or has failed to fulfil a duty to support the other spouse. A similar rule exists in many of the states. Annot., Abandonment, Desertion, or Refusal to Support on Part of Surviving Spouse as Affecting Marital Rights in Deceased Spouse's Estate, 13 A.L.R.3d 446. The standards of proof and the allocation of the burden of proof are discussed in In re Appeal of Fisher, 442 Pa. 421, 276 A.2d 516 (1971).

3. *Felonious slaying of the decedent.* In a majority of states statutes have been enacted barring a felonious slayer from taking any benefit from the estate of his victim. See, Annot., Homicide—Preclusion from Inheritance, 25 A.L.R.4th 787. This problem and a representative statute are analyzed in Bird v. Plunkett, p. 7, supra.

SECTION NINE. ADVANCEMENTS

The intestate succession statutes have traditionally contained a reservation which requires that property "advanced" to an heir before the intestate dies be charged against the advancee's share of the intestate's estate. A number of statutes follow the approach of the English Statute of Distributions of 1670 and speak only of the children of the decedent. Other statutes use more comprehensive words such as "heirs" or "descendants." It is usually held that an advancement to a parent is charged, if the advancee has predeceased the intestate, against the share going to the advancee's issue.

A simple example illustrates the operation of the doctrine. Mother in her lifetime advanced $2,000 to one son, $3,000 to her daughter and nothing to a second son. She dies intestate leaving a net estate for distribution of $13,000. The first son has predeceased her leaving two surviving children; the daughter and the second son also survive and mother's husband has been dead for many years. The computation of shares requires that the amounts advanced be added to the estate which gives a total of $18,000. The share of each child will be $6,000. The first son had been advanced $2,000 and so his children divide the remaining $4,000. The daughter has already received $3,000 and so she gets $3,000 from the estate. The second son has not received anything during his mother's life and so he gets a full share of $6,000. The $4,000, $3,000 and $6,000 add up to $13,000, the amount available for distribution.

If the amount advanced to the daughter exceeded the value of each of the children's shares, the daughter would be omitted from the distribution but would not be required to refund. Thus, if she had received $9,000 during life, the total "estate" would be $24,000, which divided into thirds makes shares of $8,000 apiece or $1,000 less than daughter has already received. The doctrine attempts to obtain a rough equality within the family of the estate on hand for distribution but does not go so far as to require advancees to return any property they have received. The estate would be distributed $7,500 to the second son and $2,750 to each of the first son's children.

In the abstract, the doctrine has a nice ring to it. Inequality of treatment among members of the same class inevitably gives rise to bitterness and family friction. It is a simple matter to avoid the problem before the fact by drafting a will or trust so that the shares are equal or, if not, by making clear the reasons for the disparity. If, however, the principle of equality of treatment is to be applied to a lifetime of inter vivos transfers, problems soon arise as to which transfers were intended to be a downpayment on the child's inheritance and which were made for other reasons.   The costs of maintenance and education are not ordinarily intended as advancements.   It must, then, be an outlay which is unusual, but the transferor may have intended it to be an outright gift or a loan. A parent is not required to treat his or her children and grandchildren the same over the years.   The doctrine does no more than take into account transfers which were intended to be an early payment of the child's inheritance.   It is unusual for a lawyer to be called in to supervise informal family transactions, and so the parent's intent remains ambiguous more often than not.   It used to be the general law and still is the rule in some jurisdictions that when the advancor is a parent and the advancee a child, a presumption will be applied favoring an advancement classification.   Cravens v. Cravens, 56 Tenn.App. 619, 410 S.W.2d 424 (1966).   The trend in recently amended statutes reverses the presumption and greatly reduces the general applicability of the doctrine by ruling that there is no advancement unless the advancor or advancee has recognized it as such in a contemporaneous, signed document.   See, for instance, N.Y.—McKinney's EPTL 2–1.5 and UPC § 2–110, set out below.

Most of the modern statutes codify the traditional rule which requires that the advancement be valued at the date the advancee takes title to it rather than at the date of the advancor's death, but the New York statute calls for the property to have the "value at which it is appraised for estate tax purposes."   The newer statutes also make the doctrine applicable to any heir and not just a child.   The general rule has been that the doctrine only applies if the decedent dies wholly intestate, but a number of recent statutes, New York for one, now make it applicable to testate as well as intestate distributions.   For a discussion of the related doctrine of "satisfaction" which applies to wills, see Chapter Five, Section 4(b), infra, at p. 358–359.   The subject of advancements is exhaustively reviewed in Elbert, Advancements, 51 Mich.L.Rev. 665 (1953), 52 Mich.L.Rev. 231 (1953) and 535 (1954).   UPC § 2–110 reads as follows:

> If a person dies intestate as to all his estate, property which he gave in his lifetime to an heir is treated as an advancement against the latter's share of the estate only if declared in a contemporaneous writing by the decedent or acknowledged in writing by the heir to be an advancement. For this purpose the property advanced is valued as of the time the heir came into possession or enjoyment of the property or as of the time of death of the decedent, whichever first occurs.   If the recipient of the property fails to survive the decedent, the property is not taken into account in computing the intestate share to be received by the recipient's issue, unless the declaration or acknowledgment provides otherwise.

Chapter Three

PROTECTION OF THE FAMILY

SECTION ONE. INTRODUCTION

From a policy perspective the law of estates is an important adjunct to the law pertaining to the family.   Wealth is a cement to hold families together, to give the capable members the maximum opportunities, and to provide care and security for the members who are old or disabled. Wealth may also be explosively divisive as disappointed expectations of inheritance may pit one member of the family against another in a fight which for intensity and bitterness makes litigation between business competitors sound like a tea party.   The law regulating the disposition of wealth must take into account this potential to shape the family structure.

In the vast majority of cases a person's wealth descends to his or her immediate family.   This result is required if the person dies intestate. The will would seem to have been designed to facilitate deviation from this pattern, but historians argue otherwise.   Professor W. D. Macdonald in his book, Fraud on the Widow's Share (1960), states at page 40:

> Indeed, it is probable that through the centuries freedom of testation has been used more as an instrument of family protection than as a weapon of disinheritance.   Maine pointed out long ago that in Roman law "it would rather seem as if the Testamentary Power were chiefly valued for the assistance it gave in *making provision* for a Family, and in dividing the inheritance more evenly and fairly than the Law of Intestate Succession would have divided it."

Contemporary studies indicate that the will is most frequently used to augment the surviving spouse's share.   As noted earlier, the fact that this is usually done at the expense of the children does not indicate any want of affection for the children but rather the conviction that the surviving spouse will take care of the children and at his or her death divide the family property among them.   The law has not been content to rely on the property owner to adopt this typical dispositive pattern wholly on his or her own.   A variety of statutes have been enacted to compel, or at the very least encourage, one spouse to reward the other spouse and his or her family.   The following brief introductory comment indicates the profusion of laws involved in the process.

121

A.   PROTECTION OF THE SPOUSE

[Historically, the wife was the first object of the law's concern.] The traditional statement of policy assumed a wife who had given up her own economic opportunities to serve her husband and family, had participated in countless intangible ways in the accumulation of his estate, was untrained at an advanced age (when death had removed him) and incapable of caring for herself, and was so destitute of property of her own that she was forced to become a charge on the state.   Almost every state has some provision in its law to protect the wife from disinheritance.   Today, these devices have been enlarged to accord like privileges to the husband in his wife's estate, although statements of policy still tend to focus on protection of the wife as the law's primary objective.   Widows outnumber widowers by 5.3 to 1.   In recognition of this statistical fact the discussion which follows is described in terms of the wife's claim to her husband's estate.   The reader should bear in mind that these roles may be reversed.

Four basic techniques are used to implement this policy—dower, the elective or indefeasible share, community property, and marital property, as defined in the recently promulgated uniform act.   These types of claims against the decedent's property vary in historical origin and method of operation.   Several fundamental differences should be noted at the outset.   The first, which receives major attention in the material that follows, involves the extent to which the husband may disinherit his wife by transferring title to his property to someone else, either outright or in trust, before he dies.   [Under the rules of dower the wife has an inchoate estate in all of the husband's realty owned during marriage, which means that any transfer of the property by him goes subject to her superior claim to dower]   The original statutes establishing the wife's right to an indefeasible share in lieu of dower took a different approach whereby the husband could do as he wished with his property during life, but his estate at death was subject to the claim of his wife for a certain share.

The conflict in policy represented by these differing approaches has not been finally resolved.   Much of the criticism of dower has been directed at the wife's inchoate estate on the ground that it adversely affects the marketability of land and makes for uncertainty in titles.   In response to this criticism all but a handful of states have abolished dower, and several of the remaining states have modified it to limit the length of time in which the wife retains her inchoate veto over property which has been transferred.   The experience of states which have enacted elective share legislation, to be examined below, demonstrates the inadequacy of an indefeasible share which only takes effect against the estate at death.   The title to assets may be transferred to a trustee and the assets are thereby removed from the estate, but the husband retains practically all the incidents of beneficial enjoyment by reserving a right to the income, the unrestricted power to remove principal and substantial control over the management of the fund.

The law is challenged as to whether it will tolerate such evasions particularly when the motive behind them is to circumvent the statutory policy against disinheritance of the wife.   A paradox is apparent: a number of states have abolished dower in favor of an indefeasible share because, among other reasons, dower gave the wife a control over inter vivos transfers, but, without that control, her indefeasible share may be nullified by an inter vivos trust which the husband may establish without even paying the penalty of losing the right of substantial enjoyment of the property for the balance of his life. New York and the Uniform Probate Code have attempted to counter such maneuvers by adding to the basic elective share provision authority in the surviving spouse to recapture a portion of the assets the other spouse gave away during life but over which he retained a measure of enjoyment or control.

As a general proposition, each spouse in a community property state retains the power to manage and control his or her own separate property, while they share equally the power to manage and control the community property. Thus, it would appear that the wife can protect her share of the community property from defeasance by her husband's inter vivos transfers. The literature on the subject suggests, however, that because some property is not treated as belonging to the community and there is a general insufficiency of remedies, the reality falls short of the ideal. In California, for example, community property business is not subject to joint control, financial institutions deal only with the named account holder, a spouse has no claim to the other spouse's separate property, and only at divorce are remedies available for improper management. The Uniform Marital Property Act, which is designed to import community property principles into common law jurisdictions, strikes a middle course, with a provision permitting one spouse to set aside a portion of certain gifts made by the other spouse but providing that a third person is secure in his or her dealings with the spouse who is the titleholder of the property.

A second area of difference among these devices for protecting the surviving spouse involves the extent to which the spouse's share takes priority over those of the decedent's creditors. Briefly stated, the wife's dower is superior to the claims of her husband's creditors; an indefeasible share only applies against the "net" estate and is therefore subordinate to the decedent's debts; and community property is liable for community debts. The subject is briefly noted in subsequent text material but is not explored in detail. This brevity of treatment is not intended to obscure the obvious fact that priority among claims may have a vital impact on the welfare of a family whose financial situation is approaching insolvency.

The legal literature in the field tends to talk about these techniques as though they were the most important, indeed, practically the exclusive methods of protecting the spouse. This is understandable in that their roots are deep in the law, they operate contrary to accepted notions of free testation, they can cause dramatic complications within individual families, and they are the source of constant concern on the part of lawyers, judges and statutory reformers. In simple truth, if the problem is described not in terms of the property of an individual family but rather as a national problem involving spouses throughout the country who are left without support by the death of the family wage-earner, it is immediately apparent that the really significant solutions are to be found in the field of retirement, disability and death programs, public and private, most notably Social Security. The coverage of these programs, both in numbers of eligible people and size and diversity of benefits, is discussed in Section Ten, infra. In any listing of available benefits note must also be taken of the pension provisions in state laws covering occupations such as teachers, police and firemen, government employees and the like. A compilation made in Illinois a number of years ago counted forty state statutes which, along with twenty federal statutes, made sixty different methods of distributing benefits to spouses and children. Many of these programs, like federal Social Security, have as an essential feature the requirement that the benefits go to the spouse (and sometimes the children) despite any attempts made by the other spouse to deprive the survivor of those benefits. Dunham, Sixty Different Succession Laws in Illinois, 46 Ill.B.J. 741 (1958).

B. PROTECTION OF THE CHILDREN

In Section Six of this Chapter, infra, at pp. 181–182, two excerpts are set out expressing opposite policy perspectives concerning the fate of a child following the death of the parents. One pictures the typical child as orphaned and pauperized; the other sees the child as being middle-aged and, by upbringing and education in a family with property, well established in his or her own right. In a given situation either one of these views might be accurate, and in that fact lies the major deficiency in legislation that establishes a forced share for the spouse or child. It would be preferable to have legislation which is selective and can allocate the decedent's resources to meet the specific, real needs of the immediate family. This approach has been rejected in this country on the ground that it would convert every estate into a lawsuit and the resulting chaos could not be administered by the courts. For spouses the legislatures have ordered differing forms of forced shares. But children have not been accorded like benefits, and, in all states except Louisiana which retains from its civil law background a form of the continental legitime, they may be completely disinherited by their parents. The law is either totally silent on the point, or, as in a number of states, is limited only to making sure that if the parent disinherits a child it is done intentionally and not by mistake or inadvertence.

C. RESTRICTIONS ON GIFTS TO CHARITIES

Up until a decade ago, a number of jurisdictions, including New York, Pennsylvania and the District of Columbia, imposed statutory limitations on bequests to charities. These statutes represented an extension of the general legislative policy of protecting the family, in this instance, by invalidating, in whole or in part, certain gifts to charity that were according to statutory standards overly generous or improvidently made. Remnants of these limitations are to be found in a few jurisdictions, but, for the most part, this form of family protection has disappeared either by repeal of the statute (e.g., New York) or its invalidation as a violation of the equal protection clause of the Constitution (e.g., Pennsylvania and the District of Columbia).

D. TAX INCENTIVES FOR FAMILY GIVING

The marital deduction provision of the federal estate and gift taxes operates on the principle that a married couple is a single economic unit for tax purposes. Thus a husband and wife can transfer their assets from one to the other without incurring either a gift or estate tax. The Internal Revenue Code does, however, strike a bargain with the taxpayer who claims the deduction—the initial transfer of property is exempted from tax on the condition that the donee-spouse receives the property with rights comparable to those of an outright owner so that the latter spouse will be subject to gift or estate tax on transferring the property to beneficiaries outside the husband-wife unit. The marital deduction constitutes a powerful incentive for inter-spousal giving. Not only is a married couple able to delay payment of the estate tax until the survivor of them dies, but also they may combine the credits authorized by the statutes to achieve a tax saving. For example, after the maximum credit is in effect in 1987, each parent may be enabled to pass $600,000 of family assets, for a total of $1,200,000, to their children or other beneficiaries without paying any gift or estate tax.

Under another application of the marital deduction principle, the gift tax contains a consent procedure for married couples whereby a gift by either spouse to a third person can be reported as though each spouse made a gift of one-half of the donated amount. This split-gift procedure makes available two unified credits rather than one and gives a married couple the opportunity to double the number of $10,000 per-donee exclusions to be deducted from the amount of the gift before computing the tax. For example, a husband and wife can join together and make annual gifts of $20,000 to each of their three children and six grandchildren and thus transfer a total of $180,000 each year free of tax to younger generations of the family. The marital deduction is examined in more detail in Chapter Ten, pp. 933–948, infra.

A number of states, New York for example, grant a similar unlimited marital deduction in their estate taxes. State inheritance taxes that do not have a marital deduction typically adjust their rates and exemptions according to the relationship of the beneficiary to the decedent—the closer the relationship the lower the tax bracket and the higher the exemption.

E. FAMILY ALLOWANCE AND HOMESTEAD

Statutes in many states provide for two methods of protecting the family which, although unknown at common law, are of long standing in this country—the family allowance and the homestead. While both of these devices developed originally to provide a measure of security to the family from the claims of creditors, they now also operate to give additional property to the spouse and family. Because they are statutory rights, they cannot be defeated by will. This brief description is included here to round out the picture of available protections for the family.

The usual purpose of the family allowance statute is to provide temporary support out of the estate of a decedent to the family during the period of administration of the estate and prior to distribution. The persons entitled to the allowance include the surviving spouse, who was entitled to receive support from the decedent, and, in some statutes, the minor children. In many but not all of these statutes, the only source of the family allowance is personal property. Some of these statutes specifically describe articles of personal property such as household furniture, wearing apparel, etc., that are to be included in the allowance. Under many of the statutes the property set apart as a family allowance is exempt from the claims of the creditors of the deceased.

The primary purpose of the homestead principle is to guarantee the continuance of a home for the family of a debtor by exempting it from the claims of creditors. In many states real property automatically becomes a homestead when it is used by a family as a home, and no formal proceedings are necessary prerequisites to its acquisition of the qualities of a homestead. In other states, however, the statutes require recordation of a declaration of homestead before the property acquires such special characteristics. While the original purpose of the homestead device was to provide an exemption from claims of creditors, the modern statutes also tend to give the family some indestructible interests in it. Some of the statutes authorize the spouse of the owner to claim the exemption of the homestead from the owner's creditors if the owner is not willing to do so. Some prevent the owner from making an effective conveyance inter vivos without the consent of his or her spouse. The statutes also quite generally provide that the death of the owner does not destroy the homestead qualities, which are continued for the benefit of the surviving spouse for life and for surviving minor children during their minority. The surviving members of the family included in the statutes may claim the exemption after the death of the owner as against his or her creditors, and in most of the states also as against his or her heirs or devisees, although some jurisdictions limit the exemption to claims of creditors of the deceased owner. Insofar as the homestead rights of the surviving members of the family have priority over the takers under the will of the deceased owner, this device, of course, operates as a restriction on testamentary disposition. Under some of the homestead statutes the home is only exempt up to a certain value and sometimes this value is so small (for example, $500 or $1,000) that the protection of the home is more theoretical than real.

The Uniform Probate Code sections are illustrative:

Section 2–401. [Homestead Allowance]

A surviving spouse of a decedent who was domiciled in this state is entitled to a homestead allowance of [$5,000]. If there is no surviving spouse, each minor child and each dependent child of the decedent is entitled to a homestead allowance amounting to [$5,000] divided by the number of minor and dependent children of the decedent. The homestead allowance is exempt from and has priority over all claims against the estate. Homestead allowance is in addition to any share passing to the surviving spouse or minor or dependent child by the will of the decedent unless otherwise provided, by intestate succession or by way of elective share.

Section 2–402. [Exempt Property]

In addition to the homestead allowance, the surviving spouse of a decedent who was domiciled in this state, is entitled from the estate to value not exceeding $3,500 in excess of any security interests therein in household furniture, automobiles, furnishings, appliances and personal effects. If there is no surviving spouse, children of the decedent are entitled jointly to the same value. If encumbered chattels are selected and if the value in excess of security interests, plus that of other exempt property, is less than $3,500, or if there is not $3,500 worth of exempt property in the estate, the spouse or children are entitled to other assets of the estate, if any, to the extent necessary to make up the $3,500 value. Rights to exempt property and assets needed to make up a deficiency of exempt property have priority over all claims against the estate, except that the right to any assets to make up a deficiency of exempt property shall abate as necessary to permit prior payment of homestead allowance and family allowance. These rights are in addition to any benefit or share passing to the surviving spouse or children by the will of the decedent unless otherwise provided, by intestate succession, or by way of elective share.

Section 2–403. [Family Allowance]

In addition to the right to homestead allowance and exempt property, if the decedent was domiciled in this state, the surviving spouse and minor children whom the decedent was obligated to support and children who were in fact being supported by him are entitled to a reasonable allowance in money out of the estate for their maintenance during the period of administration, which allowance may not continue for longer than one year if the estate is inadequate to discharge allowed claims. The allowance may be paid as a lump sum or in periodic installments. It is payable to the surviving spouse, if living, for the use of the surviving spouse and minor and dependent children; otherwise to the children, or persons having their care and custody; but in case any minor child or dependent child is not living with the surviving spouse, the allowance may be made partially to the child or his guardian or other person having his care and custody, and partially to the spouse, as their needs may appear. The family allowance is exempt from and has priority over all claims but not over the homestead allowance.

The family allowance is not chargeable against any benefit or share passing to the surviving spouse or children by the will of the decedent unless otherwise provided, by intestate succession, or by way of elective share. The death of any person entitled to family allowance terminates his right to allowances not yet paid.

Section 2–404. [Source, Determination and Documentation]

If the estate is otherwise sufficient, property specifically devised is not used to satisfy rights to homestead and exempt property. Subject to this restriction, the surviving spouse, the guardians of the minor children, or children who are adults may select property of the estate as homestead allowance and exempt property. The personal representative may make these selections if the surviving spouse, the children or the guardians of the minor children are unable or fail to do so within a reasonable time or if there are no guardians of the minor children. The personal representative may execute an instrument or deed of distribution to establish the ownership of property taken as homestead allowance or exempt property. He may determine the family allowance in a lump sum not exceeding $6,000 or periodic installments not exceeding $500 per month for one year, and may disburse funds of the estate in payment of the family allowance and any part of the homestead allowance payable in cash. The personal representative or any interested person aggrieved by any selection, determination, payment, proposed payment, or failure to act under this section may petition the Court for appropriate relief, which relief may provide a family allowance larger or smaller than that which the personal representative determined or could have determined.

SECTION TWO. CONSTITUTIONAL PROHIBITIONS OF GENDER-BASED DIFFERENCES IN BENEFITS

HALL v. McBRIDE
Supreme Court of Alabama, 1982.
416 So.2d 986.

FAULKNER, Justice.

William Hall died on May 25, 1979. On July 3, 1979, his wife, Mary E. Hall, filed for letters of administration on William Hall's estate, alleging he left no last will and testament. The letters of administration were issued on July 20, 1979. In August, Mr. Hall's sister, Anne Hall McBride, filed a petition to admit the last will and testament of Mr. Hall. The probate Court of Mobile County admitted the will to probate. Mary Hall, the widow, filed a dissent from the will pursuant to Code 1975, § 43–1–15. Anne McBride filed a motion to strike the dissent.

The Honorable John L. Moore, Probate Judge of Mobile County, granted Mrs. Hall's motion to strike the widow's dissent. The judge granted the motion to strike on the grounds that § 43–1–15 makes an unconstitutional gender-based classification. The probate court also refused to extend § 43–1–15 to those persons who were not explicitly extended protection, namely, widowers. Mary Hall, the surviving spouse, appeals.

Mary Hall married the deceased in 1945. Mrs. Hall returned to college in 1963 or 1964, and had lived apart from her husband since that time—approximately seventeen years. Her income for the past few years has been approximately $15,000.00 annually. She designated herself as being single on her income tax returns for these years.

Two issues are raised on appeal: 1) Whether § 43–1–15 provides a constitutionally impermissible gender-based classification under the equal protection provisions of the United States and Alabama constitutions. 2) If yes, whether § 43–1–15 should be totally invalidated or whether the section should be expanded to provide benefits to the entire class of persons, surviving spouses.

It is clear that a statutory classification that distinguishes between males and females is "subject to scrutiny under the Equal Protection Clause." Craig v. Boren, 429 U.S. 190, 97 S.Ct. 451, 50 L.Ed.2d 397 (1976). Nevertheless, the Supreme Court of the United States has had some difficulty in agreeing upon the proper approach and analysis in cases involving challenges to gender-based classifications. Michael M. v. Superior Court of Sonoma County, 450 U.S. 464, 101 S.Ct. 1200, 67 L.Ed.2d 437 (1981). The major area of conflict has centered on the proper level of scrutiny to apply to a statutory classification which places a burden on males which is not shared by females. Id.

The test often enunciated by the Court for determining the constitutionality of a gender-based classification is whether the classification bears a "substantial relationship" to "important governmental objectives." Id.; Orr v. Orr, 440 U.S. 268, 99 S.Ct. 1102, 59 L.Ed.2d 306 (1979); Craig v. Boren, 429 U.S. 190, 97 S.Ct. 451, 50 L.Ed.2d 397 (1976). In general, a statute will not be upheld if the statute makes "overbroad generalizations based on sex." A statute which is based on the legislature's misconceptions concerning the role of females in the home rather than in the "market place and the world of ideas" will not survive constitutional scrutiny. Craig v. Boren, 429 U.S. at 199, 97 S.Ct. at 457. A gender-based legislative classification carries "the inherent risk of reinforcing the stereotypes about the 'proper place' of women and their need for special protection." Orr v. Orr, 440 U.S. at 283, 99 S.Ct. at 1113. "Thus, even statutes purportedly designed to compensate for and ameliorate the effects of past discrimination must be carefully tailored." Id. A statute based on notions of "romantic paternalism" and which carry "the baggage of sexual stereotypes" cannot withstand constitutional scrutiny. Frontiero v. Richardson, 411 U.S. 677, 93 S.Ct. 1764, 36 L.Ed.2d 583 (1972).

On the other hand, the Equal Protection Clause does not "demand that a statute necessarily apply equally to all persons" or require "things which are different in fact * * * to be treated in law as though they were the same." Michael M. v. Superior Court of Sonoma County, 450 U.S. at 469, 101 S.Ct. at 1204 (quoting Tigner v. Texas, 310 U.S. 141, 60 S.Ct. 879, 84 L.Ed. 1124 (1940)). The court has upheld statutes in which the gender classifications "realistically reflect the fact that the sexes are not similarly situated in certain circumstances." Id.; Schlesinger v. Ballard, 419 U.S. 498, 95 S.Ct. 572, 42 L.Ed.2d 610 (1975); Kahn v. Shevin, 416 U.S. 351, 94 S.Ct. 1734, 40 L.Ed.2d 189 (1974).

Alabama's statutory scheme on descent and distribution permits a widow to dissent from her deceased husband's will and take an amount equal to a widow's intestate share in personalty, and her dower portion of realty.   Code 1975, § 43–1–15.   At common law, a widow who was not satisfied with the portion her husband gave her in his will, could seek a writ of dower *unde nihil habiut* against the tenant of the freehold.   If she established her right to the writ, she assigned her dower to the sheriff. Finally, an action of ejectment was brought against the current land holder.   See Dean v. Hart, 62 Ala. 308 (1878);   McLeod v. McDonnel, 6 Ala. 236 (1844).   The widow's right to dower was in addition to the gifts or devises to the widow by her husband.   Id.   Section 43–1–15 and its predecessors changed the common law.   The presumption is that a gift or devise by a husband in his will to his wife precludes the widow from receiving an intestate share.

The purpose of enacting § 43–1–15 is to protect the wife from a husband who would cut her from his will, leaving her with few or no assets for her support.   See McGhee v. Stephens, 83 Ala. 466, 3 So. 808 (1887);   McReynolds v. Jones, 30 Ala. 101 (1857).

"In the feudal system from which dower arose, the husband had complete control over family wealth;   consequently, the widow was forced to depend upon her deceased husband's estate for support."   Comment, Reverse Sex Discrimination Under Alabama's Law of Decedents' Estates, 32 Ala.L.Rev. 135, 150 (1980);   see Jones, Alabama Probate Law—Need for Revision of Intestate Provisions, 20 Ala.L.Rev. 121 (1967).   The purpose of § 43–1–15 is to put the claims of the widow "beyond her husband's control," thus protecting her from being left with little or no means of support.   McGhee v. Stephens, 83 Ala. 466, 3 So. 808 (1887);   McReynolds v. Jones, 30 Ala. 101 (1857).

In order to withstand scrutiny under the Equal Protection Clause, this gender-based classification must serve "important governmental objectives and must be substantially related to achievement of those objectives."   Orr v. Orr, 440 U.S. at 279, 99 S.Ct. at 1111.   Our next step is to examine the governmental objectives of the statutory scheme.

One obvious objective of the statute has its roots in romantic paternalism—protection of women because it is assumed that their role as wives and mothers leaves them financially helpless.   The statute "effectively announce[s] the State's preference for an allocation of family responsibilities under which the wife plays a dependent role, and as seeking for [its] objective the reinforcement of that model among the State's citizens."   Orr v. Orr, 440 U.S. 279, 99 S.Ct. 1111.   The United States Supreme Court has stated repeatedly that such an objective which is part of the baggage of sexual stereotypes presuming certain roles of males and females in the home and the working world cannot sustain the constitutionality of statutes.   * * *   The statute, if it is to survive constitutional attack, must be validated on some other basis.

It may be asserted that, like Alabama's gender-based alimony statutes, § 43–1–15, giving only a widow the right to dissent from the spouse's will, serves to reduce the economic disparity between men and women which is the result of our long history of discrimination against women. Furthermore, it may be asserted that § 43–1–15 serves the purpose of assisting needy spouses.   The United States Supreme Court has recognized that these are both important governmental objectives. See Orr v. Orr, 440 U.S. at 280, 99 S.Ct. at 1112; Califano v. Webster, 430 U.S. 313, 97 S.Ct. 1192, 51 L.Ed.2d 360 (1977); Kahn v. Shevin, 416 U.S. 351, 94 S.Ct. 1734, 40 L.Ed.2d 189 (1974).

The final step in our analysis under the Equal Protection Clause is to determine whether the classification contained in the statute is substantially related to the aforementioned important governmental objectives. We hold that it is not.

In general, gender is not "a reliable proxy for need." Orr v. Orr, 440 U.S. at 281, 99 S.Ct. at 1112. The statute provides aid to women who are excluded from their husbands' wills, but no aid to men who are destitute and who are inequitably excluded from their wives' wills. The statute also gives aid to widows who are not needy, to the exclusion of other needy devisees. Thus, the alleged purpose of the statute, to help needy spouses, could be fulfilled by a gender-neutral statute. "Where, as here, the State's compensatory and ameliorative purposes are as well served by a gender-neutral classification as one that gender classifies and therefore carries with it the baggage of sexual stereotypes, the State cannot be permitted to classify on the basis of sex." Orr v. Orr, 440 U.S. at 283, 99 S.Ct. at 1113.

In determining whether the classification is substantially related to the objective of reducing economic disparity between the sexes, we must ask "whether women had in fact been significantly discriminated against *in the sphere to which the statute applied* a sex-based classification, leaving the sexes '*not* similarly situated with respect to opportunities' in that sphere." Id. at 281, 99 S.Ct. at 1112 (quoting Schlesinger v. Ballard, 419 U.S. 498, 508, 95 S.Ct. 572, 577, 42 L.Ed.2d 610 (1975) (emphasis added). It is interesting to note that most commentators state that with few exceptions, the Alabama law of decedents' estates favors the widow. See Comment, Reverse Sex Discrimination, supra; Holt, Intestate Succession in Alabama, 23 Ala.L.Rev. 319 (1971); Jones, Alabama Probate Law, supra.

The statute does not achieve the goal of eliminating the economic disparity between men and women in all cases. Some widows may defy the stereotypes and be more wealthy than their husbands, and thus not need the benefit of the statute. Likewise, some widowers may have few assets; yet they cannot receive benefits under the statutory scheme. In sum, the goal of reducing the economic disparity between men and women could be achieved with a gender-neutral statute, based on need.

"[T]he statutory structure and its legislative history [reveal] that the classification was not enacted as compensation for past discrimination." Orr v. Orr, 440 U.S. at 281, n. 11, 99 S.Ct. at 1113, n. 11 (quoting Califano v. Webster, 430 U.S. at 317, 97 S.Ct. at 1194). It is clear that the widow's right to dissent had its origin in a time when women had no property rights. Women needed some protection of the law to prevent their husbands from transferring all assets that would provide women with a means of support. This is no longer the case. Women may, and do, freely build separate estates and freely transfer assets. In many cases, women may accumulate more wealth than their husbands. Thus, the historical roots of the right to dissent do not indicate that reduction of economic disparity was the purpose of the statute.

We hold that Alabama's statute permitting a widow to dissent from her husband's will is invalid, as an impermissible gender-based classification. We now turn to the second issue of whether to expand the underinclusive class.

[The court concluded by invalidating the statute rather than extending its coverage to widowers. It reasoned that because the "statutes on decedents' estates are so complex and interwoven", the court "is ill-equipped to tinker with the various parts" and that therefore the issue should be left to the legislature. Subsequently, Alabama adopted much of the elective share provisions of the Uniform Probate Code § 2–202, infra, p. 164.]

Notes

1. For similar rulings from other jurisdictions, see In re Estate of Reed, 354 So.2d 864 (Fla.1978) (family allowance payable only to widow unconstitutional); Hess v. Wims, 272 Ark. 43, 613 S.W.2d 85 (1981) and Stokes v. Stokes, 271 Ark. 300, 613 S.W.2d 372 (1981) (dower, statutory allowances and homestead rights available only to the widow unconstitutional).

2. In Kahn v. Shevin, 416 U.S. 351, 94 S.Ct. 1734, 40 L.Ed.2d 189 (1974) the Supreme Court upheld the constitutionality of a Florida statute which granted an annual $500 property tax exemption to all widows, but denied it to widowers. The Court cited economic data to prove that women had been placed at a disadvantage in the job market, and indicated that Florida's differing treatment of widows and widowers was designed to help alleviate the hardships imposed by this past discrimination. In later cases where it has been faced with benign discrimination statutes (i.e., statutes favoring women with the purpose of remedying past harm) the Court has examined the legislation with much greater scrutiny than it did in Kahn, stating that the "mere recitation of a benign, compensatory purpose is not an automatic shield which protects against an inquiry into the actual purpose underlying a statutory scheme". Weinberger v. Wiesenfeld, 420 U.S. 636, 648, 95 S.Ct. 1225, 1233 43 L.Ed.2d 514 (1975). In that case, the Court found no actual compensatory intent, and ruled that it is an impermissible classification under the due process clause of the Fifth Amendment for social security benefits which are payable to the widow on the husband's death not to be payable to the widower on the wife's death. Such a classification is based on the "archaic and overbroad generalization * * * not tolerated under the constitution * * *, namely that male workers' earnings are vital to the support of their families, while the earnings of female wage-earners do not significantly contribute to their families' support" 420 U.S. 636, 643, 95 S.Ct. 1225, 1230, 43 L.Ed.2d 514. See also Orr v. Orr, discussed in the principal case, which overturned an Alabama law imposing alimony obligations only upon husbands and not upon wives. The current validity of the type of statute upheld in Kahn has been placed into doubt by these later decisions.

LOS ANGELES DEPARTMENT OF WATER AND POWER
v. MANHART

Supreme Court of the United States, 1978.
435 U.S. 702, 98 S.Ct. 1370, 55 L.Ed.2d 657.

Mr. Justice STEVENS delivered the opinion of the Court.

As a class, women live longer than men. For this reason, the Los Angeles Department of Water and Power required its female employees to make larger contributions to its pension fund than its male employees. We granted certiorari to decide whether this practice discriminated against individual female employees because of their sex in violation of § 703(a)(1) of the Civil Rights Act of 1964, as amended.[1]

For many years the Department has administered retirement, disability, and death-benefit programs for its employees. Upon retirement each employee is eligible for a monthly retirement benefit computed as a fraction of his or her salary multiplied by years of service. The monthly benefits for men and women of the same age, seniority, and salary are equal. Benefits are funded entirely by contributions from the employees and the Department, augmented by the income earned on those contributions. No private insurance company is involved in the administration or payment of benefits.

Based on a study of mortality tables and its own experience, the Department determined that its 2,000 female employees, on the average, will live a few years longer than its 10,000 male employees. The cost of a pension for the average retired female is greater than for the average male retiree because more monthly payments must be made to the average woman. The Department therefore required female employees to make monthly contributions to the fund which were 14.84% higher than the contributions required of comparable male employees.[2] Because employee contributions were withheld from paychecks a female employee took home less pay than a male employee earning the same salary.[3]

Since the effective date of the Equal Employment Opportunity Act of 1972, the Department has been an employer within the meaning of Title VII of the Civil Rights Act of 1964. See 42 U.S.C. § 2000e (1970 ed., Supp. V). In 1973, respondents brought this suit in the United States District Court for the Central District of California on behalf of a class of women employed or formerly employed by the Department. They prayed for an injunction and restitution of excess contributions.

---

1. The section provides:

"It shall be an unlawful employment practice for an employer—

"(1) to fail or refuse to hire or to discharge any individual, or otherwise to discriminate against any individual with respect to his compensation, terms, conditions, or privileges of employment, because of such individual's race, color, religion, sex, or national origin * * *." 78 Stat. 255, 42 U.S.C. § 2000e–2(a)(1).

2. The Department contributes an amount equal to 110% of all employee contributions.

3. The significance of the disparity is illustrated by the record of one woman whose contributions to the fund (including interest on the amount withheld each month) amounted to $18,171.40; a similarly situated male would have contributed only $12,843.53.

While this action was pending, the California Legislature enacted a law prohibiting certain municipal agencies from requiring female employees to make higher pension fund contributions than males. The Department therefore amended its plan, effective January 1, 1975. The current plan draws no distinction, either in contributions or in benefits, on the basis of sex. On a motion for summary judgment, the District Court held that the contribution differential violated § 703(a)(1) and ordered a refund of all excess contributions made before the amendment of the plan. The United States Court of Appeals for the Ninth Circuit affirmed.

The Department and various *amici curiae* contend that: (1) the differential in takehome pay between men and women was not discrimination within the meaning of § 703(a)(1) because it was offset by a difference in the value of the pension benefits provided to the two classes of employees; (2) the differential was based on a factor "other than sex" within the meaning of the Equal Pay Act of 1963 and was therefore protected by the so-called Bennett Amendment; (3) the rationale of General Electric Co. v. Gilbert, 429 U.S. 125, 97 S.Ct. 401, 50 L.Ed.2d 343, requires reversal; and (4) in any event, the retroactive monetary recovery is unjustified. We consider these contentions in turn.

I

There are both real and fictional differences between women and men. It is true that the average man is taller than the average woman; it is not true that the average woman driver is more accident prone than the average man. Before the Civil Rights Act of 1964 was enacted, an employer could fashion his personnel policies on the basis of assumptions about the differences between men and women, whether or not the assumptions were valid.

It is now well recognized that employment decisions cannot be predicated on mere "stereotyped" impressions about the characteristics of males or females. Myths and purely habitual assumptions about a woman's inability to perform certain kinds of work are no longer acceptable reasons for refusing to employ qualified individuals, or for paying them less. This case does not, however, involve a fictional difference between men and women. It involves a generalization that the parties accept as unquestionably true: Women, as a class, do live longer than men. The Department treated its women employees differently from its men employees because the two classes are in fact different. It is equally true, however, that all individuals in the respective classes do not share the characteristic that differentiates the average class representatives. Many women do not live as long as the average man and many men outlive the average woman. The question, therefore, is whether the existence or nonexistence of "discrimination" is to be determined by comparison of class characteristics or individual characteristics. A "stereotyped" answer to that question may not be the same as the answer that the language and purpose of the statute command.

The statute makes it unlawful "to discriminate against any *individual* with respect to his compensation, terms, conditions, or privileges of employment, because of such *individual's* race, color, religion, sex, or national origin." 42 U.S.C. § 2000e–2(a)(1) (emphasis added). The statute's focus on the individual is unambiguous. It precludes treatment of individuals as simply components of a racial, religious, sexual, or national class. If height is required for a job, a tall woman may not be refused employment merely because, on the average, women are too short. Even a true generalization about the class is an insufficient reason for disqualifying an individual to whom the generalization does not apply.

That proposition is of critical importance in this case because there is no assurance that any individual woman working for the Department will actually fit the generalization on which the Department's policy is based. Many of those individuals will not live as long as the average man. While they were working, those individuals received smaller paychecks because of their sex, but they will receive no compensating advantage when they retire.

It is true, of course, that while contributions are being collected from the employees, the Department cannot know which individuals will predecease the average woman. Therefore, unless women as a class are assessed an extra charge, they will be subsidized, to some extent, by the class of male employees. It follows, according to the Department, that fairness to its class of male employees justifies the extra assessment against all of its female employees.

But the question of fairness to various classes affected by the statute is essentially a matter of policy for the legislature to address. Congress has decided that classifications based on sex, like those based on national origin or race, are unlawful. Actuarial studies could unquestionably identify differences in life expectancy based on race or national origin, as well as sex. But a statute that was designed to make race irrelevant in the employment market, see Griggs v. Duke Power Co., 401 U.S. 424, 436, 91 S.Ct. 849, 856, 28 L.Ed.2d 158, could not reasonably be construed to permit a take-home-pay differential based on a racial classification.

Even if the statutory language were less clear, the basic policy of the statute requires that we focus on fairness to individuals rather than fairness to classes. Practices that classify employees in terms of religion, race, or sex tend to preserve traditional assumptions about groups rather than thoughtful scrutiny of individuals. The generalization involved in this case illustrates the point. Separate mortality tables are easily interpreted as reflecting innate differences between the sexes; but a significant part of the longevity differential may be explained by the social fact that men are heavier smokers than women.

Finally, there is no reason to believe that Congress intended a special definition of discrimination in the context of employee group insurance coverage. It is true that insurance is concerned with events that are individually unpredictable, but that is characteristic of many employment decisions. Individual risks, like individual performance, may not be predicted by resort to classifications proscribed by Title VII. Indeed, the fact that this case involves a group insurance program highlights a basic flaw in the Department's fairness argument. For when insurance risks are grouped, the better risks always subsidize the poorer risks. Healthy persons subsidize medical benefits for the less healthy; unmarried workers subsidize the pensions of married workers; persons who eat, drink, or smoke to excess may subsidize pension benefits for persons whose habits are more temperate. Treating different classes of risks as though they were the same for purposes of group insurance is a common practice that has never been considered inherently unfair. To insure the flabby and the fit as though they were equivalent risks may be more common than treating men and women alike; but nothing more than habit makes one "subsidy" seem less fair than the other.

An employment practice that requires 2,000 individuals to contribute more money into a fund than 10,000 other employees simply because each of them is a woman, rather than a man, is in direct conflict with both the language and the policy of the Act. Such a practice does not pass the simple test of whether the evidence shows "treatment of a person in a manner which but for that person's sex would be different." It constitutes discrimination and is unlawful unless exempted by the Equal Pay Act of 1963 or some other affirmative justification.

II

Shortly before the enactment of Title VII in 1964, Senator Bennett proposed an amendment providing that a compensation differential based on sex would not be unlawful if it was authorized by the Equal Pay Act, which had been passed a year earlier. The Equal Pay Act requires employers to pay members of both sexes the same wages for equivalent work, except when the differential is pursuant to one of four specified exceptions. The Department contends that the fourth exception applies here. That exception authorizes a "differential based on any other factor other than sex."

The Department argues that the different contributions exacted from men and women were based on the factor of longevity rather than sex. It is plain, however, that any individual's life expectancy is based on a number of factors, of which sex is only one. The record contains no evidence that any factor other than the employee's sex was taken into account in calculating the 14.84% differential between the respective contributions by men and women. We agree with Judge Duniway's observation that one cannot "say that an actuarial distinction based entirely on sex is 'based on any other factor other than sex.' Sex is exactly what it is based on." 553 F.2d 581, 588 (1976).

* * *

III

The Department argues that reversal is required by General Electric Co. v. Gilbert, 429 U.S. 125, 97 S.Ct. 401, 50 L.Ed.2d 343. We are satisfied, however, that neither the holding nor the reasoning of *Gilbert* is controlling.

In *Gilbert* the Court held that the exclusion of pregnancy from an employer's disability benefit plan did not constitute sex discrimination within the meaning of Title VII. Relying on the reasoning in Geduldig v. Aiello, 417 U.S. 484, 94 S.Ct. 2485, 41 L.Ed.2d 256, the Court first held that the General Electric plan did not involve "discrimination based upon gender as such." The two groups of potential recipients which that case concerned were pregnant women and nonpregnant persons. " 'While the first group is exclusively female, the second includes members of both sexes.' " 429 U.S., at 135, 97 S.Ct., at 407. In contrast, each of the two groups of employees involved in this case is composed entirely and exclusively of members of the same sex. On its face, this plan discriminates on the basis of sex whereas the General Electric plan discriminated on the basis of a special physical disability.

In *Gilbert* the Court did note that the plan as actually administered had provided more favorable benefits to women as a class than to men as a class. This evidence supported the conclusion that not only had plaintiffs failed to establish a prima facie case by proving that the plan was discriminatory on its face, but they had also failed to prove any discriminatory effect.

In this case, however, the Department argues that the absence of a discriminatory effect on women as a class justifies an employment practice which, on its face, discriminated against individual employees because of their sex. But even if the Department's actuarial evidence is sufficient to prevent plaintiffs from establishing a prima facie case on the theory that the effect of the practice on women as a class was discriminatory, that the evidence does not defeat the claim that the practice, on its face, discriminated against every individual woman employed by the Department.

In essence, the Department is arguing that the prima facie showing of discrimination based on evidence of different contributions for the respective sexes is rebutted by its demonstration that there is a like difference in the cost of providing benefits for the respective classes. That argument might prevail if Title VII, contained a cost justification defense comparable to the affirmative defense available in a price discrimination suit. But neither Congress nor the courts have recognized such a defense under Title VII.

Although we conclude that the Department's practice violated Title VII, we do not suggest that the statute was intended to revolutionize the insurance and pension industries. All that is at issue today is a requirement that men and women make unequal contributions to an employer-operated pension fund. Nothing in our holding implies that it would be unlawful for an employer to set aside equal retirement contributions for each employee and let each retiree purchase the largest benefit which his or her accumulated contributions could command in the open market. Nor does it call into question the insurance industry practice of considering the composition of an employer's work force in determining the probable cost of a retirement or death benefit plan. Finally, we recognize that in a case of this kind it may be necessary to take special care in fashioning appropriate relief.

IV

The Department challenges the District Court's award of retroactive relief to the entire class of female employees and retirees. Title VII does not require a district court to grant any retroactive relief. A court that finds unlawful discrimination "may enjoin [the discrimination] * * * and order such affirmative action as may be appropriate, which may include, but is not limited to, reinstatement * * * with or without back pay * * * or any other equitable relief as the court deems appropriate." 42 U.S.C. § 2000e–5(g) (1970 ed., Supp. V). To the point of redundancy, the statute stresses that retroactive relief "may" be awarded if it is "appropriate."

In Albemarle Paper Co. v. Moody, 422 U.S. 405, 95 S.Ct. 2362, 45 L.Ed.2d 280, the Court reviewed the scope of a district court's discretion to fashion appropriate remedies for a Title VII violation and concluded that "backpay should be denied only for reasons which, if applied generally, would not frustrate the central statutory purposes of eradicating discrimination throughout the economy and making persons whole for injuries suffered through past discrimination." Id., at 421, 95 S.Ct., at 2373. Applying that standard, the Court ruled that an award of backpay should not be conditioned on a showing of bad faith. Id., at 422–423, 95 S.Ct., at 2373–2374. But the *Albemarle* Court also held that backpay was not to be awarded automatically in every case.

* * *

[The opinion concluded that "without qualifying the force of the *Albermarle* presumption in favor of retroactive relief, we conclude that it was error to grant such relief in this case." It noted the potential impact which changes in the rules governing the assessment of rates and benefits by insurance companies might have on the solvency of those companies.]

[The concurring opinions of Justices Blackmun and Marshall and the dissenting opinion of Chief Justice Burger and Justice Rehnquist have been omitted.]

Notes

1. The Manhart case rules unconstitutional differentials in contributions being made into a pension fund. In Arizona Governing Committee for Tax Deferred Annuity and Compensation Plans v. Norris, 463 U.S. 1073, 103 S.Ct. 3492, 77 L.Ed.2d 1236 (1983), the Supreme Court reaffirmed the Manhart ruling and applied it to hold that differentials in retirement benefits based on gender were also unconstitutional. See also Spirt v. Teachers Insurance & Annuity Association, 691 F.2d 1054 (2d Cir. 1982), 735 F.2d 23 (2d Cir. 1984) (use of sex-distinct mortality tables to calculate TIAA-CREF benefits a violation of the equal protection clause of Constitution). For a full examination of the issues presented in these cases, compare Brilmayer, Hokeler, Laycock and Sullivan, Sex Discrimination in Employer-Sponsored Insurance Plans: A Legal and Demographic Analysis, 47 U.Chi.L.Rev. 505 (1980) (sexually integrated actuarial tables in employer-sponsored insurance plans constitutionally required) with Benston, The Economics of Gender Discrimination in Employee Fringe Benefits:

Manhart Revisited, 49 U.Chi.L.Rev. 489 (1982) (gender is a valid predictor of life expectancy and is not invidiously used in this context); followed up by Brilmayer, Laycock and Sullivan, The Efficient Use of Group Averages as Non-discrimination: A Rejoinder to Professor Benston, 50 U.Chi. 222 (1983) and Benston, Discrimination and Economic Efficiency in Employee Fringe Benefits: A Clarification of Issues and a Response to Professors Brilmayer, Laycock, and Sullivan, 50 U.Chi. 250 (1983). These actions arose under Title VII of the Civil Rights Act, and the principles enunciated in the opinions are as applicable to private employers as to the states that maintained the pension funds there in issue. Because there is some continued use in the private sector of sex-distinct mortality tables, legislation has been introduced into Congress for the enactment of a Nondiscrimination in Insurance Act. Objections to this proposal rest in part on the McCarran-Ferguson Act, 15 U.S.C.A. § 1011, stating that regulation of insurance is a state responsibility. Note, Ending Sex Discrimination in Insurance: The Nondiscrimination in Insurance Act, 11 J. of Leg. 457 (1984). If gender is not to be used in any way to establish benefits and premium rates, all forms of insurance will be affected. For example, it has long been the case that women drivers under 25 pay substantially less in premiums for automobile insurance than do their male counterparts.

2. Prior to December 1, 1983, the Treasury in its estate and gift tax regulations used two sets of actuarial tables, one for men and one for women, to establish the value of life estates, terms for years, remainders, reversions, and private annuities. Effective on that date, the Treasury adopted unisex tables. I.R.C. Regs. §§ 20.2031–7 and 25.2512–5.

SECTION THREE.   PROTECTION OF THE SPOUSE—DOWER

RHEINSTEIN AND GLENDON, THE LAW OF DECEDENTS' ESTATES
89–92 (1971) (footnotes omitted).

2. In those states where the assets of husband and wife are treated as two separate masses of property, other techniques must be applied. It is possible for a legal system to develop rules according to which a wife has a fixed property interest, a right in rem, in all or certain of the assets owned by her husband, and a husband a corresponding interest in those owned by his wife. This right in rem must be so constructed that it is not affected by any transaction of the owner of the asset, that it endures, in particular, when the owner gives away or sells or encumbers the asset to a bona fide party, and that it is not subject to liability to the owner's creditors. Of such a nature were the estates of *dower* and *curtesy* at Common Law. They served to protect the surviving spouse both against a will and in intestacy.

a. At Common Law, *Dower* was an estate of a wife in every freehold estate of inheritance of which her husband was seised at any moment during marriage. It was acquired by the wife with the marriage if the piece of land in question was owned by the husband at the time of the marriage, and at the time of acquisition by the husband if he acquired the land during the marriage. Nothing the husband subsequently did could affect the wife's interest. If he conveyed the land her interest simply continued to encumber it in the hands of the purchaser; if the land was mortgaged by the husband the wife's dower interest was superior to that of the mortgagee; if the husband ran into debt and his land was sold by the sheriff, the purchasers would take it subject to the wife's dower interest. As long as the husband lived the wife's dower interest was "inchoate," that is, it was capable of becoming possessory only in the case of the wife's surviving her husband. If the wife died before her husband her inchoate dower interest was extinguished. If, however, the wife survived her husband, her dower interest became "consummate," that is, the wife became entitled to a life estate in one-third of each parcel of land in which she had a dower interest. This life estate, since it was but an incident of an interest which the wife had in the land already during her husband's lifetime, could in no way be affected by her husband's will. If he devised the land, the devisee took it subject to the widow's dower.

If practically feasible, the wife could demand that her dower be assigned to her in kind, so that one-third of each parcel would be set aside for her by metes and bounds to be possessed by her for life.

* * *

If assignment by metes and bounds was not feasible, the wife would be entitled for life to one-third of the income derived from the land. From all that has been said it follows that the widow could exercise her dower right against the creditors of the estate as well as against any person who might be the owner of the land at the moment of her husband's death, irrespective of whether such owner had any knowledge of the existence of any dower right at the time of his acquisition of the land.

The estate which was granted by the Common Law to a husband in the lands of his wife, the so-called *estate by the curtesy* of England, corresponded to the wife's dower in all essential aspects of legal technique. It was different, however, in some respects, of which the following two are important: first, curtesy initiate was not acquired by the husband unless issue was born alive to the marriage; second, curtesy consummate gave the surviving husband a life estate not in one-third of each parcel in which it existed but in the entire parcel. In modern legislation curtesy has been widely assimilated to dower, is now often simply called dower and will be referred to under this name in this chapter.

b. It can be readily seen that dower is a highly effective means to protect a surviving spouse against complete disinheritance, provided that the deceased spouse owned real property. It can be defeated neither by inter vivos transactions nor by creditors. However, there are disadvantages as well: The dower system is impracticable with respect to objects of a nondurable or nonstationary character, i.e., to objects other than land. Theoretically dower rights might be created in chattels or even in shares of stock, bond-holders' rights or other intangible forms of property. The obvious difficulties of enforcing such rights in personal property which is frequently transferred, however, have prevented even experimentation in this respect. Dower rights have been and still are recognized exclusively in land. They do not exist in those other forms of wealth which have become so prominent in modern civilization. Hence, dower is no protection at all to a woman whose husband does not own real estate or who owns his real estate through the medium of owning stock in a real estate holding corporation.

As to land, the existence of the institution of dower results in a clog on marketability and a threat to the security of titles. Prospective purchasers must often engage in difficult title searches involving such factual problems as the determination of the existence and the exact date of a marriage, perhaps an informal common-law marriage or a marriage of spouses no longer living together, or such intricate legal problems as the determination of the validity of an out-of-state divorce. The danger of unknown dower rights has a depressing influence upon real estate prices, and causes added expenses for title searches and title insurance.

Notes

1. Dower consummate traditionally was a life interest only. As such, it is a terminable interest and does not qualify without more for the marital deduction under the federal estate tax. I.R.C.Regs. § 20.2056(b)–1. A number of decisions have allowed the deduction when, under local law, the surviving spouse received a lump sum payment as the commuted value of the dower or as an elective share of the estate in lieu of dower. See, e.g., First National Exchange Bank of Roanoke v. United States, 335 F.2d 91 (4th Cir. 1964). Since 1981, the executor has been given a right to elect to treat a life interest (i.e., a vested right to income from a fund for life) as qualified terminable interest property and thereby make it eligible for the marital deduction. I.R.C. § 2056(b)(7); Bittker and Clark, Federal Estate and Gift Taxation, 479–483 (1984).

2. For the reasons given in the preceding text, dower in its pure form no longer exists, having been superseded in the common law states by the elective share. Elements of dower sometimes appear, however, in the statutes that define the elective share. The word "dower" is also used in a few statutes, although the estate being described limits the surviving spouse's claim to property owned at death. See e.g., Mass.Gen.Laws Ann., c. 191, § 15. Without its essential characteristic, the inchoate estate, dower becomes another form of elective share. A few statutes do not refer to dower as such but create an estate in real property quite similar to inchoate dower. See e.g., Vernon's Ann.Mo.Stat. § 474.150, infra p. 161, stating that an inter vivos conveyance of real property made by one spouse may be challenged by the other spouse, who did not consent to the conveyance, as in "fraud of the marital rights". Indeed, the provisions in New York and in the Uniform Probate Code authorizing the surviving spouse to invalidate a portion of certain lifetime transfers made by the other spouse may be likened to the estate of inchoate dower.

For a historical perspective on the estates of dower and curtesy, as well as a survey of their common law characteristics, the work of George L. Haskins is particularly noteworthy. I Amer.Law of Property, Part 5, 615–911 (1952).

SECTION FOUR. PROTECTION OF THE SPOUSE—
ELECTIVE SHARE

MACDONALD, FRAUD ON THE WIDOW'S SHARE

21–24 (1960) (footnotes omitted).

As mentioned earlier, the statutory (or "forced") share normally guarantees the surviving spouse a specified fraction of the "estate" of the deceased spouse. This share may be elected ("forced") regardless of the terms of the will. In most states the share is specifically or by implication based upon the net estate. The phrase "estate" is significant. For one thing, it ensures the widow a share in the husband's personal property as well as in his realty. In another aspect, however, it breeds confusion: in literal terms it restricts the forced share to property that forms part of the husband's estate for purposes of administration. Inter vivos transfers, in theory, are unaffected.

There is some variety in the statutory provisions. The amount recoverable may include: (a) the intestate share; (b) the intestate share limited to a defined amount or fraction of the estate; (c) a share in the realty only; (d) a combination of a share in personalty and inchoate dower; (e) a limited right to elect; (f) nothing.

The extent of the share usually varies with the number of children involved. Thus, if no children survive, the widow may receive one half or even all of the estate; but in the event of children surviving she may be relegated to a "child's share," which may be a third, or even less, depending on the number of surviving children. Aside from this mechanical variation, the over-all picture is one of fixed, unalterable, arbitrary portions. Relief is standardized; no attention is paid to individual equities or unusual circumstances.

A. DISINHERITANCE BY LIFETIME TRANSFERS

√ NEWMAN v. DORE

Court of Appeals of New York, 1937.
275 N.Y. 371, 9 N.E.2d 966, 112 A.L.R. 643.

LEHMAN, Judge. The Decedent Estate Law (Consol. Laws, c. 13, arts. 2, 3) regulates the testamentary disposition and the descent and distribution of the real and personal property of decedents. It does not limit or affect disposition of property inter vivos. In terms and in intent it applies only to decedents' estates. Property which did not belong to a decedent at his death and which does not become part of his estate does not come within its scope.

The share in the real and personal property of a decedent, not devised or bequeathed, which a husband or wife takes, is now fixed by section 83 of the Decedent Estate Law. Prior to the revision of the Decedent Estate Law which took effect on September 1, 1930, a decedent could by testamentary disposition effectively exclude a wife or husband from the share of the estate which would pass to her or him in case of intestacy. That was changed by section 18 of the revised Decedent Estate Law.   By that section (subdivision 1) "a personal right of election is given to the surviving spouse to take his or her share of the estate as in intestacy, subject to the limitations, conditions and exceptions contained in this section." These limitations and exceptions include a case where "the testator has devised or bequeathed in trust an amount equal to or greater than the intestate share, with income thereof payable to the surviving spouse for life."   Subdivision 1(b).   The Legislature has declared that its intention in enacting these sections of the revised Decedent Estate Law was "to increase the share of a surviving spouse in the estate of a deceased spouse, either in a case of intestacy or by an election against the terms of the will of the deceased spouse thus enlarging property rights of such surviving spouse."   Laws 1929, c. 229, § 20.

Ferdinand Straus died on July 1, 1934, leaving a last will and testament dated May 5, 1934, which contained a provision for a trust for his wife for her life of one-third of the decedent's property both real and personal.   In such case the statute did not give the wife a right of election to take her share of the estate as in intestacy.   She receives the income for life from a trust fund of the amount of the intestate share, but does not take the share.   That share is one-third of the decedent's estate.   It includes no property which does not form part of the estate at the decedent's death.   The testator on June 28, 1934, three days before his death, executed trust agreements by which, in form at least, he transferred to trustees all his real and personal property.   If the agreements effectively divested the settlor of title to his property, then the decedent left no estate and the widow takes nothing.   The widow has challenged the validity of the transfer to the trustees.   The beneficiary named in the trust agreement has brought this action to compel the trustees to carry out its terms. The trial court has found that the "trust agreements were made, executed and delivered by said Ferdinand Straus for the purpose of evading and circumventing the laws of the State of New York, and particularly sections 18 and 83 of the Decedent Estate Law."   Undoubtedly the settlor's purpose was to provide that at his death his property should pass to beneficiaries named in the trust agreement to the exclusion of his wife. Under the provisions of the Decedent Estate Law the decedent could not effect the desired purpose by testamentary disposition of his property. The problem in this case is whether he has accomplished that result by creating a trust during his lifetime.

The validity of the attempted transfer depends upon whether "the laws of the State of New York and particularly sections 18 and 83 of the Decedent Estate Law" prohibit or permit such transfer.   If the statute, in express language or by clear implication, prohibits the transfer, it is illegal;   if the laws of the state do not prohibit it, the transfer is legal. In strict accuracy, it cannot be said that a "purpose of evading and circumventing" the law can carry any legal consequences.   "We do not speak of evasion, because, when the law draws a line, a case is on one side of it or the other, and if on the safe side is none the worse legally that a party has availed himself to the full of what the law permits.   When an act is condemned as an evasion what is meant is that it is on the wrong side of the line indicated by the policy if not by the mere letter of the law." Bullen v. Wisconsin, 240 U.S. 625, 630, 36 S.Ct. 473, 474, 60 L.Ed. 830. In a subsequent case it was said of a defendant: "The fact that it desired to evade the law, as it is called, is immaterial, because the very meaning of a line in the law is that you intentionally may go as close to it as you can if you do not pass it." Superior Oil Co. v. State of Mississippi, 280 U.S. 390, 395, 50 S.Ct. 169, 170, 74 L.Ed. 504, both opinions by Mr. Justice Holmes. Under the laws of the State of New York, and particularly sections 18 and 83 of the Decedent Estate Law, neither spouse has any immediate interest in the property of the other. The "enlarged property right" which the Legislature intended to confer is only an expectant interest dependent upon the contingency that the property to which the interest attaches becomes a part of a decedent's estate. The contingency does not occur, and the expectant property right does not ripen into a property right in possession, if the owner sells or gives away the property. Herrmann v. Jorgenson, 263 N.Y. 348, 189 N.E. 449; Matter of McCulloch's Will, 263 N.Y. 408, 189 N.E. 473, 91 A.L.R. 1440. Defeat of a contingent expectant interest by means available under the law cannot be regarded as an unlawful "evasion" of the law. A duty imperfectly defined by law may at times be evaded or a right imperfectly protected by law may be violated with impunity, but to say that an act, lawful under common-law rules and not prohibited by any express or implied statutory provision, is in itself a "fraud" on the law or an "evasion" of the law, involves a contradiction in terms.

That does not mean, of course, that the law may not place its ban upon an intended result even though the means to effect that result may be lawful. The statute gives to a spouse a property right. [The question is, how far the statute protects that right even while it remains only expectant and contingent.] A right created by law may be protected by law against invasion through acts otherwise lawful. A wrong does not cease to be a wrong because it is cloaked in form of law. The test of legality, then, is whether the result is lawful and the means used to achieve that result are lawful. Here, we should point out that the courts below have not based their decision primarily upon the finding that the trust agreements were executed for the purpose of evading and circumventing the law of the state of New York. The courts have also found, and the evidence conclusively establishes, that the trust agreements were made for the purpose of depriving the decedent's widow of any rights in and to his property upon his death. Upon the trust agreements executed a few days before the death of the settlor, he reserved the enjoyment of the entire income as long as he should live, and a right to revoke the trust at his will, and in general the powers granted to the trustees were in terms made "subject to the settlor's control during his life," and could be exercised "in such manner only as the settlor shall from time to time direct in writing." Thus, by the trust agreement which transferred to the trustees the settlor's entire property, the settlor reserved substantially the same rights to enjoy and control the disposition of the property as he previously had possessed, and the inference is inescapable that the trust agreements were executed by the settlor, as the court has found, "with the intention and for the purpose of diminishing his estate and thereby to reduce in amount the share" of his wife in his estate upon his death and as a "contrivance to deprive * * * his widow of any rights in and to his property upon his death." They had no other purpose and substantially they had no other effect. Does the statute intend that such a transfer shall be available as a means of defeating the contingent expectant estate of a spouse?

In a few states where a wife has a similar contingent expectant interest or estate in the property of her husband, it has been held that her rights may not be defeated by any transfer made during life with intent to deprive the wife of property, which under the law would otherwise pass to her. Thayer v. Thayer, 14 Vt. 107, 39 Am.Dec. 211; Evans v. Evans, 78 N.H. 352, 100 A. 671; Dyer v. Smith, 62 Mo.App. 606; Payne v. Tatem, 236 Ky. 306, 33 S.W.2d 2. In those states it is the intent to defeat the wife's contingent rights which creates the invalidity and it seems that an absolute transfer of all his property by a married man during his life, if made with other purpose and intent than to cut off an unloved wife, is valid even though its effect is to deprive the wife of any share in the property of her husband at his death. Dunnett v. Shields & Conant, 97 Vt. 419, 123 A. 626; Patch v. Squires, 105 Vt. 405, 165 A. 919. The rule has been stated that "while the wife cannot complain of reasonable gifts or advancements by a husband to his children by a former marriage, yet, if the gifts constitute the principal part of the husband's estate and be made without the wife's knowledge, a presumption of fraud arises, and it rests upon the beneficiaries to explain away that presumption." Payne v. Tatem, supra, 236 Ky. 306, at page 308, 33 S.W.2d 2, 3.

Motive or intent is an unsatisfactory test of the validity of a transfer of property. In most jurisdictions it has been rejected, sometimes for the reason that it would cast doubt upon the validity of all transfers made by a married man, outside of the regular course of business; sometimes because it is difficult to find a satisfactory logical foundation for it. Intent may, at times, be relevant in determining whether an act is fraudulent, but there can be no fraud where no right of any person is invaded. "The great weight of authority is that the intent to defeat a claim which otherwise a wife might have is not enough to defeat the deed." Leonard v. Leonard, 181 Mass. 458, 462, 63 N.E. 1068, 1069, 92 Am.St.Rep. 426, and cases there cited. Since the law gives the wife only an expectant interest in the property of her husband which becomes part of his estate, and since the law does not restrict transfers of property by the husband during his life, it would seem that the only sound test of the validity of a challenged transfer is whether it is real or illusory. That is the test applied in Leonard v. Leonard, supra. The test has been formulated in different ways, but in most jurisdictions the test applied is essentially the test of whether the husband has in good faith divested himself of ownership of his property or has made an illusory transfer. "The 'good faith' required of the donor or settlor in making a valid disposition of his property during life does not refer to the purpose to affect his wife but to

the intent to divest himself of the ownership of the property.   It is, therefore, apparent that the fraudulent intent which will defeat a gift inter
vivos cannot be predicated of the husband's intent to deprive the wife of
her distributive   *   *   *   share as widow."   Benkart v. Commonwealth
Trust Co., of Pittsburgh, 269 Pa. 257, 259, 112 A. 62, 63.   In Pennsylvania
the courts have sustained the validity of the trusts even where a husband
reserved to himself the income for life, power of revocation, and a considerable measure of control.   Cf. Lines v. Lines, 142 Pa. 149, 21 A. 809,
24 Am.St.Rep. 487;   Potter Title & Trust Co. v. Braum, 294 Pa. 482, 144
A. 401, 64 A.L.R. 463;   Beirne v. Continental-Equitable Trust Co., 307
Pa. 570, 161 A. 721.   In other jurisdictions transfers in trust have been
upheld regardless of their purpose where a husband retained a right to
enjoy the income during his life.   Rabbitt v. Gaither, 67 Md. 94, 8 A.
744;   Cameron v. Cameron, 10 Smedes & M. (Miss.) 394, 48 Am.Dec. 759;
Gentry v. Bailey, 6 Gratt. (47 Va.) 594;   Hall v. Hall, 109 Va. 117, 63
S.E. 420, 21 L.R.A.,N.S., 533;   Stewart v. Stewart, 5 Conn. 317;   Osborn
v. Osborn, 102 Kan. 890, 172 P. 23.   In some of these cases the settlor
retained, also, a power of revocation.   In no jurisdiction has a transfer
in trust been upheld where the conveyance is intended only to cover up
the fact that the husband is retaining full control of the property though
in form he has parted with it.   Though a person may use means lawfully
available to him to keep outside of the scope of a statute, a false appearance of legality, however attained, will not avail him.   Reality, not appearance, should determine legal rights.   Cf. Jenkins v. Moyse, 254 N.Y.
319, 172 N.E. 521, 74 A.L.R. 205.

In this case the decedent, as we have said, retained not only the
income for life and power to revoke the trust, but also the right to control
the trustees.   We need not now determine whether such a trust is, for
any purpose, a valid present trust.   It has been said that, "where the
settlor transfers property in trust and reserves not only   *   *   *   a
power to revoke and modify the trust but also such power to control the
trustee as to the details of the administration of the trust that the trustee
is the agent of the settlor, the disposition so far as it is intended to take
effect after his death is testamentary.   *   *   *"   American Law Institute, Restatement of the Law of Trusts, § 57, subd. 2.   We do not now
consider whether the rule so stated is in accord with the law of this state
or whether in this case the reserved power of control is so great that the
trustee is in fact "the agent of the settlor."   We assume, without deciding,
that except for the provisions of section 18 of the Decedent Estate Law
the trust would be valid.   Cf. Robb v. Washington & Jefferson College,
185 N.Y. 485, 78 N.E. 359;   Von Hesse v. MacKaye, 136 N.Y. 114, 32
N.E. 615.   Perhaps "from the technical point of view such a conveyance
does not quite take back all that it gives, but practically it does."   That
is enough to render it an unlawful invasion of the expectant interest of
the wife.   Leonard v. Leonard, supra;   Brownell v. Briggs, 173 Mass.
529, 54 N.E. 251.

Judged by the substance, not by the form, the testator's conveyance
is illusory, intended only as a mask for the effective retention by the

settlor of the property which in form he had conveyed. We do not attempt now to formulate any general test of how far a settlor must divest himself of his interest in the trust property to render the conveyance more than illusory. Question of whether reservation of the income or of a power of revocation, or both, might even without reservation of the power of control be sufficient to show that the transfer was not intended in good faith to divest the settlor of his property must await decision until such question arises. In this case it is clear that the settlor never intended to divest himself of his property. He was unwilling to do so even when death was near.

The judgment should be affirmed, with costs.

CRANE, C. J., and HUBBS, LOUGHRAN and RIPPEY, JJ., concur.

FINCH, J., concurs in result.

O'BRIEN, J., takes no part.

Judgment affirmed.

Notes

(overstatement)

1. Although the ruling in this case has been superseded by statute in New York (N.Y.—McKinney's EPTL 5–1.1, set out infra, p. 162), the decision remains the starting point in the analysis of all courts that have dealt with the problem and remains an important influence in the field. See e.g. Montgomery v. Michaels, infra, p. 148; Staples v. King, 433 A.2d 407 (Me.1981) ("We find the reasoning of Newman v. Dore persuasive."). It and the line of authority which it spawned have been the subject of a great amount of critical comment. See Macdonald, Fraud on the Widow's Share (1960) (a book on the subject which contains many of the early citations); Symposium, The Right of Election of a Surviving Spouse Under Section 18 of the Decedent Estate Law, 32 St. John's L.Rev. 161 (1958).

2. The marriage involved in Newman v. Dore was hardly a model of domestic tranquillity. Mr. Straus was a widower, eighty years old, while his wife was in her thirties and the mother of two children whom he adopted as part of the arrangement. At his death four years after the marriage there was pending an action brought by the wife for separation with alimony on the grounds that his perverted sexual habits made it impossible for her to live with him. The record never makes clear the nature of his alleged perversions although it does include a newspaper account in which he is described as having received a transplant of monkey glands by surgical operation. In the manner of a perfectly normal, red-blooded octogenarian he was highly indignant over these charges. He brought an action for annulment of the marriage which was also pending at his death and instructed his lawyer to see to it that that "whore" and, here, at least, displaying some confusion as to genders, "son of a bitch" was not to receive any of his estate at death. The lawyer told him that in 1930 New York had enacted Section 18 of the Decedent Estate Law which made it impossible to disinherit his wife by will. A first step was to restrict her to the flat minimum required by the statute, and in May of 1934 he executed a will under which the wife was given the life income in a trust covering one third of the estate's assets. Prodded by the testator to show more ingenuity, the lawyer consulted a few friends, including a professor of law at St. John's University (who was also a bank vice-president—proof that at one time law professors were properly ap-

preciated), and came up with the idea of an inter vivos trust by which all the assets of the estate were to be conveyed away, leaving nothing against which the provisions of the will could take effect.   On June 28, 1934 Mr. Straus executed such a trust naming one Dore and another as trustees.   At his death the remainder was to pass to Emma Newman, who was the niece of his first wife and who was held in all the affection of a natural daughter.   Three days later he died.   In due time Emma Newman brought an action against Dore and his co-trustee to compel implementation of the inter vivos trust.   The widow appeared as the real party defendant to challenge the validity of the trust by which she was disinherited.

These seamy details of a tragic second marriage between a young woman and a pathetic old man two and a half times her age are included to suggest a slightly different perspective as to the kinds of marriages involved in this type of litigation from the one set forth in the usual policy statements on the subject.

MONTGOMERY v. MICHAELS

Supreme Court of Illinois, 1973.
54 Ill.2d 532, 301 N.E.2d 465, 64 A.L.R.3d 181.

DAVIS, Justice: During her lifetime, Bernice D. Montgomery created in certain banks eight savings accounts, which differed somewhat in their terms, but all were essentially the same in that she was named as trustee therein and the accounts were for the benefit of her two children by a prior marriage.   All but two of the accounts specifically provided that they were to be paid to the child or children named therein on her death. She retained control over all of these accounts during her lifetime and made deposits in and withdrawals from them.

She died intestate, and her husband, Dr. Earl Montgomery, was appointed administrator of her estate[;] as administrator and individually, he filed a citation petition in the circuit court of Lake County wherein he alleged that the trusts were a fraud on his marital rights and were illusory, and if sustained would defeat his statutory right to one third of the decedent's personal estate (Ill.Rev.Stat.1969, ch. 3, par. 11), and his right to a widower's award (Ill.Rev.Stat.1969, ch. 3, par. 178).   He prayed, among other things, that the court enter an order finding that said trusts are illusory and invalid, that said bank accounts are the property of the decedent, and that the balance of said accounts be turned over to him as administrator of the estate.

The trial court granted a motion to dismiss the petition, except as to the amount of the funeral bill, which was assessed equally against the two beneficiaries of the eight savings-account trusts.   It found that the savings-account trusts were not illusory, and that the balances therein should be paid to the named beneficiaries after payment of the funeral bill.   The appellate court affirmed (2 Ill.App.3d 821, 277 N.E.2d 739), and we granted leave to appeal.

In In re Estate of Petralia (1965), 32 Ill.2d 134, 204 N.E.2d 1, we upheld the validity of savings-account trusts or "Totten Trusts," so called because of the case entitled In re Totten (1904), 179 N.Y. 112, 71 N.E. 748.   In Petralia we held that if the settlor is also the trustee and retains complete control over the account during his or her lifetime, such a savings account is not different in substance from other revocable *inter vivos* trusts, which this court has found to be valid; that the declaration of the trust immediately creates an equitable interest in the beneficiaries even though the enjoyment of the interest is postponed until the death of the settlor and may be completely destroyed by withdrawal from the account of all of the deposits made by the settlor during his or her lifetime; and that the destructibility of the interest of the beneficiary does not negate the existence of a valid trust. Farkas v. Williams (1955), 5 Ill.2d 417, 125 N.E.2d 600; Gurnett v. Mutual Life Ins. Co. (1934), 356 Ill. 612, 191 N.E. 250.

In *Petralia*, at page 138, 204 N.E.2d at page 3, we quoted from Restatement (Second) of Trusts, sec. 58: "Where a person makes a deposit in a savings account in a bank or other savings organization in his own name as trustee for another person intending to reserve a power to withdraw the whole or any part of the deposit at any time during his lifetime and to use as his own whatever he may withdraw, or otherwise to revoke the trust, the intended trust is enforceable by the beneficiary upon the death of the depositor as to any part remaining on deposit on his death if he has not revoked the trust."

The question remains, however, whether such a trust is valid for every purpose, and particularly whether it is effective to defeat a surviving spouse's statutory share in the estate of his deceased spouse, and his right to a widower's award. Ill.Rev.Stat.1969, ch. 3, par. 178.

The Probate Act expressed the policy of protecting a surviving spouse in the expectancy which he or she may anticipate from the other's estate. The minimum statutory share of a surviving spouse in the real and personal estate of the deceased spouse is that provided in event of intestacy if there are both a spouse and descendants, namely, a one-third interest therein to the surviving spouse. The surviving spouse takes one half of the estate if there is no descendant. Ill.Rev.Stat.1971, ch. 3, pars. 11, 16.

A surviving spouse may renounce a will, and by doing so will receive this minimum share. (Ill.Rev.Stat.1963, ch. 3, par. 16.) The question in the case at bar is whether a "Totten Trust" is sufficiently testamentary in nature that by analogy the statutory policy of permitting a surviving spouse to renounce under the decedent's will and share in the proceeds of such estate should be applicable to such trust to the same extent as to an estate passing under a will.

Some cases suggest that the answer should depend upon the intent of the deceased spouse in creating the trust. This intent may be revealed by the myriad of attendant circumstances that include the secretive nature [sic] in which the decedent acted, what he may have said to others with respect to his intent, the proximity in time between the transfer and death, the size of the estate and the amount otherwise left to the surviving spouse, and, generally, all factors which might be indicative of an intent to defraud the surviving spouse of his or her statutory share. (Rose v. St. Louis Union Trust Co. (1969), 43 Ill.2d 312, 316, 317, 253 N.E.2d 417.)

At the same time, our courts have recognized that one may dispose of his property during his lifetime and thus deprive a spouse of his, or her, statutory share, so long as the disposition was sufficiently effective and complete, unless the transaction is illusory or tantamount to fraud.   Holmes v. Mims (1953), 1 Ill.2d 274, 279, 115 N.E.2d 790;   Padfield v. Padfield (1875), 78 Ill. 16, 18, 19.

The infirmities and difficulties in determining the intent of the decedent in connection with an *inter vivos* transfer of his personal property and in ascertaining whether such intent is so tainted with fraud as to cause such transfer to be ineffective in the deprivation of a spouse of his, or her, statutory share in the decedent's estate are readily apparent. Rose v. St. Louis Union Trust Co. (1969), 43 Ill.2d 312, 316, 317, 253 N.E.2d 417.

In the case at bar the settlor was also the trustee.   During her lifetime she retained absolute, unqualified control over the bank accounts, and possessed and exercised all incidents of complete ownership, including the right to receive interest payable thereon and withdraw the principal thereof.   The enjoyment of the proceeds of the accounts by the beneficiary or beneficiaries named therein would arise only upon the death of the settlor-trustee with the accounts remaining intact.

Under these circumstances, the expressed statutory policy of protecting a surviving spouse's statutory share in the estate should prevail, regardless of the intent of the deceased spouse in creating the savings-account trust.   In Blankenship v. Hall (1908), 233 Ill. 116, at page 129, 84 N.E. 192, at page 196, this court stated: "There has been a manifest desire on the part of the lawmakers of this State to provide for the support of the wife, not only during the lifetime of the husband but also after his death, until as this court said in In re Taylor's Will, 55 Ill. 252, on page 259: 'We do not go too far when we say that it has become a sort of common law in this State that this support shall be in all cases one-third of the husband's real estate for life, and one-third of the personal estate forever, which shall remain after the payment of debts.' "

In Newman v. Dore (1937), 275 N.Y. 371, 379, 9 N.E.2d 966, 968, the court, in considering the right of a surviving spouse in the property of the deceased spouse, stated: "Motive or intent is an unsatisfactory test of the validity of a transfer of property."   The court further stated, with reference to the rights of a surviving spouse, that "the only sound test of the validity of a challenged transfer is whether it is real or illusory." (275 N.Y. 371, 379, 9 N.E.2d 966, 969.)   The court held that the transfer was illusory and not sufficiently real to deprive the decedent's spouse of her statutory share in his estate.   Other cases have reached the same result.   Krause v. Krause (1941), 285 N.Y. 27, 32 N.E.2d 779;   Steixner v. Bowery Savings Bank (Sup.Ct.1949), 86 N.Y.S.2d 747;   MacGregor v. Fox (1952), 280 App.Div. 435, 114 N.Y.S.2d 286.

Text writers have concluded that the control retained over a savings-account trust is so complete that even though the trust is valid, it should not be so as against the surviving spouse.   In commenting upon dictum suggesting that a savings deposit in trust for another would be an effective method of cutting out a depositor's surviving spouse, Scott (1 A. Scott, Law of Trusts, sec. 58.5, at 546–547 (3d ed. 1967)) states:

> "It would seem that a strong argument could be made against this result, on the ground that it violates the policy of the statute which gives a distributive share of the decedent's estate to the surviving spouse. It is true that it is generally held that the creation of a revocable trust is sufficient to cut out the surviving spouse, at least if the settlor does not reserve too great a control over the property. In the case of the savings-deposit trust, however, the depositor reserves such complete control that it would seem that, even though the trust is valid as against the personal representative of the depositor, it should not be valid as against the surviving spouse. Certainly the policy underlying the statute protecting the surviving spouse is stronger than the policy underlying the statute providing for certain formalities to evidence a testamentary disposition. It may well be held that the creation of a savings deposit trust is valid but not effective to cut out the surviving spouse."

Also see: Bogert, Law of Trusts and Trustees, sec. 47, at 340–341 (2d ed. 1965).

While we recognize the general validity of "Totten" savings-account trusts for the reasons set forth above, we conclude that the savings-account trusts in question were illusory and invalid as against Dr. Montgomery and that they did not deprive him of his statutory share in his deceased spouse's estate. The trial court order, which was affirmed by the appellate court, provided that the funeral bill of the decedent be paid from the savings bank accounts in question, and that the banks distribute the balance of the said accounts to the beneficiaries named therein. This order properly directed the payment of the funeral bill from said accounts, if such funds were needed therefor.

In all other respects the order was erroneous. The balances in the savings-account trusts should be treated as the property of the decedent for the purpose of determining Dr. Montgomery's statutory share in his deceased spouse's estate, and, if necessary, he may draw upon the varying amounts in the respective trust accounts on a proportionate basis to the extent required to pay him one third of the net estate remaining after payment of all just claims. Such claims would include a surviving spouse's award, if such an award is appropriate, as well as the costs of administering the estate. (Ill.Rev.Stat.1971, ch. 3, par. 202.) Thereafter the balance remaining in the accounts should be distributed to the beneficiaries named in the trust accounts.

Accordingly, the judgment of the appellate court is reversed in part and affirmed in part, and the cause is remanded to the circuit court for further proceedings not inconsistent with the views expressed herein.

In view of the nature of the proceeding below, we believe it appropriate on remand to specify that respondents be given the opportunity to file an answer to the petition and to present evidence, if there be any, of any defense that might be available to them in view of the conclusions expressed herein.

Affirmed in part and reversed in part and remanded.

Note

A Totten trust is a deposit in a savings bank in the depositor's name "as trustee" for a named beneficiary and is freely revocable by the depositor on presentation of the pass book at any time.   On Totten trusts generally, see Chapter Seven, p. 454.

JOHNSON v. LA GRANGE STATE BANK

Supreme Court of Illinois, 1978.
73 Ill.2d 342, 22 Ill.Dec. 709, 383 N.E.2d 185.

RYAN, Justice:

These consolidated cases involve the validity of *inter vivos* transfers of property by one spouse against the marital rights of the surviving spouse in the property transferred.

Johnson v. La Grange State Bank concerns an *inter vivos* trust created by Eleanor Johnson for the ultimate benefit of several relatives and various charities.   *   *   *   The plaintiff in each case is the surviving husband.   Each has claimed his respective statutory share in the assets transferred.

[The facts of the second case are omitted.   At issue was a husband's challenge of several joint bank accounts set up and funded by his wife, with her sister-in-law as the other tenant.   The lower court denied the husband's claim, and that ruling is sustained here on the analysis used in the Johnson case.]

In the *Johnson* case, plaintiff, H. Franklin Johnson, and Eleanor Johnson had been married in 1937 and for more than 36 years enjoyed a happy marriage.   The plaintiff, who had accumulated an estate in excess of $2,000,000, was very generous towards his wife and quite frequently gave her substantial gifts of money and securities.   Mrs. Johnson relied on her husband's business acumen and followed his advice in making investments, as well as in managing the accumulated gifts which he gave her.   The trial court found, and it is not disputed, that there was no estrangement or feeling of antipathy of one spouse toward the other.

In 1966, Mrs. Johnson learned that she had cancer; she later learned that her life expectancy was less than five years.   Prior to 1969 the Johnsons, who had no children, had simple reciprocal wills which provided that in the event of the death of either of them, the survivor would receive the decedent's entire estate.   On February 5, 1969, the Johnsons executed new wills in which Johnson provided that his wife's relatives would receive 20% of his estate if his wife did not survive him, and Mrs. Johnson provided that her entire estate was left to her family if Johnson did not survive her.

In the summer of 1970, Mrs. Johnson executed a new will and again in February of 1972, seven months before her death, she executed another will and simultaneously executed a revocable *inter vivos* trust in which she placed in trust substantially all of her assets.   The will, by the residuary clause, poured the balance of her estate into the *inter vivos* trust.

By the terms of the trust, Mrs. Johnson named herself trustee of certain properties (stocks, bonds, etc.).   The entire income of the trust was to be paid to her during her lifetime, and she reserved the power to invade the principal of the trust, as she in her discretion saw fit.   She retained broad powers to invest, reinvest, divide, and distribute the trust property and likewise retained the power to alter, amend or modify the trust provisions in any manner.   The La Grange State Bank was designated as successor trustee to act upon her death or disability.   The trust instrument provided the method of determining when she would be considered disabled. Upon her death, the successor trustee was to distribute assets of the trust to Mrs. Johnson's mother, sister, niece, and certain named charities.   The trust document included a provision whereby her husband, plaintiff, was to receive so much of the income and principal to meet any emergency situation for his reasonable support, medical, and burial expenses.   The trustee, however, was advised to consider other sources available to him and the needs of Mrs. Johnson's mother and sister before making any such emergency payments.

In 1972, Mrs. Johnson moved to Florida, where she lived until her death in September 1972.   Her will was admitted to probate in Florida on October 19, 1973.   During the pendency of the Florida proceeding, the plaintiff instituted an action in the circuit court of Cook County against the trustee and the trust beneficiaries to set aside the *inter vivos* trust established by his wife, insofar as it deprived him of his marital rights in the property held in trust.   Plaintiff sought to impose a constructive trust on the trust assets to the extent of his claim.   In count I of his three-count amended complaint he alleged that, as the surviving spouse, the trust was illusory and fraudulent as to him and that he was therefore entitled to receive a statutory one-half share of the original corpus of the trust.   Count II alleged that the decedent established the trust with the intention of defeating plaintiff's marital interest in the settlor's personal estate.   Count III alleged that the decedent acted in an intentional, deliberate, and fraudulent manner for the purpose of denying plaintiff his statutory share of the decedent's estate.   The court allowed defendants' motion to dismiss counts I and II of the amended complaint, but allowed count III to stand.   Trial was held without a jury.   At the conclusion of the plaintiff's case, judgment was entered for the defendants.   The trial court also found no support for the plaintiff's contentions that decedent's actions were fraudulent and held that the plaintiff's allegations were made in bad faith and without reasonable cause, and assessed attorney's fees and costs against the plaintiff.   Plaintiff appealed from both orders.

The First District Appellate Court reversed the trial court (50 Ill. App.3d 830, 8 Ill.Dec. 670, 365 N.E.2d 1056), holding that an *inter vivos* trust may not defeat the marital rights of a settlor's surviving spouse where the settlor effectively retains ultimate control of the trust assets. Also, since the appellate court sustained the plaintiff's cause of action, the trial court's judgment assessing attorney's fees and expenses against the plaintiff as a sanction under section 41 of the Civil Practice Act (Ill. Rev.Stat.1973, ch. 110, par. 41) was accordingly reversed.

* * *

Plaintiffs in both of these cases rely on this court's opinion in Montgomery v. Michaels (1973), 54 Ill.2d 532, 301 N.E.2d 465. In *Montgomery*, the issue was whether certain savings account trusts ("Totten trusts") created by the decedent for the benefit of her children by a former marriage defrauded the surviving spouse of his marital rights. The decedent had provided that the accounts were to be paid to the named beneficiaries upon her death, but during her lifetime she retained complete control over the accounts and made deposits in and withdrawals from them. This court held that while Totten trusts were not invalid *per se* (see *In re Estate of Petralia* (1965), 32 Ill.2d 134, 204 N.E.2d 1), such trusts were ineffective to defeat a surviving spouse's statutory or forced share in the estate of his deceased spouse. The opinion stated:

> "In the case at bar the settlor was also the trustee. During her lifetime she retained absolute, unqualified control over the bank accounts, and possessed and exercised all incidents of complete ownership, including the right to receive interest payable thereon and withdraw the principal thereof. The enjoyment of the proceeds of the accounts by the beneficiary or beneficiaries named therein would arise only upon the death of the settlor-trustee with the accounts remaining intact.
>
> Under these circumstances, the expressed statutory policy of protecting a surviving spouse's statutory share in the estate should prevail, regardless of the intent of the deceased spouse in creating the savings-account trust. 54 Ill.2d 532, 536, 301 N.E.2d 465, 467."

The above-quoted language from *Montgomery* was cited by the appellate court in *La Grange State Bank*, and is significant in that court's decision that the *inter vivos* trust created by Mrs. Johnson could not serve to deprive plaintiff of his marital rights in the trust assets. The court noted that *Montgomery*, as illustrated by the above-quoted language, adopted a "retention of ownership" test to be employed by the courts to determine whether transfers may be deemed fraudulent as to the rights of surviving spouses. Basically, the "retention of ownership" test determines whether the decedent retained so much control over the property in question that it can be said that the decedent in effect only parted with that control upon death. Under such circumstances, where the donor does in effect "retain ownership" of the property subject to the transfer, the trust will be deemed substantially testamentary in character, at least insofar as the surviving spouse is concerned, so as to subject it to the claims of the surviving spouse just as if the property had passed under the decedent's will, or had otherwise been included in the probate estate. Montgomery v. Michaels (1973), 54 Ill.2d 532, 538, 301 N.E.2d 465.

The "retention of ownership" test of *Montgomery* was limited on its facts to Totten trusts. A Totten trust, in effect, purports to change ownership of the deposited funds to the designated beneficiaries upon the death of the settlor. The requirements for their establishment are very informal. The enjoyment of the beneficiaries is provisional and tentative, since there are no limitations or qualifications on the ability of the settlor to withdraw funds from the account. Inevitably, a great deal of control and ownership is reserved to the settlor over the funds. (See 1 A. Scott, Trusts sec. 58.5, at 546–47 (3d ed. 1967).) These are valid reasons for invalidating such trusts *per se* insofar as they relate to the claims of the surviving spouse. Because the degree of ownership by the trustee is customarily so great, public policy in favor of protecting surviving spouses permits the categorical conclusion that such arrangements are testamentary in character and are ineffective to deprive surviving spouses of their lawful claims.

The courts of this State have readily upheld *inter vivos* trust arrangements where the settlor has named himself trustee and retained indicia of ownership and control. (Farkas v. Williams (1955), 5 Ill.2d 417, 125 N.E.2d 600.) There is no contention in this case that the trust was not a valid *inter vivos* trust. It is only contended that it is invalid to the extent that it deprived the plaintiff of his marital rights in the property. With the exception of Montgomery v. Michaels and the rules therein concerning the validity of Totten trusts, no general principles have emerged invalidating such other *inter vivos* transfers *per se* in respect to the marital rights of surviving spouses. Rather, whether the transfer of property in trust is vulnerable to attack depends on whether the trust employed is colorable and illusory and a fraud on marital rights. (E.g., Holmes v. Mims (1953), 1 Ill.2d 274, 115 N.E.2d 790.) This determination necessarily turns on the facts of each individual case. (See Burnet v. First National Bank (1957), 12 Ill.App.2d 514, 140 N.E.2d 362.) We therefore reject the reasoning of the appellate court that our decision in *Montgomery* is controlling in this case.

In *Montgomery*, the court acknowledged that, in some instances, whether the trust is invalid as to a surviving spouse is determined by a consideration of all the facts and circumstances which might be indicative of an intent to defraud the surviving spouse of his statutory share and cited Rose v. St. Louis Union Trust Co. (1969), 43 Ill.2d 312, 253 N.E.2d 417. The defendants in this court likewise urge that *Rose* adopted the "intent to defraud" test in determining if an *inter vivos* trust is invalid as to the surviving spouse. *Rose* did in fact apply the "intent to defraud" test; however, it is important to note that *Rose* was applying Missouri law, and under the Missouri statute and decisions a voluntary conveyance which a surivng spouse may set aside as fraudulent is one that is executed with the intent and purpose of defeating the marital rights of the spouse in the property conveyed. (See Annot., 39 A.L.R.3d 14, 59–68 (1971).) In Illinois, however, and by the weight of authority in other jurisdictions, the owner of property has an absolute right to dispose of his property during his lifetime in any manner he sees fit, and he may do so even though the transfer is for the precise purpose of minimizing or defeating the statutory marital interests of the spouse in the property conveyed. (Padfield v. Padfield (1875), 78 Ill. 16; Blankenship v. Hall (1908), 233 Ill. 116, 84 N.E. 192; Hoeffner v. Hoeffner (1945), 389 Ill. 253, 59 N.E.2d 684; Annot., 39 A.L.R.3d 14 (1971); Annot., 49 A.L.R. 2d 521 (1956).) Such a gift or transfer is not vulnerable or subject to attack by the surviving spouse unless the transaction is a sham and is *strd*

"colorable" or "illusory" and is tantamount to a fraud.   Holmes v. Mims (1953), 1 Ill.2d 274, 115 N.E.2d 790.

The general rule stated by this court in *Holmes* is widely accepted (see Annot., 49 A.L.R.2d 521 (1956)) and has been generally applied by the courts of this State.   The difficulty arises, as is so often the case, in the application of the general rule.   The use of the phrase "intent to defraud" is confusing and carries a connotation not relevant to the question to be resolved.   When the cases discuss fraud on the marital rights of the surviving spouse, they are not considering fraud in the traditional sense.   Also, a minority view, in considering whether there has been a fraud on the marital property rights, has held that any conveyance made with the intent to minimize or defeat the marital rights of the surviving spouse in the property conveyed is presumed fraudulent.   As noted above, this is the rule followed in Missouri, and the rule that was followed by this court in *Rose*, applying Missouri law.   In Illinois and in a majority of jurisdictions, however, as previously noted, such a conveyance is not presumptively a fraud on the surviving spouse.

Although not applicable to this case, Public Act 80–737, approved and effective September 16, 1977 (Ill.Rev.Stat.1977, ch. 110½, pars. 601, 602), provides:

> "Sec. 1.   An otherwise valid transfer of property, in trust or otherwise, by a decedent during his or her lifetime, shall not, in the absence of an *intent to defraud,* be invalid, in whole or in part, on the ground that it is *illusory* because the deceased retained any power or right with respect to the property.   .
>
> Sec. 2.   This Act takes effect upon becoming a law and applies to savings account trusts established on or after its effective date, and as to all other transfers this Act is *declaratory of existing law.*"   (Emphasis added.)

This enactment has thus retained "intent to defraud" as necessary to be established in proving the invalidity of a transfer on the ground that it was illusory.   The Act also states that except as to savings account trusts (Totten trusts) its requirement is declaratory of existing law.   What effect the amendment had on our holding in *Montgomery* is not before us.

Since "intent to defraud" in the context of these cases does not carry the traditional meaning of fraud, and since a property owner may convey his property for the precise purpose of defeating his spouses's marital property rights, the meaning of "intent to defraud" must be construed in connection with the words "illusory" and "colorable" with which it is usually associated in the cases cited.   It has been suggested that the intent by which a transfer is to be tested should not be stated in the confusing terms of "intent to defraud," but it should be tested by the intent of the donor either to retain or to part with the ownership of property. Smith, The Present Status of "Illusory" Trust—The Doctrine on Newman vs. Dore Brought Down to Date, 44 Mich.L.Rev. 151 (1945).

The cases do not always differentiate between the terms "illusory" and "colorable."   However, it is acknowledged, within the sphere of the subject that we are now discussing, that an illusory transfer is one which takes back all that it gives, while a colorable transfer is one which appears *defns* absolute on its face but due to some secret or tacit understanding between the transferor and the transferee the transfer is, in fact, not a transfer because the parties intended that ownership be retained by the transferor. 44 Mich.L.Rev. 151, 153, 162 (1945).

The intent to defraud is found in the nature of the transfer, whether it be illusory or colorable. In either event the transfer is a fraud on the marital rights because the transferor in reality had no intent to convey any present interest in the property but, in fact, intended to retain complete ownership. Although the spouse's marital rights can be defeated by an actual transfer, a purported transfer whereby the owner does not intend to convey a present interest, but intends to retain ownership, is evidence of an intent to defraud. See Newman v. Dore (1937), 275 N.Y. 371, 9 N.E.2d 966.

In Toman v. Svoboda (1976), 39 Ill.App.3d 394, 349 N.E.2d 668, the appellate court carefully analyzed the problems involved in considering *inter vivos* transfers and reached what we find to be an acceptable understanding of the determinative factor. The court stated:

> "The confusing factor is that Illinois and the majority of American States also examine the gift looking for what they unfortunately also call fraudulent circumstances, but by which they mean circumstances indicating that the gift was not a *real* gift because there was no present donative intent (that is, no donative intent of any kind or, at most, a mere testamentary, as distinguished from a present, donative intent), for lack of which the alleged gift was simply a sham or a merely colorable transfer of legal title." (Emphasis in original.) (39 Ill.App.3d 394, 399, 349 N.E.2d 668, 673.)

The court then mentioned some of the circumstances discussed in *Montgomery* which have a bearing upon the intent of the donor in making the *inter vivos* transfer and stated:

> "All these circumstances are relevant to the existence of an intent to defraud the surviving spouse of his or her statutory marital right *by making a sham or merely colorable inter vivos donative transfer*, which *is* a sham or merely colorable because it lacks the essential element of a present donative intent; either there is no donative intent of any kind, or there is at most a mere *testamentary* donative intent. The fraud * * * relates to the absence of a present donative intent, not to the presence of an intent or purpose to minimize or defeat the statutory marital right of the now surviving spouse." (Emphasis in original.) (39 Ill.App.3d 394, 399–400, 349 N.E.2d 668, 673.)

The court then considered the effect of the retention by the donor of the present benefits in the property and stated:

> "But, where the donor does reserve to himself the life estate in the whole subject matter of the gift, the existence of his *present* intent to give now the *future* fee interest in the subject matter of the gift must be subjected to special scrutiny to make sure that his donative intent *is* present and not merely testamentary." (Emphasis in original.) (39 Ill.App.3d 394, 400, 349 N.E.2d 668, 674.)

The court further stated:

> "[W]e agree that such retention is highly relevant on the issue of the existence of a *present* donative intent. But such evidence is far from con-

trolling on that issue, because it is at least equally compatible with the retention by the donor-spouse of a present life estate in the shares, so that the precise subject matter of the gift which the donor-spouse presently intended to give was, not the full present fee interest in the shares, but rather the vested *future* fee interest *only*." (Emphasis in original.) 39 Ill.App.3d 394, 401, 349 N.E.2d 668, 675.

We conclude that an *inter vivos* transfer of property is valid as against the marital rights of the surviving spouse unless the transaction is tantamount to a fraud as manifested by the absence of donative intent to make a conveyance of a present interest in the property conveyed. Without such an intent the transfer would simply be a sham or merely a colorable or illusory transfer of legal title.

[The court here quoted with approval from the opinion in Farkas v. Williams. For the text of that opinion, see p. 49, supra.]

Thus the appellate court in *Toman* applied a present-donative-intent test in determining whether the transfer constituted a fraud on the surviving spouse's property rights similar to the intent test this court applied in *Farkas* in determining whether the *inter vivos* trusts in that case were effective transfers, or whether they were testamentary in nature and invalid. It would appear to be logical that similar criteria should govern both situations. A surviving spouse only has an interest in the property which becomes a part of the decedent's estate. (Ill.Rev.Stat.1977, ch. 110½, pars. 2–1, 2–8.) If the interest in the property passed under a valid *inter vivos* conveyance it would then not become a part of the decedent's estate and the surviving spouse would have no interest in it. This is in accord with the reasoning of the much cited case of Newman v. Dore (1937), 275 N.Y. 371, 9 N.E.2d 966.

* * *

We are satisfied that the *inter vivos* trust created by Eleanor Johnson was not colorable, illusory, or tantamount to fraud. The fact cannot be denied that as trustee of a revocable trust she retained a significant degree of control over the trust assets. However, the form of control which the donor retains over the trust does not make it invalid. (Gurnett v. Mutual Life Insurance Co. (1934), 356 Ill. 612, 191 N.E. 250.) In addition, it is well established that the retention by the settlor of the power to revoke, even when coupled with the reservation of a life interest in the trust property, does not render the trust inoperative. Kelly v. Parker (1899), 181 Ill. 49, 54 N.E. 615; Bear v. Millikin Trust Co. (1929), 336 Ill. 366, 168 N.E. 349.

Nevertheless, the facts of a particular case may show that the trust in question, while ostensibly valid, is in actuality a sham transaction, essentially testamentary in character, and therefore invalid. In this case, the facts do not support such a conclusion. Mrs. Johnson was certainly well aware of the fact that her husband had a net worth of over $2,000,000, and was, and would most likely continue to be, well provided for. She was concerned, however, with the welfare of certain of her relatives, particularly her mother, who was dependent on her. She formalized a declaration of trust, with advice of counsel, for the benefit of her relatives. The declaration of trust immediately created an equitable interest in the beneficiaries, although the enjoyment of the interest was postponed until Mrs. Johnson's death and subject to her power of revocation. This, however, did not make the transfer illusory. And the power of control that she had as trustee was not an irresponsible power; she was charged with a fiduciary duty in respect to the beneficiaries' interest, and her management and administration of the assets in trust could only be exercised in accordance with the terms of the trust. See Farkas v. Williams.

The conclusion of the appellate court that Mrs. Johnson parted with nothing during her life (50 Ill.App.3d 830, 842, 8 Ill.Dec. 670, 365 N.E. 2d 1056) is incorrect. The trust directed that the trustee, in event of the grantor's disability, was to use the income and principal of the trust estate for the grantor's benefit and for the benefit of any person dependent on her. The trust instrument provided that the successor trustee was to assume the office of trustee during her lifetime should she become disabled, and the instrument set forth the means of determining her disability. There is no evidence that Mrs. Johnson made any withdrawals from the principal or otherwise exercised any of her reserved powers to deplete the trust assets. These facts tend to show that she intended to make a valid and effective transfer at the time her declaration of trust was executed. We find that a valid transfer was effected under the trust.

We have yet to address two additional points raised by the appeal in Johnson v. La Grange State Bank. The plaintiff argues that a constructive trust should be imposed on the trust property because the assets were fraudulently obtained from the plaintiff. In this regard, he argues that he parted with the assets in the expectation that they would be returned to him upon his wife's death.

The allegations of the amended complaint, which would support the imposition of a constructive trust, were found to be not supported by the evidence both in the trial court and in the appellate court. We agree with this determination. The Johnsons had a warm and loving marriage, and the evidence shows that Johnson's frequent gifts to his wife were out of his concern for her welfare. They were made with no strings attached. He had some knowledge of his wife's contact with her attorneys for the purpose of preparing a trust instrument and a will, and the plaintiff elected not to involve himself in the matter. These facts, along with other evidentiary matter in the record, show that there was an absence of fraud in this case. The plaintiff's attempt to impose a constructive trust on the assets in question must fail.

[The court did, however, conclude that the plaintiff-husband had not acted in bad faith and should not have had the fees assessed against him.]

Notes

1. The Montgomery and Johnson cases, separated in time by only five years, demonstrate the difficulties courts have in determining the validity of inter vivos transactions that work to limit a surviving spouse's claim to an elective

share.   As the court in the Johnson case notes, supra p. 156, the Illinois leg-islature enacted in 1977 a statute stating that a savings account trust is not, "in the absence of an intent to defraud", to be invalidated "because the deceased retained any power or right with respect to the property".   Although the John-son court declined to express an opinion as to the effect of this decision on the Montgomery holding, it had earlier spoken with apparent approval of that hold-ing.   Would the result in Montgomery be the same if the case were to arise today?   To what extent does the 1977 statute clarify the issue?   What is the current test to be used in Illinois to determine whether or not a transfer is illusory?   Intent to disinherit?   Intent to benefit others?   Retention of control and enjoyment?

2. At one time, New York experienced much of this same confusion.   In its first case on the issue after Newman v. Dore, the New York Court of Appeals held that the husband's Totten trust in favor of his daughter who lived in Germany was illusory and subject to the widow's claim, thereby making a reality of the dictum in the Newman case to the effect that a transfer could be valid as a matter of property law but invalid as to the surviving spouse.   Krause v. Krause, 285 N.Y. 27, 32 N.E.2d 779 (1941).   A year later the same court upheld a joint savings account with right of survivorship against the wife's challenge on the ground that the section of the Banking Law authorizing such accounts vested title in the surviving tenant.   Inda v. Inda, 288 N.Y. 315, 43 N.E.2d 59 (1942).   In this context, there is no significant difference between a Totten trust and a joint savings account;   the depositor who retains the bank book has complete control over the funds in both instances.   In the last case coming to the Court of Appeals involving Totten trusts, the court refused to follow the precedent of Krause v. Krause and held four Totten trusts, which the husband had created naming his granddaughter Sandra as the beneficiary, not subject to the widow's claim because the decedent had a positive intent to benefit his granddaughter.   Matter of Halpern, 303 N.Y. 33, 100 N.E.2d 120 (1951).   Is an "intent to benefit" test any easier to administer than an "intent to disinherit" test?   The Halpern decision was criticized on a number of grounds and left the New York law in such a state of confusion as to make legislative intervention inevitable.

3. The Illinois court in the first case indicates that Dr. Montgomery is entitled to invalidate the Totten trusts only to the extent necessary to make up his intestate share.   The early New York cases reached a different conclusion. Matter of Halpern presented the following problem: The husband's will left the entire probate estate to his second wife and named her executrix.   A few years later as disaffection set in he put all his available cash, approximately $14,000, into three Totten trusts naming his granddaughter Sandra as the ul-timate beneficiary.   The Appellate Division held the Totten trusts illusory but voided them only to the extent necessary to make up the wife's intestate share. Thus, assuming there was $4,000 in the probate estate, the wife's share was $6,000 of which $2,000 was taken from the Totten trusts.   In re Halpern's Estate, 277 App.Div. 525, 100 N.Y.S.2d 894 (1st Dept. 1950).   The Court of Appeals, though affirming because the issue had not been preserved on appeal, said: "We see no power in the courts to divide up such a Totten trust and call part of it illusory and the other part good.   The only test is that quoted above, from Newman v. Dore, supra, and Krause v. Krause, supra, and the results of its application would necessarily be either total validity or total invalidity, as to any one transfer."   Matter of Halpern, 303 N.Y. at p. 40, 100 N.E.2d at p. 123.

4. Comprehensive surveys of decisions dealing with the problem presented in the three principal cases appear in Annot., Inter Vivos Trust—Impairing Spouse's Right, 39 A.L.R.3d 14; Annot., Savings Account Trust—Rights of Spouse, 64 A.L.R.3d 187. At least one jurisdiction has refused to follow the New York lead. Connecticut has no statutory provision covering transfers made in fraud of the spouse's share, and the Connecticut Supreme Court of Errors has expressly rejected the special privilege approach of Newman v. Dore. Cherniack v. Home National Bank & Trust Co. of Meriden, 151 Conn. 367, 198 A.2d 58 (1964).

B. STATUTORY REMEDIES TO AUGMENT THE SPOUSE'S SHARE

1. MISSOURI: VERNON'S ANN.MO.STAT. § 474.150

Gifts in Fraud of Marital Rights—Presumption on Conveyances

1. Any gift made by a person, whether dying testate or intestate, in fraud of the marital rights of his surviving spouse to share in his estate, shall, at the election of the surviving spouse, be treated as a testamentary disposition and may be recovered from the donee and persons taking from him without adequate consideration and applied to the payment of the spouse's share, as in case of his election to take against the will.

2. Any conveyance of real estate made by a married person at any time without the joinder or other written express assent of his spouse, made at any time, duly acknowledged, is deemed to be in fraud of the marital rights of his spouse, if the spouse becomes a surviving spouse, unless the contrary is shown.

3. Any conveyance of the property of the spouse of an incompetent person is deemed not to be in fraud of the marital rights of the incompetent if the probate court authorizes the guardian of the incompetent to join in or assent to the conveyance after finding that it is not made in fraud of the marital rights. Any conveyance of the property of a minor or incompetent made by a guardian pursuant to an order of court is deemed not to be in fraud of the marital rights of the spouse of the ward.

Notes

1. In determining whether an inter vivos transfer is in fraud of marital rights the courts weigh the following factors: presence or absence of consideration; proportion between the amount of the transfer and the size of the total estate; amount of control retained over the transferred property; extent to which the transfer was made openly and with frank disclosure to the other spouse; amount of time between the transfer and death; identity of the transferee as a natural object of the donor's bounty; and extent to which the surviving spouse is left without means of support. Nelson v. Nelson, 512 S.W.2d 455 (Mo.1974) (funds in a bank account in the joint names of the deceased husband and his sister held subject to widow's claim); but see Windsor v. Leonard, 154 U.S.App.D.C. 348, 475 F.2d 932 (1973) (under the Maryland law, which is applicable in the District of Columbia, wife's revocable trust held not in fraud of husband's rights).

2. Tennessee's statute makes voidable any conveyance made fraudulently with intent to defeat the surviving spouse's elective share. The leeway for

interpretation of this statute is demonstrated by a comparison of Sherrill v. Mallicote, 57 Tenn.App. 241, 417 S.W.2d 798 (1967) (irrevocable trust of stock for the benefit of husband's brothers and sisters held voidable by widow) and Warren v. Compton, 626 S.W.2d 12 (Tenn.App.1981) (decedent's gifts "to his girl friend" totalling $57,300 in value not voidable by widow).

2. NEW YORK: N.Y.—McKINNEY'S EPTL 5–1.1

(b) Inter vivos dispositions treated as testamentary substitutes for the purpose of election by surviving spouse.

(1) Where a person dies after August thirty-first, nineteen hundred sixty-six and is survived by a spouse who exercises a right of election under paragraph (c), the following transactions effected by such decedent at any time after the date of the marriage and after August thirty-first, nineteen hundred sixty-six, whether benefiting the surviving spouse or any other person, shall be treated as testamentary substitutes and the capital value thereof, as of the decedent's death, included in the net estate subject to the surviving spouse's elective right:

(A) Gifts causa mortis.

(B) Money deposited, after August thirty-first, nineteen hundred sixty-six, together with all dividends credited thereon, in a savings account in the name of the decedent in trust for another person, with a banking organization, savings and loan association, foreign banking corporation or organization or bank or savings and loan association organized under the laws of the United States, and remaining on deposit at the date of the decedent's death.

(C) Money deposited, after August thirty-first, nineteen hundred sixty-six, together with all dividends credited thereon, in the name of the decedent and another person and payable on death, pursuant to the terms of the deposit or by operation of law, to the survivor, with a banking organization, savings and loan association, foreign banking corporation or organization or bank or savings and loan association organized under the laws of the United States, and remaining on deposit at the date of the decedent's death.

(D) Any disposition of property made by the decedent after August thirty-first, nineteen hundred sixty-six whereby property is held, at the date of his death, by the decedent and another person as joint tenants with a right of survivorship or as tenants by the entirety.

(E) Any disposition of property made by the decedent after August thirty-first, nineteen hundred sixty-six, in trust or otherwise, to the extent that the decedent at the date of his death retained either alone or in conjunction with another person, by the express provisions of the disposing instrument, a power to revoke such disposition or a power to consume, invade or dispose of the principal thereof. The provisions of this paragraph shall not affect the right of any income beneficiary to the income undistributed or accrued at the date of death.

(2) Nothing in this paragraph shall affect, impair or defeat the right of any person entitled to receive (A) payment in money, securities or other

property under a thrift, savings, pension, retirement, death benefit, stock bonus or profit-sharing plan, system or trust, (B) money payable by an insurance company or a savings bank authorized to conduct the business of life insurance under an annuity or pure endowment contract, a policy of life, group life, industrial life or accident and health insurance or a contract by such insurer relating to the payment of proceeds or avails thereof or (C) payment of any United States savings bond payable to a designated person, and such transactions are not testamentary substitutes within the meaning of this paragraph.

(3) Transactions described in subparagraphs (C) or (D) shall be treated as testamentary substitutes in the proportion that the funds on deposit were the property of the decedent immediately before the deposit or the consideration for the property held as joint tenants or as tenants by the entirety was furnished by the decedent. The surviving spouse shall have the burden of establishing the proportion of the decedent's contribution. Where the other party to a transaction described in subparagraphs (C) or (D) is a surviving spouse, such spouse shall have the burden of establishing the portion of his contribution, if any. For the purpose of this subparagraph, the surrogate's court may accept such evidence as is relevant and competent, whether or not the person offering such evidence would otherwise be competent to testify.

* * *

Notes

1. The following example of § 5–1.1(b) in operation comes from the Third Report, N.Y. Temporary Commission on Estates, 139 (1964):

In computing the elective share, the amount or value of all money or other property passing to the surviving spouse by reason of the death of the decedent under like form of ownership shall be charged against such share. In addition to the amount or value of such property, the value of real property held by the decedent and the surviving spouse as tenants by the entirety at the time of his death would be charged against the elective share. To illustrate, assume that H died [testate, having willed nothing to his wife W and] leaving property in the following forms of ownership: 1) true estate $100,000; 2) two Totten trust bank accounts, one payable to W in the amount of $40,000 and one payable to his son of $60,000. The application of the proposed statute would produce the following results:

(a) The right of election would extend to the total fund of $200,000 giving W the sum of $66,667.

(b) W's Totten trust of $40,000 would be charged against her elective share, leaving $26,667 to be contributed $10/16$ ($5/8$) by the estate and $6/16$ ($3/8$) by the son's Totten trust.

2. Additional examples of the New York statute in operation appear in Arenson, Surviving Spouse's Right of Election and Its Application to Testamentary Substitutes, 20 N.Y.L.Forum 1 (1974). See also Estate of Schlosser, 73 Misc.2d 380, 342 N.Y.S.2d 808 (1973).

3. UNIFORM PROBATE CODE SECTION 2–202

[Augmented Estate.]

The augmented estate means the estate reduced by funeral and administration expenses, homestead allowance, family allowances and exemptions, and enforceable claims, to which is added the sum of the following amounts:

(1) The value of property transferred to anyone other than a bona fide purchaser by the decedent at any time during marriage, to or for the benefit of any person other than the surviving spouse, to the extent that the decedent did not receive adequate and full consideration in money or money's worth for the transfer, if the transfer is of any of the following types:

(i) any transfer under which the decedent retained at the time of his death the possession or enjoyment of, or right to income from, the property;

(ii) any transfer to the extent that the decedent retained at the time of his death a power, either alone or in conjunction with any other person, to revoke or to consume, invade or dispose of the principal for his own benefit;

(iii) any transfer whereby property is held at the time of decedent's death by decedent and another with right of survivorship;

(iv) any transfer made to a donee within two years of death of the decedent to the extent that the aggregate transfers to any one donee in either of the years exceed $3,000.

Any transfer is excluded if made with the written consent or joinder of the surviving spouse. Property is valued as of the decedent's death except that property given irrevocably to a donee during lifetime of the decedent is valued as of the date the donee came into possession or enjoyment if that occurs first. Nothing herein shall cause to be included in the augmented estate any life insurance, accident insurance, joint annuity or pension payable to a person other than the surviving spouse.

(2) The value of property owned by the surviving spouse at the decedent's death, plus the value of property transferred by the spouse at any time during marriage to any person other than the decedent which would have been includible in the spouse's augmented estate if the surviving spouse had predeceased the decedent, to the extent the owned or transferred property is derived from the decedent by any means other than testate or intestate succession without a full consideration in money or money's worth. For purposes of this subsection:

(i) Property derived from the decedent includes, but is not limited to, any beneficial interest of the surviving spouse in a trust created by the decedent during his lifetime, any property appointed to the spouse by the decedent's exercise of a general or special power of appointment also exercisable in favor of others than the spouse, any proceeds of insurance (including accidental death benefits) on the life of the decedent attributable to premiums paid by him, any lump sum immediately payable and the commuted value of the proceeds of annuity contracts under which the decedent was the primary annuitant attributable to premiums paid by him, the commuted value of amounts payable after the decedent's death under any public or private pension, disability compensation, death benefit or retirement plan, exclusive of the Federal Social Security system, by reason of service performed or disabilities incurred by the decedent, any property held at the time of decedent's death by decedent and the surviving spouse with right of survivorship, any property held by decedent and transferred to the surviving spouse by reason of the decedent's death, and the value of the share of the surviving spouse resulting from rights in community property in this or any other state formerly owned with the decedent. Premiums paid by the decedent's employer, his partner, a partnership of which he was a member, or his creditors, are deemed to have been paid by the decedent.

(ii) Property owned by the spouse at the decedent's death is valued as of the date of death. Property transferred by the spouse is valued at the time the transfer became irrevocable, or at the decedent's death, whichever occurred first. Income earned by included property prior to the decedent's death is not treated as property derived from the decedent.

(iii) Property owned by the surviving spouse as of the decedent's death, or previously transferred by the surviving spouse is presumed to have been derived from the decedent except to the extent that the surviving spouse establishes that it was derived from another source.

*   *   *

Notes

1. A person, who is determined to disinherit his or her spouse (as was Mr. Straus in Newman v. Dore), still has a number of devices available to accomplish that purpose. Both the New York and UPC recapture provisions exempt life insurance and pension benefits; New York also excepts from its coverage U.S. savings bonds. Those assets could be made payable to others, say children by a first marriage, and thus not be included in the augmented estate against which the surviving spouse's share is assessed. In New York, the Mr. Straus of today could establish an inter vivos trust with his compliant friend, Mr. Dore, as trustee and direct that the income be paid to himself for life, remainder at his death to Emma Newman, and give Dore the discretionary power to invade principal in order to maintain Straus in accordance with his customary standard of living. The New York statute appears to make voidable only a trust over which the settlor retains by the terms of the instrument a power in himself to revoke or invade principal. The UPC provision is tighter in this regard but still offers opportunities for evasion by vesting powers in a third person rather than in the settlor. See generally, Clark, The Recapture of Testamentary Substitutes to Preserve the Spouse's Elective Share: An Appraisal of Recent Statutory Reforms, 2 Conn.L.Rev. 513 (1970).

2. The statutes designed to recapture transfers for the benefit of the surviving spouse and the various death taxes differ in language and policy objectives. They do, however, share the common problem of finding a definition for transfers which are technically made during life but are, because of enjoyment and control retained, nonetheless testamentary in nature. The experience in the tax field demonstrates the difficulties a legislative draftsman has in nailing down the mercurial concept of the testamentary transfer. The New York and UPC provisions make the test whether or not the settlor has personally retained powers to control or enjoy the funds. The tax cases reveal an infinite variety

of devices used by taxpayers to avoid similar limitations that appear in the tax codes. It remains for the future to determine what, if any, impact this voluminous jurisprudence will have on the interpretation of these statutes. See In re Estate of Schwartz, 449 Pa. 112, 295 A.2d 600 (1972) (court by a divided vote refused to use federal estate tax authority as a basis for finding under former Pennsylvania statute that husband had a power to consume property given to a child in order to defeat wife's elective share).

C. SATISFACTION OF THE SPOUSE'S SHARE BY TESTAMENTARY TRUST: THE NEW YORK APPROACH

From the time of its original enactment as Section 18 of the N.Y. Decedent Estate Law, the New York statute has included a unique feature which allowed the decedent's will to satisfy the statutory requirement if it gave the surviving spouse a minimum sum outright (currently $10,000 but prior to the 1966 revision $2,500) and placed the balance necessary to make up her or his intestate share (not to exceed one-half the estate) in trust under which she or he had an indefeasible right to income for life. There is obviously a substantial difference in value for a spouse of middle age or beyond between receiving the income from one-third of the estate and taking the amount in fee. See Note on Valuation of Life Estates and Remainders, infra, p. 173. Prior to 1981, satisfaction of the spouse's statutory share by trust as authorized under the New York law did not qualify the trust property for the marital deduction under the federal estate tax, unless the surviving spouse was given a general power of appointment over the trust principal. As the tax law is now written, the executor of the testator's estate can elect to treat the trust as "qualified terminable interest property" and thereby qualify it for the marital deduction. I.R.C. § 2056(b)(7); see discussion p. 945, infra.

IN RE SHUPACK'S WILL

Court of Appeals of New York, 1956.
1 N.Y.2d 482, 154 N.Y.S.2d 441, 136 N.E.2d 513.

FULD, Judge. Irving Shupack died in October of 1953, survived by his wife, a son and a daughter. His will, admitted to probate a month later, contained an absolute legacy of $2,500 to his wife and gave the residue of his estate to a trustee (also named as executor) "to be divided into three equal parts". One part was placed in trust for the benefit of his wife for life; upon her death, it was provided, the trust was to terminate and the principal was to be divided between the other trusts. The other two parts were placed in separate trusts for the benefit of the two children, each was to receive the income until his majority, and at that time the trusts were to end and each child was to receive the principal outright. The property left by the testator consisted primarily of six corporations which he wholly owned, two engaged in manufacturing, the other four in the real estate business, their gross assets totaling about $750,000.

We must decide two questions: first, whether the widow is entitled, under section 18 of the Decedent Estate Law, Consol.Laws, c. 13, [Editors'

Note: now revised as N.Y. EPTL § 5–1.1], to elect to take her intestate share of the estate and, second, whether the executor-trustee may exercise plenary managerial control over the property held by the real estate corporations.   We answer both in the negative, and, since we agree with the Appellate Division's treatment and disposition of the second question, relating to the executor-trustee's control (see, also, dissenting opinion, 1 N.Y.2d 498–499, 154 N.Y.S.2d 453), we discuss only the first, the wife's right of election under the statute.

So far as it is pertinent, section 18 grants to a surviving spouse the right to elect to take his or her share of the estate as in intestacy, subject to the following limitation and condition:

> "(d) Where the will contains an absolute legacy or devise, whether general or specific, to the surviving spouse, of or in excess of the sum of twenty-five hundred dollars and also a provision for a trust for his or her benefit for life of a principal equal to or more than the excess between said legacy or devise and his or her intestate share, no right of election whatever shall exist in the surviving spouse."

It is the widow's claim that she has a right of election because the trust in her favor is "inadequate" and "illusory."   Her reasoning, briefly stated, is this.   As a minority holder in closed corporations, she will be at the mercy of the holders of the majority of the stock for the declaration of dividends and for their amount.   Her children, who will acquire the remaining stock upon attaining their majority, the boy in 1957, the girl in 1961, will be able to elect the directors who will decide whether to distribute or retain the corporate profits; and thus they, or any strangers to whom they might sell, will control the amount of her income.   The Appellate Division, agreeing with the widow, reversed the decree of the surrogate and held that she was entitled "to elect to take against the will as in intestacy."   [1 A.D.2d 841, 149 N.Y.S.2d 23.]

That decision rests upon an unwarranted expansion of section 18 and the legislative purpose underlying its enactment.   We have more than once declared that the statute's purpose is to assure to a surviving husband or wife the right to claim his or her full intestate share, in spite of any will, "unless the instrument should provide substantial equivalents. A testamentary gift of an equal sum * * * or a gift in trust of such a sum for the use of the surviving spouse for life" constitutes such an equivalent.   Matter of Wittner's Estate, 301 N.Y. 461, 465, 95 N.E.2d 798, 800; Matter of Byrnes' Will, 260 N.Y. 465, 470, 474, 184 N.E. 56, 57, 58, 87 A.L.R. 223, reargument denied 261 N.Y. 623, 185 N.E. 765.

Contrary to respondent's argument, the statute was not, and rationally could not have been, designed to guarantee any particular income or any particular standard of living to the surviving wife.   The widow must accept her share of what her husband owned.   If he died possessed of nothing, the widow, of course, would receive nothing.   Similarly, if the husband died possessed of unproductive, unsaleable real estate, throwing off little, if any, income, the widow could not complain when she received one third of it outright or a legacy of $2,500 plus the one third in trust. Her financial position may turn out to be disadvantageous, and cause for regret, but, unfortunately for her, section 18 was not intended to assure her more than one third of what her husband possessed when he died.

By bequeathing to respondent the sum of $2,500 outright and also a life interest in a trust of one third of the residue of the estate, the testator provided her with the requisite equivalent for her intestate share and fully complied with the demands of the statute. The possibility which she fears, that her income may be impaired by hostile majority owners, results from the character of the property left by her husband rather than from any attempt to deprive her of her lawful share in the estate. It would have been far better for respondent if her husband had owned shares in General Motors, United States Steel or some other large publicly held corporation. But, the fact is, he owned only shares in such enterprises as Harjan Realty Corporation and American Hinge Corporation of Brooklyn. All that the testator owned, all he had to dispose of, was the stock in these personally held corporations.

While there is a danger that the widow will not receive an income from her trust proportionate to that received by her husband during his life, that consequence flows from the character of his property rather than from any failure on his part to comply with the provisions of law enacted for the benefit of the surviving spouse. If she were to take her intestate share, that is, a third of the stock outright, she would still have only a minority interest in each of these small corporations and the income would still be dependent upon decisions of directors selected by the majority stockholders. In such a case, she would, it is true, possess the right to sell her one third share, but this right is seriously impaired, if not effectively destroyed, by the practical difficulty attendant upon obtaining a fair-price buyer for a minority interest in a closely held corporation such as we have here.

We agree that the right to elect against the will is not barred where the trust, although in form complying with section 18, is, in fact, illusory or not the substantial equivalent of the intestate share. But, as the case before us illustrates, "illusory" has not the same meaning as "possibly unproductive of real income." The decisions in which a testamentary trust to the surviving spouse has been branded as "illusory" have either involved a duration shorter than the life of such spouse, Matter of Byrnes' Will, supra, 260 N.Y. 465, 184 N.E. 56, 87 A.L.R. 223, or a corpus subject to invasion and reduction of amount. Matter of Wittner's Estate, supra, 301 N.Y. 461, 95 N.E.2d 798; Matter of Matthews' Will, 255 App.Div. 80, 5 N.Y.S.2d 707, affirmed 279 N.Y. 732, 18 N.E.2d 683; Matter of Schrauth's Will, 249 App.Div. 846, 292 N.Y.S. 923.

This is not to say, though, that a testator, who dies possessed of both income producing and non-income producing property, may so divide his estate as to bequeath to his wife only the unproductive portion. When we are confronted with such a case, we shall deal with it. Nor does our decision mean, or even remotely suggest, that the widow would lack a remedy if the designated trustee were to prove faithless to the trust or were so to conduct and manage its affairs as to prejudice or discriminate against her interests. See, e.g., Matter of Hubbell's Will, 302 N.Y. 246, 97 N.E.2d 888, 47 A.L.R.2d 176. All we are now holding is that, where a testator has left to his spouse one third of all of his property, fairly and equitably divided, either outright or in trust in accordance with the provisions of the Decedent Estate Law, the fear or possibility of misconduct on the part of the trustee or of the corporate directors, managing the property, does not give rise to a right of election under section 18.

The order of the Appellate Division should be modified, with costs to all parties appearing separately and filing separate briefs, payable out of the estate, and the case remitted to the Surrogate's Court for proceedings not inconsistent with this opinion.

CONWAY, Chief Judge (dissenting).

* * *

The question before us is whether the widow is entitled to elect to take her intestate share against the terms of the will under section 18 of the Decedent Estate Law.

The Surrogate below held that the widow was not entitled to so elect. Upon appeal to the Appellate Division, however, that court, in ruling that the testamentary provision for the widow's benefit did not satisfy the requirements of section 18 and that thus the widow could elect to take her intestate share, stated in part: "In the light of the facts that the children's interests are necessarily antagonistic to appellant's [the widow], that at least upon the attainment by both children of their majorities they will have effective control of the affairs of the corporations by virtue of their outright ownership of two thirds of the stock, and that the question of whether income would be available for appellant, and, if so, the amount thereof, will depend upon whether the directors of the corporations declare dividends, bearing in mind that the right to challenge directors with respect to the declaration of dividends is circumscribed, we do not believe that the trust created for the benefit of appellant is one which may be said to be of such substantial benefit as to warrant a determination that she is not entitled to elect to take against the will. Despite the fact that the capital value of the principal of a trust appears to satisfy the conditions which under section 18 of the Decedent Estate Law would operate to bar a right of election[,] if in fact because of other reasons the trust would not be of substantial benefit to the surviving spouse, the trust is illusory and the spouse would be deemed to have a right to elect to take against the will as in intestacy [citing cases]."

[Chief Judge CONWAY here reviews the New York cases and concludes as follows:]

Thus, a trust will be deemed illusory where, because of the peculiar nature of the property, or the imposition of some term of [sic. or] condition, the surviving spouse's right to receive income might *possibly* be negated, impaired or rendered insecure. In short, a trust within the contemplation of section 18 must provide with reasonable certainty a real and substantial benefit to the surviving spouse. [Citations omitted.]

As earlier stated, the bulk of the corpus of the trusts for the widow and children here consists of wholly owned stock in individually owned corporations. The corporate assets, as such, belong to the corporations; and Morrison, as trustee, will hold all of the stock. The widow and the children (during their minorities), therefore, are merely beneficiaries of trusts of corporate stock. Upon the children's attainment of their respective majorities (Harold in 1957, and Janet in 1961) their respective trusts will end, at which time, each will receive one third of the stock. The widow will never receive the corpus or any part thereof. Before both children attain their majorities, control of the corporations will reside in Morrison, as trustee. Thereafter (in 1961), the children, as two thirds' owners of the stock, will assume control over the corporations. As stockholders, the children will be in a position to sell their interests to third parties, in which event strangers will assume control of the corporations. In any event, it is clear that the widow, for her life, will merely be the income beneficiary of a trust of a one third minority interest in corporate stock.

Where corporate stock constitutes the trust *res*, income to the corporation is not necessarily income to the trust beneficiary. The stockholder—and in turn the trust beneficiary—receives income only if and when—and in the amount that—the directors of the corporation decide to declare dividends. The exercise of discretion and business judgment in this respect resides solely with such directors. United States Trust Co. v. Heye, 224 N.Y. 242, 253, 120 N.E. 645, 648; Robertson v. De Brulatour, 188 N.Y. 301, 80 N.E. 938; Matter of Schaefer, 178 App.Div. 117, 122, 165 N.Y.S. 19, 22, affirmed 222 N.Y. 533, 118 N.E. 1076; Stewart v. Phelps, 71 App.Div. 91, 98, 75 N.Y.S. 526, 530, affirmed 173 N.Y. 621, 66 N.E. 1117; Avedon v. Gem Dress House, 194 App.Div. 678, 681, 185 N.Y.S. 871, 872, affirmed 232 N.Y. 505, 134 N.E. 548. It is plain, therefore, that the widow will receive income under her trust only if and when dividends are declared by the directors of the corporations. As of 1961, the children, as the majority stockholders, will control the corporations. If they sell their stock to third parties, strangers will assume such control. Control permits of a choice of directors. The directors decide and determine corporate policy. That is, they alone decide whether corporate earnings should be distributed as dividends, or whether profits should be retained by the corporations for business expansion, liquidation of indebtedness, or for some other purpose. It follows, therefore, that as of 1961, the children or strangers will, *in practical effect*, determine whether or not dividends shall be declared and, if so, when and in what amount. The widow as beneficiary of a trust for life in stock may realize income therefrom *only in the form of dividends. Thus will the children or strangers control the income of the widow under her trust.* The children or strangers have a right to act for their own best interests. They are not required to serve as the widow's "keeper". It is conceivable, therefore, even assuming that the children or strangers (acting through the then directors) exercise honest and sound business judgment, that no dividends will be declared for several years, or, if declared, may prove to be wholly inadequate. During that period of time, the widow will be without support. It is no answer that the widow (through the trustee) would be able to maintain an action against the directors to compel a dividend declaration. Exceptionally convincing must be the showing before a court will interfere in the internal management of a corporation by ordering the declaration of a dividend. Lockley v. Robie, 276 App.Div. 291, 296, 94 N.Y.S.2d 335, 339, modified 301 N.Y. 371, 93 N.E.2d 895. The directors decide if and when a dividend shall be declared and the amount thereof, and, unless fraud, bad faith, dishonesty or a clear abuse of discretion can be established, the judgment of the directors in withholding dividends is recognized as conclusive. Gordon v. Elliman, 306 N.Y. 456, 459, 119 N.E.2d 331, 333; see, also, City Bank Farmers' Trust Co. v. Hewitt Realty Co., 257 N.Y. 62, 67–68, 177 N.E. 309, 311, 76 A.L.R. 881. Thus, in view of the tremendous burden imposed upon a stockholder in that type of action, we may fairly conclude that the bequest of a "law suit" to a surviving spouse was never intended by the Legislature as the kind of beneficial provision which bars that spouse's right of election under section 18 of the Decedent Estate Law.

In arriving at our conclusion in the present case, we are assuming that in the event the directors were to withhold dividends and thus deprive the widow of income under her trust, that such directors were acting honestly and in good faith. We are not even precluding the possibility that the directors might declare dividends regularly and in an adequate amount. It is *possible*, however, because of the peculiar nature of the trust *res*, and the potentially antagonistic interests of the children (or strange third parties, in the event the children sold their interests to them) and the widow—irrespective of whether or not the directors act properly—that the widow will receive no income or inadequate income under her trust. Viewed in the light of that possibility, it is plain that the prospects of the widow under her trust are *insecure*. It follows that the trust set up by the testator for the widow's life does not constitute with reasonable certainty a real and substantial benefit to her within the contemplation of section 18 of the Decedent Estate Law. Although, in form, it satisfactorily complies with the requirements of the statute, it is illusory in fact. It is immaterial that the testator *did not intend* that the widow should be deprived of her rights as surviving spouse. "The only pertinent inquiry is as to whether *in fact* such a result has been accomplished." Matter of Bommer's Will, 159 Misc. 511, 520, 288 N.Y.S. 419, 432, supra. We believe that the tone of section 18 was aptly pointed up by Surrogate Wingate in the Bommer case as follows, 159 Misc. 511, 519, 288 N.Y.S. 419, 430, supra: "The entire theory underlying the enactments contained in section 18 is that the widow is not to be viewed as an almoner beseeching the bestowal of the crumbs from her master's table, but as a partner and aliquot co-owner of the family property which chances to rest in the legal ownership of the nominal head of the family partnership."

It is also urged that even were the widow to receive one third of the corporate stock outright, rather than as beneficiary of a trust comprising such stock, she would be in no better a position. With that contention we do not agree. As owner of the stock outright, the widow would at least be in a position to sell her interest if she so desired, i.e., if no or inadequate dividends were forthcoming. It may be that she would realize a paltry consideration were she to sell such a minority interest in closed corporations to a third party. That, however, would not be the only alternative open to her. She might very well be able to realize a substantial consideration were she to sell her interest to either or both of her children. Furthermore, assuming the children, at some subsequent time during the life of the widow, decided to abandon the corporate businesses, an attractive offer could be made to a third-party purchaser. That is, the children and the widow, by banding their interests together, could sell all the outstanding interests in such businesses. In this way, the children, as well as the widow, could obtain a substantial remuneration for their respective interests.

In view of the foregoing considerations, we believe that the widow's trust does not measure up to the type of trust demanded by section 18 and that she, therefore, may exercise her right of election against the terms of the will as in intestacy. See, also, Matter of Halperin's Will, 201 Misc. 763, 106 N.Y.S.2d 96.

* * *

DYE, FROESSEL, VAN VOORHIS and BURKE, JJ., concur with FULD, J.

CONWAY, C. J., dissents in an opinion, in which DESMOND, J., concurs.

In each proceeding: Order modified, with costs to all parties appearing separately and filing separate briefs, payable out of the estate, and case remitted to the Surrogate's Court for proceedings not inconsistent with the opinion herein.

Notes

1. In In re Byrnes' Will, 260 N.Y. 465, 184 N.E. 56, 87 A.L.R. 223 (1933) reargument denied 261 N.Y. 623, 185 N.E. 765 (cited in both the majority and dissenting opinions) the court upheld the widow's right of election against a will which would have given her income in a trust "for life or until her remarriage." The aftermath of this case illustrates the administrative problems posed by an election which disrupts the dispositive pattern of the will. Matter of Byrnes, 149 Misc. 449, 267 N.Y.S. 627 (Surr.1933). The will contained preliminary legacies to three charities aggregating $40,000. The residue which came out to $140,000 was bequeathed in trust, income to the wife until death or remarriage, remainder to the children of testator's deceased brother Ronald "who were living at the time of the death or remarriage of the widow." The testator had no children and therefore his widow was entitled on election to one half his estate outright or $90,000. The Surrogate held that all the gifts would abate pro rata to make up the $90,000, thus leaving $20,000 to the charities and $70,000 to the trust. It was further held that the $70,000 remainder could not be accelerated and immediately distributed to the then living children of Ronald. The remainder was contingent, and by its terms the beneficiaries could only be determined on the death or remarriage of the widow.

2. The majority opinion cites Matter of Wittner's Estate, 301 N.Y. 461, 95 N.E.2d 798 (1950) in which it was held that a testamentary trust which is subject to a power of invasion exercisable for a person other than the spouse does not satisfy the requirements of the statute because the spouse does not have a guaranteed share. Even when the threat to the spouse's share is not very substantial the court has permitted the spouse to elect to take against the will. In re Estate of Plimack, 72 Misc.2d 476, 339 N.Y.S.2d 410 (1973). The spouse cannot elect against a will which gives her a choice between two alternative dispositions one of which satisfies the statutory requirements. Matter of Jacobsen, 61 Misc.2d 317, 306 N.Y.S.2d 290 (1969) affirmed 33 A.D.2d 760, 306 N.Y.S.2d 297 (1969).

Note on Valuation of Life Estates and Remainders

The actuarial value of a life estate is determined by use of an annuity formula, coupled with (a) an estimate of life expectancy that is based on mortality experience tables, and (b) more or less arbitrary assumptions as to the probable income from the property and as to the value of the use of money, i.e., interest rate.

An annuity is the right to receive a fixed periodic payment for a stipulated period—e.g., $1000 every July 1 to and including July 1, 1990; $100 on the 15th of every month for 120 months. The term is also applied where the duration of the fixed payments is measured by a life or lives— a *life annuity* being different from a *life estate* in that the latter yields the actual income of specified property whatever the income turns out to be, rather than a fixed amount. For present purposes, however, the term "annuity" is used to mean a *term annuity*, i.e., an annuity lasting for a predetermined period of months or years.

The *principal* of an annuity (i.e., its basic cost, exclusive of loading for expense and profit of the person undertaking the obligation to make the annuity payments) is related to the periodic *annuity payments* by the following formula:

$$P = A \times \frac{1 - (1+r)^{-n}}{r}$$

where P = the annuity principal
   A = the periodic payment (made at the end of each period)
   r = the interest rate for each payment period (compounded at each periodic payment date)
   n = the number of periodic payments

Example:

If $22,000 is the basic cost of an annuity whereby the annuitant will receive a fixed annual payment starting one year from now and continuing nine years thereafter, for a total period of ten years, and if the interest rate is 4% per annum, how large will each annual payment be?

P = 22,000
A = ?
r = .04
n = 10

$$22,000 = A \times \frac{1-(1+.04)^{-10}}{.04} = A \times \frac{1-\dfrac{1}{(1.04)^{10}}}{.04} = A \times \frac{1-.675567}{.04}$$

$$A = 22,000 \times \frac{.04}{1-.675567}$$

$$A = 2712.40$$

Proof:

Year	Balance at beginning of year	Annual interest (.04)	Total	Less 2712.40 (balance at end of year)
1	22000.00	880.00	22880.00	20167.60
2	20167.60	806.70	20974.30	18261.90
3	18261.90	730.48	18992.38	16279.98
4	16279.98	651.20	16931.18	14218.78
5	14218.78	568.75	14787.53	12075.13
6	12075.13	483.01	12558.14	9845.74
7	9845.74	393.83	10239.57	7527.17
8	7527.17	301.09	7828.26	5115.86
9	5115.86	204.63	5320.49	2608.09
10	2608.09	104.32	2712.41	.01

It will thus be seen that P ($22,000) is the present value of the right to receive $2712.40 a year for the next ten years.

The valuation of a life estate is based on the annuity formula. The value of n is assumed to be the life expectancy of the life tenant, as determined from some one of the many mortality experience tables that have been compiled. (The tables vary among themselves because of differences in the underlying data. The selection of the table is therefore a significant determinant. Ordinarily the selection is made by statute—on a more or less arbitrary basis.) The *actual* expectancy, e.g., in the case of a cancer sufferer, is usually deemed immaterial.

A second assumption is also made, namely, that the income of the property will be a certain percentage of its value. In the case of a life estate (unlike an annuity) this is an arbitrary assumption, since the actual income is not known precisely, at the beginning. The percentage is ordinarily prescribed by statute, again on a general and more or less arbitrary basis—the *actual* income expectancy (which would be quite low for a growth stock and might be quite high for rental real estate) being usually deemed immaterial. This percentage, when applied to the value of the property in which the life estate exists, fixes the value of A, the periodic payment.

The same percentage is customarily used as the value of r. This is not logically necessary, but is convenient and no more arbitrary than the other assumptions.

With these values of n, A and r, the annuity formula can be used to find P, which is the value of the life estate. The value of the remainder is determined by subtracting P from the value of the whole property. By use of a different formula, the value of the remainder can be computed directly; but for present purposes the foregoing analysis should be sufficient. In actual practice the attorney does not use the formula at all, but resorts to published tables—which are easily available. A representative sample will be found in Am.Jur.2d Desk Book, 339–357 (1962).

SECTION FIVE. PROTECTION OF THE SPOUSE— COMMUNITY PROPERTY

AMERICAN LAW OF PROPERTY
Vol. II, 121–122 (1952) (footnotes omitted).

The Concept of Community Property. Community of property between husband and wife in one form or another has existed as a legal system for centuries in large portions of the civilized world and is at the present time the dominant system of marital property rights in jurisdictions outside of the Anglo-American sphere. The unifying principle of a marital community with respect to property underlies the variant forms of the system despite diversity as to the kind of property owned in community and the precise nature of the individual rights of the spouses with relation thereto.

The Spanish type of community property has found root in a limited but important segment of the United States. This system may be generally described as one under which the husband and wife become co-owners of property acquired during the marriage by either or both through labor, industry, or skill. In contrast to the modernized common law system of individual ownership in the spouse individually acquiring the property, the community system creates a co-ownership in both spouses of property individually acquired by either the husband or wife other than by gift, bequest, descent or devise. Moreover, this co-ownership has no counterpart in the common law pattern of marital rights because the basic concept is one of co-ownership as conjugal partners in gains and acquisitions. This partnership or community continues during the marriage with managerial powers vested largely or exclusively in the husband. [Editors' Note: as explained below, the law has been changed to give husband and wife equal rights of management and control.] Property owned by a spouse at the time of the marriage remains the separate property of that spouse and does not become part of the community fund. On the death of a spouse one-half of the community property passes according to the testamentary disposition of the decedent or, in the event of intestacy, to those persons entitled to take under the applicable statutes; the other half goes to the survivor. [Editors' Note: the intestate succession statutes of a number of community property states give the decedent's half of the community property to the surviving spouse in addition to her or his own half. See e.g. Cal.Prob. Code § 6401(a).]

The system in the United States is almost entirely statutory, and there are substantial differences in the statutes of the several states [Editors' Note: the states include Arizona, California, Idaho, Louisiana, Nevada, New Mexico, Texas and Washington] which have received the system. As might be expected, the statutes even when similar have been given diverse interpretations by the courts in many instances, with the result that the system has become highly complex whether viewed as a whole or in relation to the law of a particular state. Despite these variations the basic framework is that outlined above.

The California Constitution does not define community property, but, in Article 1, § 21, it gives the following definition of separate property: "Property owned before marriage or acquired during marriage by gift, will, or inheritance is separate property". The presumption is that all other property belongs to the community. Not surprisingly, the concept is simpler to state than to apply. Disputes, which require characterization of an asset as separate or community, arise in a variety of contexts. Thus, for example on death or divorce it is necessary to determine the nature of commingled accounts and assets, earnings that accrued during the marriage from separate property (e.g., husband's fulltime occupation is managing the substantial estate he inherited from his mother), property located in a common law state that was acquired with community assets, and rights in the working spouse's postemployment retirement benefits, to identify but a few problem areas. Because of its origins in the civil law system, community property law is largely statutory, and therefore responses to such questions vary depending upon the laws of the particular jurisdiction. For the responses in California, see Bruch, The Definition and Division of Marital Property in California: Towards Parity and Simplicity, 33 Hastings L.J. 771 (1982).

During the decade of the seventies, all eight community property states amended their laws to give equal management rights to both spouses over their community property.* For the ways in which the previous system discriminated against the wife, see Note, Equal Rights and Equal Protection: Who Has Management and Control?, 46 S.Cal.L.Rev. 892 (1973). The new rules vary among the states, and individual statutes must be consulted. The following brief description focuses on the law of California.

---

* Had the states not taken remedial action, the Supreme Court would have mandated it. Kirchberg v. Feenstra, 450 U.S. 455, 101 S.Ct. 1195, 67 L.Ed.2d 428 (1981) (former Louisiana law giving husband managerial control over community property unconstitutional as a denial of equal protection).

Since 1975, each spouse is vested with the right to manage his or her separate property and both have the equal right to manage the community property. The statute explicitly states that community property business is under the sole control of the spouse who is operating it. In addition, banks and similar financial institutions deal only with named account holders, rendering assets in those accounts de facto separate property. In this chapter, we have been examining the division of marital property at death and the protections available to a spouse from disinheritance by the unilateral acts of the other spouse which remove assets from the marital estate. The California statute states that one spouse may not make a gift of community property in any form without the written consent of the other spouse. West's Ann.Cal.Civ. Code § 5125. Either spouse may sell community personal property for valuable consideration, but both spouses must join in the sale of household goods and in the sale, encumbrance, or lease for longer than one year of community real property. West's Ann.Cal.Civ. Code §§ 5125, 5127. The statute imposes an obligation of "good faith" on the spouse who is exercising management powers.

The application of these statutes has yet to be tested in court. If the marriage is stable, joint control of assets is not likely to create any problems. If, on the other hand, the marriage is shaky or one of the spouses is a spendthrift, community personal property may be dissipated, and the aggrieved spouse may be without an effective remedy to obtain reimbursement from the defaulting spouse's separate property. A divorce court may award an injured spouse compensation for the other spouse's deliberate misappropriation of community property, but the probate court is not vested with comparable powers. One commentator has identified a number of potential problem areas in the California law which require remedial action by the legislature. Bruch, Management Powers and Duties Under California's Property Laws: Recommendations for Reform, 34 Hastings L.J. 229 (1982) at pps. 233–234:

> Left totally unclarified by current law are the extent to which other actions by one spouse may violate the statutory good faith management duty and the nature of possible remedies during marriage for a spouse injured by a violation of the Civil Code's management standards. Several situations can be imagined in which a remedy might fairly be requested to vindicate such marital property rights. If a spouse refuses to reveal what community property he or she has, or in which form it is being held, relief should be made available by way of an action for disclosure. Further, if one spouse controls community assets in a business or account that is subject to his or her sole management and control and refuses to make those assets or some reasonable portion of them available to the other spouse for legitimate community purposes (such as the payment of outstanding obligations), an action for access to the community property for good cause shown should be authorized. Moreover, a spouse whose name has not been included on the title of a community asset should be able to insist that the title be corrected to give notice of his or her ownership interest. On the other hand, if spousal consent is required by statute but is withheld without good reason, or if one spouse is unable to consent due to physical or mental

incapacity, procedures should permit a court to dispense with the consent requirement for that transaction or course of transactions.

If there has been long-term mismanagement by one spouse, the other spouse should be permitted to request that the couple's finances be severed, or that the financially prudent spouse be made solely responsible for the management and control of the couple's community property. A division of existing community property and clarification of the parties' obligations to existing creditors should be available in conjunction with such litigation. If gifts or other transfers have been wrongfully made, or if community property has been wrongfully applied to debts for which separate property was initially liable, the injured spouse should have options available during marriage to require that the other spouse's separate property or other community property be used to redress the injury. Additionally, a number of remedies or protections against third parties are in order that would not unduly infringe upon their interests, yet would avoid serious hardship to one spouse as a result of the other spouse's irresponsibility. These remedies would include rights to rescind or to set aside unauthorized transfers of community property and a right to insist upon a fair marshalling of assets on behalf of the debtor when creditors' claims are satisfied. Finally, the mutual obligations and protections governing property management by spouses should extend into the post-divorce period for so long as common property remains undivided by agreement or court order.

Note

A court in a common law jurisdiction may have occasion to apply community property principles when determining ownership of local assets purchased with community property. For example, a California couple plans to move their domicile to New York. The husband precedes his wife and purchases a home, acquires some stock, and opens a bank account, using community property to fund each transaction. He puts title to the various assets in his own name, with the intention of making them joint following his wife's arrival, but dies before having an opportunity to do so. The situation may be further complicated if they have moved several times. A number of states (e.g., N.Y.—McKinney's EPTL §§ 6–6.1 through .7) have adopted the Uniform Disposition of Community Property Rights at Death Act (8A ULA 121–134), which provides that where the spouses have not indicated an intent to sever their community rights property acquired by or traceable to community assets will retain its character as community property. Thus, the wife is entitled to one half the New York realty and assets even though she may have been entitled to less by intestacy or under the terms of her husband's will. The commentary to the New York statute describes the uniform act as "basically a codification of existing law." § 6–6.3 states that the surviving spouse does not have a right of election in the deceased spouse's half of the property, and 6–6.5 makes secure the rights of purchasers and creditors who have relied on the title being in one spouse's name.

SECTION SIX. PROTECTION OF THE SPOUSE— UNIFORM MARITAL PROPERTY ACT

The concept of marriage creating a partnership between husband and wife, with the result that property acquired by either one of them during marriage is to be shared as if a partnership asset, is rapidly becoming a basic tenet of American property law. It finds expression in the marital deduction provisions of the federal estate and gift taxes and is the principle that underlies the statutes, now enacted in practically all of the common law states, authorizing the equitable distribution at divorce of property accumulated during the marriage, regardless of the name in which the property is held. See e.g., N.Y.—McKinney's Dom.Rel.L. § 236, Part B; Cheadle, The Development of Sharing Principles in Common Law Marital Property States, 28 U.C.L.A.L.Rev. 1269 (1981). The Uniform Marital Property Act, * adopted by the National Conference of Commissioners on Uniform State Laws in 1983, converts the sharing principle into ownership rights during the marriage so that on the termination of the marriage by divorce or death the right of each spouse to half the property is already established. While the act is designed primarily for use in common law states, it is carefully crafted to make more precise the rights and remedies of each spouse and to avoid the deficiencies which, Professor Bruch suggested in the above excerpt, exist in the California community property law.

The Act adopts the community property distinction between marital and individual property. Property acquired during marriage is marital property, while individual property consists of property owned before marriage or acquired at any time by gift or inheritance. Appreciation in the value of individual property retains its character as individual but income earned by it becomes marital property. Special rules are set out to deal with commingled individual and marital assets and with life insurance and deferred employee benefits. Both spouses are granted a present undivided one-half interest in the marital property.

Although title no longer governs ownership of the property, it does determine who has the rights of management and control. The wife has control over assets held in her name, the husband over assets in his name, and both of them over assets held jointly. Third persons who rely on title are protected. The Act does, however, contain a number of safeguards against unilateral dissipation of marital assets by one spouse.

§ 2. Responsibility Between Spouses

(a) Each spouse shall act in good faith with respect to the other spouse in matters involving marital property or other property of the other spouse. This obligation may not be varied by a marital property agreement.

(b) Management and control by a spouse of that spouse's property that is not marital property in a manner that limits, diminishes, or fails to produce income from that property does not violate subsection (a).

§ 6. Gifts of Marital Property to Third Persons

(a) A spouse acting alone may give to a third person marital property that the spouse has the right to manage and control only if the value of

---

* The full text of the Act, with explanatory notes, appears in the 1984 Pocket Part to Vol. 9A ULA 19–54.

the marital property given to the third person does not aggregate more than [$500] in a calendar year, or a larger amount if, when made, the gift is reasonable in amount considering the economic position of the spouses.   Any other gift of marital property to a third person is subject to subsection (b) unless both spouses act together in making the gift.

(b) If a gift of marital property by a spouse does not comply with subsection (a), the other spouse may bring an action to recover the property or a compensatory judgment in place of the property, to the extent of the noncompliance.   The other spouse may bring the action against the donating spouse, the recipient of the gift, or both.   The action must be commenced within the earlier of one year after the other spouse has notice of the gift or 3 years after the gift.   If the recovery occurs during marriage, it is marital property.   If the recovery occurs after a dissolution or the death of either spouse, it is limited to one-half of the value of the gift and is individual property.

§ 15. Interspousal Remedies

(a) A spouse has a claim against the other spouse for breach of the duty of good faith imposed by Section 2 resulting in damage to the claimant spouse's present undivided one-half interest in marital property.

(b) A court may order an accounting of the property and obligations of the spouses and may determine rights of ownership in, beneficial enjoyment of, or access to, marital property and the classification of all property of the spouses.

(c) A court may order that the name of a spouse be added to marital property held in the name of the other spouse alone, except with respect to:

(1) a partnership interest held by the other spouse as a general partner;

(2) an interest in a professional corporation, professional association, or similar entity held by the other spouse as a stockholder or member;

(3) an asset of an unincorporated business if the other spouse is the only spouse involved in operating or managing the business; or

(4) any other property if the addition would adversely affect the rights of a third person.

(d) Except as provided otherwise in Section 6(b), a spouse must commence an action against the other spouse under subsection (a) not later than 3 years after acquiring actual knowledge of the facts giving rise to the claim.

———

A married couple may enter into a marital property agreement that varies most provisions of the Act.   If they have not done so, each spouse has the power of testamentary disposition over his or her undivided half; to the extent he or she fails to exercise that power, his or her half will devolve by intestacy.

This Act is destined to receive a great deal of attention in the coming years.   Powerful pressure for its enactment is to be expected in the common law states, and community property states may well be asked to consider for adoption the sections of the Act that make the rights and remedies of each spouse more precise. In 1983, Wisconsin adopted the Act to become effective in 1986. For a detailed description of the Wisconsin experience and analysis of the Act's anticipated impact on existing law, see 57 Wisconsin Bar Bul. No. 7, 1–63 (July 1984).

SECTION SEVEN. PROTECTION OF CHILDREN

Compare the following statements:

The Commission has left to be considered by others whether a parent has a moral duty, which should be made a legal duty, to provide for the support and maintenance of children during the period of their dependence. Should the law compel a parent at death to provide for his helpless dependents? The right of a testator to pauperize his helpless dependents now exists under our law. When will the State step in and take away that privilege? When will such public policy be changed? The State is vitally interested in the care of minor children from both a pecuniary and a social viewpoint.

> Slater, Reforms in the New York Law of Property,
> reproduced in Report of New York Decedent
> Estate Commission, 293 (1930).

The legal right of the next of kin to inherit a part at any rate of the deceased's property—observed in cases of intestacy in England and in all cases in other Western European countries—is often thought to have some sort of moral justification, particularly where the next of kin are the widows or children of the deceased. They had a moral claim to his support during life, it is argued, and they have a moral claim to the support his property gives after death. One is expected to conjure up a picture of a penniless widow, or of orphans in their 'teens. Their father's hard-earned savings have rightly been put by for their benefit. Have they not a moral claim to these savings? Certainly no wise State, confronted with such a case, would deny that claim; it would rather hope that the savings were sufficient to pay for the orphans' upkeep, lest the ratepayers have to contribute.

But it is nonsense to suggest that the great bulk of the property bequeathed and inherited goes to sustain indigent widows and young children, who cannot fend for themselves. Most of the widows of rich men have, in fact, some property of their own; and the large majority of penniless widows have practically penniless husbands from whom they will never inherit anything substantial, whatever the law on the subject. Again, the average age of children who survive well-to-do parents is somewhere about forty. The description "children", for inheritors in the direct line of descent, is therefore apt to be misleading. The sons who inherit large estates are usually men rather beyond the prime of life, at the time of their inheritance, whose parents gave them in youth an expensive training, and who were already receiving before their inheritance a considerable income whether from earnings and savings, or from gifts of property made during their parents' lifetime. The advent of a large inheritance in such cases is only likely to deter them from exerting themselves to earn a living.

But even if all children were too young or otherwise unfitted at the time of their parents' death to earn a livelihood by their own exertions, would our sense of justice or of social expediency demand that they should be supported at a scale of living in proportion to their parents' property? Has the child of a man with £100,000 for example, a fair claim to inherit one hundred times as much as the child of the man with £1,000? For the idea that such a claim is fair and reasonable appears to underlie the Continental law of *legitim* and the English law of inheritance in cases of intestacy. The only argument for such a claim, on the grounds of social equity, would appear to be that the parent has accumulated property with the expectation that his children will inherit, that the children have been brought up with the expectation that they will inherit, and that it is unfair and causes unhappiness to disappoint such established expectations. Yet clearly such expectations are entertained because of the laws of inheritance, and if those laws did not exist, neither would the expectations exist. We are still faced with the question of whether or not such expectations are fair and reasonable in themselves, apart from the existing law on the subject.

Personally I agree with John Stuart Mill that children may reasonably claim from their parent that he should "provide, so far as depends on him, such education and such appliances and means, as will enable them to start with a fair chance of achieving by their own exertions a successful life. *To this every child has a claim*; and I cannot admit that as a child he has a claim to more. There is a case in which these obligations present themselves in their true light, without any extrinsic circumstances to disguise or confuse them: it is that of the illegitimate child. To such a child it is generally felt that there is due from the parent the amount of provision for his welfare which will enable him to make his life on the whole a desirable one. I hold that to no child, merely as such, anything more is due than what is admitted to be due to the illegitimate child; and that no child, for whom this much has been done, has, unless on the score of previously raised expectations, any grievance, if the remainder of the parent's fortune is devoted to public uses, or to the benefit of individuals on whom in the parent's opinion it is better bestowed".

If this view is accepted, it follows that, in the large majority of cases where the sons of well-to-do parents have reached maturity before the latter's death, and have previously received education, appliances and means, which were not insufficient on grounds of expense to give them a fair start, there can be no reasonable claim to any inheritance in addition—except on the score of previously raised expectations, for which the existing law and custom must be chiefly responsible.

Wedgwood, *The Economics of Inheritance*, 189–192 (1929).

Although there continue to be expressions of concern for minor children who have been disinherited by their parents (see e.g., Fourth Report, N.Y. Commission on Estates, 184 (1965); Haskell, Restraints Upon the Disinheritance of Family Members, in Halbach, Death, Taxes and Family Property 105, 114 (1977) (proposal that provision be made for support of minor children)), no state except Louisiana has enacted legislation to require shares for them. The law does intervene for certain children in a roundabout way. On the questionable assumption that the omission of children from wills is unintended, the law, under certain circumstances, will save them their intestate shares. The justification is that the law is implementing the true intent of the testators. If they really intend to disinherit their children, they must make that intent express in their wills. The Goff case, which follows, represents an application of one of these statutes. If Mr. Goff could be revived for an interview, might he be expected to express appreciation of the law's solicitude for his true intent? In the Goff case, who presumably are awarded the estate and what moral claims do they have to it?

GOFF v. GOFF

Supreme Court of Missouri, 1944.
352 Mo. 809, 179 S.W.2d 707, 152 A.L.R. 717.

BARRETT, Commissioner. This is a suit for an accounting of rents and profits, for an injunction and to try and determine title to a tract of land in Worth County. The defendants are the legatees and devisees and the executor of the estate of Charles Granville Goff who died on September 7, 1942. The plaintiffs, Marjorie Anne Goff, age twelve, and Dean Joe Goff, age ten, are the children of Joe Goff who died on December 31, 1936. The plaintiffs assert title to the land as the grandchildren and pretermitted heirs of Charles Granville Goff, neither they nor their father, Joe Goff, being named or provided for in this will. Mo.R.S.A. § 526.

Charles Granville Goff was a farmer and spent most of his life in Worth County. About five months before his death, at the age of about sixty-six years, he went to California and stayed with a nephew, Roy S. Goff. While there and about five weeks before he died he executed his will. His will appointed his brother, Silas C. Goff, executor and provided that his executor should sell all of his property "in a manner which may seem best to him and in his discretion" and that he should distribute the proceeds as follows: $5.00 to his brother George L. Goff; $1,000.00 to his brother Silas, the executor, and the remainder between his nephews, Roy S. Goff and L. Jay Goff, equally. The second [sic] clause of the will said: "I am not married and have no children." The fifth clause said: "I hereby give and bequeath to any person who might contest this will the sum of $1.00 only, in lieu of any other share or interest in my estate, either under this will or through intestate succession."

The trial court found that Charles Granville Goff was not aware of the existence of the plaintiffs, Marjorie Anne and Dean Joe, but found that he had provided for them by item five of the will and, therefore, they were not pretermitted heirs.   The respondents contend that item five shows the testator's intention but if it does not do so clearly the extrinsic evidence, including the testator's declarations, makes definitely certain his intention that these plaintiffs were in his mind and provided for by this clause of his will.   The plaintiffs contend that the language of the will is plain and unambiguous and, therefore, the court was in error in admitting extrinsic evidence to show the testator's intention to be other than that expressed in his will.   The plaintiffs contend, in any event that the court erred in holding that the plaintiffs, grandchildren unknown to the testator, were named or provided for by item five of the will.

The facts with reference to those who are specifically named in the will are that the testator, Charles Granville Goff, was survived by two brothers, Silas and George.   One brother, Edward, predeceased the testator and his son, Roy, is one of the residuary beneficiaries.   The other residuary beneficiary is Silas' son, L. Jay Goff.   Silas was appointed executor of the will and given a bequest of $1,000.   Before Granville went to California he and his brother George quarreled over a tenant George had secured for Granville's farm.   Granville experienced some difficulty in getting the tenant off the farm and the controversy between the brothers became so bitter that Granville said to Silas: "I will sure fix it so George   *   *   *   will not participate in my property."   He told Silas' daughter, Mrs. Akard, that he "didn't want Uncle George to have anything he had."   And so, in his will, he gave his brother George five dollars.   Having made the son of his deceased brother, Edward, one of his residuary beneficiaries and having given Silas $1,000 and George five dollars, the testator specifically named or provided for every blood relative, as far as this record is concerned, except Joe or these plaintiffs.

The facts with reference to the testator, Joe and Joe's mother and their relationship to one another furnish the background for this litigation and the circumstances which the respondents claim exclude the plaintiffs as pretermitted heirs under this will.   In the 1890's the testator, Granville, was a young man living on his father's farm in Worth County. David White and his family were farm neighbors, living a few miles distant.   On October 10, 1895, Granville Goff and Cassie M. White procured a marriage license in Worth County and were married in the White home by a minister, Joshua Florea. They immediately went to Granville's home to live with his people.   After four or five weeks Cassie left the Goff home or Granville took her back to her home and she instituted an action against him for divorce in the Circuit Court of Worth County. When Cassie and Granville were married Cassie was pregnant and on February 22, 1896, a son, Joe, was born.   In her divorce action she was awarded a divorce and custody of the minor child of whom she alleged she was enceinte by Granville at the time of their marriage.   Cassie and her child remained on her father's farm, in the vicinity of the Goff's home, eight or ten years.   In 1901 Cassie married J. W. McCann, with whom she lived until his death in 1932. At the time of the trial she was living in Wisconsin with her daughters and sons.

Joe Goff was reared in the McCann home. He was married on June 21, 1929 and the plaintiffs are his children. Prior to his death in 1936 he had been cashier of the Swea City and Hawkeye banks in Iowa and at the time of his death was an assistant state bank examiner.

Silas Goff testified that Granville and Cassie were married at the request of Cassie and her father. Silas called it a "shotgun" wedding. He testified that after Granville and Cassie came to their home to live they quarreled continuously. He says that they quarreled violently over whether Granville was the father of the unborn baby—Cassie contending that he was its father and Granville denying it. Silas testified that throughout his life Granville denied Joe's paternity. A neighbor, as well as Silas and Silas' daughter, Mrs. Akard, all testified that Granville was always most reluctant to discuss Joe and the marriage to Cassie. According to this record he mentioned them but two or three times in the forty-seven years, and Ezekiel Goff, a cousin of Granville's, said that when Granville was notified of Joe's death in 1936 he said: "I am not interested." We mention and call attention to the evidence reviewed in this paragraph because it furnishes a background for the plaintiffs' contention, as the court found, that Granville Goff was not even aware of Joe's children and, therefore, could not have had them in mind and did not provide for or mention them in item five, and the defendants' contrasting contention that the testator did know of the children, had them in mind and provided for them in item five.

Silas testified that just prior to the time Granville went to California Granville was telling him about his difficulties with George and the tenant. In that conversation Granville stated that he intended to fix his business before he went to California and he said: "I will sure fix it so George and Joe's children will not participate in my property." Silas says Granville referred to Joe's children three or four times in the course of five or six years. Mrs. Akard, Silas' daughter, said that she once asked Granville whether he had ever been married and he told her he had but he denied Joe's paternity and "he told me he had these two grandchildren. I have never repeated that. He didn't want it repeated." Subsequently he told her about the quarrel with his brother George and said: "I am going to take care of those who would take care of me. I don't know of anyone but you and Jay and Roy." Then Mrs. Akard testified "he said he was going to take care of the ones that would take care of him and he very definitely said he didn't want Uncle George to have anything he had and he didn't want Joe's children to have anything because Joe was not his boy."

Joe's wife, the mother of the plaintiffs, said: "To my knowledge, I don't think he (Granville) knew there were children." There was other evidence from the plaintiffs indicating that Granville did not know of Joe's two children. But, as we have said, the respondents contend that item five was designed to and did mention and provide for these children regardless of whether the testator knew of their existence or not.

Deferring to and accepting, as we do in this instance, the trial court's finding and judgment (based for the most part on the credibility, weight and probative force of the evidence) that Marjorie Anne Goff and Dean Joe Goff are the grandchildren of the testator and the children of his deceased son Joe and that "Charles Granville Goff did not know of the existence of the plaintiffs" we eliminate all questions as to the admissibility of the extrinsic evidence, as to which there may be some doubt. See and compare the annotations in 94 A.L.R. 26, 209–211; 51 L.R.A., N.S., 646; 1 Page, Wills, Sec. 530; Thomas v. Black, 113 Mo. 66, 20 S.W. 657; McCoy v. Bradbury, 290 Mo. 650, 235 S.W. 1047 and Bond v. Riley, 317 Mo. 594, 296 S.W. 401; Willard v. Darrah, 168 Mo. 660, 68 S.W. 1023, 90 Am.St.Rep. 468. But with this assumption of fact as a starting point the conclusion that they were not provided for by item five of this will within the meaning of Section 526 is inescapable.

In item five of this will Marjorie Anne's and Dean Joe's father, Joe Goff (who to the testator's knowledge predeceased him), is neither "named" nor "provided for" specifically and hence the children are not excluded by reason of their father's being named or provided for, which would clearly and on the face of the will show that the testator remembered his child and intentionally disinherited his descendants whether he knew of their existence or not, as was the fact in Lawnick v. Schultz, 325 Mo. 294, 28 S.W.2d 658, and Miller v. Aven, 327 Mo. 20, 34 S.W.2d 116. The word "child" or "grandchildren" does not appear in item five and so they were not all remembered collectively and excluded as a class or provided for as a class as was the case with McCourtney v. Mathes, 47 Mo. 533, and Ernshaw v. Smith, Mo.Sup., 2 S.W.2d 803.

The respondents say that item five is an exclusion clause and is sufficient to exclude the plaintiffs because "through intestate succession" could only mean an heir. In this respect the instance is comparable to Williamson v. Roberts, Mo.Sup., 187 S.W. 19. There the testator had five children, one of whom was an unmarried, epileptic daughter. He was particularly anxious to provide for her and devised his land to her without mentioning the other children. In a separate item of his will he said: "I desire that all the rest and residue and remainder of my estate be disposed of as the law directs" and it was urged that this language was a sufficient compliance with the statute but the court could not find from this language that the testator had the other children in mind. As was said in Pounds v. Dale, 48 Mo. 270, 272: "He had nine children, and defendant urges that it is unreasonable to suppose that he forgot the seven while naming the two. I certainly would conjecture that all were in his mind, and that he meant to disinherit them. But it is a mere guess. The will must show upon its face that he remembered them; and though they be not directly named, there must be provisions or language that point directly to them." See also Baker v. Grossglauser, Mo.Sup., 250 S.W. 377, 378, and Wyatt v. Stillman Institute, 303 Mo. 94, 103, 260 S.W. 73.

The respondents, relying on the fact that Granville always denied Joe's paternity and the testimony of Silas and his daughter, Mrs. Akard, that Granville said he did not want Joe's children to have anything or that he would fix it so they would not get anything, contend that the testator intended to disinherit the plaintiffs and that the testator's declarations clearly identify the persons to whom he intended the exclusionary clause to apply. Our acceptance of the trial court's finding that Granville was not even aware of the plaintiffs is decisive of that contention as far as these two children are concerned, it seems to us. But, even if the argument might be made as to Joe we do not think it applicable under our statute. It is true that there are two cases in Missouri which say that the statute applies only when the children or descendants were "unintentionally omitted." But the complete quotation from one of them shows what the court meant when it said, " * * * the object of it is to produce an intestacy only when the child, or the descendant of such child, is unknown or forgotten, and thus unintentionally omitted." McCourtney v. Mathes, 47 Mo. 533. And, as we have previously pointed out with reference to the Lawnick case, in both instances the testator used the word "children" and so his heirs or descendants were not unintentionally omitted.

The soundness of the reasons for, the policy of and the practical operation of the statutes with reference to pretermitted heirs are not now open to question. It is sufficient to say that such statutes are a limitation upon and modify one's unlimited and unqualified power and right to disinherit and to dispose of one's property. The policy behind the statutes [:]"Fundamentally, (it) is a desire to prevent inadvertent disinheritance." 29 Col.L.R., 748, 750. To accomplish the purpose of preventing inadvertent disinheritance, from which there was no relief at common law, two types of statutes have been enacted. One is called the Massachusetts type statute and the other is commonly called the Missouri type statute. 32 Ill.L.R. 1. The Massachusetts type statutes provide that if the testator omits to provide for any of his children or the issue of a deceased child such omitted child or issue shall take as though the testator had died intestate "unless it appears that the omission was intentional and not occasioned by accident or mistake." G.L. (Ter.Ed.) c. 191, § 20. The Missouri type statutes provide that if a person make his last will and dies leaving a child or descendants of a child "not named or provided for in such will, * * * every such testator * * * shall be deemed to die intestate" as to the omitted child or descendants. Mo.R.S.A. § 526. The Massachusetts type statutes emphasize intention and "intention is the material factor in determining its applicability." Annotation 65 A.L.R. 472, 473. It is for this reason that many of the respondents' cited cases are inapplicable; they are taken from California where a Massachusetts type statute has been enacted and "The section requires that the omission appear from the will to be intentional," there is "no requirement * * * either that a child be named in the will or that he be provided for therein." In re Estate of Lombard, 16 Cal.App.2d 526, 60 P.2d 1000, 1001; In re Estate of Allmaras, 24 Cal.App.2d 457, 75 P.2d 557; In re Estate of Kurtz, 190 Cal. 146, 210 P. 959. On the other hand, the Missouri type statutes omit all reference to intention and the statutes, by their terms, arbitrarily apply unless the child or descendant is named or provided for. Annotation 65 A.L.R. 472, 481; 1 Page, Wills, Secs. 526, 528; 16 Am.Jur., Secs. 82, 85. Under these statutes it is immaterial that the testator intended to disinherit a child or descendants of a deceased child unless there is some language or provision in his will indicative of his purpose. Annotation 94 A.L.R. 26, 211; 51 L.R.A.,N.S., 646; 1 Page, Wills, Sec. 530; Thomas v. Black, 113 Mo. 66, 20 S.W. 657. Joe, having predeceased Granville, could not have been intended or included in the phrase "or through intestate succession" and, as we have said, the court found that Granville did not know of Joe's children. Furthermore, the first [sic] clause of the will says, "I am not married and have no children," and so, obviously, he could not have had children or their descendants in mind. Even if he knew of these plaintiffs he must have regarded their status as foreclosed by Cassie's divorce or Joe's death, of which he had been informed in 1936. Wadsworth v. Brigham, 125 Or. 428, 259 P. 299, 266 P. 875; In re Parrott's Estate, 45 Nev. 318, 203 P. 258.

Finally, it is argued that the phrase "I hereby give and bequeath to any person who might contest this will the sum of $1.00 only," shows that the testator "meant to exclude someone." And the respondents argue that the will shows that "someone" meant any person not provided for in the will and included these plaintiffs or anyone who would share in his estate by intestate succession. The respondents emphasize the word "contest" and urge that the word was used in a generic sense and not in the restricted sense of a statutory will contest. But there is nothing in this record nor in the context in which the word is used to indicate that it was used with reference to the plaintiffs or anyone else occupying their relationship to the testator and the will. A pretermitted child, under the statute, takes independently of the will and has no remedy by way of attacking the will itself or its probate. Schneider v. Koester, 54 Mo. 500; Cox v. Cox, 101 Mo. 168, 13 S.W. 1055; Story v. Story, 188 Mo. 110, 86 S.W. 225; Campbell v. St. Louis Union Trust Co., 346 Mo. 200, 139 S.W.2d 935, 135 A.L.R. 316; annotation 123 A.L.R. 1073, 1084. It may be that in some uses of the word the plaintiffs "contest" the will but nevertheless the will, though it does not name pretermitted heirs, is valid in all other respects (Gibson v. Johnson, 331 Mo. 1198, 56 S.W.2d 783, 88 A.L.R. 369) and in the absence of other circumstances with reference to the clause other than the testator's general intent, not expressed in his will, it cannot be assumed that the word was used in the sense of applying to these plaintiffs.

It is our view, under the assumed facts, that neither the testator's child, Joe, nor Joe's descendants, Marjorie Anne and Dean Joe, were "named or provided for in" his will and he is "deemed" to have died intestate as to them. Thomas v. Black, supra; Williamson v. Roberts, supra; Barker v. Hayes, 347 Mo. 265, 147 S.W.2d 429.

The judgment is reversed and the cause is remanded for further proceedings consistent with this opinion.

WESTHUES and BOHLING, CC., concur.

PER CURIAM.

The foregoing opinion by BARRETT, C., is adopted as the opinion of the Court.

All concur.

Notes

1. The statutes under discussion in the Goff case protect "pretermitted" ("passed by", "omitted", "not provided for") issue of the testator, born *either before or after* the execution of the will, from inadvertent disinheritance. Such statutes, varying considerably in phraseology and construction, exist in about one-half of the states. Rees, American Wills Statutes, 46 Va.L.Rev. 856, 892–894 (1960). They should be distinguished from provisions existing in other states which protect only such children as are born *after* the making of the will. These latter statutes are roughly of two types: the after-born child effects a total revocation of the will (Conn.Gen.Stat.Ann. § 45–162) or revokes the will pro tanto to make up the amount of his or her share (Ill.—S.H.A. ch. 110½, § 4–10). The afterborn children statutes serve a similar purpose to the pretermission statutes, but, to the extent generalization is possible, operate in a slightly different manner. Unlike most omission statutes, the subsequent birth statutes apply only to the birth of a child, not children's issue, and make the intention of the testator either immaterial or require that intention to be shown by provisions in the will and not by extrinsic evidence (cf. Missouri's pretermission statute described in the Goff case). See generally, Rees, American Will Statutes, 46 Va.L.Rev. 856, 892–898 (1960); Mathews, Pretermitted Heirs: An Analysis of Statutes, 29 Col.L.Rev. 748 (1929); Evans, Should Pretermitted Issue Be Entitled to Inherit?, 31 Calif.L.Rev. 263 (1943).

2. There are decisions going both ways on the issue presented in the principal case whether testamentary provisions denying the existence of children or disinheriting "contestants" sufficiently mention children to preclude them from taking as pretermitted heirs. A sampling of recent cases that are in agreement with the Goff ruling and hold that such language does not bar a claim under a pretermission statute include: Matter of Estate of Padilla, 97 N.M. 508, 641 P.2d 539 (1982) ("I declare I have no children whom I have omitted to name or provide for herein"); Estate of Gardner, 21 Cal.3d 620, 147 Cal. Rptr. 184, 580 P.2d 684 (1978) (disinheritance of every person not named in the will); but on the other side are cases holding that a bequest of $1 to any person who makes a claim against the estate is sufficient to bar a claim under the statute: Estate of Hilton, 98 N.M. 420, 649 P.2d 488 (1982) (nominal gift to contestants sufficient to disinherit grandchildren); Estate of Hirschi, 113 Cal. App.3d 681, 170 Cal.Rptr. 186 (1981) (reviews the California cases), but see Estate of Leonetti, 113 Cal.App.3d 378, 171 Cal.Rptr. 303 (1981) (evidence admitted to show that language was not intended to disinherit grandchildren). Mere mention of a person's name is enough to render the pretermission statute inapplicable. See e.g., In re Estate of Osgood, 122 N.H. 961, 453 A.2d 838 (1982) (bequest to the "children of my son Neil" mentioned Neil and precluded him from making a claim as a pretermitted heir). The provisions in the will do not have to be precisely accurate if the court can find in the words intent to disinherit. Testator stated that he made no bequest to the "four grandchildren of my deceased son, Stewart Voden." Held, this statement was sufficient to take the deceased son's four children out of the pretermission statute. In re Estate of Robinson, 252 Or. 110, 447 P.2d 94 (1968). Another case, however,

involved a will which contained a bequest "to my step daughter Shirley McGuire Hamilton" of $1.00. Four years after the execution of this will testator formally adopted Shirley. Held that the testator referred to her only as a stepdaughter, a status in which she had no legal rights as an heir, and did not intend to exclude her as a child and that she was therefore entitled to take as a pretermitted child. In re Estate of Hamilton, 73 Wn.2d 865, 441 P.2d 768 (1968). Many statutes specifically include adopted children within the statutory coverage, but, even in the absence of a statute, the cases have generally arrived at the same result. See e.g., Estate of Marshall, 27 Wn.App. 895, 621 P.2d 187 (1980) (adult adopted child may claim as pretermitted heir); Annot., 105 A.L.R. 1176.

The debate as to which approach, that of Massachusetts or Missouri, on the admission of extrinsic evidence is preferable continues. See e.g., Crump's Estate v. Freeman, 614 P.2d 1096 (Okl.1980) (adopts the Missouri approach). It appears that Massachusetts has more adherents. See Annot., Admissibility of Extrinsic Evidence to Show Testator's Intention as to Omission of Provision for Child, 88 A.L.R.2d 616 (annotation to the leading California case, Torregano's Estate, 54 Cal.2d 234, 5 Cal.Rptr. 137, 352 P.2d 505 (1960).

3. At first reading the policy justifications for these statutes seem appealing. Questions, however, quickly come to mind. A pretermission statute assumes that the testator does not know of the existence or whereabouts of his or her children or, if they are dead, of his or her grandchildren. Does that assumption accord with modern-day probabilities? An afterborn child statute can work to distort an estate plan to the detriment of the best interests of the family. The husband executes a simple will leaving his entire estate to his wife and making no mention of the two children who are alive at the time the will is signed. Another child is born thereafter and the husband dies without having altered his will. The statute will work to save an intestate share to the one child and the rest will go to the wife under the will. Newer statutes attempt to be more discriminating in their application. The Uniform Probate Code and New York statute are illustrative:

UPC § 2-302. [Pretermitted Children]

(a) If a testator fails to provide in his will for any of his children born or adopted after the execution of his will, the omitted child receives a share in the estate equal in value to that which he would have received if the testator had died intestate unless:

(1) it appears from the will that the omission was intentional;

(2) when the will was executed the testator had one or more children and devised substantially all his estate to the other parent of the omitted child; or

(3) the testator provided for the child by transfer outside the will and the intent that the transfer be in lieu of a testamentary provision is shown by statements of the testator or from the amount of the transfer or other evidence.

(b) If at the time of execution of the will the testator fails to provide in his will for a living child solely because he believes the child to be dead, the child receives a share in the estate equal in value to that which he would have received if the testator had died intestate.

(c) In satisfying a share provided by this section, the devises made by the will abate as provided in Section 3–902.

N.Y. EPTL 5–3.2. Revocatory Effect of Birth of Child After Execution of Will

(a) Whenever a testator, during his lifetime or after his death, has a child born after the execution of a last will, and dies leaving the after-born child unprovided for by any settlement, and neither provided for nor in any way mentioned in the will, every such child shall succeed to a portion of the testator's estate as herein provided:

(1) If the testator has one or more children living when he executes his last will, and:

(A) No provision is made therein for any such child, an after-born child is not entitled to share in the testator's estate.

(B) Provision is made therein for one or more of such children, an after-born child is entitled to share in the testator's estate, as follows:

(i) The portion of the testator's estate in which the after-born child may share is limited to the disposition made to children under the will.

(ii) The after-born child shall receive such share of the testator's estate, as limited in subparagraph (i), as he would have received had the testator include [sic] all after-born children with the children upon whom benefits were conferred under the will, and given an equal share of the estate to each such child.

(iii) To the extent that it is feasible, the interest of the after-born child in the testator's estate shall be of the same character, whether an equitable or legal life estate or in fee, as the interest which the testator conferred upon his children under the will.

(2) If the testator has no child living when he executes his last will, the after-born child succeeds to the portion of such testator's estate as would have passed to such child had the testator died intestate.

(b) The after-born child may recover the share of the testator's estate to which he is entitled, either from the other children under subparagraph (a)(1)(B) or the testamentary beneficiaries under subparagraph (a)(2), ratably, out of the portions of such estate passing to such persons under the will. In abating the interests of such beneficiaries, the character of the testamentary plan adopted by the testator shall be preserved to the maximum extent possible.

The Wisconsin statute goes further and grants discretion to the court to set an appropriate amount. Wis.Stat.Ann. § 853.25(5). It reads in part:

(5) Discretionary power of court to assign different share. If in any case under sub. (1) or (2) the court determines that the intestate share is a larger amount than the testator would have wanted to provide for the omitted child or issue of a deceased child, because it exceeds the value of a provision for another child or for issue of a deceased child under the will, or that assignment of the intestate share would unduly disrupt the testamentary scheme, the court may in its final judgment make such provision for the omitted child or issue out of the estate as it deems would best accord with the probable intent of the testator, such as assignment, outright or in trust, of any amount less than the intestate share but approximating the value of the interest of other issue, or modification of the provisions of a testamentary trust for other issue to include the omitted child or issue.

4. The usual remedy is to save for the omitted child an intestate share. The New York after-born-child statute, supra, states, however, that the omitted child is to receive the same share as other children receive under the will. Mother's will left all her estate to one son, disinheriting her other five children. Subsequent to the execution of the will, a seventh child was born. Held that the after-born child is entitled to one half rather than one seventh of the estate. Estate of Newman, 114 Misc.2d 434, 451 N.Y.S.2d 637 (Surr.Ct.1982).

5. Except in Louisiana these statutes do not prohibit disinheritance. Under authority which has been described as "a general rule in this country," a will which expressly disinherits son X or daughter Y (or any other intestate successor) but does not effectively dispose of all the property will not bar X or Y from sharing in the intestate distribution of the undisposed property. Matter of Estate of Stroble, 6 Kan.App.2d 955, 636 P.2d 236 (1981); Kimley v. Whittaker, 63 N.J. 236, 238, 306 A.2d 443, 444 (1973) (it should be noted, however, that the court places more emphasis on the construction of the testator's intent than on the "general rule"); Annot., Effect of Will Provision Cutting Off Heir or Next of Kin, or Restricting Him to Provision Made, to Exclude Him from Distribution of Intestate Property, 100 A.L.R.2d 325 (1965). Other decisions have not allowed the intestate successor to share in intestate property when the intent to disinherit set out in the will was clear and unambiguous. Matter of Estate of Eckart, 39 N.Y.2d 493, 384 N.Y.S.2d 429 (1976); see also Matter of Estate of Dunlap, 649 P.2d 1303 (Mont. 1982) (disinherited child may take exempt property under the statute).

SECTION EIGHT. PROTECTION OF THE FAMILY BY LIMITATIONS ON GIFTS TO CHARITIES

Statutes restricting the property owner's power to make charitable gifts, often referred to as "mortmain statutes," are becoming increasingly rare in the United States. These statutes are predicated on the assumption that a testator, due to frailties or fear of impending death, may be subject to some variety of undue influence when making gifts immediately before death to religious or charitable organizations. Another justification frequently given for such statutes is the protection they give the testator's family against disinheritance. The statute may operate either by making voidable gifts to charity in excess of a certain percentage of the estate, see the recently repealed New York Statute, N.Y.—McKinney's EPTL § 5–3.3 (gifts to charity in excess of one half the estate voidable); by invalidating or making voidable gifts to a charity made in a will executed too near the time of death, see Fla.Stat.Ann. § 732.803 (six months before death); or by combining both of these elements by establishing some period before the testator's death during which charitable gifts are valid only to the extent that they do not exceed a certain percentage of the estate. Ohio Rev. Code § 2107.06 is representative of this latter type of statute:

Bequests to Charitable Purpose and Governmental Units

(A) If a testator dies leaving issue and by his will devises or bequeaths his estate, or any part thereof, in trust or otherwise to any municipal corporation, county, state, country, or subdivision thereof, for any purpose whatsoever, or to any person, association, or corporation for the use or benefit of one or more benevolent, religious, educational, or charitable purposes, such devises and bequests shall be valid in their entirety only if the testator's will was executed more than six months prior to the death of the testator.   If such will was executed within six months of the testator's death, such devises and bequests shall be valid to the extent they do not in the aggregate exceed twenty-five per cent of the value of the testator's net probate estate, and in the event the aggregate of the devises and bequests exceeds twenty-five per cent thereof, such devises and bequests shall be abated proportionately so that the aggregate thereof equals twenty-five per cent of the value of the testator's net probate estate.

———

Several courts have recently invalidated a number of mortmain statutes as violations of the equal protection clauses of the federal and state constitutions, holding that the classifications they create are wholly arbitrary and not reasonably related to any legitimate statutory objective. In invalidating the Pennsylvania statute, which made voidable bequests to charities in wills that were executed within 30 days of death, the court in In re Estate of Cavill, 459 Pa. 411, 416–417, 329 A.2d 503, 505–506 (1974) reasoned as follows:

Section 7(1) divides testators into two classes.   One class is composed of those testators whose wills provide for charitable gifts and who die within 30 days of executing their wills.   The other class is composed of those testators who either make no charitable gifts or survive the execution of their wills by at least 30 days.   The statute renders invalid any charitable gifts made by a testator in the first class if any person "who would benefit by its invalidity" objects.   In all other cases, one who wishes to invalidate a testamentary gift must prove lack of testamentary capacity or undue influence.

Clearly, the statutory classification bears only the most tenuous relation to the legislative purpose.   The statute strikes down the charitable gifts of one in the best of health at the time of the execution of his will and regardless of age if he chances to die in an accident 29 days later.   On the other hand, it leaves untouched the charitable bequests of another, aged and suffering from a terminal disease, who survives the execution of his will by 31 days.   Such a combination of results can only be characterized as arbitrary.

Furthermore, while the legislative purpose is to protect the decedent's family, the statute nevertheless seeks to nullify bequests to charity even where, as here, the testator leaves no immediate family.   In these circumstances, the statute would operate to "protect" only distant relatives, with whom the testator may have had little or no contact during life, against the carefully selected and clearly identified objects of the testator's bounty. This protection of a nonexistent "family" defeats the testator's expressed intent without any relation to the purpose which is sought to be promoted, further demonstrating the irrationality of the statutory classification.

Because the statute sweeps within its prohibition many testamentary gifts which present no threat of the evils which the statute purports to minimize, it is substantially over-inclusive.   Since the statute also leaves unaffected many gifts which do present such a threat, it is also substantially under-inclusive. We are thus compelled to conclude that it lacks "a fair and substantial relation" to the legislative object. Therefore, the Equal Protection Clause forbids us to give it any effect.

Note

For similar holdings, see In re Estate of French, 365 A.2d 621 (D.C.App. 1976) (District of Columbia statute invalidating bequests to clergymen or religious organizations in wills executed within 30 days of death unconstitutional); Estate of Kinyon, 615 P.2d 174 (Mont. 1980) (Montana statute unconstitutional). There are, however, earlier cases holding mortmain statutes constitutional. See e.g., Taylor v. Payne, 154 Fla. 359, 17 So.2d 615 (1944) (Florida's six-month statute constitutional), appeal dismissed 323 U.S. 666, 65 S.Ct. 49, 89 L.Ed. 541, rehearing denied 323 U.S. 813, 65 S.Ct. 113, 89 L.Ed. 647 (1944); Patton v. Patton, 39 Ohio 590 (1883) (Ohio statute constitutional). On the validity of these statutes see Note, Mortmain Statutes: Questions of Constitutionality, 52 Notre Dame Lawyer 638 (1977); Annot., Mortmain Statutes—Validity and Effect, 6 A.L.R. 4th 603.

SECTION NINE. BRITISH INHERITANCE (PROVISIONS FOR FAMILY AND DEPENDENTS) ACT 1975

The American law pertaining to the family's rights in the estate of a deceased member has been criticized as inflexible and inadequate. The share of the surviving spouse is fixed and cannot be altered to meet particular needs. No provisions are made for the decedent's dependents.

As an alternative solution, consider the following: Inheritance (Provision for Family and Dependents) Act 1975, c. 63.

Be it enacted by the Queen's most Excellent Majesty, by and with the advice and consent of the Lords Spiritual and Temporal, and Commons, in this present Parliament assembled, and by the authority of the same, as follows:—

1.—(1) Where after the commencement of this Act a person dies domiciled in England and Wales and is survived by any of the following persons:—

(a) the wife or husband of the deceased;

(b) a former wife or former husband of the deceased who has not remarried;

(c) a child of the deceased;

(d) any person (not being a child of the deceased) who, in the case of any marriage to which the deceased was at any time a party, was treated by the deceased as a child of the family in relation to that marriage;

(e) any person (not being a person included in the foregoing paragraphs of this subsection) who immediately before the death of the deceased was being maintained, either wholly or partly, by the deceased;

that person may apply to the court for an order under section 2 of this

Act on the ground that the disposition of the deceased's estate effected by his will or the law relating to intestacy, or the combination of his will and that law, is not such as to make reasonable financial provision for the applicant.

(2) In this Act "reasonable financial provision"—

(a) in the case of an application made by virtue of subsection (1)(a) above by the husband or wife of the deceased (except where the marriage with the deceased was the subject of a decree of judicial separation and at the date of death the decree was in force and the separation was continuing), means such financial provision as it would be reasonable in all the circumstances of the case for a husband or wife to receive, whether or not that provision is required for his or her maintenance;

(b) in the case of any other application made by virtue of subsection (1) above, means such financial provision as it would be reasonable in all the circumstances of the case for the applicant to receive for his maintenance.

(3) For the purposes of subsection (1)(e) above, a person shall be treated as being maintained by the deceased, either wholly or partly, as the case may be, if the deceased, otherwise than for full valuable consideration, was making a substantial contribution in money or money's worth towards the reasonable needs of that person.

2.—(1) Subject to the provisions of this Act, where an application is made for an order under this section, the court may, if it is satisfied that the disposition of the deceased's estate effected by his will or the law relating to intestacy, or the combination of his will and that law, is not such as to make reasonable financial provision for the applicant, make any one or more of the following orders:—

(a) an order for the making to the applicant out of the net estate of the deceased of such periodical payments and for such term as may be specified in the order;

(b) an order for the payment to the applicant out of that estate of a lump sum of such amount as may be so specified;

(c) an order for the transfer to the applicant of such property comprised in that estate as may be so specified;

(d) an order for the settlement for the benefit of the applicant of such property comprised in that estate as may be so specified;

(e) an order for the acquisition out of property comprised in that estate of such property as may be so specified and for the transfer of the property so acquired to the applicant or for the settlement thereof for his benefit;

(f) an order varying any ante-nuptial or post-nuptial settlement (including such a settlement made by will) made on the parties to a marriage to which the deceased was one of the parties, the variation being for the benefit of the surviving party to that marriage, or any child of that marriage, or any person who was treated by the deceased as a child of the family in relation to that marriage.

* * *

3.—(1) Where an application is made for an order under section 2 of this Act, the court shall, in determining whether the disposition of the deceased's estate effected by his will or the law relating to intestacy, or the combination of his will and that law, is such as to make reasonable financial provision for the applicant and, if the court considers that reasonable financial provision has not been made, in determining whether and in what manner it shall exercise its powers under that section, have regard to the following matters, that is to say—

(a) the financial resources and financial needs which the applicant has or is likely to have in the foreseeable future;

(b) the financial resources and financial needs which any other applicant for an order under section 2 of this Act has or is likely to have in the foreseeable future;

(c) the financial resources and financial needs which any beneficiary of the estate of the deceased has or is likely to have in the foreseeable future;

(d) any obligations and responsibilities which the deceased had towards any applicant for an order under the said section 2 or towards any beneficiary of the estate of the deceased;

(e) the size and nature of the net estate of the deceased;

(f) any physical or mental disability of any applicant for an order under the said section 2 or any beneficiary of the estate of the deceased;

(g) any other matter, including the conduct of the applicant or any other person, which in the circumstances of the case the court may consider relevant.

* * *

[§ 5 permits the court to make interim orders to meet immediate financial needs.]

[§ 6 authorizes the court to vary, discharge, suspend or revive orders providing for periodical payments.]

[§ 7 authorizes payment of lump sums by installments.]

[§§ 8 and 9 permit, subject to certain limitations, the inclusion in the decedent's net estate for the purposes of the Act of the following items: property which the decedent has nominated some other person to receive at his death; gifts causa mortis made by the decedent; and the decedent's severable share of property held in joint tenancy at the time of death.]

10.—(1) Where an application is made to the court for an order under section 2 of this Act, the applicant may, in the proceedings on that application, apply to the court for an order under subsection (2) below.

(2) Where on an application under subsection (1) above the court is satisfied—

(a) that, less than six years before the date of the death of the deceased, the deceased with the intention of defeating an application for financial provision under this Act made a disposition, and (*b*) that full valuable consideration for that disposition was not given by the person to whom or for the benefit of whom the disposition was made (in this section referred to as "the donee") or by any other person, and

(*c*) that the exercise of the powers conferred by this section would facilitate the making of financial provision for the applicant under this Act,

then, subject to the provisions of this section and of sections 12 and 13 of this Act, the court may order the donee (whether or not at the date of the order he holds any interest in the property disposed of to him or for his benefit by the deceased) to provide, for the purpose of the making of that financial provision, such sum of money or other property as may be specified in the order.

* * *

Notes

1. In its original form, Inheritance (Family Provision) Act, 1938 (1 & 2 Geo. 6, c. 45), this statute permitted the court to deal with only fractional shares of the decedent's estate, which varied depending upon the relationship of the survivors, and did not grant the court such extensive powers to redistribute the estate.   The statute's prototype was first enacted in New Zealand in 1900. Today the six states of Australia and all the common law provinces of Canada have enacted similar legislation.   The experience in New Zealand under the statute has not reflected any large increase in litigation.   Over a five-year period, according to one commentator, 4396 wills were proved on an average per year; the annual average of wills contested under the Act during that same period totaled 77.   It was pointed out that had there been no procedure as set forth in the Act a substantial proportion of the 77 cases would have ended up in contests on undue influence, lack of capacity, etc. anyway.   The courts in Australia and New Zealand have taken a generous view of their powers under these Acts.   Reports as to the English experience have not shown a similar tendency.   Professor Leach has pointed out in that regard: "In the English cases the courts have been severe in awarding costs against unsuccessful petitioners where the court feels that the application should not have been made. This is an obvious deterrent to applications based on spite or the what-can-we-lose theory."   Leach, Cases and Text on the Law of Wills, p. 36 (2d ed. 1960). The English experience with the statute is described in Bromley, Family Law, 508–517 (4th ed. 1971); Note, Dependents' Application under the Inheritance (Provision for Family and Dependents) Act 1975, 96 L.Q.Rev. 534 (1980); Bennet, Recent Cases on the Inheritance (Provision for Family and Dependents) Act 1975, 131 New L.J. 1151 (1981).

See in general Macdonald, Fraud on the Widow's Share, 290–298 (1960) (the author proposes an adaptation of the original Act for enactment by states in this country, 301–327); Atkinson, Protection of the Surviving Family: A Foreword to the British System, 35 N.Y.U.L.Rev. 981 (1960); Crane, Family Provision on Death in English Law, 35 N.Y.U.L.Rev. 984 (1960); Laufer, Flexible Restraints on Testamentary Freedom—A Report on Decedents' Family Maintenance Legislation, 69 Harv.L.Rev. 277 (1955); Dainow, Limitations on Testamentary Freedom in England, 25 Corn.L.Q. 337 (1940).

2. The New York Law Commission considered legislation based on the 1938 English statute in place of sections 18-a and 18-b of the Decedent Estate Law,

later replaced by N.Y. EPTL 5–1.1.   Such legislation was in fact introduced in the legislature to protect dependent children of a decedent, but no action was taken on it.   Fourth Report, N.Y. Temporary Commission on Estates, 184–187 (1965).   The reasons for rejecting this approach as a means of protecting the spouse appear in the Third Report, N.Y. Temporary Commission on Estates, 211–212 (1964) (footnotes omitted):

> Such legislation would require that the share of the surviving spouse, if any, would be determined by the judge to whom the application was made.   That this would promote litigation in most estates of married decedents, where the surviving spouse has not received the entire assets of the decedent or has not acquiesced in the provisions made by the decedent is evident.   Aside from the burden that this would place upon the courts, the wisdom of allowing the courts to dispose of the decedent's assets as the particular judge deems just, rather than allowing the decedent to dispose of his property as he sees fit, is open to serious objections.   We believe that our tradition of limited restraint upon the disposition of property by will has become part of our public policy.   Of course, the law should prevent a person from pauperizing his dependents but it is submitted that at least insofar as the faithful surviving spouse is concerned, a minimal statutory share will not only adequately protect him or her, but will avoid the expense and inconvenience of court proceedings to obtain maintenance from an estate which he or she probably had a hand in accumulating.

> Nor would maintenance legislation be consistent with today's emphasis on the need for estate planning.   A trust contemplated by section 18 does not necessarily qualify for the marital deduction and thus increases estate taxes, but the testator in creating such a trust balances this against his desired aims.   He knows the effects of his disposition with some certainty in advance.   Under the maintenance theory, any plan for the future would be at most a guess.

> Finally, maintenance legislation is essentially and designedly flexible and uncertain and would inherently breed litigation.   While no one can gainsay the rash of litigation which followed the enactment of section 18, who can estimate the amount of litigation which has been avoided by its certain, definite and to some extent arbitrary provisions?   It is axiomatic that the law must be certain as well as just, especially the law governing the devolution of property.   Perhaps maintenance legislation is in order for what is the rare case where a person disinherits his minor or dependent children as well as their surviving parent and a Commission Staff Report advocates its enactment.   The surviving spouse should be treated differently, however, since his or her claim is not based solely on dependency (certainly it is not insofar as the husband is concerned), but also in recognition of the partnership created by marriage.

> Nor is it an answer to say that maintenance legislation has worked well in the countries which adopted it.   Macdonald and Laufer attribute this to the nature of maintenance legislation and its inherent large discretion which discourages inheritance claims.   Except in England, no jurisdiction with as large a population as New York has adopted it.   That there is more familial harmony in England than here is reflected in the fact that the divorce rate there, while increasing, is about one-half of ours.   Statistics collected by Professor Macdonald from 10 states indicate that in nearly one

of every four marriages here one of the parties was married before. While he attributes the increase in what he calls "evasion cases" to, among other things, the frequency of remarriage and the presence of children by the first marriage, and there can be no quarrel with that conclusion, it is submitted that much of the litigation which has arisen over section 18 is caused by the same family situation. Finally, while there are no statistics available on the subject, it is doubtful if there is any country in the world as litigation-minded as the United States. While New York probably has an amount of litigation which is disproportionate even to its large population, this litigation is not restricted to controversies over the right of election. New York has a litigious population and especially where there are second marriages, it is doubtful that making the share of the surviving spouse dependent upon the discretion of a court will alleviate the burden on our courts. For this and many other reasons the maintenance legislation for the surviving spouse should not be adopted here.

SECTION TEN. PROTECTION OF THE FAMILY—FEDERAL SOCIAL SECURITY

There can be no share for the spouse or any other member of the family unless the decedent possessed property and savings against which rights arising by way of an elective share statute or from community or marital property can attach, and the extent of the protections available to the family following the death of one of its senior members will depend on how substantial these holdings are. For great numbers of widows, widowers, and families of persons dying in this country today, these devices are of little or no consequence. Social security, on the other hand, is almost universally available and provides not only retirement and disability benefits and Medicare but also substantial benefits on the death of the wage-earner to his or her spouse, minor children, and, under certain circumstances, dependent parents. Wage-earners cannot divert these death benefits from their spouses and families by designation of alternative beneficiaries, by gift or sale of accumulated credits, or by failure (except by not working) to make contributions into the system through mandatory payroll deductions. Estimates show that over 95 out of 100 spouses and children in the country are eligible to receive these monthly benefits in the event of the death of a worker in the family.

A wage-earner becomes eligible for the full amount of retirement benefits at age 65. A person who retired in 1984 and who had average earnings throughout his or her working life is entitled to a monthly payment of $542. If that person's spouse is also 65, then she or he will receive a spouse's benefit that is equal to one half the basic benefit or $271, for a total of $813. * The retiree with maximum credits is entitled to about $703, which, plus a spouse's benefit of $351.50, comes to $1054.50

---

* This method of computing spousal benefits has been under study and may be subject to future legislative change. Critics of the present system advocate an approach based on the sharing concept, i.e., the earnings of husband and wife are split equally for the purpose of computing the benefits. For a preliminary appraisal of this proposal, see N.Y. Times, Dec. 30, 1984, p. 1, col. 1.

a month or $12,654 a year. A retiree's child under 18 (under specified circumstances the age may be extended) is entitled to a benefit equal to one half the retiree's benefit, subject to an overall ceiling on the amount that can be paid to one family. Wage-earners may retire at age 62 and receive 80% of the full benefit or delay their retirement until after 65 and receive increased benefits.

If the wage-earner, for example the husband, dies, the death benefits to his widow and minor or disabled children are substantial. Each child under 18 or disabled before reaching age 22 is eligible to receive 75% of the decedent's basic benefit; the widow (or widower if the roles are reversed) is entitled to the same amount during the period that she is caring for a child who is disabled or under 16. The total amount that may be received as death benefits is subject to a maximum but is estimated to run as high as $1,553 a month for the family of a wage-earner who died in 1984. The surviving spouse's benefits stop when the children's disabilities are removed but resume at a reduced rate when she or he is 60 or at a full rate at 65. As originally written, the Social Security Act made the spouse's benefits available only to the widow. In 1975, the Supreme Court held this feature of the statute unconstitutional as an impermissible discrimination based on gender. Weinberger v. Wiesenfeld, 420 U.S. 636, 95 S.Ct. 1225, 43 L.Ed.2d 514 (1975) (widowed father who was caring for two children entitled to similar benefits); see also Califano v. Goldfarb, 430 U.S. 199, 97 S.Ct. 1021, 51 L.Ed.2d 270 (1977) (gender-based dependency requirement for widowers but not for widows unconstitutional).

The amounts set out above are subject to constant change and are used only to be illustrative. * When evaluating them, other features of social security should be borne in mind: benefits are subject to an automatic adjustment to reflect an increase in the cost of living index; benefits for most people are not subject to income tax **; credits in the system are in no way effected by a wage-earner's change of jobs; and rights under the system are backed by the United States government rather than by a single company as may be the case with an employee pension plan.†

A detailed analysis of social security is beyond the scope of this book. We do know that it is not now a complete answer. There are, for example, great numbers of current recipients who retired some time ago whose benefits are inadequate, and, tragically, many others who receive no benefits at all. It is estimated that one seventh of the over-65 population lives below the poverty level. It is obvious that restraints on a property

---

* The benefit amounts are taken from Information Please Almanac 1985, pps. 327–328. They represent benefits accruing to a person retiring or dying in 1984. The average amounts will increase for persons retiring or dying in later years.

** Starting in 1984, a single person with taxable income over $25,000 and a married couple with taxable income over $32,000 pay income tax on up to one half of their social security benefits.

† The first two items on this list (cost-of-living increases and immunity from income tax) are subject to continuing political debate, and the solvency of the system is no longer taken for granted. Nevertheless, for all its problems, social security is at this time all we've got.

owner's privilege of testation to preserve family support are of no relevance to this important segment of the population.   The statistics will improve as the coverage of the system approaches 100% of the population and as cost-of-living increases keep the benefits above the minimum-subsistence level, but there are uncertainties ahead.   A national debate over the future of social security is underway and seems likely to intensify as lawmakers struggle with the deficit.   No one can predict the outcome of this debate, but everyone concedes that the stakes are high.

Chapter Four

MENTAL CAPACITY SUFFICIENT TO
MAKE A TRANSFER

The several types of statutes outlined in Chapter Three represent the extent to which legislatures have gone in limiting the privilege of testation to protect the family. This chapter and the next deal with the various methods of ascertaining and effectuating the property owner's intent. All courts would verbally concur in the attitude expressed in Bird v. Plunkett (page 7 supra) that courts may not impose, absent legislative authority, their own ideas of equity or morality on the wealth transmission process. Consider, as you read the following cases, whether the reality is not something else again and whether sympathy for the family is not frequently a controlling principle. One legislature has admonished its courts as follows (Official Code Ga.Ann. § 53–2–9(b)):

A testator may bequeath his entire estate to strangers, to the exclusion of his spouse and children. In such a case the will should be closely scrutinized; and, upon the slightest evidence of aberration of intellect, collusion, fraud, undue influence, or unfair dealing, probate should be refused.

SECTION ONE.   TESTAMENTARY CAPACITY
BARNES v. MARSHALL
Supreme Court of Missouri, 1971.
467 S.W.2d 70.

HOLMAN, Judge.   This action was filed to contest a will and two codicils executed by Dr. A. H. Marshall a short time before his death which occurred on July 29, 1968. The plaintiff is a daughter of the testator. The defendants are the beneficiaries of the alleged will. A number are relatives of testator, but many are religious, charitable, and fraternal organizations. A trial resulted in a verdict that the paper writings were not the last will and codicils of Dr. Marshall. A number of the defendants have appealed. We will hereinafter refer to the appellants as defendants. We have appellate jurisdiction because the will devises real estate and also because of the amount in dispute.

One of the "Points Relied On" by defendants is that the verdict is against the greater weight of the credible evidence. Since this court will not weigh the evidence in a case of this nature this point, strictly speaking, would not present anything for review.   However, in considering the argument under that point we have concluded that defendants actually intended to present the contention that plaintiff did not make a submissible case and that the trial court erred in not directing a verdict for defendants, and we will so consider the point.   The petition charged that testator was not of sound mind and did not have the mental capacity to make a will.   The transcript contains more than 1,100 pages and there are a large number of exhibits.   We will state the facts as briefly as possible and we think they will clearly support our conclusion that the submission is amply supported by the evidence.

The will, executed April 30, 1968, made specific bequests of testator's home and office furniture and equipment.   The remainder of the net estate was devised to trustees, with annual payments to be made from the income to various individuals, churches, charities, and fraternal organizations.   Plaintiff, her husband and two children were to receive $5.00 each per year.   The estate was appraised in the inventory at $525,400.

The Marshalls had three children: plaintiff who lived in St. Louis, Mary Taylor Myers who lived in Dexter, Missouri, and died in May 1965, and Anetta Ester Vogel who lived near Chicago and who died about a month after her father's death.

In stating the evidence offered by plaintiff we will deal specifically with five witnesses: three lay witnesses because of contentions concerning their testimony, hereinafter discussed, and the two medical witnesses because of the importance we attribute to their testimony.   There were many other witnesses whose testimony we will endeavor to summarize in a general way.

Ward Barnes, husband of plaintiff, testified that he visited in the Marshall home frequently from the time of his marriage in 1930 until Dr. Marshall's death; that Mrs. Marshall was a very cultured, refined, patient, and accommodating woman; that he spent a great deal of time with testator and soon learned that testator would dominate the conversation in accordance with a certain pattern; that testator told him that he discontinued his medical practice at the command of the Lord so that he might use his time in saving the nation and the world; that testator had told him "that the Lord had revealed to him the secrets of heaven; that he was the only man on earth to whom the Lord had revealed these secrets; that he had told him that heaven was a glorious place and that when he went to heaven he would have a beautiful crown and a wonderful throne sitting next to Thee Lord.   He said that there were three powers in heaven, the Lord, Thee Lord, and God, and he said that this throne that he would have would be on the right hand side of Thee Lord in heaven. He said that heaven was a wonderful place, Thee Lord had revealed to him that whatever pleasures man had on earth he would have in heaven. If it was whiskey, if it was gambling, if it was women, that these would be provided him."   He stated that testator had also told him that the Lord had given him a special power of calling upon the Lord to right the wrongs which people had done to him; that many times he related instances of various people whom he had "turned over to the Lord" and the Lord had meted out justice at his instance by taking away the person's wealth, and usually that the person lost his health, had a long period of suffering, and eventually died; that when testator related stories about the men he had turned over to the Lord he would become highly emotional, would pound on the table with his fists, would call these men dirty profane names, his face would become flushed, and the veins in his neck would stand out; that testator had told him that he (testator) had run for Congress on two occasions and had run for President of the United States (although apparently never nominated by any party) on two or three occasions; that he had told him that "if he were made President of the United States he would cancel all public debt, that he would call in all government bonds and discontinue the interest on all of these obligations, and that he would then print money and control the currency, and that he would kill the damn bankers and the crooks and the thieves that were robbing the people in political office and that the world would then be able to settle down and live in peace." He stated that on one occasion testator took him to his office and showed him a number of young women who were mailing out material in the interest of his candidacy; that he had said it was costing him "thousands of dollars to mail this material out, but the Lord had told him to do it and he had no right to go counter to what the Lord had told him to do." He further stated that in one of his campaigns for President testator had purchased a new car and had many biblical quotations and sayings of his own printed all over the automobile; that he had observed him, campaigning from this car, at the corner of Grand and Lindell Boulevard in St. Louis.

Witness Barnes further testified that testator had told him that Mrs. Marshall had inherited a piece of land and that when it was sold he took part of the money and gave her a note for $3,500; that later Mrs. Marshall had pressed him for payment and had conferred with Moore Haw, an attorney, and that because of that testator had locked her out of the house; that Mrs. Marshall then filed a suit and caused him to pay her the $3,500; that eventually the Marshalls were reconciled and resumed their life together; that at the time Mrs. Marshall died he and plaintiff went immediately to Charleston and at testator's request plaintiff made the funeral arrangements; that testator went to his wife's bedroom and searched the room looking for money and called him and plaintiff in to help him; that he found only a few dollars and then became enraged, "his fists clenched * * * his hands were shaking, his body was trembling; his face was red and he was—you could see he was in a terrible emotional state as he stood there shaking his fists and shouting. He said, 'I know she had more money than that. * * * Your mother made me pay and that scoundrel Moore Haw, the dirty, low down * * * made me pay that thirty-five hundred dollars,' and he said, 'I want my money back. I want you to give it to me.'" Witness further testified that of the $3,500 testator had paid his wife in 1941 Mrs. Marshall had given plaintiff $1,500; that from the time of his wife's death until his own death testator had frequently demanded that plaintiff send him $3,500 and stated that if she didn't he would cut her out of his will; that it was his opinion that from the time he first became acquainted with him until his death Dr. Marshall was not of sound mind.

Frank Eaves testified that he had known testator for about eight years before his death; that he was Plant Supervisor for Crenshaw Packing Company and that testator would come to the plant about once a week; that he had heard testator talk about having the Lord come down on people, making them suffer, and having them killed; that he said his furnace didn't work and he had the Lord put a curse on it and it had worked good ever since; that he said he "talked directly to God and God told him things"; that when he would discuss subjects of that kind "his face would get real red, his eyes would bug out, the vessels would stand out on his neck, he would slobber and shout, and pound on anything available"; that he would sometimes come in dressed in nothing but his nightgown and his house shoes; that on one occasion he came to the plant with nothing on but a housecoat; that he was talking about a rash on his body and opened his housecoat and exposed his private parts to the female secretary and others present. Mr. Eaves was of the opinion that testator was of unsound mind over the period he had known him.

William West testified that he was a drug clerk in the Myers Drug Store in Dexter; that he had known testator from 1951 until his death; that testator came in the drug store about once a month during that period; that he had heard testator say that he talked directly to the Lord and the Lord told him the things he was to do; that one of these was that he should save the world and should be prime minister of the United States; that he also talked about turning people over to the Lord for punishment and when he did so the Lord would mete out the punishment and the men would die, or lose their wealth or something of that nature; that when he would talk about such things he used loud abusive language, his face would be flushed, and he would pound the table; that at the funeral of testator's daughter, Mrs. Myers, he (the witness) started to assist Mrs. Marshall, who was then about 80 years old, out of her chair and Dr. Marshall "slapped me on the arm and told me to keep my hands off of her"; that he was present when Mrs. Marshall was trying to get out of the car and in so doing exposed a portion of her leg and testator "bawled her out for it." Witness was of the opinion that testator, during the time he had known him, was of unsound mind.

Dr. Charles Rolwing testified that he first saw testator professionally in 1940; that at that time testator complained of heart trouble but he was unable to find any evidence of such; that he was of the opinion that he was then suffering from manic-depressive psychosis for which there is no cure and that it would gradually get worse; that he also attended testator from the first part of May 1968 until his death in July; that at that time he was suffering from a serious heart ailment; that he was at that time still suffering from manic-depressive psychosis; that he was of the opinion that on April 30, May 17, and May 24, 1968, testator was of unsound mind.

Plaintiff also presented the testimony of Dr. Paul Hartman, a specialist in psychiatry and neurology, who testified in response to a hypothetical question. This question hypothesized much of the evidence related by the other witnesses for plaintiff and utilizes ten pages of the transcript. In response thereto Dr. Hartman expressed the opinion that Dr. Marshall was of unsound mind on the dates he executed his will and codicils; that he would classify Dr. Marshall's mental disease as manic-depressive psychosis with paranoid tendencies; that it was his opinion that Dr. Marshall was incapable of generalized logical thinking.

In addition to the foregoing evidence plaintiff testified herself and offered more than a dozen other witnesses, all of whom related unusual conduct and statements of testator. Plaintiff also offered a large number of exhibits in the nature of letters from testator and various publications containing advertisements and statements written by testator. There was evidence that plaintiff had been a dutiful daughter, had been solicitous of testator and her mother, had visited them frequently and often would take prepared food which she knew they liked. A number of these witnesses testified that testator had told them of various men who had wronged him and that he had turned them over to the Lord who meted out punishment in the form of financial loss, illness, death, or all three; that when he would tell of these things he would speak loud, get excited, his face would become red, his eyes bulge out, and he would gesture violently; that testator was unreasonably jealous of his wife and often said that all women who wore short skirts, or smoked, were immoral.

There was testimony that on the Christmas before the death of his daughter, Mary Myers, the Myers and Barnes families ate Christmas dinner with the Marshalls, and after the dinner testator "jumped on" Mary about her skirt being short and continued doing so until Mary became so upset that she and her husband had to leave.

A number of witnesses testified concerning the fact that testator would go to various public establishments dressed in his nightgown and bathrobe. An article written by testator and published in a local newspaper under date of June 4, 1942, under the heading of "DR. MARSHALL SAYS," contained the following: "Providence they say always raises up a great leader in every crisis * * *. I am that great leader. I am that prophet that Moses and all the other prophets have spoken about. I am the Messiah that the people of this world have been talking and praying about and believing and hoping that he would soon show up. I am the inspired prophet."

In contending that plaintiff did not make a submissible case defendants point to the testimony of their witnesses to the effect that testator was of sound mind and was calm, quiet, and collected on the day the will was executed. The difficulty with that argument is that in determining this question "we must disregard the evidence offered by defendants unless it aids plaintiffs' case, accept plaintiffs' evidence as true, and give them the benefit of every inference which may legitimately be drawn from it." Sturm v. Routh, Mo.Sup., 373 S.W.2d 922, 923.

It is also contended that most of plaintiff's evidence dealt with testator's "sickness, peculiarities, eccentricities, miserliness, neglect of person or clothing, forgetfulness, anger, high temper, unusual or peculiar political and religious views, jealousy, mistreatment of family, unusual moral views, and repeating of stories, which are not evidence of testamentary incapacity or of unsound mind."

As we have indicated, we do not agree with defendants' contentions. We have stated a portion of the evidence and it need not be repeated here. It is sufficient to say that we think testator's stated views on government, religion, morals, and finances go beyond the classification of peculiarities and eccentricities and are sufficient evidence from which a jury could reasonably find he was of unsound mind. When we add the strong medical testimony to that of the lay witnesses there would seem to be no doubt that a submissible case was made.

Defendants also point out that there is evidence that a person suffering from manic-depressive psychosis has periods of normalcy between the abnormal periods of elation or depression and that testator was in a normal period at the time the will was executed. The mental condition of testator at the precise time the will was executed was a question for the jury to decide. The jury was obviously persuaded that he was not of sound mind and since there was evidence to support that verdict it is conclusive.

The defendants have briefed the contention that the trial court erred in sustaining objections to certain questions they desired to ask the prospective jurors on voir dire.

* * *

It is fundamental in our jury system that litigants are entitled to unbiased and unprejudiced jurors. And in order to obtain such they should be allowed a reasonable latitude in examining prospective jurors on voir dire. However, "counsel has no right on voir dire to cause the prospective jurors to pledge or speculate as to their action in certain contingencies which may later occur or arise during trial. State v. Pinkston, supra [336 Mo. 614, 79 S.W.2d 1046]; State v. Ramsey, 355 Mo. 720, 197 S.W.2d 949. The qualified and selected and instructed juror, having been attentive to the argument of counsel and to the reasoning of his fellows, should be free to reach a conclusion satisfactory to him upon the evidence introduced." State v. Heickert, Mo.Sup., 217 S.W.2d 561, 562. And, of necessity, a trial judge is vested with a broad discretion in controlling the voir dire examination and his rulings should not be disturbed unless they clearly and manifestly indicate an abuse of such discretion. Cleghorn v. Terminal Railroad Ass'n of St. Louis, Mo.Sup. 289 S.W.2d 13[16].

The questions counsel sought to propound in this case were of a type which would tend to commit the veniremen. However, in any event, we cannot see how the rulings of the trial court could be considered prejudicial because counsel thereafter was permitted, without objection, to ask very similar questions of various prospective jurors, of which the following is an example:

"Mr. Banta: Mrs. Britt, the Court will instruct you as to the law and the issues in this case. Will you follow the law, the Court's instructions, even though you may think his instructions are wrong?   Mrs. Britt: Yes, sir.   Mr. Banta: You will follow the Court's instructions, even though they might disagree with what you think the law should be?   Mrs. Britt: Yes, sir, I believe I can follow those instructions.   * * *

"Mr. Banta: Do you believe that a person, subject to the conditions and restrictions as will be given to you in the Court's instructions, should have a right to make a will as they see fit?   Mr. Burkett: If he is of sound mind, yes, sir.   Mr. Banta: And irrespective of how he disposes of his property, you think that is his right to do that as he sees fit?   Mr. Burkett: I think so.   Mr. Banta: Even though he doesn't give his children anything?   Mr. Burkett: Yes, sir.   * * *

"Mr. Banta: Do you believe, subject to the instructions as will be given to you by the Court as to the law, that a person has the right to make a will as they see fit?   Mr. Sutton: Yes, sir.   Mr. Banta: Even though they might give one of their children only five dollars, do you still believe that?   Mr. Sutton: Yes, sir.   * * *

Mr. Banta: You wouldn't have any feeling that you would have to find for his daughter because he didn't leave her something in the will? Mr. Reeves: If that is his wish.   * * *"

Under the circumstances here shown we rule that the trial court did not abuse its discretion in rulings relating to the voir dire examination and that no prejudicial error occurred in that regard.

Plaintiff's evidence relating to the mental condition of testator encompassed the period from 1940 until his death in 1968.   The next point briefed by defendants is that the court erred in admitting evidence of occurrences years prior to the execution of the will because it was too remote to have any probative value.   It is true, as defendants contend, that "[e]vidence, not too remote, of mental unsoundness either before or after the will's execution is admissible, provided it indicates that such unsoundness existed at the time the will was made."   Rothwell v. Love, Mo.Sup., 241 S.W.2d 893, 895.   There can be no question, however, but that evidence concerning testator's mental condition long prior to the execution of the will is admissible if it tends to show his condition at the time of said execution.   Holton v. Cochran, 208 Mo. 314, 106 S.W. 1035, 1. c. 1069; Buford v. Gruber, 223 Mo. 231, 122 S.W. 717[4]; Clingenpeel v. Citizens' Trust Co., Mo.Sup., 240 S.W. 177.   Dr. Rolwing testified that he treated testator in 1940 and that he was of unsound mind at that time; that he was suffering from manic-depressive psychosis, an incurable mental disease which would gradually get worse.   That testimony was certainly admissible as it would have a direct bearing on testator's mental condition at the time the will was executed.   And in view of that testimony it was appropriate to admit other evidence concerning testator's statements and conduct tending to support the submission of mental incapacity occurring during the intervening period.   This point is accordingly ruled adversely to defendants' contention.

The next point briefed by defendants is that the court erred in permitting lay witnesses Ward Barnes, Frank Eaves, and William L. West to express an opinion that testator was of unsound mind.   This for the reason that the facts related by those witnesses were not inconsistent with sanity and hence the necessary foundation was not established. The rule regarding the competency of lay witnesses to express an opinion on the issue as to whether a person is or is not of sound mind is that "a lay witness is not competent to testify that, in the opinion of such witness, a person is of unsound mind or insane, without first relating the facts upon which such opinion is based; and, when the facts have been stated by such lay witness, unless such facts are inconsistent with such person's sanity, the opinion of such lay witness that the person under consideration was insane or of unsound mind, is not admissible in evidence and may not be received. * * * In this connection it has repeatedly been determined that evidence of sickness, old age, peculiarities, eccentricities in dress or oddities of habit, forgetfulness, inability to recognize friends, feebleness resulting from illness, and other facts or circumstances not inconsistent with the ability to understand the ordinary affairs of life, comprehend the nature and extent of one's property and the natural objects of his bounty, and which are not inconsistent with sanity, cannot be used as a basis for the opinion testimony of a lay witness that a person is of unsound mind or insane. * * * 'The rule is well settled that, ordinarily, before a lay witness will be permitted to give his opinion that a person is of unsound mind, he must first detail the facts upon which he bases such opinion, but if he expresses an opinion that such person is of sound mind, he is not required to detail the facts upon which he founds his opinion. The reason for the rule is obvious. An opinion that a person is of unsound mind is based upon abnormal or unnatural acts and conduct of such person, while an opinion of soundness of mind is founded upon the absence of such acts and conduct.'" Lee v. Ullery, 346 Mo. 236, 140 S.W.2d 5, 1. c. 9, 10.

Because of this point we have heretofore detailed the testimony of these three witnesses in the factual statement and such need not be repeated here. We think it is obvious that each witness detailed sufficient facts upon which to base the opinion stated. Those facts went far beyond a mere showing of peculiarities and eccentricities. They were clearly inconsistent with the conclusion that testator was of sound mind. * * *.

The defendants also contend that the court erred in refusing to permit their witness, Harris D. Rodgers, to express an opinion that testator was of sound mind. This witness operated an abstract business in Benton, Missouri, which is about 20 miles from Charleston. However, he had known testator for about 35 years and had seen and visited with him on an average of from two to four times a year. We have concluded that we need not determine whether or not the court erred in excluding this testimony. This for the reason that it is "well settled that, if in a specific instance the evidence should not have been excluded, the error is harmless if the same evidence is found in the testimony of the same or other witnesses, given before or after the objection was sustained." Steffen v. Southwestern Bell Telephone Co., 331 Mo. 574, 56 S.W.2d 47, 48. In this instance defendants offered ten lay witnesses who were permitted to testify that in their opinion testator was of sound mind. With such an abundance of testimony on that issue it seems apparent to us that the exclusion of the opinion of one additional witness could not have been prejudicial. No reversible error appearing this point is ruled adversely to defendants.

Defendants' final contention is that the court erred in refusing to give their proffered Instruction No. P–1. They say that the instructions given were not sufficient to properly instruct the jury and that P–1 was necessary to clarify the issues. The instructions given submitted the issue as to whether testator was of sound and disposing mind and memory at the time he signed the documents. Also given was Instruction No. 8 which is MAI 15.01 and which defines the phrase "sound and disposing mind and memory."

Instruction P–1 reads as follows:

"The Court instructs the jury that, in determining the issue of whether Dr. A. H. Marshall was of sound and disposing mind and memory, you may take into consideration the instrument itself and all its provisions, in connection with all other facts and circumstances in evidence. But, under the law of the State of Missouri, Dr. A. H. Marshall was not obligated to leave any part of his estate to the plaintiff, Julia Amma Barnes, and he was not obliged to mention plaintiff in his will. A man who is of sound and disposing mind and memory as defined by Instruction No. —— has the right to dispose of his property by will as he may choose, even to the entire exclusion of those who, but for the will, would be the heirs of his estate; and if after considering all the evidence in the case, including the instrument itself and all its provisions, you believe that Dr. A. H. Marshall was of sound and disposing mind and memory, you will not further consider whether said disposition was appropriate or unappropriate [sic]. The jury should not substitute its judgment for the testator's judgment, nor should they determine the case upon the wisdom or the justice of the disposition made by the testator of his property; whether such disposition is just or right is a question for the testator, and for none other than the testator."

It will be noted that P–1 is clearly a cautionary instruction. And the rule is well established that "[t]he giving of cautionary instructions is largely within the discretion of the trial court and unless such discretion is abused it will not be interfered with on appeal." Bucks v. Hamill, 358 Mo. 617, 216 S.W.2d 423, 425. We also have the view that the instruction is somewhat argumentative in its nature. In that connection this court recently said that "Missouri Approved Instructions were adopted so that questions of fact may be accurately and concisely submitted to a jury in lieu of the vast amount of surplusage that formerly was found in many instructions." Stemme v. Siedhoff, Mo.Sup., 427 S.W.2d 461, 466. Moreover, it appears that the manner in which P–1 is prepared is out of harmony with the direction that "instructions shall be simple, brief, impartial, free from argument * * *." S.Ct. Rule 70.01(e), V.A.M.R. The ultimate issues were properly submitted to the jury and we do not consider it necessary or desirable that P–1 should have been given. The trial court did not abuse its discretion in refusing to give it and hence no reversible error occurred.

The judgment is affirmed.

All concur.

Notes

1. The classic English case on the subject of capacity is Banks v. Goodfellow, Court of Queen's Bench, L.R. 5 Q.B. 549 (1870) in which can be found the original of the following rather typical statement of the test (Atkinson on Wills, p. 232 (1953)):

> To make a valid will one must be of sound mind though he need not possess superior or even average mentality. One is of sound mind for testamentary purposes only when he can understand and carry in his mind in a general way:
>
> (1) The nature and extent of his property,
>
> (2) The persons who are the natural objects of his bounty, and
>
> (3) The disposition which he is making of his property.
>
> He must also be capable of:
>
> (4) Appreciating these elements in relation to each other, and
>
> (5) Forming an orderly desire as to the disposition of his property.
>
> As shown above, testamentary capacity is determined according to one's mental ability to make a will; one may have testamentary capacity though he is under guardianship or lacks the ability to make a contract or transact other business.

2. It is questionable whether a generalized formula of the kind quoted above is very helpful in analyzing cases or predicting results. The contestant in Barnes v. Marshall is attempting to make out a case of general incapacity rather than trying to show that the will results from a single "insane delusion" (see next case). The evidence is typical in that it describes all of the testator's idiosyncratic behavior and his deteriorating health. The subject of all this attention is by definition dead and cannot defend himself. Actions involving testamentary capacity, undue influence and fraud are not infrequently brought with the hope of forcing a settlement out of the family to avoid disclosure of family secrets. The process has been criticized as involving trials that "generally represent unrestricted fishing expeditions into the life, the inner thoughts and the intimate personal relations of the decedent," causing estates to be "consumed with fees and expenses, costs being but rarely imposed upon unsuccessful contestants." Cahn, Undue Influence and Captation, A Comparative Study, 8 Tul.L.Rev. 507, 517 (1933) (written fifty years ago but still an important reminder of the abuses that may occur).

3. A testator need have only a "modest level of competence," described in one jurisdiction as "the weakest class of sound minds," in order to make a will. Estate of Rosen, 447 A.2d 1220, 1222 (Me. 1982) (will valid, although court found support for the allegation that the testator was "ravaged by cancer and dulled by medication"). The fact that a person has been judged incapable of managing his or her affairs and that a conservator or guardian has been appointed to administer his or her property does not compel a finding that that person lacks testamentary capacity. See e.g., Matter of Maynard, 64 N.C.App. 211, 307 S.E.2d 416 (1983) (adjudication of incompetency and appointment of guardian created a presumption against testamentary capacity but presumption

rebutted by evidence that testator understood what she was doing); Matter of Estate of Sorensen, 87 Wis.2d 339, 274 N.W.2d 694 (1974) (previous adjudication of incompetency does not mean testator is incapacitated at time will executed); Rossi v. Fletcher, 135 U.S.App.D.C. 333, 418 F.2d 1169 (1969), certiorari denied 396 U.S. 1009, 90 S.Ct. 568, 24 L.Ed.2d 501 (1970). See generally, Annot., Effect of Guardianship of Adult on Testamentary Capacity, 89 A.L.R.2d 1120 (1963).

In making a case of total incapacity, no one item of proof (senility, drunkenness, use of drugs, weakened physical condition, illiteracy, etc.) is enough unless proof is made that the testator was under the control of that condition at the time the will was executed. For example, the wills in the following cases were held valid despite vigorous attack:

a. *Use of Alcohol and Drugs.* Hellams v. Ross, 268 S.C. 284, 233 S.E.2d 98 (1977) (habitual drunkard had capacity when he made will in favor of charity to the exclusion of his family); In re Estate of Kietrys, 104 Ill.App.3d 269, 60 Ill.Dec. 31, 432 N.E.2d 930 (1982) (testator, who it was alleged drank a quart of whiskey a day, not intoxicated when executed will); In re Burt's Estate, 122 Vt. 260, 169 A.2d 32, 90 A.L.R.2d 916 (1961) (testator's drunkenness and illiteracy did not invalidate will); In re Bailey's Estate, 122 So.2d 243 (Fla.App. 1960) (use of drugs not a disqualification). See generally, Annot., Testamentary Capacity as Affected by Use of Intoxicating Liquor or Drugs, 9 A.L.R.3d 15 (1966).

b. *Old Age and Weakened Physical Condition.* Thomason v. Carlton, 221 Va. 845, 276 S.E.2d 171 (1981) (88-year old woman enfeebled by several paralytic strokes and loss of memory had capacity to make will favoring son over other issue); In re Estate of Vermeersch, 109 Ariz. 125, 506 P.2d 256 (1973) (will of 94-year old woman who was almost totally blind and deaf valid); see Smith and Hager, The Senile Testator: Medicolegal Aspects of Competency, 13 Clev.-Mar.L.Rev. 397 (1964).

4. Because the legal test of capacity is articulated in terms that are both broad and vague, the outcome in a particular case will depend on the facts. One author has offered a useful grouping of the evidentiary facts into four categories: "(1) symptomatic conduct of the alleged incompetent; (2) opinion testimony of incompetency; (3) organic condition and habits of the alleged incompetent; (4) moral aspects of the transaction and its consequences." Green, Proof of Mental Incompetency and the Unexpressed Major Premise, 53 Yale L.J. 271, 275 (1944). The weight given to the testimony of the witnesses on these points appears to vary with the witness's opportunity to observe and standing in the community.

a. *Attending Physician.* The doctor has the best opportunity to observe the testator's "organic condition" and to speak with experience and authority about the testator's capabilities. The cases confirm that the party who has the medical testimony in support of his or her position has a distinct advantage. In re Estate of O'Loughlin, 50 Wis.2d 143, 183 N.W.2d 133 (1971) (will valid on testimony of two doctors, although testator had Parkinson's disease in a severe stage, caused by arteriosclerosis); In re Estate of Bennight, 503 P.2d 203 (Okl.1972) (will invalid on attending physician's testimony, corroborated by nurse, as to testator's inability to remember and understand); but see In re Estate of Kuzma, 487 Pa. 91, 408 A.2d 1369 (1979) (will upheld although two attending physicians testified that testator lacked capacity).

b. *Attorney*. Typically, the attorney who is called as a witness served as the draftsman of the will. The attorney is the best witness on the "moral aspects of the transaction" and can describe the extent to which the testator had independent advice, was free of outside influence and made a "normal" disposition under the circumstances. Blackmer v. Blackmer, 525 P.2d 559 (Mont.1974); In re Estate of Velk, 53 Wis.2d 500, 192 N.W.2d 844 (1972) (undue influence). The attorney who anticipates the problem may attempt to prepare the case for capacity while the testator is still alive. Of course, the attorney who suggests that the client undergo a psychiatric examination before the execution of the will may lose a client. If, however, the client is willing, a medical or psychiatric statement is useful. In re Estate of McGonigal, 46 Wis.2d 205, 174 N.W.2d 256 (1970) (undue influence); In re Ford's Estate, 19 Wis.2d 436, 120 N.W.2d 647 (1963). New York S.C.P.A. § 2507(1) provides: " * * * There may also be filed with the will affidavits of certified medical examiners, under the provisions of the mental hygiene law, certifying that the maker of the will was of sound mind at the time of its execution, together with any facts supporting such opinion." This provision is of limited utility inasmuch as the affidavit can only be used for purposes of cross-examination.

c. *Friends, Neighbors, Business Associates*. As the principal case illustrates, reliance must often be placed on the lay witness to describe "the idiosyncratic behavior" of the testator. The credibility of the witness diminishes as the events on which the testimony is based become further removed from the time of the will's execution. In re Estate of Milligan, 4 Ill.App.3d 38, 280 N.E.2d 244 (1972). A trial court ruling that the proof be limited to facts occurring within two years on either side of the date of execution was upheld. In re Hall's Will, 252 N.C. 70, 113 S.E.2d 1 (1960). If the particular facts are no longer capable of description, a nonexpert witness who has had an opportunity to observe the testator is usually permitted to state an opinion as to capacity. Barnes v. Marshall, supra, at p. 208–209; Annot., 40 A.L.R.2d 15 (1955).

d. *Attesting Witnesses*. The testimony of an attesting witness in support of the will is said to be entitled to great weight. Whitteberry v. Whitteberry, 9 Or.App. 154, 496 P.2d 240 (1972); Thompson v. Smith, 70 App.D.C. 65, 103 F.2d 936, 123 A.L.R. 76 (1939). An attesting witness need not know the testator nor have personal knowledge of the testator's mental capacity, although that fact will make the witness's testimony on the subject of diminished value. In re Estate of Camin, 212 Neb. 490, 323 N.W.2d 827 (1982). The attesting witness who testifies against the will is the object of judicial scorn. In re Wright's Estate, 7 Cal.2d 348, 60 P.2d 434 (1936) (" * * * their [the three attesting witnesses who appeared against the will] testimony would nevertheless be subject to the scrutiny and suspicion which courts rightfully exercise in considering the testimony of persons who out of their own mouths admit their guilt of self-stultification"); In re Warren's Estate, 138 Or. 283, 4 P.2d 635, 79 A.L.R. 394 (1931) ("The law does not leave a will wholly at the mercy of subscribing witnesses"); but see In re Estate of Nigro, 243 Cal.App.2d 152, 52 Cal.Rptr. 128 (1966) (the witnesses knew the testator well and had only reluctantly witnessed his will).

e. *Psychiatrist*. A distinction must be made between the psychiatrist who has treated the testator and the one who has not seen the testator but is called as an expert witness to give an opinion in reponse to a hypothetical question. The issues would seem to be susceptible to professional analysis by the psychiatrist who has treated the testator, but the cases frequently lay stress on the dissimilarities in the legal and psychiatric definition of incapacity and do not appear to accord particular weight to the psychiatrist's testimony. See, for instance, Webster v. Larmore, 268 Md. 153, 299 A.2d 814 (1973); In re Wagner's Estate, 75 Ariz. 135, 252 P.2d 789 (1953) (two qualified psychiatrists who had examined the testator before death and the family doctor testified that the testator was incompetent but twenty-two lay witnesses affirmed his sanity; held will validly admitted to probate). Contradictory testimony on the part of psychiatrists for either side does not give confidence that there is a scientific answer to the problem. See, for instance, Duross' Will, 395 Pa. 492, 150 A.2d 710 (1959) (no one could complain that the dispute among the psychiatrists was due to the lack of opportunity to observe—the decedent was in charge of the occupational therapy department at the Wernersville State Hospital and was well known to the entire staff). One author has concluded: "Too long have judges ignored the insights that psychiatry has to offer." Note, Testamentary Capacity in a Nutshell: A Psychiatric Reevaluation, 18 Stan.L.R. 1119 (1966) (the author proposes as a solution an antemortem examination by a psychiatric council). See generally, Leifer, The Competence of the Psychiatrist to Assist in the Determination of Incompetency: A Sceptical Inquiry into the Courtroom Functions of Psychiatrists, 14 Syr.L.Rev. 564 (1963); Mezer and Rheingold, Mental Capacity and Incompetency: A Psycho-Legal Problem, 118 Amer.J. of Psy. 827 (1962); Green, Proof of Mental Incompetency and the Unexpressed Major Premise, 53 Yale L.J. 271 (1944). The psychiatric opinion of the expert witness who has not seen the testator is given little weight. Gordon v. Levy, 362 Mass. 866, 284 N.E.2d 926 (1972); In re Estate of Bracken, 475 P.2d 377 (Okl.1970); Jackson v. Jackson, 249 Md. 170, 238 A.2d 852 (1968).

5. The point has frequently been made that the disinheritance of worthy members of the immediate family is the most decisive factor in persuading a court to invalidate a will on the grounds of incapacity. Green, Proof of Mental Incompetency and the Unexpressed Major Premise, 53 Yale L.J. 271 (1944); Note, Testamentary Capacity in a Nutshell: A Psychiatric Reevaluation, 18 Stan.L.Rev. 1119 (1966); Epstein, Testamentary Capacity, Reasonableness and Family Maintenance: A Proposal for Meaningful Reform, 35 Temp.L.Q. 231 (1962). It has been suggested that excessive concern for the family causes undue interference with the testator's freedom of testation and that the jury should not be aware of the dispositive provisions in the will when it considers the issue of capacity. Comment, A Case against Admitting into Evidence the Dispositive Elements of a Will in a Contest Based on Testamentary Incapacity, 2 Conn.L.R. 616 (1970). The traditional test for capacity requires the testator to be able to identify the natural objects of his or her bounty. It need only be shown that the testator has the "capacity to know who these objects of his bounty are * * * and not whether in fact the testator appreciates his moral obligations and duties toward such heirs in accordance with some standard fixed by society, the courts or psychiatrists." In re Estate of Weil, 21 Ariz.App. 278, 281, 518 P.2d 995, 998 (1974).

The family does not always win. See e.g. In re Langlois' Estate, 361 Mich. 646, 106 N.W.2d 132 (1960) (jury verdict invalidating the will reversed; mistress received property instead of middle-aged children with own homes who received insurance). In In re Hill's Estate, 198 Or. 307, 256 P.2d 735 (1953) the court upheld a will which disinherited a daughter in favor of a niece, saying on this point (at 198 Or. 314–315, 256 P.2d 738–739):

Many a contestant's high hopes, destined to disappointment, spring from a carelessly bandied use of that phrase which refers to them as the "natural objects of the testator's bounty." Too many seem to garner therefrom a rule of law not present nor to be implied. It confers no inferential rights, nor indeed any rights, to take from one dying testate. It compels no duty upon the part of a testator to make any provision for those comprehended by its words. The phrase "natural objects of the testator's bounty" is no more, no less, than a euphemistic way of defining what can be more simply said and with equal meaning, i.e., "next of kin", In re Walther's Estate, 177 Or. 382, 397, 163 P.2d 285, 291 (1917) or as was said in Page v. Phelps, 108 Conn. 572, 143 A. 890, 893 (1929) those who "would take in the absence of a will because they are the persons whom the law has so designated". Moreover, a will is not unnatural because it excludes one's next of kin in preference to those who may have enjoyed a closer and perhaps an affectionate relationship with the testator.

6. Although no constitutional right to trial by jury exists in a proceeding to probate or contest a will, some form of jury trial is now almost universally authorized by statute. There is considerable variation among the statutes as to whether the verdict controls or is advisory only and as to the circumstances under which a jury may be claimed. Page on Wills, Bowe-Parker Revision, §§ 26.85, 26.86 (1961). One party or the other usually feels that there is an advantage to having a jury.

The court's allocation of the burden of proof will control the order in which the facts are presented to the jury. The party with the burden bears the risk of losing if the jury is not persuaded by a preponderance of the evidence, has the obligation to go forward with the presentation of evidence and has the right to open and close the argument. The cases are about equally split as to whether the burden is on the proponent or on the contestant. One theory views capacity as an essential element of the proponent's case and places the risk of nonpersuasion on the proponent. The proponent is aided initially in going forward with the evidence by the presumption of sanity, but, if the contestant brings in contrary evidence, the proponent must proceed with proof of capacity unaided by the presumption. Wigmore on Evidence § 2500; In re Estate of Hastings, 479 Pa. 122, 387 A.2d 865 (1978); Duchesneau v. Jaskoviak, 360 Mass. 730, 277 N.E.2d 507 (1972); In re Leonard, 321 A.2d 486 (Me.1974); In re Will of Watson, 37 A.D.2d 897, 325 N.Y.S.2d 347 (1971). The other theory holds that the contestant is the moving party and that the burden traditionally falls on the one who initiates the action. Phelps v. Goldberg, 270 Md. 694, 313 A.2d 683 (1974); Thompson v. Estate of Orr, 252 Ark. 377, 479 S.W.2d 229 (1972). UPC § 3–407 requires the proponent to establish proof of due execution, but the burden is on the contestant to prove lack of intent or capacity, undue influence, fraud, duress, mistake or revocation.

7. Inter vivos transfers presuppose the existence of donative intent. Much the same tests are used to judge the capacity of the donor. If anything they are more severe and there are statements to the effect that a person may have sufficient capacity to make a will without having sufficient capacity to contract. Other courts hold that the tests are the same. See Scholting v. Scholting, 183 Neb. 850, 164 N.W.2d 918 (1969) (undue influence); Berkowitz v. Berkowitz, 147 Conn. 474, 162 A.2d 709 (1960) (undue influence); Note, Mental Incompetence As It Affects Wills and Contracts, 13 U. of Fla.L.Rev. 381 (1960) (com-

parison of the tests for wills and contracts); Green, The Operative Effect of Mental Incompetency on Agreements and Wills, 21 Tex.L.Rev. 554 (1943). The same rules apply for the revocation of a will. Hiler v. Cude, 248 Ark. 1065, 455 S.W.2d 891 (1970).

MATTER OF ESTATE OF BONJEAN
Appellate Court of Illinois, Third District, 1980.
90 Ill.App.3d 582, 45 Ill.Dec. 872, 413 N.E.2d 205.

SCOTT, Justice:

At the time of her death, Armida L. Bonjean was a very troubled woman. She left surviving her two sisters, Alice Svendsen and Ann Puhal, and one brother, Gentile Ghidina, and the nephew of a predeceased brother, Mark Ghidina. She also left a will executed on December 30, 1976, which has been admitted to probate in the Circuit Court of Peoria County and which provides the basis for this dispute. The will bequeaths the majority of her property to Mark Ghidina, to Norma Craig, her deceased husband's sister, and to Josephine Massa and Ettore Serangeli, Mrs. Craig's children. Her living sisters and brother were specifically disinherited. The sisters and brother filed a petition in the circuit court below which alleges that Mrs. Bonjean was subject to insane delusions at the time her will was executed and she was therefore lacking testamentary capacity. After hearings on the petition the court below concluded that the testatrix suffered " * * * insane delusions which arose over her misunderstanding of her family's effort to assist her in her own mental condition * * *." As a consequence, that same court voided the will. This appeal was prosecuted seeking our review.

The Probate Act provides that "[e]very person who has attained the age of 18 years and is of sound mind and memory has power to bequeath by will the real and personal estate which he has at the time of his death." (Ill.Rev.Stat.1977, ch. 110½, par. 4–1.) Interpreting the "sound mind and memory" requirement of paragraph 4–1 and its predecessor sections, the courts have held that:

> "Testamentary capacity requires sufficient mental ability to know and remember who are the natural objects of (one's) bounty, to comprehend the kind and character of (one's) property and to make disposition of the property according to some plan formed in (one's) mind. * * * Deliberate disinheritance of an heir does not establish inability to know the natural objects of testator's bounty." Beyers v. Billingsley (1977), 54 Ill.App.3d 427, 12 Ill.Dec. 306, 369 N.E.2d 1320, 1328.

It was not argued below, nor is it argued here, that the testatrix failed to meet the test set forth in the *Beyers* case. However, the petitioners point to a narrow objection to testamentary capacity which can be sustained where the testatrix knows the objects of her bounty but suffers from insane delusions regarding those objects.

The court decisions which discuss the effect of insane delusions on testamentary capacity are accurately synthesized in a published treatise:

> "An insane delusion may render a will invalid if it can be shown that the will was a product of, or influenced by, the delusion. While it is difficult

def^N

to define 'insane delusion', the Supreme Court has held it to be present where a testator, without evidence of any kind, imagines or conceives something to exist which does not exist in fact, and which no rational person would, in absence of evidence, believe to exist   *   *   *."

"The insane delusion must affect the will or enter into its execution. Even if the testator has an insane delusion on a particular subject, if the property and objects of bounty are known by the testator, and the property is disposed of according to a plan, the will will not be set aside for lack of testamentary capacity." Horner Probate Practice and Estates, 4th Ed., Vol. 3, Sec. 1384.

An insane delusion is an irrational belief. Where a testatrix has some actual grounds for the belief which she has, though regarded by others as wholly insufficient, the mere misapprehension of the facts or unreasonable and extravagant conclusions drawn therefrom do not establish the existence of such a delusion as will invalidate her will. Snell v. Weldon (1910), 243 Ill. 496, 90 N.E. 1061.

The law presumes every man to be sane and of sound mind until the contrary is proved, with the burden resting upon the party who asserts it to prove lack of testamentary capacity. Consistent with that presumption, the petitioners here had the burden of proving that Mrs. Bonjean's disinheritance of her sisters and brother was the result of an irrational belief. If that act of disinheritance, whether motivated by prejudice, dislike, or even hatred, can be explained on any rational ground, then the burden of proof necessary to set aside the will has not been met. (Jackman v. North (1947), 398 Ill. 90, 75 N.E.2d 324.) Testamentary capacity is not denied even if the testatrix dislikes and disinherits her family for bad reasons so long as the bad reasons have a rational foundation.

As we noted at the outset, Armida L. Bonjean was a troubled woman, but we do not believe that her testamentary rebuff of the petitioners, her sisters and brother, defies rational explanation.

The glimpses of Mrs. Bonjean's life as recounted by the record on appeal etch a portrait of human tragedy. The testatrix was unhappily married for nineteen years to Americo Bonjean and both parties had from time to time separated and contemplated divorce. Mrs. Bonjean sought treatment at the George A. Zeller Zone Center for "involutional melancholia" during part of 1969. Reconciled with her husband by October 26, 1971, the spouses argued with each other and Mrs. Bonjean left the apartment with her husband threatening to take his own life as she fled. She later returned to discover he had carried out his threat. Later that same year and twice in 1972 Mrs. Bonjean voluntarily entered the Zeller Center afflicted with severe guilt, grief and depression. She blamed herself for her husband's death.

On July 14, 1972, the testatrix was found comatose in her Springfield apartment. She had attempted suicide by taking drugs and placing a plastic bag over her head. This was not the first occasion, nor would it be the last, when Mrs. Bonjean would attempt to take her own life. Indeed, just a year later on July 17, 1973, the testatrix was admitted to Zeller Center after her attempt at suicide by jumping off the Murray-

Baker Bridge in Peoria. She was treated for depressive neurosis as an in-patient until October 15, 1973, when she was released to out-patient status.

After her release from in-patient care, Mrs. Bonjean became increasingly antagonistic toward family members. This antagonism caused the three petitioners to meet and to decide to have the decedent involuntarily committed. This attempt at involuntary commitment caused Mrs. Bonjean to be examined on January 9, 1974, by Dr. P. J. Perkins, who found she had "no psychosis", and "no combativeness", "was oriented", and "was not certifiable." She was released for continued out-patient counselling, and to that end she met with Dr. Ismail Tolek the next day. Contemporaneously, Dr. Tolek wrote to the circuit court in which the commitment proceeding was pending, stating that:

> "During our contacts with Mrs. Bonjean in the past it has come to our attention that a long-standing conflict has existed between her and family members. Most recently it appears though that they have threatened to use her background of previous hospitalizations in mental facilities to force her commitment to an institution at this time, which provokes the client to the extent of relating hostility and resentment to those individuals by phone and by letters; and they in turn use this against her for involuntary commitment with our system.

> " * * * It appears that the petitioner's tendency to indulge in the client's personal affairs has quite a disturbing effect on the emotional well-being of the client. I feel that I should bring this to your Court's attention for any additional legal matters being taken to avoid further harassment of this client."

Petitioners testified that they sought to place Mrs. Bonjean in Zeller Center for her own health and safety, strictly altruistic motives, but that the decedent interpreted their actions as unkind and unfair.

In March of 1975 the testatrix was hired to run the gift shop at the Greater Peoria Airport. Until she terminated her employment for health reasons in November, 1977, the decedent performed her employment in a satisfactory manner, accepting considerable responsibility and maintaining an excellent relationship with her co-workers. During this time Mrs. Bonjean spoke infrequently, if at all, of her sisters and brother, making little contact with them. This was in sharp contrast to the warm and cordial relationship among the siblings prior to 1973.

During this same period of time the testatrix wrote to public officials with letters which carried two main themes. First, the letters defended the right of an individual to take his own life as long as the individual is not psychotic or a danger to others. Second, the letters expressed the concern that the method for involuntary commitment provided for in the Mental Health Code permitted family members to intimidate one another with the threat of commitment.

On December 5, 1977, Mrs. Bonjean died at the age of 64 from ingestion of cyanide.

The petitioners argue, and we quote from their brief, that the testatrix "could not rationally turn against her sisters and brother who did nothing to her but try to help her." We disagree with that conclusion and believe the decision reached below is inconsistent with the uncontradicted evidence.

The act of suicide, or attempted suicide, is not, *per se,* proof of insanity or insane delusions. (Wilkinson v. Service (1911), 249 Ill. 146, 94 N.E. 50; In re Lingenfelter's Estate (Calif., 39 Cal.2d 571), 241 P.2d 990; In re Rein's Estate (N.J., 139 N.J.Eq. 122), 50 A.2d 380). Suicide may, however, be part of a pattern of behavior which eludes rational explanation. The actions of the testatrix in the case at bar do not defy rational explanation. The petitioners concede that although their actions toward the decedent were prompted by altruistic concerns, those actions were not always received or interpreted in the same spirit. We believe Mrs. Bonjean's resentment of her family's attempt to force her commitment provides a rational explanation for their disinheritance. The trial court found that the testatrix misunderstood her family's effort to assist her in her own mental condition. Yet, "the mere misapprehension of the facts" does not establish the existence of such a delusion as will invalidate a will. Snell v. Weldon.

We find that the facts which fostered Mrs. Bonjean's <u>hostility</u> toward her sisters and brother <u>have a rational basis.</u> The hostility is not the product of a "perverted imagination." Mrs. Bonjean's hostility toward her family can be rationally explained as deriving from a threat to her personal liberty associated with those same family members. Because this rational explanation appears uncontradicted in the record, <u>the burden of proof necessary to set aside the will has not been met.</u>

* * *

Notes

1. Certain types of delusion recur: spouse's infidelity, <u>In re Honigman's Will</u>, 8 N.Y.2d 244, 203 N.Y.S.2d 859, 168 N.E.2d 676 (1960) (4–3 decision holding that the issue had been properly submitted to the jury which invalidated the will; however, matter remanded for a new trial on other grounds), Benjamin v. Woodring, 268 Md. 593, 303 A.2d 779 (1973) (sufficient evidence of delusion to warrant submission to jury); belief that testator had not sired one or more of the children, Kingdon v. Sybrant, 158 N.W.2d 863 (N.D.1968) (sufficient evidence to warrant jury submission), Russell v. Fulton National Bank of Atlanta, 248 Ga. 421, 283 S.E.2d 879 (1981) (will valid, alleged delusion not proven); belief that testator was married and father of a child, In re Estate of Rask, 214 N.W.2d 525 (N.D.1974) (will invalid); fear that a person intends to kill or do bodily harm to testator, Rizzo v. D'Ambrosio, 2 Mass.App.Ct. 837, 310 N.E.2d 925 (1974) (delusion that niece was poisoning testator sufficient to invalidate will), Huffman v. Dawkins, 273 Ark. 520, 622 S.W.2d 159 (1981) (belief that wife intended to kill testator had some basis in fact and did not invalidate will). More exotic beliefs also arise. See e.g., Kelley v. Reed, 265 Ark. 581, 580 S.W.2d 682 (1979) (delusion that family mistreated testator because she was a cripple and worked against her reelection as county treasurer did not affect the will); Powell v. Thigpen, 230 Ga. 760, 199 S.E.2d 251 (1973) (delusion that sister had "cast a spell" on testator raised issue sufficient to go to jury). See generally, Annot., Insane Delusion as Invalidating a Will, 175 A.L.R. 882; Comment,

Psychology and Law: An Examination of the Concept of Insane Delusions, 1960 Wis.L.Rev. 54.

2. The family of a person who is becoming increasingly disabled by physical or mental illness may be compelled to make a series of difficult and painful decisions.   Consider the wrench to everyone involved in telling a beloved parent that he or she may no longer write checks, conduct business, or drive a car.   As in the principal case, legal proceedings, such as petitions for commitment or appointment of a conservator, even though inspired by the most benevolent of motives, may generate bitter resentments that become manifest in a new will, disinheriting those members of the family who are now perceived as enemies. See for example, Skelton v. Davis, 133 So.2d 432, 89 A.L.R.2d 1114 (Fla. App. 1961) (delusion theory was not specifically argued, but the case illustrates a mother's reaction to a petition filed by two of her five children to have a curator appointed to handle her affairs).

SECTION TWO.   UNDUE INFLUENCE, FRAUD, AND MISTAKE

IN RE DILIOS' WILL

Supreme Judicial Court of Maine, 1960.
156 Maine 508, 167 A.2d 571.

DUBORD, Justice.   These two cases which were tried together in the Probate Court within and for the County of Cumberland and before the Supreme Court of Probate, are before us to be heard together, upon exceptions filed by the Casco Bank & Trust Company and Bertha Tomuschat, to the findings of the Superior Court sitting as the Supreme Court of Probate for the County of Cumberland holding the will of Christos Dilios, late of Portland, Maine, as invalid because of undue influence and mistake.

Christos Dilios died on June 27, 1958.   An instrument dated and executed by him on March 14, 1958 was presented in the Probate Court within and for the County of Cumberland as and for his last will and testament.   In this purported will, he named the Casco Bank & Trust Company and Israel Bernstein, a Portland attorney, as joint executors.

By decree dated April 7, 1959, the will was disallowed by the Probate Court within and for the County of Cumberland.   This order was entered without the filing of any opinion or expressing any legal reason for the action taken.

An appeal from this decree was filed by the Casco Bank & Trust Company to the Supreme Court of Probate.   Bertha Tomuschat, a beneficiary named in the aforesaid purported will, filed a similar appeal.

Both appeals were heard together and on August 28, 1959, the sitting justice of the Superior Court, acting as the Supreme Court of Probate, filed decrees in both cases in which it was ruled that the testator, at the time of the execution of the purported will was in possession of mental capacity sufficient to execute a will, but the appeal was dismissed and the purported will held invalid, because of undue influence and mistake.

To these findings, the proponents filed their exceptions.

The issues for our determination are as follows:

(1) Was the instrument purporting to be the last will and testament of Christos Dilios procured by undue influence?

(2) Was this instrument executed by Christos Dilios under mistake and misunderstanding as to its composition?

The proponents maintain that the execution of the instrument in question was not the result of undue influence and that there was no mistake or misunderstanding on the part of the testator. These assertions are denied by the appellees and to the aforesaid issues, the appellees advance the additional argument that the findings of the Justice of the Supreme Court of Probate should not be disturbed, for the reason that such findings can be attacked only for errors of law or for abuse of judicial discretion, and that such findings are conclusive if there is any evidence to support them. Appellees contend that no such error or abuse is shown and that there was sufficient evidence to support the findings.

We start out with the premise, of course, that an instrument purporting to be a last will and testament obtained by undue influence is void; and likewise, that a mistake which defeats the intention of a testator is sufficient to invalidate a purported will.

We turn our attention, therefore, to what constitutes undue influence such as to invalidate a purported will and the burden of proof when an instrument purporting to be a last will and testament is contested on the grounds that it was obtained by undue influence.

* * *

The nature of the undue influence that will vitiate an alleged will was elaborately considered in an opinion by Chief Justice Rugg in Neill v. Brackett, 234 Mass. 367, 126 N.E. 93, 94. Here the court said:

> "Fraud and undue influence in this connection mean whatever destroys free agency and constrains the person whose act is under review to do that which is contrary to his own untrammelled desire. It may be caused by physical force, by duress, by threats, or by importunity. It may arise from persistent and unrelaxing efforts in the establishment or maintenance of conditions intolerable to the particular individual. It may result from more subtle conduct designed to create an irresistible ascendancy by imperceptible means. It may be exerted either by deceptive devices or by material compulsion without actual fraud. Any species of coercion, whether physical, mental or moral, which subverts the sound judgment and genuine desire of the individual, is enough to constitute undue influence. Its extent or degree is inconsequential so long as it is sufficient to substitute the dominating purpose of another for the free expression of the wishes of the person signing the instrument. Any influence to be unlawful must overcome the free will and eliminate unconstrained action. The nature of fraud and undue influence is such that they often work in veiled and secret ways. The power of a strong will over an irresolute character or one weakened by disease, overindulgence or age may be manifest although not shown by gross or palpable instrumentalities. Undue influence may be inferred from the nature of the testamentary provisions accompanied by questionable

conditions, as for example when disproportionate gifts or benefactions to strangers are made under unusual circumstances. When the donor is enfeebled by age or disease, although not reaching to unsoundness of mind, and the relation between the parties is fiduciary or intimate, the transaction ordinarily is subject to careful scrutiny. In such an inquiry all the attributes, sensuous, intellectual, ethical and religious, of the individuals concerned are involved. Strength or infirmity of will, natural and cultivated tastes and temperament, and tendencies to passion, resentment, obstinacy, prejudice and calm, all are elements to be considered. A strong sense of justice, determination and steadfastness of purpose are significant considerations, as are also a spirit of domination, persistent desire to rule, and deep-seated selfishness. Age, weakness and disease are always important factors. Relations of intimacy, confidence and affection in combination with other circumstances are entitled to weight.   *   *   *

"Fraud or undue influence, such as if found to have been exercised, invalidates a will, may be manifested in divers ways. It is not practicable or desirable to attempt to lay down any hard and fast rule. Whatever may be the particular form, however, in all cases of this character three factors are implied: (1) A person who can be influenced, (2) the fact of deception practiced or improper influence exerted, (3) submission to the overmastering effect of such unlawful conduct." Neill v. Brackett, supra.

*   *   *

Now, what of the facts of this case?

Christos Dilios came to this country from Greece and became a naturalized American citizen. He went into the restaurant business and was conducting an apparently successful venture in the City of Portland for a number of years prior to and at the time of his death.

He made and executed at different times in the later years of his life, three wills and a codicil to his first one. All of these instruments were highly complicated, due in large measure to the fact that at the time he executed his first will and codicil his entire family consisting of his wife, two sons and a daughter, were residents in the country of Albania; and at the time of the drafting of the last two instruments, his wife and daughter still remained in Albania, a country dominated by communistic influence and in which the ordinary modes of communication no longer existed. Because of this situation, the testator realized the difficulties in making provisions for distribution of money, first to his entire family, and then to his wife and daughter after the boys had managed to escape and come to this country.

The record discloses that it was the hope and ambition of the testator that his entire family might some day be able to leave Albania and emigrate to this country. His ambition and hope insofar as his wife and daughter were never realized, but after substantial expenditure of money and tireless effort on the part of the father, the two sons succeeded in escaping from Albania and in reaching this country. It was determined that they were American citizens by virtue of their father's naturalization.

The first name of the older son was Dhimitrios, and the first name of the younger son was Basilios. After the boys had arrived in this country, the older son became known as James and the younger son as William.

A study of the three wills and the codicil to the first one indicates, insofar as the wife and daughter are concerned, a similar pattern relating to their rights in the estate of Christos Dilios.

The first will was dated January 29, 1954. In this instrument the Casco Bank & Trust Company and Israel Bernstein were named as executors and trustees. Among the directions and powers given to the trustees was that of carrying on the restaurant business previously conducted by the testator.

The first will did not provide for any specific legacies and it is to be noted that it makes no provision of any kind for Bertha Tomuschat.

All of the estate is given to the trustees for the benefit of the testator's wife, his daughter and his two sons. There is also a provision for some support for his sister during her lifetime. It is finally provided that if any money remains in the trust fund after the death of the last survivor, that such balance shall be divided between the Hellenic Orthodox Church of Portland, Maine, and Maine General Hospital of Portland, Maine. As indicative of his interest in his two boys, it is provided that the trustees shall have authority to expend such funds as may be necessary to enable them to come to this country and the trustees are also instructed to pay for the education of William by means of increased payments to him if necessary.

On July 11, 1956, Christos Dilios executed a codicil to his will and the substance of this change is that provision was made for the payment by the trustees of $200 per month to the older boy, and in the event the older son was unable to receive the money to the younger boy, apparently upon the theory and belief on the part of the testator that his sons would take care of the other members of the family in an appropriate manner from this monthly payment.

That the testator at this time intended that eventually either or both of his sons should have his entire estate, subject to their taking care of their mother and sister, is indicated by a provision in the codicil that at the request of either or both of the sons, the trust assets should be liquidated and the proceeds paid over to the sons in equal shares, or wholly to either of the sons, as the trustees may determine. It was further specified that if either or both of the sons should come to the United States, then upon the request of either son, the trust should be determined and the assets paid over to such son or in equal shares to the sons, if both of them were in this country. The testator expressed confidence that either or both of them would take care of the other members of the family.

Up to this point we have seen, therefore, that the testator had clearly declared his intention, albeit in a complicated manner, of making sure that his estate would be used for the benefit of his wife, daughter and two sons, and eventually be shared by the two boys.

The boys arrived in this country in the summer of 1957 and it is evident that shortly after their arrival, trouble ensued between the boys and Bertha Tomuschat, who was then, and had been for many years, a cashier in the restaurant. The evidence discloses that there was a close relationship between Bertha Tomuschat and the testator, a relationship which had existed for a long period of years. There is nothing in the case to show the marital status of Mrs. Tomuschat, but it is indicated she was the mother of a seventeen year old daughter. Of course, the testator was a married man with a wife in Albania. The two sons resented this relationship between their father and this woman.

Shortly after the arrival of the two boys, it appears that trouble developed, at first between the older boy and his father, and later between the younger boy and his father. More will be said later in this opinion concerning some of the evidence and the proof which the court below had before it for consideration from the standpoint of drawing conclusions and inferences.

In any event, Christos Dilios executed a new will on December 31, 1957.

By this will he bequeathed Bertha Tomuschat the sum of $1,000, in recognition he said, of her many years of faithful and devoted service. He then requested that his executors and trustees, and a son he did not name, continue to employ her as manager or assistant manager at a salary of not less than $40 per week. The son he had in mind must have been William because in subsequent provisions in the will he specified for eventual distribution of the restaurant to him.

In this will of December 31, 1957, he cut off his elder son, James, with a bequest of only $100. The other provisions relating to the benefits for his wife, his daughter, and his son William, are somewhat similar to those contained in the prior will and codicil.

In the will of December 31, 1957 we find the following paragraphs:

"C. Anything herein to the contrary notwithstanding, I direct that if my Trustees determine that my said son, William, is capable of managing his own affairs and the business affairs of my estate, has a sense of financial responsibility, has developed maturity and good judgment, has qualities of industriousness, honesty and sincerity, and has demonstrated proper respect and consideration for his Mother and other members of our family, then they may, in the exercise of their sole discretion, when my said son, William, has reached the age of twenty-three (23), or at any time thereafter, distribute to my said son William, free of trust, at any time and from time to time, all, or any part of, the assets forming a part of my estate and upon any such distribution or distributions, my Trustees shall determine whether the right to receive all or any part of the income herein provided for my said son, William from this estate shall be determined and ended. I expressly authorize the complete termination of this trust and the distribution of all of its net assets to my said son, William, if, in the exercise of their sole discretion, my Trustees determine that William has made appropriate commitments and arrangements to provide proper support to meet the de-

terminable needs of his mother and sister who would otherwise be beneficiaries of this estate had it continued.

"D. Anything herein to the contrary notwithstanding, I direct that
within five (5) years after the date of my death the Trustees shall, in
accordance with the provisions of the foregoing Paragraph, distribute, free
of trust, to my said son, William, those assets of my estate which make up
the restaurant enterprise which I carried on during my lifetime, provided
that my estate at that time still owns and operates said restaurant enterprise. I request, but do not direct, that my Executors and Trustees carry
on my said restaurant business for such eventual distribution to my said
son, William, if at all possible.

"E. Anything herein to the contrary notwithstanding, I direct that, if
an opportunity arises for my said wife and my said daughter, or either of
them, to come to the United States, my Trustees may, without regard to
any of the other provisions of this Will and any other rights herein created,
in the exercise of their sole and uncontrolled discretion use any and all of
the funds of this estate to enable my said wife and daughter, or either of
them, to come to the United States for the purpose of establishing a permanent residence and in the hope of eventually securing United States
citizenship; and further that, if an opportunity arises for my said son,
William, to continue his education, my Trustees may, without regard to
any of the other provisions of this will or any other rights herein created,
in the exercise of their sole and uncontrolled discretion increase the payments being made to my said son, William, in such amounts and at such
time or times as they shall determine, to enable my said son, William, to
continue his education."

Although there are prior paragraphs providing for distribution of any
balance remaining after the death or remarriage of the wife, the death
of the daughter and the death of William, to the Hellenic Orthodox Church
and to Maine Medical Center of Portland, Maine, it is clear from the three
foregoing paragraphs that as of December 31, 1957, Christos Dilios, having cut off his older son with a bequest of only $100.00 showed an inten-
tion, first that his son, William, might eventually receive his entire estate, and second an expectation that the trustees named in the will were
to see that he received a proper education.

The will which was presented for probate, which is the subject of this
case, was executed on March 14, 1958, about two and one half months
after the will of December 31, 1957.

In this will be devised to Bertha Tomuschat the so-called camp property on Highland Lake in satisfaction, Dilios said, of debts owed by him
to her, and conditioned upon her giving the estate an appropriate release
and discharge of all the obligations incurred by him to her during his
lifetime. It was further provided that she be continued as manager or
assistant manager of the restaurant at not less than $40 per week.

He then gave each of his sons a legacy of $100 and this was the sole
provision made for them.

After making a few specific bequests, he then made provision for the
care of his wife, daughter and sister, still in Albania with bequests of any

residue after the death of all beneficiaries, to the Hellenic Orthodox Church and Maine Medical Center.

We propose now to digest briefly the evidence applicable to occurrences leading up to the drafting of the will of December 1957 and the final will of March 1958.

For many years, Christos Dilios had employed a firm of attorneys, one of whose members drafted the will. He had the utmost confidence in them and it is fair to recite at this point that there is nothing in the record which in any manner can point the finger of suspicion at these highly competent and honorable attorneys.

A study of the evidence of the scrivener indicates that the bringing of his sons to the United States by the testator was the culmination of a life long dream. Nobody, the scrivener said, could have been happier than he was when at last his two sons were here. However, the scrivener further said that after a very short period, Dilios came to him and talked to him and told him he was having serious problems, particularly with his oldest son. This was in the fall of 1957 and the boys, it will be noted, had been in this country at that time less than six months. The oldest boy[,] the scrivener said, was causing his father terrible heartache because he had no respect for him, would not tend to business, and would not obey instructions. He told the scrivener a story of a physical beating administered by the older boy to the younger boy at the family home, at which time when the father attempted to intervene he had been struck. This story incidentally was denied by both of the boys. The scrivener said, "to make a long story short, he came to me and said that he wanted his eldest son taken out of his will." The scrivener said he advised him to go slow, but finally at the end of the year after a serious illness on the part of the testator, he informed the scrivener that he was determined to cut off the older boy. Then about a month after this will was drawn, very early in 1958, either in January or February, the testator came to the office again and gave directions for the drafting of a new will in which the younger son was disinherited. The reasons attributed by the father for this change was that the younger son was siding with his older brother. After giving definite instructions that a will be drafted, in which both sons were given only the sum of $100, the scrivener said that the testator indicated that he hoped the boys might reform in which event, he might make a new will.

Upon being asked whether or not the testator had ever told him that part of the trouble with the oldest son was because of the cashier, he replied, that the testator told him that they did not work well in the restaurant; that they did not take his instructions; and that they did not take instructions from Mrs. Tomuschat; that they were constantly doing things which disturbed him in the restaurant. He further said that he was disturbed because the older boy insisted on having social contacts with the waitresses. He also questioned the honesty of the older boy.

It is clear from some of the remaining testimony of the scrivener that much trouble had developed because of ill feeling between Mrs. Tomuschat and the boys.

The scrivener also testified that the testator informed him that Mrs. Tomuschat had mentioned to him incidents of alleged misbehavior in the restaurant on the part of the older son.

A witness, of Greek extraction, the operator of a restaurant in Biddeford, testified that he was a close friend of Christos Dilios; that he knew that Dilios had executed a will in which he disinherited his sons, because Dilios went about broaching this information to his friends. This witness testified that in a discussion with Dilios, he told Dilios he had heard he had disinherited his sons, and asked him particularly about the younger boy. To this, he said, Dilios informed him that the executors would take care of him, and there was nothing to worry about, and he discussed with him the matter of the education which should be furnished to William. He also testified regarding the relationship between Mrs. Tomuschat and the testator, and that the sons disapproved of it.

He said Dilios made this statement to him: "I have been going around with this lady 12, 13 years; taken the best years of her life. I have received something in return. I just can't put her away now because the boys come in. I am getting old, not long to live."

Upon being asked if Dilios had told him of the problems existing between the sons and the woman, he said that the boys objected to his relationship with her. Dilios informed this witness that the boys had personally indicated their objections to their father.

He further said that upon pressing Dilios for the real reason for his action of disinheritance, Dilios replied: "You know the real reason. They can't get along with the lady."

Under cross examination he repeated that Dilios stated that the younger boy was to be taken care of by his attorneys and executors. There is, of course, no provision in the last will instructing or directing the attorneys and executors to expend money for William's education, but there was such a provision for his education in a prior will.

Another witness of Greek extraction described himself as a close friend of Dilios. As a result of talks with the testator, he attributed the trouble arising over the boys as due to Mrs. Tomuschat.

Note the following testimony:

"Q. Can you tell us what Mr. Dilios told you about the trouble he had? A. Well, Mr. Dilios and I, very, very close friends, and I took authority, I says: 'Why you have this kind of trouble with sons?' I says: 'Your big dream to bring your sons over here to United States. You spend so much money.' He says to me: 'I am pleased. Don't ask me any more questions. I am in big trouble with woman.' I says: 'All right. What kind of trouble? You throw your sons on street for one woman.' I says: 'What is trouble? Are you married legal?' I am very, very close friend and I ask many details. He says to me: 'You couldn't know, but I am big trouble. Don't ask me any more.' He started to cry."

* * *

James Dilios testified that he arrived in this country on June 8, 1957 and he recited a story of the happiness experienced by his father.

Upon being asked whether or not he ever had any trouble with Mrs. Tomuschat in the restaurant he replied: "I did not have any trouble at the beginning when we first came over here, but we did have trouble later on, when I found out my father had relations with the woman. In other words, that my father was on a friendly basis with the woman that was when the trouble started."

He denied ever having struck his father and said he had great respect for him. He said he had discussed with his father the relationship with Mrs. Tomuschat. He said that after a period of a few months, he realized his father was a sick man and he asked if it would be possible for him to learn the restaurant business to which his father said it would not be possible at that time because Mrs. Tomuschat did not approve of the idea of James working behind the counter and that the entire proposition would be disagreeable to her. He related an episode occurring at the restaurant about Mrs. Tomuschat objecting to having him behind the counter, lost her temper with him and threw all of his clothes outside, and then telephoned his father. Upon arriving at the restaurant, the father not knowing the facts, but relying entirely upon Mrs. Tomuschat's story ordered him out of the restaurant. He then called the police and informed them that his son was making trouble in the restaurant and the police took him to headquarters. A few days later he decided to go back to the restaurant to work, but before he had a chance to begin, two police officers entered, he said as a result of a telephone call, and they took him to police headquarters again. As to accusations that he took money from the cash drawer, he said that several persons had access to the cash drawer, including Mrs. Tomuschat, and that accusations about money missing, which he says were false were made by Mrs. Tomuschat. He further testified that it was a usual occurrence for Mrs. Tomuschat to make complaints to his father on various subjects always in criticism of the boys.

In telling of the relationship between his father and Mrs. Tomuschat, he said, "knowing my father's past, and after being here 5 to 6 months and seeing the very close relationship that my father had with this woman, and realizing every day we were being driven farther and farther apart from one another, my brother, and especially myself, I sat down to have a mind, to talk with him."

He then said that as a result of this talk which he instituted, an argument developed with his father.

"Q. Will you tell us in your own words, what the argument was between you and your father in 1957? A. I asked my father to tell me everything that had happened up to December, 1957, and by asking him that question, my father was deeply hurt. However, I went on and asked my father to explain the situation and to straighten out before things developed into a worse mess than what they already had been into.

"Q. Are you through?   A. From that moment on, my father sort of withdrew himself from me.   However, I continued and told him to stop going to this woman's house every day.   My father told me he was sick and he had to have someone to take care of him.   However, in return, I told him he had two sons who could take care of him if he was sick.   I did not ask my father to fire this woman from the restaurant.   I simply asked him to tell this woman not to infringe on us all the time, not to find certain things that she would throw the blame on, that is, concerning us.   My father, in return, told me that: 'I could not tell her anything because I have been with her for a good many years.   If I told her anything to that effect, she would get very mad.' "

* * *

Mrs. Tomuschat was called as a witness, but her testimony was very brief.   She was not asked to explain her marital status, but said she had been employed in this restaurant since 1943, having first started to work for the predecessor of Dilios.   She denied having trouble with the boys.   Upon being asked whether or not Dilios had trouble with the boys, she said, because she could not understand Greek, she did not know what he was saying to them.   She was evasive in her answers regarding arguments between the father and the sons and said he did not discuss with her what took place at his home.   She denied having any arguments with either or both of the boys and said that no problems existed.   Upon being asked whether or not Dilios was indebted to her, she said:

"Well, it is hard to say how it was.   I never kept track.   Sometimes he borrowed some from me when he was short, a lot of times.   I worked a lot of over time and never got paid for it.

"Q. At the time of his death, you have any indication of the amount?   A. I have no record of it.

"Q. As far as you are concerned, he owed you nothing?   A. Just from my working there, and working the way I did.

"Q. Would you hazard a guess as to what you feel he owed you for money?   A. No, I will not guess."

* * *

There was ample evidence in the record to authorize the presiding justice to find that the trouble between the father and the sons developed as a result of the machinations of Mrs. Tomuschat, the cashier in his restaurant.   The record indicates that from the very beginning, the older boy made known to his father his objections to the relationship with the cashier, and that later, the younger boy voiced the same objections.   There is evidence permitting the presiding justice to find that bitter feeling on the part of the father towards his sons developed as a result of continued accusations made by Mrs. Tomuschat to the father about alleged improper actions on the part of the sons in the restaurant, accusations which were unfounded in fact and which were concocted by Mrs. Tomuschat.

That there was a close relationship between testator and Mrs. Tomuschat is proved by the evidence of the two boys as well as by the testimony of two friends of the testator.

While illicit relationship between the testator and the person alleged to have exerted undue influence is not enough per se to raise a presumption that a will was procured by undue influence, such a relationship is a fact to be considered along with other facts relating to the question of whether or not a purported will was procured by undue influence.

It is pointed out in 54 Am.Jur., Wills, § 444, that although the existence of an illicit relationship does not of itself justify finding that undue influence was in fact exerted on the testator, that the law recognizes that the difficulty of uncovering undue influence is greatly increased where the persons involved have been in an illicit relationship, and coercion of the testator may be inferred from less evidence where the person charged therewith was in an illicit relationship with the testator.

The testimony of Mrs. Tomuschat and her demeanor upon the witness stand, may well have had a bearing upon the final conclusions of the presiding justice.   While there is no evidence in the record to show that she knew that Christos Dilios was executing new wills, it is difficult to believe, in the light of human experience, when her close relationship with the testator was so clearly shown, that she did not know that the testator was executing wills in which he was disinheriting his sons.   True, she testified that she had no trouble with the boys and that she did not know their father was having trouble with them.   However, the presiding justice did not have to believe her testimony.

Moreover, the presiding justice had for consideration the testimony of the two friends of Dilios, one of whom testified that Dilios told him that he had been going around with Mrs. Tomuschat for 12 or 13 years and had taken the best years of her life, and that he could not put her away because the boys had arrived, and that the real reason for disinheriting the boys was the fact that "they cannot get along with the lady." The testimony of the other witness was to the effect that he was in "big trouble"; that he requested this witness not to ask him any more questions and then started to cry.

While we have seen that the person who is alleged to have exerted the undue influence does not necessarily have to be a beneficiary, there was a basis for an inference on the part of the presiding justice that Mrs. Tomuschat had a motive for the disinheritance of the boys.   Not only was she given some property in payment, the will said, for money loaned by her to the testator, a fact left in serious doubt by her own testimony, but she had an expectation of a long period of employment, which without question would cease as soon as either of the boys acquired possession of the restaurant for which possession and ownership previous wills had made provision.

Christos Dilios was in a condition enfeebled by a serious illness when he executed the will of December 31, 1957 and he died a very short time after he executed the instrument which is now before us for consideration. One fact which has a bearing upon the condition of his mind at the time of the execution of the instrument in question, is that although there was no provision for taking care of the younger boy in the instrument, he nevertheless told his close friends that his lawyers were to take care of the boy.

There is no set formula to determine the workings of the human mind. The existence of the mind, its nature, and its operations, can be deduced only from the known conduct of the human being.

Here we find an unnatural and unjust testamentary disposition, and while this does not alone carry the issue of undue influence, along with other circumstances, it may well be sufficient.

We have examined the record with great care. We have been assisted by very excellent briefs filed by counsel for both sides. We arrive at the conclusion that the record indicates that there were facts proven from which the presiding justice could logically infer that when Christos Dilios executed the instrument purporting to be a last will and testament, his act was not that of a mind free and untrammelled.

Two eminent jurists have resolved the issue in similar manner. There were facts proven permitting a finding that Christos Dilios, because of his weakened physical condition and other factors, was a person whose mind could be influenced; and facts proven from which a logical conclusion could be reached that he submitted to the overmastering effect of unlawful influence, such as to invalidate the instrument now purporting to be his last will and testament. The contestants have not sustained the burden of showing that the decrees of the presiding justice of the Supreme Court of Probate upon the issue of undue influence were clearly erroneous.

Having determined that the decrees of the presiding justice below to the effect that undue influence invalidated the instrument purporting to be the last will and testament of Christos Dilios, are well founded in law and in fact, it is unnecessary for us to consider the issue of mistake.

The entry will be:

Exceptions overruled. Decrees below affirmed. Counsel fees and expenses to be awarded to counsel for proponents and contestants, the amount thereof to be fixed by the Probate Court and charged as an expense of the administration of the estate.

Notes

1. In the principal case, the lover is deprived of her legacy. There are, however, many cases in which the relationship did not disqualify the beneficiary. Parrisella v. Fotopulos, 111 Ariz. 4, 522 P.2d 1081 (1974) ("the testator, who was called Gus, was a rollicking roistering, heavy-drinking woman chaser"; will favoring mistress upheld against brother's challenge); In re Estate of Newkirk, 456 P.2d 104 (Okl.1969) (estranged wife and daughter disinherited by a will which left the entire estate to a woman who had been testator's mistress for some thirteen years). The following statement from In re Kelly's Estate, 150 Or. 598, 618, 46 P.2d 84, 92 (1935) as to the effect of the relationship on the process is representative:

As we have seen, the evidence indicates that a meretricious _(evil)_ relationship existed between P. J. Kelly and Mrs. Northrop. The mere existence

of such a relationship does not render invalid a bequest made to the par- *(slut)*
amour, because one possessed of an estate may settle his bounty upon an
immoral person if he chooses; nor does such a relationship create a presumption that the beneficiary exerted undue influence in obtaining the
testamentary recognition. But, since the relationship which arises out of
illegal amours may provide favorable opportunities for the exertion of undue
influence, proof of the relationship is admissible when undue influence is
charged. It is frequently said that the relationship casts suspicion upon
the will, and cautions the court to examine the evidence with unusual care.
Proof that the relationship existed and that the will makes an unnatural
disposition of the estate, when accompanied with only a small amount of
evidence that undue influence was exerted, may overcome positive denials
from the paramour and her witnesses. This is due to a conviction that the
usual difficulty of unmasking deceit and wrongful conduct is greatly increased when the alleged wrongdoer has employed as an aid sensual pleasures.

The cases are collected in Annot., Existence of Illicit or Unlawful Relations
Between Testator and Beneficiary as Evidence of Undue Influence, 76 A.L.R.3d
743 (1977).

2. As to undue influence affecting part of a will, the usual approach is
stated as follows in Carother's Estate, 300 Pa. 185, 150 A. 585, 69 A.L.R. 1127
(1930):

> Where a provision in a will which gives a legacy is void because of
> undue influence, the will itself is not necessarily void nor are other legacies
> unless such influence directly or impliedly affects them. Undue influence
> invalidates such part of a will as is affected by it. If the whole will is
> procured through undue influence, it is entirely void. Where, however,
> part of the will is caused by undue influence, and the remainder is not
> affected by it, and the latter can be so separated as to leave it intelligible
> and complete in itself, such part of the will is valid and enforceable.

There are a few decisions to the contrary. See e.g. In McCarthy v. Fidelity
National Bank & Trust Co., 325 Mo. 727, 30 S.W.2d 19, 69 A.L.R. 1122 (1930),
the court held:

> Since our statute requires that, in a will contest case, "an issue shall
> be made up whether the writing produced be the will of testator or not,"
> the writing so produced must be shown to be the testator's will in its entirety
> or it is not his will at all. When there is undue influence on the part of
> one legatee, which results in a provision of the purported will beneficial to
> said legatee, such undue influence vitiates the entire will and renders it
> invalid in its provisions as to other beneficiaries, although they did not
> participate in bringing undue influence to bear upon testator.

The cases are collected in Annot., Partial Invalidity of Will, 64 A.L.R.3d
261 (1975). See also for a discussion of the issue Williams v. Crickman, 81
Ill.2d 105, 39 Ill.Dec. 820, 405 N.E.2d 799 (1980).

3. Can a will invalid for want of testamentary capacity or undue influence
be made valid by later codicil? See Annot., Validation by Codicil, 21 A.L.R.2d
821 (1952).

HAYNES v. FIRST NATIONAL STATE BANK OF NEW JERSEY

Supreme Court of New Jersey (1981).
87 N.J. 163, 432 A.2d 890.

HANDLER, J.

This is a will contest in which the plaintiffs, two of the decedent's six grandchildren, seek to set aside the probate of their grandmother's will and two related trust agreements. The major issue presented is whether the will is invalid on the grounds of "undue influence" attributable to the fact that the attorney, who advised the testatrix and prepared the testamentary instruments, was also the attorney for the principal beneficiary, the testatrix's daughter, in whom the testatrix had reposed trust, confidence and dependency. A second question concerns the enforceability of a "non-contestability" or *in terrorem* clause in the testamentary documents under New Jersey common law since the decedent died before the effective date of the new probate code, N.J.S.A. 3A:2A–32, which invalidates such clauses in wills.

In an unreported opinion upholding the probate of the will and related trusts, the trial court held that the circumstances created a presumption of undue influence but that this presumption had been rebutted by defendants. It ruled further that the *in terrorem* clause was unenforceable. The case was appealed to the Appellate Division, which affirmed the trial court as to the lack of undue influence, sustaining the probate of the will and its judgment upholding the related trust agreements, but disagreed with the trial court's ruling that the *in terrorem* clause was unenforceable. Plaintiffs then filed their petition for certification which was granted. 85 N.J. 99, 425 A.2d 264 (1980).

I

The issues raised by this appeal, particularly whether the contested will was invalid as a result of "undue influence," require a full exposition of the facts.

Mrs. Isabel Dutrow, the testatrix, was the widow of Charles E. Dutrow, an employee of Ralston Purina Co. who had acquired substantial stock in that corporation. Upon his death the stock, aggregating almost eight million dollars, was distributed to his widow and their two daughters, both outright and in trust.

Betty Haynes, one of the daughters of Charles and Isabel Dutrow, came with her two sons to live with her parents in the Dutrow family home in York, Pennsylvania in 1941 while Betty's husband was in military service during World War II. Following Charles Dutrow's death in 1945 and her own divorce, Betty and her sons continued to live with Mrs. Dutrow in York. The relationship between mother and daughter were extremely close, Mrs. Dutrow having deep affection for Betty, as well as her grandsons whom she practically raised. The two boys, however, left the York home sometime around 1968 to the considerable aggravation and disappointment of their grandmother.[1]   But Betty remained with her mother until Betty's death in June 1973.

At the time of Betty's death, she had been living with her mother for more than 30 years.   Mrs. Dutrow was then 84 years old and suffered from a number of ailments including glaucoma, cataracts and diverticulitis, and had recently broken her hip.   Mrs. Dutrow, distraught over the death of her closest daughter and somewhat alienated from the Haynes children, decided to move in with her younger daughter, Dorcas Cotsworth, and Dorcas' husband, John, who had homes in Short Hills and Bay Head, New Jersey.   This decision was a reasonable one, freely made by Mrs. Dutrow, who despite her age, physical condition and feelings of despair was and remained an alert, intelligent and commanding personality until the time of her death.

During her lifetime, Mrs. Dutrow executed a great many wills and trust agreements.   All of these instruments, as well as those her husband had executed prior to his death, were prepared by the longstanding family attorney, Richard Stevens, of Philadelphia.   By June 1967 Stevens had prepared five wills and several codicils for Mrs. Dutrow.

As of the time she moved in with the Cotsworths, Mrs. Dutrow's estate plan reflected a basic disposition to treat the Haynes and the Cotsworth family branches equally.   During the last four years of her life, however, while living with daughter Dorcas, Mrs. Dutrow's will went through a series of changes which drastically favored Dorcas and her children while diminishing and excluding the interests of the Haynes brothers.   These changes, and their surrounding circumstances, bear most weightily upon the issue of undue influence.

Shortly after moving in with Dorcas, following a conference between her daughter and Stevens, the first of many will and trust changes was made by Mrs. Dutrow on July 25, 1973.   Under the new provisions of the will, Mrs. Dutrow's residuary estate was to be divided into two equal trusts, one for Dorcas, the principal of which Dorcas could invade up to certain limits and the other a trust with income to each of the Haynes boys without a power of invasion.   A new will and an inter vivos trust with almost identical provisions, including approximately 60,000 shares of Ralston Purina stock, were later executed on November 24, 1973 and December 4, 1973, respectively.   Mrs. Dutrow also gave Dorcas 5,000 shares of stock outright to compensate her for the expense of having Mrs. Dutrow live with her.

During the time these instruments were being drawn, Dorcas and her husband, John Cotsworth, began actively to express their views about Mrs. Dutrow's estate plans to Stevens.   In a meeting between Stevens, Mrs. Dutrow, and the Cotsworths on November 13, 1973 at the Cotsworth home in Short Hills, John Cotsworth gave Stevens two charts of Mrs. Dutrow's estate which Cotsworth had prepared.   According to Stevens'

---

1.   The Haynes children apparently undertook lifestyles which caused both their mother and grandmother great anguish;   one son resisted military service and took refuge in Canada during the Vietnam war and both had live-in girlfriends whom they eventually married.

testimony at trial, the import of the charts was to make "substantial outright gifts to the members of the Cotsworth family and similar gifts to [plaintiffs, the Haynes children]." Stevens further testified that Mrs. Dutrow had told him at this meeting that the pressure upon her by the Cotsworths to change her will was enormous. On November 19, 1973, John Cotsworth wrote Stevens a long letter in which he summarized what he, Cotsworth, saw as Mrs. Dutrow's "objectives" with regard to her estate plans and then detailing in over five pages the calculations as to how these "objectives" could be achieved. An important aspect of his proposal was to deplete substantially the estate to simplify Mrs. Dutrow's "money worries." Cotsworth further noted at the beginning of this letter to Stevens that

[o]ur joint obligation—you and the family—is to accomplish these objectives with minimum tax effects upon the total estate. Obviously you are in a far better position to work out the details than I am, but you appear reluctant to go as fast or as far as I have suggested for reasons that are not clear to us.

Then, on November 26, 1973, Cotsworth proceeded to consult Grant Buttermore, his own lawyer, regarding Mrs. Dutrow's estate plans. Buttermore had been the attorney for the Cotsworth family and the Cotsworth family business, the Berry Steel Corporation, for six to seven years and had provided substantial legal advice concerning the corporation. He had also prepared wills for both Mr. and Mrs. Cotsworth and some of their children. For all intents and purposes, Buttermore can be viewed as having been the family attorney for the Cotsworths.

On November 29, 1973, following the initial contact by her husband, Dorcas Cotsworth went to Buttermore concerning the trust agreement of November 24 that Stevens had prepared for her mother. As a result, Buttermore called Stevens while Dorcas was in his office and discussed the matter of Mrs. Dutrow's domicile. This subject, in addition to a proposal concerning "gifting" by Mrs. Dutrow, had earlier been broached to Buttermore by John Cotsworth. Both lawyers agreed that Mrs. Dutrow's domicile should be changed to New Jersey for tax purposes and Buttermore made the change on the instrument by hand. Later that day Buttermore wrote to Stevens to confirm the results of the call, as well as the fact that the Cotsworths were personally involved in Mrs. Dutrow's estate planning, *viz.*:

We are in the process of reviewing Mrs. Dutrow's estate with her and Mr. and Mrs. Cotsworth along the lines suggested by Mr. Cotsworth in his outline heretofore submitted to you.

Buttermore concluded this letter by relaying Mrs. Dutrow's request to Stevens to provide "a compete list of all [her] assets * * * in order that we may make a proper analysis."

Stevens immediately responded, writing separate letters to Buttermore and Mrs. Dutrow on November 30. He gave Buttermore a skeletal list of Mrs. Dutrow's assets with no detail. At the same time he also undertook to make some technical corrections of Mrs. Dutrow's will, which was executed, as noted, on December 4. In the letter accompanying the will, he mentioned his conversation with Buttermore and his "assumption" that Mrs. Dutrow wanted him to give Buttermore the information he was requesting.

The response to this communication was a letter written to Stevens on December 3, 1973 in Dorcas Cotsworth's handwriting on her personal stationary, and signed by Dorcas and Mrs. Dutrow, which contained the following:

> These are my mother's observations as she sits here besides me—and she insists she is *not* being pressured.   *   *   *

> Mother and I have discussed this so often—now she says get it over and let me forget it—as it worries her with everything undone.

> Her desire and intent is to have Dorcas rewarded while alive—to have an Irrevocable Trust set up to let Dorcas have income and right to sprinkle money to Grandchildren when necessary.   *   *   *

> When Dorcas dies then the per stirpes takes over.   *   *   *

> Mother approves of Mr. Grant Buttermore knowing all details and keeping in this estate.

A meeting of Buttermore and John Cotsworth with Stevens was scheduled for December 13, 1973.   Prior to this meeting Buttermore met with Mrs. Dutrow alone, as he testified was his customary practice, "so that I could get the intent directly from   *   *   *   the testatrix." During this two hour conference, according to Buttermore, he explained various legal and tax aspects of estate planning to Mrs. Dutrow.   He also told her "that intent was much more important and controlled over the other two items, meaning taxation and liquidity."   Buttermore also reviewed at length Mrs. Dutrow's assets and her present will and trusts.   Among other things, Mrs. Dutrow, according to Buttermore's testimony, said that "her first priority was to make sure she had enough to last during her lifetime," for which purpose Mrs. Dutrow said she would need $26,000 per year.   Buttermore also explained to Mrs. Dutrow that the practical effect of the per stirpes disposition of the November 24 trust agreement would be to enable the two plaintiffs, the Haynes brothers, ultimately to "receive twice as much as each of the other grandchildren," to which Mrs. Dutrow responded, according to Buttermore, "I didn't realize that."

Buttermore testified that he told Stevens at the December 13 meeting that Mrs. Dutrow "wanted to go to the per capita basis equally among the grandchildren."   Stevens, according to Buttermore, was very skeptical that Mrs. Dutrow wanted to do this and asked Buttermore to doublecheck it with her.   Buttermore replied that "[i]n my mind she'd already made that decision after our talk on December the eleventh."

On December 17 and 18, a concerned Stevens wrote Buttermore letters confirming the discussion of December 13, and on December 18, specifically adverted to the possibility of "undue influence."   There is no indication in the record that Buttermore responded to Stevens on this matter.

Buttermore, in response to a call from Dorcas Cotsworth, again met alone with Mrs. Dutrow in Short Hills on January 11 to discuss a problem concerning some back dividends.   While he was with her, Buttermore, at his own initiative, told her what had happened during his December 13 meeting with Stevens and John Cotsworth and reviewed with her Stevens' letter of December 17 concerning her estate plans.   Following that exchange, Buttermore related, Mrs. Dutrow instructed him to "draw the papers."   Although Stevens had previously asked Buttermore to write him in Vermont, where he was vacationing, if there were any further developments concerning Mrs. Dutrow's estate planning, Buttermore did not do so, apparently believing that Mrs. Dutrow, who complained of Stevens' absence, did not desire or need Stevens to be further involved. Thus, Buttermore, still the Cotsworths' attorney, also stepped in, exclusively, as Mrs. Dutrow's attorney for purposes of planning her estate.

Significantly, at this juncture, drastic changes in Mrs. Dutrow's estate planning materialized.   According to Buttermore, he and Mrs. Dutrow then proceeded to discuss in detail her wishes for a new will and trust agreements.   Mrs. Dutrow assertedly indicated that she wanted "to leave [her estate] equally   *   *   *   between the grandchildren," and did not care about the adverse tax consequences which Buttermore claimed he had explained to her.   Buttermore also seemed to minimize the effect of the proposed change allegedly requested by Mrs. Dutrow by pointing out to her that altering the particular trust in question would not accomplish her goals;   although all six grandchildren would inherit equally under the particular trust in question, the consequence of other trusts already in existence would be that the two Haynes grandchildren would "still be getting greater in the end" than Mrs. Cotsworth's children.   During that meeting, Buttermore also apparently showed Stevens' letter of December 18 concerning undue influence to Mrs. Dutrow.

These discussions resulted in the near total severance of the Haynes children from their grandmother's estate.   Assertedly, at Mrs. Dutrow's request, Buttermore promptly prepared two new trust agreements, which provided for the payment of income with full right of invasion of principal to Dorcas Cotsworth during her lifetime and that, upon Dorcas' death, "the then remaining balance in said trust shall be divided equally among settlor's grandchildren."   In addition, Mrs. Dutrow's new will provided for the bequest of all her tangible personal property to Dorcas Cotsworth, "or if she does not survive me to my grandchildren who survive me, equally."   These instruments were executed by Mrs. Dutrow on January 16, 1974.

On January 19 Buttermore sent Stevens copies of the new instruments along with a letter in which he explained that after going over everything "meticulously with Mrs. Dutrow," the new instruments had been prepared "along the lines we have discussed" and that, in Stevens' absence, Mrs. Dutrow had become "quite upset with the Fidelity Bank and decided that she wanted to immediately revoke" the existing trust agreements and will.   Stevens testified to astonishment at the proposed distribution.   He also expressed surprise about the provision in both trust agreements, which permitted Dorcas Cotsworth to withdraw the principal each year so that, if exercised, there might be nothing left when she died.

In early May 1974 Buttermore again met with Mrs. Dutrow to make some changes in the trust agreements. The most important change allowed the corporate trustee First National Bank of New Jersey to distribute principal, "in its sole discretion," to Dorcas Cotsworth and any of Mrs. Dutrow's grandchildren (i.e., plaintiffs as well as Dorcas' children). This was in contrast to the original terms of this trust agreement, as executed by Mrs. Dutrow in January 1974, which allowed for such discretionary distribution by the bank only to Mrs. Cotsworth and her children, not to plaintiffs. According to Buttermore's testimony, this change was clearly Mrs. Dutrow's idea.

On April 24, 1975, Mrs. Dutrow amended the revocable trust agreement and added a codicil to her will in order to add *in terrorem* clauses to each instrument. Both the amendment and the codicil were prepared by Buttermore. At trial, Buttermore said that Mrs. Dutrow had decided to add the clause after reading that J. Paul Getty had included such a clause in his will to prevent litigation.

Buttermore next met with Mrs. Dutrow to discuss her estate on December 11, 1975. At this meeting, according to Buttermore's testimony, Mrs. Dutrow told him that she had decided to give her estate, other than special bequests or amounts, to Dorcas Cotsworth, to enable Dorcas to enjoy it during Dorcas' lifetime. Buttermore testified that he was "taken by surprise" by this proposal and tried to explain to Mrs. Dutrow that this change would result in additional taxes of between $700,000 and $800,000 when Dorcas died. But, according to Buttermore, Mrs. Dutrow insisted on making the change. The necessary amendments to the revocable trust agreement were prepared by Buttermore and executed by Mrs. Dutrow on January 9, 1976, providing for distribution of the principal to Dorcas upon Mrs. Dutrow's death, or, if Dorcas was not then living, equally among Mrs. Dutrow's grandchildren. A new will executed the same day provided, as had previous wills, that Dorcas would inherit all of Mrs. Dutrow's tangible personal property. The final change made by Mrs. Dutrow in her estate plans before she died in September 1977, was to amend the revocable trust to give $10,000 to each of her grandchildren at her death, apparently realizing that otherwise the Haynes children would likely not inherit anything.

The last testamentary document executed by the testatrix was a will dated April 8, 1976. It contained no further major changes in her dispositions. Mrs. Dutrow died on September 27, 1977 and her final will was admitted to probate by the Surrogate of Ocean County on October 12, 1977, with the First National State Bank of New Jersey as executor.

II

In any attack upon the validity of a will, it is generally presumed that "the testator was of sound mind and competent when he executed the will." Gellert v. Livingston, 5 N.J. 65, 71, 73 A.2d 916 (1950). If a will is tainted by "undue influence," it may be overturned. "Undue influence" has been defined as "mental, moral or physical" exertion which has destroyed the "free agency of a testator" by preventing the testator "from following the dictates of his own mind and will and accepting instead the domination and influence of another." In re Neuman, 133 N.J.Eq. 532, 534, 32 A.2d 826 (E. & A. 1943). When such a contention is made

> the burden of proving undue influence lies upon the contestant unless the will benefits one who stood in a confidential relationship to the testatrix and there are additional circumstances of a suspicious character present which require explanation. In such case the law raises a presumption of undue influence and the burden of proof is shifted to the proponent. [In re Rittenhouse's Will, 19 N.J. 376, 378–379, 117 A.2d 401 (1955)]

* * *

The first element necessary to raise a presumption of undue influence, a "confidential relationship" between the testator and a beneficiary, arises

> where trust is reposed by reason of the testator's weakness or dependence or where the parties occupied relations in which reliance is naturally inspired or in fact exists. * * * [In re Hopper, 9 N.J. 280, 282, 88 A.2d 193, 194 (1952)]

Here, the aged Mrs. Dutrow, afflicted by the debilitations of advanced years, was dependent upon her sole surviving child with whom she lived and upon whom she relied for companionship, care and support. This was a relationship sustained by confidence and trust. The determination of the trial court, in this case, that there was a confidential relationship between the testatrix and the chief beneficiary of her will is unassailable.

The second element necessary to create the presumption of undue influence is the presence of suspicious circumstances which, in combination with such a confidential relationship, will shift the burden of proof to the proponent. Such circumstances need be no more than "slight." * * *

In this case there were suspicious circumstances attendant upon the execution of the will. There was a confidential relationship between the testatrix and her attorney, who was also the attorney for the daughter and the daughter's immediate family. Furthermore, following the establishment of the confidential relationship of the daughter's attorney with the testatrix, there was a drastic change in the testamentary dispositions of the testatrix, which favored the daughter. These factors collectively triggered the presumption that there was undue influence in the execution of the will.

On this record, the trial court correctly posited a presumption of undue influence that shifted the burden of proof on this issue to the proponents of the will. The court concluded ultimately on this issue, however, that the proponents, the defendants, had overcome the presumption of undue influence. The trial judge determined that Mrs. Dutrow was of firm mind and resolve, that the final testamentary disposition, though markedly different from previous plans, was not unnatural or instinctively unsound and it represented her actual intent. Further, the court found the explanation for Mrs. Dutrow's final testamentary disposition to be candid and satisfactory.

The plaintiffs argue vigorously that the trial court's findings of fact and conclusions are not supported by sufficient evidence. They contend that in view of the strength of the presumption of undue influence created by the confidential relationships and the peculiarly suspicious circumstances of this case, there is an unusually heavy burden of proof required to disprove undue influence, which defendants failed to meet.

In this jurisdiction, once a presumption of undue influence has been established the burden of proof shifts to the proponent of the will, who must, under normal circumstances, overcome that presumption by a preponderance of the evidence. In re Week's Estate, supra, 29 N.J.Super. at 538–539, 103 A.2d 43. * * * As stated by Judge Clapp in In re Week's Estate, supra:

> In the case of a presumption of undue influence, apparently because the presumption is fortified by policy, the proponent must, according to the language of the cases, prove, to the satisfaction of the trier of fact, that there was no undue influence. In connection with this presumption, unlike other presumptions, the courts do not speak as to the burden of going forward with the evidence. However, we conclude, the moment this presumption is erected, both the burden of proof * * * and the burden of going forward with proof, shift to the proponent and are identical and coincident. To meet each of these assignments, the proponent must establish by the same quantum of proof—that is, by a preponderance of the proof—that there is no undue influence. [29 N.J.Super. at 538–539, 103 A.2d 43 (citations omitted)]

In re Week's Estate, supra, recognized, however, that there were situations calling for a stronger presumption of undue influence and a commensurately heavier burden of proof to rebut the presumption. While in that case the presumption of undue influence was deemed to be rebuttable by a preponderance of evidence, the court acknowledged other

> cases where the presumption of undue influence is so heavily weighted with policy that the courts have demanded a sterner measure of proof than that usually obtaining upon civil issues. That is the situation, for instance, where an attorney benefits by the will of his client and especially where he draws it himself. [29 N.J.Super. at 539, 103 A.2d 43.]

It has been often recognized that a conflict on the part of an attorney in a testimonial situation is fraught with a high potential for undue influence, generating a strong presumption that there was such improper influence and warranting a greater quantum of proof to dispel the presumption. Thus, where the attorney who drew the will was the sole beneficiary, the Court required "substantial and trustworthy evidence of explanatory facts" and "candid and full disclosure" to dispel the presumption of undue influence. In re Blake's Will, 21 N.J. 50, 58–59, 120 A.2d 745 (1956). And, where an attorney-beneficiary, who had a preexisting attorney-client relationship with the testatrix, introduced the testatrix to the lawyer who actually drafted the challenged will, this Court has required evidence that was "convincing or impeccable," In re Rittenhouse's Will, supra, 19 N.J. at 382, 117 A.2d 401, "convincing," In re Hopper, supra, 9 N.J. at 285, 88 A.2d 193, and, "clear and convincing," In re Davis, supra, 14 N.J. at 170, 101 A.2d 521. * * *

In imposing the higher burden of proof in this genre of cases, our courts have continually emphasized the need for a lawyer of independence and undivided loyalty, owing professional allegiance to no one but the testator.   In In re Rittenhouse's Will, supra, 19 N.J. at 380–382, 117 A.2d 401, the Court questioned the attorney's independence and loyalty in view of the attorney-beneficiary's role in bringing the draftsman and the testatrix together, noting that the beneficiary had been "unable to give a satisfactory explanation of the relationship" between himself, the draftsman and the testatrix, *viz:*

> [I]t would appear the testatrix did not independently choose [the draftsman] as the scrivener of her will.   It is fair to assume from the record that she was influenced to do so by [the beneficiary].

Similarly, in In re Davis, supra, 14 N.J. at 171, 101 A.2d 521, the Court observed:

> We wish to reiterate what has been said repeatedly by our courts as to the proprieties of a situation where the testatrix wishes to make her attorney or a member of his immediate family a beneficiary under a will. Ordinary prudence requires that such a will be drawn by some other lawyer of the testatrix' own choosing, so that any suspicion of undue influence is thereby avoided.   Such steps are in conformance with the spirit of *Canons* 6, 11, of the Canons of Professional Ethics promulgated by this court.   * * *

It is not difficult to appreciate the policy reasons for creating an especially strong presumption of undue influence in cases of attorney misconduct.   Such professional delinquency is encompassed by our official rules governing the professional ethics of attorneys.   Our disciplinary rules cover all gradations of professional departures from ethical norms, and, the existence of an ethical conflict exemplified in this case is squarely posited under DR 5–105.[2]   This ethical rule prohibits an attorney from engaging in professional relationships that may impair his independent and untrammeled judgment with respect to his client.   This disciplinary stricture

---

2.   DR 5–105 Refusing to Accept or Continue Employment if the Interests of Another Client May Impair the Independent Professional Judgment of the Lawyer.

(A) A lawyer shall decline proffered employment if the exercise of this independent professional judgment in behalf of a client will be or is likely to be adversely affected by the acceptance of the proffered employment, except to the extent permitted under DR 5–105(C).

(B) A lawyer shall not continue multiple employment if the exercise of his independent professional judgment in behalf of a client will be or is likely to be adversely affected by his representation of another client, except to the extent permitted under DR 5–105(C).

(C) In situations covered by DR 5–105(A) and (B) except as prohibited by rule, opinion, directive or statute, a lawyer may represent multiple clients if he believes that he can adequately represent the interests of each and if each consents to the representation after full disclosure of the facts and of the possible effect of such representation on the exercise of his independent professional judgment on behalf of each.

(D) If a lawyer is required to decline employment or to withdraw from employment under DR 5–105, no partner or associate of his or his firm may accept or continue such employment

[In the Model Rules of Professional Conduct, adopted by the House of Delegates of the American Bar Association, August 1983, this rule reads:

should be practically self-demonstrative to any conscientious attorney.   There is nothing novel about the ethical dilemma dealt with by DR 5–105.   A lawyer cannot serve two masters in the same subject matter if their interests are or may become actually or potentially in conflict.   [In re Chase, 68 N.J. 392, 396, 346 A.2d 89 (1975)]

* * *

Accordingly, it is our determination that there must be imposed a significant burden of proof upon the advocates of a will where a presumption of undue influence has arisen because the testator's attorney has placed himself in a conflict of interest and professional loyalty between the testator and the beneficiary.   In view of the gravity of the presumption in such cases, the appropriate burden of proof must be heavier than that which normally obtains in civil litigation.   The cited decisions which have dealt with the quantum of evidence needed to dispel the presumption of influence in this context have essayed various descriptions of this greater burden, *viz:* "convincing," "impeccable," "substantial," "trustworthy," "candid," and "full."   Our present rules of evidence, however, do not employ such terminology.   The need for clarity impels us to be more definitive in the designation of the appropriate burden of proof and to select one which most suitably measures the issue to be determined.   See, e.g., In re Week's Estate, supra.   Only three burdens of proof are provided by the evidence rules, namely, a preponderance, clear and convincing, and beyond a reasonable doubt.   Evid.R. 1(4).   The standard in our evidence rules that conforms most comfortably with the level of proofs required by our decisions in this context is the burden of proof by clear and convincing evidence.   In re Davis, supra, 14 N.J. at 170, 101 A.2d 521;   cf. Sarte v. Pidoto, 129 N.J.Super. 405, 411, 324 A.2d 48 (App.Div.1974) (*de facto* use of a standard stricter than preponderance of the evidence entails proof by clear and convincing evidence under rules of evidence).   Hence, the presumption of undue influence created by a professional conflict of interest on the part of an attorney, coupled with confidential relationships between a testator and the beneficiary as well as the attorney, must be rebutted by clear and convincing evidence.

Applying these principles to this case, it is clear that attorney Buttermore was in a position of irreconcilable conflict within the common

---

RULE 1.7 Conflict of Interest: General Rule

(a) A lawyer shall not represent a client if the representation of that client will be directly adverse to another client, unless:

(1) the lawyer reasonably believes the representation will not adversely affect the relationship with the other client;   and

(2) each client consents after consultation.

(b) A lawyer shall not represent a client if the representation of that client may be materially limited by the lawyer's responsibilities to another client or to a third person, or by the lawyer's own interests, unless:

(1) the lawyer reasonably believes the representation will not be adversely affected;   and

(2) the client consents after consultation.   When representation of multiple clients in a single matter is undertaken, the consultation shall include explanation of the implications of the common representation and the advantages and risks involved.   Eds.]

sense and literal meaning of DR 5–105.   In this case, Buttermore was required, at a minimum, to provide full disclosure and complete advice to Mrs. Dutrow, as well as the Cotsworths, as to the existence and nature of the conflict and to secure knowing and intelligent waivers from each in order to continue his professional relationship with Mrs. Dutrow.   DR 5–105(C).   Even these prophylactic measures, however, might not have overcome the conflict, nor have been sufficient to enable the attorney to render unimpaired "independent professional judgment" on behalf of his client, DR 5–105(B);   see Lieberman v. Employers Ins. of Wausau, supra, 84 N.J. at 338–340, 419 A.2d 417.   Any conflict, of course, could have been avoided by Buttermore simply refusing to represent Mrs. Dutrow. DR 5–105(A), (B);   see In re Davis, supra, at 171, 101 A.2d 521.   But, Buttermore was apparently insensitive or impervious to the presence or extent of the professional conflict presented by these circumstances.   He undertook none of these measures to eliminate the dual representation or overcome the conflict.[3]   Consequently, a strong taint of undue influence was permitted, presumptively, to be injected into the testamentary disposition of Mrs. Dutrow.

Accordingly, the attorney's conduct here, together with all of the other factors contributing to the likelihood of wrongful influence exerted upon the testatrix, has engendered a heavy presumption of undue influence which the proponents of the will must overcome by clear and convincing evidence.

This determination that clear and convincing evidence must be marshalled to overcome the presumption of undue influence appropriately requires that the matter be remanded to the trial court for new findings of fact and legal conclusions based upon application of this burden of proof.   We remand, recognizing that there is considerable evidence in the record as to Mrs. Dutrow's intelligence, independence and persistence, of her alienation, to some extent, from the Haynes children, and as to her natural intent primarily to benefit her children, rather than her grandchildren.   Moreover, all of this evidence is based upon the credibility of witnesses, which we cannot independently evaluate.   We are also mindful that the trial court found that the explanation for Mrs. Dutrow's testamentary disposition was candid and satisfactory.

Nevertheless, the trial court does not appear to have given full weight to the additional significant factor generating the heightened presumption of undue influence in this case, namely, that occasioned by the con-

---

3. In this case, we recognize that Buttermore believed in good faith that he was taking proper precautions to overcome or avoid the consequences of the improper conflict and did not believe or perceive that his position involved an impermissible conflict of interest in light of these measures.   He also expressed the view that frequently estate planning involves members of an entire family and therefore no conflict exists for an attorney who has professional relationships with members of the family, in addition to the testator.   This position is, of course, inconsistent with our explicit holding that such conduct, as exemplified by the facts of this case, violates DR 5–105.   Since this application of DR 5–105 to such situations has not been generally acknowledged, we do not think it fair that ethical sanctions be pursued retroactively in this case for such conduct, since there are no additional aggravating circumstances.   See In re Smock, 86 N.J. 426, 432 A.2d 34 (1981).

flict of interest on the part of the attorney drafting the will, whose testimony was crucial to the outcome of this case. Most importantly, the court's conclusion was premised upon an application of the conventional standard of proof entailing only a preponderance of the evidence. We therefore cannot with any certitude predict that the trial court's findings of fact and resultant conclusion would be the same were he to reassess the evidence, imposing upon the proponents of the will the burden of proof of lack of undue influence by clear and convincing evidence. Consequently, the fair disposition, which we now direct, is to remand the matter to the trial court for a redetermination of facts and conclusions based upon the record.

III

The second issue involves the enforceability of the *in terrorem* clauses challenged by the plaintiffs. The trial court noted that under the State's common law, *in terrorem* clauses are enforceable when the contest is based upon an allegation of undue influence, even if probable cause and good faith are present. The trial judge nonetheless declared the clauses unenforceable because the new probate code, N.J.S.A. 3A:2A–32, admittedly not controlling in this case because of the date of Mrs. Dutrow's death, "provides that *in terrorem* clauses are unenforceable if probable cause exists" and, following the lead of the new code on this point, the court refused to enforce the clauses, noting that its ruling was "in accord with the authoritative view and the modern trend."

On this latter issue, the Appellate Division found that there was no basis in law for the trial court's decision, and that although the new probate code, N.J.S.A. 3A:2A–32, changed the law with respect to wills, the change applied only to wills of decedents who died on or after September 1, 1978, nearly a year after Mrs. Dutrow's death. In addition, the Appellate Division found no indication that the new statute is meant to apply to trusts. Furthermore, the court said in support of reversal on this issue, "[e]nforcement of the *in terrorem* clause is particularly equitable here."

As noted earlier, on April 24, 1975, Mrs. Dutrow amended the revocable trust agreement and added a codicil to her will in order to add *in terrorem* clauses to each instrument. The clause in the amendment to the revocable trust agreement, almost identical to that in the will, provided:

> If any beneficiary under this trust shall contest the validity of, or object to this instrument, or attempt to vacate the same, or to alter or change any of the provisions hereof, such person shall be thereby deprived of all beneficial interest thereunder and of any share in this Trust and the share of such person shall become part of the residue of the trust, and such person shall be excluded from taking any part of such residue and the same shall be divided among the other persons entitled to take such residue.[4]

---

4. If enforced, the result would be to deprive each of the two plaintiffs of $10,000 which they were to receive under this trust agreement as modified by the fourth amendment thereto of April 7, 1976.

In 1977 the Legislature enacted N.J.S.A. 3A:2A–32 as part of the new probate code.[5] This statute renders *in terrorem* clauses in wills unenforceable if probable cause for a will contest exists:

> A provision in a will purporting to penalize any interested person for contesting the will or instituting other proceedings relating to the estate is unenforceable if probable cause exists for instituting proceedings.

In Alper v. Alper, 2 N.J. 105, 65 A.2d 737 (1949), the Court said that the existence of probable cause to bring the challenge to the will should result in nonenforcement of an *in terrorem* clause "where the contest of the will is waged on the ground of forgery or subsequent revocation by a later will or codicil." However, where typical grounds of challenge were advanced—"fraud, undue influence, improper execution or lack of testamentary capacity"—the clause was deemed to be enforceable, notwithstanding probable cause, as a safeguard against deleterious, acrimonious and wasteful family litigation. Id. at 112–113, 65 A.2d 737.   *   *   *

The new statute, N.J.S.A. 3A:2A–32, however, abolishes the distinction drawn by the Court in *Alper* between cases in which *in terrorem* clauses in wills shall be enforced, and those in which they shall not, stating quite simply that *whenever* there is probable cause to contest a will, the clause should not be enforced. While the statute applies neither to the will in this case, which was probated prior to the statute's effective date, nor to the trust agreement, since the statute applies only to wills, the statute is indicative of a legislative intent to create a policy less inhibitory to the bringing of challenges to testamentary instruments. There does not appear to be any logical reason why the purpose of the statute should not be presently recognized and be applied equally to trust instruments or should not be applied in the circumstances of this case.

There are public policy considerations both favoring and disfavoring the enforcement of *in terrorem* clauses. On the one hand, such provisions seek to reduce vexatious litigation, avoid expenses that debilitate estates and give effect to a testator's clearly expressed intentions.   *   *   *

On the other hand, a majority of jurisdictions have declined to enforce *in terrorem* clauses where challenges to testamentary instruments are brought in good faith and with probable cause. [Citations to cases from other jurisdictions have been omitted.]

Given this relative equipoise of considerations, it is entirely appropriate for the courts to be sensitive and responsive to the Legislature's perception of the public interest and policy in these matters.   *   *   * The assessment, balancing and resolution of these concerns by the Legislature, now reflected in the statute law, is, of course, not binding upon the judiciary's decisional authority in a matter not governed by such enactments. Nevertheless, the legislative handling of the subject is, and should be, strongly influential in the judicial quest for the important

---

5. N.J.S.A. 3A:2A–32 is identical to Uniform Probate Code (U.L.A.) § 3–905 (1969). The Uniform Probate Code has been adopted in its entirety by fourteen states and two others, of which New Jersey is one, have adopted some portions of it.

societal values which are constituent elements of the common law and find appropriate voice in the decisions of the court expounding the common law.   *   *   *

We therefore decline to enforce an *in terrorem* clause in a will or trust agreement where there is probable cause to challenge the instrument. The trial court concluded that the plaintiffs in this case "proceeded in good faith and on probable cause."   That finding is amply supported by evidence of record.

IV

We have determined that *in terrorem* clauses in the will and trust instruments are not enforceable.   We have also directed, for reasons set forth in this opinion, that the case be remanded for new findings of fact and legal conclusions with respect to the major issue of undue influence in the execution of the will.

Accordingly, the judgment below is reversed and the matter remanded.   Jurisdiction is not retained.

CLIFFORD, J., dissenting in part.

I am in full accord with the majority's meticulous treatment of the "undue influence" issue, but I part company on its decision concerning the *in terrorem* clauses.

On April 24, 1975, when Mrs. Dutrow added the challenged clauses to the testamentary instruments, enforcement of *in terrorem* clauses was perfectly in keeping with the public policy of this state, as it was at the time of the testator's death in 1977.   As the Court acknowledges, ante at 903, that policy was to give effect to such clauses where, as here, the instrument was contested on the ground of undue influence.

*   *   * As *Alper* instructs us, an *in terrorem* clause is

a reasonable safeguard against attempted overthrow of the testamentary dispositions by a disappointed heir, striving for an undue advantage, and a device to lessen the wastage of the estate in litigation and the chance of increasing family animosities by besmirching the reputation of the testator when he is no longer alive to defend himself and to discourage the contesting of wills as a means of coercing a settlement.   [2 N.J. at 112, 65 A.2d 737.]

Mrs. Dutrow's intentions in insisting on such a provision comported entirely with the judicially-declared public policy as of the time she made her testamentary dispositions and as of the time of her death.

Instead of honoring the testator's manifest wishes, however, the court looks for guidance to a statute not effective until a year after her death. *   *   * The majority bows to this "legislative handling" of the subject as an aid in the "judicial quest for the important societal values that are the constituent elements of the common law   *   *   *."   Quite apart from the tardy surfacing of this newly recognized public policy is the shaky foundation upon which it rests.   The Legislature, clearly in error (as forthrightly conceded by plaintiffs), believed that N.J.S.A. 3A:2A–32 codifies existing New Jersey case law on the subject.   See Statement of Assembly Comm. on Judiciary, Law, Public Safety and Defense, Assembly

Doc. No. 1717, L.1977, c. 412 (1977). As demonstrated above, the statute does no such thing. It runs directly contrary to the case law.

We may view an *in terrorem* clause in a less charitable fashion than did the *Alper* court, perhaps as a device to wreak revenge on a disgruntled object of one's testamentary disposition. We may see such clauses as representing the most disagreeable impulses of a testator. They may lay bare one's mean, uncharitable, impervious, suspicious, hostile, downright churlish nature—and then some. I do *not* suggest that Mrs. Dutrow manifested any of those characteristics, but I *do* suggest that testators are allowed to exhibit all of them, and worse, without fear that a court will disregard their final wishes.

In keeping with both the testator's unambiguously-declared intent and the public policy of this state at the time of her death, I would give effect to the *in terrorem* clauses.

For reversal—Justices SULLIVAN, PASHMAN, CLIFFORD, SCHREIBER and HANDLER—5.

For affirmance—None.

Notes

1. The opinion makes clear that Mrs. Dutrow was a wealthy woman, but it does not specify the precise amount of her net estate against which the death taxes were assessed. Her husband died in 1945, leaving an estate of approximately $8 million to Mrs. Dutrow and their two daughters. In a family situation of this kind, it is fair to speculate that the widow received the largest share, that her inheritance appreciated substantially between 1945 and 1977, and that she may have owned wealth derived from sources other than her husband. Had she, like her husband, left an $8 million estate at her death in 1977, her estate would have had to pay a federal estate tax of approximately $4,600,000. The same estate in 1987 will pay about $1 million less in federal tax due to the 1981 amendments to the statute which increased the unified credit and reduced the top marginal rate from 70% to 55% (50% as of 1988) on estates in excess of $2,500,000. See Chapter Ten, pages 893–896 infra. In addition to the federal estate tax, the Dutrow estate was also liable for a substantial state death tax, although this liability was offset by a credit against the federal tax for a portion of the state death tax.

A number of references in the opinion raise points that are discussed elsewhere in the book. Mrs. Dutrow changed her domicile from York, Pennsylvania, to Short Hills, New Jersey. In so doing she had to sever completely her settled connections with her original domicile to insure that her estate would not face liability for two sets of domiciliary death taxes, as did the estate of John T. Dorrance. Mr. Dorrance, the chief executive of the Campbell Soup Company, maintained two homes, one in New Jersey and a second in Pennsylvania. Following his death, each state claimed that Dorrance was domiciled within its jurisdiction and on that basis assessed full death taxes upon his estate, amounting to more than $14 million in Pennsylvania and $12 million in Jersey. The United States Supreme Court refused to resolve the conflicting claims of domicile, although in legal theory a person can possess only one domicile at any given time. For a discussion of the *Dorrance* rulings and of related cases, see

Chapter Eight, Sec. A. The Decedent in a Federal System: Domicile, pages 582–590, infra.

Mrs. Dutrow was urged by her daughter and son-in-law to make inter vivos gifts. At that time, a donor was entitled to give $3,000 to each donee, each year, without incurring any gift tax. Under present law, this amount, known as the annual exclusion, has been increased to $10,000 per donee. Thus Mrs. Dutrow would have been able to make gifts each year to her daughter and six grandchildren, totaling $21,000, without tax. On the subject of gifts and the annual exclusion, see Chapter Ten, pages 890–893, infra.

In its final form, Mrs. Dutrow's estate plan was set out in two documents: a revocable inter vivos trust covering her intangible property, including her Ralston Purina stock, and a will that bequeathed to her daughter her tangible personal property such as jewelry and antiques. Because she retained control over the trust, the trust principal was subject to tax just as if she continued to own it in fee. Mrs. Dutrow was warned by Attorney Buttermore that a disposition of the estate outright to her daughter, who was apparently independently wealthy, would add $700,000 to $800,000 to the daughter's estate taxes at the daughter's death. The attorney probably had in mind as an alternative disposition that Mrs. Dutrow leave the property in trust, giving the daughter the right to income during her life, with the remainder passing free of the estate tax to the grandchildren at the daughter's death. On the present status of transfers designed to skip generations for tax purposes, see Chapter Ten, pages 959–961, infra.

2. Clients frequently find the inclusion of an in terrorem or no-contest clause reassuring. Is a word of caution from the attorney appropriate? Consider again the competing views on the subject set out in the concurring judge's opinion, supra.

The statute, enacted in 1977 as described in the principal opinion, brought New Jersey into line with the majority of jurisdictions, holding that an in terrorem clause is unenforceable if probable cause exists for initiating the proceedings. The issue of probable cause will only arise if the contest has failed to invalidate the will. What is the test of probable cause under such circumstances? To the extent no-contest clauses are enforceable, secondary questions may arise as to their applicability to a person who seeks a construction of the will to ascertain whether it contains a violation of the rule against perpetuities, to an infant beneficiary whose guardian joins the contest, or to a person who refuses to initiate the contest but is made a party to it. The cases are collected in Annot., Will-Forfeiture by Contesting Beneficiary, 23 A.L.R.4th 369 (1983). See generally, Jack, No Contest or In Terrorem Clauses in Wills—Construction and Enforcement, 19 Sw.L.J. 722 (1965); Selvin, Comment: Terror in Probate, 16 Stan.L.Rev. 355 (1963); Pfaltz, "In Terrorem" Ne Terreamus, 52 Ky.L.J. 769 (1964); Leavitt, Scope and Effectiveness of No-Contest Clauses in Last Wills and Testaments, 15 Hast.L.J. 45 (1963).

3. The court in the principal case applies the traditional rule which assigns the burden in cases involving undue influence and fraud to the contestant with the obligation of going forward with the production of evidence shifted to the proponent after it has been shown that a confidential relationship existed between the proponent and the testator. This court requires that the proponents rebut the "heavy presumption" by "clear and convincing" evidence. See also Franciscan Sisters Health Care v. Dean, 95 Ill.2d 452, 69 Ill.Dec. 960, 448 N.E.2d

872 (1983) (detailed discussion of the operation of the presumption). Once rebutted, the presumption has no continuing force, and the trial proceeds on the facts, with the burden of going forward with the evidence and the risk of non-persuasion on the contestant. The relationship between the parties is, of course, a fact from which the trier may draw an inference of undue influence. See generally, Wigmore on Evidence § 2502; Annot., Effect of Presumption as Evidence or Upon Burden of Proof, Where Controverting Evidence Is Introduced, 5 A.L.R.3d 19, 79.

4. What relationships have the potential for control that justifies a characterization of "confidential" and the creation of a presumption of undue influence?

a. Testator's *attorney* is the most obvious candidate for suspicion. As is illustrated in the principal case, the attorney may be under a heavy duty to explain his or her representation of the testator even when not named as a beneficiary in the will. The attorney who drafts a will that contains a bequest in his or her favor not only has little or no chance to receive the bequest but may also be subject to disciplinary proceedings for unethical conduct. See e.g. In re Anderson, 52 Ill.2d 202, 287 N.E.2d 682 (1972) (drafting documents from which personal profit was gained, in addition to a number of other violations of the code of ethics, justified a five-year disbarment of testator's attorney). The suspicion extends to bequests to members of the attorney's family. See e.g. In re Estate of Peterson, 283 Minn. 446, 168 N.W.2d 502 (1969) (will favoring attorney's children disallowed); Annot., Presumption or Inference of Undue Influence from Testamentary Gift to Relative, Friend, or Associate of Person Preparing Will or Procuring Its Execution, 13 A.L.R.2d 381.

Upon discovery of the testator's desire to benefit him or her, the attorney is obligated to refer the testator to another attorney for independent advice and assistance in drafting the will. Franciscan Sisters Health Care v. Dean, 95 Ill.2d 452, 69 Ill.Dec. 960, 448 N.E.2d 872 (1983) (lawyer-draftsman rebutted presumption of undue influence by showing that testator had consulted another attorney about the will). The attorney has not, however, always been able to avoid a challenge by having another attorney draft the will. See e.g. In re Will of Moses, 227 So.2d 829 (Miss.1969) (divided court upheld lower court order refusing probate to will favoring testator's attorney, who was also her lover, even though testator had secured independent advice from two different attorneys); In re Estate of Komarr, 46 Wis.2d 230, 175 N.W.2d 473 (1970), certiorari denied 401 U.S. 909, 91 S.Ct. 867, 27 L.Ed.2d 806 (1971) (fact that beneficiary-attorney retained another lawyer to draft will not sufficient to overcome inference of undue influence). There are cases where the attorney has been able to satisfy the duty of explanation and to take the legacy. See e.g. In re Gold's Estate, 408 Pa. 41, 182 A.2d 707 (1962) (lawyer allowed to retain three-fifths of estate because decedent not in a weakened condition); Costello v. Conlon, 344 Mass. 754, 182 N.E.2d 532 (1962) (lawyer who did not draw the will allowed to take $16,000 out of a $114,000 estate); Cline v. Larson, 234 Or. 384, 383 P.2d 74 (1963) (lawyer's secretary who typed the will and who had befriended the testatrix allowed to take against a strong dissent decrying the erosion of the rule); In re Paul's Estate, 407 Pa. 30, 180 A.2d 254 (1962) (lawyer allowed to take although his statement to testator that stock was only worth $50 per share rather than true value of $800 led to his bequest equalling 33 per cent of the estate rather than 3); but see In re Hurst's Estate, 406 Pa. 612, 179 A.2d

436 (1962), certiorari denied 37 U.S. 862, 83 S.Ct. 118, 9 L.Ed.2d 99 (1962) (lawyer who had only known testatrix four weeks, when testatrix stricken with grief over death of son, not allowed to take). It is not improper for persons involved in the planning and drafting of a will to be named executor of the estate. Brown v. Commercial National Bank of Peoria, 42 Ill.2d 365, 247 N.E.2d 894 (1969), certiorari denied 396 U.S. 961, 90 S.Ct. 436, 24 L.Ed.2d 425 (1969) (bank-executor not guilty of undue influence); State v. Gulbankian, 54 Wis.2d 605, 196 N.W.2d 733, 57 A.L.R.3d 696 (1972) (disciplinary proceedings against two attorneys for inserting provisions in wills naming themselves as executors or attorneys for estates dismissed, although court warned that active solicitation of this kind of business is unethical). On the subject generally see Annot., Undue Influence in Gift to Testator's Attorney, 19 A.L.R.3d 575.

b. A *guardian* or *conservator,* appointed to manage the property of a person debilitated by illness, injury or age, occupies a sensitive position. See e.g. Pepin v. Ryan, 133 Conn. 12, 47 A.2d 846 (1946) (conservator failed to sustain burden of proving will that favored her while disinheriting testator's nieces and nephews). Guardians have sometimes successfully sustained the burden of explanation and the wills have been probated. See In re Estate of Garfield, 192 Neb. 461, 222 N.W.2d 369 (1974); Whitteberry v. Whitteberry, 9 Or.App. 154, 496 P.2d 240 (1972). Testator may have been particularly susceptible to the influence of a *financial adviser* or *business associate.* See e.g. Salisbury v. Gardner, 515 S.W.2d 881 (Mo.App.1974) (bank president failed to rebut presumption of undue influence arising from his confidential relationship to testator); Paskvan v. Mesich, 455 P.2d 229 (Alaska 1969) (business partner fails to sustain burden).

c. A *clergyman* may be over-zealous in presenting the financial needs of his or her religious community to the testator, causing the courts to shift the burden of explanation to the clergyman. In re Estate of Cox, 383 Mich. 108, 174 N.W.2d 558 (1970) (two cousins successfully attacked the will of a 98-year old woman leaving the residue of the estate to her church because attorney and rector unduly influenced her); but see, Gingrich v. Bradley, 232 Ark. 884, 341 S.W.2d 33 (1960) (31-year old minister and wife had not influenced 78-year old testator); see generally, Annot., Undue Influence in Gift to Clergyman, Spiritual Adviser, or Church, 14 A.L.R.2d 649.

d. A *spouse* may be guilty of influence, but a court is not likely to classify it as "undue". "The evidence adduced going to this issue [wife's alleged undue influence] indicated that any activity by the decedent and his wife with respect to the will [she tore up his former will] was well within the great latitude which is and should be given to a wife in counseling and persuading her husband with respect to the making of a will." In re Rasnick, 77 N.J.Super. 380, 186 A.2d 527 (1962); see also Matter of Estate of Robinson, 231 Kan. 300, 644 P.2d 420 (1982) (no presumption arises from the marital relationship; "it would be monstrous to deny to a woman who is generally an important agent in building up domestic prosperity, the right to express her wishes concerning its disposal"). The wife does not, however, always win. See e.g. In the Matter of Will of Andrews, 299 N.C. 52, 261 S.E.2d 198 (1980) (jury verdict denying probate upheld; wife had unduly influenced her husband to the detriment of his son by a previous marriage); Matter of Estate of Waters, 629 P.2d 470 (Wyo.1981) (will of testator who "was suffering from the ravages of alcohol" set aside because of wife's undue influence). The wife has been described as "the darling of the probate court", a characterization that suggests a powerful sense of sympathy for a widow. By her behavior, she may, however, forfeit the court's special regard. See e.g. Matter of Estate of Hamm, 262 N.W.2d 201 (S.D.1978) (widow, who was described as a prostitute, who at one time had "taken off for other climes with his [husband-testator's] car and a portion of his money", and who had been convicted of conspiracy in the murder of her stepson, failed in her contest of husband's will which favored his attorney and a nursing home in which the attorney had an interest).

e. The position of the *lover* is discussed in Note 1, page 231, supra.

f. The *owner or operator of a nursing or foster home* has the opportunity to influence elderly and vulnerable patients. See Matter of Estate of Brandon, 55 N.Y.2d 206, 448 N.Y.S.2d 436, 433 N.E.2d 501 (1982) (inter vivos gifts set aside; evidence of two prior judgments holding that the owner of the nursing home, "Friendly Acres", had exerted undue influence on patients properly admitted); but see Estate of Podgursky, 271 N.W.2d 52 (S.D.1978) (will admitted to probate over dissent that pointed out practice of foster home owners to manipulate elderly patients to the owners' financial advantage).

g. *Friendship* is not a sufficient basis to raise a presumption of undue influence without a showing that the testator was particularly dependent on the friend, that the will was executed under suspicious circumstances, or that the disposition was unnatural or unjust. See e.g. Matter of Ferrill, 97 N.M. 383, 640 P.2d 489 (1981) (82-year old testatrix put confidence in friend and gave him her power of attorney); In re Estate of Button, 459 Pa. 234, 328 A.2d 480 (1974) (testator in weakened mental condition). Courts cast a suspicious eye on a relationship between an elderly testator and a young friend. In re Estate of Van Aken, 281 So.2d 917 (Fla.App.1973) (will of 78-year old man whose wife of 57 years had recently died not accepted for probate inasmuch as the sole beneficiary was a secretary who had been in his employ for two months, to the exclusion of his daughters); but see Casper v. McDowell, 58 Wis.2d 82, 205 N.W.2d 753 (1973) (nurse-housekeeper who was fifty years testator's junior allowed to inherit); Sweeney v. Eaton, 486 S.W.2d 453 (Mo.1972) (will of widow in her seventies leaving estate to a 31-year old dry cleaning delivery man upheld although evidence was presented that his motive was to "see every one of his children have a dollar bill in one hand and a candy bar in the other").

h. During the course of treatment, a patient may become totally dependent on a *psychiatrist*. The nature and extent of that dependency is discussed in Katz, The Silent World of Doctor and Patient, pages 142–143 (Free Press 1984):

Early in his work with patients, Freud observed the development of an "intense emotional relationship between the patient and the analyst which [cannot] be accounted for by the actual situation." [Freud, S., 20 Standard Edition of the Complete Psychological Works of Sigmund Freud, page 42, (Hogarth Press, 1959)]. He noted that "[i]t can be of a positive or of a negative character and can vary between the extreme of a passionate, completely sensual love and the unbridled expression of an embittered defiance and hatred." He called this phenomenon, of which patients initially are largely unaware, "transference." By this term he sought to capture patients' proclivity to endow their analyst with many of the characteristics of their earliest caretakers rather than to view the analyst solely as who he is. The process of transference leads patients to project onto the analyst all kinds of magical expectations, hopes, and fears that are intrinsically irrational because they emerge out of confusion not only of past and present but also of fantasy and reality.

* * *

Transference feelings become more intense when persons are ill and beset by fears and anxieties. Patients' basic modes of expression of such feelings are in many ways predictable and stereotypical, but their finely tuned manifestations also reveal facets of an individual's uniqueness and essence, of his or her personality as it has evolved in interactions with parents and other important persons during childhood years. Thus, manifestations of transference constitute a mixture of highly individualized personal reactions, as well as universal human adult and childlike longings, that possess both rational and irrational components. Transferences can guide and misguide persons—the latter more in times of stress, when infantile hopes and fears surface most insistently.

One psychiatrist has reported on his experiences, following the death of a patient who left a large bequest to him and named him executor of her estate. Eissler, The Psychiatrist and the Dying Patient, pages 198–240 (International Universities Press 1955). Although he had been unaware of her intentions and she had received independent advice, the psychiatrist refused the bequest, stating that it would be a breach of ethics to accept it, but he did reluctantly agree to serve as executor in order to prevent a family controversy. A contest alleging the psychiatrist's undue influence was settled. Dr. Eissler comments on the powerful effect "transference" may have on the patient's state of mind (pages 230–231):

Transference, particularly in psychotherapy, may rise to an inordinate intensity. All the latent strivings of a positive nature, desires of giving and of expressing affection might become mobilized and focus upon the therapist. The intensity of these strivings in its relationship to the strength of the ego can be compared to a hypnotic state. Without any stimulation from the outside in the form of the therapist's unconscious acting out or in the form of the therapist's unconscious wishes, the patient's transference wish still may find a symbolic and factual gratification in giving the therapist a gift. In the situation of the dying this may easily lead to the psychiatrist's inclusion in the will of the patient who looks at him as an object of his bounty. The question arises whether from the point of view of modern psychology this makes the will invalid, notwithstanding the laws admitting the physician as a natural object of the patient's bounty. I believe this question must be answered in the negative. A will does not become invalid merely by the fact that a patient acts out the transference in the form of making the treating psychiatrist a beneficiary. It would actually lead to an infringement upon the patient's freedom if he could make a valid will only by excluding his psychiatrist. But from the point of view of modern psychology, the psychiatrist is not permitted to *accept* the inheritance. In this moment of refusal the "undue influence" under which the patient stood—if the constellation is viewed in terms of modern psychology—is canceled out; the psychiatrist returns the inheritance to the estate and the consequences of his treatment, which had left a trace in the patient's will, have been eliminated. If a patient left his whole estate to the psychiatrist, it would become incumbent upon the court to decide its further disposition.

5. Can an undue influence action be predicated on fears that the legatee may not prove faithful to her oral promises to the testatrix? Wilhoit v. Fite, 341 S.W.2d 806 (Mo.1960). Testatrix's son predeceased testatrix leaving a minor son by his first wife, and also leaving a second wife. Testatrix was very close to her second daughter-in-law who acted substantially as her business manager. The will left everything to the daughter-in-law but with the oral understanding that the daughter-in-law would see to the grandson's education and support. The daughter-in-law has had no opportunity to show her good or bad faith. What result?

6. A will (or particular provisions in it) that has been procured by fraud may be set aside. Although the line of demarcation between fraud and undue influence frequently becomes blurred in cases where a will is challenged as having been wrongfully procured, the two concepts are theoretically distinct. Fraud requires proof that a person has made a false representation, knowing it to be false, with the intention that the testator rely on it, which in fact the testator has done, with the result that the will does not truly represent the testator's intent. Fraud may be practiced on an intelligent person who is in no way susceptible to undue influence. In In re Ford's Estate, 19 Wis.2d 436, 120 N.W.2d 647 (1963), for example, the testator was strong minded and could not be influenced, but statements made to him that several of his relatives were making claims to his property, if intentionally false, could be a sufficient fraud to have the will invalidated. The court held, however, that the statements were not fraudulent because they may have been true.

The contest will fail unless it can be shown that the will was induced by the fraud. In In re Carson's Estate, 184 Cal. 437, 194 P. 5, 17 A.L.R. 239 (1920), testatrix bequeathed something over $100,000 in value to "my husband J. Gamble Carson." Carson's previous marriage had not been terminated, making his marriage to testatrix a fraud. The contest was remanded to the trial court to determine whether testatrix left the bequest to Carson because she believed him to be her husbnd or because she wanted him to have it whether he was or was not her husband.

In In re Newhall's Estate, 190 Cal. 709, 214 P. 231, 28 A.L.R. 778 (1923), testatrix died at the age of eighty leaving a will which bequeathed $5 to Grace Ryder, one of two daughters of testatrix's first marriage, and the bulk of her estate to two daughters of a second marriage. The record revealed that one daughter of the second marriage had falsely told her mother that Mrs. Ryder had caused a guardianship proceeding to be instituted against the mother (a proceeding that the mother bitterly resented) and that Mrs. Ryder "was an immoral woman, that she was no good, and that she was not decent." An order to admit the will to probate was reversed, and the matter was remanded for a new trial on the issue of whether the will had been procured by fraud. On the retrial, what would be the result if the jury found that the daughter had actually believed that her information about Mrs. Ryder was true?

MATTER OF SNIDE

Court of Appeals of New York, 1981.
52 N.Y.2d 193, 437 N.Y.S.2d 63, 418 N.E.2d 656.

WACHTLER, Judge.

This case involves the admissibility of a will to probate. The facts are simply stated and are not in dispute. Harvey Snide, the decedent, and his wife, Rose Snide, intending to execute mutual wills at a common execution ceremony, each executed by mistake the will intended for the other. There are no other issues concerning the required formalities of execution (see EPTL 3–2.1), nor is there any question of the decedent Harvey Snide's testamentary capacity, or his intention and belief that he was signing his last will and testament. Except for the obvious differences in the names of the donors and beneficiaries on the wills, they were in all other respects identical.

The proponent of the will, Rose Snide, offered the instrument Harvey actually signed for probate. The Surrogate, 96 Misc.2d 513, 409 N.Y.S.2d 204 decreed that it could be admitted, and further that it could be reformed to substitute the name "Harvey" wherever the name "Rose" appeared, and the name "Rose" wherever the name "Harvey" appeared. The Appellate Division, 74 A.D.2d 930, 426 N.Y.S.2d 155, reversed on the law, and held under a line of lower court cases dating back into the 1800's, that such an instrument may not be admitted to probate. We would reverse.

It is clear from the record, and the parties do not dispute the conclusion, that this is a case of a genuine mistake. It occurred through the presentment of the wills to Harvey and Rose in envelopes, with the envelope marked for each containing the will intended for the other. The attorney, the attesting witnesses, and Harvey and Rose, all proceeding with the execution ceremony without anyone taking care to read the front pages, or even the attestation clauses of the wills, either of which would have indicated the error.

Harvey Snide is survived by his widow and three children, two of whom have reached the age of majority. These elder children have executed waivers and have consented to the admission of the instrument to probate. The minor child, however, is represented by a guardian ad litem who refuses to make such a concession. The reason for the guardian's objection is apparent. Because the will of Harvey would pass the entire estate to Rose, the operation of the intestacy statute (EPTL 4–1.1) after a denial of probate is the only way in which the minor child will receive a present share of the estate.

The gist of the objectant's argument is that Harvey Snide lacked the required testamentary intent because he never intended to execute the document he actually signed. This argument is not novel, and in the few American cases on point it has been the basis for the denial of probate (see Nelson v. McDonald, 61 Hun. 406, 16 N.Y.S. 273; Matter of Cutler, Sur., 58 N.Y.S.2d 604; Matter of Bacon, 165 Misc. 259, 300 N.Y.S. 920; see, also, Matter of Pavlinko, 394 Pa. 564, 148 A.2d 528; Matter of Goettel, 184 Misc. 155, 55 N.Y.S.2d 61). However, cases from other common-law jurisdictions have taken a different view of the matter, and we think the view they espouse is more sound (Matter of Brander, 4 Dom.L.Rep. 688 [1952]; Guardian, Trust & Executor's Co. of New Zealand v. Inwood, 65 N.Z.L.Rep. 614 [1946] [New Zealand]; see Wills, 107 U. of Pa.L.Rev. 1237, 1239–1240; Kennedy, Wills-Mistake-Husband and Wife Executing

Wills Drawn for Each Other—Probate of Husband's Will With Substitutions, 31 Can.Bar.Rev. 185).

Of course it is essential to the validity of a will that the testator was possessed of testamentary intent (Matter of May, 241 N.Y. 1, 148 N.E. 770; 64 N.Y.Jur., Wills, § 11; see EPTL 1–2.18), however, we decline the formalistic view that this intent attaches irrevocably to the document prepared, rather than the testamentary scheme it reflects. Certainly, had a carbon copy been substituted for the ribbon copy the testator intended to sign, it could not be seriously contended that the testator's intent should be frustrated (Matter of Epstein, Sur., 136 N.Y.S.2d 884, see 81 ALR2d 1112, 1120 1121). Here the situation is similar. Although Harvey mistakenly signed the will prepared for his wife, it is significant that the dispositive provisions in both wills, except for the names, were identical.

Moreover, the significance of the only variance between the two instruments is fully explained by consideration of the documents together, as well as in the undisputed surrounding circumstances. Under such facts it would indeed be ironic—if not perverse—to state that because what has occurred is so obvious, and what was intended so clear, we must act to nullify rather than sustain this testamentary scheme. The instrument in question was undoubtedly genuine, and it was executed in the manner required by the statute. Under these circumstances it was properly admitted to probate (see Matter of Pascal, 309 N.Y. 108, 113–114, 127 N.E.2d 835).

In reaching this conclusion we do not disregard settled principles, nor are we unmindful of the evils which the formalities of will execution are designed to avoid; namely, fraud and mistake. To be sure, full illumination of the nature of Harvey's testamentary scheme is dependent in part on proof outside of the will itself. However, this is a very unusual case, and the nature of the additional proof should not be ignored. Not only did the two instruments constitute reciprocal elements of a unified testamentary plan, they both were executed with statutory formality, including the same attesting witnesses, at a contemporaneous execution ceremony. There is absolutely no danger of fraud, and the refusal to read these wills together would serve merely to unnecessarily expand formalism, without any corresponding benefit. On these narrow facts we decline this unjust course.

Nor can we share the fears of the dissent that our holding will be the first step in the exercise of judicial imagination relating to the reformation of wills. Again, we are dealing here solely with identical mutual wills both simultaneously executed with statutory formality.

For the reasons we have stated, the order of the Appellate Division should be reversed, and the matter remitted to that court for a review of the facts.

JONES, Judge (dissenting).

I agree with the Appellate Division that the Surrogate's Court had no authority to reform the decedent's will and am of the conviction that the willingness of the majority in an appealing case to depart from what has been consistent precedent in the courts of the United States and England will prove troublesome in the future. This is indeed an instance of the old adage that hard cases make bad law.

Our analysis must start with the recognition that any statute of wills (now articulated in this State at EPTL 3–2.1) operates frequently to frustrate the identifiable dispositive intentions of the decedent. It is never sufficient under our law that the decedent's wishes be clearly established; our statute, like those of most other common-law jurisdictions, mandates with but a few specific exceptions that the wishes of the decedent be memorialized with prescribed formality. The statutes historically have been designed for the protection of testators, particularly against fraudulent changes in or additions to wills. "[W]hile often if may happen that a will truly expressing the intention of the testator is denied probate for failure of proper execution, it is better that this should happen under a proper construction of the statute than that the individual case should be permitted to weaken those provisions intended to protect testators generally from fraudulent alterations of their wills" (64 N.Y. Jur., Wills, § 198, p. 348).

Next it must be recognized that what is admitted to probate is a paper writing, a single integrated instrument (codicils are considered integral components of the decedent's "will"). We are not concerned on admission to probate with the substantive content of the will; our attention must be focused on the paper writing itself. As to that, there can be no doubt whatsoever that Harvey Snide did not intend as his will the only document that he signed on August 13, 1970.

Until the ruling of the Surrogate of Hamilton County in this case, the application of these principles in the past had uniformly been held in our courts to preclude the admission to probate of a paper writing that the decedent unquestionably intended to execute when he and another were making mutual wills but where, through unmistakable inadvertence, each signed the will drawn for the other. Nor had our courts blinkingly invoked a doctrine of equitable reformation to reach the same end. * * *

On the basis of commendably thorough world-wide research, counsel for appellant has uncovered a total of 17 available reported cases involving mutual wills mistakenly signed by the wrong testator. Six cases arise in New York, two in Pennsylvania, three in England, one in New Zealand and five in Canada. With the exception of the two recent Surrogate's decisions (*Snide* and *Iovino*) relief was denied in the cases from New York, Pennsylvania and England. The courts that have applied the traditional doctrines have not hesitated, however, to express regret at judicial inability to remedy the evident blunder. Relief was granted in the six cases from the British Commonwealth. In these cases it appears that the court has been moved by the transparency of the obvious error and the egregious frustration of undisputed intention which would ensue from failure to correct that error.

Under doctrines both of judicial responsibility not to allow the prospect of unfortunate consequence in an individual case to twist the application of unquestioned substantive legal principle and of *stare decisis,* I perceive no jurisprudential justification to reach out for the disposition adopted by the majority. Not only do I find a lack of rigorous judicial reasoning in this result; more important, I fear an inability to contain the logical consequences of this decision in the near future. Thus, why should the result be any different where, although the two wills are markedly different in content, it is equally clear that there has been an erroneous contemporaneous cross-signing by the two would-be testators, or where the scrivener has prepared several drafts for a single client and it is established beyond all doubt that the wrong draft has been mistakenly signed? Nor need imagination stop there.

For the reasons stated, I would adhere to the precedents, and affirm the order of the Appellate Division.

JASEN, FUCHSBERG and MEYER, JJ., concur with WACHTLER, J.

JONES, J., dissents and votes to affirm in a separate opinion in which COOKE, C. J., and GABRIELLI, J., concur.

Notes

1. The "settled principles" to which the majority opinion refers are embodied in the traditional rule holding that there is no remedy to reform mistakes of law or fact made by a testator in the execution of a will or in the drafting of its provisions. See e.g. Gifford v. Dyer, 2 R.I. 99, 57 Am.Dec. 708 (1852) (testatrix did not omit only child who had been absent many years by mistake, but court indicated that in any event mistake is only remediable if apparent on face of a will which also shows what the disposition would have been but for the mistake); Sadler v. Sadler, 184 Neb. 318, 167 N.W.2d 187 (1969) (wife entitled to elect against will although husband mistakenly believed that he had fulfilled his obligation to her by inter vivos settlement); cf. Ga.Code § 53–2–8, authorizing a remedy for certain mistakes, but see Herrin v. Herrin, 224 Ga. 579, 163 S.E.2d 713 (1968) (no remedy for error of judgment after testator has or should have investigated the facts). The no reformation rule has been applied where the mistake was more that of the attorney than the testator. See e.g. Mahoney v. Grainger, 283 Mass. 189, 186 N.E. 86 (1933) ("heirs at law" limited to maternal aunt, to the exclusion of 25 first cousins whom testator had instructed her attorney to make the beneficiaries; draftsman's error did not authorize court to reform fully executed will); In re Estate of Pavlinko, 394 Pa. 564, 148 A.2d 528 (1959) (court denied remedy on facts similar to those in the *Snide* case; a different rule, i.e. a grant of reformation for mistake, would render the Wills Act a "meaningless scrap of paper" and would open the door to "countless fraudulent claims").

Courts refuse to reform wills on the ground that they cannot accept extrinsic statements of testator's intent which have not been formally attested in accordance with the requirements of the Statute of Wills. Construction of the language of a will to determine its true meaning is often required; the process is not, however, to be used to alter the terms of the disposition. See for further discussion of the construction process and of the admissability of extrinsic evidence to resolve latent ambiguities, Chapter Eight, page 630, infra; Annot., Effect of Mistake of Draftsmen in Drawing Will, 90 A.L.R.2d 924. The line separating construction from reformation is sometimes indistinct. See e.g.

Estate of Taff, 63 Cal.App.3d 319, 133 Cal.Rptr. 737 (1976) (extrinsic evidence of testatrix's intent used to define "heirs" to exclude persons who were entitled to share in the estate under the California intestacy laws); Engle v. Siegel, 74 N.J. 287, 377 A.2d 892 (1977) (evidence of intent used to avoid operation of anti-lapse statute).

On the subject generally, see Henderson, Mistake and Fraud in Wills, 47 B.U.L.Rev. 303, 461 (1967).

2. Hope has been expressed that the decisions in Snide, Taff, and Engle v. Siegel represent a modern trend toward relaxation of the no-reformation rule which will in time culminate in the complete repudiation of the rule. Langbein and Waggoner, Reformation of Wills on the Ground of Mistake: Change of Direction in American Law?, 130 U. of Pa.L.Rev. 521 (1982). The authors do not believe that the rule is necessary to protect wills from unreliable evidence as is demonstrated in the cases where routine use of extrinsic evidence is made to reform instruments implementing such nonprobate transfers as deeds of gift, inter vivos trusts, and life insurance. They spell out, at pages 577–588, criteria for the administration of a general doctrine of reformation that includes allocation of the burden of proof to the contestant to prove the mistake by clear and convincing evidence.

For other areas of the law of wills where remedies are available to correct mistakes, see the doctrine of dependent relative revocation, pages 348–352, infra, and the use of cy pres to correct violations of the rule against perpetuities, pages 836–837, infra. Wills have been reformed in order to make their provisions qualify for tax advantages that the testator thought he or she was getting. See e.g. Mittleman's Estate v. Commissioner, 522 F.2d 132 (D.C.Cir. 1975).

3. Mistakes by an attorney of the type illustrated in the cases where reformation is sought may give rise to a malpractice action. See Annot., Attorney's Liability, to One Other than His Immediate Client, for Consequences of Negligence in Carrying Out Legal Duties, 45 A.L.R.3d 1181, 1195–1200.

LATHAM v. FATHER DIVINE

Court of Appeals of New York, 1949.
299 N.Y. 22, 85 N.E.2d 168, 11 A.L.R.2d 802.

DESMOND, Judge. The amended complaint herein has, in response to a motion under rule 106 of the Rules of Civil Practice, been dismissed for insufficiency. Its principal allegations are these: plaintiffs are first cousins, but not distributees, of Mary Sheldon Lyon, who died in October, 1946, leaving a will, executed in 1943, which gave almost her whole estate to defendant Father Divine, leader of a religious cult, and to two corporate defendants in some way connected with that cult, and to an individual defendant (Patience Budd) said to be one of Father Divine's active followers; that said will has been, after a contest instituted by distributees, probated under a compromise agreement with the distributees, by the terms of which agreement, to which plaintiffs were not parties, the defendants just above referred to will receive a large sum from the estate; that after the making of said will, decedent on several occasions expressed "a desire and a determination to revoke the said will, and to execute a new will by which the plaintiffs would receive a substantial portion of the estate", "that shortly prior to the death of the deceased she had certain attorneys draft a new will in which the plaintiffs were named as legatees for a very substantial amount, totalling approximately $350,000"; that "by reason of the said false representations, the said undue influence and the said physical force" certain of the defendants "prevented the deceased from executing the said new Will"; that, shortly before decedent's death, decedent again expressed her determination to execute the proposed new will which favored plaintiffs, and that defendants "thereupon conspired to kill, and did kill, the deceased by means of a surgical operation performed by a doctor engaged by the defendants without the consent or knowledge of any of the relatives of the deceased."

Nothing is better settled than that, on such a motion as this, all the averments of the attacked pleading are taken as true. For present purposes, then, we have a case where one possessed of a large property and having already made a will leaving it to certain persons, expressed an intent to make a new testament to contain legacies to other persons, attempted to carry out that intention by having a new will drawn which contained a large legacy to those others, but was, by means of misrepresentations, undue influence, force, and indeed, murder, prevented, by the beneficiaries named in the existing will, from signing the new one. Plaintiffs say that those facts, if proven, would entitle them to a judicial declaration, which their prayer for judgment demands, that defendants, taking under the already probated will, hold what they have so taken as constructive trustees for plaintiffs, whom decedent wished to, tried to, and was kept from, benefiting.

We find in New York no decision directly answering the question as to whether or not the allegations above summarized state a case for relief in equity. But reliable texts, and cases elsewhere, see 98 A.L.R. 474 et seq., answer it in the affirmative. Leading writers, 3 Scott on Trusts, pp. 2371–2376; 3 Bogert on Trusts and Trustees, part 1, §§ 473–474, 498, 499; 1 Perry on Trusts and Trustees [7th ed.], pp. 265, 371, in one form or another, state the law of the subject to be about as it is expressed in comment *i* under section 184 of the Restatement of the Law of Restitution: *"Preventing revocation of will and making new will.* Where a devisee or legatee under a will already executed prevents the testator by fraud, duress or undue influence from revoking the will and executing a new will in favor of another or from making a codicil, so that the testator dies leaving the original will in force, the devisee or legatee holds the property thus acquired upon a constructive trust for the intended devisee or legatee."

A frequently-cited case is Ransdel v. Moore, 153 Ind. 393, at pages 407–408, 53 N.E. 767, at page 771, 53 L.R.A. 753, where, with listing of many authorities, the rule is given thus: "when an heir or devisee in a will prevents the testator from providing for one for whom he would have provided but for the interference of the heir or devisee, such heir or devisee will be deemed a trustee, by operation of law, of the property, real or personal, received by him from the testator's estate, to the amount or extent that the defrauded party would have received had not the intention of the deceased been interfered with.   This rule applies also when an heir prevents the making of a will or deed in favor of another, and thereby inherits the property that would otherwise have been given such other person."   To the same effect, see 4 Page on Wills [3d ed.], p. 961.

While there is no New York case decreeing a constructive trust on the exact facts alleged here, there are several decisions in this court which, we think, suggest such a result and none which forbids it.   Matter of O'Hara's Will, 95 N.Y. 403, 47 Am.Rep. 53;   Trustees of Amherst College v. Ritch, 151 N.Y. 282, 45 N.E. 876, 37 L.R.A. 305;   Edson v. Bartow, 154 N.Y. 199, 48 N.E. 541, and Ahrens v. Jones, 169 N.Y. 555, 62 N.E. 666, 88 Am.St.Rep. 620, which need not be closely analyzed here as to their facts, all announce, in one form or another, the rule that, where a legatee has taken property under a will, after agreeing outside the will, to devote that property to a purpose intended and declared by the testator, equity will enforce a constructive trust to effectuate that purpose, lest there be a fraud on the testator.   In Williams v. Fitch, 18 N.Y. 546, a similar result was achieved in a suit for money had and received.   In each of those four cases first above cited in this paragraph, the particular fraud consisted of the legatee's failure or refusal to carry out the testator's designs, after tacitly or expressly promising so to do.   But we do not think that a breach of such an engagement is the only kind of fraud which will impel equity to action.   A constructive trust will be erected whenever necessary to satisfy the demands of justice.   Since a constructive trust is merely "the formula through which the conscience of equity finds expression" Beatty v. Guggenheim Exploration Co., 225 N.Y. 380, 386, 122 N.E. 378, 380;   see 3 Bogert on Trusts and Trustees, part 1, § 471; Lightfoot v. Davis, 198 N.Y. 261, 91 N.E. 582, 29 L.R.A., N.S. 119, 139 Am.St.Rep. 817, 19 Ann.Cas. 747;   Falk v. Hoffman, 233 N.Y. 199, 135 N.E. 243;   Meinhard v. Salmon, 249 N.Y. 458, 164 N.E. 545, 62 A.L.R. 1;   also, see, Warren in 41 Harv.L.Rev. 309 et seq., its applicability is limited only by the inventiveness of men who find new ways to enrich themselves unjustly by grasping what should not belong to them.   Nothing short of true and complete justice satisfies equity, and, always assuming these allegations to be true, there seems no way of achieving total justice except by the procedure used here.

The Appellate Division held that Hutchins v. Hutchins, (7 Hill 104), decided by the Supreme Court, our predecessor, in 1845, was a bar to the maintenance of this suit.   Hutchins v. Hutchins, supra, was a suit at law, dismissed for insufficiency in the days when law suits and equity causes had to be brought in different tribunals;   the law court could give nothing but a judgment for damages, see discussion in 41 Harv.L.Rev. 313, supra.   Testator Hutchins' son, named in an earlier will, charged that defendant had, by fraud, caused his father to revoke that will and execute a new one, disinheriting plaintiff.   The court sustained a demurrer to the complaint, on the ground that the earlier will gave the son no title, interest or estate in his father's assets and no more than a hope or expectancy, the loss of which was too theoretical and tenuous a deprivation to serve as a basis for the award of damages.   See, also, Simar

v. Canaday, 53 N.Y. 298, 302, 303, 13 Am.Rep. 523. Plaintiffs' disappointed hopes in the present case, held the Appellate Division, were similarly lacking in substance. But disappointed hopes and unrealized expectations were all that the secretly intended beneficiaries, not named in the wills, had in Matter of O'Hara's Will, supra; Trustees of Amherst College v. Ritch, supra and Edson v. Bartow, supra, but that in itself was not enough to prevent the creation of constructive trusts in their favor. Hutchins v. Hutchins, supra, it seems, holds only this: that in a suit at law there must, as a basis for damages, be an invasion of a common-law right. To use that same standard in a suit for the declaration and enforcement of a constructive trust would be to deny and destroy the whole equitable theory of constructive trusts.

Nor do we agree that anything in the Decedent Estate Law, Consol. Laws, c. 13, § 1 et seq., or the Statute of Frauds stands in the way of recovery herein. This is not a proceeding to probate or establish the will which plaintiffs say testatrix was prevented from signing, nor is it an attempt to accomplish a revocation of the earlier will as were Matter of Evans' Will, 113 App.Div. 373, 98 N.Y.S. 1042 and Matter of McGill's Will, 229 N.Y. 405, 411, 128 N.E. 194, 195, 196. The will Mary Sheldon Lyon did sign has been probated and plaintiffs are not contesting, but proceeding on, that probate, trying to reach property which has effectively passed thereunder. See Ahrens v. Jones, 169 N.Y. 555, 561, 62 N.E. 666, 667, 668, 88 Am.St.Rep. 620, supra. Nor is this a suit to enforce an agreement to make a will or create a trust or any other promise by decedent, Personal Property Law, Consol.Laws, c. 41, § 31; see Frankenberger v. Schneller, 258 N.Y. 270, 179 N.E. 492; Bayreuther v. Reinisch, 264 App.Div. 138, 34 N.Y.S.2d 674, affirmed 290 N.Y. 553, 47 N.E.2d 959; Blanco v. Velez, 295 N.Y. 224, 66 N.E.2d 171. This complaint does not say that decedent or defendants promised plaintiffs anything or that defendants made any promise to decedent. The story is, simply, that defendants, by force and fraud, kept the testatrix from making a will in favor of plaintiffs. We cannot say, as matter of law, that no constructive trust can arise therefrom.

The ultimate determinations in Matter of O'Hara's Will, supra and Edson v. Bartow, supra, that the estate went to testator's distributees do not help defendants here, since, after the theory of constructive trust had been indorsed by this court in those cases, the distributees won out in the end, but only because the secret trusts intended by the two testators were, in each case, of kinds forbidden by statutes.

We do not agree with appellants that Riggs v. Palmer, 115 N.Y. 506, 22 N.E. 188, 5 L.R.A. 340, 12 Am.St.Rep. 819, completely controls our decision here. That was the famous case where a grandson, overeager to get the remainder interest set up for him in his grandfather's will, murdered his grandsire. After the will had been probated, two daughters of the testator who, under the will, would take if the grandson should predecease testator, sued and got judgment decreeing a constructive trust in their favor. It may be, as respondents assert, that the application of Riggs v. Palmer, supra, here would benefit not plaintiffs, but this testator's distributees.   We need not pass on that now.   But Riggs v. Palmer, supra, is generally helpful to appellants, since it forbade the grandson profiting by his own wrong in connection with a will; and, despite an already probated will and the Decedent Estate Law, Riggs v. Palmer, supra, used the device or formula of constructive trust to right the attempted wrong, and prevent unjust enrichment.

The reference to a conspiracy in the complaint herein makes it appropriate to mention Keviczky v. Lorber, 290 N.Y. 297, 49 N.E.2d 146, 146 A.L.R. 1410.   Keviczky, a real estate broker, got judgment on findings that a conspiracy by defendants had prevented him from earning a commission which he would otherwise have gotten.   All sides agreed that he had not in fact performed the engagement which would have entitled him to a commission as such; thus, when the conspiracy intervened to defeat his efforts, he had no contractual right to a commission but only an expectation thereof which was frustrated by the conspirators. Thus again we see, despite the broad language of Hutchins v. Hutchins, supra, that it is not the law that disappointed expectations and unrealized probabilities may never, under any circumstances, be a basis for recovery.

This suit cannot be defeated by any argument that to give plaintiffs judgment would be to annul those provisions of the Statute of Wills requiring due execution by the testator.   Such a contention, if valid, would have required the dismissal in a number of the suits herein cited.   The answer is in Ahrens v. Jones, 169 N.Y. 555, 561, 62 N.E. 666, 668, 88 Am.St.Rep. 620, supra: " 'The trust does not act directly upon the will by modifying the gift, for the law requires wills to be wholly in writing; but it acts upon the gift itself as it reaches the possession of the legatee, or as soon as he is entitled to receive it.   The theory is that the will has full effect by passing an absolute legacy to the legatee, and that then equity, in order to defeat fraud, raises a trust in favor of those intended to be benefited by the testator, and compels the legatee, as a trustee ex maleficio, to turn over the gift to them.' "

The judgment of the Appellate Division, insofar as it dismissed the complaint herein, should be reversed, and the order of Special Term affirmed, with costs in this court and in the Appellate Division.

LOUGHRAN, C. J., and CONWAY and FULD, JJ., concur with DESMOND, J.

LEWIS and DYE, JJ., dissent and vote for affirmance upon the grounds stated by VAUGHAN, J., writing for the Appellate Division.

Judgment reversed, etc.

Notes

1. Numerous decisions have recognized a cause of action in a court of general jurisdiction for wrongful interference with an expected inheritance, remediable by an award of damages against the wrongdoer or by the imposition of a constructive trust on the assets that the wrongdoer has received from the estate.   The typical action is brought by an intestate successor who has been disinherited by a will but who, for some reason, does not have an adequate remedy by way of a contest against the will in the probate court.   See e.g.

Robinson v. First State Bank of Monticello, 104 Ill.App.3d 758, 60 Ill.Dec. 488, 433 N.E.2d 285 (1982) (disinherited heirs granted cause of action on their allegation that testator's attorney, who benefited from the will, had not disclosed all the facts at the time the heirs entered into a financial settlement not to contest the will); Barone v. Barone, (W.Va. 1982) 294 S.E.2d 260 (daughter may maintain action for punitive damages and constructive trust against brother on the basis of information of his wrongdoing discovered after estate distributed); Cyr v. Cote, 396 A.2d 1013 (Me.1979) (heirs entitled to action when their expected inheritance was reduced by inter vivos transfers but here failed to prove fraud or duress). Statutes limiting the time within which a probate court order may be contested or appealed are not applicable to actions based on fraud in courts of general jurisdiction. If, however, adequate remedies are available in the probate proceedings, the parties will be required to exhaust those remedies before pursuing an action for tortious interference elsewhere. DeWitt v. Duce, 408 So.2d 216 (Fla.1981); see also Dragan v. Miller, 679 F.2d 712 (7th Cir. 1982) (so-called "probate exception" to federal diversity jurisdiction applies, confining action to state court; Illinois probate procedures not to be circumvented by calling will contest an action in tort).

A nonheir who was named as a beneficiary in an earlier will has standing to bring an action for malicious interference with the expected legacy. See Nemeth v. Banhalmi, 99 Ill.App.3d 493, 55 Ill.Dec. 14, 425 N.E.2d 1187 (1981); Davison v. Feuerherd, 391 So.2d 799 (Fla.App.2d Dist. 1980) (same, beneficiary of a revocable trust). The Latham decision is unique in extending standing to persons who were neither heirs nor beneficiaries of a previously executed will.

See generally citations compiled in Barone v. Barone, supra; Annots., Liability in Damages for Interference with Expected Inheritance or Gift, 22 A.L.R.4th 1229; Rights and Remedies Against One Who Interferes in the Making, Changing or Revoking of a Will, 11 A.L.R.2d 808.

2. Is the constructive trust remedy available only to recapture property from a wrongdoer or may it also be used to award the property to a person whom the court believes the testator meant to benefit? For example, in the Latham case the intestate successors' contest of the will had been terminated by a settlement before the plaintiffs, who were not intestate successors, brought their action against Father Divine. Assume that the contest had not been compromised but had proceeded to a successful conclusion, with the will being voided and the estate being distributed to the intestate successors. Would the plaintiffs have then been entitled to claim that the intestate successors were holding $350,000 as constructive trustees for them because the testatrix intended them to have that amount? A typical statement of the rule indicates that the action lies only against "one who, by fraud, actual or constructive, by duress or abuse of confidence, by commission of wrong, or by any form of unconscionable conduct, artifice, concealment, or questionable means, or who in any way against equity or good conscience, either has obtained or holds the legal right to property which he ought not, in equity and good conscience, hold and enjoy." 76 Am.Jur.2d 446 (1975). It has been held that remedies are not available against a person whose statement caused a codicil not to be executed when that person was not a beneficiary of the estate and was not aware that the statement was false. Lowe Foundation v. Northern Trust Co., 342 Ill.App. 379, 96 N.E.2d 831 (1951).

A wrongdoer may, however, be required to hold the property as constructive trustee for an intended beneficiary. The Latham opinion cites in this regard the so-called secret trust cases: " * * * where a legatee has taken property under a will, after agreeing outside the will, to devote that property to a purpose intended and declared by the testator, equity will enforce a constructive trust to effectuate that purpose, lest there be a fraud on the testator." Page 264, supra. See also § 45 Restatement, Second, Trusts (remedy for breach of an oral trust of land in favor of third party). See generally, Langbein and Waggoner, Reformation of Wills on the Ground of Mistake: Change of Direction in American Law?, 130 U. of Pa.L.Rev. 521, 571–577 (1982).

Chapter Five

WILLS

SECTION ONE. FORMALITIES OF TRANSFER

A. POLICY

GULLIVER AND TILSON, CLASSIFICATION OF GRATUITOUS TRANSFERS

51 Yale L.J. 1, 2–10 (1941) (footnotes omitted).

guiding princp = effect teste's intent (> formality)

One fundamental proposition is that, under a legal system recognizing the individualistic institution of private property and granting to the
owner the power to determine his successors in ownership, the general
philosophy of the courts should favor giving effect to an intentional exercise of that power.   This is commonplace enough, but it needs constant
emphasis, for it may be obscured or neglected in inordinate preoccupation
with detail or dialectic.   A court absorbed in purely doctrinal arguments
may lose sight of the important and desirable objective of sanctioning
what the transferor wanted to do, even though it is convinced that he
wanted to do it.

If this objective is primary, the requirements of execution, which
concern only the form of the transfer—what the transferor or others must
do to make it legally effective—seem justifiable only as implements for
its accomplishment, and should be so interpreted by the courts in these
cases.   They surely should not be revered as ends in themselves, en-
throning formality over frustrated intent.   Why do these requirements
exist and what functions may they usefully perform?   If all transfers
were required to be made before the court determining their validity, it
is probable that no formalities except oral declarations in the presence
of the court would be necessary.   The court could observe the transferor,
hear his statements, and clear up ambiguities by appropriate questions.
But such a procedure does not correspond with existing mores and would
be entirely impracticable in our present society for various rather obvious
reasons.   The fact that our judicial agencies are remote from the actual
or fictitious occurrences relied on by the various claimants to the property,
and so must accept second hand information, perhaps ambiguous, perhaps
innocently misleading, perhaps deliberately falsified, seems to furnish

265

the chief justification for requirements of transfer beyond evidence of oral statements of intent.

In the first place, the court needs to be convinced that the statements of the transferor were deliberately intended to effectuate a transfer. People are often careless in conversation and in informal writings. Even if the witnesses are entirely truthful and accurate, what is the court to conclude from testimony showing only that a father once stated that he wanted to give certain bonds to his son, John? Does this remark indicate finality of intention to transfer, or rambling meditation about some possible future disposition? Perhaps he meant that he would like to give the bonds to John later if John turned out to be a respectable and industrious citizen, or perhaps that he would like to give them to John but could not because of his greater obligations to some other person. Possibly, the remark was inadvertent, or made in jest. Or suppose that the evidence shows, without more, that a writing containing dispositive language was found among the papers of the deceased at the time of his death? Does this demonstrate a deliberate transfer, or was it merely a tentative draft of some contemplated instrument, or perhaps random scribbling? Neither case would amount to an effective transfer, under the generally prevailing law. The court is far removed from the context of the statements, and the situation is so charged with uncertainty that even a judgment of probabilites is hazardous. Casual language, whether oral or written, is not intended to be legally operative, however appropriate its purely verbal content may be for that purpose. Dispositive effect should not be given to statements which were not intended to have that effect. The formalities of transfer therefore generally require the performance of some ceremonial for the purpose of impressing the transferor with the significance of his statements and thus justifying the court in reaching the conclusion, if the ceremonial is performed, that they were deliberately intended to be operative. This purpose of the requirements of transfer may conveniently be termed their ritual function.

Secondly, the requirements of transfer may increase the reliability of the proof presented to the court. The extent to which the quantity and effect of available evidence should be restricted by qualitative standards is, of course, a controversial matter. Perhaps any and all evidence should be freely admitted in reliance on such safeguards as cross-examination, the oath, the proficiency of handwriting experts, and the discriminating judgment of courts and juries. On the other hand, the inaccuracies of oral testimony owing to lapse of memory, misinterpretation of the statements of others, and the more or less unconscious coloring of recollection in the light of the personal interest of the witness or of those with whom he is friendly, are very prevalent; and the possibilities of perjury and forgery cannot be disregarded. These difficulties are entitled to especially serious consideration in prescribing requirements for gratuitous transfers, because the issue of the validity of the transfer is almost always raised after the alleged transferor is dead, and therefore the main actor is usually unavailable to testify, or to clarify or contradict other evidence concerning his all-important intention. At any rate, whatever the ideal solution may be, it seems quite clear that the existing requirements of transfer emphasize the purpose of supplying satisfactory evidence to the court. This purpose may conveniently be termed their evidentiary function.

Thirdly, some of the requirements of the statutes of wills have the stated prophylactic purpose of safeguarding the testator, at the time of the execution of the will, against undue influence or other forms of imposition. As indicated below, the value of this objective and the extent of its accomplishment are both doubtful. It may conveniently be termed the protective function.

The Functions of the Statutes of Wills

Formal Wills

Ritual Function. Compliance with the total combination of requirements for the execution of formal attested wills has a marked ritual value, since the general ceremonial precludes the possibility that the testator was acting in a casual or haphazard fashion. The ritual function is also specifically emphasized in individual requirements. It furnishes one justification for the provision that the will be signed by the testator himself or for him by some other person. Under the English Statute of Wills of 1540, specifying a will "in writing," no signature was expressly required. In construing this statute, the courts gave effect to various informal writings of the testator or others, even though the circumstances furnished no assurance that the testator intended them to be finally operative. These decisions are said to have been influential in the enactment of the provisions of the Statute of Frauds, which were the first to require a signature. The signature tends to show that the instrument was finally adopted by the testator as his will and to militate against the inference that the writing was merely a preliminary draft, an incomplete disposition, or a haphazard scribbling. The requirement existing in some states that the signature of the testator be at the end of the will has also been justified in terms of this function; since it is the ordinary human practice to sign documents at the end, a will not so signed does not give the impression of being finally executed. The occasional provisions that the testator publish the will or that he request the witnesses to sign also seem chiefly attributable to this purpose, since such actions indicate finality of intention.

Evidentiary Function. The absence of any procedure for determining the validity of a will before the death of the testator has two important consequences relevant to this function. First, as has already been stated, the testator will inevitably be dead and therefore unable to testify when the issue is tried. Secondly, an extended lapse of time, during which the recollection of witnesses may fade considerably, may occur between a statement of testamentary intent and the probate proceedings. Both factors tend to make oral testimony even less trustworthy than it is in cases where there is some likelihood of the adverse party being an available witness and where the statute of limitations compels relative promptness in litigation. The statute of wills may therefore reasonably incorporate unusual probative safeguards requiring evidence of testamentary intent to be cast in reliable and permanent form.   The requirement that a will be in writing has, of course, great evidentiary value.   A written statement of intention may be ambiguous, but, if it is genuine and can be produced, it has the advantage of preserving in permanent form the language chosen by the testator to show his intent.   While, for the purpose of preventing frustration of intent through accident or design, the contents of a lost or destroyed will may usually be probated on satisfactory secondary evidence, such cases are relatively infrequent.   The requirement of the testator's signature also has evidentiary value in identifying, in most cases, the maker of the document.   While the typical statutory authorization of a signature made by another for the testator, and the generally recognized rule that the testator's signature need not be his correct name, both indicate lack of complete adherence to this purpose, such cases are probably quite rare in view of the usual custom in a literate era of signing documents with a complete name.   The possibility of a forged signature must be controlled by the abilities of handwriting experts.   There is judicial support for the theory that the requirement that the will be signed at the end has an evidentiary purpose of preventing unauthenticated or fraudulent additions to the will made after its execution by either the testator or other parties.

The important requirement that this type of will be attested obviously has great evidentiary significance.   It affords some opportunity to secure proof of the facts of execution, which may have occurred long before probate, as contrasted with the difficulties that might otherwise arise if an unattested paper purporting to be a will executed, according to its date, thirty or forty years before, were found among the papers of the testator after his death.   Of course, this purpose is not accomplished in every case since all of the attesting witnesses may become unavailable to testify because of death or some other reason, and their unavailability will not defeat probate of a will.   The high evidentiary value placed by the courts and legislatures on the testimony of those chosen by the testator as attesting witnesses is shown by the requirement, unusual under the philosophy of the general rules of evidence which leave the calling of witnesses to the initiative of the parties, but regularly accepted for wills, that one or more of the attesting witnesses must be produced at probate if available.

The provision existing in some states that the will be signed or acknowledged by the testator in the presence of the attesting witnesses may be justified as having some evidentiary purpose in requiring a definitive act of the testator to be done before the witnesses, thus enabling them to testify with greater assurance that the will was intended to be operative.

Protective Function.   Some of the requirements of the statutes of wills have the objective, according to judicial interpretation, of protecting the testator against imposition at the time of execution.   This is difficult to justify under modern conditions.   First, it must be reiterated that any requirement of transfer should have a clearly demonstrable affirmative value since it always presents the possibility of invalidating perfectly genuine and equitable transfers that fail to comply with it; there are numerous decisions interpreting these requirements, particularly with reference to the competency of attesting witnesses, wholly or partially invalidating wills that do not seem from the opinions to be in any way improper or suspicious. Secondly, there are appropriate independent remedies for the various forms of imposition, and these prophylactic provisions are therefore not, in the long run, of any essential utility except in instances where the imposition might not be detected. Thirdly, as indicated below, it is extremely doubtful that these provisions effectively accomplish any important purpose. Fourthly, they are atypical; no similar purpose is indicated in the requirements for inter vivos dispositions. Why should there be a differentiation between inter vivos and testamentary transfers in this respect? The purely legal elements of the two categories suggest no justification; in fact, the automatic revocability of a will presents a simpler and more uniformly prevalent means of nullifying the effect of imposition than exists for inter vivos transfers. In spite of the benevolent paternalism expressed in some of the decisions interpreting these requirements, the makers of wills are not a feeble or oppressed group of people needing unusual protection as a class; on the contrary, as the owners of property, earned or inherited, they are likely to be among the more capable and dominant members of our society. It is probable that the distinction originally arose because of a difference in the factual circumstances customarily surrounding the execution of the two types of transfer. The protective provisions first appeared in the Statute of Frauds, from which they have been copied, perhaps sometimes blindly, by American legislatures. While there is little direct evidence, it is a reasonable assumption that, in the period prior to the Statute of Frauds, wills were usually executed on the death bed. A testator in this unfortunate situation may well need special protection against imposition. His powers of normal judgment and of resistance to improper influences may be seriously affected by a decrepit physical condition, a weakened mentality, or a morbid or unbalanced state of mind. Furthermore, in view of the propinquity of death, he would not have as much time or opportunity as would the usual inter vivos transferor to escape from the consequences of undue influence or other forms of imposition. Under modern conditions, however, wills are probably executed by most testators in the prime of life and in the presence of attorneys. If this assumption is correct, the basis for any general distinction disappears. For these reasons, this article will proceed on the hypothesis that, while the provisions of the statutes of wills seeking to fulfill the protective function must be reckoned with doctrinally as part of our enacted law, this function is not sufficiently important in the present era to justify any more emphasis than these provisions require.

LANGBEIN, SUBSTANTIAL COMPLIANCE WITH THE WILLS ACT

88 Harv.L.Rev. 489, 498–99, 513, 524–26 (1975) (footnotes omitted).

What is peculiar about the law of wills is not the prominence of the formalities, but the judicial insistence that any defect in complying with them automatically and inevitably voids the will. In other areas where legislation imposes formal requirements, the courts have taken a purposive approach to formal defects. The common examples are the judicial doctrines which sustain transactions despite noncompliance with the Statute of Frauds—the main purpose and part performance rules. The essential rationale of these rules is that when the purposes of the formal requirements are proved to have been served, literal compliance with the formalities themselves is no longer necessary. The courts have boasted that they do not permit formal safeguards to be turned into instruments of injustice in cases where the purposes of the formalities are independently satisfied.

Why has the Wills Act not been interpreted with a similar purposiveness? There are factors which distinguish Wills Act defects from Statute of Frauds violations, but we submit that none of them really justifies the harsher treatment of Wills Act defects.

* * *

The substantial compliance doctrine is a rule neither of maximum nor of minimum formalities, and it is surely not a rule of no formalities. It applies to any Wills Act, governing the consequences of defective compliance with whatever formalities the legislature has prescribed. Our major theme is that substantial compliance fits easily into the existing doctrinal structure and judicial practice of the law of wills.

Proper compliance with the Wills Act, so-called due execution, is the basis in modern law for certain presumptions which shift the burden of proof from the proponents of a will to any contestants. Unless the contestants advance disproof, the proponents need establish no more than due execution. Because there are usually no contestants, the effect of the presumptions is to limit the proofs in the probate proceeding to the question of due execution, and there are further presumptions which allow due execution to be easily inferred from seeming regularity of signature and attestation.

These presumptions are extremely wise and functional. They routinize probate. They transform hard questions into easy ones. Instead of having to ask, "Was this meant to be a will, is it adequately evidenced, and was it sufficiently final and deliberate?," the court need only inquire whether the checklist of Wills Act formalities seems to have been obeyed. In all but exceptional cases, a will is simply whatever complies with the formalities.

The substantial compliance doctrine would permit the proponents in cases of defective execution to prove what they are now entitled to presume from due execution—the existence of testamentary intent and the fulfillment of the Wills Act purposes. * * * .

* * *

The Wills Acts govern the transmission of "millions of estates and billions of dollars in assets." The substantial compliance doctrine must necessarily impair something of the channeling function, because it permits the proponents of noncomplying instruments to litigate the question of functional compliance, an issue which the rule of literal compliance presently forecloses.   If testation were transformed from routine administration into routine adjudication, the social cost and the cost to estates and distributees would be intolerable.

We assert therefore a fundamental point when we say that the substantial compliance doctrine would have no effect whatever upon primary conduct.   The incentive for due execution would remain.   Precisely because the substantial compliance doctrine is a rule of litigation, it would have no place in professional estate planning.   Today lawyers in holograph jurisdictions have their clients' wills executed as attested wills; that is, they opt for maximum formality, in order to be in the best possible position to defend the will against any claim of imposition or want of finality.   The counselor's job is to prevent litigation.   Only when the lawyer has bungled his supervision of the execution of a will would he have occasion to fall back on substantial compliance.

Hence, the substantial compliance doctrine would apply overwhelmingly to homemade wills.   We know from long and sad experience that the rule of literal compliance with the Wills Act does not deter laymen from drafting and executing their own wills without professional advice.   The substantial compliance doctrine would not attract the reliance of amateurs, nor increase the number of homemade wills.   Anyone who would know enough about the probate process to know that the substantial compliance doctrine existed would know enough not to want to rely upon it.

The substantial compliance doctrine would pertain not to every will, but to that fraction of wills where the testator, acting without counsel or with incompetent counsel, has failed to comply fully with the Wills Act formalities.   Two important factors would operate to diminish the incidence and the difficulty of such litigation.   First, by no means would every defectively executed instrument result in a contest.   On many issues the proponents' burden of proof would be so onerous that they would forego the trouble and expense of hopeless litigation;   and on certain other issues the proponents' burden would be so light that potential contestants would not bother to litigate.   Evidentiary and cautionary formalities like signature and writing are all but indispensable, whereas omitted protective formalities like competence of witnesses are easily shown to have been needless in the particular case.

Second, the litigation which would occur would for the most part raise familiar issues which the courts have demonstrated their ability to handle well.   We have seen that the elements of the substantial compliance doctrine arise in other contexts in current litigation when courts examine whether purported wills evidence testamentary intent and were executed freely and with finality.

The substantial compliance doctrine would not simply add to the existing stock of probate litigation, but would to some extent substitute one type of dispute for another.   The rule of literal compliance can produce results so harsh that sympathetic courts incline to squirm.   Many of the formalities have produced a vast, contradictory, unpredictable and sometimes dishonest case law in which the courts purport to find literal compliance in cases which in fact instance defective compliance.   Is a wave of the testator's hand a publication or an acknowledgement?   Was the signature "at the end"?   When the attesting witnesses were in the next room, were they in the testator's presence?   The courts now purport to ask in these cases: did the particular conduct constitute literal compliance with the formality?   The substantial compliance doctrine would replace that awkward, formalistic question with a more manageable question: did the conduct serve the purpose of the formality?   By substituting a purposive analysis for a formal one, the substantial compliance doctrine would actually decrease litigation about the formalities.   The standard would be more predictable, and contestants would lose their present incentive to prove up harmless defects.

Notes

1. The Uniform Probate Code represents a significant attempt to make the statutes setting out the formalities for the execution of wills less rigid.   As is developed in the material that follows, under the Code, witnesses need not forfeit their legacies in order to be competent, the will is not invalidated if the testator fails to sign at the end, witnesses need not sign in the presence of the testator and each other, and more.   UPC § 1–102 states that the Code provisions are to be "liberally construed and applied to promote its underlying purposes and policies", which include, inter alia, "to discover and make effective the intent of a decedent in distribution of his property".   Recent amendments from several other states are also designed to introduce greater flexibility into the statutes. See e.g. N.Y.—McKinney's EPTL § 3–2.1, infra p. 276.   As yet no American states have followed the lead of two Australian states and Israel in adopting the "substantial compliance" approach, i.e. the court may admit an instrument to probate if it is in substantial compliance with the required formalities.   See Langbein, Crumbling of the Wills Act: Australians Point the Way, 65 A.B.A.J. 1192 (1979).

Without similar enabling acts in this country, most courts continue to set as the test against which the facts are to be analyzed the necessity for strict compliance with the statutes.   As stated in one recent opinion: "The frustration of decedent's apparent testamentary intent by her own failure to observe the proper formalities may seem at first a harsh result, but it is a result which is required by our Legislature and which this Court may not alter."   Estate of Proley, 492 Pa. 57, 422 A.2d 136, 138 (1980) (3–3 decision upholding ruling of the Orphan's Court sitting en banc that will was invalid because not signed by the testator at the end; dissent described the result as a "rather blatant frustration of testatrix's intent").   See also, Estate of Zaharis, 91 A.D.2d 737, 457 N.Y.S.2d 995 (3d Dep't. 1982) (will invalid because signature in wrong place); Wich v. Fleming, 652 S.W.2d 353 (Tex.1983) (will invalid because witnesses signed self-proving affidavit and not the will); Estate of Johnson, infra p. 299 (holographic will denied probate on technical grounds).   It should, however, be noted that in all but the last of the above cases there were strong dissents arguing for a more flexible application of the statutes.   Recall the use of the substantial compliance approach by the Illinois court in upholding the inter vivos trusts in Farkas v. Williams, supra p. 49.   Why should the courts be more flexible in dealing with lifetime transfers of property than with testamentary transfers?

2. If a will is declared invalid for failure to satisfy all the statutory requirements, the attorney who supervised its execution may be held liable for damages in negligence. Potential liability extends not only to the client-testator but also to a person named as a beneficiary in the will who loses his or her legacy. For example, solicitors mailed the will as requested to the testator with a covering letter giving instructions on executing it but failing to warn the testator that the witnesses must not have a financial interest in the will. (This is the competency of witness doctrine discussed infra pp. 291–298). After testator's death, the will, which had been executed out of the presence of the solicitors, was probated, but legacies to the plaintiff were purged under the statute because plaintiff's husband was a witness to the will. Plaintiff was allowed to recover damages in the amount of the legacies plus costs against the solicitors for their negligent failure to warn the testator on the law. Ross v. Caunters, (1979) 3 All E.R. 580. See also, Licata v. Spector, 26 Conn.Sup. 378, 225 A.2d 28 (1966) (lawyer who used two witnesses when statute required three subject to suit for negligence); Biakanja v. Irving, 49 Cal.2d 647, 320 P.2d 16 (1958) (notary held liable in damages when will denied probate because the witnesses did not sign in the presence of the testator or each other). See generally, Johnston, Legal Malpractice in Estate Planning—Perilous Times Ahead for the Practitioner, 67 Iowa L.Rev. 629 (1982).

B. HISTORICAL BACKGROUND

It seems that the Anglo-Saxon disposition which accomplished the purposes of a testamentary transfer of real or personal property differed from the modern will in most legal respects. See Whitelock, Anglo-Saxon Wills (1930), reviewed by Plucknett, 43 Harv.L.Rev. 1331 (1930) and in 46 L.Q.Rev. 372 (1930); 2 P. & M. 316–23 (2d ed. 1905); 2 Holds. 90–97 (4th ed. 1936). The Norman Conquest probably occasioned no sudden change in the law of testamentary succession, but by the thirteenth century there was established the same division in jurisdiction as in the case of intestate succession. From then until the nineteenth century, wills of realty were within the jurisdiction of the law courts, while the validity of testaments of personalty was determined in the ecclesiastical courts.

By the thirteenth century, the law courts had adopted the rule that no will of real property could be made. The reasons for and methods of evasion of this doctrine can be discussed more intelligibly in connection with the system of uses. (See Chapter Seven on Trusts, infra, at p. 419.) The rule was changed in 1540, when the first English Statute of Wills was passed. That statute, with later amendments, authorized wills of land provided that they were in writing, but required no other formalities.

The Statute of Frauds (1676) contained the first provisions that resemble those of the modern American statutes, many of which copied it. Prior to the statute the ecclesiastical courts recognized the power to make an oral testament of personalty without imposing any strict requirements as to its form. The Statute of Frauds did put some limitations on oral wills of personalty, but was primarily concerned with wills of real prop-

erty.   The Wills Act of 1837, however, imposed uniform requirements
for wills of both real and personal property, and is still the basis of the
English law of wills.   Its provisions are copied in some of the American
statutes.   2 P. & M. 314–356 (2d ed. 1905); 3 Holds. 75–6, 535–50 (4th
ed. 1936);   Reppy and Tompkins, Historical and Statutory Background
of the Law of Wills, 4–47 (1928);   Bordwell, An Introduction to Wills and
Administration, 14 Minn.L.Rev. 1 (1929).

In the United States, the law of wills is based entirely on statute.
Generally speaking, the requirements for the valid execution of a will
are far more numerous and detailed than is true of any other form of
disposition of property.   Page on Wills, Chapters 62 and 65 (1963 Bowe-
Parker ed.) includes a variety of forms for wills and codicils, and also
reprints in full the wills of a number of wealthy and prominent testators.
Interesting books, the contents of which are indicated by their titles, are
Harris, Ancient, Curious and Famous Wills (1911) and Collins and Weaver,
Wills of the U.S. Presidents (1976).   See, along the same lines, Gest,
Some Jolly Testators, 8 Temp.L.Q. 297 (1934);   Hibschman, Whimsies of
Will-Makers, 66 U.S.L.Rev. 362 (1932);   Million, Humor in or of Wills,
11 Vand.L.Rev. 737 (1958).

C.   REPRESENTATIVE STATUTES

Statute of Frauds.   29 Car. 2, c. 3 (1976)

V. And be it further enacted by the Authority aforesaid, That   *   *   *
all Devises and Bequests of any Lands or Tenements   *   *   *   shall be
in Writing, and signed by the Party so devising the same, or by some
other Person in his Presence and by his express Directions, and shall be
attested and subscribed in the Presence of the said Devisor by three or
four credible Witnesses, or else they shall be utterly void and of none
Effect.

*   *   *

XIX. And for the Prevention of fraudulent Practices in setting up
Nuncupative Wills, which have been the Occasion of much Perjury; (2)
Be it enacted by the Authority Aforesaid, That   *   *   *   no Nuncupative
Will shall be good, where the Estate thereby bequeathed shall exceed the
Value of thirty Pounds, that is not proved by the Oaths of three Witnesses
(at the least) that were present at the Making thereof; (3) nor unless it
be proved that the Testator at the Time of pronouncing the same did bid
the Persons present, or some of them, bear Witness, that such was his
Will, or to that Effect; (4) nor unless such Nuncupative Will were made
in the Time of the last Sickness of the Deceased, and in the House of his
or her Habitation or Dwelling, or where he or she hath been Resident for
the Space of ten Days or more next before the making of such Will, except
where such Person was surprized or taken sick, being from his own Home,
and died before he returned to the Place of his or her Dwelling.

XX. And be it further enacted, That after six Months passed after
the speaking of the pretended Testamentary Words, no Testimony shall
be received to prove any Will Nuncupative, except the said Testimony,

or the Substance thereof, were committed to Writing within six Days after the making of the said Will.

XXI. And be it further enacted, That no Letters Testamentary or Probate of any Nuncupative Will shall pass the Seal of any Court, till fourteen Days at the least after the Decease of the Testator be fully expired; (2) nor shall any Nuncupative Will be at any Time received to be proved, unless Process have first issued to call in the Widow, or next of Kindred to the Deceased, to the End that they may contest the same, if they please.

* * *

XXIII. Provided always, That notwithstanding this Act, any Soldier being in actual Military Service, or any Mariner or Seaman being at Sea, may dispose of his Moveables, Wages and Personal Estate, as he or they might have done before the making of this Act.

* * *

Wills Act. 7 Wm. 4 & 1 Vict., c. 26 (1837)

Be it enacted * * * That the Words and Expressions herein-after mentioned, which in their ordinary Signification have a more confined or a different Meaning, shall in this Act, except where the Nature of the Provision or the Context of the Act shall exclude such Construction, be interpreted as follows; (that is to say) the Word "Will" shall extend to a Testament, and to a Codicil, * * * and to any other Testamentary Disposition * * *.

* * *

IX. *And be it further enacted*, That no Will shall be valid unless it shall be in Writing and Executed in manner herein-after mentioned; (that is to say,) it shall be signed at the Foot or End thereof by the Testator, or by some other Person in his Presence and by his Direction; and such Signature shall be made or acknowledged by the Testator in the Presence of Two or more Witnesses present at the same Time, and such Witnesses shall attest and shall subscribe the Will in the Presence of the Testator, but no Form of Attestation shall be necessary.

* * *

XI. *Provided always, and be it further enacted*, That any Soldier being in actual Military Service, or any Mariner or Seaman being at Sea, may dispose of his Personal Estate as he might have done before the making of this Act.

* * *

XIII. *And be it further enacted*, That every Will executed in manner herein-before required shall be valid without any other Publication thereof.

* * *

McKinney's New York Estates, Powers and Trusts Law

§ 3–2.1   Execution and Attestation of Wills; Formal Requirements

(a) Except for nuncupative and holographic wills authorized by 3–2.2, every will must be in writing, and executed and attested in the following manner:

(1) It shall be signed at the end thereof by the testator or, in the name of the testator, by another person in his presence and by his direction, subject to the following:

(A) The presence of any matter following the testator's signature, appearing on the will at the time of its execution, shall not invalidate such matter preceding the signature as appeared on the will at the time of its execution, except that such matter preceding the signature shall not be given effect, in the discretion of the surrogate, if it is so incomplete as not to be readily comprehensible without the aid of matter which follows the signature, or if to give effect to such matter preceding the signature would subvert the testator's general plan for the disposition and administration of his estate.

(B) No effect shall be given to any matter, other than the attestation clause, which follows the signature of the testator, or to any matter preceding such signature which was added subsequently to the execution of the will.

(C) Any person who signs the testator's name to the will, as provided in subparagraph (1), shall sign his own name and affix his residence address to the will but shall not be counted as one of the necessary attesting witnesses to the will.   A will lacking the signature of the person signing the testator's name shall not be given effect; provided, however, the failure of the person signing the testator's name to affix his address shall not affect the validity of the will.

(2) The signature of the testator shall be affixed to the will in the presence of each of the attesting witnesses, or shall be acknowledged by the testator to each of them to have been affixed by him or by his direction. The testator may either sign in the presence of, or acknowledge his signature to each attesting witness separately.

(3) The testator shall, at some time during the ceremony or ceremonies of execution and attestation, declare to each of the attesting witnesses that the instrument to which his signature has been affixed is his will.

(4) There shall be at least two attesting witnesses, who shall, within one thirty day period, both attest the testator's signature, as affixed or acknowledged in their presence, and at the request of the testator, sign their names and affix their residence addresses at the end of the will. There shall be a rebuttable presumption that the thirty day requirement of the preceding sentence has been fulfilled.   The failure of a witness to affix his address shall not affect the validity of the will.

(b) The procedure for the execution and attestation of wills need not be followed in the precise order set forth in paragraph (a) so long as all the requisite formalities are observed during a period of time in which, satisfactorily to the surrogate, the ceremony or ceremonies of execution and attestation continue.

§ 3-2.2 Nuncupative and Holographic Wills

(a) For the purposes of this section, and as used elsewhere in this chapter:

(1) A will is nuncupative when it is unwritten, and the making thereof by the testator and its provisions are clearly established by at least two witnesses.

(2) A will is holographic when it is written entirely in the handwriting of the testator, and is not executed and attested in accordance with the formalities prescribed by 3-2.1.

(b) A nuncupative or holographic will is valid only if made by:

(1) A member of the armed forces of the United States while in actual military or naval service during a war, declared or undeclared, or other armed conflict in which members of the armed forces are engaged.

(2) A person who serves with or accompanies an armed force engaged in actual military or naval service during such war or other armed conflict.

(3) A mariner while at sea.

(c) A will authorized by this section becomes invalid:

(1) If made by a member of the armed forces, upon the expiration of one year following his discharge from the armed forces.

(2) If made by a person who serves with or accompanies an armed force engaged in actual military or naval service, upon the expiration of one year from the time he has ceased serving with or accompanying such armed force.

(3) If made by a mariner while at sea, upon the expiration of three years from the time such will was made.

(d) If any person described in paragraph (c) lacks testamentary capacity at the expiration of the time limited therein for the validity of his will, such will shall continue to be valid until the expiration of one year from the time such person regains testamentary capacity.

(e) Nuncupative and holographic wills, as herein authorized, are subject to the provisions of this chapter to the extent that such provisions can be applied to such wills consistently with their character, or to the extent that any such provision expressly provides that it is applicable to such wills.

Uniform Probate Code

Section 2-502. [Execution]

Except as provided for holographic wills, writings within Section 2-513 [a separate writing referred to in the will that disposes of tangible personal property], and wills within Section 2-506 [a will valid under the laws of another jurisdiction], every will shall be in writing signed by the testator or in the testator's name by some other person in the testator's presence and by his direction, and shall be signed by at least 2 persons each of whom witnessed either the signing or the testator's acknowledgment of the signature or of the will.

Comment

The formalities for execution of a witnessed will have been reduced to a minimum. Execution under this section normally would be accomplished by signature of the testator and of two witnesses; each of the persons signing as witnesses must "witness" any of the following: the signing of the will by the testator, an acknowledgment by the testator that the signature is his, or an acknowledgment by the testator that the document is his will. Signing by the testator may be by mark under general rules relating to what constitutes a signature; or the will may be signed on behalf of the testator by another person signing the testator's name at his direction and in his presence. There is no requirement that the testator publish the document as his will, or that he request the witnesses to sign, or that the witnesses sign in the presence of the testator or of each other. The testator may sign the will outside the presence of the witnesses if he later acknowledges to the witnesses that the signature is his or that the document is his will, and they sign as witnesses. There is no requirement that the testator's signature be at the end of the will; thus, if he writes his name in the body of the will and intends it to be his signature, this would satisfy the statute. The intent is to validate wills which meet the minimal formalities of the statute.

A will which does not meet these requirements may be valid under Section 2–503 as a holograph.

Section 2–503.   [Holographic Will]

A will which does not comply with Section 2–502 is valid as a holographic will, whether or not witnessed, if the signature and the material provisions are in the handwriting of the testator.

Section 2–505.   [Who May Witness]

(a) Any person generally competent to be a witness may act as a witness to a will.

(b) A will or any provision thereof is not invalid because the will is signed by an interested witness.

————

Although now inaccurate in some particulars because of amendments to the statutes, several summaries make evident the variety, detail and technicality of the requirements for the execution of wills throughout the country. Rees, American Will Statutes, 46 Va.L.Rev. 613 (1960); Kossow, Probate Law and the Uniform Code: "One for the Money", 61 Geo. L.J. 1357, 1394–1400 (1973).

D. FORMAL WILLS—WITNESSES—ORDER OF SIGNING

HOPSON v. EWING

Court of Appeals of Kentucky, 1962.
353 S.W.2d 203, 91 A.L.R.2d 733.

PALMORE, Judge. Following the death of Ike Weathers in July of 1957 the Jefferson County Court admitted to probate as his will the instrument hereinafter copied in full. A contest in the circuit court resulted in a directed verdict for the proponents. The contestants appeal on two main grounds, (1) that the instrument is insufficient in form and substance to constitute a will and (2) that it was not proved to have been executed in accordance with KRS 394.040.

Except for the signatures and date at the foot the document in question was written by typewriter. It reads as follows:

"Sadie Rose, Mary Rose and Joe Ellis

443 South 7th Street

1124 South 8th Street

3208–3210 Southern Avenue

(2) Lots—3608–3610 Grand Avenue

City Truck—Jewelry—Bank Account—(1) Three Karat Diamond Ring.

Alonzo Dorsey—

524 South Ninth Street

Mary C. Duncan

All contents at 3606 Grand Avenue and 1120 South 36th Street

My home and everything.

She shall take care of George Smith as long as he lives.

/s/ Preston O. Davis

/s/ Thomas Manier

/s/ Ike Weathers

Nov. 20–1951"

"Of all instruments a will is least governed by form, the form being unimportant, except as indicating intent." Dixon v. Dameron's Adm'r, 1934, 256 Ky. 722, 77 S.W.2d 6, 7; 57 Am.Jur. 51 (Wills, § 20). "The absence of dispositive words such as 'give,' 'devise,' or 'bequeath' does not necessarily stamp an instrument as nontestamentary." Id., p. 54, § 21. We have no difficulty in concluding that the paper before us in this case was intended as a will and was sufficient in form and substance for that purpose.

Our conclusion is supported by the evidence. The items of property listed on the instrument actually were owned by Weathers at the time of its execution. Davis, one of the attesting witnesses, testified that Weathers had told him beforehand he wanted him to witness his will. Manier, the other witness, said that while he and Davis were accompanying Weathers on the way to the place where the paper was executed he asked what was the purpose at hand and Davis, in the presence of Weathers, answered, "Ike's going to make a will." Where a nondescript instrument not in the usual form of a will is of ambiguous import on its face, extrinsic evidence is admissible to establish testamentary intent. 57 Am.Jur. 581 (Wills, § 874); Boggess v. McGaughey, 1948, 306 Ky. 319, 207 S.W.2d 766; Nelson v. Nelson, 1930, 235 Ky. 189, 30 S.W.2d 893, 896; 1 Bowe-Parker: Page on Wills, § 5.16, p. 204. See also annotation at 21 A.L. R.2d 319, 324.

* * *

Now as to the matter of execution. Weathers apparently was a man of little education, but of distinct commercial acumen, who had accumulated his estate from the bail bond business, the operation of a dump truck around the city hall in Louisville, and various other trading activities. He had the will prepared by some friend or lay empiricist in the city clerk's office. He arranged with his old friends "Red Mike" Manier and "Fats" Davis to meet in the vicinity of the city hall at an appointed time. They all went to a big office with a long desk where a man handed him some papers. Then and there, in the presence of each other, they all signed. Both witnesses identified the will in question as the paper they signed. From the arrangement of the signatures it would appear, and the shifting testimony of the two witnesses indicated, that the testator signed last. He did not at any time on that occasion or thereafter refer to the instrument as a will, nor did he so acknowledge it by any manifestation beyond what we have recited here.

We do not have here a question of acknowledgment. KRS 394.040 requires that a non-holographic will be signed *or* acknowledged in the presence of the witnesses. Since Weathers signed the will in the presence of Manier and Davis, whether he acknowledged it is immaterial. Bennett v. Craycraft, Ky.1956, 290 S.W.2d 615; Darnaby v. Halley's Ex'r, 1948, 306 Ky. 697, 208 S.W.2d 299 (in which case the statute was held satisified by subscription before one witness and separate later acknowledgment before another).

Where the testator subscribes the will in the presence of the witnesses there is no requirement relating to the order in which the signatures are affixed, so long as each attesting signature is made in the testator's presence. See the leading case of Swift v. Wiley, 1840, 1 B.Mon. 114, 40 Ky. 114 (where two of three witnesses, though present when the testator signed the will, had affixed their own signatures some hours before); and Sechrest v. Edwards, 1862, 4 Metc. 163, 61 Ky. 163. Even in the case of acknowledgment, vis-à-vis subscription, where it may be argued with some force that there is no will to be acknowledged until the testator has signed, it has been held that if the whole transaction is substantially contemporaneous the order of precedence is of no moment. Robertson v. Robertson, 1930, 232 Ky. 572, 24 S.W.2d 282. See also annotations at 39 A.L.R. 933 and 57 A.L.R. 833. So in this case nothing can be made of the point that one or both witnesses signed ahead of the testator.

The appellants raise further questions of a technical nature. In a pretrial deposition Preston O. "Fats" Davis evidently had given testimony indicating that he and Weathers signed before the arrival of Manier, the other witness. At the trial the propounders proved the execution of the will by the testimony of Manier alone. Davis was put on the stand by the contestants. He disappointed them by corroborating the evidence given by Manier except as to the time of day when the transaction took place. Without objection counsel for the contestants proceeded to question him concerning the contradictory statements made in the deposition. But the witness was nimble as an eel, and held fast to his later testimony. In fact, we are not satisfied after a study of the transcript that he ever really admitted that he had made the statements read from the deposition, and if he did so he nevertheless did a good job of explaining the discrepancies away. But anyway, counsel for the proponents did not ask the court to admonish the jury as to the effect of the contradictory statements, and the contestants now contend that they should have been taken as substantive testimony creating a conflict in the evidence and precluding a directed verdict.

We agree with the position taken by the learned trial judge. It is difficult to see under what rational theory testimony that the law specifically limits to such minimizing influence as it may have on the credibility of the witness could be treated as having probative force. Among other reasons, the very fact that the witness declines to ratify it on the witness stand destroys whatever weight it might otherwise possess. Its greatest possible consequence could be to erase the force of the witness' later testimony at the trial, and if we apply that theory to this case we are left with all the evidence still on one side. True, the burden of showing proper execution of the will was on the propounders, Poindexter's Adm'r v. Alexander, 1939, 277 Ky. 147, 125 S.W.2d 981; Speshiots v. Coclanes, 1949, 311 Ky. 547, 224 S.W.2d 653, but the proof laid down by them in this case was such that reasonable men could arrive at but one conclusion. Hence the peremptory was in order.

Judgment affirmed.

Notes

1. What is the specific responsibility of the witnesses? To certify the authenticity of the testator's signature? To guarantee that all the formalities of testation are satisfied? To know the contents of the will? The Kentucky statute in the Hopson case (Ky.Rev.Stat. § 394.040) requires the witness to "subscribe" the will. Does an additional requirement that he "attest" it alter his responsibilities? Courts have described the objective of the process as giving the witnesses an opportunity to observe the attestation so that at a later probate proceeding they can "give testimony as to the essential elements of the two statutory issues of due execution and testamentary capacity sufficient, if cred-

ited by the jury, to prove both issues". Wheat v. Wheat, 156 Conn. 575, 244 A.2d 359 (1968) (the court recognized, however, that because the witnesses are usually laymen who often do not understand or appreciate their function, other competent evidence is admissible on the issues); Young v. Young, 20 Ill.App. 3d 242, 313 N.E.2d 593 (1974) (will not entitled to probate: witnesses must see testator sign or hear him acknowledge his signature in order to focus on his ability to execute the will and on the regularity of the proceedings). The witness's understanding of the transaction may be significant. See e.g. Weaver v. Grant, 394 So.2d 15 (Ala.1981) (witness must intend to witness some document, although need not know that it is a will). It has been held that a will is not properly executed when the witnesses signed only the self-proving affidavit attached to the will and not the will itself. Wich v. Fleming, 652 S.W. 2d 353 (Tex.1983). The holding is premised on the theory that the two acts require different types of intent on the part of the witness. "The attesting witness is expressing his present intent to act as a witness. The witness executing a self-proving affidavit is swearing to the validity of an act already performed." 652 S.W.2d at p. 354.

2. The typical statute states that a person eighteen or over may make a will. The testator in the Hopson case was described as a man of little education. Illiterates or persons suffering from a physical incapacity are not deprived of the privilege of making a will because they are unable to sign their names. A mark or an abbreviated name will suffice if the will can be identified as the testator's. See e.g., Mitchell v. Mitchell, 245 Ga. 291, 264 S.E.2d 222 (1980) ("X" sufficient signature of testator who was capable of writing a few words including his name). Statutes exist in all but a handful of states permitting someone else to sign for the testator. There are varying safeguards stipulated in the statutes with an almost universal requirement that the third person be under the direction and in the presence of the testator. A number of statutes require that the person who signs the testator's name must also sign his own name, but the will is not universally invalidated if he fails to comply.

A number of states have adopted by statute the "substituted judgment" doctrine whereby the guardian or conservator of an incompetent person is authorized to make gifts of the ward's property to persons whom the ward is legally, morally, or equitably obligated to support or to charities, if it is likely that the ward would make such gifts if legally competent to do so. It has been held under a statute of this kind that a conservator may take extensive steps to implement an estate plan on behalf of the ward, including the creation inter vivos of a revocable trust and an irrevocable charitable remainder trust, but that the statute cannot be expansively construed to permit the conservator to execute a will for the ward. Matter of Jones, 379 Mass. 826, 401 N.E.2d 351 (1980). If a person is disabled (other than for reasons of minority) and in need of protection, UPC § 5–407(b)(3) grants the court all the powers over the person's property "which the person could exercise if present and not under disability, except the power to make a will".

3. A number of statutes require that the testator sign the will "at the end." In other jurisidictions the requirement that the will be "subscribed" has been construed as requiring a signing at the end. The decisions locate this point at the "logical end of the language used by decedent in expressing his testamentary purpose." In re Estate of Treitinger, 440 Pa. 616, 269 A.2d 497, 44 A.L.R.3d

691 (1970). The same court is able to be both flexible and rigid on the question. Compare In re Estate of Stasis, 452 Pa. 425, 307 A.2d 241 (1973) (will validly executed although signed in upper margin at top of reverse side of page which was the only space left on the document sufficiently large to take the signature) with In re Estate of Weiss, 444 Pa. 126, 279 A.2d 189 (1971) (will invalid because testator signed in the side margin of a form will rather than on the line designated on the form as the place of the signature). The debate in Pennsylvania continues. See In re Estate of Proley, 492 Pa. 57, 422 A.2d 136 (1980) (decision by Orphan's Court holding that form will signed on title page but not in space for testator's signature was invalid affirmed by 3–3 vote). The cases are collected in Annot., Wills: When Is Will Signed at "End" or "Foot" as Required by Statute?, 44 A.L.R.3d 701 (1972). The appearance of significant material (which usually refers to an added dispositive provision) after the signature has traditionally invalidated the will. Matter of Winters, 277 App.Div. 24, 98 N.Y.S.2d 312 (1st Dept.1950) (the will was held invalid where the nomination of the executor appeared after the testator's signature, with a strong dissent by Justice Shientag), affirmed 302 N.Y. 666, 98 N.E.2d 477 (1951), 302 N.Y. 845, 100 N.E.2d 43; legislatively overruled by N.Y. EPTL 3–2.1(a)(1)(A), supra, p. 276. The New York approach now is to validate the will but to hold the provisions following the signature ineffective. A misplaced signature may, however, still render a will invalid. See Estate of Zaharis, 91 A.D.2d 737, 457 N.Y.S.2d 995 (3rd Dep't.1982) (will on single file card signed in the righthand margin of front page not entitled to probate). A number of jurisdictions, Virginia for instance, have adopted the New York approach without statutory prompting. Fenton v. Davis, 187 Va. 463, 47 S.E.2d 372 (1948). In that case, the post-signature language was stripped from a holographic will, on the ground that the signature was not clearly intended as an authentication of it.

4. South Carolina and Vermont require three witnesses. Except for some special provisions in Louisiana, all the other states require two witnesses. The Pennsylvania statute (20 Pa.C.S.A. § 2502) does not require the witnesses to sign the will (although they customarily do), unless the will was signed by the testator with his or her mark or by another person on the testator's behalf, but two witnesses are needed to prove the will at probate. Ligo v. Dodson, 301 Pa. 124, 151 A. 694 (1930). Many jurisdictions require that the witnesses sign in the presence of the testator. See e.g., In re Weber's Estate, which follows. In a few states the witnesses are required to sign in the presence of each other. As in the Hopson case, the order of signing is generally not treated as significant as long as the testator and witnessses sign in a single transaction. In Marshall v. Mason, 176 Mass. 216, 57 N.E. 340 (1900), however, Chief Justice Holmes, writing for the Massachusetts Supreme Judicial Court, held that the will was invalid where the witnesses signed before the testator. The Massachusetts statute (which has been carried forward as Mass.Gen.Laws Ann. c. 191 § 1 (1978)) required that the will must be "signed by him [the testator] or by a person in his presence and by his express direction, and attested and subscribed in his presence by [two] or more competent witnesses * * *." Accord, Jackson v. Jackson, 39 N.Y. 153 (1868). But cf. In re Jones' Estate, 157 Misc. 847, 285 N.Y.S. 894 (Surr.Ct. Oneida 1936) (" * * * the rule may be departed from under circumstances which show a complete compliance with the statute in one transaction, even though the testator signs last.").

E.   FORMAL WILLS—WITNESSES—PRESENCE

IN RE WEBER'S ESTATE

Supreme Court of Kansas, 1963.
192 Kan. 258, 387 P.2d 165.

WERTZ, Justice.   This was a proceeding to admit a document to probate as the last will and testament of Henry H. Weber.   The facts are undisputed and are substantially as follows:

Henry H. Weber, the decedent, died November 21, 1960.   At the time of his death he was seventy-three years of age, lawfully married to Rosa Weber, who had been adjudicated an incompetent person, and who, on the above-mentioned date, was, and had been for several years prior thereto, hospitalized at Topeka State Hospital.

Shortly after 12:00 p. m. on November 16, 1960, Henry Weber went to the home of Ben Heer in Riley.   Mr. Heer was not at home but his wife was, and Mr. Weber advised Mrs. Heer he was ill and needed help to get into the hospital.   He stated he wished to go the Riley County Hospital in Manhattan.   Mrs. Heer telephoned the hospital and made arrangements to have Mr. Weber admitted.

After arrangements were completed Mrs. Heer offered to put Mr. Weber's clothes in a suitcase and otherwise help him prepare to go to the hospital.   Next, she called a neighbor who in turn went to where Mr. Heer was working, which was about four miles from Riley, and told Mr. Heer that Henry Weber was at Heer's home and wanted to see him.   Heer went immediately to his home.   When he arrived Weber advised Heer of his illness and of his desire to make a will leaving one-half of his estate to his wife and one-half to his niece, Lillian Price.   Heer and Weber then decided to go to see Harold Holmes, president of the Riley State Bank, to have the will prepared.

The distance from the Heer residence to the bank was three or four blocks.   The two men drove to the bank, each in his own automobile.   Mr. Weber parked his car at an angle against the curb of the street and beneath a window on the north side of the bank and asked Mr. Heer, who had parked on the east side and had come over to the Weber car, to see if Mr. Holmes would come out to the car and talk to him.   Weber remained in his car and Heer went into the bank and talked to Holmes who then came out and got into the front seat of Weber's car.   At Weber's request Heer got into the back seat of the automobile.   It was a chilly November day and the car windows were kept closed.   Weber explained to Holmes how he desired to dispose of his property, one-half to be left to his wife and one-half to his niece, and that he wanted Heer to be his executor.   Holmes took notes as Weber talked.   After Holmes concluded taking notes he went back into the bank and prepared the purported will on a printed form captioned "Last Will and Testament" by filling in a portion of the blank spaces thereof with the information contained in the notes he had made, except that he failed to mention Weber's wife in the purported will.

The third paragraph of the will reads:

> "Third.　I give, devise and bequeath to *My Niece, Lillian Price of Junction City, Kansas My share of land situated in the Eureka Valley in Ogden and Manhattan Townships also My share of all Real estate located in Madison Township, Riley County Kansas* and I do devise and bequeath all the rest and residue of may estate both real, personal and mixed to *My Niece Lillian Price, any and all, money, stocks or Bonds, any and all personal property which I may possess at my death, whatsoever."*

The italicized portion of the above quotation was that part typed from Holmes' notes onto the printed will form.

While Holmes was inside the bank he directed three bank employees, Mr. and Mrs. Chamberlain and Mrs. Carlson, to go to and stand in front of a closed window in the bank in order that they could serve as witnesses to the signing of the will.　The window was approximately eight to ten feet from where Weber was sitting in his closed automobile.

About fifteen minutes later Holmes returned to Weber's automobile with a clipboard to which the purported will was fastened.　Holmes re-entered Weber's automobile and handed the document to him.　Weber read the document, Holmes and Heer being in the automobile at this time.

Holmes and Weber having previously discussed the need for witnesses, Holmes directed Weber's attention to the window of the bank where the above-named bank employees were standing.　By waving to them, Weber indicated he saw them, and they in turn waved back to him. After looking the purported will over, Weber placed the clipboard on the steering wheel of his automobile where it could be seen through the closed windows by the witnesses, and signed the document.

Holmes then returned to the bank with the document, and there, standing before the bank window as heretofore described, the witnesses signed their names.　The table upon which the signing occurred was against the window but the table top was a foot to a foot and a half beneath the window sill. Hence Weber could see the witnesses in the window as they signed but could not see the pen or the purported will on the table at the time of signing.　Only that portion of the body of each witness in the window could be seen by him.

After the three witnesses signed the purported will Holmes took it back out to Weber's automobile, showed it to him, Weber looked it over, and at Weber's request Holmes retained the document at the bank.

The record disclosed that all three witnesses were acquainted with Weber prior to November 16, 1960, and knew his signature when they saw it.　They recognized Weber's signature on the purported will.　However, none of the witnesses could read any of the writing or printing on the document while it was being signed by Weber in his automobile.

It is noted from the record that at no time was there any type of communication between Weber and the witnesses other than their waving to one another;　no verbal communication whatsoever.　Weber never entered the bank building during this period of time and heard nothing of what was said inside the building;　and even more important, the witnesses never left the building, so they couldn't possibly have heard any of the conversation that occurred in Weber's automobile.

The transaction at the bank took approximately one to one and a half hours to complete. Weber then proceeded to drive his automobile, unaccompanied, approximately twenty miles to the Riley County Hospital where the earlier admittance arrangements had been made, and it was there on November 21, 1960, just five days later, he died.

At the conclusion of the evidence the trial court made findings of fact and concluded as a matter of law that the will was duly executed by the decedent and attested by two competent witnesses in conformity with the provisions of G.S.1949, 59–606; that it was a valid will of the decedent and should be admitted to probate as the last will and testament of Henry H. Weber, deceased; and entered judgment accordingly.

From an order overruling his motion for a new trial, R. R. Bennett, guardian of the person and estate of Rosa Weber, an incompetent person, has appealed.

The determinative question in this case is whether or not the purported will was duly executed and attested in accordance with the provisions of G.S.1949, 50–606, which reads:

> "Every will, except an oral will as provided in section 44 [59–608], shall be in writing, and signed at the end thereof by the party making the same, or by some other person in his presence and by his express direction, and shall be attested and subscribed in the presence of such party by two or more competent witnesses, who saw the testator subscribe or heard him acknowledge the same."

The mentioned statute, insofar as is pertinent to the issues involved, contains the following elements: (1) The will must be attested and subscribed by two competent witnesses in the presence of the testator; (2) the witnesses must have either seen the testator subscribe or have heard him acknowledge the will. It is apparent that the statute clearly requires two essential factors: (1) presence, and (2) sight or hearing. There must be presence and sight or presence and hearing. Presence only, sight only, hearing only, or sight and hearing only are not sufficient. It is quite possible that one could see a testator subscribe to his will, i.e., by television, or one could hear the testator acknowledge his will, i.e., by telephone, but in either instance the witnesses would not be in the presence of the testator as contemplated by our statute. Conversely, one could be in the testator's presence and yet not see him sign or hear him acknowledge his will. The witnessing of a will is a matter of great importance and solemnity, and this is especially so because dispute about it does not arise until the testator's lips are sealed. (Rice v. Monroe, 108 Kan. 526, 527, 196 P. 756.)

In In re Estate of Bond, 159 Kan. 249, 252, 153 P.2d 912, 914, we stated:

> "The fact is that aside from an oral will, as provided in G.S.1943 Supp. 59–608, there is only one way to make a will in Kansas and that is by signing in the presence of two witnesses who saw the testator sign or heard him acknowledge it."

In Fuller v. Williams, 125 Kan. 154, 163, 264 P. 77, 81, this court stated:

"One who attests and subscribes a will as a witness should do so with the understanding that he is competent to testify on the probate of the will that the testator had mental capacity to make a will and was not under restraint or undue influence. Lawrie v. Lawrie, 39 Kan. 480, 18 P. 499; Hospital Co. v. Hale, 69 Kan. 616, 619, 77 P. 537; McConnell v. Keir, 76 Kan. 527, 531, 92 P. 540. The attesting witnesses to a will must not only witness the signing or publishing of it by the testator, but it is also their duty to satisfy themselves that the testator is of sound and disposing mind and memory and capable of executing a will. Smith et al. v. Young et al., 134 Miss. 738, 99 So. 370, 35 A.L.R. 69; In re Swan's Estate, 51 Utah 410, 170 P. 452. 'A witness to a will must * * * satisfy himself * * * of his (the testator's) testamentary capacity.' 40 Cyc. 1110; Dunkeson v. Williams (Mo.Sup.) 242 S.W. 653; Schouler on Wills (6th Ed.) §§ 229, 514; Page on Wills (2d Ed.) § 332. And see cases collected in annotation 35 A. L.R. 79. This duty necessarily requires that the attesting witnesses to a will should know and understand that the instrument they are signing as witnesses is a will, and they should do so prepared to testify to the testamentary capacity of the testator and that he is free from restraint and undue influence.

"We are aware there is a line of authorities to the effect that a witness to a will need not know whether he is witnessing a will or some other instrument, but we do not regard such authorities as being in accord with the duties required by an attesting and subscribing witness to a will under our statute, in accordance with the decision of our court."

In In re Estate of Bond, supra, it was stated that we prefer the strict construction of the statute to one which would tend to break down the formalities with which our legislature has seen fit to cloak the passing of property by devise. This strict construction rule was reaffirmed in the case of In re Estate of Davis, 168 Kan. 314, 322, 212 P.2d 343. It is possible that at times an honest attempt to execute a last will and testament is defeated by the failure to include some one or more of the statutory requirements. However, it is far more important that this should happen under a proper construction of the statute than that the individual case should be permitted to weaken the legislative mandate calculated to protect testators generally from fraud, duress, bad faith, overreaching, or undue influence in the making of their wills. The right to make a testamentary disposition of property is wholly statutory and the testator's intent to execute a valid will is not by itself sufficient to give validity to an instrument not executed in accordance with the statutory requirements.

The proponent of the will (the executor) in his brief invites our attention to Kitchell v. Bridgeman, 126 Kan. 145, 267 P. 26. However, in that case the will was executed by the testator in his room before two witnesses who saw him sign the will. In re Estate of Davis, 168 Kan. 314, 212 P.2d 343, is cited to us. In this case the testator signed in the presence of one witness and subsequently the second witness was brought into the room where the testator acknowledged to her and the witness signed in the testator's presence.   The proponent also cites Humphrey v. Wallace, 169 Kan. 58, 216 P.2d 781, where the witnesses did not see the testatrix sign but did in their presence hear her acknowledge her signature and that it was her last will and testament.   Attention is invited to Moore v. Glover, 196 Okl. 177, 163 P.2d 1003, where the testatrix handed the witnesses the will and stated that it was her will and requested the witnesses to sign as witnesses to her will.   The witnesses clearly heard testatrix acknowledge it as her will, and after they signed as witnesses returned it to her.   None of these cases supports the very liberal construction which the proponent wishes to place upon the statute under the facts of the instant case.

The statute was designed to require the attestation to be made in the presence of the testator so as to prevent the substitution of a surreptitious will.   The testator must be able to see the wtinesses attest the will;   or, to speak with more precision, their relative position to him at the time they are subscribing their names as witnesses must be such that he may see them, if he thinks it proper to do so, and satisfy himself by actual view that they are witnessing the very paper he signed to be his last will. In the instant case there is evidence that Weber told Mr. Heer and Banker Holmes that he wanted one-half of his property to go to his wife and one-half to his niece.   The document, as prepared, failed to mention the wife in any manner.   It is further noted that Holmes took some time in preparing the purported will, placed it upon a clipboard and then stationed three of his employees at the window and had them remain there while he took the instrument through the door and into the closed car where the witnesses saw Weber sign a paper, or document, which Holmes advised the witnesses was Weber's will.   A statement by the person who supervises the execution of the document that it is the testator's will and the like does not amount to an acknowledgment by testator if he does not hear such statement.   (2 Bowe-Parker: Page on Wills, § 19.115, p. 224.) The witnesses testified that there was no communication whatsoever between Weber and themselves.   There is nothing in the record to show that the witnesses read the provisions of the purported will but only knew Weber's signature appeared thereon.

Appellee seems to place much stress upon conscious presence and substantial compliance.   However, where the execution of a will in testator's presence is at issue, neither words nor intentions suffice.   The rule is that the burden of proof rests upon proponent of a will to establish that the will was executed according to the provisions of the statute.   To hold that the requirements of the statute were complied with in the instant case would subvert the purpose and intent of the statute and would amount to a disregard of its substance.   Failure to halt here under the facts in the instant case would permit substantial compliance and conscious presence to run wild so that if in any given case the intention of the testator is ascertained his will may be sustained.   Application of the rule of substantial compliance or conscious presence under the facts in the instant case is to ignore the statute intended to prevent fraud.

While it is unfortunate in this case that Lillian Price must suffer from the lack of legal ability and understanding of a scrivener who sought to perform a legal act of great importance and solemnity, that of drafting a will and purporting to supervise the execution thereof, it is better that she be denied her would-be beneficial intersts in the will than to open the door and set a pattern, by those not versed in the law of wills and in utter disregard to [sic] the plain provisions of the statute, for the drafting of future wills so as to permit fraud, undue influence, overreaching and bad faith which might in some other instances be practiced upon the weak, aged or infirm testators in the disposition of their worldly goods.

We are of the opinion that the facts of the instant case disclose the proximity between the witnesses and the testator was not sufficient to establish "presence," and, therefore, the will does not meet the necessary requirements of G.S.1949, 59–606, authorizing its admission to probate as the last will and testament of Henry H. Weber, deceased.   The judgment of the trial court is reversed and the case is remanded with instructions to set aside the judgment admitting the will to probate.

It is so ordered.

PARKER, C.J., and PRICE and FATZER, JJ., dissent.

Notes

1. Two types of "presence" may be required: (a) the testator signs in the presence of the witnesses; (b) the witnesses sign in the presence of the testator. The first of these two types is not universally required.   Frequently (as in Kansas), the testator's acknowledgment of his or her signature will suffice.   See e.g. Norton v. Georgia Railroad Bank & Trust Co., 248 Ga. 847, 285 S.E.2d 910 (1982) (acknowledgment may be inferred from testator's conduct).   The requirement that the witnesses sign in the presence of the testator continues to be honored in many jurisdictions, although variation exists in the cases in the degree of strictness with which it is applied.   The New York statute and the Uniform Probate Code do not require the witnesses to sign the will in the presence of the testator.   N.Y. EPTL § 3–2.1(a)(4), supra p. 276 (testator signs in the presence of the witnesses or acknowledges the signature and witnesses sign "within one thirty day period"); UPC § 2–502, supra p. 277 (acknowledgment of signature sufficient).

2. The courts tend to reiterate, without adequate explanation or analysis, the statement that the purpose of the requirement that the witnesses attest in the presence of the testator is to prevent the witnesses from substituting some other paper for the will executed by the testator.   To evaluate the functional validity of this stated purpose, analyze the following possibilities in terms of the probability of their being attempted (consider difficulties of preparation) or, if attempted, being successful (consider chances of detection—if the testator detects the substitution, he can destroy the spurious document and execute a genuine will unless he dies too soon; if the substitution is detected after his death, remedies for his intended beneficiaries would be available):

a. The witnesses forge the testator's signature to a spurious will in favor of themselves, and, when they are out of the testator's presence, they attest the forged will and return it to the testator instead of the genuine will.

b. Some people other than the witnesses forge the testator's signature to a spurious will in favor of themselves, and then bribe the witnesses to attest it and return it to the testator instead of the genuine will.

c. The witnesses (or others who have bribed them) are beneficiaries under a former will, but not under the will now being executed, which revokes the former will. The former will is substituted for the genuine one.

d. The witnesses (or others who have bribed them) are intestate successors and substitute an inoperative document for the intended will.

3. In what way might the requirement that the witnesses sign in the testator's presence aid in the successful prosecution of a dishonest claim? Or as a device to obtain a more "equitable" distribution of the estate?

4. The court in the classic case of Reed v. Roberts, 26 Ga. 294, 300–01, 71 Am.Dec. 210 (1858), said in the conclusion of an opinion in which the will was invalidated:

> Why a desire to favor the wills of testators made *in extremis* should exist in this State, we do not very well understand. Ordinarily, our statute of distribution makes the fairest disposition of a dead man's property. Here a man advanced in life, weakened by disease, and racked with pain, is supported in bed while he subscribes his will. While in the act of executing his will, by which he bequeaths an estate of from $20,000 to $35,000 to the children by a second marriage, he forgets the amount of the pittance with which he cuts off the offspring of a former marriage, first saying, when the will was read to him, that he thought he had left to them $10 instead of $100, and then upon the second reading $5 instead of $10! And yet, the salutary safeguards of the statute of frauds are to be broken down and disregarded, to set up such a will! It is going quite far enough to say, in such a case, that the law is satisfied by the testator being in such a situation that he *may*, from that situation, and without change of position, and without aid from others, supervise the attestation.

5. The usual test of presence is stated in terms of whether the testator could have seen the witnesses attest the will or not and how much effort was required to enable him to do so. There are wide variations in the application of the requirement. Some opinions try to give some meaning to a "conscious presence rule." In re Tracy's Estate, 80 Cal.App.2d 782, 182 P.2d 336 (1947) (" * * * the testator need not actually view the act of signing by the witnesses, but * * * these elements must be present: (1) the witnesses must sign within the testator's hearing, (2) the testator must know what is being done, and (3) the signing by the witnesses and the testator must constitute one continuous transaction." 80 Cal.App.2d at 783–84); In re Demarris' Estate, 166 Or. 36, 110 P.2d 571 (1941) ("But we do not believe that sight is the only test of presence. We are convinced that any of the senses that a testator possesses, which enable him to know whether another is near at hand and what he is doing, may be employed by him in determining whether the attesters are in his presence as they sign his will. * * * It is unnecessary, we believe, that the attestation and execution occur in the same room. And, as just stated, it is unnecessary that the attesters be within the range of vision of the testator when they sign. If they are so near at hand that they are within the range of any of his senses, so that he knows what is going on, the requirement has been met." 166 Or. at 71–72, 110 P.2d at 585). See also In re Lane's Estate, 265 Mich. 539, 251 N.W. 590 (1933) (where the Michigan court, emphasizing that there was no claim of incompetency, fraud or undue influence and that the document had been returned to the testator after the attestation, proclaimed

itself in favor of a liberal construction of the requirement); accord, Glenn v. Mann, 234 Ga. 194, 214 S.E.2d 911 (1975). Literal compliance is however, frequently required. Jefferson's Will, 349 So.2d 1032 (Miss.1977) (attorney signed as witness in presence of testator but returned to office to have his partner sign as a second witness); Morris v. Estate of West, 643 S.W.2d 204 (Tex.App. 1982) (testator remained in conference room of attorney's office, while witnesses took will and codicil to secretarial office to sign); In re Hill's Estate, 349 Mich. 38, 84 N.W.2d 457 (1957) (witnesses knew testatrix's signature but signed 40 or 50 feet away from her in another room); In re Palmer's Estate, 255 Iowa 428, 122 N.W.2d 920 (1963) (will invalid where witnesses signed outside testator's room and out of his sight); How can "presence" be determined in the case of a blind testator? See Welch v. Kirby, 255 F. 451, 9 A.L.R. 1409 (1918) certiorari denied 249 U.S. 612, 39 S.Ct. 386, 63 L.Ed. 801 (1919).

See generally, Annot., Presence: What Constitutes the Presence of the Testator in the Witnessing of His Will?, 75 A.L.R.2d 318 (1961); Gulliver and Tilson, Classification of Gratuitous Transfers, 51 Yale L.J. 1, 10–11 (1941).

F.　FORMAL WILLS—COMPETENCY OF WITNESSES

Probably the most significant feature of the statutory provisions for formal wills is the requirement that they be attested by witnesses. Attestation was not necessary under the Statute of Wills of 1540, but it was required for devises by the Statute of Frauds in 1676 and for wills of both real and personal property by the Wills Act of 1837. Except in the special cases where holographic or nuncupative wills are permitted, attestation is an almost universal requirement for the validity of a will in this country.

Compliance with the competency requirements for attesting witnesses is especially important, because the interest of the witness will, in practically all cases, appear on the face of the will. There is, therefore, less chance of the will being probated in spite of a violation of the statute of wills here than there is in cases where such a violation would not come to the attention of the court in the absence of testimony by some witness.

The common law cases on the question of the competency of attesting witnesses to a will arose at a time when the disqualification of witnesses in ordinary lawsuits was far more extensive than it is at the present day. Parties to the action and other interested persons were barred from testifying—a rule severely criticized by Bentham in 1827 and abolished by statute in England in 1843 as to interested witnesses and in 1851 as to parties. Disqualification for interest has also been generally abolished in the United States as far as the usual type of lawsuit is concerned; the interest of the witness may be considered in determining his credibility but is no longer a ground for excluding his or her testimony.

The assumption that a financial interest will necessarily result in deliberately or unconsciously erroneous testimony seems unwarranted, and the common law disqualification would often exclude important evidence, particularly if the parties to the suit were the ones who knew most about the facts. 2 Wigmore, Evidence §§ 575–577; 9 Holds. 193–196.

A husband or a wife was also disqualified at common law from testifying *in favor of* the other spouse, though this doctrine was not extended to other family relationships such as parent and child. Under this rule, the spouse of a party, or of one interested in the event of a lawsuit, was barred from testifying. This rule was also criticized by Bentham and abolished in England for civil actions by statutes in 1853 and 1869. It has also been abolished in most American jurisdictions for the usual type of lawsuit, by the so-called "enabling acts." 2 Wigmore, op. cit. §§ 600–603, 606–607; 9 Holds. 197. The rule just stated should be distinguished from the privilege not to testify *against* one's husband or wife, which is still rather generally sanctioned in the United States. 8 Wigmore, op. cit. §§ 2227–28, 2245; 9 Holds. 197–198.

It was against this background that the early cases on competency of attesting witnesses to wills were decided. The Statute of Frauds (1676) required attestation "by three or four credible witnesses." In 1699 it appears to have been held that a will was invalid if one of the necessary witnesses was a devisee, on the theory that because of his interest in the event (he would profit by the will being sustained), the devisee could not be a "credible witness." Hilliard v. Jennings, 1 Ld.Raym. 505, 91 Eng. Rep. 1237. In the middle of the eighteenth century, there arose a famous controversy as to whether the competency of testamentary witnesses should be judged as of the time of attestation or as of the time when, after the testator's death, they actually testified about the execution of the will. If the latter were adopted as the criterion, then it would be possible for a devisee-witness to release his interest in the will after the testator's death and before the validity of the will was tried, thereby rendering himself competent to help sustain the will. In 1746, it was held that the Statute of Frauds required competency at the time of attestation, the purpose being to safeguard the testator at the time of the execution of the will. Holdfast d. Anstey v. Dowsing, 2 Strange 1253, 93 Eng.Rep. 1164. This decision is said to have occasioned great alarm as threatening to upset many wills; this was particularly true under the then existing rules by which a creditor of the testator would be an interested party if the will charged the testator's real estate with the payment of his debts. 2 Bl.Com. 377. Under the common law rule (now made obsolete by the modern procedure allowing creditors to be paid from realty), creditors of a deceased person could not satisfy their claims out of his real property unless it had been charged by the deceased with liability for the payment of his debts. A creditor attesting a will charging realty with the payment of debts would thus have a bias in favor of the will, since his recourse against what would at that time probably be the valuable property of the deceased would depend on the will's validity. Since many testators might, in fairness to their creditors, incorporate such charges in their wills, and since it was probable that at least one of the necessary witnesses would be a creditor of the testator at the time of attestation (e.g., a servant, a doctor, a nurse, a lawyer, or others to whom the testator owed money), it is easy to understand the fear of the destructive effect on wills of a rule requiring witnesses to be competent at the time when the will was executed.

This led to the first "purging" statute in 1752, which removed the interest of the witness by providing that, if any beneficiary under a will also attested it, the gift to him in the will should be void and he should be a competent witness. It also made creditors, whose debts were charged on the testator's land by the will, competent attesting witnesses. 25 Geo. II, c. 6.

In the United States, many states have "purging" statutes, similar to that of George II, supra. The latter statute was repealed in England by the Wills Act of 1837 (7 Wm. 4 & 1 Vict., c. 26), which, however, substantially reenacted its provisions, along with certain additions. The provisions of the Wills Act of 1837 on this subject are:

XIV. *And be it further enacted*, That if any Person who shall attest the Execution of a Will shall at the Time of the Execution thereof or at any Time afterwards be incompetent to be admitted a Witness to prove the Execution thereof, such Will shall not on that Account be invalid.

XV. *And be it further enacted*, That if any Person shall attest the Execution of any Will to whom or to whose Wife or Husband any beneficial Devise, Legacy, Estate, Interest, Gift, or Appointment, of or affecting any Real or Personal Estate (other than and except Charges and Directions for the Payment of any Debt or Debts), shall be thereby given or made, such Devise, Legacy, Estate, Interest, Gift or Appointment shall, so far only as concerns such Person attesting the Execution of such Will, or the Wife or Husband of such Person, or any Person claiming under such Person or Wife or Husband, be utterly null and void, and such Person so attesting shall be admitted as a Witness to prove the Execution of such Will, or to prove the Validity or Invalidity thereof, notwithstanding such Devise, Legacy, Estate, Interest, Gift, or Appointment mentioned in such Will.

XVI. *And be it further enacted*, That in case by any Will any Real or Personal Estate shall be charged with any Debt or Debts, and any Creditor, or the Wife or Husband of any Creditor, whose Debt is so charged, shall attest the Execution of such Will, such Creditor notwithstanding such Charge shall be admitted a Witness to prove the Execution of such Will, or to prove the Validity or Invalidity thereof.

XVII. *And be it further enacted*, That no Person shall, on account of his being an Executor of a Will, be incompetent to be admitted a Witness to prove the Execution of such Will, or a Witness to prove the Validity or Invalidity thereof.

———

The Uniform Probate Code § 2–505 (see supra p. 278 and discussion, note 1, infra p. 296) and the laws of a few states (see e.g., Va. Code 1950, § 64.1–51) no longer require that a witness be financially disinterested in the will. The doctrine is critically reviewed in Gulliver and Tilson, Classification of Gratuitous Transfers, 51 Yale L.J. 1, 11–13 (1940); Evans, The Competency of Testamentary Witnesses, 25 Mich.L.Rev. 238–243, 264–267 (1926). The English rules are described in Bodkin, Gifts to Attesting Witnesses, 26 Sol. 91 (1959).

✓
DORFMAN v. ALLEN
Supreme Judicial Court of Massachusetts, 1982.
386 Mass. 136, 434 N.E.2d 1012.

O'CONNOR, Justice.

We are presented with a will dispute and a constitutional challenge to G.L. c. 191, § 2, which voids bequests to spouses of necessary subscribing witnesses.

By a will executed on March 24, 1965, and a codicil executed on November 1, 1976, William Herbits left one-half of the residue of his estate to his wife on the condition that she survive him by thirty days, and "one-half (or all, if my said wife shall not survive me thirty days) in equal shares to my daughters, MURIEL HARRIET ALLEN and IRIS SHEILA CHANDLER, and their issue by right of representation." The codicil leaves $1,000 to William's son, Charles, and "intentionally [makes] no further provision for him." Both instruments were subscribed to by three witnesses. In each instance one of these was Muriel's husband. William died on December 28, 1976. His wife did not survive him by thirty days. At the time of William's death, Muriel had two issue, Peter A. Allen and Richard L. Allen.

General Laws c. 191, § 2, as amended by St.1920, c. 2, was in effect on the dates the will and codicil were executed and William died, and governs both instruments. It provided, in pertinent part, that "a beneficial devise or legacy to a subscribing witness or to the husband or wife of such witness shall be void unless there are three [1] other subscribing witnesses to the will who are not similarly benefited thereunder." Section 2 voids the residuary bequest to Muriel. Rosenbloom v. Kokofsky, 373 Mass. 778, 369 N.E.2d 1142 (1977).

The Probate and Family Court reported two questions pursuant to G.L. c. 215, § 13. The first question is whether G.L. c. 191, § 2, is constitutional. Muriel and her children, Peter and Richard, argue that § 2 violates the equal protection and due process guarantees of the Federal and State Constitutions; Iris, Charles, and the Attorney General as amicus curiae, disagree. No other constitutional question is argued. The second question is whether, if § 2 is constitutional, the legacy to Muriel passes by the law of intestate succession, so that Charles, Iris, and Muriel are each entitled to one third, or by the will, to Peter and Richard, Muriel's children. G.L. c. 190, § 3.

* * *

Constitutionality. Muriel contends that § 2 differentiates between two classes of persons (spouses and all others) without a rational basis,

---

1. Statute 1976, c. 515, § 5, by § 35 made effective July 1, 1978, amended G.L. c. 191, § 2, by substituting "two" for "three." By St.1977, c. 76, § 2, the effective date of the amendment was advanced to January 1, 1978.

deprives her of property without a rational basis, and creates an irrebuttable presumption[2] that is not necessarily true.

Section 2 creates a class of spouses of necessary subscribing witnesses
and voids bequests to members of that class. The provision does not
implicate a suspect class or a fundamental interest. In this context,
Muriel's consitutional challenges, which derive from the State and Federal equal protection and due process guarantees, give rise to essentially
the same inquiry: whether the statute is rationally related to a permissible legislative objective. If it is, the statute's classification survives
equal protection attack, and its irrebuttable presumption survives due
process attack. Weinberger v. Salfi, 422 U.S. 749, 768–769, 776–777,
95 S.Ct. 2457, 2468, 2472, 45 L.Ed.2d 522 (1975) (irrebuttable presumption
analysis under the Federal Constitution). Dandridge v. Williams, 397
U.S. 471, 485, 90 S.Ct. 1153, 1161, 25 L.Ed.2d 491, (1970) (Federal equal
protection). Pinnick v. Cleary, 360 Mass. 1, 14 & n.8, 271 N.E.2d 592
(1971) (Federal and State due process). McQuade v. New York Cent.
R.R., 320 Mass. 35, 38, 68 N.E.2d 185 (1946) (Federal and State equal
protection). See L. Tribe, American Constitutional Law § 16–32 (1978).

Section 2 advances at least two permissible objectives: reduction of
the potential for perjury and protection of testators from overreaching or
coercion by the subscribing witnesses who, through their spouses, will
benefit from the testator's bounty. Voiding the spouse's interest is certainly a rational way of achieving these ends. That the statute does not
void bequests to other relatives of a necessary witness, such as a child or
parent, does not render it invalid. "[A] State [need not] choose between
attacking every aspect of a problem or not attacking the problem at
all." Dandridge, supra 397 U.S. at 486–487, 90 S.Ct. at 1162–63. Section 2 is therefore constitutional.

Distribution. While § 2 voids Muriel's residuary interest, the statute is silent as to where that bequest devolves. The general rule is that
a void residuary bequest to a legatee who is not a member of a donee
class passes according to the law of intestate succession. * * * However, where the testator has created a gift over, the bequest passes according to the terms of that gift. * * *

William left the residue to Muriel and Iris "and their issue by right
of representation." "Right of representation" is defined by statute to
involve nonsurvival. G.L. c. 190, § 8. Williams clearly created a gift
over to Muriel's children in the event that Muriel did not survive him.
The question is whether the will demonstrates William's intention to
create a gift over to Muriel's children in the event that the gift to Muriel
fails even though she survives him. It is the court's duty to effectuate
the testator's intent unless some positive rule of law forbids. Old Colony
Trust Co. v. Treadwell, 312 Mass. 214, 217, 43 N.E.2d 777 (1942). Although it is apparent that William did not contemplate failure of his
bequest to Muriel except by her predeceasing him, we believe that the

---

2. The alleged presumption is that a necessary subscribing witness to a will will overreach
the testator where the spouse of the witness is a legatee.

language of the residuary clause demonstrates his intention that Muriel's issue should be substituted for Muriel if she should be unable to take the bequest. It is apparent from William's attempted disposition of all his property that he desired to avoid intestacy. The result we reach is consistent with the settled principle that "a construction of a will resulting in intestacy is not to be adopted unless plainly required." Lyman v. Sohier, 266 Mass. 4, 8, 164 N.E. 460 (1929).

* * *

Because the will provides for a gift over to Muriel's issue, her issue alive at William's death are entitled to her share of the residue. See Hubbard v. Lloyd, 6 Cush. 522 (1850).

Notes

1. In practical effect, the competency doctrine creates an irrebuttable presumption that a legatee or the spouse of a legatee, who witnesses a will, is dishonest. The Court gives the traditional justification for the rule as a means of reducing the "potential for perjury" and of providing "protection of testators from overreaching or coercion by the subscribing witnesses". How real is the danger? Does the competency rule give geniune protection to the testator? The official comment explains the reasons for the removal of the requirement in the § 2–505 of the Uniform Probate Code:

> This section simplifies the law relating to interested witnesses. Interest no longer disqualifies a person as a witness, nor does it invalidate or forfeit a gift under the will. Of course, the purpose of this change is not to foster use of interested witnesses, and attorneys will continue to use disinterested witnesses in execution of wills. But the rare and innocent use of a member of the testator's family on a homedrawn will would no longer be penalized. This change does not increase appreciably the opportunity for fraud or undue influence. A substantial gift by will to a person who is one of the witnesses to the execution of the will would itself be a suspicious circumstance, and the gift could be challenged on grounds of undue influence. The requirement of disinterested witnesses has not succeeded in preventing fraud and undue influence; and in most cases of undue influence, the influencer is careful not to sign as witness but to use disinterested witnesses.

> An interested witness is competent to testify to prove execution of the will, under Section 3–406.

2. The rule disqualifies a witness who receives a legacy that is of direct pecuniary benefit, i.e., the type of benefit for which a person would commit fraud. See e.g., Cox, Appellant, 126 Me. 256, 137 A. 771, 53 A.L.R. 208 (1927) (membership in club does not render witness incompetent when club is testamentary beneficiary because interest too indirect and slight).

Does a gift to a corporation, town or church disqualify a witness who is a stockholder, taxpayer or parishioner? A few purging statutes specifically exempt gifts of this kind. See Conn.Gen.Stat. § 45–172; see also In re Koop's Estate, 143 So.2d 693 (Fla.1962) (bequest to bank as trustee valid even though employee-stockholders of the bank were witnesses).

Is the person nominated in the will as executor or trustee an incompetent witness? The statutes of a few states follow the example of the English Wills

Act of 1837 in providing that the executor of a will is a competent attesting witness. It is the usual holding, in the absence of such a statute, that an executor or testamentary trustee has not a sufficient interest, as such, to render him or her incompetent. Giacomini's Estate, 4 Kan.App.2d 126, 603 P.2d 218 (1979); In re Fay's Estate, 353 Mich. 83, 90 N.W.2d 837 (1958). A commission set out in the will which exceeds that allowed by statute will be purged. In re Estate of Small, 346 F.Supp. 600 (D.C.1972). See generally Annot., Competency of Named Executor as Subscribing Witness to Will, 74 A.L.R.2d 283 (1960).

A testamentary direction to the executor to employ a named person as the attorney for the estate is not deemed to be binding on the executor and therefore the attorney is not disqualified as an attesting witness. See Pavletich v. Pavletich, 78 N.M. 93, 428 P.2d 632 (1967) and the cases cited in Annot., 30 A.L.R.3d 1361 (1970).

Financial interest is not the only basis on which a witness' competency may be challenged. As in other areas of the law, a witness to a will must have sufficient capacity and maturity to observe, recall, and narrate the events that took place at the attestation of the will. A few statutes set a minimum age. See e.g., Iowa Code Ann. § 633.280 (sixteen); Utah Code Ann.1953, § 75–2–505 (eighteen). For an analysis of the age factor absent a statute, see Dejmal's Estate, 95 Wis.2d 141, 289 N.W.2d 813 (1980) ("Certainly nineteen is not such a tender age that it would preclude one from testifying in court to the facts relating to execution of a will."). A person who has been convicted of an "infamous" crime such as perjury has been declared a competent witness, because, to hold otherwise, would create a "needless trap for the unwary testator who, by failing to discover an attesting witness' prior criminal record, risks having his will declared void." McGarvey v. McGarvey, 286 Md. 19, 405 A.2d 250, 255 (1979).

3. Some purging statutes, N.Y.—McKinney's EPTL § 3–3.2 for example, do not disqualify the spouse who acts as a witness to a will in which the other spouse is a beneficiary. Accordingly, it was held in a case where the testator devised realty to husband and wife that the wife, who was a witness to the will, forfeited her devise, but her husband was entitled to take title to the entire lot. Matter of Flynn, 68 Misc.2d 1087, 329 N.Y.S.2d 249 (1972). In Rosenbloom v. Kokofsky, cited in the principal case, the Supreme Judicial Court was asked to interpret the statute so as to bring the Massachusetts rule into line with the "more liberal view" held in states like New York. It was argued that to purge the interest of the witness' spouse defeated the testator's intent and was based on "an out-moded concept of the legal identity of spouses". The Court appeared to be sympathetic to the argument but refused to intervene, stating that the statute was clear and unambiguous and could only be altered by the legislature. Courts are not prepared to expand the reach of the doctrine. See e.g., Berndtson v. Heuberger, 21 Ill.2d 557, 173 N.E.2d 460 (1961) (witness who marries the devisee after the execution of the will is not incompetent and devise need not be purged). Neither the statutes nor the common law hold that a parent, who witnesses a will in which his or her child is a beneficiary, is an incompetent witness. See e.g., Sparhawk v. Sparhawk, 92 Mass. 155 (1865).

4. If one of three witnesses is a beneficiary and the local statute only requires two witnesses, the interested witness, being superfluous, need not forfeit his or her legacy. There appears to be no escape from the purging statute

when two of three witnesses are beneficiaries.   Thus, it has been held, where witnesses A and B are beneficiaries but witness C is disinterested, that A and C cannot join to validate B's legacy, nor B and C to validate A's legacy.   Both A and B must forfeit their legacies.   Estate of Watts, 67 Ill.App.3d 463, 23 Ill. Dec. 795, 384 N.E.2d 589 (1979).

The typical statute of wills requires that two witnesses attest the will at the time the testator executes it.   Because, in the interim between the time the will was signed and the time it is probated, witnesses may be rendered unavailable by death, insanity, absence from the jurisidiction, or other cause, a second statute, dealing with probate procedures, may require that only one witness be produced to testify at the probate hearing.   Indeed, procedures are available to probate the will on proof of the handwriting of the testator and witnesses when no attesting witness can be produced to testify.   If the purging statute is concerned only that the witness who testifies at the probate proceeding is competent, the legacy of an attesting witness who is not needed to testify may be saved.   A purging statute that voids the legacy or devise of a witness when "the will cannot be proved except by his testimony" has been construed to make the competency requirement only applicable to witnesses who are testifying at the time of probate.   Rogers v. Helms, 69 Ohio St.2d 323, 432 N.E.2d 186 (1982) (will and bequest to witness valid; witnesses need not be financially disinterested at time of attestation under the general enabling act and witness not needed to testify at probate proceedings); see also In re Walters' Estate, 285 N.Y. 158, 33 N.E.2d 72 (1941) (legislatively overruled by an amendment to N.Y. EPTL § 3–3.2 requiring witnesses to be competent at the time of attestation as well as at probate).

5. Suppose that an attesting witness who is a beneficiary in the will would have received property worth $100,000 if the testator had died intestate.   The purging statute may exempt an heir of the testator from its operation.   See e.g., Conn.Gen.Stat.Ann. § 45–172.   The more common approach is that used in N.Y.—McKinney's EPTL § 3–3.2 which saves to the intestate successor the amount that he would have received had there been no will, not to exceed the value of the legacy.

(a) Under the New York type of purging statute, what would the witness receive if the will gave him

(1) Nothing?

(2) $50,000?

(3) $100,000?

(4) $150,000?

(b) A witness to a will, who was not an heir to the testator, was allowed to take her $10,000 legacy because an earlier will that would have been controlling had this will been ineffective contained an identical legacy.   In re Estate of Johnson, 359 So.2d 425 (Fla.1978).   Would the result be the same under the Connecticut statute?   Suppose under 5(a) supra there was an earlier will that disinherited the witness?

(c) Would the share receivable by the witness come to him by intestacy or under the will?   Cf. Matter of Ehrlich, 158 Misc. 540, 287 N.Y.S. 313 (1936). Suppose that the will set up a trust to pay the income to the witness for life, and that the figures given in note 5(a) supra represented the present value of the right to receive this income; would the witness take his share outright or subject to the trust?

G. HOLOGRAPHIC WILLS

Holographic wills originated in the Roman Law, were authorized by the Code Napoleon, and are recognized in a number of foreign countries. They were never recognized as such in England. They are recognized in approximately half the states, but the statutory provisions vary. The question of their validity may, of course, arise in other states, under the rules of conflict of laws. By the statement that "holographic wills are recognized" it is meant that they are considered in a class by themselves, exempted from the statutory requirements for formal wills (the most important of which is attestation), and only required to comply with the statute expressly applicable to holographic wills alone. There is, of course, no objection to a formal will being written in the handwriting of the testator, but no special significance is attached to that fact in jurisdictions not recognizing holographic wills. See generally, Bird, Sleight of Handwriting: The Holographic Will in California, 32–1 Hastings L.J. 605 (1981); Rees, American Wills Statutes, 46 Va.L.Rev. 613, 634–636 (1960).

GULLIVER AND TILSON, CLASSIFICATION OF GRATUITOUS TRANSFERS

51 Yale L.J. 1, 13 (1941) (footnotes omitted).

The exemption of holographic wills from the usual statutory requirements seems almost exclusively justifiable in terms of the evidentiary function. The requirement that a holographic will be entirely written in the handwriting of the testator furnishes more complete evidence for inspection by handwriting experts than would exist if only the signature were available, and consequently tends to preclude the probate of a forged document. While it may be argued that the requirement tends to prevent fraud in the execution, since the testator would normally sign the will immediately after he had finished writing it, and, there is, therefore, less likelihood of his signing a different document, there seems no substantial guarantee of the performance of the protective function, since no effort is made to prevent other forms of imposition such as undue influence. A holographic will is obtainable by compulsion as easily as a ransom note. While there is a certain ritual value in writing out the document, casual offhand statements are frequently made in letters. The relative incompleteness of the performance of the functions of the regular statute of wills, and particularly the absence of any ritual value, may account for the fact that holographic wills are not recognized in the majority of the states, and for some decisions, in states recognizing them, requiring the most precise compliance with specified formalities.

ESTATE OF JOHNSON

Court of Appeals of Arizona, Division 1, Department A 1981.
129 Ariz. 307, 630 P.2d 1039.

WREN, Chief Judge.

This appeal involves the question of whether the handwritten portions on a printed will form, submitted to the trial court as a holographic will, were sufficient to satisfy the requirements of A.R.S. § 14–2503 that the material provisions of such a will must be entirely in the handwriting of the testator.

Arnold H. Johnson, the decedent, died on January 28, 1978 at the age of 79. One of his sons, John Mark Johnson, was appointed personal representative of the estate. In addition to John, the decedent was survived by five other children. Approximately three weeks following appointment of the personal representative, appellants, Barton Lee McLain and Marie Ganssle, petitioned for formal probate of an instrument dated March 22, 1977. The personal representative objected to the petition and filed a motion for summary judgment on the grounds that the instrument was invalid as a will, in that it was not attested by any witnesses as required by A.R.S. § 14–2502, and did not qualify as a holographic will under A.R.S. § 14–2503, since the material provisions thereof were not in the handwriting of the testator.

Appellants filed a cross-motion for summary judgment, urging that the document did constitute a holographic will. The trial court disagreed with appellants and granted the motion of the personal representative. We affirm.

The document claimed by appellants to be decedent's last will and testament was a printed will form available in various office supply and stationery stores. It bore certain printed provisions followed by blanks where the testator could insert any provisions he might desire. The entire contents of the instrument in question are set forth below, with the portions underscored which are in the decedent's handwriting.

THE LAST WILL AND TESTATMENT

I Arnold H. Johnson a resident of Mesa Arizona of Maricopa County, State of Arizona, being of sound and disposing mind and memory, do make, publish and declare this my last WILL AND TESTAMENT, hererby revoking and making null and void any and all other last Wills and Testaments heretofore by me made.

FIRST—My will is that all my just debts and funeral expenses and any Estate or Inheritance taxes shall be paid out of my Estate, as soon after my decease as shall be found convenient.

SECOND—I give devise and bequeath to My six living children as follows
To John M. Johnson ⅛ of my Estate

Helen Marchese	⅛
Sharon Clements	⅛
Mirriam Jennings	⅛
Mary D. Korman	⅛
A. David Johnson	⅛
To W. V. Grant, Souls Harbor Church	
3200 W. Davis Dallas Texas	⅛
To Barton Lee McLain	
and Marie Gansels	
Address 901 E. Broadway	⅛
Mesa	

I nominate and appoint <u>Mirriam Jennings my Daughter</u> of <u>Nashville Tenn.</u> as execut<u>ress</u> of this my Last Will and Testament Address <u>1247 Saxon Drive</u> <u>Nashville Tenn.</u>

IN TESTIMONY WHEREOF, I have set my hand to this, My Last Will and Testament, at _____this <u>22</u> day of <u>March,</u> in the year of our Lord, One Thousand Nine Hundred <u>77</u>

The foregoing instrument was signed by said Arnold H. <u>Johnson</u> in our presence, and by _____published and declared as and for _____ Last Will and Testament, and at _____request, and in _____ presence, and in presence of each other, we hereunto subscribe our Names as Attesting Witnesses, at _____This <u>22</u> day of <u>March, 1977</u>

My Commission expires   <u>Ann C. McGonagill</u>
Jan. 16, 1981

(Notary public seal)

Sections 14–101 to 14–134, Arizona Revised Statutes, 1956, and Amendments thereto

Initially it is to be noted that Arizona has adopted the Uniform Probate Code, the holographic will provisions being contained in § 2–503, and found in A.R.S. § 14–2503:

> A will which does not comply with § 14–2502 is valid as a holographic will, whether or not witnessed, if the signature and the material provisions are in the handwriting of the testator.

The statutory requirement that the material provisions be drawn in the testator's own handwriting requires that the handwritten portion clearly express a *testamentary* intent. Estate of Morrison, 55 Ariz. 504, 103 P.2d 669 (1940). Appellants argue that the purported will here should thus be admitted to probate, since all the key dispositive provisions essential to its validity as a will are in the decedent's own handwriting; and further, when all the printed provisions are excised, the requisite intent to make a will is still evidenced. We do not agree. In our opinion, the only words which establish this requisite testamentary intent on the part of the decedent are found in the *printed* portion of the form.

The official comment to § 2–503 of the Uniform Probate Code (U.L.A.) sheds some light upon the situation where, as here, a printed will form is used:

> By requiring only the "material provisions" to be in the testator's handwriting (rather than requiring, as some existing statutes do, that the will be "entirely" in the testator's handwriting) a holograph may be valid even though immaterial parts such as date or introductory wording be printed or stamped. A valid holograph might even be executed on some printed will forms if the printed portion could be eliminated and the handwritten portion could evidence the testator's will. For persons unable to obtain legal assistance, the holographic will may be adequate.

Prior to the adoption of § 14–2503 in 1974, In re Estate of Schuh, 17 Ariz.App. 172, 496 P.2d 598 (1972), permitted probate, as a holographic will, the handwritten language on a stationer's will form, where the printed words on the form were found not to be essential to the meaning of the handwritten portion. The court held that the printed portions did not deprive the document of validity as a holograph.

This court, in In re Estate of Mulkins, 17 Ariz.App. 179, 180, 496 P.2d 605, 606 (1972) traced earlier Arizona decisions and determined that the "important thing is that the *testamentary* part of the will be wholly written by the testator and of course signed by him" (citing Estate of Morrison, supra) (emphasis in original). *Mulkins* also found that the printed words of the will * * * were not essential to the meaning of the handwritten words and could not be held to defeat the intention of the deceased otherwise clearly expressed.

It is thus clear that, under the terminology of the statute and the comment thereto, an instrument may not be probated as a holographic will where it contains words not in the handwriting of the testator if such words are essential to the testamentary disposition. However, the mere fact that the testator used a blank form, whether of a will or some other document, does not invalidate what would otherwise be a valid will if the printed words may be entirely rejected as surplusage.

In support of their position appellants rely on Estate of Blake v. Benza, 120 Ariz. 552, 587 P.2d 271 (App.1978). In *Blake* this court upheld the trial court's admission to probate, as a valid holograph the postscript to a personal letter:

P.S. You can have my entire estate. /x/ Harry J. Blake (SAVE THIS).

There having been no contention that the letter was not written and signed by the decedent, it was held that the postscript was more than a mere casual statement, and was deemed sufficient to demonstrate a testamentary intent. Analogizing to *Blake* which held that the use of the word "estate" by the decedent inferred that he was making a disposition of his property to take effect upon his death, appellants point to that portion of the document here which states:

TO (the name of the respective person) ⅛ of my estate.

as being sufficient to likewise establish the requisite intent. Again, we do not agree.

Blake did not rely solely upon the use of the word "estate" to determine that the testator had a testamentary intent. The opinion focused upon the emphasized words "SAVE THIS" to support the position that the letter was to have a future significance. The fact that the formal signature following the dispositive clause bore the testator's name in full as opposed to simply "Your Uncle Harry", as in previous letters, was also supportive of a testamentary intent. Finally, the dispositive clause itself in *Blake* contained the phrase "you can have," which clearly imported a future connotation.

Contrasting the *Blake* will to the handwritten segments of the purported will before us, we find a marked difference. Though the decedent here used the word "estate", this word alone is insufficient to indicate an *animus testandi*.

In *Webster's New Collegiate Dictionary*, G & C Merrian & Company, Springfield, 1975 at 391, one of the definitions of the word, "estate" is, "the assets and liabilities left by a person at death." However, the same word is also defined as:

> the degree, quality, nature, and extent of one's interest in land or other property. POSSESSIONS, PROPERTY *esp*: a person's property in land and tenements.

Clearly then the word "estate" is not the *sine qua non* of an intent to draft a will. Likewise, the word "TO", by itself, has neither a present nor a future meaning. We are thus unable to determine from the handwritten portions of the will form whether it was meant by decedent to have a testamentary significance and thus hold that the trial court did not err in refusing to admit it to probate.

Admittedly, as pointed out in the special concurrence, our decision here might well do violence to the intent of the decedent, Arnold H. Johnson. However, as was stated by our Supreme Court in Estate of Tyrrell, 17 Ariz. 418, 153 P. 767 (1915):

> If the statute requires the testator to sign the instrument and he omits to sign it, although he intended to do so, such omission may not be cured by his intention. The omission is fatal to the validity of the will. The omission of any of the requirements of the statute will not be overlooked on the ground that it is beyond question that the paper was executed by decedent as his will while he possessed abundant testamentary capacity, and was free from fraud, constraint or undue influence, and there is no question of his testamentary purpose, and no obstacle to carrying it into effect had his will been executed in the manner prescribed by the statute. (Citations omitted) 17 Ariz. at 422, 153 P. at 768.

Further, quoting from In re Walker's Estate, 110 Cal. 387, 42 P. 815, 52 Am.St.Rep. 104, 30 L.R.A. 460, 42 P. 815, *Tyrrell* went on to state:

> When a will is proved every exertion of the court is directed to giving effect to the wishes of the testator therein expressed, but in the *proving* of the instrument the sole consideration before the court is whether or not the legislative mandates have been complied with. id. (emphasis added).

We thus have stringent requirements for finding that a document, which might appear in a thousand different forms, is a valid and authentic holographic will.

This document having failed as a will, we dismiss appellants' argument that we may look to extrinsic evidence to determine the testator's intent. * * *

Judgment affirmed.

CONTRERAS, Judge, specially concurring:

I find myself compelled to concur in this decision because established legal principles clearly indicate that the trial court did not err in refusing to admit the document to probate. Nonetheless, I feel similarly compelled to tender the observation that the intended simplification of our statutes regarding holographic wills has perhaps created more problems than it has solved.

The most basic purpose of the Uniform Probate Code is to "discover and make effective the intent of a decedent in distribution of his property."

U.P.C. § 1–102(b)(2). With respect to the execution of wills, the purpose of the Code is to simplify the requirements of execution and validate the will whenever possible. The general comment to the Uniform Probate Code Part 5 relating to wills provides in part:

> If the will is to be restored to its role as the major instrument for disposition of wealth at death, its execution must be kept simple. The basic intent of these sections is to validate the will whenever possible.

The result in this case is contrary to all of these expressed purposes. The document before us is clearly denominated as "THE LAST WILL AND TESTAMENT" and the first paragraph in which the decedent, in his own handwriting, placed his name and residence in the appropriate blanks, clearly and unequivocally establishes testamentary intent. However, when the printed portion of the first paragraph is excised, testamentary intent is not established and the document fails as a valid will. Based upon case law and the official comment relating to the holographic will section of the probate code, this is the legal result which must obtain. But it is an illogical result which defeats the intent of the decedent and fails to uphold the proffered will. In addition, it ignores the practical consideration of a lay person who desires to dispose of his small estate without the assistance of an attorney. Such a person would consider a form will to be a viable alternative to seeking the services of an attorney, but unless that document is witnessed, it will fail to dispose of the decedent's estate as he desired. See A.R.S. § 14–2502. And since the material provisions are not in the testator's handwriting, the document fails to meet the requirements as set forth in A.R.S. § 14–2503 in order to serve as a valid holographic will.

The result in this case defeats the purposes of effectuating the intent of the decedent and simplifying the execution of wills and, in my opinion, justifies a reappraisal of the statutorily expressed requirements of a holographic will in light of realistic and practical considerations.

Notes

1. Recall that the requirement that a holographic will be in the handwriting of the testator is to insure that the document is authentic. Was there any question on that score in the principal case? It appears that the holding here is opposite the one that the Uniform Probate Code seeks to promote. In your opinion, does UPC § 2–503 mandate the invalidation of the will as the court holds? If so, how might the Code be amended to better implement the stated desire to validate legitimate expressions of a testator's intent?

Form wills are not only available at legal stationery stores, but may also be purchased by answering mass-media advertisements. West's Ann.Cal.Pro. Code § 53 states that a "holographic will is one that is entirely written, dated and signed by the hand of the testator himself." The cases, several of them involving form wills, had consistently construed this statute to invalidate a holographic will when the testator intended to make the printed matter a part of the will by physically incorporating it therein, even if the printed material was not essential to establish the testator's intent. See e.g. Estate of Helmar, 33 Cal.App.3d 109, 109 Cal.Rptr. 6 (1973); Estate of Christian, 60 Cal.App.3d 975, 131 Cal.Rptr. 841 (1976). In 1982, the California Supreme Court reexamined this interpretation of the statute. Estate of Black, 30 Cal.3d 880, 181 Cal.Rptr. 222, 641 P.2d 754. In a 4–3 decision, a majority of the Court rejected what it called the "hypertechnical application" of the statute and held that the printed matter could be disregarded as surplusage unless it was relevant to the substance of the will. The dissent traced the origins and development of the California law and concluded that the surplusage approach did not conform to the statutory requirement that a will be entirely in the testator's handwriting and that the adoption of a new interpretation of the law would bring uncertainty to the administration of the holographic will statute. See generally on the subject, Annot., Requirement That Holographic Will Be Entirely in Handwriting of Testator as Affected by Appearance of Printed Matter or Handwriting of Another, 89 A.L.R.2d 1198 (1963).

2. As stated in the principal case, a court must find that the instrument was intended by the testator to be a will, or, as it is frequently postulated in the cases, that the testator possessed *animus testandi* at the time of writing the document. Many bizarre documents are offered for probate; not all of them are accepted. See e.g. McDonald v. Petty, 262 Ark. 517, 559 S.W.2d 1 (1977) (sketch on back of used envelope not a will); compare Estate of Teubert, 298 S.E.2d 456 (W.Va.1982) (handwritten list of assets accepted as a will) with In re Estate of Ritchie, 480 Pa. 57, 389 A.2d 83 (1978) (list of assets in contemplation of a later will not entitled to probate); see also the case reported in 26 Can.B. Rev. 1242 (1948) (describing the results where the will was written on the fender of a tractor). Writings may be accepted as wills even though words are misspelled, the syntax confused, the handwriting illegible, and the disposition set out in a few words. See e.g. Estate of Logan, 489 Pa. 29, 413 A.2d 681 (1980) (review of many wills written by people who had little formal education); Estate of Grobman, 635 P.2d 231 (Colo.App.1981) (will may be probated although writing appeared to be illegible).

3. Informal letters are often upheld as holographic wills if they manifest the necessary testamentary intent. Annot., Letters as a Will or Codicil, 40 A.L.R.2d 698 (1955). Problems may arise as to the completeness of such documents and the location of the testator's signature. Wilson v. Polite, 218 So.2d 843 (Miss.1969); Annot., Place of Signature of Holographic Wills, 19 A.L.R.2d 926 (1951). A first name, nickname or initials are held sufficient if they identify the testator. In re Briggs' Estate, 148 W.Va. 294, 134 S.E.2d 737 (1964); Annot., Sufficiency, as to Form, of Signature to Holographic Will, 75 A.L.R.2d 895 (1961). A sampling of some of these documents highlights the problems that confront the courts in determining whether a letter is intended to be a will. In In re Kimmel's Estate, 278 Pa. 435, 437, 123 A. 405, 31 A.L.R. 678 (1924) the following document was accepted for probate:

Johnstown, Dec. 12

The Kimmel Bros. and Famly We are all well as you can espec fore the time of the Year. I received you kind & welcome letter from Geo & Irvin all OK gald you poot your Pork down in Pickle it is the true way to keep meet every piece gets the same, now always poot it down that way & you will not miss it & you will have good pork fore smoking you can keep it from butchern to butchern the hole year round. Boys, I wont agree with you about the open winter I think we are gone to have one of the hardest. Plenty of snow & Verry cold verry cold! I dont want to see it this way but it will will come see to the old sow & take her away when the time comes well I cant say if I will come over yet.   I will wright in my next letter it may be to ruff we will see in the next letter if I come I have some very valuable papers I want you to keep fore me so if enny thing hapens all the scock money in the 3 Bank liberty lones Post office stamps and my home on Horner St goes to George Darl & Irvin Kepp this letter lock it up it may help you out.   Earl sent after his Christmas Tree & Trimmings I sent them he is in the Post office in Phila working.

Will clost your Truly

Father

4. A holographic will may be admitted to probate in a state which does not allow such wills if the will was validly executed in another state.   In re Robinson's Estate, 20 Wis.2d 626, 123 N.W.2d 515 (1963) (applying the Uniform Foreign Wills Act).

ESTATE OF RUDOLPH

California Court of Appeals, First District, Division 4 (1980).
112 Cal.App.3d 81, 169 Cal.Rptr. 126.

POCHE, Associate Justice.

This is an appeal from an order denying probate to a handwritten instrument purporting to be the Last Will and Testament of the deceased.

Aline Bonenfant Rudolph died August 16, 1978.   In an uncontested proceeding her formally executed will and codicil signed in 1956 and in 1960 respectively were admitted to probate and respondent was appointed administrator with the will annexed.   Four months later appellant, decedent's sister, petitioned both for revocation of that order and for admission to probate of the holograph which does not mention a month of execution.   It is dated simply "Monday 26, 1978."

Without objection the trial court took judicial notice that in the year 1978 only once did the 26th day of a month occur on a Monday: in June. Nevertheless, the petition was denied on the sole ground the document did not contain an "entire" date.

We reverse.

It has long been recognized that the statutory requirement of a date serves two purposes: (1) it allows evaluation of testamentary capacity as of the specific time the instrument was executed, and (2) in situations like this where more than one document is offered for probate, it permits determination of which is in fact the *last* will.   (See e.g., Estate of Wilkinson (1931) 113 Cal.App. 645, 298 P. 1037.)

Although some decisions contain language which if read out of context require inscription of the month, the day, and the year (cf., e.g., Estate of Vance (1916) 174 Cal. 122, 162 P. 103) each California case finding dating insufficient involves a situation where reference could be to more than one day.   In such circumstances the purposes of the Probate Code could not be met.   (See for example, Estate of Carpenter (1916) 172 Cal. 268, 156 P. 464 ["10 1912"];   Estate of Vance, supra, 174 Cal. 122, 162 P. 103 ["22nd day of March in the year of our Lord, one thousand"];   Estate of Moody (1953) 118 Cal.App.2d 300, 257 P.2d 709 ["Nov. 21 Thanksgiving Day"]; Estate of Carson (1959) 174 Cal.App.2d 291, 344 P.2d 612 ["May 1948"]; Estate of Hazelwood (1967) 249 Cal.App.2d 263, 57 Cal.Rptr. 332 ["1965"].) Not one of the cases involves a dating which could refer to only one day.

Judicial notice to complete technically incomplete dates on holographic wills is not unusual. (See for example, Estate of Lakemeyer (1901) 135 Cal. 28, 66 P. 961 ["Nov. 22, 97"]; Estate of Chevallier (1911) 159 Cal. 161, 113 P. 130 ["4–14–07"].) Here, such notice of the 1978 calendar has corrected the facially incomplete dating. Thus, without resort to extrinsic evidence, the inscription "Monday 26, 1978" becomes "Monday, June 26, 1978." Both capacity and chronology may now be appropriately determined.

The order denying probate of the document dated Monday, 26, 1978 is reversed. The matter is remanded to the trial court for proceedings not inconsistent with this opinion.

Note

Although the court here speaks of it as language taken out of context, previous California cases, including those cited in the opinion, appear to require a complete date, including a day, month, and year, and do not accept extrinsic evidence to fill in a missing element, although such evidence is admissible to clarify a full date. The argument supporting this approach contends that the word "entirely" in the statute (Cal. Probate Code § 53, note 1, p. 304, supra) governs the word "dated" and that there is therefore a legislative mandate that the will be entirely (i.e., completely) dated. This mechanical approach does, however, give rise to a number of anomalies. For instance, a holographic will need not be entirely signed by the full name of the testator (see authorities cited in note 3, p. 305, supra) nor does a complete date that is incorrect invalidate the will if extrinsic evidence is available to establish the time of execution. See Estate of Fay, 145 Cal. 82, 78 P. 340 (1904); Kanable v. Birch, 86 Nev. 558, 471 P.2d 237 (1970). The approach in the Rudolph case introduces a measure of flexibility into the process, but it has its obvious limitations. See e.g. Succession of Raiford, 404 So.2d 251 (La.1981) ("Monday 8, 1968" insufficient date; eighth day of the month occurred on a Monday three times in 1968). The statutes in a number of states do not require a date. See e.g. UPC § 2–503, supra p. 278. It should be noted in this connection that formal wills are not required to be dated, although they customarily are. A few decisions have adopted the substantial compliance approach, holding that a partial date suffices when no issue is presented that requires for its resolution knowledge of the exact time of execution. See e.g. In re Irvine's Estate, 114 Mont. 577, 139 P.2d 489 (1943). The Irvine case demonstrates the capacity of this seemingly inconsequential issue to inflame passions. The will in issue there was of uncertain meaning, covering an estate of less than $100. The majority, in a lengthy opinion, upheld the will as being substantially dated with the inscription "May, 1938." The Chief Justice, in an equally lengthy dissent, saw this interpretation as a gross distortion " * * * of a government of men for a government of laws, by the unconstitutional judicial usurpation of legislative power in place of the constitutionally authorized fair judicial interpretation of legislative enactments." 114 Mont. at 608, 139 P.2d at 502. See also Succession of Boyd,

306 So.2d 687 (La.1975) (extrinsic evidence established that "2–8–72" meant February 8, 1972; extensive review of the cases dealing with abbreviated dates).

H. NUNCUPATIVE WILLS

GULLIVER AND TILSON, CLASSIFICATION OF GRATUITOUS TRANSFERS
51 Yale L.J. 1, 14 (1941) (footnotes omitted).

In order to afford a dying man who has no opportunity to make a formal will the privilege of making a last minute oral disposition, many states, following the English Statute of Frauds, have enacted statutes authorizing nuncupative wills in the last illness, provided that numerous detailed requirements are complied with.   The desirability of attempting to insure compliance with the ritual function seems to justify the requirement that the testator ask some person or persons present to bear testimony to such disposition as his will, since such a statement indicates that he intends a serious disposition and is not conversing in a purely haphazard manner.   The evidentiary function seems responsible for the requirement of a reduction to writing, which tends to prevent a variation between the testator's statement and subsequent testimony owing to lapse of memory, and also for the requirement that the will be proved by more than one witness, which makes it possible for the misinterpretation of one witness to be cleared up by another witness.   The protective function is exemplified in statutes requiring the witnesses to be competent and disinterested and decisions to the same effect in the absence of an expressed statutory requirement.   Because of the detailed requirements for the validity of these nuncupative wills and the restrictions on the type and value of the property that may be transferred by them, they are probably rarely employed.   There is very little litigation concerning them, and they are, therefore, not of great importance in a general survey of the exercise of the testamentary power in this country.

Notes

1. Twenty-five years ago a majority of the states had statutes authorizing nuncupative wills, although in ten of those states the device was only available to soldiers and sailors.   Rees, American Wills Statutes, 46 Va.L.Rev. 613, 636–46 (1960).   Since that time, the number has been significantly reduced, as states, for example Pennsylvania in 1974 and California in 1983, have repealed their statutes.   The Uniform Probate Code does not recognize the nuncupative will as a method of making a testamentary disposition.   The statutes that remain differ as to details but typically require that the testator be in his or her "last sickness" at the time of making the will and that the oral statement be heard by several competent witnesses, who are asked by the testator to serve as witnesses and who must within a perscribed period record in writing the proceedings.   The will is generally only effective to pass personal property, and the statutes in many states impose a maximum limit, ranging from $200 to several thousand dollars, on the amount of property that can be transferred. Courts have traditionally defined "last sickness" to require that the testator be in such extreme circumstances as to be unable to make a written will.   See

e.g. McClellan's Estate, 325 Pa. 257, 189 A. 315 (1937) (oral will witnessed by a nurse, doctor, and friend not entitled to probate; 33-year old testatrix, who entered the hospital with encephalitis on the 22nd, became delirious and incoherent on the 24th, had 3 hours of lucidity on the 25th during which she gave instructions about the distribution of her property, and died on the 27th, had time to make a written will). Decisions of this kind seem to have rendered the nuncupative device useable only in situations of extreme emergency such as an automobile accident followed by death within a few hours. There have been virtually no reported cases involving nuncupative wills in recent years.

2. Both the Statute of Frauds and the English Wills Act of 1837 specifically excepted from their requirements wills of personal property made by soldiers "in actual military service" or sailors while "at sea". Somewhat similar provisions exist in many of the states. See e.g. N.Y.—McKinney's EPTL § 3–2.2, set out supra, p. 277. The New York statute authorizes the use by soldiers, civilians who accompany the armed forces into combat, and sailors of both the nuncupative and holographic will. This is the only exception made in the New York wills statute. Note that the statute imposes no limitations on the type or amount of property that may be disposed of, but does specify that a soldier's will is valid for only one year after discharge from the services and a sailor's will for only three years after it was made. Special solicitude for members of the armed services seems unnecessary today. The services provide ample opportunity for will making to their personnel by having available at every base headquarters form wills and advice as to how to use them.

I. LIVING WILLS AND DURABLE POWERS OF ATTORNEY

For almost any condition that renders a person terminally ill, some medical intervention is available that will postpone the moment of death. A competent person, who is fully informed of all the facts, has a right, as a general rule, to refuse medical treatment that will prolong his or her life, but the decision to forego treatment for incompetent persons has to be made by doctors, usually, but not always, in consultation with the patient's family. Meyers, Medico-Legal Implications of Death and Dying, 352–353 (1981). This state of affairs creates many uncertainties. On the one hand, persons contemplating advancing age and the possible loss of capacity, are fearful that they will be kept alive by use of heroic measures when they are no longer sensate, and, on the other, doctors, hospitals, and families see themselves as exposed to possible liability when making life-and-death decisions for incompetent persons. Indeed, in a number of well-publicized suits, patients, members of the family, physicians, and hospitals have sought court permission to withdraw treatment even when there was general agreement that withdrawal was justified. See e.g., Satz v. Perlmutter, 362 So.2d 160 (Fla.App.1978) (competent patient, who was suffering from Lou Gehrig's disease, granted right to order respirator removed); Matter of Quinlan, 70 N.J. 10, 355 A.2d 647 (1976), certiorari denied, 429 U.S. 922, 975 S.Ct. 319, 50 L.Ed.2d 289 (1976) (father of Karen Ann Quinlan appointed her guardian with power to make decisions with regard to her medical treatment); John F. Kennedy Memorial Hospital v. Bludworth, 452 So.2d 921 (Fla.1984) (patient died while hospital sought declaratory judgment, although patient had signed a living will and wife as guardian and doctors wanted to terminate extraordinary life supports).

In order to give persons some measure of self determination over the future course of their medical treatment and to afford doctors and hospitals protection from liability, many states have passed legislation authorizing persons to execute advance directives. See Deciding to Forego Life-Sustaining Treatment, A Report on the Ethical, Medical, and Legal Issues in Treatment Decisions by the President's Commission for the Study of Ethical Problems in Medicine and Biomedical and Behavorial Research, 136–153 (1983) (comprehensive study of issues from many perspectives with citation to the voluminous literature on the subject). These directives take two forms: 1. the instruction directive (so-called living will) in which persons specify the type of care they do or do not want should they become incompetent; and 2. the proxy directive (so-called durable power of attorney) in which persons designate surrogates to make decisions should they ever be unable to do so.

Fourteen states and the District of Columbia have enacted Natural Death Acts which set out the requirements for a living will. See Deciding to Forego Life-Sustaining Treatment, supra, Appendix D. The word "will" in this context is misapplied. The document is intended to become operative while the declarant is still alive, it need not be probated, and it does not pertain to the disposition of property. The statutes do, however, typically require that the document be attested by two disinterested witnesses and be executed in much the same maner as a testamentary instrument. See e.g. Ark. Stats. § 82–37802 set out below. Although differing somewhat in details, these statutes have several characteristics in common: 1. they purport to bind the physician (in California and several other states the physician is only bound if the document is executed two weeks after the patient has notice of the terminal diagnosis) to the terms of the directive, although only five states specify penalties, usually "professional discipline", for failing to implement the directive or transferring the patient to a doctor who will implement it; 2. medical personnel and institutions are protected from civil and criminal liability if acting within the terms of the directive; 3. the directive becomes operative when the patient's condition is diagnosed as terminal and death is imminent regardless of treatment and in a number of the statutes this fact must be certified by at least two physicians; and 4. the directive may be revoked at any time.

A form living will appears in the Model Medical Treatment Decision Act, sponsored by the Society for the Right to Die, 250 West 57th Street, New York, New York 10107, reprinted in Deciding to Forego Life-Sustaining Treatment, supra, 314–315:

DECLARATION

Declaration made this _____ day of _____ (month, year). I, _____, being of sound mind, willfully and voluntarily make known my desire that my dying shall not be artificially prolonged under the circumstances set forth below, do hereby declare:

If at any time I should have an incurable injury, disease, or illness certified to be a terminal condition by two physicians who have personally examined me, one of whom shall be my attending physician, and the physicians have determined that my death will occur whether or not life-sustaining procedures are utilized and where the application of life-sustaining procedures would serve only to artificially prolong the dying process, I direct that such procedures be withheld or withdrawn, and that I be permitted to die naturally with only the administration of medication or the performance of any medical procedure deemed necessary to provide me with comfort care.

In the absence of my ability to give directions regarding the use of such life-sustaining procedures, it is my intention that this declaration shall be honored by my family and physician(s) as the final expression of my legal right to refuse medical or surgical treatment and accept the consequences from such refusal.

I understand the full import of this declaration and I am emotionally and mentally competent to make this declaration.

Signed _____

City, County and State of Residence

_____

The declarant has been personally known to me and I believe him or her to be of sound mind.

Witness _____

Witness _____

All fifty states have statutes authorizing durable powers of attorney under which the agent's authority continues even when his or her principal has become incompetent. Traditionally, these statutes operate to permit transactions in property. There does not appear to be authority for using them to justify the agent making a medical decision for the principal, and some commentators have speculated that medical decision-making may be too personal to be delegated. See Note, Appointing an Agent to Make Medical Treatment Choices, 84 Col.L.Rev. 985 (1984) (author weighs the arguments and concludes that the statutes do permit medical decisions). A number of states have removed the ambiguity: five have provisions either in their natural death acts or their durable power statutes explicitly authorizing an individual to appoint an agent to make medical decisions in the event the principal becomes incompetent; two (see e.g. Ark.Stats. § 82–8302 set out below) list persons who may act as an incompetent person's agent to execute a living will, if there is no prior declaration; and six have statutes designating relatives who are empowered to give substituted consent for an incompetent. See Deciding to Forego Life-Sustaining Treatment, supra Appendix E. Does the attorney make the decision that he or she believes the patient would have made if competent or the decision that is in the patient's best interests to the extent that that fact may be objectively determined?

The Arkansas statute, §§ 82–3801 through 4, authorizes both types of advance directives:

Right to Die With Dignity or to Have Life Prolonged

Every person shall have the right to die with dignity and to refuse and deny the use or application by any person of artificial, extraordinary, extreme or radical medical and surgical means or procedures calculated to prolong his life. Alternatively, every person shall have the right to request that such extraordinary means be utilized to prolong life to the extent possible.

Written Request

Any person, with the same formalities as are required by the laws of this State for the execution of a will, may execute a document exercising such right and refusing and denying the use or application by any person of artificial, extraordinary, extreme or radical medical or surgical means or procedures calculated to prolong his life. In the alternative, any person may request in writing that all means be utilized to prolong life.

Who May Execute Written Request for Another

If any person is a minor or an adult who is physically or mentally unable to execute or is otherwise incapacitated from executing either document, it may be executed in the same form on his behalf:

(a) By either parent of the minor;

(b) By his spouse;

(c) If his spouse is unwilling or unable to act, by his child aged eighteen [18] or over;

(d) If he has more than one [1] child aged eighteen [18] or over, by a majority of such children;

(e) If he has no spouse or child aged eighteen [18] or over, by either of his parents;

(f) If he has no parent living, by his nearest living relative; or

(g) If he is mentally incompetent, by his legally appointed guardian.

Provided, that a form executed in compliance with this Section must contain a signed statement by two [2] physicians that extraordinary means would have to be utilized to prolong life.

No Liability for Actions in Accordance With Request

Any person, hospital or other medical institution which acts or refrains from acting in reliance on and in compliance with such document shall be immune from liability otherwise arising out of such failure to use or apply artificial, extraordinary, extreme or radical medical or surgical means or procedures calculated to prolong such person's life.

Notes

1. These statutes have yet to be tested in the courts. A poll of physicians after one year's experience under the California natural death act indicated that the legislation had partially achieved its goal of giving terminally ill patients some control over their own treatment. Nearly two-thirds of the doctors reported that some of their patients had made directives, and many of the doctors stated that they felt more secure when making decisions because of the act's protection and that the act made it easier for them to honor a patient's directive.

On the other hand, few of the directives affected the disposition of the case, as only 6.5% of the doctors reported that they withheld treatment which they would have administered had the act not been in force.   (It appears that because of the brief experience with the statute the sample upon which these results were based was small.)   There was even some evidence of a negative affect, as a number of doctors indicated that because of their uncertainty as to the act's legal implication they had given treatment in situations in which they would have previously withheld it.   The authors conclude that the limited results of one year's experience were due to limitations in the act itself, particularly the provision that made the directive binding only if executed two weeks after notification of the terminal illness, the doctors' unfamiliarity with the specifics of the act, and insufficient attention to helping patients take advantage of the act.   Note, The California Natural Death Act: An Empirical Study of Physicians' Practices, 31 Stan.L.Rev. 913 (1979).

2. Human bodies, in whole or in part, are used in many areas of modern medical science, including teaching, research, therapy and transplantation. The parts of the body which may be transplanted include skin, bones, blood, corneas, kidneys, livers, arteries and hearts.   The need is great, and many people are willing to be donors.   The Uniform Anatomical Gift Act, 8 ULA 15 (1972), which has now been enacted in all fifty states, regularizes the procedures and forms for making a gift:

§ 4. [Manner of Executing Anatomical Gifts]

(a) A gift of all or part of the body under Section 2(a) [by a person 18 or over who gives all or part of his body] may be made by will.   The gift becomes effective upon the death of the testator without waiting for probate. If the will is not probated, or if it is declared invalid for testamentary purposes, the gift, to the extent that it has been acted upon in good faith, is nevertheless valid and effective.

(b) A gift of all or part of the body under section 2(a) may also be made by document other than a will.   The gift becomes effective upon the death of the donor.   The document, which may be a card designed to be carried on the person, must be signed by the donor in the presence of 2 witnesses who must sign the document in his presence.   If the donor cannot sign, the document may be signed for him at his direction and in his presence in the presence of 2 witnesses who must sign the document in his presence. Delivery of the document of gift during the donor's lifetime is not necessary to make the gift valid.

(c) The gift may be made to a specified donee or without specifying a donee.   If the latter, the gift may be accepted by the attending physician as donee upon or following death.   If the gift is made to a specified donee who is not available at the time and place of death, the attending physician upon or following death, in the absence of any expressed indication that the donor desired otherwise, may accept the gift as donee.   The physician who becomes a donee under this subsection shall not participate in the procedures for removing or transplanting a part.

(d) Notwithstanding Section 7(b) [the physician who attends the death shall not remove the organ], the donor may designate in his will, card, or other document of gift the surgeon or physician to carry out the appropriate procedures.   In the absence of a designation or if the designee is not available, the donee or other person authorized to accept the gift may employ or authorize any surgeon or physician for the purpose.

(e) Any gift by a person designated in Section 2(b) [the spouse, adult son or daughter, parent, adult brother or sister, guardian of the person or person authorized to dispose of the body] shall be made by a document signed by him or made by his telegraphic, recorded telephonic, or other recorded message.

The Act removes many of the legal problems that may arise and gives appropriate protection to the surgeon and others involved in implementing the gift. It leaves to the attending physician the responsibility of pronouncing a person dead and thereby avoids the thorny problem of defining death. The Act makes it easier to make an effective gift, but it has not relieved the critical shortage of bodies or body parts. Various proposals, including the purchase of organs and the enactment of legislation which makes the removal of organs routine unless the decedent or the next of kin objects, have been advanced as ways of increasing the supply. See, Dukeminier, Supplying Organs for Transplantation, 68 Mich.L.R. 811 (1970); Sanders and Dukeminier, Medical Advance and Legal Lag: Hemodialysis and Kidney Transplantation, 15 U.C.L.A.L.Rev. 357 (1968). A number of states have printed forms on the back of their drivers licenses, permitting the operator to make a gift of all or specific parts of his or her body on death. Competent adults may during life make an effective gift of such non-vital organs as "one kidney, the spleen, bone marrow, three to six feet of small bowel, small pieces of skin, part of the thyroid, one parathyroid, one adrenal gland and one gonad" (the author notes that the list is not intended to be exclusive). Note, The Sale of Human Body Parts, 72 Mich.L.R. 1182, 1193 n. 73 (1974) (a comprehensive review of the entire subject).

SECTION TWO.   ILLUSTRATIVE WILL

I, John Sprat, a resident of and domiciled in the Town of Hamden, County of New Haven and State of Connecticut, do hereby make, publish and declare this as and for my Last Will and Testament.

ARTICLE ONE: I direct that all of my just debts (including unpaid charitable pledges whether or not the same are enforceable obligations of my estate), my funeral expenses and the costs of administration of my estate be paid as soon as practicable after my death. In his sole discretion, my executor may pay from my domiciliary estate all or any portion of the costs of ancillary administration and similar proceedings in other jurisdictions.

[Dispositive Provisions]

ARTICLE TWO: I give and devise my summer home, Ahab's Retreat, located in Whitefish, West Carolina, to my mother, Ferocia Sprat, if she survives me. In the event that my said mother does survive me, I direct my executor to pay off and discharge any mortgage or other encumbrances or liens upon any interest in said property which my mother shall own at my death by operation of this Article, and to pay any interest which is due or may become due thereon.

ARTICLE THREE: I give and bequeath the following articles of personal property to the following persons:

See defns p. 359

1. My engraved Winchester hunting rifle to my brother, Hammerhead Sprat. *"Specific" devise*

2. The portrait of mother painted by Charles Haddock to my sister, Minnie Sprat Karp.

3. Three thousand dollars ($3,000) to my mother, Ferocia Sprat, and I direct that my sailboat, Moby Dick, be sold and the proceeds applied to payment of this gift. *"demonstrative bequest"*

ARTICLE FOUR: I give and bequeath all the rest of the tangible personal property which I shall own at my death to my wife, Enorma Sprat, if she shall survive me. I hope, but do not require, that she will distribute certain articles out of this property to my children, children-in-law, and grandchildren in accordance with a memorandum which I shall leave addressed to her.

precatory terms — words of req.

ARTICLE FIVE: I give and bequeath the following amounts of money to the following persons or organizations:

"general bequest"

1. One Thousand Dollars ($1,000) to each of my grandchildren who shall survive me.

2. Five Thousand Dollars ($5,000) to my son, Chub Sprat, if he shall survive me.

3. Five Thousand Dollars ($5,000) to my daughter, Sunny Sprat, if she shall survive me.

4. Five Thousand Dollars ($5,000) to the Church of St. Elmo, Walton Pike, New Haven, Connecticut.

If the total of gifts in this Article shall exceed fifteen per cent (15%) of the amount available for distribution by my executor, then all gifts in this Article shall be ratably reduced so that the total of such gifts does not exceed such fifteen per cent (15%). In making this determination the decision of my executor as to the value of assets available for distribution shall be conclusive.

ARTICLE SIX: All the rest, residue and remainder of my estate, real, personal and mixed, of whatsoever nature and wheresoever situate, of which I shall die seized or possessed, or to which I shall be in anywise entitled at the time of my death, including any legacies which may lapse or be invalid or for any reason fail to take effect, and including all property over which I shall have at the time of my death any power of appointment or disposal, which I shall not have otherwise exercised or released, I give, devise, bequeath and appoint to my wife, Enorma Sprat, or, if she shall not survive me, in equal shares to any children of mine who may survive me, but if any child of mine shall predecease me leaving issue who shall survive me, such issue shall take *per stirpes* the share which such deceased child would have taken had he or she survived me.

Big Winners

ARTICLE SEVEN: If any of the persons who take under this will is under the age of twenty-one (21) years at the time title vests in him or her, I authorize my executor in his discretion to retain his or her share, to manage, invest and reinvest the same and apply the net income therefrom or such portion thereof and such portion of the principal as my executor may deem necessary for the proper education, support and general welfare of such minor until he or she attains the age of twenty-one (21) years, at which time I direct my executor to transfer or pay to such minor the accumulated income, if any, and the balance of the principal. My executor is authorized to retain any part of such income not so used and to reinvest the same.

In lieu of making application of the net income and principal, if any, for the benefit of any such minor, I authorize my executor to make payment thereof to a parent of the minor or to any other person having the care of the minor or directly to the minor, without obligation to look to the proper application thereof by the person receiving it.

[Administrative Provisions]

ARTICLE EIGHT: I confer upon my executor, with respect to the management and administration of any property, real or personal, including property held under a power in trust, the following discretionary powers, without limitation by reason of specification:

1. To retain any such property for such period of time as he may deem advisable without liability for depreciation or loss; to deposit any moneys at any time constituting a part of my estate in one or more banks, savings or commercial, in such form of account, whether or not interest-bearing, and without limitation as to the amount of any such account, or in the discretion of my executor, to hold any such moneys uninvested.

2. To lease real property for such period, with or without an option to purchase, and upon such terms as he may deem advisable.

3. To borrow money for any purpose whatsoever and to mortgage real property and pledge personal property as security for such loans.

4. To sell, exchange or otherwise dispose of any or all of my property, real or personal, at public or private sale, at any time and from time to time, for such consideration and upon such terms, including terms of credit, as he shall deem advisable.

5. In his discretion to vote, in person or by proxy, or consent for any purpose, in respect of any stocks or other securities constituting assets of my estate; to exercise or sell any rights of subscription or other rights in respect thereof.

6. In making distribution of any property to persons entitled thereto hereunder, to convey, transfer, or pay over the same in kind or in money, or partly in kind and partly in money, and for such purposes to transfer and assign undivided interests in any such property.

ARTICLE NINE: In the event that any beneficiary under this Will and I shall die in a common accident or disaster or under such circumstances that it is difficult or impracticable to determine who survived the other, then I direct that for the purpose of this Will such beneficiary shall be deemed to have predeceased me.

[Payment of Taxes]

ARTICLE TEN: I direct that there shall be no apportionment among the persons beneficially interested of any estate, transfer, succession or other inheritance taxes or any interest thereon imposed by the United States or any state thereof or any foreign country in so far as such taxes and interest are imposed with respect to any property or interests passing under this Will, any insurance on my life, any trusts, gifts or other transfers created or made by me or any property or accounts owned jointly by me and any other person or persons.   All such taxes shall be paid by my executor and treated as an expense of administering my estate.

[Appointive Provisions]

ARTICLE ELEVEN: A. I hereby nominate and appoint my friend and lawyer, Snapper T. Piranha, as my executor hereunder.   In the event that he shall fail for any reason to qualify or, having qualified, shall cease for any reason to act, then I nominate and appoint THE TITANIC NATIONAL BANK of New Haven, Connecticut, to act as executor in the place and stead of said Snapper T. Piranha.

B. Any corporation into which The Titanic National Bank may be merged or with which it may consolidate, or any corporation resulting from any merger, consolidation or reorganization to which The Titanic National Bank shall be a party, or any corporation which shall succeed to all or substantially all of the business or assets of The Titanic National Bank, shall be substituted hereunder for The Titanic National Bank.

C. I direct that no bond or other security shall be required of any executor acting hereunder for the faithful performance of his or its duties, any law of any state or jurisdiction to the contrary notwithstanding.

[Afterborn Children Clause]

ARTICLE TWELVE: In making this Will I have considered the possibility that there may be children born to me hereafter and I intend to make no provision for any such children other than those made hereinabove by this Will.

[Revocation Clause]

ARTICLE THIRTEEN: I hereby revoke all wills and codicils heretofore made by me.

[Witness Clause]

IN WITNESS WHEREOF, I John Sprat, have hereunto set my hand and seal and have signed my initials on each of the _____4_____ preceding pages this _____ day of _____, A.D.   One thousand nine hundred and eighty-five.

_____[L.S.]

[Attestation Clause]

The foregoing instrument was signed, sealed, published and declared by John Sprat the above-named Testator, as and for his last Will and Testament in our presence, all being present at the same time, and thereupon we, at his request and in his presence and in the presence of each other, have initialed each of the _____ previous pages and have hereunto subscribed our names as witnesses this _____ day of _____ ,

"3x present recitation"

A.D. One thousand nine hundred and eighty-five, at the Town of Hamden and State of Connecticut.

_____ residing at _____

_____ residing at _____

[Affidavit for Self-Proved Will]*

I, _____, the testator, sign my name to this instrument this ___ day of _____, 19___, and being first duly sworn, do hereby declare to the undersigned authority that I sign and execute this instrument as my last will and that I sign it willingly (or willingly direct another to sign for me), that I execute it as my free and voluntary act for the purposes therein expressed, and that I am eighteen years of age or older, of sound mind, and under no constraint or undue influence.

_____
Testator

We, _____, _____, the witnesses, sign our names to this instrument, being first duly sworn, and do hereby declare to the undersigned authority that the testator signs and executes this instrument as his last will and that he signs it willingly (or willingly directs another to sign for him), and that each of us, in the presence and hearing of the testator, hereby signs this will as witness to the testator's signing, and that to the best of our knowledge the testator is eighteen years of age or older, of sound mind, and under no constraint or undue influence.

_____
Witness
_____
Witness

The State of _____

County of _____

Subscribed, sworn to and acknowledged before me by ____, the testator, and subscribed and sworn to before me by ____, and ____, witnesses, this ____ day of ____ .

(Seal)

(Signed) _____

_____
(Official capacity of officer)

Notes

1. The sample will set out above is designed only to illustrate, in simple form, some recurring types of clauses. It is not intended as a model for ad-

---

* This form is taken from UPC § 2–504 which directs that:

Any will may be simultaneously executed, attested, and made self-proved, by acknowledgment thereof by the testator and affidavits of the witnesses, each made before an officer authorized to administer oaths under the laws of the state where execution occurs and evidenced by the officer's certificate, under official seal, in substantially the [above form].

aptation to specific situations. Any litigation or other problems which arise after a property owner's death means that the lawyer has failed to do a thorough job of planning the estate or drafting the instruments. The term "estate planning" is much in vogue today. It has no essentially new meaning but rather refers to a function which lawyers have been performing for centuries. Admittedly, today, the task of providing wisely for the family's financial welfare has become more difficult with the increased complexities of modern tax laws. The successful planner must have a solid background in property, tax, insurance, business, conflicts and domestic relations law, the ability to marshal those facts about the property owners, their families and property which are sometimes so sacred that clients will not confide them even to their spouses, and finally, the technical competence to draft the instruments which properly implement the plan. While the informational background can in part be acquired in law school, the techniques cannot. Proficiency in drafting can only come with a great deal of actual experience.

2. By the self-proved will procedure, the witnesses' (and testator's) sworn testimony is taken at the time of execution, thereby relieving the witnesses of the obligation to appear at the probate proceeding, unless called to testify on some issue in dispute by one of the parties. It has been held that a self-proved will may not be contested in regard to signature requirements and makes conclusive the presumption of proper execution that arises from the presence of an attestation clause. Testamentary incapacity is not, however, a component of due execution and may therefore be the basis of a contest of the will's validity. Estate of Flider, 213 Neb. 153, 328 N.W.2d 197 (1982). UPC § 2–504(b) sets out a similar procedure and form to be used when the will is made self-proveable subsequent to the time of its execution. A number of states that have not adopted the Uniform Probate Code have statutes authorizing self-proved wills. See e.g. Conn.Gen.Stat.Ann. § 45–166.

3. Over half the jurisdictions in the United States have statutes providing that a will is valid if executed according to the law either of the testator's domicile or of the place where the will was executed. See, for instance, UPC § 2–506. Even in the absence of a statute, the traditional choice of laws approach offers the same alternative. Appeal of Jarboe, 91 Conn. 265, 99 A. 563 (1917). It is a wise precaution for the lawyer to follow standard procedures and to word an attestation clause in such a way as to satisfy the diverse requirements of formality of every state. See, for example, the attestation clause on p. 317, supra. Professor Leach has some suggestions on the value of an attestation clause and the choice of witnesses. Leach, Cases and Text on the Law of Wills, 44–46 (1960 ed.). See also 7 Powell ¶ 960 (1974).

4. A will is unique in the number and variety of formalities required for its execution and in the requirement which is followed in most jurisdictions that the witnesses be produced in court before the will is declared operative. Critics of the status quo have observed: (1) the vast majority of wills do not need such elaborate safeguards; (2) the more obstacles interposed the more likely genuine expressions of a property owner's intent will be upset; (3) the various formalities and requirements are of doubtful value in catching real crooks and schemers. As is developed in Chapter Four supra, a will may also be subject to challenge on the ground that the testator lacked capacity or that it was procured by undue influence and fraud. All too often, a disappointed heir attacks a will on one or more of these grounds at the probate hearing when the testator is

dead and no longer able to defend him or herself. Frequently, the contestant initiates the action in hopes that the family will settle to avoid the expense, delay, and publicity of a trial. The attorney may start at the time the will is executed putting together a defense against such strike actions by preparing for the records an affidavit describing the events that occurred during the attestation proceedings and the testator's demeanor and conduct and by securing supporting affidavits from the witnesses, the family physician, and a psychiatrist who has been treating the testator, friends and the like. Some attorneys have gone a step further and videotaped the proceedings.

A number of commentators have argued that many of these problems could be avoided by probating the will when the testator is still alive and able to rebut spurious claims. See e.g. Cavers, Ante Mortem Probate: An Essay in Preventive Law, 1 U.Chi.L.Rev. 440 (1934). For a brief period, 1883–85, Michigan had a statute authorizing ante-mortem probate of wills, but the Michigan Supreme Court struck it down, contending that such a procedure was outside the court's authority because there was no judicially cognizable controversy between a living man and his heirs. Fink, Ante-Mortem Probate Revisited: Can an Idea Have a Life After Death?, 37 Ohio St.L.J. 264 (1976). Professor Fink, after analyzing in depth the Michigan experience and concluding that the invalidating decision rested on a rationale that would not be controlling today, advocated enactment of a declaratory judgment procedure to be initiated by the testator to determine the validity of the will and the issue of testamentary capacity.

Several states have enacted such statutes. See e.g. Ark.Stats. §§ 62–2134 through 37; N.D.Cent.Code 30.1–08.1–1–01 through 04; Ohio Rev. Code §§ 2107.081 through .085. These statutes in practical effect authorize the testator to institute a will contest of his or her own will, by giving notice to the persons who would be the interested parties (i.e. intestate successors, takers under earlier wills, etc.) had the testator died at the moment the suit commenced and thereby to require them to proceed with the contest in the testator's presence. A number of flaws in the procedure have been cited: the ultimate heirs, who cannot be finally determined until the testator dies, may not have received notice of the ante-mortem probate and thus may not have had an opportunity to make their claims; the contestants have no incentive to participate (nor to incur the expenses of litigation), since the testator may revoke the will after the proceeding is concluded; the testator may not wish to disclose the contents of the will; and it may be difficult and costly to determine who is entitled to notice. Recommendations to remedy these problems have been forthcoming. See Langbein, Living Probate: The Conservatorship Model, 77 Mich.L.Rev. 63 (1978) (recommending the appointment of a conservator to represent all the persons who might be contestants, with the testator paying the conservator's reasonable costs); Alexander and Pearson, Alternative Models of Ante-Mortem Probate and Procedural Due Process Limitation on Succession, 78 Mich.L.Rev. 89 (1979) (recommending an administrative proceeding to which only the guardian ad litem, representing all interested parties, receives notice and in which the contents of the will are not necessarily made public).

5. In 1977, the Commissioners on Uniform State Laws adopted the Uniform International Wills Act for enactment by the states, either as part of the Uniform Probate Code or as separate legislation. The purpose of the Act is to provide

testators with a method of executing wills that will be valid as to form in all states and countries that adopt the Act. As stated in a Prefatory Note, "the objective would be achieved through uniform local rules of form, rather than through local or international law that makes recognition of foreign wills turn on choice of law rules involving possible application of foreign law". The Act, which appears as UPC §§ 2–1001 through 19, sets out requirements for writing, attestation, presence, position of the signature, execution by some other person under the testator's direction, and the like. States and countries adopting the Act are encouraged to make additional provisions for the registering and safe-keeping of international wills. The origins and purposes of the Act are described in Prefatory Note, 8 ULA 178.

SECTION THREE. WHAT CONSTITUTES THE WILL?

Documents and language that purport to dispose of a person's property at death must conform to the requirements of the local wills statute in order to be operative. Cases arise on the basis of this principle in which challenges are made to the validity of material that has not been signed by the testator or attested by witnesses but which is arguably intended to be a part of the will. Three doctrines relate to this issue.

Integration. In the case of a formal, witnessed will, the rule requires that a set of unconnected papers must have been intended by the testator to constitute a single will and the papers must have been in existence and present as a will at the time of execution. Proof of intent may consist of evidence that the papers were at one time attached together (i.e. by staple, paper clip, etc. or included in a single envelope) or that there is a connection of language or a "coherence of sense", carrying over from page to page. It is common practice today, although not required by statute, for the testator to sign his or her initials at the bottom of each page to make clear that neither afterthoughts nor spurious pages have been added to the will after its execution.

The holographic will adds another dimension to the problem. The will may consist of a disorganized, multi-page letter or a series of letters written over a period of time. The modern view treats all the papers as a will if the holographic testator so intended, regardless of the time and place of their writing. See e.g. In re Moore's Estate, 143 Cal.App.2d 64, 300 P.2d 110 (1956) (holographic will need not be made on single day nor the pages attached together where they reflect a continuous chain of thought). See generally, Atkinson on Wills § 139 (1953); Evans, Incorporation by Reference, Integration, and Non-Testamentary Act, 25 Colum.L.Rev. 879 (1925); Mechem, The Integration of Holographic Wills, 12 N.C.L.Rev. 213 (1934); Annot., Validity of Will Written on Disconnected Sheets, 38 A.L.R.2d 477 (1954).

Incorporation by reference. A will may direct that the estate, or a portion thereof, be distributed in accordance with the terms of an inter vivos trust, deed, letter, or other memorandum. Unless the outside material has been signed and witnessed in the manner of a will, it is vul-

nerable to challenge as violative of the statute of wills.   UPC § 2–510
permits the incorporation of any writing in existence when the will is
executed "if the language of the will manifests this intent and describes
the writing sufficiently to permit its identification."   A few states, of
which New York and Connecticut are notable examples, have rejected
the doctrine of incorporation by reference.   Booth v. Baptist Church, 126
N.Y. 215, 28 N.E. 238 (1891);   Hatheway v. Smith, 79 Conn. 506, 65 A.
1058 (1906).   Both states have, however, enacted the Testamentary Additions to Trusts Act.   N.Y. EPTL 3–3.7;   Conn.Gen.Stat. § 45–173.

Frequently a person who owns a great variety of items of property
such as jewelry, antiques, art objects and the like desires to leave a letter
(which can be easily amended if circumstances change) setting out the
dispositive scheme for those items.   While the desire is understandable,
the device may needlessly invite litigation.   Only an existing document
may be incorporated by reference, and a letter, written after the will was
executed, would not qualify.   For examples of the difficulties that may
be encountered, see Walsh v. St. Joseph's Home for Aged, 303 A.2d 691
(Del.Ch.1973) (the court admitted that there could be no serious dispute
that the decedent intended to leave designated bonds to the named charities, but her intent failed because there was no way of knowing whether
the designations had been made before or after the will was executed).
The intent may be expressed in non-mandatory form.   See Illustrative
Will, Article Four, p. 315, supra.   UPC § 2–513 allows such writings for
tangible personal effects:

> Whether or not the provisions relating to holographic wills apply, a
> will may refer to a written statement or list to dispose of items of tangible
> personal property not otherwise specifically disposed of by the will, other
> than money, evidences of indebtedness, documents of title, and securities,
> and property used in trade or business.   To be admissible under this section
> as evidence of the intended disposition, the writing must either be in the
> handwriting of the testator or be signed by him and must describe the items
> and the devisees with reasonable certainty.   The writing may be referred
> to as one to be in existence at the time of the testator's death;   it may be
> prepared before or after the execution of the will;   it may be altered by the
> testator after its preparation;   and it may be a writing which has no sig-
> nificance apart from its effect upon the dispositions made by the will.

The pour-over will is a popular and useful device whereby the testator
directs that the distributable probate estate, in whole or in part, be added
to a trust which the testator or someone else (a spouse, for instance) has
previously established.   See discussion p. 58, supra.   This device is now
sanctioned by statute, either the uniform act set out below or similar
legislation, in almost every jurisdiction in the country.   Prior to the
enactment of such statutes, the courts quite regularly upheld the pour-
over arrangement by stating that the inter vivos trust was incorporated
by reference into the will.   By this theory, the trust, as an existing
document, could be incorporated into the will even if defectively executed
or if subject to the settlor's power to revoke, alter, or amend, although
difficulties did arise if the trust was actually amended after the date of

the will's execution. See e.g. Montgomery v. Blankenship, 217 Ark. 357, 230 S.W.2d 51, 21 A.L.R.2d 212 (1950); but see Matter of Estate of Daniels, 665 P.2d 594 (Colo. 1983) (will did not pour over estate into inter vivos trust because testator never intended trust to become effective). See generally, Palmer, Testamentary Disposition to the Trustee of an Inter Vivos Trust, 50 Mich.L.Rev. 33 (1951).

Section 1 of the Uniform Testamentary Additions to Trusts Act (incorporated as § 2–511 of the Uniform Probate Code) reads:

> A devise or bequest, the validity of which is determinable by the law of this state, may be made by a will to the trustee or trustees of a trust established or to be established by the testator or by the testator and some other person or persons or by some other person or persons (including a funded or unfunded life insurance trust, although the trustor has reserved any or all rights of ownership of the insurance contracts) if the trust is identified in the testator's will and its terms are set forth in a written instrument (other than a will) executed before or concurrently with the execution of the testator's will or in the valid last will of a person who has predeceased the testator (regardless of the existence, size, or character of the corpus of the trust). The devise or bequest shall not be invalid because the trust is amendable or revocable, or both, or because the trust was amended after the execution of the will or after the death of the testator. Unless the testator's will provides otherwise, the property so devised or bequeathed (a) shall not be deemed to be held under a testamentary trust of the testator but shall become a part of the trust to which it is given and (b) shall be administered and disposed of in accordance with the provisions of the instrument or will setting forth the terms of the trust, including any amendments thereto made before the death of the testator (regardless of whether made before or after the execution of the testator's will), and, if the testator's will so provides, including any amendments to the trust made after the death of the testator. A revocation or termination of the trust before the death of the testator shall cause the devise or bequest to lapse.

Facts of Independent Significance. This doctrine recognizes that the contents of a will, as to both beneficiaries and assets disposed, may change because of acts by the testator or others which occur after the execution of the will. Examples include legacies "to the persons who are in my employ at the time of my death", or "of all the furnishings in my summer home", etc. The events which may occur to change the will are not done with exclusively testamentary purpose and are not, therefore, treated as invalid amendments to or revocations of the will. See Atkinson on Wills, § 81 (1953).

The incorporation by reference doctrine requires that the document be in existence at the time the will is made. An inter vivos trust fails this test if it has been altered after the will's execution. The uniform act makes specific provision for this possibility. Prior to the act's enactment, courts tended to uphold wills that poured over property into an amended trust by treating the amendment as an act of independent significance that did not require attestation under the statute of wills.

See e.g. Second Bank-State Street Trust Co. v. Pinion, 341 Mass. 366, 170 N.E.2d 350 (1960) and authorities cited therein.

SECTION FOUR.   REVOCATION

A.   POWER TO REVOKE

1.   *Joint Wills*

IN RE WIGGINS ESTATE

Supreme Court of New York, Appellate Division, Fourth Department, 1974.
45 A.D.2d 604, 360 N.Y.S.2d 129, affirmed without opinion, 39 N.Y.2d 791,
385 N.Y.S.2d 287, 350 N.E.2d 618 (1976).

SIMONS, Justice: In 1948 Fred and Helen Wiggins executed a joint will.   Mr. Wiggins died in 1948.   In 1968 and 1969 Helen Wiggins executed two codicils changing the testamentary disposition of her estate. She died in 1969.

The issue before the court is whether the codicils were effective to alter the dispositions contained in the Will of Mr. and Mrs. Wiggins. Upon a petition requesting reprobate of the Will, probate of the two codicils and construction of the conflicting provisions contained in the instruments, the Surrogate admitted both the Will and the codicils to probate and held that the bequests in the codicils were to be given effect, finding that the Will did not constitute a contract between the two testators for joint disposition of their estates.

The Will provided that the estate of the first to die was to pass to the survivor and upon the death of the survivor, certain specific legacies totalling about $1800 were to be paid.   The residue was bequeathed to the First Baptist Church of Warsaw, New York for scholarships and general church purposes.   The two codicils bequeathed specific legacies totalling approximately $27,000.

At the time of Fred Wiggins' death the value of the estate was approximately $60,000.   The couple had no children and Mrs. Wiggins had been employed during their marriage and had contributed some of her earnings to their joint property.   In addition, Mrs. Wiggins had inherited property worth about $27,000 from her relatives, prior to her husband's death.   It is alleged that the value of the joint estate has increased as the result of careful management and the predictable influence of inflation during the 21 year period between Mr. Wiggins' death and the death of his wife and now exceeds $200,000.[3]

---

3.   The property in issue was derived from the original estate in 1948.   The dissent refers to it as "after-acquired property", but it is after-acquired only in the sense that it reflects and includes appreciation in value and savings from the earnings of the estate after the husband's death.

The positions of the Surrogate and the dissent are grounded upon Paragraph *Second*[4] of the Will which provided in part:

> " * * *   the survivor of us shall have the full use and the power to consume the principal of the decedent's estate during his or her lifetime, *except the right to dispose of the same by Will.*"   (Emphasis added.)

The Surrogate, noting that this paragraph referred to the "decedent's estate" rather than "our property", held that no contract was created by the joint Will and that disposition was restricted only with respect to the estate of the first testator to die.   The dissent relies upon the same language but, conceding a contract, contends that this language limits its application to the assets of both parties as they existed at the time of Mr. Wiggins' death in 1948.

We hold that the parties entered into a binding contract for the distribution of their collective assets, that Mrs. Wiggins' promised performance became irrevocable upon the death of her husband in 1948 and that the entire estate of the two parties as it existed at the time of Mrs. Wiggins' death is to be distributed in accordance with the Will, the bequests contained in the later codicils notwithstanding.

The joint Will contains familiar indicia of the parties' intention to make a contract and states reciprocal promises for the disposition of the parties' collective property binding upon the survivor.   The entire context of the instrument is plural.   Thus, it provided that "we" make this "our" last Will devising "all our property", stated that it was the Will of "each one of us and both of us" and employed similar language throughout (see, Rastetter v. Hoenninger, 214 N.Y. 66, 72, 108 N.E. 210, 211).   The Will does not contain an absolute gift of property to the survivor but only life use of the joint estate (see, Rubenstein v. Mueller, 19 N.Y.2d 228, 232, 278 N.Y.S.2d 845, 847, 225 N.E.2d 540, 542; Rich v. Mottek, 11 N.Y.2d 90, 94, 226 N.Y.S.2d 428, 431, 181 N.E.2d 445, 447; Tutunjian v. Vetzigian, 299 N.Y. 315, 320, 87 N.E.2d 275, 277, and cf. Matter of Zeh, 24 A.D.2d 983, 265 N.Y.S.2d 257, affd., 18 N.Y.2d 900, 276 N.Y.S.2d 635, 223 N.E.2d 43).   Furthermore, Paragraph *Third* provided:

> " * * *   [i]t is the will and desire of each of us and our mutual desire that, upon the death of whichever one of us that survives the other, that all of the remainder of our property, either real or personal * * * shall be divided and we give, devise and bequeath the same as follows * * *."

---

4.   The entire paragraph reads:

"It is the will and desire of each of us and each gives, devises and bequeaths to the other, upon the death of either of us, all of the property, both real and personal and where so ever the same may be situate, of the deceased party for the use of the surviving party so long as the said survivor shall live, and the said survivor shall have the right to invade the principal or corpus of the *decedent's estate*, both real and personal, as he or she shall in his or her own discretion require for his or her proper maintenance, support and comfort during the survivor's lifetime, and the survivor shall have the full power and authority during his or her lifetime, to sell and transfer any and all real and personal property of which the decedent died seized, and the said survivor may invest the same and the proceeds thereof, without regard to the laws for the investment of trust funds.   It is the mutual wish and desire of each of us that the survivor of us shall have the full use and the power to consume the principal of *the decedent's estate* during his or her lifetime, *except the right to dispose of the same by Will.*"   (Emphasis added.)

This language brings the instrument well within the form of those wills which the courts have held to be contracts providing for a joint disposition of the parties' collective assets.   Having found that, the governing rules are easily applied.   The reciprocal promises of the Will are irrevocably binding on the survivor after the death of one of the testators. Mrs. Wiggins was at liberty to use the property during her lifetime as her own and as she saw fit but she could not alter the testamentary disposition contained in the will (Rich v. Mottek, supra, 11 N.Y.2d 93, 226 N.Y.S.2d 430, 181 N.E.2d 446; Rastetter v. Hoenninger, supra, 214 N.Y. 73, 108 N.E. 211) and if she attempted to do so after the death of her husband, the beneficiaries of the will could maintain an action in equity to enforce its terms.   While this is an appeal from a construction proceeding and not an equitable action, we may not recognize rights here which must later be undone by separate action in equity.

The dissent would construe the phrase "all of the remainder of our property" found in Paragraph Third to mean only the property owned by testators, either jointly or singly, at the death of the first of them and that Mrs. Wiggins' property should be bound by the contract only to the extent of its value at the time of her husband's death in 1948.   This interpretation of the will is not only in conflict with the language it relies upon from Paragraph Second but it also construes an isolated phrase in a way which is at odds with the testamentary plan established by the whole Will and which does violence to the concept of joint wills by destroying the mutuality of the parties' promises.   We should not adopt such an extraordinary interpretation without a clear indication in the instrument that it represents the intention of the testators.   The will is not to be construed from the reading of a single word or sentence, but "from a sympathetic reading of the will as an entirety and in view of all the facts and circumstances   *   *   * "   (Matter of Fabbri, 2 N.Y.2d 236, 240, 159 N.Y.S.2d 184, 187, 140 N.E.2d 269, 271).

The manifest purpose of the parties was to provide for the security of the survivor and to remember the legatees, principally the church, after the last death.   Mrs. Wiggins' codicils recognized this commitment because the provisions of the codicils did not alter the original plan significantly, they merely attempted to increase the size of some of the specific legacies [5] and add a few more.   No doubt her actions were prompted by the increase in the value of the estate but this was a natural consequence of the joint will in view of the lengthy interval separating the two deaths.   Such a possibility is a necessary consideration in all estate planning and may not justify altering the fixed disposition of the assets. The problems the dissent anticipates by a remarriage of the surviving spouse are matters within her control and easily resolved by proper planning.   The imprecision of its proposed rule limiting the operation of the Will to those assets existing or contemplated at the time of the Will's

---

5.   The similarity of the names of the specific legatees in the will and some of those named in the codicils 20 years later would suggest that the subsequent legatees were heirs or survivors of those originally named.

execution would only magnify such difficulties and others frequently arising from the use of joint wills.

Finally, the dissent contends that equitable considerations support the result it proposes. It is not clear what equitable considerations mandate such a strained construction of the Will. The testamentary plan to which we give effect is precisely that agreed upon by the parties, a plan by which the great proportion of the estate goes to the Church, with friends, remote relatives and other charities receiving relatively small financial gifts. The facts that Mrs. Wiggins was not profligate with the funds and that there was no fraud on her part or unjust enrichment do not change her promise or alter the terms of the contract contained in the joint Will.

The Will and the codicils, having been duly executed, should be admitted to probate but the codicils were without legal effect to alter the terms of the Will, and the Surrogate's construction of the instruments to the contrary should be reversed.

Decree modified in accordance with opinion and as modified affirmed with costs to respondent payable out of the estate.

MARSH, P. J., and MAHONEY and DEL VECCHIO, JJ., concur.

CARDAMONE, J., dissents and votes to affirm the Judgment in the following Opinion.

CARDAMONE, Justice (dissenting):

The question presented on this appeal is whether property acquired by a surviving wife *after* the death of her husband is impressed with a trust for the benefit of those provided for under the terms of the joint will. In my view, law and equity both require that this question be answered in the negative.

A joint will is an instrument that when viewed solely as a will is revocable at pleasure, but when considered as a contract, if supported by adequate consideration, may be enforceable in equity (Rastetter v. Hoenninger, 214 N.Y. 66, 71, 108 N.E. 210, 211). The majority have concluded that this joint will contains a contractual promise which binds the disposition of the after-acquired property of the surviving spouse. I disagree. We all agree that there is a joint will between decedent husband and his wife who survived. But its language and the surrounding circumstances do not clearly spell out any promise to have its terms binding on more than the property contemplated by the parties at the time of the death of the first of them. On the contrary, the last sentence in the second paragraph of the joint will expresses an intent to bind merely the decedent's estate as follows: "It is the mutual wish and desire of each of us that the survivor of us shall have the full use and power to consume the principal of the *decedent's estate* during his or her lifetime, except the right to dispose of the *same* by Will" (emphasis supplied). Similar references to the estate of the decedent are contained in the first sentence of the same paragraph.

It has long been settled that the mere execution of joint or mutual wills does not by itself establish a contract prohibiting alteration or revocation without clear and convincing evidence that such a provision was made. [citations omitted] In this case, the promise related to the estate of the decedent which equity should enforce, but there exists no clear and convincing evidence of a promise binding upon after-acquired property of the survivor (cf. Tutunjian v. Vetzigian, 299 N.Y. 315, 87 N.E.2d 275). In *Tutunjian*, for example, the will expressly referred to after-acquired property. Absent such kind of evidence equity will impress a trust only "[a]s to property received by (the survivor) under the joint will" (Rubenstein v. Mueller, 19 N.Y.2d 228, 233, 278 N.Y.S.2d 845, 849, 225 N.E.2d 540, 543; Rastetter v. Hoenninger, 214 N.Y. 66, 74, 108 N.E. 210, 212).

The majority's holding seems unduly inflexible, especially when it is bottomed on such slim proof of a contractual promise.

With respect to equitable considerations, the Attorney General on behalf of the charitable residuary beneficiary, petitioned the Surrogate to exercise its equitable power to impress a trust upon the proceeds of the codicils. The elements which would compel a court to impress such constructive trust, e.g., fraud and unjust enrichment are not present in this case. The two codicils of the surviving wife which are at issue here do not alter specific bequests of the joint will, nor may they be construed as an attempt by the survivor to enrich herself or her relatives to the detriment of the decedent husband or his relatives. In fact, the most substantial additional bequest is one of $20,000 to a cousin of the husband. The codicils carry out the intent of the joint will and do not diminish the gift to the residuary legatee. It receives, giving effect to the codicils, a substantially larger bequest (approximately three times as much) than it would have received at the time the joint will was executed. Nor is there any indication that the survivor wife abused a confidential relationship. There must be a "sympathetic reading of the will as an entirety and in view of all the facts and circumstances under which the provisions of the will were framed" (Matter of Fabbri, 2 N.Y.2d 236, 240, 159 N.Y. S.2d 184, 187, 140 N.E.2d 269, 271). Thus, the intent of the joint will is to be gathered not merely from the language of the instrument itself, "but also from the conditions and circumstances extrinsic to it" (Spencer v. Childs, 1 N.Y.2d 103, 107, 150 N.Y.S.2d 788, 790, 134 N.E.2d 60, 61). Considering the expressed intent of the makers of the joint will to leave modest but significant bequests to their only relatives and the long passage of time during which the value of those bequests depreciated with the value of money, it is highly unlikely that the decedent husband would have disposed of his property differently had he contemplated the codicil modifications made in favor of his and his wife's relatives. It is consonant with sound construction then, considering these facts, conditions and circumstances, to grant the codicils legal effect.

Subsequent to the husband's death the size of the estate increased, due solely to the surviving wife's prudent investments and frugal life style. Thus, on the facts recited, it is plain that the surviving wife committed no fraud, nor was she guilty of self-enrichment. On the contrary, to deny effect to the codicils of her will would unjustly enrich the charitable beneficiary at the expense of the living relatives of both the decedent husband and the surviving wife as makers of the joint will. This result the Surrogate, in the exercise of his equitable power, properly refused to carry out.   To illustrate the inequity of the rule adopted by the majority, if the surviving wife had remarried after her husband's death, had children and then inherited a large estate from her second husband, it would be plainly unjust and inequitable to distribute the after-acquired property from the second husband in accordance with the prior joint will.

The judicial policy has been one of great reluctance to restrict the ambulatory nature of a will—be it joint or mutual—absent convincing evidence of such a clear intent.   [citations omitted]   A proper rule for the disposition of the after-acquired property and one in accordance with the intent of the joint will would impress a trust on the surviving wife's property only to the extent of its value at the time the husband died (Olsen v. Olsen, 189 Misc. 1046, 70 N.Y.S.2d 838).   For these reasons I dissent and vote to affirm the judgment of the Surrogate.

Notes

1. The weight of authority holds that the fact that a will is joint and contains reciprocal provisions does not of itself establish a contract of irrevocability.   An agreement that the will is not to be revoked by the survivor of the two testators may be express and found either in the will or in a separate document.   In the absence of an express agreement, the contract may be established by implication from the language of the will and from extrinsic evidence which bears on the parties' intent.   In such an inquiry, the fact that it is a single document which makes reciprocal provisions, uses the plural pronouns "we" and "our," and speaks of the dispositions as being "forever" will be persuasive evidence of a contract forbidding revocation by the survivor.   See e.g. Rauch v. Rauch, 112 Ill.App.3d 198, 67 Ill.Dec. 785, 445 N.E.2d 77 (1983) (contract established); but see Estate of Bainer, 71 A.D.2d 728, 419 N.Y.S.2d 228 (1979) (contract not established; use of "we" not decisive).   A few courts have ruled that the existence of a joint and mutual will creates a presumption of irrevocability.   In re Estate of Chayka, 47 Wis.2d 102, 176 N.W.2d 561 (1970) ("contract may be conclusively presumed from the fact of the joint will being executed"); In re Edwards' Estate, 3 Ill.2d 116, 120 N.E.2d 10 (1954) (rebuttable presumption).   A contract of irrevocability was found, by applying the same analysis, in a case of inter vivos revocable trusts which had been executed by a husband and wife as will substitutes.   Reznik v. McKee, 216 Kan. 659, 534 P.2d 243 (1975).   If the contract involves land or is otherwise within the technical scope of the Statute of Frauds, the courts have shown a readiness to stress the fact that the survivor has accepted benefits from the will of the first party to die and to permit proof of an oral agreement on part performance, estoppel or unjust enrichment grounds.   See, for instance, Crail v. Blakely, 8 Cal.3d 744, 106 Cal.Rptr. 187, 505 P.2d 1027 (1973).

2. If the joint will is found to be irrevocable but the survivor of the two testators revokes it and makes a new will, what is the appropriate remedy? The usual authority requires the beneficiary of the joint will to proceed in contract.   The Kansas court in In re Estate of Chronister, 203 Kan. 366, 454 P.2d 438, 440 (1969) described the dilemma as follows:

By way of preliminary comment, we pause here to reiterate * * * that a single instrument may be both a will contractual in character, and a contract testamentary in nature; as a will it is revocable but as a contract it is enforceable; and although a contractual will revoked by execution of a second will, cannot be probated, it may nonetheless be enforced as a contract against the estate of the testator breaching it.

See also Shimp v. Shimp, 287 Md. 372, 412 A.2d 1228 (1980) (husband, who survived wife, entitled to a declaratory decree permitting him to revoke the joint and mutual will, but binding contract between husband and wife continues and at his death will be enforceable specifically or by an action in damages).

There is, however, some authority for refusing probate to the second will and distributing the estate in accordance with the joint will which is accepted as the official will. In re Edwards' Estate, 3 Ill.2d 116, 120 N.E.2d 10 (1954). Can the surviving testator circumvent the prohibition by giving away the property inter vivos rather than by a new will? The court in In re Estate of Chayka, 47 Wis.2d 102, 176 N.W.2d 561 (1970) ordered a second husband to return to his wife's estate the property which she had given him during the marriage in violation of an agreement with her first husband not to revoke, and to account for property not still in his possession. By the terms of the will, was Mrs. Wiggins in the principal case free to give away the property by inter vivos gift? By revocable trust? See Mansour v. Rabil, 277 N.C. 364, 177 S.E.2d 849 (1970). It has been held that the interest of an ultimate beneficiary of a joint will comes into being at the death of the first spouse to die so that his death after that date but before the second spouse's death does not cause the legacy to lapse. Rauch v. Rauch, supra note 1.

3. The argument that a joint will cannot be revoked by the survivor has led the Internal Revenue Service to deny the marital deduction to the surviving spouse on the ground that the property passing to her (or him) is a terminable interest. Bittker and Clark, Federal Estate and Gift Taxation, 465–466 (5th ed.1984). While the Service has not had notable success in proving that the applicable state law forbids revocation by the survivor, the frequency with which it has tried should give added pause to the lawyer who is about to draft a joint will for his or her clients.

2. Mutual Wills

[handwritten: Author "Greatest Story ever told" (@ bible)]

OURSLER v. ARMSTRONG

Court of Appeals of New York, 1961.
10 N.Y.2d 385, 223 N.Y.S.2d 477, 179 N.E.2d 489.

VAN VOORHIS, Judge. Charles Fulton Oursler had two children by his first wife and two children by his second wife. In 1951 Oursler and his second wife, Grace Perkins Oursler, executed wills at the same time before the same attesting witnesses. His will provided that his residuary estate would go to Grace; but if he survived her it would go to the four children of both his marriages, or their children; the will of Grace provided that her residuary should go to Oursler but, if she survived him, the property coming to her from Oursler would go to the same four children of both marriages, or to their children.

Oursler died in 1952. Grace survived him. On January 21, 1955, in the year of her death, she made a new will which was admitted to probate in which she left everything to her two children and nothing to the children of Oursler's first marriage. In this action in the Supreme Court the children of the first marriage and their children seek to impress a trust on the property received by Grace under Oursler's will.

The trial court impressed such a trust on the basis of a promise found to have been made by Grace Oursler that she would deal with the property received by her under her husband's will so that the children of both marriages would share alike in the property. The Appellate Division affirmed, stating that "On the whole record we are thus of opinion that Grace took the property by Fulton's will in a relationship of confidence from which Fulton believed she would dispose of the property 'as he would do it himself'; and that it was the implicit understanding between them that such a distribution was an obligation, based on confidence, which Grace undertook. The imposition of a constructive trust upon the estate of Grace is thus well grounded in equitable principle." One Justice dissented on the ground that the proof did not support a promise by Grace on which a constructive trust could be founded. We are in accord with the latter view.

Grace may have had a moral obligation to give the property which she inherited from Fulton to all four of the children, but a moral obligation alone is not enough to set the court in motion in a case of this kind (Amherst College v. Ritch, 151 N.Y. 282, 45 N.E. 876, 37 L.R.A. 305). The only basis on which a court can intervene is that a promise was made by Mrs. Grace Oursler not to alter or revoke her 1951 will and that by reason of her promise to that effect her husband gave and bequeathed to her what he did. The power to dispose of one's property by will is not lightly to be denied even if Judges think that the testatrix should have disposed of her estate differently. No express promise or representation was proved in writing or orally to have been made by Grace Oursler that she would not change her testamentary intent as expressed in the will which she executed contemporaneously with the will of her husband. Nor does the evidence from which such a promise is sought to be implied establish anything more than a 1951 intention on Mrs. Oursler's part to dispose of her property as she provided by her 1951 will.

The law does not view the renunciation of the right to alter or revoke a will as a casual matter (Matter of Bekker, 283 App.Div. 609, 129 N.Y. S.2d 126) and, regardless of whether the Statute of Frauds (Personal Property Law, § 31, subd. 7) controls this case, as quite possibly it does not (Sinclair v. Purdy, 235 N.Y. 245, 139 N.E. 255; Foreman v. Foreman, 251 N.Y. 237, 167 N.E. 428; Wood v. Rabe, 96 N.Y. 414; O'Boyle v. Brenner, 189 Misc. 1058, 73 N.Y.S.2d 687, mod. on other grounds 273 App.Div. 683, 79 N.Y.S.2d 84, 278 App.Div. 900, 105 N.Y.S.2d 386, mod. 303 N.Y. 572, 104 N.E.2d 913; Lawrence v. Mildenberger, 30 Misc.2d 1012, 92 N.Y.S.2d 519, affd. 276 App.Div. 1079, 97 N.Y.S.2d 195; Matter of Buehler, 186 Misc. 306, 59 N.Y.S.2d 766, affd. 272 App.Div. 757, 70 N.Y.S.2d 139), the spirit of it as well as the decisional law requires clear evidence of the existence of a promise of this nature (see opinion by Dore, J., in Bayreuther v. Reinisch, 264 App.Div. 138, 34 N.Y.S.2d 674, affd. 290 N.Y. 553, 47 N.E.2d 959; Rubin v. Irving Trust Co., 305 N.Y. 288, 113 N.E.2d 424; Meltzer v. Koenigsberg, 302 N.Y. 523, 99 N.E.2d 679; Matter of Levin, 302 N.Y. 535, 99 N.E.2d 877; West v. Day Trust Co., 328 Mass. 381, 103 N.E.2d 813, 29 A.L.R.2d 1224). In Edson v. Parsons, 155 N.Y. 555, 571, 50 N.E. 265, 269, after mentioning the similarity in lives, thoughts, emotions and testamentary plan of two elderly maiden sisters whose wills were executed on the same day before the same witnesses, the court said in regard to a subsequent change in the will of the survivor: "Was the surviving sister not to be free, in all the contingencies of life, with all the possible mutations in her relations to others, or in the worthiness of the destined objects of their bounty, to make such other testamentary dispositions as might seem wise, or in better accord with her sentiments? These are most serious questions for consideration upon the plaintiff's appeal to a court of equity for relief."

The Appellate Division appears to have realized the weakness of the evidence in this record of any binding agreement or promise by Grace Oursler to renounce her future power of testamentary disposition. The opinion at the Appellate Division states that "it is clear that there is no remedy for plaintiffs to be laid in contract; they are unable to show either an enforcible contract by Grace to make a will for their benefit; or an enforcible contract by Grace to assume a trust in their interest."

The opinion then states: "The theory of constructive trust does not depend necessarily upon proof of the actual undertaking of a trust obligation by the party charged. He may have intended to become a trustee, and the proof of his undertaking either is barred by statutory or other rules of evidence, or direct proof of intent may be absent altogether. On the other hand he may have had no intention at all of becoming a trustee." This is followed by the statement that a constructive trust may embrace situations "where all reasonable probabilities point to an intended trust which cannot be proved," as well as "situations in which equity spells out a trust not at all intended by the trustee."

Thus a constructive trust for the testamentary disposition of assets received from another is equated with a quasi contract implied in law, contrary to actual fact, as thus described in Miller v. Schloss, 218 N.Y. 400, 407, 113 N.E. 337, 339: "A *quasi* or constructive contract rests upon the equitable principle that a person shall not be allowed to enrich himself unjustly at the expense of another. In truth it is not a contract or promise at all. It is an obligation which the law creates, in the absence of any agreement, when and because the acts of the parties or others have placed in the possession of one person money, or its equivalent, under such circumstances that in equity and good conscience he ought not to retain it, and which *ex aequo et bono* belongs to another. Duty, and not a promise or agreement or intention of the person sought to be charged, defines it. It is fictitiously deemed contractual, in order to fit the cause of action to the contractual remedy."

This is evidently the reasoning behind the statement by the Appellate Division in the case at bar that "It is the weight of judicial power that imposes the constructive trust; it is a trust fashioned by the moral mandate of equity."

This is all very well in instances where a defendant is charged as a trustee *ex maleficio* without intending to become a trustee in fact in instances where he has misappropriated property belonging to another. It has no application to the present case where no property has been misappropriated and it is admitted that a moral obligation alone is not enough to set a court in motion to compel the devolution of property in a certain way (Amherst College v. Ritch, supra; Oursler v. Armstrong, 8 A.D.2d 194, 197, 186 N.Y.S.2d 829, 831, citing Wood v. Rabe, supra, 96 N.Y. p. 421).

Although at one point it was stated that on the whole record "it was the implicit understanding between them that such a distribution was an obligation, based on confidence, which Grace undertook" (8 A.D.2d 194, 200, 186 N.Y.S.2d 829, 836), the decision of this appeal depends upon the existence of an actual promise by Grace, express or implied, that she would not afterward change her will. Any conclusion based on analogy with the law of quasi contract is inadmissible. Courts do not have that much power over the devolution of other people's property. That is made clear by the cases which are cited in support of the existence of a confidential relationship in order to escape the impact of the Statute of Frauds, such as Sinclair v. Purdy (supra) and Foreman v. Foreman (supra), where, in writing the opinion, Judge Cardozo repeated the language used by him at Special Term in Golland v. Golland, 84 Misc. 299, 306, 147 N.Y.S. 263, 268, that "It is not the promise only, nor the breach only, but the promise and the breach combined with the extortion of property from the owner upon the faith of the engagement, which puts the court in motion." The existence of a promise, express or implied, is a vital necessity; the mere fact of a confidential relationship is not enough. In the present instance Grace Oursler appropriated no property belonging to others, within the rule of quasi contract. She had the legal right to dispose of her property by will as she chose, unless she obtained her deceased husband's estate on the strength of a promise that she would bequeath it equally among his four children, in which event only could a constructive trust come into being covering what she inherited from him.

Where a testator has received property from others, now deceased, equity will intervene under certain circumstances to declare the surviving testator a trustee in order to carry out a promise on the strength of which the property has been received (Ahrens v. Jones, 169 N.Y. 555, 62 N.E. 666; Amherst College v. Ritch, supra); the existence of a joint will where the same document is signed by both husband and wife has been held to constitute a sufficient basis for the existence of such a promise (Rastetter v. Hoenninger, 214 N.Y. 66, 108 N.E. 210; Tutunjian v. Vetzigian, 299 N.Y. 315, 87 N.E.2d 275). An antenuptial contract has been held sufficient to the purpose (Phalen v. United States Trust Co., 186 N.Y. 178, 78 N.E. 943, 7 L.R.A., N.S., 734). Nevertheless, "To attribute to a will the quality of irrevocability demands the most indisputable evidence of the agreement which is relied upon to change its ambulatory nature, and that presumptions will not, and should not, take the place of proof." (Edson v. Parsons, supra, 155 N.Y. p. 568, 50 N.E. p. 268; Lally v. Cronen, 247 N.Y. 58, 63, 159 N.E. 723, 726; Wallace v. Wallace, 216 N.Y. 28, 109 N.E. 872; Matter of Bekker, supra). The same is true of the existence of a promise, express or implied from circumstances, in the case of a constructive trust of the nature sought to be established in this case. Such a promise is not established by the mere confidentiality of the relationship between the persons involved.

None of the testimony adduced to sustain the judgment establishes a promise by Grace Oursler to renounce her power of testamentary disposition. The witnesses Farrar and Denker merely testified to conversations of a general nature, which have no tendency to establish a promise by Grace. The testimony of the attorney, Mr. Morris L. Ernst, indicates that there was a friendly relationship between Fulton and his two children by his first wife. Mr. Ernst did not testify to any promise made by Grace nor did he even testify that the memorandum which Grace sent to him outlining the contents of portions of her 1951 will was ever seen or mentioned by Fulton Oursler. If the intention had been that Mrs. Grace Oursler was renouncing her power to alter or revoke her 1951 will, as regards the property which she stood to inherit from her husband, it is remarkable that it was not put in writing or even mentioned orally in joint consultation by so experienced and competent a lawyer as Mr. Ernst. Instead of there being a promise to sustain a constructive trust of this kind, binding Grace Oursler during the rest of her life to the same testamentary disposition, it is plain that Fulton Oursler gave his property to her by will absolutely believing that in her own good judgment she would do whatever was the right thing. Many another husband has done the same.

The circumstance that Fulton Oursler once discussed the formation of a corporation to do a television production of "The Greatest Story Ever Told" whereas such corporation was never formed has no operative effect, nor the preincorporation agreement embodying an arrangement at one time desired by him. Nothing in the memorandum which Grace Oursler submitted to their attorney, Mr. Ernst, amounts to a promise that she would refrain from later exercising her prerogative of revoking or altering her 1951 will to which it relates. This memorandum has no more probative force than the will itself, the substance of portions of which it incorporates. The mere inclusion of statements that her 1951 will is "as he would wish it", or that "Should he not survive me then I would wish my estate handled as he would wish matters to be handled, except that anything of my own would go directly to my own children and grandchildren, knowing that my husband's loved ones have been, are and will be well remembered", do not alter the situation. She was stating her present wish with regard to the contents of her 1951 will. The mere circumstance that she executed this will contemporaneously with the will of her husband, and that both contained similar provisions with respect to the gift over to Fulton Oursler's children in 1951, does not constitute an agreement as was recognized by the Appellate Division's citing Edson v. Parsons (supra) (8 A.D.2d 196, 186 N.Y.S.2d 831).

The judgment appealed from should be reversed and the complaint dismissed, with costs in all courts.

FROESSEL, BURKE and FOSTER, JJ., concur with VAN VOORHIS, J.

DESMOND, C. J., and DYE and FULD, JJ., dissent and vote to affirm upon the opinion of Justice Bergan in the Appellate Division.

Judgment reversed, etc.

A: Grace made no promise!

Notes

1. As an interesting sidelight it might be noted that the opinion of the Appellate Division which is reversed here was written by Justice Bergan. In 1963 he succeeded Judge Foster on the Court of Appeals. Had the case come up thereafter, the 4–3 decision would have presumably gone the other way.

2. Assume that A, in consideration of B's promise to take care of A in his old age, promises to leave his property to B by will. Is the agreement enforceable? What remedies are available?

Such contracts are viewed "with misgivings and suspicion." In re Estate of Vajentic, 453 Pa. 1, 306 A.2d 300 (1973). The court in Cook v. Cook, 80 Wash.2d 642, 644, 497 P.2d 584, 587 (1972), explained why:

> The genesis of the concept that this type of case requires proof beyond the usual civil rule of preponderance of the evidence lies in the very nature of the problem. The right to devolve one's estate is a valuable right and these cases arise after death has silenced the only person who actually knows the decedent's true intent. Thus, courts must look to objective facts—the actions and statements made by the deceased promissor during his lifetime—to determine the existence of an agreement. In assessing the evidence, the trier of the facts must be mindful of the elements of probable self-interest of those still living and seeking the benefits of an asserted agreement; that statements made by the decedent to disinterested parties must be tested in light of the time and circumstances existing at the time; and the countervailing equities of the contesting parties. In short, courts strive to determine whether or not the contract did in fact exist and, within the obvious limitations of proof in these cases, the trier of the facts must be convinced that it is highly probable that there was such an agreement as is asserted by the proponents of the contract.

If the contract involves land, it is within the Statute of Frauds and must be in writing. As to personalty, an oral agreement, if it can be proved, is usually enforceable (but see N.Y. EPTL 13–2.1). Courts may disagree on the form of the remedy. Specific performance is theoretically available but many courts view it as inconsistent with the concept of a will as a freely revocable instrument. The inconsistency is frequently resolved by allowing probate of the last will and granting the claimant compensation for the reasonable value of the services rendered, 2 Corbin on Contracts § 314. A constructive trust remedy may also be available. 7 Powell ¶ 963. A written contract not to leave property to a particular person is also valid and enforceable. Roberts v. Conley, 626 S.W.2d 634 (Ky.1981).

3. As the principal case makes evident, courts are not as quick to imply a contract of irrevocability from the execution of mutual wills as they are in the case of a joint will. If, however, the contract is express, it will be enforced and the surviving spouse cannot make an inter vivos transfer of the property in defiance of its terms. Schwartz v. Horn, 31 N.Y.2d 275, 290 N.E.2d 816 (1972).

B. METHODS OF REVOCATION

1. Physical Destruction or Mutilation

Fifteen states follow the language of the Statute of Frauds in providing for revocation by "burning, cancelling, tearing, or obliterating". Other states use similar language. The relevant section of the Statute of Frauds, 29 Car. 2, c. 3 (1676) reads:

"VI. And moreover, No Devise in Writing of Lands, Tenements or Hereditaments, nor any Clause thereof, shall at any Time after the said four and twentieth Day of *June* be revocable, otherwise than by some other Will or Codicil in Writing, or other Writing declaring the same, or by Burning, Cancelling, Tearing or Obliterating the same by the Testator himself, or in his Presence and by his Directions and Consent; (2) but all Devises and Bequests of Lands and Tenements shall remain and continue in Force, until the same be Burnt, Cancelled, Torn or Obliterated by the Testator, or his Directions, in Manner aforesaid, or unless the same be altered by some other Will or Codicil in Writing, or other Writing, of the Devisor, signed in the Presence of three or four Witnesses, Declaring the same; any former Law or Usage to the contrary notwithstanding."

IN RE BAKHAUS' ESTATE
Supreme Court of Illinois, 1951.
410 Ill. 578, 102 N.E.2d 818.

FULTON, Justice. William F. Bakhaus, a resident of Crete, Illinois, died on July 9, 1947. A document purporting to be his last will and testament was found in a drawer in the harness shop which he operated in the basement of his home on July 14, 1947. The instrument consisted of two pages of typewriting, and is as follows:

PAGE 1

"Know All Men By These Presents, That I, William F. Bakhaus, of Crete, Illinois, being of sound and disposing mind and memory do hereby make, publish and declare, this to be my Last Will and Testament, hereby revoking all Wills by me at anytime heretofore made.

"First; I order and direct, that my Executor hereinafter named pay my funeral expenses and just debts as soon after my decease as conveniently may be.

"Second; I give, devise and bequeath unto my beloved wife Bertha Bakhaus, all of my personal property and belongings, that I may die possessed of or may be entitled to.

"Third; My Home described as, Lot Number Two (2) in Seggebruchs Subdivision, in the Village of Crete, County of Will and State of Illinois, with the buildings thereon, I give, devise and bequeath unto my beloved wife Bertha Bakhaus, for her sole use during her lifetime and after her death, the same shall become the property of my Nephew, William Bakhaus, of Grant Park, Illinois. Subject however to the payment of the following bequests which are to be paid after the death of my beloved wife, Bertha Bakhaus, as follows:

To my brother Fred Bakhaus, One Hundred Dollars

To my brother August Bakhaus, One Hundred Dollars

To my sister Emma Engelking, One Hundred Dollars

To my niece Velma Bakhaus, One Hundred Dollars

and I charge the aforesaid Real Estate with the payment of the above bequests.

"Fourth; I hereby nominate and appoint, my nephew William Bakhaus of Grant Park, Illinois, sole Executor of this my Last Will and Testament and I do hereby exempt him from giving any Surety on any Bond that may be required of him as such Executor.

"In Witness Whereof, I have hereunto set my hand and affixed my seal this _27th_ day of October, A.D. 1941.

PAGE 2

"The within instrument, consisting of two sheets of paper including this sheet, was at the date thereof, signed, sealed, published and declared, by the said Testator, William F. Bakhaus as and for his Last Will and Testament, in the presence of us and we at his request and in his presence and in the presence of each other, have affixed our names as witnesses thereto, the day and year first above written.

"Witnesses	Address
Johanna Rohe	_Crete, Ill._
Fred A. Rohe	_Crete, Ill._"

It was on legal size paper and the signature of the testator had been cut from the will. The cutting had apparently been done by a sharp instrument straight across the bottom of the page, and the cutting had removed not only the bottom of the first page together with the signature, but also the bottom of the second page of the will.

The executor named in the will offered the same for probate. The attesting witnesses appeared before the probate court and testified to the proper execution of the will by the testator, and that court admitted the will to probate. Two of the heirs appealed from the action of the probate court to the circuit court of Will County and after another hearing in that court the will was held to have been properly admitted to probate. These two heirs have brought this appeal contending that the will was improperly admitted to probate. A freehold being involved, the appeal has been taken directly to this court.

William F. Bakhaus, the testator, was a widower and was the owner of a house in Crete, where he lived, in the basement of which he conducted a harness shop. His wife had died in 1946 and after her death his nephew

William Bakhaus and his nieces, Velma Bakhaus and Beatrice Bakhaus, children of his deceased brother, came and resided with him in this home. He was afflicted with palsy and during the last few months of his life he was quite shaky and had to be assisted while eating or cutting his food by his niece and at times it was necessary for her to assist him in the harness shop. The proponent of the will offered the testimony of the two attesting witnesses as to the due execution of the will on October 27, 1941, showing that the will was duly and properly executed in Crete, at the office of a real-estate broker who had prepared it at the request of the testator. After the execution of the will it appears that the testator took the will with him to his home and that it remained there until his death. No evidence was submitted by any of the parties as to the circumstances attending the mutilation of the will. The proponent, however, did introduce testimony of several witnesses who testified to statements and declarations made by the testator during his lifetime that he wanted his home to go to his nephew, the proponent, and that the deceased held the proponent in high regard. It was further shown by the evidence that the will was found in a drawer in the harness shop, while his other valuable papers were found in a safe which the testator kept in his bedroom closet. Evidence was admitted indicating that the harness shop was a gathering place for testator's many customers and numerous friends, that the entrance to the harness shop was unlocked and that persons other than the testator had access to the shop.

Two witnesses testified in behalf of the contestants. These witnesses were nieces of testator and daughters of one of the contestants. They testified that in December, 1946, about 7 months prior to testator's death, he stated to them that the home was not going to the nephew but that he desired to have all of his property divided equally between his heirs. Fred Rohe, the man who drew the will, testified that the last time the testator spoke to him about his affairs in detail was when the will was drawn in 1941, but that, about a week before testator died, testator had a conversation with him in which he told Rohe he wanted to see him sometime and that he would let him know when he should come, since he thought he might make some changes in his will.

The contestants argue that the will was revoked by the testator and therefore should not have been admitted to probate. They contend that where a will remains in the testator's possession until his death and is then found among his papers or effects with erasures, alterations or mutilations, the law presumes that the will was revoked by the testator with the proper intention. The proponent contends that the will was properly admitted to probate because the will was established as having been validly executed and, before the presumption of revocation by the testator exists, it must be established that the will was in the exclusive possession and control of the testator up until the time of death. He further argues that any presumption of destruction by the testator is a rebuttable one which can be overcome by declarations of the testator and other evidence. Likewise, he contends that this case presents purely a question of fact and that the decision of the trial court will not be disturbed unless manifestly against the weight of the evidence.

Our statute on wills provides (Ill.Rev.Stat.1949, chap. 3, par. 194) "Every will by which any real or personal estate is devised or bequeathed shall be reduced to writing, shall be signed by the testator or by some person in his presence and by his direction, and shall be attested in the presence of the testator by two or more credible witnesses."

Our statute also provides the mode in which a will may be revoked. (Ill.Rev.Stat.1949, chap. 3, par. 197.) "A will may be revoked only (a) by burning, cancelling, tearing, or obliterating it by the testator himself or by some person in his presence and by his direction and consent, (b) by some other will declaring the revocation, (c) by a later will to the extent that it is inconsistent with the prior will, or (d) by an instrument in writing declaring the revocation and signed and attested in the manner prescribed by this Article for the signing and attestation of a will."

It has been held that this provision of the statute permitting the revocation of the will by tearing also permits revocation by cutting the will and that such cutting need not be the cutting of the entire will. Fleming v. Fleming, 367 Ill. 97, 10 N.E.2d 641; Burton v. Wylde, 261 Ill. 397, 103 N.E. 976.

We have held that even though one of the requisite methods of revocation is followed by the testator, the act is ineffectual unless there is an intent to revoke the will.   Gorrell v. Boyd, 376 Ill. 132, 33 N.E.2d 190.   We have also held that the intent to revoke the will may be made to appear from the nature of the act of revocation.   Board of National Missions v. Sherry, 372 Ill. 272, 23 N.E.2d 730; Martin v. Martin, 334 Ill. 115, 165 N.E. 644, 67 A.L.R. 1127.

Cases wherein a will is torn or cut normally fall in two categories, first, cases wherein certain provisions or portions of the will are removed by cutting or tearing, and second, cases where the signature is removed or obliterated.   In the first type of case we have held that the tearing or cutting of a portion of the will was similar to cases wherein lines have been drawn through certain portions of the will.   In these instances it has been held that the drawing of a line through certain portions of the will, or the cutting of a certain portion of it, was an attempt to revoke so much of the will as was crossed out or removed and that, in the absence of evidence of an intention on the part of the testator to revoke the entire will, such crossing out or cutting would be disregarded and the will admitted to probate as it originally existed, so far as legible.   Fleming v. Fleming, 367 Ill. 97, 10 N.E.2d 641; Casey v. Hogan, 344 Ill. 208, 176 N.E. 257; Schmidt v. Bauermeister, 279 Ill. 504, 117 N.E. 49.

In the latter type of case the court has held that, where a signature of a testator had been cut from the codicil to the will, the codicil was revoked and, depending upon the intention of the testator as to the will itself, the whole will could be revoked by such action.   Burton v. Wylde, 261 Ill. 397, 103 N.E. 976, 978.

In the case of Burton v. Wylde, we held that, if declarations by the testator are admissible to prove a lost will, they were admissible to explain the acts of revocation or to show the intent of the testator, and we stated, "If declarations of this nature are admissible to show the total destruction or cancellation of the will, there can be no escape from the conclusion that they are admissible to show partial mutilation, cancellation or tearing of the will."

In the case of Burton v. Wylde many statements had been made by a testatrix to various people, some indicating that she had destroyed her will and some indicating that she had a will. In that case, after discussing the various contentions of the parties and the conflicting evidence this court stated, "Intelligent, careful woman that she was shown to be, How should she expect the will to remain in force if she cut a portion out of it, even though that portion might be small? In view of all the evidence in the record, in the light of the condition in which the will was found among the papers of the testatrix at her death, we can reach no other conclusion, under the authorities, than that she herself cut out her signature with the intention of revoking the entire document."

It would appear to us from the record of this case that the cutting of the signature from the will must certainly be taken as an act of revocation. The signature is the most important part of the will and if one not familiar with the statute were to revoke a will, the cutting of the signature from the will would be an ordinary mode to adopt, since the cutting of signatures from documents is frequently used to indicate their cancellation.

Proponent has argued that the will was not in the possession or control of the testator until his death, and has attempted to avoid the presumption that when the will is found in the possession and control of testator in a mutilated condition the law presumes that the mutilation was done by the testator with the requisite intention. He asserts that, the will having been kept in a drawer in the harness shop, it was not in the exclusive possession of the testator as it would have been had it been in the testator's safe in his bedroom. We do not agree with this contention because we do not feel that the exclusive possession of the testator means that it must be kept under lock and key or in a safety-deposit box. This will appears to have been kept in a drawer where he kept other papers in connection with his business. The fact that the place where he kept the will was not as safe a place as he had available to him does not mean that the will was not in his exclusive possession and control. If the keeping of the will in the drawer rather than the safe means anything, it could easily mean that the testator, having revoked the will, thought that it was no longer a valuable paper and therefore did not keep it in his safe but rather in a drawer in his harness shop where he could look at it and decide whether or not he wanted to make a new will.

Under all of the circumstances shown by this record, we believe that the will should not have been admitted to probate, in view of the fact that it did not contain the signature thereon of the testator and it appearing that the will had, since its execution, remained in his possession and control.

The right of a person to dispose of his property by will did not always exist but was originally created by statute. In view of the fact that a will operates contrary to the statute of descent and permits a person to dispose of his property contrary to the way the law prescribes, we believe that the proponent of a will disposing of property contrary to the statute of descent has the burden of showing the will to be validly executed and effective, and that the presumption against the validity of a will which has been mutilated should not be lightly set aside. This court can see that in the case at bar it could well have been the intention of the testator to give his home to his nephew and namesake, and, while such an intention might be considered commendable, such an intention is contrary to the statute of descent and, therefore, any will which attempts to accomplish that purpose must be established by such evidence as to leave little doubt as to its validity.

For the reasons stated in this opinion, the judgment of the circuit court of Will County is reversed and the cause remanded, with directions to enter an order denying the probate of said will.

Reversed and remanded, with directions.

Notes

1. Attorneys are seldom in attendance when a will is revoked by physical destruction, and it is not surprising to find the courts confronted by a bewildering array of situations involving actions which fall short of total destruction but which might be construed as a burning, tearing, cancelling, or obliterating. Compare Jessup v. Jessup, 221 Va. 61, 267 S.E.2d 115 (1980) (destruction of three of eleven pages and a paragraph from another page constituted a revocation of holographic will, remaining pages intended as instructions for a new will) with Estate of Eglee, 119 R.I. 786, 383 A.2d 586 (1978) (red pencil interlineation through every word and signature, plus the word "obliterated" with testator's initials and a date written diagonally across each clause of the will, did not constitute a revocation under the statute where will remained legible). See generally, Annot., Effect of Testator's Attempted Physical Alteration of Will After Execution, 24 A.L.R.2d 514.

A partial revocation by destruction of a paragraph, sentence or name is theoretically possible. The courts usually require a complete elimination of the name. Compare In re Estate of Newell, 119 Ill.App.2d 385, 256 N.E.2d 53 (1970) (names of two residuary beneficiaries were "pencilled through" but still legible; held acts do not constitute an obliteration and full will entitled to probate) with In re Estate of Bogner, 184 N.W.2d 718 (N.D.1971) (lines drawn through son-in-law's name held an effective obliteration; evidence showed that testator knew that son-in-law had been "participating in depraved moral conduct, including incestuous relationships with one of his daughters"). A holographic will may be partially revoked by cutting out a clause in it as long as the remainder sets out an understandable testamentary disposition. Seeley v. Estate of Seeley, 627 P.2d 1357 (Wy.1981) (will taped back together by testator after material cut out). An attempt to write in a new name will not be effective unless independently signed and witnessed. As an extension of that same theory, courts make difficult the wide use of the partial revocation doctrine by imposing the limitation that the revocation cannot effect a new disposition of the property. Walpole v. Lewis, 254 Ark. 89, 492 S.W.2d 410 (1973); Oliver v. Union National Bank of Springfield, 504 S.W.2d 647 (Mo.App.1974). If that restriction were taken literally no partial revocation would be accepted, but the courts have held that an enlargement of the residuary estate is not a new testamentary act requiring compliance with the statute of wills.   Estate of Becklund, 7 Wash.App. 10, 497 P.2d 1327 (1972).

The statutes permit a third person to destroy the will if under the direction and in the presence of the testator.   In re Estate of Bancker, 232 So.2d 431 (Fla.App.1970) (revocation not effective because persons were not in testator's presence when they, at his bidding, tore up the will and flushed it down the toilet in another room off testator's bedroom).   Estate of Haugk, 91 Wis.2d 196, 280 N.W.2d 684 (1979) (will of wife who was in kitchen not revoked when husband burnt it in basement incinerator;   trial court's finding that she, being thirteen steps away, was in husband's "constructive presence" overturned).

2. There is a presumption that a mutilated will has been revoked.   The presumption is rebuttable.   In McKenzie v. Frances, 214 Va. 104, 197 S.E.2d 221 (1973), the court admitted the will to probate after it was shown by use of an ultraviolet ray that it had been soaked while in a sealed envelope and testimony was introduced that the testator had said she had dropped a drink on it.   For a case in which the presumption was not rebutted, see Jessup v. Jessup, supra note 1.

3. Statutes exist permitting probate of lost or unintentionally destroyed wills.   N.Y.—McKinney's SCPA § 1407 sets as the prerequisites: (1) that it be established that the will was not revoked;   (2) that execution of the will be proven;   and (3) that the provisions of the will are "clearly and distinctly proved by each of at least two credible witnesses or by a copy or draft of the will proved to be true and complete."   For an analysis of facts sufficient to overcome the presumption that a lost will has been revoked, see Estate of Wasco, 444 Pa. 184, 281 A.2d 877, (1971) (original will, retained in files of attorney, lost when attorney predeceased testator).   See Annot., Failure to Replace Lost Will and Revocation, 61 A.L.R.3d 958.

2.   Subsequent Written Instrument

Section 2–507 of the Uniform Probate Code
[Revocation by Writing or by Act.]

A will or any part thereof is revoked

(1) by a subsequent will which revokes the prior will or part expressly or by inconsistency;   or

(2) by being burned, torn, canceled, obliterated, or destroyed, with the intent and for the purpose of revoking it by the testator or by another person in his presence and by his direction.

Notes

1. The case of Harchuck v. Campana, 139 Conn. 549, 550–51, 95 A.2d 566, 567 (1953) presented the following undisputed facts:

John G. Harchuck died on July 21, 1949, leaving an estate and eight surviving children, two sons and six daughters.   On August 24, 1945, he had executed a will leaving all of his property to his two sons, the plaintiffs, and naming them executors of the will.   On March 25, 1949, while ill in Bridgeport Hospital, he signed a paper bearing that date which read: "I, John George Harchuck here by revoke any wills or codicils which I have here to fore made."   The paper also bore the signatures of two witnesses.   On July 29, 1949, the day before the plaintiffs filed their application for the probating of the will, one of the decedent's other heirs, in an application to the court, stated that the decedent had left no will and asked that she be appointed administratrix of the estate.

The trial court found that the will had been revoked by a "cancelling." The Supreme Court of Errors reversed, holding that the attempted revocation was by a subsequent instrument which was ineffective because witnessed by only two rather than the required three witnesses. (The Connecticut Statute has since been changed to require only two witnesses.)

2. If the statute permits revocation by "some other writing" or is silent on the point, nontestamentary writings have sometimes been accepted as a revocation of the will. Annot., Revocation of Will by Nontestamentary Writing, 22 A.L.R.3d 1346 (1968). But see Kronauge v. Stoecklein, 33 Ohio App.2d 229, 293 N.E.2d 320 (1972) (a statement in the margin, "This will is void" plus an explanation as to why it was void and a date did not effect a revocation).

N.Y.—McKinney's EPTL § 3–4.3 states: "A conveyance, settlement or other act of a testator by which an estate in his property, previously disposed of by will, is altered but not wholly divested does not revoke such disposition, but the estate in the property that remains in the testator passes to the beneficiaries pursuant to the disposition. However, any such conveyance, settlement or other act of the testator which is wholly inconsistent with such previous testamentary disposition revokes it." An issue arose under this statute whether the provisions of a separation agreement between a husband and wife were "wholly inconsistent" with the terms of decedent's will so as to cause a revocation of his will in her favor. (Had the parties divorced, that fact would have revoked provisions for her in his will under N.Y.—McKinney's EPTL § 5–1.4). The Court of Appeals held that the general release in the separation agreement waived only the spouse's statutory claims against her husband's estate and did not cover voluntary bequests to her. The last sentence of N.Y.—McKinney's EPTL § 3–4.3 was given a strict reading to apply only when the agreement either "explicitly renounces" any testamentary dispositions made before the agreement became effective or "unequivocally manifests an intent on the part of the spouses that they are no longer beneficiaries under each other's wills". Estate of Maruccia, 54 N.Y.2d 196, 445 N.Y.S.2d 73, 429 N.E.2d 751 (1981). See also Estate of Coffed, 46 N.Y.2d 514, 414 N.Y.S.2d 893, 387 N.E.2d 1209 (1979) (separation agreement abrogated contract to execute reciprocal wills but did not revoke the will executed pursuant to that contract).

IN RE CABLE'S WILL

Supreme Court of New York, Appellate Division, Third Department, 1925.
213 App.Div. 512, 210 N.Y.S. 187, affirmed mem. 242 N.Y. 510,
152 N.E. 405 (1925).

VAN KIRK, J. On November 16, 1923, Newell Cable died, leaving a last will and testament, dated January 15, 1912, to which were physically attached codicils numbered consecutively from 1 to 11. In his will he gave his residuary estate to a niece, Bertha W. Williams. By the third codicil he revoked this residuary clause, and gave the residue, share and share alike, to his nephews and nieces. By the fourth codicil he revoked the part of the third codicil which gave the residue to nephews and nieces, and in place thereof gave the residue to six churches named.   In the fifth codicil he revoked the bequest in the fourth codicil to the First Baptist Church of Walton, and gave it to the Free Methodist Church.   There was another codicil, not numbered [and not included in the eleven numbered codicils attached to the will. Ed.], which was executed by Newell Cable February 3, 1923, between the dates of the ninth and tenth [numbered] codicils.   By this codicil he revoked the provisions of the fourth and fifth codicils giving the residue to the six churches, and in place thereof gave to each of seven churches $1,000 and the residue of his estate to 13 nephews and nieces, one of whom was Bertha W. Williams.   At that time Newell Cable was an old man, sick at his home, where he had for many years been living with Bertha W. Williams.   She told testator's attorney, John G. More, who drew the will and all of the codicils, that Mr. Cable wished to make a codicil to his will, and gave the instructions as to its contents.   More so prepared it.   She shortly thereafter telephoned More to come up to make out the income tax reports for Mr. Cable and to bring the codicil.   After the income tax reports had been completed, the codicil was produced and was executed by Newell Cable.   So far as appears, he had never seen or heard of it before.

About two weeks later Mr. Cable went to the home of Mary Cable in Walton.   Attorney More was called to the house, and Mr. Cable said to him that he had not wanted to sign the paper which he signed the other morning;   he had never told More to draw it up, and More replied, "that is true;"   he did not want to make any changes;   his will was as he wanted it;   he got to town just as soon as he was able.   He sent More to his office to get the paper, and on More's return said, "I want it burned up."   In the presence of three witnesses it was burned, and Mr. Cable then said, "I have the thing back as I want it now."   The surrogate has found that this destroyed codicil was executed in compliance with the statute (Decedent Estate Law, § 21) and was a valid testamentary paper.   Every codicil contained this introductory paragraph:

> "I, Newell Cable, of Walton, Delaware county, New York, having made my last will and testament bearing date the 15th day of January, 1912, do now make, publish and declare this codicil thereto, which is to be taken as an addition to, and a part of my said last will and testament."

Also this clause:

> "And I hereby ratify and confirm my said last will and testament in every respect save so far as any part of the same is inconsistent with this codicil."

This is the wording in the first codicil.   Mr. More says that in drafting each codicil he used the same form;   in all the later codicils the scrivener has evidently by oversight changed the word "save" to "in," except that in the second, third, fourth, and fifth codicils he inserts, after the words "last will and testament," the words "and codicil thereto."   The above facts are undisputed, except that the residuary legatees under the fourth and fifth codicils claim that, when the destroyed codicil was executed, Newell Cable acted under undue influence and restraint.   The surrogate has admitted the will and the 11 codicils to probate.

Assuming that the destroyed codicil was a valid testamentary instrument, the first question we consider is whether the fourth and fifth codicils, revoked by the destroyed codicil, had been revived and were at the time of Newell Cable's death a part of the testamentary disposition of his estate. This revocation did not revive the fourth and fifth codicils, which had been thus revoked; nor were the declarations of the testator at the time and after the destruction of the paper sufficient to revive these codicils. To revive a will it must be republished in compliance with the statutory requirements for the publication of a will. Matter of Kuntz, 163 App.Div. 125, 148 N.Y.S. 382. If those codicils be revived, it resulted from the publication of the tenth and eleventh [numbered] codicils. In section 2 of the Decedent Estate Law is this definition:

> "The term 'will,' as used in this chapter, shall include all codicils, as well as wills."

Section 41 of the Decedent Estate Law provides:

> *"Canceling or Revocation of Second Will Not to Revive First.*—If, after the making of any will, the testator shall duly make and execute a second will, the destruction, canceling or revocation of such second will shall not revive the first will, unless it appear by the terms of such revocation, that it was his intention to revive and give effect to his first will; or unless after such destruction, canceling or revocation, he shall duly republish his first will."

This statute provides specifically for the reviving of a prior will (including codicil), which had been revoked[,] by republishing it. Under section 41 a republishing is not simply a redeclaration or a reacknowledgment of a prior or valid will, but it accomplishes the revival of a revoked or dead will. If, then a codicil is a part of the will, it is revived when the will is revived, unless a contrary intent is disclosed. It is established in our courts that a codicil duly executed becomes a valid, integral part of the testamentary disposition; it does not revoke the will, except in the particular respects stated in the codicil, or in those respects in which the codicil is absolutely inconsistent with provisions of the will. It modifies or changes in part the will, and with the will is to be read and executed as one entire instrument. Bloodgood v. Lewis, 209 N.Y. 95, 102 N.E. 610; Ward v. Ward, 105 N.Y. 68, 11 N.E. 373.

The tenth and eleventh codicils [numbered] were duly executed with all the statutory formalities. So far as our statute and our decisions require, everything was done by this testator to revive these two codicils. In our view, the execution of the tenth and eleventh codicils was a republication of the fourth and fifth codicils, and revived them, if such was the intention of the testator. Brown v. Clark, 77 N.Y. 369; Matter of Campbell's Will, 170 N.Y. 84, 62 N.E. 1070. Whether a former codicil is revived depends upon the testator's intention, which is to be deduced from all the circumstances. Williams v. Williams, 142 Mass. 515, 8 N.E. 424.

The plain intent of the testator must control, when it does not run counter to established law or public policy. Evidently the testator believed that, when he burned the codicil of February 3d, he revived the fourth and fifth codicils, and left the disposition of his estate at that time as provided in his will and the nine codicils, and such was his intent. This intent is not only shown by the circumstances, but is disclosed by the undisputed declarations of the testator at the time he burned the codicil. It is true that such declarations are inadmissible to aid the interpretation of the provisions of the will. If admitted for such purpose, they might tend to overthrow the words of the written instrument, and oral declarations cannot be authenticated in the manner required for a valid testamentary disposition of property. Wigmore, § 2471. But the declarations are admissible to show intent, motive, or plan, if they are statements "of a present existing state of mind" accompanying the act in question, and "appear to have been made in a natural manner and not under circumstances of suspicion."

The intention or plan in mind can generally be shown by some act or speech only, and when the person is dead, evidence thereof is often not only the best, but the only, evidence of what was in his mind at the time. Wigmore, § 1725; Commonwealth v. Trefethen, 157 Mass. 180, 185, 31 N.E. 961, 24 L.R.A. 235. A design to do or not to do a specific act is always relevant to show that the act named was or was not done. Wigmore, § 1735. Under our statute, supra, these declarations were not sufficient to show that the revoked codicils were revived. They are relevant to show the intent with which the revocation of the burned codicil was made. It is said in Matter of Kennedy's Will, 167 N.Y. 163, 173, 60 N.E. 442, 445:

> "The general rule is that, where an act is done, to which it is necessary or important to ascribe a motive or a cause, what was said by the actor at the time, from which the motive or the cause may be collected, is part of the res gestae, and may be given in evidence."

These two codicils, as is true of all save the burned codicil, were never detached from the will; in the majority of them the testator simply revoked a $1,000 bequest, because he had advanced the payment of it; he could not have intended to republish the will itself, and not republish these codicils. He intended to republish all the codicils at the time attached to his will; with the will they stated his completed testamentary plan.

The burned codicil stands differently. There is no proof in the case that the instructions for the preparation or the contents of the burned codicil were ever given by the testator; the evidence shows the contrary. As soon after its execution as he was able to reach Mr. More, he demanded the paper and that it be burned, and, having been burned, he declared in substance that his will was then as he wanted it to be; that the burned codicil was never his will. Though in law it was properly executed, in fact he never intended it to express his testamentary wish. There is nothing in the record tending to show that he ever changed this intention so unequivocally demonstrated. The burned codicil was never attached to his will and was not in existence. He had not simply revoked it by a later codicil, as was his practice; he burned it; he meant to be rid forever of the paper he never desired to execute. We think it is a fair inference that this pronounced intent and plan continued.   On what can it be found that he ever changed this intent, or that he intended to revive or recognize the burned codicil?   In 40 Cyc. 1217, is this:

> "A codicil may, by referring in adequate terms to a revoked will, revive that will if it be in existence, but not if it has been burnt or otherwise destroyed."

Rule

Had the testator intended to revive the burned codicil, he would certainly have rewritten it, and would not have left its provision to the uncertainty of memory.

We have concluded that, by publishing the tenth and eleventh codicils, he revived and gave effect to the fourth and fifth codicils, but did not revive the burnt codicil.   It would involve a curious inconsistency of intent to hold that he intended to revive the two codicils, and at the same time and by the same act he intended to revive the codicil which would on the instant revoke them.   Of this testator's intention there can be no doubt;   this plain intention, no law or statute forbidding it, we conclude should be made effective.   We find no sufficient reason for denying him his will.   See Matter of Fowles' Will, 222 N.Y. 222, 232, 233, 118 N.E. 611, Ann.Cas.1918D, 834.

Since we have reached this conclusion, it is not necessary to determine whether or not there was evidence which should have been submitted to the jury tending to show that the destroyed codicil was executed under restraint or undue influence.   If it were, the result would be the same as above reached.

As to the English cases cited, we quote from Matter of Conway's Will, 124 N.Y. 455, 460, 26 N.E. 1028, 1030 (11 L.R.A. 796):

> "A brief reference to the state of the law relating to the execution of wills in England will make it apparent that neither the decisions of its courts nor the rules deduced therefrom by English textwriters can be made applicable to cases arising under our statute."

We find no errors in the record which were prejudicial.   The decision of the surrogate should be affirmed, with costs to the executor payable out of the estate.

HINMAN and McCANN, JJ., concur.

COCHRANE, P. J., concurs in result.

HENRY T. KELLOGG, J., dissents.

Notes

1. The rule in the English common law courts was that a first will which had not been physically destroyed but had been revoked by a second will was revived by the revocation of the second will.   The ecclesiastical courts held that a will of personal property was only revived if the testator's intent, as gleaned from all the circumstances, favored revival.   The matter is now governed in England by a statute similar to New York's.   The cases from jurisdictions without statutes in this country follow one or the other of the two original English rules.   See Atkinson on Wills, 474 (1953).   The New York statute has been reworded but is basically unchanged as to substance.   N.Y. EPTL 3–4.6.

UPC § 2–509 is in accord and permits the admission of "testator's contemporary or subsequent declarations" to assist in determining intent. See generally, Annot., Codicil as Reviving Revoked Will or Codicil, 33 A.L.R.2d 922 (1954).

2. Careful planning and drafting is necessary to make sure that the provisions in the will and in the codicil are not in conflict. A codicil should refer to the will in explicit terms, identify the parts to be changed, set forth the new (substituted or additional) provisions, and reaffirm and republish the will except as so modified. 7 Powell ¶ 966 (1974). It is generally advisable to use a codicil only to effect minor changes in the dispositive scheme.

LACROIX v. SENECAL

Supreme Court of Errors of Connecticut, 1953.
140 Conn. 311, 99 A.2d 115.

BROWN, Chief Justice. The plaintiff, a niece of the testatrix, who was left nothing under her aunt's will and codicil, brought this action for a declaratory judgment as heir and next of kin. She asked in effect for a decree that one-half of the residuary estate of the testatrix is intestate and that she, as heir, is entitled to that one-half interest. The plaintiff's claim of intestacy is predicated upon the fact that one of the three subscribing witnesses of the codicil was the husband of the defendant Aurea Senecal, to whom one-half of the residue was given by the express terms of both instruments. The court held that the residuary devise and bequest to the defendant under the codicil was void but that there was no resulting intestacy as to that portion of the residue, because the gift thereof under the will is valid. The plaintiff has appealed.

The testatrix, Celestine L. Dupre, died in Putnam on April 19, 1951, leaving as her heir at law and next of kin her niece, the plaintiff. The testatrix left a will dated March 26, 1951, and a codicil thereto dated April 10, 1951. These instruments were admitted to probate on May 22, 1951. Item five of the will reads as follows: "All the rest, residue and remainder of my property of whatsoever the same may consist and wheresoever the same may be situated, both real and personal, I give, devise and bequeath one-half to my nephew, Nelson Lamoth of Taftville, Connecticut, to be his absolutely; the other one-half to Aurea Senecal of 200 Providence Street, Putnam, Connecticut, to be hers absolutely."

The codicil reads as follows: "1. I hereby revoke Item Five of said will and substitute for said Item Five the following: Item Five: All the rest, residue and remainder of property of whatsoever the same may consist and wheresoever the same may be situated, both real and personal, I give, devise and bequeath one-half to my nephew Marcisse Lamoth of Taftville, Connecticut, also known as Nelson Lamoth, to be his absolutely; the other one-half to Aurea Senecal of 200 Providence Street, Putnam, Connecticut to be hers absolutely. 2. I hereby republish and confirm my said will in all respects except as altered by this Codicil."

Aurea Senecal is not related to the testatrix. One of the three subscribing witnesses to the codicil was Adolphe Senecal, who at the time he witnessed the codicil was, and still is, the husband of Aurea Senecal. Section 6952 of the General Statutes, so far as material, provides as

*hvsb with cod,
but Not orig will!*

follows: "Every devise or bequest given in any will or codicil to a subscribing witness, or to the husband or wife of such subscribing witness, shall be void unless such will or codicil shall be legally attested without the signature of such witness * * * ; but the competency of such witness shall not be affected by any such devise or bequest." As the court pointed out in its memorandum of decision, any bequest to Aurea Senecal in item five of the codicil was void because her husband was a subscribing witness. The question left to be answered, therefore, was whether the devise or bequest to the defendant Aurea under item five of the original will stands. It is to be noted that the only difference between item five of the will and item five of the codicil is the substitution for the words "my nephew, Nelson Lamoth of Taftville, Connecticut," in the former, of the words "my nephew, Marcisse Lamoth of Taftville, Connnecticut, also known as Nelson Lamoth," in the latter. It is also to be noted that by the second paragraph of the codicil the testatrix confirmed the will "in all respects except as altered by this Codicil."

I

The defendants' brief suggests that the issue on this appeal is whether the doctrine of dependent relative revocation may be invoked to sustain a gift by will, when such gift has been revoked in a codicil which substantially reaffirmed the gift but was void as to it, under § 6952, by reason of the interest of a subscribing witness. The gist of the doctrine is that if a testator cancels or destroys a will with a present intention of making a new one immediately and as a substitute and the new will is not made or, if made, fails of effect for any reason, it will be presumed that the testator preferred the old will to intestacy, and the old one will be admitted to probate in the absence of evidence overcoming the presumption. 1 Page, Wills (Lifetime Ed.) p. 885; 1 Schouler, Wills, Executors & Administrators (6th Ed.) § 632; 57 Am.Jur. 356, § 514; note, 24 A.L.R.2d 514, 554. The rule has been more simply stated in these words: "[W]here the intention to revoke is conditional and where the condition is not fulfilled, the revocation is not effective." Matter of Macomber's Will, 274 App.Div. 724, 725, 87 N.Y.S.2d 308, 310. As is stated in that opinion at page 727, the doctrine has had wide acceptance in both England and the United States. It is a rule of presumed intention rather than of substantive law; McIntyre v. McIntyre, 120 Ga. 67, 70, 47 S.E. 501; notes, 62 A.L.R. 1367, 1401, 115 A.L.R. 710, 721, 57 Am.Jur. 357, § 515; and is applicable in cases of partial as well as total revocation. Gardner v. Gardiner [sic. Gardiner], 65 N.H. 230, 232, 19 A. 651, 8 L.R.A. 383; Schneider v. Harrington, 320 Mass. 723, 726, 71 N.E.2d 242; In re Roeder's Estate, 44 N.M. 578, 588, 106 P.2d 847; 57 Am.Jur. 358, § 516. That it can only apply when there is a clear intent of the testator that the revocation of the old is made conditional upon the validity of the new is well brought out in Sanderson v. Norcross, 242 Mass. 43, 45, 136 N.E. 170, and in Estate of Kaufman, 25 Cal.2d 854, 858, 155 P.2d 831, where many cases are cited.

Rule

The doctrine has long been accepted in Connecticut, notwithstanding the plaintiff's claim that we should adopt the contrary view. In 1898, Justice Simeon E. Baldwin stated in a case involving a question of this nature: "It being [the testator's] manifest intention to revoke the provision in the will only for this purpose, so far as the purpose fails of effect, the revocation must fall with it.   *   *   *   The revocation of his former provision   *   *   *   was indissolubly coupled with the creation of the substituted provision.   It may be given effect so far as the substitution is valid, but no further, because so only can the plain purpose of the testator be attained, and the mutual dependence of the two articles   *   *   * preserved.   The whole instrument was a single testamentary act, and must be read as if the testator had expressly declared that he revoked the gift made   *   *   *   in his will simply in order to put it in a different form.   Rudy v. Ulrich, 69 Pa. 177, 183;   Stickney v. Hammond, 138 Mass. 116, 120;   Powell v. Powell, L.R. 1 Prob. & Div. 209.   The rule of construction upon which we proceed is analogous to that governing a revocation which is grounded on a state of facts which proves not to exist. It falls when its foundation falls.   Dunham v. Averill, 45 Conn. [61] 62." Security Co. v. Snow, 70 Conn. 288, 293, 39 A. 153, 155.

In a later case involving the principle, we stated: "The case, therefore, is within the reason of the rule that a writing purporting to revoke a will on account of the existence of a certain fact does not revoke it if there be no such fact.   Dunham v. Averill, 45 Conn. 61, 80.   It is true that the mistake is, at bottom, one of law.   [The testatrix] supposed that her unsigned and unattested will would have full effect upon her decease. In law it had no effect.   But as respects a question of this nature, it is immaterial whether the mistake under which the act of revocation was done were one of fact or law.   The act was nothing unless done with the intent of revocation.   If the intent to revoke was, as in this case, clearly dependent on a reliance upon a certain legal consequence attributed to certain circumstances, an error in attributing that effect to them is as effectual a bar to an actual revocation as if it were a pure error of fact. Security Co. v. Snow, 70 Conn. 288, 294, 39 A. 153;   Stickney v. Hammond, 138 Mass. 116, 120;   Clarkson v. Clarkson, 2 Sw. & Tr. 497." Strong's Appeal, 79 Conn. 123, 125, 63 A. 1089, 6 L.R.A.,N.S., 1107.   The plaintiff's contention that the principle adopted by this court in the above cases was overruled by Blakeman v. Sears, 74 Conn. 516, 51 A. 517, is unwarranted.   Not only did the court make no reference therein to the doctrine of dependent relative revocation but in 74 Conn. at page 519, 51 A. at page 518, it expressly pointed out that the disposition of the corpus of the testator's estate as "made in the will he radically changed in the codicil."

So far as the factual situation is concerned, it would be difficult to conceive of a more deserving case for the application of the doctrine of dependent relative revocation than the one before us.   There is no room for doubt that the sole purpose of the testatrix in executing the codicil was, by making the very minor change in referring to her nephew, to eliminate any uncertainty as to his identity.   Obviously, it was furthest from her intention to make any change in the disposition of her residuary estate.   When the will and codicil are considered together, as they must be, to determine the intent of the testatrix, it is clear that her intention to revoke the will was conditioned upon the execution of a codicil which would be effective to continue the same disposition of her residuary estate. Therefore, when it developed that the gift under the codicil to the defendant Aurea was void, the conditional intention of the testatrix to revoke the will was rendered inoperative, and the gift to Aurea under the will continued in effect. The situation is well summed up in this statement by the court in a case on all fours with the one at bar: "When a testator repeats the same dispositive plan in a new will, revocation of the old one by the new is deemed inseparably related to and dependent upon the legal effectiveness of the new." Estate of Kaufman, 25 Cal.2d 854, 860, 155 P.2d 831, 834. In short, in the words of the court in Matter of Macomber's Will, 274 App.Div. 724, 728, 87 N.Y.S.2d 308, 312, "the facts here fit well within the classic pattern of the rule in its most reliable aspect, and it ought to be applied to the facts of this case."

It only remains to consider the plaintiff's further claim that, even though the doctrine of dependent relative revocation does prevail in Connecticut, it cannot be applied in the present case because of the reason for the invalidity of the gift under the codicil to the defendant Aurea. The claim is that, since the history of § 6952 shows that from the beginning its purpose was to prevent the subversion of wills, the doctrine considered above cannot be utilized as a means of defeating the very purpose of this express statutory provision. There very likely could be a case where on the facts there would be force to this argument. However, this cannot be said to be so here. The history of the statute as traced in the plaintiff's brief shows that the subversion of wills which it was designed to prevent was that which results from the scheming activities of persons in a position to utilize the capacity of attesting witnesses to take advantage of testators by overpersuading them to make wills in favor of the scheming persons. There is no intimation of any such improper attempt or achievement in the case before us. As has already been pointed out, no change of beneficiaries or in the amount or nature of any of the gifts under the will was made by the codicil. The sole motivating cause of its execution was an attempt by the testatrix to confirm and make more certain the gift to her nephew which she had already expressly provided for in the will. Under these circumstances, the purpose of § 6952 is neither challenged nor thwarted by applying the doctrine of dependent relative revocation in order to realize the obvious testamentary intent of this testatrix. As was well pointed out in a closely analogous case: "The doctrine of dependent relative revocation is basically an application of the rule that a testator's intention governs; it is not a doctrine defeating that intent. It should be applied in this case." Linkins v. Protestant Episcopal Cathedral Foundation, 87 U.S.App.D.C. 351, 187 F.2d 357, 360, 28 A.L.R.2d 521.

Since the defendants expressly stated that no claim is made under their cross appeal in the event that the plaintiff fails to prevail on her appeal, the former calls for no consideration.

There is no error.

In this opinion the other judges concurred.

Notes

1. The doctrine of dependent relative revocation is most frequently used in instances where the revocation was induced by some mistaken assumption of law or fact on the part of the testator. It was initially applied in cases involving revocation by physical act but is now regularly extended to cases where the revocation was by subsequent instrument. See e.g. Estate of Shelly, 484 Pa. 322, 399 A.2d 98 (1979) (invalid later will did not revoke earlier will); Carter v. First United Methodist Church, 246 Ga. 352, 271 S.E.2d 493 (1980) (earlier will valid under the doctrine, although testator had drawn pencil line through the dispositive provisions). The doctrine has been described as follows: "In the main the doctrine is a fictional process which consists of disregarding revocation brought about by mistake on the feigned grounds that the revocation was conditional." Atkinson on Wills, 454 (1953). To the effect that the doctrine is not an arbitrary rule of law but rather is a rule of presumed intention and is only to be applied in furtherance of testator's intent, see Estate of Patten, 179 Mont. 299, 587 P.2d 1307 (1978). See generally Palmer, Dependent Relative Revocation and Its Relation to Relief for Mistake, 69 Mich.L.Rev. 989 (1971).

2. A revocation clause may be conditional on an express condition in which case the revocation does not go into effect until the condition has been satisfied. In like manner the will itself may be subject to a condition precedent before it becomes operative. In Eaton v. Brown, 193 U.S. 411, 24 S.Ct. 487, 48 L.Ed. 730 (1904), the will opened: "I am going on a Journey and may, not ever return. And if I do not, this is my last request." Justice Holmes for the Court held that a reading of the document and a consideration of the facts indicated that her bounty was not conditional on her failure to return from her journey. If the will uses conditional language, the court must determine whether the language represents the inducement or occasion for making the will or whether it was intended as a condition precedent to the operation of the document. Modern authority prefers the former construction. Mason v. Mason, 268 S.E.2d 67 (W. Va.1980) (recovery from surgery did not render will inoperative). Even if the condition is expressed in unambiguous terms, courts may find from an examination of the will as a whole that the testator meant it to be absolute and not conditional. See e.g. Estate of Gardner, 615 P.2d 1215 (Utah 1980) ("In the event my husband precedes me in death I leave all etc." did not cause will to fail because husband survived testator).

3. Despite the mistake of the testatrix as to her nephew's name, the bequest in the principal case would probably have gone to the proper party even without the attempted corrective codicil. Courts do not hold themselves to rigid standards of literal interpretation in cases of this nature, since primary concern must be directed towards the substance of a testator's disposition, rather than the formal accuracy of a beneficiary's name. Indulgence has generally been shown to the intentions of testators who designate beneficiaries generally known by names other than their true names (including nicknames), and there have been some cases which hold that clear mistakes in the description of a beneficiary may be judicially corrected. See, e.g., Siegley v. Simpson, 73 Wash. 69, 131 P. 479 (1913) (testator naming Richard Simpson as beneficiary, found to have meant H. Simpson—otherwise known as "Rotary Bill"). See Restatement of Property §§ 241–43, and, in particular, § 242, Comment *d*.

3. *Revocation by Operation of Law—Change in Family Situation*

The statutes of a number of jurisdictions present a variety of provisions calling for revocation of the will, in whole or in part, when the composition of the immediate family changes after execution. The following are representative:

Conn.Gen.Stat. § 45–162(a)

If, after the making of a will, the testator marries or is divorced or his marriage is annulled or dissolved or a child is born to the testator or a minor child is legally adopted by him, or a child is born as a result of A.I.D. as defined in section 45–69f, to which the testator has consented in accordance with subsection (a) of section 45–69g, and no provision has been made in such will for such contingency, such marriage, divorce, annulment, dissolution, birth or adoption of a minor child shall operate as a revocation of such will, provided such divorce, annulment or dissolution shall not operate as a revocation of such will if the spouse of the testator was not a beneficiary under such will. * * *

Uniform Probate Code § 2–508
[Revocation by Divorce; No Revocation by Other Changes of Circumstances.]

If after executing a will the testator is divorced or his marriage annulled, the divorce or annulment revokes any disposition or appointment of property made by the will to the former spouse, any provision conferring a general or special power of appointment on the former spouse, and any nomination of the former spouse as executor, trustee, conservator, or guardian, unless the will expressly provides otherwise. Property prevented from passing to a former spouse because of revocation by divorce or annulment passes as if the former spouse failed to survive the decedent, and other provisions conferring some power or office on the former spouse are interpreted as if the spouse failed to survive the decedent. If provisions are revoked solely by this section, they are revived by testator's remarriage to the former spouse. For purposes of this section, divorce or annulment means any divorce or annulment which would exclude the spouse as a surviving spouse within the meaning of Section 2–802(b). A decree of separation which does not terminate the status of husband and wife is not a divorce for purposes of this section. No change of circumstances other than as described in this section revokes a will.

Notes

1. It should be noted that these statutes give way to a showing of intent in the will contrary to their provisions. Thus, for example, in Connecticut if the will makes a gift to the afterborn child or specifically disinherits him or her, the statutory revocation does not become effective. Illustrative Will, Article Twelve, p. 317, supra. Difficult problems of construction may arise as to whether a general provision which disinherits anyone who may contest the will applies to afterborn children in such a way as to bar the revocation. See Goff v. Goff, supra, p. 183; Van Strien v. Jones, 46 Cal.2d 705, 299 P.2d 1 (1956). Statutes revoking a will by testator's subsequent marriage are frequently con-

ditioned on there being no contrary provision in the will or provision by marriage contract. A, the husband, divorced B, making a divorce settlement in her favor. He then executed a will in which his daughter was the principal beneficiary. He subsequently remarried B, dying soon thereafter. The will was not revoked by his remarriage to B because in this context the divorce settlement constituted a marriage contract. Riesterer v. Dietmeier, 98 Nev. 279, 646 P.2d 551 (Nev. 1982).

2. A statute that revokes provisions in a will favoring a divorced spouse has been construed to revoke as well an inter vivos life insurance trust which was executed on the same day as the will and into which the probate estate was to pour. Miller v. First National Bank & Trust Co., 637 P.2d 75 (Ok.1981) (5–3 decision). In the absence of statute, the courts are divided on the effect of divorce on an existing will. See the discussion of the opposing positions in the majority and dissenting opinions in Luff v. Luff, 359 F.2d 235 (C.A.D.C.1966), adopting for the District of Columbia the rule that divorce accompanied by a property settlement revokes a prior will (in the absence of a contrary manifestation of intent). The rule cannot, however, be expanded to revoke a will favoring testator's stepchildren when testator's divorced wife (mother of the children) predeceased him. Matter of Rice, 118 N.H. 528, 390 A.2d 1146 (1978).

4. *Revocation by Operation of Law—Change in Property Holdings*

a. *Ademption*

IN RE ESTATE OF NAKONECZNY
Supreme Court of Pennsylvania, 1974.
456 Pa. 320, 319 A.2d 893.

NIX, Justice. Michael Nakoneczny died testate on January 26, 1970, leaving a Will dated November 5, 1956, an insurance agreement executed the same day and two codicils dated May 4, 1966 and March 27, 1967 respectively. The Will and codicils were admitted to probate and an inventory and appraisement were filed showing a gross estate of $545,483.21. This is an appeal from the denial of exceptions filed to the Opinion, Order and Decree of Distribution by appellants, Paul Nakoneczny, son of testator, and his wife, Stella. The exceptions were dismissed and the Decree of the auditing judge was affirmed by the Court en banc on April 25, 1972.

ADEMPTION OF THE SPECIFIC DEVISE
OF THE PREMISES
3039 PREBLE AVENUE

In paragraph four of his will testator provided:

"FOURTH: I give, devise and bequeath that certain parcel of real estate situate at 3039 Preble Avenue, Pittsburgh, Pennsylvania, which is presently operated as a tavern, together with all fixtures forming a part of the said realty and all equipment necessary to the operation of the said tavern, to my son, PAUL NAKONECZNY, if he survives me. It is my desire that my Executor secure, if at all possible, the transfer of the liquor license to my son, PAUL NAKONECZNY, if he is then living."

In November of 1956, testator owned the building situated at 3039 Preble Avenue, Pittsburgh. A portion of these premises was used in the operation of a restaurant and barroom by testator and the remainder served as a dwelling for him and his family. Decedent operated this business until January 1960 when he gave the business, equipment, supplies and liquor license to his son, the appellant, Paul Nakoneczny. In May of 1968, the property was acquired by the Urban Redevelopment Authority and the bulk of the proceeds were used by decedent to purchase certain bonds which he retained and remained in his possession until his death. The auditing judge found that there had been an ademption and denied appellants' claim to the bonds that had been purchased with the proceeds derived from the sale of the Preble Avenue property. We agree.

It has long since been decided in this jurisdiction that a specific legacy or devise is extinguished if the property is not in existence or does not belong to the testator at the time of his death. Soles' Estate, 451 Pa. 568, 304 A.2d 97 (1973); McFerren's Estate, 365 Pa. 490, 76 A.2d 759 (1950); Horn's Estate, 317 Pa. 49, 175 A. 414 (1934); Harshaw v. Harshaw, 184 Pa. 401, 39 A. 89 (1898); Hoke v. Herman, 21 Pa. 301 (1853); Blackstone v. Blackstone, 3 Watts 335 (1834). Testator's intent is not relevant where the property devised or bequeathed in his will is not part of his estate at death. Where the legacy has been determined to be specific "[t]he legatee is entitled to the very thing bequeathed if it be possible for the executor to give it to him; but if not, he cannot have money in place of it. This results from an inflexible rule of law applied to the mere fact that the thing bequeathed does not exist, and it is not founded on any presumed intention of the testator." * * * This rule is equally applicable where the specifically devised or bequeathed property is removed from testator during his lifetime by an involuntary act or by operation of law.[6] Harshaw v. Harshaw, supra; Pleasants' Appeal, 77 Pa. 356 (1875). Thus, where it is established that the bequest or devise was specific and the nonexistence of the item in the testator's estate at the time of death, an ademption results.

The only issue crucial to the resolution of the problem presented is whether the devise of the realty in this case was specific. A specific devise is a gift by will of a specific parcel which is identified and distinguished from all other parcels of land, and which may be satisfied only by delivery of the particular parcel of property. Soles' Estate, supra, 451 Pa. 573, 304 A.2d 97; Snyder's Estate, 217 Pa. 71, 66 A. 157 (1907). Appellant first argues that this was a demonstrative devise and thus not subject to ademption. He argues that paragraphs seven[7] and eight[8]

---

6. "It was once thought that ademption was dependent on intention, and it was, therefore, held in old days that when a change was effected by public authority, or without the will of the testator, ademption did not follow. But for many years, that has ceased to be law. * * * What courts look to now is the fact of change. That ascertained, they do not trouble themselves about the reason for the change." In Re Brann, 219 N.Y. 263, 114 N.E. 404, 405 (1918) (Cardozo J.)

7. "Paragraph Seventh: Subject to the provisions of Paragraphs Third and Fourth, I authorize my Executor to sell any and all real estate of which I die seised, at public or private sale, for such prices and upon such terms and conditions as it shall deem advisable, and to make, execute and deliver good and sufficient deed or deeds there [sic]."

8. "Paragraph Eighth: Subject to the provisions of Paragraphs Third and Fourth, I authorize my Executor to make distribution of my estate in kind, in cash or partly in kind and partly in cash, as my Executor shall believe advisable."

evidence a clear intention on the part of decedent to assure Paul's right to the proceeds in the event the Preble Avenue property was sold. Although, as has been stated, <u>intention is not relevant on the question of ademption,</u> it is relevant when the issue to be determined is whether the legacy is demonstrative or specific. Shearer's Estate, 346 Pa. 97, 29 A.2d 535 (1943); Walls v. Stewart, 16 Pa. 275, 281–282 (1851). Further, that intention must be gathered not only from the language used in creating the bequest or devise but from the provisions of the will as a whole, and if there is doubt, courts are inclined to find a demonstrative rather than a specific legacy, devise or bequest. Shearer's Estate, supra, 346 Pa. at 101, 29 A.2d 535. See also Crawford's Estate, 293 Pa. 570, 574, 143 A. 214 (1928). Here, however, the language of paragraph four leaves no question of the intent to create a specific devise. Nor do we find any merit in the suggestion that paragraphs 7 and 8 in any way alters [sic] this conclusion. Clearly paragraphs 7 and 8 were merely limiting the power of the Executor to prevent the sale of the property that was designated in paragraph 4 as the subject of the specific devise provided that the property was an asset of the estate at the time of death. In our judgment, these paragraphs strengthen rather than weaken the view that testator intended a specific devise.

Appellant's reliance upon *Shearer's Estate*, supra, is misplaced. In *Shearer's Estate*, the testator created by will a trust for the benefit of his son, for and during the lifetime of the son. After describing his farm along with the stock and personal property thereon as the corpus of the trust, testator provided:

> "[t]he value of the said farm and contents I fix at the sum of Six Thousand Dollars, so that my said son shall receive the use and benefit of said amount out of my estate."

From other provisions in the document it was clear that testator was attempting to equalize the distributions among his children. This Court there properly held:

> " * * * it is quite obvious that the intention of testator was that his son Clayton should, in all events, receive the benefit of an amount of $6,000, his paramount desire being to equalize the shares of his children after taking into consideration the amounts that some of them had received in his lifetime. As Jacob had already obtained $6,000, and each daughter $2,000, he gave to each daughter $4,000 more and to Clayton the farm and its contents, the value of which he expressly fixed at the sum of $6,000 'so that my said son shall receive the use and benefit of *said amount* out of my estate.'" 346 Pa. at 101, 29 A.2d at 537.

As evident as testator's "demonstrative" intent was in *Shearer*, the intent of this testator to make a specific devise is equally as apparent. The fourth paragraph fails to express any intention to carry with it the proceeds from a possible sale of the subject real estate.

Appellant's reliance upon Frost's Estate, 354 Pa. 223, 47 A.2d 219 (1946) is also of no avail. In Frost's Estate, supra, where testatrix provided a gift to her brother and sisters of the <u>proceeds</u> of her General Motors stock and prior to death sold the stock, however the funds were traceable, we held that the gift was not adeemed. Our decision in *Frost* was a recognition of a distinction between a gift of stock and a gift of its proceeds. Consistent with the decisions in a number of other jurisdictions we held in the latter instance where the money can be traced the gift is not adeemed and the legatee is entitled to the proceeds. Here, however, there was not a gift of the proceeds from the sale of the realty but rather a gift of the realty itself.

Finally, appellant argues that Section 14 of the Wills Act of 1947 is applicable. This section provides:

"(17) Ademption. A specific devise or bequest shall not be adeemed when the testator or the testator's estate receives an asset in exchange for the subject of the devise or bequest and the act which otherwise would have caused the ademption occurs while the testator is an adjudged incompetent. In such case the devise or bequest shall be deemed to apply to whatever was received in exchange. Added 1965, Dec. 22, P.L. 1194, § 1.

Appellant attempted to demonstrate that the decedent became incompetent shortly after the sale of the subject real estate and was therefore unable to make a new Will. To the contrary, there was substantial testimony in the record that indicates decedent continued to conduct his personal affairs competently for many months after the June 1968 sale. In any event there was never an adjudication of incompetency and thus this statutory provision is inapplicable. We therefore affirm the Court en banc's ruling that the devise set forth in paragraph four of the will was adeemed.

[The Court rejected the argument made by testator's son that a contract between his father and himself required transfer of the bonds to him and the further argument that the daughter-in-law had a claim for housekeeping, bookkeeping and clerical services.]

Decree affirmed. Costs to be borne by the appellants.

Notes

1. In declaring that testator's intent is not relevant, the court is applying the "identity" theory of ademption. This approach is followed in the majority of jurisdictions, but signs of dissatisfaction continue to appear. See, for instance, the debate between the majority and dissenters in Newbury v. McCammant, 182 N.W.2d 147 (Ia.1970). The experience in New York is revealing. New York has been described as the leading jurisdiction in the United States for strict application of the identity doctrine. The doctrine has, however, been partially abrogated by three statutes. N.Y. EPTL 3–4.4 states that if property, which has been specifically disposed of in the will, has been sold by the committee of an incompetent, the beneficiary will receive any proceeds remaining at the death of the incompetent (overruling In re Ireland, 257 N.Y. 155, 177 N.E. 405 (1931)). Section 3–4.5 requires that insurance paid after testator's death for the accidental loss of specifically devised or bequeathed property shall pass to the beneficiary (overruling on this issue In re Wright's Will, 7 N.Y.2d 365, 197 N.Y.S.2d 711, 165 N.E.2d 561 (1960)). Section 3–4.3, discussed supra p. 343, declares that an act by the testator which alters but does not wholly divest property which has been specifically disposed of in the will does not revoke the disposition. It has been argued that New York should go all the way and make

intent the test.   Note, Ademption in New York: The Identity Doctrine and the Need for Complete Abrogation by Legislation, 25 Syr.L.Rev. 978 (1974).   Wisconsin has enacted such a statute.   Wis.Stat.Ann. § 853.35.   See also UPC §§ 2–607 and 2–608.   The court in the principal case cites the statute which declares that the property is not adeemed when it is sold while the testator is adjudged an incompetent.   (See also the New York statute described supra).   Some courts arrive at the same result even when there is no controlling statute. In re Estate of Graham, 216 Kan. 770, 533 P.2d 1318 (1975); Grant v. Banks, 270 N.C. 473, 155 S.E.2d 87 (1967).

2. A 1957 will bequeathed 25 shares of A.T. & T. stock to a named beneficiary.   In 1959 the stock was split three for one and in 1964 two for one. Testator died in 1965.   Does the beneficiary receive 25 or 150 shares of A.T. & T. stock?   Bostwick v. Hurstel, 304 N.E.2d 186 (Mass.1973) (150);   accord, Morriss v. Pickett, 503 S.W.2d 344 (Tex.Civ.App.1973).   If before death testator has sold real property but taken back a mortgage on it, a devise of that property is adeemed, and the beneficiary does not receive the note and mortgage in substitution for the property.   Estate of Taylor, 480 Pa. 488, 391 A.2d 991 (1978);   accord, Estate of Reposa, 121 N.H. 114, 427 A.2d 19 (1981).

b. Satisfaction

BECK v. McGILLIS

Supreme Court of New York, Albany Special Term, 1850.
9 Barb. 35, 56–57 (Extract from opinion).

Some confusion has arisen on this subject, from the failure even of elementary writers, to keep in view the distinction which I suppose exists between what is, strictly, the ademption of a legacy and its satisfaction. *Ademption*, as I understand the term, is only predicable of a specific legacy.   It takes place, as the term imports, when the thing which is the subject of the legacy, is *taken away*, so that when the testator dies, though the will purports to bestow the legacy, the thing given is not to be found to answer the bequest.   It has been extinguished, if a specific debt, by having been paid to the testator himself; if an article of property, by its sale or conversion.   This is ademption—whether or not it has taken place is a conclusion of law, and does not depend upon the intention of the testator.   Whether or not a particular legacy is a specific or a general pecuniary legacy, is, indeed, very much a question of intention.   It is not always easy to determine whether a testator intended to give, to the object of his bounty, a specific thing, as some specified debt then due to him, or a general legacy to be paid out of such specified debt.   In the one case, the collection of the debt by the testator would be an ademption of the legacy.   In the other, the legacy would be a charge upon his estate generally.   Upon this subject, Chancellor Kent remarks that "the courts are so desirous of construing the bequest to be general, that if there be the least opening to imagine that the testator meant to give a sum of money, and referred to a particular fund only as that out of which he meant it to be paid, it shall be construed to be a pecuniary legacy, so that it may not be defeated by the destruction of the security."   [Citation omitted.] When this question is settled, and it is determined that it was the intention of the testator to give a specific thing, and not a general legacy, then the intention of the testator has nothing further to do with the question of ademption. This is entirely a rule of law, and the rule is, that the legacy is extinguished, if the thing given is gone.

Satisfaction, on the other hand, is predicable, as well of a general, as a specific legacy. It takes place when the testator, in his lifetime, becomes his own executor, and gives to his legatee what he had intended to give by his will. Thus it may happen, in respect to a *specific* legacy, that it has been both *adeemed* and *satisfied*; adeemed, because the thing is gone when the testator dies; *satisfied*, because the legatee has received it. And this, unlike that of ademption, is purely a question of intention. Upon this question, with a view to ascertain whether, in fact the testator, in making an advance to his legatee, intended it as a satisfaction, either *in toto* or *pro tanto*, extrinsic evidence is admissible.

Note

If A makes an inter vivos gift of Blackacre to B, the devise of Blackacre to B in A's will is adeemed, which may be doctrinally explained as either ademption by extinction or by satisfaction. If, on the other hand, A's will includes a legacy of $50,000 to B and A gives B $25,000 before he dies, the legacy is not extinguished but may, depending on A's intent, be declared partially satisfied. Whether A intended the $25,000 as a downpayment on the legacy is a question of fact which may be determined by reference to extrinsic evidence. The fact that the property given is not of the same value or nature as the property described in the will is evidence that ademption by satisfaction was not intended but that fact is not conclusive. The traditional view holds that if the testator is the parent of the legatee, the subsequent gift to the legatee is presumed to be in satisfaction of the legacy. At work here is the same policy against double portions that underlies the principle of advancements in the case of intestacy. A discussion of the rules relating to advancements appears supra pp. 119–120. As is true in the case of advancements, the trend in recently amended statutes abolishes the presumption and reduces the general applicability of the doctrine by ruling that there is no satisfaction unless the testator or legatee has recognized it as such in a contemporaneous, signed document. See e.g. N.Y.—McKinney's EPTL § 2–1.5 and UPC § 2–612.

c. Abatement

Dispositions under a will are classed as specific, demonstrative, general or residuary. They are defined as follows:

(1) A *specific* devise or bequest is a gift of some particular item of property that is capable of being designated and identified.

(2) A *demonstrative* bequest is one of a certain amount or quantity to be satisfied primarily out of a certain fund or particular property, but, if this is impossible, payable generally from the estate. (A demonstrative devise is theoretically possible, but is uncommon.)

(3) A *general* bequest is one which is payable out of general assets of the estate and which does not require the delivery of any specific thing or satisfaction from any designated portion of testator's property.

(4) A *residuary* gift is a gift of whatever is left after the satisfaction of other dispositions.

facts to exist @ time of death

The classification of testamentary dispositions is important for purposes of ademption (supra p. 354) and abatement: (a) If a testamentary gift is specific, a disposition of the property prior to death will adeem it. Demonstrative and general bequests are not adeemed. (b) Unless a different order is prescribed in the will, property in the estate will be applied to the payment of debts, taxes and expenses in the following order:

1. Intestate property, if any.

2. Residuary gifts.

3. General bequests and demonstrative bequests (if the designated source is not available).

4. Demonstrative bequests (if the designated source is available), specific bequests and specific devises.

It will be seen that demonstrative dispositions have the best of both worlds. For purposes of ademption they are treated like general bequests but for purposes of abatement they are treated like specific gifts. The borderline between specific and demonstrative disposition is sometimes uncertain. A gift of "my gold watch" won't cause much trouble, but how about a gift of "my 100 shares of General Motors stock"? On these problems see Powell, ¶ 978; Mechem, Specific Legacies of Un-Specific Things, 87 U.Pa.L.Rev. 546 (1939).

5. *Death of a Legatee—Lapsed and Void Bequests*

At common law, an attempted testamentary gift was ineffective if the intended donee predeceased the testator. If the intended donee's death occurred after execution of the will, the gift was said to lapse; if before execution of the will, the gift was said to be void. Almost all states now have statutes partially avoiding the effect of this rule, unless the testator manifests a contrary intent.

The statutes vary considerably in the following respects:

(1) *Required relationship between the testator and the intended donee.* Some states require the intended donee to be a child of the testator; some require him to be a relative within a prescribed class of near relatives; some require only that he be a relative, no matter how distant; and some omit the requirement.

(2) *Required relationship between the intended donee and the substitute taker.* Nearly all states preserve the gift only for descendants of the intended donee, but a few preserve the gift for his intestate successors generally.

(3) *Application to void as well as lapsed gifts.* Most states preserve only lapsed gifts, but some preserve void gifts also (i.e., they apply where the intended donee died before the will was executed).

(4) *Application to class gifts.* Most states interpret their anti-lapse statutes as preserving for the substitute taker of a deceased member of a class, the share of the class gift that the deceased member would have taken if he had survived the testator. Other states take the position that a class gift, being made to an impersonal category rather than to

identified individuals, is intended to include only those persons who are in the category at the testator's death; that a deceased member is therefore not an intended donee; and that there is thus no lapse for the statute to operate on. Some statutes specifically deal with this question.

The Uniform Probate Code anti-lapse provision is § 2–605, which provides:

> If a devisee who is a grandparent or a lineal descendant of a grandparent of the testator is dead at the time of execution of the will, fails to survive the testator, or is treated as if he predeceased the testator, the issue of the deceased devisee who survive the testator by 120 hours take in place of the deceased devisee and if they are all of the same degree of kinship to the devisee they take equally, but if of unequal degree than those of more remote degree take by representation. One who would have been a devisee under a class gift if he had survived the testator is treated as a devisee for purposes of this section whether his death occurred before or after the execution of the will.

As noted above an anti-lapse statute will not override the expression by the testator of a contrary intent. Whether a will manifests such an intent is sometimes a difficult question. See, e.g., In Re Estate of Corbett at p. 435, infra. On the application of anti-lapse statutes to powers of appointment, see p. 873, infra.

Chapter Six

GIFTS

SECTION ONE. REAL PROPERTY

The evolution of the Anglo-American methods of conveying land falls chronologically into three periods: first, that of the common law conveyances, most important of which was the feoffment; next, that of conveyances under the Statute of Uses; and, at the present time, that of conveyances under modern statutes prescribing forms for deeds in the different states. 3 Am.L.Prop. § 12.1–12.2 (1953). The first two periods will be further discussed in connection with the history of trusts.

The modern idea of consideration had not been formulated at the early period of the common law conveyances, and no similar concept seems to have played any part in their doctrinal development. It can be argued ex post facto that the equivalent of consideration was present in the incidents of the resulting feudal tenure. 4 Kent Com. 465. But the usual statement is that no consideration was necessary, at least for the validity of a feoffment as between the parties to it, its vital element being a transfer of possession. Brewster, The Conveyance of Estates in Fee by Deed § 53 (1904); 2 P. & M. 82; 3 Holds. 221.

The conception that transfer of title to land required consideration was introduced with the system of uses. Consideration was essential to the validity of a bargain and sale, and therefore also of a lease and release operating under the Statute of Uses (as to which see p. 429, and cf. pp. 415–416, infra). English decisions in the latter sixteenth and the seventeenth centuries reduced this requirement to a mere form. 7 Holds. 358. The value of the consideration was immaterial and a purely nominal one would suffice. Case of Sutton's Hospital, 10 Co.Rep. 1a, 34a, 77 Eng.Rep. 937, 975 (twelve pence rent reserved sufficient for bargain and sale); Barker v. Keate, 2 Vent. 35, 86 Eng.Rep. 293, 1 Freem. 249, 89 Eng.Rep. 179, 1 Mod. 262, 86 Eng.Rep. 868, 2 Mod. 249, 86 Eng.Rep. 1054 (rent of a peppercorn reserved sufficient for bargain and sale of lease, making tenant capable of taking release without entry, and thus effectuating lease and release conveyance). Actually a gift of land could be made by a bargain and sale deed properly reciting a consideration, since such recital was conclusive and no evidence was admissible to contradict it, so far as the validity of the deed as between the parties to it

362

was concerned. Fisher v. Smith, Moore, 569, 72 Eng.Rep. 764 (1559) (dictum); Smith v. Lane, 1 Leon. 170, 74 Eng.Rep. 157 (1586). American cases showed the same tendency to uphold the conveyance if possible. Jackson ex dem. Hudson v. Alexander, 3 Johns. 484, 3 Am.Dec. 517 (N.Y., 1808) (recital "for value received" sufficient to sustain deed as bargain and sale under the Statute of Uses; review of English authorities). In this case, Kent, Ch. J. said: "The rule requiring a consideration to raise a use, has become merely nominal, and a matter of form; for if a sum of money be mentioned, it is never an inquiry whether it was actually paid, and the smallest sum possible is sufficient: nay, it has been solemnly adjudged, that a pepper-corn was sufficient to raise a use. * * * Since, then, the efficacy of the rule is so completely gone, we ought, in support of deeds, to construe the cases, which have modified the rule, with the utmost liberality. * * * Value received does, in judgment of law, imply money, or its equivalent. The grantor must be estopped by this express averment in his deed."

The normal way of making a gift of land today is by statutory deed. American statutes generally do not include consideration in their requirements for deeds of real property. 3 Am.L.Prop. § 12.43 (1953). That is, the absence of consideration will not usually affect the validity of the deed as between the parties to it. It may, of course, be material for other purposes. If creditors of the grantor seek to set aside the conveyance as one in fraud of creditors, its gratuitous character will usually assist them. A donee of land is obviously not an innocent purchaser for value for the purpose of protection against prior equities or under the recording acts. A donee usually cannot obtain reformation of a deed against the donor on the ground of mistake. In jurisdictions altering the common law efficacy of the seal, the grantor's covenants in the deed may be unenforceable if the transaction is gratuitous.

While the assumption that consideration is not necessary to pass title to the grantee of a modern statutory deed is supported by the provisions of the statutes and by dicta, there seem to be comparatively few actual decisions on the point. This may be due partly to the fact that the statutes are too clear to afford any basis for argument. Furthermore, it is customary to recite a consideration even in a gratuitous deed. Such a recital will permit the deed to be sustained as a bargain and sale if, for any reason, it fails to comply with the statutory form, since the courts are willing to place a conveyance in a different category from that contemplated by the grantor for the purpose of making it effective. A recital of consideration, while open to contradiction for most purposes, is generally conclusive on the parties to the deed on the issue of its effectiveness as a transfer between them. The general custom of reciting consideration, therefore, precludes grantors from raising the question of absence of consideration and thus diminishes litigation on the point.

The New York Law is representative. The statutory requirements for conveyance of real property do not mention consideration. N.Y.— McKinney's Gen.Oblgs.Law, § 5–703, Real Prop.Law, § 243. While the statutory forms include a recital of consideration, the section prescribing such forms is merely permissive and does not prevent the use of other forms, Real Prop. Law § 258; Goldberg v. Norek, 101 Misc. 371, 166 N.Y.S. 1023 (Sup.Ct., King's Co. 1917). There does not seem to be any satisfactory New York decision on the validity of a gratuitous statutory deed not reciting consideration, although there is language in one early case to the effect that the revised statutes eliminated the requirement of consideration previously existing under the Statute of Uses. Cunningham v. Freeborn, 11 Wend. 240, 247 (1833); but see Morris v. Ward, 36 N.Y. 587 (1867). The absence of decisions on the point is probably due to the fact that a recital of consideration binds the grantor. Grout v. Townsend, 2 Denio 336 (1845) (at 340, the court said: "I apprehend * * * that it would be unheard of to allow a grantor to avoid his own conveyance * * * by proving that the consideration which he had acknowledged had not in fact been paid; unless in connection with such proof he offered to shew fraud in the transaction."); Meriam v. Harsen, 2 Barb.Ch. 232, 267 (1847); Winans v. Peebles, 31 Barb. 371, 380 (1860), reversed on other grounds 32 N.Y. 423 (1865). And, as stated in Morris v. Ward, supra, at 598, "The practice to insert a pecuniary consideration of small amount, in gratuitous conveyances, which nominal sum is not generally paid, is * * * so general, that it may almost be pronounced universal."

HEUER v. HEUER
Supreme Court of North Dakota, 1934.
64 N.D. 497, 253 N.W. 856.

NUESSLE, Judge. The plaintiff William Heuer brought this action to quiet title to a quarter section of land in Cass county as against a mortgage thereon held by the defendant Henry Heuer. The case was tried to the court without a jury. Judgment was ordered and entered for the plaintiff. Defendant, perfecting this appeal, demands a trial de novo in this court.

Carl Heuer was a long-time resident of Cass county. In 1910 he bought the land which is the subject of this action. The plaintiff William Heuer is the son of Carl Heuer. William Heuer married in 1912. He and his wife lived with his father for a year. Then in April, 1913, they moved onto the land here involved. They lived there continuously up to the time of the trial of this action in 1933. William Heuer paid the taxes and kept the place in repair. He made additional improvements thereon, set out fruit and ornamental trees, built fences, a garage, a smokehouse, a cistern, and dug an expensive well. In short, William Heuer and his wife created there a home for themselves and their family of eleven children.

In 1913 before William Heuer went to live on the farm his father said to him: "This is your farm Bill. Farm it the way you want to. I will hold the deed to save it for you so you don't lose it or sell it or get rid of it." It was pursuant to this conversation that plaintiff moved onto the farm. Thereafter he regarded and treated the land as his own, he farmed it as he saw fit, and paid the taxes every year execept for the year 1917.

He made no accounting to his father or to any one for the rents and profits. When he went upon the land there was a mortgage of $2,800 against it. He paid the interest on this mortgage in the sum of $168 annually until 1919, when his father discharged it. In 1919, Carl Heuer bought another piece of land. He borrowed the purchase price of $19,000 from his brother Henry Heuer, the defendant. To secure this loan he mortgaged the land so purchased. He kept up the taxes on the land, paid the interest on the loan, and reduced the principal somewhat so that in 1929 there remained unpaid thereon the sum of $16,000. In 1929 at the request of Henry Heuer, Carl Heuer executed a new note for the amount of the loan then remaining unpaid and secured this note by a mortgage on the land which had been the original security and on the quarter section involved in the instant action. This action is brought to quiet title as against the mortgage.

In 1929 Carl Heuer sold and deeded a right of way through the land for a state highway and received and retained the consideration therefor.

In 1926, Carl Heuer was not in good health. In that year he deeded the tract here involved, together with other lands belonging to him, to his wife, the mother of the plaintiff. He died intestate in May, 1930. The deed was not filed for record until after his death.

There is also evidence in the record that at various times after the plaintiff took possession of the land and prior to the execution of the mortgage to Henry Heuer in 1929, Carl Heuer said the land belonged to the plaintiff; that he (Carl Heuer) was holding the title so that plaintiff's creditors could not get it and so that the plaintiff would not lose it or otherwise dispose of it. He said this to strangers as well as to various members of his own family. Among others, he told this to the notary at the time he executed the deed to his wife, saying that he was deeding it to her so as to save it for plaintiff as against his creditors. It is undisputed that the defendant who lived in the vicinity knew the plaintiff resided with his family upon the land here involved. And it was commonly reputed in the neighborhood that this land belonged to the plaintiff.

Plaintiff contends that he is the owner of the land; that it became his by and through an executed gift to him from his father; that relying upon the gift he went into possession of the land, made improvements thereon, and occupied it openly and adversely as the owner; that thereby the equitable title passed to him. On the other hand, the defendant insists that giving the evidence its greatest effect, there is, nevertheless, not such a certainty with respect to the gift as the law requires; that though the plaintiff occupied the land from 1913 on, his father at all times regarded it as his own; that all of the circumstances indicate that while he might have intended at some time in the future to give the land to the plaintiff, he did not do so, but considered and treated it as his own; that if there was an attempted gift it was by parol and therefore void under the statute of frauds; that any improvements that may have been put upon the land by the plaintiff were inconsiderable, worth much less than the rental value of the premises, and so not sufficient to take the transaction out of the statute of frauds; that there is no competent evidence

Clark, Lusky, Murphy Grat. Tr. 3rd ACB—10

as to the gift; and that the evidence offered as to the statements of the deceased, Carl Heuer, is inadmissible either under section 7871, C.L.1913, or as attempting to establish a transfer of realty by a parol agreement.

Thus the question here is as to whether a valid title may be predicated upon the facts and circumstances established in the record. This question must be considered in the light of the following statutory provisions:

"An estate in real property other than an estate at will for a term not exceeding one year, can be transferred only by operation of law or by an instrument in writing, subscribed by the party disposing of the same or by his agent thereunto authorized by writing." Section 5511, C.L.1913.

"An agreement for the leasing for a longer period than one year, or for the sale of real property, or of an interest therein, * * * is invalid, unless the same, or some note or memorandum thereof, is in writing and subscribed by the party to be charged, or by his agent." Section 5888, C.L.1913.

"No agreement for the sale of real property, or of an interest therein, is valid unless the same, or some note or memorandum thereof, is in writing and subscribed by the party to be charged, or his agent thereunto authorized in writing; but this does not abridge the power of any court to compel the specific performance of any agreement for the sale of real property in case of part performance thereof." Section 5963, C.L.1913.

The trial court, who saw and heard the witnesses, found that there was an oral gift of the land to the plaintiff by his father. Pursuant to and in reliance upon this gift, the plaintiff went into possession in 1913. He has at all times since then openly exercised all the acts of proprietorship which are ordinarily exercised by an owner, paid the taxes (except for 1917), made substantial improvements upon the land, and in all things used the land as his own and as a home for himself and his family. If these findings are sustainable on the record, then the judgment must be affirmed.

The fact that the gift was by parol does not necessarily avoid it. Where a vendee is placed in possession of land under a contract of sale, makes valuable improvements, and pays part of the purchase price, the fact that the requirements of the statute of frauds were not complied with in making the contract will not defeat an action for the specific performance thereof. Mitchell v. Knudtson Land Company, 19 N.D. 736, 124 N.W. 946. There is no good reason why a gift should not be subject to the same rules as a sale, and the cases so hold. See Urbanec v. Urbanec, 43 N.D. 127, 174 N.W. 880; Wylie v. Charlton, 43 Neb. 840, 62 N.W. 220; 27 C.J. 208. Thus where under a parol gift of land the donee takes possession and makes improvements in reliance on the gift so it would work a substantial injustice to hold the gift void, the transaction is taken out of the statute of frauds. [Citations omitted.] It seems to us clear that this rule must be applied in the instant case.

It is objected, however, that the improvements made by the plaintiff here were inconsiderable in value and worth much less than the value of the rents and profits of the land during the period of the plaintiff's occupancy; that therefore the rule cannot be invoked. The record does not show the value of the rents and profits during the time plaintiff has been in possession of the land. It does show that the improvements, exclusive of labor, were worth about $1,000. Spread over the whole period of the plaintiff's occupancy this may be regarded as an inconsiderable amount. If expended in a single year this would not be so. But, in any event, it seems to us the case cannot turn upon the dollar and cent value of the improvements alone. The point is that it would work a substantial injustice to hold the gift void under the circumstances disclosed. Dollars and cents cannot make a man whole if he be deprived of the home he has created and occupied with his family for nearly twenty years in good faith reliance upon a gift. See, in this connection, West v. Bundy, 78 Mo. 410; Ford v. Steele, 31 Neb. 521, 48 N.W. 271; Halsey v. Peters' Ex'r, 79 Va. 65.

Presumptively, since the title to this land stood in Carl Heuer's name on the public records, plaintiff's occupancy thereof was under and in subordination to this title. Section 7365, C.L.1913. But this presumption was not conclusive. Of course, the plaintiff has the burden of establishing such an interest in the land as will entitle him to maintain the action. But this is a civil action and he need not establish the facts essential to his case beyond a reasonable doubt. It is sufficient if his evidence establishes these facts with reasonable certainty. Wylie v. Charlton, supra; Hargreaves v. Burton, supra; Neale v. Neale, supra. The defendant insists that the plaintiff's proofs are not sufficient to do this. There is no dispute as to the plaintiff's occupancy of the land or as to what he has done while thus in possession of it. The case must hinge, then, on whether such occupancy and possession was under a gift from his father or otherwise. In view of the relationship existing between Carl Heuer and plaintiff, the latter's use and occupancy of the land are not necessarily inconsistent with title and ownership in Carl Heuer. Many sons reside on their fathers' land, exercise the prerogatives of ownership, and pay no rent for the use of it. But neither were Carl Heuer's acts with respect to the land necessarily inconsistent with the plaintiff's contention that his father had given the land to him and that he went into possession of it because of and in reliance upon this gift, for oftentimes there is delay and negligence and disregard of ordinary business methods in entering into and completing transactions between father and son. And a father's desire to insure to his son the enjoyment of his gift is most natural. So the intention of Carl Heuer when he put the plaintiff into possession becomes important. If he intended to make a present gift of the land to the plaintiff and reserve title in himself for some reason of his own, then under the facts and circumstances shown the gift was valid and effective. On the other hand, if he merely intended at some time in the future to give the land to the plaintiff and not to make a present gift, then the plaintiff cannot prevail. Plaintiff sought to establish the intention to make a present gift by evidence of the statements of Carl Heuer to him at the time of the making of the alleged gift and thereafter. * * *

[The court here discussed, and rejected, the objection that evidence of Carl Heuer's statements was inadmissible under the dead man statute.]

* * * Thus the evidence was properly received, and we think that it amply evidences an intention on the part of Carl Heuer to give the land to his son at the time he put him into possession thereof. It dissipates any uncertainty that may have arisen on account of the acts of Carl Heuer with respect to the land after the purported gift to the plaintiff.

Some contention is made that defendant is a bona fide holder of the mortgage here involved and took the same for value without notice of the plaintiff's equities in the land. But the plaintiff was in possession. The defendant stands in the shoes of Carl Heuer as of the time of the execution of his mortgage with respect to equities of which he had notice. If at that time plaintiff could have maintained his claim that he held the land under a valid executed gift against Carl Heuer, he can maintain it now as against the defendant. Plaintiff's possession was notice to the defendant of plaintiff's rights in the land. See O'Toole v. Omlie, 8 N.D. 444, 79 N.W. 849; Earnest v. First National Bank, 56 N.D. 309, 217 N.W. 169.

Accordingly, viewing the whole record, we hold, as did the trial court, that the plaintiff has sustained the burden that was placed upon him and has established his case by that weight of the evidence which the law requires.

Finally, the defendant insists that the judgment as ordered and entered is too broad, in that it quiets title generally in the plaintiff. Of course, any judgment for the plaintiff in this action must be limited in its effect to canceling and vacating the defendant's mortgage and quieting title as against it. We think that the judgment as entered was intended to have that effect, and in so far as it does so, and no further, such judgment must be, and it is, affirmed.

BURR, C. J., and BURKE and CHRISTIANSON, JJ., concur.

MOELLRING, J., did not participate.

Notes

1. As to the improvements required under the doctrine announced in the principal case, see Glass v. Tremellen, 294 Pa. 436, 439, 144 A. 413, 414 (1928) ("necessary repairs * * * such as a tenant might be expected to make" insufficient); Turner v. Rogers, 106 S.W.2d 1078, 1079–80 (Tex.Civ.App.1937) ("The improvements made are required to be of a permanent nature, and of such value, in comparison with the nature and value of the property upon which the improvements are made, as to enhance the value of such property to a substantial degree." If three tracts claimed, improvements on one tract will not bring other two tracts within doctrine "unless the usages and location of the separate tracts of land are of such a nature as to definitely constitute an entity, one farm or one homestead."); Nugent v. Dittel, 213 Iowa 671, 674–75, 239 N.W. 559, 560 (1931) ("Papering, varnishing, some painting, the planting of some shrubbery and perennials, and providing a gas connection for the laundry stove," involving "trivial outlays," held insufficent. Improvements "were not of a substantial nature, but temporary in character to make the home more livable to her as an occupant."). Cf. Annot., 33 A.L.R. 1489 (1924).

The usual test as announced above is in terms of corroborating the intent that a gift was made. Another test is sometimes used which stresses the elements of equity and fairness behind the part performance doctrine. In Rarry v. Shimek, 360 Pa. 315, 320–21, 62 A.2d 46, 48–49 (1948) the court put it this way:

> * * * The testimony was that, after taking possession, Shimek cemented the basement, put up partitions there for a laundry room, fruit cellar, coal bin and furnace room, installed a sink and a lavatory, built a linen closet in the bathroom, dug a water-well, dug driveways and laid cement sidewalks around the house, graded the lawn, sowed grass seed on it and planted trees and shrubbery. It is true that he obtained the material for these improvements either as gifts or at small expense, but he himself performed the necessary labor, working nights and at odd hours when not on duty for the Riffles. Plaintiffs deprecate the importance of the improvements on the ground that they were neither valuable nor incapable of being adequately compensated in damages; they were, however, of a permanent nature and of such an extent as to render any attempted revocation of the gift unjust and inequitable. Improvements that might be deemed inconsequential in connection with a property which was itself extremely valuable might properly be regarded as of comparatively large value when made upon a $9000 house, and, since Shimek made them by his own labor performed at various odd times, his contention would seem reasonable that compensation therefor in damages must necessarily be inadequate; the requirement of the law that the improvements be such that compensation would be inadequate does not mean, of course, that no amount of compensation, however large, would be sufficient, but that it would be impracticable, if not impossible, to determine such amount with any fair degree of accuracy by ordinary and available standards. There is peculiarly apposite to the present case what was said in Greenwich Coal & Coke Co. v. Learn, 234 Pa. 180, 187, 83 A. 74, that "where a man under circumstances like these has spent the best part of his life improving a piece of land for a home, compensation in damages is not adequate."

2. Gifts of real property have been predicated upon informal letters which do not satisfy the legal requirements of a deed. Barnes v. Banks, 223 Ill. 352, 79 N.E. 117 (1906). Compare Hill v. Bowen, 8 Ill.2d 527, 134 N.E.2d 769 (1956). An oral gift of land renders the donee's possession of the land adverse to the donor's and has been held to give rise to a successful claim of title by adverse possession. Humphrey v. Harrison, 646 S.W.2d 340, 342 (Ky.1982) ("An entry under a parole gift of an undivided interest, though permissive and friendly in the popular sense, is hostile and adverse to the donor's exclusive title in the legal sense, because there is an assertion of ownership in the donee").

SECTION TWO. PERSONAL PROPERTY

Gifts Inter Vivos

Conceptions of Ownership

The simplest and most innate conception of ownership is materialistic and is identified with physical control. In the trade among young children in those innumerable and diverse chattels which seem to fall into their possession, the standard and obvious way to "transfer title" is to hand the thing over. And it would hardly occur to a child who had been tortiously dispossessed to seek comfort in the thought that he was still the true owner. In this way of thinking, the owner is the one who has physical control; if you want to make some one else owner, you must make a physical transfer of the subject-matter; and, if you lose possession, you are no longer the owner. You haven't got a thing if you haven't got it. It is probable that these ideas are shared by many adults not accustomed to thinking in legal terms. How many laymen would comprehend, or take kindly to, a lawyer's distinction between title and possession? Are they not more likely, unless stirred by theft or other impairment of their rights, to dismiss the matter as a boring bit of legal metaphysics?

More sophisticated legal reasoning has now freed the idea of ownership from the confines of pure materialism and places it on a more abstract plane. Ownership is popularly defined as a "bundle of rights" (Maitland, The Mystery of Seisin, 2 L.Q.Rev. 481, 489 (1886)) or as a group of legal relations, the nature of which of course varies with the interest involved. Transfer of ownership is therefore, by definition, a transfer of legal relations. Legal relations are in turn concepts that are useful in the description and analysis of what courts have done in the past and in the prediction of what they may do in the future. The statement that ownership (as thus defined) has been transferred is therefore a shorthand expression of legal opinion, convenient in the quick communication of ideas, and not a description of a factual occurrence, except in so far as the phrase may incidentally connote certain actions of the parties. Such abstractions as ownership and legal relations are, of course, not susceptible of physical transfer. Nor should the phrase "transfer of ownership" be read literally to mean that the legal relations of the transferee will be precisely identical with the previous legal relations of the transferor, since those will vary according to the terms of the transfer and the applicability of legal rules such as those relating to good faith purchase. But the phrase serves well enough to state the opinion that they will be substantially similar, or, in other words, that after the "transfer," the courts will treat the transferee in about the same way that, before it, they would have treated the transferor. What proof the courts will require as prerequisite to an effective transfer under this analysis is a question of legal judgment, to be determined more by considerations of policy than by the idea that a physical transfer is a sine qua non.

These two conceptions of ownership seem to influence a large part of the law of gifts inter vivos of personal property. The materialistic attitude obviously stresses physical transfer of a tangible object. The modern notion of ownership shifts the emphasis to the functional criterion of what the courts should require before putting one person in the shoes of another with reference to any particular type of property. Under this criterion, a physical transfer is not indispensable and will only be of importance if it accomplishes some useful purpose. In this manner, however, materialism, because of its natural and widespread character, will find a place in a functional approach. Thousands of gifts are made daily in this country by laymen with only the simplest ideas of ownership, and probably, except in rare instances, without benefit of legal advice. To many people who would not think of considering a will or a trust without going to an attorney, it might not even occur that there was a legal problem involved in gifts of personalty. They have been giving presents all their lives without having to pay a lawyer. And, very likely, to most of them "giving" means "handing over." Functional criteria cannot neglect these typical human habits, or the materialistic assumptions underlying them, without leading to arbitrary and intent-defeating results. For an example of an attempt to formulate legal doctrine in the light of ordinary human reactions, see the opinion of Lord Esher in an important English case, which reads in part:

> " * * * Upon long consideration, I have come to the conclusion that actual delivery in the case of a 'gift' is more than evidence of the existence of the proposition of law which constitutes a gift, and I have come to the conclusion that it is a part of the proposition itself. * * * The proposition before the Court on a question of gift or not is—that the one gave and the other accepted. * * * The one cannot give, according to the ordinary meaning of the word, without giving; the other cannot accept then and there such a giving without then and there receiving the thing given. * * * Short of these things being done, the donee could not get possession without bringing an action against the donor to force him to give him the thing. But if we are to force him to give, it cannot be said that he has given. Suppose the proposing donor offers the thing saying, 'I give you this thing—take it'; and the other says, 'No, I will not take it now; I will take it tomorrow.' I think the proposing donor could not in the meantime say correctly to a third person, 'I gave this just now to my son or my friend.' The answer of the third person would (I think rightly) be: 'You cannot say you gave it to him just now; you have it now in your hand.' All you can say is: "That you are going to give it to him tomorrow, if then he will take it.' I have come to the conclusion that in ordinary English language, and in legal effect, there cannot be a 'gift' without a giving and taking. The giving and taking are the two contemporaneous reciprocal acts which constitute a 'gift.' They are a necessary part of the proposition that there has been a 'gift.' They are not evidence to prove that there has been a gift, but facts to be proved to constitute the proposition that there has been a gift." Cochrane v. Moore, 25 Q.B.Div. 57, 75–6 (1890).

Evolution of the Law of Gifts

Notwithstanding the comparative scarcity of original sources, historians agree that, in the thirteenth century, in accordance with the general emphasis on possession, the only possible method of making a gift of a chattel was by delivering the chattel to the donee. Delivery of a deed of gift without delivery of the subject-matter of the gift was ineffectual, and the concept of constructive delivery was unknown. 2 P. & M. 180; 3 Holds. 353; Cochrane v. Moore, 25 Q.B.Div. 57, 65 (1890) (the opinion of Fry, L. J. in this case traces the history of gifts of personalty). In 1468, however, it was held that a gift could be effectuated by a deed of gift even though the subject-matter was not delivered. Y.B. 7 Ed. IV, fol. 20, pl. 21. The report merely contains a brief statement of the result, but Holdsworth suggests that it was based on the analogy of the binding effect of a promise under seal. At this period, a deed had the characteristics of both contract and conveyance, between which two concepts there was as yet no clear distinction. If a promise under seal to pay money gave a cause of action to the promisee, why should not a promise to convey or a conveyance under seal give the donee the right to the chattel? That the materialistic attitude of the early law no longer completely prevailed is shown by the alteration, at the same period, of the early rule that no title could pass in the sale of chattels until delivery. 3 Holds. 354–58. Under this explanation, and in all probability, the effectiveness of a deed of gift of personalty at common law was entirely dependent on the presence of a seal and on the ritualistic and irrebuttable character of a sealed instrument at that time. If a man stated under seal that persons gave a chattel, they could not later deny it, and the gift was therefore effectual. This factor cannot be overlooked today in arguing the question of whether an unsealed instrument of gift is operative. Mechem, Delivery in Gifts of Chattels, 21 Ill.L.Rev. 568, 576 (1927). In view of the confusion on the question in some modern decisions, it is extremely important to remember that, as stated, the English law, as early as the fifteenth century, recognized two alternative methods of delivery in gifts of personalty: (1) delivery of the subject-matter, *or* (2) delivery of a deed of gift, it being essential that the deed be under seal. A deed of gift, like other deeds, must of course be "delivered" (a term of varying content and meaning) in order to be effectual. Assuming satisfactory evidence of donative intent, necessary in any gift case, the donee could prevail on proof of either of these two forms of delivery.

It is difficult to reach the origin of the concept that "constructive," as distinguished from actual, delivery will effectuate a gift. No English judicial discussion of this concept has been found earlier than the eighteenth century. While no final decision on the point in that century has been found, several cases assume or expressly state its existence. Jones v. Selby, Prec. Ch. 300, 24 Eng.Rep. 143 (1710) (possibility of gift of contents of trunk by delivery of key to trunk apparently assumed without discussion in reversing on other grounds a decree below in favor of the donee); Ryall v. Rowles, 1 Ves.Sen. 348, 362, 27 Eng.Rep. 1074, 1082 (1750) (statement, in another context, that "a delivery of the key of a warehouse is a delivery of those goods, which are bulky, being the only immediate delivery the things are capable of"); Ward v. Turner, 2 Ves. Sen. 431, 442–3, 28 Eng.Rep. 275, 282 (1752) (rather frequently quoted dictum that "delivery of a mere symbol" would be insufficient, but that delivery of a key giving access to bulky goods "has been allowed as delivery of the possession, because it is the way of coming at the possession, or to make use of the thing," citing only Jones v. Selby and Ryall v. Rowles, supra). The matter is further complicated by the fact that the idea of constructive delivery of chattels is material in other situations than that of gifts inter vivos. Pollock and Wright, Possession in the Common Law, 60–70 (1888). In view of the inconclusive character of these authorities, one can only guess that the concept was present in eighteenth century litigation but was probably non-existent at any much earlier period. At any rate, there seems to be no historical basis for any assumption that the reason for the validity of a deed of gift (recognized in the fifteenth century) was that it was a "constructive delivery" of the subject-matter (a considerably more recent doctrine). The idea of constructive delivery appears more clearly in the later English cases. In re Mustapha-Mustapha v. Wedlake, 8 T.L.R. 160 (1891) (delivery by donor on deathbed of key to wardrobe containing key to safe held sufficient to effectuate gift causa mortis of bonds in safe); In re Wasserberg (1915) 1 Ch. 195 (delivery at donor's home, just before operation, of key to box kept at bank held sufficient to effectuate gift causa mortis of securities contained in box).

During the nineteenth century, some doubts arose concerning the necessity of delivery. The existing law had been clearly reasserted in Irons v. Smallpiece, 2 B. & A. 551 (1819) (oral gift held invalid because no delivery of either subject-matter or deed of gift), and this decision was followed in a number of the later cases. But dicta stating definitely that a gift should rest purely on the question of intention, and that delivery should not be a prerequisite, but that its presence or absence should only be material as evidence relating to intention, also appeared. In re Harcourt, Danby v. Tucker, 31 W.R. 578 (1883); In re Ridgway, 15 Q.B.Div. 447 (1885). It is interesting to note, however, in considering the evidentiary value of delivery, that in both of these cases claims of alleged donees were denied because the court was not satisfied that there was an intention to give the undelivered articles. These doubts were effectively silenced by the famous case of Cochrane v. Moore, 25 Q.B.Div. 57 (1890), which, although only in dictum, considered the matter in great detail and strongly reaffirmed the necessity of delivery of either the subject-matter or a deed of gift, in terms of both history and modern policy. On this development, see 7 Holds. 503–09.

The necessity of delivery in gifts of personal property has always been generally adhered to in the United States. The typical American law may therefore be stated as follows: To succeed in establishing a gift inter vivos of personalty, the claimant must prove (1) the alleged donor's intent to give and (2) delivery of either (a) the subject-matter of the gift or (b) an instrument of gift. While this statement may convey an initial illusion of simplicity, it obviously contains words of art such as "delivery", which mean different things in different contexts.

Gifts Causa Mortis

As its name indicates, a gift causa mortis is a gift made in contemplation of death, for the purpose of effectuating a final disposition of the property involved if death occurs. Story called it "a sort of amphibious gift between a gift inter vivos and a legacy." Story, Equity Jurisprudence, § 606 (11th ed., 1873). This seems an apt description, for, as developed in England and America, this form of transfer resembles a will in objectives and general effect, but is classified as a transfer inter vivos for the purpose of the requirements of transfer.

The following are the characteristics of the modern concept of a gift causa mortis:

    1. It is only applicable to transfers made in apprehension of death, because the concept by definition is restricted to that situation. It is there-

fore similar in factual surroundings to a nuncupative will in the last illness. But the basis for the requirement is entirely different in the two cases. The nuncupative will is only permitted on the theory that the testator was too near death to have time to execute a formal will, and the courts are therefore quite strict in those cases in insisting on proximity to death. Here the courts are less interested in the exact lapse of time between the gift and the death of the donor, the purpose being to provide a factual setting appropriate for the intent postulated to exist in this type of transfer, rather than to justify an unusual relaxation of formalities.

2. A gift causa mortis will become inoperative if the donor recovers from the illness from which he or she was suffering at the time of the gift. It has always been an essential element of the concept that this result be intended by the donor. It is the main basis for classifying a transfer in this category rather than as a gift inter vivos, which is not subject to any such condition. There is again a similarity in circumstances to a nuncupative will in the last illness, since an illness is not a "last illness" if the testator recovers from it. But, on the same basis as in (1) supra, the rationale differs. The reason for holding a nuncupative will inoperative if the testator recovers, is that he or she will then have time to make a formal will, and the justification for relaxation of formalities does not exist. Here, it is a question of the intent required by the definitions of the concept.

3. It is always stated that a gift causa mortis is revocable by the donor, although there is little actual litigation on the point. It is not likely to arise frequently. If the donor recovers, the gift becomes automatically inoperative on that ground and the issue of revocation by the donor is immaterial. If the donor dies, there will be little time for revocation, and usually little likelihood of the circumstances changing sufficiently in the brief period between the gift and death to furnish any reason for it. Since the intent to give is generally established in these cases by proof of oral declarations of the donor, there seems to be no reason for any special formality in revocation, and it is generally assumed that none exists. The gift causa mortis here resembles a will in being revocable, rather than a gift inter vivos, which is irrevocable unless a power of revocation is expressly and effectively reserved.

4. A gift causa mortis will become inoperative if the donee fails to survive the donor. In this respect, it has no similarity to a gift inter vivos, where the death of the donee, before or after that of the donor, has no effect on the validity of the original gift, but merely passes on the donee's title to his or her successors. This characteristic of a gift causa mortis is due to the incorporation in that concept of the doctrine of lapse, regularly employed in will cases. While entirely permissible from a functional point of view, since the courts are here authorizing a transfer that has the general purpose and effect of a will, the analogy seems technically inaccurate. The lapse of a legacy is theoretically justifiable on the reasoning that a will passes no title until death, and a dead person cannot receive title; therefore, a predeceased legatee cannot take title by will. This explanation would only be appropriate here if the usual theory were that a gift causa mortis passed no title until the death of the donor, which, as appears infra, is probably not the case. This characteristic again is largely the product of

dicta; it is not likely that a donee will predecease a donor who is dying at the time of the gift.

5. The property transferred by a gift causa mortis is automatically subject to the claims of the donor's creditors, if the property passing by will and intestacy is not sufficient to satisfy them—i.e., if the decedent's estate is insolvent. Here again, the analogy is to property passing by will, in which creditors always have a priority over beneficiaries, and not to property given inter vivos, which can be reached by creditors only by proving the gift to have been made while the donor was insolvent. There are few actual decisions on this point.

6. A gift causa mortis is effectuated by delivery, and for this and other purposes of formalities of transfer is treated as an inter vivos and not a testamentary disposition. It need not comply with the statute of wills. It is not probated. The claim of the donee is adverse to, and not under, the personal representative, who, far from holding the property as a fiduciary for the donee, is frequently the party disputing the donee's claim. In this respect, therefore, there is no analogy whatever to a will.

7. It is usually held in this country that a gift causa mortis passes title to the donee at the time of the gift, subject to be divested by the operation of the conditions subsequent of recovery, revocation, predecease, and liability to creditors. This seems the only explanation consistent with the undisputed proposition that it is a transfer inter vivos for the purpose of the requirements of transfer. Some courts, probably to assist in reaching the result desired in the particular case, have stated that title passes to the donee on the death of the donor. See Hatcher v. Buford, 60 Ark. 169, 29 S.W. 641 (1895) (theory that donor's death is condition precedent to vesting of title used to give donor's widow share in property covered by gift, under statute guaranteeing widow one-third of property owned by husband at his death). But this, being a repetition of the definition of a will, makes it logically impossible, on a doctrinal level, to hold a gift causa mortis valid when it does not comply with the statute of wills; yet, it is always tested by delivery and not by that statute. See Basket v. Hassell, 107 U.S. 602, 2 S.Ct. 415, 27 L.Ed. 500 (1882). In many cases, this technical question is not raised by the issues. In others, the court's attitude is obscured by such general statements as that the gift "is conditional on death." This may mean either that death is a condition precedent to the passing of any interest or merely that, until death occurs, there is a possibility of the donee's title being divested by the condition subsequent.

One reason for the general agreement on the doctrinal structure of a gift causa mortis is that the concept is one of long standing, having been taken by the English from the Roman law, and its character has not varied greatly since the days of Justinian. The Roman donatio causa mortis clearly had the first five characteristics enumerated above. Inst. 2, 7, 1, translated 2 Scott, Civil Law, 49 (1932); and Sandars, Institutes of Justinian, 218 (1st Am.Ed., 1876); Dig. 39, 6, 17, translated 9 Scott, op. cit. 37. No exact parallels can be drawn on the last two characteristics, because of differences in the two systems of law, because the Roman authorities are not entirely clear, and because the concept was then in the process of evolution producing uncertainty as to whether it should be classed as inter vivos or testamentary for the purpose of formalities of transfer. Both theories of passage of title were employed.

Bracton, writing in the thirteenth century, referred to gifts causa mortis. De Legibus, f. 60. But much of his dicusssion is taken almost verbatim from the Roman Law. Woodbine, The Roman Element in Bracton's De Adquirendo Rerum Dominio, 31 Yale L.J. 827, 837 (1922); Scrutton, Roman Law and the Law of England, 92 (1885). It has been contended that Bracton was in the habit of using Roman law on subjects on which there was no English law at the time, in order to give completeness to his exposition. Scrutton, op. cit., 82. While there is disagreement concerning Bracton's use of the Roman law, there seems to be good reason for the contention with respect to a gift causa mortis, since it is now generally agreed that the concept did not appear in the actual decisions in England until the eighteenth century. The Statute of Frauds, enacted in 1677, put an end to informal wills by its provisions regulating nuncupative wills. One widely accepted view holds that the concept of causa mortis gifts emerged at that time in order to validate transfers rendered ineffective by the new statute. This history is recounted in Rundell, Gifts of Choses in Action, 27 Yale L.J. 643, 647 (1918); Schouler, Oral Wills and Death-Bed Gifts, 2 L.Q.Rev. 444, 447 (1886).

SCHERER v. HYLAND

Supreme Court of New Jersey, 1977.
75 N.J. 127, 380 A.2d 698.

PER CURIAM.

Defendant, the Administrator *ad litem* of the Estate of Catherine Wagner, appeals from an Appellate Division decision, one judge dissenting, affirming a summary judgment by the trial court holding that Ms. Wagner had made a valid gift *causa mortis* of a check to plaintiff. We affirm.

The facts are not in dispute. Catherine Wagner and the plaintiff, Robert Scherer, lived together for approximately fifteen years prior to Ms. Wagner's death in January 1974. In 1970, the decedent and plaintiff were involved in an automobile accident in which decedent suffered facial wounds and a broken hip. Because of the hip injury, decedent's physical mobility was substantially impaired. She was forced to give up her job and to restrict her activities. After the accident, plaintiff cared for her and assumed the sole financial responsibility for maintaining their household. During the weeks preceding her death, Ms. Wagner was acutely depressed. On one occasion, she attempted suicide by slashing her wrists. On January 23, 1974, she committed suicide by jumping from the roof of the apartment building in which they lived.

On the morning of the day of her death, Ms. Wagner received a check for $17,400 drawn by a Pennsylvania attorney who had represented her in a claim arising out of the automobile accident. The check represented settlement of the claim. Plaintiff telephoned Ms. Wagner at around 11:30 a.m. that day and was told that the check had arrived. Plaintiff noticed nothing unusual in Ms. Wagner's voice. At about 3:20 p.m., decedent left the apartment building and jumped to her death. The police, as part of their investigation of the suicide, asked the building superintendent to admit them to the apartment. On the kitchen table they found the check, endorsed in blank, and two notes handwritten by the decedent. In one, she described her depression over her physical condition, expressed her love for Scherer, and asked him to forgive her "for taking the easy way out." In the other, she indicated that she "bequeathed" to plaintiff all of her possessions, including "the check for $17,400 * * *." The police took possession of the check, which was eventually placed in an interest-bearing account pending disposition of this action.

Under our wills statute it is clear that Ms. Wagner's note bequeathing all her possessions to Mr. Scherer cannot take effect as a testamentary disposition. N.J.S.A. 3A:3–2. A *donatio causa mortis* has been traditionally defined as a gift of personal property made by a party in expectation of death, then imminent, subject to the condition that the donor die as anticipated. Establishment of the gift has uniformly called for proof of delivery.

The primary issue here is whether Ms. Wagner's acts of endorsing the settlement check, placing it on the kitchen table in the apartment she shared with Scherer, next to a writing clearly evidencing her intent to transfer the check to Scherer, and abandoning the apartment with a clear expectation of imminent death constituted delivery sufficient to sustain a gift *causa mortis* of the check. Defendant, relying on the principles established in Foster v. Reiss, 18 N.J. 41, 112 A.2d 553 (1955), argues that there was no delivery because the donor did not unequivocally relinquish control of the check before her death. Central to this argument is the contention that suicide, the perceived peril, was one which decedent herself created and one which was completely within her control. According to this contention, the donor at any time before she jumped from the apartment roof could have changed her mind, re-entered the apartment, and reclaimed the check. Defendant therefore reasons that decedent did not make an effective transfer of the check during her lifetime, as is required for a valid gift *causa mortis*.

* * *

There is general agreement that the major purpose of the delivery requirement is evidentiary. Proof of delivery reduces the possibility that the evidence of intent has been fabricated or that a mere donative impulse, not consummated by action, has been mistaken for a completed gift. Since "these gifts come into question only after death has closed the lips of the donor," the delivery requirement provides a substantial safeguard against fraud and perjury. See Keepers v. Fidelity Title and Deposit Co., 56 N.J.L. 302, 308, 28 A. 585 (E. & A.1893). In *Foster,* the majority concluded that these policies could best be fulfilled by a strict rule requiring actual manual tradition of the subject-matter of the gift except in a very narrow class of cases where "there can be no actual delivery" or where "the situation is incompatible with the performance of such ceremony."

18 N.J. at 50, 112 A.2d at 559.   Justice Jacobs, in his dissenting opinion
(joined by Justices Brennan and Wachenfeld) questioned the reasonableness of requiring direct physical delivery in cases where donative intent
is "freely and clearly expressed in a written instrument." Id. at 56, 112
A.2d at 562.   He observed that a more flexible approach to the delivery
requirement had been taken by other jurisdictions and quoted approv-
ingly from Devol v. Dye, 123 Ind. 321, 24 N.E. 246, 7 L.R.A. 439 (Sup.
Ct.1890).   That case stated:

> [G]ifts *causa mortis* * * * are not to be held contrary to public policy,
> nor do they rest under the disfavor of the law, when the facts are clearly
> and satisfactorily shown which make it appear that they were freely and
> intelligently made.   Ellis v. Secor, 31 Mich. 185.   While every case must
> be brought within the general rule upon the points essential to such a gift,
> yet, as the circumstances under which donations *mortis causa* are made
> must of necessity be infinite in variety, each case must be determined upon
> its own peculiar facts and circumstances.   Dickeschild v. Bank, 28 W.Va.
> 341; Kiff v. Weaver, 94 N.C. 274.   The rule requiring delivery, either
> actual or symbolical, must be maintained, but its application is to be mil-
> itated and applied according to the relative importance of the subject of the
> gift and the condition of the donor.   The intention of a donor in peril of
> death, when clearly ascertained and fairly consummated within the mean-
> ing of well-established rules, is not to be thwarted by a narrow and illiberal
> construction of what may have been intended for and deemed by him a
> sufficient delivery * * *.

The balancing approach suggested in Devol v. Dye has been articulated in the following manner:

> Where there has been unequivocal proof of a deliberate and well-considered
> donative intent on the part of the donor, many courts have been inclined
> to overlook the technical requirements and to hold that a "constructive" or
> "symbolic" delivery is sufficient to vest title in the donee.   However, where
> this is allowed the evidence must clearly show an intention to part presently
> with some substantial attribute of ownership.   [Gordon v. Barr, 13 Cal.2d
> 596, 601, 91 P.2d 101, 104 (Sup.Ct.Cal.1939)]

In essence, this approach takes into account the purposes served by the
requirement of delivery in determining whether that requirement has
been met.   It would find a constructive delivery adequate to support the
gift when the evidence of donative intent is concrete and undisputed,
when there is every indication that the donor intended to make a present
transfer of the subject-matter of the gift, and when the steps taken by
the donor to effect such a transfer must have been deemed by the donor
as sufficient to pass the donor's interest to the donee.   We are persuaded
that this approach, which does not minimize the need for evidentiary
safeguards to prevent frauds upon the estates of the deceased, reflects
the realities which attend transfers of this kind.

In this case, the evidence of decedent's intent to transfer the check
to Robert Scherer is concrete, unequivocal, and undisputed.   The circumstances definitely rule out any possibility of fraud.   The sole question,
then, is whether the steps taken by the decedent, independent of her
writing of the suicide note, were sufficient to support a finding that she

effected a lifetime transfer of the check to Scherer.   We think that they were.   First, the act of endorsing a check represents, in common experience and understanding, the only act needed (short of actual delivery) to render a check negotiable.   The significance of such an act is universally understood.   Accordingly, we have no trouble in viewing Ms. Wagner's endorsement of the settlement check as a substantial step taken by her for the purpose of effecting a transfer to Scherer of her right to the check proceeds.   Second, we note that the only person other than the decedent who had routine access to the apartment was Robert Scherer. Indeed, the apartment was leased in his name.   It is clear that Ms. Wagner before leaving the apartment placed the check in a place where Scherer could not fail to see it and fully expected that he would take actual possession of the check when he entered.   And, although Ms. Wagner's subsequent suicide does not itself constitute a component of the delivery of this gift, it does provide persuasive evidence that when Ms. Wagner locked the door of the apartment she did so with no expectation of returning.   When we consider her state of mind as it must have been upon leaving the apartment, her surrender of possession at that moment was complete.   We find, therefore, that when she left the apartment she completed a constructive delivery of the check to Robert Scherer.   In light of her resolve to take her own life and her obvious desire not to be deterred from that purpose, Ms. Wagner's failure manually to transfer the check to Scherer is understandable.   She clearly did all that she could do or thought necessary to do to surrender the check.   Her donative intent has been conclusively demonstrated by independent evidence.   The law should effectuate that intent rather than indulge in nice distinctions which would thwart her purpose.   Upon these facts, we find that the constructive delivery she made was adequate to support a gift *causa mortis*.

Defendant's assertion that suicide is not the sort of peril that will sustain a gift *causa mortis* finds some support in precedents from other jurisdictions.   E.g., Ray v. Leader Federal Sav. & Loan Ass'n, 40 Tenn. App. 625, 292 S.W.2d 458 (Ct.App.1953).   See generally Annot., "Nature and validity of gift made in contemplation of suicide," 60 A.L.R.2d 575 (1958).   We are, however, not bound by those authorities nor do we find them persuasive.   While it is true that a gift *causa mortis* is made by the donor with a view to impending death, death is no less impending because of a resolve to commit suicide.   Nor does that fixed purpose constitute any lesser or less imminent peril than does a ravaging disease. Indeed, given the despair sufficient to end it all, the peril attendant upon contemplated suicide may reasonably be viewed as even more imminent than that accompanying many illnesses which prove ultimately to be fatal.   Cf. Berl v. Rosenberg, 169 Cal.App.2d 125, 336 P.2d 975, 978 (Dist. Ct.App.1959) (public policy against suicide does not invalidate otherwise valid gift *causa mortis*).   And, the notion that one in a state of mental depression serious enough to lead to suicide is somehow "freer" to renounce the depression and thus the danger than one suffering from a physical illness, although it has a certain augustinian appeal, has long since been replaced by more enlightened views of human psychology.   In re

Van Wormer's Estate, 255 Mich. 399, 238 N.W. 210 (Sup.Ct.1931) (melancholia ending in suicide sufficient to sustain a gift *causa mortis*). We also observe that an argument that the donor of a *causa mortis* gift might have changed his or her mind loses much of its force when one recalls that a *causa mortis* gift, by definition, can be revoked at any time before the donor dies and is automatically revoked if the donor recovers.

Finally, defendant asserts that this gift must fail because there was no acceptance prior to the donor's death. Although the issue of acceptance is rarely litigated, the authority that does exist indicates that, given a valid delivery, acceptance will be implied if the gift is unconditional and beneficial to the donee. See, e.g., Sparks v. Hurley, 208 Pa. 166, 57 A. 364, 366 (Sup.Ct.1904); Graham v. Johnston, 243 Iowa 112, 49 N.W.2d 540, 543 (Sup.Ct.1951). The presumption of acceptance may apply even if the donee does not learn of the gift until after the donor's death. Taylor v. Sanford, 108 Tex. 340, 344, 193 S.W. 661, 662 (Sup.Ct.1912) (assent to gift of deed mailed in contemplation of death but received after grantor's death should be presumed unless a dissent or disclaimer appears). A donee cannot be expected to accept or reject a gift until he learns of it and unless a gift is rejected when the donee is informed of it the presumption of acceptance is not defeated. See id. at 344, 193 S.W. at 662. Here the gift was clearly beneficial to Scherer, and he has always expressed his acceptance.

Judgment affirmed.

Notes

1. The purposes that are served by the delivery requirement are analyzed in Gulliver and Tilson, Classification of Gratuitous Transfers, 51 Yale L.J. 1 (1941); Mechem, the Requirement of Delivery in Gifts of Chattels and of Choses in Action Evidenced by Commercial Instruments, 21 Ill.L.Rev. 341, 457 (1926–27); Rohan, The Continuing Question of Delivery in the Law of Gifts, 38 Ind. L.J. 1 (1962); Fuller, Consideration and Form, 41 Colum.L.Rev. 799 (1941).

2. There are three types of delivery: manual delivery of the subject-matter of the gift; delivery of an instrument of gift (see Kintzinger v. Millin and Thatcher v. Merriam, the last two cases in this chapter); and constructive delivery. This latter type of delivery contemplates the handing over of some object which will open up access to the subject-matter of the gift. The key to a safe-deposit box, a chest, or a jewelry box is the classic example. See for example Carlson v. Bankers Trust Co., 242 Iowa 1207, 50 N.W.2d 1 (1951). It is a doctrinal prerequisite to this form of delivery that manual delivery of the object itself be "difficult, impracticable, inconvenient or impossible" owing to the excessive bulk or the inaccessibility of the subject-matter. Hatch v. Atkinson, 56 Me. 324, 96 Am.Dec. 464 (1868); Newman v. Bost, 122 N.C. 524, 29 S.E. 848 (1898). This prerequisite can be explained in terms of the functions of delivery, that if the subject-matter can easily be transferred the delivery of a key in its place makes equivocal the donative intent. If the donor delivers one key to a safe deposit box while retaining a duplicate, the requisite confirmation of donative intent would seem to be lacking. In re Estate of Stahl, 13 Ill.App.3d 680, 301 N.E.2d 82 (1973) (intent equivocal and therefore no delivery); but see Winsor v. Powell, 209 Kan. 292, 497 P.2d 292 (1972) (donor and donee's

wife had duplicate keys but the stock in the box had been registered in donee's name and the gift was held valid).

Inasmuch as a key is a tangible object, its delivery satisfies to some extent the common law materialistic concept of vesting ownership by gift. Some of the situations which are analogous to delivery of a key do not have this latter characteristic. The fact that courts have nevertheless sustained the gifts demonstrates the more modern attitude of emphasizing the functions rather than the actualities of delivery. See for example Clark v. O'Neal, 555 S.W.2d 68 (Mo.App.1977) (oral instructions from the hospital bed sufficient delivery of certificates of deposit and promissory note located in donor's home, on analogy to delivery of a key); Waite v. Grubbe, 43 Or. 406, 73 P. 206 (1903) (disclosure of five locations where money was buried held good constructive delivery); Teague v. Abbott, 51 Ind.App. 604, 100 N.E. 27 (1912) (disclosure of combination to safe upheld).

The delivery of a key to a house has been held sufficient to sustain a gift of the furnishings and other personal property in the house. Libel v. Corcoran, 203 Kan. 181, 452 P.2d 832 (1969). Delivery of a car key may constitute a gift of the car. In re Line's Estate, 21 Misc.2d 699, 201 N.Y.S.2d 290 (1959); Antos v. Bocek, 9 Ariz.Supp. 368, 452 P.2d 2533 (1969) (gift denied on other grounds). What are the donee's chances of getting a new registration without litigating the question of title? A public announcement to the newspapers of a gift of a valuable private library to the Hebrew University plus the crating of the books for shipping was held to constitute an effective constructive delivery. Hebrew University Ass'n. v. Nye, 26 Conn.Super. 342, 223 A.2d 397 (1966) (superseding on the submission of additional evidence Hebrew University Association v. Nye, 148 Conn. 223, 169 A.2d 641 (1961)).

3. In situations where the donor is in extremis, it is open to the parties to show that he intended the gift to be final whether he lived or died and that therefore it is an inter vivos rather than a causa mortis gift. Newell v. National Bank of Norwich, 214 A.D. 331, 212 N.Y.S. 158 (1925). The label may be important in determining the outcome of the litigation. Because courts see the doctrine of causa mortis gifts as a threat to the integrity of the statute of wills, a number of rather arbitrary limitations have sometimes been imposed upon such gifts:

(a) If the donee is already in possession of the subject-matter of the gift there must nonetheless be a redelivery to effect a valid causa mortis gift. Drew v. Hagerty, 81 Me. 231, 17 A. 63 (1889) (a case famous for its analysis of delivery as evidence of deliberation and intention and as a guard against frauds). Not so if the gift is classified as inter vivos. Halisey v. Howard, 148 Conn. 466, 172 A.2d 379 (1961); In re Gorden's Will, 238 Iowa 580, 27 N.W.2d 900 (1947). See generally Annot., Necessity of Delivery Where Subject of Gift Is Already in Possession of Donee, 103 A.L.R. 1110 (1936).

(b) It is generally held that an attempted gift causa mortis of real property is void. Reh's Estate, 196 Mich. 210, 162 N.W. 978 (1917); Norman v. Norman, 131 Ind.App. 67, 169 N.E.2d 414 (1960). However, a deed of realty made and delivered at a time when the grantor fears the possibility of death may be sustained by classifying it as a gift inter vivos. Prendergast v. Drew, 103 Conn. 88, 130 A. 75 (1925).

(c) In a few cases, courts have shown a reluctance to accept delivery of an informal written instrument as sufficient to effectuate a gift causa mortis. See for example Foster v. Reiss, cited and discussed in the principal case, and cases cited in Annot., 48 A.L.R.2d 1405, 1422 (1956).

4. The motivation for making a gift causa mortis is frequently the same as for making a will. Traditional doctrine requires that title pass to the donee at delivery. If the transfer is classified as a gift causa mortis the title is subject to divestment if the donor revokes or recovers. A non-lawyer may have difficulty in appreciating the difference between the operation of a gift causa mortis and a will. (So may a lawyer). The outcome of litigation on the validity of the gift has turned on whether the donor said, "When I die these are yours" or "These are yours—if I recover I may want them back." Compare Van Pelt v. King, 22 Ohio App. 295, 154 N.E. 163 (1926) (donor's statement that "if he did not return from the hospital they were hers" meant that the delivery did not pass present title and the gift failed) with In re Newland's Estate, 47 Ohio Abs. 252, 70 N.E.2d 238 (1946) (similar language construed to constitute present gift). One court has denied the distinction and held that the gift is valid whether it is said to vest on the fulfillment of a condition precedent or subject to a condition subsequent. In re Nol's Estate, 251 Wis. 90, 28 N.W.2d 360 (1947). There are a few cases in which the donor has attempted to dispose of his entire estate by a gift causa mortis. Some early authority suggested that this was impermissible because the distinction between a gift and a will must be preserved. This view appears to have been rejected by modern authority. See Elliott's Estate, 312 Pa. 493, 167 A. 289, 90 A.L.R. 360 (1933).

5. The apprehension of death requirement would seem to serve the benevolent purpose of establishing a foundation for the implication of the conditions of revocability during life and by recovery which are justified as being what the donor would desire under the circumstances. But this requirement has also been used as an arbitrary device to nullify the gift. For instance, some authority suggests that the donor must die of the illness of which he was apprehensive (difficult problems of proof involving medical diagnosis and the subjective fears of a person now dead), although most modern authority rejects the necessity of making any such showing. Ridden v. Thrall, 125 N.Y. 572, 26 N.E. 627 (1891); but see, Antos v. Bocek, 9 Ariz.App. 368, 452 P.2d 533 (1969). A gift in contemplation of a surgical operation is held the valid basis for a causa mortis gift even if the donor voluntarily submits to it. Adcock v. Bishop, 309 Ky. 502, 218 S.W.2d 52 (1949). The validity of gifts made in contemplation of suicide is discussed in the principal case.

6. Donative intent is intent to surrender dominion and control over the property and may be present for any type of gift even when the donor harbors hostile feelings toward the donee. See Schultz v. Schultz, 637 S.W.2d 1 (Mo.1982) (donor made valid gift by throwing stock certificates on brother's desk with instructions "to stick them * * *"). Delivery of the subject-matter of the gift with intent to benefit the donee may not suffice if the donor retains control over the property. Gibson v. Boling, 274 Ark. 53, 622 S.W.2d 180 (1981). Failure to re-register the stock on the books of the issuing company, to file gift tax returns, or to affix transfer stamps on the stock may be evidence that a gift was not intended, but such evidence is in no way conclusive. See e.g., Estate of Cristo, 86 A.D.2d 700, 446 N.Y.S.2d 555 (3d Dep't 1982) (gift upheld).

The donee may return the donated articles to the donor without nullifying the gift if the original intent to make the gift is clear. Barham v. Jones, 98 N.M. 195, 647 P.2d 397 (1982) (donee returns rings to donor with words "you are just not you without them"). Once established, donative intent cannot be repudiated at a later date by the donor who changes his or her mind. See e.g., Ashley v. Ashley, 482 Pa. 228, 393 A.2d 637 (1978).

7. The only other event in a person's life which is considered sufficiently analogous to death to warrant the implication of a condition of divestment if the event does not occur is marriage. Thus, substantial gifts such as an engagement ring, clothes, a home, money, jewelry, etc., given in anticipation of marriage, have been held divested if the donee causes the marriage not to occur. Results vary depending on which party, donor or donee, is at fault. Thus pilot-donor, who removed his deceased fiancee's engagement ring at the scene of the crash, must return it to her estate because his negligence caused the crash and prevented the marriage. Hahn v. United States, 535 F.Supp. 132 (S.D.1982). The conditional gift doctrine has been used to effect a restitution of property following the break-up of a relationship between two unmarried persons. See for example In re Marriage of Heinzman, 198 Colo. 36, 596 P.2d 61 (1979). There is, however, no recovery if when the gifts were made the donee was married to some one other than the donor. Hooven v. Quintana, 44 Colo.App. 395, 618 P.2d 702 (1980).

At one time the New York courts held that the statute abolishing actions for breach of contract to marry (N.Y. Civil Rights Law § 80–a) also did away with all other actions arising directly or indirectly out of such breach. Andie v. Kaplan, 263 App.Div. 884, 32 N.Y.S.2d 429 (2d Dep't 1942), affirmed without opinion 288 N.Y. 685, 43 N.E.2d 82 (1942). In 1965 the legislature overruled this holding by enacting § 80–b which permits recovery of gifts made in consideration of marriage without regard to fault when the marriage does not occur. A married man who gives the woman whom he intends to marry after getting a divorce a $60,000 ring has been denied the benefit of the statute as a basis for recovering the ring following the woman's "second thoughts" about the marriage because the underlying arrangement was void as against public policy. Lowe v. Quinn, 27 N.Y.2d 397, 318 N.Y.S.2d 467, 267 N.E.2d 251 (1971). Other courts have held that statutes abolishing actions for breach of contract to marry do not abrogate the right of recovery. See for example Piccininni v. Hajus, 180 Conn. 369, 429 A.2d 886 (1980); Gikas v. Nicholis, 96 N.H. 177, 71 A.2d 785 (1950). See generally, Annot., 46 A.L.R.3d 578 (1972).

Transfer of Choses in Action

FARRELL v. PASSAIC WATER CO.

Court of Chancery of New Jersey, 1913.
82 N.J.Eq. 97, 88 A. 627.

STEVENS, V. C. This is a bill filed by the administratrix of Catherine Farrell against the Passaic Water Company and the executors of James Atkinson. It is alleged that Mr. Atkinson was engaged to be married to Miss Farrell, and that about the year 1895, and while so engaged, he handed her a coupon bond of the Passaic Water Company for $1,000, intending to make her a gift of it. The bond was, at the time of the alleged gift, and still is, registered, as to principal, in the name of Atkinson. The principal sum is payable in July, 1937. Miss Farrell drew the interest coupons during her life, and died in 1909. Atkinson died in 1902. Since the death of Miss Farrell, the bond has been in the possession of either her next of kin or her administratrix. On its face it provides that it is payable to the bearer or registered holder thereof, and that it "may at any time be registered in the name of the owner on the books of the company, * * * after which this bond shall be transferable only upon the books of the company, until it shall, at the request of the holder, be registered as payable to bearer, which shall restore transferability by delivery." The bill prays that the bond may be declared to be a part of the estate of Catherine Farrell, and that the company may be decreed to register it in the name of her administratrix.

The defense is, first, that no gift is proven, and, second, that, if an intention to give has been shown, such gift was imperfect without registry, and a court of equity will not lend its aid to perfect it.

Nothing is better settled than that there is no equity to perfect an imperfect gift, says Sir George Jessel, M.R., in Richards v. Delbridge, L.R. 18 Eq. 11. "The principle is a very simple one. A man may transfer his property without valuable consideration in one of two ways: He may either do such acts as amount in law to a conveyance or assignment of the property, and thus completely divest himself of the legal ownership, in which case the person who by those acts acquires the property takes it beneficially or on trust as the case may be; or the legal owner of the property may by one or other of the modes recognized as amounting to a valid declaration of trust constitute himself a trustee, and, without an actual transfer of the legal title, may so deal with the property as to deprive himself of its beneficial ownership, and declare that he will hold it from that time forward in trust for the other person."

There is nothing in this case to indicate that Atkinson declared that he held the bond in controversy as trustee for Miss Farrell. What he did was, not to set it aside among his own papers, and to declare in any way that from that time forth he held it for her benefit, but to give her the possession of it, and, as far as appears, concern himself no further about it. "If," says the Master of the Rolls, "in the case cited, the gift is intended to take effect by transfer, the court will not hold the intended transfer to operate as a declaration of trust, for then every imperfect instrument would be made effectual by being converted into a perfect trust." If, then, the complainant has a valid title, it must be because Atkinson completely divested himself of all title.

I think considerable confusion has resulted from the use, in some of the later cases, of the term "equitable" in connection with the title of the assignee to a chose in action. If by "equitable" is meant such a title as only a court of equity can give effect to the assumption is manifestly erroneous. If a right is recognized and protected by a court of law (of course I am speaking of those jurisdictions in which the courts of law and equity are still constitutionally distinct), and if such a court has come to be the proper tribunal in which to enforce it, it is a misuse of terms to call the right equitable in contradistinction to legal.

The history of the law on this subject is somewhat curious. In the time of Coke, the property in the paper on which an obligation was written and in the wax with which it was sealed could be divorced from the property in the debt which the paper manifested. He says (folio 232b, § 377): "It is implied that, if a man hath an obligation, though he cannot grant the thing in action, yet he may give or grant the deed, viz., the parchment and wax, to another who may cancel and use the same at his pleasure." This distinction constituted the basis of decision by the Lord Justices in Rummens v. Hare (1 Exch.Div. 169) as late as 1876.

Property in the debt evidenced by the paper stood on a different footing. As the advantages arising from commerce began to be felt, the custom of merchants whereby a foreign bill of exchange was assignable by the payee to a third person so as to vest in him the legal as well as the equitable title was recognized and supported by the English law courts as early as the fourteenth century, and a like custom rendering an inland bill transferable was established in the seventeenth century. Chitty on bills, *10. Promissory notes were put upon the footing of inland bills by the statute of 7 Anne. Other choses in action long stood upon a different footing. Lord Coke (214a) says that it is one of the maxims of the common law that no right of action can be transferred, "because under color thereof pretended titles might be granted to great men, whereby right might be trodden down, and the weak oppressed, which the common law forbiddeth."

But the necessities of trade and commerce were too strong for this maxim, and courts of equity at an early period began to recognize the interest of the assignee. During this period the title of the assignee was equitable, and equitable only. Then the law courts began, indirectly at first, to recognize his right. In Winch v. Keely, 1 Term Rep. 619 (A.D.1787), they did so for the first time explicitly. There a suit was brought in the name of the assignor for the use of the assignee. The defense was that the assignor had become bankrupt and that his title had passed to his assignee in bankruptcy. It was held that the title had not passed, and that the suit would lie. Having recognized and protected the assignee's right, it became, at least to some extent, a mere question of procedure whether the suit should be brought in the one name or the other. This was the view of Buller, J., in Master v. Miller, 4 Term R. p. 341 (A.D.1791). He says: "It must be admitted that, though the courts of law have gone the length of taking notice of choses in action and acting upon them, yet in many cases they have adhered to the formal objection that the action shall be brought in the name of the assignor and not in the name of the assignee. I see no use or convenience in preserving that shadow when the substance is gone, and that it is merely a shadow is apparent from the later cases in which the courts have taken care that it shall never work injustice." Still, in England the action continued for many years to be brought in the name of the assignor. But it became mere form, for, said Hornblower, C. J., in Allen v. Pancoast, 20 N.J.Law, 68, "it has long since been held that an assignment of a chose in action carries with it by implication a right to use the name of the assignor, even against his consent, and in opposition to his release or defeasance of the debt or security assigned."

It is going pretty far to call the right of such an assignee, so protected, an *equitable* in contradistinction to a *legal* right. But when our Legislature in 1797 (Paterson's Laws 1703–1800, p. 254) enacted that the "assignment of bills, bonds and other writings obligatory, for the payment of money, shall be good and effectual in law, and an assignee of any such may thereupon maintain an action of debt in his own name," the only excuse for calling the assignee's title equitable vanished (Reed v. Bainbridge, 4 N.J.Law, 358). The legal title to the wax and paper had always been in the assignee; the legal title to the debt was now also in the assignee.

It thus conclusively appears that the aid of a court of equity to perfect the title of an assignee to a sealed bond for the payment of money is unnecessary, for the right is perfect already. Agreements to assign stand upon quite another footing. If based upon valuable consideration, equity may sometimes enforce them; if not so based, it will not.

Then a perfectly distinct question arises. By what formalities may title be vested in an assignee? At first it was held that an instrument under seal could only be assigned by an instrument of equal dignity. Wood v. Partridge, 11 Mass. 488; but this view has been abandoned, and it is now held that instruments such as bonds, mortgages, and policies of insurance may be assigned without seal, or even by parol accompanied by delivery. Vreeland v. Van Horn, 17 N.J.Eq. 137; Travelers' Insurance Co. v. Grant, 54 N.J.Eq. 208, 33 A. 1060; Allen v. Pancoast, 20 N.J. Law, 71. The effect of the assignment is precisely the same in any of these forms—it vests the legal title in the assignee. The proof of it may be more difficult in the case of an assignment by parol, but in any mode the debt theretofore owing to the obligee passes to the assignee; he is the creditor, and the only creditor.

These several modes of assignment are as applicable to the case of gifts as to those of transfers for value. The gift is just as completely vested by the one mode as by the other, and it is settled law that the fact that the bond is not payable to bearer or that the instrument is not negotiable does not prevent a valid gift of it by manual tradition without writing. Executors of Egerton v. Egerton, 17 N.J.Eq. 421; Corle v. Monkhouse, 50 N.J.Eq. 537, 25 A. 157; Travelers' Insurance Co. v. Grant, 54 N.J.Eq. 208, 33 A. 1060; Thompson v. West, 56 N.J.Eq. 660, 40 A. 197. Proof of delivery, coupled with proof of intent to pass a present interest by way of gift, has precisely the same effect as a formal written transfer. A moment's consideration will show that this is necessarily so. The instrument given remains, in either case, unchanged. If payable by A. to B., it remains so payable on the face of it, whether transferred by writing or not; but by the effect of the transfer what theretofore was payable to B. has in law become payable to C., the transferee. In the case of Green v. Tulane, 52 N.J.Eq. 169, 28 A. 9, the question was not before the court.　I do not think it can be fairly gathered from what Pitney, V. C., said that he thought that a writing was necessary; but, if he there so expressed himself, when the point came squarely before him, in the insurance case, he held otherwise.　The question, then, is, Did Atkinson make a gift; that is, a perfect gift?　Two objections are made; First, it is said that the proof fails to show delivery accompanied with a declaration of intent; and, secondly, that the instrument itself forbids the making of a gift in the manner in which it is alleged to have been made.

As to the first objection: The evidence is that Atkinson, a business man of mature years, possessed of considerable property, while engaged to be married to Miss Farrell, parted with the bond in question; how or when does not appear.　Although he lived for six or seven years after it came into Miss Farrell's possession, he did not reclaim it; reclamation being all the more easy because of the fact that the bond stood registered in his name.　He told a friend that he had made Miss Farrell a present of a bond of that description.　She took the interest accruing upon it for 10 or 12 years before her death.　It was natural that, situated as they were, he should have made a gift, and there is no evidence against it. Under these circumstances I think the inference that a gift was actually made is the only fair inference from the proofs.

But counsel argues that, conceding that an intention to give is proved, the gift remains incomplete because of the clauses in the bond which provide that it is payable to the bearer or registered holder, and that, if registered, it shall be transferable only on the books of the company, until it shall, at the request of the holder, be registered payable to bearer, *"which shall restore transferability by delivery."*

There are two kinds of corporation bonds in common use to-day: Those that are negotiable, and those that are merely assignable.　It seems quite apparent that the object of the clause in question was to give the owner the option of having either the one form of obligation or the other at his pleasure.　It is hardly to be supposed that the company was endeavoring to put upon the market a new kind of obligation, viz., one, *title* to which would not pass from one man to another unless or until there was an actual transfer on the books.　The implied prohibition against transfer would be just as effective in the case of a written assignment, even an assignment under seal, as in the case of a verbal one.　There might, indeed, be a question whether such a limitation could be made effective; but here I do not think it was intended to impose it.　The clause was probably suggested by the similar one put in the ordinary stock certificate, as to which Chancellor Green said: "The title of the holder is in no wise affected by a provision in the charter or by-laws of the corporation that the stock is transferable only on the books of the corporation.　Such a provision is intended merely for the protection and benefit of the corporation."　The fact that in the one case the provision is intended chiefly to protect the company and in the other the bondholder can make no difference, so far as the point under consideration is concerned.　It is well settled that, as between the transferor and transferee, title to the stock certificate is completely vested without transfer on the books.   Matthews v. Hoaglund, 48 N.J.Eq. 455, 21 A. 1054.

But it is said that the failure to direct the company to make a transfer on its books is evidence that Atkinson did not intend his gift to be irrevocable.   If the facts justify the inference that he did so intend, proof that he failed to authorize the company by power of attorney to make a transfer is immaterial.   He had, I have shown, the option of making the gift with or without writing.   Such failure might indeed be a circumstance militating against the gift, if coupled with other circumstances throwing doubt upon it.   Standing by itself, it is without significance as long as it is the doctrine of this court that a valid gift may be made by parol.   Proof of failure to make in one way is no proof of failure to make in another.

Considering, as I do, that the question as between the administratrix of Miss Farrell and the executor of Mr. Atkinson is one of legal title— title of which the law courts take cognizance—it would seem to follow that, if there were a real doubt as to who was legal owner, that doubt would have to be, under our system, settled by the law courts.   There is, however, no dispute as to the material facts, and no reasonable doubt as to the inference to be drawn from them.   The case seems really to be one between the administratrix and the water company;   Atkinson's executors being proper parties, because their testator stands upon the company's books as registered owner.   There is proof that a request to register was made by the administratrix, and that such request was refused.   If a court of equity has jurisdiction to decree a registry of stock (Archer v. American Water Co., 50 N.J.Eq. 50, 24 A. 508; Reilly v. Absecon Land Co., 75 N.J.Eq. 71, 71 A. 248), I see no good reason why it may not compel performance of the company's agreement to register the bond.   A suit for damages based on a refusal to do so would not be a complete or satisfactory remedy.

Under the peculiar circumstances of the case, neither party should have costs.

Notes

1. The proposition that a gift of a chose in action may be effectuated by handing over written evidence of the obligation is illustrated in the following cases:

(a) Stocks and bonds as exemplified by the principal and the next cases. See generally, Israels, Investment Securities as Negotiable Paper—Article 8 of the Uniform Commercial Code, 13 Bus.Law. 676, 681–683 (1958); Annot., Necessity of Delivery of Stock Certificate to Complete Valid Gift of Stock, 23 A.L.R.2d 1171 (1952).

(b) It is generally held that a gift of the rights represented by bills of exchange, promissory notes, checks and certificates of deposit payable to the donor, may be effectuated by handing over the written instrument, whether or not it is indorsed by the donor.   See e.g. Elkins v. Vana, 25 Ariz.App. 122, 541 P.2d 585 (1975) (principle recognized but gift failed on other grounds); Annots., 25 A.L.R. 642 (1923), 40 A.L.R. 508 (1926).

These cases must be distinguished from those where the donor is the maker of the note or the drawer of the check, and attempts to make a gift by delivering such an instrument payable to the donee. Gratuitous delivery of the donor's own note is inoperative, since the promise to pay is a contractual obligation requiring consideration. For a collection of the cases see Annot., Donor's Own Check as Subject of Gift, 38 A.L.R.2d 594 (1954); Suske v. Straka, 229 Minn. 409, 39 N.W.2d 745 (1949); Woods v. Sturges, 116 Miss. 412, 77 So. 186 (1917). While the normal way of making a gift of the whole or part of a checking account is by check, it is usually held that the check is not an assignment but merely an order to pay, which, if gratuitous, is revocable before presentation for payment. Such a gift is, therefore, not complete until payment or certification, and, until then, is revocable by stopping payment or by the donor's death. Holsomback v. Akins, 134 Ga.App. 543, 215 S.E.2d 306 (1975); Griffin v. Louisville Trust Co., 312 Ky. 145, 226 S.W.2d 786 (1950); In re Yale's Estate, 164 Kan. 670, 191 P.2d 906 (1948). There are a few cases contra. Smith v. Clark, 219 Ark. 751, 244 S.W.2d 776 (1952); Hale v. Hale, 313 Ky. 344, 231 S.W.2d 2 (1950). It has also been held that a gratuitous check is an immediate assignment if it covers the entire deposit. Varley v. Sims, 100 Minn. 331, 111 N.W. 269 (1907).

(c) It is generally held that an oral gift of the rights of the donor under a life insurance policy on his own life may be effectuated by handing over the written policy. For a collection of the cases see Annot., Gift of Life Insurance Policy, 33 A.L.R.2d 273 (1954); Davis v. Gillespie, 507 S.W.2d 179 (Ky.1974); McGlynn v. Curry, 82 App.Div. 431, 81 N.Y.S. 855 (2d Dep't 1903) (provision in policy requiring written assignment held not to bar oral gift, since intended only for protection of company); Schlesinger, Gifts of Life Insurance, 103 Trusts & Estates 738 (1964).

(d) Delivery of a savings bank book will effectuate a gift of a deposit in a savings bank. Ridden v. Thrall, 125 N.Y. 572, 26 N.E. 627 (1891) (a famous case on the whole subject of causa mortis gifts).

Why then does delivery of a personal check book fail to effect a gift of the checking account? Brophy v. Haeberle, 220 App.Div. 511, 221 N.Y.S. 698 (4th Dept. 1927); Havighurst, Gifts of Bank Deposits, 14 N.C.L.Rev. 129 (1936).

2. Courts, with uncommon unanimity, have held that clauses in bonds to the effect that, if the bond is registered, it shall be transferable only on the books of the company are of limited effect. They are designed to protect the issuing company and may be relied on by it for questions concerning ownership of the bond, but they have no effect on the rights as between donors and donees and a valid gift may be made by manual delivery of the bond without a change in the registration. In this regard United States Series E savings bonds have presented a particular problem. The Treasury Regulations require that such bonds can only be transferred by re-registration. State courts have held that such regulations are binding upon them with the force of federal law and must be literally adhered to. Annot., United States Saving Bonds as Subject of Valid Gift, 40 A.L.R.2d 788 (1955); Connell v. Bauer, 240 Minn. 280, 61 N.W.2d 177 (1953); Brown v. Vinson, 188 Tenn. 120, 216 S.W.2d 748 (1949); Fidelity Union Trust Co. v. Tezyk, 140 N.J.Eq. 474, 55 A.2d 26, 173 A.L.R. 546 (1947); contra, Marshall v. Felker, 156 Fla. 476, 23 So.2d 555, 161 A.L.R. 167 (1945). The Supreme Court has held that the registered co-owner of a U.S. savings bond could not make an effective gift by physically delivering it to the other registered

co-owner and that therefore the bond remained in the donor's estate and was subject to the federal estate tax.   The regulations, which require that a transfer can only be made by reissuance of the bond in the new owner's name, override any inconsistent state property law.   United States v. Chandler, 410 U.S. 257, 93 S.Ct. 880, 35 L.Ed.2d 247 (1973).

It has been held, however, that a sole owner, as distinguished from a co-owner, may make a valid inter vivos gift by delivery of the bond, because the regulations are only concerned with bonds that are registered in two or more names as joint tenants with rights of survivorship.   In re Klarfeld's Estate, 38 Misc.2d 688, 237 N.Y.S.2d 424 (1963) (and the cases discussed therein).   Similar authority for gifts causa mortis was acknowledged by language added in 1954 to the regulations (31 C.F.R. § 315.13a), reading as follows: "Payment or reissue will be made to the donee of a gift causa mortis of a savings bond if the donor was not survived by a co-owner or beneficiary and the gift is established to the satisfaction of the Secretary of the Treasury by judicial proceedings or otherwise."   19 Fed.Reg. 3223 (1954).

KINTZINGER v. MILLIN

Supreme Court of Iowa, 1962.
254 Iowa 173, 117 N.W.2d 68.

GARFIELD, Chief Justice.   This is a probate proceeding involving the validity of testator's inter vivos gift of 3700 shares of corporate stock to his son, James W. Millin, one of three co-executors under the will of LaVern G. Millin, deceased.   Following trial to the court it was decreed the gift was invalid because the stock was not delivered to the donee. He, as an executor and individually, together with David W. Kintzinger, another executor, has appealed.

The issues arose upon an application of Kintzinger and James W. Millin, executors, and Millin, individually, for authority to sell preferred stock of Western Printing & Lithographing Co. (herein called "Western" or "the company") in order to pay debts, taxes and costs of administration. The largest of these items is the federal estate tax.   Bernice P. Millin, testator's divorced wife to whom the preferred stock was bequeathed, Chloe M. Calkins, daughter of Bernice and testator (she is also a sister of James W. Millin), and Willard D. Calkins, Chloe's husband, as the third co-executor, filed objections to the application.   They alleged the 3700 shares of Western common stock was rightfully part of testator's residuary estate and it was chargeable with the liabilities of the estate before resort could be had to the preferred stock bequeathed to Bernice.

By reply to the above objections, applicants-appellants alleged in part that testator did not own the 3700 shares of common stock when he died October 21, 1959, but had made a completed gift of it to his son James W. in January of that year.

Most of the evidence offered on the trial consisted of depositions of Western's officers in an attempt to establish there were valid restrictions against ownership of the stock by nonemployees.   Testator was a retired employee of Western but his son James was never connected with it.   The trial court, as indicated, placed his decision on the sole ground the gift to James failed for want of delivery of the stock and found it unnecessary to decide the validity of the claimed restrictions on its transfer.

I. On January 8, 1959, testator LaVern G. Millin and his son James went to a bank in Dubuque, where LaVern lived, and saw Mr. Peryon, vice-president. Testator had with him an envelope containing 17 certificates representing 3700 shares of Western common stock. He asked Peryon to witness his signature on the certificates and send them to Western at Racine, Wisconsin, so they might be transferred to his son. Testator signed the transfer form on each certificate, leaving blank the name of the transferee, and Peryon signed each of them as a guarantor of testator's signature. Testator asked the banker to transfer the certificates to James and instruct Western to mail them to his son.

Peryon wrote and signed a letter on the bank's letterhead to Western as testator directed. The latter read it and was given a copy. He was satisfied with the letter which, with the certificates, was mailed to Western at Racine the same day. The letter read, "We are enclosing herewith 3700 shares of stock issued in the names of L. G. Millin and LaVern G. Millin, who are one and the same person. Please reissue these shares in the name of James W. Millin and forward same to him at 1069 Lombard Ave., St. Paul, 5, Minnesota. We understand this transfer has already been discussed with you."

Mr. Benstead, a top officer of Western, wrote testator in Dubuque on January 12, acknowledging receipt of the bank's letter and the stock certificates, declining to transfer the stock and asserting that when testator was in Racine the preceding week it was understood testator intended to assign certain of his common stock to a trustee with the understanding Western's treasurer would vote the stock and it would be sold back to Western after testator's death. "When such a trust * * * is completed, we will be glad to transfer your stock, but to transfer it pursuant to the letter from the bank is, first contrary to our agreement with you and, second, the request comes from a party not in interest. We would be disposed to return your certificates with this letter but inasmuch as they are endorsed and in negotiable form, we will hold them in safe keeping, awaiting your advice as to their disposition."

On January 17, 1959, Mr. Kintzinger, as attorney for testator and his son James, wrote Benstead. Essential parts of the letter are: "Mr. Millin wants his said stock transferred to his son, James W. Millin Sr., and enclosed herewith as your authority for completing said transfer is a separate Assignment of Stock, duly executed by Mr. Millin, which together with the assignments already signed by him, should give you ample legal authority to *complete the assignment immediately.* * * *

"Mr. Millin does not desire to establish a trust as proposed by you at the present time, nor does he or his son propose to work against the interests of you or the company in any way.

"If there is any legal reason why this transfer should not be completed promptly by you, please advise me the details of same. If there is some agreement, as you speak of in your letter, please let me know all of the details. Mr. Millin does not understand that he agreed to set up a trust as suggested by you, but his understanding is that he was merely discussing the matter with you and that he did not make any binding agreement supported by consideration.

"Please issue the new stock certificate promptly and send it to me as attorney for James W. Millin, Sr."

Enclosed with Kintzinger's letter to Benstead was an "Assignment of Stock," dated January 16, 1959, signed by LaVern G. Millin in Kintzinger's presence and with his signature guaranteed by the Dubuque bank previously referred to. Body of the assignment reads: "FOR VALUE RECEIVED, Lavern G. Millin, also known as L. G. Millin, does hereby sell, assign and transfer unto James W. Millin Sr., 1069 Lombard Ave., St. Paul 5, Minnesota thirty-seven hundred (3,700) shares of Common Stock of the Western Printing and Lithographing Co. (Racine, Wisconsin) standing in my name on the books of said corporation represented by various Stock Certificates which have recently been forwarded to the corporation for transfer, and I do hereby irrevocably constitute and appoint ——— attorney to transfer the said stock on the books of the within named Company with full power of substitution in the premises."

On January 29 Benstead wrote Kintzinger a letter, sending a copy to testator, his son and daughter. The letter is too long to reproduce here. It expresses surprise testator would attempt to transfer his stock to a nonemployee of the company without giving an employee the right to vote the stock and again urges creation of a trust "in a manner consistent with the wishes of the company as to the ultimate disposition of the stock."

Benstead testified in his deposition it was a condition of owning the stock that it would be offered back to the company if the employee became employed by a competing company and that upon the employee's death it would be offered back to Western in a manner suitable to the employee. There is no claim testator was ever employed by a competing company. There is other evidence the stock was to be offered back to Western if the owner merely left its employ before reaching retirement age. There was no restriction on transfer of the stock in the articles of incorporation or bylaws or on the stock certificates themselves prior to July 26, 1960, when the articles were amended to provide for different classes of stock and changing the corporate name to Western Publishing Co., Inc. There was no written agreement between the company and testator or other stockholder restricting transfer of the stock.

The week before testator and his son went to the Dubuque bank on January 8 they visited the company office in Racine. Benstead testified testator told him then he was not going to live long and had "enough stock here to take care of my wife and children and I would like to get the thing settled. I want to have Jim act for me in the matter." (After he and Bernice were divorced testator married Nancy Elizabeth who survived as his widow.) According to Benstead he told testator he might accomplish his purpose by setting up trusts for his heirs that would carry out his wishes and not violate the conditions under which he owned the stock[;] Benstead showed him a trust agreement he had made regarding his own stock and testator said that was satisfactory to him as a means of accomplishing his purpose.

After testator's stock certificates were sent the company three quarterly dividends on it were declared and paid to testator before he died October 21, 1959.

On July 13, 1960, the three executors, the widow, the divorced wife, the son and daughter, who include all the heirs and beneficiaries under the will, signed a written consent that the 3700 shares be forthwith transferred absolutely and delivered to the son James "in accordance with the assignment of said shares made to (him) by LaVern G. Millin under date of January 16, 1959." James, in turn, assigned 1110 shares to his sister Chloe M. Calkins. The company then (July, 1960) transferred 2590 shares to James and 1110 to Chloe.

The attitude of the company toward transfer of the stock to James prior to July, 1960, was thus expressed by Mr. Benstead, "We object to James owning stock, not as an individual, but because he is not an employee."

II. We think the first question is the validity of the claimed restriction on transfer of the stock. This is solely a question of law. It is clear the stock would have been transferred on the company books and a new certificate issued to the son James except for this restriction on the transfer. It is unimportant just what the precise terms of the restriction were.

This question is to be determined by Wisconsin law. It is contended the restriction was orally agreed to by testator and other stockholders. The company is a Wisconsin corporation. Its place of business where the stock was issued and where testator worked was in that state. Testator lived there until his retirement. If, as contended, testator made an agreement restricting transfer of his stock it was made and to be performed in Wisconsin.

The law of the place of contracting determines the legality of the contract, especially where such place is also the place of performance. Liljedahl v. Glassgow, 190 Iowa 827, 830–831, 180 N.W. 870; McDaniel v. Chicago & N.W.R. Co., 24 Iowa 412, 417; Restatement, Conflict of Laws, section 332(e); 11 Am.Jur., Conflict of Laws, sections 116, 117; 15 C.J.S. Conflict of Laws § 11b, pages 883–886.

At the time this stock was issued to testator section 15 of the Uniform Stock Transfer Act was in effect in Wisconsin, W.S.A. 183.14. So far as now pertinent it provides: " * * * there shall be no restriction upon the transfer of shares so represented (by certificate) by virtue of any by laws of such corporation, *or otherwise,* unless the * * * restriction is stated upon the certificate." (Emphasis added).

Further, the Wisconsin Supreme Court had held a corporate bylaw containing a less restrictive provision than the one now before us did not bind the purchaser of stock because it was not stated upon the stock certificate and he could compel the corporation to transfer the stock on its books. Magnetic Mfg. Co. v. Manegold (1930), 201 Wis. 154, 229 N.W. 544.

The case just cited was followed by Larson v. Superior Auto Parts (1955), 270 Wis. 613, 72 N.W.2d 316, 318–319, where the restriction was agreed to by all stockholders. It was there contended the restriction was binding upon a stockholder who had actual notice of it even though not stated on the certificate and that the above statute did not apply to restrictions on transfers created by mutual agreement. Both contentions were rejected and the purported contract was held to be void.

Appellant's reply to appellees' objections refers to the Wisconsin statute and these two decisions by plain designation and the trial court's attention was called to them, as contemplated by rule 94, Rules of Civil Procedure, 58 I.C.A. The Wisconsin statute and decisions leave no room for doubt that the claimed restriction upon the transfer of testator's 3700 shares was in violation of Wisconsin law and therefore void because not stated upon any of the certificates.

The Uniform Stock Transfer Act is in effect in Iowa (chapter 493A, Codes, 1950–1962, I.C.A.; chapter 252, Laws 52d General Assembly, 1947) and all other states. Kansas and North Dakota, however, omitted section 15 of the Act from their enactments. Hopwood v. Topsham Telephone Co., 120 Vt. 97, 132 A.2d 170, 173; Anno. 29 A.L.R.2d 901. The Wisconsin precedents, supra, accord with several on the points there considered, notably Costello v. Farrell, 234 Minn. 453, 48 N.W.2d 557, 560–563, 29 A.L.R.2d 890, 897–900, a leading case. See Anno., supra, at pages 901–902; Hopwood v. Topsham Telephone Co., supra; Sorrick v. Consolidated Telephone Co., 340 Mich. 463, 65 N.W.2d 713, 716.

Appellees admit Larson v. Superior Auto Parts and Costello v. Farrell, both supra, are contrary to their contention the claimed restriction on transfer was valid. They rely upon Baumohl v. Goldstein (1924), 95 N.J.Eq. 597, 124 A. 118, 121, and Doss v. Yingling (1930), 95 Ind.App. 494, 172 N.E. 801. The Baumohl case makes the statement that section 15 of the Uniform Act "was designed for the protection of innocent purchasers of stock." No authority is cited for this. Doss v. Yingling repeats the statement on the authority of the Baumohl opinion. Neither decision is from the highest court of the state. Both antedate several decisions which reach a contrary result. In connection with Doss v. Yingling see Hoosier Chemical Works v. Brown, 200 Ind. 535, 165 N.E. 323, 325, which the former considers.

Baumohl v. Goldstein and Doss v. Yingling are discussed in Costello v. Farrell, supra, which Larson v. Superior Auto Parts, supra, approves. The annotation, supra, in 29 A.L.R.2d 901, 904–905, explains the Baumohl and Doss cases on the basis of the peculiar facts in each which made it inequitable for the corporate officer to invoke section 15 of the Uniform Act. "It is doubtful that these cases would be followed except under similar conditions. It seems certain, at any rate, that it cannot be assumed from these cases that mere knowledge of the restriction will make it effective even though there is a lack of compliance with section 15 of the statute (page 904)."

There are at least three reasons why we decline to approve the statement in the Baumohl opinion, repeated in Doss v. Yingling, that section

15 of the Act was designed merely for the protection of innocent purchasers of stock; (1) the facts in those cases differ widely from those here. (2) As Costello v. Farrell, supra, 234 Minn. 453, 48 N.W.2d 557, 561, 29 A.L.R.2d 890, 898, observes, "If the authors of the uniform act and the legislature had intended that the benefit of the provision (section 15) * * * should be limited to a purchaser for value in good faith without notice of the restrictive by-law, they undoubtedly would have said so. They simply said that there should be no restriction unless (it) was stated upon the certificate." (3) The Wisconsin court has declared the law of that state, with which we are concerned on this issue, to be contrary to the statement on which appellees rely.

It is unnecessary to decide appellants' claim that the restriction was void as against public policy.

III. We think the question whether there was a valid delivery of the 3700 shares is one of law. The facts bearing on the issue are not disputed nor susceptible of different inferences. No question of credibility of witnesses or weight of the evidence is presented. The only reasonable conclusion to be fairly drawn from this record is that there was sufficient delivery of the stock and the gift may not be invalidated on the ground of nondelivery. Tucker v. Tucker, 138 Iowa 344, 348, 116 N.W. 119; In re Estate of Hanson, 205 Iowa 766, 218 N.W. 308; In re Estate of Higgins, 207 Iowa 95, 97, 222 N.W. 401.

Division I hereof states the controlling facts. Testator signed the transfer form on each stock certificate in the presence of his son and the banker Peryon and gave them to the latter, directing him to send them to the company with instructions to reissue the stock in the son's name and forward it to James at his given address. The banker did as directed to testator's satisfaction. As stated, it is clear the stock would have been reissued to the son except for a restriction on its transfer we have held void.

Upon being advised of the company's refusal to transfer the stock and its retention of the certificates, testator executed a separate document containing a written assignment and power of attorney in blank to transfer the stock on the company books. Upon receipt of this document and accompanying request for issuance of a new certificate in the son's name, the company again refused the request because of the void restriction on transfer of the stock.

There is no substantial evidence casting doubt on testator's intention that James have this stock at the time testator parted with it. Such intent appears from writings that are not questioned. It may be conceded delivery is essential to a gift inter vivos. But delivery may be constructive or symbolic as well as actual. It was not necessary, under the circumstances here, that testator physically hand these stock certificates to his son who was present at the bank when the former gave them to the banker and retained no control over them.

We have held corporate stock may be transferred, as between the parties, by written assignment thereof without manual delivery of the stock certificates. Delivery of the separate instrument is deemed delivery of the stock. Especially should this be true where, as here, the owner has parted with possession of the certificates by having them sent to the corporation for transfer of the stock on its books.

See in support of these views Leedham v. Leedham, 218 Iowa 767, 769, 254 N.W. 61, 62, where the certificates themselves were not delivered to the donee-son nor to the attorney with whom the assignment was left. This holding is approved in Petty v. Mutual Benefit Life Ins. Co., 235 Iowa 455, 464, 15 N.W.2d 613, 615, and Home for Destitute Crippled Children v. Boomer, 308 Ill.App. 170, 31 N.E.2d 812, 820–821. See also In re Fenton's Estate, 182 Iowa 346, 357, 165 N.W. 463, which supports the view that the written assignment here was a confirmation of the delivery already made of the stock. These precedents express the general rule. 24 Am.Jur. Gifts § 81; 38 C.J.S. Gifts § 22b, page 802; Annos. 48 A.L.R.2d 1405, 1407–1408; 23 A.L.R.2d 1171, 1190; 99 A.L.R. 1077, 1078, 1084; 63 A.L.R. 537, 545–546.

According to our decisions and the weight of authority, transfer of the stock on the corporate books was not essential to a valid gift thereof as between the parties. [Citations omitted.]

Appellees' assertion that Leedham v. Leedham, supra, has been over-ruled by Code section 493A.1 of our Uniform Stock Transfer Act cannot be accepted. They maintain the law of Iowa governs the validity of the transfer. Since appellants concede this, insofar as it involves the question of delivery, we assume it to be true, without so deciding.

Section 493A.1 provides: "How transferred. Title to a certificate and to the shares represented thereby can be transferred only, (1) by delivery of the certificate indorsed either in blank or to a specified person by the person appearing by the certificate to be the owner of the shares represented thereby, or (2) by delivery of the certificate and a separate document containing a written assignment of the certificate or a power of attorney to sell, assign, or transfer the same or the shares represented thereby, signed by the person appearing by the certificate to be the owner of the shares represented thereby. Such assignment or power of attorney may be either in blank or to a specified person."

In the first place, certificates for 1620 of the 3700 shares were issued prior to February 21, 1947, and chapter 493A, including section 493A.1, does not apply to these certificates (section 493A.23).

In the second place, "delivery of the certificate," as used in 493A.1, quoted above, should not be held to mean merely delivery to the donee *personally*, as appellees seem to assume. The statute is not so limited in terms and we should not engraft such a limitation upon it. If there is delivery of the certificate indorsed in blank or accompanied by a separate document as referred to in (2) signed by the person appearing by the certificate to be the owner, the statute is complied with. " 'Delivery' means voluntary transfer of possession from one person to another." 493 A.22. There was a delivery here within the terms of 493 A. 1. See in this connection 29 Chicago-Kent Law Review 342; Young v. Cockman, 182 Md. 246, 34 A.2d 428, 149 A.L.R. 1006, 1010. We will return to this point.

In the third place, although some decisions are to the contrary[,] by what we think is the weight of authority which we are persuaded to follow, the rights of the parties as between themselves are not affected by the provisions of the Uniform Act. They were enacted for the protection of the corporation, so it might safely deal in payment of dividends or otherwise with the person in whose name the stock was registered. [Citations omitted.]

See also Annos. 23 A.L.R.2d 1171, 1194–1196; 48 A.L.R.2d 1405, 1416 ("In several of the later cases the courts have (held) * * * the provisions of the statute are for the protection of the corporation issuing the stock, and do not preclude a gift of the shares evidenced only by a separate written instrument which would be effective, as between the parties thereto, in the absence of the statute.")

We have said the Uniform Act, even if applicable, does not require delivery to the donee personally. Nor does the law, independent of the statute. "The rule is well settled that delivery to a third person as agent or trustee for the use of the donee, and under such circumstances as indicate that the donor relinquishes all control over the property and intends to vest title in the donee, is quite as effectual as manual delivery directly to him." [Citations omitted.]

Appellees argue the company was testator's agent for the purpose of delivery of the stock and cite a few precedents from other jurisdictions claimed to support this view. It is true generally that delivery to a donor's agent is not deemed absolute since he holds the property for the donor subject to recall. It is otherwise where delivery is to a third person as agent or trustee for the benefit of the donee. Annos. 23 A.L.R.2d 1171, 1179–1183; 48 A.L.R.2d 1405, 1419–1421; 38 C.J.S. Gifts § 25; 24 Am. Jur. Gifts § 30.

Our decisions make it clear that by causing the stock to be sent to the company for transfer on its records to James testator did not intend to retain the title in himself nor cause the stock to be held subject to his right of recall. He is deemed rather to have constituted the company agent or trustee for the son's benefit. In no other way could the stock be transferred on the corporate records. [Citations omitted.]

We have said the person to whom delivery is made for the benefit of the donee is presumed, in the absence of countervailing circumstances, to take the property as trustee for the donee, not as agent of the donor. [Citations omitted.]

One other fact deserves further mention. As stated, after the stock was sent [to] the company it declared and paid testator three quarterly dividends prior to his death. We think this insufficient on which to base a finding the stock was not delivered.

Testator's name stood on the corporate records as owner of the stock. Payment of dividends to him would therefore necessarily follow. Re Connell's Estate, supra, 282 Pa. 555, 128 A. 503, 38 A.L.R. 1362, 1364.

The gift having been completed when the assigned certificates and the separate assignment were sent the company, the son's title could not be affected by testator's receipt of the dividends. Indeed any act of a donor after a completed gift, not consented to or acquiesced in by the donee, will not affect the latter's title. [Citations omitted.]

An article in 20 Rocky Mountain Law Review 67, 68, entitled Application of the Uniform Stock Transfer Act to Gifts of Stock, states: "If the donor's only purpose is to make an effective inter vivos gift of corporate stock, he should:

"1. Indorse the certificate and tender it to the issuing company for transfer with instructions to register the shares in the name of the donee and to mail a new certificate to the donee;

"2. Instruct the donee to exercise voting rights, receive dividends, and retain possession of the certificate."

Testator strictly complied with the first of these statements. Compliance with the second is not shown. Testator had no occasion to comply therewith because of the company's refusal to reissue the stock.

This from Strout v. Burgess, 144 Me. 263, 68 A.2d 241, 12 A.L.R.2d 939, 952, directly supports our holding on the issue of delivery: "It is evident that Charles T. Burgess made sufficient delivery of these endorsed certificates of stock to transfer title. Both the transferee and the transferor were present at the bank with these stock certificates endorsed in blank. The stock certificates in the presence of both parties were delivered to the Cashier of the bank to forward for transfer on the books of the various corporations by whom they had been issued, in accordance with directions given to him. This constitutes sufficient delivery by a the transferor to the transferee. Had the transfer been of the entire interest no one could question the sufficiency of the delivery to pass title from the transferor to the transferee."

Reversed and remanded.

* * *

Notes

1. The Uniform Stock Transfer Act, various provisions of which are discussed in the principal decision, has been superseded by the Uniform Commercial Code, which has, in turn, been enacted generally throughout the United States. The Code continues the requirement that a transfer of a security requires delivery of the certificate although the statutory language has been simplified from that used in Section 1 of the Uniform Stock Transfer Act (see § 493A.1 of the Iowa Code quoted in the opinion at p. 396). The language of the Uniform Commercial Code is as follows:

§ 8–309. Effect of Indorsement Without Delivery

An indorsement of a certificated security, whether special or in blank, does not constitute a transfer until delivery of the certificated security on which it appears or, if the endorsement is on a separate document, until delivery of both the document and the certificated security.

§ 8–103. Issuer's Lien

A lien upon a security in favor of an issuer thereof is valid against a purchaser only if:

(a) the security is certificated and the right of the issuer to the lien is noted conspicuously thereon; or

(b) the security is uncertificated and a notation of the right of the issuer to the lien is contained in the initial transaction statement sent to the purchaser or, if his interest is transferred to him other than by registration of transfer, pledge, or release, the initial transaction statement sent to the registered owner or the registered pledgee.

§ 8–204.   Effect of Issuer's Restrictions on Transfer

A restriction on transfer of a security imposed by the issuer, even if otherwise lawful, is ineffective against any person without actual knowledge of it unless:

(a) the security is certificated and the restriction is noted conspicuously thereon; or

(b) the security is uncertificated and a notation of the restriction is contained in the initial transaction statement sent to the person or, if his interest is transferred to him other than by registration of transfer, pledge, or release, the initial transaction statement sent to the registered owner or the registered pledgee.

2. It is held that delivery of an unindorsed certificate effects a gift. In re McVicker's Estate, 39 Ill.App.2d 389, 188 N.E.2d 731 (1963) (but the fact that it is unindorsed may raise questions concerning donative intent); In re Hill's Estate, 30 Ill.App.2d 243, 174 N.E.2d 233 (1961). Can there be a valid gift where the stock is registered in the donee's name but the certificate is retained by the donor? As with the recordation of land conveyances, this is usually held to constitute a valid transfer if a transfer was really intended. See Estate of Ross v. Ross, 626 P.2d 489 (Utah 1981) (and cases discussed therein). But registration of a savings bank account in someone else's name without a surrender of the savings bank book does not necessarily mean that a court will find a gift. Tanner v. Robinson, 411 So.2d 240 (Fla.App.1982) (gift of joint brokerage account upheld). Annot., Opening Savings Account in Sole Name of Another, Without Surrender of Passbook, as a Gift, 1 A.L.R.2d 538 (1948).

Note should be taken of the volume of cases involving the joint holding with express rights of survivorship of stocks, bonds, bank accounts and the like. The question of ownership arises when the person who contributed all the property and who usually retained all the indicia of ownership dies first. Does his estate or the surviving tenant have the superior claim to the property? The traditional view holds that the survivor will take the property if a gift of it was intended. Annot., Creation of Joint Savings Account or Savings Certificate as Gift to Survivor, 43 A.L.R.3d 971 (1972). The issue frequently arises whether a joint bank account with right of survivorship has been opened for the convenience of the parties (i.e., a parent makes a daughter or son a joint tenant in order to manage the funds) without intending to make a gift to the survivor. See e.g., Desrosiers v. Germain, 12 Mass.App.Ct. 852, 429 N.E.2d 385 (1981) (no gift to the survivor intended). In re Estate of Sipe, 492 Pa. 125, 422 A.2d 826 (1980) (not just a convenience account, as gift to survivor intended). The signing of a joint signature card is prima facie evidence of a gift to the survivor, placing the burden on the contestant to rebut the presumption of gift by convincing evidence. See Banko v. Malanecki, 499 Pa. 92, 451 A.2d 1008 (1982) (gift to survivor of co-habitants upheld).

3. The principal case discusses briefly the important doctrinal area concerning the effect of making delivery to a third person rather than to the donee. The situation arises when the donor hands the object to a friend with instructions to deliver it to the donee. Complications arise when the donor gives further instructions to give it to the donee only when the donor dies. The issue is whether there is a valid divestment at the time when the delivery was made, and that is said to turn on whether the third person is "trustee" for the donee or the "agent" of the donor. The former label means that the delivery was effective and the gift valid while the latter label means that there was no delivery (unless the third person has handed the object over to the donee) and that the agency is revoked by the principal's death. The word "trustee" in this context is not being used in its true technical sense but rather as a convenient title for the donee's alter ego. See In re Gardner's Estate, 82 Ohio Abs. 185, 162 N.E.2d 579, 582 (1959).

In the flow of cases on the point it appears, for the most part, that the two labels are totally conclusionary, applied only to explain a decision which has already been made as to whether or not a gift was intended. It has been suggested that the following types of evidence may be relevant to the characterization of the third person:

(a) The donor's instruction. The donor's statement that he might ask for the object back (in other words, the retention of the power to revoke) is very persuasive that the third person is the agent of the donor. It is ironic that if the gift is held to be causa mortis such a power would be implied without invalidating the gift. Retention of other types of control or supervision over the third person suggests an agency. The instructions not to deliver until after death do not necessarily destroy the gift—the issue turns again on whether only possession awaits the death of the donor, in which case title passed at delivery and the gift is good, or whether death is a condition precedent to the passing of title, in which case the transfer is void as testamentary.

(b) Reasons for making a gift through an intermediary. The unavailability or infancy of the donee, for instance, explain the necessity of a third person on grounds other than the retention of control by the donor.

(c) The previous relationship between the donor and the third person. If the third person had been the donor's lawyer or business agent a court may hold that the agency relationship continued.

On the validity of delivery to a third person, compare Estate of Cristo, 86 A.D.2d 700, 446 N.Y.S.2d 555 (3d Dep't 1982) (delivery to donor's accountant upheld) and Malloy v. Smith, 265 Md. 460, 290 A.2d 486 (1972) (delivery to donor's friend to be turned over to donee at donor's death effective delivery) with First National Bank of Lockhaven v. Fitzpatrick, 29 A.D.2d 450, 289 N.Y.S.2d 314 (1968) (delivery to a nephew ineffective because still under the donor's control). See generally, Annot., Delivery to Third Person as Valid Gift, 57 A.L.R.3d 1083 (1974).

THATCHER v. MERRIAM

Supreme Court of Utah, 1952.
121 Utah 191, 240 P.2d 266.

HOYT, District Judge. In this case the administrator and heirs of Joseph F. Livingston, deceased, sue to have declared void an instrument entitled "Assignment" by which Joseph F. Livingston, in consideration of love and affection purported to give and assign a certain promissory note, together with a deed of trust and a chattel mortgage securing payment of same, to his three sisters, subject to certain terms and conditions set out in the assignment. The instrument of assignment was delivered by Livingston personally in his lifetime at the home of one of the assignees in the presence of all three of them. The promissory note, deed of trust and a certified copy of the chattel mortgage (the original being filed with the county recorder) remained in Livingston's possession until his death, which occurred nineteen days after he delivered the assignment to the three sisters. The promissory note referred to was for the principal sum of $70,476.92 and was a renewal of a previous note given at the time the deed of trust and chattel mortgage were executed. The whole amount of the renewal note remained owing at the time of Livingston's death. The material parts of the instrument of assignment are as follows:

"ASSIGNMENT

"In consideration of the love and affection which I hold for the assignees herein, I, Joseph F. Livingston, of Salt Lake City, Salt Lake County, State of Utah, hereby give and assign fifty (50%) per cent of the following described property to my sister, Isabelle Mirriam [sic], of Manti, Utah, twenty-five (25%) percent of the following described property to my sister, Lillian Robertson, of Fountain Green, Utah, and twenty-five (25%) per cent of the following described property to my sister Ellen Cook, of Salt Lake City, Utah, subject to the terms and conditions hereinafter set forth, said property being more particularly described as follows:

"One Deed of Trust covering 5,260 acres of real property   *   *   * in which instrument one Loren Dewayne Mirriam [sic] conveyed said property in trust to the undersigned, Joseph F. Livingston, to secure the payment of his promissory note made payable to the undersigned, upon which there was a balance due as of November 1st, 1947, of the sum of $70,476.92, which promissory note said Deed of Trust secures.

together with said promissory note, which the undersigned hereby assigns to the assignees herein in the percentages herein reserved unto them, provided, however, that the undersigned assignor hereby reserves unto himself during his lifetime all amounts becoming due on the principal of said promissory note and all amounts in excess of the amounts periodically becoming due thereon which the maker thereof under the terms of said note may choose to pay on said principal during the lifetime of the assignor herein; the interest on said principal amount to be paid as said interest shall accrue, to the assignees herein in the percentages hereinabove reserved, i.e., 50% of said interest accruing to be paid to said Isabelle Mirriam [sic], 25% of said interest accruing to be paid to said Lillian Robertson, and 25% of said interest accruing to be paid to said Ellen Cook, the undersigned hereby authorizing the maker of said note and mortgage to make payment of the amounts herein assigned to the persons named in the percentages herein mentioned; [Then follows a similar recital with reference to a chattel mortgage given to secure the same note.]

"In Witness Whereof, I have hereunto set my hand at Salt Lake City, Utah, this 27th day of March, 1948.

"/s/ Joseph F. Livingston

"Signed in the Presence of:

"/s/ A. S. Anderson.   *   *   *"

The instrument bears a notary's certificate of acknowledgment but the evidence shows that the assignor did not appear before the notary to acknowledge it.

The plaintiffs (appellants herein) contend (1) That by the language of the assignment Joseph F. Livingston retained such dominion and control over the subject matter of the attempted gift, or at least as to the installments of principal, that the assignment was inoperative; (2) That, since the promissory note was not endorsed, and the note, deed of trust and chattel mortgage were retained in Livingston's possession until his death, there was no transfer of ownership of the note or security; (3) That the court erroneously received in evidence a deposition of one of the defendants in violation of the so-called dead man statute, Section 104–49–2(3) U.C.A.1943.

With reference to point No. 3, it is claimed by plaintiff that the defendant, Isabelle Merriam, was disqualified to testify by reason of the so-called dead man statute, and that the court erred in receiving in evidence her deposition relative to transactions had with Livingston in his lifetime. In answer to this the defendants assert that there was ample evidence without the testimony of Mrs. Merriam to prove delivery of the assignment to which she testified and that, if the court erred in receiving the deposition, the error was harmless. We think the record shows defendants' contention to be correct as to there being ample evidence, without the testimony of Isabelle Merriam, to support the finding of the trial court that there was a delivery of the assignment. We therefore hold that the error, if conceded, was insufficient to constitute any ground for reversal, the case having been tried without a jury.

As to plaintiff's first point, the language of the assignment, including the reservation clause, is free from ambiguity and recites a clear and unequivocal intention on the part of Livingston to make a present gift to his sisters of the interest becoming due on the note in his lifetime and of whatever principal remained owing at the time of his death. Does the fact that the reservation gave him the right to receive principal installments becoming due during his lifetime together with "all amounts in excess of the amounts periodically becoming due thereon which the maker thereof under the terms of said note may choose to pay on said principal during the lifetime of the assignor" require the court to defeat the expressed intention of the donor? We think it does not. We do not agree with counsel for plaintiffs that this constituted a reservation of complete dominion over the principal of the gift. It is true that the maker of the note might, at his option, pay the entire principal in the lifetime of the payee and thereby defeat the gift, but that contingency was not within Mr. Livingston's control. He could not force payment prior to maturity of the respective installments and it was not within his power to prolong his sojourn in mortality so as to make certain of receiving the installments of principal as they respectively became due. The further argument of plaintiffs that, insofar as the principal was concerned, it was an attempt to make a gift effective upon death of the donor and was thereby invalid because of the statutes relating to testamentary disposition of property is in our opinion without merit. There was a clearly expressed present gift of such part of the principal as did not become due and was not paid during the lifetime of the donor. The fact that the maker might, at his option, pay before maturity and before the death of the donor, did not invalidate the gift in case the maker did not so exercise that option. It should also be remembered that the maker of the note was a son of one of the donees and presumably would not be likely to exercise an option so as to defeat the gift to his mother. The language of the assignment cannot be construed as a gift subject to revocation during the lifetime of the donor. The fact that the gift was of installments of principal becoming due after his death did not make it any less binding upon him than if it had been of unpaid installments falling due after a definite designated date or after the happening of any designated contingency which was bound to happen.

*   *   *

Referring now to plaintiff's second point, that the instrument of assignment was ineffective because of retention of possession of the note and deed of trust by Livingston, it appears that that contention is opposed to the great weight of authority and cannot be reconciled with the views expressed by this court in the case of Johnson v. Beickey, 64 Utah 43, 228 P. 189, 191. In that case a note had been pledged by the payee to a bank to secure a debt of the payee. He thereafter executed and delivered to another party, to whom he was indebted, a writing by which he assigned all his right in the note. Before the note was collected by the bank, a garnishment was served upon it, by which a third creditor of the payee attempted to attach his interest in the note. There was a surplus of proceeds of the note, above the amount owing the bank, and the suit was between the garnishing creditor and the assignee named in the assignment. It was contended there, as here, that the assignment by a separate writing without delivery of the instrument was inoperative. This court held otherwise, quoting with approval the following from 8 Cyc. p. 383: *"Like an ordinary chose in action, a bill or note may be transferred by assignment* or by mere delivery with the usual incidents of such a transfer, and this rule is not changed by the negotiable instrument law. *   *   * It may be formal or informal; *   *   * it may be by a *separate instru-*

ment, or in the absence of a statute to the contrary, by parol." (Italics added.)   See to same effect 8 C.J. 383, § 568;   10 C.J.S., Bills and Notes, § 227, p. 719.

That the rule applies in cases of gifts as well as in cases of transfer for a consideration is evident from the authorities: "The courts have quite generally held, where there is an assignment or conveyance in writing that is delivered to the donee, that the gift is not defeated because the note itself remains in possession of the donor."   26 A.L.R. at 671, citing Walker v. Crews, 1882, 73 Ala. 412;   and Burkett v. Doty, 1917, 176 Cal. 89, 167 P. 518, 520.

In the last mentioned case, as in the case at bar, there was an assignment in writing executed by the owner of a note secured by mortgage, the assignment being delivered to the assignee in the lifetime of the assignor but the note and mortgage remaining in possession of the assignor up to the time of her death.   The assignment recited that it was not to be recorded until after the death of the donor.   The assignment was without consideration and was intended as a gift to the assignee who was a niece of the assignor.   After the death of the assignor, the administrator of her estate refused to deliver the note to the assignee and claimed title to it.   The trial court upheld the claim of the administrator but the Supreme Court, by unanimous decision, reversed the judgment saying:

"It must be remembered that, as between donor and donee it is not necessary to the validity of a gift inter vivos, if made by a written instrument transferring the title to the donee, that possession of the thing given be passed to the donee."   See also annotation in 63 A.L.R. 537.

"While it has been held, where there is a note, bond, or other written obligation evidencing the debt, that there must be a delivery of the instrument, it is generally held that delivery is not necessary if the assignment is proved by other satisfactory evidence.   Thus, where an assignment of a chose in action is made by a separate paper it will be valid, although the written evidence of the chose in action is not delivered".   6 C.J.S., Assignments, § 48, p. 1095, citing In re Smith, 191 Mich. 694, 158 N.W. 148;   5 C.J. 903 note 81.

Appellants did not argue in their brief the effect of Sec. 61–1–17 Utah Code Annotated 1943, which is Sec. 16 of the Uniform Negotiable Instruments Act and which provides that: "Every contract on a negotiable instrument is incomplete and revocable until delivery of the instrument for the purpose of giving effect thereto.   As between immediate parties, and as regards a remote party other than a holder in due course, the delivery in order to be effectual must be made either by or under the authority of the party making, drawing, accepting or indorsing, as the case may be;   and in such case the delivery may be shown to have been conditional or for a special purpose only, and not for the purpose of transferring the property in the instrument."

A casual reading of that section might seem to prevent the passing of title to a negotiable instrument which is retained in the possession of an assignor, even though he signs and delivers a written assignment of title. But the section should be read in conjunction with Section 191 of the Uniform Act, which is Sec. 61–4–1 of Utah Code Annotated 1943, and which recites that: " 'Delivery' means transfer of possession, actual or constructive, from one person to another."

In this case, where the payee executed and delivered to the assignees a written assignment of a part interest in the note, but reserved to himself the right to receive installments of principal falling due in his lifetime, he should be considered to be holding the note for himself and the assignees and to have made a constructive delivery to them so as to satisfy the statute.

"There may be a delivery notwithstanding the maker keeps the note in his possession, where it is apparent that he intended to hold it for the benefit and as the agent of the payee". 10 C.J.S., Bills and Notes, § 78, p. 513, note 69; 8 C.J. 205, note 90.

"The delivery of a bill or note to one of two or more payees will operate as a delivery to all." 10 C.J.S., Bills and Notes, § 78, p. 514, note 94, 8 C.J. 210, note 60.

The judgment of the trial court is affirmed, respondents to recover costs.

WOLFE, C. J., and WADE, McDONOUGH,, and CROCKETT, JJ., concur.

HENRIOD, Justice, being disqualified, did not participate herein.

Notes

1. For a collection of cases on instruments of gift see Annot., Delivery as Essential to Gifts of Tangible Chattels or Securities by Written Instrument, 48 A.L.R.2d 1405 (1956). For a case which denies the gift on facts very similar to those of the principal case see Levas v. Dewey, 33 Wash.2d 232, 205 P.2d 356 (1949). On the subject generally see 4 Corbin on Contracts, § 921 (1951); 21 Ill.L.Rev. 568–86 (1927); Carey v. Jackson, 603 P.2d 868 (Wyo.1979) (gift of jewelry, spode china, and antique glassware effectively given by two written assignments, although articles remained in donor's possession until her death; cases on the subject reviewed).

2. Valuable gifts may be effectuated by informal letters. Speelman v. Pascal, 10 N.Y.2d 313, 222 N.Y.S.2d 324, 178 N.E.2d 723 (1961) (a piece of My Fair Lady was effectively given by a letter to the donee even though delivery occurred before the show was produced). See also Hawkins v. Union Trust Co. of New York, 187 App.Div. 472, 175 N.Y.S. 694 (1st Dep't 1919) (gift of a yacht); In re Kaufman's Estate, 201 Misc. 905, 107 N.Y.S.2d 681 (Surr.Ct., N.Y.Co. 1951) (gift good although letter received in the mails after donor's death); Humble v. Gay, 168 Cal. 516, 143 P. 778 (1914) (chatty letter too informal to show intent to give a valuable collection of Indian rugs); Lewis v. Burke, 248 Ind. 297, 226 N.E.2d 332 (1967) (gift of household furnishings and contents effected by letter sustained over a vigorous dissent). The donor must, however, have the necessary mental capacity to understand the gift, and the transaction must be free from fraud. In re Dodge, 50 N.J. 182, 234 A.2d 65 (1967) (a claimed gift of a $1,700,000 art collection to a college failed); Matter of Estate of Saathoff, 206 Neb. 793, 295 N.W.2d 290 (1980) (gift by 81-year old donor of her

intestate share in deceased son's estate valid and not procured by undue influence).

SECTION THREE. GIFTS TO MINORS

Since minors are legally incompetent to engage in property transactions, minors holding legal title or full title can only sell, lease, mortgage, or otherwise deal with their property (at common law) through guardians appointed to act on their behalf. This is an expensive, cumbersome, and relatively inflexible type of arrangement. For example, a fidelity bond, with surety, must be filed with the appointing court along with the application for guardianship. Ordinarily the guardian must file a periodic accounting every year or two (depending on the jurisdiction) and a final accounting when the ward reaches majority or dies. The guardian is authorized to disburse only income; authority to sell an asset must be obtained by special application.

A direct gift of property to a minor involves serious practical difficulties, particularly upon sale of the property during minority. If, for example, the property consists of securities, then brokers, banks, issuers and transfer agents deal with the minor at their peril. After majority, the minor may disaffirm the sale and hold them liable for any loss suffered as a result of the transaction.

For these reasons, estate planners have for a long time taken pains to avoid the vesting of legal title in minors. Whenever some benefit was to be provided for a minor, it was made available through the medium of a trust so that the minor received a beneficial interest only, not legal title.

In 1955, states began to enact statutes simplifying gifts of securities to minors and the subsequent administration of the property during minority. Since then, more and more states have enacted such statutes and existing statutes have been broadened in various ways. At present, every jurisdiction has some such statute, for the most part based on one of the versions of the Uniform Gifts to Minors Act. Key sections of the 1966 Revised Act, 8A ULA 317–404, read:

§ 2. [Manner of Making Gift]

(a) An adult person may, during his lifetime, make a gift of a security, a life insurance policy or annuity contract or money to a person who is a minor on the date of the gift:

(1) if the subject of the gift is a security in registered form, by registering it in the name of the donor, another adult person [an adult member of the minor's family, a guardian of the minor] or a trust company, followed, in substance, by the words: "as custodian for _____ under the [name of enacting state] Uniform Gifts to Minors Act";

(2) if the subject of the gift is a security not in registered form, by delivering it to an adult other than the donor [an adult member, other than the donor, or of the minor's family, a guardian of the minor] or a

trust company, accompanied by a statement of gift in the following form, in substance, signed by the donor and the person designated as custodian:

"GIFT UNDER THE [NAME OF ENACTING STATE] UNIFORM GIFTS TO MINORS ACT

      I, _____ hereby deliver to _____ as custodian for _____ under the [name of enacting state] Uniform Gifts to Minors Act, the following security(ies): (insert an appropriate description of the security or securities delivered sufficient to identify it or them)

_____

_____ hereby acknowledges receipt of the above described security(ies) as custodian for the above minor under the [name of enacting state] Uniform Gifts to Minors Act.

Dated: _____   _____ "

      (3) if the subject of the gift is money, by paying or delivering it to a broker or a [domestic] financial institution for credit to an account in the name of the donor, another adult [an adult member of the minor's family, a guardian of the minor] or a trust company, followed, in substance, by the words: "as custodian for _____ under the [name of enacting state] Uniform Gifts to Minors Act".

      (4) if the subject of the gift is a life insurance policy or annuity contract, by causing the ownership of the policy or contract to be registered with the issuing insurance company in the name of the donor, another adult [an adult member of the minor's family, a guardian of the minor] or a trust company, followed, in substance, by the words: "as custodian for _____ under the [name of enacting state] Uniform Gifts to Minors Act".

      (b) Any gift made in a manner prescribed in Subsection (a) may be made to only one minor and only one person may be the custodian.

      (c) A donor who makes a gift to a minor in a manner prescribed in Subsection (a) shall promptly do all things within his power to put the subject of the gift in the possession and control of the custodian, but neither the donor's failure to comply with this Subsection, nor his designation of an ineligible person as custodian, nor renunciation by the person designated as custodian affects the consummation of the gift.

§ 3. [Effect of Gift]

      (a) A gift made in a manner prescribed in this act is irrevocable and conveys to the minor indefeasibly vested legal title to the security, life insurance policy, annuity contract or money given, but no guardian of the minor has any right, power, duty or authority with respect to the custodial property except as provided in this act.

      (b) By making a gift in a manner prescribed in this act, the donor incorporates in his gift all the provisions of this act and grants to the custodian, and to any issuer, transfer agent, bank, financial institution, life insurance company, broker or third person dealing with a person designated as custodian, the respective powers, rights and immunities provided in this act.

§ 4. [Duties and Powers of Custodian]

(a) The custodian shall collect, hold, manage, invest and reinvest the custodial property.

(b) The custodian shall pay over to the minor for expenditure by him, or expend for the minor's benefit, so much of or all the custodial property as the custodian deems advisable for the support, maintenance, education and benefit of the minor in the manner, at the time or times, and to the extent that the custodian in his discretion deems suitable and proper, with or without court order, with or without regard to the duty of himself or of any other person to support the minor or his ability to do so, and with or without regard to any other income or property of the minor which may be applicable or available for any such purpose.

(c) The court, on the petition of a parent or guardian of the minor or of the minor, if he has attained the age of fourteen years, may order the custodian to pay over to the minor for expenditure by him or to expend so much of or all the custodial property as is necessary for the minor's support, maintenance or education.

(d) To the extent that the custodial property is not so expended, the custodian shall deliver or pay it over to the minor on his attaining the age of twenty-one or, if the minor dies before attaining the age of twenty-one years, he shall thereupon deliver or pay it over to the estate of the minor.

(e) The custodian, notwithstanding statutes restricting investments by fiduciaries, shall invest and reinvest the custodial property as would a prudent man of discretion and intelligence who is seeking a reasonable income and the preservation of his capital, except that he may, in his discretion and without liability to the minor or his estate, retain a security given to the minor in a manner prescribed in this act or hold money so given in an account in the financial institution to which it was paid or delivered by the donor.

(f) The custodian may sell, exchange, convert, surrender or otherwise dispose of custodial property in the manner, at the time or times, for the price or prices and upon the terms he deems advisable. He may vote in person or by general or limited proxy a security which is custodial property. He may consent, directly or through a committee or other agent, to the reorganization, consolidation, merger, dissolution or liquidation of an issuer of a security which is custodial property, and to the sale, lease, pledge or mortgage of any property by or to such an issuer, and to any other action by such an issuer. He may execute and deliver any and all instruments in writing which he deems advisable to carry out any of his powers as custodian.

(g) The custodian shall register each security which is custodial property and in registered form in the name of the custodian, followed, in substance, by the words: "as custodian for _____ under the [name of enacting state] Uniform Gifts to Minors Act". The custodian shall hold all money which is custodial property in an account with a broker or in an insured [domestic] financial institution in the name of the custodian, followed, in substance, by the words: "as custodian for _____ under the [name of enacting state] Uniform Gifts to Minors Act". The custodian shall keep all other custodial property separate and distinct from his own property in a manner to identify it clearly as custodial property.

(h) The custodian shall keep records of all transactions with respect to the custodial property and make them available for inspection at reasonable intervals by a parent or legal representative of the minor or by the minor, if he has attained the age of fourteen years.

(i) A custodian has [and holds as powers in trust], with respect to the custodial property, in addition to the rights and powers in this act, all the rights and powers which a guardian has with respect to property not held as custodial property.

(j) If the subject of the gift is a life insurance policy or annuity contract, the custodian:

(1) in his capacity as custodian, has all the incidents of ownership in the policy or contract to the extent as if he were the owner, except that the designated beneficiary of any policy or contract on the life of the minor shall be the minor's estate and the designated beneficiary of any policy or contract on the life of a person other than the minor shall be the custodian as custodian for the minor for whom he is acting; and

(2) may pay premiums on the policy or contract out of the custodial property.

* * *

Notes

1. The original version of the Uniform Gifts to Minors Act appeared in 1956 and closely followed a model "Act concerning Gifts of Securities to Minors" which was sponsored by the New York Stock Exchange and the Association of Stock Exchange Firms. The 1966 revision expanded the types of financial institutions which could serve as depositories of custodial funds, facilitated the designation of successor custodians, and added life insurance policies and annuity contracts to the types of property that could be made the subject of a gift under the Act. Since 1966, many states have amended their versions of the Uniform Act to expand the kinds of property that may be given and the types of transfers that may be made to a custodian. In recognition of these developments and in the interest of encouraging uniformity among the states, the Commissioners on Uniform State Laws in 1983 adopted further revisions to the Gifts to Minors Act and republished the Act, now entitled Uniform Transfers to Minors Act, See 1984 Pocket Part to 8A ULA 63–84. As of the end of 1984, this version of the Act had been adopted by California, Colorado, and Idaho. A prefatory note explains the ways in which the Transfers Act differs from the 1966 Gifts Act:

This Act follows the expansive approach taken by several states and allows any kind of property, real or personal, tangible or intangible, to be made the subject of a transfer to a custodian for the benefit of a minor

(SECTION 1(6)). In addition, it permits such transfers not only by lifetime outright gifts (SECTION 4), but also from trusts, estates and guardianships, whether or not specifically authorized in the governing instrument (SECTIONS 5 AND 6), and from other third parties indebted to a minor who does not have a conservator, such as parties against whom a minor has a tort claim or judgment, and depository institutions holding deposits or insurance companies issuing policies payable on death to a minor (SECTION 7). For this reason, and to distinguish the enactment of this statute from the 1956 and 1966 versions of UGMA, the title of the Act has been changed to refer to "Transfers" rather than to "Gifts," a much narrower term.

As so expanded, the Act might be considered a statutory form of trust or guardianship that continues until the minor reaches 21. Note, however, that unlike a trust, a custodianship is not a separate legal entity or taxpayer. Under SECTION 11(b) of this Act, the custodial property is indefeasibly vested in the minor, not the custodian, and thus any income received is attributable to and reportable by the minor, whether or not actually distributed to the minor.

The expansion of the Act to permit transfers of any kind of property to a custodian creates a significant problem of potential personal liability for the minor or the custodian arising from the ownership of property such as real estate, automobiles, general partnership interests, and business proprietorships. This problem did not exist under UGMA under which custodial property was limited to bank deposits, securities and insurance. In response, SECTION 17 of this Act generally limits the claims of third parties to recourse against the custodial property, with the minor insulated against personal liability unless he is personally at fault. The custodian is similarly insulated unless he is personally at fault or fails to disclose his custodial capacity in entering into a contract.

Nevertheless, the Act should be used with caution with respect to property such as real estate or general partnership interests from which liabilities as well as benefits may arise. Many of the possible risks can and should be insured against, and the custodian has the power under SECTION 13(a) to purchase such insurance, at least when other custodial assets are sufficient to do so. If the assets are not sufficient, there is doubt that a custodian will act, or there are significant uninsurable risks, a transferor should consider a trust with spendthrift provisions, such as a minority trust under Section 2503(c), IRC, rather than a custodianship, to make a gift of such property to a minor.

2. Under I.R.C. § 2503 of the federal gift tax, a donor is allowed each year to give up to $10,000, known as the "exclusion," to each donee free of the gift tax. A married couple may combine their exclusions to make a total of $20,000 (regardless of which spouse is the economic source of the property) to each donee each year. The statute requires, however, that the gift be of a present, as opposed to a future, interest. The Treasury has ruled that a gift made pursuant to the Uniform Act is a present interest and qualifies for the exclusion. Rev. Rul. 59–357, 1959–2 C.B. 212. Tax difficulties may arise if a parent, who is the custodian of property for his or her child, dies while the child is a minor. Because the parent-custodian may use the property to support the child, the property may be attributed to the parent for estate tax purposes. See e.g., Prudowsky's Estate v. Commissioner, 55 T.C. 890 (1971), affirmed per curiam,

465 F.2d 62 (7th Cir. 1972) (I.R.C. § 2036(a)(1) applies); Stuit v. Commissioner, 452 F.2d 190 (7th Cir. 1971) (powers given by Uniform Act equivalent to powers to alter, amend, revoke and terminate taxable under I.R.C. § 2038 of the estate tax).

Chapter Seven

TRUSTS

SECTION ONE. INTRODUCTION: USES, AND THE NATURE, UTILITY, AND CLASSIFICATION OF TRUSTS

The trust concept as such is essentially quite simple. It merely involves the idea of one person (the trustee) holding the legal title to certain property (the res or subject-matter) for the benefit of another person (the cestui or beneficiary) whose interest is equitable. While it may seem unfortunate to use the terms "legal" and "equitable" in view of the efforts of modern codes to merge law and equity, the idea that the trustee is recognized as the sole owner at law, and the cestui's interest is only recognized in equity, is such a fundamental element of the reasoning in many trust cases that it would be difficult, if not impossible, to understand the development and utility of the trust device without appreciating this traditional division of title. From a functional viewpoint, the effect of the division of title is to allocate the burdens of property ownership to the trustee, and to allocate its benefits (except for the commission paid to the trustee for his services) to the beneficiary.

The chief emphasis here will be on the utility of the trust device in gratuitous disposition of property; but this is by no means its sole purpose, as will appear from other courses. In both England and America it has been employed to accomplish a large variety of results. Its simplicity and unrestricted generality tend to make it an adaptable device actually or potentially applicable to many diverse situations. It is extensively used in business as well as non-commercial transactions; it has been employed under various circumstances as part of the reasoning by which defendants are required to conform to the equitable standard of fairness; remedies against tortfeasors are made more effectual by calling them trustees; people who, by strict legal doctrine, would be entitled to retain property are forced to give it up in the name of the trust if the court thinks that it would be unjust for them to keep it. These are merely examples, and of course not intended to constitute an exhaustive catalogue of the functions of the trust device. See Scott, The Trust as an Instrument of Law Reform, 31 Yale L.J. 457 (1922); Arnold, The Restatement of the Law of Trusts, 31 Colum.L.Rev. 800, 1266 (1931) (it is desirable to read these two interesting articles for the purpose of formulating some philosophy of the subject); Maitland, The Unincorporate Body, 3 Coll.Pap. 271 (1911). Lepaulle, Traité Théorique et Pratique des Trusts (1932) at 114, remarks: "Le trust est l'ange gardien de l'Anglo-Saxon."

Trusts have traditionally been classified as express, constructive, and resulting. The conceptual distinction between the express and the constructive trust is analogous to that between the concepts of express contract and quasi-contract. The ideas of both constructive trust and quasi-contract took an established formula from its existing context for the purpose of employing it to remedy injustice. While quasi-contractual obligations were enforced at law, the results achieved and the methods of reaching those results have a distinctly equitable character, and it is desirable to bear in mind the analogy of the quasi-contract to the constructive trust and other equitable remedies performing similar functions. Theoretically the express trust, like the express contract, is an intent-enforcing mechanism; that is, the court acts on the theory that the defendant has previously manifested an intention to assume the obligation for the breach of which he is held responsible, as in a case where a trustee is sued for failure to pay over income from a trust fund as he has agreed to do. The constructive trust, however, like the quasi-contract, is theoretically a remedial device in no way dependent upon the defendant's intention to assume the obligation imposed. If a thief is compelled to transfer to his victim the proceeds of sale of the stolen property, either on a quasi-contractual theory or on the ground that he is a constructive trustee, the court is surely not employing an intent-enforcing device; in the average case, it would seem fantastic to assume that a thief intended to restore to his victim the proceeds of his wrong. At any rate, the ascertainment of his intention is an immaterial inquiry if relief is given on a constructive trust theory. The constructive trust is an equitable device utilized for the purpose of preventing unjust enrichment. "A constructive trust is the formula through which the conscience of equity finds expression. When property has been acquired in such circumstances that the holder of the legal title may not in good conscience retain the beneficial interest, equity converts him into a trustee." Cardozo, J. in Beatty v. Guggenheim Exploration Co., 225 N.Y. 380, 386, 122 N.E. 378 (1919). See also Cardozo, The Nature of the Judicial Process, 40 (1921).

It is extremely difficult, even on a conceptual plane, to define the idea of the resulting trust in terms of its essential nature. Decisions based on the theory of a resulting trust seem in part to utilize it as a remedial device and in part to emphasize the intention of the parties. Perhaps the idea of the resulting trust can be made most intelligible by enumerating the three situations in which it has been employed: (1) The resulting trust on a gratuitous conveyance (now largely obsolete) was formerly imposed, under certain circumstances, for the benefit of the grantor, on the grantee of land gratuitously transferred. (2) The purchase money resulting trust exists where A conveys to B, C paying A the purchase price; under certain circumstances, B is said to hold on a resulting trust for C. (3) The resulting trust on failure or termination of an express trust exists for the benefit of the creator of the trust, or his transferees, in the event of entire or partial failure of the express trust, or its termination before the expiration of the trustee's legal title. It is with this third category that we shall be chiefly concerned. For discussions of the classification of trusts, see Arnold, supra; Stone, Resulting Trusts and the Statute of Frauds, 6 Colum.L.Rev. 326 (1906); Costigan, The Classification of Trusts as Express, Resulting and Constructive, 26 Harv.L.Rev. 437 (1914); Scott, Resulting Trusts Arising Upon the Purchase of Land, 40 Harv.L.Rev. 669–74 (1927); Mait.Eq. 53, 75; Tiffany, §§ 106–8.

The trust idea, the development and extensive use of which are believed by some legal scholars to represent perhaps the greatest achievement of Anglo-American law, has not been recognized as such in other legal systems. Trusts therefore did not exist in Louisiana, due to the civil law basis of the law of that jurisdiction, until authorized by statute in 1920. However, other systems of law accomplish similar results by employing different concepts and theories. Lepaulle, Civil Law Substitutes for Trusts, 36 Yale L.J. 1126 (1927); Lepaulle, An Outsider's View of Trusts, 14 Corn.L.Q. 52 (1928); De Wulf, The Trust and Corresponding Institutions in the Civil Law (1965). English and American lawyers have become so accustomed to thinking in terms of the trust device, both in situations to which it is technically applicable and in others for which it seems to furnish an appropriate metaphor, that perhaps there is a tendency to consider it an inevitable part of our legal system. This, however, seems obviously not so. The concept of the trust evolved through a development to which a number of accidental factors of a political and historical nature contributed. If it had not happened to grow as it did, some other device or devices might have been adapted to perform similar functions.

Historical Importance of Uses

The unique character of the Anglo-American trust is fundamentally due to the existence of its prototype, the use, and to the dual system of law and equity which made the latter possible. Maitland has said that "it is absolutely impossible for one to speak of trusts, even at the present day, without speaking first of uses." Mait.Eq. 36. The system of uses as such is and should be largely obsolete today; there is comparatively little necessity for courts today to resort to the ancient learning. Cf. Arnold, supra, 31 Colum.L.Rev. at 813; Rood, The Statute of Uses and the Modern Deed, 4 Mich.L.Rev. 109 (1905); Maitland, The Law of Real Property, 1 Coll.Pap. 162, 191 (1911); Bordwell, The Repeal of the Statute of Uses, 39 Harv.L.Rev. 466 (1926). But some general understanding of the origin and development of the use device contributes considerably to intelligent comprehension of the modern law of trusts, as well as other elements of property law, particularly future interests. From the historical point of view, the development was of course momentous, as seems apparent from a recital of some of its permanent effects. The system of uses was not merely responsible for the trust and all the services that the latter performs today; it revolutionized the methods of conveying land, furnishing the transition between the old conveyances by transfer of possession and the modern conveyance by deed; it was probably the most important event in the evolution of the law of future interests, contributing simple and liberal doctrines which so greatly mitigated the severity of the rigidly technical common law scheme as to necessitate the formulation of the Rule against Perpetuities, itself of course of great modern significance; it made possible testamentary dispositions of land, at that time the most important form of wealth; it contributed, with general approval and consent, a large volume of business to the Chancellor during the early struggles of Chancery to maintain itself as a separate court, without which the dual system of law and equity might not have survived. See Bordwell, supra; Mait.Eq. 23, 36; Maitland, Outlines of English Legal History, 2 Coll.Pap. 417, 492 (1911); Maitland, Trust and Corporation, 3 Coll.Pap. 321, 334 (1911); 1 Holds. 454; 4 Holds. 473; 7 Holds. 119, 354. An attempt will therefore be made here to describe the development of uses in general terms in so far as it appears to contribute to an understanding of the law of trusts. In doing so, however, we must include some details not strictly relevant to trusts as such in order to make the description intelligible.

The Common Law Conveyances

Since, for reasons to be explained later, the original use transactions involved transfers of land rather than personal property, the common law methods of conveying land should be recalled at the outset. They seem in general to disclose two major characteristics. First, in common with the other permissible transfers of the period, the primary requisite was a change in physical possession. The second outstanding feature was the insistence on publicity—a policy the desirability of which, in an age which knew no recording system, seems obvious.

The possible forms of conveyance of an absolute fee simple interest in land at common law were four: the feoffment, the fine, the common recovery, and the lease and release. Of these, of course the feoffment, with livery of seisin (delivery of possession), was the one most commonly employed. While the feoffment was often accompanied by a charter of feoffment, the original purpose of such a writing was merely to preserve in written form the terms of the transfer; it was "an evidentiary, not a dispositive document. Its language will be not 'I hereby give' but 'know ye that I have given.'" 2 P. & M. 82. The vital operative fact was the delivery of possession—the feoffee entering upon the land and the feoffor leaving it—often including the symbolic ceremony of handing over a twig or piece of turf—"they are the land in miniature, and thus the land passes from hand to hand." 2 P. & M. 84. And some degree of publicity was assured by the change in possession and all the drama and ritual of the feoffment which would serve to impress the transaction upon the minds of the witnesses to it and probably, in most cases, call the attention of the neighbors to the transfer of ownership. 2 Bl.Com. *310–317; 2 P. & M. 82–90; 3 Holds. 221–234.

The term "fine" was an abbreviation of "finalis concordia" (final settlement), and this type of conveyance employed the form of the compromise of a lawsuit (usually fictitious) for the real purpose of transferring title to land, the terms of the compromise containing an admission by the transferor of the transferee's ownership of the land. The common recovery also used the medium of a fictitious lawsuit, not compromised like the fine, but prosecuted to judgment for the "recovery" of the land, and depending for its efficacy upon the doctrine of vouching to warranty; it was chiefly used to bar an estate tail. The complexities of these two obsolete fictional devices are of no modern importance, but it should be noted that publicity was achieved by the transfer's being publicly recorded, and that the notion of a physical transfer appears in the early requirement that the sheriff deliver possession to the transferee. 2 Bl. Com. *348–364; 2 P. & M. 94–106; 3 Holds. 118–120, 236–246; Challis, Real Property 304–313 (3d ed. by Sweet, 1911).

The lease and release was, as the name indicates, a double conveyance. If A wished to transfer a fee simple to B, A could first lease to B for one year. There was no requirement of writing for a lease for years prior to the Statute of Frauds, but as a matter of practice such a lease was usually made by deed in order to give the lessee an action of covenant against the lessor. Since a term of years was not a freehold estate, livery of seisin as such was not required (the mere deed or oral agreement gave the lessee no estate in the land, but merely an interesse termini—a right of entry); but, in accordance with the usual requirement of transfer of possession, it was necessary for the lessee to enter on the land in order to perfect his estate and entitle him to take a release. After B had taken possession under his lease, A would release his reversion by deed to B and, by the merger of the term of years and the reversion, B would acquire a fee simple estate. For the release, no livery of seisin was required because the transferee, B, was already in possession of the land, and, as in the case of an inter vivos gift of a chattel to a donee already in possession, the unnatural ceremony of the transferee's yielding possession in order to become formally repossessed was considered unnecessary. The lease and release was used as an alternative to the feoffment, but was not so frequently employed. It will be noted that here, as in the feoffment, a change of physical possession with its accompanying publicity was required. Perhaps the major significance of the common law release and release is that it was the pattern for the important conveyance of the same name after the Statute of Uses. 2 Bl.Com. *314, *324–325; 2 P. & M. 90–91; 3 Holds. 232, 248–249.

Origin and Enforcement of Uses

There is nothing at all complicated or unique about the basic idea of the original use device, which simply involved a transfer of property from A to B for certain purposes, A trusting B to carry out those purposes. The precise origin of this conception presents a more complex problem, but, while the early writers attributed it to the Roman law, most modern historians have followed the lead of Mr. Justice Holmes in maintaining that the Roman law analogies were superficial.   They maintain, rather, that the actual prototype of the feoffee to uses (as well as of the executor) was the Germanic Salman or Treuhand, a person to whom property was transferred for certain purposes to be executed either in the lifetime or after the death of the transferor.   Holmes, Early English Equity, 1 L.Q. Rev. 162 (1885), reprinted Holmes, Coll.Leg.Pap. 1 (1921), and 2 Select Essays in Anglo-American Legal History 705 (1908);   Ames, The Origin of Uses and Trusts, 21 Harv.L.Rev. 261 (1907), reprinted Ames, Lectures on Legal History 233 (1913), and 2 Select Essays in Anglo-American Legal History 737 (1908);   3 Holds. 563;   4 Holds. 410;   Maitland, The Origin of Uses, 8 Harv.L.Rev. 127 (1894), reprinted 2 Coll.Pap. 403 (1911);   2 P. & M. 230;   Maitland, Trust and Corporation, 3 Coll.Pap. 321, 327, 332, 335 (1911).   A French commentator, however, thinks it highly improbable that either theory is correct, or that those who were really doing nothing more unusual than trusting their friends, in an arrangement that the courts would not enforce, would have to seek a precedent for this normal human habit in the jurisprudence of a foreign country.   Lepaulle, Traité Théorique et Pratique des Trusts 14 (1932).

For the express creation of a use, it was originally necessary to employ one of the common law conveyances.   For the purpose of simplicity of statement, the example of the feoffment (the most common transfer) will be taken, but uses might also be created by using the other common law conveyances.   4 Holds. 421.   If A wished C to have the benefit of the use device, A would enfeoff B, B agreeing to hold the land to the use (i.e., for the benefit) of C.   A would be called the "feoffor to uses" (corresponding to the settlor of the modern trust);   B the "feoffee to uses" (corresponding to the trustee of the modern trust);   and C the "cestui que use" (corresponding to the cestui que trust, or beneficiary, of the modern trust).

The beginning of uses in England is obscure, but they were certainly in operation at least by the thirteenth century.   For about the first two centuries of its existence, the use device probably had no legal significance.   That is, the feoffment in the hypothetical case just stated would of course transfer the legal title to the land to B, but B's agreement to hold it for C's benefit was unenforceable.   The courts of common law refused to recognize it.   It was merely a gentlemen's agreement depending for its efficacy upon the trustworthiness of B.   However, the scheme apparently worked well enough to be popular, even without the assistance of any court.   A would scarcely part with his land under such an arrangement unless he had implicit confidence in B, and disloyal feoffees to uses were probably comparatively rare.   A similar device—the unenforceable trust—is employed for some purposes in this country today. Leaphart, The Use, A Factor in the Law Today, 79 U.Pa.L.Rev. 253 (1931). Petitions to the Chancellor just before 1400, requesting enforcement of the use, are extant, and it is probable that he gave relief early in the fifteenth century, though it seems that no recorded decree in favor of a cestui que use before 1445 has been found.   Whenever it happened, this was a most significant step. The effect was to separate the benefits of property ownership from its burdens, and that is the distinguishing characteristic of the trust.

The Chancellor probably acted originally on simple ethical grounds. This original use transaction looks much like a modern contract. In consideration of the receipt of the land from A, B promised A to deal with that land in a certain way. Speaking in modern terms, consideration for this promise would seem to be present; the conception of bargain is now flexible enough to cover a conveyance made in reliance on the transferee's promise, even though the transferee received no benefit. Today, the enforcement of B's promise would seem obviously proper. So in the early days the Chancellor considered it only fair to compel B to live up to his agreement, though it would be anachronistic to assume that he reasoned in terms of the modern doctrines of consideration, which had not yet then been formulated. The disloyal feoffee to uses did not conform to the equitable standard of morality. The common law afforded no remedy; under its doctrines the feoffee was absolute owner. The basis for the Chancellor's intervention therefore seems clear enough. Thus began what was probably the most permanently important branch of the equitable jurisdiction. Ames, supra; Mait.Eq. 29; 1 Holds. 454; 4 Holds. 414–420; 2 P. & M. 235–239; Barbour, Some Aspects of Fifteenth-Century Chancery, 31 Harv.L.Rev. 834, 849 (1918); Selden Society, Select Cases in Chancery XXXVI (1896); Scott, supra, 31 Yale L.J. at 458.

Any detailed discussion of the characteristics of the cestui's interest as developed in Chancery would necessarily be long and complex. The Chancellor followed some of the doctrines of the common law; others, in order to further the purposes of the use device, he discarded. The importance of uses was largely due to the latter process, the Chancellor's progressive liberality furnishing a means of escape from the rigidity of the common law. The use agreement was informal and could be informally created, either orally or in writing. While originally uses only arose on a common law conveyance, the latter was necessary solely for the purpose of transferring legal title to the feoffee to uses. As above stated, it was the receipt of that title that made the breach of the agreement, pursuant to which it was received, seem unfair, and induced the Chancellor to intervene. For the creation of the use itself, however, no common law conveyance or other formality was necessary. The usual obligations of the feoffee to uses may be summarized as three: first, he was obliged to allow the cestui que use to enjoy the land; second, he was under the duty of transferring the legal title to such persons and for such estates as the cestui might orally or in writing direct; third, he was required to take all necessary proceedings to protect the legal title against disseisors or other adverse claimants. The cestui could not bring such actions, since his interest was not recognized at law. The feoffee was entitled to be reimbursed by the cestui que use for expenses incurred by him in fulfilling these obligations. It will thus be appreciated that the feoffee to uses was in reality a dummy depositary of the legal title, and that this typical arrangement was the prototype of what was subsequently described as the passive trust.   4 Holds. 422, 431.

Functions and Reasons for Popularity of Uses

The functions of the use device were numerous.   It was probably first extensively employed (in the thirteenth century) to solve the predicament of the Franciscan friars, whose vow of poverty, forbidding them to own property, was found to be inconsistent with the material necessities of life.   This dilemma was avoided by the adoption of a subtle distinction between ownership and use; they could not hold legal title, but they were permitted to be the beneficiaries of the use device, the use not being "property" for this purpose.   In order to give them lodging when they came to a town as missionaries, land would therefore be conveyed to the borough community to their use.   Similarly, the provisions of the mortmain statutes, prohibiting the acquisition of legal title to land by religious corporations, were circumvented by a transfer to the use of the latter. It was also possible to defeat creditors by means of the use; the debtor would convey legal title to another to his own use, and the land could not be seized by his creditors, because it no longer was legally his.   It is interesting to note that the employment of the use device for the two latter purposes was so widespread and efficacious as to require legislative control even before the use became enforceable in Chancery; the first of a series of statutes to prevent the defrauding of creditors by means of the use was enacted in 1377, and evasion of the mortmain acts by the use was prohibited by statute in 1392.   The Statute of Uses was thus not the first to deal with uses; in the respects just indicated and otherwise, the legislature interfered, long before that statute, to prevent the employment of the use device for purposes considered contrary to public policy.

The great value of the use arrangement lay in the fact that it enabled a person to escape the unfortunate consequences which technical legal ownership might entail, and yet enjoy the benefits of ownership.   And the Chancellor's intervention of course greatly increased the efficacy and popularity of the plan; thereafter, the enjoyment of this practical though non-legal ownership was sanctioned by equitable enforcement and no longer solely dependent on the personal honesty of the feoffees to uses. Moreover, though the cestui que use was thereafter protected in Chancery and therefore had what may be called "equitable title," the law courts refused to recognize his interest, and therefore the escape from the disadvantages of "legal" (as distinguished from equitable) ownership continued to be effective.   Thus the dual system of law and equity made possible the convenient though curious situation in which one person, in reality only a dummy, was recognized in the law courts as sole owner with all the legal consequences which the accumulated doctrines of the common law had attached to ownership, while the beneficiary enjoyed protection in Chancery free and clear of those consequences except in so far as the Chancellor might wish to follow the previous doctrines of the common law.   This opportunity of sloughing off from practical ownership antiquated or unpopular legal doctrines seems the basic reason for the amazing popularity and utility of the use device.

Of all the causes of the widespread employment of uses, the most important and influential was the desire to make a will of land. From the thirteenth century until 1540, the law courts adhered to the rule that no will of real property could be made. Several possible reasons for this doctrine may be suggested. It compensated the heir for the abolition of the rule requiring his consent to an inter vivos transfer. It furthered the interests of the feudal system—to allow a will of land would decrease the value of the feudal incidents and greatly reduce the likelihood of the lord's obtaining the land by escheat, and the scheme of intestate succession was supposedly framed, in part at least, to meet the needs of feudalism. It was harmonious with the then existing notions of transfer— a will by definition has no dispositive effect until death and therefore would not fit into the prevailing forms of conveyance, which were predicated upon the assumption that title passed on delivery of possession. To make the two conceptions compatible it would seem necessary for the feoffor to expire conveniently at the precise moment of transferring possession. Furthermore, since wills were usually semi-secret death-bed transactions, often influenced by the clergy, they would infringe upon the policy of open publicity. And the law courts wished to protect the heir against ecclesiastical greed and the otherworldliness of dying men. 2 P. & M. 328; 3 Holds. 75.

However reasonable the prohibition of the devise might seem to the law courts, it was unpopular with the populace at large. There was a widespread desire to avoid the doctrine of primogeniture, by which the eldest son would receive all the land in an age when land was the chief form of wealth; without a will, it would be impossible for the dying man to provide adequately for his daughters and younger sons. And he would also probably wish to devote some of the land to charitable uses for the good of his soul. Another very important factor in the development of uses, also influential in promoting the desire to make a will, was the wish to escape the onerous feudal incidents which attached on the death intestate of the owner of land, much as people today attempt to avoid death taxation.

The Typical Use Arrangement

Both of these ends—the testamentary gift of land and the avoidance of feudal incidents—were achieved by what, because of the widespread importance of these two factors, became the typical use arrangement. The feoffor would enfeoff, not one, but several feoffees (e.g., six or more) as joint tenants of the legal title, to the use of the feoffor himself. These feoffees would agree to allow the feoffor to use the land and to transfer the title to whomever he should designate at any time. By this device, the feoffor could in effect make a will by then or thereafter instructing the feoffees to transfer the legal title after the feoffor's death to such persons as he desired to have the land after he died. More often than not, the directions for the post-mortem disposition of the land were ac-

tually contained in the feoffor's last will.   In the law courts there was
no testamentary disposition here.   The subject matter of the will was
the use interest of the feoffor and in the law courts this interest was not
recognized and might as well have been non-existent for this purpose;
therefore this was no violation of the rule prohibiting the devise.   And
there was no testamentary disposition of the legal title;   unless one were
willing to look through form to substance—and the law courts were not—
the only dispositions of the legal title were two inter vivos transfers, the
first by the feoffor to the feoffees and the second by the feoffees to the
ultimate cestuis que use.   Eliminating the use agreement from the picture, as the law courts did, there was no basis for prohibiting these transfers;   there was no rule against a man conveying land inter vivos to
whomever he might desire.   By the same device, the feudal incidents
were avoided.   Again the law courts shut their eyes to the use interest
and therefore it could give rise to no feudal incidents.   True, the cestuis
que use and not the feoffees were the practical owners;   but there was
no rule prohibiting the legal owner from allowing somebody else to enjoy
his land.   Prevention of feudal incidents on the death of one of the feoffees, holding the title recognized by the law courts, was achieved by
conveying to them as joint tenants.   The chief characteristic of joint
tenancy is the doctrine of survivorship, by which on the death of one joint
tenant, no interest passes from him by intestacy, but the other surviving
joint tenants remain as owners of the entire estate.   Therefore, on the
death of one of these joint tenant feoffees, no intestate succession resulted
and no feudal incidents attached.   To preclude the eventuality of the
death of a single surviving joint tenant (in which event, there would be
intestate succession) the ranks of the feoffees were assiduously replen-
ished;   if the number became dangerously low, more feoffees would be
added as joint tenants by feoffment and re-feoffment.   In this way, the
legal title was kept free not merely of feudal incidents but also of dower
and of the possibility of escheat in the event of the feoffee's death without
heirs.   So popular did this arrangement become that it is said that, by
about the year 1500, almost all of the land in England was held to uses.
For discussion of these and other causes of the popularity of uses, see 4
Holds. 416–17, 521–24, 436–44;   Mait.Eq. 25–27;   2 P. & M. 231, 238;
Maitland, Trust and Corporation, 3 Coll.Pap. 321, 335 (1904);   Turner,
Uses Before the Statute of Uses, 3 Va.L.Rev. 439 (1916);   Scott, supra.

Rarity of Use for Personalty

On the existing historical evidence, it seems that this original use
arrangement was seldom employed in dealing with chattels.   In the first
place, testamentary dispositions of personalty were permissible, the executor performing many of the functions of the feoffee to uses of land,
and the major reasons for the employment of the use with respect to land
did not apply to chattels.   Second, while the extreme rigidity of the
common law of real property precluded recognition of the interest of the
cestui que use, the law of personal property of this period was in a considerably more fluid state and afforded adequate legal remedies to those

for whose use chattels were held.　There was therefore less necessity for the liberalizing influence of the equitable use in the law of personal property.　Third, chattels at the early period were a comparatively unimportant form of wealth, consisting chiefly of perishable articles, and therefore not likely either to be the subject of the rather permanent use arrangement or to contribute particularly to such a widespread and significant development as uses.　4 Holds. 412–14, 420–21; Ames, supra, 90; Maitland, The Unincorporate Body, op. cit. supra, 3 Coll.Pap. at 273; but see Barbour, supra, 31 Harv.L.Rev. at 850.

Reasons for Refusal of Law Courts to Recognize Uses

Several reasons have been advanced to explain the refusal of the courts of law to recognize the use.　In the first place, the law courts did not recognize the use as an estate in land.　It seems apparent that the common law rules could not have done so without occasioning a substantial upheaval in their existing doctrine.　The land law had at this period been cast into rigid form and was not adaptable to new devices, particularly one so antagonistic to the existing system as the use.　And obviously, if the law courts had gone so far as to recognize the use as a legal estate, the bottom would have fallen out of the entire structure, since its major purpose was to accomplish precisely the opposite result and give the cestui the advantages of ownership without subjecting him to the disadvantages attached to the legal title.　Secondly, the law courts did not enforce the obligation of the feoffee to uses on a contractual theory, in spite of the analogy already noted between the original use transaction and the modern conception of contract.　In part this was due to the accidental chronological development.　At the time of the inception of uses, the modern theory of contract had not yet been formulated—promises were at that time unenforceable at law unless contained in a sealed instrument, and the typical use agreement was not so formal.　After the development of assumpsit in the fifteenth century, the obligation of the feoffee might have been enforced at law on a contractual theory, but by that time the Chancellor's jurisdiction had become established, and the law courts did not interfere.　And it should be noted that, in addition to technical difficulties, to force uses into the category of contracts at law would have entailed unfortunate consequences.　First, the interest of the cestui would then be considered a chose in action and inalienable according to the then existing law; this would have decreased greatly the value of the practical ownership of the cestui que use.　One of the major advantages of ownership is the power to transfer one's interest, and the Chancellor favored this end by holding the interest of the cestui freely and informally assignable.　Second, if the use had been considered a contract, only the feoffor, the promisee, could have enforced the arrangement, since a cestui que use, if other than the feoffor, would probably be a third party beneficiary and at that time third party beneficiaries could not sue—whereas the efficacy of the use would in many cases depend upon the power of such a third party cestui to hold the feoffee to uses responsible.　Third, the cestui que use would not want damages for breach of contract, but specific enjoyment of the land. Recognition of the use as a legal contract would therefore have substantially diminished its utility. Thus originated the distinction between trust and contract, which plays a large part in our law today.

It is probable that the law courts did not desire to take the jurisdiction over uses away from the Chancellor, and made no effort to adjust their machinery to that end. It seems at first sight curious, in view of their traditional jealousy of the Chancellor and of the controversies between the two courts in the early days, that the law courts should not have attempted at least to diminish the large amount of business that jurisdiction over uses gave to the Chancellor. If the latter had been denied this jurisdiction, it is quite possible, as above stated, that Chancery would not ultimately have emerged victorious. For that matter, it also seems strange that the Chancellor, the King's right hand man, should have been mainly responsible for a scheme which substantially diminished the King's revenue by the evasion of feudal obligations. The explanation of both of these paradoxes probably lies in the enormous popularity and utility of uses, which made the furtherance of the scheme dominant over less important issues. The common lawyers favored the development probably in part because they appreciated its progressive and beneficial character and in part because they themselves were landowners and personally resorted to the device. Both Henry V and Thomas Littleton employed the use device, to make a will of land. So the common lawyers kept their hands off, though it would result in overthrowing many of their established doctrines and in furnishing much support to their rival, the Chancellor. If they had not done so, the trust would probably not have emerged in its present form. 4 Holds. 414–16, 418–19, 430, 448; Mait.Eq. 27–31; Barbour, supra, 31 Harv.L.Rev. at 838; 2 P. & M. 232; Maitland, Outlines of English Legal History, op. cit. supra, 2 Coll.Pap. at 492; Maitland, The Unincorporate Body, op. cit. supra, 3 Coll.Pap. at 274; Maitland, Trust and Corporation, op, cit. supra, 3 Coll.Pap. at 340–44.

The Statute of Uses

While most of the British nation seemed favorable to the use development, there was one person who chiefly suffered from it and that was the King. Although other landowners would, as feudal lords, lose by the evasion of feudal incidents, the same individuals would also gain as feudal tenants. And the feudal regime by this time had long outlived its utility and become largely a system of unpopular monetary exactions. The King alone, at the top of the feudal land-holding structure, would always lose and never gain—he was feudal lord over all and tenant to none. The widespread employment of uses resulted in serious diminution of the revenue of the crown, but during the disturbed period of the fifteenth century the monarchy had been too weak to make effective objection. When the accession of Henry VII restored the strength of the crown, there were some superficial legislative attempts to remedy the difficulty. Under Henry VIII, the situation came to a head. After a long series of negotiations and consideration of draft measures, Henry VIII, by threat and diplomacy, ultimately secured, in 1535, the passage of the famous Statute of Uses (27 Hen.8, c. 10) which read in part as follows:

Where by the Common Laws of this Realm, Lands, Tenements and Hereditaments be not devisable by Testament, (2) nor ought to be transferred from one to another, but by solemn Livery and Seisin, Matter of Record, Writing sufficient made *bona fide,* without Covin or Fraud; (3) yet nevertheless divers and sundry Imaginations, subtle Inventions and Practices have been used, whereby the Hereditaments of this Realm have been conveyed from one to another by fraudulent Feoffments, Fines, Recoveries and other Assurances craftily made to secret Uses, Intents and Trusts; (4) and also by Wills and Testaments, sometime made by *nude parolx* and Words, sometime by Signs and Tokens, and sometime by Writing, and for the most Part made by such Persons as be visited with Sickness, in their extreme Agonies and Pains, or at such Time as they have scantly had any good Memory or Rememberance; (5) at which Times they being provoked by greedy covetous Persons lying in wait about them, do many Times dispose indiscreetly and unadvisedly their Lands and Inheritances; (6) by reason whereof, and by Occasion of which fraudulent Feoffments, Fines, Recoveries and other like Assurances to Uses, Confidences and Trusts, divers and many Heirs have been unjustly at sundry Times disherited, the Lords have lost their Wards, Marriages, Reliefs, Harriots, Escheats, aids *pur fair fitz chivalier & pur file marier,* (7) and scantly any Person can be certainly assured of any Lands by them purchased, nor know surely against whom they shall use their Actions or Executions for their Rights, Titles and Duties; (8) also men married have lost their Tenancies by the Curtesy, (9) Women their Dowers, (10) manifest Perjuries by Trial of such secret Wills and Uses have been committed; (11) the King's Highness hath lost the Profits and Advantages of the Lands of Persons attainted, (12) and of the Lands craftily put in Feoffments to the Uses of Aliens born, (13) and also the Profits of Waste for a Year and a Day of Lands of Felons attainted, (14) and the Lords their Escheats thereof; (15) and many other Inconveniences have happened, and daily do increase among the King's Subjects, to their great Trouble and Inquietness, and to the utter Subversion of the ancient Common Laws of this realm; (16) for the extirping and Extinguishment of all such subtle practiced Feoffments, Fines, Recoveries, Abuses and Errors heretofore used and accustomed in this Realm, to the Subversion of the good and ancient Laws of the same, and to the Intent that the King's Highness, or any other his Subjects of this Realm, shall not in any wise hereafter by any Means or Inventions be deceived, damaged or hurt, by reason of such Trusts, Uses or Confidences: (17) It may please the King's most Royal Majesty, that it may be enacted by his Highness, by the Assent of the Lords Spiritual and Temporal, and the Commons, in this present Parliament assembled, and by the Authority of the same, in Manner and Form following: that is to say, [18] That *where any Person or Persons* stand or be *seised,* or at any Time hereafter shall happen to be seised, of and in any Honours, Castles, Manors, Lands, Tenements, Rents, Services, Reversions, Remainders or other Hereditaments, *to the Use,* Confidence or Trust *of any other Person or Persons,* or of any Body Politick, by reason of any Bargain, Sale, Feoffment, Fine, Recovery, Covenant, Contract, Agreement, Will or otherwise, by any manner [or] Means whatsoever it be; that in every such Case, all and every *such Person and Persons,* and Bodies Politick, *that have or hereafter shall have any such Use,* Confidence or Trust in Fee-simple, Feetail, for Term of Life or for Years or otherwise, or any Use, Confidence or Trust in Remainder or Reverter, *shall from henceforth* stand and *be seised,* deemed and adjudged in lawful Seisin, Estate and Possession of and in the same Honours, Castles, Manors, Lands, Tenements, Rents, Services, Reversions, Remainders, and Hereditaments, with their Appurtenances, to all Intents, Constructions and Purposes in the Law, *of and in such like Estates as they had or shall have in Use,* Trust or Confidence of or in the same; (19) *and* that *the estate,* Title, Right and Possession *that was in such Person or Persons that were,* or hereafter shall be *seised* of any Lands, Tenements or Hereditaments, *to the Use,* Confidence, or Trust *of any such Person or Persons,* or of any Body Politick, *be from henceforth* clearly *deemed* and adjudged *to be in him or them that have, or hereafter shall have, such Use,* Confidence or Trust, after such Quality, Manner, Form, and Condition as they had before, in or to the Use, Confidence or Trust that was in them. (Italics after [18] added. Ed.)

The entire statute is printed in 15 Complete Stats. of Eng. 51 (1930).

It will be noted that the preamble to this statute (the first sixteen items) attempts to state the case against uses as strongly as possible, emphasizing the supposed evils of the evasion of the common law requirements of transfer and of the rule prohibiting the devise, and relegates to a comparatively subordinate position any indication of the real motive force behind its enactment—Henry's desire to replenish the King's revenue. This preamble "is far from being a sober statement of historical fact." 4 Holds. 460. It was rather an astute attempt to justify a measure which was bound to be unpopular, and to secure the passage of which it had been necessary for Henry alternately to frighten and to conciliate both the lawyers and the landowners, the two most powerful groups in the House of Commons. His method of securing the consent of the common lawyers was typical. In part they would be persuaded, in view of their traditional jealousy of Chancery, by the prospect of the statute's transferring from the Chancellor to the law courts the important business of uses. But Henry also intimidated the lawyers by listening to a petition complaining of such apparently enduring abuses as the law's delay, graft, excessive fees charged by lawyers, and reliance by them upon technicalities.

The latter portion of the Statute, supra, contains its important enactment. Its basic purpose was to extinguish the seisin or legal estate of the feoffees to uses and give it to the cestui que use instead, and thereby to abolish the former dual ownership and prevent evasion of the common law by making the cestui the legal owner and thus subjecting him to the liabilities of legal ownership. In other words, the system of uses was not abolished as such, but use interests were "executed" by the statute and turned into legal estates. Thereafter, if A enfeoffed B in fee to the use of C in fee, B's legal estate would be taken from him by the statute and vested in C, who would thus be made fee simple owner at law.

While the statute would probably have been unpopular merely because it was a revenue measure, its attempt, by turning the equitable into a legal estate, to abolish the power to devise land, was the chief cause of immediate hostility. Influenced by this, Henry restored this power in 1540 by securing the enactment of the first statute of wills. It is interesting to note that in this statute the King reserved his rights to the feudal incidents, making them applicable to devises as they had formerly been to intestate succession. On this entire development, see Holdsworth, The Political Causes Which Shaped the Statute of Uses, 26 Harv.L.Rev. 108 (1912); 4 Holds. 446–67; Mait.Eq. 34–36; Bordwell, supra.

Uses Not Executed by Statute of Uses

The survival of the trust or use device is due to the fact that the Statute of Uses did not apply to all use transactions and therefore left a residue of jurisdiction in the Chancellor which developed into his important and broad supervision over trusts. The types of uses that were not executed by the statute and therefore remained equitable interests subject to the jurisdiction of the Chancellor, were three in number.

In the first place, the statute did not apply to *uses of personal property*. As already stated, chattels played no significant part in the use development, and the statute was apparently passed to cover the typical case. It will be noted that the statute expressly applies only where one person is "seised" to the use of another, and by this time the word "seisin" had come to apply only to freehold estates in real property. The statute therefore did not apply when one person was merely "possessed" of chattels real or personal to the use of another. Thus, if A held either a personal chattel or a term of years to the use of B, the statute did not apply, and B continued to have an equitable interest enforceable by the Chancellor. It should be realized that this requirement of a freehold estate only applied to the person who would formerly have been legal owner. If A were "seised" in fee to the use of B for one year, B's use would be executed into a legal estate by the express wording of the statute, which covers a use "for term of life or for years." If, however, A did not have a freehold, but was merely "possessed" of a term for one year to the use of B, then, as above stated, B's interest would remain equitable. With the subsequent increase of the importance of personal property as a form of wealth, the Chancellor thus acquired a significant branch of jurisdiction. 4 Holds. 463, 476; Mait.Eq. 37–8.

The second exception to the statute was the *active use* or *trust,* and the Chancellor's retention of jurisdiction over this was the most important factor contributing to the growth of the modern trust. The distinction between the active and the passive trust is significant today and will be developed in connection with the cases infra. The active trust is the normal trust today, the trustee having active duties to perform, and the retention by him of the "legal" title being essential to carry out the purposes of the trust. One explanation of the non-execution of the active use or trust by the Statute of Uses is that it would defeat the objects of the trust to execute it, since that would take the title out of the trustee and thus remove him from the picture and convert the trust gift into an absolute gift. The validity of this as an explanation of the early as distinguished from the more recent cases has, however, been disputed on the ground that the courts would not at that time have been much concerned with the intention of the creator of the trust when construing a statute the object of which was to defeat rather than carry out the purposes of the use transactions. 17 Mich.L.Rev. 87 (1918). Perhaps a more satisfactory solution of the problem is to say that the statute was aimed primarily at the typical use arrangement, the passive use, under which the feoffee to uses was a dummy holding the legal title and the cestui was in possession and enjoying all the practical benefits of ownership. That was the situation that made evasion of the legal doctrines popular and occasioned the evils asserted in the preamble. On the other hand, any scheme resembling the modern active trust was exceedingly rare and probably would not be considered as giving the cestui the equivalent of ownership; the feoffee to uses would be in possession and control and the cestui would be thought of as having merely a right to an accounting. And it may be argued that the statute showed by its terms an intention to exclude the latter by employing the words "estates *   *   * in use." Whatever the reasons, the courts excepted active trusts from the operation of the statute and thereby allowed the Chancellor to develop the modern trust. 4 Holds. 463; Mait.Eq. 38.

The third exception to the statute was the *use on a use,* which was an attempt to give two contemporaneous use interests in the same property, as in a case where A enfeoffed B in fee to the use of C in fee to the use of D in fee—D's interest would be the use of (or "on") a use. The limitation of two successive use interests—as in a case where A enfeoffed B to the use of C until D returned from Rome and then to the use of D— would not be a use on a use, but a "shifting use." The doctrines of "shifting" and "springing" uses will be further referred to in Chapter Nine, at p. 740, infra. They are not relevant to that part of the law of trusts which is considered in this section, but the concept of the use on a use should not be confused with that of the shifting use. The exclusion of the use on a use from the statute has occasioned much discussion and sarcasm; Lord Hardwicke said that "by this means a statute made upon great consideration, introduced in a solemn and pompous manner *   *   * has had no other effect than to add at most, three words to a conveyance." Hopkins v. Hopkins, 1 Atk. 581, 591 (1738). In other words, the insertion of the words "use of C" in the above case would vest the legal estate in C under the statute, but would prevent D's use from being executed by the statute and allow D's use to be enforced by the Chancellor, thereby accomplishing the same result as would have been reached before the statute if A had enfeoffed C to the use of D. But, while this was a true description of the state of affairs in 1738, the process was neither so simple and sudden nor so out of harmony with the purpose of the statute as Hardwicke's statement would imply. It is probable that prior to the

Statute of Uses the use on a use was considered void as repugnant to the first use.   So if land were conveyed to the use of C to the use of D, the two contemporaneous uses would be considered incompatible and C would have the equitable use and D would have nothing.   The statute then provided that uses should be turned into legal estates.   But D had no use before the statute and so, after the statute, had nothing that could be turned into a legal estate.   It was therefore held that a use on a use was void at law, as it had previously been in equity, and was not executed by the statute.   Tyrrel's Case, 2 Dyer 155 (1557).   The Chancellor did not immediately take advantage of this to increase his jurisdiction.   The use on a use continued to be held void in Chancery also, and it was not until a hundred years after the Statute of Uses that the Chancellor recognized and began to enforce the second use.   Sambach v. Dalston, Tothill, 188 (1634).   The Chancellors, during this intervening century, probably realized that, if they should enforce the use on a use, the Statute of Uses would be nullified in the manner suggested by Hardwicke, and, out of sympathy for both the King's interests and the purposes of the statute, they refrained from doing so at least until the incidents of tenure had become obsolete.   Upon Chancery's recognition of the use on a use, however, that was of course added to the equitable jurisdiction over uses and trusts that persisted in spite of the statute.   Ames, supra;   Mait.Eq. 41–42;   4 Holds. 468–73;   5 Holds. 307–09;   6 Holds. 641–42;   7 Holds. 135;   Bordwell, supra, 39 Harv.L.Rev. at 471–73.

Conveyances Under Statute of Uses

Finally, a brief description of the conveyances made possible by the Statute of Uses is necessary to complete the picture.   These conveyances furnished the transition between the common law transfers and the modern deed, and, while they are chiefly important in the law of conveyancing, they also provide some analogies for the law of trusts.   They were three in number: the bargain and sale, the covenant to stand seised, and the lease and release.

Of these three, the *bargain and sale* was the only one in existence prior to the Statute of Uses.   It was recognized by the Chancellor as a method of creating a use, about the year 1500.   If A, for a valuable consideration, either orally or in writing, agreed to sell land to B, the Chancellor, prior to the statute, held that A was seized to the use of B.   An analogy for this was furnished by the already existing common law doctrine that a similar bargain and sale of a chattel would "pass the property" in the chattel and give B an action of detinue.   And, as the Chancellor had previously considered it unfair for the feoffee to uses to go back on the agreement pursuant to which he had received the land, so here he considered it unfair for A, who had the purchase money in his pocket, not to live up to his contract.   In the case of a feoffment to uses, it was the receipt of the land that charged the conscience of the feoffee; here it was the receipt of the consideration that charged the conscience of the seller.   And, while the Chancellor did not require a writing for a bargain and sale, he did originally require a valuable consideration; he refused to follow common law analogies to the extent of holding a gratuitous sealed instrument operative to raise a use. This requirement of consideration later became a mere form. After the Statute of Uses, the bargain and sale would transfer legal title because the former use would be executed by the Statute into a legal estate. This result was foreseen, and to secure publicity and reliability of evidence in this form of transfer, the Statute of Enrollments was passed at the same time as the Statute of Uses. 27 Hen. VIII, c. 16. A far more elaborate and universal scheme for the registration of conveyances had been proposed, but Parliament failed to pass it, possibly for no more complicated reason than exhaustion from the laborious and controversial consideration of the Statute of Uses. "Whatever the truth may be, it is clear that a great opportunity was lost forever when this bill was rejected." 4 Holds. 460. Instead of a comprehensive scheme of registration which might have greatly simplified the land law at the inception of its modern stage, the Statute of Enrollments was enacted and only stimulated ingenious evasion of its provisions. It merely required a bargain and sale of a freehold to be under seal and enrolled (i.e. recorded). In this way, the transfer of legal title by deed was introduced into the law.

The *covenant to stand seised* appears to have been initiated by the court of Queen's Bench in 1565 in an action of trespass at law. Sharington v. Strotton, 1 Plowd. 298, 75 Eng.Rep. 454 (1565). In that case it was held that a gratuitous covenant under seal to stand seised of land to the use of the covenantor's brother and the latter's wife was sufficient to pass title to the covenantees. This was not on the ground that no consideration was necessary, but on the theory that Baynton's (the covenantor's) "desire that the land should continue in the blood and name of Baynton, and the brotherly love" constituted sufficient consideration. While this language was followed in later statements to the effect that in such a case natural love and affection for a relative furnished the consideration, such an explanation seems fictional. There was in fact no consideration in the usual sense of the word, but the requirement of consideration in a bargain and sale was departed from probably because it seemed reasonable to permit gifts of land by this method to members of the family of the donor, and to recognize the already existing employment of uses in the creation of family settlements. In 1597, an oral agreement to stand seised to the use of a son was held invalid in the Exchequer Chamber because not under seal. Callard v. Callard, Moore K.B. 950, 72 Eng.Rep. 841 (1597). This decision was probably due to a desire to secure reliable evidence, since the covenant to stand seised was not within the Statute of Enrollments. As a result of these two cases, legal title could be transferred by the covenant to stand seised provided that: (1) it was under seal; (2) the transferee was related by blood or marriage to the transferor.

The *lease and release* conveyance operating under the Statute of Uses was first recognized in 1620. Lutwich v. Mitton, Cro.Jac. 604 (1620).

This operated in the same way as the common law lease and release with one exception, namely, that the term of years was created by a bargain and sale deed instead of the common law method. If the grantor was seised of a freehold estate, the use for a term of years would, as above explained, be executed by the statute into a legal estate, enabling the grantee to receive a release of the reversion. This was therefore a mongrel conveyance, the lease operating under the Statute of Uses and the release under the common law. Its advantage over the common lease and release was that it dispensed with the necessity of the grantee's taking possession. Its advantage over the bargain and sale was that it was not within the Statute of Enrollments, evasion of which was the chief reason for its invention. As above stated, that statute only applied to a bargain and sale of a freehold, and the bargain and sale in this transfer was of a term of years, a non-freehold estate. Because of these and other advantages, the lease and release became the most common type of conveyance in England. On conveyances operating under the Statute of Uses, see 4 Holds. 424–27, 460; 7 Holds. 353–62; Ames, supra; Mait.Eq. 35–36; Bordwell, supra, 39 Harv.L.Rev. at 468, 470; Tiffany, § 100; Bacon, Reading on the Statute of Uses, 3 Works of Francis Bacon 299 (New Ed., 1841).

Methods of Creating Trusts

In conclusion, it should be said, by way of transition to trusts, that there are at the present day, two general methods of creating trusts inter vivos. The first is a *transfer in trust*, the expression used to describe a case where A (settlor) transfers to B (trustee) in trust for C (cestui); this is similar to the creation of a use on a feoffment or other common law conveyance. The second is a *declaration of trust*, which describes a case where A, the owner of the property, instead of transferring it to B, another person as trustee, declares himself trustee of that property for the benefit of C, the cestui; this is similar to the creation of a use by bargain and sale or covenant to stand seised. A testamentary declaration of trust would of course be impossible, since the instrument would not go into effect until the testator was dead and unable to act as trustee for that rather obvious reason. The creation of a trust by will is similar to a transfer in trust inter vivos.

Notes

1. The passive trust still has some legitimate uses. For example, a real estate developer who is married and does business in a dower state may well prefer to take title in the name of a passive trustee, who can resell without obtaining a release of dower for each parcel. (Conceivably, however, such a trusteeship might be held to be active; see the cases in the next section.)

Can you think of any other situations in which dummy ownership can legitimately be used?

2. Many a modern deed contains a habendum clause, even though latter-day statutes dispense with the need for such clauses. A typical habendum clause might read as follows: "To have and to hold the said property to the use

of the grantee, his heirs and assigns forever." Why do you suppose the habendum clause came into common usage?

SECTION TWO. ACTIVE AND PASSIVE TRUSTS

McKENZIE v. SUMNER

Supreme Court of North Carolina, 1894.
114 N.C. 425, 19 S.E. 375.

Appeal from superior court, Rowan county: Jacob Battle, Judge.

Bill in equity by C. H. McKenzie and wife against Julian E. Sumner. From a decree for plaintiffs, defendant appeals. Affirmed.

Thomas J. Sumner devised to defendant certain land, in trust for plaintiff, "to have and to hold, to her and her heirs, in fee simple, forever." He also bequeathed to defendant, in trust for plaintiff, 50 shares of stock in a manufacturing company. Plaintiff is a married woman, and sues to have the legal title to this property vested in her, and the trust terminated.

SHEPHERD, C. J. As to the real estate devised to the defendant for the benefit of the plaintiff, there is no reason why the legal title is not vested in the plaintiff by the statute of uses, as the land is not conveyed to her "sole and separate use" (see authorities collected in Malone, Real Prop.Tri. 544), nor is the trustee charged, in any manner whatever, with any special duties in respect to the same. The case does not fall within either of the three well-known exceptions to the operation of the statute, and it would seem clear that the legal estate is executed in the plaintiff. 1 Perry, Trusts, 298, and the numerous authorities cited in the note. The statute, however, does not apply to personal property, such as notes and bank stock; and the legal title remains in the trustee until it is, in some way, transferred to the equitable owner. Is there any reason why the court, exercising its equitable jurisdiction, should not have directed the assignment of the legal title in this instance? We can see none. The plaintiff being the absolute equitable owner, there are no ulterior limitations to be protected; and under the terms of the will the trustee has nothing but a bare, naked, legal estate, unaccompanied, as we have remarked, with a single, specified duty. As the plaintiff's separate estate is fully protected against the interference of her husband by the provisions of the constitution, and as the trustee has no power to withhold from her either the property or its income, we are unable to see why the legal title should remain in him, unless it be to enable him to charge the 5 per cent commissions which he claims for "simply collecting and paying over the dividends upon the stock." We do not deem it necessary to enter into an elaborate discussion of the subject, but will simply refer to the following authorities, which, although perhaps not exactly in point, fully sustain, upon principle, the ruling of his honor: [Citations omitted] We will add the following extract from Lewin on Trusts (page 18): "The simple trust is where property is vested in one person upon trust for another, and the nature of the trust, not being prescribed by the settler [sic] (and such is the case here), is left to the construction of law. In this case the cestui que trust has jus habendi, or the right to be put into actual possession of the property, and jus disponendi, or the right to call upon the trustee to execute conveyances of the legal estate as the cestui que trust directs." This is so clearly a simple trust that, under our decisions, the property, prior to the present constitution, would have belonged to the husband. Ashcraft v. Little, 4 Ired.Eq. 236; Heartman v. Hall, 3 Ired.Eq. 414. We have examined the authorities cited by the intelligent counsel for the appellant, but they do not satisfy us that the judgment below was erroneous. The judgment, in all respects, is affirmed.

Note

In Penney v. White, 594 S.W.2d 632 (Mo.App.1980), the court declared that although a passive trust of personalty is not covered by the Statute of Uses, such a trust is executed by the separate principle that equity does not tolerate the continuance of a useless thing.

KINZER v. BIDWILL
Supreme Court of Wisconsin, 1972.
55 Wis.2d 749, 201 N.W.2d 9.

Appellant, Richard A. Kinzer, and his then wife purchased a lakefront lot on Lake Geneva from the respondents in 1955. The Kinzers also purchased from respondents an undivided one-sixth interest in a 75-acre parcel of land, not fronting on the lake, hereinafter termed the "back property." This parcel of "back property" was located across the road and behind the lakefront lots owned individually by respondents and Kinzers.

Prior to the sale to the Kinzers, the respondents had owned the back property subject to a claimed agreement that: (1) No party would attempt to sell or partition his interest without first offering to sell it to the other parties at cost; and (2) no improvements would be made on the back property without the unanimous consent of the parties. Respondents were advised that putting the back property in trust was a better way to carry out their agreement or understanding.

Thereafter the back property was transferred to a land trust with the First Wisconsin Trust Company named as trustee. When the sale to the Kinzers took place, the trust company conveyed the back property back to the respondents. They then joined in a deed conveying a one-sixth interest to the Kinzers. The respondents and Kinzers then deeded the property back to the trust company subject to the terms of a land trust agreement.

The Kinzers built a home on the lakefront property and occupied it until 1968. At that time they put up for sale the lakefront property and their interest in the back property. In December of 1968, a party by the name of Schwimmer made an offer to purchase the Kinzers' lakefront property and their interest in the back property, agreeing also to become a party to the land trust. The Kinzers accepted the offer. However, before the deal was closed, respondent Bidwill called prospective purchaser Schwimmer's real estate agent and stated that the Kinzers were bound by an agreement prohibiting the sale of the undivided one-sixth interest in the back property without first offering it to the respondents at cost. The sale of the back property was not consummated.

Appellant Kinzer then brought suit against respondents seeking partition of the back property. (Mrs. Kinzer had deeded her interest in the back property to appellant pursuant to a property settlement in a divorce action.) The trial court held that the land trust was void; that the parties owned the back property as tenants in common; that appellant was entitled to partition of his one-sixth interest in the back property; that, while void, the trust was nevertheless a valid agreement creating an equitable servitude prohibiting development of the back property until 1980. From an interlocutory judgment and order, appellant and respondents appeal.

ROBERT W. HANSEN, Justice. The trial court here did three things:

(1) Held the land trust to be void, finding it to be a passive trust;

(2) Found the parties to the trust to be tenants in common, each entitled to bring suit for partition;

(3) Held the trust, while void, to be a valid agreement, and reformed such agreement to prohibit development of the back property until 1980.

Appellant challenges the trial court's reforming the agreement of the parties to create an equitable servitude banning development of the back property until 1980.

Respondents contend that the trial court should have further reformed the agreement of the parties to prohibit partition, and that appellant should be estopped from asserting his right to partition.

However, the rights of the parties as tenants in common under an agreement and the right of the court to reform such agreement on the basis of mutual mistake are before the trial court only if the land trust is void. If the trust is a valid one, its provisions determine and control the rights of the parties for the life of the trust. So the initial inquiry must be as to whether this land trust is void or valid.

The trial court held that, by its terms and on its face, the land trust here was a passive trust. A trust is passive if the trustee has no active duties to perform, and in this state passive trusts have been abolished and legal title goes to the beneficiaries of the trust. Trusts in this state have been held to be passive where the trustee had no active duties to perform, and where the trust instrument stated the beneficiaries should have the management and control of the property, and the trustee was to have no duties to perform.

While specific findings or reasons are not spelled out, it is clear that the trial court held that the various provisions of the trust dealing with leasing, development, selling or mortgaging the property made it a passive trust. In such major areas, the trust provides that the trustee can act only after being directed to do so by four-sixths of the shareholders. The trial court concluded: "Basically the trustee has no duties regarding said real estate without and until such time as directed by ⅚ of the beneficiaries in writing.   *   *   *"

One begins with the evident purpose of this trust to maintain the 75-acre tract of land in its natural or undeveloped state, at least until four-sixths of the beneficiaries agree to a particular use or development.   Ordinarily, it is true, it is the duty of a trustee under a land trust to maximize income, collect rents and promote commercial use of the property placed in trust.   Here both purpose and result are to maintain the ecological status quo, the property to be kept by the trustee undeveloped unless four-sixths of the shareholders direct otherwise.   The land in question is by the trust kept out of the possession, use and control of the individual shareholders.   Possession, use and control are placed in the trustee and it is to administer the corpus in such a way as to carry out the purpose of the trust and maximize the benefits to all of the beneficiaries.   There is evidence that the purpose of the trust was to administer the back property so as to "protect" the beneficiaries' lakefront property.   But, aside from that, a trust intended and resulting in the likely maintenance of property in its natural, undeveloped state is not made "passive" by that fact.   Where the individual beneficiaries have no right to possession, use or control of the property, the duty of the trustee to prevent development, partition or sale by individual beneficiaries, unless directed by four-sixths so to do, is an active responsibility, not an absence of responsibility.

Additionally, the trustee under this trust does have active duties, and is actually performing such duties.   Article V of the trust instrument provides that: "Subject to the provisions of Articles III and IV, the Trustee is empowered to do any act it considers to be for the best interest of the trust estate.   *   *   *"   Testimony of the assistant secretary to the trust company, serving as trustee, uncontradicted, establishes that the trustee maintains liability insurance on the property, checks the taxes and pays the taxes each year, handled inquiries from parties desiring to buy or list the property for sale, bills and collects moneys from the beneficiaries for the payment of taxes, insurance and tree removal.   This court has held that the single act of enforcing payment of rent and taxes was sufficient to make a trust an active trust.

Many years ago, this court stated the rule or standard to be: "   *   *   * If there are any active duties for the [trustee] to perform with respect to administering the property, and the primary use be expressly or impliedly, by reason of such active duty, vested in the trustee, the trust is necessarily active.   *   *   *"   Here the trustee had active duties to perform and did perform them.   Here the individual shareowner relinquished to the trust the right to sell, lease or partition, subject only to directions given to the trustee by four-sixths of the shareholders.   Here the purpose and result of the trust was to prevent sale, lease or development of portions of the 75-acre tract.   Put together, we hold the trust here to be an active trust, not passive and not void.

It follows that the rights of appellant and respondents are not those of tenants in common, but those of shareholders and beneficiaries of a valid land trust agreement. · It follows that appellant is not entitled to bring suit for partition while the trust is in effect, *to wit,* until 1980. It follows that appellant's right to dispose of his one-sixth beneficial interest in the trust is to be controlled by the terms of the trust agreement. It follows that there is no reason to determine what the status of the parties would be if the trust was void, and no right to reform any agreement of the parties found to exist with the trust held void.

Judgment and order reversed, with directions to dismiss the complaint of plaintiff in suit for partition.

Notes

1. The subject of active and passive trusts and the Statute of Uses is discussed in 1 Scott on Trusts (3d ed.) § 69; Evans, The Termination of Trusts, 37 Yale L.J. 1070, 1084, 1099 (1928); Annot., 97 A.L.R. 729; Restatement, Second, Trusts §§ 67–73, 88.

As to the extent to which the Statute of Uses is operative in this country, see Bordwell, The Repeal of the Statute of Uses, 39 Harv.L.Rev. 466, 477 (1926); Rood, The Statute of Uses and the Modern Deed, 4 Mich.L.Rev. 109 (1905).

2. Recent cases on the distinction between active and passive trusts include: Hatcher v. Southern Baptist Theological Seminary, 632 S.W.2d 251 (Ky.1982); Penney v. White, 594 S.W.2d 632 (Mo.App.1980); Johnson v. Thornton, 264 S.C. 252, 214 S.E.2d 124 (1975); Clement v. Charlotte Hospital Association, Inc., 137 So.2d 615 (Fla.App.1962); Matter of Fischer, 307 N.Y. 149, 120 N.E.2d 688 (1954); Finch v. Honeycutt, 246 N.C. 91, 97 S.E.2d 478 (1957); Fishel and Taylor v. Grifton United Methodist Church, 22 N.C.App. 647, 207 S.E.2d 330 (1974).

SECTION THREE.   THE EXPRESS TRUST

Restatement, Second, Trusts

§ 2—Definition of Trust

A trust, (as the term is used in the Restatement of this Subject, when not qualified by the word "charitable," "resulting" or "constructive,") is a fiduciary relationship with respect to property subjecting the person by whom the title to the property is held to equitable duties to deal with the property for the benefit of another person, which arises as a result of a manifestation of an intention to create it.

A.   TRUSTS CREATED BY PRECATORY WORDS

IN RE ESTATE OF CORBETT

Supreme Court of Pennsylvania, 1968.
430 Pa. 54, 241 A.2d 524.

Before BELL, C. J., and MUSMANNO, JONES, COHEN, EAGEN, O'BRIEN and ROBERTS, JJ.

ROBERTS, Justice.

[handwritten: " handwritten"]*

This is an appeal from a decree of the Orphans' Court of Chester County. The testator, Reverend Dennis A. Corbett, died September 7, 1956 leaving a holographic will dated December 22, 1925. Two small pecuniary bequests were followed by the presently contested residuary clause: "All the remainder of my estate, of whatever nature, I give and bequeath to my two sisters, Catherine Corbett, and Julia Corbett, and to my brother, John Corbett—two parts to each of said sisters, and one part to said brother—*who are instructed as to my charitable wishes."* (Emphasis supplied.) At the time this will was executed testator's two sisters and brother named in the residuary clause were living. Another brother, Patrick J. Corbett, had died exactly one year before the date of execution.

[handwritten left margin: "intent to create a trust ?"]

All of the specified beneficiaries predeceased the testator, the last of the three having passed away in 1948. Catherine and Julia Corbett died unmarried and without issue; John Corbett was survived by James Corbett, his adopted son,[1] the appellee. Patrick J. Corbett, the one brother not mentioned in the residuary clause, was survived by two daughters, Mae K. Corbett and Margaret P. Suria, the appellants. The sole issue presented by this appeal is the proper distribution of the residue of decedent's estate. The auditing judge awarded the entire residue to James Corbett. However, the appellants insist that an intestacy should have been declared and that they are therefore each entitled to one-third of decedent's residual property with the remaining third given to appellee.

Appellants advance, albeit somewhat tentatively, the suggestion that the phrase "who are instructed as to my charitable wishes" evidences an intention of testator to create a testamentary trust. If such is the case, they argue, the property bequeathed in the residuary clause must pass by intestacy because the trust is incapable of effectuation. We hold, however, that the quoted phrase does not create a trust and, in fact, is not even indicative of an intent to create one.

[handwritten left margin: "H"]

We begin with the proposition that the word "wish" (or, in this case, "wishes") is generally classified as precatory. Calder's Estate, 343 Pa. 30, 21 A.2d 907 (1941). However, such a word may be mandatory when expressive of an intention of the testator to be carried out without the intervention of another's will and when used "in direct reference to the estate." Id. at 37, 21 A.2d at 911.[2] Stinson's Estate (No. 1), 232 Pa. 218, 221, 81 A. 207, 208, 36 L.R.A.,N.S., 504 (1911), perhaps the leading case in this area, enunciates this rule:

"[W]hen precatory words are used merely for the purpose of advising or influencing, or as expressive of a wish or desire that the legatee make a certain use of the testator's bounty, they are not obligatory upon those to

---

1. The fact that appellee is an adopted child is of no consequence in this litigation. See Act of April 24, 1947, P.L. 80, § 8, 20 P.S. § 1.8; Act of April 24, 1947, P.L. 89, § 14, as amended by the Act of February 17, 1956, P.L. (1955) 1070, § 1, 20 P.S. § 180.14(6) (Supp.1966).

2. The *Calder* Court noted that this rule often runs contra to the principle that, where there is an absolute gift, later words in the same instrument will not operate to reduce the estate already bequeathed unless it is reasonably certain that such was the intention of the testator. It is clear that were it not for the words "who are instructed as to my charitable wishes," the gift to the residuary legatees is absolute. Under many of the cases cited in *Calder* the quoted language would thus be deemed not to reduce the estate previously given.

whom they are addressed; but when used to express his manifest intention to control or direct, they are mandatory, and will be so construed in saying what effect is to be given to them: [Citations omitted] * * *."

That the phrase employed in Rev. Corbett's residuary clause falls within the italicized *Stinson* language and is thus completely precatory is amply illustrated by Herskovitz's Estate No. 1, 81 Pa.Super. 379 (1923). After leaving his estate to his wife, Dr. Herskovitz directed that she "must * * * comply with my last requests, which is [sic] as follows: * * *." Then followed a series of pecuniary gifts to various charities. Testator, in an attempt to insure that his requests were honored, added: "I hereby hope, wish and demand that every point of my last will shall be wholly fulfilled by my lawful wedded wife to a T." The Superior Court held that the quoted directions and demands were precatory and not sufficient to create a charitable trust. Certainly, if Dr. Herskovitz's directions were precatory, then the considerably milder comment that Rev. Corbett's legatees were "instructed as to * * * [his] charitable wishes" must be.[3]

This conclusion is reinforced by our belief that testator's direction was legally insufficient to create a trust.[4] A trust, charitable or otherwise, cannot be created unless the purported settlor manifests an intention to impose enforceable duties. Restatement 2d, Trusts § 25 and § 351 (1959). Illustration 1, appended to section 25 of the Restatement, is apt: "A bequeaths $10,000 to B 'desiring that he should use it for such purposes as he might think the testator would deem wise.' In the absence of other evidence [and there is no other here], B is entitled beneficially to the money and does not take it in trust." See also comment (b), § 25; comment (c), § 351.

We next turn to appellants' second contention—the phrase "who are instructed as to my charitable wishes" demonstrates that testator intended that only the three named legatees should take under the residuary clause and that, since none survived testator, an intestacy results. Both parties cite a myriad of guides to the construction of wills: a layman's will is to be construed as if written by a layman, Ziegler Estate, 356 Pa. 93, 51 A.2d 608 (1947); each word of a will is to be, if possible, given effect. England Estate, 414 Pa. 115, 200 A.2d 897 (1964); rules of construction are not employed unless the will is ambiguous or testator's intent uncertain, Houston Estate, 414 Pa. 579, 201 A.2d 592 (1964); all, of course, are cited as an aid to the ultimate determination, i.e., what intent is manifested by the language employed.[5]

---

3. At least one court has suggested that the case law shows a tendency to construe provisions in a will as precatory when such a construction will operate to the benefit of a close family relation. See Shober Estate, 67 Pa.Dist. & Co.R. 251 (O.C.Philadelphia Cty.1949). Assuming that this observation is valid, then our predilection should favor a decision that testator's instructions were precatory since the residuary legatees were his closest family.

4. As to the requirements for the creation of a trust, see generally Brubaker v. Lauver, 322 Pa. 461, 185 A. 848 (1936).

5. Appellant relies heavily upon the rule of construction that the law leans toward equality among heirs. See *Ziegler Estate*, supra. The court below and appellee counter this rule with another: the presumption that a testator wished to die testate. See Grier Estate, 403 Pa. 517, 170 A.2d 545 (1961). These rules, tending to produce opposite conclusions in the same case, seem to be of little aid here.

Section 14 of the Wills Act of 1947, Act of April 24, 1947, P.L. 89, 20 P.S. § 180.14(8) and (10), provides:

"In the absence of a contrary intent appearing therein, wills shall be construed as to real and personal estate in accordance with the following rules:

* * *

"(8) Lapsed and void devises and legacies.—Substitution of issue. A devise or bequest * * * to * * * [testator's] brother or sister * * * shall not lapse if the beneficiary shall fail to survive the testator and shall leave issue surviving the testator but shall pass to such surviving issue * * *

* * *

"(10) Lapsed and void devises and legacies.—Shares in residue. When a devise or bequest * * * shall be included in a residuary clause of the will and shall not be available to the issue of the devisee or legatee under the provisions of clause (8) hereof, * * * it shall pass to the other residuary devisees or legatees, if any there be, in proportion to their respective shares or interests in the residue."

Both parties agree, and well they should, that, absent the phrase "who are instructed as to my charitable wishes", appellee would unquestionably be entitled to the entire residue. [Citations omitted] By the operation of subsection (8) the bequests to the two sisters lapsed for they died without issue; the bequest to John Corbett, however, does not lapse since he was survived by issue, the appellee. Since the lapsed bequests to testator's sisters were contained in a residuary clause, subsection (10) dictates that appellee, whose father's bequest did not lapse, is entitled to the entire residue. Appellants' contention thus reduces to the proposition that the phrase "who are instructed as to my charitable wishes" is a sufficient manifestation of a "contrary intent" on the part of testator to prevent the operation of the anti-lapse provisions of section 14. We do not agree.

The question of what language is sufficient to show an intent that the anti-lapse statute should not be applied is one that has been the subject of relatively frequent litigation. See Annot., Testator's Intention as Defeating Operation of Antilapse Statute, 63 A.L.R.2d 1172 (1959). The general rule, as developed primarily in California, appears to be that the intention of the testator to render the statute inoperative must be plainly indicated.[6] This intention need not manifest itself by a specific provision in the will dealing expressly with the question of lapse, for testator's intention can be deduced by implication from other aspects of the will. Thus, in other jurisdictions some cases hold that testator's desire to disinherit an individual or a clause expressing an intention to exclude from participation persons not mentioned in the will is sufficient to indicate that the anti-lapse provisions should not be applied to the

---

6. Some states place the burden of proof upon the individual seeking to show the non-operation of the anti-lapse statute, while others merely state that the testator is presumed to have known of the statute and its effect.

putative beneficiaries of the statute. See id. at 1181–90. Since Rev. Corbett included no *express* provision as to lapse, appellants must rest on the theory that the phrase in question *impliedly* requires that the anti-lapse statute not apply.

To the extent that the problem of an implied intention to prevent the application of the anti-lapse provisions has been considered, Pennsylvania cases *seem* to hold that the statute is rendered inoperative only when testator specifically provided for disposition of lapsed bequests.[7] [Citations omitted] While we do not here decide what words, estate plan or other circumstance would be sufficient to exclude by implication the operation of the anti-lapse statute, we are convinced that Wright Estate, 380 Pa. 106, 110 A.2d 198 (1955) compels a conclusion that Rev. Corbett's manifestation of intent was not sufficient.

At the time his will was executed, Wright had three living sisters. Accordingly, he left the residue of his estate "to be divided between [sic] my three sisters." One of these sisters died; Wright thereupon crossed out the word "three" in his will and substituted next to it the word "two." We held that this interlineation could not be probated but that there was a partial cancellation of the will so that the residuary clause in legal effect now read: "the rest to be divided between my sisters." Wright was survived by his two sisters and the daughter of the predeceased sister. Under section 14, the gift to the predeceased sister did not lapse but rather passed to her surviving daughter. It was contended, however, that the interlineation at least demonstrated that Wright intended that only his two surviving sisters should share in the residue and that, therefore, he manifested an intent that the anti-lapse provisions not apply. We rejected this contention and held that an invalid bequest could not operate to show an actual intent.

Wright's interlineation indicating that only his surviving sisters should benefit was thus deemed insufficient.[8] We thus fail to see how Rev. Corbett's clearly less substantial manifestation of intent, i.e., "who are instructed as to my charitable wishes," can be held sufficient.

The decree of the Orphans' Court of Chester County is affirmed. Each party to pay own costs.

BELL, C. J., dissents.

COHEN, J., files a dissenting opinion.

DISSENTING OPINION

COHEN, Justice. The majority opinion reaches a result by applying artificial rules of construction which, in my view, directly contravenes the obvious intention of the deceased.

---

7. We do not here intimate that only an express provision in the will covering a possible lapse will be sufficient to show testator's contrary intent.

8. The reverse but analogous, situation is presented by McFerren Estate, 365 Pa. 490, 76 A.2d 759, 22 A.L.R.2d 451 (1950). We there held that the mere fact that the testatrix made specific provision that certain legacies (otherwise saved by the statute) would lapse did not demonstrate an intent that legacies not covered by the statute would not lapse. We there said that it would be conjecture to assume that by providing for lapse in some bequests, testatrix therefore intended that other bequests should not lapse.

In Ziegler Estate, 356 Pa. 93, 51 A.2d 608 (1943), we said that in construing a layman's will, the language must be considered without reference to technical rules of construction. Obviously, the purpose of employing the phrase "who are instructed as to my charitable wishes" was sufficient to indicate that testator intended that at least part of the residue of his estate should be used for charitable purposes. It is also clear that the only persons advised and instructed as to these charitable wishes were those beneficiaries named in the will, all of whom predeceased the testator. Nevertheless, in the guise of the rule concerning precatory language, and the application of the anti-lapse statute, the majority opinion permits someone who was not informed or instructed as to testator's charitable desires to be the recipient *under the will* of the entire residue of his estate.

While I agree with the majority that testator's use of precatory words was legally insufficient to create a trust or impose any enforceable duties, I cannot agree that such language does not indicate an actual intention of the testator to transfer the residue of his estate to only those persons apprised of his charitable wishes. Appellee certainly does not possess the knowledge of how much and to whom part or all of the residue [sic] the testator intended to give to particular charitable institutions. Testator's actual intent under the will being frustrated and incapable of fulfillment due to the death of all the named beneficiaries, the residue of his estate should not pass under the will, but should be distributed as if testator died intestate.

Moreover, in apparent disregard to what I think is the clear intention of the testator, the majority seeks to buttress its resolution by resorting to Section 14 of the Wills Act of April 24, 1947, P.L. 89, 20 P.S. §§ 180.14(8) and (10) which provides in pertinent part as follows:

[Statutory quotations omitted]

The majority determines that the phrase "who are instructed as to my charitable wishes" is not a sufficient manifestation of a contrary intent to prevent the operation of the anti-lapse statute. I disagree for the reasons previously stated. It is inconceivable that the testator intended that the residue of his estate should pass to the surviving issue of the named beneficiaries in the will, since the surviving issue could not in any way fulfill testator's charitable intentions being completely unaware of those wishes.

In my opinion, the words "who are instructed as to my charitable wishes" are a sufficient expression of a contrary intent rendering inoperative the anti-lapse provision under the Wills Act of 1947. The majority in concluding otherwise, relies almost exclusively upon Wright Estate, 380 Pa. 106, 110 A.2d 198 (1955), which case I find inapplicable to the present situation. In *Wright,* we held that an illegal revocation or invalid substitutionary gift could not affect or operate to show an actual intent to defeat a prior valid bequest, nor could it be used to show a contrary intent that the anti-lapse statute should not apply. However, the *Wright* case can be distinguished from the instant case in several respects. First, the anti-lapse statute by its terms did not apply in *Wright,* since it could not be successfully argued that the word inserted ("two") evidenced a contrary intent *appearing in the will*. Since the insertion was deemed an invalid substitutionary gift, the will had to be read as if testator provided "the rest to be divided between my sisters." Consequently, no expression of a contrary intent actually appeared in the will. Here the words "who are instructed as to my charitable wishes" were not invalidly inserted in the will, but rather were merely incapable of enforcement. Although unenforceable, the words quite properly appear in the will and should be used, unlike in *Wright,* for the purpose of ascertaining testator's intent. Secondly, in *Wright* we only proscribed the *use* of an invalid bequest to demonstrate a contrary intent and not as the majority suggests that the invalid bequest failed to sufficiently manifest the necessary contrary intent. Here no such situation exists. Appellants are not offering an invalid bequest or devise so as to affect or operate to defeat a prior valid disposition of testator's property, but on the contrary offer an expression of intent appearing in the will which for reasons other than its invalidity cannot be enforced. Moreover, our Court in *Wright* was faced with a very practical problem due to the fact that if we were to have held that the invalid insertion could be used to indicate a contrary intent we would have simply arrived at the same result as if we allowed the invalid substitutionary gift to be an effective disposition of Wright's property. This practical problem also fails to exist in the instant case.

For these reasons I am firmly convinced that we should use this expression of intent to resolve the crux of the issue before us, namely, the actual and obvious intent of the testator. Since the avowed purposes of the residuary clause cannot possibly be effectuated *under the will*, I would distribute the proceeds of this estate in accordance with the rules of intestate succession.

I dissent.

LEVIN v. FISCH

Court of Civil Appeals of Texas, 1966.
404 S.W.2d 889.

COLLINGS, Justice. Laura Fisch brought suit against Suzanne Cohen Levin and Jay Howard Cohen, individually and as independent executors of the estate of Bertha Cohen, deceased. Plaintiff, a sister of the deceased, claimed that she had an interest in said estate under the provisions of the last will and testament of Bertha Cohen. Defendants are the children of Bertha Cohen, deceased. It was stipulated that Bertha Cohen died on November 28, 1959, in Houston, Harris County, Texas, that the last will and testament of Bertha Cohen, dated April 11, 1958, was admitted to probate on January 27, 1960 by the Probate Court of Harris County, Texas, and that the defendants are the duly appointed and acting independent executors of the estate of Bertha Cohen, deceased. Both plaintiff and defendants filed motions for summary judgment urging that no genuine issue as to any material fact existed. Plaintiff contended that under the pleadings, the language of the will, considered with her ex parte affidavit and stipulations, she was entitled to judgment as a matter of law.   Defendants contended that they were entitled to judgment, as a matter of law, because the provision of the will relied upon by plaintiff[was precatory in nature and not mandatory] and amounted, in effect, to only the expression of a wish on the part of the testatrix.   The court overruled defendants' motion for summary judgment, sustained plaintiff's motion and rendered judgment for the plaintiff.   The defendants have appealed.

The will provided for specific bequests to appellants.   In addition to the provision for specific bequests, paragraph V of the will, the interpretation of which is here in controversy, is as follows:

> "All of my other property of whatsoever nature, real, personal, or mixed, I give, devise and bequeath to my two children, Suzanne Cohen Levin and Jay Howard Cohen, to be divided equally between them so that each shall receive an equal share with the other in said property.   It is my desire that each year out of the annual rent proceeds, rents and revenues from such property during such year so received by my said daughter and son they pay to my sister Mrs. Laura Fisch the sum of $2,400.00, provided such net proceeds, rents and revenues, received by them from such property for such year is sufficient to meet such payment.   In the event the net revenues from such property for any given year should be insufficient to meet such payment for such year, then the amount of the payment to my said sister for such year should be reduced in the amount of such deficiency.   It is my desire that my children continue such payments during the remainder of my said sister's life time provided that should my sister LAURA FISCH get married, then my said children should not, after the date of such marriage continue such payment.   In the event my said sister should marry, then the payment to her during the year of such marriage, should be prorated as of the date of such marriage."

Appellants present one point of error contending the court erred in overruling appellants' motion for summary judgment, and in sustaining appellee's motion for summary judgment and rendering judgment thereon, for the reason that paragraph V of the last will and testament of Bertha Cohen is clearly precatory in nature and not mandatory, and amounts only to a wish on the part of the testatrix and does not express a mandatory bequest to appellee, or devise or bequeath to appellee any interest whatsoever in the estate of Bertha Cohen, deceased, which the appellants, or either of them, either individually or as independent executors, are, as a matter of law required to recognize, honor or pay.

Appellants point out that the testatrix Bertha Cohen unequivocally devised and bequeathed to appellants all of her property not theretofore devised.   Appellants contend that the phrase "It is my desire" considered in connection with the language used "within the four corners of the instrument", is not ambiguous, and should be given its ordinary and natural meaning, and should not be interpreted as a bequest or a mandatory instruction to appellants to pay to her sister, Mrs. Fisch, the $2,400.00 annual payment indicated in the will.   Appellants contend that if Bertha Cohen had intended to bestow upon her sister, Laura Fisch, any right to the annual net rents and revenues from the properties which she had previously and unequivocally devised to appellants, she would have directed appellants in their capacity as executors to make such distribution. The word "desire" in its ordinary and primary meaning is precatory, but is often construed when used in a will as directive or mandatory when it clearly appears that such was the intention of the testator from a consideration of the instrument as a whole and the surrounding circumstances.

In support of the judgment appellee relies upon Colton v. Colton, 127 U.S. 300, 8 S.Ct. 1164, 32 L.Ed. 138 (1888). In that case the testator devised and bequeathed to his wife all of his estate, both real and personal, and then continued as follows: "I recommend to her the care and protection of my mother and sister, and request her to make such gift and provision for them as in her judgment will be best." In discussing the question of whether the above provision was precatory or mandatory the court stated:

"According to its context and manifest use, an expression of desire or wish will often be equivalent to a positive direction, where that is the evident purpose and meaning of the testator. * * * And in such a case as the present, it would be but natural for the testator to suppose that a request, which, in its terms, implied no alternative, addressed to his widow and principal legatee, would be understood and obeyed as strictly as though it were couched in the language of direction and command. * * *"

The applicable rule in such cases was stated to be as follows:

"The object * * * of a judicial interpretation of a will is to ascertain the intention of the testator, according to the meaning of the words he has used, deduced from a consideration of the whole instrument and a comparison of its various parts in the light of the situation and circumstances which surrounded the testator when the instrument was framed."

The record in this case which is not disputed shows the following facts and circumstances surrounding the testator when the will was executed. The deceased, Bertha Cohen and the appellee Laura Fisch were sisters. Appellants are the children of Bertha Cohen. On April 11, 1958, when Bertha Cohen executed the will she and Laura Fisch were both widows, approximately fifty years of age. Bertha Cohen owned property of the value of approximately one million dollars, and the value of property owned by Laura Fisch was approximately Twenty-five Thousand Dollars. The appellant Cohen was twenty years of age and appellant Levin was twenty-five years old. Appellants had one year previously inherited from their father property of the approximate value of one million dollars. For two years prior to her death Bertha Cohen paid appellee the sum of $200.00 per month. She also made other gifts to appellee and her daughter of clothing and money. The record shows that appellee was in poor health and unable to work full time, and that her income was approximately $300.00 per month.

Appellants rely principally on Byars v. Byars et al., 143 Tex. 10, 182 S.W.2d 363, (Sup.Ct.1944), in which it was held that the word "request" in its ordinary or natural meaning when used in a will is precatory and not mandatory. Our Supreme Court in that case noted the statement of *iprecatory unless facts prove otherwise* [handwritten margin note]

the rule set out in the Colton case, supra, and then distinguished the facts in the Byars case as follows:

> "No facts are presented in this case, as in Colton v. Colton, 127 U.S. 300, 8 S.Ct. 1164, 32 L.Ed. 138, showing the situation of the testator when the will was drawn and the circumstances of the surviving wife and the other persons named, from which the inference might be drawn that the precatory paragraph of the will was intended to be mandatory. There is the single circumstance that the request is by the husband to the surviving wife. * * *"

In 95 C.J.S. Wills § 602b the rule which in our opinion is applicable in Texas is stated as follows:

P + Rule [handwritten margin note]

> "Whether Precatory or Mandatory. In determining whether particular words are to be construed as precatory or mandatory, the court will look to the expressed intent of the testator, as found from the context of the will and surrounding circumstances; and words which, in their ordinary meaning, are precatory will be construed as mandatory only when it is evident that such was the testator's intent."

[Citations omitted]

The trial court correctly found that there was no genuine issue of fact in the case. Based upon the rule announced in the above cited cases and authorities it is our opinion that it was the intention of the testatrix that the words of "desire" as used in the will were a positive directive and imposed an obligation on appellants to comply therewith. The provision of the will for the payment to appellee of $2,400.00 annually was set out specifically as well as the desire or direction of the testatrix that such payments should be discontinued in certain specified contingencies. The language in question considered in context and in connection with the language of the will as a whole, and the surrounding facts and circumstances is in our opinion more clearly mandatory than that of the Colton case. The court properly entered summary judgment in favor of appellee, Laura Fisch.

The judgment is affirmed.

Notes

1. The Court cites and discusses the famous case of Colton v. Colton, 127 U.S. 300, 8 S.Ct. 1164, 32 L.Ed. 138 (1888), which is often cited but rarely followed in litigation involving the precatory trust doctrine. The estate in the Colton case was in excess of a million dollars. How would you frame a decree to carry out the Court's mandate in that case? Was the wife apt to be a suitable trustee for her mother- and sister-in-law after that litigation?

2. These cases show that words such as "trust" and "trustee" need not be used in order to create a trust. Likewise, the use of such words does not guarantee that a trust will be found if other characteristics of the arrangement are not present. Restatement 2d Trusts, § 25. Burton v. Irwin, 212 Va. 104, 181 S.E.2d 624 (1971).

3. The recent cases tend strongly away from the older view that precatory words such as "wish" and "desire" are presumptively mandatory, and instead inquire whether the words and the factual context reveal an intention to impose

legally enforceable obligations on the transferee. A sampling of recent cases on the effectiveness *vel non* of words claimed to be precatory:

Held not effective: Page v. Buchfinck, 202 Neb. 411, 275 N.W.2d 826 (1979); Haltom v. Austin National Bank, 487 S.W.2d 201 (Tex.Civ.App.1972); Alexander v. Botsford, 439 S.W.2d 414 (Tex.Civ.App.1969); Estate of Beauchamp, 256 C.A.2d 563, 64 Cal.Rptr. 340 (1967); Ivanoff v. Johnson, 6 Mich. App. 272, 148 N.W.2d 882 (1967); Estate of Hogan, 259 Iowa 887, 146 N.W.2d 257 (1966); Estate of Lubenow, 146 N.W.2d 166 (N.D.1966); Quickel v. Quickel, 261 N.C. 696, 136 S.E.2d 52 (1964); Matter of Warren, 11 N.Y.2d 463, 230 N.Y.S.2d 711, 184 N.E.2d 304 (1962); In re Estate of Welter, 253 Iowa 87, 111 N.W.2d 282 (1961); Agan v. United States National Bank, 227 Or. 619, 363 P.2d 765 (1961); Cahill v. Monahan, 58 N.J.Super. 54, 155 A.2d 282 (1959); Estate of Tucker, 130 C.A.2d 699, 279 P.2d 760 (1955).

Held effective: Trustees of First Methodist Church v. Attorney General, 359 Mass. 658, 270 N.E.2d 905 (1971); Farmer v. Broadhead, 230 So.2d 779 (Miss.1970); Cooney v. Montana, 347 Mass. 29, 196 N.E.2d 202 (1964); Waesche v. Rizzuto, 224 Md. 573, 168 A.2d 871 (1961); Estate of Liginger, 14 Wis.2d 577, 111 N.W.2d 407 (1961); Anders v. Anderson, 246 N.C. 53, 97 S.E.2d 415 (1957); Spencer v. Childs, 1 N.Y.2d 103, 150 N.Y.S.2d 788, 134 N.E.2d 60 (1956); Williams v. Williams' Committee, 253 Ky. 30, 68 S.W.2d 395 (1933).

B. DECLARATION OF TRUST

KNAGENHJELM v. RHODE ISLAND HOSPITAL TRUST CO.

Supreme Court of Rhode Island, 1921.
43 R.I. 559, 114 A. 5.

STEARNS, J.   This is a suit in equity brought by the complainant, a citizen of Norway, against the respondent corporation as administrator d. b. n. c. t. a. of the estate of Theodore M. Davis and as trustee under a deed of trust made by Davis to the respondent.

The bill asserts the right of complainant to 422 shares or interests in a corporation, Keweenaw Land Association, Limited, each in the name of Theodore M. Davis, trustee, which came into the possession of respondent as administrator after the death of Mr. Davis, and the relief sought is that complainant may be declared to be the owner of said certificates at the death of Mr. Davis, and entitled to receive all income derived therefrom since that time, and that respondent be required to transfer and deliver to complainant said certificates, and to account for all dividends and profits received, with interest. Complainant bases her claim upon a written declaration of trust, also upon a subsequent deed of assignment made by Mr. Davis.

In its answer the respondent denies the right of complainant to the stock, and claims the right to hold the same as a part of the remainder of the personal estate bequeathed to the respondent as trustee, by said Davis.

* * *

The essential facts are not in dispute.   Mr. Davis was a man of large wealth, who had retired from the active practice of the law and settled in Newport.   He was married, but had no children.   For many years he had been the friend of complainant's father, and had been associated with him at different times in business and legal matters.   The complainant, whose name before marriage was Eleanor S. Wilson, from her early childhood had been a particular favorite of Mr. Davis.   So strong was his affection for the child that he sought the consent of her parents to adopt her legally as his daughter.   Complainant's parents would not consent, but did allow their daughter to spend her summers at Newport and to travel extensively with Mr. Davis and his family.   Mr. Davis was generous in his gifts to his relatives and friends, and enjoyed giving freely and often to those for whom he cared.

In 1894 the complainant received a proposal of marriage from Mr. Knagenhjelm, who at the time was in the diplomatic service of Norway and a temporary resident of this country.   Under the rules of his government Mr. K. was not permitted to marry without a substantial independent income in addition to his salary.   In order that this obstacle to the marriage might be removed, Mr. Davis, after an interview with Mr. K., in Newport in July, 1895, told complainant that he had arranged everything with Mr. K., and that she should have $5,000 a year, and the engagement was then at once announced by Mr. Davis, at a dinner in his own house.   On the same day, or shortly thereafter, Mr. Davis, at his residence in Newport, signed a declaration of trust in the presence of a witness.   The document, which is in the handwriting of Mr. D. is as follows:

"Newport, R.I., July 16–1895

"The four hundred and ninety-seven (497) 'Interests in the Capital of the Keweenaw Association, Limited,' which stands in my name as Trustee, and Certificate for which I herewith inclose, I hereby declare to be held in trust for Eleanor S. Wilson, and in case of my death, she surviving me, are to be delivered to her as her property, and duly Transferred to her, or as she may direct.

"Theo. M. Davis

"Witness:

"John R. Procter, Jr."

On the same day he indorsed in blank two certificates in the association, standing in his name as trustee, numbered A77 and A78, for 100 and 397 interests, respectively, and placed them, together with the declaration of trust, in an envelope upon which he wrote the following inscription:

"497 shares of 'Interests in the Capital of the Keweenaw Association, Limited,' held in trust for Eleanor S. Wilson, daughter of Nath. Wilson, Esq., of Washington, D.C.   To be delivered to her, she surviving my death.   Theo. M. Davis."

This envelope was placed and kept in Mr. Davis' safe deposit in the Newport Trust Company, where it was found shortly before his death. At some time, which has not been definitely fixed, the word "ninety" in the declaration was scratched out and the words "four hundred forty-seven (447) T. M. Davis," were written by Mr. Davis above and before the word "Interests" and on the envelope the number "497" was scratched out and the number "447" was written above it.

Complainant was married early in September, 1895. At the time of the wedding Mr. Davis told complainant he had made the trust for her benefit, that it was his wedding present to her, and that the Keweenaw interests he held in trust for her were in his safe deposit box in Newport. Mrs. Knagenhjelm testifies that often thereafter Mr. Davis on different occasions told her not to worry over the future, that he had created a trust in these interests for her, and also on several occasions he referred to the trust in his letters to her. He always referred to the number of interests as 500, and complainant did not know that the number was reduced by him to 422 interests, or his reason for doing this.

Two of the dividends on the interests paid after the date of the marriage were deposited by Mr. D. in complainant's bank account. Complainant and her husband then went abroad to live, and thereafter the dividends were deposited to Mr. Davis' own account, and the fact that the dividends were from the trust interests was noted in the deposit book. Mr. D. sent to complainant regularly $5,000 a year, and subsequently increased the amount of the allowance to $10,000. Complainant was always told that the dividends were taken into consideration in making the allowance. Mr. D. made further provision for complainant in his will, and so informed her, but she was always made to understand that the provision for the Keweenaw interests was separate and apart, and was additional to any benefit she was to receive by the terms of his will.

In 1902 Mr. K. was seriously ill, and as a consequence was unable to continue in the diplomatic service. By the advice of Mr. D., and at his expense, complainant made a change of residence, in the hope that her husband would be benefited thereby. Mr. K. did not improve, but failed steadily in health, and finally died in 1907. Mr. D. during this period continued to visit the family whenever he went abroad, and at his suggestion complainant incurred many additional expenses, payment for which was made by Mr. D.   *   *   *

*   *   *

The respondent's contention is that in order to distinguish a voluntary trust on the one hand and an intent or attempt to make a testamentary disposition on the other hand, there must be some transfer of present interest to the donee; that the so-called declaration of trust did not transfer any present beneficial interest to Mrs. K., but was an attempt to make a gift to take effect upon the death of the donor, and consequently was void because it was not executed as a will; that the vital question in regard to the declaration of trust is not the intent of Mr. Davis, but whether or not he did enough to "execute" the trust.

Respondent has cited numerous cases from different jurisdictions, showing that the authorities are not uniform in the requirements held to be necessary to establish a voluntary trust. Without attempting to discuss or to differentiate the different decisions we think the law as stated in Ray v. Simmons, Adm'r, 11 R.I. 266, 23 Am.Rep. 447 (1875), is decisive of the case at bar, and we see no reason, either on principle or authority, to depart from the law as thus established in this state.

* * * At page 268 of 11 R.I. (23 Am.Rep. 447), the court, speaking through Durfee, C. J., said:

> "A person need use no particular form of words to create a trust, or to make himself a trustee. It is enough if, having the property, he conveys it to another in trust, or, the property being personal, if he unequivocally declares, either orally or in writing, that he holds it in praesenti in trust, or as a trustee for another."

After citing authorities, the court continues:

> "And the creation of the trust, if otherwise unequivocal, is not affected by the settlor's retention of the instrument of trust, especially where he is himself the trustee."

* * * Respondent calls our attention to certain statements of Mr. Davis, made after the execution of the deed of trust, to his acts in taking and disposing of some of the stock originally dedicated to the trust, and to his conduct in regard to the dividends. Regarded alone and without reference to the admitted facts a doubt perhaps might be raised in regard to the donor's intentions, but considered as they properly should be in the light of the entire evidence in the case, they fail to change our conclusion.

The amount of the trust was not large from the point of view of the donor. Considering the relations of the parties and the fact that the donor regularly gave to complainant much more than the amount of the dividends, his failure to give complainant each dividend as it was received is of no particular importance. His actions, if the most unfavorable view be taken, appear to be technical breaches of trust, rather than an attempted repudiation or denial of the trust. We are satisfied that the donor intended to give complainant a present interest in the subject-matter of the trust. The words, "I hereby declare to be held in trust," show an intention to give the beneficial interest in praesenti. We cannot believe that the donor, when he told complainant on her wedding day that he had made her a wedding present, meant that he had given her something in his will. He was an experienced lawyer, and presumably was familiar with the requirements necessary to make a testamentary disposition of his property. A present beneficial interest having been created, the character of the trust was not changed by the fact that the beneficiary was not entitled to receive possession of the trust property until the death of the donor. In Atkinson, Petitioner, 16 R.I. 413, 16 Atl. 712, 3 L.R.A. 392, 27 Am.St.Rep. 745 (1889), * * *, Durfee, C. J., said:

> "There are cases which hold otherwise, but it seems to us that the courts which decided them did not sufficiently distinguish between a gift, which requires a delivery of the thing given, actual or symbolical, and the creation of a voluntary trust which requires for its conservation [sic], not a delivery of the trust to the beneficiary, but a retention of it by the trustee

for the beneficiary's benefit; and, of course, where the donor makes himself the trustee, a retention of it by the donor as trustee for his benefit."

In Gobeille v. Allison et al., 30 R.I. 525, 76 Atl. 354 (1910), this court affirmed the cases of Ray v. Simmons and Petition of Atkinson. In the Gobeille Case a mother made a deposit in a bank in her own name as trustee to the credit of her daughter, and a deposit book was given to the mother in the like form. At the time of making the deposit the mother informed the bank that she wished to retain control of these deposits during her life, as she might change her mind and do something else with the deposits. Later the bank book was delivered to the daughter, who subsequently returned it to her mother, in whose possession it remained until her death. It was held that a trust was not created at the time of the deposit, because the mother did not intend to make an absolute and binding trust at that time, but that the subsequent conduct of the mother in delivering the book to the daughter and informing her of the trust amounted to a declaration on the part of the mother that she held the fund in praesenti in trust for the daughter, and that a valid trust was constituted which was irrevocable. This case does not support respondent's contention, and in no way weakens the authority of the Simmons Case. The delivery of the bank book was not the essential thing to constitute the trust, but was evidence which, in connection with the information given to the daughter, established the intention to then make a trust. There was no change made in the res, which was the right to demand a fixed amount of money from the bank, nor was there at the time the trust became effective any deposit made or transfer of legal title. The intention to create a trust is the essential thing; this intention must be expressed, and must be clearly established by proof, the nature of which naturally varies in different cases. In the case at bar we find the intention to establish a trust in praesenti, the expression of this intention by the written declaration of trust; the subject-matter of the trust was designated and set apart in such a manner that it could be identified, and the beneficiary was informed of the creation of the trust. There was but little, if anything, more which the donor could have done to make a valid trust. The donor was entitled to retain the stock in his possession, also to retain the deed of trust. It was not necessary to make any delivery to the beneficiary. By the declaration of the trust the beneficiary acquired at once a beneficial interest in the res, and of necessity the donor at the same time parted with such beneficial interest. In a certain sense it may be said that there was then a transfer of the beneficial interest from the donor to the beneficiary, but such transfer resulted by operation of the declaration of trust and as a result thereof, and required no further or other act.

Our conclusion is that the complainant was entitled to the 422 interests at the death of Mr. Davis, and so much of the decree appealed from as establishes her right thereto is affirmed, and the appeal of the respondent is dismissed.

* * *

Notes

1. The court's discussion of a deed of assignment to Mrs. Knagenhjelm executed in 1902, is omitted since the court considered it immaterial in view of the holding that the prior declaration of trust was valid.

2. Mr. Davis had reduced the number of shares from 497 to 422 by (a) giving the 100-share certificate to Mrs. Knagenhjelm's father (who then gave it to her) and putting two 25-share certificates in the safe deposit box; and, later, (b) giving one of the 25-share certificates to his butler. The court treated these acts as of no significance because the complainant waived any claim to the 75 shares by reason of "Mr. D's great kindness and generosity to her." If she had not so waived, would she have had an action against Mr. Davis's estate for breach of trust?

3. Was this trust active or passive (a) during the settlor's lifetime? (b) after his death?

4. If the res is land the Statute of Frauds requires that the trust be in writing. See Section Six of this Chapter, infra, p. 540. A declaration of trust of personalty is ordinarily not required to be in writing but may well be put in writing to secure more enduring evidence of the terms of the trust. Because the requirements for a valid declaration of trust are not precise, the situations where securities are found after the decedent's death set aside among his possessions and marked as being held for some designated person have elicited varying responses from the courts depending on how the decedent had used the property after the alleged transfer, the extent he had communicated his intent to the outside world, the value of the securities in relationship to the overall estate, the identity of the parties and like considerations. Contrast: Govin v. De Miranda, 76 Hun 414, 27 N.Y.S. 1049 (1894), second appeal, 79 Hun 286, 29 N.Y.S. 345 (1894) (trust not sustained—"In no case has it ever been held as yet that a party may, by transferring property from one pocket to another, make himself a trustee." 76 Hun at 419); Estate of Smith, 144 Pa. 428, 22 A. 916 (1891) (envelope containing 13 bonds worth $1,000 apiece held for a nephew, sustained as a trust and not made part of an estate valued in excess of $1,000,000). A more modern analysis sustaining the declaration of trust appears in Ridge v. Bright, 244 N.C. 345, 93 S.E.2d 607 (1956).

5. The factual context in which the validity of a declaration of trust is in issue frequently involves attempted transfers to minor children, grandchildren, or other close relatives. The methods of making gifts to minors and of holding the property during their minority have been regularized by Gifts to Minors statutes which were originally sponsored by the New York Stock Exchange and the Association of Stock Exchange Firms in 1956, more modern versions of which have been enacted in every state. See for the history of the Uniform Act and several key provisions pp. 406–11, supra.

✓EX PARTE PYE;   EX PARTE DUBOST
Chancery, 1811.
18 Ves.Jr. 139, 34 Eng.Rep. 271.

William Mowbray by his will, dated the 10th of April 1806, giving his wife the residue of his property after payment of his debts, except the sums after mentioned, among other legacies gave as follows: "I give and bequeath the sum of £4000 sterling to Louisa Hortensia Garos daughter of John Louis Garos formerly of Berwick Street Westminister; the like sum of £4000 to Emily Garos her sister and £4000 to Julia Garos her other sister; and in case of the death of one of the three I desire that the legacy may be divided equally betwixt the two surviving sisters; and in case of the death of two of them I desire the whole £12,000 may be paid to the surviving sister."

The testator also gave to John Louis Garos £600; and "to Marie Genevieve Garos his wife the sum of £2500 sterling for her own use, and over which her husband is not to have any power: he having lived abroad for many years; and she in this country; and no correspondence having passed between them during that time. Her own receipt shall be a sufficient authority to my executors for paying her the above legacy."

The testator died on the 8th of June 1809. His widow became a lunatic: the petitioner Pye was the Committee under the Commission; and upon her death took out administration to her, and administration de bonis non to the testator.

The Master's Report stated from the examination of the petitioner Pye, that Louisa Hortensia, Emily, and Julia Garos were the three natural daughters of the testator by Marie Genevieve Garos the wife of John Louis Garos; and that since the date of the Will Louisa Hortensia Garos married Christopher Dubost; * * *

* * * that by a letter, written by the testator to Christopher Dubost in Paris, on the 25th of November 1807, the testator authorized him to purchase in France an annuity of £100 for the said Marie Genevieve Garos for her life, and to draw on him for £1500 on account of such purchase; and under that authority Dubost purchased an annuity of that value; but that, as she was married at the time, and also deranged, the annuity was purchased in the name of the testator; and the testator sent to Dubost by his desire a power of attorney authorizing him to transfer to Marie Genevieve Garos the said annuity, dated the 10th of June 1808.

The Report further found upon the affidavit of Dubost and the copy of the deed, that the first intimation he received of the death of the testator, who died in June 1809, was in November 1809; and that, in ignorance of such death Dubost on the 21st of October 1809, exercised the power, vested in him, by executing to Marie Genevieve Garos, her late husband being then dead, and she of sound mind, a deed of gift of the said annuity; and the Master found, that by the Law of France, if an attorney be ignorant of the death of the party, who has given the power of attorney, whatever he has done, while ignorant of such death, is valid. The Master therefore stated his opinion, that the annuity was no part of the personal estate of William Mowbray.

The first petition, prayed, that so much of the Report as certifies the French annuity to be no part of the testator's personal estate may be set aside; and that it may be declared, that the said annuity is part of his personal estate.

* * *

Sir Arthur Piggott, Mr. Richards, Mr. Wingfield, Mr. Horne, and Mr. Wear, for different parties, in support of the first Petition. The French annuity being purchased in the testator's name, and no third person interposed as a trustee, the interest could not be transferred from him without certain acts, which were not done at the time of his death. It was therefore competent to him during his life to change his purpose, and to make some other provision for this lady by funds in this country; conceiving perhaps, that she might return here. The authority, given to purchase this annuity, could not have been enforced against him during his life by a person, claiming as a volunteer: nor can it be established against his estate after his death: the act, which would have given the benefit of it against the personal representative, not having been completed. (Cotteen v. Missing, 1 Madd. 176.) Where a question is to be decided by a foreign Law, the first step is an inquiry by the Master, to ascertain, what is the Law of that country.

* * *

The other question involves, not only the construction of the French law, and the point, whether that has been sufficiently investigated, but farther, whether the power of attorney amounts here to a declaration of trust? It is clear that the Court will not assist a volunteer: yet, if the act is completed, though voluntary, the Court will act upon it. It has been decided, that upon an agreement to transfer stock this Court will not interpose: but if the party had declared himself to be the trustee of that stock, it becomes the property of the *cestui que trust* without more; and the Court will act upon it. (18 Ves. 99.)

The Lord Chancellor [Eldon]. These petitions call for the decision of points of more importance and difficulty than I should wish to decide in this way, if the case was not pressed upon the Court. With regard to the French annuity, the Master has stated his opinion as to the French law perhaps without sufficient authority, or sufficient inquiry into the effect of it, as applicable to the precise circumstances of this case: but it is not necessary to pursue that; as upon the documents before me it does appear, that, though in one sense this may be represented as the testator's personal estate, yet he has committed to writing what seems to me a sufficient declaration, that he held this part of the estate in trust for the annuitant.

* * *

Under this Judgment the Order was pronounced, dismissing the first petition. * * *

Notes

1. What was it that was construed as a declaration of trust in this case? What was the subject-matter of the trust? Was the trust active or passive?

2. The practice of the English courts, following Ex parte Pye, of sustaining imperfect transfers as declarations of trust is said to have been terminated by the decision in Richards v. Delbridge, L.R. 18 Eq. 11, 14–15 (Chancery, 1874) in which the court said:

The principle is a very simple one. A man may transfer his property, without valuable consideration, in one of two ways: he may either do such acts as amount in law to a conveyance or assignment of the property, and thus completely divest himself of the legal ownership, in which case the person who by those acts acquires the property takes it beneficially, or on trust, as the case may be; or the legal owner of the property may, by one or other of the modes recognized as amounting to a valid declaration of trust, constitute himself a trustee, and, without an actual transfer of the legal title, may so deal with the property as to deprive himself of its beneficial ownership, and declare that he will hold it from that time forward on trust for the other person. It is true he need not use the words, "I declare myself a trustee," but he must do something which is equivalent to it, and use expressions which have that meaning; for, however anxious the Court may be to carry out a man's intention, it is not at liberty to construe words otherwise than according to their proper meaning.

*   *   *

The true distinction appears to me to be plain, and beyond dispute: for a man to make himself a trustee there must be an expression of intention to become a trustee, whereas words of present gift shew an intention to give over property to another, and not retain it in the donor's own hands for any purpose, fiduciary or otherwise.

3. The modern American Rule is stated as follows in Restatement, Second, Trusts:

§ 28. *Consideration for Declaration of Trust*

The owner of property can create a trust of the property by declaring himself trustee of it although he receives no consideration for the declaration of trust.

§ 31. *Conveyance Inter Vivos to a Person for His Own Benefit*

If the owner of property makes a conveyance inter vivos of the property to another person to be held by him for his own benefit and the conveyance is not effective to transfer the property, no trust is created.

Comment

a. *Methods of giving property.* If the owner of property wishes to give to another the beneficial interest in the property, he can do so in any one of three ways: (1) he can transfer the property to the other as an outright gift; (2) he can transfer the property to a trustee in trust for the other; (3) he can declare himself trustee for the other.

If the owner manifests an intention to give the beneficial interest in the property to another by employing one of these three methods, and the disposition is ineffective because of his failure to comply with the requirements for an effective disposition by that method, the disposition will not be upheld merely because it would have been effective if he had manifested an intention to employ one of the other methods. An ineffective gift, therefore, will not be upheld as a declaration of trust. *   *   *

See Mechem, The Requirement of Delivery in Gifts of Chattels, 21 Ill.L.Rev. 341, 352 (1926); Labatt, The Inconsistencies of the Laws of Gifts, 29 Am.L.Rev. 361 (1895); Pound, Juristic Science and Law, 31 Harv.L.Rev. 1047, 1053 (1918); Pound, Consideration in Equity, 13 Ill.L.Rev. 667 (1918); McWilliams, Consideration and the Law of Trusts, 14 Calif.L.Rev. 188 (1926).

C.　TOTTEN TRUSTS

IN RE RODGERS' ESTATE

Supreme Court of Pennsylvania, 1953.
374 Pa. 246, 97 A.2d 789, 38 A.L.R.2d 1238.

ALLEN M. STEARNE, Justice.　Did Elizabeth M. Rodgers revoke either during her lifetime or by will the tentative trust which she had established for her sister, Martha B. Rodgers?　This is the single question presented by the appeal.

The issue is raised by the petition of John J. Mitchell, Jr., Esq., executor of the will of Elizabeth Rodgers, for a citation directed to the guardian of the estate of Martha B. Rodgers, incompetent, and to the Beneficial Saving Fund Society, to show cause why the fund on deposit in that society in an account entitled "Elizabeth M. Rodgers in trust for sister Martha B. Rodgers" should not be paid to the executor.　After answer on the merits the matter was referred for hearing to a master who concluded in an exhaustive report that the trust had been revoked and that the fund should be awarded to the executor as part of the decedent's estate.　Exceptions were argued in the orphans' court and the matter referred back to the master for a further finding.　The master affirmed his earlier conclusion in a second report, and this was approved by the orphans' court in banc.　This appeal followed.

The doctrine of tentative trusts was evolved by the courts of New York in what Justice (later Chief Justice) Schaffer described as "an effort to retain for the depositor the complete control of the fund during his life and yet secure to the beneficiary any balance standing in the account at the death of the depositor".　In re Scanlon's Estate, 313 Pa. 424, 427, 169 A. 106, 108.　In that case we adopted the New York rule as the law of Pennsylvania, quoting as follows from In re Totten, 179 N.Y. 112, 71 N.E. 748, 70 L.R.A. 711 [1904]:

"'*　*　*　A deposit by one person of his own money in his own name as trustee for another, standing alone, does not establish an irrevocable trust during the lifetime of the depositor.　It is a tentative trust merely, revocable at will, until the depositor dies or completes the gift in his lifetime by some unequivocal act or declaration, such as delivery of the passbook or notice to the beneficiary.　In case the depositor dies before the beneficiary without revocation, or some decisive act or declaration of disaffirmance, the presumption arises that an absolute trust was created as to the balance on hand at the death of the depositor.'"

Since then, despite some criticism of the rule, see e.g., dissenting opinion of Mr. Justice Bell in Re Ingels' Estate, 372 Pa. 171, 182, 92 A.2d 881, it has become an integrated part of our jurisprudence and has been applied time and again by our appellate courts and courts of first instance.　[Citations omitted.]

Our decisions have repeatedly acknowledged the New York origin of the rule and have adverted to the reports of that state for guidance in exploring its many ramifications.　On the question of revocation now before us, we once again find no definitive authority in Pennsylvania but a number of decisions in New York. The latter cases have been concisely summarized in a recent opinion of the Surrogate's Court of Kings County, In re Koster's Will, 119 N.Y.S.2d, at pages 4, 5:

Rule

"It has been held that, among other means, a tentative trust may be revoked: ① by a transfer of the form of the deposit; ② by the terms of a will of a depositor, Moran v. Ferchland, 113 Misc. 1, 184 N.Y.S. 428; Matter of Brazil's Estate, 127 Misc. 288, 216 N.Y.S. 430; Matter of Schrier's Estate, 145 Misc. 593, 260 N.Y.S. 610; Matter of Beck's Estate, 260 App. Div. 651, 23 N.Y.S.2d 525; In re Shelley's Estate, Sur., 50 N.Y.S.2d 570; Walsh v. Emigrant Industrial Savings Bank, 106 Misc. 628, 176 N.Y.S. 418, affirmed 192 App.Div. 908, 182 N.Y.S. 956, affirmed 233 N.Y. 512, 135 N.E. 897; ③ by the depositor's unequivocal act or declaration of disaffirmance, Walsh v. Emigrant Industrial Savings Bank, supra; Matter of Beagan's Estate, 112 Misc. 292, 183 N.Y.S. 941; Matter of Richardson's Estate, 134 Misc. 174, 235 N.Y.S. 747; Cf. Matter of Halpern's Estate, 303 N.Y. 33, 100 N.E.2d 120; and ④ by facts and circumstances resulting in inadequacy of the estate assets to satisfy the testamentary gifts, funeral and administration expenses, taxes and other charges. Matter of Murray's Estate, 143 Misc. 499, 256 N.Y.S. 815; Matter of Mannix' Estate, 147 Misc. 479, 264 N.Y.S. 24; Matter of Beagan's Estate, supra; Matter of Reich's Estate, 146 Misc. 616, 262 N.Y.S. 623."

The master and the learned court below found that revocation had been accomplished in the present case by either of the last two of the four means above enumerated.

Such decision does not rest upon New York authority alone. The Restatement of Trusts definitely supports the same view in the following excerpts from the comment to sec. 58:

"b. *Revocation of tentative trust.* A tentative trust of a savings deposit in a bank can be revoked by the depositor at any time during his lifetime, by a manifestation of his intention to revoke the trust. *No particular formalities are necessary to manifest such an intention.*" (latter italics ours)

"A tentative trust of a savings deposit can be revoked by the depositor by his will. It is so revoked where by will he makes a disposition of the bank deposit in favor of anyone other than the beneficiary. It is also revoked where by will he makes a disposition of his property which cannot be carried out except by using the deposit, as for example where he leaves no other property than the deposit."

Indeed, the original statement of the Totten rule quoted in Re Scanlon's Estate, supra, clearly implies that revocation may be accomplished by "some decisive act or declaration of disaffirmance." Implied recognition of the right to revoke orally is also found in Re Krewson's Estate, 154 Pa.Super. 509, at page 511, 36 A.2d 250, at page 251, wherein it is said through Judge Baldrige:

"The alleged oral statements made by the decedent * * * were not sufficiently clear and unambiguous to constitute a parol revocation of the written declaration of trust made with the deposit."

What was the evidence of oral revocation which satisfied the master and the orphans' court in banc in the present case? Mr. Mitchell, the executor, a reputable member of the bar of Philadelphia county, was the scrivener of the will. He was permitted to testify to his conversations with the testatrix leading to the preparation of her will. This testimony was admitted over the objection of the appellants, who contended that the will was clear and unambiguous and not subject to oral explanation. We agree with this contention of appellants and would exclude the testimony if it were offered only as explanation of the will. In re Mizener's Estate, 262 Pa. 62, 105 A. 46; Prime's Petition, 335 Pa. 218, 6 A.2d 530. But, as above stated, the creator of a tentative trust has power to revoke it by oral declarations, and the testimony of testatrix's attorney was clearly admissible to show her intention that the trust be revoked, entirely apart from any question of interpretation of the written will. Testatrix told Mr. Mitchell that her sister Martha was the prime object of her bounty, that Martha was sole beneficiary under an earlier will but was now " * * * infirm mentally and physically * * * can't look after things for herself, and somebody will have to look after her in case I go first". She approved the attorney's suggestion of a trust for maintenance and support with power to invade principal and discussed with him, without reaching any definite conclusion, the Catholic charities to whom she would bequeath the remainder. According to Mr. Mitchell's testimony, she then described the property which would be the subject of this trust as follows: " ' * * * we have some stocks and we own the property we live in at 1805 Wylie Street,' and she said, 'my money is on deposit at the Beneficial Saving Fund Society.' " It is undisputed that the only money which testatrix had on deposit at that bank was the tentative trust fund in question. Unless she was referring to that fund when she spoke of her money on deposit at the Beneficial, her words were meaningless. Hence this conversation with the scrivener constitutes a clear declaration by the decedent of her desire to revoke the tentative trust and with that money make more appropriate arrangements for the care of her failing sister.

Furthermore, we agree with the court below that the will itself was sufficient to effect a revocation by the fourth means referred to in In re Koster's Will, supra. Findings of fact by the master to which no exceptions were taken establish that at the time of the making of the will, decedent's only assets other than the savings fund account were approximately $500 in cash, fractional interests in real estate worth about $2,000, an expectancy of a legacy of about $2,000 and joint ownership with her sister of securities stated to be small in value and a checking account of about $300. It requires no legal or financial expert to conclude that after payment of her own debts and funeral and administration expenses, her assets other than the savings account in dispute would be pitifully inadequate for the establishment of a trust for maintenance and support. It would be ascribing extraordinarily poor judgment to testatrix to suppose that she went to the trouble of creating an elaborate testamentary trust for the relatively small assets she possessed outside the savings account and yet intended the fund which comprised the bulk of her estate to go to the sister absolutely. This account contained $34,356.30.

Appellants also argue that, because the parties lived together sharing all expenses, had reciprocal wills and reciprocal tentative trusts with common possession of the pass books, the trusts which they created were irrevocable. The master and the court below found these circumstances inadequate to justify an inference that the sisters intended to make their trusts irrevocable. We are entirely in accord with this conclusion. We recently had occasion to discuss the quantum of evidence necessary to establish that a settlor intended to impart a quality of irrevocability to a tentative trust. In re Ingels' Estate, 372 Pa. 171, 92 A.2d 881. The circumstantial evidence here present falls far short of the standard we there established; viz., " 'clear and unambiguous language or conduct' indicating that [settlor] intended to make the tentative trust irrevocable." 372 Pa. at page 177, 92 A.2d at page 884.

This tentative trust was revoked by testatrix in her lifetime by her oral declarations. But in any event the decedent by her will by establishing a testamentary scheme whereunder her assets would have been wholly inadequate, likewise disclosed an unequivocal intent of such revocation since her scheme failed unless the trust fund was included.

Decree affirmed; costs to be paid out of the fund.

BELL, J., dissents.

Notes

1. If the case holds that Miss Rodgers' statement to her lawyer was enough to revoke her Totten trust, query whether the Rodgers decision opens the way to fraud. Can any apparently disinterested perjurer throw a Totten deposit into the residue? Concern over that possibility may account for the assertion in Estate of Vittorio, 290 Pa.Super. 329, 434 A.2d 777 (1981) that the first rationale in the Rodgers opinion is questionable. On the other hand, it has been followed elsewhere (see, e.g., Concannon v. Winship, 94 Nev. 432, 581 P.2d 11 (1978)); and in New York it gave rise to so much litigation that in 1975 N.Y.—McKinney's EPTL 7–5.2(2) was enacted, providing:

stat that recognz totten trusts

> A [Totten] trust can be revoked, terminated or modified by the depositor's will only by means of, and to the extent of, an express direction concerning such trust account, which must be described in the will as being in trust for a named beneficiary in a named financial institution. Where the depositor has more than one trust account for a particular beneficiary in a particular financial institution, such a direction will affect all such accounts, unless the direction is limited to one or more accounts specifically identified by account number in addition to the foregoing requirements. A testamentary revocation, termination or modification under this paragraph can be effected by express words of revocation, or by a specific bequest of the trust account, or any part of it, to someone other than the beneficiary. A bequest of part of a trust account shall operate as a pro tanto revocation to the extent of the bequest.

See Estate of Newman, 106 M.2d 135, 431 N.Y.S.2d 256 (Surr.Ct.1980); Estate of Silberkasten, 102 M.2d 227, 423 N.Y.S.2d 141 (Surr.Ct.1979); and practice commentary on N.Y.—McKinney's EPTL 7–5.2(2) by Dean Patrick J. Rohan.

2. At common law, many states refused to recognize tentative trusts of savings accounts as non-testamentary dispositions. See, e.g., Cazallis v. Ingraham, 110 Me. 240, 110 A. 359 (1920). All of them except Ohio, however, have now adopted the Totten rule by statute. See BlueValley Federal Savings

& Loan Association v. Burrus, 617 S.W.2d 111 (Mo.App.1981). Note that a
number of such statutes apply the rule to any "time or demand deposit," which
would seem to include checking as well as savings accounts. The Connecticut
statute establishes a "conclusive presumption," subject to certain specified safeguards, that the depositor intends to create a trust for the named beneficiary
if the latter survives him. Conn.Gen.Stat.Ann. § 36–110.

3. In the absence of special circumstances, a Totten trust terminates, and
the depositor holds the deposit free of the trust, if he survives the beneficiary.
Annot., Death of beneficiary as terminating or revoking trust of savings bank
account over which settlor retains right of withdrawal or revocation, 64 A.L.R.3d
221 (1975).

IN RE ESTATE OF CAPOCY

Appellate Court of Illinois, First District, First Division, 1981.
102 Ill.App.3d 609, 58 Ill.Dec. 880, 430 N.E.2d 1131.

GOLDBERG, Justice:

This appeal involves disposition of the assets of a savings account
trust executed by Charles Capocy (settlor) for the benefit of his niece,
Josephine Piper, and deposited at Talman Federal Savings and Loan
Association of Illinois (Talman). Upon motion of the independent administrator of the settlor's estate, the trial court directed Talman to release the proceeds of the account to the administrator for distribution to
the Capocy heirs. Talman and the heirs of Josephine Piper appeal.

The savings account in question was opened on October 5, 1976. The
account was in the name of the settlor as trustee for the benefit of Josephine Piper (beneficiary). Concurrent with the opening of the account,
settlor executed a form trust agreement. The settlor made several deposits and withdrawals but never revoked nor modified the trust agreement or the savings account. The front of the trust agreement identified
the settlor. The reverse side, also signed by the settlor, provided:

"TRUST AGREEMENT

"The funds in the account identified on the reverse side hereof, together
with earnings thereon, and any future additions thereto, are by these presents hereby assigned, transferred, conveyed and delivered to the trustee
(identified on reverse side) for the benefit of the beneficiary or beneficiaries
named (on reverse side). The conditions of said trust are: (1) The trustee
is authorized to hold, manage, invest and re-invest said funds in his sole
discretion; (2) The undersigned Settlor reserves the right to revoke said
trust in part or in full at any time, and any partial or complete withdrawal
by the original trustee, if he is the Settlor, shall be a revocation to the
extent of such withdrawal, but no other revocation shall be valid unless
written notice by the Settlor is given to the Association; (3) This trust,
subject to the right of revocation, shall continue for the life of the Settlor,
and thereafter as hereinafter specified: (a) If, upon the death of the Settlor,
the beneficiary has reached his legal majority, the trust shall terminate
and the proceeds delivered to the beneficiary; (b) If, upon the death of the
Settlor, the beneficiary has not reached his legal majority, then the legally
appointed guardian of the estate of the beneficiary, shall act as successor

trustee hereunder for the support, education and maintenance of the minor, provided, however, if the balance of funds accountable to the minor be less than $1,000.00 any adult with whom the minor resides may act as successor trustee, upon application to and acceptance of such adult by the Association; said successor trustee shall, in addition to his powers to administer this trust as successor trustee, have the full power to terminate this trust and take possession of the funds as Guardian (or Custodian if under $1,000 provision applies) of the minor beneficiary's estate, and the receipt of such guardian shall be a complete discharge to the Association. In any event, this trust shall terminate and the proceeds shall be delivered to the beneficiary when he reaches his legal majority, subject to the condition precedent that the Settlor is then deceased; (4) Two or more named beneficiaries shall have equal interests, one such share for each beneficiary living at the time of distribution. If any beneficiary shall die before distribution, his interest shall abate and be paid on an equal basis to the surviving beneficiaries unless such deceased beneficiary shall have one or more descendants then living, in which case the deceased beneficiary's share shall be divided, per stirpes, among said descendants. The word descendants, as used herein, shall include those persons legally adopted into such status as well as those born therein. If, upon the death of the Settlor, there should be a complete failure of the beneficiaries of this trust, then the funds shall be considered owned in their entirety by the Settlor and shall be part of his estate; (5) The original trustee is authorized at the discretion of said trustee, to delegate by written power of attorney, an attorney in fact to act on behalf of said trustee and upon any such appointment, the Association is authorized to act with respect to the account upon the signature of either the trustee or the attorney. Any such power granted shall terminate upon written notice to the Association by the trustee, or upon the death or incompetency of the original trustee, and the provisions of this trust shall govern the disposition of the funds; (6) The Association is authorized to pay the same or act in any respect affecting said account before or after the termination of this trust upon the signature of the trustee or successor trustee, or any attorney in fact, and has no responsibility to follow the application of the funds.

"In this instrument, the singular includes the plural and the masculine includes the feminine and the neuter.

"Dated ___10/5/76___ Settlor _Charles Capocy_ "

On November 14, 1979, the beneficiary died leaving five heirs. Approximately four and one-half months later, on March 26, 1980, the settlor died. The question before this court is whether the proceeds of this account become part of the estate of the settlor, or that of the beneficiary.

Initially, the administrator of the settlor's estate suggests the savings account trust is a "Totten" trust. In Re Totten (1904), 179 N.Y. 112, 125, 71 N.E. 748, first recognized the type of property disposition now referred to as a "Totten trust."

* * *

Because generally the beneficial interest in a Totten trust does not vest until the death of the settlor, the general rule developed in other jurisdictions (the issue has apparently not yet arisen in Illinois) that if the beneficiary predeceases the settlor, the trust fails and the corpus of the trust reverts to the estate of the settlor.   [Citations omitted.]

However, in the case at bar, the savings account trust is not a Totten trust.   As we stated in In Re Estate of Anderson (1966), 69 Ill.App.2d 352, 363, 217 N.E.2d 444:

> "In the case before us, we have more than mere accounts in the name of the depositor as trustee.   We have the specific trust declarations containing definite terms and provisions regarding the deposit and disposition of funds and the change, alteration, modification and termination of the trust.   These trust accounts, therefore, cannot be considered 'Totten or tentative' trusts but,   * * *, they are express inter vivos trusts."

See also In Re Estate of Petralia (1965), 32 Ill.2d 134, 204 N.E.2d 1.

The language of the instant trust agreement evidences intent to establish an immediate trust.   The agreement opens with the language: "The funds in the account identified on the reverse side hereof * * * are by these presents hereby assigned, transferred, conveyed, and delivered to the trustee * * * for the benefit of the beneficiary or beneficiaries named (on reverse side)."   The agreement expresses no condition or requirement that the beneficiary survive the settlor.   On the contrary, the trust becomes operative immediately upon execution.   Thus, the trust is not "tentative" but is rather a valid, revocable inter vivos trust.   Therefore, any rule governing the disposition of Totten trusts is inapplicable here.

In what appears to be the most recent analogous case, the Appellate Court of Michigan reached the same conclusion.   In May v. American Savings Association (1973), 46 Mich.App. 668, 675, 208 N.W.2d 619, the court held a savings account trust coupled with the execution of a form trust agreement established a valid inter vivos trust.   Furthermore, the court held that when the beneficiary predeceases the settlor, the corpus of the trust becomes part of the estate of the beneficiary unless that disposition is incompatible with the language of the trust agreement. The court reasoned (46 Mich.App. 668, 676, 208 N.W.2d 619):

> "The beneficial interest of [the beneficiary] was expressly conditioned upon the absence of revocation by the grantor.   But this fact alone does not mean that this Court should imply another and distinct condition, that of survival of the grantor.   Though contingent, [the beneficiary's] interest was transferable and became upon her death an asset of her estate."

The same result was reached by the Appellate Court of California 40 years earlier in Sherman v. Hibernia Savings & Loan Society (1933), 129 Cal.App.Supp. 795, 20 P.2d 138.   See also Randall v. Bank of America National Trust & Savings Association (1941), 48 Cal.App.2d 249, 119 P.2d 754.

We agree with the courts of California and Michigan.   We conclude that if the beneficiary of a revocable inter vivos savings account trust predeceases the settlor, upon death of the settlor, the corpus of the trust will pass to the estate of the beneficiary.   This presumption will not govern if the settlor amends or revokes the trust during his lifetime, or if the language of the trust agreement indicates an alternate distribution.

In the case at bar, the settlor clearly never revoked the trust. Therefore, we must look to the pertinent language of the trust agreement.

The only arguably relevant provision of the trust agreement is section (4) above quoted. The parties disagree as to the relevance and interpretation of this language.

The heirs of the beneficiary contend the provision applies only when at least two beneficiaries are designated in the trust and here the settlor named only one beneficiary. Talman urges the provision does apply to the instant situation, and accordingly interprets the language as establishing the descendants of the beneficiary as a class of contingent beneficiaries. Thus, the contingent interest of the heirs of the designated beneficiary became vested upon her death before the death of the settlor.

[The court held § 4 to be inapplicable]

For these reasons the judgment appealed from is reversed and the cause is remanded with directions that the trust estate and all avails thereof shall pass to the estate of the deceased beneficiary.

Reversed and remanded with directions.

McGLOON and O'CONNOR, JJ., concur.

Notes

1. To the same effect, see Matter of Chandler's Estate, 90 Ill.App.3d 674, 46 Ill.Dec. 46, 413 N.E.2d 486 (1980). For a full discussion, see Salvio v. Salvio, 186 Conn. 311, 441 A.2d 190 (1982).

2. In the case of a savings account trust that does not qualify as a Totten trust, a provision for revocation only by withdrawal or by written notice to the bank is fully effective. Funk v. Funk, 24 Wash.App. 19, 598 P.2d 792 (Wash. App.1979). Contrariwise, in the case of a Totten trust such a provision is quite generally held to be for the protection of the bank only; only the bank can invoke it. E.g., In re Agostini's Estate, 311 Pa.Super. 233, 457 A.2d 861 (1983); Terner v. Rand, 417 So.2d 303 (Fla.App.1982); Jones v. First National Bank of Rome, 142 Ga.App. 18, 234 S.E.2d 794 (Ga.App.1977).

D.   TRUSTS TO BEGIN IN THE FUTURE—THE TRUST RES (Corpus)

FARMERS' LOAN & TRUST CO. v. WINTHROP

Court of Appeals of New York, 1924.
238 N.Y. 477, 144 N.E. 686.

CARDOZO, J.   On February 3, 1920, Helen C. Bostwick executed her deed of trust to the Farmers' Loan & Trust Company as trustee. It is described as the 1920 deed, to distinguish it from an earlier one, made in 1918, which is the subject of another action. By the later of the two deeds she gave to her trustee $5,000, "the said sum, and all other property hereafter delivered to said trustee as hereinafter provided," to be held upon the trusts and limitations therein set forth. The income was to be paid to her own use during life, and the principal on her death was to be divided into two parts—one for the benefit of the children of a deceased son, Albert; the other for the benefit of a daughter, Fannie, and the children of said daughter. The donor reserved "the right, at any time and from time to time during the continuance of the trusts, * * * to deliver to said trustee additional property to be held by it" thereunder. She reserved also a power of revocation.

At the date of the execution of this deed, a proceeding was pending in the Surrogate's Court for the settlement of the accounts of the United States Trust Company as trustee of a trust under the will of Jabez A. Bostwick. The effect of the decree, when entered, would be to transfer to Mrs. Bostwick money, shares of stock, and other property of the value of upwards of $2,300,000. The plan was that this property, when ready to be transferred, should be delivered to the trustee, and held subject to the trust. On February 3, 1920, simultaneously with the execution of the trust deed, three other documents, intended to effectuate this plan, were signed by the donor. One is a power of attorney whereby she authorized the Farmers' Loan & Trust Company as her attorney "to collect and receive any and all cash, shares of stock and other property" to which she might "be entitled under any decree or order made or entered" in the proceeding above mentioned. A second is a power of attorney authorizing the Farmers' Loan & Trust Company to sell and transfer any and all shares of stock then or thereafter standing in her name. A third is a letter, addressed to the Farmers' Loan & Trust Company, in which she states that she hands to the company the powers of attorney just described, and in which she gives instructions in respect of the action to be taken thereunder:

> "My desire is and I hereby authorize you to receive from the United States Trust Company of New York all securities and property coming to me under the decree on the settlement of its account and to transfer such securities and property to yourself as trustee under agreement of trust bearing even date herewith executed by me to you."

The decree in the accounting proceeding was entered March 16, 1920. It established the right of Helen C. Bostwick to the payment or transfer of shares of stock and other property of the market value (then or shortly thereafter) of $2,327,353.70. On April 27, 1920, a representative of the Farmers' Loan & Trust Company presented the power of attorney to the United States Trust Company and stated that he was authorized to receive such securities as were ready for delivery. Shares of stock having a market value of $856,880 were handed to him then and there. No question is made that these became subject to the provisions of the deed of trust. The controversy arises in respect of the rest of the securities, $1,470,473.70 in value, which were retained in the custody of the United States Trust Company, apparently for the reason that they were not yet ready for delivery. During the night of April 27, 1920, Helen C. Bostwick died. She left a will, appointing the Farmers' Loan & Trust Company executor, and disposing of an estate of the value of over $20,000,000. The securities retained, as we have seen, in the custody of the United States Trust Company, were delivered on or about July 13, 1920, to the executor under the will. Conflicting claims of ownership are made by the legatees under the will and the remaindermen under the deed.

just begun; incomplete

We think, with the majority of the Appellate Division, that the gift remained inchoate at the death of the donor. There is no occasion to deny that in the setting of other circumstances, a power of attorney, authorizing a donee to reduce to possession the subject of a gift, may be significant as evidence of a symbolical delivery. We assume, without deciding, that such effect will be allowed if, apart from the power, there is established an intention that the title of the donor shall be presently divested and presently transferred. The assumption ignores difficulties not to be underestimated (cf. Young v. Young, 80 N.Y. 422, 36 Am.Rep. 634; Beaver v. Beaver, 117 N.Y. 421, 22 N.E. 940, 6 L.R.A. 403, 15 Am. St.Rep. 531; Augsbury v. Shurtliff, 180 N.Y. 138, 72 N.E. 927), but we pass them over for the purpose of the argument, and treat them as surmounted. Even so, the basic obstacle remains that there is here no expression of a purpose to effectuate a present gift. The power of attorney, standing by itself, results, as all concede, in the creation of a revocable agency. Hunt v. Rousmanier, 8 Wheat. 174, 5 L.Ed. 589; Farmers' Loan & Trust Co. v. Wilson, 139 N.Y. 284, 34 N.E. 784, 36 Am.St.Rep. 696.

eg where poa is considered a declaration of trust (Pye)

No pwrs to Co as trustee; merely as agent.

If something more was intended, if what was meant was a gift that was to be operative at once, the expression of the meaning will have to be found elsewhere, in the deed of trust or in the letter. Neither in the one, however, nor in the other, can such a purpose be discerned. Deed and letter alike are framed on the assumption that the gift is executory and future, and this though the addition of a few words would have established it beyond cavil as executed and present. In the deed there is a present transfer of $5,000 and no more. This wrought, there is merely the reservation of a privilege to augment the subject-matter of the trust by deliveries thereafter. The absence of words of present assignment is emphasized when we consider with what simplicity an assignment could have been stated. All that was needed was to expand the description by a phrase: *"The trust res shall include..."*   *↳ of the trust res*

"The right, title, and interest of the grantor in the securities and other property due or to become due from the United States Trust Company as trustee under the will."

The deed and the other documents, we must remember, were not separated in time. They were parts of a single plan, and were executed together. In these circumstances, a present transfer, if intended, would naturally have found its place in the description of the deed itself. If omitted for some reason there, the least we should expect would be to find it in the letter. Again words of present transfer are conspicuously absent. What we have instead is a request, or at best a mandate, incompetent without more to divest title, or transfer it, serving no other purpose than a memorandum of instructions from principal to agent as a guide to future action. Harris v. Clark, 3 N.Y. 93, 51 Am.Dec. 352; Gerry v. Howe, 130 Mass. 350; Welch v. Henshaw, 170 Mass. 409, 49 N.E. 659, 64 Am.St.Rep. 309. Deed and documents were prepared by counsel learned in the law. With industrious iteration, they rejected the familiar formulas that would have given unmistakable expression to the transfer of a present title. With like iteration, they chose the words and methods appropriate to a gift that was conceived of as executory and future. We must take the transaction as they made it. The very facility with which they could have made it something else is a warning that we are not at liberty, under the guise of construction, to make it other than it is. Matter of Van Alstyne, 207 N.Y. 298, 309, 310, 100 N.E. 802. They were willing to leave open what they might readily have closed. Death overtook the signer before the gap was filled.

Viewed thus as a gift, the transaction was inchoate. An intention may be assumed, and indeed is not disputed, that what was incompetent at the moment should be completed in the future. The difficulty is that the intention was never carried out. Mrs. Bostwick remained free (apart from any power of revocation reserved in the deed of trust) to revoke the executory mandate, and keep the property as her own. Very likely different forms and instrumentalities would have been utilized, if she or her counsel had supposed that death was to come so swiftly. We might say as much if she had left in her desk or memorandum expressing her resolutions for the morrow. With appropriate forms and instrumentalities available, she chose what the course of events has proved to be the wrong one. The court is without power to substitute another. Hunt v. Rousmanier, supra; Young v. Young, supra; Beaver v. Beaver, supra.

The transaction, failing as a gift, because inchoate or incomplete, is not to be sustained as the declaration of a trust. Beaver v. Beaver, supra; Matter of Crawford, 113 N.Y. 560, 566, 21 N.E. 692, 5 L.R.A. 71; Wadd v. Hazelton, 137 N.Y. 215, 33 N.E. 143, 21 L.R.A. 693, 33 Am.St.Rep. 707. The donor had no intention of becoming a trustee herself. The donee never got title, and so could not hold it for another.

There was no equitable assignment. Equity does not enforce a voluntary promise to make a gift thereafter.

There was no power in trust. Such a power may be created only by a will, or by an instrument sufficient to pass an estate or interest in the property to which the power relates. Real Property Law (Consol.Laws, c. 50) § 140, re-enacting in substance 1 R.S. 735, § 106; Jennings v. Conboy, 73 N.Y. 230, 234.

One other question is in the case. It concerns the right of the executor to charge a proportionate part of the estate and inheritance taxes upon the interest of the remaindermen under the 1920 deed of trust. For the reasons stated in another action between the same parties involving the 1918 deed, the federal taxes are to be borne by the residuary estate.

The judgment of the Appellate Division should be modified, so as to affirm the judgment entered on the report of the referee in respect of the payment of the federal estate taxes, and, as so modified, affirmed, with a separate bill of costs to each party or set of parties appearing by separate attorney and to the several guardians ad litem, all payable out of the estate.

HISCOCK, C. J., and POUND, MCLAUGHLIN, CRANE, ANDREWS, and LEHMAN, JJ., concur.

Judgment accordingly.

Notes

1. It appears from the opinion below, 207 App.Div. 356, 202 N.Y.S. 456 (1923), that by Mrs. Bostwick's will, one-fourth of the residuary estate was given to the children of her son and three-fourths to the children of her daughter. See 33 Yale L.J. 666 (1924); 24 Colum.L.Rev. 545 (1924); 10 Cornell L.Q. 252 (1925).

2. Accord, Adams v. Hoshauer, 29 Ill.App.2d 2, 172 N.E.2d 399 (1961). Recent cases refusing to convert an imperfect gift into a trust include: Hebrew Univ. Ass'n v. Nye, 148 Conn. 223, 169 A.2d 641 (1961). This opinion does stand for the proposition for which it is cited, but it was superseded on the submission of additional evidence by a decision giving the library to the Hebrew University as a gift. See discussion, supra, page 381; Davis v. National Bank of Tulsa, 353 P.2d 482 (Okl.1960); Matter of Levine, 26 Misc.2d 307, 203 N.Y.S.2d 643 (1960).

3. In Estate of Collins, 84 Cal.App.3d 928, 149 Cal.Rptr. 65 (1978) decedent, shortly before his death signed an application to open a Totten trust account at Bank A. He deposited no funds but signed a sight draft directing Bank B to deliver to Bank A the proceeds of a savings account in Bank B. Before the draft was honored, he died. Held, no Totten trust account was created.

4. The Restatement, Second, Trusts declares:

§ 74. The Necessity of Trust Property. A trust cannot be created unless there is trust property.

§ 75. Non-existent Interests. An interest which has not come into existence or which has ceased to exist cannot be held in trust.

§ 76. Indefinite Subject Matter. A trust cannot be created unless the subject matter is definite or definitely ascertainable.

§ 78. Transferable Property. Any property which can be voluntarily transferred by the owner can be held in trust.

§ 79. Non-transferable Property. [With two narrow exceptions,] property which the owner cannot transfer cannot be held in trust.

§ 82. Intangible Things. Interests in intangible things, if transferable, can be held in trust.

    Comment: a. Chose in action. A creditor's interest in a debt or a contract right, if transferable, can be held in trust. * * *

    b. Life insurance. The interest of a person named as beneficiary of a life insurance policy may be held in trust. * * *

    c. Patent or Copyright. A patent or copyright can be held in trust.

    d. Good-will or trade-mark. The good-will of a business or a trade-mark can be held in trust. * * *

    e. Trade secret. A trade secret can be held in trust. * * *

    f. Literary production. An uncopyrighted literary production, for example, a novel or a poem, can be held in trust.

    g. Invention. An unpatented invention can be held in trust. * * *

§ 83. Equitable Interests. An equitable interest, if transferable, can be held in trust.

§ 86. Expectancies. An expectation or hope of receiving property in the future cannot be held in trust.

§ 87.   Obligor as Trustee.   An obligor cannot be trustee of the duties which he owes to the obligee; but if a valid trust has been created, the fact that the trustee becomes obligor does not relieve him from his duties as trustee.

5. See, also, on express and constructive trusts of intangible interests, 46 Harv.L.Rev. 861 (1933) (invention); 81 U.Pa.L.Rev. 636 (1933) (same); 17 Minn.L.Rev. 558 (1933) (same); 16 A.L.R. 1195 (1922) (same); cf. 42 Harv. L.Rev. 254, 257 (1928) (trade secret).

6. See In re Gurlitz, 105 Misc. 30, 172 N.Y.S. 523 (Surr.Ct.N.Y.Cty.1918), modified sub nom. In re Lynde's Estate, 175 N.Y.S. 289 (1919), affirmed mem. 190 App.Div. 907, 179 N.Y.S. 933 (1st Dep't. 1919), holding that an assignment of an expectancy to a trustee was a mere promise to create a trust, which, made without consideration, cannot be enforced.   See also Bowden v. Teague, 276 Ala. 142, 159 So.2d 844 (1964).   A promise made for consideration to create a trust in the future is enforcible even if the res in not yet in existence.   Penney v. White, 594 S.W.2d 632 (Mo.App.1980);   Restatement, Second, Trusts § 30; Brainard v. Commissioner, 91 F.2d 880 (Cir. 7th 1937) certiorari granted 302 U.S. 682, 58 S.Ct. 480, 82 L.Ed. 526, certiorari dismissed 303 U.S. 665, 58 S.Ct. 748, 82 L.Ed. 1122; In re Turcan, 40 Ch.D. 5 (1888).   An extensive review of the cases appears in Annot., "Creation of express trust in property to be acquired in future," 3 A.L.R.3d 1416 (1965).

7. Suppose that A, named as legatee in B's existing will, assigned, during B's life, A's expectancy to S for value; and that S, after the assignment, but still during B's life attempted to assign S's interest in A's expectancy gratuitously to T in trust for C, would a trust be created?   Compare In re Baker, 13 F.2d 707 (C.C.A.6 1926), certiorari denied 273 U.S. 733, 47 S.Ct. 242, 71 L.Ed. 864 (1926); Note, 36 Yale L.J. 272 (1926).

E.   INSURANCE TRUSTS

GURNETT v. MUTUAL LIFE INSURANCE CO.

Supreme Court of Illinois, 1934.
356 Ill. 612, 191 N.E. 250.

DEYOUNG, Justice.   Daniel W. Gurnett and four other persons, partners, doing business under the firm name and style of Gurnett & Co., filed their amended and supplemental bill of complaint in the circuit court of Cook county against the Mutual Life Insurance Company of New York, the Penn Mutual Life Insurance Company, the Central Republic Bank & Trust Company, as successor trustee under a life insurance trust agreement, the executors of the last will and testament of Knowlton L. Ames, deceased, and his heirs at law.   The relief prayed for was: (1) To have the trust agreement and the amendments thereto entered into by Knowlton L. Ames and the Central Trust Company of Illinois, as trustee, declared void; (2) to enjoin the two named insurance companies from paying to the trustee the proceeds of certain policies they had issued; (3) to restrain the trustee from disposing of the proceeds of other policies paid to it; and (4) to order the trustee to hold the proceeds of the several policies under a resulting trust in favor of the estate of Ames and to pay such proceeds to the executors of his will.   Motions to dismiss the bill were made by all the defendants, and, after an extended hearing upon these motions, the chancellor found that the agreement and amendments thereto constituted a valid trust agreement, and that the amended and supplemental bill was without equity. The complainants elected to abide by their bill, and the court entered a decree dismissing it for the want of equity. Upon appeal, the Appellate Court for the First district affirmed the decree. The cause is here upon a writ of certiorari for a further review.

The complainants, in their amended and supplemental bill, alleged that they were stockbrokers engaged in business in Boston, Mass.; that under various agreements, relative to the purchase and sale of stocks and other securities, Ames became indebted to them in the sum of $324,361.83, — with interest thereon; that, although they had instituted legal proceedings against Ames in the superior court of Cook county for the recovery of this sum, with interest, the suit was undisposed of and pending when he died on December 23, 1931; that his estate, in the process of administration in the probate court of Cook county, was insufficient to pay the claims of creditors; that the proceeds of certain life insurance policies subject to a life insurance trust agreement dated December 2, 1930, and two amendments thereto, had been paid to the trustee designated therein, but that a sum in excess of $300,000 payable under the policies issued by the Mutual Life Insurance Company of New York and the Penn Mutual Life Insurance Company and also subject to the trust had not been paid to the trustee; that Ames had not assigned the policies to the trustee; that prior to his death Ames treated the policies as his sole property; and that he borrowed money from insurance companies upon some of the policies after December 2, 1930. It is further alleged that the agreement and amendments thereto did not conform to the legal requirements for the disposition of property inter vivos, because there was no disposition by Ames during his lifetime of any interests in the life insurance policies to the trustee; that there was no actual corpus of the trust while Ames lived, as the result of which the trust failed; and that the proceeds of the policies rightfully belong to the executors and should be impressed with a resulting trust in favor of the estate. It is charged that the executors, the Central Republic Bank & Trust Company and John Dawes Ames, are disqualified from bringing the suit because of interest as the trustee and a beneficiary, respectively, of the trust, and that, owing to their failure to institute legal proceedings to have the trust declared void, the complainants have filed their amended and supplemental bill, for and in the place of the executors, and on behalf of claimants, creditors, the legatees and heirs of the decedent as well as in their own behalf. Fraud is not alleged, nor are there any allegations that the transaction contravenes any statute or the public policy of the state or any provision of the various contracts of insurance.

The trust agreement, including a schedule of the policies initially deposited with the trustee thereunder, and amendments dated April 2, 1931, and June 25, 1931, respectively, were attached to and made a part of the bill. The schedule discloses that beginning in 1906 and continuing through 1927, Ames acquired thirty-three policies of life insurance from ten different companies for a total exceeding $1,000,000. By the trust agreement Ames is designated as the assured, and the Central Trust Company of Illinois, a corporation authorized to accept and execute trusts, as the trustee. The agreement sets forth that Ames deposited the policies with the trustee and agreed to make the trustee the beneficiary of all the policies. Ames thereafter caused the companies, including the two made defendants to this suit, to change the beneficiaries in conformity with the provisions of the trust agreement. Where the trustee previously had not been named as the beneficiary, the companies noted the change on the face of the policies. The agreement further provided that Ames should continue to pay all premiums, assessments, and other charges required to keep the policies in force, and that he retain the power to exercise any right, option, or privilege given to him by any of the policies, including the right to change the beneficiary, to borrow money in accordance with the respective policy provisions, to use any of the policies as security for any purpose whatsoever, to receive any dividends, earnings, or other payments on the policies, and to surrender any policy for its cash surrender value. In addition to the powers reserved with respect to the policies, the agreement provided that Ames should have the right to terminate it in whole or in part, or to modify or amend it. The latter power was twice exercised. The trustee agreed to hold the policies until Ames should in writing otherwise request or direct. If so requested or directed, and upon the payment to it of reasonable compensation for its past services, the trustee was required to deliver the policies demanded. The agreement imposed no other duties upon the trustee during the lifetime of Ames. The trustee agreed, upon his death, to collect the policies and to administer and dispose of the proceeds in conformity with the detailed directions prescribed in the trust agreement. For the performance of these duties after Ames' death, the agreement provided that the trustee would be entitled to compensation.

The plaintiffs in error contend that the agreement of December 2, 1930, did not create a valid trust because the settlor neither relinquished the power to change the beneficiary named in the policies nor assigned any of the policies to the trustee. To support the decree sustaining the validity of the trust, the defendants in error maintain, first, that the trust agreement passed property rights or interests of the settlor in the policies to the trustee during the lifetime of the settlor, and, second, that, by the execution of the agreement and the nomination of the trustee as the beneficiary of the policies, the settlor manifested his intention to transfer the title to, as well as the physical possession of, the policies to the trustee.

A trust is an obligation arising out of a confidence reposed in a person, for the benefit of another, to apply property faithfully and according to such confidence. [Citations omitted] It may be created in any property, real or personal, legal or equitable, which is in existence, and which in the eye of a court of equity is of value. [Citations omitted] Choses in action, contingent interests, and expectancies may be assigned and a valid trust created in them. Although not assignable at law, they may be transferred, so as to be binding in equity, by a contract made in good faith and for a valuable consideration. [Citations omitted] To constitute a valid trust of personal property, there must be a declaration by a person competent to create it, a trustee, designated beneficiaries, a certain and ascertained object, a definite fund or subject-matter, and its delivery or assignment to the trustee. [Citations omitted]

Requisites to create a valid trust

A life insurance policy is property and may constitute the subject-matter of a trust. [Citations omitted] The designated beneficiary of the policy may, by the provisions of a collateral trust agreement, be named as the trustee. Vance on Insurance (2d Ed.) p. 606. When the beneficiary promises the insured to pay either the whole or a portion of the proceeds of the policy to a third person, the proceeds will be impressed with a trust to the extent of the promise made. [Citations omitted]

Ames, the creator of the trust assailed, made his insurance policies payable to a trustee and contemporaneously executed a trust agreement providing for the administration and disposition of the proceeds of the policies. The trustee promised to perform the duties of administering the trust according to the provisions of the agreement, and the policies were placed in its possession. The policies were contracts between the insured and the insurers for the payment of stipulated sums by the latter to the trustee as the nominee of the insured upon the happening of a certain contingency; namely, the death of Ames. 1 Biddle on Insurance, p. 5; 1 Joyce on Insurance (2d Ed.) § 7. The premiums paid by Ames constituted the consideration for the promises made by the insurers. Their obligations to pay and the right of the trustee to receive the proceeds of the policies, upon the happening of the contingency specified, were determined when the companies noted upon the face of the policies the exercise, by the insured, of his right or privilege to change the beneficiaries. The date of the death of the insured merely fixed the time when the obligation of the insurers to pay and the right of the beneficiary to receive the proceeds of the policies became enforceable. [Citation omitted] The trust agreement and the change of beneficiaries, however, became effective during the lifetime of the settlor. The continuing right to receive the proceeds of an insurance policy is not impaired by the unexercised right or privilege of the insured to designate another beneficiary. [Citations omitted] The designation of a beneficiary in a policy of life insurance creates an inchoate gift of the proceeds of the policy, which, if not revoked by the insured in his lifetime, vests in the beneficiary at the time of the former's death. [Citation omitted] A policy of life insurance is not deemed an asset of the estate of the insured unless it is made payable to him, his executors or administrators. The mere fact that the insured may change the beneficiary does not make the policy or its proceeds a part of his estate. Neither the policies nor their proceeds constituted a part of the estate of Knowlton L. Ames, deceased. Since his death, the trust agreement is merely evidence of the trustee's contract under which it must collect the policies and hold the proceeds for the purposes of the trust.

A trust in the proceeds of an insurance policy was enforced in Otis v. Beckwith, 49 Ill. 121, a case in which the policy was not delivered to the trustee, and the existence of an assignment was first discovered following the death of the insured. Edward Sacket requested Thomas S. Beckwith to act as trustee of the proceeds of a life insurance policy for the benefit of Sacket's three sons by his first marriage. Upon the written acceptance by Beckwith of the trusteeship, Sacket executed an assignment of the policy to him and attached the assignment to the policy. The assignment was made in conformity with the provisions of the contract of insurance, and was noted upon the insurer's books. Sacket did not, however, deliver either the policy or the assignment to the trustee. After Sacket's death, the trustee and the administrator of his estate each claimed the proceeds of the policy. In a bill filed for the purpose of compelling the administrator to surrender the policy and to pay the proceeds to the trustee, it was alleged that the intention of Sacket was to vest the title to the policy in Beckwith as trustee for his three sons, and that Sacket, from the time of the assignment until his death four years later, considered it as belonging absolutely to Beckwith, as such trustee. Sacket's widow contended that her husband retained possession and control of the policy and the assignment during his lifetime so that the title to the policy should not vest in the trustee absolutely, and that he might make a different disposition of it if he so desired. In her answer, she averred that he failed to effect any legal transfer and that the title to the policy, regardless of her husband's intention, never vested in the trustee. This court held that, since the policy was actually assigned and the assignment accepted in writing and noted on the books of the insurer, these acts were equivalent to an actual delivery of the assignment to the trustee. In affirming the decree of the trial court directing the administrator to pay the proceeds of the policy to the trustee, this court emphasized the intention of Sacket and observed that he created a fund for his children; that he did all within his power to confer upon the trustee the necessary authority to receive the fund; that, by the payment of premiums, he kept the policy in force; and that he never manifested any repentance of his act. The intention of Ames, in the present case, is equally clear, for he created the fund, continued to pay premiums on the policies, and did not revoke the trust. It follows that upon his death the obligations of the insurance companies were owing to the trustee.

The case of Bose v. Meury, 112 N.J.Eq. 62, 163 A. 276, is similar to the case at bar. Arnold J. Meury named a trust company as trustee of the proceeds of all his life insurance policies. A trust agreement provided for the payment of the income from the proceeds of the policies to his wife, with the remainder to his children. Meury reserved the right to add or to withdraw policies and to revoke the trust. He exercised that power by withdrawing two policies aggregating $25,000 and pledging them with Edward Bose as security for a loan. The beneficiary, however, was not changed. Upon Meury's death, the proceeds of these two policies were paid to Bose, who deposited the excess above his claim in court upon an interpleader bill. The estate was insolvent, and the trustee, the widow as administratrix, and creditors claimed the surplus. It was contended that, by the reserved right to withdraw policies and to revoke the trust, control of the subject-matter was retained and that the trust was testamentary. In denying these contentions, the court said: "Whatever merit there may be to the points were the res in trust the property of the trustor, they are beside the question where, as here, the res is the proceeds of insurance on the life of the trustor which never were his property. The proceeds are the fulfillment of promises by the insurance company to the Montclair Trust Company, trustee, to pay the stipulated sums, upon the death of the insured. The insured paid the consideration for the promises and he had the right, under the terms of the policies, to change the promises at will, but when the day came—the insured's death—the obligations of the insurance company were due to the Montclair Trust Company, trustee. Its source of title was the promise in the policies, not the trust agreement. The trust agreement is no more than a declaration of trust by the trustee that it would hold the proceeds of the policies for the benefit of the insured's wife and children, and whether it had physical possession of the policies or whether there was a stripping of interest by the 'donor,' or that the trust deed was testamentary, is wholly immaterial."

Likewise, in the case of Hirsh v. Auer, 146 N.Y. 13, 40 N.E. 397, 398, it appeared that the insured at any time could have changed the beneficiary of his certificate of insurance. In impressing the proceeds of the policy with the trust created by an agreement between the insured and the beneficiary, the court said: "The statutes of this state do not define the objects for which trusts in personal property may be created, and if they are not against public policy, and do not contravene any existing provisions of law, they will be enforced. The fact that the trust dealt with a contingent interest of the insured in the certificate of insurance is of no moment. That interest became vested at the death of the insured, and, the beneficiary having collected the insurance money, the trust, under the agreement creating and acknowledging it, attached to the fund. A trust of this character is not to be distinguished from assignments of contingent interests, which courts of equity recognize as valid. Field v. Mayor of New York, 6 N.Y. 179 [57 Am.Dec. 435]; Stover v. Eycleshimer, *42 N.Y. [3 Keyes] 620."

The reservation of the power to revoke an entire trust does not invalidate the agreement presently creating it or render it testamentary. [Citations omitted] The plaintiffs in error concede the validity of the provision reserving power to the settlor to terminate the trust agreement in whole or in part. Naming new beneficiaries in one or more of the policies would have produced precisely the same effect as the termination of the trust with respect to such policies. The power to designate another beneficiary in an insurance policy is a privilege personal to the insured. The powers and privileges reserved do not affect the obligations of the insurers to pay the proceeds of the policies to the trustee upon the death of the insured.

It is not alleged in the bill of complaint that any insurance contract subject to the trust agreement required an assignment to transfer the policy. If such a requirement was prescribed, it was for the benefit of the insurance company, which alone could complain that it had not been observed. The insurers did not challenge the validity of the transaction attacked by the plaintiffs in error. All the insurance companies recognized the title of the trustee either by the payment of the policies prior to the commencement of this suit or by motions to dismiss the amended and supplemental bill. The plaintiffs in error were neither parties to the trust agreement nor to any of the contracts of insurance, and they claim no lien on any of the policies. Moreover, the intention of the insured with respect to the payment of a policy was as effectually manifested by the designation of a new beneficiary as by the assignment of the policy. [Citations omitted]

The allegations of the amended and supplemental bill disclose that Ames could have named his wife and children the direct beneficiaries of the policies in which they were not so designated. His intention to provide financial security for his family through the medium of a life insurance trust is clear. The contentions urged by the plaintiffs in error do not warrant the frustration, by the interposition of a court of equity, of that intention.

The judgment of the Appellate Court is affirmed.

Judgment affirmed.

Note

1. Mr. Ames appears to have died insolvent. Very possibly he remained solvent, however, until shortly before his death; in 1931 the road from riches to rags was often short. If he had paid life insurance premiums while insolvent, or if the payments had rendered him insolvent, his creditors would not have been entirely without remedy. See, e.g., Bose v. Meury, 112 N.J.Eq. 62, 65, 163 A. 276, 277 (Chancery 1932):

> There is proof that the insured was insolvent when the trust was created. The creditors are entitled to the sum of the premiums paid during the period of insolvency as disclosed by the testimony, not exceeding six years prior to the filing of the claim for relief. Lanning v. Parker, 84 N.J. Eq. 429, 94 A. 64 (Chancery 1915).

Can you devise a theory that would give the creditors more complete relief than was granted in that case?

2. Insurance trusts are held nontestamentary (almost as a matter of course) on either or both of two theories. Often the court declares that the execution of the trust agreement, and the performance of present duties under it, results in transfer of an interest to the insurance beneficiary *then*. See, e.g., In re Estate of Herron, 237 So.2d 563 (Fla.App.1970). Except in the rare situation where it makes a difference *when* the insurance trust came into existence, there is a simpler reason for rejecting the contention that it is void as a testamentary transfer without testamentary formalities. See, e.g., In re Albert Anderson Life Ins. Trust, 67 S.D. 393, 398, 293 N.W. 527, 529 (1940):

> We are concerned here with a trust res which never was the property of the insured and which came into existence only after his death. We are not here concerned with the policy of insurance as such or the rights of the beneficiary in such policy. We are concerned only with the funds which the insurance companies paid to the bank, the title to which funds never was in Anderson. The transaction that here appears, is that Albert An-

derson named the bank as beneficiary in the policy, and in consideration for this designation the bank declared the trust in the proceeds of the policy to which it acquired title upon the death of Albert Anderson. See Scott on Trusts, § 86.

The principal case is typical in utilizing both theories indiscriminately. See also Connecticut General Life Insurance Company v. First National Bank of Minneapolis, 262 N.W.2d 403 (Minn.1977); Gordon v. Portland Trust Bank, 201 Or. 648, 271 P.2d 653, 53 A.L.R.2d 1106 (1954).

3. In the cases where the designated beneficiary of the insurance policy is an individual who has promised to give all or part of the proceeds to others an additional theory is frequently invoked. Under a constructive trust doctrine, the beneficiary may not be allowed to go back on his promise. See, for an example, Voelkel v. Tohulka, 236 Ind. 588, 141 N.E.2d 344 (1957), certiorari denied 355 U.S. 891, 78 S.Ct. 263, 2 L.Ed.2d 189 (1957).

4. Are there any functional differences between the interest of a beneficiary of a life insurance policy on the life of a living person and the expectant interest under the will of a living testator? See Vance, The Beneficiary's Interest in a Life Insurance Policy, 31 Yale L.J. 343, 358 (1922); Brown's Estate, 384 Pa. 99, 119 A.2d 513 (1956), noted, 18 U.Pitt.L.Rev. 337 (1957). The argument has been frequently made and almost invariably rejected to the effect that a life insurance trust is an invalid testamentary transfer. Prudential Insurance Co. v. Gatewood, 317 S.W.2d 382 (Mo.1958); Koziell Trust, 412 Pa. 348, 194 A.2d 230 (1963); Sigal v. Hartford Nat. Bank & Trust Co., 119 Conn. 570, 177 A. 742 (1935); 53 A.L.R.2d 1112 (1957); 72 A.L.R.2d 924 (1960).

5. Various types of transactions generally described as "life insurance trusts" are extensively utilized. Broadly speaking, they may be classified in two categories. One category includes life insurance policies with agreements purporting to make the insurance company issuing the policy a trustee of the proceeds thereof. The other category includes the cases where a trust company or other third party, named by the insured as the beneficiary of the policy, agrees to hold the proceeds in trust. Insurance trusts of the latter type are classified on the basis of the method of payment of premiums as "funded" or "unfunded". In the funded life insurance trust, the insured settlor not only names the trust company or other trustee as trustee to hold the proceeds in trust after his death, but also delivers property to the trustee in trust to use the same or the income thereof to pay the insurance premiums during his life. The agreement may provide that any unexpected balance of the property thus devoted to the payment of premiums shall, at the death of the insured-settlor, be held in trust on the same terms as the proceeds of the policy. In the unfunded life insurance trust, the insured-settlor pays the premiums on the policy himself. The funded type is less frequent, for the reason, among others, that it requires a substantial outlay of capital.

6. On the uses of life insurance trusts in estate planning, see generally, Adams and Bieber, Irrevocable Life Insurance Trusts, 12 Cumb.L.Rev. 283 (1981/1982) (can be used to avoid estate tax and minimize gift and income taxes); Stoeber, Effective Uses of Life Insurance Trusts, 18 J.Am.Soc. C.L.U. 118 (1964); Moses, Irrevocable Life Insurance Trusts in Estate Planning, 16 J.Am.Soc. C.L.U. 117 (1962); Friedman and Wheeler, New Look at Insurance Trusts: Tax and Other Considerations in Choice of Policy Transfers, 100 Trusts & Estates 396

(1961);   Beatty, Insurance Proceeds in Trust, 28 Tenn.L.Rev. 344 (1961);   10 S.D.L.Rev. 128 (1965).

PIEROWICH v. METROPOLITAN LIFE INSURANCE CO.

Supreme Court of Michigan, 1937.
282 Mich. 118, 275 N.W. 789.

CHANDLER, Justice.   The appellee, on September 15, 1931, issued a policy of life insurance on the life of Dan Pierowich, in which his wife was named beneficiary.   Subsequently the parties were divorced and during the pendency of the proceedings the insured changed the policy and named his two minor sons, Alex and James, age eight and ten respectively, as the beneficiaries.   On November 23, 1934, the insured executed and delivered to appellee the following:

"Policy No. 7288571—A

"To the Metropolitan Life Insurance Company, New York, New York.

"I hereby direct that in the event either of my sons, Alex Pierowich, born 5/9/1924, and James Pierowich, born 2/1926, the beneficiaries of record shall survive me but shall not have attained the age of 21 years at the time of my death, the amount payable under the said policy upon my death, to such son, shall be retained by the Company and interest thereon at the rate which the Company may each year declare on such funds (but at no less rate than three and one-half per centum per annum) shall be compounded annually at the end of each year until such child shall have attained the age of 21 years when his share, together with the interest then accumulated thereon, shall be paid at once in one sum to him.

"Provided, however, in the event that either of my said sons shall survive me but shall die before attaining the age of 21 years, his share, together with the interest then accumulated thereon, shall be paid at once in one sum to the executors or administrators of such deceased son.

"And I hereby further direct that neither of my said sons shall have the right to withdraw any of the amount retained by the Company, except as hereinbefore provided, nor the right to assign or encumber any payment hereunder.

"Provided, however, that the foregoing directions shall not apply to the share of either of my said sons who shall predecease me or who shall not be a beneficiary of record at the time of my death or who shall have attained the age of 21 years at the time of my death.

"The right to cancel the foregoing directions by written notice to the Home Office of the Metropolitan Life Insurance Company of New York, New York, is reserved.

"Dated at Hamtramck, Mich.   Nov. 23, 1934

"Insured Dan Pierowich.

"Witness

"L. M. Locianoures."

Dan Pierowich died on June 18, 1935, and thereafter appellee, upon surrender of the policy, delivered to each of the beneficiaries a supplemental contract providing for payment of the proceeds of the policy in exact accordance with the directions given by the insured in his lifetime and set forth above.

The mother of Alex and James filed her bill in equity as guardian of said minors alleging that she is without sufficient funds with which to properly maintain and educate the children, and prayed for a decree ordering appellee to pay her for this purpose such sums from the proceeds of the policy as the court found necessary. The trial court dismissed the bill.

Whether or not a trust was created must depend upon the intention of the insured in providing for the disposition of the proceeds of the policy in the manner which he instructed and whether the necessary requisites to the creation of a trust were observed. In Equitable Trust Co. v. Milton Realty Co., 261 Mich. 571, 246 N.W. 500, 502, we held that: "To create a trust, there must be an assignment of designated property to a trustee with the intention of passing title thereto, to hold for the benefit of others. There must be a separation of the legal estate from the beneficial enjoyment."

We are unable to find from an examination of the evidence the essential element of intent to create a trust. Although not decisive, the provision for the payment of interest on the fund held by appellee, together with the fact that there was no designation or segregation of any particular fund from which payment was to be made, are of interest in determining the intent, and are not indicative of the trust relationship. The supplemental agreements executed by appellee which in terms specifically incorporate the insured's directions appear to be no more than contracts containing a promise to pay the proceeds of the policy in such a manner as the contingencies therein expressed shall command. We fail to find that the fund was assigned from the appellee as debtor to the appellee as trustee as is contended by appellants. The relationship existing is that of debtor and creditor rather than that of trustee and cestui que trust.

The case is not unlike that of McLaughlin v. Equitable Life Assurance Soc. of the U.S., 112 N.J.Eq. 344, 164 A. 579, 580, where the policy contained an agreement that, in the event of the death of the insured prior to the beneficiary attaining the age of 18 years, the proceeds thereof should be held by the insurer and be paid in installments upon the beneficiary reaching the mentioned age. It further provided for the payment of interest and that any payments due during the minority of the beneficiary should be paid to the insured's wife as trustee. A bill was filed to reach a portion of the fund in question for the support, education, and maintenance of the beneficiary. In denying relief, the court said:

"The defendant below appeals to this court on the ground that the policy of insurance and the claim which resulted thereunder by reason of the death of the insured did not create a trust and that the relation of the parties to the suit was not that of trustee and cestui que trust, and also for the reason that there was no evidence before the Vice Chancellor which justified him in decreeing that the defendant should pay the guardian of the infant $25. a week. We are of the opinion that the court below erred in respect to the construction which it placed upon the contract of insurance. The policy of insurance was a contract, and under its terms the insurance company was bound to carry out its provisions. The intention of the insured was to provide a fund for the education, support, and maintenance of his son, John F. McLaughlin, in the event that the insured died before his son attained the age of eighteen years and that he should not have access to such fund except as provided in the contract of insurance until he attained the designated age. This fund, therefore, did not become a trust fund until it was paid over by the insurance company under the term of the contract of insurance to the trustee, and this was not to take place until the beneficiary arrived at the age of eighteen years, when it should be paid in installments covering a period of four years.

"We are of the opinion that the court could not change the terms of this contract and that the insurance company cannot be compelled to agree to any other terms than the terms set forth therein. It is, therefore, not necessary to consider the other point raised by the appellant.

"The decree below is, therefore, reversed."

Appellant further contends that, even though no trust relationship appears, the facts are such as to warrant the interference of a court of equity to grant the desired relief. In support of this position, testimony was introduced establishing the indigent circumstances of the family and the lack of funds claimed necessary to properly provide for the support and education of the beneficiaries. Although in certain circumstances an advancement will be allowed from a trust fund for such purposes as are relied upon in the instant case, Post v. Grand Rapids Trust Co., 255 Mich. 436, 238 N.W. 206, we do not find this rule to be applicable here. The disposition of the property has been fixed by contract, and this court cannot alter the terms thereof even in view of the changed now existing conditions.

The decree is affirmed, with costs to appellee.

FEAD, C. J., and NORTH, WIEST, BUTZEL, BUSHNELL, SHARPE, and POTTER, JJ., concur.

Notes

1. Would a trust have been created if the insurance company had agreed to hold the proceeds of the policy "in trust" for the purpose of making the payments specified by the insured? As the principal case illustrates, different remedies are available depending on whether the arrangement is classified as a trust or contract. Acceleration of trust funds under circumstances similar to those set out here is sometimes permitted. See Note, 51 Harv.L.Rev. 365 (1937); 2 Scott on Trusts § 168; but see New York Life Ins. Co. v. Conrad, 269 Ky. 359, 107 S.W.2d 248 (1937) (no deviation from the terms allowed though insurance company held the proceeds "in trust").

2. It is interesting to speculate as to whether the Metropolitan Life Insurance Company viewed its role in this litigation as a passive stakeholder or whether it was moved by self-interest to oppose strenuously the guardian's petition. Consider the differences in responsibility between a payor on a deferred payment contract and a trustee of a minority trust. Even if the insurance contract refers to the company as trustee of the proceeds, the fine print in the

contract will remove practically all the traditional fiduciary duties by establishing a fixed rate of return and payment schedule, permitting commingling with general assets, waiving additional compensation as trustee and the like. A number of states have statutes concerning these matters. See, for example, Conn.Gen.Stat.Ann. § 38–162 authorizing a domestic life insurance company to act as trustee of the proceeds of any policy issued by it and to hold such proceeds as a part of its general assets without segregating them.

3. Insurance company contracted to serve as trustee of the proceeds of three insurance policies issued by it and to pay 240 monthly installments of $50 each to the widow as first beneficiary and in the event of her death to the children. At the death of the insured the company denied liability on the policies claiming they were fraudulently procured. On defendants' motion the insurance company was removed as trustee because its interest was antagonistic to its responsibility as trustee and a trust company was appointed as successor trustee. New York Life Ins. Co. v. O'Brien, 27 F.2d 773 (W.D.Mich.1927). If the insurance policies are held valid how is the trust company to administer the trust in order to carry out the terms of the contract?

SECTION FOUR. ALIENABILITY OF THE BENEFICIARY'S INTEREST

A. INTRODUCTION

In the absence of a restriction in the trust instrument or an applicable statute, the interest of a trust beneficiary is as transferable as any other property. Except in a few states, the settlor may, however, make the beneficiary's income interest inalienable, in which case the interest is not only not subject to voluntary transfer by the beneficiary but may be unreachable in whole or part by the beneficiary's creditors.

This kind of trust, somewhat misleadingly called "spendthrift," had stormy beginnings and, despite its present wide acceptance in this country, remains a subject of considerable controversy. The history, as well as other aspects, of spendthrift trusts, and their cousins support trusts and discretionary trusts, is the subject of a classic treatise by Dean Griswold. Griswold, Spendthrift Trusts (2d ed. 1947).

The policy considerations underlying the conflict have been described as follows (Second Report, N.Y. Temporary Commission on Estates 459, 461, 464 (1963)) (footnotes omitted):

> The first, and the one upon which spendthrift trusts are usually justified is based on the maxim *cujus est dare, ejus est disponere.* "The law rests its protection of what is known as a spendthrift trust fundamentally on the principle of *cujus est dare, ejus est disponere.* It allows the donor to condition his bounty as suits himself, so long as he violates no law in so doing. When a trust of this kind has been created, the law holds that the donor has an individual right of property in the execution of the trust; and to deprive him of it would be a fraud on his generosity. For the law to appropriate a gift to a person not intended would be an invasion of the donor's private dominion. * * * It is always to be remembered that consideration for the beneficiary does not even in the remotest way enter into the policy of the law; it has regard solely to the rights of the donor.

Spendthrift trusts can have no other justification than is to be found in considerations affecting the donor alone."

* * *

The second philosophy, which is in conflict with the rule that a settlor or testator should be permitted to dispose of his property as he sees fit so long as he violates no rule of law or public policy[,] is that followed in states which do not permit spendthrift trusts on the ground that they are violative of public policy and in fraud of the rights of creditors. The rationale of this is stated in an early Rhode Island case in which it was said[:] "Certainly, no man should have an estate to live on, but not an estate to pay his debts with. Certainly, property available for the purposes of pleasure or profit, should also be amenable to the demands of justice." In the report of the Decedent Estate Commission it was stated that a spendthrift trust has been defined as one which permits the life beneficiary to live at the same time in luxury and in debt. So far as New York is concerned neither of these strictures any longer apply, as will be shown.

In a number of states, the creation and the characteristics of spendthrift trusts are governed by statute. See, e.g., Mont.Rev.Codes § 86–112; Ala.Code, Tit. 58 § 1; Indiana Code § 30–4–3–2; Nev.Rev.Stat. Ch. 166. In New York, by statute, all trusts to receive the rents and profits of real property or the income of personal property are spendthrift unless otherwise provided by the trust instrument, but certain assignments of income exceeding $10,000 per year are permitted (N.Y.— McKinney's EPTL 7–1.5). Moreover, the decision in Estate of McManus, 68 A.D.2d 758, 407 N.Y.S.2d 180 (2d Dep't 1978), affirmed memo 47 N.Y.2d 717, 417 N.Y.S.2d 55, 390 N.E.2d 773 (1979) indicates the definite possibility that broad powers routinely conferred on trustees in instruments drafted by lawyers may result in the inadvertent creation of discretionary rather than spendthrift trusts in New York. The difference is most likely to be material in the event of an attempt at premature termination. See pp. 517–539, infra.

B. VOLUNTARY ALIENABILITY

HOW FAR SHOULD FREEDOM OF DISPOSITION GO?
By Richard R. Powell

THE SECOND MORTIMER H. HESS MEMORIAL LECTURE
DELIVERED BEFORE THE ASSOCIATION OF THE BAR OF
THE CITY OF NEW YORK ON OCTOBER 8, 1970
26 Record of the Association of the Bar
of the City of New York 8 (Jan. 1971).

There is inescapably great gratification to me

1. in this opportunity to return to the scene of my many former crimes;
2. in observing the growth in stature—and in status—and in girth of so many whom I first met in class;
3. in this invitation to give the second Mortimer Hess Memorial Lecture, with its implicit recognition that the approach of one's eightieth birthday is no barrier to potential usefulness.

Throughout the last half century I have found myself constantly querying how far it is socially desirable to permit one who has accumulated wealth *to use,* or *to dispose* of his property *exactly* as he chooses. *Two* aspects only of this great basic problem will be discussed by me tonight. * * * *First,* how far is there social justification for the setting of a limit on the *projection of a disposer's desires into the future,* as is done by a rule against perpetuities in the form now had by New York? *Second* how sound, socially, is the *spendthrift trust concept,* embodied in the present statutes and decisions of this State?

* * *

I shall now proceed to discuss the second facet of our general topic, namely, the social desirability of curtailing the power of an owner of property to create beneficial interests under a trust and to deny to the recipient of such interest both the power to alienate such interest *and the liability to have such interest reachable by the creditors of such recipient.* In other words, we shall be discussing the social desirability of the spendthrift trust concept and, the limitation, if any, with which it should be permitted to function.

A bit of historical background is essential. Austin Scott, in his great book on Trusts [3d Ed. § 132] traces the complete absence of restraints on the alienability of the interest of the beneficiary of both uses and trusts. So our point of departure is the *complete* invalidity of *any* attempted restraint on the ability of the owner of any beneficial trust interest either to alienate his interest or to subject his interest to the legitimate claims of his creditors. * * *

The earliest break in the law's hostility to restraints on alienation occurred late in the eighteenth and early in the nineteenth century, with the judicial manufacture of what came to be called the "equitable separate property of married women." Fond and wealthy fathers, well represented in the English judiciary, desired to assure the financial safety of their daughters and their daughters' progeny against dissipations or subtle persuasions of those selected by their daughters as husbands. So the life interests, created by such trusts in favor of the married daughters, were held to be inalienable by the girls and unreachable by any creditors of the daughters or their spouses. This earliest form of a spendthrift trust has become completely obsolete in the United States by the enactment in all states of the so-called "Married Womens' Acts."

The New York Revised Statutes of 1830 permitted trusts "to receive and apply income" for the benefit of a named person, and, in terms, directed that the beneficiary of such a trust could not alienate his interests; adding in the oft neglected clause that "the right and interest of the beneficiary of any *other* trust * * * may be transferred." This provision has been continuously a part of the law of New York from 1830 to this present moment. It is now N.Y. EPTL 7–1.5. Thus, the New York statutes generated a spendthrift trust, *without inquiry* as to the *desires* of either the *creator* of the trust or its *beneficiary.* This rule was made applicable, first by decisions, and, later by a confirmatory statute, to trusts of both land and personalty. Note, however that this New York deviation from the all-inclusive background of hostility to restraints on alienation *was* confined to *income* provisions. So far as our statutes are concerned, this position is still law. * * *

Wholly separate and apart from the statutory spendthrift trust as to *income,* which originated in *New York,* was the *judicially evolved* spendthrift trust as to *income* which originated in *Pennsylvania.*

Dean Griswold, in his most excellent book on Spendthrift Trusts [2d Ed. 1947, § 26] traced this evolution to a wholly unwarranted generalization from decisions in Pennsylvania caused by the procedural absence of equity powers in the Courts of that Commonwealth. Since, *at law,* creditors could not reach the life interest of a trust beneficiary, it was irrationally generalized into a rule that creditors could not, *in any way,* reach the life interest of a trust beneficiary. Hence came the dicta of Mr. Justice Miller, in 1875, when he decided the much cited case of Nichols v. Eaton [91 U.S. 716].

Griswold also points out that Mr. Justice Miller was a self-made man, living in an era when the philosophical viewpoint was that "what a man owned was his own; with it he could do as he liked." Thus, the concept of the *absoluteness of property* rights, served to obsure, and eventually to eliminate, the idea that restraints on the alienability of income interests were anti-social.

John Chipman Gray published the first edition of his book on Restraints on Alienation in 1883. At page X of his preface, he took the position that "spendthrift trusts have no place in the system of the Common Law." He stressed their paternalistic effect. Gray was fighting against the concept of the absoluteness of property rights. He was out of step with the thinking at the end of the nineteenth century. As a result, spendthrift trusts as to *income, without the aid of any statute* gained quick acceptance in more than 20 of our states. A few jurisdictions have adhered to the common law prohibition of these and other restraints on alienation, *as for example, Kentucky, New Hampshire, and Rhode Island.*

With the turn of the century there began a basic change in underlying thought.

The pendulum had begun its return trip from the complete validity of spendthrift trusts as to income, back towards the freedom of alienation accorded to the beneficiary of all trusts in earlier years.

How far has New York gone in this swing of the pendulum? Is it far enough? If not, what more is needed?

From the beginning of the New York statutory spendthrift trust as to income, creditors of a trust beneficiary have had the "station-in-life" route available to them. It is still present in EPTL Section 7–3.4 and in our present CPLR 5205(e) and 5256. By this route, as applied by our courts, a creditor can reach the income of a beneficiary-debtor, to the extent that it can be proved that such income *exceeds that which the beneficiary needs to continue living in the manner to which he is accustomed!* This "station-in-life" rule has seldom given a creditor any payment on his claim, either in New York or in other states having a similar provision. If one thinks but a moment, this lack of productivity is to be expected. Trusts of this type are usually created by persons of substantial wealth for the benefit of a wife or of children, all of whom have been accustomed to relatively luxurious living. No provable surplus above that needed to continue the accustomed mode of life is to be expected.

A small supplement to the normally valueless station-in-life rule came, in New York, just after the beginning of the century, by a statute permitting the creditor to garnishee the trust income. This is still a part of our law, in CPLR 5231.

* * *

The litigation in the Vought case [25 N.Y.2d 163, 303 N.Y.S.2d 61, 250 N.E.2d 343, July 1969] rested back on the will of Chance Vought, the great airplane designer, executed June 16, 1930. The testator died a month later [*July 25, 1930*]. Note that date! He was survived by a wife married ten years before and two infant sons. After outright gifts to his widow Ena and to his two parents, a trust was created as to a large residue. As to *one-half* of this residue the principal was distributed in 1946 and no question remains. As to the *second-half* of the residue, the income was to be paid to widow Ena for life, and on her death, (which occurred October 14, 1965), the corpus went in equal shares to the two sons of the testator. The corpus of this second half amounted to nearly $2,000,000. The sons' interest[s] were declared by the Court to have vested indefeasibly on the father's death in 1930. In Article VII of the will appeared the usual spendthrift trust clause as to *income* plus the following language:

> "* * * the principal shall not be assignable, nor can the income or principal of said trust funds become attached by garnishment or other legal proceedings while in the hands of the Trustees, except to the extent permitted by law."

It is usual to determine the validity and effect of a will's language by the law operative when the will spoke. This was the year *1930*. The Restatement of Trusts, prepared by Austin Scott was published in 1935, five years after this testator died. By it, this attempted restraint on the alienability of the indefeasibly vested remainder interest of each son in the second half of this residuum was stated to be wholly invalid. [See Restatement of Trusts, 1st, § 153, published in 1935]. This position was supported by many authorities in the first edition of Mr. Scott's great Treatise on Trusts published in 1939. This accumulated evidence as to the American non-statutory law of 1930 was completely disregarded by the Court of Appeals.

The record does not make clear what happened to the son, Chance Vought, Jr. in the late 1950's. In one of the Briefs it is stated that he was then engaged in "bitter matrimonial litigation" with his then wife Eugenia, and has spent some time in jail for failure to provide court ordered support. During ten months, beginning in October, 1959, he made four "assignments" of his indefeasibly vested remainder. The first three were in dollar amounts, and the fourth was for "the balance" of his

interest.   In one of the Briefs it is stated that he received for these
assignments "only 9 cents on the dollar."   [Brief of Siegmund, as Spec.
Guardian for two children].   Early in 1964 Chance Vought, Jr. died,
survived by a widow, a divorced wife and four children.   *If the four assignments were valid,* those ladies and children would receive *nothing*
from this trust.   If, on the other hand, the four assignments were *invalid,*
the family of Chance Vought, Jr. would get these assets and the "mon-
eylenders,"   who had bought the assignments would suffer a loss of approximately $100,000.   Incidentally, I find no one as yet advancing the
claim of these purchasers for "restitution" of that money!   Why not?   All
of the pulls of human emotion were favorable to the spouses and children
and hostile to the business entrepreneurs.   Never has there been a more
striking example of the cliché that hard cases make bad law.   Surrogate
Di Falco, in August, 1967 found the will restraint on the alienation of
the principal valid.   The Appellate Division affirmed without opinion
[30 App.Div.2d 805].   Leave to go the the Court of Appeals was obtained
and, the Court of Appeals, in an opinion written by Judge Charles Breitel,
and concurred in by all members of the court except Chief Judge Stanley
Fuld, affirmed the Surrogate.   The family was safeguarded, but the law
of New York suffered a loss.

* * *

I respectfully urge upon you a prompt reconsideration of the social
wisdom of your law on spendthrift trusts;   and that this reconsideration
concern itself with:

1. the *abandonment* of the present rule that every trust of the most
commonly created type *must* be spendthrift in character whether the
settlor wishes it or does not;   confining permissible spendthrift trust[s]
to those set up pursuant to the express manifestation by settlor that
such is his desire; *

2. the *rounding out* of the rule now stated in N.Y.—McKinney's EPTL
7–1.5[d] so as not only to authorize the beneficiary of a spendthrift
trust to transfer his income to or for the benefit of his dependents;
but also expressly to authorize such persons to reach the trust income
for maintenance and support;

3. the *confining* of the doctrine of spendthrift trusts exclusively to
income, thus reversing the recent decision in the Vought case;   (this
position constitutes Section 4 of Erwin Griswold's model statute [§ 565],
proposed in 1936 and enacted into Law in LA Laws, 1938, Art. § 28).

4. The allowance of the creation of a spendthrift trust only for the
benefit of a relation by blood or marriage of the settlor;   (this restriction is now law in Alabama and North Carolina).

5. (and this is the most important of my suggestions) The establishment of a ceiling, stated either in terms of corpus (maybe $200,000,

---

* In 1973 the New York Law was amended to permit the creation of a non-spendthrift trust.
See p. 478, supra.   Ed.

as is now the rule in Virginia) or of income (maybe $10,000, as is now the rule in Louisiana) upon the amount *which* any one person can put into a spendthrift trust for another.   This would need careful safeguarding against multiple trusts of this character for the same beneficiary.   All this was done in Erwin Griswold's model statute (§ 565) proposed in 1936 and enacted into law in 1938 in Louisiana.

Notes

1. Even though the beneficiary's interest is non-assignable, an assignment by him is effective "as a revocable authorization to the trustee to make the payments."   Scott, Trusts § 152.3.   And of course, once the payment is received by the beneficiary, it is free of restrictions.   Minot v. Minot, 319 Mass. 253, 66 N.E.2d 5 (1946).

2. Can a valid distinction be drawn between an assignment of income and a contract to pay over income when received?   Contrast Bixby v. St. Louis Union Trust Co., 323 Mo. 1014, 22 S.W.2d 813 (1929) with Kelly v. Kelly, 11 Cal.2d 356, 79 P.2d 1059 (1938).   See Griswold, Spendthrift Trusts §§ 372–73 (2d ed. 1947).

3. If the settlor or testator prohibits voluntary alienation, saying nothing about involuntary alienation, the effect is to make the trust spendthrift (just as if both had been prohibited).   In re Wilson, 1 B.R. 439 (Btcy.Ct.W.D.Va.1980).   The same is true if involuntary alienation is alone prohibited.   Eaton v. Boston Trust Co., 240 U.S. 427, 36 S.Ct. 391, 60 L.Ed. 723 (1916).   Demonstrate how these results are logically necessary.

C.   INVOLUNTARY ALIENABILITY

ERICKSON v. BANK OF CALIFORNIA

Supreme Court of Washington, En Banc, 1982.
97 Wash. 2d 246, 643 P.2d 670.

DORE, Justice.

The trustee in bankruptcy for George Leslie Schafer appealed a summary judgment of the trial court dismissing his complaint, which attempted to reach the bankrupt's interest in the assets of a spendthrift trust.   The cotrustees of the trust refused to submit to an accounting of Schafer's interest in the trust.   The Court of Appeals set aside the trial court's summary judgment dismissal and remanded for a factual determination of whether the withholding of payment to the creditors was an abuse of the cotrustees' discretion in denying payments for "necessities". In doing so, the Court of Appeals held that RCW 30.30.120 was not intended to restrict the common law as it relates to spendthrift trusts and that a spendthrift trust does not vest by operation of law in the trustee in bankruptcy under section 70(a)(5) of the former Bankruptcy Act.   Erickson v. Bank of Cal., 28 Wash.App. 337, 623 P.2d 721 (1981).

The appellate court applied section 70(c) of the Bankruptcy Act, holding that a creditor who has furnished necessary goods or services to a beneficiary of a spendthrift trust may reach the beneficiary's interest in the trust if (1) the settlor intended that such necessities of life would be provided by trust funds *and* (2) the trustee of the spendthrift trust has authorized payment.

On appeal to this court, the cotrustees contend that all spendthrift trust provisions created by a settlor in a trust instrument are valid and enforceable, and that a trustee in bankruptcy cannot under any circumstances reach the income of the trust. In contrast, petitioner bankruptcy trustee urges that section 70(c) of the Bankruptcy Act gives him the same right to reach the spendthrift trust as a creditor holding a judgment against the bankrupt on the date of bankruptcy. Upon the expiration of the trust, any such creditor could obtain an order subjecting the vested remainder of the trust to execution for the debts of a remainderman.

FACTS

George Schafer filed a petition in bankruptcy on April 13, 1978. He and his siblings are beneficiaries of his mother's testamentary trust, clause 6, paragraph 4 of which provides that the cotrustees were given discretionary power to provide as much of the income and principal of the trust as necessary for the maintenance, support and education of each child until they each attain the age of 22.[9] Paragraph 5 of clause 6 of the testamentary trust in pertinent part provides as follows:

> If at any time the Co-Trustees, in their judgment, after taking into consideration all other resources, if any, which may then be known to the Co-Trustees to be available for each child, deem any child over twenty-two (22) years of age to be in need of maintenance, support and education, the Co-Trustees, in their discretion, may pay to or use for the benefit of such child so much of the trust estate then remaining as the Co-Trustees deem advisable for such needs. * * *

Clause 7 of the testamentary trust contains the following spendthrift provision:

> 4. The beneficial interest (in principal or income hereunder) of any beneficiary hereof shall not be subject to claims of the respective beneficiary's creditors or others, nor to legal process, and shall not be voluntarily or involuntarily assigned, alienated or encumbered;

---

9. Clause 6, paragraph 4 provides:

"The Co-Trustees shall use so much of the net income and principal of the trust estate or the remainder thereof as in their sole discretion is necessary for the maintenance, support and education of each living child, to-wit: GEORGE SCHAFER, ROBERTA SCHAFER, JOAN SCHAFER, and KENNETH SCHAFER, but when such child under twenty-two (22) attains such age, all payments hereunder to or for the benefit of such child shall cease, except as hereinafter provided; the Co-Trustees need not effect equal apportionment among such children under twenty-two (22) years of age, but can take into consideration the greater need of one child over the other, the availability of other income to support said child and the ability of said child to support himself or herself;"

Paragraph 6 of Clause 6 goes on to provide further:

"At such time as all of my children shall attain the age of twenty-two (22) years, my Co-Trustees shall * * * divide the trust estate then remaining into equal shares, one share for each then living child, and one share for each then deceased child having then living child or children. Such share shall * * * constitute separate trusts and shall be held, paid and distributed * * *

* * *

"Thereafter, when such child attains twenty-seven (27) years of age, the then remaining balance of the trust estate, principal accrued income, if any, shall be distributed to such child;"

Schafer filed his petition for bankruptcy at the age of 27, and his youngest sibling did not become 22 until 6 months later. Therefore, on the date on which the petition was filed, Schafer was not entitled to receive his portion of the trust assets.

I

We turn first to the issue of the validity of spendthrift trusts in Washington. Although unreasonable restraints on the alienation of real property are invalid, reasonable restraints on alienation have been upheld where justified by the legitimate interests of the parties. Bellingham First Fed. Sav. & Loan Ass'n v. Garrison, 87 Wash.2d 437, 553 P.2d 1090 (1976). RCW 6.32.250[10] has been said to have the "practical effect * * * to clothe every active trust with statutory spendthrift provisions, at least in so far [sic] as attempts by creditors of a beneficiary to reach his interest by legal process are concerned". Seattle First Nat'l Bank v. Crosby, 42 Wash.2d 234, 243, 254 P.2d 732 (1953).

In Milner v. Outcalt, 36 Wash.2d 720, 722, 219 P.2d 982 (1950), we upheld express spendthrift provisions in trust instruments, stating:

> We are of the opinion that the restraint on alienation of the principal or income of the trust is valid. * * * The essential idea of a spendthrift trust is that the beneficiary cannot deprive himself of the right to future income under the trust. * * * The intention of the settlor that the beneficiary should receive the trust property free and clear of liens and other charges, should be given effect. In view of the nature of these trusts, creditors of Outcalt were on notice of the restraints on alienation.

Ordinarily, a property owner has the power to dispose of his property as he wishes, as long as he does not violate public policy. The owner and donor of the property should be free to select the trust beneficiary who will enjoy his bounty, and should be able to put enforceable provisions in the trust which will prevent his trust beneficiary from voluntarily conveying or assigning his interest, thus precluding any creditor from taking that interest away from the beneficiary.

II

We turn next to the issue of whether the interest of the beneficiary in a spendthrift trust may be reached by a trustee in bankruptcy. Section 70(c) of the Bankruptcy Act, 11 U.S.C. § 110(c) (1976) provides in part:

> The trustee shall have as of the date of bankruptcy the rights and powers

---

10. RCW 6.32.250 provides:

"Property exempt from seizure. This chapter does not authorize the seizure of, or other interference with, any property which is expressly exempt by law from levy and sale by virtue of an execution, or any money, thing in action or other property held in trust for a judgment debtor where the trust has been created by, or the fund so held in trust has proceeded from, a person other than the judgment debtor; or the earnings of the judgment debtor for his personal services rendered within sixty days next before the institution of the special proceeding, where it is made to appear by his oath or otherwise that those earnings are necessary for the use of a family wholly or partly supported by his labor."

of: (1) a creditor who obtained a judgment against the bankrupt upon the date of bankruptcy, whether or not such a creditor exists, (2) a creditor who upon the date of bankruptcy obtained an execution returned unsatisfied against the bankrupt, whether or not such a creditor exists, and (3) a creditor who upon the date of bankruptcy obtained a lien by legal or equitable proceedings upon all property, whether or not coming into possession or control of the court, upon which a creditor of the bankrupt upon a simple contract could have obtained such a lien, whether or not such a creditor exists.

Petitioner also based his argument upon RCW 30.30.120, which provides:

Nothing in RCW 6.32.250 shall forbid execution upon the income of any trust created by a person other than the judgment debtor for debt arising through the furnishing of the necessities of life to the beneficiary of such trust; or as to such income forbid the enforcement of any order of the superior court requiring the payment of support for the children under the age of eighteen of any beneficiary; or forbid the enforcement of any order of the superior court subjecting the vested remainder of any such trust upon its expiration to execution for the debts of the remainderman.

The trustee contends specifically that (1) the bankrupt's interest was a vested remainder and that RCW 30.30.120 should apply; and (2) a creditor who furnishes necessities of life may reach the spendthrift trust, and a bankruptcy trustee may, likewise, reach the bankrupt's interest in the trust.

Petitioner's argument that RCW 30.30.120 should apply to § 70(c) is not persuasive. As the Court of Appeals noted, although the language of RCW 30.30.120 restricts the broad application of RCW 6.32.250, there is no indication that it was meant to restrict the common law as it relates to spendthrift trusts. Therefore, it is not applicable to a trust which contains an express spendthrift provision as permissible under common law.

The trustee in bankruptcy's argument that a creditor can assert a claim for necessities of life against the bankrupt beneficiary's interest in a spendthrift trust under section 70(c) of the Bankruptcy Act, however, is controlling. This "strong arm" provision's predecessor was said to confer upon the bankruptcy trustee the status of "the ideal creditor, irreproachable and without notice, armed cap-a-pie with every right and power which is conferred by the law of the state upon its most favored creditor who has acquired a lien by legal or equitable proceedings". In re Waynesboro Motor Co., 60 F.2d 668, 669 (S.D.Miss.1932). While the issue of whether the trustee is entitled to such a status is a federal question to be answered under the Bankruptcy Act, the extent of the trustee's rights, remedies and powers as a lien creditor are measured by the substantive law of the jurisdiction governing the property in question. See 4B W. Collier, Bankruptcy ¶70.49, at 602–03 (14th ed. 1978).

The Restatement (Second) of Trusts § 157 (1959) provides:

Although a trust is a spendthrift trust * * * the interest of the beneficiary can be reached in satisfaction of an enforceable claim against the beneficiary,

*   *   *

(b) for necessary services rendered to the beneficiary or necessary supplies furnished to him   *   *   *

In Knettle v. Knettle, 197 Wash. 225, 84 P.2d 996 (1938), this court held that under section 157, even a spendthrift trust may be subjected to the support of a wife or child, or the alimony awarded to the divorced wife of the beneficiary. The rationale for this exception—that the beneficiary is legally obligated on the debt and spendthrift trusts are sanctioned for the purpose of providing the beneficiary with living expenses—applies equally to suppliers of necessities. See G. Bogert, Trusts and Trustees § 224 (rev.2d ed. 1979).

The ultimate question thus becomes whether or not the trustee of the bankrupt estate can "step into the shoes" of such a hypothetical creditor described in section 70(c). This issue appears to be one of first impression, both here in Washington and in other jurisdictions. Several cases from other jurisdictions have held that if there are judgment creditors under state law who can garnish a certain portion of the income of the trust which would otherwise be exempt or inalienable, the trustee in bankruptcy may secure that portion of the trust through his powers under section 70(c). See cases in 4A W. Collier, Bankruptcy ¶ 70.26, at 370 n.8 (14th ed. 1978), including In re Irving Trust Co., 267 N.Y. 102, 195 N.E. 811, appeal dismissed and cert. denied, 296 U.S. 539, 56 S.Ct. 139, 80 L.Ed. 383 (1935); Sarver v. Towne, 285 N.Y. 264, 34 N.E.2d 313 (1941); Jenks v. Title Guarantee & Trust Co., 170 App.Div. 830, 156 N.Y.S. 478 (1915).

Although these cases appear to deal only with general judgment creditors, rather than creditors having "special claims," the policy is equally, if not more, applicable in cases of suppliers of necessities and alimony and child support claims. As a hypothetical lien creditor, the trustee in bankruptcy may "step into the shoes" of any creditor who *could* (but not necessarily *does*) exist under the terms of the trust. He may, therefore, invade the spendthrift trust in the place of the creditors who furnished "necessities" to Schafer as discussed above.

In this case, the settlor of the trust intended that necessities of life would be provided by trust funds. Suppliers of necessary goods and services to the beneficiary should be able to reach the beneficiary's interest in the trust, whether or not the withholding of payment is properly within the discretion of the cotrustees. We, therefore, decline to take the approach of In re Estate of Dodge, 281 N.W.2d 447 (Iowa 1979),[11] which the Court of Appeals relied upon in reaching its decision.

---

11. In In re Estate of Dodge, 281 N.W.2d 447, 451 (Iowa 1979) [p. 498 infra, Ed.], the court applied the Restatement (Second) of Trusts § 157(b) (1979) stating: "We do not adopt the § 157(b) standard without qualification and would require an additional showing similar to that made in this case, i.e., that (1) the claim is for necessary goods or services, not officiously rendered, which the settlor intended to be provided the beneficiary by trust funds; and (2) the withholding of payment for goods and services is not properly within the discretion granted the trustee by the instrument, before a creditor's claim may be enforced against the trustee of a support trust subject to a spendthrift clause."

The facts of this case further support our decision not to allow the trust beneficiary to defraud creditors by hiding behind a spendthrift trust provision. Section 70(a) of the Bankruptcy Act provides that all property which vests in the bankrupt within 6 months after bankruptcy by bequest, devise or inheritance shall vest in the bankruptcy trustee. Schafer incurred debts for numerous necessities such as doctors, ambulance services, telephone services, utilities and hospitals.[12] He then deliberately filed his petition in bankruptcy 6 months and 6 days before he believed his beneficial interest in the trust would vest, thus attempting to make his interest nontransferable to the bankruptcy trustee under federal law. Had Schafer filed bankruptcy just *7 days* later, his creditors could have secured the assets he received under the spendthrift trust. We cannot condone this obvious attempt to benefit from obtaining necessary goods and services without paying for them. The settlor of this trust would also undoubtedly disapprove of Schafer's effort to defraud the suppliers of necessities for which the settlor intended to provide.

CONCLUSION

We modify the Court of Appeals decision by holding that the ability of the trustee in bankruptcy to reach a beneficiary's interest in a spendthrift trust is not dependent upon the exercising of the trustee's discretionary power. Section 70(c) of the Bankruptcy Act allows the trustee in bankruptcy, as a hypothetical lien creditor holding a judgment against the debtor on the date of bankruptcy, to reach the spendthrift trust for debts incurred by Schafer for *necessities* of life. The settlor provided for the necessities of life for her children, and her intentions should not be arbitrarily violated. This is the only just and equitable conclusion in this matter. To hold otherwise would be to hand spendthrift trust beneficiaries an active sword for defrauding creditors against the public policy of this state.

We modify the Court of Appeals' reversal of the trial court's summary judgment of dismissal, and remand for a determination of whether the goods purchased were "necessities". If they were, and the amounts paid were reasonable, such purchases shall be paid from assets of the spendthrift trust.

BRACHTENBACH, C. J., and ROSSELLINI, STAFFORD, UTTER, DOLLIVER, WILLIAMS and DIMMICK, JJ., concur.

KELLER v. KELLER

Appellate Court of Illinois, First District, 1936.
284 Ill.App. 198, 1 N.E.2d 773.

MATCHETT, Justice. This appeal is by defendant trustees from a decree entered July 13, 1935, directing them to apply a portion of the income of a certain trust fund in their hands, otherwise payable to Theo-

---

12. See Bankruptcy Petition of George Schafer, Clerk's Papers, at 98–99, listing persons to whom he owed debts.

dore P. Keller, to the satisfaction of orders entered by the superior court of Cook county against him for the support of his minor children, Lloyd George and Edith Jane, during their minority. The cause was heard upon a stipulation of facts, and the question for our consideration concerns the law applicable thereto.

The summarized facts would appear to be that plaintiff, Marion Keller, and defendant Theodore P. Keller, were married January 17, 1917, and Lloyd George and Edith Jane were born of that marriage. May 17, 1926, Marion Keller sued Theodore P. Keller for separate maintenance in the superior court of Cook county, and May 28, 1927, she filed her amended bill praying for divorce. June 17, 1927, a decree in her favor was entered as prayed. The decree gave to her the care, custody, and education of these minor children, but no provision was made in the decree for the payment of alimony or for the support of the children. However, the day following the entry of the decree, Theodore P. Keller executed and delivered a trust indenture by which he conveyed to the Northern Trust Company and Marion Keller, as trustees, certain improved real estate situated in Chicago and known as 1245 Jarvis avenue; the express intention being thereby to provide adequate support for their children. At the time of the conveyance the real estate was incumbered by a mortgage for $17,000, and shortly after June 2, 1930, the income became insufficient to pay interest and expenses of upkeep, whereupon the trustees on April 16, 1934, in order to avoid the expense of foreclosure (and with the consent of Theodore P. Keller), conveyed the premises in satisfaction of the mortgage indebtedness. These minor children have lived with plaintiff, their mother, and have been supported by her, she being permitted to occupy one of the apartments at 1245 Jarvis avenue, but as she was unable to pay rent she has been compelled to vacate.

The father of Theodore P. Keller was Theodore C. Keller of Chicago, who died testate September 6, 1930, a resident of Cook county, and leaving a substantial estate. His will created a trust fund from which Theodore P. Keller is entitled to receive an income amounting to approximately $4,400 per annum.

The third paragraph of the will devises and bequeaths all the rest, residue, and remainder of his estate, subject to certain provisions of the first article, to his wife, Jessie P. Keller, and the National Bank of the Republic of Chicago, as trustees for the uses and purposes therein set forth. Paragraph 7 of the will provides for the payment of the income from the trust fund to the testator's children, including Theodore P. Keller, and provides, with respect to the payment of all income: " * * * Such payments to be made in installments, as often as found convenient by my trustees, but not less than twice in each year; each installment to be paid personally to the child entitled thereto, and not to be capable of anticipation or assignment." The will was executed about three years after the entry of the divorce decree against Theodore P. Keller. The question for determination is whether the court erred in subjecting this income of Theodore P. Keller to the support of his minor children.

The courts of different jurisdictions are not in harmony on the question of the validity of so-called "spendthrift trusts." In England, such trusts are held invalid as unlawful restraints on the alienation of property. Brandon v. Robinson, 18 Ves. 429. The courts of some American states have adopted the English rule upon the same reasoning. Tillinghast v. Bradford, 5 R.I. 205, and Smith v. Moore, 37 Ala. 327, are illustrative. The Supreme Court of the United States, however, gave the weight of its approval to the validity of such trusts in Nichols v. Eaton, 91 U.S. 716, 23 L.Ed. 254, the Supreme Court of Massachusetts likewise in Broadway Nat. Bank v. Adams, 133 Mass. 170, 43 Am.Rep. 504, and the Supreme Court of Pennsylvania in Overman's Appeal, 88 Pa. 276. These earlier decisions and many others from courts of different jurisdictions are discussed in Professor Gray's treatise on "Restraints on the Alienation of Property," published in 1883. The author presents with vigor arguments against the validity of such trusts as being contrary to good morals and against public policy. These objections, however, have not generally prevailed in American jurisdictions, which have usually approved such trusts as valid. The Supreme Court of Illinois declared in favor of the validity of such trusts in Steib v. Whitehead, 111 Ill. 247, decided in 1884. From that time the courts of this state have consistently adhered to the view that trusts of this kind are valid, as in Congress Hotel Co. v. Martin, 312 Ill. 318, 143 N.E. 838, 33 A.L.R. 562, where such trust was held valid, although consisting of property far exceeding the amount necessary to maintain the beneficiary according to her station in life. In Hopkinson v. Swaim, 284 Ill. 11, 119 N.E. 985, where such a trust created in favor of a daughter and which provided that the property should be "exempt from the power and control of any husband and from liabilities for any debts or engagements," was held valid. In Hartley v. Heirs of Wyatt, 281 Ill. 321, 117 N.E. 995, 996, the court said it was not necessary to use the word "spendthrift" in order to create such a trust, nor was it necessary that the writing should contain an express provision against the alienation of the trust property. "If," said the court, "it appears from the whole will that the testator intended to create such a trust, such an intention will be given effect." Cases to the same effect are Bennett v. Bennett, 217 Ill. 434, 75 N.E. 339, 4 L.R.A.(N.S.) 470; Wallace v. Foxwell, 250 Ill. 616, 95 N.E. 985, 50 L.R.A.(N.S.) 632; Jouvenat v. Continental Nat. Bank & Trust Co., 253 Ill.App. 400.

However, in the states affirmatively adhering to the doctrine of the validity of such trusts, there has appeared a determination to limit the cases in which the rule will be recognized by creating exceptions in certain classes of cases, where it is held upon various theories that the rule should not be applied. In 1 Bogert's Trusts & Trustees, § 223, p. 727, the author states: "Great efforts have been made to get courts and legislatures to make exceptions to their doctrine about spendthrift trusts, in favor of certain creditors with peculiarly powerful claims on the sympathy of courts. Restatement of the Law of Trusts, Tentative Draft § 183. To a certain extent these attempts have been successful. Perhaps the most striking example is found in the case of a spendthrift trust for a married man with a wife and children, where there is a failure to support his family, or there has been a divorce with a decree for the payment of alimony by the husband. It has been urged that the duty to support the wife and children is not a debt but a common law obligation placed upon the husband entirely outside contract principles, and attorneys for the wife have also argued that a spendthrift trust for a married man impliedly includes his wife and children as cestuis, so that an effort to get part of the income on their part is not an effort to break the trust but to have it carried out. Some support for these contentions is to be found in the common law decisions." A large number of these decisions, too numerous to be reviewed in this opinion, are cited in a footnote.

In Restatement of the Law of Trusts, vol. 1, § 157, p. 389, the prevailing doctrine is stated as follows:

"Although a trust is a spendthrift trust or a trust for support, the interest of the beneficiary can be reached in satisfaction of an enforceable claim against the beneficiary,

"(a) by the wife or child of the beneficiary for support, or by the wife for alimony;

"(b) for necessary services rendered to the beneficiary or necessary supplies furnished to him;

"(c) for services rendered and material furnished which preserve or benefit the interest of the beneficiary."

In a caveat the author states that the enumeration of situations in which the interest of the beneficiary of a spendthrift trust can be reached is not necessarily exclusive.

The leading case holding that such a trust fund may be reached for the support of a wife or child is that of In re Moorehead's Estate, 289 Pa. 542, 137 A. 802, 52 A.L.R. 1251. The court there concluded, after reviewing all the facts, that it was not the intention of the testatrix to impose such restrictions upon her estate, but other factors tending to the same conclusion were that such exemption would be contrary to public policy as releasing the husband from his primary obligations to society to support his family, and also destructive of the legal unity which common law recognized as existing between husband and wife. The latter argument does not seem quite persuasive when, as here, the trust is created after the unity of the family has been destroyed by a decree of divorce, but the biological reasons which demand that a father support his children were not destroyed by such a decree, and was given due weight in the opinion of the court.

The courts of California have reached a contrary conclusion. San Diego Trust & Savings Bank v. Heustis, 121 Cal.App. 675, 10 P.(2d) 158, decided in 1932. The opinion of the court there considers and disapproves of the reasoning in the Moorehead Case, and describes the Pennsylvania court as "laboring" to reach the result. The question, so far as the briefs disclose, has never been considered by the Supreme Court of Illinois, but that court and the Appellate Courts have indicated in no uncertain terms that the duty of a father to support his children is not regarded in the light of a merely contractual obligation. On the contrary, the nurture and the training of children of divorced parents in Kelley v. Kelley, 317 Ill. 104, 147 N.E. 659, 662, were held to be matters of vital interest to the state; the court pointing out that children are of the parents' blood, that it is not their fault that their parents may have been divorced, and that a divorce decree does not destroy their right to be given care "by those who brought them into the world until they are old enough to take care of themselves." That doctrine is expressed in innumerable cases of which we cite a few: Brand v. Brand, 252 Ill. 134, 96 N.E. 918; Walgreen Co. v. Industrial Commission, 323 Ill. 194, 153 N.E. 831, 48 A.L.R. 1199; Union Bank of Chicago v. Wormser, 256 Ill.App. 291. Indeed, the failure of a father to support his minor children under certain circumstances has been denounced by the Legislature of the state as a crime. Smith-Hurd Ann.St. c. 68, § 24, Ill.Rev.Stat.1935, c. 38, par. 2. There are many cases in the books which have sustained convictions for such offense in this and other states. State v. Miller, 111 Kan. 231, 206 P. 744, 22 A.L.R. 795, with Bluebook of Supplemental Decisions. People v. Baker, 222 Ill.App. 451.

Substantially the same question here presented was raised in England v. England, 223 Ill.App. 549. It was there contended by the trustees that the income from a spendthrift trust which had been created by the last will and testament of Albert T. England could not be subjected to the lien for alimony against the beneficiary, his son, Albert C. England. The opinion, based upon the theory that an intention on the part of the trustor to exclude the wife was not apparent from a consideration of the whole instrument, held that the obligation of the husband to support the wife was not founded upon a debt or contract, but was a social obligation, based on public policy and for the good of society.

In the later case of Tuttle v. Gunderson, 254 Ill.App. 552, the claim of a wife for alimony and for an allowance for the support and maintenance of her minor child from the proceeds or increment of a fund which had been left in trust to her husband was upheld as against the trustees, although the trust provided that the income and increment should be paid to the beneficiary "in person and not upon any written or verbal order, nor upon any assignment or transfer" by the beneficiary. The court reviewed the authorities in this and other states, and said: "The principles stated in Re Moorehead's Estate, in so far as they apply to the instant case are in accord with England v. England. In the notes to In re Moorehead's Estate, 52 A.L.R. 1259, the author says: 'Except where the trust was a spendthrift trust of the strictest sort, requiring the income to be paid to the beneficiary in person, and no one else (as in Board of Charities & Corrections v. Lockard (1901) 198 Pa. 572, 48 A. 496, 82 Am.St.Rep. 817) the courts have uniformly construed provisions for the protection of the beneficiary from the claims of creditors of the consequences of his own improvidence, as not preventing the income of the trust from being subjected to the support of the beneficiary's wife and minor children. See England v. England, supra; Gardner v. O'Loughlin (1912) 76 N.H. 481, 84 A. 935; Eaton v. Eaton (1924) 81 N.H. 275, 125 A. 433, 35 A.L.R. 1034; Id. on subsequent appeal (1926) 82 N.H. 216,

132 A. 10; Pruyn v. Sears (1916) 96 Misc. 200, 161 N.Y.S. 58; In re Moorehead's Estate (reported herewith) [289 Pa. 542, 137 A. 802, 52 A.L.R. 1251]; Decker v. Directors of Poor (1888) 120 Pa. 272, 13 A. 925; Board of Charities & Correction v. Moore (1888) 6 Pa.Co.Ct.R. 66, 19 Phila, 540, 45 Leg.Int. 216; Board of Charities & Correction v. Kennedy (1894) 3 Pa.Dist.R. 231, 34 Wkly. Notes Cas. 83.' After a careful consideration of the instant contention of the appellants, we have reached the conclusion that it is without merit."

The trustees here rely upon section 49 of the Chancery Act (Smith-Hurd Ann.St. c. 22, § 49, Cahill's Ill.Rev.Stat.1933, c. 22, par. 49), but the provisions of that statute are applicable only to merely contractual obligations.

The trustees contend also that even if a creditor of a beneficiary of a trust could obtain satisfaction in equity out of funds in the hands of the trustees, it would be improper to decree future payments by the trustees which the beneficiary did not then owe to the creditor. In this class of cases the court retains jurisdiction and will be able to decide each situation as it arises upon equitable principles.

We hold that because the will creating this trust fund does not expressly disclose an intention to the contrary, because the claim for support of children is one which transcends any contractual obligation, and because of the recognition in our law of the unity of the family, the court did not err in subjecting the income from this trust fund to the support of the minor children of the beneficiary. The weight of authority sustains this determination. Griswold Spendthrift Trusts, 1936, p. 292, Chap. V., §§ 331–340.

The decree is therefore affirmed.

Affirmed.

MCSURELY, P. J., and O'CONNOR, J., concur.

Notes

1. In Matt v. Matt, 105 Ill.2d 330, 85 Ill.Dec. 505, 473 N.E.2d 1310 (1985) The rule of the principal case was held to be reinforced by the 1983 Illinois Non-Support of Spouse and Children Act. The Restatement position was expressly rejected in Erickson v. Erickson, 197 Minn. 71, 266 N.W. 161 (1936). In accord with Keller v. Keller, however, see e.g. Bacardi v. White, 463 So.2d 218 (Fla.1985); Wife, J.G.B. v. Husband, P.J.G., 286 A.2d 256 (Del.Ch.1971).

2. On the alienability of due but unpaid distribution, see Sproul-Bolton v. Sproul-Bolton, 383 Pa. 85, 117 A.2d 688 (1955); Erickson v. Erickson, supra, note 1.

3. As to restraints on alienation of the beneficiary's interest in principal, the Restatement, Second, Trusts declares:

> § 153. *Restraint on Alienation of Principal*
>
> (1) Except as stated in §§ 156 [self-settled trusts] and 157 [see supra p. 486–87 and infra p. 495], if by the terms of a trust the beneficiary is entitled to have the principal conveyed to him at a future time, a restraint on the voluntary or involuntary transfer of his interest in the principal is valid.

(2) If the beneficiary is entitled to have the principal conveyed to him immediately, a restraint on the voluntary or involuntary transfer of his interest in the principal is invalid.

(3) If the principal is not to be conveyed to the beneficiary during his lifetime, a restraint on the voluntary transfer of his interest in the principal is invalid.

But see Erickson v. Erickson supra note 1.

ZOUCK v. ZOUCK
Court of Appeals of Maryland, 1954.
204 Md. 285, 104 A.2d 573.

HAMMOND, Judge.   The appeal in this case is from a decree ordering Henry Charles Zouck, one of the appellants, to perform the obligation he had assumed in a separation agreement executed several years before by him and his wife, Betty Long Zouck, the appellee.   A consideration of the agreement was the dismissal of a bill for divorce by the wife and a cross-bill by the husband, which had been filed in Baltimore, the matrimonial domicile.   The agreement provided that the custody of the daughter, then seven years old, would continue in the mother, that the father was to pay $25 a week for the support of the child and to assign certain insurance policies to the daughter and execute a will, under which there would pass to her his remainder interests in three trust estates. One of the trust estates was created by deed from the husband's father to the Safe Deposit and Trust Company, Trustee, the other appellant. The husband has not paid a cent since the execution of the agreement in 1949 and has never complied with any other of its terms, having thrown his executed copy into a trash can as he left the lawyer's office where it was signed.

The decree of the lower court directed the husband to pay up the arrearages in a lump sum and, thereafter, to pay $25 a week, as well as to assign the policies and to execute the will, as agreed.   It awarded custody of the daughter to the mother.

The trust held by the Safe Deposit and Trust Company, as Trustee, is a spendthrift trust.   Nevertheless, the court, in order to enforce compliance with its decree, held that jurisdiction of the court attached to the interest of the husband in the trust, both as to principal and income—in other words, that the spendthrift trust could be invaded for the satisfaction of the court's decree.

Both the husband and the wife are nonresidents of Maryland.   She lives in North Carolina, where she has supported herself and her daughter since the separation.   He, an engineer by profession, has worked in various places in this country and abroad.   * * *

It is earnestly contended by Zouck that whatever the power of the chancellor to require specific performance of the agreement, the court was without authority to authorize invasion of the spendthrift trust for enforcement of the decree.   The trustee makes a similar contention and urges beyond this, that as a matter of policy, the courts of Maryland should not lend their aid to the invasion of a domestic spendthrift trust, at the suit of a non-resident wife. The trust, by its terms, terminated in February of this year, when the youngest beneficiary became thirty-five. Whatever the rule elsewhere as to whether a trust for a short term of years is spendthrift as to principal, it seems clear that the language in the deed of trust is sufficient under the Maryland cases to make the trust spendthrift as to principal and income. Medwedeff v. Fisher, 179 Md. 192, 17 A.2d 141, 138 A.L.R. 1313.

Next to be considered then is whether the court erred in decreeing that the spendthrift trust could be reached to satisfy the decree for support, representing as it did, judicial approval of the agreement to pay, as fair, just and reasonable, and so entitled to specific performance. In Bauernschmidt v. Safe Deposit and Trust Co., 176 Md. 351, 4 A.2d 712, Maryland failed to treat as alimony an award of money granted by a California decree, which confirmed a separation agreement, although such a decree was effective as alimony in California. This Court held that the wife under the California decree was an ordinary contract creditor of the husband, and as such, could not reach his interest in a spendthrift trust. A different result was reached as to alimony in Safe Deposit and Trust Co. of Baltimore v. Robertson, 192 Md. 653, 65 A.2d 292, 295. There the Court quoted the Restatement of Trusts, Section 157, wherein it is set forth: " 'Sec. 157. Particular Classes of Claimants. Although a trust is a spendthrift trust or a trust for support, the interest of the beneficiary can be reached in satisfaction of an enforceable claim against the beneficiary, (a) by the wife or child of the beneficiary for support, or by the wife for alimony; * * *' " Judge Henderson said for the Court, quoting 1 Scott, Trusts, paragraph 157.1, that: " 'Even though ordinary contract creditors cannot reach the interest of the beneficiary of a spendthrift trust, it has been held in a number of cases that his interest can be reached by his wife or children to enforce their claims against him for support. * * *' " There followed a thorough analysis of the grounds on which this decision had been reached and applied in the various jurisdictions. The Court continued: "We think the view expressed in the *Restatement* is sound." The opinion pointed out that alimony is an obligation which continues during the joint lives of the parties and is a duty, not a debt. The opinion continued: "We think the rule that gives legal effect to spendthrift provisions as against contract creditors should not be extended to claims for support or alimony. In such situations the wife is a favored suitor, and her claim is based upon the strongest grounds of public policy. * * * We rest our decision upon grounds of public policy, not upon any interpretation of the instruments in question, * * *."

The Robertson case was followed by Hitchens v. Safe Deposit and Trust Co., 193 Md. 62, 66 A.2d 97, 99, where there was a separation agreement entitling the wife to "permanent alimony". This court held that the trial court was correct in refusing to permit its payment from a spendthrift trust, saying: "The appellant's claim is not based upon a lien or judgment, but merely upon an agreement to pay certain sums as 'permanent alimony,' and to pay one-third of the amount distributed to him after settlement of the estate. * * * In any event, we think the claim is barred by the spendthrift trust provisions. * * * The appellant is only a contract creditor and has not brought herself within the exception as to alimony laid down in Safe Deposit & Trust Co. [of Baltimore] v. Robertson [192 Md. 653], 65 A.2d 292."

The monetary claim in the present case is based, in essence, upon the statutory obligation of the father, declaratory of the common law, to support his child. It is true that under Article 72A, Section 1, of the Code 1951, the obligation of support is jointly and severally that of the father and the mother, but by the agreement in this case, the father bindingly obligated himself to meet that obligation by the payment of $25 a week, and to this extent, exonerated the mother from her obligation. The fact that the father has recognized his obligation and has agreed in writing to meet it in a specified amount, does not change his duty to a debt nor does it create the relationship of ordinary contract debtor and creditor between the father and the child, or the father and the mother, as the representative of or trustee for the child. Marsh v. Scott, 2 N.J.Super. 240, 63 A.2d 275, Shaw v. Shaw, 24 Del.Ch. 110, 9 A.2d 258, and Tullis v. Tullis, 138 Ohio St. 187, 34 N.E.2d 212. His obligation remains the same whether it be calculated and required by original order of court, by voluntary agreement, or by voluntary agreement specifically ordered to be performed by order of court. Nor is it significant that the mother for some years has met the obligation which the father violated, so that the money he promised to pay week by week, would now be paid, under court order, in a lump sum. Paragraph 10 of the separation agreement, after reciting the consideration moving from one to the other of the parties, including the abandonment by the wife of any claim to support, other than the nominal payment of $1.00 a week, sets forth that the daughter was: " * * * the principal beneficiary of the covenants and agreements herein contained." It was further provided that the real consideration was to require the husband: " * * * adequately to provide for the support of his minor child and to provide further for her upon the demise of the husband." The fundamental nature of the support looked for by the agreement is not changed because the husband is now required to pay at one time what he should have paid week by week.

We will not extend the holdings that a wife entitled to support by virtue of an agreement is a contract creditor only, who may not invade a spendthrift trust, but rather, here hold that a contract by a father to support a child, found by a court to be fair and reasonable, and so, judicially decreed to be enforced, is the equivalent of the decree of a court awarding support to the child or alimony to a wife, and as such, comes within the rule of public policy announced and followed in the Robertson case. There are differences between an agreement by a wife for support and such an agreement as to a child. The wife is *sui juris* and can make an agreement which, if otherwise valid, waives or concedes rights to whatever extent she desires. On the other hand, by such an agreement, she can exact from the husband concessions far beyond those which alimony would give her. Easy to foresee is a broken marriage where a grasping wife secures an agreement for the payment of exorbitant separate maintenance. The agreement might well be valid and so, enforceable, at the suit of the wife; yet, if its satisfaction were permitted from a spendthrift trust, not only would the will of the creator be frustrated, but the requirements of public policy be far exceeded because of the unreasonableness of the allowance. In the case of a child, the obligation of the father to support, imposed by law, cannot be bargained away or waived. Any provision of an agreement for the child may be disregarded by a court, which can increase or decrease an allowance for support. Article 16, Section 37 of the Code 1951; Boggs v. Boggs, 138 Md. 422, 114 A. 474, and Melson v. Melson, 151 Md. 196, 134 A. 136. We find then that the agreement by a parent to support a child, declared to be reasonable and proper, and so, enforceable by a court, constitutes an obligation which justifies the invasion of a spendthrift trust for its fulfillment. The public policy which underlies this holding certainly does not run counter to the recent trend of public policy in related matters. In 1950—after the decisions in the Bauernschmidt, Robertson, and Hitchens cases—the people amended Article III, Section 38, of the Constitution of Maryland, so that it reads: "No person shall be imprisoned for debt, *but a valid decree of a court of competent jurisdiction or agreement approved by decree of said court for the support of a wife or dependent children, or for alimony, shall not constitute a debt within the meaning of this section.*" (Italicized portion added by amendment.) Two things are significant: first, an agreement for support or alimony, approved by a court of competent jurisdiction, is equated to a decree of such court for support or alimony, neither being a debt; second, the agreement in the case before us was approved by a court of competent jurisdiction. A second evidence of the trend of public policy—and this would seem to answer the argument of the trustee that a non-resident wife is not to be favored as against a domestic spendthrift trust—is found in the Uniform Reciprocal Enforcement of Support Act, codified as Article 89C of the Code 1951. By the enactment of that law, the Legislature showed a policy of liberality towards the enforcement in Maryland of the claims of non-resident wives and children entitled to support. See also State v. James, 203 Md. 113, 100 A.2d 12. Indeed, the common law rule has been said to be that a wife could reach for support property of a husband in a state in which neither she nor he resided. George v. George, 23 A.2d 599, 20 N.J.Misc. 41. The chancellor was justified, therefore, in passing the decree as to payments of income and principal to make up the arrearages and for the deposit of the balance of Zouck's share of the trust estate in the registry of the court, subject to its further order. Article 16, Section 222 of the Code 1951; Oles Envelope Corp. v. Oles, 193 Md. 79, 94, 65 A.2d 899, Johnson v. Johnson, Md., 97 A.2d 330, and Ricketts v. Ricketts, 4 Gill 105. Of course, future orders of the court in respect to the impounding of the funds, should not require the holding of more than enough to meet the weekly payments until the child passes her minority.

*   *   *

Case remanded for passage of a decree in conformity with this opinion. Costs to be paid by the appellants.

HENDERSON, J., dissents in part.

D. DISCRETIONARY AND SUPPORT TRUSTS

MATTER OF ESTATE OF DODGE

Supreme Court of Iowa, 1979.
281 N.W.2d 447.

REES, Justice.

This is an appeal by Hunter L. Scott, trustee under the will of Carolyn L. Dodge from the order and judgment of the trial court requiring him to reimburse Eleanor Scott Paine for expenditures personally made by her for the support of the trust beneficiary, Margaret Scott Bowers.

The will of Carolyn L. Dodge, who died in 1954, provided for the establishment of several trusts. The trust involved herein was to be administered for the use and benefit of the testator's niece, Margaret Scott Bowers, by her brother, Hunter L. Scott. The will granted the trustee "the right to disburse or use any portion of the principal for the care and maintenance" of the beneficiary and, inter alia, contained an additional spendthrift provision:

The interests of the beneficiaries in the trust created in this Will as to principal and income shall not be * * * subject to any legal process, nor subject in any manner to the interference, control or claims of creditors, nor be liable for the debts of the beneficiaries.

In 1971 appellee Eleanor Scott Paine, the guardian and sister of Margaret, filed objections to the 1970 and 1971 annual reports of the trustee, alleging that Hunter L. Scott should be required to invade the principal of the trust due to the insufficiency of the income therefrom to meet the needs of Margaret, who was suffering from mental illness and required care in a rest home. No hearings were held on the objections to the reports, nor were orders entered disposing of them.

Margaret Scott Bowers died in April of 1976 and in July of the same year the trustee filed his final report and requested discharge. Eleanor filed an objection to the report on August 16, alleging that Margaret had incurred unpaid expenses which should have been satisfied out of the trust principal.

On March 3, 1977, subsequent to commencement of this action, the court made an adjudication of law points pursuant to rule 105, Iowa Rules of Civil Procedure, in which it held that Eleanor could pursue her claim as a creditor in her own right and that, despite the spendthrift provision of the trust instrument, "necessary" items provided by or paid for by Eleanor could be the proper subject of her claim.

On May 17, 1977, Eleanor amended her objection to state that she had advanced substantial funds for the support and maintenance of Margaret, including a summary of such expenditures. At the hearing before the trial court in December of 1977, Eleanor testified that she had paid for expenses of Margaret such as nursing home care, doctor bills, hospital expenses and personal items. On February 9, 1978 the trial court entered its order allowing Eleanor's claim for $40,783.81 against the trust for necessary expenditures made by Eleanor for Margaret's support.

The trustee filed a motion for a new trial on February 21, 1978, which was overruled. He then perfected timely appeal to this court.

Eleanor Scott Paine has since died and the executors of her estate have been substituted herein as appellees.

The appellant states the following issues for review:

(1) Was the trust administered by Hunter L. Scott not a discretionary trust as to principal such that a creditor could not compel payment for any claim by the trustee?

(2) Would not the spendthrift clause of the trust instrument preclude payment of Eleanor's claim as a creditor?

(3) Should Eleanor have been required to reduce her claim against the beneficiary to judgment before attempting to enforce her claim against the trust?

* * * As noted by the defendant, rule 105 does limit subsequent reference or objection to those points of law already adjudicated. For purposes of determining whether error has been preserved in this case, we must examine the arguments of parties prior to the adjudication of points of law and those points passed upon by the court.

We conclude that the only issue which the defendant urges on appeal and which was both argued to and decided by the trial court concerns the effect to be given the spendthrift clause of the trust instrument. While the trial court did find the trust to be one for the support of the beneficiary rather than a classic discretionary trust, the precise issue presented by the pleadings was whether there had been an abuse of discretion by the trustee. It was not directly asserted that the trust was purely discretionary. This is a fine distinction and it may reasonably be argued that characterization of the trust is a necessary preliminary step to establishing a standard for review. On the merits we concur in the trial court's determinations that the requisite grant of unfettered or unlimited discretion necessary to find a discretionary trust was lacking and that the instrument evidences an intent to support the beneficiary. See Restatement (Second) of Trusts § 155, comment c (1979); G. Bogert, The Law of Trusts and Trustees § 227, 715–17 (2d ed. 1965); II A. Scott, The Law of Trusts § 155, 1181–83 (3d ed. 1967); E. Griswold, Spendthrift Trusts § 430 (1936). The discretion which a trustee may exercise in discharging his or her duties is clearly distinguishable from the virtually unlimited grant of discretion which characterizes a purely discretionary trust.

Nowhere in the pleadings does the defendant contend that the plaintiff's action must fail due to the claim not having been reduced to judgment; nor does it appear that the trial court passed upon this proposition. As this argument is being pressed for the first time on appeal, we will not pass upon its merits.

III. We thus reach the sole issue properly preserved and presented by this appeal: the effect to be given the spendthrift clause of the trust instrument. The defendant alleges this clause bars the assertion of claims of creditors against the beneficiary's interest in the trust. A literal application of the clause would defeat recovery in this case. The trial court permitted recovery, based upon the exception expressed in Restatement (Second) of Trusts § 157:

> Although a trust is a spendthrift trust or a trust for support, the interest of the beneficiary can be reached in satisfaction of an enforceable claim against the beneficiary * * * (b) for necessary services rendered to the beneficiary or necessary supplies furnished to him. * * * " [13]

The court found the consistency of the support purpose of the trust with the nature of the services rendered to compel recovery despite the spendthrift clause. We agree.

Spendthrift provisions in trust instruments are generally valid in Iowa. See, e.g., In re Bucklin's Estate, 243 Iowa 312, 51 N.W.2d 412 (Iowa 1952). We have not previously been faced with the position stated by Restatement § 157(b), although we have in the past rejected § 157(a) which would make available support or spendthrift trust funds for the support or alimony of the beneficiary's children or wife. In re Bucklin's Estate; Roorda v. Roorda, 230 Iowa 1103, 300 N.W. 294 (1941); DeRousse v. Williams, 181 Iowa 379, 164 N.W. 896 (1917). In so doing, we acknowledged the power of the donor to limit or place conditions on the disbursement of trust funds.

We find the trust instrument in the case before us here sufficiently distinguishable from those regarding child support and alimony to allow recovery by the plaintiff. Here the trust was one expressly for the support of the beneficiary which left much less discretion to the trustee than had been granted to the trustee in either *Bucklin* or *Roorda*. The discretion vested in the trustees in *Bucklin* and *Roorda* was much more akin to that of a true discretionary trust. Here the instrument requires use of the trust income for the maintenance of the beneficiary and permits invasion of the trust corpus to achieve that end. Our reading of the whole of the trust instrument leads us to conclude that the testator intended the trust principal to be applied, as necessary, for the support and maintenance of Margaret Scott Bowers. We therefore also conclude, as did the trial court, that the trustee abused his discretion in not invading the trust principal.

Construction of the trust instrument to determine the intent of the testator is essential to our resolution of this issue. Other courts, in deciding whether to apply Restatement § 157(b) in particular situations, have focused on whether such a result would be consistent with the testator's intent as evidenced by the terms of the instruments and the degree of discretion granted the trustee. See, e.g., In re McLoughlin, 507 F.2d 177 (5th Cir. 1975); American Security and Trust Co. v. Utley, 127 U.S. App.D.C. 235, 382 F.2d 451 (1967); In re Lackmann's Estate, 156

---

13. As this trust is one for support with a spendthrift provision, it contains elements of both of the trusts discussed by the *Restatement*. Section 157 is therefore definitely applicable.

Cal.App.2d 674, 320 P.2d 186 (1958); In re Estate of Hinckley, 195 Cal.App.2d 164, 15 Cal.Rptr. 570 (1961); City of Bridgeport v. Reilly, 133 Conn. 31, 47 A.2d 865 (1946); In re Mayer's Will, 59 N.Y.S.2d 561 (Sur.1945); State v. Rubion, 158 Tex. 43, 308 S.W.2d 4 (1958); Smith v. Plainview Hospital and Clinic Foundation, 393 S.W.2d 424 (Tex.Civ. App.1965). If the payment of the claim is consistent with the donor's discernable intent and the discretion granted the trustee is not such that payment could properly be withheld, enforcement of the claim has generally been allowed despite the existence of a support trust or spendthrift clause. American Security and Trust Company v. Utley, 453 of 382 F.2d ("We view the primary purpose of such a trust to assure that the beneficiary will be provided for independent of his own improvidence. To accomplish this the income need not be made immune from debts incurred for the necessities of life, indeed to allow such claims is entirely compatible with the purpose of the trust.") In re Lackmann's Estate; State v. Rubion. As noted earlier, the purpose of this trust and the resulting degree of discretion granted Hunter L. Scott distinguishes this case from the prior decisions of this court where spendthrift clauses were found to bar the claims asserted and application of Restatement § 157(a) was rejected.

We hold, on the facts of this case and the language of the trust instrument, that the trial court did not err in applying Restatement (Second) of Trusts § 157(b). We do not adopt the § 157(b) standard without qualification and would require an additional showing similar to that made in this case, i.e., that (1) the claim is for necessary goods or services, not officiously rendered, which the settlor intended to be provided the beneficiary by trust funds; and (2) the withholding of payment for the goods and services is not properly within the discretion granted the trustee by the instrument, before a creditor's claim may be enforced against the trustee of a support trust subject to a spendthrift clause.

In so holding, we do not call into question the continued general validity of spendthrift clauses in Iowa nor of the Iowa precedents upholding such clauses. We continue to give primary attention to the language of the trust instrument and the intent of the testator or settlor expressed therein.

Credit was extended to the beneficiary for services, largely nursing home expenses, necessary for her support and maintenance, the purpose for which the trust was established. Several trusts were established by the will in question, all subject to the spendthrift clause. In resolving the tension between the support purpose of the specific trust and the instrument's general spendthrift clause, we think it best and more consistent with the settlor's intent to affirm the trial court's allowance of the claim. See People v. Casias, 549 P.2d 803 (Colo.App.1976). To bar this claim for necessary services rendered the deceased beneficiary would unjustly enrich the trust corpus at the expense of the creditor, a result contrary to the intent of the testator which would effectively vest the trustee with greater discretion than that granted by the trust instrument.

The judgment and decree of the trial court is therefore affirmed.

Notes

Handwritten margin note: NO, just this one!

1. The court in the principal case evidently assumes that a support trust cannot also be a discretionary trust. In Abravanel, Discretionary Support Trusts, 68 Iowa L.Rev. 273 (1983), it is argued that the hybrid form should be accorded wider recognition than it has so far received.

Handwritten margin note: Intent = to allow debts, that's reason for descent

2. Show how a creditor has more bargaining power against the beneficiary of a discretionary trust than against the beneficiary of a spendthrift or support trust.

3. Even where the trustee is given "absolute discretion" he is subject to judicial control to prevent abuse of his discretion since the discretionary power is held in a fiduciary capacity. In some circumstances the court will even order a distribution; see, e.g., In re Chusid's Estate, 60 Misc.2d 462, 466, 301 N.Y.S.2d 766, 771–72 (Surr.Ct.1969).

4. A trust can be both discretionary and spendthrift. *[handwritten: — provision — form]*

5. Sections 154 and 155 of the Trusts Restatement do not adequately distinguish between discretionary and support trusts. Support trusts involve a restriction of the trustee's power, whereas discretionary trusts involve its expansion. Support trusts generally have all the characteristics of spendthrift trusts (but, unlike them, do not require the use of language prohibiting alienation or rendering creditor process ineffective), and are generally enforced as such even in states not otherwise recognizing the effectiveness of spendthrift restrictions.

6. In England and a few of the American states, where spendthrift trusts are not recognized, forfeiture restraints (whereby attempted assignment of the interest, or a creditor's attempt to reach it, will cause it to terminate) are nevertheless enforced. For an example of an instrument creating a forfeiture restraint, see In re Villar, Chapter Nine, Section Three, infra, p. 756.

E.   SELF-SETTLED TRUSTS

SECURITY TRUST CO. v. SHARP

Delaware Court of Chancery, New Castle County, 1950.
32 Del.Ch. 3, 77 A.2d 543.

SEITZ, Vice Chancellor. In this action plaintiff seeks instructions from the court as to the validity of an assignment of trust income to certain educational and charitable institutions by the largest income beneficiary of the trust.

On December 14, 1931 Isabella duPont Sharp entered into a trust agreement with plaintiff trustee establishing a trust with respect to 500 shares of stock. Under a provision thereof, the trust income was payable to her husband, Hugh Rodney Sharp, for his lifetime, and upon his death if she should survive him, to her for her lifetime. On the same date Hugh Rodney Sharp entered into an agreement with plaintiff establishing an identical trust (mutatis mutandis) in respect of 500 shares of the same stock. The income was payable to Mrs. Sharp for her lifetime and upon her death, if Mr. Sharp survived her, to him for his lifetime. The remainders went to their children or their survivors.

On December 30, 1935 these agreements were amended by the parties in interest to provide that a certain amount of income of each trust should be paid to the sons of Mr. and Mrs. Sharp, the remainder of the income to be paid as theretofore directed.

Mrs. Sharp died testate on December 17, 1946. Thereafter the executors encountered certain difficulties with the Bureau of Internal Revenue. After the enactment of the so-called "Technical Changes Act" of October 25, 1949, 26 U.S.C.A. § 811(c), the only important legal question remaining between the Bureau and the executors was the applicability of the "reciprocal trust" theory, i.e., the doctrine that each of the two trusts such as the two Sharp trusts is created in consideration of the other, and therefore the creator of trust A is to be deemed in law the "settlor" of trust B and has made a transfer under which he "has retained for his life * * * the income from the property" transferred; from which it follows that trust B is includible in his estate under the provisions of the Joint Resolution of March 3, 1931, 46 Stat.L. 1516, 26 U.S.C.A.Int. Rev.Acts, page 227.

From the commissioner's determination that the trusts were reciprocal the executors on January 26, 1950 appealed to the Tax Court. Thereafter a settlement consented to by all parties was reached. This settlement was embodied in a stipulation and two agreements. For purposes of this settlement the two trusts were considered to be reciprocal. Mrs. Sharp was considered to have furnished the consideration for Mr. Sharp's trust and to have been the settlor thereof. Accordingly, a portion of Mr. Sharp's trust was included in Mrs. Sharp's gross estate. The tax was determined on the basis of these documents. No part of the trust created by Mrs. Sharp was included in her gross estate.

On June 3, 1950 Mr. Sharp executed and delivered to the plaintiff trustee an instrument of assignment, assigning to eight educational or charitable institutions in certain designated amounts all the trust income payable to him from the trust created by Mrs. Sharp. All of the assignees have accepted the gifts. Thereafter plaintiff trustee filed this suit for instructions seeking to ascertain whether such assignment is valid. The named defendants are Mr. Sharp and the assignees. They have all filed answers admitting jurisdiction and admitting, with few exceptions, the averments of the complaint. By stipulation of the parties, the case is being heard and determined upon the facts alleged in the complaint and admitted in the answer of the defendant Sharp plus certain additional facts set forth in a stipulation of the parties. Since all defendants contend that the assignment is valid, amici curiae were appointed to present arguments against its validity.

The ultimate question before the court is whether Mr. Sharp's assignment is invalid because of the provisions of the first paragraph of Paragraph Tenth of Mrs. Sharp's trust of December 14, 1931. This paragraph reads as follows:

"Tenth: It is hereby agreed between the Settlor and the Trustee that the trusts hereby created are irrevocable, and that no part of the principal or income of the Trust Estate hereby created shall be subject to control,

Spendthrift provsn

debts, liabilities and/or engagements of any of the beneficiaries thereof, and no part of said principal or income shall be subject to assignment or alienation by them, or any of them, or to execution or process for the enforcement of judgments or claims of any sort against such beneficiaries, or any of them."

Defendants' principal argument in favor of the validity of the assignment goes like this: The prohibition in a trust agreement against the alienation of income by a beneficiary does not apply where the beneficiary is also the settlor. This is so because public policy does not permit one to create a spendthrift trust with his own property for his own benefit. This rule is unaffected by the existence of a statute validating spendthrift trusts. He who furnishes the consideration for the creation of a trust is deemed to be the settlor thereof; in the case of "reciprocal trusts", each is deemed to be the consideration for the other, and the nominal creator of one is deemed to be the real settlor of the other. Mr. Sharp having furnished the consideration for Mrs. Sharp's trust, the two trusts being reciprocal, he should here be treated as the real settlor of Mrs. Sharp's trust.

The amici curiae make the following answer to this contention: Even if the trusts here are reciprocal, Mrs. Sharp is the settlor of the trust in question because (1) the property transferred in trust by her was her own. She imposed the limitations on the right of the beneficiaries to control. Mr. Sharp, as a beneficiary, accepted the trust on the conditions stated and acquiesced therein for more than 15 years. Mr. Sharp and his assignees are therefore estopped to deny the validity of the provision prohibiting assignment of income. And (2), the reciprocal trust theory which treats the beneficiary as the settlor of the trust of which he is beneficiary, is confined to tax cases and is not applicable to situations involving general trust law.

All of the defendants' legal arguments are premised on the assumption that Mr. Sharp should be here treated as the settlor of Mrs. Sharp's trust. In discussing the legal principles, I shall make the same assumption and thereafter decide the point assumed.

In the not unusual case, a person creates a so-called spendthrift trust for his own benefit by transferring his own property in trust for himself. He may do the same thing by providing the consideration for a conveyance by another person to the trustee. In the latter case the interest of the person who furnishes the consideration for the creation of the trust will be treated, at least for certain purposes, the same as if it had resulted from a conveyance of his own property directly to the trustee. See Griswold Spendthrift Trusts (2d Ed.) Sec. 487; 1 Scott on Trusts Sec. 156.3.

This court has ruled that a settlor-beneficiary of a spendthrift trust in which no other party is interested may terminate it at will. This is true even though the trust agreement contains a prohibition against termination. See Weymouth v. Delaware Trust Co., Del.Ch., 45 A.2d 427; and compare Wilmington Trust Co. v. Carpenter, Del.Ch., 75 A.2d 815. It has likewise been generally held that a settlor-beneficiary of a life estate in a trust containing a prohibition against assignment may, nevertheless, assign his interest. See Griswold Spendthrift Trusts (2d Ed.) Sec. 494. This rule is based on public policy which does not permit one to create a spendthrift trust with his own property for his own benefit. This appears to be justified on the theory that one should not be permitted to have the substantial benefits of ownership without its burdens. Since the law does not permit him to use the trust to escape the burdens of ownership, the courts do not hold him to his self-imposed restraint on his own property. This seems reasonable. See Byrnes v. Commissioner, 3 Cir., 110 F.2d 294. Considering the matter apart from our spendthrift trust statute, I conclude that the settlor-beneficiary of a life estate may assign his interest even though the trust instrument contains a prohibition against assignment of income. I see no reason to differentiate between his right to terminate his interest and his right to assign it.

Does our spendthrift trust statute validate the provision of the trust agreement prohibiting assignment of income? The statute [14] provides: "The creditors of a beneficiary of a trust shall have only such rights against such beneficiary's interest in the trust property or the income therefrom as shall not be denied to them by the terms of the instrument creating or defining the trust or by the laws of this State; provided, however, that if such beneficiary shall have transferred property to the trust in defraud of his creditors the foregoing shall in no way limit the rights of such creditors with respect to the property so transferred. Every interest in trust property or the income therefrom which shall not be subject to the rights of the creditors of the beneficiary, as aforesaid, shall be exempt from execution, attachment, distress for rent, and all other legal or equitable process instituted by or on behalf of such creditors. Every assignment by a beneficiary of a trust of his interest in the trust property or the income therefrom which is, by the terms of the instrument creating or defining the trust unassignable, shall be void."

The language of the statute is not circumscribed in terms and might be said to impliedly embrace settlor-beneficiary interests. However, I believe, in the light of the common law applicable to the settlor-beneficiary situation when the statute was passed (1933), the statute should not be held applicable to settlor-beneficiary trust interests. The reasons for this construction are more apparent in cases where creditors have attacked self-imposed prohibitions on alienation. See Schenck v. Barnes, 156 N.Y. 316, 50 N.E. 967, 41 L.R.A. 395. However, in view of the strong, perhaps "judicially" created, public policy against restraints on alienation, I conclude that the statute does not apply to the interest of a settlor-beneficiary. Compare Schenck v. Barnes, supra. In view of its overall implications I would want to see the most explicit statutory language before I would feel justified in concluding that the statute encompassed settlor-beneficiary interests. Compare Tracey v. Franklin, Del., 67 A.2d 56; Wilmington Trust Company v. Carpenter, supra.

14. Revised Code of Delaware 1935, Paragraph 4415. Although Mrs. Sharp's trust was created prior to the enactment of this statute, I shall assume, without deciding, that the validity of the assignment requires a consideration of the statute.

I need not consider what would have been the law in Delaware prior to the adoption of the spendthrift trust statute because it is not contended that such law would have validated the provision prohibiting the assignment of a settlor-beneficiary's interest.

It follows from the foregoing legal principles which I have here adopted that the assignment is valid if Mr. Sharp is to be considered the settlor of Mrs. Sharp's trust. Should Mr. Sharp be treated here as though he were the settlor of Mrs. Sharp's trust?

As to the trust of which Mrs. Sharp is the nominal settlor, did Mr. Sharp furnish the consideration for the transfer of the stock made to the trust by Mrs. Sharp? In order to answer this question, consideration must be given to the facts surrounding the creation of the trust in question.

Mrs. Sharp, with the assistance of an attorney, executed the trust agreement in question on December 14, 1931. She transferred to Security Trust Company, trustee, 500 shares of common stock which she owned in Delaware Realty and Investment Company. Under the terms of the trust agreement Mrs. Sharp was the nominal settlor. The trust income was payable to her husband, Hugh Rodney Sharp, for his lifetime and upon his death, if she survived him, to her for her lifetime. Under certain circumstances, if the trust continued, the income was payable to the Sharp children or their survivors in equal shares. Upon the death of the survivor of certain individuals, the trust was to terminate and the assets were to be distributed in equal shares to the Sharp children or their survivors.

By an agreement of the same date Mr. Sharp, with the assistance of the same attorney, created a trust with the same trust company. He also conveyed to the trustee 500 shares of common stock which he owned in Delaware Realty Investment Company. His wife was to receive the income for life and upon her death, if Mr. Sharp survived her, it was payable to him for his lifetime. Under the same certain circumstances as appeared in Mrs. Sharp's trust, if the trust continued, the income was to be divided equally among the Sharp children or their survivors. It was provided that upon termination of the trust the assets should be divided in equal shares among the Sharp children or their survivors.

On the basis of the undisputed facts just narrated, I conclude that Mrs. Sharp executed her trust agreement in consideration of Mr. Sharp's executing his trust agreement and vice versa. These trusts are what are known as reciprocal trusts. I base my conclusion on the identity of creation dates, similarity of terms, identity of trustees and attorney, sizes of the trusts, similarity of assets, and the relationship of the parties and the beneficiaries. Compare Orvis v. Higgins, 2 Cir., 180 F.2d 537. It thus becomes unnecessary to consider whether the proceedings in the Tax Court of the United States constituted a determination here binding as to the reciprocal nature of these trusts.

In certain tax fields one reciprocal trust is deemed to constitute the consideration for the other and the nominal creator of one is deemed to be the real settlor of the other. See Lehman v. Commissioner, 2 Cir.,

109 F.2d 99; In re Perry's Estate, 111 N.J.Eq. 176, 162 A. 146. Defendants urge that this rule should be applied in the field of general trust law so that Mr. Sharp would be considered here to be the settlor of Mrs. Sharp's trust.

Amici curiae argue that the principle applied to tax cases involving reciprocal trusts should not be adopted in the trust law field generally. They point out that it has a practical justification in tax law, that it has not been recognized in any case involving a nontax situation and that its general application would result in certain bizarre consequences where the trust instrument imposes duties on the settlor.

It is unnecessary to discuss the reasons for the application of the principle in so-called reciprocal trust tax cases. It is sufficient to say that the courts have decided that the form will not be permitted to obscure the substance of the transaction. However, the fact that the trusts are reciprocal is not in and of itself the vital point because, as the court said in the Lehman case, "The fact that the trusts were reciprocated or 'crossed' is a trifle, quite lacking in practical or legal significance." [109 F.2d 100.] The important fact in such situations is that one trust was executed in consideration of the execution of the other. Being practically identical in both purpose and objective, the court—looking to substance—will say that each party, by indirection, created a trust for his own benefit. Moreover, it is not unlikely that the same approach would be taken by the courts when such trusts are attacked by creditors. See the dictum in Provident Trust Co. v. Banks, 24 Del.Ch. 254, 9 A.2d 260.

Since the court will look through form to substance, in order to impose burdens on the interest of a settlor-beneficiary, I think it would be highly inequitable to insist that he be bound by what are in reality self-imposed restraints on the alienability of his interest. In other words I think the equities warrant the court in concluding that the principle recognized in the so-called reciprocal trust tax cases and creditors' cases should also be applied when the question of alienability of income is involved. The same result is justified when the substance of the transaction is examined in the light of general trust principles. See 1 Restatement of the Law of Trusts Sec. 156e.

The argument of amici curiae that Mrs. Sharp's expressed intention should control cannot be accorded substantial weight here when the basic objectives sought to be reached by the creation of the two trusts are brought into sharp focus. For the same reasons, it would be inequitable to impose an estoppel against Mr. Sharp and his assignees. I recognize that there is much substance to the estoppel argument when the case arises as it does here, but the law has stripped this type of trust of much of its substance. Having done so, the basis for upholding the validity of the provisions in the present situation loses much of its force. Thus, I conclude that Mr. Sharp and his assignees are not estopped to attack the validity of the provision prohibiting the assignment of income.

The question as to the identity of the settlor for purposes of performing other trust duties will be determined when and if the matter is ever presented. Other arguments of counsel need not be considered.

I conclude that the assignment by Hugh Rodney Sharp is valid and the trustee is to be governed accordingly.

Order on notice.

Notes

1. The same result is reached by statute in a number of states, e.g., Illinois, Tennessee, and Washington.

2. Why should it be impossible for a person to establish a spendthrift trust for himself? See, e.g., Griswold, Spendthrift Trusts at 644–5; Note, 64 Colum. L.Rev. 1323 (1964); Johnson v. First National Bank of Jackson, p. 531 infra; cf. Watterson v. Edgerly, 40 Md.App. 230, 388 A.2d 934 (1978).

SECTION FIVE. TERMINATION OF TRUSTS

A. TERMINATION PURSUANT TO THE TRUST INSTRUMENT

GABEL v. MANETTO

Superior Court of New Jersey, Appellate Division, 1981.
177 N.J.Super. 460, 427 A.2d 71.

JOELSON, J. A. D.

H: YES

The question in this case is whether an express *inter vivos* trust of real property can be revoked orally. It is an issue which apparently has not been decided in this State. The trial judge ruled that such an *inter vivos* trust cannot be revoked orally. We disagree and reverse.

Joseph Manetto executed a trust agreement on March 7, 1964 relating to rental property owned by him in Bloomfield. On the same day he executed a bargain and sale deed conveying the same property to his son, Peter Manetto, as trustee. Both the trust agreement and the deed were recorded several weeks later in the Essex County Register's Office. The trust agreement, which was specifically referred to in the deed, provided that the settlor and his wife were each to be paid one-half of the net income from the property during their joint lives, and that all of the net imcome should be paid to the surviving spouse in the event of the death of either of them. After the death of both spouses, the property was to be sold and the proceeds to be distributed equally to the settlor's four children: Peter Manetto, Anna Puppo, Eleanor Gianetti and Gloria Gabel. (Gloria Gabel was settlor's child by a second marriage.)

Paragraph 8 of the trust agreement provided as follows:

> Settlor may amend, alter or revoke this Trust in whole or in part during his lifetime. Upon the death of Settlor, this Trust shall become irrevocable. The power to amend, alter or revoke herein retained by Settlor may be released by an instrument in writing executed by Settlor for such purpose and delivered to Trustee. Upon delivery of such instrument, this Trust shall become irrevocable.

The settlor died in November, 1976, his spouse having died in 1974 at a time when the husband and wife were estranged. This action was instituted by Gloria and her husband after her father's death. It sought either partition of the property or that the property be sold and the proceeds be divided pursuant to the trust. All defendants other than the judgment creditors filed a joint answer, alleging that the trust had been revoked. They also counterclaimed, seeking an order that each child except Gloria should be declared to have a one-third interest in the property pursuant to a will made by their father on September 23, 1975. This will left testator's property, real and personal, in equal shares to the children of his first marriage, but only $2,000 in cash to Gloria. At the time he made the will and at the time of his death, he owned no other real property.

Legal authorities have stated generally that where no method of revocation is specified in the instrument creating an *inter vivos* trust, it may be revoked by any method which sufficiently proves the intention of the settlor to revoke it. Restatement, Trusts 2d, § 330, comment i at 138 (1959); 4 Scott on Trusts (3 ed. 1967), § 330.7 at 2605; Bogert, Trusts and Trustees (2 ed. 1962), § 1001 at 494; 76 Am.Jur.2d, Trusts, § 78 at 327; 89 C.J.S., Trusts, § 91a at 917. However, plaintiffs contend that since the *res* of the trust was real property, any revocation of the trust was required to be in writing. In this respect, plaintiffs rely on the Statute of Frauds, particularly N.J.S.A. 25:1–2 and N.J.S.A. 25:1–3. We find these statutes inapplicable.

N.J.S.A. 25:1–3 provides that "all declarations and creations of trust * * * in real estate shall be manifested or proved by some writing. * * *." Since we are dealing with the revocation of a trust rather than its declaration and creation, the statute does not apply. N.J.S.A. 25:1–2 provides that no estate or interest in real estate "shall be assigned, granted or surrendered unless it be by deed or note in writing. * * *." We do not regard the revocation of a trust interest in real estate as an assignment, grant or surrender of that interest. We are dealing with an alleged extinguishment of an interest by the original grantor of that interest. The case relied upon by plaintiffs, Moses v. Moses, 140 N.J.Eq. 575, 53 A.2d 805 (E. & A. 1947), is inapposite. It dealt with an unenforceable oral express trust of land and a consequent constructive trust. The court held that in those circumstances the purported oral surrender by a *cestui* of a beneficial interest was ineffectual. In our view, that is far different from the extinguishment of a concededly revocable trust by the settlor.

Plaintiffs contend, further, that even if the statute of frauds does not govern, paragraph 8 of the trust agreement quoted above requires that any revocation must be in writing. They draw this conclusion from the provision in paragraph 8 that "the power to amend, alter or revoke herein retained by the settlor may be released by an instrument in writing. * * *." While acknowledging that this requirement does not apply to the revocation itself but only to the power to revoke, they state in their brief that they "believe it compelling to believe that if the settlor required formality for the release of the power of revocation there should be no less formality for the revocation itself." We believe that more reasonable is the argument to the contrary, that since the settlor required that the

'If he so intended, he would have stated so —

release of his power to amend, alter or revoke be accomplished in writing, but did not so require as to amendment, alteration or revocation itself, his intention to retain the power to make the change orally is manifest. An affirmative expression ordinarily implies a negation of any other alternative. *Expressio unius est exclusio alterius.* *Moses*, supra at 583, 53 A.2d 805. The settlor so prized his right to amend, alter or revoke that he directed that such power could only be ceded in writing, but that does not negate his intention to be able orally to effect these changes.

π   Next, plaintiffs assert that under a concept of "equal dignity," a written instrument should not be permitted to be revoked unless the revocation is in writing also. However, there is no general prohibition against parol revocation of an agreement in writing. Thus, someone who makes a written offer to enter into a contract may legally revoke that offer by oral notice to the offeree, before acceptance. 1 Corbin, Contracts, § 39 at 164 (1963). A competent lawyer would no doubt advise a revocation in writing in such case to avoid difficulties of proof. Yet the oral revocation of the written offer would be effective if legally proved.

We are not unmindful of the fact that in the case before us the agreement of trust and the deed to the trustee were recorded. However, we are not called upon to decide the rights of anyone who might have relied on these recorded documents to his detriment. We are rather considering the relative rights of parties whose status would have been the same whether or not the documents had been recorded. The records can be corrected if necessary.

The trial judge tried this nonjury case to conclusion after hearing all the evidence. However, in his written opinion he dealt only sketchily with the facts because he ruled as a matter of law that an oral revocation of the *inter vivos* trust could not be legally accomplished. In view of our disagreement with the judge on this question of law, we remand the matter. The burden of proof of revocation shall be on the party asserting it, and must be proved by clear and convincing evidence.

We base our requirement respecting the canon of proof on an analogy with Aiello v. Knoll Golf Club, 64 N.J.Super. 156, 165 A.2d 531 (App.Div. 1960) where a claim was made of a parol gift of realty under circumstances where the grantor was alleged to be estopped from pleading the statute of frauds because of the grantee's expenditures for improvements to the property. We pointed out in that case that the requirement of proof by clear and convincing evidence represented a compromise between the strong policy of the statute of frauds and equity's paramount goal of fair disposition, and was necessary to forestall trumped-up prayers for relief. Id. at 161 and 164, 165 A.2d 531. In order to dispose fairly of the matter before us, we have ruled that the written *inter vivos* trust could have been revoked orally despite the fact that the trust *res* was real estate. However, in order to insure to the greatest extent possible against a fabricated claim of revocation, we adopt a burden of proof "commensurate with the dimensions of fraud perceived in the particular case or situation." Merenoff v. Merenoff, 76 N.J. 535, 554, 388 A.2d 951 (1978).

The judge in reaching his determination will, of course, consider all the evidence including the alleged acrimony between Gloria and her father, the testimony that the lawyer physically destroyed the original trust agreement in the presence of the settlor and the trustee, the lawyer's disclaimer of any such incident, and all other relevant evidence. However, the will itself should not be considered to be a revocation of the trust. Since a will does not take effect until after a testator's death, it is not the proper instrument to revoke a trust when the power to do so is an *inter vivos* power. In re Kovalyshyn's Estate, 136 N.J.Super. 40, 343 A.2d 852 (Cty.Ct.1975); In re Henning's Estate, 116 N.J.Super. 491, 282 A.2d 786 (Ch.Div.1971). Fidelity Union Trust Co. v. Hall, 125 N.J.Eq. 419, 6 A.2d 124 (Ch.1939). Thus, the trial judge's consideration of the will should only be with regard to any light it may cast upon the underlying question of whether the settlor revoked the trust prior to his death.

Reversed and remanded for further proceedings in accordance with the foregoing. In view of the fact that we have applied law not heretofore established in New Jersey, we consider it to be only fair that either party may supplement the record with additional proofs directed towards an application of that law. We do not retain jurisdiction.

Notes

1. See also Cahill v. Armatys, 185 Neb. 539, 177 N.W.2d (1970). Responding to a contention that the trust was passive because the will made the testator's two daughters trustees for themselves, the court said:

> A trust is ordinarily passive if there is no separation of the equitable and legal interest. In order that there may be a valid trust created by a will, there must be a trustee, an estate devised to him, and the trustee and beneficiary must be separate and distinct entities. However, this exception does not apply if there is more than one trustee and the trustees and the beneficiaries are identical. [Case citation] Consequently, the fact that the trustees and the beneficiaries are identical is of no moment herein.

2. Although no formality is required unless called for by the terms of the trust, the revocatory intent must be manifested; the mere execution of an unwitnessed will is not a sufficient revocation. Gamage v. Liberty National Bank & Trust Co., 598 S.W.2d 463 (Ky.App.1980).

Restatement, Second, Trusts

Gen'l Rule

§ 331. Modification of Trust by Settlor

(1) The settlor has power to modify the trust if and to the extent that by the terms of the trust he reserved such a power.

(2) Except as stated in §§ 332 [reformation for mistake] and 333 [rescission for fraud, illegality, etc.], the settlor cannot modify the trust if by the terms of the trust he did not reserve a power of modification.

Comment:

* * *

g. *Whether power to revoke includes power to modify.* It is a question of interpretation to be determined in view of the language used and all the circumstances whether a power to revoke the trust includes a power to modify it. Ordinarily a general power to revoke the trust will be interpreted as authorizing the settlor not only to revoke the trust in part by withdrawing a part of the trust property from the trust (see § 330, Comment *n*), but also to modify the terms of the trust, and it will be unnecessary for the settlor first to revoke the trust and then to create a new trust. If, however, the effect of the modification is to add to or vary the duties of the trustee, this is a ground for permitting the trustee to resign as trustee. See § 106. If the settlor reserves power to revoke the trust "as an entirety," he cannot modify the trust, although he can revoke the trust and if he so desires create a new trust.

Note

See Stahler v. Sevinor, 324 Mass. 18, 84 N.E.2d 447 (1949); Hinds v. Hinds, 126 Me. 521, 140 A. 189 (1928).

B. TERMINATION BY COMPLETION OF PURPOSE

FROST NATIONAL BANK OF SAN ANTONIO
v. NEWTON

Court of Appeals of Texas, Waco, 1976.
543 S.W.2d 196.

HALL, Justice.

The Frost National Bank of San Antonio is independent executor of the will of Louise M. Cozby, deceased, and trustee of the trust estate created in the will. The Bank brought this suit in both capacities seeking a declaratory judgment as to whether, under the terms of the will, the trust has terminated or should be terminated.

The will was executed by Mrs. Cozby on August 25, 1965. Following several bequests and the devise of a life estate in the testatrix's homestead to her husband, Rexford S. Cozby, the will provides in parts relevant to this appeal as follows:

"TRUST ESTATE

"I hereby give, devise and bequeath unto the Frost National Bank of San Antonio, as Trustee, in trust for the following beneficiaries and for the uses and purposes hereinafter set forth, * * * all of the residue and remainder of my property and estate * * * all of which property will be hereinafter referred to as the "Trust Estate," and is to be held, managed, controlled and disposed of by said Bank as Trustee, as hereinafter provided.

"The said Trust * * * shall continue in force and effect during the remainder of the lifetime of the last survivor of the following named three beneficiaries, viz: Rexford S. Cozby, Karolen Newton and Louise Purvis, and shall terminate upon the date of death of the last survivor of said three last-named beneficiaries. Provided, however, that said Trustee shall have the right, at its option, to sooner terminate said Trust in the event the income from the trust property shall hereafter cease to be sufficient in amount to justify the further continuance of such Trust, in the opinion of the Trustee.

*   *   *

"During the entire existence of the term of said Trust, the said Trustee is directed to pay, out of said Trust funds, to or for the use and benefit of the following named respective beneficiaries the following periodical payments:

"One-third (⅓) of the net income from said Trust Estate shall be by said Trustee paid to my husband, Rexford S. Cozby, during the remainder of his lifetime; and the remaining two-thirds (⅔) of said net income from said Trust Estate (plus such portions of the principal thereof as the Trustee may deem necessary) shall be applied to the payment of the expenses incident to: (a) The support and education through high school and college of my great-nephew, Warren S. Wilkinson, Jr., so long as he may attend and continue in school or college during the term of said Trust; and (b) the support and education through college of my great-niece, Susan Arnette, so long as she may attend and continue in college during the term of said Trust; and (c) the support and education through college of my great-niece, Karolen (Lyn) Wilkinson, so long as she may attend and continue in college during the term of said Trust; and (d) if, as, and when any one or more of said three student beneficiaries shall, during the term of said Trusts, obtain a college degree, he or she shall be paid by said Trustee the sum of $1,000.00 in cash out of the interest or principal of said two-thirds (⅔) of said total Trust Estate, as a graduation present.

"The payments of net income which are to be so paid by the Trustee to or for the use and benefit of the respective beneficiaries above-named shall be so paid in monthly installments, or in such other periodical installments as the Trustee may determine, and the respective proportionate amounts of the principal payments to be so paid to or for the benefit of my said great-nephew and great-nieces for educational purposes, out of the said two-thirds (⅔) of the total net income from the entire Trust Estate, shall be left to the discretion of and shall be determined by the Trustee according to the needs of each of said three student beneficiaries, and need not be in equal proportions. Such payments may be made direct to said student beneficiaries, regardless of their minority, or may be made to any other person or persons for any such beneficiary's use and benefit.

"If at any time during the term of said Trust the net income from said two-thirds (⅔) of said Trust Estate shall be insufficient to pay the expenses incident to a college education for said last-named three beneficiaries, or any of them, then in such event the Trustee shall have the right to pay any excess amount needed for said purposes out of the principal of said two-thirds (⅔) share of said entire net Trust Estate; and in the event their said proportionate share of said net income shall be more than sufficient to pay for their college education as aforesaid, then any such excess amount thereof shall be by the Trustee, from time to time, paid in equal shares thereof to Louise Purvis and Karolen Newton at such times and in such installments as the Trustee may determine.

"Upon the final termination of said Trust Estate all of the property then comprising said Trust Estate, and all of the remainder and residue of my property and estate, if any, not hereinabove otherwise disposed of, I hereby give, devise and bequeath to the following named ultimate beneficiaries, in equal shares, an undivided one-half (½) to each, viz: Karolen Newton and Louise Purvis. If either one of said last-named beneficiaries be not living at the time of the final termination of the Trust Estate above provided for, then the share

Kids'
interest

of my estate which such deceased beneficiary would be otherwise entitled to receive if living shall go to and vest in her then living children, in equal shares."

The testatrix died in December, 1967. Her husband, Rexford S. Cozby, predeceased her, having died in January, 1967. They had no children. The other beneficiaries named in the trust survived the testatrix. Karolen Newton and Louise Purvis were the nieces of the testatrix. Their relationship with Mrs. Cozby was like that of mother and daughters. Warren S. Wilkinson, Jr., Susan Arnette, and Karolen (Lyn) Wilkinson (now Karolen Dittmar), are the only children of Louise Purvis. These surviving beneficiaries, and the three children of Karolen Newton were named by the bank as defendants. Later, Mrs. Alibel M. Pardue, who is the surviving sister of the testatrix and is the mother of Karolen Newton and Louise Purvis, was brought into the case as a defendant. All of these defendants are adults. Additionally, a guardian ad litem was appointed to represent the unborn and unadopted children of Karolen Newton and Louise Purvis.

The case was heard by the court without a jury. During the course of the trial, Karolen Newton and Louise Purvis and their six children made and introduced into evidence an agreement in which they released and waived all their claims and rights under the trust, released and discharged the Bank as Trustee from all responsibility, and requested the court to terminate the trust and order distribution of the trust assets "to the two ultimate beneficiaries," Karolen Newton and Louise Purvis. Mrs. Pardue filed an answer in which she adopted the pleadings of her daughters requesting termination of the trust and distribution of the trust assets to them.

After the hearing the court terminated the trust and ordered the assets delivered to Karolen Newton and Louise Purvis. It made the following findings and conclusions, among others, in support of its rulings: that the primary purposes of the trust were (1) to provide a lifetime income for the testatrix's husband, Rexford S. Cozby, and (2) to provide for the education of Warren S. Wilkinson, Jr., Susan Arnette, and Karolen Wilkinson; that the provision for income to Karolen Newton and Louise Purvis was only an incidental purpose of the trust; that the three educational beneficiaries of the trust have either completed their education or elected not to accept benefits under the trust; that all of the direct and contingent beneficiaries of the trust have consented to its termination; and that no primary purpose of the trust would be frustrated by terminating the trust and distributing the assets to Karolen Newton and Louise Purvis in accordance with the agreement of the beneficiaries.

LC

The Bank and the guardian ad litem are the appellants. They do not question the finding that the three educational beneficiaries have completed their schooling and renounced any right of further benefits under the trust. However, they do question the court's determination that the provision for income to Karolen Newton and Louise Purvis was merely an incidental purpose of the trust. Rather, they say that a primary purpose of the trust was to provide for payment of income to each of those two beneficiaries during their lifetimes. They base this contention on assumptions that under the terms of the trust it must continue "during the remainder of the lifetime of the last survivor of * * * Rexford S. Cozby, Karolen Newton, and Louise Purvis" unless terminated earlier only at the option of the Bank because of insufficient income, and that the direction in the last paragraph of the trust for distribution of assets to Karolen Newton and Louise Purvis on "final termination" refers only to a termination by the Bank for want of sufficient income. We disagree with this construction of the will.

We have set forth the pertinent parts of the will virtually in full because we believe they plainly show that the primary purposes for which Mrs. Cozby created the trust were to provide income for her husband during the remainder of his lifetime, and to provide for the education through college for each of the three student beneficiaries. These purposes have been fulfilled. The trust also plainly shows that the payment of income benefits to Karolen Newton and Louise Purvis was merely a minor or incidental purpose. They are not named as lifetime income beneficiaries. The testatrix did not intend to guarantee continuing, regular support from the income, or any support, for Karolen Newton and Louise Purvis during the term of the trust, as she did for the other beneficiaries. This is evidenced by the provision that any income payments to them must come only from any excess remaining after the needs of the student beneficiaries are met. It is evidenced also by the fact that the provision for payment of "excess income" to them was not included in the same paragraph in which the provisions for regular income expenditures are contained.

The present value of the trust estate is $450,000. The appellants argue that the trust has not terminated because Karolen Newton and Louise Purvis are not deceased and because there are sufficient assets to justify the continuance of the trust. They base this argument on the language contained in the second paragraph of the trust set forth, above. The appellants' construction of this language places it directly in conflict with the "ultimate beneficiaries" status accorded Karolen Newton and Louise Purvis in the last paragraph of the trust to receive the assets remaining on "final termination" of the trust, and would mean that these two beneficiaries specifically designated by Mrs. Cozby to finally receive the corpus of the trust would never do so. We cannot agree with this construction. To follow it would simply permit the Bank to continue the trust for an incidental purpose and collect an annual fee as Trustee after the primary purposes of the Trust have been accomplished. If the main object of a trust has been attained, the trust will not be continued in order to achieve an incidental or minor purpose. Equity will decree its termination. Alamo National Bank of San Antonio v. Daubert, 467 S.W.2d 555, 561 (Tex.Civ.App., Beaumont 1971, writ ref. n. r. e.). Additionally, a trust may be terminated upon the application of all beneficiaries when they are sui juris and no subversion of the wishes of the trustor will be caused by the termination. 57 Tex.Jur.2d 417, Trusts, § 35; 76 Am.Jur.2d 324, Trusts, § 76; Restatement of Trusts, Second Edition, § 337; Bogert, Trusts And Trustees (2d ed. 1962), § 1007. For these reasons, the trust in question was properly terminated by the court.

The appellants' points and contentions are overruled.   The judgment is affirmed.

Note

Compare Work v. Central Bank & Trust Company, 260 Iowa 898, 151 N.W.2d 490 (1967), where termination was denied because a secondary purpose had not been accomplished.

C. TERMINATION BY SUPERVENING IMPOSSIBILITY OR ILLEGALITY

Restatement, Second, Trusts

§ 335. Accomplishment of Purposes Becoming Impossible or Illegal

If the purposes for which a trust is created become impossible of accomplishment or illegal, the trust will be terminated.

IN THE MATTER OF THE ESTATE OF LENA FRANK

Surrogate's Court, Kings County, 1968.
57 Misc.2d 446, 293 N.Y.S.2d 16.

EDWARD S. SILVER, J.   In this construction proceeding, petitioner seeks a determination that the proceeds of sale of certain real property are presently distributable to the beneficiaries named in the will.   Testatrix died on September 13, 1954 leaving a will dated October 18, 1941 which was subsequently admitted to probate.   She left her surviving two children, Anna, the petitioner herein, and Daniel who died intestate in 1957 survived by a spouse and issue.

Under article third of the will, testatrix devised a specific parcel of improved real property to her trustees in trust "to furnish my daughter, Anna * * * with one of the apartments in said premises * * * rent free during her lifetime," and to pay the balance of the net income therefrom in equal shares to Anna and Daniel, with Daniel's share of the income payable to his issue if he predeceased Anna.   Upon the death of Anna it was provided that the realty become part of the residuary estate, which passes in equal shares to Daniel and Anna, with gifts over if either failed to survive testatrix.   The will nominated them as coexecutors and trustees, but Daniel renounced his appointment and Anna has acted in both capacities.

It is alleged that in 1964 Anna vacated the apartment provided her by the will, and that in 1965, because of the continued vacancy of the building and the general deterioration of the surrounding area, the trust realty was sold with the consent of the interested parties.   In this proceeding the court must determine whether the proceeds of the sale are distributable outright to the persons interested therein or are to be held in further trust pursuant to the terms of the will.   No objection has been raised by any of the interested parties to the petitioner's proposed outright distribution.

The court initially finds that a valid trust was created by article third of the will (Matter of Goldenberg, 27 Misc.2d 425). When, however, the purpose for which a trust is created has been accomplished or has become impossible of accomplishment, or if continuance of the trust is unnecessary to carry out the purpose of the trust, termination may be ordered before the period fixed by the creator (4 Scott, Trusts [3d ed.], § 335). It is evident from the language of the will in question that the primary and dominant purpose of the testatrix was to furnish Anna with an apartment in the family home rent free for life. Once the apartment was vacated by Anna and the property thereafter sold, the necessity for continuance of the trust ceased. Under these circumstances, and bearing in mind the fact that Anna is the trustee, and together with her brother's estate the only parties interested in the fund, there is no compelling reason why the trust should be continued. Additionally, the administration of such a trust would be economically unsound in view of the limited moneys available for the funding thereof.

In the light of the purpose for which the trust was intended, and the facts and circumstances present herein, the court holds that the trust created by article third of testatrix' will has terminated and the proceeds realized from the sale of the property are presently distributable in equal shares to testatrix' daughter, Anna, and the estate of testatrix' son, Daniel (cf. Real Property Law, § 109, now McKinney's N.Y. EPTL 7–2.2).

Note

In Selig v. Wexler, 355 Mass. 671, 247 N.E.2d 569 (1969) a voting trust was terminated for frustration of purpose because one of the three trustees, chosen because of his supposed impartiality, proved to be biased in favor of another trustee.

D. TERMINATION BY CONSENT

Restatement, Second, Trusts

§ 337. Consent of Beneficiaries

(1) Except as stated in Subsection (2), if all of the beneficiaries of a trust consent and none of them is under an incapacity, they can compel the termination of the trust.

(2) If the continuance of the trust is necessary to carry out a material purpose of the trust, the beneficiaries cannot compel its termination.

Comment:

a. General rule. The beneficiaries of a trust, if all consent and none is under an incapacity, can compel its termination if the continuance of the trust is not necessary to carry out a material purpose of the trust, although the period fixed by the terms of the trust for its duration has not expired. On the other hand, even though they all consent, they cannot compel the termination of the trust if its continuance is necessary to carry out a material purpose of the trust.

* * *

f. Successive beneficiaries—Purposes accomplished. The mere fact that the settlor has created a trust for successive beneficiaries does not of itself indicate that it was a material purpose of the trust to deprive the beneficiaries of the management of the trust property for the period of the trust. If a trust is created for successive beneficiaries, in the absence of circumstances indicating a further purpose, the inference is that the only purpose of the trust is to give the beneficial interest in the trust property to one beneficiary for a designated period and to preserve the principal for the other beneficiary, and if each of the beneficiaries is under no incapacity, and both of them consent to the termination of the trust, they can compel the termination of the trust. Similarly, if the beneficiary who is entitled to the income acquires the interest of the remainderman, or the remainderman acquires the interest of the beneficiary entitled to the income, or the beneficiary entitled to the income disclaims with the result that the interest of the remainderman is accelerated, or if a third person acquires the interests of both, the beneficiary who thus becomes the sole beneficiary can compel the termination of the trust.

§ 338. Consent of Beneficiaries and Settlor

(1) If the settlor and all of the beneficiaries of a trust consent and none of them is under an incapacity, they can compel the termination or modification of the trust, although the purposes of the trust have not been accomplished.

(2) Although one or more of the beneficiaries of a trust do not consent to its modification or termination or are under an incapacity, the other beneficiaries with the consent of the settlor can compel a modification or a partial termination of the trust if the interests of the beneficiaries who do not consent or are under an incapacity are not prejudiced thereby.

Comment:

a. Scope of the rule. The rule stated in this Section is applicable where the settlor and the beneficiaries consent to a reconveyance of the trust property to the settlor and also where they consent to a conveyance of the trust property to the beneficiaries or to a third person. It is applicable whether or not the settlor is one of the beneficiaries. As to the termination of the trust where the settlor is the sole beneficiary, see § 339.

The rule stated in this Section is applicable although the settlor does not reserve a power of revocation, and even though it is provided in specific words by the terms of the trust that the trust shall be irrevocable.

If the settlor is dead, the consent of his heirs or personal representatives is not sufficient to justify the termination of the trust under the rule stated in this Section. The rule is not applicable to trusts created by will, or to trusts created inter vivos if the settlor has died.

* * *

d. Spendthrift trust. Although by the terms of the trust or by statute the interest of one or more of the beneficiaries is made inalienable by him, if all of the beneficiaries and the settlor, none of them being under an incapacity, consent to terminate the trust, the trust will be terminated, although the beneficiaries without the consent of the settlor could not compel the termination of the trust. See § 337(2) and the Comment *l* thereon.

Notes

1. In England the rule is otherwise; all beneficiaries can compel termination even if the settlor's purpose is thereby defeated. In re Courtourier, 1 Ch. 470 (1907).

2. The requirement that beneficiaries consent is not satisfied by their mere passive acquiescence. Sundquist v. Sundquist, 639 P.2d 181 (Utah 1981). Other recent decisions applying the principles of §§ 337 and 338 to deny premature termination include Heritage Bank North v. Hunterdon Medical Center, 164 N.J.Super. 33, 395 A.2d 552 (App.Div.1978) and Clayton v. Behle, 565 P.2d 1132 (Utah 1977).

3. In applying the common law Rule against Perpetuities, to be treated in Chapter Nine, women are deemed capable of bearing children regardless of their age and physical condition. That strict rule is not applied in trust termination cases. See, e.g., Estate of Weeks, 485 Pa. 329, 333, 402 A.2d 657, 659 (1979):

> If there is any bar to early termination of this trust, it can only be the existence of contingent beneficiaries, that is additional grandchildren. This Court, however, has long held that distribution of trust funds is governed by principles of equity rather than the conclusive common law presumption of "fertility unto death." * * * Briefs for both parties aver that the surviving life beneficiaries are all women over sixty years of age.

Termination of the trust was permitted.

IN RE BAYLEY TRUST

Supreme Court of Vermont, 1969.
127 Vt. 380, 250 A.2d 516.

Before HOLDEN, C. J., and SHANGRAW, BARNEY and KEYSER, JJ.

HOLDEN, Chief Justice. This is an appeal by the trustee from an order of the probate court, directing partial termination of the testamentary trust established by Charles H. Bayley. Mr. Bayley, who resided at Newbury, Vermont, died January 28, 1928. His will was established and allowed by the probate court for the district of Bradford.

The testator bequeathed the residue of his estate to the First National Bank of Boston in trust. In substance, the will directed the trustee to pay one-half the annual gross income to Laura Morse Bayley, the surviving widow. Provided the widow received an annual net income of not less than $12,000, the remaining income was to be expended to certain specified relatives and to four annuitants for charitable uses—The First Congregational Church, the Tenney Memorial Library, the Ox-Bow Cemetery, all of Newbury, and the Mary Hitchcock Memorial Hospital of Hanover, New Hampshire.

The will provides that the "trust hereby created shall be terminated upon the death of the last surviving life beneficiary hereinbefore mentioned * * *." Upon the termination of the trust, the trustee was directed to pay a bequest to the Mary Hitchcock Memorial Hospital and establish four separate trusts to continue the benefit of the charity specified above and provide income to be paid to the town for the maintenance of the Village Common and shade trees.

The will then follows:

> All the rest, residue and remainder of my estate, of every name and nature, both real and personal, of which I may die seised and possessed, or to which I may be entitled at the time of my decease, or which may fall into the said rest and residue of my estate, as hereinbefore provided, I give, devise and bequeath to the Museum of Fine Arts, located in said Boston, and its successors, the same to be held by it as a separate and permanent fund to be known as the "Charles H. Bayley Picture and Painting Fund", the income only to be expended in the purchase of pictures and paintings for said Museum of Fine Arts.

Mrs. Bayley died on February 7, 1963. Only two of the life beneficiaries are now living—Margaret C. Fabyan and Dorothy Chamberlin Robinson. Under the terms of the will, these annuitants receive $2,000 and $1,000 annually. With the income payable to the charities during the life of these beneficiaries, the total income distributed by the trustee is $5,500.

On December 31, 1966, the market value of the trust estate was $6,856,081.08. Since the death of Mrs. Bayley the trustee has accumulated more than $600,000 from income, beyond that required to pay the annuities, adding an average of $200,000 to the principal each year.

On October 21, 1966, all of the surviving beneficiaries under the will joined in an agreement to petition the probate court to terminate the trust as to that part of the estate which is not necessary to provide the income required for the annuities specified in the instrument. The agreement provides for setting aside sufficient funds to increase the annuity of Margaret C. Fabyan from $2,000 to $3,000, and that of Dorothy Chamberlin Robinson from $1,000 to $1,750 during their respective lives. The share to be distributed to the Mary Hitchcock Memorial Hospital is increased from $10,000 to $25,000. The separate trust estates for the benefit of each of the charities in Newbury are also enlarged to provide increased income to those beneficiaries. The agreement provides that upon the setting apart of these sums,—the Trustee shall forthwith pay over, transfer and deliver the remainder of the residuary trust fund, held by it under the will, to the Museum to be received by it for the purposes set forth in the residuary clause of the will. Subject to these changes, the entire trust estate is to be distributed, as provided in the will, upon the termination of the trust at the death of the last surviving life beneficiary.

In accordance with its stipulation, the agreement of the beneficiaries was presented to the probate court for the district of Bradford by petition of the Museum of Fine Arts. The trustee and the attorney general of

Vermont were cited before the court with the several beneficiaries. The case was submitted on agreed facts.

After hearing, the court determined that the trust created under the will of Charles H. Bayley was not a spendthrift trust. It was further determined that no lawful restriction imposed by the testator and no ascertainable purpose of his will would be nullified or disturbed by the court's approval of the agreement of the beneficiaries. The court found that the life expectancies of the living annuitants, Margaret C. Fabyan and Dorothy Chamberlin Robinson, as of July 31, 1968, were 9.63 and 9.15 respectively.

Other findings of the court establish that since the death of the testator, particularly in the last ten years, the scarcity of paintings and pictures of high quality, desirable for acquisition, has been subject to extraordinary and continuing increase. The prices required to purchase such works of art will continue to increase in the foreseeable future. The purchasing power of the dollar has declined substantially since the death of the testator. The court also found that all parties to the proceedings will be substantially benefitted by carrying out the agreement of the beneficiaries and that this is especially true of the Museum of Fine Arts. The agreement will enable this beneficiary to purchase paintings and pictures of high quality at prevailing prices and before these works of art are permanently removed from the market. Upon these considerations, the probate court approved the agreement of the beneficiaries and issued its decree in substantial compliance with its terms.

In these proceedings the trustee, the First National Bank of Boston, has assumed the posture of a stakeholder, without urging either the adoption of the agreement or adherence to the literal terms of the Bayley will. To make certain that the decree issued by the probate court is effective and binding and insure proper performance of its duties under the trust, the trustee brings this appeal. Two questions are presented—(1) Does the probate court for the district of Bradford have jurisdiction to hear and act upon the petition? (2) May the beneficiaries of the Bayley trust, by mutual agreement and with the approval of the probate court, accelerate the distribution of a substantial portion of the trust estate in the manner demonstrated in the record?

The jurisdictional question presented by the trustee seems to arise from its precautionary attitude that there is competing or conflicting authority between the courts of probate and chancery in the field of testamentary trusts. Such is not the case.

Courts of probate have plenary and exclusive jurisdiction in the settlement of the estates of deceased persons which continues until the estate is fully administered. Murray v. Cartmell's Executor, 118 Vt. 178, 180, 102 A.2d 853. In re Estate of Curtis, 109 Vt. 44, 49, 192 A. 13. Inherently, as well as by statute, they have general equity powers to hear and determine matters relating to testamentary trusts that develop in the settlement of estates. 14 V.S.A. § 2327; In re Will of Prudenzano, 116 Vt. 55, 61, 68 A.2d 704; First National Bank of Boston v. Harvey Comm.

of Texas, 111 Vt. 281, 295, 16 A.2d 184;   Robinson v. Swift, Admr., 3 Vt. 283, 289.

The careful pen of the late Justice Blackmer has defined the area for the intervention of the courts of equity in this domain.   "The jurisdiction of the court of chancery in probate matters is not original, but special and limited, and only in aid of the probate court when the powers of that court are inadequate.   *   *   *   It must appear, among other things, that the probate court cannot reasonably and adequately handle the question."   In re Will of Prudenzano, supra, 116 Vt. at 61, 68 A.2d at 709. Thus, where the probate court is wanting in authority to grant adequate equitable relief concerning persons or claims beyond its reach, equity jurisdiction may be invoked to provide essential assistance.   Manley v. Brattleboro Trust Co., 116 Vt. 460, 464, 78 A.2d 488;   Heirs of Adams v. Adams' Admrs., 22 Vt. 50, 58.

The concern of the present proceedings is the trust and trust funds that were established under the will of Charles H. Bayley.   The trust estate, its trustee and all beneficiaries in being, are presently before the probate court for the district of Bradford.   Since the estate has not come to an end, the powers of that court are entirely adequate to deal with the questions presented.   Abbott v. Abbott, 112 Vt. 449, 452, 28 A.2d 375.

 The remaining question is whether that tribunal had the legal authority to accelerate the operation of the residuary clause in the manner provided by the agreement of all the beneficiaries. We think it did.

The postponement of the distribution was principally designed to protect the interest of the testator's widow and, incidently, that of the surviving life beneficiaries.   The provision that the widow is to receive one-half the annual income, but in no event less than $12,000, clearly indicates the testator did not foresee the bountiful accumulations that now prevail.   However that may be, Mrs. Bayley is now deceased.   The other life beneficiaries, who have survived, have agreed to the partial termination of the original trust and join the other beneficiaries to urge that the probate decree be affirmed.   Their life interests are adequately secured.   The design of the agreement and the scheme of the will are entirely compatible.   In the present inflationary economy, the agreement promotes the objectives of the testator's bounty and is in no way discordant with his interest.

When all the beneficiaries of a trust desire to terminate it in part, they can compel that result unless the continuation of the entire trust estate is necessary to carry out a material purpose of the trust.   Davis v. Goodman, 17 Del.Ch. 231, 152 A. 115, 117;   Welch v. Trustees of Episcopal Theological School, 189 Mass. 108, 75 N.E. 139, 140;   Ames v. Hall, 313 Mass. 33, 46 N.E.2d 403;   Harlow v. Weld, R.I., 104 A. 832;   Restatement, Trusts 2d § 337, comment p;   Scott, Trusts (Third Ed.) § 337.8;

 Continuation of the entire trust estate is not essential to the purpose of the trust.   To the contrary, the facts presented demonstrate that partial termination and acceleration of the remaining trusts will serve the testator's ultimate objective and promote the interests of those he sought to protect by the postponement.

Decree affirmed.

HATCH v. RIGGS NATIONAL BANK

United States Court of Appeals, District of Columbia Circuit, 1966.
361 F.2d 559.

LEVENTHAL, Circuit Judge. Appellant seeks in this action to obtain modification of a trust she created in 1923. The income terms of the trust instrument are of a spendthrift character, directing the trustees to pay to the settlor for life all the income from the trust estate "for her own use and benefit, without the power to her to anticipate, alienate or charge the same * * *." Upon the death of the settlor-life tenant, the trustees are to pay over the corpus as the settlor may appoint by will; if she fails to exercise this testamentary power of appointment, the corpus is to go to "such of her next of kin * * * as by the law in force in the District of Columbia at the death of the * * * [settlor] shall be provided for in the distribution of an intestate's personal property therein." No power to appoint the corpus by deed, nor any power to revoke, alter, amend or modify the trust, was expressly retained by appellant, and the instrument states that she conveys the property to the trustees "irrevocably."

Appellant does not claim that the declaration of trust itself authorizes her to revoke or modify the trust. In effect she invokes the doctrine of worthier title, which teaches that a grant of trust corpus to the heirs of the settlor creates a reversion in the settlor rather than a remainder in his heirs. She claims that since she is the sole beneficiary of the trust under this doctrine, and is also the settlor, she may revoke or modify under accepted principles of trust law.

The District Court, while sympathizing with appellant's desire to obtain an additional stipend of $5000 a year, out of corpus, "to accommodate recently incurred expenses, and to live more nearly in accordance with her refined but yet modest tastes," [15] felt that denial of the requested relief was required by this court's decision in Liberty National Bank. v. Hicks, 84 U.S.App.D.C. 198, 173 F.2d 631, 9 A.L.R.2d 1355 (1948). Summary judgment was granted for appellees. We affirm.

I

The *Hicks* case involved a spendthrift trust created by Hicks in which all income was reserved to the settlor for life; at his death, half of the

---

15. In her complaint, appellant also sought an additional $50,000 from corpus to purchase a residence, but dropped this request at the hearing. The District Court found that there was "no suggestion of extravagance" in appellant's way of life or in her request for additional funds. She now lives in a one-bedroom apartment in a modest residential section of Long Beach, California, and has no assets except limited jewelry, furniture, personal effects, and a medium-priced automobile.

corpus was to go, by detailed provisions not relevant here, to his children or their issue, and the other half according to his will or, lacking a will, to his heirs at law according to the statutes of descent of the District of Columbia. The trust, by the terms of the trust agreement, was irrevocable. Hicks subsequently executed an instrument revoking the trust and demanded that the trustees turn over the corpus to him. The bank refused, and Hicks brought an action to have the trust declared void as a spendthrift trust against public policy. The court, noting that any rules against spendthrift provisions were for the protection of creditors, held that the settlor could not invoke the invalidity of his own trust to revoke it. It further held that revocation was not effected because, with request [sic] to both halves of the trust, Hicks had not obtained the consent of all beneficiaries.[16] With respect to the second half of Hicks' trust, analogous to the one set up by appellant in the case at bar, the court stated (84 U.S.App.D.C. at 202, 173 F.2d at 635):

> * * * Hicks reserved no right of disposition except by last will, in the absence of (failing) which it is to pass to his heirs-at-law. This provision of the trust shows, we think, that as to it Hicks intended to and did reserve only the right to dispose of it by testamentary appointment. This right continues, but, except as it provides, Hicks in creating this trust retained no control or estate, save his life interest in the income. His present effort, contrary to the terms of the trust, to alter and amend its limitations, must, therefore, be held for naught. This is the rule applied by the Maryland Court of Appeals in Allen v. Safe Deposit & Trust Co., 177 Md. 26, 7 A.2d 180, which we adopt and approve.

In neither the *Hicks* case nor the *Allen* case which it followed did the court address itself to the doctrine of worthier title. The abbreviated discussion in *Hicks* may be taken as an implied rejection of that doctrine, though it was not discussed, for if the doctrine of worthier title were applicable, then the gift over to heirs-at-law would not be effective to create a remainder interest making their consent, as beneficiaries, a condition to revocation of the trust. This appeal squarely raises the question, and we deem it appropriate that we rely not on the aura of *Hicks*, but on an express consideration of the applicability of the doctrine of worthier title.

The doctrine of worthier title had its origins in the feudal system which to a large extent molded the English common law which we inherited. In its common law form, the doctrine provided that a conveyance of land by a grantor with a limitation over to his own heirs resulted in a reversion in the grantor rather than creating a remainder interest in the heirs. It was a rule of law distinct from, though motivated largely by the same policies as, the Rule in Shelley's Case. Apparently the feudal

---

16. "[A] trust once validly constituted may not thereafter be terminated without the consent of all the cestuis que trust. This includes not only those specially named but those then unborn who may take on the expiration of the trust according to the terms." 84 U.S.App.D.C. at 210, 173 F.2d at 634. The court relied on an earlier opinion to the same effect in Hurt v. Gilmer, 59 App.D.C. 282, 40 F.2d 794 (1930).

overlord was entitled to certain valuable incidents when property held by one of his feoffees passed by "descent" to an heir rather than by "purchase" to a transferee. The doctrine of worthier title—whereby descent is deemed "worthier" than purchase—remained ensconced in English law, notwithstanding the passing of the feudal system, until abrogated by statute in 1833.[17]

The doctrine has survived in many American jurisdictions, with respect to inter vivos conveyances of both land and personalty, as a common law "rule of construction" rather than a "rule of law." In Doctor v. Hughes, 225 N.Y. 305, 122 N.E. 221 (1919), Judge Cardozo's landmark opinion reviewed the common-law history of the doctrine and concluded that its modern relevance was as a rule of construction, a rebuttable presumption that the grantor's likely intent, in referring to his own heirs, was to reserve a reversion in his estate rather than create a remainder interest in the heirs. Evidence might be introduced to show that the grantor really meant what he said when he spoke of creating a remainder in his heirs. "Even at common law," wrote Cardozo, "a distinction was taken between grants to the heirs as such, and grants where the reference to heirs was a mere *descriptio personarum*." But to overcome the presumption that a reversion rather than a remainder was intended, "the intention to work the transformation must be clearly expressed." 122 N.E. at 222.

In the decades that followed, the worthier title doctrine as a rule of construction with respect to inter vivos transfers won widespread acceptance.[18] The "modern" rationale for the rule is well stated in an opinion of the Supreme Court of California:

> It is said that where a person creates a life estate in himself with a gift over to his heirs he ordinarily intends the same thing as if he had given the property to his estate; that he does not intend to make a gift to any particular person but indicates only that upon his death the residue of the trust property shall be distributed according to the general laws governing succession; and that he does not intend to create in any persons an interest which would prevent him from exercising control over the beneficial interest. * * * Moreover, this rule of construction is in accord with the general policy in favor of the free alienability of property, since its operation tends to make property more readily transferable.[19]

While the weight of authority, as just indicated, supports the retention of the doctrine of worthier title (unlike its common-law brother, the

17. 3 & 4 Wm. IV, ch. 106, § 3. For more detailed discussion of the evolution of the doctrine of worthier title at common law, see Annot., 125 A.L.R. 548, 549–550 (1940); Doctor v. Hughes, 225 N.Y. 305, 122 N.E. 221 (1919); In re Burchell's Estate, 299 N.Y. 351, 87 N.E.2d 293, 296 (1949).

18. See Restatement, Property, § 314(1) (1940); Restatement (Second), Trusts, § 127 Comment b (1959); Annot., 16 A.L.R.2d 691 (1951).

19. Bixby v. California Trust Co., 33 Cal.2d 495, 202 P.2d 1018, 1019 (1949). See also McKenna v. Seattle-First Nat. Bank, 35 Wash.2d 662, 214 P.2d 664, 16 A.L.R.2d 679 (1950).

Rule in Shelley's Case) as a rule of construction, there has been substantial and increasing opposition to the doctrine.[20]

The views of the critics of the doctrine, which we find persuasive against its adoption, and borne out by the experience of the New York courts in the series of cases which have followed Doctor v. Hughes, supra, may be summarized as follows. The common-law reasons for the doctrine are as obsolete as those behind the Rule in Shelley's Case.[21] Retention of the doctrine as a rule of construction is pernicious in several respects.

First, it is questionable whether it accords with the intent of the average settlor. It is perhaps tempting to say that the settlor intended to create no beneficial interest in his heirs when he said "to myself for life, remainder to my heirs" when the question is revocation of the trust, or whether creditors of the settlor's heirs should be able to reach their interest. But the same result is far from appealing if the settlor-life beneficiary dies without revoking the trust and leaves a will which makes no provision for his heirs-at-law (whom he supposed to be taken care of by the trust). In short, while the dominant intent of most such trusts may well be to benefit the life tenant during his life, a subsidiary but nevertheless significant purpose of many such trusts may be to satisfy a natural desire to benefit one's heirs or next of kin. In the normal case an adult has a pretty good idea who his heirs will be at death, and probably means exactly what he says when he states in the trust instrument, "remainder to my heirs."

It is said that the cases in which such is the grantor's intent can be discerned by an examination into his intent; the presumption that a gift over to one's heirs creates a reversion can thereby be rebutted in appropriate cases. But the only repository of the settlor's intent, in most cases, will be the trust instrument itself. Nor would it be fruitful or conducive to orderly and prompt resolution of litigation to engage in searches for other sources of intent. In the typical case of this genre—a stark, unqualified "to myself for life, remainder to my heirs"—the instrument will send forth no signals of contrary intent to overcome the presumption that only a reversion was intended. Yet this is precisely the class of cases in which settlors are likely to have intended to create beneficial interests in their heirs.

A lengthier document may send forth more signals, but they may well be murky. Where other indicia of intent can be discovered in the trust instrument, with the aid of ingenious counsel, the result, as the New York cases have demonstrated, is a shower of strained decisions

---

20. See, e.g., Simes, Fifty Years of Future Interests, 50 Harv.L.Rev. 749, 756 (1937); Note, 48 Yale L.J. 874 (1939); Note, 39 Colum.L.Rev. 628, 656 (1939); Comment, 34 Ill.L.Rev. 835, 850–51 (1940). A recent study of the subject by Professor Verrall of the University of California, under the auspices of the California Law Revision Commission, resulted in a strong condemnation of the doctrine. Verrall, The Doctrine of Worthier Title: A Questionable Rule of Construction, 6 U.C.L.A.L.Rev. 371 (1959).

21. The Rule in Shelley's Case (1 Coke Rep. 104) has been abolished by statute in the District of Columbia. D.C.Code § 45–203 (1961 ed.).

difficult to reconcile with one another and generative of considerable confusion in the law.[22]   After three decades of observing the New York courts administer the rule of construction announced in Doctor v. Hughes, supra, Professor Powell of Columbia observed that "there were literally scores of cases, many of which reached the Appellate Division, and no case involving a substantial sum could be fairly regarded as closed until its language and circumstances had been passed upon by the Court of Appeals * * *.   This state of uncertainty was the product of changing an inflexible rule of law into a rule of construction."[23]

An excellent example of this confusion is the effect to be given the fact that, as in the case at bar, the settlor has reserved the power to defeat the heirs' interest by appointing the taker of the remainder by will.   One might well think that the reservation of a power of appointment was an index of intent which buttressed the presumption of a reversion by demonstrating that the settlor did not wish to create firm interests or expectations among his heirs, but intended to retain control over the property. Most courts, including the New York Court of Appeals in its most recent pronouncement on the subject, have disagreed, albeit over the voice of dissent.[24]   They have reasoned that the retention of the testamentary power of appointment confirms the intent to create a remainder in the heirs, since the settlor would not have retained the power had he not thought he was creating a remainder interest in the heirs.

We see no reason to plunge the District of Columbia into the ranks of those jurisdictions bogged in the morass of exploring, under the modern doctrine of worthier title, "the almost ephemeral qualities which go to prove the necessary intent."[25]   The alleged benefit of effectuating intent must be balanced against the resulting volume of litigation and the diversity and difficulty of decision.[26]   We are not persuaded that the policy of upholding the intention of creators of trusts is best effectuated by such a rule of construction, with its accompanying uncertainty.

The rule we adopt, which treats the settlor's heirs like any other remaindermen, although possibly defeating the intention of some settlors, is overall, we think, an intent-effectuating rule.   It contributes to certainty of written expression and conceptual integrity in the law of trusts. It allows heirs to take as remaindermen when so named, and promises less litigation, greater predictability, and easier drafting.   These considerations are no small element of justice.

---

22.   The New York cases are admirably summarized and discussed in Verrall, op.cit. supra note [20], at 374–387.

23.   Powell, Cases on Future Interests 88 n. 14 (3d ed. 1961).

24.   In re Burchell's Estate, 299 N.Y. 351, 361, 87 N.E.2d 293, 297 (1949); see Comment, 34 Ill.L.Rev. 834, 844–45 (1940).

25.   In re Burchell's Estate, supra, 299 N.Y. at 361, 87 N.E.2d at 297 (1949).

26.   These results led Judge Fuld to call for "clarifying legislation."   Dissent in In re Burchell's Estate, supra note [17].

We hold, then, that the doctrine of worthier title is no part of the law of trusts in the District of Columbia, either as a rule of law or as a rule of construction. Any act or words of the settlor of a trust which would validly create a remainder interest in a named third party may create a valid remainder interest in the settlor's heirs. It follows that the District Court was correct·in granting summary judgment for appellees in this case, since appellant's action is based on the theory that she was the sole beneficiary and hence could revoke the "irrevocable" trust she had created.

II

Appellant's invocation of worthier title was premised in part on the injustice alleged to result in many cases from holding such a trust irrevocable. The irrevocability was supposed to be riveted into the trust by the impossibility of obtaining consent to revocation from all the beneficiaries, since some of them are still unborn. Appellant's argument reflects a misunderstanding of the consequence of the judgment of the District Court.

It is hornbook law that any trust, no matter how "irrevocable" by its terms, may be revoked with the consent of the settlor and all beneficiaries.

The beneficiaries of the trust created by appellant are herself, as life tenant, and her heirs, as remaindermen. Her heirs, if determined as of the present time, are her two sisters. There is no assurance that they will in fact be the heirs who take the remainder under the trust; appellant might survive one or both. Yet their consent is necessary, we think, to revocation, since they are at least the persons who would be beneficiaries if the settlor died today.[27]

In addition, it is necessary to protect the interests of those additional persons, both living and unborn, who may, depending on circumstances, be members of the class of heirs at the time the corpus is distributed. We think that upon an adequate showing, by the party petitioning to revoke or modify the trust, that those who are, so to speak, the heirs as of the present time consent to the modification, and that there is a reasonable possibility that the modification that has been proposed adequately protects the interests of those other persons who might be heirs at the time the corpus is to be distributed, the District Court may appoint a guardian ad litem to represent the interests of those additional persons.

Although the question has not been previously discussed by this court we think basic principles of trust law are in accord with appointment of a guardian ad litem to represent interests of unborn or unascertained beneficiaries, for purposes of consent to modification or revocation of a trust. This use of a guardian ad litem is not uncommon in other jurisdictions. In a number of states authority for such appointments is pro-

---

27. One of the sisters is not *sui juris*. In referring to her consent, we do not mean to exclude consent by her guardian ad litem.

vided by statute.[28] These statutes reflect a broad sentiment of the approaches that are consistent with the Anglo-American system of law and adopted to promote the objective of justice. Where it is at least debatable whether rulings must await express legislative authorization, this court must take into account the fact that the legislature for the District of Columbia is primarily concerned with awesome questions of national policy, and we should be more ready to accept our obligation as a court to refine and adapt the corpus of law without waiting for a legislative go-ahead. Here we are certainly in a field where it is not inappropriate for courts to act without statutory foundation, as appears from the well-considered authority cited in the margin.[29] "Courts of justice as an incident of their jurisdiction have inherent power to appoint guardians ad litem."[30] The efficacy of a guardian ad litem appointed to protect the interests of unborn persons is no different whether he be appointed pursuant to statute or the court's inherent power. Given such protection, the equitable doctrine of representation embraces the flexibility, born of convenience and necessity, to act upon the interests of unborn contingent remaindermen to the same effect as if they had been *sui juris* and parties.

The use of guardians ad litem to represent interests of unborn and/ or otherwise unascertainable beneficiaries of a trust seems to us wholly appropriate. Though the persons whose interests the guardian ad litem represents would be unascertainable as individuals, they are identifiable as a class and their interest, as such, recognizable.

The settlor seeking to revoke or modify the trust may supplement his appeal to equity with a quid pro quo offered to the heirs for their consent. In many cases it may well be consistent with or even in furtherance of the interest of the heirs to grant such consent. The case at bar provides a good example. Here the interest of all heirs is contingent, since ap-

---

28. E.g., Cal.Code Civ.Proc. § 373.5; Ill.Rev.Stat. ch. 22, § 6 (1959); Restatement, Property § 182, Comment c (1936). The leading case upholding such appointments is Gunnell v. Palmer, 370 Ill. 206, 18 N.E.2d 202, 120 A.L.R. 871 (1938), noted in 34 Ill.L.Rev. 101 (1939), where the court viewed the statute as providing the same protections to unborn persons as traditional doctrines of equitable representation. See also Wogman v. Wells Fargo Bank & Union Trust Co., 123 Cal.App.2d 657, 267 P.2d 423, 429 (1954); Reynolds v. Remick, 327 Mass. 465, 99 N.E.2d 279 (1951). Compare Mullane v. Central Hanover Bank & Trust Co., 339 U.S. 306, 317–318, 70 S.Ct. 652, 94 L.Ed. 865 (1950).

29. Peoples Nat. Bank v. Barlow, 235 S.C. 488, 112 S.E.2d 396, 398–399 (1960). A few courts have held, to the contrary, that no guardian ad litem for the interests of unborn beneficiaries may be appointed in the absence of express statutory authorization. E.g., Moxley v. Title Ins. & Trust Co., 154 P.2d 417 (Cal.Dist.Ct.App.1945), decided before the California statute, supra note [28], was passed. That decision, it should be noted, was affirmed by the California Supreme Court, 27 Cal.2d 457, 165 P.2d 15, 163 A.L.R. 838 (1946), with no discussion of this point; Justice Traynor, dissenting, relied on an earlier California holding that appointment of a guardian ad litem for unborn beneficiaries was proper. 165 P.2d at 26. The Restatement expressly takes no position as to whether the general power of equity, apart from statute, includes the power to appoint such a guardian. Restatement, Property, § 182, Comment e (1936).

30. Mabry v. Scott, 51 Cal.App.2d 245, 124 P.2d 659, 665, cert. denied sub nom. Title Ins. & Trust Co. v. Mabry, 317 U.S. 670, 63 S.Ct. 75, 87 L.Ed. 538 (1942). See also Smith v. Lamb, 103 Ga.App. 157, 118 S.E.2d 924, 927 (1961) (power to appoint guardian ad litem an "incident of courts"); 27 Am.Jur., Infants § 120, pp. 840–41 ("The power to appoint a guardian ad litem is inherent in every court of justice."). Compare Rule 17(c), Fed.R.Civ.P.

pellant can defeat their remainder by exercising her testamentary power of appointment. If the modification agreed upon not only increased the annual income of the life tenant but also transferred assets in trust for the benefit of the heirs, without any power of alteration in the settlor, the heirs' remainder interest would be secure, and accordingly more valuable than it is now. The pattern of such a modification is clearly available where the remaindermen of a trust are specific named persons, and, we think, should also be available where the remaindermen are recognizable as a class even though the members of the class are not now individually ascertainable.

Appellant, proceeding on a different theory, has not taken steps to obtain the consent of heirs. We think it important to make clear that, in rejecting the doctrine of worthier title, we do not mean to put settlors and life tenants of trusts in which the remaindermen are the settlor's heirs at an unwarranted disadvantage with respect to legitimate efforts to modify trust arrangements concluded largely for their own benefit. Our affirmance of the judgment for appellees is without prejudice to a future submission by appellant on such a basis.

Affirmed.

Notes

1. New York does not follow the common law rule with respect to unborn potential beneficiaries because N.Y. EPTL 7–1.9, as interpreted, dispenses with the need for their consent as a condition of consensual early termination. See, e.g., Application of Roth, 73 A.D.2d 560, 423 N.Y.S.2d 25 (1979). As was said in Matter of Schroll, 297 N.W.2d 282, 282 (Minn.1980):

> Appellant contends that modification should be permitted where the settlor and all *living* beneficiaries are in agreement, urging us to adopt the New York principle that persons not in existence are not "beneficially interested" so as to constitute necessary parties to its modification or termination. [New York citations]

> However, the New York rule is based on the interpretation of New York statutes and runs contrary to the common law rule under which unborn issue may be beneficiaries of a trust. See Restatement § 127. Our statutes comport with the common law and recognize that a party "unascertained or not in being" may be a party interested in a trust. See Minn.Stat. § 501.36 (1978).

> Here, the settlor created future interests in favor of the issue of appellant and his siblings. See 1 L. Simes & A. Smith, The Law of Future Interests § 1 (2d ed. 1956). While the interests of unborn beneficiaries are contingent, id. §§ 152, 153, they may not be disregarded. (Emphasis in original; footnote omitted)

2. For an exhaustive analysis and appraisal of the worthier title doctrine in general, and the principal case in particular, see Note, Trusts: Modification of Irrevocable Trusts Through Appointment of a Guardian for Unborn Heirs— Repudiation of Worthier Title Doctrine, 66 Colum.L.Rev. 1552 (1966).

JOHNSON v. FIRST NATIONAL BANK OF JACKSON

Supreme Court of Mississippi, 1980.
386 So.2d 1112.

BROOM, Justice, for the Court:

Terminability of a trust agreement is the chief issue of this case in which the appellant, Mary Moore Johnson (trustor) seeks termination. She sued the trustee, First National Bank of Jackson (FNB), in the Chancery Court of the First Judicial District of Hinds County for termination of the trust and now appeals from a decree adverse to her. We reverse.

Mary Moore Johnson and FNB entered into a trust agreement dated August 5, 1976, and styled "Irrevocable Trust Agreement." By the agreement, Moore [sic] assigned unto FNB most of her rights and interest derived from the estate of her deceased father, Lee White Johnson, M. D. In June of 1978, she sent to FNB a Revocation of Trust Agreement form. In this form, Johnson claimed that she was: the "settlor and sole beneficiary" of the trust; *sui juris*; suffering from no incapacity whatsoever; and desired to have all of the corpus of the trust returned to her control.

Johnson is 25 years old and has never been married. She attended college one year during which she attended three different colleges. Her collegiate studies included no courses in economics or related to handling or investing money or anything of that nature. Johnson has held various unskilled jobs, but none for a substantial length of time.

Her testimony was that she had entered into the trust agreement on the advice of her mother and a friend named Charlton Anderson, an FNB trust officer. She also had advice from Harold James, a CPA, who told her that he thought it would be a good thing. Further, she stated that she recognized the fact that at the time she had come into a large inheritance from her father's estate but lacked the ability to handle that kind of money. Now, her testimony is that she is more responsible, older, wiser, and able to handle her affairs.

During this time period, Johnson has become associated with the Church of Scientology in Florida to the extent that in the past three or four years she has donated it approximately $30,000. Ten thousand dollars of this money was borrowed from Johnson's grandmother which, at this time, has not been repaid.

There is no need to detail all of the transactions. Documentary evidence showed that during the approximately two years between the entering into the trust agreement and the filing of the revocation document, Johnson had made numerous demands to the trustee for money which would have had to come from the corpus of the trust. Some of the requests were granted and some were not. Evidence also showed that when Johnson did receive these sums, she may not have managed them with expertise.

At the close of the hearing, the chancellor entered an opinion favorable to FNB in which he noted that apparently Mississippi has not yet passed on the question of whether a supposedly irrevocable trust can be revoked at any time by the settlor who is the sole beneficiary of the trust. Johnson's bill was dismissed.

DID THE LOWER COURT ERR IN HOLDING THAT JOHNSON, EVEN THOUGH SERVING AS BOTH TRUSTOR AND SOLE BENE- FICIARY OF THE WRITTEN INTER VIVOS IRREVOCABLE TRUST AGREEMENT, COULD NOT TERMINATE SUCH AN AGREEMENT?

The problem involves three main questions: (1) as sole beneficiary of the trust, may the settlor compel termination of the trust even though the trust was apparently established to be irrevocable; (2) if the settlor can compel the termination of the trust generally, are there any reasons for not following the general rule which permits termination; and (3) if the first two questions are answered affirmatively, is there a reason in the case at bar for now allowing the settlor to terminate this trust?

In response to the first question above, we have not found nor has any Mississippi case directly in point been cited. Deposit Guaranty National Bank v. Walter E. Heller & Co., 204 So.2d 856 (Miss.1967) held that a spendthrift trust for the benefit of the grantor is void. Restatement (Second) of the Law of Trusts, § 339 (1959) states:

§ 339. Where Settlor is Sole Beneficiary. If the settlor is the sole ben- eficiary of a trust and is not under an incapacity, he can compel the ter- mination of the trust, although the purposes of the trust have not been accomplished.

Also, G. Bogert, Trusts and Trustees, § 1004 (2d Ed. 1962) states:

If the trustee refuses the settlor's request and insists on continuing the trust administration, the court should and does order him to comply and thus to terminate the trust. It is true that this is not carrying out the intent which the settlor had when he created the trust and when he decided to have his property managed for him and to take its benefits indirectly. But that original intent ought to be of no importance when the settlor has changed his mind and formed new plans with regard to the enjoyment of his own property. His present intent should be carried out.

As further pointed out in *Bogert*, supra, no one has standing to object to the ending of the trust in cases of this type where the settlor demands that the trustee return the trust property to him and the trustee ac- quiesces. 4 A. W. Scott, The Law of Trusts, § 339 (3d Ed. 1967) is to the same effect.

Our conclusion is that we should, and now do, adopt the general rule that a settlor who is the sole beneficiary of a trust may have the trust revoked and set aside even though it was initially set up in the form of an irrevocable trust. There may arise future cases on different facts where we will recognize exceptions to the general rule.

Final question to be resolved here is whether or not the lower court's de- termination that it would not be in "the best interest of the complainant" to terminate the trust is controlling. The testimony and evidence showed that Johnson may not be an astute business woman, nor very proficient in managing her money. For example, after buying a Chevrolet Camaro in Mississippi for $5,400, she then went back to Florida and sold the car some two or three months later for $4,400. She made large contributions to the Church of Scientology, and the proof showed that she intended to spend a great deal more of the money for courses and training with that entity. However, she has never been adjudged to be a person of unsound mind, has never been under a guardianship, or under any other legal disability whatsoever.

It might very well be in her best interest to have someone look after her financial affairs, as is true of many individuals. Nevertheless, in our opinion, this Court and the other courts of this state should not attempt to shield persons from their own folly, where there is no showing of lack of mental capacity. One of the maxims of equity is that "when parties are disabled, equity will act for them." (Griffith, Mississippi Chancery Practice, § 45 [1950]). This maxim was *never* intended to mean that the courts of equity would attempt to guard a person from his own folly as determined by the standards of society. In the case before us, it was shown that trustor Johnson had given considerable money to the Church of Scientology, and intended to give it much more. While the chancellor carefully avoided stating this as a ground for his decision, we think it is fairly obvious that it played at least some part in his opinion. We do not imply that the chancellor related his ruling to the particular church to which the appellant donated her money, but rather that she donated such vast amounts over such a short period of time.

How a person who is not under a legal disability chooses to spend her money is not and should not be subject to review by courts. If she chooses, and so long as she is under no legal disability, Johnson is perfectly free to donate everything she has to any entity including the Church of Scientology. As was stated by Mr. Justice Jackson, dissenting in United States of America v. Ballard, 322 U.S. 78, 94, 64 S.Ct. 882, 890, 88 L.Ed. 1148 (1944), "I doubt if the vigilance of the law is equal to making money stick by over-credulous people."

Further, Johnson may not create a spendthrift trust for herself in this case, i.e., she may not place this money in trust to remove it from the reach of her creditors. Deposit Guaranty National Bank v. Walter E. Heller & Co., supra. Even if this Court were to determine that it would not be "in the best interest" of Johnson to terminate or revoke this trust, she may in effect revoke it herself. For example, she may borrow money equal to the amount of the money of the corpus of the trust, donate this amount to the Church of Scientology, and her creditors would then be able to proceed against the corpus of the trust. Our view is that, unless Johnson is determined judicially to be of unsound mind (which has not been done) under the general rule stated above, she has the right to revoke and terminate this trust and dispose of the money.

It may be said of this case that FNB and the chancellor made a noble effort to protect the appellant from herself, but we are unwilling to say that they have a legal right to do so. The mere fact that a person has done or attempted to do something with her money which is considered foolish by society is not sufficient reason for an equity court to invoke its power.

Reversed and rendered.

Note

To the same effect as the principal case, see Matter of Harbaugh's Estate, 231 Kan. 564, 646 P.2d 498 (1982); Waldron v. Commerce Union Bank, 577 S.W.2d 669 (Tenn.App.1978).

AMBROSE v. FIRST NATIONAL BANK OF NEVADA
Supreme Court of Nevada, 1971.
87 Nev. 114, 482 P.2d 828.

THOMPSON, Justice. This appeal is from an order of the district court refusing to terminate an inter vivos trust. The petition to terminate was presented to the court by the sole beneficiary, Elizabeth Ann Ambrose, and was based upon the proposition that the trust had become a dry trust since its material purpose had been accomplished. The trust was created in 1953 by the petitioner's mother, Elizabeth Fenno Ambrose, for the declared purpose of preventing the dissipation of her assets and contains a spendthrift provision that "no beneficiary of the income or principal of the trust property or any share or any part thereof may at any time assign, transfer, anticipate or create any lien upon the principal or income of the trust property or any interest therein." The First National Bank of Nevada was named trustee and was given the power to invade the principal for the support and maintenance of the settlor and her daughter, Elizabeth Ann, until the daughter became 21 years old. Thereafter, no provision was made for the support of the daughter except upon direction of her mother, the settlor. The trust was to continue after the death of the settlor, and when the daughter became 28 years old she was to receive one half of the corpus and upon attaining the age of 35 she was to receive the remainder, and the trust would end.

When the mother died in 1969 her daughter was sui juris and under no physical or mental disability. Since the trust instrument did not provide for the daughter's support after she had reached the age of 21 and until she became 28, the Bank petitioned the court for an order allowing the payment of discretionary sums to the daughter, asserting that the trust instrument was ambiguous as to whether such payments could be made. The petition did not state in what respect the instrument was ambiguous, nor did the court, in granting the Bank's petition, point to any ambiguity. The daughter, who had notice of that proceeding, did not object to the Bank's request for authority to pay discretionary sums for her support. She did, however, at age 23, commence the instant proceeding to terminate the trust. The adversaries agree that the sole beneficiary of a trust, who is not under an incapacity, may compel its termination before the period fixed for its duration has expired, if continuance of the trust is not necessary to carry out a material purpose. Rest. Second Trusts § 337, Comment a at 158 (1959). Moreover, they agree that the attempt by the mother to create a spendthrift trust for herself was ineffective since such a trust may only be created for a person or persons other than the settlor.[31] NRS 166.040.[32] However, the Bank does contend that a valid spendthrift trust was created with respect to the daughter and that its purpose had not been realized and termination before the period fixed for its duration has expired is, therefore, improper. This contention rests mainly upon two words of the spendthrift clause that "no beneficiary" may assign, transfer, anticipate, etc. Since the daughter is a beneficiary, the spendthrift clause applies to her. The trust instrument is otherwise void of language suggesting that the daughter who was six years old when the trust was created, might become a spendthrift after reaching the age of 21 years, and that the settlor desired to protect her against that eventuality. We do not decide whether the Bank's position on this point has merit since the trust instrument as drawn removes this particular trust from the Spendthrift Trust Act with the result that the daughter, as sole beneficiary, may compel an early termination. We turn to explain why this is so.

1. The Ambrose Trust is deemed to have been drawn in the light of the Spendthrift Trust Act, and the provisions thereof control the construction, operation and enforcement of the trust. NRS 166.060. Several provisions of the Act point to a precondition that provision must be made for the support and maintenance of the beneficiary before a valid restraint upon the transfer of a beneficiary's interest may be imposed. For example, NRS 166.090 provides that "provision for the beneficiary will be for the support, education, maintenance and benefit of the beneficiary alone * * *." NRS 166.100 states that "provision for the ben-

---

31. The mother's desire to protect her estate against her own propensity to spend recklessly is firmly established by the preamble of the trust instrument, executed when her daughter was but six years of age. The preamble reads:

"WHEREAS, George K. Livermore has in his custody and under his management and control the property and securities, except for the real property, listed in 'Schedule A', attached hereto and made a part hereof, and has from time to time invested and reinvested the securities in said 'Schedule A' and has paid over from time to time the net income from said securities to the Grantor; and

"WHEREAS, the said property and securities listed in said schedule are the sole property of the Grantor; and

"WHEREAS, the Grantor has incurred numerous debts and liabilities over the past few years and at the present time, and in payment of such debts and liabilities has expended large sums over and above the income received from her securities, and has required said George K. Livermore to sell large quantities of her securities and deliver the proceeds to her for the payment and discharge of said debts and liabilities, with the result that the property and securities belonging to the Grantor have been dissipated and their value diminished by not under One Hundred and Ninety Thousand dollars during the past nine years; and

"WHEREAS, the Grantor has a daughter, Elizabeth Ambrose, aged six, who is dependent on the Grantor for her entire support and maintenance; and

"WHEREAS, if the Grantor continues to have access to the property and securities listed in said 'Schedule A' she will, at the present rate of dissipation of said assets, very soon exhaust her property and securities still remaining, with the result that both she and her daughter may become public charges."

32. NRS 166.040 reads: "Any person competent by law to execute a will or deed may, by writing only, duly executed, by will, conveyance or other writing, create a spendthrift trust in real, personal or mixed property for any other person or persons."

eficiary will extend to all of the income of the trust estate   *   *   *." Finally, NRS 166.120(1) excepts from the Act a trust that "does not provide for the application for or the payment to any beneficiary of sums out of capital or corpus or out of rents, profits, income, earnings or produce of property, lands or personalty."   A trust that does not so provide may be anticipated, assigned or aliened by the beneficiary voluntarily.   The mentioned statutory sections of the Act compel the conclusion that a trust which does not provide for the support and maintenance of the beneficiary may not qualify as a spendthrift trust under ch. 166 and is subject to general law regarding early termination.   Since the Ambrose Trust does not provide for the support and maintenance of the daughter after she becomes 21 years old and until she attains the age of 28, the trust must fail as a spendthrift trust within the contemplation of the Act.

2. The Bank contends that the prior district court order allowing the Bank to pay discretionary sums to the beneficiary for her support somehow precludes the beneficiary from seeking an early termination of the trust in this proceeding.   This contention is not sound.   The validity of the trust as a spendthrift trust was not raised in the prior proceeding. Neither was the right of the beneficiary to compel an early termination an issue.   Consequently, the doctrines of res adjudicata and collateral estoppel are not involved and the beneficiary is not foreclosed from asserting her right to an early termination.   Clark v. Clark, 80 Nev. 52, 389 P.2d 69 (1964).   The prior order did not cure the defect in the trust instrument nor was it intended to do so.   The trust did not become a valid spendthrift trust for the daughter by reason of court authorization for her support.   At that point in time the daughter enjoyed the right to compel an early termination and receive the entire trust estate.   She had not yet asserted that right.   The court possessed the power to provide for her support until she elected to exercise her right to terminate the trust, since her right to the entire corpus embraces her right to support.

3. We perceive no material purpose to be served by the continuation of this trust.   Since it does not qualify as a spendthrift trust for reasons already expressed, the beneficiary may anticipate, assign or alienate her interest therein.   NRS 166.120(1).   Were she to do so the settlor's intent would, perhaps, be frustrated.   With this in mind it would appear absurd to refuse termination for fear of frustrating the settlor's intent, when the net result of such refusal is to continue the trust for the sole benefit of the trustee.

We are not persuaded that the doctrine of the leading American case of Claflin v. Claflin, 149 Mass. 19, 20 N.E. 454 (1889), should rule the trust before us.   That case announced the principle that a court will not direct termination prior to the time fixed therefor, even though the beneficiary desires to terminate, since this would be contrary to the purpose of the settlor.   This, we think, is an arbitrary view when applied automatically and without regard to all of the settlor's underlying motives. Here, the overriding purpose of the settlor was to protect her estate against her own improvidence.   This forcefully appears from the recitals of the trust instrument.   No reason is expressed in the trust instrument for delaying the daughter's enjoyment following the settlor's death. No provision is made therein for the daughter's support between the ages of 21 and 28. Should the daughter die during that period of time she would be denied enjoyment of the corpus. All of these factors together with a strong public policy against restraining one's use and disposition of property in which no other person has an interest [Warner v. Keiser, 93 Ind.App. 547, 177 N.E. 369 (1931); Simmons v. Northwestern Trust Co., 136 Minn. 357, 162 N.W. 450 (1917); Rector v. Dalby, 98 Mo.App. 189, 71 S.W. 1078 (1903); In re Africa's Estate, 359 Pa. 567, 59 A.2d 925 (1948)] leads us to conclude that termination should be decreed and the beneficiary spared the expense incident to the continued administration of the trust. The Bank, within a reasonable time, shall furnish to the beneficiary a final accounting in accordance with appropriate provisions of the Uniform Trustees Accounting Act and this trust shall thereafter be terminated and the trust estate delivered and transferred to Elizabeth Ann Ambrose, the sole beneficiary.

Reversed, with direction to enter judgment in accordance with this opinion. Costs are allowed to the appellant.

BATJER and GUNDERSON, JJ., concur.

ZENOFF, Chief Justice, and MOWBRAY, Justice (dissenting).

We respectfully dissent. The trust in question is a valid spendthrift trust as regards the appellant; a material purpose of the trust remains to be accomplished; and the appellant is collaterally estopped from asserting the trust does not provide for payments to her. For these reasons, the decision of the lower court should be affirmed.

1. Appellant urges that the trust is invalid since it was invalid as regarded her mother as an attempt to establish a spendthrift trust for oneself. Appellant does not argue that the trust was void *ab initio*, however, so the question is not determined by its earlier validity or invalidity with regard to her mother. Coughran v. First Nat'l Bank of Baldwin Park, 19 Cal.App.2d 152, 64 P.2d 1013 (Cal.App.1937); 2 G.Bogert, Law of Trusts and Trustees, § 223 (2d ed. 1965). The sole question with respect to this issue is whether the trust is a spendthrift trust as regards the appellant.

The answer to this question is determined by the Spendthrift Trust Act (NRS Chapter 166). NRS 166.020 defines a "spendthrift trust" as "a trust in which by the terms thereof a valid restraint on the voluntary and involuntary transfer of the interest of the beneficiary is imposed." Appellant does not question the validity of the trust as regards herself (for example as a fraud against creditors), and as was indicated, its validity or invalidity as regarded her mother does not determine this question. Instead, she asserts that the trust was not intended to operate as a spendthrift trust as to her.

Though the preamble to the trust speaks only of the intent to restrain her mother's spending, the body of the trust instrument was fashioned to restrain the appellant's spending also. She is to receive money out of the trust only at the discretion of the trustee until she reaches age 28, and she is precluded from assigning, transferring, anticipating or creating a lien upon her interest in the trust. NRS 166.050 indicates that no magic words are necessary for the creation of a spendthrift trust.[33]

2. By use of these words, a restraint is imposed on the voluntary and involuntary transfer of the appellant's interest within NRS 166.020. The material purpose of the trust remains to be accomplished so the appellant may not terminate it even though she is the sole living beneficiary. IV A. Scott, Law of Trusts, § 337.3 (3d ed. 1967). Under NRS 166.090 the existence of a spendthrift trust does not depend upon the character, capacity, incapacity, competency or incompetency of the beneficiary. It is not for us to decide the wisdom of the creation of the spendthrift trust as to the appellant, nor are those cases pertinent that allow beneficiaries to terminate an "ordinary" trust where the beneficiaries consent to a termination because the purposes of the trust are fulfilled. A spendthrift trust is "special," one that is established usually to prevent the beneficiary from becoming impoverished.

The purpose of this trust, at least it so appears, was to protect the daughter from experiencing what was happening to her mother. Such material purpose does not allow the beneficiary to reach the trust fund. The material purpose of this trust has not been served as to the daughter, and for that reason alone she cannot terminate the trust. Some states have judicially declared policies against spendthrift trusts (see G. Bogert, Law of Trusts and Trustees, §§ 222, 224 (2d ed. 1965)) but the legislature in this state has chosen to sanction them and we must follow that direction.

3. Furthermore, the only statutory exception to the general rule of anticipation of the trust according to NRS 166.120 exists when the trust does not provide for payments to the beneficiary.[34] Appellant contends that even if the trust is a valid spendthrift trust as regards her, she may anticipate her interest in it because it does not provide for payments to her. The answer to this contention is that the trust does provide for the necessary payments. In November, 1969, a judgment was entered in the Second Judicial District Court, Washoe County, declaring that the respondent was empowered to pay the appellant discretionary sums under the trust instrument. The judgment recites that the appellant had notice

---

33. NRS 166.050. *No specific language necessary for creation of trust.* No specific language is necessary for the creation of a spendthrift trust. It is sufficient if by the terms of the writing (construed in the light of this chapter if necessary) the creator manifests an intention to create such a trust.

34. NRS 166.120. *Principle governing construction: Restraints on alienation.*

1. A spendthrift trust as defined in this chapter restrains and prohibits generally the assignment, alienation, acceleration and anticipation of any interest of the beneficiary under the trust by the voluntary or involuntary act of the beneficiary, or by operation of law or any process or at all. *An exception is declared, however, when the trust does not provide for the application for or the payment to any beneficiary of sums out of capital or corpus or out of rents, profits, income, earnings, or produce of property, lands or personalty. In such cases, the corpus or capital of the trust estate, or the interest of the beneficiary therein, may be anticipated,* assigned or aliened * * * . (Emphasis added.)

of the respondent's petition to the court.　She did not contest the propriety of that judgment and may not now act in disregard of it.

In Clark v. Clark, 80 Nev. 52, 56, 389 P.2d (1964), this court stated: "On the other hand, collateral estoppel (estoppel by record) may apply even though the causes of action are substantially different, if the same fact issue is presented."　See also Anno. 25 A.L.R.3d 318 (1969).　This rule applies here to bar the appellant's right to claim relief under NRS 166.120(1).

The November, 1969, judgment declared that the trustee was empowered to pay the appellant discretionary sums out of the trust under the ambiguous trust instrument.　The appellant's assertion that she may anticipate recovery of her interest in the trust is founded upon the contention that the trust makes no provision for payments to her.　She thus attacks collaterally the earlier judgment made in a proceeding of which she had notice.　Allowing her to do so flies in the face of the well-reasoned rule announced in *Clark*.　While it is true, as the majority indicates, that the earlier judgment did not determine the right of the appellant to compel an early termination of the trust, that judgment did make a finding which determines the outcome of this action.

It is well settled that judgments entered in probate proceedings are entitled to be treated as *res judicata*.　Lucich v. Medin, 3 Nev. 93 (1867); 1 Banc.Prob.Prac. § 129 (1950);　46 Am.Jur.2d, Judgments § 623 (1969). The appellant thus may not relitigate this question merely because she was a noncontesting party to a probate proceeding.

This case is comparable to In re Freman's Estate, 185 Cal.App.2d 527, 8 Cal.Rptr. 311 (1960), where the beneficiary was barred from contesting the propriety of the trustee's first accounting on the assertion that it had improperly refused to make retroactive payments out of the trust. The trustee had earlier sought court instructions on the distribution of the trust and was told to make distributions prospectively only.　The later attack upon the trustee's accounting was viewed as a collateral attack on the earlier judgment and as such was held to be prevented by collateral estoppel.　So also should the collateral attack presented here be prevented.

For the foregoing reasons, we respectfully dissent and urge that the judgment of the trial court should be affirmed.

Note

Cases denying termination by beneficiaries where a material purpose of the creator of the trust would be frustrated, include St. Louis Union Trust Co. v. Conant, 499 S.W.2d 761 (Mo.1973);　Estate of Davis, 449 Pa. 505, 297 A.2d 451 (1972);　Mumma v. Huntington National Bank, 9 Ohio App.2d 166, 223 N.E.2d 621 (Ct.App.1967);　Lafferty v. Sheets, 175 Kan. 741, 267 P.2d 962 (1954);　Fowler v. Lanpher, 193 Wash. 308, 75 P.2d 132 (1938) (termination of a second trust allowed, however, with settlor's consent).

SECTION SIX. STATUTE OF FRAUDS,
CONSTRUCTIVE AND RESULTING TRUSTS

For the creation of trusts inter vivos, statutes in the majority of the states follow the English Statute of Frauds in requiring express trusts of land to be in writing, but express trusts of personal property may be created orally. [There is no requirement that the evidence giving rise to either a constructive or a resulting trust be in writing.)

In approximately one-quarter of the American jurisdictions, there is no statute expressly requiring a writing for the validity of a trust. Some of these states, however, like Connecticut, require a writing for an express trust of land even in the absence of such a statute. Dean v. Dean, 6 Conn. 285 (1826); Wilson v. Warner, 84 Conn. 560, 80 A. 718 (1911). Others have permitted oral express trusts of land in some or all cases. See Lord and Van Hecke, Parol Trusts in North Carolina, 8 N.C.L.Rev. 152 (1950); Madden, Trusts and the Statute of Frauds, 31 W.Va.L.Q. 166 (1925) (West Virginia cases); Benson, Parol Trusts in Real Estate, 1 Va.L.Reg. (n.s.) 81 (1915); 61 U.Pa.L.Rev. 687 (1913); 5 Tex.L.Rev. 186 (1927) (Texas cases).

See 1 Scott on Trusts § 40.1, for the historical background of the Statute of Frauds; see also 6 Holds. 379; Hening, The Original Drafts of the Statute of Frauds, 61 U.Pa.L.Rev. 283 (1913).

* * *

Restatement, Second, Trusts

§ 41. When and by Whom the Memorandum Should Be Signed—Declaration of Trust

Where the owner of an interest in land declares himself trustee of the interest, a memorandum properly evidencing the trust is sufficient to satisfy the requirements of the Statute of Frauds, if it is signed by him

(a) prior to or at the time of the declaration; or

(b) subsequent to the time of the declaration but before he has transferred the interest.

§ 42. When and by Whom the Memorandum Should Be Signed—Transfer in Trust

Where the owner of an interest in land transfers it inter vivos to another person in trust, a memorandum properly evidencing the trust is sufficient to satisfy the requirements of the Statute of Frauds, if it is signed

(a) by the transferor prior to or at the time of the transfer; or

(b) by the transferee

(i) prior to or at the time of the transfer; or

(ii) subsequent to the transfer to him but before he has transferred the interest to a third person.

§ 43.　Performance of an Oral Trust

Where an oral trust of an interest in land is created inter vivos, the trustee can properly perform the trust if he has not transferred the interest, although he cannot be compelled to do so.

* * *

§ 46.　What Memorandum Must Contain

A memorandum properly signed is sufficient to satisfy the requirements of the Statute of Frauds if, but only if, it sets forth with reasonable definiteness the trust property, the beneficiaries and the purposes of the trust.

* * *

§ 50.　Part Performance

Although a trust of an interest in land is orally declared and no memorandum is signed, the trust is enforceable if, with the consent of the trustee, the beneficiary as such enters into possession of the land or makes valuable improvements thereon or irrevocably changes his position in reliance upon the trust.

§ 51.　Who Can Take Advantage of Failure to Comply with Statute

Although a trust of an interest in land is orally declared and no memorandum is signed, no one except the trustee or persons succeeding to his interest can take advantage of the unenforceability of the trust.

Notes

1. The application of §§ 43 and 51 is illustrated by In re German, 193 F.Supp. 948 (S.D.Ill.1961), a bankruptcy proceeding. Mr. and Mrs. Sersig had conveyed realty to Mrs. German on an oral trust, the purpose being to enable Mr. and Mrs. German to build a duplex dwelling for occupancy by both couples and then convey it to the Sersigs. The plan was frustrated by entry of a judgment against the Germans by a pre-existing creditor, which interfered with construction financing. The realty was thereupon reconveyed to the Sersigs, without consideration; and, less than two months later, the Germans (who had been insolvent since before the conveyance on oral trust) became voluntary bankrupts.

The Sersigs claimed ownership of the realty. The Germans' judgment creditor resisted the claim, contending that the oral trust of realty was void and that the reconveyance to the Sersigs was both a fraudulent conveyance and a voidable preference. The reconveyance was held valid, and the judgment creditor's claim was rejected.

To the same effect, see Ward v. Grant, 9 Mass.App. 364, 401 N.E.2d 160 (1980).

2. Even if the titleholder becomes insolvent and the property has been attached or is subject to a tax lien, his recognition of the oral trust in writing makes the trust effective from the date of the original transfer and immunizes the property from the claims of his creditors. Zwaska v. Irwin, 52 N.J.Super.

27, 144 A.2d 554 (1958); United States v. Johnson, 200 F.Supp. 589 (D.Ariz. 1961). If the creditor has relied on the specific title being in the trustee, however, recognition of the trust does not remove the property from execution. Bryant v. Klatt, 2 F.2d 167 (S.D.N.Y.1924).

RASDALL'S ADMINISTRATORS v. RASDALL

Supreme Court of Wisconsin, 1859.
9 Wis. 379.

By the Court, PAINE, J. This suit was brought by the plaintiffs as administrator and administratrix of the estate of Abel Rasdall, deceased, to enjoin the defendant from proceeding in a suit to recover possession of certain real estate in the city of Madison, and to compel a conveyance by him to the plaintiffs. The grounds set forth for relief are that the plaintiffs' intestate, having in a personal encounter in 1843, dangerously wounded a man named Smith, and being apprehensive of arrest and prosecution, and desirous to so arrange his affairs that he might escape from the country, conveyed the property in question to the defendant, who was his brother; and that although the deed was absolute on its face, and purported to be for the consideration of $2,000, yet that it was without consideration, and that the defendant agreed to hold the property in trust, for the use and benefit of the deceased and his heirs. * * *

We have no doubt, from the evidence presented, that the conveyance was made by the deceased under the circumstances, and with the understanding set forth in the bill, though this is denied by the answer. And were this evidence proper to be received, it would fully sustain the decision of the court below. But it was parol evidence, and was all objected to by the defendant's counsel, and the objection is fatal.

It is one of those cases where the real merits and justice of the matter create a strong desire to escape from the application of the stern rule of law, which prohibits an inquiry by means of parol evidence. But the barrier is too strong to be broken over; and while it restrains us, furnishes its own justification in the fact, that though, in individual instances like the present, it may work hardship, yet in the main it promotes private security and the general good.

We do not feel called upon to cite authorities, to show that in the absence of fraud, accident, or mistake, parol evidence cannot be received to prove that a deed, absolute on its face, was given in trust for the benefit of the grantor; and we have not been able to find anything in this case to make it an exception. We cannot see why, if this evidence is to be received to establish this trust, every other deed in the state may not be shown by parol to have been given upon trust, and the statute of frauds be entirely annulled.

But the counsel for the complainants, seeming conscious of the difficulty of sustaining the admissibility of this evidence for the purpose of establishing the trust, yet contended that although inadmissible for that purpose directly, it should be admitted, and the relief granted, on the ground of fraud. This presents a question of very great importance, and in view of the authorities on the subject, of no little difficulty. There is no doubt that if any fraud had been alleged, by means of which the defendant procured the conveyance from his brother to himself, or any mistake, by which the instrument was made absolute, instead of expressing the trust intended, parol evidence would have been admissible to show such fraud or mistake. This conveyance would thus stand upon the same footing with all other contracts, and come within the conceded power of courts of equity to inquire, by parol evidence, into frauds or mistakes in their procurement or execution.

But no such fraud or mistake is alleged here. On the contrary, it appears from the whole tenor of the complaint, that the conveyance was made by Abel Rasdall, upon his own motion, and without any solicitation or instigation of the defendant, and that it was intended to be, as it is, absolute on its face.

The only fraud alleged, therefore, is that of the defendant's now claiming the property in violation of the parol trust, and whether that constitutes such a fraud, as will justify a court of equity in overturning the written contract of the parties upon parol evidence, is the question presented.

It cannot be denied that if the court can, by any legal means, arrive at the existence of the parol trust, then the violation of it by the defendant, in wresting their inheritance from the family of his dead brother, is most grossly fraudulent. And to avoid such injustice, courts of equity have frequently seized upon the slightest circumstances connected with the procurement of the conveyance, to avoid the operation of the statute of frauds. And there are cases, the principle of which would warrant the assertion that the attempt by the defendant to claim the rights which this deed, on its face, gives him, contrary to the parol trust, is such a fraud as would justify the relief upon parol evidence. But I confess my inability to see how, upon principle, this position can be sustained, consistently with a due observance of the statute. Placing the relief in such cases upon the ground of fraud, is implied by admitting that the parol evidence cannot be admitted to establish the trust, for the purpose of enforcing it, directly as a trust. And this is also expressly admitted. But it seems apparent to my mind that to say, in such a case, it shall be admitted to establish the fraud, is equally a violation of the statute. Because the fraud consists only in the refusal to execute the trust. The court, therefore, cannot say that there is a fraud, without first saying that there is a trust. And the parol evidence, if admitted, must be admitted to establish the trust, in order that the court may charge the party with fraud in setting up his claim against it. Conceding then, that they cannot execute the trust directly in such case, because it cannot be proved by parol, is it not a mere evasion of the statute to say that they will allow it to be proved by parol for the purpose of enforcing it indirectly, by charging the party with fraud for refusing to execute it? Such a course does not relieve the court from the charge of violating the statute, but subjects it to the odium of an attempted, but unsuccessful evasion.

It may be said that fraud ought not to be tolerated. That is very true, but that is not the question. The question is, whether the court, without violating the law, can get at the fraud. There is no doubt that trusts ought to be enforced; but that is not a sufficient reason for admitting parol evidence to establish them. When the party offers this, the court says no; the law forbids it.

So, however desirable it may be to prevent fraud, if the fraud cannot be established, except by first showing a trust by parol, is not the same answer equally applicable? If not, it is difficult to see that the statute of frauds is to have any practical effect; for although trusts and agreements contrary to the written contracts of parties, cannot be proved by parol so as to be enforced as such, yet they may be proved and held of sufficient force to charge the party with fraud in not observing them. And the result is practically the same. It is for courts to say to the parties, "These agreements are not valid, not binding; we cannot compel you to observe them; yet if you do not observe them without being compelled, we will hold that to be a fraud on your part, and for the fraud, will compel you to execute them."

It is impossible to reconcile with principle very many of the adjudications upon the statute of frauds. Courts seem to have been so intent upon administering justice in the particular case, that they have frequently lost sight of its provision, and their action has often amounted to little less than the exercise of the right to appeal [sic] or suspend its operation whenever they deemed that the real justice of the case required it. But the progress of adjudication upon the subject has been marked by many strong protests against the wide departure from principle, and the regrets expressed by courts that it had ever obtained. And the current of modern authority is in favor of returning to the due observance of the provisions of this law, according to their obvious intent.

But the distinction between fraud in procuring a conveyance, and that which arises only from the refusal to execute a parol trust or agreement, connected with a conveyance obtained without fraud, is not only clear upon principle, but is not without sanction.

* * *

In the cases of Dean v. Dean et al., 6 Conn. 284; Bandor v. Snyder, 5 Barb.S.C.Rep. 63; Lathrop v. Hoyt, 7 id. 59, and other similar cases which might be cited, the hardship of enforcing the statute was equally great as in this case, and in some of them the courts expressed their willingness to escape from its application if possible. But there was no suggestion that the mere refusal of the defendants to execute the parol trusts, was such a fraud as would take the case out of its provisions.

But the strongest support that seems to exist for the opposite view, may perhaps be derived from the cause of decision admitting parol evidence to show that a deed absolute on its face was given as security, and thereby converting it into a mortgage. * * *

* * * And in determining this question, I can see no distinction between an express trust and a parol agreement making a deed a mort-

gage. If the refusal to abide by the latter is to be held on principle, to be such a fraud as takes the case out of the rule, and justifies parol evidence, I can see no reason why a refusal to execute an express trust, evidenced only by parol, should not be so held. The injustice, the wrong and the fraud are not only as great, but greater in the latter case than in the former. For in the former the party would only get the land for the money he had loaned, while in the latter he would get it for nothing. And if these cases are to be held correct upon principle, we can see so reason why the refusal by any party to perform a parol agreement, within the statute of frauds, should not be held such a fraud as would take the case out of the statute whenever such refusal would work hardship and injustice upon the opposite party. But we must say that we think these decisions cannot be sustained upon principle, and that, if established by authority too firmly to be shaken, it must be regarded as an invasion upon the statute which cannot justify still further encroachment. And it is perhaps not so settled on authority as to be beyond question.

* * *

But we will not pursue this part of the subject further. We do not of course purpose to pass upon the question, whether in the absence of fraud or mistake in its execution, an absolute deed can be converted by parol evidence into a mortgage. That question is not before us, but it is so nearly allied to the one before us, that we could not well determine the latter, without inquiring how it was affected by the decisions to which we have alluded. And as we think the rule they have established does not rest upon principle, however it may be determined upon authority, we do not feel warranted in following the rule which they would by analogy suggest. And we must hold that as the deed was made absolute to the defendant without any mistake, or fraud on his part, his mere refusal to perform the trust, is not such a fraud as will justify the admission of parol evidence, and the enforcement of the trust. The reason is, that the law forbids us to be informed that there was a trust by that kind of evidence. It may and does undoubtedly work hardship in this case, and that we regret; but if parties will, in face of the positive provisions of the statute, risk their interests upon the honor or justice of others, and the security fails them, they have no right to ask courts to violate the law to furnish relief.

[margin note: P: Precedent]

* * *

We are compelled therefore upon the whole case, to _reverse_ the judgment of the court below, and direct a decree to be entered dismissing the complaint. At the same time we may express the hope that the defendant's conscience, to which his brother has trusted, may not suffer him so far to violate that trust, as to detain their just inheritance from his wife and children.

Notes

1. The great majority of the American decisions are at least verbally in accord. Graham v. Williams, 92 R.I. 102, 166 A.2d 412 (1961); Ledbetter v. Ledbetter, 271 Ala. 629, 126 So.2d 477 (1961); Rosen v. Rosen, 384 Pa. 547,

121 A.2d 89 (1956). The courts have persisted in the real or apparent inconsistency, criticized in the principal case, in cases involving restitution on payment of an oral mortgage or for other forms of unfair dealing with real property. See Restatement of the Law of Restitution §§ 62, 108, 180.

2. The *Rasdall* case poses starkly the flat conflict between the policy of the Statute of Frauds and the policy against dishonesty. In most cases, the only evidence of unfair dealing is the oral promise to hold the property in trust and proof of that promise is forbidden by the Statute of Frauds. The English courts have had little trouble dealing with that conflict and decree a reconveyance from the grantee to the grantor if the grantee fails to keep his oral promise to hold the land for, or reconvey to, the grantor without more, on the theory that the grantee is a constructive (not express) trustee for the grantor and the Statute of Frauds expressly excludes constructive trusts from its operation. Haigh v. Kaye, L.R. 7 Ch.App.C. 469 (Chancery, 1872); Davies v. Otty, 35 Beav. 208 (Chancery, 1865). In the latter case the court said: "I am of the opinion that it is not honest to keep the land." In the United States, the courts are less ready—at least in theory—to bypass the Statute of Frauds. If there is fraud in the procurement of the title to the land or a confidential relationship between the transferor and the transferee a constructive trust will be imposed. Koizim v. Koizim, 181 Conn. 492, 435 A.2d 1030 (1980); Fuller v. Fuller, 606 P.2d 306 (Wyo.1980); Dove v. White, 211 Md. 228, 126 A.2d 835 (1956); Kachanian v. Kachanian, 100 N.H. 135, 121 A.2d 566 (1956); Marston v. Myers, 217 Or. 498, 342 P.2d 1111 (1959); White v. White, 16 N.J. 458, 109 A.2d 418 (1954); Gammel v. Enochs, 353 P.2d 1106 (Okl.1960). There must be proof that the transferee agreed to hold the land for the transferor, before the fraud in the procurement or a confidential relationship will be made the basis for a remedy. Gruenwald v. Mason, 139 Colo. 1, 335 P.2d 879 (1959); Light v. Ash, 174 Neb. 44, 627, 115 N.W.2d 903, 119 N.W.2d 90 (1963).

3. The Restatement, Second, Trusts summarizes the rule:

§ 44. *Effect of Failure of Oral Trust for the Settlor*

(1) Where the owner of an interest in land transfers it inter vivos to another in trust for the transferor, but no memorandum properly evidencing the intention to create a trust is signed, as required by the Statute of Frauds, and the transferee refuses to perform the trust, the transferee holds the interest upon a constructive trust for the transferor, if

(a) the transfer was procured by fraud, duress, undue influence or mistake, or

(b) the transferee at the time of the transfer was in a confidential relation to the transferor, or

(c) the transfer was made as security for an indebtedness of the transferor.

(2) Where the owner of an interest in land transfers it inter vivos to another in trust for the transferor, and the transferor's intention to create a trust but not the identity of the beneficiary is properly manifested, and the transferee refuses to perform the trust, the transferee holds the interest upon a resulting trust for the transferor.

* * *

Sinclair v. Purdy, 235 N.Y. 245, 139 N.E. 255 (1923) illustrates the operation of the "American rule" in a case of confidential relationship. ("Here was a man transferring to his sister the only property he had in the world. He was transferring it in obedience to advice that embarrassment would be avoided if he put it in her name. He was doing this, as she admits, in reliance upon her honor." 235 N.Y. at 254.)

4. The rule is different where the settlor is not the intended beneficiary. The Restatement, Second, Trusts declares:

§ 45. *Effect of Failure of Oral Trust for a Third Person*

(1) Where the owner of an interest in land transfers it inter vivos to another in trust for a third person, but no memorandum properly evidencing the intention to create a trust is signed, as required by the Statute of Frauds, and the transferee refuses to perform the trust, the transferee holds the interest upon a constructive trust for the third person, if, but only if,

(a) the transferee by fraud, duress or undue influence prevented the transferor from creating an enforceable interest in the third person, or

(b) the transferee at the time of the transfer was in a confidential relation to the transferor, or

(c) the transfer was made by the transferor in anticipation of death.

(2) Except under the circumstances stated in Subsection (1, a, b, c), where the owner of an interest in land transfers it inter vivos to another in trust for a third person, and the transferor's intention to create a trust but not the identity of the beneficiary is properly manifested, and the transferee refused to perform the trust, the transferee holds the interest upon a resulting trust for the transferor.

* * *

See comments, Breach of Oral Agreement between Persons in a Confidential Relationship, 31 N.C.L.Rev. 242 (1953); The Confidential Relationship Theory of Constructive Trusts—An Exception to the Statute of Frauds, 29 Ford. L.Rev. 561 (1961); Imposition of a Constructive Trust in New England, 41 B.U.L.Rev. 78 (1961). Compare Oursler v. Armstrong, 10 N.Y.2d 385, 179 N.E.2d 489 (1961) (supra page 330).

5. On these issues generally, see Scott, Conveyances Upon Trusts Not Properly Declared, 37 Harv.L.Rev. 653 (1924); Ames, Constructive Trusts Based Upon the Breach of an Express Oral Trust of Land, 20 Harv.L.Rev. 549 (1907), reprinted in Lectures on Legal History, 425 (1913); Stone, Resulting Trusts and the Statute of Frauds, 6 Colum.L.Rev. 323 (1906); Costigan, Trusts Based on Oral Promises, 12 Mich.L.Rev. 423, 515 (1914); Bogert, Confidential Relations and Unenforcible Express Trusts, 13 Cornell L.Q. 237 (1928).

Note On Constructive Trusts

Our concern with constructive trusts in this section is with its use as a device for effectuating oral express trusts which would otherwise fail under the Statute of Frauds. The constructive trust is not a true trust but a remedial device available to prevent unjust enrichment in a wide variety of situations most of which do not involve express trusts. E.g., Bird v. Plunkett, supra p. 7; Latham v. Father Divine, supra p. 258; In Re Wiggins Estate, supra p. 324. The essential elements of the device are illustrated in the following extract from the Restatement of Restitution.

Restatement, Second, Restitution
Tentative Draft No. 2 (1984)

§ 30. Constructive Trust and Equitable Lien

(1) A constructive trust or an equitable lien as described in this Chapter is a right to restitution from property, conferred as a means of preventing unjust enrichment. Such a trust or lien attaches only to the extent that the property is held by a person who owes restitution to the claimant.

* * *

Comment:

a. Constructive trust and equitable lien compared. A principal use of constructive trust is to award to a claimant a gain produced by an investment of property that was acquired from him by wrongdoing such as fraud; another is to charge a fiduciary for gain he acquired by breach of loyalty to the claimant. Imposing a constructive trust is also a means of requiring specific restitution to the claimant. In contrast, imposing an equitable lien on an asset does not vest ownership in the claimant and does not afford him specific restitution. The lien assures the claimant that the asset will be devoted to satisfying his right to restitution in preference to the claims of ordinary creditors of the person owing restitution. When a sum of money has been acquired from the claimant by fraud and partly dissipated, the claimant has a right to restitution greater in amount than the money remaining in the wrongdoer's control. That is a proper case for an equitable lien. The claimant can get a judgment for the amount acquired by the wrongdoer (with interest as appropriate) and an order that the money remaining with the wrongdoer be applied to the judgment. The claimant can get comparable relief if the wrongdoer has made a losing investment of the money he acquired by fraud; property acquired by the wrongdoer through the investment will be subjected to an equitable lien. If the claimant wants specific restitution of that property, and the requirements of § 10 are satisfied [i.e., if it is shown that retention of the property would unjustly enrich the wrongdoer (or a successor in interest)], a constructive trust is an appropriate form of relief.
* * *

In general, a claimant whose property has been misappropriated and exchanged for other property of less value will be best served by enforcing an equitable lien on the latter and preserving, as a deficiency claim, any unsatisfied part of his right to restitution. Asserting a constructive trust on property of a wrongdoer (or of a successor in interest) will give the claimant more complete relief only when the value of the property includes a gain by investment, appreciation, or natural increase. * * *

b. Basis in unjust enrichment. Both constructive trusts and equitable liens are means of redressing unjust enrichment. * * * They are based on the ground that unless a person is held to account for property, or an interest in property, either he or someone claiming under him will be unjustly enriched. The occasions for such relief are as various as are the grounds for personal liability to make restitution. If unjust enrichment results from tortious conduct, or from the abuse of a fiduciary or confidential relationship, a constructive trust or an equitable lien may be an appropriate remedy. * * * If it results from mistake, such a remedy may likewise be appropriate. * * * These are the most usual instances. * * *

Notes

1. For a recent case applying the foregoing principles, see Namow Corp. v. Egger, 668 P.2d 265 (Nev.1983). See also Provencher v. Berman, 699 F.2d 568 (1st Cir. 1983); Chase Manhattan Bank v. Israel-British Bank, 2 W.L.R. 202 (Ch.Div.1979); In Re Stix & Co., Inc. 27 B.R. 252 (E.D.Mo.1983).

2. Subjecting the ill-gotten gains to a constructive trust is fairly easy where the original property is still intact. Where it has been sold and the proceeds invested in other property a difficult problem of "tracing" may be encountered. On the subject of tracing, see Ayers v. Fay, 187 Okla. 230, 102 P.2d 156, 158–59 (1940):

> It has long been a fundamental concept of English law that a change in the form of a thing which is owned does not change the ownership. Derived from and based upon this concept is the rule that the equitable owner of trust property is entitled to that which arises out of such property by sale, exchange or otherwise. This rule is, in many instances, effectuated by a device known as "tracing", meaning nothing more nor less than identification, by the cestui, of the trust or its avails in the hands of the trustee or a third person not a bona fide purchaser. A majority of the courts require the cestui, seeking to follow trust property, to convince the court that the fund or property in the hands of the trustee or another not a bona fide purchaser is either all of, part of, or was produced by the original trust res. Volume 4, Bogert, "Trusts & Trustees", § 921.

> Early cases tended to impose on the cestui the unbearable burden of specifically identifying even coins and bills claimed subject to the original trust. But the more modern and certainly the more practical view is that trust funds have been sufficiently traced when it is shown they entered a mass of cash and have remained there. As stated in Massey v. Fisher, C.C., 62 F. 958, 959, "It is sufficient to trace it into the bank's vaults, and find that a sum equal to it (and presumably representing it), continuously remained there until the receiver took it. The modern rules of equity require no more". See, also, 65 C.J. 973, where it is stated sufficient proof is made if the cestui " * * * can show the particular fund or mass into which the trust money has gone, such as an individual bank account of the trustee". And where a trustee has commingled trust funds with his own, the cestui may recover, to the extent of the trust fund, the lowest balance to which the mass has been depleted. The trustee is presumed to have used his own funds first, so that the remainder is sufficiently identified as the trust fund, 65 C.J. 975.

Note on Resulting Trusts

The constructive trust is implied in *law*, i.e. imposed on a transaction regardless of the intent of the parties. The resulting trust is implied in *fact* in three types of situations: (1) where a trust (private or charitable) has become impossible of fulfillment, e.g. Evans. v. Abney, supra p. 19; (2) where a (private or charitable) trust is fully performed without exhausting the trust property; (3) where one person pays the consideration for property and directs that title be transferred to another. The first two types of resulting trust are the equitable analogue of the possibility of reverter (see p. 800, infra). The third type—the "purchase money resulting trust"—is of immediate interest because it sometimes serves the same purpose as the constructive trust, effectuating an oral express trust which would otherwise fail under the Statute of Frauds. Like the constructive trust the resulting trust is not subject to the Statute of Frauds, a fact which may explain the courts' tendency to treat them interchangeably. See e.g. Askins v. Easterling, 141 Colo. 83, 347 P.2d 126 (1959).

The Restatement, Second, Trusts outlines the doctrine as follows:

§ 440. General rule

Where a transfer of property is made to one person and the purchase price is paid by another, a resulting trust arises in favor of the person by whom the purchase price is paid, except as stated in §§ 441, 442 and 444 [illegal purpose].

§ 441. Rebutting the resulting trust

A resulting trust does not arise where a transfer of property is made to one person and the purchase price is paid by another, if the person by whom the purchase price is paid manifests an intention that no resulting trust should arise.

§ 442. Purchase in the name of a relative

Where a transfer of property is made to one person and the purchase price is paid by another and the transferee is a wife, child or other natural object of bounty of the person by whom the purchase price is paid, a resulting trust does not arise unless the latter manifests an intention that the transferee should not have the beneficial interest in the property.

§ 443. Rebutting the presumption of a gift to a relative

Where a transfer of property is made to one person and the purchase price is paid by another, and the transferee is a wife, child or other natural object of bounty of the person by whom the purchase price is paid, and the latter manifests an intention that the transferee should not have the beneficial interest in the property, a resulting trust arises.

* * *

The origins of the purchase money resulting trust doctrine are obscure. Some commentators assume that the presumption arose at the same time and for the same reasons as the presumption of a resulting use on a gratuitous conveyance. Ames, Constructive Trusts Based upon the Breach of an Express Oral Trust of Land, 20 Harv.L.Rev. 549 (1907), reprinted Lectures on Legal History, 425 (1913); Costigan, The Classification of Trusts as Express, Resulting, and Constructive, 27 Harv.L.Rev. 437 (1914). It is a plausible hypothesis that this presumption also originated because of a general practice of holding land to the use of another, since a purchaser of land under such a practice would probably have title conveyed to a dummy.   On the basis of this assumption, Ames, in the article just cited, argued that there was no reason for the continuance of the purchase money resulting trust presumption after the Statute of Uses had changed the land-holding customs.   That is, Ames felt that there was no longer any more justification for this presumption than for the presumption of a resulting trust on a gratuitous conveyance, and that the proper assumption, in the absence of evidence to the contrary, was that the grantee was intended to take absolutely.   Professor Scott has argued that, because of a variety of situations in which the purchase money resulting trust presumption corresponds with the intent of the parties, the continuance of the presumption is justifiable.   Scott, Resulting Trusts Arising upon the Purchase of Land, 40 Harv.L.Rev. 669 (1927).   A number of states have followed the Ames view and abolished the presumption by statute.   See, for example, McKinney's N.Y. EPTL 7–1.3.   For a discussion of the statutes on the subject see 40 Harv.L.Rev. 668, 675 (1927).   The titleholder may, however, still be held as a constructive trustee under the confidential relationship or fraud in the inducement theories.   Foreman v. Foreman, 251 N.Y. 237, 167 N.E. 428 (1929).   Because most of the statutes (though not New York's) only apply to realty, the presumption of a purchase money resulting trust remains available for personalty notwithstanding the enactment of the statute. See McQuaide v. McQuaide, 92 Ind.App. 370, 168 N.E. 500 (1921).

It should be noted that the relationships which give rise to a presumption of gift are usually very narrowly defined.   See McCafferty v. Flinn, 14 Del.Ch. 307, 125 A. 675 (1924) (analysis of the reasons for the presumption of gift).   The fact that the grantee is the wife or the child of the payor does not always guarantee that he will take the land as a gift.   Shores v. Shores, 134 Colo. 319, 303 P.2d 689 (1956);   Krager v. Waage, 76 S.D. 395, 79 N.W.2d 286 (1956);   Leyva v. Pachecho, 163 Tex. 638, 358 S.W.2d 547 (1962);   Jackson v. Jackson, 150 Ga. 544, 104 S.E. 236 (1920).

SECTION SEVEN.   THE BENEFICIARY— CHARITABLE AND HONORARY TRUSTS

A.   IN GENERAL

MORICE v. BISHOP OF DURHAM

Chancery, 1804.

9 Ves.Jr. 399, 32 Eng.Rep. 656;   10 Ves.Jr. 522, 32 Eng.Rep. 947 (1805).

Ann Cracherode by her Will, dated the 16th of April 1801, and duly executed to pass real estate, after giving several legacies to her next of kin and others, some of which she directed to be paid out of the produce of her real estate, directed to be sold, bequeathed all her personal estate to the Bishop of Durham, his executors, etc., upon trust to pay her debts and legacies, etc.;   and to dispose of the ultimate residue to such objects of benevolence and liberality as the Bishop of Durham in his own discretion shall most approve of; and she appointed the Bishop her sole executor.

The bill was filed by the next of kin, to have the Will established, except as to the residuary bequest; and that such bequest may be declared void. The Attorney General was made a Defendant. The Bishop by his answer expressly disclaimed any beneficial interest in himself personally.

* * *

The Master of the Rolls [Sir W. Grant]. The only question is whether the trust, upon which the residue of the personal estate is bequeathed, be a trust for charitable purposes. That it is upon some trust, and not for the personal benefit of the Bishop is clear from the words of the Will; and is admitted by his Lordship; who expressly disclaims any beneficial interest. (See Gibbs v. Rumsey, 2 Ves. & Bea. 194). That it is a trust, unless it be of a charitable nature, too indefinite to be executed by this Court, has not been, and cannot be, denied. There can be no trust, over the exercise of which this Court will not assume a control; for an uncontrollable power of disposition would be ownership, and not trust. If there be a clear trust, but for uncertain objects, the property, that is the subject of the trust, is undisposed of, and the benefit of such trust must result to those, to whom the law gives the ownership in default of disposition by the former owner. But this doctrine does not hold good with regard to trusts for charity. Every other trust must have a definite object. There must be somebody, in whose favour the Court can decree performance. But it is now settled, upon authority, which it is too late to controvert, that, where a charitable purpose is expressed, however general, the bequest shall not fail on account of the uncertainty of the object: but the particular mode of application will be directed by the King in some cases, in others by this Court.

Then is this a trust for charity? Do purposes of liberality and benevolence mean the same as objects of charity? That word in its widest sense denotes all the good affections, men ought to bear towards each other; in its most restricted and common sense, relief of the poor. In neither of these senses is it employed in this Court. Here its signification is derived chiefly from the Statute of Elizabeth (stat. 43 Eliz. c. 4). Those purposes are considered charitable, which that Statute enumerates, or which by analogies are deemed within its spirit and intendment; and to some such purpose every bequest to charity generally shall be applied. But it is clear liberality and benevolence can find numberless objects, not included in that statute in the largest construction of it. The use of the word "charitable" seems to have been purposely avoided in this Will, in order to leave the Bishop the most unrestrained discretion. Supposing, the uncertainty of the trust no objection to its validity, could it be contended to be an abuse of the trust to employ this fund upon objects, which all mankind would allow to be objects of liberality and benevolence; though not to be said, in the language of this Court, to be objects also of charity? By what rule of construction could it be said, all objects of liberality and benevolence are excluded, which do not fall within the Statute of Elizabeth?   The question is, not whether he may not apply it upon purposes strictly charitable, but whether he is bound so to apply it?   I am not aware of any case, in which the bequest has been held charitable, where the testator has not either used that word, to denote his general purpose, or specified some particular purpose, which this Court has determined to be charitable in its nature.   (10 Ves. 540.)

* * * But here there is no specific purpose pointed out, to which the residue is to be applied: the words "charity" and "charitable" do not occur: the words used are not synonymous: the trusts may be completely executed without bestowing any part of this residue upon purposes strictly charitable.   The residue therefore cannot be said to be given to charitable purposes; and, as the trust is too indefinite to be disposed of to any other purpose, it follows, that the residue remains undisposed of; and must be distributed among the next of kin of the testatrix.

[This decree was affirmed on appeal in 10 Ves.Jr. 522, 32 Eng.Rep. 947 (1805) by Lord Chancellor Eldon.   The following are excerpts from his opinion.   Ed.]

The question then is entirely, whether this is according to the intention a gift to purposes of charity in general, as understood in this Court: such, that this Court would have held the Bishop bound, and would have compelled him, to apply the surplus to such charitable purposes as can be answered only in obedience to decrees, where the gift is to charity, in general: or is it, or may it be according to the intention, to such purposes, going beyond those, partially, or altogether, which the Court understands by "charitable purposes"; and, if that is the intention, is the gift too indefinite to create an effectual trust, to be here executed? * * * It is not contended, and it is not necessary, to support this decree, to contend, that the trustee might not consistently with the intention, have devoted every shilling to uses, in that sense charitable, and of course a part of the property.   But the true question is, whether, if upon the one hand he might have devoted the whole to purposes, in this sense charitable, he might not equally according to the intention have devoted the whole to purposes benevolent and liberal, and yet not within the meaning of charitable purposes, as this Court construes those words; and, if according to the intention it was competent to him to do so, I do not apprehend, that under any authority upon such words the Court could have charged him with mal-administration, if he had applied the whole to purposes, which according to the meaning of the testator are benevolent and liberal; though not acts of that species of benevolence and liberality, which this Court in the construction of a Will calls charitable acts.

* * * But the question is, whether, according to the ordinary sense, not the sense of the passages and authors alluded to, treating upon the great and extensive sense of the word "charity," in the Christian religion, this testatrix meant by these words to confine the Defendant to such acts of charity or charitable purposes as this Court would have enforced by decree, and reference to a Master.   I do not think, that was the intention; and, if not, the intention is too indefinite to create a trust. But it was the intention to create a trust; and the object being too in-

definite, has failed. The consequence of Law is, that the Bishop takes the property upon trust to dispose of it, as the Law will dispose of it: not for his own benefit, or any purpose this Court can effectuate. I think, therefore, this decree is right.

Notes

1. Would the same result have been reached if there had been an outright bequest to the Bishop followed by such language as: "I request the Bishop of Durham to dispose of the ultimate residue to such objects of benevolence and liberality as he in his own discretion shall most approve of, not intending, however, to impose any obligation upon him to carry out this request"?

In Norman v. Prince, 40 R.I. 402, 101 A. 126 (1917), property was left to a trustee in trust to pay the income for a designated period "in whole or in part at such time or times as the trustee shall select to testator's said son Hugh or to Hugh's wife or to any child or children of Hugh or to any other person or persons whomsoever, as the trustee for the time being in the uncontrolled absolute discretion or pleasure of said trustee shall see fit". Hugh died without issue, and his widow released all claims against the estate. The court, emphasizing the broad and arbitrary power of disposition, held that no trust was created, and that the original and successor trustees might dispose of the income as they desired.

In In re Ralston's Estate, 1 Cal.2d 724, 37 P.2d 76, 96 A.L.R. 953 (1934), the will gave the entire estate to the executor "in trust" with "absolute authority to dispose of this my entire estate as he may see fit". The court held that the property passed by intestacy, the dissenting judge expressing the opinion that the will made an absolute gift to the executor.

See 45 Yale L.J. 1515 (1936); 35 Colum.L.Rev. 954 (1935); 34 Mich.L.Rev. 582 (1936); 31 Harv.L.Rev. 661 (1918); 14 Minn.L.Rev. 310 (1930); 28 Mich. L.Rev. 943 (1930); 1 Scott on Trusts §§ 123, 125; 3 ibid. §§ 411, 411.1, 417; Restatement, Second, Trusts §§ 125, 411, 417.

2. Why is the trust in the principal case invalid as

(a) A private trust?

(b) A charitable trust?

The use of vague general terms describing the purposes of the trust, such as "benevolent", "liberal", "utilitarian", "public", "deserving", "worthy", "patriotic", etc., is, of course, highly unfortunate. Even if the trust is not ultimately held void, such words naturally invite litigation. In Chichester Diocesan Fund v. Simpson, [1944] A.C. 341, the House of Lords affirmed the view that the word "benevolent" is not synonymous with "charitable." Not all American courts, however, have agreed. See 115 A.L.R. 1123; 3 Scott on Trusts § 398.1; Restatement, Second, Trusts § 398.

3. Assuming that no trust was effectively created in the situation of the principal case, and assuming further that the court could determine what were "objects of benevolence and liberality", is there any way in which the Bishop of Durham might have been held privileged to carry out the intent of the testatrix, and also be subject to control at the suit of some person or persons if he failed to devote the property to the objects specified in the will?

For discussion of the issues raised by this case, see Ames, The Failure of the Tilden Trust, 5 Harv.L.Rev. 389 (1892), reprinted in Lectures on Legal

History, 285 (adverse criticism of Morice v. Bishop of Durham); Gray, Gifts for a Non-Charitable Purpose, 15 Harv.L.Rev. 67 (1902); Gray, The Rule against Perpetuities, Appendix H (3d Ed., 1915); Scott, Control of Property by the Dead, 65 U.Pa.L.Rev. 527, 538 (1917); 1 Scott on Trusts §§ 112, 119–125; 3 ibid. §§ 348–348.4, 364, 368–377, 391, 398–398.2; Restatement, Second, Trusts §§ 112, 119–25, 348, 364, 368–77, 391, 398.

"Stat of Elizabeth"

Charitable Purpose

In Morice v. Bishop of Durham the Master of the Rolls cited the 1601 Statute of Charitable Uses, 43 Eliz. c. 4, as the chief guide to the meaning of charitable purpose. The preamble to that statute listed a number of typical charities:

> * * * some for relief of aged, impotent and poor people, some for maintenance of sick and maimed soldiers and mariners, schools of learning, free schools, and scholars in universities, some for repair of bridges, ports, havens, causeways, churches, sea-banks and highways, some for education and preferment of orphans, some for or towards relief, stock or maintenance for houses of correction, some for marriages of poor maids, some for supportation, aid and help of young tradesmen, handicraftsmen and persons decayed, and others for relief or redemption of prisoners or captives, and for aid or ease of any poor inhabitants concerning payments of fifteens, setting out of soldiers and other taxes * * *

Subject to the general requirement noted below, of benefit to the public at large or a substantial segment of it, gifts for purposes that fit within or are closely analogous to one or more of the purposes recited in the 1601 statute are usually held to be charitable *per se*, without extensive inquiry as to the public value of the particular gift. The statutory enumeration did not purport to be exhaustive, however, and other purposes of public value have also been held charitable. The Restatement of Trusts, Second, after denominating as charitable the relief of poverty, the advancement of education, the advancement of religion, the promotion of health, and governmental or municipal purposes (§§ 369–373), adds the following catch-all:

> § 374. Promotion of Other Purposes Beneficial to the Community
>
> A trust for the promotion of purposes which are of a character sufficiently beneficial to the community to justify permitting property to be devoted forever to their accomplishment is charitable.

Not surprisingly, judicial appraisal of community benefit is to some extent a function of time and place. Jackson v. Phillips, 96 Mass. 539 (1867), though holding trusts for opposition to slavery and aid to fugitive slaves to be charitable, held non-charitable a trust "to secure the passage of laws granting women, whether married or unmarried, the right to vote; to hold office; to hold, manage, and devise property; and all other civil rights enjoyed by men." Accord: Garrison v. Little, 75 Ill.App. 402 (1898). Compare Register of Wills for Baltimore City v. Cook, 241 Md. 264, 216 A.2d 542 (1966), holding charitable a $10,000 trust to pay $100 a year for ten years to the Maryland Branch of the National Women's Party and to use the rest of the trust property "to help further the passage of and enactment into law of the EQUAL RIGHTS AMENDMENT to the Constitution of the United States."

Astonishing advances in technology have led modern courts to be fairly open-minded with respect to the possibility of further advances. Holding charitable a trust to pay the annual net income "as an award to the individual, or team, who, during the year * * *, has contributed most toward the solution of the problem of alcoholism" and to deliver the corpus to whoever should "solve the problem of alcoholism whereby alcoholics can ingest alcohol without the concomitant allergy of the body and obsession of the mind," the Court in Pierce v. Tharp, 58 Tenn.App. 362, 376, 430 S.W.2d 787, 793 (1968), reversed as to attorney fees, 224 Tenn. 328, 455 S.W.2d 145 (1970)—though confronted by "a vast amount of testimony * * * that it is impossible for an alcoholic to be cured so that he can become a social drinker"—said:

> Even that may be possible, however, in the future. As was said by the learned Chancellor in his opinion: "A devise or bequest made fifty years ago to reward the first person who lands on the moon, probably would have been held unenforceable and therefore void, but certainly it would not be so held today."

A subsequent report of the Rand Corporation, to the effect that a significant percentage of alcoholics can return to moderate drinking without relapsing into alcohol abuse, suggests that the Court's optimism may prove to be justified. New York Times, June 10, 1976, p. 1, col. 1.

A distinction must be drawn between the "purpose" of the gift and the motivation of the giver. The charitability of the purpose is determined not on the subjective basis ordinarily connoted by the term, but by the objective standard of benefit to the community or a sizeable part of it. It is immaterial that the gift was prompted by a selfish motive such as the desire to perpetuate one's own memory; many charitable gifts, if not most of them, are selfishly motivated in this sense.

The limitation of benefits to a small class will render a gift noncharitable even though the nature of the benefits fits into an accepted charitable category. Establishment and maintenance of a public park is ordinarily a charitable purpose. See, e.g., Kentucky v. Isaac W. Bernheim Foundation, 505 S.W.2d 762 (Ky.1974). The contrary was held, however, where the park was for the exclusive benefit of purchasers of lots in a 500-acre tract of land owned by the settlor. Butler v. Shelton, 408 S.W.2d 530 (Tex.Civ.App.1966). A testamentary trust for "the promotion and/or publication of my late husband's compositions" was held charitable, on the ground that the purpose was entertainment and education of the public. Matter of Manschinger, 74 Misc.2d 373, 343 N.Y.S.2d 426 (Surr.Ct.1973). But in Wilber v. Asbury Park National Bank & Trust Co., 142 N.J.Eq. 99, 59 A.2d 570 (1948) aff'd 2 N.J. 167, 65 A.2d 843 (1949) a testamentary trust for the typing, editing, and distribution of the testator's "Random Scientific Notes Seeking the Essentials in Place and Space" was held non-charitable. The court found as a fact that the Notes were irrational, unintelligible, and of no scientific or other value, so that the expenditure of the $15,000 corpus for their dissemination would be a waste of money—in other words, that there would be no public benefit.   Compare Fidelity Title & Trust Co. v. Clyde, 143 Conn. 247, 121 A.2d 625 (1956), a similar case with the same outcome (more doubtful, because the Court seems to have been influenced less by lack of literary merit than by the nature of the writings, which it characterized as pornographic).

Superficially it might seem that a trust to award annual prizes to individuals would benefit too small a group to qualify as a charity.   The courts have taken a broader view, holding such trusts to be charitable if the availability of the prizes offers an incentive to accomplishments that will benefit the community.   See, e.g., In re Harmon's Will, 80 N.Y.S.2d 903 (Surr.Ct.1948) (trust to award Harmon aviation trophies held charitable as designed to promote world peace);   Annot., Validity, As Charitable Trust, of Gift for Prize or Award to Person or Persons Accomplishing Specified Result, 7 A.L.R.3d 1281 (1966).   Likewise, a trust to endow a professorial chair, or to pay or supplement a minister's salary, is charitable even though the particular incumbents are few;   the gift also aids the school or church by relieving it of a financial burden.   IV Scott on Trusts §§ 370, 371.1 (3d ed. 1967).   Bequests for masses or other religious services for the deceased testator are held noncharitable by some courts as being for the sole benefit of the testator (though allowable as funeral expense if reasonable in amount).   E.g., Chelsea National Bank v. Our Lady Star of the Sea, 105 N.J.Eq. 236, 147 Atl. 470 (1929).   Most courts hold such bequests to be charitable, however, as gifts to the religious institution.   E.g., Matter of Connolly, 40 Misc.2d 673, 243 N.Y.S.2d 727 (Surr.Ct.1963);   Matter of Klein, 39 Misc.2d 960, 242 N.Y.S.2d 241 (Surr.Ct. 1963) (Jewish memorial services);   Obrecht v. Pujos, 206 Ky. 751, 268 S.W. 564 (1925).

Two limitations on charitable purposes find some support in the earlier law but no longer have much significance.   First, decisions can be found denying charitable status to trusts supporting good works in another state or nation.   The modern cases take a less parochial view.   E.g., Bogdanovich v. Bogdanovich, 360 Mo. 753, 230 S.W.2d 695 (1950) (trust for school in Yugoslavia);   Matter of Antoni, 186 Misc. 988, 61 N.Y.S.2d 349 (Surr.Ct.1946) ("trust for widows and orphans of my native village" in Germany).   Second, it has occasionally been held that trusts to promote changes in existing law are not charitable.   E.g., Jackson v. Phillips, supra.   The great weight of modern authority is to the contrary.   Annot., Validity of Charitable Trust to Promote Change in Laws or Systems or Methods of Government, 22 A.L.R.3d 886 (1968).   Federal tax deductions are denied, by express legislation, to contributions to charities substantially engaged in legislative programs or political campaigns;   but this has no effect on their status as a matter of property law.   For an overview of this subject and charitable purpose generally, see Clark, "The Limitation on Political Activities: A Discordant Note in the Law of Charities," 46 Va.L.Rev. 439 (1960).

✓LEFKOWITZ, ATTORNEY GENERAL
v. CORNELL UNIVERSITY

New York Supreme Court, Appellate Division, Fourth Department, 1970.
35 A.D.2d 166, 316 N.Y.S.2d 264.

MARSH, Justice: Defendants, Cornell University (Cornell), Cornell Aeronautical Laboratory, Inc. (CAL) and EDP Technology, Inc. (EDP) appeal from a judgment whereby it was ordered and adjudged that all of the defendants be permanently enjoined from consummating the proposed sale of CAL to EDP; and that defendants Cornell and CAL be permanently enjoined from conveying CAL or any of its capital stock or its land, buildings, or facilities, except upon notice to the Attorney General and approval by the Supreme Court.

In late 1945, Curtiss-Wright Corporation was the owner of research laboratory facilities, together with an uncompleted wind tunnel, located in the Town of Cheektowaga, Erie County. Due to the conclusion of World War II and also because of a planned move by Curtiss-Wright to Columbus, Ohio, Curtiss-Wright felt there was little prospect of its using the wind tunnel to the extent originally contemplated. It therefore considered making a charitable gift of the Cheektowaga facilities in order to obtain a tax saving for the year 1945, a year in which it could derive the maximum benefit from a tax deduction.

After the facilities had been offered to and rejected by at least one other university, Curtiss-Wright began preliminary negotiations with Cornell concerning the disposition of the lab. Thereafter, on December 13, 1945, Curtiss-Wright presented a formal proposal to Cornell. By the terms of the proposal, Curtiss-Wright was to:

(1) donate to Cornell the wind tunnel and research facilities located at Cheektowaga;

(2) donate the sum required to complete the wind tunnel;

(3) make available for employment by Cornell, insofar as possible, such members of the laboratory and wind tunnel staff as Cornell might designate.

In return, Cornell was to:

(1) conduct such further research and development upon certain of Curtiss-Wright's inventions as were then in existence as Curtiss-Wright might request and at reasonable charge;

(2) continue research and development work then being performed at the facility by Curtiss-Wright for others; and

(3) enter into separate agreements with Curtiss-Wright for the performance of such additional research and development work as Curtiss-Wright might require subsequent to the transfer of the facilities, it being understood that Curtiss-Wright would receive terms at least as favorable as those granted to anyone else.

An underlying condition of the entire proposal was that the gift be consummated for tax purposes before January 1, 1946.

Cornell accepted the proposal and the facilities were transferred to it by deed and bill of sale. Both the deed and bill of sale recite that the transfer was made in consideration of $1.00 "and the advancement of science and education."

In addition to the property received from Curtiss-Wright, Cornell also received cash gifts totalling $675,000 from several eastern aircraft manufacturers, the money to be utilized to provide working capital for the laboratory. This money had been solicited by Cornell prior to its acceptance of the laboratory and wind tunnel facilities in order to insure that the laboratory would not become a financial drain on the University.

The laboratory was leased by Cornell to Cornell Research Foundation, Inc. and was operated as a division of the Foundation from January 1, 1946 until May 31, 1948. On March 4, 1948, CAL was incorporated and soon thereafter, on June 1, 1948, it acquired the laboratory and wind tunnel facilities in exchange for the issuance of its 100 shares of stock to Cornell. All of the stock issued by CAL has been continuously owned and held by Cornell and the ultimate control of the operation of the laboratory was and is in Cornell.

During the more than 20 years of its ownership of the lab, Cornell has maintained a policy of operating it on a non-profit basis. With the exception of a total sum of $1,698,882 which was used for such purposes as fellowships, professorships and CAL's share of administrative expenses, all of the profits have been plowed back into the laboratory. As a result of this policy CAL has grown considerably over the years. At the time the facilities were acquired from Curtiss-Wright, they had a value of approximately $5,000,000. CAL's present value is approximately $25,000,000 to $30,000,000. In 1969 it had a gross income of over $30,000,000 and a net profit of over $1,400,000.

In addition, CAL has expanded its research operations so that in addition to aeronautical research, which at one time was almost its sole preoccupation, it now conducts research into such fields as air and water pollution, automobile safety, urban transportation problems and fingerprint identification.

Apparently as a result of pressure from certain student and faculty groups a committee was appointed to study Cornell-CAL relationships. The committee found that student utilization of CAL has been small and that potential conflict exists betwen CAL's overseas research efforts and Cornell's large and expanding program of international studies. It therefore concluded that CAL should be separated from Cornell.

After receiving offers from 5 prospective purchasers of CAL, the Executive Committee of the Board of Trustees, on September 17, 1968, voted to accept EDP's offer of $25,000,000 and entered into a formal contract of sale approximately one year later.

After becoming aware of the proposed sale of CAL to EDP, the Attorney General, by a complaint dated November 8, 1968 commenced this action pursuant to Article 8 of the Estates, Powers, and Trusts Law. As the statutory representative of beneficiaries of charitable trusts, the Attorney General seeks: (1) a permanent injunction against the proposed sale of CAL to EDP; (2) a permanent injunction against the sale of CAL to any person except a non-profit organization, and then, only upon notice to the Attorney General and approval by the court; and (3) a direction that Cornell use the proceeds of any sale for similar educational, research and scientific purposes in the field of aeronautics and allied fields.

The Attorney General seeks to block the sale of CAL on two grounds: (1) that the laboratory and wind tunnel facilities were given to Cornell "for a charitable use in the nature of a public trust for educational, research and scientific purposes" and

(2) that even if the facilities weren't originally given in the nature of a trust, Cornell, by its actions and statements over the years concerning CAL, has itself dedicated and rededicated the facilities as a public trust for scientific and educational purposes.

The basis for the latter assertion is that Cornell and CAL have made many statements over the years that CAL would be operated as a non-profit institution and would continue to be an instrument of service to the aircraft industry, to education and to the public at large. These statements, most of them made by CAL rather than Cornell, were made at dedication ceremonies, in applications by CAL for tax exemptions, in policy statements of CAL, in minutes of CAL board of director meetings and in publications distributed by CAL for purposes of recruiting personnel and obtaining research contracts.

The court below, after stating that the formal documents transferring the facilities did not express the entire agreement of the parties, examined the facts and circumstances surrounding the gift and held (62 Misc.2d 95, 100, 308 N.Y.S.2d 85, 91) that:

> "From the evidence relating to the circumstances surrounding the gift of the laboratory from Curtiss-Wright to Cornell and the clear understanding of the parties, it appears that a 'charitable trust' was created for the restricted purpose of conducting a laboratory to conduct scientific research and not for the purpose of supporting the general educational programs of Cornell."

and further that:

> "Although it is not necessary for a determination of this action, it is the opinion of the Court that Cornell by its actions and the use of the laboratory for research purposes over the years and the use of the income almost entirely for research purposes as [sic] the laboratory itself created a charitable trust or use for that purpose, which now prevents the diversion of the laboratory or the income therefrom to an entirely different purpose."

The court also stated that there was no showing that the sale of CAL would in any way promote the carrying out of the purposes of the charitable trusts.

New York courts have held that where a gift is made to a charitable corporation subject to the restriction that it be used for a specific purpose which is one of its corporate purposes, no trust is created in the technical sense. St. Joseph's Hospital v. Bennett, 281 N.Y. 115, 22 N.E.2d 305; 7 N.Y.Jur., Charities, § 62. However, the cases have held that a trust will be implied in the sense that the gift will be required to be devoted to the purposes for which it was given. St. Joseph's Hospital v. Bennett, supra; Sherman v. Richmond Hose Co., 230 N.Y. 462, 130 N.E. 613; 7 N.Y.Jur., Charities, §§ 62, 79. The laboratory was given to Cornell for the "advancement of science and education." The "advancement of science and education" being one of Cornell's corporate purposes (Laws of New York 1865, ch. 585, § 1 as amended Education Law §§ 5701–5702), the issue is not whether a charitable trust was created in the technical sense, but whether the gift of the laboratory was made subject to a restriction that it be forever used as a research laboratory.

In order to find that a restriction has been placed upon the use of a gift to a charitable corporation such restriction must be clearly expressed. St. Joseph's Hospital v. Bennett (supra); Restatement of Trusts 2d § 351. In the instant case there is no clear expression of intent that the gift to Cornell was subject to the restriction that it be forever used as a research laboratory for the public benefit.   In fact, an examination of the deed, bill of sale and the list of proposals submitted to Cornell by Curtiss-Wright leads one to the opposite conclusion.

By letter dated December 13, 1945, Curtiss-Wright submitted a list of proposals to Cornell in respect of the contemplated gift. An underlying condition of the entire proposal was that the gift be consummated prior to January 1, 1946. By the proposals which were submitted to and accepted by Cornell, Cornell was obligated to operate the laboratory only until the completion of work upon inventions of Curtiss-Wright which were then in existence and completion of work then being performed by Curtiss-Wright pursuant to contracts with others. In view of the precision with which Curtiss-Wright spelled out the conditions of the gift, it seems clear that if Curtiss-Wright had intended to restrict Cornell's use of the laboratory to the extent that Cornell would be forever obligated to operate it as a research laboratory for the public benefit, it would have done so in the same clear and precise language. Thus, the implication is that no such restriction was ever intended.

The language used in the deed further supports this conclusion.   In addition to reciting that the consideration of the conveyance was $1.00 and the "advancement of science and education", the deed further recites that Curtiss-Wright does hereby remise, release and quitclaim to (Cornell), its *successors* and *assigns* forever." (emphasis added) The habendum clause on page 3 of the deed also recites "TO HAVE AND TO HOLD the premises herein granted unto the party of the second part, its successors and assigns forever".   In addition, the bill of sale also uses the words "successors and assigns".   It would appear that the use of these words is inconsistent with an intent that Cornell be forever obligated to operate the lab in trust for the public benefit.   Additionally, there is no evidence that Cornell received the gift of the laboratory as a result of representations on its part that it would forever operate it for the public benefit.

Accordingly, we find that Cornell received the laboratory facilities free from a restriction that it forever operate it as a public trust.

Also the fact that Cornell solicited and received contributions from several aircraft manufacturers does not alter this result.   While these cash gifts were made for the express purpose that they be used as operating capital for the laboratory, it is undisputed that the money was used for the purpose for which it was given and has long since been exhausted. In none of the letters from the aircraft companies is it stated that the gifts were conditioned upon Cornell's perpetual operation of the laboratory. Thus, while Cornell may have been obligated to operate the laboratory for some period of time during which the reasonably anticipated objectives of the donating airline companies might be fulfilled, it has fulfilled its obligations by continuously operating the lab for almost 25 years.

We also find that no trust was created by Cornell's conduct and actions with respect to the laboratory. While a charitable trust may be created by a declaration of the owner of the property that he holds it upon a charitable trust (Restatement, Trusts 2d § 349), no trust is created unless the donor manifests an intent to impose enforceable duties. Restatement, Trusts 2d § 351. While no particular words are required to create the trust, "the words and acts relied on must be unequivocal in nature and admit of no other interpretation than that the property is held in trust." Matter of Fontanella, 33 A.D.2d 29, 30, 304 N.Y.S.2d 829, 831. The evidence in the instant case is insufficient to show that Cornell ever intended to create a trust. Apparently, the court below based its holding mainly upon the fact that over the years Cornell both used the laboratory for research purposes and continually "plowed back" almost all of the profits into the laboratory. While these actions reflect Cornell's policy with respect to the operation of the laboratory, they do not show that Cornell took steps to impose upon itself the legal obligation to continue such policies. In short, these actions do not show "beyond reasonable doubt that a trust was intended" to be created by Cornell. Matter of Fontanella, supra at 30–31, 304 N.Y.S.2d at 831.

It would further appear that such statements as were made at dedication ceremonies to the effect that CAL was a nonprofit institution operated as an instrument of service to the aircraft industry, education and the public at large did not manifest an intent to create a trust of the property but were merely expressions of Cornell's then present and contemplated future policies with respect to the operation of the laboratory.

It is clear that Cornell did not operate the laboratory as a separate corporation for purposes of establishing a trust. Rather, the decision to separate it from the University was the result of many factors, including limitation of financial risk on the part of the University and the nature of the contracts that the laboratory entered into. Cornell never passed any formal resolutions restricting the use of the income of the laboratory to research purposes.

Accordingly, we conclude that Cornell does not hold the laboratory facilities as a public trust but may sell them subject only to the restriction that it use the proceeds of the sale for the "advancement of science and education."

In accordance with the foregoing the judgment should be reversed and the complaint dismissed.

Judgment unanimously reversed on the law and facts, with costs, and complaint dismissed.

GOLDMAN, P. J., and WITMER, MOULE and HENRY, JJ., concur.

Note

As held in the principal case and in the leading case of St. Joseph's Hospital v. Bennett which it cites, even a restricted gift to a charitable corporation does not in itself create a charitable trust; but the Attorney General will enforce restrictions attached to the gift, and cy pres is available if they turn out to defeat its general purpose. Recent cases include Estate of McKenna, 114 M.2d 304, 451 N.Y.S.2d 617 (Surr.Ct.1982); In re Estate of Criswell, 20 Ariz.App. 157, 510 P.2d 1062 (1973); Mayor and Aldermen of City of Annapolis v. West Annapolis Fire and Improvement Co., 264 Md. 729, 288 A.2d 151 (1972); Y. W. C. A. v. Morgan, 281 N.C. 485, 189 S.E.2d 169 (1972). See Scott on Trusts § 348.1 (3d ed. 1967).

B. CY PRES

TRAMMELL v. ELLIOTT

Supreme Court of Georgia, 1973.
230 Ga. 841, 199 S.E.2d 194.

HAWES, Justice. The appeal here is from an order of the Superior Court of DeKalb County entered on motion for summary judgment in a case brought by the executor of the estate of Miss Clem Boyd seeking construction of her will and direction from the court.

* * *

5. We now approach the central issue of this appeal. In Item X of the will of Clem Boyd, there is recorded the desire that an educational scholarship fund be established in memory of the deceased's parents. This provision is, in its entirety, as follows: "All funds remaining after the aforementioned bequests are made or set aside, I wish made into an Endowment or Scholarship Fund in memory of my parents, the late William and Frances McCord Boyd, of Newton County, Georgia, said fund to be known as the Boyd-McCord Memorial Scholarship and placed with the Trustees of the Georgia Institute of Technology, Emory University, and Agnes Scott College, in equal proportions, to manage and keep reports on same. This scholarship is set aside *for benefit of deserving and qualified poor white boys and girls*, and interest only is to be used for said scholarships. However, should any proven descendant of my parents qualify and apply for benefits of this scholarship, it is my desire that they be given preference, and, if need be, go into the principal to the amount of $500.00 per scholastic year of four years for said descendant if earnestness is indicated and courses taken leading to a degree." (Emphasis supplied.) Although two of the named universities to act as trustees of the funds are private institutions, the Attorney General representing the Board of Regents of the University System of Georgia has conceded the requisite state interest with regard to the trust administration on behalf

of the Georgia Institute of Technology.   We proceed, therefore, on the basis that there is sufficient state action involved to invoke the strictures of the Fourteenth Amendment of the United States Constitution and that the racial restrictions in the devise may not be enforced save in violation of equal protection of law.   Evans v. Newton, 382 U.S. 296, 86 S.Ct. 486, 15 L.Ed.2d 373 (1966); Pennsylvania v. Board of Directors of City Trust, 353 U.S. 230, 77 S.Ct. 806, 1 L.Ed.2d 792 (1957).   See, also, Sweet Briar Institute v. Button, 280 F.Supp. 312 (W.D.Va.1967).   The single issue before the court with regard to the devise is whether the trial court erred in applying the doctrine of *cy pres* to exclude the offensive and discriminatory classification of the beneficiaries of the trusts and to effectuate the devise on the basis of an otherwise nondiscriminatory administration of the trusts.

The rule of law commonly termed the doctrine of *cy pres* is codified in the law of Georgia in two separate sections of the Code.   These sections are as follows: "When a valid charitable bequest is incapable for some reason of execution in the exact manner provided by the testator, donor, or founder, a court of equity will carry it into effect in such a way as will as nearly as possible effectuate his intention."   Code § 108–202.   "A devise or bequest to a charitable use will be sustained and carried out in this State; and in all cases where there is a general intention manifested by the testator to effect a certain purpose, and the particular mode in which he directs it to be done shall fail from any cause, a court of chancery may, by approximation, effectuate the purpose in a manner most similar to that indicated by the testator."   Code § 113–815.

The public policy expressed in these provisions favoring the validation of charitable trusts is supported by the longstanding rule of construction of this court by which forfeitures because of restrictive conditions attached to grants or devises of property are not favored, and as well by related Code provisions immunizing such trusts from the Georgia law against perpetuities.   Code Ann. § 85–707.   See Hardage v. Hardage, 211 Ga. 80, 84 S.E.2d 54 (1954).

As a general rule, the doctrine of *cy pres* is applied in cases (1) where there is the presence of an otherwise valid charitable grant or trust; that is, one that has charity as its purpose and sufficiently offers benefits to an indefinite public; (2) where the specific intention of the settlor may not be legally or practicably carried into effect; and (3) where there is exhibited a general charitable intent on the part of the settlor.   See, e.g., Creech v. Scottish Rite Hospital for Crippled Children, 211 Ga. 195, 84 S.E.2d 563 (1954); Moss v. Youngblood, 187 Ga. 188, 200 S.E. 689 (1938); Goree v. Georgia Industrial Home, 187 Ga. 368, 200 S.E.2d 684 (1938); Restatement, Second, Trusts Vol. 2, § 399, p. 297, and Note, Cy Pres, Discriminatory Charitable Trusts in Georgia, 6 Ga.S.B.J. 428 (1970).   In determining at the outset whether there is exhibited a valid charitable purpose, the court is to look to Code § 108–203 wherein are listed the legitimate subjects of charity in Georgia.   This Code provision includes, for example, for purposes of this appeal, "1. Relief of aged, impotent, diseased, or poor people.   2. Every educational purpose", among other legitimate subjects.   Secondly, the court is to consider, from the instrument itself, whether there is exhibited a general charitable intent.   See Hines v. Village of St. Joseph, Inc., 227 Ga. 431, 181 S.E.2d 54 (1971). The existence of a general charitable intent is inferred upon the establishment that the grant conforms in subject matter to any of the legitimate subjects of charity described in Code § 108–203.   However, in deference to the intent of the testator, *cy pres* will not be applied where there is demonstrated an intention of the settlor contrary to the inference of general charitable intent that the property should be applied exclusively to the purpose which is or has become impracticable or illegal.   Evans v. Abney, 224 Ga. 826, 165 S.E.2d 160 (1968).   See, also, Restatement, Second, Trusts Vol. 2, § 399 Comment c, p. 299, and IV Scott, Trusts § 399.2 (3d ed. 1967).   In view of the public policy expressed in Code §§ 108–202 and 113–815 favoring the effectuation of charitable grants promoting the public good and our own rule disfavoring forfeitures, such demonstration of a specific intent of the settlor as would result in a failure of the devise must be clear, definite, and unambiguous.   In such event the trust will fail, and a resulting trust will be implied for the benefit of the testator or his heirs.   Code § 108–106.

In viewing the will of Clem Boyd, the trusts established in Item X conformed in subject matter to those legitimate subjects of charity as found in Code § 108–203, being for the poor and for educational purposes. The purpose was one which offered a benefit to the general community, thereby qualifying as a public trust even though a preference is given to the relatives of the testator.   Cp. Hardage v. Hardage, 211 Ga. 80, 84 S.E.2d 54, supra.   We infer from this that the testatrix possessed the requisite charitable intent as would authorize the use of cy pres to remove the discriminatory classification of the beneficiaries.

The appellant has argued on the basis of Evans v. Abney, 224 Ga. 826, 165 S.E.2d 160, supra, however, that the mere existence of the racial classification was sufficient to rebut the inference of general charitable intent.   This argument is not, we believe, of substance.   In *Evans* we held that from the contents of the will, in addition to the provision for racial restrictions on the use of a park, there was exhibited an intention on the part of the testator which would preclude the use of such park in any manner except that as exclusively and clearly demanded by the testator.   *Evans*, therefore, upon its facts, stood for the recognized exception in the use of cy pres whereby from the will the specific intent of the testator conclusively negated any general charitable intention.

The will in the present case did not contain language by which the testatrix intended that the charitable trusts be administered exclusively in the manner prescribed.   Other evidence supportive of the establishment of a specific and exclusive intention was also absent from the will, for there was no provision in the devise, for example, for a reverter clause or an alternative gift over in the event of a failure of the grant.   On the other hand, in other parts of the will, the testatrix indicated strongly that she desired that no provision of the will should fail and the funds as set aside revert to her heirs.   In Item IX, she noted in this regard that "Adults do not need my life's earnings, and the children who need a college education are the ones who interest me most."

We conclude from the foregoing that the evidence on summary judgment was conclusive of the trial court's finding of a general charitable intent on the part of the testatrix and that the doctrine of cy pres was correctly applied in excluding the illegal racial classification from the charitable grant.

6. Under the foregoing ruling, it is unnecessary to pass upon the remaining contention of the appellant that the devise under Item X of the will violates the rule against perpetuities.

Judgment affirmed.

All the Justices concur except JORDAN, J., who dissents from Division 5 and the judgment of affirmance.

Notes

1. To the same effect, see Matter of Gerber, 652 P.2d 937 (Utah 1982) (failure of cooperation by charitable corporation named as trustee); Will of Porter, 310 Pa.Super. 299, 447 A.2d 977 (1982) (insufficient funds); Estate of Puckett, 168 Cal.Rptr. 311, 111 Cal.App.3d 46 (1980) (surplus funds); Campbell v. Board of Trustees, 220 Va. 516, 260 S.E.2d 204 (1979) (prior accomplishment of charitable purpose); Dunbar v. Board of Trustees of George W. Clayton College, 170 Colo. 327, 461 P.2d 28 (1969). In In re Estate of Vanderhoofven, 18 Cal.App.3d 940, 96 Cal.Rptr. 260 (1971) the Court evinced a willingness to apply cy pres in a similar situation if the testatrix were shown to have had a general charitable purpose, and remanded the case for admission of extrinsic evidence on that issue.

2. Courts will commonly apply cy pres when the particular charitable purpose indicated by the testator cannot be accomplished because of:

    a. insufficient or surplus funds;

    b. prior accomplishment of the charitable purpose;

    c. impossibility;

    d. refusal of a trustee or third person to cooperate;

    e. nonexistence of named charitable corporation or association;

    f. unsuitability of premises devised for charitable purpose.

See generally, Scott on Trusts § 399.2.

3. Some states, by statute, give the living settlor a veto power on resort to cy pres. See, e.g., McKinney's N.Y. EPTL 8–1.1(c).

4. Even as to private trusts, which are not aided by cy pres, courts have inherent equitable power to authorize *limited* departure from the literal terms of the trust instrument, in order to accommodate new circumstances not foreseen by the settlor. Restatement, Second, Trusts § 167. This power can also be exercised with respect to charitable trusts. First Nat. Bank v. Elliott, 406 Ill. 44, 92 N.E.2d 66, 76 (1950).

5. With some qualifications, charitable trusts are exempt from the Rule against Perpetuities. See Chapter Nine, at pp. 794–801, infra.

MATTER OF ESTATE OF WILSON

Court of Appeals of New York, 1983.
59 N.Y.2d 461, 465 N.Y.S.2d 900, 452 N.E.2d 1228.

COOKE, Chief Judge.

These appeals present the question whether the equal protection clause of the Fourteenth Amendment is violated when a court permits the administration of private charitable trusts according to the testators' intent to finance the education of male students and not female students. When a court applies trust law that neither encourages, nor affirmatively promotes, nor compels private discrimination but allows parties to engage in private selection in the devise or bequest of their property, that choice will not be attributable to the State and subjected to the Fourteenth Amendment's strictures.

I

The factual patterns in each of these matters are different, but the underlying legal issues are the same. In each there is imposed a decedent's intention to create a testamentary trust under which the class of beneficiaries are members of one sex.

In Matter of Wilson, article eleventh of Clark W. Wilson's will provided that the residuary of his estate be held in trust (Wilson Trust) and that the income "be applied to defraying the education and other expenses of the first year at college of five (5) young men who shall have graduated from the Canastota High School, three (3) of whom shall have attained the highest grades in the study of science and two (2) of whom shall have attained the highest grades in the study of chemistry, as may be certified to by the then Superintendent of Schools for the Canastota Central School District." Wilson died in June, 1969 and for the next 11 years the Wilson Trust was administered according to its terms.

In early 1981, the Civil Rights Office of the United States Department of Education received a complaint alleging that the superintendent's acts in connection with the Wilson Trust violated title IX of the Education Amendments of 1972 (U.S. Code, tit. 20, § 1681 et seq.), which prohibits gender discrimination in Federally financed education programs. The Department of Education informed the Canastota Central School District that the complaint would be investigated. Before the investigation was completed, the school district agreed to refrain from again providing names of students to the trustee. The trustee, Key Bank of Central New York, initiated this proceeding for a determination of the effect and validity of the trust provision of the will.

The Surrogate's Court, 108 Misc.2d 1066, 439 N.Y.S.2d 250, held that the school superintendent's co-operation with the trustee violated no Federal statute or regulation prohibiting sexual discrimination, nor did it implicate the equal protection clause of the Fourteenth Amendment. The court ordered the trustee to continue administering the trust.

A unanimous Appellate Division, 87 A.D.2d 98, 451 N.Y.S.2d 891, Third Department, modified the Surrogate's decree. The court affirmed the Surrogate's finding that the testator intended the trust to benefit male students only and, noting that the school was under no legal obligation to provide the names of qualified male candidates, found "administration of the trust according to its literal terms is impossible." (87 A.D.2d, p. 101, 451 N.Y.S.2d 891.) The court then exercised its cy pres power to reform the trust by striking the clause in the will providing for the school superintendent's certification of the names of qualified candidates for the scholarships. The candidates were permitted to apply directly to the trustee.

Matter of Johnson also involves a call for judicial construction of a testamentary trust created for the exclusive benefit of male students. By a will dated December 13, 1975, Edwin Irving Johnson left his residuary estate in trust (Johnson Trust). Article sixth of the will provided that the income of the trust was to "be used and applied, each year to the extent available, for scholarships or grants for bright and deserving young men who have graduated from the High School of [the Croton-Harmon Union Free] School District, and whose parents are financially unable to send them to college, and who shall be selected by the Board of Education of such School District with the assistance of the Principal of such High School."

Johnson died in 1978. In accordance with the terms of the trust, the board of education, acting as trustee, announced that applications from male students would be accepted on or before May 1, 1979. Before any scholarships were awarded, however, the National Organization for Women, filed a complaint with the Civil Rights Office of the United States Department of Education. This complaint alleged that the school district's involvement in the Johnson Trust constituted illegal gender-based discrimination.

During the pendency of the Department of Education's investigation, a stipulation was entered into between the executrix of the will, the president of the board of education, and the Attorney-General. The parties sought "to avoid administering the educational bequest set forth in Article Sixth in a manner which is in conflict with the law and public policy prohibiting discrimination based on sex". The stipulation provided that "all interested parties agree to the deletion of the word 'men' in Article Sixth of the Will and the insertion of the word 'persons' in its place." The Attorney-General then brought this proceeding by petition to the Surrogate's Court to construe article sixth of the will.

The Surrogate found that the trustee's unwillingness to administer the trust according to its terms rendered administration of the trust impossible. The court, however, declined to reform the trust by giving effect to the stipulation. Rather, it reasoned that the testator's primary intent to benefit "deserving young men" would be most closely effected by replacing the school district with a private trustee.

A divided Appellate Division, 93 A.D.2d 1, 460 N.Y.S.2d 932, Second Department, reversed, holding that under the equal protection clause of the Fourteenth Amendment, a court cannot reform a trust that, by its own terms, would deny equal protection of law. The court reasoned that inasmuch as an agent of the State had been appointed trustee, the trust, if administered, would violate the equal protection clause. Judicial reformation of the trust by substituting trustees would, in that court's view, itself constitute State action in violation of the Fourteenth Amendment. The court determined that administration of the trust was impossible and, in an exercise of its cy pres power, reformed the trust by eliminating the gender restriction.

II

On these appeals, this court is called upon to consider the testators' intent in establishing these trusts, evaluate the public policy implications of gender restrictive trusts generally, and determine whether the judicial reformation of these trusts violates the equal protection clause of the Fourteenth Amendment.

There can be no question that these trusts, established for the promotion of education, are for a charitable purpose within the meaning of the law (see EPTL 8–1.1; see, also, Russell v. Allen, 107 U.S. 163, 172, 2 S.Ct. 327, 27 L.Ed. 397; Butterworth v. Keeler, 219 N.Y. 446, 114 N.E. 803; see, generally, Bogert, Trusts and Trustees [rev 2d ed.], § 375; 4 Scott, Trusts [3d ed.], § 370). Charitable trusts are encouraged and favored by the law (see Bogert, op. cit., § 361), and may serve any of a variety of benevolent purposes (see EPTL 8–1.1). Among the advantages the law extends to charitable trusts are their exemption from the rules against perpetuities (see EPTL 9–1.1; Matter of MacDowell, 217 N.Y. 454, 112 N.E. 177) and accumulations (EPTL 8–1.7) and their favorable tax treatment (see Bogert, Trusts and Trustees [rev 2d ed.], § 246.25; 9B Rohan, N.Y.Civ.Prac., pars. 8–1.7[3]—8–1.7[6]). Moreover, unlike other trusts, a charitable trust will not necessarily fail when the settlor's specific charitable purpose or direction can no longer be accomplished.

When a court determines that changed circumstances have rendered the administration of a charitable trust according to its literal terms either "impracticable or impossible", the court may exercise its cy pres power to reform the trust in a manner that "will most effectively accomplish its general purposes" (EPTL 8–1.1, subd. [c]). In reforming trusts pursuant to this power, care must be taken to evaluate the precise purpose or direction of the testator, so that when the court directs the trust towards another charitable end, it will "give effect insofar as practicable to the full design of the testator as manifested by his will and codicil" (Matter of Scott, 8 N.Y.2d 419, 427, 208 N.Y.S.2d 984, 171 N.E.2d 326; see Bogert, Trusts and Trustees [rev. 2d ed.], § 442).

The court, of course, cannot invoke its cy pres power without first determining that the testator's specific charitable purpose is no longer capable of being performed by the trust (see, e.g., Matter of Scott, supra; Matter of Swan, 237 App.Div. 454, 261 N.Y.S. 428, affd. sub nom. Matter of St. Johns Church of Mt. Morris, 263 N.Y. 638, 189 N.E. 734; Matter of Fairchild, 15 Misc.2d 272, 178 N.Y.S.2d 886). In establishing these trusts, the testators expressly and unequivocally intended that they provide for the educational expenses of male students. It cannot be said that the accomplishment of the testators' specific expression of charitable intent is "impossible or impracticable." So long as the subject high schools graduate boys with the requisite qualifications, the testators' specific charitable intent can be fulfilled.

Nor are the trusts' particular limitation of beneficiaries by gender invalid and incapable of being accomplished as violative of public policy. It is true that the eradication in this State of gender-based discrimination is an important public policy. Indeed, the Legislature has barred gender-based discrimination in education (see Education Law, § 3201–a), employment (see Labor Law, §§ 194, 197, 220–e; General Business Law, § 187), housing, credit, and many other areas (see Executive Law, § 296). As a result, women, once viewed as able to assume only restricted roles in our society (see Bradwell v. State, 16 Wall [83 U.S.] 130, 141, 21 L.Ed. 442), now project significant numbers "in business, in the professions, in government and, indeed, in all walks of life where education is a desirable, if not always a necessary, antecedent" (Stanton v. Stanton, 421 U.S. 7, 15, 95 S.Ct. 1373, 1378, 43 L.Ed.2d 688). The restrictions in these trusts run contrary to this policy favoring equal opportunity and treatment of men and women. A provision in a charitable trust, however, that is central to the testator's or settlor's charitable purpose, and is not illegal, should not be invalidated on public policy grounds unless that provision, if given effect, would substantially mitigate the general charitable effect of the gift (see 4 Scott, Trusts [3d ed.], § 399.4).

Proscribing the enforcement of gender restrictions in private charitable trusts would operate with equal force towards trusts whose benefits are bestowed exclusively on women. "Reduction of the disparity in economic condition between men and women caused by the long history of discrimination against women has been recognized as * * * an important governmental objective" (Califano v. Webster, 430 U.S. 313, 317, 97 S.Ct. 1192, 1194, 51 L.Ed.2d 360). There can be little doubt that important efforts in effecting this type of social change can be and are performed through private philanthropy (see, generally, Commission on Private Philanthropy and Public Needs, Giving in America: Toward a Stronger Voluntary Section [1975]). And, the private funding of programs for the advancement of women is substantial and growing (see Bernstein, Funding for Women's Higher Education: Looking Backward and Ahead, Grant Magazine, vol. 4, No. 4, pp. 225–229; Ford Foundation, Financial Support of Women's Programs in the 1970's [1979]; Yarrow, Feminist Philanthropy Comes Into Its Own, *NY Times*, May 21, 1983, p. 7, col. 2). Indeed, one compilation of financial assistance offered primarily or exclusively to women lists 854 sources of funding (see Schlacter, Directory of Financial Aids for Women [2d ed., 1981]; see, also, Note, Sex Restricted Scholarships and the Charitable Trust, 59 Iowa L.Rev. 1000, 1000–1001, & nn. 10, 11). Current thinking in private philanthropic institutions advocates that funding offered by such institutions and the opportunities within the institutions themselves be directly responsive to the needs of particular groups (see Ford Foundation, op. cit., at pp. 41–44; Fleming, Foundations and Affirmative Action, 4 Foundation News No. 4, at pp. 14–17; Griffen, Funding for Women's Programs, 6 Grantmanship Center News, No. 2, at pp. 34–45). It is evident, therefore, that the focusing of private philanthropy on certain classes within society may be consistent with public policy. Consequently, that the restrictions in the trusts before this court may run contrary to public efforts promoting equality of opportunity for women does not justify imposing a per se rule that gender restrictions in private charitable trusts violate public policy.

Finally, this is not an instance in which the restriction of the trusts serves to frustrate a paramount charitable purpose.   In Howard Sav. Inst. v. Peep, 34 N.J. 494, 170 A.2d 39, for example, the testator made a charitable bequest to Amherst College to be placed in trust and to provide scholarships for "deserving American born, Protestant, Gentile boys of good moral repute, not given to gambling, smoking, drinking or similar acts."   Due to the religious restrictions, the college declined to accept the bequest as contrary to its charter.   The court found that the college was the principal beneficiary of the trust, so that removing the religious restriction and thereby allowing the college to accept the gift would permit administration of the trust in a manner most closely effectuating the testator's intent (see, also, Matter of Hawley, 32 Misc.2d 624, 223 N.Y.S.2d 803;   Coffee v. Rice Univ., 408 S.W.2d 269 [Tex.Civ.App.]).

In contrast, the trusts subject to these appeals were not intended to directly benefit the school districts.   Although the testators sought the school districts' participation, this was incidental to their primary intent of financing part of the college education of boys who attended the schools. Consequently, severance of the school districts' role in the trusts' administration will not frustrate any part of the testators' charitable purposes. Inasmuch as the specific charitable intent of the testators is not inherently "impossible or impracticable" of being achieved by the trusts, there is no occasion to exercise cy pres power.

Although not inherently so, these trusts are currently incapable of being administered as originally intended because of the school districts' unwillingness to co-operate.   These impediments, however, may be remedied by an exercise of a court's general equitable power over all trusts to permit a deviation from the administrative terms of a trust and to appoint a successor trustee.

A testamentary trust will not fail for want of a trustee (see EPTL 8–1.1;   see, also, Matter of Thomas, 254 N.Y. 292, 172 N.E. 513) and, in the event a trustee is unwilling or unable to act, a court may replace the trustee with another (see EPTL 7–2.6;   SCPA 1502;   see, also, Matter of Andrews, 233 App.Div. 547, 253 N.Y.S. 590;   2 Scott, Trusts [3d ed.], § 108.1).   Accordingly, the proper means of continuing the Johnson Trust would be to replace the school district with someone able and willing to administer the trust according to its terms.

When an impasse is reached in the administration of a trust due to an incidental requirement of its terms, a court may effect, or permit the trustee to effect, a deviation from the trust's literal terms (see 9A Rohan, NY Civ.Prac., pars. 7–2.4[3]—7–2.4[4]).   This power differs from a court's cy pres power in that "[t]hrough exercise of its deviation power the court alters or amends administrative provisions in the trust instrument but does not alter the purpose of the charitable trust or change its dispositive provisions" (Bogert, Trusts and Trustees [rev. 2d ed.], § 394, p. 249; see, e.g., Trustees of Sailors' Snug Harbor v. Carmody, 211 N.Y. 286, 105 N.E. 543; Matter of Bruen,83 N.Y.S.2d. 197; Matter of Godfrey, 36 N.Y.S.2d 414, affd. no opn. 264 App.Div. 885, 36 N.Y.S.2d 244). The Wilson Trust provision that the school district certify a list of students is an incidental part of the trust's administrative requirements, which no longer can be satisfied in light of the district's refusal to co-operate. The same result intended by the testator may be accomplished by permitting the students to apply directly to the trustee. Therefore, a deviation from the Wilson Trust's administrative terms by eliminating the certification requirement would be the appropriate method of continuing that trust's administration.

III

It is argued before this court that the judicial facilitation of the continued administration of gender-restrictive charitable trusts violates the equal protection clause of the Fourteenth Amendment (see U.S. Const., 14th Amdt., § 1). The strictures of the equal protection clause are invoked when the State engages in invidious discrimination (see Moose Lodge No. 107 v. Irvis, 407 U.S. 163, 173, 176–177, 92 S.Ct. 1965, 1971, 1973, 32 L.Ed.2d 627; Burton v. Wilmington Parking Auth., 365 U.S. 715, 721, 81 S.Ct. 856, 859, 6 L.Ed.2d 45; Civil Rights Cases, 109 U.S. 3, 3 S.Ct. 18, 27 L.Ed. 835). Indeed, the State itself cannot, consistent with the Fourteenth Amendment, award scholarships that are gender restrictive (see Mississippi Univ. for Women v. Hogan, 458 U.S. 718, 102 S.Ct. 3331, 73 L.Ed.2d 1090; Kirchberg v. Feenstra, 450 U.S. 455, 101 S.Ct. 1195, 67 L.Ed.2d 428; Stanton v. Stanton, 421 U.S. 7, 95 S.Ct. 1373, 43 L.Ed.2d 688, supra).

The Fourteenth Amendment, however, "erects no shield against merely private conduct, however discriminatory or wrongful." (Shelley v. Kraemer, 334 U.S. 1, 13, 68 S.Ct. 836, 842, 92 L.Ed. 1161; see Blum v. Yaretski, 457 U.S. 991, 1002, 102 S.Ct. 2777, 2785, 73 L.Ed.2d 534; Jackson v. Metropolitan Edison Co., 419 U.S. 345, 349, 95 S.Ct. 449, 452, 42 L.Ed.2d 477; Moose Lodge No. 107 v. Irvis, 407 U.S. 163, 171–179, 92 S.Ct. 1965, 1970–74, 32 L.Ed.2d 627, supra; Evans v. Abney, 396 U.S. 435, 445, 90 S.Ct. 628, 633, 24 L.Ed.2d 634). Private discrimination may violate equal protection of the law when accompanied by State participation in, facilitation of, and, in some cases, acquiescence in the discrimination (see, e.g., Burton v. Wilmington Parking Auth., 365 U.S. 715, 81 S.Ct. 856, 6 L.Ed.2d 45, supra; Reitman v. Mulkey, 387 U.S. 369, 87 S.Ct. 1627, 18 L.Ed.2d 830; Shelley v. Kraemer, 334 U.S. 1, 68 S.Ct. 836, 92 L.Ed. 1161, supra). Although there is no conclusive test to determine when State involvement in private discrimination will violate the Fourteenth Amendment (see Reitman v. Mulkey, supra, 387 U.S. at p. 378, 87 S.Ct. at p. 1632), the general standard that has evolved is whether "the conduct allegedly causing the deprivation of a federal right [is] fairly attributable to the state" (Lugar v Edmondson Oil Co., 457 U.S. 922, 937, 102 S.Ct. 2744, 2754, 73 L.Ed.2d 482). Therefore, it is a question of "state responsibility" and "[o]nly by sifting facts and weighing circumstances can the * * * involvement of the State in private conduct be attributed its true significance" (Burton v. Wilmington Parking Auth., 365 U.S. 715, 722, 81 S.Ct. 856, 860, 6 L.Ed.2d 45, supra).

* * *

The State generally may not be held responsible for private discrimination solely on the basis that it permits the discrimination to occur (see Flagg Bros. v. Brooks, 436 U.S. 149, 164, 98 S.Ct. 1729, 1737, 56 L.Ed.2d 185; Jackson v. Metropolitan Edison Co., 419 U.S. 345, 357, 95 S.Ct. 449, 456, 42 L.Ed.2d 477, supra; Moose Lodge No. 107 v. Irvis, 407 U.S. 163, 176, 92 S.Ct. 1965, 1973, 32 L.Ed.2d 627, supra; Evans v. Abney, 396 U.S. 435, 90 S.Ct. 628, 24 L.Ed.2d 634, supra). Nor is the State under an affirmative obligation to prevent purely private discrimination (see Reitman v. Mulkey, 387 U.S. 369, 376, 377, 87 S.Ct. 1627, 1631, 1632, 18 L.Ed.2d 830, supra). Therefore, when the State regulates private dealings it may be responsible for private discrimination occurring in the regulated field only when enforcement of its regulation has the effect of compelling the private discrimination (see Flagg Bros. v. Brooks, supra; Moose Lodge No. 107 v. Irvis, supra; Shelley v. Kraemer, 334 U.S. 1, 68 S.Ct. 836, 92 L.Ed. 1161, supra; cf. Adickes v. Kress & Co., 398 U.S. 144, 170, 90 S.Ct. 1598, 1615, 26 L.Ed.2d 142).

In Shelley v. Kraemer (supra), for example, the Supreme Court held that the equal protection clause was violated by judicial enforcement of a private covenant that prohibited the sale of affected properties to "people of Negro or Mongolian Race." When one of the properties was sold to a black family, the other property owners sought to enforce the covenant in State court and the family was ordered to move from the property. The Supreme Court noted "that the restrictive agreements standing alone cannot be regarded as violative of any rights guaranteed to petitioners by the Fourteenth Amendment. So long as the purposes of those agreements are effectuated by voluntary adherence to their terms, it would appear clear that there has been no action by the State and the provisions of the Amendment have not been violated" (334 U.S., at p. 13, 68 S.Ct. at p. 842). The court held, however, that it did [not] have before it cases "in which the States have merely abstained from action leaving private individuals free to impose such discriminations as they see fit. Rather, these are cases in which the States have made available to such individuals the full coercive power of the government to deny petitioners, on the grounds of race or color, the enjoyment of property rights" (id., at p. 19, 68 S.Ct. at p. 845). It was not the neutral regulation of contracts permitting parties to enter discriminatory agreements that caused the discrimination to be attributable to the State. Instead, it was that the State court's exercise of its judicial power directly effected a discriminatory act.

* * *

A court's application of its equitable power to permit the continued administration of the trusts involved in these appeals falls outside the ambit of the Fourteenth Amendment. Although the field of trusts is regulated by the State, the Legislature's failure to forbid private discriminatory trusts does not cause such trusts, when they arise, to be attributable to the State (see Flagg Bros. v. Brooks, 436 U.S. 149, 165, 98 S.Ct. 1729, 1738, 56 L.Ed.2d 185, supra; see, also, Evans v. Abney, 396 U.S. 435, 458, 90 S.Ct. 628, 640, 24 L.Ed.2d 634 [Brennan, J., dissenting], supra). It naturally follows that, when a court applies this trust law and determines that it permits the continued existence of private discriminatory trusts, the Fourteenth Amendment is not implicated.

In the present appeals, the coercive power of the State has never been enlisted to enforce private discrimination. Upon finding that requisite formalities of creating a trust had been met, the courts below determined the testator's intent, and applied the relevant law permitting those intentions to be privately carried out. The court's power compelled no discrimination. That discrimination had been sealed in the private execution of the wills. Recourse to the courts was had here only for the purpose of facilitating the administration of the trusts, not for enforcement of their discriminatory dispositive provisions.

This is not to say that a court's exercise of its power over trusts can never invoke the scrutiny of the Fourteenth Amendment. This court holds only that a trust's discriminatory terms are not fairly attributable to the State when a court applies trust principles that permit private discrimination but do not encourage, affirmatively promote, or compel it.

The testators' intention to involve the State in the administration of these trusts does not alter this result, notwithstanding that the effect of the courts' action respecting the trusts was to eliminate this involvement. The courts' power to replace a trustee who is unwilling to act as in Johnson or to permit a deviation from an incidental administrative term in the trust as in Wilson is a part of the law permitting this private conduct and extends to all trusts regardless of their purposes. It compels no discrimination. Moreover, the minimal State participation in the trusts' administration prior to the time that they reached the courts for the constructions under review did not cause the trusts to take on an indelible public character (see Evans v. Newton, 382 U.S. 296, 301, 86 S.Ct. 486, 489, 15 L.Ed.2d 373; Commonwealth of Pennsylvania v. Brown, 392 F.2d 120).

In sum, the Fourteenth Amendment does not require the State to exercise the full extent of its power to eradicate private discrimination. It is only when the State itself discriminates, compels another to discriminate, or allows another to assume one of its functions and discriminate that such discrimination will implicate the amendment.

Accordingly, in Matter of Wilson, the order of the Appellate Division should be affirmed, with costs payable out of the estate to all parties appearing separately and filing separate briefs.

In Matter of Johnson, the order of the Appellate Division should be reversed, with costs payable out of the estate to all parties appearing separately and filing separate briefs and the decree of the Surrogate's Court, Westchester County, reinstated.

MEYER, Judge (concurring in Matter of Wilson and dissenting in Matter of Johnson).

I would affirm in both cases. Although the Constitution does not proscribe private bias, it does proscribe affirmative State action in furtherance of bias.

In Matter of Wilson the trust is private and the only involvement of a public official (the superintendent of schools) is his certification of a student's class standing, information which is, in any event, available to any student applying to the trustee for a scholarship. There is, therefore, no State action.

In Matter of Johnson, however, the trustee is the board of education, a public body. The establishment of a public trust for a discriminatory purpose is constitutionally improper, as Presiding Justice Mollen has fully spelled out in his opinion. For the State to legitimize that impropriety by replacement of the trustee is unconstitutional State action. The only permissible corrective court action is, as the Appellate Division held, excision of the discriminatory limitation.

SIMMONS v. PARSONS COLLEGE

Supreme Court of Iowa, 1977.
256 N.W.2d 225.

LeGRAND, Justice.

This declaratory judgment action was brought to construe the will of Lester Morgan Wells as it relates to two trusts established for the education of needy students at Drake University and Parsons College.

The will was executed on August 15, 1969. Lester Morgan Wells died on January 3, 1974. After the execution of the will but prior to the testator's death, Parsons College became bankrupt. It no longer operates as an educational institution.

The action was brought by Dorothy Simmons, Executor of the estate of Lester Morgan Wells. Parsons College (and its trustee in bankruptcy), Drake University, and the heirs at law of the decedent were made defendants. The trial court held the trust established for Parsons College students failed and the testator's heirs at law were entitled to take the property which would otherwise have gone to Parsons College as trustee.

Parsons College has filed a disclaimer and is not a party to this appeal. The heirs at law, of course, do not appeal. The sole appellant is Drake University (Drake), and our discussion is limited accordingly. We affirm the trial court.

We set out the controversial provision of decedent's will:

"Fourth: All the rest of my estate and the assets thereof, I give, devise and bequeath, subject to the provisions of the Fifth Paragraph of this will, to Drake University of Des Moines, Iowa, and Parsons College of Fairfield, Iowa, in equal shares, for SCHOLARSHIP PURPOSES ONLY. Such funds shall be held in a permanent trust by each institution, which shall be known as the LESTER MORGAN WELLS TRUST, and only the income therefrom

shall be used to assist needy students to receive a college education and the same shall be paid to such persons and in such amounts as the respective colleges shall determine, but the principal is to be kept intact and properly invested as a permanent trust fund; said institutions are not required to give bond.

"It is my wish and desire, but not mandatory, that the trust fund herein established and devised for Parsons College of Fairfield, Iowa, be used for the benefit of students seeking a college education who reside in Jefferson County, Iowa, or in the vicinity thereof, which shall include the State of Iowa but not beyond.

"If either or both of said institutions should fail to faithfully carry out the provisions of the Fourth Paragraph of this will, then said trust or trusts shall fail and shall stand cancelled and revoked and the principal thereof I will, devise and bequeath to my legal heirs at law who may be living at that time and as may be determined by the laws of the State of Iowa, said heirs to be determined as of the date of my death."

Several codicils were executed later, but they are unimportant to the issues raised on this appeal.

Although Drake poses a number of questions to be answered, the sole issue presented is whether the doctrine of cy pres should be applied to the Parsons College trust in view of that institution's inability to carry out the trust purposes. Drake says we should apply cy pres and urges us to let it serve as trustee for the entire fund. Otherwise, Drake argues, that portion of the funds left to Parsons College will revert to numerous collateral heirs whom the testator did not know and whom he did not intend to benefit.

Cy pres is a doctrine which literally means "as near as may be." Hodge v. Wellman, 191 Iowa 877, 882, 179 N.W. 534, 536 (1920); 9 Drake L.Rev. 90, 94 (1959). It is applicable only to charitable trusts and then only when the trust established by a testator fails, no alternative disposition of the property has been made, and the general trust purposes may be accomplished by permitting it to be administered in a way different from, but closely related to, the testator's plan.

The doctrine is stated this way in Restatement (Second) Trusts, § 399 (1959):

> "*Failure of Particular Purpose Where Settlor Had General Charitable Intention. The Doctrine of Cy Pres.*
>
> "If property is given in trust to be applied to a particular charitable purpose, and it is or becomes impossible or impracticable or illegal to carry out the particular purpose, and if the settlor manifested a more general intention to devote the property to charitable purposes, the trust will not fail but the court will direct the application of the property to some charitable purpose which falls within the general charitable intention of the settlor."

While charitable trusts are favored by the law (In Re Estate of Small, 244 Iowa 1209, 1225–1227, 58 N.W.2d 477, 485 (1953)), courts may not ignore the testator's intent in order to give effect to doubtful trust provisions by invoking the doctrine of cy pres. Cy pres is simply a liberal rule of construction used to carry out, not defeat, the testator's intent.

In Re Estate of Staab, 173 N.W.2d 866, 870 (Iowa 1970); Hodge v. Wellman, supra, 191 Iowa at 882, 179 N.W. at 536.

The cy pres doctrine is inapplicable when the testator has anticipated the possible failure of the trust and has made alternative disposition of his property to meet that contingency. Under such circumstances the testamentary intent may be ascertained without such extrinsic help. [Citations]

Although Drake argues otherwise, the testator made such alternative disposition in the event either Parsons or Drake was unable to administer the trust. He said unequivocally the assets which would have gone to the trust should then go to his heirs at law.

This was the basis for the trial court's ruling that the cy pres doctrine was not applicable. We hold this conclusion was correct. We have reviewed all of the authorities relied on by Drake. None of them afford substantial support for its position.

We are told the case is stronger in favor of cy pres because the trust failed at the outset rather than after it had been under administration for some time. The authorities are to the contrary. The doctrine is more reluctantly resorted to under such circumstances. See Restatement (Second) Trusts § 399, Comment "i", at 302 and 14 C.J.S. Charities § 52c. at 516.

We hold the bequest to Parsons College in trust for the purposes set out in the Fourth Paragraph of decedent's will has failed because Parsons College is unable to administer the trust. We further find that the last will of Lester Morgan Wells provides the designated trust property under such circumstances should go to his heirs at law.

The judgment of the trial court is affirmed.

Notes

1. Even in the absence of a gift over upon failure of the trust, cy pres is inappropriate if the absence of general charitable purpose is shown. Matter of Syracuse University, 3 N.Y.2d 665, 171 N.Y.S.2d 545, 148 N.E.2d 671 (1958).

2. Other recent cases holding that a gift over tends strongly to disprove general charitable intent are: Burr v. Brooks, 75 Ill.App.3d 80, 30 Ill.Dec. 744, 393 N.E.2d 1091 (1979), affirmed 83 Ill.2d 488, 48 Ill.Dec. 200, 416 N.E.2d 231 (1981); Nelson v. Kring, 225 Kan. 499, 592 P.2d 438 (1979); First Church in Somerville v. Attorney General, 375 Mass. 332, 376 N.E.2d 1226 (1978); Smyth v. Anderson, 238 Ga. 343, 232 S.E.2d 835 (1977).

C. STANDING TO ENFORCE CHARITABLE TRUSTS

Notes

1. When the particular purpose of a charitable trust cannot be realized, the settlor or his successor has standing to oppose the court's application of cy pres and claim a reverter. If, however, the court does decide to apply cy pres, then, in the absence of a statute to the contrary (see, e.g., N.Y.—McKinney's EPTL § 8–1.1(c)), the settlor or his successor has no standing to object to the court's choice of alternative use.

Identifiable beneficiaries with a specific interest, such as the incumbents of endowed professorial chairs, have standing to enforce a charitable trust; but unidentifiable beneficiaries without a specific interest ordinarily do not. See, however, Parsons v. Walker, 28 Ill.App.3d 517, 328 N.E.2d 920 (1975). In any event, the Attorney General does have standing and is an indispensable party in all cy pres cases. Persons with no specific identifiable interest may sometimes petition the Attorney General to institute a suit to enforce a charitable trust, and bring a derivative action in his name if he refuses, but they may have to assume the responsibility for costs. See 37 Yale L.J. 533 (1928).

2. The doctrine of cy pres can be applied only by a court, never by the trustees acting alone. See generally, Scott on Trusts § 391 (3d ed. 1967).

D. "HONORARY" TRUSTS

IN RE THOMPSON

Chancery Division, 1934.
[1934] 1 Ch. 342.

ADJOURNED SUMMONS. The testator, who was a member of Trinity Hall in the University of Cambridge and died on August 21, 1932, by his will made on December 14, 1904, bequeathed a legacy of 1000£ to his friend George William Lloyd to be applied by him in such manner as he should in his absolute discretion think fit towards the promotion and furthering of fox-hunting and devised and bequeathed his residuary estate to Trinity Hall in the University of Cambridge to be applied by the Master and Fellows thereof in such manner as they should deem best for the benefit of the college as therein more particularly mentioned.

This was an originating summons by the executors of the testator's will for the determination of the question whether the legacy was a valid bequest or failed for want of a definite object or for uncertainty or on other grounds.

* * *

J. V. Nesbitt for the defendant G. W. Lloyd. The legatee makes no claim to any beneficial interest in the legacy and is anxious to carry out the testator's wishes so far as he is entitled so to do. This is not a trust for charitable purposes. The trust being one for the mere encouragement of a particular sport and not having for its object a general public purpose is not a charitable trust: In re Nottage. [(1895) 2 Ch. 649.] True, there is no cestui que trust who can enforce the application of the legacy, but that is immaterial: In re Dean. [(1889) 41 Ch.D. 552.] The object to which the legacy is to be applied is sufficiently defined to be enforced.

[CLAUSON, J. The college, as residuary legatees, seem to have an interest in the legacy, as, but for the trust for its application, they would be entitled to it. The procedure adopted by Knight Bruce V. C. in Pettingall v. Pettingall, 11 L.J. (Ch.) 176, cited in Jarman on Wills, 7th ed., vol. 2, p. 877, might be followed in this case.]

J. M. Paterson for Trinity Hall, Cambridge. The college, as the residuary legatees under the testator's will, are anxious that the wishes of the testator in respect to the legacy to his friend should be carried out; but being in the position of trustees they feel it to be their duty to submit that the bequest was not valid on the ground that there is no cestui que trust to enforce the trust; there must be somebody in whose favour the court can decree performance: Morice v. Bishop of Durham. [(1805) 9 Ves. 399, 405.]

CLAUSON, J. The testator, who was a member of Trinity Hall, Cambridge, by his will dated December 14, 1904, bequeathed a legacy of 1000£ to his friend George William Lloyd, who is also a member of the same college, to be applied by him in such manner as he should in his absolute discretion think fit towards the promotion and furthering of fox-hunting. In the first place, it is clear that Mr. Lloyd is not entitled to the legacy for his own benefit nor indeed does he so claim it, but he is anxious to carry out the testator's expressed wishes, if and so far as he lawfully may do so. No argument has been put forward which could justify the Court in holding this gift to be a gift in favour of charity, although it may well be that a gift for the benefit of animals generally is a charitable gift: but it seems to me plain that I cannot construe the object for which this legacy was given as being for the benefit of animals generally. In my judgment the object of the gift has been defined with sufficient clearness and is of a nature to which effect can be given. The proper way for me to deal with the matter will be, not to make, as it is asked by the summons, a general declaration, but, following the example of Knight Bruce V. C. in Pettingall v. Pettingall [11 L.J. (Ch.) 176], to order that, upon the defendant Mr. Lloyd giving an undertaking (which I understand he is willing to give) to apply the legacy when received by him towards the object expressed in the testator's will, the plaintiffs do pay to the defendant Mr. Lloyd the legacy of 1000£; and that, in case the legacy should be applied by him otherwise than towards the promotion and furthering of fox-hunting, the residuary legatees are to be at liberty to apply.

Notes

1. Restatement, Second, Trusts:

§ *124. Specific Non-charitable Purposes*

Where the owner of property transfers it in trust for a specific non-charitable purpose, and there is no definite or definitely ascertainable beneficiary designated, no enforceable trust is created; but the transferee has power to apply the property to the designated purpose, unless such application is authorized or directed to be made at a time beyond the period of the rule against perpetuities, or the purpose is capricious.

Comment:

a. *No duty to apply*. Where property is transferred to a person upon an intended trust for a specific non-charitable purpose, and there is no definite or definitely ascertainable beneficiary, the transferee is not under a duty and cannot be compelled to apply the property to the designated purpose, since there is no beneficiary to enforce the intended trust. See § 112. It is not enforceable as a charitable trust by the Attorney General, or other officer of the State, since the purposes are not charitable purposes. See § 398.

b. *Power to apply property to the intended purpose.* The devisee or legatee can properly apply the property to the designated purpose, if the purpose is not capricious and there is no violation of the principle of the rule against perpetuities. If he refuses to apply it to the designated purpose, he will be compelled to hold it upon a resulting trust for the settlor or his estate. He can either apply the property to the designated purpose or surrender it to the settlor or his estate; in no event will he be permitted to keep it. If he has not applied the property to the designated purpose, the court can properly decree that he reconvey it to the settlor or his estate unless within such reasonable time as the court may fix he shall apply it to the designated purpose.

As to the resulting trust which arises where the devisee or legatee fails to apply the property to the designated purpose, see § 418.

c. *"Honorary trust."* Since an intended trust for a specific non-charitable purpose is not enforceable because there is no beneficiary to enforce it, it is not a trust, as the term is used in the Restatement of this Subject. Where the transferee has power to apply the property for such a purpose, the intended trust is sometimes called an "honorary trust." Since, however, the transferee has only a power and not a duty to apply the property, and since in the Restatement of this Subject the term "trust" connotes the existence of duties which will be enforced in the courts, it is more accurate to state that the trustee has a power than it is to state that he holds upon trust, whether honorary or otherwise.

* * *

f. *Rule against perpetuities.* If by the terms of the intended trust the devisee or legatee is authorized to apply the property to the designated purpose for a period longer than the period of the rule against perpetuities, the devisee or legatee cannot properly apply the property to the designated purpose even though he is willing so to apply it. The period of the rule against perpetuities is, in the absence of a statute otherwise providing, a period of the lives of designated persons in being at the time of the transfer and twenty-one years. Thus, if a testator bequeaths property to a person to apply the income forever for the maintenance of a tomb or grave, the legatee cannot properly apply the income for the purpose, but he holds the property upon a resulting trust for the estate of the testator. So also, where the devisee or legatee is authorized to apply the property for the maintenance of one or more animals during the lives of the animals, the provision is invalid since the period of the rule against perpetuities is measured by lives of persons and not lives of animals, whether or not the normal duration of the life of the animal is shorter than that of a human being. Whether in such cases the devisee or legatee can properly apply the property for a period of twenty-one years, on the ground that the annual payments are to be treated as separable, is not within the scope of the Restatement of this Subject.

By statute in many States dispositions of property for the perpetual maintenance of graves, tombs and monuments are permitted.

As to the application of the rule against perpetuities or a similar rule to honorary trusts, see Restatement of Property, § 379.

To the effect that the lives which can be used in measuring the permissible period under the rule against perpetuities must be lives of human beings, see Restatement of Property, § 374, Comment h.

* * *

2. Common types of honorary trusts include those for:

a. the erection of tombs, monuments, and graves;

b. the saying of masses (though such trusts are regarded as charitable in some states);

c. the benefit of specific animals.

See generally, Scott on Trusts § 124.

3. N.Y.—McKinney's EPTL 8–1.5 is an example of a statute which accords charitable trust treatment to trusts " *   *   *   for the purpose of perpetual care, maintenance, improvement or embellishment of cemeteries or private burial lots   *   *   * ".

4. On "trusts" for the promotion of sport, see Bogert, Trusts and Trustees (2d ed. 1964) § 379; 74 U.Pa.L.Rev. 101 (1925).

Chapter Eight

ADMINISTRATION OF DECEDENT
AND TRUST ESTATES

SECTION ONE. JURISDICTION

A. THE DECEDENT IN A FEDERAL SYSTEM: DOMICILE

The theory underlying a federal structure of government holds that if the power over citizens is divided between two sovereigns, both of whom occupy the same geographical area, neither one of them can become arbitrary or tyrannical. The citizens pay a price for this protection. Consider the case of the wealthy and mobile couple who own a winter home in New York, a summer home in Maine, a hunting lodge in Georgia, and a factory in Connecticut. In their younger days they divided most of their time between Connecticut and New York. With advancing age they spent more and more of their time in Maine and Georgia. During life this dispersal of self and resources created few problems; they could move both as the situation required. But at death the status of each of them and the situs of their property became fixed. An enlightened system of law should provide for a single, unified administration of this estate. That is the theoretical ideal. The reality is the subject matter of Section One of this Chapter.

Restatement, Second, Conflict of Laws (1971)

§ 314. Where Will May Be Probated and Representative Appointed

The will of a decedent will customarily be admitted to probate and an executor or administrator appointed in a state

    (a) where the decedent was domiciled at the time of his death; or

    (b) where there are assets of the estate at the time of the decedent's death or at the time of the appointment of the executor or administrator; or

    (c) where there is jurisdiction over the person or property of one who is alleged to have killed the decedent by his wrongful act, if the statute under which recovery is sought permits suit by an executor or administrator appointed in that state.

§ 315. Where Administrator May Be Appointed in Case of Intestacy

An administrator will customarily be appointed in the case of intestacy in any state in which a will would have been admitted to probate.

§ 11. Domicil

(1) Domicil is a place, usually a person's home, to which the rules of Conflict of Laws sometimes accord determinative significance because of the person's identification with that place.

(2) Every person has a domicil at all times and, at least for the same purpose, no person has more than one domicil at a time.

RILEY v. NEW YORK TRUST CO.

Supreme Court of the United States, 1942.
315 U.S. 343, 62 S.Ct. 608, 86 L.Ed. 885.

Mr. Justice REED delivered the opinion of the Court.

Coca-Cola International Corporation, incorporated in Delaware, filed a bill of interpleader in a Delaware Court of Chancery against Julian Riley and Hughes Spalding, petitioners here, the Executors of Mrs. Julia M. Hungerford, with letters testamentary issued by the Court of Ordinary of Fulton County, Georgia, and against The New York Trust Company, the respondent, a New York corporation, as temporary administrator (afterward administrator c. t. a.) of the same decedent, appointed by the Surrogate's Court for New York County, New York.

The Georgia executors and the New York administrator each claim the right to have transferred to them in their representative capacity stock in the Coca-Cola corporation now on its books in the name of the decedent. The outstanding certificates are in Georgia in the hands of the Georgia executors. The parties are agreed, and it is therefore assumed that Delaware is the situs of the stock. In accordance with the prayer of the bill, the Delaware court directed the adversary claimants to interplead between themselves as to their respective claims.

The Georgia executors assert that original domiciliary probate of Mrs. Hungerford's will in solemn form was obtained by them in Georgia with all beneficiaries and heirs at law of testatrix, including her husband, Robert Hungerford, actual parties by personal service. These, it is conceded, were all the parties under the law of Georgia entitled to be heard on the probate of the will. The respondent administrator c. t. a. was not a party. The record of probate includes a determination by special finding, over the objection of the caveator, the husband, that the testatrix was domiciled in Georgia. The special finding was specifically approved as an essential fact to determine the jurisdiction of the Court of Ordinary by the highest court of Georgia in its affirmance of the probate. Hungerford v. Spalding, 183 Ga. 547, 189 S.E. 2.

These facts were alleged by petitioners in their statement of claim to the stock filed below in response to the decree of interpleader. Exemplified copies of the probate record of the several Georgia courts were pleaded and proven as were the applicable Georgia statutes governing domiciliary probate. From the facts alleged, petitioners inferred the conclusive establishment of the place for domiciliary distribution against "all persons" and prayed the issue to them of new certificates. An offer was made to pay all Delaware taxes or charges on the stock. At the trial petitioners relied upon Article IV, Section 1, of the Federal Constitution,[1] the full faith and credit clause, as determinative of their right to the new certificates. The pleading and trial contention adequately raised the Constitutional question. Tilt v. Kelsey, 207 U.S. 43, 50, 28 S.Ct. 1, 3, 52 L.Ed. 95.

Respondent admitted that all parties entitled under the law of Georgia to be heard in opposition to probate were actually before the Georgia courts. It denied that Mrs. Hungerford was domiciled in Georgia or that the Georgia judgment of domicile and probate was binding on it, and averred testatrix' domicile at death was New York. It further averred that there were New York creditors of the estate interested in the proper and lawful administration of the estate, and that New York had certain claims for inheritance and estate taxes. Its own subsequent appointment by the Surrogate's Court of New York County, New York, on the suggestion of testatrix' husband and the State Tax Commission, was pleaded with applicable provisions of New York probate and estate tax law. By stipulation it was established that petitioners and the heirs and beneficiaries of testatrix, except her husband who was an actual party, were notified of the New York proceedings for probate only by publication or substituted service of the citation in Georgia and did not appear. As a domiciliary administrator c. t. a. the respondent prayed the issue to it of new certificates for the stock in controversy.

The trial court concluded from the evidence adduced at the hearings that the testatrix was domiciled in Georgia. It was therefore, as the court stated, unnecessary for it to consider the binding effect of the Georgia judgment.[2] The Supreme Court of Delaware reversed this finding of fact, determined that New York was testatrix' domicile and denied petitioners' contention that Article IV, Section 1, of the Constitution required the award of the certificates of stock to the Georgia executors. The Coca-Cola Corporation was directed to issue its stock certificate to the respondent, the New York administrator c. t. a. New York Trust Co. v. Riley, Del.Sup., 16 A.2d 772. Because of the importance of issues previously undecided by this Court, certiorari was granted to review the alleged error, to wit, the asserted denial of full faith and credit to the Georgia judgment. 313 U.S. 555, 61 S.Ct. 1105, 85 L.Ed. 1517.

The constitutional effect of the Georgia decree on a claim in his own name in another state by a party to the Georgia proceedings is not here

1. "Full Faith and Credit shall be given in each State to the public Acts, Records, and Judicial Proceedings of every other State. And the Congress may by general Laws prescribe the Manner in which such Acts, Records and Proceedings shall be proved and the Effect thereof."

2. Coca-Cola International Corp. v. New York Trust Co., Del.Ch., 2 A.2d 290; Id., Del.Ch., 8 A.2d 511.

involved.   The question we are to decide is whether this Georgia judgment on domicile conclusively establishes the right of the Georgia executors to demand delivery to them of personal assets of their testatrix which another state is willing to surrender to the domiciliary personal representative when another representative, appointed by a third state, asserts a similar domiciliary right.   For the purpose of this review the conclusion of Delaware that the testatrix was in fact domiciled in New York is accepted.   The answer to the question lies in the extent to which Article IV, section 1, of the Constitution, as made applicable by R.S. § 905, nevertheless controls Delaware's action.

This clause of the Constitution brings to our Union a useful means for ending litigation.   Matters once decided between adverse parties in any state or territory are at rest.   Were it not for this full faith and credit provision, so far as the Constitution controls the matter, adversaries could wage again their legal battles whenever they met in other jurisdictions. Each state could control its own courts but itself could not project the effect of its decisions beyond its own boundaries.   Cf. Pennoyer v. Neff, 95 U.S. 714, 722, 24 L.Ed. 565.   That clause compels that controversies be stilled so that where a state court has jurisdiction of the parties and subject matter, its judgment controls in other states to the same extent as it does in the state where rendered.   Roche v. McDonald, 275 U.S. 449, 451, 48 S.Ct. 142, 72 L.Ed. 365, 53 A.L.R. 1141.   This is true even though the cause of action merged in the judgment could not have been enforced in the state wherein the enforcement of the judgment is sought. Christmas v. Russell, 5 Wall. 290, 302, 18 L.Ed. 475;   Fauntleroy v. Lum, 210 U.S. 230, 236, 28 S.Ct. 641, 643, 52 L.Ed. 1039.   By the Constitutional provision for full faith and credit, the local doctrines of res judicata, speaking generally, become a part of national jurisprudence, and therefore federal questions cognizable here.

The Constitution does not require,   * * *   nor does Delaware provide that the judgments of Georgia have the force of those of her own courts.   A suit in Delaware must precede any local remedy on the Georgia judgment.   Subject to the Constitutional requirements, Delaware's decisions are based on Delaware jurisprudence.   Her sovereignty determines personal and property rights within her territory.   Subject to Constitutional limitations, it was her prerogative to distribute the property located in Delaware or to direct its transmission to the domiciliary representative of the deceased.   State of Iowa v. Slimmer, 248 U.S. 115, 121, 39 S.Ct. 33, 34, 63 L.Ed. 158.   The full faith and credit clause allows Delaware in disposing of local assets to determine the question of domicile anew for any interested party who is not bound by participation in the Georgia proceeding.   * * *   It must be admitted that this reexamination may result in conflicting decisions upon domicile, but that is an inevitable consequence of the existing federal system which endows its citizens with the freedom to choose the state or states within which they desire to carry on business, enjoy their leisure or establish their residences.   Worcester County Trust Co. v. Riley, 302 U.S. 292, 299, 58 S.Ct. 185, 187, 82 L.Ed. 268.   But while allowing Delaware to determine domicile for itself, where any interested party is not bound by the Georgia proceedings, the full faith and credit clause and R.S. § 905 * * * do require that Delaware shall give Georgia judgments such faith and credit "as they have by law or usage" in Georgia.

We note, but need not discuss at length, the respondent's contention that our application of Georgia law is limited to the statutes, decisions and usages of that state pleaded or proven in the Delaware proceedings and that for such further rules of law, as may be needed to reach a conclusion here, we must necessarily, in reviewing a Delaware judgment, rely upon the law which, in the absence of proof of other Georgia law, properly guided the state courts, that is the Delaware law. At any rate, the cases relied upon by petitioners to establish the Georgia law, Tant v. Wigfall, 65 Ga. 412, and Wash v. Dickson, 147 Ga. 540, 94 S.E. 1009, are cited in the opinion of the Supreme Court of Georgia pleaded in these proceedings. We think they may be considered by us under the Delaware law. No objection below was made by respondent to the citations. The opinion of the Georgia Supreme Court was properly in the record and, in the absence of a contrary ruling by Delaware, we are of the view that they may be properly considered here.

We find nothing in either of these cases, however, which would lead to the conclusion that in Georgia, the New York administrator c. t. a. was in privity, so far as the sequestration of assets for the payment of death taxes or indebtedness of decedent or her estate is concerned, with any parties before the Georgia court, or that the New York representative could not take steps in Georgia courts which might result in its getting possession of any assets which under the Georgia law of administration would be properly deliverable to a foreign domiciliary administrator. In the Tant case, Georgia refused to permit a collateral attack on a judgment of probate allegedly entered without jurisdiction of the subject matter. It was held that such attack must be made in the court where judgment was rendered. The effect of a judgment entered without jurisdiction of the persons whose rights were purportedly affected was not discussed. In the Wash case, there was simply a ruling that a judgment of the court of ordinary could not be collaterally attacked by parties or privies, unless the record negatived the existence of necessary "jurisdictional facts." Whom the court would classify as "privies" to a judgment *in personam* does not appear, and the opinion of the court below makes it amply plain that there was no privity under Delaware law. Hence, if the Georgia judgment is to bind the New York administrator, it can be considered to do so only *in rem*.

By Section 113–602, Georgia Code of 1933, set up by petitioner as a basis for his contention as to the finality of the Georgia judgment in Delaware, it is provided that the Court of Ordinary is given exclusive jurisdiction over the probate of wills and that "such probate is conclusive upon all the parties notified, and all the legatees under the will who are represented in the executor." All the parties entitled to be heard in opposition to the probate, including Mr. Hungerford, were actually before the Court of Ordinary. It may be assumed that the judgment of probate and domicile is a judgment in rem and therefore as "an act of the sovereign power," "its effect cannot be disputed" within the jurisdiction. But this does not bar litigation anew by a stranger of facts upon which the decree in rem is based. Hence it cannot be said, we think, that because respondent would have no standing in Georgia to contest the probate of a will and, we assume, the preliminary determination of domicile, held necessary in Hungerford v. Spalding, 183 Ga. 547, 550, 189 S.E. 2, 3, thereafter respondent could not file a claim in Delaware, dependent upon domiciliary representation of testatrix, for assets in the latter state. While the Georgia judgment is to have the same faith and credit in Delaware as it does in Georgia, that requirement does not give the Georgia judgment extra-territorial effect upon assets in other states. So far as the assets in Georgia are concerned the Georgia judgment of probate is in rem; so far as it affects personalty beyond the state, it is in personam and can bind only parties thereto or their privies. This is the result of the ruling in Baker v. Baker, Eccles & Co., 242 U.S. 394, 400, 37 S.Ct. 152, 154, 61 L.Ed. 386.

Phrased somewhat differently, if the effect of a probate decree in Georgia in personam was to bar a stranger to the decree from later asserting his rights, such a holding would deny procedural due process.

It seems quite obvious that the administrator c. t. a. appears in Delaware as an agency of the State of New York, and not as the alter ego of the beneficiaries of the Hungerford estate. In its answer to the petitioners' statement of claim it established its status by alleging that not merely the beneficiaries but creditors residing in New York and the State of New York were interested in the estate, that its appointment as temporary administrator had been sought by the New York Tax Commissioner "to protect the claim of the State of New York to inheritance and succession taxes," that the State of New York was asserting such claims in substantial amount on the theory that the domicile was New York, and that under New York law, as evidenced by statutes likewise pleaded, an administrator was "vested by law with the right to possession and control over and to exercise all manner of dominion over all of the goods and chattels and personal property of every kind and description of the estate of a decedent."

A state is interested primarily not in the payment of particular creditors, nor in the succession of heirs or beneficiaries, as such, but in the administration of the property of its citizens, wherever located, and that of strangers within its boundaries. In a society where inheritance is an important social concept, the managing of decedents' property is a sovereign right which may not be readily frustrated.

Georgia and New York might each assert its right to administer the estates of its domiciliaries to protect its sovereign interests and Delaware was free to decide for itself which claimant is entitled to receive the portion of Mrs. Hungerford's personalty within Delaware's borders.

Affirmed.

[Mr. Chief Justice STONE concurred specially.]

Notes

1. The Georgia court had in personam jurisdiction over Mr. Hungerford. Does that fact mean that Mr. Hungerford can be barred from appearing in the New York administration and making claim under the New York statutes to an elective share against the Coca-Cola stock? For a general discussion of the problems presented herein see Hopkins, The Extraterritorial Effect of Probate Decrees, 53 Yale L.J. 221 (1944).

2. The Court points out that there may be "conflicting decisions upon domicile." A number of significant privileges accrue to the domiciliary state, so that the determination is of great importance to the executor of a substantial estate of a decedent who during life had contacts with several different states. The Supreme Court takes the view that the Constitution only requires it to guarantee a fair trial on the issue of domicile, not consistent results. Thus the Pennsylvania court held that a decedent died domiciled in its state and that a domiciliary inheritance tax in excess of $14 million was properly levied. Dorrance's Estate, 309 Pa. 151, 163 A. 303 (1932), certiorari denied 287 U.S. 660, 53 S.Ct. 222, 77 L.Ed. 570 (1932); same case 172 A. 900 (1933), certiorari denied 288 U.S. 617, 53 S.Ct. 507, 77 L.Ed. 990 (1933). Subsequently, the New Jersey court upheld a similar domicilary tax in excess of $12 million on the same estate. In re Estate of Dorrance, 115 N.J.Eq. 268, 170 A. 601 (1934), affirmed per curiam sub nom, Dorrance v. Martin, 13 N.J.Misc. 168, 176 A. 902 (1935), affirmed per curiam 116 N.J.L. 362, 184 A. 743 (1936), certiorari denied 298 U.S. 678, 56 S.Ct. 949, 80 L.Ed. 1399 (1936), rehearing denied 298 U.S. 692, 56 S.Ct. 957, 80 L.Ed. 1410. The Supreme Court refused to resolve the conflicting claims. New Jersey v. Pennsylvania, 287 U.S. 580 (1933); Hill v. Martin, 296 U.S. 393, 56 S.Ct. 278, 80 L.Ed. 293 (1935).

A Massachusetts executor attempted to get a definitive determination of the issue by interpleading, under the Federal Interpleader Act, the tax authorities of Massachusetts and California. The Supreme Court held that the Eleventh Amendment prohibited the action against the California tax official and that his threatened domiciliary tax was not an unconstitutional act outside the Amendment's protection. Worcester County Trust Co. v. Riley, 302 U.S. 292, 58 S.Ct. 185, 82 L.Ed. 268 (1937).

In one case, Texas v. Florida, 306 U.S. 398, 59 S.Ct. 563, 83 L.Ed. 817, 121 A.L.R. 1179 (1939) the Supreme Court did make a determination of domicile. Because of a substantial danger that the tax claims of four states (all based on domicile) and the federal estate tax would exceed the amount available in a $42 million estate to make payment, the Supreme Court took original jurisdiction under its power to resolve a controversy among the states as authorized in 28 U.S.C. § 2151(a).

The Court had an opportunity to reexamine these decisions when in 1977 California asked leave to file a complaint to have the Court exercise its original jurisdiction under the authority of Texas v. Florida and determine whether millionaire Howard Hughes was domiciled in California or Texas. (There were grounds for contending that Hughes was domiciled in Nevada, but, because that state imposes no death tax, it was not a necessary party to this litigation.) California, in support of its complaint, asserted that the combined marginal tax rates of the two states and the federal estate tax totaled 101%, and that the death taxes, if levied as threatened, would cause a total depletion of the estate and give rise to a "controversy" between the states as defined in Texas v. Florida.

The Court denied this motion without opinion, although four Justices expressed in concurring statements their belief that Worcester County Trust Company v. Riley was no longer "a bar against the use of federal interpleader by estates threatened with double taxation because of possible inconsistent adjudications of domicile". Three Justices went further and stated that Texas v. Florida was wrongly decided and should be overruled, because there was no "controversy" until the states had reduced their tax claims to money judgments and it had been demonstrated that the estate was insufficient to make full payment. California v. Texas, 437 U.S. 601, 98 S.Ct. 3107, 57 L.Ed.2d 464 (1978).

Picking up on this invitation to pursue an alternate course of action, the administrator of the Hughes estate brought a statutory interpleader, asking the district court in Texas to adjudicate the competing claims of domicile. On review, a majority of the Supreme Court shut the door opened by the earlier concurrence, reaffirming Worcester County Trust Company v. Riley to the effect that interpleader is not available because the taxing officials of both states were acting within their authority and thus were rendered immune from suit by the Eleventh Amendment. Cory v. White, 457 U.S. 85, 102 S.Ct. 2325, 72 L.Ed.2d 694 (1982). In the companion action, the majority granted the renewed California motion to invoke the Court's original jurisdication to adjudicate the domicile issue. California v. Texas, 457 U.S. 164, 102 S.Ct. 2335, 72 L.Ed.2d 755 (1982). There were dissents in both actions, arguing that the landmark decisions should be reversed and that federal interpleader was the appropriate remedy for estates threatened by inconsistent claims of domicile. The action was, however, discontinued as the two states reached a settlement agreement whereby they divided an estimated $169 million in inheritance taxes. Washington Post, Aug. 30, 1984, sec. C, p. 1. At the conclusion of this confused history, it appears that the status quo has prevailed, but that the margin of its support is sufficiently narrow to suggest that some future Supreme Court may yet find justification for a federal role in the resolution of competing claims by the states to a decedent's domicile. For an analysis of the issues, written prior to the decisions in Cory v. White and the second round of California v. Texas, see Zervopoulos, Double Domicile and Federal Interpleader Revisited, 22 SW.L.J. 1241 (1980).

3. The Uniform Probate Code § 3–202 vests responsibility for making the determination in the first court to take jurisdiction:

> If conflicting claims as to the domicile of a decedent are made in a formal testacy or appointment proceeding commenced in this state, and in a testacy or appointment proceeding after notice pending at the same time in another state, the Court of this state must stay, dismiss, or permit suitable amendment in, the proceeding here unless it is determined that the local proceeding was commenced before the proceeding elsewhere. The determination of domicile in the proceeding first commenced must be accepted as determinative in the proceeding in this state.

4. Not infrequently successful business or professional people who have amassed all their wealth in one of the large northern urban centers wish to retire to a warmer climate. They move south into an apartment, club, hotel or house which they may have purchased, execute new wills declaring themselves domiciliaries of their new home, and remain south for much of the year although they may visit their children and grandchildren throughout the country, go north for the summer, and make periodic stops at their original home—

to visit friends, go to the theater, and take care of business, banking, legal or medical problems. The tax authorities of the original domicile are understandably reluctant to concede domicile to another state when these people die in a few years. For wealthy persons to change their domicile they must sever all connections with their original homes. Guterman, Avoidance of Double Taxation of Estates and Trusts, 95 U.Pa.L.Rev. 701, 704–708 (1947); Schmoker, Minimizing State Death Taxes; Domicile; Tax Situs of Various Assets, 41 N.Y.U. Inst. on Fed. Taxation, 45–1 (1983).

5. May decedents mitigate some of the problems caused by mutiple residences by designating in the will the state whose law shall govern disputed issues, assuming they have some minimal contacts with the state so selected? N.Y. EPTL § 3–5.1(h) demonstrates a statutory approach to the question:

> Whenever a testator, not domiciled in this state at the time of death, provides in his will that he elects to have the disposition of his property situated in this state governed by the laws of this state, the intrinsic validity, including the testator's general capacity, effect, interpretation, revocation or alteration of any such disposition is determined by the local law of this state. * * *

In In re Renard, 56 N.Y.2d 973, 453 N.Y.S.2d 625, 439 N.E.2d 341 (1982), the decedent, a French domiciliary but a long-time resident of New York, left her New York property to charities, stating in her will that the will's validity and effect were to be governed by New York law. Decedent's son, who held both American and French citizenship and was domiciled in California, asserted that distribution of the estate should be governed by French law under which he was entitled to a forced share equal to half the estate. The son's claim was denied. The statute was given full effect and thus the distribution of property was to be governed by New York rather than French law. Difficulty arises in reconciling this result with the outcome in an earlier case involving a spouse's elective share. Estate of Clark, 21 N.Y.2d 478, 288 N.Y.S.2d 993, 236 N.E.2d 152 (1968). In the latter case, decedent, domiciled in Virginia, died possessing an estate of $23 million, the bulk of which consisted of securities on deposit with a New York bank. His will satisfied the widow's elective share rights of New York but not of Virginia. Despite a directive that the will was to be governed by New York law, the court held that Virginia law, granting the widow a right of election, prevailed and that Decedent's Estate Law § 47, the forerunner of N.Y. EPTL § 3–5.1(h) containing similar but not precisely identical language, did not apply because the disposition of property was required by a statute and not by the will. It remains for future cases to determine whether Renard has overruled Clark for all practical purposes or whether Clark will be continued as an exception to the general rule but limited to the spouse's elective share. See discussion in Turano, In re Renard, 123 Trusts & Estates 35 (Jan.1984).

B. THE FIDUCIARY IN A FEDERAL SYSTEM: ANCILLARY ADMINISTRATION

Happily, the cases where two or more states claim the decedent as a domiciliary are rare. It is obvious that if the states persist in their claims, any kind of unified administration is impossible. The more frequent situation involves the decedent who was domiciled in one state but who owned property situated in other states. Separate administrations are sometimes necessary in the states of situs as well as in the domiciliary state. This duplication of administrations means inconvenience, delay and additional expense. It does not, however, add up to anarchy as in the cases of multiple domicile. A fair measure of cooperation is achieved among the various jurisdictions. The state of domicile is recognized as the administration-in-chief, the states where property is located being but ancillary to it. This proposition becomes meaningful as the latter states defer to the former on many matters pertaining to the personal estate of the decedent. The General Comment to Article IV of the Uniform Probate Code gives expression to the modern policy by stating that the provisions relating to the administration of estates of non-residents "are designed to coerce respect for domiciliary procedure and administrative acts to the extent possible." To achieve this objective it helps to have the domiciliary executor qualify in the other jurisdictions as ancillary administrator if an ancillary administration is deemed necessary. Unfortunately, some states have found it necessary to reproclaim their sovereignty (and incidentally to channel business to local fiduciaries) by enacting statutes which bar non-residents from qualifying as fiduciaries. See Annot., Executors—Requirement of Residency, 9 A.L.R.4th 1223 (1981).

ALBUQUERQUE NATIONAL BANK v. CITIZENS NATIONAL BANK OF ABILENE

Court of Appeals of the United States, Fifth Circuit, 1954.
212 F.2d 943.

RIVES, Circuit Judge. The controversy is between two banks, one in Texas and one in New Mexico, each named as executor and as trustee in the will of Ellis A. Hall, deceased, over which shall administer certain corporate stock constituting the major asset in his estate. This appeal is from an interlocutory order granting an injunction, appealable under 28 U.S.C.A. § 1292(1), and the questions raised by the appellant relate to the jurisdiction of the district court and to the propriety of the injunction.

On August 8, 1953, evidently anticipating the dangers incident to a long trip by airplane, Ellis A. Hall executed his last will and testament. Nine days later, on August 17, 1953, Hall, his wife, Virginia H. Hall, a daughter, a daughter of his wife by a former marriage, and a young friend were all killed while Hall was flying his own airplane over Alaska.

By the terms of his will, Hall devised and bequeathed unto the Texas bank, The Citizens National Bank of Abilene, Texas, as trustee, "all the real and personal property I may own or be entitled to in the State of Texas at the time of my death." He devised and bequeathed unto the New Mexico bank, Albuquerque National Bank of Albuquerque, New Mexico, as trustee, "all the real and personal property I may own or be entitled to in the State of New Mexico at the time of my death." The terms of the trusts are identical and the surviving beneficiaries are the same, namely: the four Hall children, Richard A. Hall, age 24, James

E. Hall, age 18, Charles Layton Hall, age 14, and Betty Jean Hall, age between 2 and 3.* As to executors, the will provided as follows:

"I hereby nominate and appoint Albuquerque National Bank, of Albuquerque, New Mexico, and Virginia Hockenhull Hall, as Co-Executors under this will, to serve without bond, giving and granting unto them full and complete power to do any and all things requisite to carry out the terms hereof; and in the event it shall be necessary to have ancillary administration in Texas, I hereby nominate Citizens National Bank of Abilene, Texas, to serve as Executor for the purpose of administration in Texas, without bond."

The will was executed at Albuquerque, New Mexico, and described the testator as residing at that place, and it is not questioned by any of the parties that that was his domicile at the time of the execution of the will and at the time of his death.

A very large part of the estate of the decedent consisted of shares of stock in the Condor Petroleum Company, a Texas corporation, which shares of stock had a value of several million dollars. The certificates representing the shares were in the decedent's safety deposit box in the New Mexico bank, and after his death passed into the possession of that bank. The New Mexico bank obtained possession of the will and on or about September 23, 1953, filed it for probate in the probate court of the County of Bernalillo, New Mexico, and had the hearing for probate set for October 20, 1953. Without awaiting that hearing, the New Mexico bank had itself appointed as special administrator by said probate court and on October 3 made written request upon Condor Petroleum Company to transfer the shares of stock of said corporation registered in the name of the decedent, Ellis A. Hall, to three named individuals and to the New Mexico bank as special administrator; and further requested that a stockholder's meeting be called in Abilene, Texas, on October 10, 1953, for the purpose of electing four new directors. On October 5, 1953, the Condor Petroleum Company returned the certificates to the New Mexico bank, stating that "upon the advice of our attorneys, we are not at this time in position to transfer the above certificates of stock as outlined in your letter of October 3, 1953."

On October 20, 1953, the will was probated, and immediately thereafter the New Mexico bank filed in the same probate court a "Petition for Construction of Will and Directions to Executor", in which it called for decision of the question as to whether the shares of stock in Condor Petroleum Company, and also other shares of stock in other Texas corporations, passed under the will to the Texas bank, as trustee, or to the New Mexico bank, as trustee. This action was later transferred to the District Court of Bernalillo County, New Mexico, where it is still pending.

On the same day, October 20, 1953, and a short time before the petition for construction of the will was filed in New Mexico, the Texas bank

---

* On rehearing (212 F.2d 951), this passage was corrected to read: " * * * the three Hall children, Richard A. Hall, age 24, James E. Hall, age 18, Charles Layton Hall, age 14, and Catherine Brandenburg, age between 2 and 3, a step-granddaughter of Ellis A. Hall." Ed.

had itself appointed temporary administrator of the estate in Texas and obtained an ex parte order authorizing it to take possession of and to preserve the estate in Texas, and to bring suits for injunction against the Condor Petroleum Company and the New Mexico bank with respect to the shares of stock in Condor Petroleum Company. Later on the same day, but still before the petition for construction of the will was filed in New Mexico, the Texas bank filed in the District Court of Taylor County, Texas, a bill seeking to assure its possession of the estate located in Texas, to enjoin Condor Petroleum Company from issuing new certificates to the New Mexico bank, and to enjoin the New Mexico bank from transferring, selling or assigning said shares of stock or the certificates which represent them. The bill prayed also that the plaintiff have judgment for general relief. On the same day, the judge of the Texas state court entered an ex parte order commanding the New Mexico bank to appear on October 30, 1953, to show cause why a temporary injunction should not be granted. On October 29, 1953, the New Mexico bank removed this suit to the United States District Court for the Northern District of Texas, and it was in this suit that the judgment here appealed from was subsequently rendered.

On the same day on which it removed the Texas state court case to the United States District Court for the Northern District of Texas, October 29, 1953, the New Mexico bank filed in the United States District Court for the District of New Mexico a Civil Action seeking to establish its title to and to remove a cloud on its title to the certificates of stock representing shares of Condor Petroleum Company, and, also, to certificates of stock representing shares in two Texas banks. Pursuant to 28 U.S.C.A. § 1655, said District Court ordered the Texas bank to appear or plead to the complaint by November 23, 1953.

On November 9, 1953, the Texas bank filed its amended complaint in the United States District Court for the Northern District of Texas in which it sought to enjoin the New Mexico bank from prosecuting either of the suits then pending in the State of New Mexico and sought to enforce the Texas bank's claim and title to the shares of stock as temporary administrator, as executor, and as trustee, free from any claims of the New Mexico bank. The next day, November 10, 1953, was the day that had been set for the hearing of the construction of will suit in the district court of Bernalillo County, New Mexico. Also, on November 9, 1953, the Condor Petroleum Company filed in the cause then pending in the United States District Court for the Northern District of Texas its answer in the nature of a bill of interpleader, asking that the court order the administration of the personal property belonging to the estate in Texas to include the stock of Condor Petroleum Company and praying that both banks be enjoined and restrained from further prosecuting the suits then pending or any other suits they might file. The judge of the District Court of the United States for the Northern District of Texas thereupon on the same day, November 9, 1953, issued a temporary restraining order, restraining the New Mexico bank from continuing the prosecution of the construction of will suit pending before the District Court of Bernalillo

County, New Mexico, and of the Civil Action brought by the New Mexico bank in the United States District Court for the District of New Mexico, and an order to show cause returnable on November 20, 1953, as to why the New Mexico bank should not be temporarily enjoined from prosecuting any other suit or proceeding involving the issues before the court in said case.

On November 20 and 21, 1953, a full hearing was had in the United States District Court for the Northern District of Texas on the matter of the granting vel non of the interlocutory injunction, and at the conclusion of that hearing the District Court granted the interlocutory injunction enjoining the New Mexico bank, its officers, agents, employees and attorneys, from continuing the prosecution of the construction of will suit before the District Court of Bernalillo County, New Mexico, and the Civil Action filed by said bank before the United States District Court for the District of New Mexico, or from filing or prosecuting any other suit or proceeding other than the action in which the injunction was issued insofar as the same involves the issue of title and right to possession of shares of stock in Condor Petroleum Company. There were further related terms of the injunction. This appeal is from that order granting an interlocutory injunction.

It appears that subsequent to the granting of that injunction, the judge of the United States District Court for the District of New Mexico took cognizance of the fact that the New Mexico bank and its attorneys were enjoined from continuing the prosecution of the case in that Court, appointed other attorneys as *amicus curiae*, heard evidence produced by them, and entered a default judgment against the Texas bank and a judgment quieting title to the certificates of stock in the New Mexico bank as executor. In a memorandum accompanying the judgment, the judge of the United States District Court for the District of New Mexico, expressed his opinion also that there was no ambiguity as to the ownership of the stock by the New Mexico bank as trustee, "In fact, an examination of the will itself appears to be sufficient to answer the question. The language is clear and the intention of the testator is not in doubt. Ambiguity does not exist."

To the direct contrary, the United States District Court for the Northern District of Texas, in the order granting the interlocutory injunction, had said:

> "The Court finds upon considering the terms of the will of Ellis A. Hall, Deceased, dated August 8, 1953, and the surrounding circumstances of the decedent, that it was the intention of the Testator that the shares of stock held by the decedent in corporations domiciled and doing business in Texas, including shares in Condor Petroleum Company, The Citizens National Bank in Abilene, and Farmers and Merchants National Bank, Abilene, Texas, be considered as property which the decedent 'owned' or 'was entitled to in the State of Texas' and as such that same passed to The Citizens National Bank in Abilene as Trustee and as Ancillary Executor."

That Court had added the following limitation: "The finding of the Court herein as to the intention of the Testator, however, is only made incident to the Court's jurisdiction with reference to the location of the property."

The property of a person while living, wherever such property may be located and of whatsoever it may consist, is for many purposes considered as a unit. So, for practical purposes, the estate of a deceased person is often considered as a whole; and difficulty of administration is encountered if that portion of it in each state is to be treated as a completely separate affair. Without cooperation between the states, and between the administrators or executors in different states, the expense and difficulty of administration often operate to the serious detriment of the estate as a whole due to the fact that our States are for most purposes entirely separate legal sovereignties. * * *

Insofar as lands or immovables are concerned, it is universally recognized that, apart from statute, administration of them must be had at the situs. * * * Lands are not directly involved in the controversy between the present parties, but the fact that a considerable part of the estate consists of income producing lands in Texas demonstrates the necessity for administration in that State.

As to movables, it is necessary that we keep in mind "the independence of the two questions, what happens to the ownership of chattels upon the death of the owner, and what happens to the administered estate ripe for distribution." 2 Beale, Conflict of Laws, Sec. 300.1, p. 1028. For that purpose, Professor Beale employs the words "administration" and "distribution", the former as meaning the collection of assets, particularly personal assets, and with them paying debts, including taxes and costs of administration, until all are paid or the assets exhausted; then, "If after full administration a balance remains, the payment of the balance to those entitled to it is here called distribution." 3 Id. Sec. 465.1, p. 1444. In the present case we are in the stage of the administration of the estate, though we must look forward to its ultimate distribution in considering the propriety of the injunction against the New Mexico bank from continuing the prosecution of the action in the District Court of Bernalillo County, New Mexico, for the construction of the will.

Each state has the right to control and administer the personal assets of a deceased person found within its borders and to satisfy debts and obligations due to its own citizens. Baker v. Baker, Eccles & Co., 242 U.S. 394, 401, 37 S.Ct. 152, 61 L.Ed. 386. The New Mexico bank derives its appointment as executor from a New Mexico court and, at least during the administration stage, it is not entitled to recognition of its status in Texas nor to possession of assets located in Texas. * * * "To the extent that he is entitled to receive the assets after administration here, his title is recognized. But he will not be permitted to intermeddle while the courts of this state are exercising their jurisdiction." Saner-Ragley Lumber Co. v. Spivey Tex.Com.App., supra, 238 S.W. [912,] at page 915.

Whether as a matter of strict jurisdiction, or by comity so well recognized as to have the same practical effect, the probate of a will at the recognized domicile of the testator is binding on all questions as to the legality of the will with regard to personal estate elsewhere. 57 Am.Jur.,

Wills, Sec. 956; 3 Beale, Conflict of Laws, Sec. 469.1, p. 1463. The validity of Mr. Hall's will is not questioned by anyone, but its construction, meaning, and effect are sharply in dispute. The Texas courts have declared, "It is a universal rule recognized in this state that, as a matter of comity, the laws of the domicile of the intestate will control in the succession of movable or personal property of his estate." Saner-Ragley Lumber Co. v. Spivey, 238 S.W. at page 915. As to the construction of a foreign will, the A.L.I., Restatement, Conflict of Laws, Sec. 308, states the rule as follows:

> "The meaning of words used in a will of movables, in the absence of controlling circumstances to the contrary, is determined in accordance with the usage at the domicile of the testator at the time of making the will."
>
> * * *

The domiciliary law and also the facts pertinent to construction of a will as an entirety and in each of its parts can ordinarily be best determined and applied by the courts of the state of the domicile, and accordingly a judgment by a competent court in the state of domicile, insofar as the judgment relates to movables, will generally, if not always, be followed by the courts in other states on questions as to the construction of the will and the rights of persons claiming under it. * * * It would be premature for us to hold that the judgment of the New Mexico state court charged with the construction of the will under the laws of that State will be controlling as to the distribution of the movables located in Texas. It is enough for present purposes to say that that judgment, when fairly rendered, will at least be highly persuasive, and that there is no present conflict of jurisdiction between the New Mexico state court and the federal district court in Texas. Even if we assume that the two courts have concurrent jurisdiction, and that the federal district court in Texas first took possession of the res, we are governed by what was said in Penn General Casualty Co. v. Pennsylvania, 294 U.S. 189, 198, 55 S.Ct. 386, 390, 79 L.Ed. 850:

> "While it is often said that, of two courts having concurrent jurisdiction in rem, that one first taking possession acquires exclusive jurisdiction, * * * it is exclusive only so far as its exercise is necessary for the appropriate control and disposition of the property. The jurisdiction does not extend beyond the purpose for which it is allowed, to enable the court to exercise it appropriately and to avoid unseemly conflicts. * * * The other court does not thereby lose its power to make orders which do not conflict with the authority of the court having jurisdiction over the control and disposition of the property."

There is no effort in the New Mexico state court to gain possession of any property, nor to interfere with the administration proper of the estate in Texas. We think it clear, therefore, that the district court erred in enjoining the New Mexico bank, its officers, agents, employees and attorneys, from continuing the prosecution of the action before the District Court of Bernalillo County, New Mexico.

We think that the action pending in the United States District Court for the Northern District of Texas is an action in rem and has been such since it was first instituted in the Texas state court, and that adequate provisions for service of process in such an action upon non-residents of the State of Texas appear in the Texas Statutes and Rules, Articles 1975, 1976, Vernon's Ann. Civil Statutes of Texas, and Rule 108 of Texas Rules of Practice and Procedure, and also in 28 U.S.C.A. § 1655. The action in the United States District Court for the District of New Mexico is professedly strictly a suit in rem. The rule as to actions in rem has been stated in Palmer v. State of Texas, 212 U.S. 118, 125, 29 S.Ct. 230, 232, 53 L.Ed. 435, as follows:

> "If a court of competent jurisdiction, Federal or state, has taken possession of property, or by its procedure has obtained jurisdiction over the same, such property is withdrawn from the jurisdiction of the courts of the other authority as effectually as if the property had been entirely removed to the territory of another sovereignty."

*   *   *

It remains to determine whether the shares of stock in Condor Petroleum Company had such a situs in Texas as would justify an administrator appointed there to take possession and as would sustain the in rem jurisdiction of the Federal District Court in Texas. There are cases which hold that corporate shares have a dual existence, a situs both in the state of incorporation and in the state where the stockholder resides and the certificate is located. *   *   * The rule in the majority of jurisdictions is stated in 21 Am.Jur., Executors and Administrators, Sec. 52, p. 403:

> "The general rule appears to be well settled that regardless of the place where the certificates happen to be, the state in which a corporation has been organized is the situs of its shares of stock, for purposes of administration, rather than the state of the decedent's domicil, and particularly so if the corporation also conducts its business in the state where it has been organized."

*   *   *

Further considerations peculiar to Condor Petroleum Company localized the situs of its shares in Texas for purposes of administration. Each of the certificates was held subject to an option to purchase by the corporation itself. On January 25, 1936 there was adopted

> "An amendment to the charter of Condor Petroleum Company to provide that the corporation shall have a first option to purchase shares of common non-par stock at the bona fide price agreed upon by the stockholder and the prospective purchaser, the stockholder having the right to dispose of his stock to others should the corporation fail to exercise its option to purchase the stock within thirty days after receipt of the written offer from the stockholder."

The corporation was not only organized in Texas, but it conducted all of its business in that State.

We hold that the District Court for the Northern District of Texas acquired jurisdiction of the res to the exclusion of the United States District Court for the District of New Mexico.

This Court, of course, has no jurisdiction to review any proceedings had in the United States District Court for the District of New Mexico. As to the order of the Texas Federal District Court, we think that it was erroneous for that Court to express even a tentative opinion on the construction of the will and on whether the shares of stock in Texas corporations passed to the Texas bank as trustee. The question before the court was merely the situs of the shares for purposes of administration, a question entirely independent from the construction of the will. The terms of the will itself drew a sharp distinction between the administration and the distribution of the estate. Administration of the estate was entrusted to the New Mexico bank as executor, and, if ancillary administration should be necessary, then to the Texas bank as executor for the purpose of administration in Texas. Independently of the terms of the will, we have indicated our view that ancillary administration in Texas is necessary, and we can see no escape from that conclusion in view of the presence in Texas of both movable and immovable assets. As to the distribution of the estate in Texas, any decree by the District Court for the Northern District of Texas should await the final conclusion of the construction of will suit pending in the New Mexico state court. We note in passing that counsel for the New Mexico bank conceded on oral argument that, in their opinion, the New Mexico bank would be bound by such a decree rather than by the judgment rendered by the District Court of the United States for the District of New Mexico.

The New Mexico bank has urged upon us that, as the domiciliary executor of such a large estate, it must raise over six million dollars to pay the federal estate tax by its due date, November 19, 1954, or the estate will suffer a considerable loss in interest. It may be that a duty as to the estate tax is imposed on all administrators and executors, wherever located. See 26 U.S.C.A. § 821(a), 930, Regulations of Internal Revenue Commissioner 105, Sec. 81.64. However that may be, the will expresses the testator's wish that both banks cooperate, and under the law it is their duty to work together for the benefit of the estate. Each bank stands in a position of trust to the beneficiaries. It is the duty of each to place the welfare of the beneficiaries above its own private interest. If either should fail to do so, it would be legally responsible for any resultant damage. It may be that, as to the litigation which has already ensued, the court or courts having jurisdiction of the accounting of the respective banks as administrator or as executor may determine that either or both of the actions filed in the respective Federal courts were unnecessary from the point of view of the welfare of the beneficiaries and that the attorney's fees and court costs of such action, or a part thereof, should not properly be charged against the estate. That is a question on which we have no authority to pass and on which no court could properly pass without more complete information than is contained in the present record. We merely note the question to call it to the attention of the guardian *ad litem* or representative of the minor children and of the court having jurisdiction of the accounting of the respective executors and administrators.   We further entertain the hope that a consideration by each bank of the paramount duty owed to the estate and to the beneficiaries and of the possible consequences of a breach of such duty may result in more effective cooperation between these two banks in the future.

As indicated in the opinion, the judgment appealed from is reversed in part and affirmed in all other parts, and the cause is remanded for further proceedings not inconsistent with this opinion.

Reversed in part and affirmed in part.

Notes

1. Some confusion may arise in the mind of the reader because of the failure to distinguish between two types of "conflicts" questions which arise.   The first involves the basis for jurisdiction and the extraterritorial effect of out-of-state probate decrees;   the second deals with the choice-of-law problem as to which of two state laws is to govern.   Both questions appear in the principal case. The first is answered by the court with its holding that there is sufficient property in Texas to support the jurisdictional claim for a Texas ancillary proceeding.   With regard to the second or choice-of-law problem, the court applies the usual rule that the law of the domiciliary state controls questions involving personal estate which may be said to have a situs elsewhere.   On the basis of these two holdings might it be said that in the principal case Texas won a battle but lost the war?   Could The Citizens National Bank of Abilene now go into the Texas court and ask it, applying the New Mexico law, to find that "location" must be given content in accordance with Mr. Hall's intent, and that Hall believed the property to be located in Texas?   The rule that the law of the domicile governs in resolving issues involving intangible personal property has been criticized.   The law of the state with the "paramount interest in the distribution" has been suggested as an alternative point of reference.   Weintraub, An Inquiry into the Utility of "Domicile" as a Concept in Conflicts Analysis, 63 Mich.L.Rev. 961, 972 (1965) and authorities cited therein.

2. The situs of land takes priority over the decedent's domicile in controlling questions of both jurisdiction and choice of law involving the land.   In addition, the law of the situs will govern all problems of devolution even though the situs has only minimal contacts with the people involved.   An Ohio domiciliary executed a will shortly before death leaving Texas mineral properties to Ohio charities.   The timing of the will rendered the charitable devises invalid under an Ohio law prohibiting deathbed transfers to charities.   The children, the immediate survivors, were citizens of Ohio.   The court applied Texas law and held the devises valid.   Toledo Society for Crippled Children v. Hickok, 152 Tex. 578, 261 S.W.2d 692, 43 A.L.R.2d 553 (1953), certiorari denied 347 U.S. 936, 74 S.Ct. 631, 98 L.Ed. 1086 (1954);   analyzed and criticized in Hancock, "In the Parish of St. Mary le Bow, in the Ward of Cheap," 16 Stan.L.Rev. 561 (1964);   see also Hancock, Full Faith and Credit to Foreign Laws and Judgments in Real Property Litigation: The Supreme Court and the Land Taboo, 18 Stan. L.Rev. 1299 (1966).

3. The necessity for ancillary proceedings stems from the notion that a personal representative's authority is coextensive with the jurisdiction which

appointed him and goes no farther. He does not then, as a general proposition, have the capacity to sue or to give valid discharge in any other state. As the exceptions to this notion indicate, there is no inexorable principle which compels this conclusion. Adherence is justified in two ways: (a) " *   *   * The dominant policy of the forum is to protect local creditors (and perhaps local distributees) whenever it is within the power of the courts of the forum to do so." ; (b) " *   *   * various kinds of personal property have, in the development of Conflict of Laws principles, come to be recognized as 'localized' in some one appropriate jurisdiction   *   *   *".   Beale, Conflict of Laws § 471.1 (1935). These reasons are critically examined in Currie, The Multiple Personality of the Dead: Executors, Administrators, and the Conflict of Laws, 33 U.Chi.L.Rev. 429 (1966); Lerner, The Need for Reform in Multistate Estate Administration, 55 Tex.L.Rev. 303 (1977). The rules as to when an ancillary administration is required are not clearly established; consider the following excerpt from Alford, Collecting a Decedent's Assets without Ancillary Administration, 18 Sw.L.J. 329, 330–332 (1964) (footnotes omitted):

> In times past, the domiciliary representative could look in the other direction, ignore the assets in the foreign state, and leave the next of kin to their own resources to get the property from the ancillary administrator. One could learn to live with multiple administrations. No clear-cut fiduciary duty had developed which required him to collect assets outside the state of his appointment. However, this situation exists no longer. The domiciliary personal representative now is liable for the full federal estate tax on land and personal property no matter where the assets are located. He has to be familiar with this property in order to pay the tax, and he must know enough about the business of the decedent in other states to file his income tax returns and to determine his gift tax liability. Pressure probably will be brought to bear upon the personal representative to develop liquid assets in order to pay taxes and other estate obligations. These forces compel the domiciliary personal representative to discover and to recover any foreign assets that he can.

> State taxes also present a problem in reducing the overall tax impact upon the estate. States of both "domicile" and "business" situs may impose inheritance taxes upon intangible personal property. Tangibles are taxable where situated. To avoid multiple taxation, the domiciliary personal representative usually is pushed to recover as much of the personal estate of the decedent as he can legitimately without subjecting it to crippling local tax blows. If an ancillary administration is commenced, it is assured that local taxes will be imposed upon the property.

> Since good and sufficient reasons exist to cut ancillary administration to the bare minimum, it is disconcerting that so many ancillary administrations apparently are conducted In the writer's opinion, many domiciliary personal representatives blunder into ancillary administrations through ignorance, although many judicial officers have been known to give kindly guidance to the wayward. Some of the administrations arise through references to lawyers to collect foreign assets. For example, the local practitioner who is to collect debts without exact knowledge of the existence of local creditors may be inclined to seek ancillary letters for his own protection. Also, corporate fiduciaries may seek to avoid conflicts with their professional competitors in other states.

Some ancillary administrations clearly may be necessary. Perhaps title to foreign land must be cleared by elimination of creditor claims in the situs jurisdiction. A debtor may refuse to pay without a receipt from a local administrator. The biography of the decedent may be so obscure that neither his assets nor his debts in other states can be discovered with certainty without a formal administration. Also it is an unfortunate fact that some domiciliary fiduciaries lack the competence to be permitted to collect debts and to pay creditors without the supervision a judicial officer in a foreign state can provide.

4. If an ancillary administration is to be avoided, then a way must be found for fiduciaries to marshal the assets of estates which have a situs outside the state of their appointment. A note, 50 Colum.L.Rev. 518 (1950), annotates a number of situations where the case law has permitted a foreign representative to sue without qualifying in the state of suit: (a) action on a negotiable instrument payable to bearer which is in his possession; (b) suit on a judgment previously rendered in favor of the representative in another jurisdiction; (c) action on a contract made by the representative on behalf of the estate; (d) action to recover property reduced to his possession in the state of his appointment but subsequently removed to another jurisdiction; (e) actions for the wrongful death of the decedent where the recovery goes exclusively to the decedent's family. See also McDowell, Foreign Personal Representatives, 30–78 (1957). For the results if a debtor makes payment to the personal representative without an official discharge, see Mersch, Voluntary Payment to a Foreign Administrator, 18 Geo.L.J. 130 (1929). In Wiener v. Specific Pharmaceuticals Inc., 298 N.Y. 346, 351, 83 N.E.2d 673, 675 (1949) there is a discussion of the wrongful death action:

> We come, then, to an important question—hitherto expressly left open by this court, * * * as to whether a foreign administrator, suing as special statutory trustee to recover damages for wrongful death, has the legal capacity to maintain such a suit in our courts.

> It has been repeatedly observed that the reason for insisting that a foreign administrator obtain ancillary letters before suing in another State is to assure that the decedent's domestic creditors shall have their claims paid out of any fund recovered for the benefit of the debtor's estate. * * *

> The point need not be further labored. The rule barring foreign administrators from our courts is just and reasonable *only* if applied in cases, first, where there are domestic creditors, and second, where the foreign administrator sues to recover a fund in which such creditors may share. Obviously, no prejudice threatens local creditors of the decedent if the wrongful death statute makes no provision for recovery on behalf of the general estate and, in fact, bars creditors' claims against the proceeds. Suing under such a statute, plaintiff acts, not as an officer of the foreign court appointed by it as alter ego for the estate, but as a trustee for the designated beneficiaries, the actual and real parties in interest. In such a case, the amount recovered truly constitutes a special fund for their exclusive benefit, and, since it is not subject to the claims of others, no danger exists that failure to require local qualification may harm or prejudice domestic creditors. With the primary and, perhaps, only reason for the rule thus removed, the rule itself has no sensible application and should not be invoked in this class of case.

Note should be made that the common law rule of incapacity to sue has been modified by statute as to certain particulars in many states, McDowell, Foreign Personal Representatives, 67–75 (1957); Note, The Extraterritorial Authority of Executors and Administrators to Sue and Collect Assets, 52 Iowa L.Rev. 290 (1966). For an example of such a statute, see N.Y. EPTL 13–3.5. Persuasive argument has been made for the appointment of a universal administrator with nationwide powers. Currie, The Multiple Personality of the Dead: Executors, Administrators, and the Conflict of Laws, 33 U.Chi.L.Rev. 429 (1966). Other fiduciaries, such as a statutory successor to a corporation, have standing to sue throughout the country. Cheatham, The Statutory Successor, the Receiver and the Executor in Conflict of Laws, 44 Colum.L.Rev. 549 (1944).

The Uniform Probate Code allows a domiciliary foreign representative to file copies of his appointment in the ancillary state, if no local administration is pending, UPC § 4–204. By so doing, the domiciliary foreign personal representative "may exercise as to assets in this state all powers of a local personal representative and may maintain actions and proceedings in this state subject to any conditions imposed upon nonresident parties generally." UPC § 4–205. Thus, it may be possible to avoid administration in any state other than that in which the decedent was domiciled, although an "application or petition for local administration of the estate terminates the power of the foreign personal representative to act under Section 4–205." UPC § 4–206.

See, Vestal, Multiple-State Estates Under the Uniform Probate Code, 27 Wash. & Lee L.Rev. 70, 77 (1970).

If situs is the basis for an ancillary administration, there remains a question to be determined under conflict of laws principles as to where personal property, as for instance a debt, is located. See in general, Hopkins, Conflict of Laws in the Administration of Decedents' Estates, 28 Iowa L.Rev. 422, 613 (1943). The statement in the principal case that the situs of stocks is the place of incorporation has been described as the majority rule. Pomerance, The "Situs" of Stock, 17 Corn.L.Q. 43 (1931); but see Restatement, Second, Conflict of Laws, §§ 324, 325. While it is ordinarily considered that a debt is an asset at the debtor's domicile, the rule appears to be otherwise with respect to the debts of the federal government, where "the domicile for the purpose of founding administration is at the domicile of the creditor." Diehl v. United States, 438 F.2d 705, 710 (5th Cir. 1971) (income tax refund was payable at decedent's domicile and therefore California rather than Texas had jurisdiction over the debt). On the above issues generally, see Schoenblum, Multistate and Multinational Estate Planning, Chapter 16 (1982).

5. As the personal representative does not have standing to sue outside the state of his appointment, it is the usual rule that he is likewise immune from out-of-state suits brought by others to recover on an obligation of the decedent unless he is subject to the other state's in personam jurisdiction. The origins of this rule, the reasons for and against its continuance, a thorough analysis of the critical comment concerning it, and the statutory changes which have resulted appear in Currie, The Multiple Personality of the Dead: Executors, Administrators, and the Conflict of Laws, 33 U.Chi.L.Rev. 429 (1966).

States have expanded the reach of their in personam jurisdiction by the enactment of long-arm statutes. N.Y. SCPA § 210 is representative of statutes designed to secure personal jurisdiction over foreign fiduciaries:

Jurisdictional Predicate

1. **Traditional bases.** The [Surrogate's] court shall exercise jurisdiction over persons and property as heretofore or hereafter permitted by law.

2. **Additional bases.**

(a) The court may exercise personal jurisdiction over any non-domiciliary, or his fiduciary, as to any matter within the subject matter jurisdiction of the court arising from any act or omission of the non-domiciliary within the state, either in person or through an agent.

(b) The receipt and acceptance of any property paid or distributed out of and as part of the administration of an estate subject to the jurisidiction of the court shall constitute a submission by such recipient to the jurisdiction of the court as to any matter concerning the payment or distribution, including proceedings for the recovery thereof.

The Uniform Probate Code similarly establishes jurisdiction over a foreign personal representative in a state where the representative files a certificate of his or her appointment, receives payment of money or receives delivery of personal property (the extent of the jurisdiction is limited to the value of the money or property), or does an act that would have given the state jurisdiction over the representative as an individual. UPC § 4–301. § 4–302 states in addition that a foreign fiduciary is subject to the jurisdiction of the state "to the same extent that his decedent was subject to jurisdiction immediately prior to death".

In Rush v. Savchuk, 444 U.S. 320, 327, 100 S.Ct. 571, 576 , 62 L.Ed.2d 516 (1980), the majority decision set out the ground rules for the administration of statutes of this kind:

> * * * a state may exercise jurisdiction over an absent defendant only if the defendant has "certain minimum contacts with [the forum] such that the maintenance of the suit does not offend 'traditional notions of fair play and substantial justice.' " International Shoe Co. v. Washington, 326 U.S. 310, 316, 66 S.Ct. 154, 158, 90 L.Ed. 95 (1945). In determining whether a particular exercise of state-court jurisdiction is consistent with due process, the inquiry must focus on "the relationship among the defendant, the forum, and the litigation." Shaffer v. Heitner, *supra*, 433 U.S., at 204, 97 S.Ct., at 2580.

Under these rules, a domiciliary executor may be subject to in personam jurisdiction if the cause of action arose out of an act done or transaction consummated in the forum state or if the executor had regular and substantial contacts in that state. For an application of these principles to the activities of a fiduciary, see Hanson v. Denckla, 357 U.S. 235, 78 S.Ct. 1228, 2 L.Ed.2d 1283 (1958) (insufficient nexus between a Delaware corporate trustee and decedent's Florida domicile to support Florida's claim to jurisdiction, even though the estate and the principal beneficiaries were located in Florida). See generally, Currie, The Multiple Personality of the Dead: Executors, Administrators, and the Conflict of Laws, 33 U.Chi.L.Rev. 429 (1966); Lewis, A Brave New World for Personal Jurisdiction: Flexible Tests Under Uniform Standards, 37 Vand.L.Rev. 1 (1984); Annot., Application of Longarm Statute to Personal Representative of Deceased Nonresidents, 19 A.L.R.3d, 171 (1968). Personal service on an ancillary administrator in one state does not constitute service on the domiciliary executor in the state of domicile.　Wisemantle v. Hull Interprises, Inc., 103 Ill.App.3d 878, 59 Ill.Dec. 827, 432 N.E.2d 613 (1981).

6.　In Mullane v. Central Hanover Bank & Trust Co., 339 U.S. 306, 70 S.Ct. 652, 94 L.Ed. 865 (1949), the bank had brought a proceeding for the judicial settlement of its accounts as trustee of a common trust fund.　The Court held that statutory notice by publication setting forth the name and address of the bank, name and date of establishment of the common trust fund, and a list of all participating estates, trusts or funds was sufficient notice to beneficiaries whose location or interests could not with due diligence be discovered or whose interests were conjectural or future.　The Court said, 339 U.S. at 313–314, 70 S.Ct. at 657, 94 L.Ed. at 873:

> *　*　*　It is sufficient to observe that, whatever the technical definition of its chosen procedure, the interest of each state in providing means to close trusts that exist by the grace of its laws and are administered under the supervision of its courts is so insistent and rooted in custom as to establish beyond doubt the right of its courts to determine the interests of all claimants, resident or nonresident, provided its procedure accords full opportunity to appear and be heard.

> *　*　*

> Personal service of written notice within the jurisdiction is the classic form of notice always adequate in any type of proceeding.　But the vital interest of the State in bringing any issues as to its fiduciaries to a final settlement can be served only if interests or claims of individuals who are outside of the State can somehow be determined.　A construction of the Due Process Clause which would place impossible or impractical obstacles in the way could not be justified.

The Court went on, however, to say (339 U.S. at 318, 70 S.Ct. at 659, 94 L.Ed. at 875):

> As to known present beneficiaries of known place of residence, however, notice by publication stands on a different footing.　Exceptions in the name of necessity do not sweep away the rule that within the limits of practicability notice must be such as is reasonably calculated to reach interested parties.　Where the names and post-office addresses of those affected by a proceeding are at hand, the reasons disappear for resort to means less likely than the mails to apprise them of its pendency.

> The trustee has on its books the names and addresses of the income beneficiaries represented by appellant, and we find no tenable ground for dispensing with a serious effort to inform them personally of the accounting, at least by ordinary mail to the record address.

In a recent decision, a majority of the Supreme Court held on the authority of the Mullane case that a county, when conducting a sale of real property for delinquent taxes, must notify a mortgagee, whose name and address are known, of the impending sale either by personal service or mailed notice.　Mennonite Board of Missions v. Adams, 462 U.S. 791, 103 S.Ct. 2706, 77 L.Ed.2d 180 (1983). Service by publication is used frequently in the administration of estates.　It now appears that this method of service is likely to be declared constitutionally deficient when applied to a party in a proceeding that affects that party's property interests, because the party is entitled to actual notice as long as his or her identity and location are reasonably ascertainable.　For the impact of this stricter rule of service on the administration of non-claim statutes, see p. 647 infra.

IN RE ESTATE OF BRAUNS

Supreme Court of Michigan, 1936.
276 Mich. 598, 268 N.W. 890, 106 A.L.R. 889.

NORTH, Chief Justice. The question of law presented by this appeal is this: Are nonresident creditors entitled to have their claims presented for allowance in an ancillary administration in this state, the estate of the deceased, as a whole, being insolvent but there being assets in excess of local claims in Michigan.

Domiciliary administration of the estate of August E. Brauns, deceased, is pending in the state of Washington. Ancillary administration is pending in the probate court of Dickinson county, Mich. Mr. Brauns died seized of both real and personal property located in Michigan. The appraised value of this property is somewhat in excess of claims allowed to Michigan creditors in the ancillary administration; but claims allowed in the domiciliary administration are very much in excess of the appraised value of the estate located in that jurisdiction. The estate as a whole is insolvent.

The appellees, the First National Bank of Appleton, Wis., and Edna Slater Holden, are respectively residents of the states of Wisconsin and Washington. In the Michigan ancillary administration the former presented a claim of $12,895 and the latter one of $6,670.35. These claims, if allowed, would render the ancillary estate insolvent. From an order of the probate court disallowing the nonresident claims, an appeal was taken to the circuit court. The circuit judge allowed these nonresident claims, but reserved to the court the question of the right of such claimants to participate pro rata or otherwise with any other creditors whose claims were allowed in Michigan. The First National Bank of Norway, a Michigan creditor, and the Michigan ancillary administrator have appealed.

Appellants assert that to the extent necessary the assets of the ancillary estate should first be applied in payment of the costs of ancillary administration and then to payment in full of Michigan creditors; and that thereupon the excess, if any, in the hands of the ancillary administrator, should be accounted for by him to the domiciliary estate. But appellees contend that they have a right to have their claims allowed in the ancillary administration and to participate pro rata in the Michigan assets; and that in any event the Michigan creditors should not be paid a larger percentage of their claims than is paid to all other creditors of the same class; and, if necessary to accomplish this result, any funds in excess of the amount necessary to make pro rata payment to Michigan creditors (after payment of ancillary administration costs) should be accounted for to the domiciliary estate.

Some states have controlling statutory provisions. Formerly there were such provisions in Michigan. See Rev.Stat.1838, c. 8, §§ 21–25. The statute was subsequently changed. See Rev.Stat.1846, c. 68, § 24, now found in Comp.Laws 1929, § 15546. At the present time the Michigan statute contains no provision for filing claims of nonresident creditors which differs in any way from the procedure prescribed for presenting claims of resident creditors, nor do we find a decision of this court which involves the identical question of law presented in the instant case. In support of their contention that local creditors should be paid in full from local assets appellants cite the following cases: In re Stevens' Estate, 171 Mich. 486, 137 N.W. 627; In re Colburn's Estate, 153 Mich. 206, 116 N.W. 986, 18 L.R.A.(N.S.) 149, 126 Am.St.Rep. 479; Jones v. Turner, 249 Mich. 403, 228 N.W. 796. In the cited cases, and possibly in some other decisions of this court, there are statements which seem to support appellants' contention; but these statements are found in cases which do not appear to involve insolvent estates. Here we are concerned with the rights of nonresident creditors of an insolvent estate. This, we think, renders the portions of the cited opinions upon which appellants rely of little, if any, authoritative value, because the exact legal question here involved was not there presented nor considered.

The first question for determination is this: Was the circuit judge correct in holding that nonresident creditors had a right to present their claims for allowance in the ancillary administration? As noted above, in Michigan the statutory provisions for filing claims against estates apply alike to resident and nonresident creditors, and also alike to domiciliary and ancillary administration. We direct attention to the provisions contained in various sections of the Compiled Laws of 1929. In section 15585 provision is made for the administration of the estates of persons who at the time of death were inhabitants of this state, and also for the administration of estates of which persons died seized who were nonresidents. Subject to certain exceptions with which we are not here concerned, section 15674 provides for the appointment of commissioners, "to receive, examine and adjust all claims and demands of all persons against the deceased." Section 15699, after making provision for payment of preferred claims in an estate wherein the assets in the hands of the executor or administrator are not sufficient to pay debts in full, directs the payment of debts due to other creditors (other than preferred creditors); making no distinction between resident and nonresident creditors. We quote section 15700: "If there shall not be assets enough to pay all the debts of any one (1) class, each creditor shall be paid a dividend in proportion to his claim; and no creditor of any one (1) class shall receive any payment until all of those of the preceding class shall be fully paid."

Section 15701 directs that the probate court shall order payment of the debts "among the creditors, as the circumstances of the estate shall require, according to the provisions of this chapter." Here again it is to be noted that no distinction is made between resident and nonresident creditors.

The American Law Institute's Restatement of the Law on Conflict of Laws contains the following which is pertinent to the question under consideration:

"Except as stated in Sec. 496, (referring to cases where there are no local creditors in the ancillary jurisdiction) all creditors, regardless of where they are domiciled can prove their claims in any state in which administration proceedings have been instituted." Section 495.

"All creditors of a decedent who have proved their claims in a competent court in which there are administration proceedings of the estate of that decedent are entitled to share pro rata in any application of the assets of the local administrator to the payment of claims irrespective of the source of such assets or of the residence, place of business, domicile or citizenship of the creditors. * * *" (Exceptions not here material are noted.) Section 497.

Under the above section the following comment is made:

"(a) Under the Constitution of the United States a State cannot give a preference to its citizens as against the citizens of other States of the United States."

"In the payment of creditors of an insolvent estate, the court in each state will, so far as possible, secure pro rata payment of all claims." Section 501.

"If the entire estate is insolvent, the court in each state in paying claimants who have proved their claims therein will pay only such proportion of each claim as, added to what the claimant has theretofore received in other states, will put him on an equality with the other creditors paid in the local court." Section 502.

"Where the entire estate is insolvent, the court in which the administration proceedings are carried on will as far as possible marshal the assets under its control in such a manner as to secure to all creditors a pro rata percentage of their claims." Section 503.

In Corpus Juris the law is thus stated: "In a few jurisdictions it is held that only local creditors can prove their claims in the ancillary jurisdiction; but the general rule is that nonresidents as well as residents may prove their claims in the ancillary jurisdiction, leaving the question of payment to be dealt with afterward when the solvency or insolvency of the whole estate is to be considered." 24 C.J. 1124.

Consideration is given to the manner in which insolvency affects payment of claims against an estate in 11 R.C.L. p. 444, § 546. We make a partial quotation: "Where the ancillary estate is insolvent and the principal estate solvent, it seems that nonresident creditors should look to the latter for payment; but where both estates are insolvent nonresident creditors may share in both, although apparently they will not be permitted to receive, in the aggregate, a larger per cent than resident creditors receive from the ancillary estate."

In the instant case Mr. Brauns died seized of both real and personal property subject to ancillary administration in Michigan. In Goodall v. Marshall, 11 N.H. 88, 35 Am.Dec. 472, the advisability, if not the necessity, of permitting nonresident creditors to file claims in ancillary administration proceedings wherein the assets in part consist of real estate is convincingly pointed out. We forego lengthy quotation from the above case, and content ourselves with calling attention to it by citation.

An instructive note on the subject under consideration, including comment on the difficulties attendant upon carrying out ancillary administration in conjunction with administration in other jurisdictions, will be found in 44 A.L.R. 801. We quote a single sentence: "The delay would undoubtedly be considerable, but this would not be so great an evil as either sending our citizens abroad, upon a forlorn hope, to seek for the fragments of an insolvent estate, or paying the whole of their debts out of the property without regard to the claims of foreign creditors."

Primarily the object of ancillary administration is to secure to local creditors their just proportion of payment from the estate of the deceased without being subjected to the inconvenience and expense of presenting their claims to a court of foreign jurisdiction. But the great weight of authority is to the effect that resident creditors of insolvent estates are entitled to receive only pro rata payment of their claims, the same as other creditors. An attempt to provide by statute or to hold by judicial determination that local creditors of an insolvent estate were entitled to be paid in full while other creditors were not would clearly seem to violate the following provisions of the Federal Constitution:

"The Citizens of each State shall be entitled to all Privileges and Immunities of Citizens in the several States." Article 4, § 2.

"No State shall make or enforce any law which shall abridge the privileges or immunities of citizens of the United States; * * * nor deny to any person within its jurisdiction the equal protection of the laws." Fourteenth Amendment, § 1.

The question under consideration was reviewed by the Supreme Court of California. We quote: "The last contention which appellant advances is that administration in this state being ancillary, no claim of a citizen of a foreign state can here be recognized at all, * * * but that such claim must be transferred to the court of primary jurisdiction. * * * In Blake v. McClung, 172 U.S. 239, 19 S.Ct. 165, 43 L.Ed. 432, it was declared that a state statute giving to residents of that state a priority over nonresidents in the distribution of the assets of a foreign corporation is violative of article 4 of the Constitution of the United States, giving equal privileges and immunities to the citizens of the several states, and as denying to every person within its jurisdiction the equal protection of the law. We find no statute of our state which, in terms, denies to a creditor and resident of a sister state the right to present his claim here, whether the administration in our courts be primary or ancillary, and, in view of the provision of the Constitution of the United States above referred to, we should doubt the validity of such a statute if found upon our books. However, upon this matter it is necessary here to say no more than that, since our statutes do not forbid, comity will dictate that such a claim should be entertained." McKee v. Dodd, 152 Cal. 637, 93 P. 854, 856, 14 L.R.A. (N.S.) 780, 125 Am.St.Rep. 82.

In accord with the authorities hereinbefore cited, we affirm the decision of the circuit judge that appellees, although they were nonresidents, were entitled to present their claims for allowance in the ancillary administration proceedings in this state. But in the Michigan ancillary administration local creditors should be paid their pro rata to the full extent that other creditors will be paid out of the estate of the deceased before nonresident creditors are permitted to participate in Michigan assets.

Judgment entered in the circuit court is affirmed, with costs to appellee.

FEAD, WIEST, BUTZEL, BUSHNELL, SHARPE, and TOY, JJ., concur.

POTTER, J., took no part in this decision.

Notes

1. It has been held that the non-claim statute (as to which see p. 644, infra) of the state of domicile need not be given extraterritorial effect and that a creditor with a claim against a nonresident decedent is not barred from recovering against the foreign administrator in a state other than the domicile by his failure to present the claim in the state of domicile within the prescribed time. Toner v. Conqueror Trust Co., 131 Kan. 651, 293 P. 745, 72 A.L.R. 1018 (1930). The ancillary administrator applies the laws of the state of his appointment including the allowance of any priorities granted by such laws. Duehay v. Acacia Mutual Life Insurance Co., 70 App.D.C. 245, 105 F.2d 768, 124 A.L.R. 1268 (1939).

See generally, Schoenblum, Multistate and Multinational Estate Planning § 16.14 (1982); Annots., 164 A.L.R. 765 (basis of distribution among unsecured creditors where estate insolvent); 90 A.L.R. 1043 (remission of assets by ancillary administrator to domiciliary executor); 106 A.L.R. 893 (right of nonresident creditor to file claim in ancillary proceeding); 92 A.L.R. 596 and 127 A.L.R. 504 (priority among creditors); 81 A.L.R. 665 (availability of land outside domiciliary state for payment of debts).

2. After local claims, taxes and expenses have been discharged, how does the ancillary fiduciary dispose of the remaining estate in his hands? Compare In re Estate of Radu, 35 Ohio App.2d 187, 301 N.E.2d 263 (1973) (ancillary administrator ordered to distribute the estate to heirs or legatees, whether Ohio residents or not, and not to turn it over to the domiciliary executor) with UPC § 3–815 (balance of local assets to be transferred to domiciliary representative); Finch v. Reese, 28 Conn.Sup. 599, 268 A.2d 409 (1970) (proceeds of the sale of Connecticut real property turned over by ancillary Connecticut trustee to the New Jersey domiciliary trustee). See Note, The Extraterritorial Authority of Executors and Administrators to Sue and Collect Assets, 52 Iowa L.Rev. 290, 302–09 (1966) (arguing that the "expediency of a unified administration" outweighs "the convenience of [local creditors] presenting their claims in a local forum").

C. JURISDICTION TO TAX

1. *Tangible personal property* and *real property* are subject to death taxation by the state where the property has its situs, and only by that state. In Frick v. Pennsylvania, 268 U.S. 473, 45 S.Ct. 603, 69 L.Ed. 1058, 42 A.L.R. 316 (1925), the Supreme Court held that the state of domicile could not constitutionally tax tangible property (in the main, a famous art collection) which had an actual situs in another state. The Court said, 268 U.S. at 492, 45 S.Ct. at 605–606, 69 L.Ed. at 1063–1064:

> The Pennsylvania statute is a tax law, not an escheat law. This is made plain by its terms and by the opinion of the state court. The tax

which it imposes is not a property tax but one laid on the transfer of property on the death of the owner. This distinction is stressed by counsel for the State. But to impose either tax the State must have jurisdiction over the thing that is taxed, and to impose either without such jurisdiction is mere extortion and in contravention of due process of law. Here the tax was imposed on the transfer of tangible personalty having an actual situs in other States—New York and Massachusetts. This property, by reason of its character and situs, was wholly under the jurisdiction of those States and in no way under the jurisdiction of Pennsylvania. True, its owner was domiciled in Pennsylvania, but this neither brought it under the jurisdiction of that State nor subtracted anything from the jurisdiction of New York and Massachusetts. In these respects the situation was the same as if the property had been immovable realty. The jurisdiction possessed by the States of the situs was not partial but plenary, and included power to regulate the transfer both inter vivos and on the death of the owner, and power to tax both the property and the transfer.

The Frick holding was reaffirmed in Treichler v. Wisconsin, 338 U.S. 251, 70 S.Ct. 1, 94 L.Ed. 37 (1949). Definitional problems may arise involving the meaning of "tangible" and "situs." See Bittker, The Taxation of Out-of-State Tangible Property, 56 Yale L.J. 640 (1947).

2. *Intangible personal property* was at one time held immune from taxation in every state except that of the decedent's domicile. This constitutional immunity from multiple taxation was abolished in Curry v. McCanless, 307 U.S. 357, 59 S.Ct. 900, 83 L.Ed. 1339 (1939). In State Tax Commission of Utah v. Aldrich, 316 U.S. 174, 62 S.Ct. 1008, 86 L.Ed. 1358, 139 A.L.R. 1436 (1942) it was held that, because the state of incorporation extends benefits and protection, it, as well as the state of the decedent's domicile, can impose a death tax on the value of corporate stock owned by the decedent. The Court said, 316 U.S. at 181–182, 62 S.Ct. at 1012, 86 L.Ed. at 1370–1371:

> * * * we repeat that there is no constitutional rule of immunity from taxation of intangibles by more than one State. In case of shares of stock "jurisdiction to tax" is not restricted to the domiciliary State. Another State which has extended benefits or protection or which can demonstrate "the practical fact of its power" or sovereignty as respects the shares * * * may likewise constitutionally make its exaction.

Cooperative action by the states has, however, eliminated for the most part multiple taxation of a decedent's intangible personal property, except in the rare case where several states claim to be the decedent's domicile. Eighteen states grant an unqualified exemption for intangible property owned by non-domiciliary decedents; twenty-nine states have enacted reciprocal exemption provisions whereby they do not tax the property of a non-domiciliary decedent if decedent's domicile extends a similar exemption or an unqualified exemption to the estates of decedents of the situs state (in most of these states the statute is either the Uniform Reciprocal Transfer Tax Act, 7A ULA 357 (1985 Supp. Pamphlet) or similar to it); two states and the District of Columbia exempt a non-domiciliary's property, excepting intangible property having a business situs in the state; and Nevada imposes no death tax. Note, Problematic

Definitions of Property in Multistate Death Taxation, 90 Harv.L.Rev. 1656 (1977).

In spite of these statutes, the possibility of double taxation of intangibles arises in three areas. (1) *Conflicting categorization of assets.* The situs state may classify an asset as realty or tangible personalty and thereby subject to its tax, while the state of domicile calls the same asset intangible personalty. For example, in Estate of Swanson, 124 Ill.App.3d 276, 79 Ill.Dec. 604, 463 N.E.2d 1379 (1984), the decedent, a resident of Florida, owned a beneficial interest in an Illinois land trust which the latter state sought to tax as real property. The Illinois court rejected the claim, holding that the trust interest was personalty and hence taxable exclusively by Florida. Accord, Department of Revenue v. Baxter, 486 P.2d 360 (Alaska 1971) (Washington domiciliary's interest as vendor in three executory contracts for the sale of Alaska realty held to be personal property and not taxable by Alaska).

(2) *Dissimilar provisions in reciprocal exemption statutes.* The exemption in many statutes is conditioned on the domiciliary state affording nonresidents a "similar, reciprocal exemption". Thus state A may tax the intangible property (assuming state A has given "benefit or protection" to the property) of a citizen of state B if B's statute does not offer as comprehensive an exemption as does the statute in state A. The exemption may not, however, be withheld by state A when its statute is reciprocal, while state B grants a more generous, unqualified exemption. Indiana Department of State Revenue v. American National Bank, —— Ind.App.——, 419 N.E.2d 177 (1981) (statutes need not be identical as long as both statutes exempt the same property).

(3) *Double domicile.* The state of domicile has jurisdiction to impose a death tax on the intangible estate wherever those assets may be said to be located. As has been previously discussed, note 2, p. 588, supra, there is no easy procedure to resolve conflicting claims of domicile by several states. The executor will attempt in such a situation to persuade the taxing authorities of the several states to compromise their claims by sharing a single tax. To that end, a number of states have adopted the Uniform Interstate Compromise of Death Taxes Act, 8A ULA 535 (procedure for compromising multiple tax claims) and Uniform Interstate Arbitration of Death Taxes Act, 8A ULA 521 (procedure for the arbitration of competing claims of domicile). In the alternative, the executor may prevail on the tax officials of one state to enter an appearance in the courts of the other state and obtain a determination of domicile that is binding on all the parties. The Connecticut commissioner followed this procedure in New York and won. Matter of Trowbridge, 266 N.Y. 283, 194 N.E. 756 (1935).

3. *Trust property* may be taxed by any state providing protection or benefits to the trust. Greenough v. Tax Assessors of Newport, 331 U.S. 486, 67 S.Ct. 1400, 91 L.Ed. 1621 (1947). A minimum listing of such states would include the domicile of a trustee or of a beneficiary and the state in which the evidences of the trust are located. Note, Taxation: Trusts: Multiple Taxation of Trust Property, 33 Corn.L.Q. 305 (1947).

A deterrent to multiple taxation may result from the difficulty the tax authority encounters in collecting the tax. The Supreme Court in Milwaukee County v. M. E. White Co., 296 U.S. 268, 56 S.Ct. 229, 80 L.Ed. 220 (1936) held, however, that a tax judgment in one state must be given full faith and credit in other states. This rule presupposes a judgment in the first state and requisite jurisdiction to enter the judgment. Cf. Riley v. New York Trust Co., p. 583, supra (Delaware need not give the Georgia decree full faith and credit after finding New York to be the domicile). In the absence of a full faith and credit requirement, courts may refuse to enforce foreign tax claims. See e.g. City of Philadelphia v. Cohen, 11 N.Y.2d 401, 230 N.Y.S.2d 188, 184 N.E.2d 167 (1962), certiorari denied 371 U.S. 934, 83 S.Ct. 306, 9 L.Ed.2d 270 (1962).

Today, however, practically all the states have enacted statutes (or have case law to the same effect) making it no longer necessary to obtain a judgment in the taxing state before filing a claim in another state. All that is required in the second state is proof that the tax was lawfully imposed. One commentator has stated that this procedure is, however, seldom used because of the expense and inconvenience of litigating in a distant forum. Taxing authorities prefer to sue at home, using long-arm statutes whenever possible to obtain personal jurisdiction over taxpayers or their estates. Leflar, Out-of-State Collection of State and Local Taxes, 29 Vand.L.Rev. 443 (1976).

D. STATUTORY JURISDICTION OF THE PROBATE COURT

A probate court's jurisdiction is derived usually from statute and therein lies another type of limitation on its powers. Unless the court is acting within the scope of its express powers or those which can be implied from specific grants of power, its actions are in effect ultra vires. The probate court has no residuum of power as does a court of general jurisdiction. A dramatic example of the effect of this limitation may be found in the cases where the court has administered the estate of a living person. Because a probate court has only been granted by statute the authority to administer decedents' estates, its mistaken assumption of jurisdiction over a living person's estate is ineffective, and titles which have resulted from the administration have been held void even as to bona fide purchasers for value without notice. Scott v. McNeal, 154 U.S. 34, 14 S.Ct. 1108, 38 L.Ed. 896 (1894); Cunnius v. Reading School District, 198 U.S. 458, 25 S.Ct. 721, 49 L.Ed. 1125 (1905). This dubious and unsatisfactory result has caused many states to vest jurisdiction in the probate court to administer absentees' as well as decedents' estates. For an example of such a statute see Uniform Absence as Evidence of Death and Absentees' Property Act, 8A ULA 1.

During the course of an administration, a variety of problems may arise demanding adjudication outside the probate court. Typically, a tort or contract claim involving the estate is litigated in the court that regularly handles such claims. Although the problem in its general terms is universal, the lines of demarcation vary in each state. To use Connecticut as an example, the probate court lacks such basic powers (this list is not all-inclusive) as the powers to "entertain proceedings having for their primary object the trial of titles; construction of wills or enforcement of contracts"; to adjudicate claims against the estate; to "render a money judgment, or issue attachments, executions or the like, or grant injunctions or decree specific performance." See Locke & Kohn, Connecticut Probate Practice, Vol. I, Ch. III (1950); Conn.Gen. Stat. 45–4.

In the interests of greater efficiency and convenience to the parties, it would seem appropriate to vest in the probate court all the powers which are necessary to administer the estate completely. A major obstacle to such a reform is the wide variation which exists in this country in the professional competence of these courts. In general terms there are three categories of courts: first, a group of states, of which New York is one, have established separate probate courts with a place in the overall court system more or less equal to that of the court of general jurisdiction; second, there is the system typified by California where the court of general jurisdiction embodies both the trial and probate courts; third, in a number of states, the probate court is a separate court but relegated to an inferior position in the hierarchy of courts. In most of the states in this last category there is no requirement that a probate judge be legally trained. Since it is unlikely that a legislature would vest in a system staffed by part-time, lay judges the power to give a definitive trial to a controverted matter, an increase in the court's jurisdiction can only be achieved after the court has been made over into a truly professional tribunal. A descriptive breakdown of American probate court systems may be found in Simes & Basye, Organization of the Probate Court in America, 42 Mich.L.Rev. 965, 43 id. 113 (1944). See also Atkinson, Organization of Probate Courts and Qualifications of Probate Judges, 23 J.Am.Jud.Soc. 93, 137, 183 (1939, 1940). A brief description of Connecticut's unique probate system appears in Clark & Clark, Court Integration in Connecticut: A Case Study of Steps in Judicial Reform, 59 Yale L.J. 1397, 1409–1413 (1950).

The probate court system within a state is typically organized on a county or district basis. The venue for the probate of a will and for administration is in the county or district where the decedent had his domicile at the time of his death or, if he had no domicile in the state, where his property was located. Basye, The Venue of Probate and Administration Proceedings, 43 Mich.L.Rev. 471 (1944); N.Y. SCPA 206.

SECTION TWO.   ESTABLISHING THE VALIDITY OF THE WILL

A.   THE NECESSITY AND EFFECT OF PROBATE

The first step in the administration of a testate estate is the presentation of the will for probate and a request for authorization to serve as executor or administrator. The procedure is similar for intestate estates, with a finding of intestacy taking the place of the decree of probate. The various types of formal and informal procedures used throughout the country to probate wills, determine heirs in intestacy, and appoint fiduciaries are described in the next section. Typically, the executor makes the offer of the will. This is not a fixed requirement; any person interested in having the will probated may initiate the proceedings. Anyone who has possession of the will is under a duty to come forward with it. In some jurisdictions there is criminal liability for suppression. The probate proceedings are an inquiry into the validity of the instrument and are not adversary in the manner of a usual civil action. After filing, for instance, the proponent cannot withdraw the will without cause.

The distinction between probate and construction proceedings must be understood at the outset. The probate proceeding establishes the external validity of the will, including its due execution in accordance with the statutory formalities, the capacity of the testator, and the fact that it is the genuine and the last formal expression of the testator's intent. The court at the probate proceeding is not concerned with what the will says. It has been held, for instance, that the fact that the sole devisee, sole legatee and sole named executrix had all predeceased the testatrix and that therefore the will would not have any practical effect was not grounds for denying probate. Matter of Davis' Will, 182 N.Y. 468, 75 N.E. 530 (1905). In like manner, a will should have been admitted to probate even though intervening circumstances negated the effectiveness of its provisions except for a revocation of earlier wills and a direction for cremation. In re Estate of Schumann, 125 N.J.Super. 56, 308 A.2d 375 (1973). Moreover, it was held not to be a proper ground for denying probate to a will that its execution revoked a prior will in violation of an agreement making the prior will irrevocable. The proper remedy was an action in equity to enforce the contract. In re Estate of Schultz, 53 Wis.2d 643, 193 N.W.2d 655 (1972). Inquiry into the validity and meaning of the language in the will must await a construction proceeding after the will has been probated.

HAUSEN v. DAHLQUIST
Supreme Court of Iowa, 1942.
232 Iowa 100, 5 N.W.2d 321, 141 A.L.R. 1304.

[On June 24, 1940, plaintiff-appellee initiated a partition action, alleging ownership in fee simple of a two-fifteenths interest in land, the major portion of which was devised to her under the terms of her father's will. At the time the action was commenced the will had not been probated. It was finally admitted to probate on November 17, 1941. This is an appeal from the March 8, 1941 rejection of defendant's motion to dismiss. References to a trust, not here relevant, are omitted.]

BLISS, J. * * * The first point which the appellants argue as a ground for reversal is that at the time the petition was filed, and when the order appealed from was entered, the will of the testator had not been admitted to probate in Iowa. They rely upon section 11882, Code of Iowa,

1939, which provides that wills, foreign or domestic, shall not be carried into effect until admitted to probate. We find no merit in this contention. The rights of all parties to this suit, with respect to at least two thirds of the real estate, are based upon the will of the testator. It is fundamental law that a will speaks from the death of the testator, and the rights of the parties hereto accrued at that time. Proof of the probate of that will may be necessary in establishing those rights, but such proof was not a condition precedent to the commencement of the suit. In Otto v. Doty, 61 Iowa 23, 26, 15 N.W. 578, 579, a like contention was made. In disposing of it, the court said:

> "We reach the conclusion, then, that there is no valid objection either to the will or the probate thereof. It is objected by the defendants, however, that the admission of the will to probate in the circuit court of Story county was too late. This action, it seems, had already been commenced. The defendants' theory is that at the time the plaintiff commenced her action she had no cause of action. But, in our opinion, the most that can be said is that at that time she merely lacked the means of proof. Her title vested at the death of the testator. To prove it, however, it was necessary for her to put in evidence the will; and to do that, it was necessary that it should be probated, not only in Tennessee, but in Iowa. We think that it was sufficient that the will had been so probated at the time it was offered in evidence."

Probate of a will is the statutory method of establishing the proper execution of the instrument, but it is, nevertheless, a valid instrument before and independent of such proof, and while the probate of a will is necessary to perfect it as an instrument of title, yet without probate it is capable of conveying an interest in land. * * *

An amendment to the abstract, which has not been challenged in any way, shows that the will has now been duly admitted to probate in the district court of Montgomery county, Iowa.

* * *

[Affirmed.]

Notes

1. Probating a will "is essentially a formal validation of the property interests which came into existence upon the death of the testator. * * * probate is title-accommodating rather than interest-creating." Jenkins v. United States, 428 F.2d 538, 548 (5th Cir. 1970), certiorari denied 400 U.S. 829 (1970). It is a generally accepted principle that an unprobated will does not constitute evidence of title. But see Bouton v. Fleharty, 215 App.Div. 180, 213 N.Y.S. 455 (2d Dept. 1926), affirmed 242 N.Y. 591, 152 N.E. 440 (1926); UPC § 3–102. If the will is not probated within a time limit fixed by a local statute, the title cannot be established. In re Estate of Zimmerman, 207 Kan. 354, 485 P.2d 215 (1971) (five years). Under the theory that title passes at death, the devisee or heir rather than the executor is the party in interest to bring or defend actions pertaining to real property. Wood v. Wood, 23 N.C.App. 352, 208 S.E.2d 705 (1974); Brill v. Ulrey, 159 Conn. 371, 269 A.2d 262 (1970). The devisee's title is subject to the executor's lawful power to sell the property

to satisfy debts or to make a sale under a discretionary power set out in the will. DeLong v. Scott, 217 N.W.2d 635 (Iowa 1974).

2. Title to personal property at the death of the owner passes to his or her personal representative, to be available for the purposes of administration. The authority as to real property is summarized in 3 American Law of Property 576–579 (1952) (footnotes omitted):

> Contrary to the present state of the law in England, neither statutes nor decisions in America have uprooted the basic tenet of the common law that title to a decedent's realty passes at once on his death to his heirs or devisees and not to his personal representatives. * * *

> The common law concept is still basic in American law. It is true that land is here universally liable for the decedent's debts, and in almost all states it can be applied by the personal representative for this purpose under statutory power of sale. In some jurisdictions the personal representative has statutory powers of sale for other purposes. Statutes sometimes give the latter the right of possession to decedent's land and the right to the rents and profits, at least where these may be necessary for payment of debts. Finally, some statutes contemplate that the personal representative will distribute the decedent's land to the heirs or devisees, or that a decree of the court will determine this matter and operate as a muniment of title. In particular regards the common law rule is thus, in effect, abrogated or is almost a mere empty shell. Still it is the principle upon which American courts must proceed, and they depart therefrom only to the extent that there is statutory authority. Important manifestations of the common law rule remain, notably the right of the heir or devisee to enjoy immediate possessory rights unless or until the personal representative has exercised his statutory powers.

ECKLAND v. JANKOWSKI
Supreme Court of Illinois, 1950.
407 Ill. 263, 95 N.E.2d 342, 22 A.L.R.2d 1002.

Mr. Chief Justice SIMPSON delivered the opinion of the court.

Appellant, Charles J. Eckland, claims to be the owner of an undivided one-half interest, as devisee of Thorwald Hegstad, deceased, in the premises occupied by appellees under a deed from the heirs-at-law of the decedent. An amended complaint for partition of the premises was filed in the circuit court of Cook County. A hearing on the merits resulted in a decree dismissing the amended complaint for want of equity. A direct appeal has been perfected to this court, a freehold being involved.

Thorwald Hegstad died January 23, 1945. At that time he was the owner of the premises described in the amended complaint for partition. Soon after his death proceedings for the administration of his estate were commenced, the estate was duly administered and the administrator finally discharged on August 14, 1946. Thereafter, on November 30, 1946, the heirs-at-law of Thorwald Hegstad, in consideration of the sum of $12,000, conveyed the real estate in question to Louis Berland and Gudrun Berland. These persons, on February 8, 1947, conveyed the premises to the appellees for the sum of $13,000. Approximately six months after appellees acquired title to the premises, through the heirs of Thorwald Hegstad, appellant found a receipt showing the existence and where-abouts of a will of Thorwald Hegstad. On December 10, 1947, almost three years after the death of Thorwald Hegstad, and slightly more than a year after the heirs had conveyed the premises, the will was admitted to probate in the probate court of Cook County. Under the provisions of the will, appellant was devised a one-half interest in the premises while the other one-half interest was devised to Garman Hegstad, one of the heirs of Thorwald Hegstad, who had previously joined in the conveyance to appellees' predecessors in title.

It is the contention of appellant that when the will was admitted to probate he became vested with the title to the premises in question; that his title relates back to the moment of the death of the testator; and that the conveyance of the premises by the heirs-at-law of the testator was absolutely void and conveyed no title to appellees' predecessors in title. Appellees contend that they are innocent purchasers for value without any notice or knowledge of the existence of the will; that the will was not effective to pass any title to appellant until it had been admitted to probate; and that the probate of the will was ineffectual to relate back to the date of death of the testator and divest title previously acquired by an innocent purchaser for value from the lawful heirs of the testator.

At the time appellees acquired their conveyance of the premises in question, Thorwald Hegstad had been deceased for more than two years. His estate had been administered upon as intestate property, and he was shown to be the last owner of the record title to the premises. The probate court found that he died intestate and declared his heirship. It was not until after the administration proceedings had been concluded that the premises were conveyed by the heirs-at-law. The controversy is one of law, namely, whether under the facts as above set out in substance, the appellant, as devisee in the will, is the owner of a one-half interest in the property in question, or whether appellees, claiming title by purchase through the heirs of Thorwald Hegstad before they had any knowledge of the existence of said will, are the owners.

Section 53 of the Probate Act, Ill.Rev.Stat.1949, chap. 3, par. 205, provides that every will when admitted to probate as provided by the act is effective to transfer the real estate of the testator devised therein. A devisee, however, cannot assert his title to land devised to him unless the will is probated and made a matter of record in accordance with the applicable statutes of our State. Barnett v. Barnett, 284 Ill. 580, 120 N.E. 532; Stull v. Veatch, 236 Ill. 207, 86 N.E. 227. The will of Thorwald Hegstad, therefore, could not become effective to vest title in appellant until it had been probated in the probate court of Cook County and made a matter of record in that county.

Section 33 of the act concerning conveyances, Ill.Rev.Stat.1949, chap. 30, par. 32, provides as follows: "All original wills duly proved, or copies thereof duly certified, according to law, and exemplifications of the record of foreign wills made in pursuance of the law of congress in relation to records in foreign states, may be recorded in the same office where deeds and other instruments concerning real estate may be required to be recorded; and the same shall be notice from the date of filing the same for record as in other cases, and certified copies of the record thereof shall be evidence to the same extent as the certified copies of the record of deeds." The only effect of recording a duly authenticated copy of a will in the office of the recorder of deeds, as provided in this act, is to give constructive notice to all persons of the contents of the will. Plenderleith v. Edwards, 328 Ill. 431, 159 N.E. 780. The section, however, does not apply to a domestic will for the reason that the probate of a domestic will of itself constitutes constructive notice of the effect of the will on real estate affected by it, in the county where it is probated.

A purchaser of land is charged with constructive notice not only of whatever is shown in the records of the office of the recorder of deeds, but in addition, with matters affecting the title of the land which appear in the records in the circuit, probate, and county courts in the county where the land is situated. Clark v. Leavitt, 335 Ill. 184, 166 N.E. 538. It is the duty of a purchaser of land to examine the record and he is chargeable with notice of whatever is shown by the record. Blake v. Blake, 260 Ill. 70, 102 N.E. 1007. In considering the cases of Bliss v. Seeley, 191 Ill. 461, 61 N.E. 524, and Harrison v. Weatherby, 180 Ill. 418, 54 N.E. 237, we held, in Catholic University of America v. Boyd, 227 Ill. 281, 81 N.E. 363, that the purpose of requiring foreign wills to be recorded in this State was to give notice, and that filing a copy without proper authentication could not be considered notice, and in the absence of notice of a will in a foreign State, either actual or constructive, a conveyance by the heirs of the testator, of land in this State was good as against the devisees subsequently filing a copy of the will for record. A like result was reached in the case of Cassem v. Prindle, 258 Ill. 11, 101 N.E. 241, strongly relied upon by appellees, in which we sustained a decree protecting the title of a *bona fide* purchaser for value against the claim of a devisee under a domestic will probated subsequent to his conveyance.

The right to take property, either real or personal, is purely a statutory right which rests wholly within legislative enactment, and the State, by appropriate legislation, may regulate and control its devolution. Jahnke v. Selle, 368 Ill. 268, 13 N.E.2d 980. Under the Statute of Descent of this State, the heir-at-law of a person who dies intestate acquires an absolute interest in the intestate's realty, although he cannot convey it to the prejudice of the rights of creditors of the decedent. Ill.Rev.Stat. 1949, chap. 3, par. 162; Neuffer v. Hagelin, 369 Ill. 344, 16 N.E.2d 715.

The object of the heirship proceedings in the probate court was to find upon whom the laws of this State had cast the estate of the intestate decedent. George v. Moorhead, 399 Ill. 497, 78 N.E.2d 216. At the time appellees obtained a conveyance to the premises, there was nothing upon record which would give them actual or constructive notice of the existence of the will, or that anyone other than those persons designated by the Statute of Descent had any interest in the premises. An examination of the record in the recorder's office would then have disclosed that Thorwald Hegstad was the owner of the record title at the time of his death and would show no transfers from him. Appellees were bound to know the law with reference to the descent of property. The records of the probate court at that time disclosed that Thorwald Hegstad had died intestate, and a finding of his heirship was included in the administration proceedings. The claims against the estate of the decedent were paid and the administrator discharged.

Under the Statute of Descent the heirs-at-law of Thorwald Hegstad had succeeded to the ownership of his real estate. The will of Thorwald Hegstad was not discovered until several months after the real estate had been conveyed by his heirs. There was no notice, either actual or constructive, as to the existence or contents of the will. Appellees had the right to rely on the devolution of title shown by the record. Under the facts and circumstances appearing of record, we conclude that the conveyance to appellees, who are admitted to be *bona fide* innocent purchasers for value, should prevail as against appellant, a devisee in the will subsequently discovered and admitted to probate.

The decree of the circuit court of Cook County is accordingly affirmed.

Decree affirmed.

Notes

1. The traditional view holds that probate and administration are necessary to establish title to personal property. An administration proceeding is also required to discharge debts owed by or to the estate. In In re Collins Estate, 102 Wash. 697, 699–700, 173 P. 1016–1017 (1918) the court said:

> This court has held that a claim against an estate is not barred by lapse of time, where no notice to creditors has been published as required by law. * * * So it is plain that there may be debts; and, if there are debts against the estate which were not barred before the death of the intestate, such debts are not now barred, because no administrator has been appointed and no notice to creditors has been published. Since the fact of no debts can be established only by the appointment of an administrator and notice to creditors, it follows that there was no proof that there are no debts, and the heirs of the deceased were not authorized to make an assignment of the note and mortgage at the time they did. When the appellant pays the note he is entitled to have the mortgage satisfied by one authorized to do so, in order that he may not again be liable to pay the note or any part thereof.

2. If the will is uncontested, the probate hearing is a simple affair. The proponent submits proof of death, jurisdiction, proper notice, due execution and testamentary capacity. The latter two points are ordinarily proved on the testimony of one or more of the attesting witnesses, if available. Statutes exist in most jurisdictions which may make the physical presence of a witness or witnesses unnecessary. For instance, their appearance may be avoided if there are no issues in dispute upon submission of an affidavit executed by them. N.Y. SCPA § 1406. If the witnesses are dead or cannot be found, the will may be probated on proof of the genuineness of their signatures. N.Y. SCPA § 1404–05. Procedures are available to probate a lost or destroyed will. N.Y. SCPA § 1407; see discussion note 3, p. 342, supra.

3. Except in states which permit probate in the common form (see p. 623, infra), notice of the proceedings must be given to interested persons (legatees, devisees, intestate successors, trustees, guardians, the state attorney-general if the will contains a charitable trust). Probate proceedings being essentially in rem, notice by publication is frequently used. Simes, The Administration of a Decedent's Estate as a Proceeding in Rem, 43 Mich.L.Rev. 675 (1945); Daft v. John and Elizabeth Whiteley Foundation, 363 Mich. 6, 108 N.W.2d 893 (1961). It now appears that under the Supreme Court's ruling in Mennonite Board of Missions v. Adams, see note 6, p. 604, supra, and note 5, p. 647, infra, notice by publication may be insufficient to satisfy due process requirements in the case of persons whose identity and location are known or are reasonably ascertainable. Even without the Court's prompting, state court decisions have sometimes held that the circumstances required either personal service or mailed notice. See e.g. In re Estate of DuVal, 133 Vt. 197, 332 A.2d 802 (1975) (publication in small town newspaper insufficient when out-of-state address known); In re Estate of Lemke, 216 N.W.2d 186 (Iowa 1974) (mailed notice not adequate). A number of state statutes require personal service upon persons who can be reached within the jurisdiction.

UPC § 1–401 stipulates as a general matter that notice be given by mail or delivery to any interested person at least fourteen days before a hearing or, if the address or identity of the person is not known and cannot be discovered with reasonable diligence, by publication at least once a week for three consecutive weeks in a general circulation newspaper. By the authority set out in UPC § 3–204, any person who has a financial or property interest in the estate may file a demand for notice with the court. Thereafter, the personal representative, who fails to give the required notice, may be liable for damages, but orders issued from a proceeding of which the person was not notified remain valid. UPC § 3–204.

Notice requirements under the Code differ depending on the nature of the proceeding. For a formal testacy proceeding, the petitioner must give notice to interested parties in advance of the hearing as prescribed in § 1–401, supra. In contrast, the moving parties in an informal probate proceeding or in a proceeding for a declaration of universal succession are only required to give notice to other persons with an interest in the estate within thirty days after the informal probate or universal succession order has been issued. UPC §§ 3–306, 3–319. Question has been raised about the adequacy of such informal, after-the-fact notice. Parker, Non-Notice Probate and Non-Intervention Administration under the Code, 2 Conn.L.Rev. 546 (1970). The notice requirements are defended in Wellman, The Uniform Probate Code: Blueprint for Reform in the 70's, 2 Conn.L.Rev. 453, 496–500 (1970).

4. If a dispute arises over the will, may all the interested parties enter into a compromise agreement which establishes a different dispositive scheme from the one set out in the will? UPC § 3–1101 takes the position that compromises are to be encouraged and provides that after formal court approval such agreements are binding on all the parties including those who are unborn, are unascertained or cannot be located. Family settlements are particularly favored. In re Probate of Will of Seabrook, 90 N.J.Super. 553, 218 A.2d 648 (1966). The policy of fostering compromises is also applicable to nonfamily parties. First National Bank of Birmingham v. Brown, 287 Ala. 240, 251 So.2d 204 (1971). If the distribution set out in the will coincides with that of the intestate succes-

sion statute and the estate has no debts, may the family refuse to probate the will in order to save the costs of the nominated executor's compensation? Dover v. Horger, 225 Or. 492, 358 P.2d 484 (1960) (yes); In re Estate of Harper, 202 Kan. 150, 446 P.2d 738 (1968) (no). Wisconsin formerly held compromise agreements void as against public policy, at least insofar as they operate to deny probate to the will. Will of Dardis, 135 Wis. 457, 115 N.W. 332 (1908) (testator has an interest which must be protected); but a 1951 statute has authorized court-approved compromises. See Wis.Stat.Ann. § 879.59. Cf. In re Hulett's Estate, 6 Wis.2d 20, 94 N.W.2d 127 (1959). See generally Note, The Effect of an Adjudicated Compromise of a Will Contest or Controversy upon the Right to Dispose of Property by Will, 37 Ind.L.J. 528 (1962); Annot., Compromise of Will Contests, 42 A.L.R.2d 1319 (1955).

5. Not infrequently in terrorem or no-contest clauses are inserted into wills. These clauses direct that any person who contests the will is to receive no benefits under it or by intestacy. The interpretation and effect of these clauses are discussed in Haynes v. First National State Bank of New Jersey, supra, p. 233, at pp. 244–247, and in note 2, supra, p. 248.

B. ADMINISTRATION OF ESTATES WITH A MINIMUM OF COURT SUPERVISION

The formal adminstration of estates under the supervision of a probate court has been frequently criticized as being unnecessarily time-consuming and expensive, involving overly complex and archaic laws and procedures, existing primarily for the benefit of lawyers and probate judges and performing a useful function only in the rare instances when a controverted issue arises. The charges have not just appeared in professional journals, nor has the debate been confined to bar association meetings and legislative halls. A paperback by Mr. Norman F. Dacey, entitled How to Avoid Probate, published in 1965, sold 670,000 copies by mid-1967 and was first on the nonfiction best-seller list in late 1966.* Anyone who has done any estate planning knows that much of the client interest in inter vivos trusts and joint tenancies stems from the fact that these forms of property holding keep the assets from inclusion in the probate estate.

The Uniform Probate Code accepts the charge that basic reforms are required and offers in substitution for existing procedures a flexible system by which non-controverted estates may, at the option of the parties, be administered free of court supervision. Thirteen states, Alaska, Arizona, Colorado, Idaho, Maine, Minnesota, Montana, Nebraska, New Jersey, New Mexico, North Dakota, Pennsylvania, and Utah have adopted the Code or its major procedural premise. Wellman, Recent Developments in the Struggle for Probate Reform, 79 Mich.L.Rev. 501, 503 (1981). The significance of the Code's innovations are not, however, to be judged alone by the fundamental changes that they have brought in the way

---

* The story has been told and its meaning for the legal profession perceptively analyzed in Wellman, The Uniform Probate Code: A Possible Answer to Probate Avoidance, 44 Ind.L.J. 191 (1969). Ed.

that probate business is conducted in those states. The Code has also ignited a national debate over the pros and cons of unsupervised versus supervised administration of decedents' estates. In recent years, the opposition, centered mainly within the legal profession itself (see infra, p. 627), has proven formidable, and the drive to enact the Code appears to be stalled temporarily. Recognizing the political obstacles to enactment of the full Code, a number of states have enacted partial measures, seeking to bring some simplification to the administration process. It is likely that the course of future developments will depend on the experience that the Code states have with the new procedures. If it can be demonstrated that the administration of estates is quicker and cheaper and that the opportunities for fraud and embezzlement are not increased, the public pressure in favor of the Code's reforms may become too powerful to be denied.

Prior to the advent of the Code, a number of procedures were in existence whereby certain estates could be administered with few, if any, contacts with a court. Indeed, the Code is in many respects a logical extension of these prototypes. Procedures that either eliminate the necessity of administration or effect a simplification of it may be summarized under five broad headings: *

1. Administration of Family Property and Small Estates

States typically authorize the immediate distribution to spouse and children, without court intervention, of certain kinds of property, including, for example, wages, bank deposits, savings and loan shares, insurance and other death benefits, and motor vehicles. These items may, however, be part of the estate for the purpose of tax and creditors' claims. Other statutes make available to the spouse and children homestead property and a family allowance (to provide maintenance of the spouse and children during administration) free of creditors' claims. For a description of these statutes and the relevant sections of the Uniform Probate Code, see Family Allowance and Homestead, pp. 125–128, supra.

States also have procedures to dispense with or simplify administration of small estates. The California statutes provide an example. An estate of personal property, owned by a decedent who leaves no real property, which does not exceed $30,000 in value, may be marshalled and distributed without an administration or probate of a will by the members of the family who are entitled to it by intestacy, or by the trustee of a trust executed by the decedent during life of which the members of the family are the primary beneficiaries and have a right to succeed to the estate, or by the beneficiary or beneficiaries under decedent's will, regardless of whether or not they are related to the decedent. West's Ann.

---

* Undoubtedly many estates are settled privately by the decedent's family. For example, no one is likely to read of a gangster's will being probated or his estate being publicly administered. Certainty in the successors' title to decedent's property must await the passage of limitation periods. See A.B.A. Committee on Administration and Distribution of Decedents' Estates, Clearing Titles of Heirs to Intestate Real Property, 10 Real Prop. Probate and Trust J. 454 (1975); see also the discussion of the "do-nothing" option under the Uniform Probate Code, infra.

Cal. Probate Code § 630. If the total net value of the estate over liens, encumbrances, and homestead interests does not exceed $20,000, the court, upon petition and notice to interested parties, may distribute the estate to the surviving spouse or minor children and close the proceedings. West's Ann.Cal. Probate Code § 640. See Basye, Dispensing With Administration, 44 Mich.L.Rev. 329 (1945) (a seminal article on informal administration of estates).

2. *Probate in the Common Form*

The English ecclesiastical courts (jurisdiction over wills of personal property only) allowed two types of probate—probate in the common form and probate in the solemn form. The former was a summary proceeding without notice to anyone, the will often being proved on the oath of the executor alone. The procedure was administrative rather than judicial, and, as a consequence, it was open to contest by any interested party at any time. (Some authorities suggest that there was a thirty-year limitation.) Probate in the solemn form required notice to interested parties, was a formal judicial proceeding in which questions of validity were litigated, and was final in the manner of any judicial decree. See Fratcher, Fiduciary Administration in England, 40 N.Y.U.L.Rev. 12 (1965).

A number of non-Code states authorize the use of the common form procedure whereby the will is admitted to probate without notice to the parties or a formal hearing. The validity of the will remains subject to challenge after the initial probate, however, by an aggrieved party (disinherited intestate successor, taker under an earlier will, and, if the state has an interest, the attorney-general) during a contest period that runs typically six months to a year in duration. See Levy, Probate in Common Form in the United States: The Problem of Notice in Probate Proceedings, 1952 Wis.L.Rev. 420. The Uniform Code's informal probate proceedings represent an adaptation of the common form approach, expanded to eliminate any need during the administration for court intervention. In contrast, the personal representative in non-Code states may continue to have some contact with the probate court for such purposes as review of an inventory or final account.

3. *Pre-Code Systems for Non-Intervention Administration*

Prior to the promulgation of the Uniform Probate Code, Arizona, Idaho, Texas, and Washington permitted the personal representative to administer the estate without court supervision if the testator in his or her will authorized the procedure. The fiduciary then had the option of using the procedure or following the traditional course of formal administration. The court, at the request of a beneficiary or creditor, could for cause withhold permission for a non-intervention administration. The statutes are collected in Parker, No-Notice Probate and Non-Intervention Administration under the Code, 2 Conn.L.Rev. 546, 559–60 (1970); see also, Fletcher, Washington's Non-Intervention Executor—Starting Point for Probate Simplification, 41 Wash.L.Rev. 33 (1966); Winn, Non-Judicial Administration of Estates in Texas, 17 S.W.L.J. 384 (1963).

Arizona and Idaho have now adopted the Code, with its more extensive options for administration without court supervision.   Texas and Washington have amended their statutes to expand the opportunities for non-intervention administration.   As now written, the statutes make the procedure available to intestate estates and to estates governed by wills that do not expressly authorize the procedure.   V.A.T.S. Probate Code, ch. 6, § 145;   West's RCWA 11.68.010–11.68.120.   Both statutes impose some court control on the process and require the personal representative to file documents like an inventory, list of claims, etc. with the court.

4.   *The Uniform Probate Code*

About the origins of the Code, Professor Richard V. Wellman, the Chief Reporter, has said: "The basic scheme is not very original   *   *   *. The idea is to offer the various major features of the different probate systems presently followed in our fifty states, as options, in a single system."   Wellman, The Uniform Probate Code: A Possible Answer to Probate Avoidance, 44 Ind.L.J. 191, 198 (1969).   Despite this disclaimer, the Code does break radically with the American tradition by making non-intervention probate and administration the norm rather than the infrequently used exception.   A court-supervised administration remains an option, but it must be specifically requested by an interested party. "The Code accepts the proposition that the probate court's proper role in regard to settlement of estates is to answer questions which parties want answered rather than to impose its authority when it is not requested *   *   *."   Wellman, 44 Ind.L.J. at p. 199.

The Code leaves it up to the interested parties, which in the vast majority of cases means the decedent's immediate family but may sometimes include non-family members who are named in a will as beneficiaries or fiduciaries, to decide the extent to which the court is to play a role in the process, with the options including no role, a spot role in order to adjudicate specific issues, or a traditional role, in which the court supervises the administration from probate of the will to the final distribution of the estate.   As Professor Wellman has observed: "The state has no greater interest in enforcing the substantive rules of inheritance than it has in enforcing the rules governing contracts, trusts and other property arrangements controlling private wealth."   Wellman, Recent Developments in the Struggle for Probate Reform, 79 Mich. 501, 509 (1981).   True to this concept, the parties only turn to the courts when a dispute arises that requires resolution by adjudication.

Although the Code may be adapted to any existing probate court organization, it works at maximum efficiency in a two-tier system: the lower tier, consisting of a clerical office staffed by a registrar, in which an informal administration and universal succession are initiated, and an upper tier, consisting of a court presided over by a judge, in which an administration may be supervised and controversies adjudicated.   Volume 1 of the Uniform Probate Code Practice Manual, pps. 189, 203–204, 239–241 (2d ed., edited by Richard V. Wellman, 1977) describes six options by which the parties may obtain an estate settlement:

1. *Survivors Take No Action of Any Sort.* The members of the family or others, who are entitled to the estate by will or intestacy, may take possession of the estate assets, UPC § 3–101 vesting title in them at decedent's death subject to administration, and do nothing else. They will be dispossessed of the estate if an interested party brings a successful petition for the appointment of a personal representative within three years of decedent's death, but, if no such action is forthcoming, the inheritance is seemingly settled in the heirs at the end of the limitation period. Proceedings to probate a will or appoint a representative are no longer possible, and unsecured creditors, who must file their claims with a personal representative, are barred when no such fiduciary can be appointed. The three-year limitation period is, however, specifically made inapplicable to a proceeding to determine heirs under intestacy statutes. It follows that settlement of an inheritance by inaction does not afford complete protection to the heirs in possession because they may have to forfeit the estate to a personal representative within the three-year period following decedent's death and, even after the period has run, do not qualify as "distributees" under § 1–201(10) and therefore cannot pass a marketable title to a good-faith purchaser.

2. *Informal Probate Only.* The parties may submit decedent's will to the registrar for probate, but not seek the appointment of a personal representative. Advance notice to interested parties is not required (see note 3, p. 620, supra), but the registrar has the discretion to deny probate if, for example, jurisdiction is lacking or the document does not satisfy the statutory formalities. As in option one supra, the takers under the will may not retain the estate as against the demand of a duly appointed personal representative who may claim the property for administration purposes. In addition, an informally probated will may be challenged in a formal probate proceeding brought to the court within three years of decedent's death or one year after the informal probate was granted, whichever period is the longer. After the limitation period has run, however, the devisees under the will may convey marketable title to purchasers.

3. *Informal Probate with Administration, or Administration in Intestacy Without Formal Testacy Proceeding.* Under this option, the parties petition the registrar for an informal probate of the will (or file a statement that there is no will) and request the appointment of a personal representative (either the fiduciary designated in the will or the person eligible in accordance with the priorities set out in § 3–203). Assuming that no one initiates a formal testacy proceeding within the limitation period, the personal representative has full control of the estate assets and the authority to settle creditors' claims, give marketable title, and make distribution to the heirs. These steps may be taken without further contact with the court, although the personal representative may turn to the court if necessary to resolve a controverted issue, obtain a construction of the will, or secure protection from future liability.

It is the expectation that the procedure outlined herein will be the way the vast majority of estates are settled. Professor Wellman cites as its advantages: the role of the court system in estate settlement, as in the implementation of contracts, is kept to a minimum; succession to family wealth is treated as a private matter; and the inheritance process occurs with a minimum of red tape, cost, and delay. Wellman, supra, 79 Mich.L.Rev. at pps. 508–510; see also Martin, Justice and Efficiency under a Model of Estate Settlement, 66 Va.L.Rev. 727 (1980) (analysis concluding that the Code provides the best procedure to resolve probate disputes). On the sensitive subject of the role of professionals in the process, Professor Wellman makes the following observation at p. 510:

> * * * Procedures that permit families to agree about estate settlements should eliminate extended and expensive legal proceedings and reduce probate costs and delays. Also, these procedures transform the role of lawyers, court officials, bondsmen, and appraisers from one that is unnecessary and forced, to one that interested survivors identify as helpful. The UPC encourages fee agreements between survivors and experts to whom they turn for assistance; fee competition should develop. Make-work and excessive fees should be curtailed. In time, and depending largely on how well or badly the legal profession functions, nonlawyers may begin to play a useful role in advising survivors about how they should handle their out-of-court affairs.

4., 5., and 6. These options involve various degrees of court supervision over the administration process. Option 6, entitled *Supervised Administration,* sets out the procedures for a formal administration of the traditional sort, including a court adjudication, following prior notice to interested parties (see note 3, p. 620, supra), of the will's validity, court orders to authorize distributions, and judicial review of accounts. There is little incentive for the parties to select this option, and it is likely to be invoked only in unusual family situations, as, for example, where the decedent has been married more than once and leaves rival sets of contentious and suspicious claimants to his substantial estate.

Options 4 and 5 offer the parties an opportunity to get a judicial adjudication of the will's validity (or a determination of heirs in intestacy) and/or a formal proceeding for the appointment of the personal representative. The parties will select these options when, for instance, the circumstances suggest that a definitive hearing is necessary to resolve disputes over the identity of the beneficiaries or fiduciaries. After initiating the administration with these formal proceedings, the personal representative may proceed with the administration and distribution of the estate as in option three, with the assurance that his authority will not be interrupted by anyone else petitioning for a formal probate or appointment.

Except under the do-nothing option, the Code puts the responsibility for the administration on the personal representative. Critics have suggested that without judicial oversight the representative has the opportunity to commit fraud and embezzlement without detection. The Code, however, imposes criminal and civil penalties for intentional misrepresentations, and liabilities attach to misuse of assets, including procedures for accountability to the decedent's creditors and successors.

In 1982 a new option was added to the Code which eliminates the personal representative from routine settlement of estates. The procedure, known as *Universal Succession* and set out as UPC §§ 3–212 to 3–322, enables the intestate successors or residuary devisees under a will to become universal successors, with the authority to settle and distribute the estate without court supervision, unless they need to invoke the jurisdiction of the court to resolve a specific issue. Application to become successors must be directed to the registrar who shall issue a "statement of universal succession" if the simple conditions set out in § 3–314, to the effect that there is no impediment to this form of procedure such as want of venue, passage of the three-year limitation period, previous administration pending, disability of the parties, etc. are satisfied. After appointment, the successors must give notice to interested parties as in the case of an informal administration by a personal representative and assume personal liability for administration expenses, death taxes, decedent's debts and other legacies or shares owing to persons entitled to participate in the inheritance. At the end of the limitation period, assuming all the claims against the estate have been satisfied and no successful application for an informal or formal administration has been made, the successors have full ownership of their respective shares of the assets and may convey marketable title to purchasers. The proponents of this new option express the hope that it will not become mired in politics to the same degree as have the other procedural provisions of the Code. They point out that the statute is brief, simple and easily understood by lay people, and can be enacted without causing major disruption to an existing probate code. Wellman, supra, 79 Mich.L.Rev. at p. 546.

5. *Post-Code Legislation to Achieve Probate Simplification*

From the outset, the Code's procedural proposals were met with what has been described as "fierce and entrenched political opposition from bench, bar, and certain commercial interests." * The published arguments in opposition emphasize the necessity of court-supervised procedures to safeguard the interests of beneficiaries and creditors from loss by fraud, embezzlement, or neglect. In moments of candor, however, attorneys will admit that much of their concern, and that of probate judges, is based on economic self-interest, that is that the Code will be successful in the promise made by its proponents to provide less expensive service, without frequent recourse to the courts and the need for continuous legal assistance. As one commentator put it: "What are the negatives? The one about which lawyers *worry most* and *talk least* relates to fees. Everyone knows that percentage fees in probate have put money in lawyers' pockets. They assume that enactment of the Code will spell the end to this happy circumstance." ** Opposition has also come from

---

* The quote and the substance of the remainder of the paragraph are taken from Martin, Justice and Efficiency Under a Model of Estate Settlement, 66 Va.L.Rev. 727, 728 (1980). In footnote 34, pps. 735–736, Professor Martin describes in detail, with citations, the opposition to the Code.

** Wellman, Lawyers and the Uniform Probate Code, 26 Okl.L.Rev. 548, 554 (1973).

two commercial groups who have a vested interest in the existing system: surety companies, which benefit from statutes requiring that fiduciaries be bonded, and newspapers, many of which derive substantial income from the publication of legal notices.

Political considerations have undoubtedly been an important factor in the decision of many state law revision agencies to chart an independent course from the Code in search of probate and administration simplification.   Professor Wellman summarizes recent developments as follows (79 Mich.L.Rev. at pp. 504–506, footnotes omitted):

> * * *   California, Florida, Hawaii, Iowa, Kentucky, Ohio, Oregon, and South Dakota have new codes or recent amendments that enlarge the authority of estate fiduciaries, while adhering to the concept of mandatory fiduciary accountability to the probate court.   Illinois, Indiana, Kansas, Michigan, Missouri, and Wisconsin have added procedures, * * *, that purport to offer new opportunities to select independent administration as an alternative to supervised administration.   An important new statute in the District of Columbia, * * *, includes some reform provisions but takes back much more than it gives.   Several states, including Delaware, Massachusetts, Nevada, and Wyoming, have new probate laws that do little to improve probate procedures.

The specifics of these recently-enacted codes are described in the text and notes of the Wellman article.   The common thread in much of the legislation is to offer new, optional modes of settling estates as alternatives to some of the requirements of court-supervised administration. Professor Wellman sets out a checklist of fourteen principles (distillations of the major procedural provisions of the Code) to serve as the objectives that all reform legislation should seek to implement (79 Mich.L.Rev. at pps. 511–513).   He compares the new codes against these standards and finds many of the principles compromised and the overall results disappointing.   A powerful case is made that the people will be better served by the adoption, nation-wide, of the Code procedures, whereby a decedent's family may select the probate and administration procedures that best meet its needs.

C. FINALITY OF PROBATE DECREES

A court order, following notice to interested parties and a hearing, is a final judgment subject only to appeal.   No such finality attaches to the actions of a personal representative who administers the estate without referring any matters to the court.   The Uniform Probate Code Section 3–108 recognizes that a non-intervention system requires a time limitation after which the informal actions of the personal representative can no longer be challenged and sets the period at three years from the date of decedent's death.   In a state like Connecticut where the probate judge need not be a lawyer and the court is not vested with the power to give a definitive trial, the appeal from all probate decrees takes the form of a trial de novo in the court of general jurisdiction.   While a trial by jury is generally not guaranteed in probate matters as a constitutional right, it is usually available by statute at the request of a party on issues

involving the validity of the will.   After the contest and appeal periods
have run, the decrees of the probate court are final and can only be upset
on a showing of fraud, accident or mistake "lying at the very basis of the
decree."   Miller v. McNamara, 135 Conn. 489, 66 A.2d 359 (1949).   See
Simes, The Function of Will Contests, 44 Mich.L.Rev. 503 (1946).

ALLEN v. DUNDAS
Court of King's Bench, 1789.
100 Eng.Rep. 490, 3 Term Rep. 125.

This was an action on the case for money had and received to the use
of the intestate, and to the use of the plaintiff as administrator: to which
the defendant pleaded the general issue.   And on the trial a special
verdict was found, stating in substance as follows.   The defendant, as
Treasurer of the Navy, was indebted to the intestate in his lifetime in
58£, 13s. 6d. for money had and received to his use.   Priestman died on
the 2d of June 1784:   on the 13th of August 1785, one Robert Brown
proved in the Prerogative Court of the Archbishop of Canterbury, a forged
paper writing, dated the 18th of May 1784, purporting to be the last will
of Priestman, otherwise Handy;   whereby he was supposed to have appointed Brown the sole executor thereof;   and a probate of that supposed
will issued in due form of law, under the seal of that Court, on the same
day, in favour of Brown.   The defendant, not knowing the will to have
been forged, and believing Brown to be the rightful executor, on Brown's
request paid him 58£. 13s. 6d. being the whole balance then due from the
defendant to Priestman.   On the 21st of July 1787, Brown was called by
citation, at the suit of John Priestman the father, and next of kin of the
deceased, in the Prerogative Court of the Archbishop of Canterbury,
touching the validity of such supposed will;   and such proceedings were
thereupon had in that Court, that the will and probate were declared null
and void;   that Thomas Priestman died intestate;   and that John Priestman the father was his next of kin.   And on the 31st of March 1788,
letters of administration of the goods, &c. of Thomas Priestman were
granted by that Court in due form of law to the plaintiff, as attorney of
John Priestman.   But whether, &c.

ASHHURST, J.—I am of opinion that the plaintiff has no right to call
on the defendant to pay this money a second time, which was paid to a
person who had at that time a legal authority to receive it.   It is admitted,
that if he had made this payment under the coercion of a suit in a Court
of Law, he would have been protected against any other demand for it:
but I think that makes no difference.   For as the party to whom the
payment was made had such authority as could not be questioned at the
time, and such as a Court of Law would have been bound to enforce, the
defendant was not obliged to wait for a suit, when he knew that no defense
could be made to it: this therefore cannot be called a voluntary payment.
This is different from payments under forged bonds or bills of exchange;
for there the party is to exercise his own judgment, and acts at his peril:
a payment in such a case is a voluntary act, though perhaps the party is
not guilty of any negligence in point of fact.   But here the defendant

acted under the authority of a Court of Law; every person is bound to pay deference to a judicial act of a Court having competent jurisdiction. Here the Spiritual Court had jurisdiction over the subject matter; and every person was bound to give credit to the probate till it was vacated. The case of a probate of a supposed will during the life of the party may be distinguished from the present; because during his life the Ecclesiastical Court has no jurisdiction, nor can they inquire who is his representative; but when the party is dead, it is within their jurisdiction. Besides, the distinction taken by the defendant's counsel between cases where a will is set aside on an appeal, or on a citation, seems to have some foundation: in the former the original sentence is as if it had never existed; in the latter, the will is only repealed, and all acts under it till the repeal are good. But the foundation of my opinion is, that every person is bound by the judicial acts of a Court having competent authority: and during the existence of such judicial act, the law will protect every person obeying it.

*   *   *

Judgment for the defendant.

Notes

1. It is usually held that a will can be offered for probate even if the estate has been fully administered under an earlier will or the laws of intestate succession. In re Elliott's Estate, 22 Wn.2d 334, 156 P.2d 427, 157 A.L.R. 1351 (1945). The principle announced in Allen v. Dundas is applied, however, with the result that a bona fide purchaser for value whose title was established by the first proceeding, and a debtor who has paid the original representative, are protected. Eckland v. Jankowski, supra, p. 616. The beneficiaries of a second will may recover against the distributees under the first administration. In re Cecala's Estate, 104 Cal.App.2d 526, 232 P.2d 48 (1951).

2. Statutes of a few states set time limits ranging from three to twenty years for the probate of a will, but some of these statutes are to be applied in the discretion of the probate court and therefore do not operate as an absolute bar. See, for example, Conn.Gen.Stat.Ann. § 45–200.

3. Decrees of the probate court may be set aside if procured by fraud. UPC § 1–106 establishes as the appropriate procedure an action against the perpetrator of the fraud or an action for restitution from any person, whether innocent or not except for a bona fide purchaser for value, benefitting from the fraud. The action against the wrongdoer must be brought within two years after the discovery of the fraud and against all others within five years after the time of the fraud's commission. An estate was reopened and the distribution order set aside on allegations of fraud, misrepresentation, and failure to satisfy the UPC notice requirements in Matter of Estates of Cahoon, 102 Idaho 542, 633 P.2d 607 (1981).

Note on Construction

The New Jersey Supreme Court has summarized the guidelines for ascertaining the testator's intent, as follows:

The court will read the testament in the light of all of the surrounding facts and circumstances and will strain towards carrying out the testator's probable intent. * * * So far as the situation fairly permits, it will ascribe to the testator those impulses which are common to human nature and will construe his testament so as to effectuate those impulses. * * * Though direct statements by the testator as to his intentions are still being excluded by most courts, other utterances by him which may bear on the construction of his will are sensibly being received more and more freely by the courts. * * * Not only may the circumstances surrounding the execution of the will be admitted but so also may the circumstances from then on until the testator's death. * * * And not only may the testator's practical construction of his will be received in evidence but so also may the practical construction by the other interested parties.

In re Cook, 44 N.J. 1, 6–7, 206 A.2d 865, 867–868 (1965). The rule that direct statements of intent by the testator are excluded is sometimes said to be based on the parol evidence rule, and is sometimes ascribed to the Statute of Wills prohibition against giving effect to unexecuted wills. In particular cases this rule may exclude the evidence that is most relevant to the issues involved. A latent ambiguity may be resolved by introducing direct statements of the testator's intent. The Supreme Court of Pennsylvania described the process: "Where the words of a will are on its face plain, consistent and certain, and where the uncertainty arises from extrinsic facts or circumstances in relation to the property bequeathed, there exists by definition a latent ambiguity. This court has repeatedly held that where a latent ambiguity does exist, parol evidence [including testimony as to direct statements of the testator's intent] is admissible to explain or clarify the ambiguity." In re Estate of Thomas, 457 Pa. 546, 551, 327 A.2d 31, 34 (1974). See, generally, 9 Wigmore on Evidence § 2425 (1940); Annot., Admissibility of Extrinsic Evidence to Aid Interpretation of Wills, 94 A.L.R. 26 (1935); Power, Wills: A Primer of Interpretation and Construction, 51 Iowa L.Rev. 75 (1965); Warren, Interpretation of Wills, 49 Harv.L.Rev. 689 (1936); Chafee, The Disorderly Conduct of Words, 41 Colum.L.Rev. 381 (1941); Holmes, The Theory of Legal Interpretation, 12 Harv.L.Rev. 417 (1899). On the related issue of using extrinsic evidence in an action to reform a will for mistake, see Matter of Snide, supra, p. 253, and Langbein and Waggoner, Reformation of Wills on the Ground of Mistake: Change of Direction in American Law?, 130 U. of Pa.L.Rev. 521 (1982).

A common motive today for bringing a construction proceeding is to obtain an interpretation of the language which will make the property disposition eligible for favorable tax treatment. Should testator's tax objectives be relevant to a determination of the meaning of the words used? Compare State Tax Commission v. Loring, 350 Mass. 568, 571, 215 N.E.2d 751, 754 (1966) ("The accomplishment of identifiable tax objectives * * * frequently may be an aid to the interpretation of trust instruments * * *") with In re Estate of Benson, 447 Pa. 62, 72, 285 A.2d 101, 106 (1971) (" * * * courts cannot be placed in the position of estate planners, charged with the task of reinterpreting deeds of trust and testamentary dispositions so as to generate the most favorable possible tax consequences for the estate"). The Internal Revenue Service, even though it is not a party, is bound by the construction given to a will or trust by the highest court in the state. Decisions of state trial courts are not, however, controlling and need only be given "proper regard" in determining the state law. Commissioner v. Estate of Bosch, 387 U.S. 456, 87 S.Ct. 1776, 18 L.Ed.2d 886 (1967).

SECTION THREE.   THE FIDUCIARY

The matters included under this title are subject to statutory control in every jurisdiction. New York Surrogate's Court Procedure Act, because of its comprehensive coverage, has been used herein to provide illustrations.

A.   APPOINTMENT AND QUALIFICATION

The instrument which effects the transfer of property, whether a will or an inter vivos trust, may specify the individual or corporate person or persons on whom the testator or settlor wishes to place the responsibility of administering the estate as executor, or the trust as trustee. See Sample Will, supra, p. 317. Many questions may be involved in the selection of a fiduciary for which testators will seek lawyers' advice. Should they name a corporate fiduciary? On the one hand, it is argued that a corporate fiduciary offers permanence, continuity and expert management, but, on the other, tends to "play it by the book" with a safe and conservative investment portfolio and to lack a personal understanding of the problems of the decedent's family. Shattuck and Farr, An Estate Planner's Handbook, 142–148 (1953); Gilman, Trustee Selection: Corporate vs. Individual, 123 Trust and Estates 29 (June 1984). Should they name their spouse or eldest child? A beneficiary of a trust who has powers over it may be subjected to unnecessary tax burdens. Pennell, Estate Planning: Drafting and Tax Considerations in Employing Individual Trustees, 60 N.C.L.Rev. 799 (1982). If testator plans to name an individual, should he or she name more than one? Multiple fiduciaries may raise problems involving the division of responsibility and the possibility of disagreement as to policy. In addition, the testator must be advised to name successor fiduciaries in the event that the primary nominee predeceases the testator or dies before the responsibilities are completed, and also to nominate a guardian of the person and property of minor children.

If there is no will the court will appoint an administrator in accordance with statutory priorities:

N.Y. SCPA

§ 1001.   Order of Priority for Granting Letters of Administration

1. Letters of administration must be granted to the persons who are distributees of an intestate and who are eligible and qualify, in the following order:

(a) the surviving spouse,

(b) the children,

(c) the grandchildren,

(d) the father or mother,

(e) the brothers or sisters,

(f) any other persons who are distributees and who are eligible and qualify, preference being given to the person entitled to the largest share in the estate, except as hereinafter provided.

Where there are eligible distributees equally entitled to administer the court may grant letters of administration to one or more of such persons.

[Authorization is given in paragraphs 2–7 for the appointment of the fiduciary or committee of an infant or incompetent when no other distributee is eligible, and for appointment of an individual or bank agreed upon by all the eligible distributees.]

8. When letters are not granted under the foregoing provisions and an appointment is not made by consent as hereinbefore provided then letters of administration shall be granted in the following order:

(a) to the public administrator, or the chief fiscal officer of the county, or

(b) to the petitioner, in the discretion of the court,

(c) to any other person or persons.

§ 707. Eligibility to Receive Letters

Letters may issue to a natural person or to a person authorized by law to be a fiduciary except as follows:

1. Persons ineligible

(a) an infant

(b) an incompetent

(c) a non-domiciliary alien, except in the case of a foreign guardian as prescribed in 1716(4) [sets out circumstances under which ancillary letters may be granted a foreign guardian]

(d) a felon

(e) one who is incompetent to execute the duties of his office by reason of drunkenness, dishonesty, improvidence or want of understanding.

2. Persons ineligible in court's discretion. The court may declare ineligible to act as fiduciary a person unable to read and write the English language.

Note

A minor died intestate in Idaho on March 29, 1967. His adoptive parents, who had separated prior to his death, filed competing petitions with the probate court to be appointed administrator of their son's estate. The Idaho Code provided that "of several persons claiming and equally entitled to administer, males must be preferred to females, and relatives of the whole to those of the half blood." Although the two parents appeared equally qualified, the Idaho courts declared the statute to be mandatory and named the father as administrator. The United States Supreme Court overruled the appointment and declared the arbitrary preference in favor of males unconstitutional as denying equal protection of the laws under the Fourteenth Amendment.   Reed v. Reed, 404 U.S. 71, 92 S.Ct. 251, 30 L.Ed.2d 225 (1971).

IN RE FOSS' WILL

Supreme Court of New York, Appellate Division, First Department, 1953.
282 App.Div. 509, 125 N.Y.S.2d 105.

BREITEL, J.   Objectants, legatees under a will, appeal.   Their objections to the issuance of letters testamentary to a coexecutor named in the will were dismissed without the taking of proof.   The basis for the objections is the existence of a diversity or conflict of interest between the coexecutor in his representative and in his individual capacities.

The facts, for purposes of this appeal, are not in dispute.

Testator for many years was employed by a book publishing corporation.   Upon his retirement in 1944 he was its president.   When he retired the corporation agreed to pay him a retirement "salary" of $25,000 a year for life.   Testator was also the owner of 1,300 shares of noncumulative preferred stock in the corporation, not subject to call for redemption.

Late in 1944, the corporation instituted a plan for its capital reorganization.   The plan required an exchange of new preferred stock for the class held by testator.   The new stock was subject to call for redemption.   Testator objected to the plan.   After negotiating with the corporation he consented to the exchange of stock, on condition that the corporation would not call the new stock for redemption during his lifetime.

Thereafter, in February, 1947, in violation of its agreement, the corporation reduced his retirement salary from $25,000 to $12,000 a year. In October, 1947, the corporation, again in violation of its agreement, called for redemption the new stock issued to testator in exchange for his former holdings.

Thus, testator's estate presumably has causes of action arising out of the transactions summarized above.   This is the circumstance giving rise to the conflict in interest of the coexecutor.   The coexecutor, a lawyer, is an officer and director of the corporation, and is also its "house-counsel". He held these offices at the time of the negotiations between testator and the corporation, and at the time of the agreements between them.   He is said to have participated not only in these negotiations, but in the decisions of the corporation to reduce testator's salary and to call his stock for redemption.

The Surrogate granted the coexecutor's motion to strike the objections on the ground that the adversity of interest said to exist was not sufficient within the meaning of section 94 of the Surrogate's Court Act to require denial of the appointment.   The grounds specified in that section were held to be exclusive, the Surrogate being without discretion to deny appointment on additional grounds.

Concededly, the objections do not cover grounds specified in section 94 of the Surrogate's Court Act rendering a person absolutely incompetent to serve as an executor. These grounds are minority; adjudicated incompetency; alienage; felony; incompetency by reason of drunkenness, dishonesty, improvidence or want of understanding. The further grounds, specified in that section, for a finding of conditional disqualification (circumstances not affording security to interested persons, and nonresidence) are also without application here.

It has been uniformly held heretofore that the grounds for disqualification set forth in section 94 are exclusive, and that the Surrogate's power to refuse letters is limited by that statute, Matter of Flood, 236 N.Y. 408, 140 N.E. 936; Matter of Leland, 219 N.Y. 387, 114 N.E. 854; Matter of Latham, 145 App.Div. 849, 130 N.Y.S. 535. The texts agree. "If the candidate cannot be slotted in any subdivision listing a disqualifying cause he may act" (2 Jessup-Redfield on Surrogate's Law and Practice [1947], § 1284. Accord, 2 Butler on New York Surrogate Law and Practice [1941], § 1161; 2 Warren's Heaton on Surrogates' Courts [1952], § 128, par. 1, subd. [a]).

The rule was fully stated by Judge Pound, writing for the Court of Appeals, in Matter of Leland, 219 N.Y. 387, 393–394, 114 N.E. 854, 856:

> "It may be broadly stated that the common law favors the rule that no restriction should be placed upon the choice of an executor, even though unsuitable persons are allowed to exercise the trust to the possible prejudice of creditors and legatees. Modern legislation enlarges the control of probate courts over improper testamentary appointees. In New York the necessary qualifications of an executor are described with minuteness. Code Civil Procedure, §§ 2564–2567. But the testator still enjoys the right to determine who is most suitable among those legally qualified to settle his affairs and execute his will, and his solemn selection is not lightly to be disregarded. Appointment is not to be refused merely because the testator's selection does not seem suitable to the judge. * * * The courts will not undertake to make a better will nor name a better executor for the testator. They will not add disqualifications to those specified by statute, nor disregard testator's wishes by too liberal an interpretation of the specified disqualifications".

Objectants assert that there are sources other than section 94 of the Surrogate's Court Act whence that court derives power to deny appointment to the nominated executor. Section 40 of the Surrogate's Court Act is claimed to be one of these, empowering the Surrogate to "administer justice in all matters relating to the affairs of decedents". The authorities previously cited do not suggest the existence of such power in this case.

Objectants seek also to invoke the court's jurisdiction and control over the conduct of attorneys. Whatever the extent of that power, the nominated executor here is involved in his capacity as such, and not as lawyer. Moreover, the possibility of conflict between the several capacities of an executor is not peculiar to lawyers who are executors. There is no reason why lawyers should be subject to a special disabling rule.

In any event, it is not essential to the determination of this case that we reconsider the scope of the rule limiting disqualification to the grounds specified in section 94, or that we rest it alone upon that ground. There are other cogent reasons why the court should not in this case displace the coexecutor chosen by the testator.

It will be recalled that when the testator executed his will in 1952 he was aware of his nominee's position with the corporation, and of his own disputes with the corporation. He named him nevertheless. Testator's knowledge of a possible conflict of interest militates against denying appointment to his choice. Cf. Matter of Cohen, 164 Misc. 98, 102, 298 N.Y.S. 368, 373, affd. 254 App.Div. 571, 2 N.Y.S.2d 764, affd. 278 N.Y. 584, 16 N.E.2d 111.

In the event that the coexecutor's apparent conflict of interest should lead to misconduct—the presumption being strongly to the contrary, Matter of Place, 42 Hun 658, 4 N.Y.St.Rep. 533, 534, General Term, First Dept., 1886, affd. 105 N.Y. 629; Matter of Forte, 149 Misc. 327, 334, 267 N.Y.S. 603, 612, Surr.Ct., Kings Co., 1933—objectants will not be left without remedy. Surrogate's Ct.Act, § 99.

In Matter of Place, 4 N.Y.St.Rep. 533, 534, supra, appointment of an administratrix was resisted because the remaining unadministered asset of the estate was a claim against her husband. The claim was then in suit, and an appeal from a judgment in the husband's favor was pending. General Term disposed of the objection as follows: "The presumption on the other hand, is that she will discharge the duties which the law enjoins upon her as the administratrix of the estate. This will not require her personal services beyond the employment of skilful and competent counsel, who will be able to understand and present the case, for the decision of the appellate tribunal. And without proof that she will disregard this duty, it is not to be inferred that any danger exists of the least neglect or dereliction on her part. But if as a matter of fact she should fail to discharge this duty, then under subdivision 2 of section 2685 of the Code of Civil Procedure, the surrogate has been authorized to remove her from her office. For wherever an executor, or administrator, shall improvidently manage the estate, or property, committed to his, or her, charge, there the surrogate has been empowered to remove the delinquent person from the office to which he or she may have been appointed."

It would be a serious matter to make any claim of conflict of interest a ground for disqualifying designated executors. Not only would it threaten to substitute the legatees' desires and views for the views of the testator, it would also undoubtedly engender a multitude of proceedings. Few estates would be certain to be free from such attack. Many estates would be subjected to extended proof-taking to determine whether the claimed conflict in fact existed.

Misconduct, not conflict in interest, merits removal of a fiduciary [SCPA § 711]. The statute provides for resolving claims between the estate and its representative [SCPA § 1805]. This is reasonable. Any other view would automatically disqualify from appointment as executor a partner, a joint owner of property, a legatee, a creditor, a debtor, a distributee, a spouse, or one who is a party to an executory contract with the testator. Few would remain eligible.

The order dismissing the objections and vacating the stay of the issuance of letters testamentary should be affirmed.

PECK, P. J., COHN, BASTOW and BOTEIN, JJ., concur.

Order unanimously affirmed, with $10 costs and disbursements to the respondent.

Notes

1. The traditional view holds that courts may not deny appointment except on grounds specified in the statute. Decedent in his will named as executrix a woman who had been his mistress for twenty years. The court denied the petition of the wife and four children objecting to the appointment. It stated that the mistress was not disqualified under the statute and that the statutory grounds were exclusive. In re Estate of Nagle, 40 Ohio App.2d 40, 317 N.E.2d 242 (1974); but see In re Estate of Henne, 66 Ohio St.2d 232, 421 N.E.2d 506 (1981) (nominated executor denied appointment as unsuitable because her personal interests were adverse to the beneficiaries of the estate; dissent argues for the traditional rule). The statutes establishing priorities for appointment as administrator have also been held to be mandatory. See e.g. In re Estate of Weaver, 214 Kan. 550, 520 P.2d 1330 (1974); contra, In re Estate of Shorter, 444 A.2d 954 (D.C.App.1982) (probate court has some discretion to deviate from statutory guidelines in appointing administrators).

May the beneficiaries under a will join together and veto the appointment of the executor nominated in the will for reasons other than the nominee's competency and capacity to serve, such as personal animus or the desire to save fees? The usual response, stressing the necessity of honoring testators' intent, has been in the negative. See e.g. State ex rel. First National Bank & Trust Co. of Racine v. Skow, 91 Wis.2d 773, 284 N.W.2d 74 (1979) (probate court cannot disqualify nominated bank as unsuitable to be executor merely because beneficiaries prefer a personal representative who did not charge fees); see generally, Whitman and Alvord, What If All Beneficiaries Object to the Executor of a Will?, 119 Trusts & Estates 30 (Dec.1980) (authors argue for a more flexible approach).

2. The court cites Matter of Cohen's Will, 164 Misc. 98, 298 N.Y.S. 368 (1937), affirmed 254 App.Div. 571, 2 N.Y.S.2d 764 (1938), affirmed 278 N.Y. 584, 16 N.E.2d 111 (1938). There, testator had nominated his three sons with the following results: Morris had been convicted of forgery in the first degree and was denied letters as a felon; Isidore, who had been convicted of petty larceny and was under indictment for perjury, was denied but was granted leave to reapply if he was acquitted on the perjury indictment; Hyman was convicted of making false oath in a federal bankruptcy proceeding which, although it resulted in a year and a day in the penitentiary, was not a "state" felony and therefore did not disqualify him from appointment. The court also pointed out that the testator knew of Hyman's federal conviction before making the will.

3. How much intelligence is required of the nominee? Just sufficient wit to hire a good lawyer? In Matter of Leland, 219 N.Y. 387, 114 N.E. 854 (1916),

the court held that the surrogate was authorized to deny the appointment of the nominated executor (the only one of three who was available) who was 63 years old, had suffered two strokes of apoplexy, was partially paralyzed and was in such mental and physical condition that he could not engage in active work. The court, however, cautioned (219 N.Y. at 393–94, 114 N.E. at 856):

> The test of incompetency should be applied with caution to cases where inability intelligently to discharge the duties of the trust arises from bodily disease resulting in permanent impairment of mental and physical ability. * * * The courts will not undertake to make a better will nor name a better executor for the testator. They will not add disqualifications to those specified by the statute, nor disregard testator's wishes by too liberal an interpretation of the specific disqualifications, nor consider the size and condition of the estate, except as a minor consideration. Where the ties of kindred and long acquaintanceship lead the testator to choose the inexperienced wife or friend rather than the modern trust company the relative advantage to the beneficiaries will not justify a judicial veto on such choice. Every executor is entitled to have the aid of counsel learned in the law.

4. The statutes of some states deny appointment to a nominee who is a nonresident. The statutes vary as to their coverage: some apply only to foreign corporations, even those that are authorized to do business in the state; some release from the prohibition close relatives of the decedent who are domiciled out of state; and some make nonresidence a ground for the exercise of discretion by the probate judge in whether to approve the appointment. These statutes have been attacked as violative of the equal protection and due process clauses of the fourteenth amendment and the privileges and immunities clause of Article IV, section 2. These attacks have for the most part been unsuccessful. See e.g. In re Estate of Greenberg, 390 So.2d 40 (Fla.1980) (majority of court, applying the minimum scrutiny test, found residence a sufficiently rational classification to uphold as constitutional the Florida statute barring unrelated nonresidents from appointment); In re Emery, 59 Ohio App.2d 7, 391 N.E.2d 746 (1978) (Ohio statute barring nonresident banks constitutional); contra, Fain v. Hall, 463 F.Supp. 661 (M.D.Fla.1979) (right to name one's personal representative "fundamental", which can only be overridden by a "compelling state interest"; Florida statute unconstitutional). A majority of the Florida Supreme Court in the Greenberg case, supra, dismissed the decision in Fain v. Hall as "wholly unpersuasive". See generally Annot., Executors—Requirement of Residency, 9 A.L.R.4th 1223 (1981). A number of states have statutes accepting the appointment of foreign corporations as fiduciaries only where the state of the corporation's domicile accords the same privilege to corporations of the forum state. See Annot., Eligibility of Foreign Corporation to Appointment as Executor, Administrator, or Testamentary Trustee, 26 A.L.R.3d 1019, 1029 (1969). A state may condition the appointment of a nonresident, individual fiduciary on that fiduciary appointing the local probate judge as agent to accept process. See e.g., Conn.Gen.Stat.Ann. § 52–61.

5. Provisions in a will naming an attorney to represent the executor in the administration of the estate are generally held to be precatory and not binding on the executor. The relationship between client and attorney being personal and one of mutual trust, the executor is entitled to select an attorney of his or her own choosing. Annot., Attorney Selected by Testator, 166 A.L.R. 491. If,

however, the appointment of the executor is expressly made conditional on the executor hiring a named attorney, the condition will be enforced, and the executor must refuse the office if he is unwilling to accept the attorney. In re Estate of Devroy, 109 Wis.2d 154, 325 N.W.2d 345 (1982) (condition that executor must hire attorney who drafted the will not void as against public policy).

6. The statutes usually require that a fiduciary take an oath (or under certain circumstances "an acknowledged consent to accept appointment") and post a bond. N.Y. SCPA § 708. In most states the will may waive the bond. New York goes a step farther and provides that no bond is required of the executor unless the will specifically demands it or the nominee is a "nondomiciliary" or "does not possess the degree of responsibility required of a fiduciary." N.Y. SCPA § 710.

B. REMOVAL AND RESIGNATION

A fiduciary may be removed by the court which appointed him for malfeasance in his office, breach of his duties, or if, because of "dishonesty, drunkenness, improvidence or want of understanding, he is unfit for the execution of his office." N.Y. SCPA § 711. It is, however, recognized that the decision to remove a fiduciary is a "drastic action" which should only be taken when the estate is endangered. In re Estate of Quinlan, 441 Pa. 266, 273 A.2d 340 (1971).

In addition, procedures are available for fiduciaries to petition to resign before the work of their office is completed. N.Y. SCPA §§ 715, 716. Before a resignation will be accepted fiduciaries must account, and turn over all the property and papers of the estate or trust to their successors. Because of the complications to accountability, compensation and title which result, the courts are not receptive to the request for the resignation of a trustee who pleads personal inconvenience or overwork. Petitions relying on old age and physical infirmities are usually granted, as are those alleging strained relationships between the trustee and the beneficiaries. Note, Resignation of a Trustee, 28 N.Y.U.L.Rev. 1298 (1953). It has also been held that a corporate trustee, which was bound by the instrument to receive less than one half the compensation to which it was by law entitled, could resign. Oregon Bank v. Hendricksen, 267 Or. 138, 515 P.2d 1328 (1973).

The fact that the primary beneficiaries of a trust have moved out of the state in which the trust was originally located and in which the trustee was appointed may be ground for removing the trust assets to the new domicile and terminating the original appointment. See Hendrickson, Change of Situs of a Trust, 118 Trusts and Estates 19 (Jan.1979) (first of ten-part series appearing in consecutive issues; Part IV on eligibility of trustees appears in the April, 1979, issue at p. 36). A trustee who moved out of the state of his appointment was removed from his trusteeship. King v. King, 228 Ga. 818, 188 S.E.2d 502 (1972).

The appointment of a successor fiduciary may follow any one of a number of courses: (a) The will nominates a successor; (b) the surviving fiduciary or fiduciaries continue without any new appointment; (c) the will names a person or persons who are to nominate a successor; (d) the court fills the vacancy.   The practice on the death of a fiduciary whereby his executor or administrator takes his place is generally obsolete today. See Restatement, Second, Trusts, §§ 104, 105.

C. COMPENSATION

A number of states have enacted statutory fee schedules.   See, for example, the New York statutes set out infra.   Other jurisdictions provide in general terms that fiduciaries shall be given reasonable compensation for their services.   In actual fact, customary rates have developed in many of these latter jurisdictions which tend to become almost as fixed as in states with statutory schedules.   It was common practice for bar associations to publish schedules of minimum fees, based on a percentage of the estate, to be charged by fiduciaries.   The Supreme Court, by holding in Goldfarb v. Virginia State Bar, 421 U.S. 773, 95 S.Ct. 2004, 44 L.Ed.2d 572 (1975), that a minimum fee schedule for doing a title search published by the county bar association constituted price-fixing in violation of Section 1 of the Sherman Anti-Trust Act, made it clear that there could no longer be uniform adherence to a set fiduciary fee schedule which had been established by bar groups or lawyers acting in concert.   Although the decision pertained to attorneys' fees, similar objections were applicable to fees set out for fiduciaries by trade associations.   The Goldfarb decision did not, however, proscribe use by individual lawyers of their own percentage fee schedules (rather than charging at their hourly rate) so long as they did not arrive at the percentages by concerted action with other lawyers.   Corcoran, Fees of Legal Representatives and Their Attorneys—Six Years after Goldfarb, 67 Ill.B.J. 618 (1979).   Nor apparently did the Court prohibit the development of purely advisory fee schedules to be used by attorneys as general guidelines.   A study made a few years after the Goldfarb decision was rendered concluded that its impact on estate administration fees was minimal.   There was some evidence that attorneys' fees had decreased in larger estates and increased in smaller estates and that in reasonable compensation jurisdictions some attorneys had changed their method of fee determination.   Overall, however, "the continued tacit reliance by many attorneys upon the old fee schedules has served to negate even this effect [of Goldfarb] to a great extent." Fiduciary and Probate Counsel Fees in the Wake of *Goldfarb,* 13 Real Prop., Probate, and Trust J. 238, 250 (1978).

N.Y. SCPA

§ 2307. Commissions of Fiduciaries Other Than Trustees

1. On the settlement of the account of any fiduciary other than a trustee the court must allow to him the reasonable and necessary expenses actually paid by him and if he be an attorney of this state and shall have rendered legal services in connection with his official duties, such compensation for his legal services as appear [sic] to the court to be just and reasonable and in addition thereto it must allow to the fiduciary for his services as fiduciary, and if there be more than one, apportion among them according to the services rendered by them respectively the following commissions:

(a) For receiving and paying out all sums of money not exceeding $100,000 at the rate of 5 per cent.

(b) For receiving and paying out any additional sums not exceeding $200,000 at the rate of 4 per cent.

(c) For receiving and paying out any additional sums not exceeding $700,000 at the rate of 3 per cent.

(d) For receiving and paying out any additional sums not exceeding $4,000,000 at the rate of 2½ per cent.

(e) For receiving and paying out all sums above $5,000,000 at the rate of 2 per cent.

2. The value of any property, to be determined in such manner as directed by the court and the increment thereof, received, distributed or delivered, shall be considered as money in computing commissions. But this shall not apply in case of a specific legacy or devise. Whenever any portion of the dividends, interest or rent payable to a fiduciary other than a trustee is required by any law of the United States or other governmental unit to be withheld by the person paying it for income tax purposes, the amount so withheld shall be deemed to have been received and paid out.

[Paragraphs 3 and 4 make additional provisions for guardians.]

5. If the gross value of the principal of the estate accounted for amounts to $300,000 or more each fiduciary is entitled to the full compensation on principal and income allowed herein to a sole fiduciary unless there be more than 3, in which case the compensation to which 3 would be entitled must be apportioned among them according to the services rendered by them respectively unless the fiduciaries shall have agreed in writing among themselves to a different apportionment which, however, shall not provide for more than one full commission for any one of them.

[The balance of paragraph 5 provides that co-fiduciaries of an estate less than $100,000 apportion the full fee of one fiduciary according to the services rendered by them and of an estate of more than $100,000 but less than $300,000 the full fee of two fiduciaries.]

* * *

N.Y. SCPA § 2309, as amended effective August 6, 1984, provides that on the settlement of the account of an individual trustee:

* * * the court must allow to him his reasonable and necessary expenses actually paid by him and if he be an attorney of this state and shall have rendered legal services in connection with his official duties, such compensation for his legal services as shall appear to the court to be just and reasonable and in addition thereto it must allow to the trustee for his services as trustee a commission from principal for paying out all sums of money constituting principal at the rate of 1 per cent.

2. In addition to the commission allowed by subdivision 1 hereof a trustee shall be entitled to annual commissions at the following rates:

(a) $8.50 per $1,000 or major fraction thereof on the first $400,000 of principal.

(b) $4.50 per $1,000 or major fraction thereof on the next $600,000 of principal.

(c) $3.00 per $1,000 or major fraction thereof on all additional principal.

[The balance of paragraph 2 deals with methods of computing the amounts.]

3. Unless the will otherwise explicitly provides the annual commissions allowed by subdivision 2 shall be payable one-half from the income of the trust and one-half from the principal of the trust.

* * *

[Paragraph 6 sets out the methods of compensating multiple trustees along the lines set out for co-executors in § 2307.]

* * *

The amended New York statute further provides that a corporate trustee is entitled to reasonable commissions, subject to court review, and specifies that for trusts having a gross principal value of not more than $400,000 annual commissions at the rate of not more than $10 per $1,000 are deemed reasonable. A corporate trustee may continue to claim the statutory rates instead of reasonable compensation. In conjunction with this legislation increasing trustees' fees, an addition to N.Y. EPTL § 11-2.2(a) was enacted to provide: "A fiduciary having special investment skills shall exercise such diligence in investing the funds for which the fiduciary is responsible, as would customarily be exercised by a prudent man of discretion and intelligence having such special investment skills". It should also be noted that paragraph 10 of § 2309 states that where the instrument provides a "specific compensation" the trustee is not entitled to any additional compensation. For an application of this limitation, see Lehman v. Irving Trust Co., 55 N.Y.2d 97, 447 N.Y.S.2d 897, 432 N.E.2d 769 (1982).

Notes

1. One variable in establishing the fee of an executor or administrator in a statutory fee state is the value of the estate, which will, in turn, depend on what property is held to be within the estate. In New York, for instance, the estate does not include and therefore the executor does not receive any fee in connection with life insurance payable to a named beneficiary (or trustee), real estate (unless sold by the executor), or specific legacies. Doyle, An Executor's 40 Steps, 105 Trusts & Estates 419, 425 (1966). In reasonable compensation jurisdictions, all assets, including those that are not included in the probate estate such as insurance, survivorship property, Totten trusts, employee benefit plans and the like, are considered in arriving at a "reasonable" fee. In most statutory fee schedule jurisdictions, additional fees are allowed upon a showing that "extraordinary services," necessary to the proper administration of the estate, were rendered. Examples of such services include managing decedent's business and litigating contested creditor or tax claims. See for a general review of methods for determining fiduciary and attorney fees, Fiduciary and Probate Counsel Fees in the Wake of *Goldfarb,* 13 Real Prop., Probate and Trust J. 238 (1978).

2. The Uniform Probate Code has adopted the reasonable compensation approach. Consistent with its aim to simplify procedures by putting the responsibility for administration in the hands of decedent's family, the Code seeks to encourage fee agreements between the survivors and the professionals who assist them for specific work done. § 3–719 states:

> A personal representative is entitled to reasonable compensation for his services. If a will provides for compensation of the personal representative and there is no contract with the decedent regarding compensation, he may renounce the provision before qualifying and be entitled to reasonable compensation. A personal representative also may renounce his right to all or any part of the compensation. A written renunciation of fee may be filed with the Court.

3. In a number of states, statutes set out a fee schedule for attorneys representing estates, but, in the majority, attorneys are compensated for the reasonable value of the services they render. See e.g. N.Y.—McKinney's SCPA 2110; Annot., Amount of Attorneys' Compensation in Absence of Contract or Statute Fixing Amount, 56 A.L.R.2d 13. In the determination of reasonableness, variables include time spent, size of the estate, difficulty of issues, degree of skill required, extent of responsibilities assumed, and results obtained. Bar schedules may be used as some evidence of customary practice in the community. In re Estate of Freeman, 34 N.Y.2d 1, 355 N.Y.S.2d 336, 311 N.E.2d 480 (1974). The number of hours spent is not to be used as the sole factor in setting a fee. In re Estate of Bush, 304 Minn. 105, 230 N.W.2d 33 (1975) ($710,000 plus expenses awarded to attorneys who represented the executors for six years in a complex estate of an approved value of $126,875,868); Matter of Shalman, 68 A.D.2d 940, 414 N.Y.S.2d 70 (1979) (objectants "placed too much emphasis on the time clock approach despite ample legal precedent to the contrary").

It was the rule at common law, predicated on the policy against self-dealing, that fiduciaries could not compensate themselves for any legal service rendered by them to the estate. The modern rule existing in most jurisdictions allows an attorney-fiduciary to receive separate compensation for each function performed. The states are described as about equally divided between those in which attorneys rarely serve in the dual capacities and those in which such service is common practice. See Fiduciary and Probate Counsel Fees in the Wake of *Goldfarb,* supra, at pps. 249–250.

4. The New York statutes, supra, establish rules for allowances to multiple fiduciaries. Other states leave it up to the court to award compensation in proportion to each fiduciary's contribution to the enterprise, even if the total thereby awarded exceeds the amount that a single fiduciary would have received. For an interesting analysis of the issues as viewed over sixty years ago, see Hayward v. Plant, 98 Conn. 374, 119 A. 341 (1923) (on a $36,271,814.42 estate the following awards were made to five co-executors: $135,000, $120,000, $120,000, $30,000 and $30,000).

5. UPC § 3–719, supra, and N.Y. SCPA § 2307, par. 5, provide that an executor may renounce any compensation prescribed for him by the will, and claim the statutory fee. This option to renounce is based on the assumption that the testator would prefer to have the nominated person at a full fee than a stranger appointed by the court. Suverkrup v. Suverkrup, 106 Ind.App. 406, 18 N.E.2d 488 (1939); Comment, Effect of Testamentary Provisions on Executors' Fees, 38 Mich.L.Rev. 381 (1940). Fiduciaries are bound by the stipulated

compensation if they accept the office without having questioned the compensation. Marks v. Marks, 51 Hawaii 548, 465 P.2d 996 (1970). One commentator has noted, however, a trend by the courts to liberalize the grounds on which a trustee may obtain relief from an earlier, imprudent agreement fixing compensation. Reynolds, Increasing Trustees' Compensation to Meet Inflation and Accomplish Trust Purposes, 113 Trusts & Estates 494 (1974).

SECTION FOUR. CREDITORS

A. INVENTORY

Notes

1. The states that require a formal administration often have a statute which makes it the responsibility of the personal representative to file with the probate court within a few months after appointment an inventory of the estate's assets. The requirement of an inventory tends to serve the purpose of having the fiduciary pull together and organize the estate at the beginning of the administration. Variables include the time within which the inventory must be filed, the property to be included, and the qualifications of the appraisers. A few states omit real property from the inventory. (Inasmuch as realty is universally available today for creditors, this omission would seem unjustified.) Two reasons have been cited for requiring an inventory. "The first is to serve as a basis of computation for the representative's intermediate and final accounts. The second is to furnish information for the benefit of the beneficiaries, creditors and others interested in the estate." Atkinson on Wills, 630 (2d ed. 1953). For this latter reason, the testator may not by direction in the will relieve the executor of the duty to file an inventory. Parker v. Robertson, 205 Ala. 434, 88 So. 418 (1921). Nor may the beneficiaries waive it. Dant's Executors v. Cooper, 123 Ky. 359, 96 S.W. 454 (1906). Failure to file an inventory has been held ground for removal and loss of compensation.

In an estate of sufficient size to require the personal representative to file an estate or inheritance tax return, the inventory requirement is largely redundant, full disclosure of the estate's assets having been made on the tax return. The requirement also means that a public record must be made of the family's assets, although many families prefer to keep such information private. UPC § 3–706 requires the personal representative to mail an inventory of decedent's property, with market values, to "interested persons who request it", but does not require that it be filed in court. New York does not require an inventory unless the court orders it on the petition of an interested party. N.Y.—McKinney's SCPA 2101, 2102.

2. The fiduciary is under a duty to clear up disputes as to title to property and may, if necessary, resort to court processes to do so. Litigation of this type is almost always conducted in the courts of general jurisdiction. In aid of collecting the assets many states have statutes permitting the representative to bring some form of discovery proceedings in the probate court. A few probate courts have jurisdiction to give more extensive relief.

B. PRE-DEATH CREDITORS

Uniform Probate Code

Section 3–803. Limitation on Presentation of Claims

(a) All claims against a decedent's estate which arose before the death of the decedent, including claims of the state and any subdivision thereof, whether due or to become due, absolute or contingent, liquidated or un-liquidated, founded on contract, tort, or other legal basis, if not barred earlier by other statute of limitations, are barred against the estate, the personal representative, and the heirs and devisees of the decedent, unless presented as follows:

(1) within 4 months after the date of the first publication of notice to creditors if notice is given in compliance with Section 3–801 [notice once a week for 3 successive weeks in a general circulation news-paper]; provided, claims barred by the non-claim statute at the de-cedent's domicile before the first publication for claims in this state are also barred in this state.

(2) within [3] years after the decedent's death, if notice to cred-itors has not been published.

(b) All claims against a decedent's estate which arise at or after the death of the decedent, including claims of the state and any subdivision thereof, whether due or to become due, absolute or contingent, liquidated or unliquidated, founded on contract, tort, or other legal basis, are barred against the estate, the personal representative, and the heirs and devisees of the decedent, unless presented as follows:

(1) a claim based on a contract with the personal representative, within four months after performance by the personal representative is due;

(2) any other claim, within 4 months after it arises.

(c) Nothing in this section affects or prevents:

(1) any proceeding to enforce any mortgage, pledge, or other lien upon property of the estate; or

(2) to the limits of the insurance protection only, any proceeding to establish liability of the decedent or the personal representative for which he is protected by liability insurance.

Notes

1. All but a few states have non-claim statutes similar to the above statute, barring absolutely claims which are not filed within the requisite time. In a few states the claim is not finally barred, but the statute creates an order of priority for payment. In New York, for instance, the fiduciary may proceed to pay legacies and claims which have been timely filed without being accountable or chargeable for the assets so distributed to late-filing creditors. N.Y. SCPA § 1802. A statute which allows claims against estates covered by insurance to be filed within eighteen months, instead of within the four months required in the basic non-claim statute, is based upon a rational classification and is not unconstitutional. Belancsik v. Overlake Memorial Hospital, 80 Wn.2d 111, 492 P.2d 219 (1971).

2. Any description of the types of claims barred by the non-claim statutes must take into account the many variations in statutory language. The stat-utes run from the comprehensive phrase, "all claims," to such more limited formulas as "claims arising out of contract." In the main, a claim which is founded on the personal obligation of the decedent and which would have been

the basis of an in personam action against the decedent had he lived is within the non-claim proscription. A claim for the recovery of property which is in rem in nature is held not to be barred. Occasionally, the formulation is made on the basis of whether the action is legal or equitable; the former is within the non-claim period while the latter is not. These several approaches are described in Padula v. Padula, 138 Conn. 102, 82 A.2d 362 (1951). Attempts to recharacterize claims for money damages as equitable claims to impress a constructive trust on property in order to avoid the nonclaim statute have been ineffective. Breen v. Phelps, 186 Conn. 86, 439 A.2d 1066 (1982). Tort claims are not always required to be filed. Comment, Filing Tort Claims Against Decedent's Estates Within Non-Claim Statutes: A Survey, 47 Marq.L.Rev. 230 (1963). Secured creditors need not file claims with the fiduciary in order to protect their security. If, however, they wish to make a claim for a deficiency against the estate, the security being insufficient to cover the full amount of the obligation, they must file this claim in the usual manner. Jones v. Mc-Lauchlin, 293 Ala. 31, 299 So.2d 723 (1974). The State of Connecticut's claim for the costs of treatment and services given to the decedent was denied because it was not filed within the time prescribed by statute. State v. Goldfarb, 160 Conn. 320, 278 A.2d 818 (1971) (authority from other states collected and analyzed). To the same effect see Department of Public Welfare v. Anderson, 377 Mass. 23, 384 N.E.2d 628 (1979).

3. Contingent obligations (which may never come into existence, such as an agreement by the decedent to go surety on another person's debt) and unmatured obligations (which are in existence but on which payment is not yet due) present special problems. Many statutes do not require that such claims be filed, in which case they will exist as claims against the distributees if and when they materialize. If they are specifically within the non-claim statute, several methods are available for their payment. One procedure requires that the obligation be given some present value and then paid off at that figure. Such a device may be satisfactory for unmatured claims, but it is of doubtful validity for contingent claims. The Federal Bankruptcy Law, 11 U.S.C.A. § 93(d) (see also § 103), utilizes this procedure where practicable for both types of obligations. In the alternative, the executor may be required to retain a reserve fund against the possibility of future liability on a contingent claim. This also has its shortcomings. See In re Reilly's Will, 175 Misc. 597, 24 N.Y.S.2d 213 (1941) (contingent claimant sought to have more than 40% of the estate set aside as a reserve fund). Comment, Right of Creditors of a Decedent to Recover from Distributees After the Estate is Closed, 41 Mich.L.Rev. 920 (1943).

4. The personal representative may allow or disallow a claim depending on his evaluation of its validity. If the claim is disallowed the claimant may bring an action to have its validity established within a further time period set out by the statute. Generally, such litigation is administered in the court of general jurisdiction. Some states do grant the probate court a measure of jurisdiction over those claims which must be presented to the personal representative. The fiduciary has the power to compromise claims if it is in the best interest of the estate. Some statutes require that any such compromise must be approved by the court. If the personal representative allows a claim that should have been disallowed he may be held personally liable therefor (i.e., not given credit for payment of the claim on his account). Shaffer, Fiduciary Power to Compromise Claims, 41 N.Y.U.L.Rev. 528 (1966).

5. The statutes typically authorize notice to be given to decedent's creditors by publication in a local newspaper. See e.g. UPC § 3–801. In Mennonite Board of Missions v. Adams, 462 U.S. 791, 103 S.Ct. 2706, 77 L.Ed.2d 180 (1983), the Supreme Court held such notice to be violative of the due process clause of the fourteenth amendment when applied to a party whose identity and location are either known or may be ascertained with reasonable diligence. See discussion in note 6, p. 604 supra.

Continental Insurance Co. had a civil action pending against a Nevada decedent at the time of her death but failed to file its claim against the estate until two days after the time for filing claims had expired. The executor, although she knew of Continental's claim, made no special effort to notify the Company of the death but rather relied on general notice by publication as representing a full satisfaction of her responsibilities to creditors. The Nevada Supreme Court, holding that an expeditious administration of estates justifies the policy that "notices to creditors [be] somewhat circumscribed," refused to vacate the order barring the Company's claim. Continental Insurance Co. v. Moseley, 98 Nev. 476, 653 P.2d 158 (1982). The United States Supreme Court, however, granted certiorari and remanded the case to the Nevada court for further consideration in light of the Mennonite Board of Missions case. 463 U.S. 1202, 103 S.Ct. 3530, 77 L.Ed.2d 1383 (1983). The Nevada Supreme Court then reversed its earlier ruling and held that under the circumstances (i.e. the executor's actual knowledge of the claim) "more than service by publication was required in order to afford due process to appellant". Continental Insurance Co. v. Moseley, — Nev. —, 683 P.2d 20 (1984). It appears that nonclaim statutes throughout the country will have to be amended to provide for personal service or service by mail for creditors who are either known or whose identity and location can be ascertained with reasonable diligence.

C. POST-DEATH CREDITORS

ONANIAN v. LEGGAT

Appeal Court of Massachusetts, Middlesex County, 1974.
2 Mass.App.Ct. 623, 317 N.E.2d 823.

ROSE, Justice. The defendant appeals from a decree of the Superior Court in which the plaintiff was declared entitled to the payment of a sum of money, with interest, in lieu of specific performance of an agreement for the purchase of certain real property from the defendant.

* * *

On July 17, 1970, the defendant qualified as executor under the will of one L. Francis F. Knowles. The will devised the decedent's real property to certain persons, but conferred a power of sale thereof upon the defendant as executor. The defendant received at least two offers to purchase the real property, one of which was from the plaintiff. During the last week of November, 1970, the plaintiff and the defendant executed an agreement for the purchase and sale of the property (the agreement) for $32,500, title to pass on or before January 1, 1971. The agreement was in typical form, but contained the following provision: "This conveyance is subject to and contingent upon the issuance of a license to sell

from the Probate Court for Middlesex County in the Estate of L. Francis
F. Knowles."

On December 3, 1970, the defendant filed a petition in the Probate
Court for Middlesex County in which he represented that "an advantageous offer for the purchase of said real estate ha[d] been made to [him]
in the sum of [$32,500]" and prayed that he "may be licensed to sell said
real estate   *   *   *   at private sale in accordance with said offer or for
a larger sum   *   *   *." The defendant also filed documents signed by
each of the devisees assenting to the "petition for license to sell real estate
for the sum of $32,500 without further notice to me." On December 15
a judge of the Probate Court entered a decree to the effect that the defendant be licensed to sell the property "at private sale in accordance
with said offer or for a larger sum, or at public auction, if he shall think
best so to do   *   *   *."

By a letter dated December 29, 1970, the defendant informed the
plaintiff that the license had been obtained. In the same letter, however,
the defendant stated that another prospective purchaser was interested
in the property and that it would be sold to the highest bidder on January
4, 1971. The plaintiff filed his bill in equity on December 31, 1970,
seeking specific performance of the agreement and other relief, but, without waiving his rights under the agreement, submitted a bid to the defendant in the amount of $35,155, and obtained title to the property for
that price during the pendency of this suit. The decree appealed from
declared the defendant indebted to the plaintiff for the difference between
that price and the contract price of $32,500, with interest from December
31, 1970.

We are uncertain whether the thrust of the defendant's argument is
that his agreement with the plaintiff was not binding upon him or that
a condition to which his obligation thereunder was subject was not fulfilled. Under either interpretation the argument is without merit.

1. Under the first of these interpretations, the defendant is contending that because he was under a duty to obtain the highest possible price
for the property, he was excused from performing the agreement when a
higher offer than the plaintiff's was received. The first of these propositions is unquestionably true, Newhall, Settlement of Estates (4th ed.)
§ 120. But the second proposition does not inevitably follow from it.
The fiduciary duty of an executor or administrator is separate and distinct
from the contractual duty he may incur when he enters into agreements
with third persons. The first is owed to and enforceable by the beneficiaries of the estate, while the second is owed to and enforceable by a
stranger to the estate. And, with a few exceptions not here material
(see Wilder Grain Co. v. Felker, 296 Mass. 177, 5 N.E.2d 207 [1936], and
cased cited), an executor or administrator is liable on contracts he makes
for the benefit of the estate, if at all, individually and not in his representative capacity. [Citations omitted.] Thus, the two types of duties
are enforceable *by* different persons and, in the eyes of the law, *against*
different persons. See Eaton v. Walker, 244 Mass. 23, 30–32, 138 N.E.
798 (1923). The executor or administrator, of course, is entitled to reim-

bursement for expenses reasonably and necessarily incurred for the benefit of the estate. Tomlinson v. Flanagan, supra, 287 Mass. at 45, 190 N.E. 785. But whether he can obtain such reimbursement is a question to be answered by the Probate Court in the settlement of his account, a separate proceeding which is not before us (Luscomb v. Ballard, supra), and as to which we make no comment (O'Brien v. Dwight, 363 Mass. 256, 294 N.E.2d 363 [1973]).

That the contracts of an executor or administrator are enforceable in an action at law, however improvident they may be from the standpoint of the estate, is well settled by the cases cited in the preceding paragraph. It has been said that personal liability attaches even where the fiduciary entering into such a contract lacks authority to perform it in accordance with its terms. Dresel v. Jordan, 104 Mass. 407, 414 (1870). Additionally, where he has authority to sell a decedent's real property (contrast Dresel v. Jordan, supra), has entered into a contract to do so (compare Weinstein v. Green, 347 Mass. 580, 199 N.E.2d 310 [1964]), and his obligation thereunder has become unconditional (contrast Grennan v. Pierce, 229 Mass. 292, 293–294, 118 N.E. 301 [1918]), the contract may well be specifically enforceable against him. See Justice v. Soderlund, 225 Mass. 320, 322–324, 114 N.E. 623 (1916); O'Neill v. Niccolls, 324 Mass. 382, 384–385, 86 N.E.2d 522 (1949). We need not decide whether the plaintiff could have obtained a decree ordering the defendant to convey the property, however, as no such decree was necessary. Having already acquired title to the property, the plaintiff received by the decree what amounts to nothing more than money damages in the nature of a refund of the excess of the price he paid over the price stipulated in the agreement— which he could just as well have recovered in an action at law.

It has been suggested that an executor or administrator can escape such personal liability to third persons by an agreement exempting himself therefrom. Anglo-American Direct Tea Trading Co. v. Seward, 294 Mass. 349, 351, 2 N.E.2d 448 (1936). Reilly v. Whiting, 332 Mass. 745, 746–747, 127 N.E.2d 567 (1955). But the agreement in the present case contains no provision purporting to grant such an exemption. The fact that the defendant is identified in the opening clause of the agreement as "Executor u/w/o L. Francis F. Knowles" and that his signature is followed by the abbreviation "Execr." is insufficient to protect him against personal liability. Reilly v. Whiting, supra; Marsh v. Drowne, 307 N.E.2d 595 (1974). Nor is it of any consequence that the defendant may have understood the agreement as affording him such protection, especially where as here, he was its draftsman. No such mistake of law on the defendant's part can free him from liability. Scirpo v. McMillan, 355 Mass. 657, 660, 247 N.E.2d 368 (1969). Rather, his liability is governed by "[t]he general rule * * * that * * * one who signs a written agreement is bound by its terms whether he reads and understands it or not * * *". Spritz v. Lishner, 355 Mass. 162, 164, 243 N.E.2d 163, 164 (1969).

2. If the defendant's argument is interpreted as one that his obligation under the agreement was conditional upon his not receiving a

higher offer for the property, it must also fail. There was no evidence of any antecedent understanding between the parties in this regard. There was nothing in the agreement itself expressly relieving the defendant of liability upon receipt of a higher offer. The defendant seems to argue, however, that the provision making his obligation conditional upon obtaining a license from the Probate Court impliedly had this effect.

[The court rejected defendant's argument.]

3. We note that the defendant is characterized in the pleadings and the decree of the Superior Court as "executor". For the reasons previously stated he is properly before the Superior Court only as an individual, and we treat the bill as having been brought against him in that capacity, the word "executor" being surplusage. See Newhall, Settlement of Estates (4th ed.) § 254. Since the identification of the defendant in the decree ("as he is the Executor of the Will of L. Francis F. Knowles") might be susceptible of misinterpretation, the decree is to be modified by striking the quoted words therefrom.

*   *   *

The decree as modified is affirmed.

So ordered.

<h2 style="text-align:center">VANCE v. ESTATE OF MYERS</h2>
Supreme Court of Alaska, 1972.
494 P.2d 816.

CONNOR, Justice. The central question in this case concerns the liability of an estate for the torts of a trustee, executor, or administrator.

Appellant brought a tort action against the administrator of the appellee's estate. The action was filed shortly before the superior court discharged the administrator, thus terminating the administration of the estate. Appellant moved to set aside the decree of discharge and reinstate the administrator until the tort action could be concluded. Appellant's motion was denied. The issue on appeal is whether the court erred in refusing to set aside its decree of discharge.

Charles O. Myers died in Fairbanks, Alaska, on May 3, 1969. Shortly thereafter Howard E. Holbert was appointed administrator of the estate. By court order Holbert was allowed to operate the business owned by the decedent, Chuck's Corner Bar, in Nenana, Alaska.

On June 1, 1970, Holbert filed a petition for settling final account, distribution and discharge. In an order of July 16, 1970, the court approved the accounting and found that the administrator should be discharged, after paying expenses and making distribution of the estate.

The final distribution, leaving no funds of the estate in the hands of Holbert, was accomplished on August 20, 1970. On August 31, 1970, a request was made by the sole beneficiary of the estate that the administrator be discharged. This request included a statement of satisfaction with the disbursements made by the administrator. On September 22,

1970, the administrator submitted a second supplement to his final accounting and petitioned for discharge.   This was granted by order of the superior court on September 25, 1970.

On August 31, 1970, the appellant filed suit against several persons, including Holbert as administrator of the estate of Myers.   The complaint alleges that appellant's husband, for whom she is suing as guardian ad litem, was physically injured in an altercation in Chuck's Corner Bar on June 5, 1970.   It is alleged that the injuries resulted, in part, from the actions of the administrator and an employee of the administrator in that they served drinks to John Vance, when Vance was already intoxicated. The complaint further alleges that this rendered Vance incapable of caring for his own safety, that the employee assisted in dragging Vance to the street outside the bar after Vance had been beaten by another person in the bar, and that the employee failed to protect Vance from being beaten in the bar while Vance was in a helpless condition.   An amended complaint, stipulated by the parties as part of the record, but as yet unfiled, also asserts that Holbert was negligent in failing to obtain insurance covering the operation of the bar.

Holbert was served with the complaint on September 6, 1970.   A copy of the complaint was sent to the probate master on September 14, 1970.   The superior court was aware of the pending tort action at the time it granted the discharge.

Appellant argues that the estate should not have been closed and the administrator discharged while a tort action was pending against it, relying upon Dunn v. Lindsey, 68 N.M. 288, 361 P.2d 328 (1961).   But that case is quite distinguishable.   There the cause of action was based upon the conduct of the decedent himself, not that of the executor.   In the present case the claim relates entirely to the alleged negligence of the administrator in his operation and management of the assets of the estate. We must consider, therefore, whether those assets can be subjected directly to liability for the alleged torts of the administrator.   Preliminarily it should be observed that in the area we are treating no distinction exists between a decedent's estate and a trust estate.

Under the traditional rule a trustee, executor, or administrator was normally liable for torts committed by him or his servants in the administration of the trust or estate.   But such torts did not result in the imposition of direct liability upon the assets of the trust or estate.   Kirchner v. Muller, 280 N.Y. 23, 19 N.E.2d 665 (1939); Brown v. Guaranty Estates Corp., 239 N.C. 595, 80 S.E.2d 645 (1954); Barnett v. Schumacher, 453 S.W.2d 934 (Mo.1970); A. Scott, "Liabilities Incurred in the Administration of Trusts," 28 Harv.L.Rev. 725 (1915).   The orthodox view, still adhered to in a great number of jurisdictions, is that the person to whom the trustee has incurred liability in the administration of the trust must bring an action against the trustee personally, but not in his representative capacity.   The claimant may not reach the trust estate directly and apply it to the satisfaction of his claim.

The personal liability of the trustee or executor for torts of his agents is now generally qualified, however, by allowing the executor or trustee to obtain reimbursement from the assets of the estate when he is personally without fault. Restatement 2d, Trusts, § 247. If the claim against the trustee is uncollectible, it is generally recognized that the plaintiff may then reach the trust assets to the extent of the trustee's right to reimbursement. Restatement 2d, Trusts, § 268; H. Stone, "A Theory of Liability of Trust Estates for the Contracts and Torts of the Trustee," 22 Column.L.Rev. 527 (1922). In some jurisdictions, when the trustee's right to reimbursement is clear, the courts have allowed suit against the trustee in his representative capacity, thus avoiding circuity of action. Ewing v. Wm. L. Foley, Inc., 115 Tex. 222, 280 S.W. 499 (1926); Dobbs v. Noble, 55 Ga.App. 201, 189 S.E. 694 (1937); Smith v. Coleman, 100 Fla. 1707, 132 So. 198 (1931).

One of the original principles underlying the basic rule was that the trustee had an obligation to the trust beneficiaries to manage the estate without fault. Trust property should not be impaired or dissipated through wrongdoing of the trustee. This is, of course, a sound principle where the trustee acts outside the scope of his authority. It evolved at a time when the administration of trusts and estates was relatively passive and seldom required active management of a business enterprise. In much of the earlier case law the courts seem to be concerned exclusively with protecting the estate and the beneficiaries from the acts of reckless and improvident fiduciaries. Parmenter v. Barstow, 22 R.I. 245, 47 A. 365 (1900); Birdsong v. Jones, 222 Mo.App. 768, 8 S.W.2d 98 (1928). Little thought seems to have been given to the plight of the tort victim for harms done to him by the operation of a business enterprise.

Where the trustee's wrongful acts or omissions occur within the general scope of his authority to manage trust assets, and more particularly when the trustee himself has no appreciable assets, the impact of the traditional rule has been perceived as unjust. For this reason the courts have sought mechanisms, described above, by which the claimants in these circumstances could ultimately reach the assets of the estate. Many of the resulting decisions represent only a partial solution to the problem. Circuity of action is still often required, suit being filed first against the trustee, and only when collection against the trustee has been exhausted and proved futile is enforcement allowed against the estate directly. Kirchner v. Muller, supra; Schmidt v. Kellner, 307 Ill. 331, 138 N.E. 604 (1923). Even that procedure assumes that the trustee has a right to be exonerated out of the estate for the liability he has incurred, which is not always the case even when the trustee's tort was committed within the scope of his authority. Reimbursement may be denied to the trustee when he is personally at fault.

* * *

The traditional rule and its exceptions have been criticized by recognized scholars and jurists as being inadequate and unfair to the tort creditor. Dean, later Chief Justice, Harlan Fiske Stone pointed out fifty years ago in a salient law review article that the traditional rule was premised upon theories which were untenable. The trustee's right to indemnity should not be the measure of the plaintiff's rights against the assets of the trust for this leads to uneven results based solely upon the criterion of whether the trustee was or was not personally at fault. The true reason for reaching the assets of the estate should be the policy of casting the economic loss resulting from the trustee's tort upon the estate, rather than upon the tort victim. This would bring the law of trust liability into harmony with the modern doctrine that an economic enterprise should bear the burden of the losses caused by it, including actionable personal injuries which result from its operations. H. Stone, op. cit., 542–545. To the same effect are the penetrating analyses and conclusions found in C. Fulda & W. Pond, "Tort Liability of Trust Estates," 41 Colum.L.Rev. 1332 (1941).

In 1937 the Commissioners on Uniform State Laws proffered one solution to the problem in the Uniform Trusts Act. Section 14 of that act provides that the trustee may be sued in his representative capacity and collection may be had directly from the trust assets if "the tort was a common incident of the kind of business activity in which the trustee or his predecessor was properly engaged for the trust." This provision has been adopted in several states. U.L.A., Uniform Trusts Act (1957). But it is not necessary that a statute be enacted in order to bring this standard into being. The basic rule was the product of common law decision. It can be altered in the same manner.

One of the current reasons advanced for perpetuating the traditional rule is that if the tort claimant is allowed to sue the trustee in his representative capacity, the beneficiaries may not be adequately represented. That is, a conflict can exist between the trustee as an individual and the trustee in his official capacity, for often he will be named a party defendant in both those capacities. Johnston v. Long, 30 Cal.2d 54, 181 P.2d 645 (1947). But this problem can be minimized by the appointment of a special representative to protect the interests of the estate and beneficiaries when such a conflict between the estate and the fiduciary appears. In re Estate of Gregory, 487 P.2d 59, 63 (Alaska 1971).

Other courts have held that the trustee may be sued in his representative capacity in cases such as the one before us. Miller v. Smythe, 92 Ga. 154, 18 S.E. 46 (1893); Smith v. Coleman, 100 Fla. 1707, 132 So. 198 (1931); Carey v. Squire, 63 Ohio App. 476, 27 N.E.2d 175 (1939). We are convinced this is the right result. It should be recognized that in respect to tort liability a trustee acting within the general scope of his authority can subject the estate to liability, in the same manner as could an agent acting on behalf of an ordinary principal. That the estate lacks legal personality is true. But that factor should not be a roadblock to achieving realistic justice. See commentary, Restatement 2d, Trusts, § 271A, comment a.–c. at 23.

We hold that an administrator, executor, or trustee may be sued in his representative capacity, and collection may be had from the trust assets, for a tort committed in the course of administration, if it is determined by the court that the tort was a common incident of the kind of business activity in which the administrator, executor, or trustee was properly engaged on behalf of the estate. It follows that appellant's action against appellee was proper.

* * *

We must reverse the denial of appellant's motion to set aside the decree of discharge and to reinstate the administrator until the tort action can be concluded, and we must remand for proceedings consistent with this opinion.

Reversed.

Notes

1. As both the principal cases make clear, most courts still verbally concur in the rule that claimants, whether their claims are founded in tort or contract, must sue the executor, administrator, guardian, or trustee in their personal capacities rather than as fiduciary (in which case the action would lie directly against the estate or trust). 3 Scott on Trusts §§ 261 through 279 (3d ed. 1967). The principle is based on the refusal of the common law courts to recognize the existence of the trust, but courts have argued that modern policy justifies its continuation. In Johnston v. Long, 30 Cal.2d 54, 63–64, 181 P.2d 645, 650–651 (1947) the court said:

> Moreover, even if it be assumed possible by some procedure to hold the estate directly liable for the torts of employees without any right against the executor personally, where the executor is not personally at fault, there are practical objections to such a procedure. Under the existing system of administration such a procedure would not afford the heirs adequate protection. The only method available for reaching the assets of the estate is an action against the executor in his representative capacity. * * * If the plaintiff could recover directly from the estate in an action against the executor in his representative capacity, the heirs would have no assurance that the question of the personal fault of the executor would be properly tried. It would not be to the interest of either the plaintiff, who would be attempting to recover out of the assets of the estate, or the defendant, whose interest as an individual and as an executor would be in conflict (see Kirchner v. Muller, 280 N.Y. 23, 28, 19 N.E.2d 665, 127 A.L.R. 681), to show personal fault on the part of the executor. Under the general rule that the executor is personally liable for the torts committed by him or his agents in the course of administration, the plaintiff may recover a judgment against the executor personally and the question of the executor's fault is determined in the probate court, where the interest of the heirs may properly be protected.

The rule has its critics. Johnston, Developments in Contract Liability of Trusts and Trustees, 41 N.Y.U.L.Rev. 483 (1966); Stone, A Theory of Liability of Trust Estates for the Contracts and Torts of the Trustee, 22 Colum.L.Rev. 527 (1922).

2. Professor Scott suggests that the modern tendency is to make the trust estate responsible for contracts and torts incurred during the administration and describes four situations in which the courts have allowed a third party claimant to bring a direct action against the trust. 3 Scott on Trusts §§ 267–271 A. 3 (3d ed. 1967):

(a) If the trustee is insolvent or is absent from the state, the third party may, through a bill in equity, succeed to the trustee's right of exoneration (i.e., indemnity) out of the trust assets. Any defenses which the trust has against the trustee will be available against the third party who, under this procedure, is proceeding in the place of the trustee. Scott § 268.

(b) When a third party has conferred a benefit on the estate (either through a contract or as a result of a tort), such person has been allowed equitable relief against the estate for the value of the benefit conferred. The general theory of the action is unjust enrichment. Scott § 269.

(c) Some cases indicate that the third party may have a direct action where the testator has indicated in his will that the estate is to bear the liability. The theory here is not based on subrogation to the fiduciary's rights of reimbursement. Thus the action will lie even though the fiduciary is in default to the estate. Scott § 270.

(d) The cases generally give effect to a provision in a contract that the fiduciary is to be liable in his representative capacity and not personally. Scott § 271.

3. The Uniform Probate Code continues in the tradition of the Uniform Trusts Act (quoted in the *Vance* case, supra) and makes the estate initially responsible for torts and contracts. Section 3–808 reads:

(a) Unless otherwise provided in the contract, a personal representative is not individually liable on a contract properly entered into in his fiduciary capacity in the course of administration of the estate unless he fails to reveal his representative capacity and identify the estate in the contract.

(b) A personal representative is individually liable for obligations arising from ownership or control of the estate or for torts committed in the course of administration of the estate only if he is personally at fault.

(c) Claims based on contracts entered into by a personal representative in his fiduciary capacity, on obligations arising from ownership or control of the estate or on torts committed in the course of estate administration may be asserted against the estate by proceeding against the personal representative in his fiduciary capacity, whether or not the personal representative is individually liable therefor.

(d) Issues of liability as between the estate and the personal representative individually may be determined in a proceeding for accounting, surcharge or indemnification or other appropriate proceeding.

UPC § 7–306 adopts a similar rule for trustees. For a discussion of these provisions and a comprehensive review of the law governing the liability for tort of the fiduciary and the estate, see Cook v. Holland, 575 S.W.2d 468 (Ky. App.1978).

4. Decedents' contracts generally are held to survive their deaths unless they involve a type of personal service that can only be performed by the promisor. Compare In re Estate of Spann, 257 Ark. 857, 520 S.W.2d 286 (1975) (executor must employ necessary farm help to complete a large contract for the sale of cotton) with Farnon v. Cole, 259 Cal.App.2d 855, 66 Cal.Rptr. 673 (1968) (contract with the popular singer, Nat King Cole, terminated by his death) and Kowal v. Sportswear by Revere, Inc., 351 Mass. 541, 222 N.E.2d 778 (1967) (contract with a salesman personal and did not survive his death).

5. Assume that decedent, when alive, was a contractor by trade and at the time of his death had a number of outstanding contracts for the construction of

buildings. His executor faces a difficult dilemma. If he breaches the contracts and allows the estate to be held liable for damages he may find himself held surchargeable for failure to protect the assets of the estate. If on the other hand he completes the contracts, he will be personally liable for the labor and material expenses and may find the estate insufficient to reimburse him. There is authority both ways on whether the executor's initial responsibility is to complete the contract. Compare Exchange National Bank v. Betts' Estate, 103 Kan. 807, 176 P. 660, 3 A.L.R. 1604 (1918), with In re Burke's Estate, 198 Cal. 163, 244 P. 340, 44 A.L.R. 1341 (1926) and Didier v. American Casualty Co., 261 Cal.App.2d 742, 68 Cal.Rptr. 217 (1968).

Personal representatives breach their duty to liquidate the estate if they carry on the decedent's business for a time longer than reasonably necessary to make an orderly disposition of the asset. The will or a court order may authorize a continuation for a longer period. It may be of significance to people who extend credit to an unincorporated business whether or not the executor is in breach. If the executor has the authority to continue the business, business debts may be classified as expenses of administration and given a top priority. If executors are in breach, creditors may have to look to them personally for payment. Comment, Continuation of a Decedent's Business: Rights of Subsequent Creditors, 35 Va.L.Rev. 358 (1949). Executors must, however, preserve the value of decedent's business during the period of administration by actively supervising its management. See e.g., Estate of Baldwin, 442 A.2d 529 (Me. 1982) (corporate executor held surchargeable for failure to oversee operation of decedent's general store).

SECTION FIVE. THE FIDUCIARY AND THE BENEFICIARIES

A. THE SUPERVISORY ROLE OF THE COURT

For fiduciaries, the principal threat of liability does not come from the outside world, the occasional third person who either through tort or contract acquires a claim against the trust or the estate. Their concern is with the beneficiaries. Accordingly, the focus shifts to problems of internal management and to the nature of the fiduciary's obligation to the beneficiaries. [The term "fiduciary" includes the executor (and administrator), the trustee and the guardian.] Their functions and powers differ, and therefore the imposition of liability may vary depending upon the capacity in which the fiduciary is serving, but the basic fiduciary duties governing the use and management by one person of property in which some other person has rights of beneficial enjoyment remains constant throughout. Most of the cases which follow involve trustees. The principles discussed therein are for the most part, however, applicable to all fiduciaries.

ESTATE OF STILLMAN

Surrogate's Court, New York County, 1980.
107 Misc.2d 102, 433 N.Y.S.2d 701.

MILLARD L. MIDONICK, J.

The central issue in this proceeding is this: at what point does an "absolute and uncontrolled" discretion of trustees to withhold invasion of principal become an unreasonable abuse of that discretion?

The petitioners here, Guy Stillman and Dr. James Stillman, are grandsons of the testator James Stillman. They are income beneficiaries of two trusts under article SEVENTH of the will of the testator. Each of them complains of the failure on the part of the trustees* of their respective trusts to invade principal requested in 1977, particularly for $145,000 requested by Guy Stillman and $150,000 requested by Dr. James Stillman.

Whatever interest the six children of Guy Stillman and the six children of Dr. James Stillman may have as remaindermen, they have been cited, and they have defaulted to the extent of the issues involved before me now. A contingent remainderman appears by counsel, who approves of the accounting in all respects and supports the trustees as not having abused their discretion to withhold principal invasions and as not having been imprudent in investment policies.

The testator James Stillman died in 1918 leaving one third of his residuary estate to his son, James A. Stillman, for his life, and provided that upon his death, which occurred in 1944, his issue should become income beneficiaries of equal shares of James A. Stillman's trust. James A. Stillman's trust commenced with a fund of approximately $9,000,000 in value in 1918. At the time of his death in 1944, this trust was split into four separate trusts as the will provided, for his four children, three grandsons and a granddaughter. Each of these four trusts was funded in 1944 with the amount of about $2,000,000. Each of the two trusts for the two complaining grandsons before me now is valued at approximately $8,500,000. (In 1977 Guy Stillman's trust approximated $8,370,000 and Dr. James Stillman's trust approximated $8,670,000.) From these, the two grandsons, petitioners, have derived income in excess of $300,000 annually in 1977 and in 1979 of approximately $425,000 annually, from each of their respective trusts.

Also in issue is the objection by the same two income beneficiaries, to the trustees' account in respect to what proportion of each of these trusts should be devoted to income tax-free investments. Approximately one third of the principal of the trusts has been invested by this time in tax-exempt income-producing securities, which these beneficiaries complain is inadequate in proportion to the entire corpus. The income beneficiaries' evidence places the tax-exempt income close to 20% of the total income. After deliberation, the court hereby rules favorably to the trustees whose judgment cannot be found to be improvident with respect to investment policies under the circumstances of this particular case. Essentially, the trustees have convinced the court that they have been fair to both the income beneficiaries with respect to the amount and character of the income, including the proportion which is tax exempt, and they have been equally fair to the presumptive remaindermen and the contingent remaindermen who are more interested in the preservation and appreciation of the principal than in the size of the income.

---

* [The trustees are not identified nor described in the reports other than the reference in the opinion to one of them as "an important banking institution." Eds.]

* * *

With respect to the most vigorously contested issue in this proceeding, we return now to the problem whether the trustees have acted correctly in refusing to invade principal of Guy Stillman's trust to the extent of the $145,000 last requested of them by him and to invade principal of Dr. James Stillman's trust to the extent of the $150,000 last requested of them by him.

In order to frame the problem, we turn to the invasion article of the will, paragraph TENTH, which reads in its entirety:

"I.   Upon any grandson of mine attaining the age of twenty-five years, during the continuance of a Trust hereunder for his benefit, I authorize and empower my said Trustees, if, in their absolute and uncontrolled discretion, they deem it advisable to do so, to convey, transfer and pay over to such grandson, out of the principal of the Trust, held for his benefit, property of the reasonable value, in the judgment of my said Trustees, of one-fifth, or of any less part, of the share so held for him.

"II.   Upon any grandson of mine attaining the age of thirty years, during the continuance of a Trust hereunder for his benefit, I authorize and empower my said Trustees, if, in their absolute and uncontrolled discretion, they deem it advisable to do so, to convey, transfer and pay over to such grandson, out of the principal of the Trust, held for his benefit, property of the reasonable value, in the judgment of my said Trustees, of two-fifths, or of any less part, of the share so held for him.

"III.   Upon any grandson of mine attaining the age of thirty-five years, during the continuance of a Trust hereunder for his benefit, I authorize and empower my said Trustees if, in their absolute and uncontrolled discretion, they deem it advisable to do so, to convey, transfer and pay over to such grandson, out of the principal of the Trust held for his benefit, property of the reasonable value, in the judgment of my said Trustees, of one-fifth, or of any less part, of the share so held for him.

"IV.   Upon any grandson of mine attaining the age of forty years, during the continuance of a Trust hereunder for his benefit, I authorize and empower my said Trustees if, in their absolute and uncontrolled discretion, they deem it advisable to do so, to convey, transfer and pay over to such grandson, the whole or any part of the remainder of the principal of the Trust held for his benefit."

The paramount consideration resolves itself to the basic intention of the testator concerning invasions and whether the trustees have deviated from the testator's plan.   (Matter of Flyer, 23 N.Y.2d 579, 584, 297 N.Y.S.2d 956, 245 N.E.2d 718; cf. Matter of Fabbri, 2 N.Y.2d 236, 240, 159 N.Y.S.2d 184, 140 N.E.2d 269).   The question here is whether the above language when read together with the entire instrument evidenced any condition for the invasion, such as need, or whether invasion was unconditional and equal to the right of petitioners to principal upon attaining various ages, or whether the trustees' "absolute and uncontrolled discretion" was intended by the testator to be based upon considerations neither of maturity of the life beneficiaries alone, nor of need alone, but upon those and other additional circumstances which the trustees have unreasonably disregarded.

In the case at bar, principal was to be disbursed at ages 25, 30, 35 and 40, i.e., ages of maturity, if in their "absolute and uncontrolled discretion, they deem it advisable to do so". These two grandsons have now attained the age of 62 in the case of Guy Stillman and of 76 in the case of Dr. James Stillman. Despite their advanced ages and obvious maturity, Dr. James Stillman has never received any principal of his $8,500,000 trust and Guy Stillman has received only $230,000 in 1974 of his $8,500,000 trust.

Upon receiving requests for invasion by each of these grandsons of the testator, the trustees used as their criterion for decision a relatively restrictive standard as the basis on which to measure and consider the purposes for which each grandson wished to have this principal.

In 1974, Guy Stillman advised that he wished to buy land adjoining a plantation he owns in Hawaii in order to profit from sugar cane farming. The trustees proceeded to employ independent business advisors who warned that a nearby sugar mill was about to close and that the business of sugar cane farming would not be profitable as a result. Guy Stillman responded that he could use a distant mill profitably. He also informed the trustees that in case it would not prove feasible to plant sugar cane, he could resort to a cattle-feeding crop. The trustees granted his request, and he used the $230,000 to acquire some but not all of the land specified, and to fund a farming project on his Hawaiian property. The nearby mill thereafter closed as he had been warned, and he found that he could not profitably transport any sugar cane as he had told the trustees he had intended to do. After 1974 when he resumed his efforts, now in dispute, for further invasion about 1977, the trustees discovered that his cash flow problem stemmed from his having planted macadamia nut trees on his Hawaiian land rather than following either of the plans he had outlined in 1974. Since those trees had not come to production, his low tax write off and high upkeep costs were compelling him in 1977 to convert his home in Scottsdale, Arizona, into a commercial enterprise and to build another home with more moderate upkeep problems; he planned to use the $145,000 that he was requesting in 1977 for this purpose.

The trustees rejected the request for $145,000 in 1977 on the ground that Guy Stillman was able to manage without this money by using his own funds and by mortgage borrowing, and although this is disputed, perhaps on the further ground that he had shown fallible business judgment in respect to the use of the previous invasion money.

Similar criteria were used to reject Dr. James Stillman's request for $150,000 since the trustees found on the basis of net worth, his income tax returns, and his own assertions, that he could manage the conversion of his beach house in Texas into commercial purposes by using his own funds and by obtaining mortgage loans.

Apparently, no real consideration was given by the trustees to the essential plan of the testator to be derived from the terms of his will probated in 1918. [Those purposes stand out quite clearly and the court finds that the intent of the testator to have been different from the standards that the trustees have been using in considering invasion.] The purpose that the testator had in mind for his grandsons were those of a careful testator intending to protect his then immature grandsons (Guy was then *en ventre sa mere,* as yet unborn; James was then about 14) from creditors of every kind.   As the years went by, the taxing authorities became one kind of potential creditor, perhaps the most depleting of all. This typical invasion language at ages 25, 30, 35 and 40, emphasizing uncontrolled and absolute discretion on the part of the trustees, constitutes more an urging of the trustees to invade than a restraint against invasion except for limited protective purposes.   This is especially the case where a series of ages is set forth in the will for permitted partial cumulative distributions at which times the trustees are enabled to dispose to grandsons of an entire estate in stages culminating at age 40.

* * *

It would be therefore a matter of questionable judgment for these trustees or income beneficiaries to extract excessive amounts of principal, because upon the deaths of these income beneficiaries, their estates will be subject to estate tax on such principal whereas no estate tax will be due on the principal if the respective trust continues to hold the principal. Apparently, the income beneficiaries are well aware of this problem because they have been quite modest in their requests for invasion, and their personal net worth is relatively modest compared to each trust's value of about $8,500,000.   Indeed, Guy Stillman testified that his children are well cared for by his trust, but his personal net worth leaves his wife relatively less financially secure in the event of his death.   He gives this concern for his wife as one reason why he requests $145,000 of invasion.   He has gone ahead by other means, such as mortgaging, to build a home in Scottsdale, Arizona, without the help of the trustees' invasion and that home cost him approximately $360,000.   Presumably, the $145,000 he is asking for will reduce or eliminate such mortgage and increase his net worth by that relatively modest amount.   He points out that $145,000 constitutes less than 2% of the principal of his trust.

Similar considerations seem to apply to Dr. James Stillman's request which was also turned down by the trustees because of lack of need and because of his ability to finance his Texas beach house conversion into a commercial enterprise through other means.   Indeed, he informed the trustees that he could and would go ahead with such plan, even if the trustees would not help him by a contribution of $150,000.   He, in fact, so acted.

The two trustees who testified agree in effect that the amounts requested and the purposes of the requests were reasonable but were not needed and were not economically feasible to produce income.   The difficulty with the trustees' standards is that they do not conform with the plan set forth in the will of the grandfather of these income beneficiaries. It is quite clear that the trustees, one of which is an important banking institution, are applying standards to these grandsons almost as though they were lending them money which is bound to be returned as in a banking transaction, or as though these income beneficiaries are themselves fiduciaries who are required to be prudent and to avoid speculative investments.

Clearly there was no such condition to the invasion intended by the decedent.　Moreover, there is no duty on the part of Guy Stillman or Dr. James Stillman as envisioned by the will to be infallible in business transactions or to be prudent in the sense that they are protecting other people's money as fiduciaries.　It was their grandfather's intention that they be reasonably comfortable as well as free of creditors, including creditors in the form of unnecessary tax liabilities.　These two Stillman grandsons seem to have conducted their lives financially in such a way as to avoid such pitfalls and they have attained ages 62 and 76 with their relatively modest property intact.

* * *

For all of these reasons the court hereby finds that the trustees quite innocently have misconstrued the testator's will and therefore have abused so-called absolute and uncontrolled discretion to withhold principal in these two instances.　["If discretion is conferred upon the trustee in the exercise of a power, the court will not interfere unless the trustee in exercising or failing to exercise the power acts dishonestly, or with an improper even though not a dishonest motive, or fails to use his judgment, or acts beyond the bounds of a reasonable judgment."]　(Restatement, Trusts 2d, § 187, Comment *e;* * * *

The trustees have overprotected these beneficiaries contrary to the intention expressed by the testator in his will.　That intention is essentially that invasion of principal shall be favorably considered, after stated ages of grandsons, if such invasion will, on balance, enhance the quality of the lives of such grandsons, by benefiting them rather than creditors of any kind.

The fact that the trustees have thus abused their discretion, but in good faith, makes it clear that there is no need to remove these trustees. The fine record of the trustees in enhancing the equity of these trusts while earning substantial income, also persuades the court of the wisdom of retaining their services as fiduciaries.

* * *

* * * Nothing in this opinion, however, can be construed as compelling the trustees to comply with future invasion requests or demands, however moderate;　this decision rules only upon the current requests, leaving future requests for invasion still subject to the absolute and uncontrolled discretion of the majority of the trustees, short of their unreasonably abusing their testamentary mandate.

[In the concluding paragraphs, the Surrogate overruled the objections made by the two income beneficiaries to the amount of attorneys' fees, payment of them out of the trust, and payment to the trustees of their statutory commissions "because they have done a commendable job by way of investments and equity appreciation, and because they have in good faith pursued their decisional duties with respect to invasions even though they have been too restrictive in respect to the two current requests for principal invasions." Eds.]

Notes

1. The Restatement, Second, Trusts, puts the proposition this way:

§ 187. Control of Discretionary Powers

Where discretion is conferred upon the trustee with respect to the exercise of a power, its exercise is not subject to control by the court, except to prevent an abuse by the trustee of his discretion.

* * *

Comment:

d. *Factors in determining whether there is an abuse of discretion.* In determining the question whether the trustee is guilty of an abuse of discretion in exercising or failing to exercise a power, the following circumstances may be relevant: (1) the extent of the discretion conferred upon the trustee by the terms of the trust; (2) the purposes of the trust; (3) the nature of the power; (4) the existence or non-existence, the definiteness or indefiniteness, of an external standard by which the reasonableness of the trustee's conduct can be judged; (5) the motives of the trustee in exercising or refraining from exercising the power; (6) the existence or non-existence of an interest in the trustee conflicting with that of the beneficiaries.

2. Cases abound in which courts describe their function as policing, not usurping, the discretion of the trustee. Should Surrogate Midonick have set out the parameters within which the trustees were to exercise their discretion and then have remanded the matter back to them to set the actual dollar amount?

3. An invasion of principal means a reduction in the amount of corpus available to earn future income and to be distributed to the remaindermen at the termination of the trust. Even though the will authorizes the invasion, the trustee may be put to some hard choices by the competing claims of the several beneficiaries. In Emmert v. Old National Bank of Martinsburg, 162 W.Va. 48, 246 S.E.2d 236 (1978), one of two brothers, who were the income beneficiaries under a testamentary trust created by their father, petitioned the trustee to exercise its discretion under the will to invade the corpus in his behalf to an amount of $100,000. He argued that he was "necessitous", because he suffered from an incurable disease that made it impossible for him to work and had incurred debts of $48,000 for hospital and other medical bills. The trustee refused primarily on the grounds that it would have to make a similar distribution of $100,000 to the other brother, which would reduce the $230,000 corpus to $30,000 and thus greatly reduce the trust's capacity to earn future income and practically eliminate the interests of the contingent remaindermen. There was additional evidence that the petitioning brother had squandered monies that he had received from the trust in the past. The trial court's order sustaining the trustee's decision was reversed on appeal. The court directed that the interests of the non-petitioning brother be protected by dividing the corpus into two trusts and remanded the matter to the trial court to make an invasion subject to the following guidelines (246 S.E.2d at 244–45):

Finally, we come to the question of appellant's needs. Having determined that The Old National Bank of Martinsburg, as trustee, has abused its discretion in refusing to make principal distributions to Frank S. Emmert, we are remanding this case to the Circuit Court of Berkeley County for a hearing to determine the frequency and amount of principal distributions. The circuit court should consider all the evidence concerning the appellant's assets, liabilities, and available financial resources. It is the present needs of the appellant and not his past extravagances that should control the court's determination. At the same time, blind approval of appellant's demand for $100,000 should not be given because it is the amount necessary for comfort and support and not what the beneficiary desires that is controlling. The court can easily determine support but meaning must also be given to "comfort." The circuit court should keep in mind that comfort is not a "mere quantum sufficient to eat, to drink and to wear * * *" but that it denotes whatever is necessary to give security from want, including reasonable physical, mental and spiritual fulfillment. A meager distribution might not fulfill the testator's intentions, but at the same time one too large could cause detriment to the beneficiary himself. The court should weigh the possibility that too rapid a reduction of principal could leave the beneficiary in want later in life (contrary to the testator's intention that he be provided for) and at the same time consider the beneficiary's needs and his station in life. Furthermore the bank should consider the probable life expectancy of Frank Emmert and the maximum benefit which combined interest and principal can provide him during his remaining life in the event that he is totally destitute of other sources of income.

We hope the hearing fairly accommodates all the competing interests of existing and contingent beneficiaries, is faithful to the testator's intent, and is just under all the circumstances. We hope that it marks the end of protracted and expensive litigation in this case, but we cannot say that in the event of some extraordinary and unanticipated circumstances the appellant's needs may not change. In such event we hope the trustee will voluntarily exercise its discretion to increase the distributions if the appellant's needs are greater, and we hope the appellant will voluntarily accept a reduction in the principal if the circumstances warrant.

See also for the resolution of a similar problem, First National Bank of Beaumont v. Howard, 149 Tex. 130, 229 S.W.2d 781 (1950) (invasion of principal for need upheld as to one sister but denied as to second sister).

B. DEVIATION FROM THE TERMS OF THE INSTRUMENT

COLONIAL TRUST CO. v. BROWN

Supreme Court of Errors of Connecticut, 1926.
105 Conn. 261, 135 A. 555.

On a suit to determine the construction of the will, the parties agreed to a statement of facts which reads in part:

Robert K. Brown died in 1916, leaving a will made five months before in which, after making a few small bequests, he gave all his property to the plaintiff in trust, directing it to pay certain annuities, and providing for the distribution of the residue among the heirs of the blood of his father *per stirpes*. * * * His estate consisted principally of the two pieces of property referred to in the ninth paragraph of his will as the Exchange Place property and the Homestead.

The Exchange Place property was acquired by testator's father in 1848, and at his death in 1881, by the testator. It is located in the heart of the financial and retail business district of Waterbury, is as valuable as any land in the city, and most favorably adapted for buildings containing stores and offices. There is, and for a long time has been, upon it a group of several old buildings. They are costly to maintain, expenditures for this purpose during the last seven years absorbing more than fifty per cent. of the gross rentals. Their condition, arrangement and appearance are such that the lower floors are not desirable for use for retail stores and the upper floors are ill-adapted to commercial or business purposes. So long as the height of buildings upon the property is restricted to three stories, it cannot be improved so as to get the best income return and the restriction is likely to have a more serious effect in the future. Even if the properties were improved, the best income return cannot be secured, so long as leases can be given only for one year, and this restriction, too, is likely to have a more serious effect in the future; it in fact diminishes the ground floor rentals by at least twenty per cent., and about seventy per cent. of the gross income from the property is derived from these rentals. Tenants of the most desirable class cannot be secured for the property, and could not be, even if the properties were improved, unless leases for more than one year could be given. This reacts upon rental values and the character of the business done in the neighborhood and retards the normal development of the property in use and value. At the testator's death the property was assessed for taxation at $418,300, and in 1924, at $746,000, its fair market value being approximately $1,000,000. There is a mortgage upon it which amounted at his death to $181,500, but which has since been reduced by a payment of $6,000.

The Homestead property was in part acquired by the testator from his father in 1876 and in part purchased by him in 1889. The land is occupied by several dwelling-houses, which have been substantially unchanged since the testator acquired them, except that the use of one has had to be abandoned, and by a brick barn, which since the testator's death has been converted into an automobile service station and salesroom. The property cannot be improved, so long as the height of buildings upon it is restricted to three stories, or, if improved, cannot be rented so long as leases upon it are restricted to one year, so as to secure the best income return from it, and the effect of these restrictions is likely to be more serious in the future. This property was assessed for taxation at the testator's death in 1914 (sic) at $50,000, and in 1924 at $80,400, its market value now being approximately $100,000.

The effect which would be caused by the restrictions as to height of buildings and length of leases to be given, inserted in the will, was apparent when the testator executed it and thereafter until his death was known to him. The net income received from the two properties for the three years before the date of the will averaged $20,000. Since then, although the annuities provided in the will have been paid, and $6,000 has been applied on the mortgage, there has been an accumulation of excess income to such an extent that, with certain other funds added, the trustee, on December 31st, 1925, held personal property to the amount of $288,469.63.

MALTBIE, J.   *   *   *

We are asked to advise whether the provision in the fourth article, restricting leases of the property to one year and forbidding any promises of longer leases, and that in the eleventh article, directing that no new buildings placed upon the Exchange Place property and the Homestead shall exceed three stories in height, are binding upon the trustee. In Holmes v. Connecticut Trust & Safe Deposit Co., 92 Conn. 507, 514, 103 Atl. 640, 642, in holding invalid certain conditions attached to the enjoyment of a trust estate by the cestui que trust, as fraught with danger to the proper conduct of the marital relationship, we said:

> "As a general rule, a testator has the right to impose such conditions as he pleases upon a beneficiary as conditions precedent to the vesting of an estate in him, or to the enjoyment of a trust estate by him as cestui que trust. He may not, however, impose one that is uncertain, unlawful or opposed to public policy."

So it may be said of the directions and restrictions which a testator may impose upon the management of property which he places in a trust, that they are obligatory upon the trustee unless they are uncertain, unlawful or opposed to public policy. Lewin on Trusts (12th Ed.) 90. In the instant case, the length of time during which the testator directed that the property should remain in the trust and the complete uncertainty as to the individuals to whom it would ultimately go, preclude any thought of an intent on his part to forbid the cumbering of the property by long leases or the burdening of it with large buildings, lest the beneficiaries be embarrassed in the development of it along such lines as they might themselves prefer. The only other purpose which can reasonably be attributed to him is to compel the trustee to follow his own peculiar ideas as to the proper and advantageous way to manage such properties. That the restrictions are opposed to the interests of the beneficiaries of the trust, that they are imprudent and unwise, is made clear by the statement of agreed facts, but that is not all, for their effect is not confined to the beneficiaries. The Exchange Place property is located at a corner of the public square in the very center of the city of Waterbury, in the heart of the financial and retail business district, is as valuable as any land in the city, and is most favorably adapted for a large building containing stores and offices, and the Homestead is located in a region of changing character, so that its most available use cannot now be determined. To impress the restrictions in question upon these properties, as the statement of agreed facts makes clear, makes it impossible to obtain from them proper income return or to secure the most desirable and stable class of tenants, requires for the maintenance of the buildings a proportion of income greatly in excess of that usual in the case of such properties, and will be likely to preclude their proper development and natural use. The effect of such conditions cannot but react disadvantageously upon neighboring properties, and to continue them, as the testator intended, for perhaps seventy-five years or even more, would carry a serious threat against the proper growth and development of the parts of the city in which the lands in question are situated. The restrictions militate too strongly against the interests of the beneficiaries and the public welfare to be sustained, particularly when it is remembered that they are designed to benefit no one, and are harmful to all persons interested, and we hold them invalid as against public policy.   *   *   *

Notes

1. This case is unusual because the testator knew the probable effects of the restrictions he sought to impose. In most cases where courts allow deviation from the terms of the instrument, an unforeseen change of circumstances is found. The courts then reason that the testator would have authorized the deviation from the terms of the instrument if he could have foreseen the change of conditions. Matter of Pulitzer, 139 Misc. 575, 249 N.Y.S. 87 (Surr.Ct., N.Y. County 1931), affirmed 237 App.Div. 808, 260 N.Y.S. 975 (1st Dept. 1932). (Trustees released from prohibition in the will of Joseph Pulitzer against sale of New York newspaper following years of losses), affirmed 237 App.Div. 808, 260 N.Y.S. 975 (1932). In a number of cases, courts have been asked to remove a testator's direction against investing trust funds in common stocks on the grounds that prudent investment in equities was required in order to permit growth of principal to keep up with inflation. See e.g., In re Trusteeship Agreement with Mayo, infra, p. 709 (restriction removed); contra, Stanton v. Wells Fargo Bank, 150 Cal.App.2d 763, 310 P.2d 1010 (1957) (no emergency shown and thus restriction in will stands). Does an amendment in the tax laws constitute such a change of circumstances as to justify a modification of specific terms of the instrument? Compare Davison v. Duke University, 282 N.C. 676, 194 S.E.2d 761 (1973) (yes as to the investment power) and Givens v. Third National Bank in Nashville, 516 S.W.2d 356 (Tenn.1974) (no as to payments of undistributed income to the remaindermen).

2. The courts are particularly reluctant to authorize a deviation from the dispositive terms of the instrument. If the income beneficiary is in the normal course of events also to receive the principal some time in the future, the courts have sometimes allowed an anticipation of principal payments to meet particular needs of the beneficiary. The court will not authorize such an invasion in favor of a person other than the designated remainderman, at least unless all the other beneficiaries consent. Petition of Wolcott, 95 N.H. 23, 56 A.2d 641, 1 A.L.R.2d 1323 (1948); see 2 Scott on Trusts § 168 (3d ed. 1967).

C. THE FIDUCIARY'S DUTIES AND LIABILITY

Fiduciaries derive their powers to manage the property from the terms of the instrument, statutes, and principles which can be fairly implied from the purposes for which they are holding the property. In the exercise of those powers there are certain duties that they cannot violate without rendering themselves liable for any resulting loss. The traditional duties include: the duty to make no profit (except for their fees) and to take no personal advantage of their position (the duty of loyalty); not to delegate; to keep and render accounts; to exercise reasonable care and skill; to retain control of and preserve the property; to enforce claims; to keep the property earmarked and separate from their own and others' property; to make the property productive; and to deal impartially with the beneficiaries. 2 Scott on Trusts, §§ 169 through 185 (3d ed. 1967).

NILES, A CONTEMPORARY VIEW OF LIABILITY FOR BREACH OF TRUST
114 Trusts & Estates, 12 and 82 (1975) (at page 12).

There are two general trends observable and they seem to go in opposite directions. First there is a trend toward strict liability or accountability wherever a fiduciary has made an unauthorized profit out of the property which he has been entrusted to manage. He must yield up this profit even if he has not been guilty of a breach of trust, even if he has not been conscious of any fault, and even if he has not caused any damage to his principal. This trend is clearly recognizable not only in the law of trusts but is being extended to an ever increasing number of other fiduciary relationships.

The other trend is toward narrowing and ameliorating the law of strict liability where a trustee, who has acted without conscious fault, is asked to pay out of his own resources for a loss suffered by the trust estate or to compensate the estate for profits that might have been made. In this branch of the subject, while liability without fault is retained for breaches of special danger, the trend is toward limiting liability for compensatory damages to cases where there is proof of wrongdoing and of the casual [sic] relation between fault and injury.

There may be an incipient trend away from personal fault toward institutionalizing or socializing some of the risks inherent in trust management. If so, this trend is largely for the future. For the present the two trends to be considered are, first, toward taking the profit out of fiduciary management, and, second, toward restricting compensatory damages to the consequences of provable fault.

1. Duty of Loyalty

MATTER OF ROTHKO
Court of Appeals of New York, 1977.
43 N.Y.2d 305, 401 N.Y.S.2d 449, 372 N.E.2d 291.

Cooke, J.

Mark Rothko, an abstract expressionist painter whose works through the years gained for him an international reputation of greatness, died testate on February 25, 1970. The principal asset of his estate consisted of 798 paintings of tremendous value, and the dispute underlying this appeal involves the conduct of his three executors in their disposition of these works of art.   In sum, that conduct as portrayed in the record and sketched in the opinions was manifestly wrongful and indeed shocking.

Rothko's will was admitted to probate on April 27, 1970 and letters testamentary were issued to Bernard J. Reis, Theodoros Stamos and Morton Levine.   Hastily and within a period of only about three weeks and by virtue of two contracts each dated May 21, 1970, the executors dealt with all 798 paintings.

By a contract of sale, the estate executors agreed to sell to Marlborough AG., a Liechtenstein corporation (hereinafter MAG), 100 Rothko paintings as listed for $1,800,000, $200,000 to be paid on execution of the agreement and the balance of $1,600,000 in 12 equal interest-free installments over a 12-year period.   Under the second agreement, the executors consigned to Marlborough Gallery, Inc., a domestic corporation (hereinafter MNY), "approximately 700 paintings listed on a Schedule to be prepared", the consignee to be responsible for costs covering items such as insurance, storage, restoration and promotion.   By its provisos, MNY could sell up to 35 paintings a year from each of two groups, pre-1947 and post-1947, for 12 years at the best price obtainable but not less than the appraised estate value, and it would receive a 50% commission on each painting sold, except for a commission of 40% on those sold to or through other dealers.

Petitioner Kate Rothko, decedent's daughter and a person entitled to share in his estate by virtue of an election under EPTL 5–3.3, instituted this proceeding to remove the executors, to enjoin MNY and MAG from disposing of the paintings, to rescind the aforesaid agreements between the executors and said corporations, for a return of the paintings still in possession of those corporations, and for damages.   She was joined by the guardian of her brother Christopher Rothko, likewise interested in the estate, who answered by adopting the allegations of his sister's petition and by demanding the same relief.   The Attorney-General of the State, as the representative of the ultimate beneficiaries of the Mark Rothko Foundation, Inc., a charitable corporation and the residuary legatee under decedent's will, joined in requesting relief substantially similar to that prayed for by petitioner.   On June 26, 1972 the Surrogate issued a temporary restraining order and on September 26, 1972 a preliminary injunction enjoining MAG, MNY, and the three executors from selling or otherwise disposing of the paintings referred to in the agreements dated May 21, 1970, except for sales or dispositions made with court permission.   The Appellate Division modified the preliminary injunction order by increasing the amount of the bond and otherwise affirmed.   By a 1974 petition, the Attorney-General, on behalf of the ultimate charitable beneficiaries of the Mark Rothko Foundation, sought the punishment of MNY, MAG, Lloyd and Reis for contempt and other relief.

Following a nonjury trial covering 89 days and in a thorough opinion, the Surrogate found: that Reis was a director, secretary and treasurer of MNY, the consignee art gallery, in addition to being a coexecutor of the estate; that the testator had a 1969 *inter vivos* contract with MNY to sell Rothko's work at a commission of only 10% and whether that agreement survived testator's death was a problem that a fiduciary in a dual position could not have impartially faced; that Reis was in a position of serious conflict of interest with respect to the contracts of May 21, 1970 and that his dual role and planned purpose benefited the Marlborough interests to the detriment of the estate; that it was to the advantage of coexecutor Stamos as a "not-too-successful artist, financially", to curry favor with Marlborough and that the contract made by him with MNY within months after signing the estate contracts placed him in a position where his personal interests conflicted with those of the estate, especially leading to lax contract enforcement efforts by Stamos; that Stamos acted negligently and improvidently in view of his own knowledge of the conflict of interest of Reis; that the third coexecutor, Levine, while not acting in self-interest or with bad faith, nonetheless failed to exercise ordinary prudence in the performance of his assumed fiduciary obligations since he was aware of Reis' divided loyalty, believed that Stamos was also seeking personal advantage, possessed personal opinions as to the value of the paintings and yet followed the leadership of his coexecutors without investigation of essential facts or consultation with competent and disinterested appraisers, and that the business transactions of the two Marlborough corporations were admittedly controlled and directed by Francis K. Lloyd. It was concluded that the acts and failures of the three executors were clearly improper to such a substantial extent as to mandate their removal under SCPA 711 as estate fiduciaries. The Surrogate also found that MNY, MAG and Lloyd were guilty of contempt in shipping, disposing of and selling 57 paintings in violation of the temporary restraining order dated June 26, 1972 and of the injunction dated September 26, 1972; that the contracts for sale and consignment of paintings between the executors and MNY and MAG provided inadequate value to the estate, amounting to a lack of mutuality and fairness resulting from conflicts on the part of Reis and Stamos and improvidence on the part of all executors; that said contracts were voidable and were set aside by reason of violation of the duty of loyalty and improvidence of the executors, knowingly participated in and induced by MNY and MAG; that the fact that these agreements were voidable did not revive the 1969 *inter vivos* agreements since the parties by their conduct evinced an intent to abandon and abrogate these compacts. The Surrogate held that the present value at the time of trial of the paintings sold is the proper measure of damages as to MNY, MAG, Lloyd, Reis and Stamos. He imposed a civil fine of $3,332,000 upon MNY, MAG and Lloyd, same being the appreciated value at the time of trial of the 57 paintings sold in violation of the temporary restraining order and injunction. It was held that Levine* was liable for $6,464,880 in damages, as he was not in a dual position acting for his own interest and was thus liable only for the actual value of paintings sold MNY and MAG as of the dates of sale, and that

---

* Mr. Levine was at the time a professor and head of the anthropology department at Fordham University. Ed.

Reis, Stamos, MNY and MAG, apart from being jointly and severally liable for the same damages as Levine for negligence, were liable for the greater sum of $9,252,000 "as appreciation damages less amounts previously paid to the estate with regard to sales of paintings." The cross petition of the Attorney-General to reopen the record for submission of newly discovered documentary evidence was denied. The liabilities were held to be congruent so that payment of the highest sum would satisfy all lesser liabilities including the civil fines and the liabilities for damages were to be reduced by payment of the fine levied or by return of any of the 57 paintings disposed of, the new fiduciary to have the option in the first instance to specify which paintings the fiduciary would accept.

The Appellate Division, in an opinion by Justice LANE, modified to the extent of deleting the option given the new fiduciary to specify which paintings he would accept. Except for this modification, the majority affirmed on the opinion of Surrogate MIDONICK, with additional comments. Among others, it was stated that the entire court agreed that executors Reis and Stamos had a conflict of interest and divided loyalty in view of their nexus to MNY and that a majority were in agreement with the Surrogate's assessment of liability as to executor Levine and his findings of liability against MNY, MAG and Lloyd. The majority agreed with the Surrogate's analysis awarding "appreciation damages" and found further support for his rationale in Menzel v. List, 24 N.Y.2d 91, 298 N.Y.S.2d 979, 246 N.E.2d 742.

* * *

In seeking a reversal, it is urged that an improper legal standard was applied in voiding the estate contracts of May, 1970, that the "no further inquiry" rule applies only to self-dealing and that in case of a conflict of interest, absent self-dealing, a challenged transaction must be shown to be unfair. The subject of fairness of the contracts is intertwined with the issue of whether Reis and Stamos were guilty of conflicts of interest. Scott is quoted to the effect that "[a] trustee does not necessarily incur liability merely because he has an individual interest in the transaction * * * In Bullivant v. First Nat. Bank [246 Mass. 324, 141 N.E. 41] it was held that * * * the fact that the bank was also a creditor of the corporation did not make its assent invalid, *if it acted in good faith and the plan was fair*" (2 Scott, Trusts, § 170.24, p. 1384 [emphasis added]), and our attention has been called to the statement in Phelan v. Middle States Oil Corp., 220 F.2d 593, 603, 2 Cir., cert. den. sub nom. Cohen v. Glass, 349 U.S. 929, 75 S.Ct. 772, 99 L.Ed. 1260 that Judge Learned Hand found "no decisions that have applied [the no further inquiry rule] inflexibly to every occasion in which the fiduciary has been shown to have had a personal interest that might in fact have conflicted with his loyalty".

These contentions should be rejected. First, a review of the opinions of the Surrogate and the Appellate Division manifests that they did not rely solely on a "no further inquiry rule", and secondly, there is more than an adequate basis to conclude that the agreements between the Marlborough corporations and the estate were neither fair nor in the best interests of the estate.   This is demonstrated, for example, by the comments of the Surrogate concerning the commissions on the consignment of the 698 paintings (see 84 Misc.2d 830, 852–853, 379 N.Y.S.2d 923, 947–948) and those of the Appellate Division concerning the sale of the 100 paintings (see 56 A.D.2d, at pp. 501–502, 392 N.Y.S.2d, at pp. 872–873).   The opinions under review demonstrate that neither the Surrogate nor the Appellate Division set aside the contracts by merely applying the no further inquiry rule without regard to fairness.   Rather they determined, quite properly indeed, that these agreements were neither fair nor in the best interests of the estate.

To be sure, the assertions that there were no conflicts of interest on the part of Reis or Stamos indulge in sheer fantasy.   Besides being a director and officer of MNY, for which there was financial remuneration, however slight, Reis, as noted by the Surrogate, had different inducements to favor the Marlborough interests, including his own aggrandizement of status and financial advantage through sales of almost one million dollars for items from his own and his family's extensive private art collection by the Marlborough interests (see 84 Misc.2d, at pp. 843–844, 379 N.Y.S.2d at pp. 939–940).   Similarly, Stamos benefited as an artist under contract with Marlborough and, interestingly, Marlborough purchased a Stamos painting from a third party for $4,000 during the week in May, 1970 when the estate contract negotiations were pending (see 84 Misc.2d at p. 845, 379 N.Y.S.2d at p. 941).   The conflicts are manifest. Further, as noted in Bogert, Trusts and Trustees (2d ed.), "The duty of loyalty imposed on the fiduciary prevents him from accepting employment from a third party who is entering into a business transaction with the trust" (§ 543, subd. [S], p. 573).   "While he [a trustee] is administering the trust he must refrain from placing himself in a position where his personal interest or that of a third person does or may conflict with the interest of the beneficiaries" (Bogert, Trusts [Hornbook Series—5th ed.], p. 343).   Here, Reis was employed and Stamos benefited in a manner contemplated by Bogert (see, also, Meinhard v. Salmon, 249 N.Y. 458, 464, 466–467, 164 N.E.2d 545, 547–548; Schmidt v. Chambers, 265 Md. 9, 33–38, 288 A.2d 356).   In short, one must strain the law rather than follow it to reach the result suggested on behalf of Reis and Stamos.

Levine contends that, having acted prudently and upon the advice of counsel, a complete defense was established.   Suffice it to say, an executor who knows that his coexecutor is committing breaches of trust and not only fails to exert efforts directed towards prevention but accedes to them is legally accountable even though he was acting on the advice of counsel (Matter of Westerfield, 32 App.Div. 324, 344, 53 N.Y.S. 25, 39; 3 Scott, Trusts [3d ed.], § 201, p. 1657).   When confronted with the question of whether to enter into the Marlborough contracts, Levine was acting in a business capacity, not a legal one, in which he was required as an executor primarily to employ such diligence and prudence to the care and management of the estate assets and affairs as would prudent persons of discretion and intelligence (King v. Talbot, 40 N.Y. 76, 85–86), accented by "[n]ot honesty alone, but the punctilio of an honor the most sensitive"

(Meinhard v. Salmon, 249 N.Y. 458, 464, 164 N.E. 545, 546, supra). Alleged good faith on the part of a fiduciary forgetful of his duty is not enough (Wendt v. Fischer, 243 N.Y. 439, 443, 154 N.E. 303, 304). He could not close his eyes, remain passive or move with unconcern in the face of the obvious loss to be visited upon the estate by participation in those business arrangements and then shelter himself behind the claimed counsel of an attorney (see Matter of Niles, 113 N.Y. 547, 558, 21 N.E. 687, 689; Matter of Huntley, 13 Misc. 375, 380, 35 N.Y.S. 113, 116; 3 Warren's Heaton, Surrogates' Courts [6th ed.], § 217, subd. 3, par. [b]).

Further, there is no merit to the argument that MNY and MAG lacked notice of the breach of trust. The record amply supports the determination that they are chargeable with notice of the executors' breach of duty.

The measure of damages was the issue that divided the Appellate Division (see 56 A.D.2d, at p. 500, 392 N.Y.S.2d at p. 872). The contention of Reis, Stamos, MNY and MAG, that the award of appreciation damages was legally erroneous and impermissible, is based on a principle that an executor authorized to sell is not liable for an increase in value if the breach consists only in selling for a figure less than that for which the executor should have sold. For example, Scott states:

> "The beneficiaries are not entitled to the value of the property at the time of the decree if it was not the duty of the trustee to retain the property in the trust and the breach of trust consisted *merely* in selling the property for too low a price" (3 Scott, Trusts [3d ed.], § 208.3, p. 1687 [emphasis added]).

> "If the trustee is guilty of a breach of trust in selling trust property for an inadequate price, he is liable for the difference between the amount he should have received and the amount which he did receive. He is not liable, however, for any subsequent rise in value of the property sold". (Id., § 208.6, pp. 1689–1690.)

A recitation of similar import appears in Comment *d* under Restatement, Trusts 2d (§ 205): *"d.* Sale for less than value. If the trustee is authorized to sell trust property, but in breach of trust he sells it for less than he should receive, he is liable for the value of the property at the time of the sale less the amount which he received. If the breach of trust consists *only* in selling it for too little, he is not chargeable with the amount of any subsequent increase in value of the property under the rule stated in Clause (c), as he would be if he were not authorized to sell the property. See § 208." (Emphasis added.) However, employment of "merely" and "only" as limiting words suggests that where the breach consists of some misfeasance, other than solely for selling "for too low a price" or "for too little", appreciation damages may be appropriate. Under Scott (§ 208.3, pp. 1686–1687) and the Restatement (§ 208), the trustee may be held liable for appreciation damages if it was his or her duty to retain the property, the theory being that the beneficiaries are entitled to be placed in the same position they would have been in had the breach not consisted of a sale of property that should have been retained. The same rule should apply where the breach of trust consists of a serious conflict of interest—which is more than merely selling for too little.

The reason for allowing appreciation damages, where there is a duty to retain, and only date of sale damages, where there is authorization to sell, is policy oriented. If a trustee authorized to sell were subjected to a greater measure of damages he might be reluctant to sell (in which event he might run a risk if depreciation ensued). On the other hand, if there is a duty to retain and the trustee sells there is no policy reason to protect the trustee; he has not simply acted imprudently, he has violated an integral condition of the trust.

"If a trustee in breach of trust transfers trust property to a person who takes with notice of the breach of trust, and the transferee has disposed of the property * * * [i]t seems proper to charge him with the value at the time of the decree, since if it had not been for the breach of trust the property would still have been a part of the trust estate" (4 Scott, Trusts [3d ed.], § 291.2; see, also, United States v. Dunn, 268 U.S. 121, 132, 45 S.Ct. 451, 69 L.Ed. 876). This rule of law which applies to the transferees MNY and MAG also supports the imposition of appreciation damages against Reis and Stamos, since if the Marlborough corporations are liable for such damages either as purchaser or consignees with notice, from one in breach of trust, it is only logical to hold that said executors, as sellers and consignors, are liable also *pro tanto*.

Contrary to assertions of appellants and the dissenters at the Appellate Division, Menzel v. List, 24 N.Y.2d 91, 298 N.Y.S.2d 979, 246 N.E.2d 742, supra is authority for the allowance of appreciation damages. There, the damages involved a breach of warranty of title to a painting which at one time had been stolen from plaintiff and her husband and ultimately sold to defendant. Here, the executors, though authorized to sell, did not merely err in the amount they accepted but sold to one with whom Reis and Stamos had a self-interest. To make the injured party whole, in both instances the quantum of damages should be the same. In other words, since the paintings cannot be returned, the estate is therefore entitled to their value at the time of the decree, i.e., appreciation damages. These are not punitive damages in a true sense, rather they are damages intended to make the estate whole. Of course, as to Reis, Stamos, MNY and MAG, these damages might be considered by some to be exemplary in a sense, in that they serve as a warning to others (see Reynolds v. Pegler, 123 F.Supp. 36, 38, D.C., affd. 223 F.2d 429, 2 Cir., cert. den. 350 U.S. 846, 76 S.Ct. 80, 100 L.Ed. 754), but their true character is ascertained when viewed in the light of overriding policy considerations and in the realization that the sale and consignment were not merely sales below value but inherently wrongful transfers which should allow the owner to be made whole (see Menzel v. List, 24 N.Y.2d 91, 97, 298 N.Y.S.2d 979, 982, 246 N.E.2d 742, 744, supra; see, also, Simon v. Electrospace Corp., 28 N.Y.2d 136, 144, 320 N.Y.S.2d 225, 231, 269 N.E.2d 21, 25, supra).

The decree of the Surrogate imposed appreciation damages against Reis, Stamos, MNY and MAG in the amount of $7,339,464.72—computed as $9,252,000 (86 works on canvas at $90,000 each and 54 works on paper at $28,000 each) less the aggregate amounts paid the estate under the two rescinded agreements and interest. Appellants chose not to offer evidence of "present value" and the only proof furnished on the subject was that of the expert Heller whose appraisal as of January, 1974 (the month previous to that when trial commenced) on a painting-by-painting basis totaled $15,100,000. There was also testimony as to bona fide sales of other Rothkos between 1971 and 1974. Under the circumstances, it was impossible to appraise the value of the unreturned works of art with an absolute certainty and, so long as the figure arrived at had a reasonable basis of computation and was not merely speculative, possible or imaginary, the Surrogate had the right to resort to reasonable conjectures and probable estimates and to make the best approximation possible through the exercise of good judgment and common sense in arriving at that amount. * * * This is particularly so where the conduct of wrongdoers has rendered it difficult to ascertain the damages suffered with the precision otherwise possible (Story Parchment Co. v. Paterson Co., supra, 282 U.S. at p. 563, 51 S.Ct. 248; Eastman Co. v. Southern Photo Co., supra, 273 U.S. at p. 379, 47 S.Ct. 400). Significantly, the Surrogate's factual finding as to the present value of these unreturned paintings was affirmed by the Appellate Division and, since that finding had support in the record and was not legally erroneous, it should not now be subjected to our disturbance.

* * *

We have considered the other alleged errors urged by the parties, and find those arguments to be without merit. In short, we find no basis for disturbing the result reached below.

Accordingly, the order of the Appellate Division should be affirmed, with costs to the prevailing parties against appellants, and the question certified answered in the affirmative.

Chief Judge BREITEL and Judges JASEN, GABRIELLI, JONES, WACHTLER and FUCHSBERG concur.

Notes

1. The Restatement, Second, Trusts imposes liability even if there is no breach of trust:

§ 203. *Accountability for Profits in the Absence of a Breach of Trust*

The trustee is accountable for any profit made by him through or arising out of the administration of the trust, although the profit does not result from a breach of trust.

Comment:

a. *Scope of the rule.* If the trustee enters into a transaction in connection with the administration of the trust for the purpose of acquiring a profit for himself in violation of his duty of loyalty to the beneficiary, he commits a breach of trust under the rule stated in § 170, and is liable under the rule stated in § 206. Even if he enters into the transaction without intending to make a profit for himself and commits no breach of trust in so doing, nevertheless he is not permitted to retain the profit.

* * *

d. *Profit made through use of trustee's individual property.*　Even if the profit is made by the use of the trustee's individual property and he does not commit a breach of trust in making the profit, he may be accountable for the profit.　Thus, if the trustee with his own funds purchases an encumbrance upon the trust property for the purpose of protecting the trust property, he is accountable for any profit he makes thereby.

Illustration:

1. A devises Blackacre to B in trust.　Blackacre is subject to a first mortgage for $10,000 and a second mortgage for $5000.　In order to prevent a foreclosure of the second mortgage, B with his own money purchases the second mortgage for $3000.　On the foreclosure of the first mortgage Blackacre sells for $16,000.　B is entitled only to $3000 and interest out of the proceeds of the sale.　See § 170, Comment *j.*

For an application of the above principle, see Home Federal Savings and Loan Association v. Zarkin, 89 Ill.2d 232, 432 N.E.2d 841 (1982) (corporate trustee's purchase of certificate of sale covering trust property that was sold under decree of foreclosure a breach of the duty of loyalty; trustee's defense that it needed to preserve the property as its security on a collateral loan denied; trustee's loan to beneficiaries may be set aside unless trustee proves fairness).

2. The court's award of appreciation damages in the Rothko case has been criticized as not clearly supported by authority and as creating a precedent that will operate as a "threat of severe penalties", adding "unacceptable legal costs to honest administration—costs that cannot be justified as a means of deterring undesirable conduct."　Wellman, Punitive Surcharges Against Disloyal Fiduciaries—Is Rothko Right?, 77 Mich.L.Rev. 95 (1978).　See also Note, Trustee Liability for Breach of the Duty of Loyalty: Good Faith Inquiry and Appreciation Damages, 49 Ford.L.Rev. 1012 (1981) (trustee who proves that sale was made in good faith should not be assessed appreciation damages).

3. The Court holds, quoting Scott on Trusts, that a beneficiary may pursue property which has been sold to a third person when that person took with notice that the sale constituted a breach of trust.　This rule is analyzed and applied in Kline v. Orebaugh, 214 Kan. 207, 519 P.2d 691 (1974).

4. In Stern v. Lucy Webb Hayes National Training School for Deaconesses and Missionaries, 381 F.Supp. 1003, 1014, 1019 (D.C.1974), although the court found that the trustees of a hospital had knowingly allowed the hospital to enter into profitable business arrangements with firms in which individual trustees were officers, it did not remove the trustees or otherwise penalize them except to require them to sign a pledge not to repeat their offenses.　The "less stringent corporate rule" was applied to charitable corporations rather than the stricter rule of accountability applied to trustees.　See also Uniform Management of Institutional Funds Act § 36, 7A ULA 421.　It has been indicated that the corporate standard of best business judgment is also applicable to union trustees under federal law, with a presumption of reasonableness of their decisions.　If, however, undisclosed self-dealing is alleged, the union trustees must prove the transaction's fairness.　Morrissey v. Curran, 650 F.2d 1267 (2d Cir. 1981).

5. In a later proceeding in *Rothko,* the Surrogate approved an award of legal fees payable to four firms that participated in the successful action against the trustees, totaling $3,200,000, reduced from a requested $8,635,000.　The

lion's share of the award, $2,600,000, went to the attorneys for decedent's daughter Kate. Estate of Rothko, 98 Misc.2d 718, 414 N.Y.S.2d 444 (1979).

IN RE BOND AND MORTGAGE GUARANTEE CO.
Court of Appeals of New York, 1952.
303 N.Y. 423, 103 N.E.2d 721.

FROESSEL, Judge. This proceeding was initiated in July, 1948, by application of a so-called Shackno Act trustee, L.1933, ch. 745, McK. Unconsol.Laws § 4871 et seq., for an order (a) settling his final account; (b) granting an allowance to him and his attorneys, and (c) granting other related relief. The trustee was appointed in 1935 for the benefit of holders of first mortgage certificates on the Half Moon Hotel in Coney Island, and he operated the property until 1947, when said hotel was sold for $855,000. When the trustee made the present application, appellants-respondents, certificate holders, opposed the granting of any fee to his attorneys on the basis that, by having purchased certificates, said attorneys forfeited the right to be compensated for their services. The question of their right to compensation, however, is not before us on these cross appeals.

[The Special Term ordered the attorneys to surrender all their certificates to the Trustee and account for all distributions and profits. The Appellate Division modified the order to require only that the former certificate holders from whom the certificates were purchased be made parties and be given notice of their possible claims against the attorneys.]

The Half Moon Hotel was constructed in 1928 and 1929 at an alleged cost of over $2,500,000. The Title Guarantee and Trust Company issued first mortgage participation certificates in a mortgage in the sum of $690,000 covering the premises. The Bond and Mortgage Guarantee Company guaranteed the payment of the bond secured by the aforesaid mortgage to the owners and holders of said bond and mortgage and/or participating certificates therein. The business and property of Bond and Mortgage Guarantee Company were taken over by the Superintendent of Insurance in 1933, pursuant to the provisions of article XI, now art. XVI, of the Insurance Law, Consol.Laws, c. 28, and the Mortgage Commission of the State of New York took over the mortgage investments. The Superintendent of Insurance thereupon sought and obtained judicial approval of a plan for readjustment, modification and reorganization of the rights of the holders of the guaranteed mortgage participation certificates. In pursuance of this plan, the Mortgage Commission foreclosed the mortgage, and title to the Half Moon Hotel was transferred to the trustee.

The order of the Supreme Court, Kings County, dated October 7, 1935, provided, among other things, that "Walter McMeekan shall be appointed Trustee by the Court *of all the property of every description securing or intending to secure the certificates issued by Title Guarantee and Trust Company against the mortgage which is the subject-matter of this proceeding* and guaranteed by Bond and Mortgage Guarantee Company. * * * Upon the execution of the said Declaration of Trust, the Trustee shall become vested with title to the said trust estate and shall hold the same in trust *for the benefit of certificate holders solely to liquidate the same in an orderly businesslike manner"*. (Emphasis supplied.)

* * *

The hotel had been operated by a receiver for two and a half years before the trustee took possession in December, 1935. The attorneys for the trustee have acted as such since that time. Between September 25, 1941, and June 21, 1944, the attorneys made a total of five purchases of certificates of the face amount of $47,489.42 at a cost of $3,995.42, or on the average less than 8½ cents on the dollar. On July 1, 1946, they purchased additional certificates in the face amount of $9,000 for which they paid $5,040. Thus their total average cost was less than 16 cents on the dollar. Distributions thus far made have amounted to nearly 56 cents on the dollar, and the attorneys' profit has amounted to well over $22,000. In addition, the attorneys have received thus far over $10,000 for their legal services, and on the present accounting request approximately an additional $25,000. The objecting certificate holders purchased their certificates of the face value of some $103,000 at various times in 1939, 1941, 1942, 1944, 1946 and 1947 at an average price of more than 43 cents on the dollar.

There is no claim of actual fraud, bad faith, or manipulation of the trust dealings by the attorneys. The attorneys assert they did not buy any of the certificates from certificate holders; they bought from dealers and brokers only. They bought in their own name without attempt at concealment. The attorneys stated they never solicited certificates for sale either from certificate holders or brokers. They also state that they did not rely on any "inside or secret information" in buying the certificates. Of course, by reason of their situation, they could not help but have the fullest information concerning the trust. The attorneys also claimed that in response to many inquiries from certificate holders, they always advised them to hold on rather than to sell at the then depressed market values. It does not appear, however, that the attorneys informed such holders that they were buying certificates, nor how many inquired.

The trustee knew about the attorneys' purchases because, after a sale was completed, the certificate was sent to him for transfer. He stated that "they had a perfect right to do it", although neither he nor any of his family directly or indirectly participated in any purchases. However, it is stated in the referee's report—and undisputed here—that the attorneys "admit their dealings in certificates were never disclosed in any way to the judges who made the allowances to them for services or to the justices in charge of reorganization and rehabilitation matters with whom they were frequently in contact as set forth in their detailed claim for fees."

We are of the view that the attorneys did breach their fiduciary obligation. The duty of the trustee, as defined by court order, was to hold the hotel in trust "for the benefit of certificate holders solely to liquidate the same in an orderly businesslike manner". One of the most fundamental duties of a trustee in any case is complete unselfishness and inflexible loyalty to the interests of the beneficiaries of the trust. This duty stems from human frailty when confronted with conflicting interests, evidenced by the centuries-old scriptural passage: "No man can serve two masters".

The attorneys, concededly in the same position as the trustee, owed an equally high degree of fidelity, and so both courts below held, the Appellate Division stating that, "by reason of their status as attorneys for the trustee, [they] were no less fiduciaries than was the trustee himself." 277 App.Div. 1132, 101 N.Y.S.2d 217, 219. Thus the attorneys, like the trustee, owed to these certificate holders "the duty of the finest loyalty", "something stricter than the morals of the market place." Meinhard v. Salmon, 249 N.Y. 458, 463–464, 164 N.E. 545, 546–547, 62 A.L.R. 1. The attorneys put themselves in a position "in which *thought of self was to be renounced,* however hard the abnegation"; their loyalty to the certificate holders was to be *"undivided and unselfish";* indeed, for them this *"rule of undivided loyalty"* was *"relentless and supreme".* Meinhard v. Salmon, supra, 249 N.Y. at pages 467, 468, 164 N.E. at page 546, emphasis supplied; * * *

Moreover, the question of bad faith or damage is irrelevant to our inquiry. As was said in Wendt v. Fischer, 243 N.Y. 439, 443–444, 154 N.E. 303, 304: "we are told that the brokers acted in good faith, that the terms procured were the best obtainable at the moment, and that the wrong, if any, was unaccompanied by damage. This is no sufficient answer by a trustee forgetful of his duty. The law 'does not stop to inquire whether the contract or transaction was fair or unfair. It stops the inquiry when the relation is disclosed, and sets aside the transaction or refuses to enforce it, at the instance of the party whom the fiduciary undertook to represent, without undertaking to deal with the question of abstract justice in the particular case.' Munson v. Syracuse, G. & C., R. R. Co., supra [103 N.Y. 58], at page 74, 8 N.E. 355; cf. Dutton v. Willner, 52 N.Y. 312, 319. Only by this uncompromising rigidity has the rule of undivided loyalty been maintained against disintegrating erosion."

Measured by these standards, we think it clear that these attorneys placed themselves in a situation wherein their own personal purposes *might* well conflict with the purposes of the trust beneficiaries, the certificate holders. Countless illustrations of such conflict suggest themselves on slight reflection. In every detail of legal advice and legal action with respect to the trust estate, the attorneys would consciously or unconsciously have in mind their own investment in the trust property. If all went well, the difficulty might not be great, but if the trust estate were in great danger, and the market price of certificates again began to decline, the temptation to protect themselves with respect to their own investment would have a tendency to affect their best judgment, advice and action. They would find it difficult to obliterate a divided loyalty, and the endangering process of "disintegrating erosion" would quickly present itself. Hence the uncompromising rigidity of the rule, and it applies irrespective of good or bad faith. There is no shadowy borderline or twilight zone. Where doubt exists, full and complete disclosure, and authorization from the court upon due notice, are the fair and simple remedies.

That the attorneys could have influenced the course of the liquidation is too plain for controversy; indeed, they could not help but influence it in one way or another, as evidenced by the affidavit of one of the attorneys in connection with the negotiations surrounding the Navy lease. The same affidavit discloses that the attorneys, when several prospects indicated an interest in buying the hotel, were "continuously consulted [by the trustee] * * * as to the manner of procedure, the type of contracts to be entered into, the terms of any sale and other related matters." How could the attorneys give an absolutely unbiased opinion on such matters when their own profits and losses were involved? That their advice and action in this case may have been correct, despite their personal interest in the trust estate, is beside the point. In another case it may be otherwise. The law cannot always discover and measure the influence of a trustee or his attorneys. The basic vice is the existence of a personal interest, entangling their private claims with those of their beneficiaries, thus creating the danger of biased judgments and opening the way to fraud and wrong. That is sufficient to brand this conduct as a breach of fiduciary obligation under the circumstances here presented.

[The court then discussed and refused to follow the holdings in Donnelly v. Consolidated Investment Trust, 99 F.2d 185 (1 Cir. 1938) and Victor v. Hillebrecht, 405 Ill. 264, 90 N.E.2d 751 (1950), certiorari denied 339 U.S. 980, 70 S.Ct. 1026, 94 L.Ed. 1384 (1950).]

We agree with the Appellate Division's order insofar as it directs that the former certificate holders from whom the attorneys purchased certificates be brought in and given notice of the possibility of their ownership of claims, and insofar as it remits the matter to Special Term for further proceedings. However, we do not agree with the Appellate Division insofar as it struck out Special Term's direction that the attorneys' certificates be delivered and surrendered to the trustee, and that their profits be accounted for. As we see it, the attorneys in no event may keep the certificates and the profits, but must account therefor to the trust estate as upon a constructive trust, subject to the rights of the former certificate holders.

* * *

LOUGHRAN, C. J., and LEWIS, CONWAY, DESMOND, DYE, and FULD, JJ., concur.

Ordered accordingly.

Notes

1. See Niles, The Divided Loyalty Rule, Proceedings of Probate and Trust Law Division of American Bar Association Convention, 10 (1952); Haggerty, Conflicting Interests of Estate Fiduciaries in New York and the No Further Inquiry Rule, 18 Fordham L.Rev. 1 (1949). See also Mosser v. Darrow, 341 U.S. 267, 71 S.Ct. 680, 95 L.Ed. 927 (1951).

2. The New York Court of Appeals has also held corporate officers accountable for profits derived from inside information even though no allegations

of financial damage to the corporation were made. Diamond v. Oreamuno, 24 N.Y.2d 494, 301 N.Y.S.2d 78, 248 N.E.2d 910 (1969).

3. A commercial banking department, in the course of analyzing a corporation's financial status before making it a loan, acquires a wealth of confidential information about that corporation's operations and prospects. Is the trust department obligated to use this inside information to improve or protect the investments of trusts which it is managing as trustee? Professor Niles poses the following hypothetical:

> T Trust Co. is trustee under the will of A and holds securities in trust for B for life, remainder to B's descendants. T Co. as trustee holds a block of the common stock of X Manufacturing Company, Inc., which is listed on the New York Stock Exchange. A vice president of T Co. receives information from a vice president of X Inc. that the earnings of X Inc. have declined substantially and that the earnings report will be issued in a week. T Co. analysts realize that the report will cause a substantial drop in the market price of X Inc. stock. The T Co. officers know that they have inside information, not known to the public. What should the officers do?

Professor Niles points out that a trustee must use all his skills and all his knowledge in the administration of the trust. On the other hand, the Securities and Exchange Commission's Rule 10b–5 prohibits making untrue statements of a material fact or omitting statements of material facts in purchasing or selling any security. The objective is to protect the investing public from exploitation by the use of inside information by corporate issuers and insiders. The T Trust Co. may find itself "liable to pay compensatory damages to the purchaser of the X Inc. stock or, indeed, a larger amount to the investing public." Niles, A Contemporary View of Liability for Breach of Trust, 114 Trusts & Estates 12, 82, 84 (1975).

There is no obvious answer to the dilemma. One approach is to erect a "Chinese Wall" between the lending and trust departments so that the latter department will not be privy to the inside information of the former. Within a single corporation is it possible for one department not to be in communication with another? Herzel and Collins, The Chinese Wall Revisited, 6 Corp.L.Rev. 116 (1983). Lipton and Mazur, The Chinese Wall Solution to the Conflict Problems of Securities Firms, 50 N.Y.U.L.Rev. 459 (1975).

RENZ v. BEEMAN

United States Court of Appeals, Second Circuit, 1978.
589 F.2d 735, certiorari denied 444 U.S. 834, 100 S.Ct. 65, 62 L.Ed.2d 43 (1979).

Gurfein, Circuit Judge:

This is an action based on diversity of citizenship, filed on September 24, 1974 in the District Court for the Northern District of New York (Hon. James T. Foley, Chief Judge) in which plaintiffs seek to impose a constructive trust on 2000 shares of voting preferred stock in Finch, Pruyn and Co., Inc. (Finch-Pruyn), purchased by Mary Beeman through negotiations conducted by her husband, Lyman A. Beeman, on August 8, 1962, and to remove the Beemans as trustees of certain trusts. The plaintiffs are Mary Whitney Renz, suing individually, and her husband, Franklin W. Renz, suing as executor of the estate of Mary H. Whitney, Mrs. Renz's mother. The Beemans are trustees of several *inter vivos* trusts executed simultaneously in 1954 (referred to compositely as the "1954 Trust"), under which appellant Mary Renz is now a beneficiary. After trial on the merits, the District Court held, inter alia, that the Beemans did not breach their fiduciary duty to the plaintiffs by purchasing the Finch-Pruyn stock, and that the plaintiffs' claim is barred under New York's Statute of Limitations. We agree that the action is barred by limitations and affirm on that ground.

On the standard of fiduciary responsibility to be applied, we agree with the District Court in some respects but differ in others. To state the issues summarily, the District Court recognized that the trustees owed a general duty of undivided loyalty to the trust beneficiaries. Judge Foley found, though somewhat equivocally, that there was not enough circumstantial evidence to support a finding that the life tenants, who also had powers of appointment, had relieved the fiduciaries of their duty by consenting to the purchase of the 2000 shares. He ruled, however, that certain clauses in the trust instrument exculpated the trustees with respect to this transaction. The court, accordingly, applied the lesser standard of good faith rather than the greater standard of undivided loyalty that it might have applied in the absence of exculpation or consent.

Since the trial court heard the witnesses, including the parties, and assessed their credibility, we cannot say that the court's finding that Lyman Beeman and Mary Beeman acted "in good faith" was clearly erroneous, and we shall accept the conclusion as a finding of fact when we consider the statute of limitations. On the other hand, we find neither exculpation nor consent, and we are convinced that the duty of the Beemans should have been measured by the higher standard of undivided loyalty rather than good faith. We will, therefore, consider the statute of limitations from that point of view as well.

[In 1954 on the termination of an earlier trust, 5334 shares of Finch-Pruyn Co., which constituted two-thirds of the outstanding shares of the voting preferred stock, were owned by two sisters and the two children of a deceased sister as follows: Nell Pruyn Cunningham 1778 ⅔ shares; Charlotte Pruyn Hyde 1777 ⅔ shares; Mary Hoopes Beeman 888 ⅚ and Samuel P. Hoopes, Jr. 888 ⅚ shares. Mrs. Cunningham, Mrs. Hyde, and Mary Beeman (as to 777 ⅚ shares) entered into an agreement, dated June 14, 1954, placing their respective shares into three inter vivos trusts as set out in a single trust instrument called the 1954 trust. Each settlor reserved an income interest and a testamentary power of appointment in her interest. Mary Beeman and her husband, Lyman Beeman, who was the President of Finch-Pruyn Co., were named trustees and are the primary defendants herein. Neither Mrs. Cunningham nor Mrs. Hyde exercised their powers. Mrs. Hyde's interest in the trust descended at her death in 1963 to her daughter, Mary Hyde Whitney, who in turn died in 1971 leaving the Hyde interest to her two children, Louis Whitney (who does not appear to be involved in the litigation) and Mary Renz, who along with her husband, Franklin Renz, an executor of his mother-in-law's estate, are the plaintiffs herein. Mrs. Cunningham died childless in 1962, with her interest being divided equally (i.e., 592 8/9 shares each) among the remaindermen of the trust, Mary Beeman, Samuel Hoopes Jr., and Mary Whitney (her children, Louis Whitney and Mary Renz, succeeded to this interest in 1971). Eds.]

The key triggering event for this action filed on September 24, 1974 is Mary Beeman's purchase on August 8, 1962, twelve years earlier, of 2000 additional shares of Finch-Pruyn voting preferred. Helen Finch Foulds, one of the heirs of the Finch side of the business, died in November 1958. She bequeathed 2000 shares of voting preferred and 6300 shares of non-voting common stock to the Metropolitan Museum of Art in New York City. Shortly after probate, Metropolitan's agent, J. P. Morgan & Co., wrote to Lyman Beeman in his capacity as President of Finch-Pruyn to advise him of Metropolitan's acquisition. A series of letters was exchanged which the District Court characterized as the "initial steps toward negotiating the purchase of the Fould[s] stock." Lyman Beeman acted as negotiator for the purchase, though it is not clear on whose behalf he was negotiating.

In December 1958, only a month after Mrs. Foulds' death, Elmer White, Vice-President of Finch-Pruyn, wrote to a co-executor of the Foulds estate: "We note that the 2000 shares of preferred stock has been appraised at $120. per share and we believe that this is a realistic value. In the event this stock is placed on the market, we are interested in purchasing same at this price." The "we" unmistakably refers to the corporation. The letter was signed "Finch, Pruyn and Company, Incorporated, Elmer S. White, Vice-President." Nor was Mr. White in 1958 a trustee of the 1954 trusts. The record does not indicate a reply to the *corporation's* offer concerning the voting preferred shares, nor does it disclose when or to whom Mary Beeman was first proposed as a purchaser in place of the corporation.

It appears that the Metropolitan wished to sell both the voting preferred and the non-voting common stock as a single block. After 3½ years, an agreement was reached under which the Finch-Pruyn Company purchased the non-voting common stock at $140 per share and Mary Beeman purchased the voting preferred at $120 per share. The District Court determined that these prices were fair and we see no reason to disturb that finding. Lyman Beeman, who was at that time co-trustee with his wife of the 1954 Trust, acted as negotiator for both purchases. The purchase of the common stock was approved by Finch-Pruyn's Board of Directors on August 21, 1962, but the minutes reflect neither that the 2000 shares of voting stock were also available for purchase nor that Mrs. Beeman was buying them. The shares acquired by Mrs. Beeman in these circumstances were not put into the 1954 Trust but were held by her outright. As will later be discussed, we consider the purchase by Mrs. Beeman to have been in breach of trust.

[Two additional events were alleged to constitute breaches of fiduciary duty. First, in 1967–1968 the certificate of incorporation was amended to alter voting procedures. The trial court's finding that these amendments were made in good faith and in furtherance of a corporate purpose was accepted.   Second, Mary Beeman and her brother, Samuel Hoopes, Jr., entered into an agreement in 1969, known as the Management Trust, whereby they guaranteed voting control of Finch-Pruyn Co. in the Hoopes side of the family until 1990 unless terminated by the trustees earlier.   The court held that Mary Beeman's use of the disputed 2,000 shares in this trust did not constitute an independent breach of trust but was an extension of the breach that occurred when the shares were acquired.]

As we mentioned at the outset, Judge Foley found it unnecessary to pass on the fiduciary obligations with respect to the Foulds stock that would be implied by the standard of undivided loyalty.   In a thoughtful opinion, he appraised the termination of the testamentary trust and the simultaneous creation of the 1954 Trust as the product of a desire to extend Pruyn family control of Finch-Pruyn;   and as evidence of "the confidence which the senior members of the Pruyn family placed in Lyman A. Beeman's stewardship" of the company.   He found that purchase of the 2000 Foulds shares did not contravene the Beemans' duties in carrying out these purposes, because (1) there was no attempt at concealment of the transaction;   (2) although no express consent to the purchase was proven, such consent could be implied from the circumstances;   and (3) the purchase was within the discretion afforded to the trustees by exculpatory language in the trust agreements.

With regard to the court's evaluation of the purposes behind the 1954 Trust, we cannot say that, as applied to the *present* generation, the finding of purpose was clearly erroneous.   When the 1954 trusts were created, Beeman had already been President of Finch-Pruyn for six years and had shown his ability to run the company.   We find no evidence, however, to support the conclusion that the settlors intended the Hoopes branch to control exclusively in succeeding generations, when Beeman's descendants might not be as capable of running the business, but could nevertheless refuse to yield to a competent *non-family* president.

The court concluded that negotiations had been conducted "with no attempt at concealment."   We see no evidence to support the subsidiary finding that there were "numerous prior general discussions within the company" (if this was meant to include *directors* of the company who were not also associated with Beeman as corporate officers), but the experienced and able trial judge was in a position to weigh credibility.   Though the circumstantial evidence is equivocal, we accept his assessment of credibility and let stand his finding that there was no attempt to conceal.

On the other hand, we think the finding of implied consent to the purchase by Mrs. Hyde and Mrs. Cunningham was clearly erroneous. Though the Judge did not find that there was *express* consent, he did find consent implied from the circumstances.   In Judge Foley's view, this independently exonerated the Beemans from liability.   Cf. Central Hanover Bank & Trust Co. v. Russell, 290 N.Y. 593, 48 N.E.2d 704 (1943). The Judge based his holding on the following: First, he found a pattern of intra-family discussions of Finch-Pruyn Co. affairs.   Second, he found a pattern of courteous and responsive treatment by Lyman Beeman of family inquiries concerning trust matters. Third, he inferred a vote of continued confidence in Lyman Beeman from the settlors' non-exercise of their testamentary powers of appointment under the 1954 Trust. Finally, the court relied on a letter from Lyman Beeman to Mary Hyde Whitney, in which the extent of Mrs. Beeman's personal holdings, including the Foulds stock, is disclosed.

This evidence is insufficient to support the inference of permission for the purchase that the District Court drew. Consent to self-dealing requires a more specific showing. It must be "clearly proved" and "made with a full knowledge of all the material particulars and circumstances," including the full extent of the cestui's legal rights. Adair v. Brimmer, 74 N.Y. 539, 554 (1878); accord Matter of Ryan, 291 N.Y. 376, 417, 52 N.E.2d 909 (1943). Accepting as proper the trial court's exclusion of evidence rendered incompetent by New York's Dead Man's Statute, N.Y. Civ.Prac.Law § 4519 (McKinney 1963 & Supp. 1978) (CPLR), we hold that the record falls short of clear proof. Neither general confidence in Lyman Beeman nor his general courtesy spell consent to personal advantage in a conflict of interest with the beneficiaries of the trust. Moreover, the letter, which we discuss in more detail when we reach the statute of limitations, though it raises other implications, is not persuasive evidence of actual consent.

Under the higher standard of undivided loyalty, the law "stops the inquiry when the relation is disclosed, and sets aside the transaction or refuses to enforce it, at the instance of the party whom the fiduciary undertook to represent, without undertaking to deal with the question of abstract justice in the particular case." Munson v. Syracuse, Geneva & Corning R.R., 103 N.Y. 58, 74, 8 N.E. 355, 358 (1886); * * * The main support for the District Court's application of a good faith standard instead of an "undivided loyalty" standard comes, however, from its conclusion that the trustees were permitted to engage in self-interested transactions by virtue of the *exculpatory* provisions in the 1954 trust agreement. It is true that even a trustee's duty of "utmost loyalty" can be reduced by means of language in the trust instrument permitting certain transactions involving self-interest, O'Hayer v. de St. Aubin, 30 A.D.2d 419, 424, 293 N.Y.S.2d 147 (1968); Matter of Balfe, 245 App.Div. 22, 280 N.Y.S. 128 (1935), or by express consent of the settlor, Central Hanover Bank & Trust Co. v. Russell, supra, 290 N.Y. at 594, 48 N.E.2d 704; * * * Such an exculpatory clause or agreement does reduce the standard of duty to one of good faith and permits a court to weigh the merits of the transaction. Matter of Balfe, supra.

We do not agree, however, that the exculpatory clauses cited below justified a lowering of the standard of the trustee's obligation. Only the most explicit language can protect a fiduciary from liability in a conflict of interest with his *cestuis*. See, e.g., Matter of Hubbell, 302 N.Y. 246, 255, 97 N.E.2d 888 (1951). Courts may not read exculpatory language broadly, lest they unwittingly permit erosion of the fiduciary duty itself. * * *

The clauses in the agreement relied on below concern matters relating to management of the trust corpus. They give the trustees broad discretion to exercise powers and rights incident to ownership of the trust property, and we assume (though we need not decide) that they establish a good faith business judgment in the handling of trust investments. Nowhere in the agreement, however, do we find a provision granting to the trustees the right to prefer their own interests to those of the trust, or to appropriate for their own account trust opportunities. We think, rather, that the trustees were given such broad powers in managing the trust *because* there was implicit faith in their undivided loyalty. See Matter of Durston, 297 N.Y. 64, 71–72, 74 N.E.2d 310 (1947). That conclusion is accented by the willingness of the settlors to accept Lyman Beeman as a "disinterested" trustee who would protect *all* the beneficiaries without favoring his own wife.

The present case differs markedly from O'Hayer v. de St. Aubin, supra. There the trust instrument expressly stated the settlor's intent that he and his son, as trustees, should be free to profit from their trusteeships. Id., 30 A.D.2d at 423–24, 293 N.Y.S.2d 147. In addition, the trust instrument expressly gave the trustees power to engage in self-dealing in the stock of the corporation whose shares comprised the corpus of the trust. Id. at 424, 293 N.Y.S.2d 147. Matter of Balfe, supra, is also different. Under the will "the trustee was authorized to act in respect of the securities in the estate without regard to whether or not the trustee had a personal interest in these same kinds of securities or the companies to which they related." Id., 245 A.D. at 24, 280 N.Y.S. at 130.

The exculpatory language involved in this case more closely resembles provisions in Matter of Durston, supra, which conferred power to act " 'with all the authority, and powers in connection with the same, I would possess, if living.' " The Court of Appeals held that such power is "to be exercised, however, in the manner and subject to the obligations and duties of trustees. If the testator intended that all these things could be done without regard to the fundamental rule of absolute loyalty and fidelity prohibiting any purchase or retention of securities involving a divided loyalty, the authority should have been stated." Id., 297 N.Y. at 72, 74 N.E.2d at 313. We discern no express exculpation in the 1954 Trust permitting competition with the trust in the purchase of voting stock that is the core of control and comprises the *corpus* of the trust. We turn, therefore, to consider the position of the trustees without benefit of an effective exculpatory provision.

In the absence of an express exculpatory clause and a lack of proof of clear consent, the central question is the obligation, under New York law, of a trustee of a family trust which controls a family corporation through ownership of a majority of the voting stock, where more than a single branch has a beneficial interest.

Absent exculpation or clear consent, it is the existence of the conflict alone that establishes the obligation. * * * Conflict can arise when a trustee becomes a competitor with the trust for a business opportunity.

* * * Favoring one beneficiary over others may also be a source of conflict. * * *

* * *

As far as this appeal is concerned, we deal with only a single large purchase which could, as indeed it did, give unchallengeable control of Finch-Pruyn to the Hoopes branch for generations to come. The absolute control of the Finch-Pruyn corporation was an asset of the trust. It is to the preservation of the joint control created by the settlors that the trustee had a fiduciary obligation. By putting the shares for control into a single basket, the settlors pledged the trustee not to disarrange the balance of control that had been created. His fiduciary obligation was enhanced because he was a member of the family whose welfare he had taken upon himself to preserve. To be sure, he had an obvious opportunity for a different conflict of interest in his position as president of the corporation and as trustee of a trust which controlled the corporate entity. But that potential conflict was known to the settlors and they were content to let Beeman serve in that dual capacity despite the remote possibility of conflict between his duties as president and as trustee. In any event, we have affirmed the finding that the apportionment of price between the corporation's purchase of the common stock and Mrs. Beeman's purchase of the preferred stock was both fair and based upon appraisal. No breach of duty can thus be inferred from his dual role. * * *

It is true also that the trustee never dealt with the shares which were in the corpus of the trust. In that sense Mr. Beeman may have been an exemplary trustee. But the absence of self-dealing does not measure the limit of the fiduciary obligation. The trust possessed an intangible asset which was to be free of competition from its fiduciary. An opportunity for purchase that comes to him in a fiduciary capacity compels the trustee to give a right of first refusal to his trust estate if the opportunity fits the purpose of the trust. Wootten v. Wootten, supra, 151 F.2d at 150. See Restatment (Second) of Trusts, § 170, comment k. When the trust is settled by two branches of a family, who jointly own control of a family company, the chancellor will insist that a trustee with ties to one branch should not disfavor the other. To upset the balance of control for selfish gain is to commit a breach of the high fiduciary duty of undivided loyalty. * * *

Under the testamentary trust Mary Whitney Renz would have become a direct distributee free of trust restraint. At the instance of the settlors, including her mother, the dissolution and recreation of the 1954 *inter vivos* trusts reduced Mrs. Whitney to the position of a remainderman and ultimate life-tenant. As we have noted, the purpose was to keep the Beemans in charge. There is no claim of fraud or overreaching in the creation of the 1954 trust itself.

It thus appears that the plaintiff herself, who succeeded to a mere life tenancy, could never gain outright control during her lifetime of the shares of her grandmother, Mrs. Hyde, unless either Lyman Beeman terminated the 1954 Trust, or Mrs. Hyde exercised her power of appointment in favor of the plaintiff.

It could hardly be clearer that Mrs. Hyde, by failing to exercise her power of appointment before her death in 1963, did express her wish that appellant should never have voting power over the trust shares. When an opportunity came to buy Mrs. Foulds' 2000 shares from the Metropolitan Museum of Art, such a purchase by the trust, even if it had been financially able to make it, would not have enhanced appellant's position with respect to control, but would only have affected her dividends as a life-tenant of the Hyde and Cunningham trusts. To buy the 2000 shares, either the Hyde or Cunningham trust would have had to borrow on its only asset, the preferred shares in the trust. Such borrowing would hardly have been supported by the aged life-tenants, whose dividends might have been cut as a result.

Thus, while Mary Beeman was theoretically in competition with the Hyde trust when she bought the shares from the Metropolitan, she was not in practical competition with appellant herself, for appellant was locked in.

This does not take into account, however, the position of the children of Mary Whitney Renz and Louis Whitney and succeeding generations. Upon the death of appellant, her children will succeed to an outright interest in Mary Renz's shares in the Hyde and Cunningham trusts. When that happens, they will still not control the corporation. The children of Mary Renz and Louis Whitney together will own 1777$\frac{2}{3}$ shares derived from the Hyde trust and 592$\frac{8}{9}$ shares from the Cunningham trust, for a total of 2370$\frac{5}{9}$ shares. The Hoopes side without the Foulds purchase would have had 999$\frac{5}{6}$ shares directly from Mary Beeman and Samuel P. Hoopes, Jr., plus 777$\frac{5}{6}$ shares from the Mary Beeman 1954 Trust, plus 1185$\frac{7}{9}$ shares from the Cunningham trust, for a total of 2963$\frac{4}{9}$ shares. Thus, *together* the two families would command a two-thirds majority of the outstanding shares. Alone, although the Hoopes family would have had a slight edge, neither family would have had a majority of the shares.

Such a stalemate could have resulted eventually in a new trust arrangement, with each side participating in the selection of new trustees, or in the creation of a voting trust. It is this eventuality, which the 1954 Trust may be said to contemplate, that the Beemans' stock purchase eliminated. By purchase of the 2000 Foulds shares, Lyman and Mary Beeman succeeded in taking for themselves and their family absolute control of the voting stock forever. When the Management Trust terminates in 1990, the Hoopes family will continue to control to the exclusion of the Hydes by outright ownership of a majority of the voting shares. They may be able, moreover, to demand a premium for themselves if they sell their shares as a "control" block.

When the Foulds stock became available, it was the duty of Beeman, as trustee, to notify the life-tenants, who because of their powers of appointment could have given binding consent to the purchase, see, e.g., Central Hanover Bank & Trust Co. v. Russell, supra, 290 N.Y. at 594, 48 N.E.2d 704 * * *; and to offer the stock to the Finch-Pruyn Company as a means of preserving the balance of control between the Hyde and Hoopes families. If the company had been willing to buy the preferred stock at what the District Court has found to be a fair price, the company purchase would have left the balance of control unaffected. There was no such offer by the trustee to Finch-Pruyn, however, and the District Court inferentially so found. If the corporation was unwilling to make the purchase, the opportunity should have been offered to the trust, or to the beneficiaries in proportion to their interest, Wootten v. Wootten, supra, 151 F.2d at 150. At the least, the trustees should have petitioned for court approval for Mrs. Beeman to make the purchase. See Matter of Scarborough Properties Corp., 25 N.Y.2d 553, 307 N.Y.S.2d 641, 255 N.E.2d 761 (1969).[3]

We hold then, that the fiduciary duty of the Beemans was higher than that applied by the District Court. It was an obligation which was not to be measured by fairness or merit but by a standard of strict prohibition against the acts of a trustee which could disserve the future interests of some of his beneficiaries. It was, at least, the standard that would have been imposed on an independent trustee who was permitted to favor neither side.

The rule was well-stated in Matter of Shehan, 285 A.D. 785, 791, 141 N.Y.S.2d 439, 444 (1955):

> The duty of a trustee is easily defined because it is absolute. "The rule is inflexible that a trustee shall not place himself in a position where his interest is or may be in conflict with his duty". (Matter of Lewisohn, 294 N.Y. 596, 608, 63 N.E.2d 589.)

We hold there is no exculpatory clause in this trust specific enough to dilute the rule. Nor do we find evidence to support a finding that the trust beneficiaries knew of the conflict and clearly gave their consent to Mrs. Beeman's purchase of the Foulds shares. The trustees committed a breach of trust when Mary Beeman purchased the Foulds shares in 1962. On the other hand, we cannot find clearly erroneous the finding below that there was no fraudulent intent.

[The court went on, however, to uphold the District Court's decision that the New York statute of limitations was a bar to recovery for the breach of trust. The Beemans had committed a breach of trust, but they were not guilty of intentional fraud of the type necessary to stay the running of the statute.]

MOORE, Circuit Judge (concurring):

---

3. We cannot say that disinterested directors would necessarily have purchased the Foulds preferred stock. That would have depended on their judgment of whether the saving of dividend payments on 2000 preferred shares was worth the purchase price to be paid. But they should have been given the opportunity by the trustee, if only in the hope that the family balance of power entrusted to the trustee's care might be thus preserved.

The steps required by the trustee, if taken, would not have been purely formal gestures. By the time the actual purchase was made, Mrs. Whitney, plaintiff's mother, was already a vested beneficiary by devolution from Mrs. Cunningham, who had died a month earlier. Mrs. Whitney had expressed her concern for the welfare of her children and might well have spoken up, if given notice, either by purchasing an aliquot share or by challenging the right of Mary Beeman to buy the stock without a court proceeding.

I concur in Judge Gurfein's opinion that the statute of limitations bars this action.

* * *

I differ with Judge Gurfein's opinion as to the fiduciary-trustee issue on his application of the law to the facts or possibly better the facts to the law. I agree that the highest standards of trust loyalty should apply but I am equally mindful of Justice (then Chief Judge) Cardozo's precept in Meinhard v. Salmon, 249 N.Y. 458 at 466, 164 N.E. 545, at 547 (1928): "Little profit will come from a dissection of the precedents". Decision in each case must rest on its own facts.

I do not place any reliance upon the exculpatory clause. On the other hand I see no justifiable reason for Lyman Beeman to have used F–P assets to purchase a preferred stock for the company when it had no business reason for so doing. To me the reasons for not buying the stock for the Trust are equally clear. It had no assets with which to make the purchase. To have borrowed the money for the purchase, pledging F–P stock, might well have been a breach of trust had the beneficiaries chosen to complain that their interests were adversely affected thereby.

In short, Judge Foley heard all witnesses called by plaintiffs, found that there was no proof of corporate mismanagement, and no fraudulent concealment of Mrs. Beeman's stock purchase. To the contrary he found the fair inferences to be otherwise. Upon the law and the facts, I would affirm Judge Foley's decision in its entirety * * *

Notes

1. The effect of exculpatory clauses and of the beneficiaries' informed consent on fiduciary liability is discussed further at p. 716, infra.

2. Judge Moore in the concurring opinion states that there was no business reason for the Beemans to purchase the stock for the corporation. Note the potential in cases involving family corporations for the trustees to be liable for breach of their obligations not only to the trust beneficiaries but also to the corporation and other stockholders. See discussion in Matter of Hubbell, 302 N.Y. 246, 97 N.E.2d 888 (1951). Are trustees who hold the controlling interest in a corporation obliged to vote themselves onto the board and to assume active management lest they be accused of wrongfully delegating their responsibilities to others? Trustees who are in this dual capacity may find themselves confronted by a no-win decision as, for instance, where they must vote dividends to obtain income for the income beneficiaries but their best business judgment tells them to reinvest the assets in furtherance of the company's continued growth. For a discussion of the rights and remedies of the parties in a situation of this kind, see In re Shupack's Will, supra, p. 166. Objections may be raised to a fiduciary receiving two compensations, one as trustee and a second as manager of the corporation, for performing substantially similar tasks. A distinction has been drawn between the corporate officer who is named by the testator to be trustee and the outsider who uses his position as trustee to vote himself into a position of authority in the corporation; only the latter trustee is in a position of conflict and subject to possible loss of compensation as corporate officer. Childs v. National Bank of Austin, 658 F.2d 487 (7th Cir. 1981) (chair-

man of the trustee-bank must account to the trust for compensation he received as chairman of the board of family corporation held in the trust).

3. Courts have ruled in favor of trustees when the testator has put them in positions of conflict between self-interest and obligation to the trust.   See e.g., Goldman v. Rubin, 292 Md. 693, 441 A.2d 713 (1982) (no self-dealing when testator's will placed four personal representatives who were directors of family corporation in a position of conflict when they sold stock to the corporation to pay taxes and expenses);   Rosencrans v. Fry, 12 N.J. 88, 95 A.2d 905 (1953) (testator's will gave the trustee who ran the business an option to buy any or all of the stock in the trust corpus at its par value;   trustee could exercise the option despite the objections of the co-trustee-widow);   In re Flagg's Estate, 365 Pa. 82, 73 A.2d 411 (1950) (redemption of stock by controlling trustee allowed even though the company's investment of the funds realized by the redemption might mean a reduction in the trust income).

2.   *Duty to Earmark and the Prohibition Against Commingling*

Restatement of the Law of Trusts 2d § 179.

Duty to Keep Trust Property Separate

The trustee is under a duty to the beneficiary to keep the trust property separate from his individual property, and, so far as it is reasonable that he should do so, to keep it separate from other property not subject to the trust, and to see that the property is designated as property of the trust.

Comment:

a. Extent of duty.   It is ordinarily the duty of the trustee (1) to keep the trust property separate from his own property;   (2) to keep the trust property separate from property held upon other trusts;   (3) to earmark the trust property as property of the trust.

b. Duty not to mingle trust funds with his own.   It is the duty of the trustee not to mingle trust funds with his own funds.   Thus, it is improper for the trustee to deposit trust money in his individual account in a bank.

c. Duty not to mingle funds of separate trusts.   It is ordinarily the duty of the trustee not to mingle property held upon one trust with property held upon another trust, whether the two trusts are created by separate settlors or by the same settlor.

* * *

Notes

1. The common law prohibition against commingling has been partially abrogated in practically every jurisdiction to permit a corporate fiduciary to hold property of trusts of which it is trustee in a common trust fund.   See Uniform Common Trust Fund Act, 7 ULA 83.   State statutes set out the conditions under which a common trust fund is to be administered.   National banks are subject to federal regulations.   Reg. 9, Comptroller of the Currency (1964) under authority set out in 76 Stat. 668, 12 U.S.C.A § 92a.   The statutes are listed in 3 Scott on Trusts § 227.9 (3d ed. 1967).   For the use of commingled funds maintained by insurance companies, banks and brokerage firms for the

investment of pension funds, see Pianko, Investment by Employee Benefit Plans in Real Estate, 41 N.Y.U. Inst. on Fed. Tax. § 22 (1983).

2. It is the usual rule that a corporate trustee cannot properly invest trust funds in the purchase of its own stock. 2 Scott on Trusts § 170.15 (3d ed. 1967). There is divided opinion as to whether a corporate executor or trustee may properly deposit cash, temporarily in its possession, in its own commercial banking department. 2 Scott § 170.18. The practice is sanctioned in § 3(c)(6) Trustees' Powers Act, 7A ULA 766.

3. *Prohibition Against Delegation of Fiduciary Obligations*

IN RE ESTATE OF SPIRTOS

Court of Appeal, Second District, 1973.
34 Cal.App.3d 479, 109 Cal.Rptr. 919.

STEPHENS, Acting Presiding Justice.

This appeal is from an order surcharging appellant Tulla Spirtos (the removed administratrix of the estate of her husband, George N. Spirtos) in the total amount of $117,841.76. Also, a motion to dismiss appeal was filed by respondents.

George N. Spirtos died intestate on August 8, 1966, survived by his wife, Tulla, and four children. On August 10, 1966, appellant filed her petition for letters of administration, alleging that she was decedent's wife; that four children issued from the marriage; and that the total estimated assets of decedent consisted of cash ($5,000), personal property (consisting mainly of decedent's medical practice) ($59,000), and annual income from other sources ($1,000), amounting to $65,000. On August 24, 1966, an order appointing her as special administratrix was issued and the qualifying bond was set at $65,000.

By written agreement dated September 16, 1966, appellant sold decedent's medical practice to Doctor Cuilty for $122,000, payable at $25,000 down and the balance in equal monthly payments of $1,464.02, carrying interest at 7% per annum. No security for the unpaid balance was obtained from Cuilty. No notice of the sale was either posted or published, and no attempt was made to obtain court approval of the sale. Appellant received the $25,000 down payment and 13 monthly payments thereafter, for a total of $44,032. Cuilty was subsequently adjudicated a bankrupt, and the claim for the balance owing to the estate was discharged, thus resulting in a loss to the estate of $78,468.

On May 5, 1967, an inventory and appraisement was filed showing assets totaling $123,500, which included the medical practice appraisal at its sales price. On February 5, 1969, pursuant to a petition by respondent-creditor Lindsay (whose claim had been approved but remained unpaid), a citation to compel an accounting (Prob.Code §§ 921 and 922) was issued and served. On May 27, 1969, a first account current and petition for settlement were filed on behalf of appellant by her attorneys. In this accounting, appellant charged herself with amounts for the inventory, supplemental inventory, and receipts from the practice prior to the sale to Cuilty, and claimed that the sales price for the medical practice, except for that portion thereof received ($44,032), was now uncollectible due to Cuilty's bankruptcy. By this first account current, appellant first raised the grounds upon which she now seeks reversal, i.e., that "Upon the advice and instructions of said former attorney, Tulla Spirtos executed, Exhibit I hereto [the sales agreement with Cuilty]." At the hearing of objections by respondent-creditor Lindsay to this account, counsel for appellant orally asked the court to approve the sale of the practice. The court refused to approve the account or confirm the sale of the medical practice,[4] and Lindsay's objections were sustained.

On March 12, 1970, appellant filed a first and final account. Objections to this account were again filed by respondent Lindsay. After a hearing, the objections were sustained and appellant was surcharged in the amount of $105,185.19. This order, however, was set aside on the ground that two tax claims had been omitted from the first and final account. Appellant thereafter filed a supplemental accounting.

On January 8, 1971, pursuant to a petition by respondent Lindsay for removal of the administratrix and for appointment of a successor administrator, an order revoking appellant's letters of administration was filed and on March 4, 1971, the Public Administrator was appointed as her successor.

On March 8, 1971, the removed administratrix filed her final account. Objections were again filed by respondent Lindsay, and were joined in by the Public Administrator. On November 11, 1971, the order sustaining objections to the final account corrected the accounting to show charges in favor of the estate in the amount of $151,518.23, and credits in favor of appellant in the amount of $33,676.47; appellant was surcharged for the amount of the difference, $117,841.76. The order also denied appellant's claim for statutory commissions and fees and ordered that the following claims be paid out of the funds to be received by the Public Administrator:

Owen W. Lindsay	$22,000.00
Marie Hellman	434.00
Franchise Tax Board, together with interest as allowed by law	4,284.19
Internal Revenue Service, together with interest as allowed by law	5,726.33
James M. Hall, Inheritance Tax Appraiser	4.24
Stuart S. Rough & Associates, Bond Premium	182.00

---

4. Prob.Code, § 755: "Except as provided by sections 770 and 771 of this code, all sales of property must be reported to the court and confirmed by the court before the title to the property passes. The report must be verified. Such report and a petition for confirmation of the sale must be made within thirty days after each sale * * *."

Prob.Code § 770: "Perishable property and other personal property which will depreciate in value if not disposed of promptly, or which will incur loss or expense by being kept, and so much other personal property as may be necessary to provide the family allowance pending the receipt of other sufficient funds, may be sold without notice, and title shall pass without confirmation; but the executor, administrator or special administrator is responsible for the actual value of the property *unless, after making a sworn return, and on a proper showing, the court shall approve the sale.*" (Emphasis added.)

[In a later footnote that is omitted, the court stated that no explanation was given as to why confirmation under § 770 was not sought.]

These obligations, totaling $32,630.76, are the only outstanding obligations of the estate, other than statutory commissions and fees owed to appellant, her attorneys, and the successor administrator and his attorney.

The transactions which resulted in the surcharge to appellant arose as a result of appellant's placing the management of the estate in the hands of her first attorneys, Caras and Evangelatos. Appellant testified that she had no knowledge of the legal steps necessary to probate an estate. At the time of decedent's death, appellant was advised by her counsel that the major asset of the estate (decedent's medical practice, weight reduction) had to be sold immediately as otherwise the patients would go elsewhere and within a month the practice would be worth nothing. Complicating the situation was the position of the lessor of the property upon which the weight-reduction facility was located; he was contending that decedent's death had terminated the lease and was threatening to bring in his own doctor and take over the medical practice. Evangelatos began negotiations with the lessor for the sale of the medical practice, and received an offer of $37,500 from the lessor. On August 24, 1966, after appellant's appointment as special administratrix, she and Evangelatos took control of the medical practice and at that time both felt that a quick sale was necessary because they were afraid that they would be evicted at any moment. Within a few days appellant found a new location for the practice, leased it for a term of three years at a total rent of $10,950, and made improvements and expenditures amounting to $15,000. Thereafter, appellant found Doctor Cuilty, who agreed to purchase the practice and move it to the new location, and Evangelatos negotiated the sale according to the terms above set forth.[5]

Evangelatos' reasons for not giving notice of sale and not opening the subject-practice to public bid were: (1) he felt that if a petition were filed with the court, the original landlord would learn of it and immediately evict them; and (2) Cuilty wanted immediate possession so that he could familiarize himself with the practice prior to moving to the new location. Cuilty subleased the new premises; however, he never occupied them, but remained at decedent's old location until Cuilty was adjudicated a bankrupt.

*   *   *

Appellant contends that there is no substantial evidence supporting the court's finding that the losses to the estate in the sum of $117,841.76 were caused by appellant's negligence. We believe that the resolution of this issue is governed by our recent decision in Estate of Guiol, 28 Cal. App.3d 818, 824–825, 105 Cal.Rptr. 35, 38–39, from which we quote at length:

---

5. According to appellant, the sale to Cuilty necessitated the securing of a lease at a different location and substantial expenditures for refurbishing. Respondent Lindsay attacked these disbursements on the grounds that they were speculative and dissipated assets of the estate. Appellant contends that they were made upon the advice of her counsel and therefore, whether or not she should be surcharged therefor must be resolved under the same principles that govern the determination of appellant's liability for the loss engendered by the sale itself.

" * * * [I]t is necessary to first recognize the primary duty of the administratrix, which was to 'take into [her] possession all the estate of the decedent, real and personal * * *.' (Prob.Code § 571.) To assure that this protection is given the creditors and beneficiaries of the estate, there is a legal requirement that the administratrix file a bond to insure the integrity of administration (' * * * [the administratrix] shall faithfully execute the duties of the trust according to law'). (Prob.Code § 541.) As complete exoneration of her failure to safeguard the estate's assets, Chandler claims reliance upon her attorney.

* * * In the instant case, the administratrix turned over possession and control of the money belonging to the estate to another person, her attorney. In doing so, she breached the duty of an estate representative. Even though the selection of the attorney was without negligence, the surrender of all of the duties of the administration of the estate without the administratrix' becoming responsible to the distributees for any losses sustained would negate the purpose of bonding the estate representative to assure administrative integrity; were such to become the rule, both the estate representative *and* the attorney would have to be bonded to give adequate safeguard to distributees. The applicable rule is set forth in Gaver v. Early, 191 Cal. 123, 127, 215 P. 394, 395: 'If a trustee confide the application of a trust fund to the care of another, whether a stranger or his own attorney or solicitor, or even cotrustee, he will be held personally responsible for any loss that may result. *Under such circumstances a trustee may employ attorneys or agents, according to the usual course of business, to reduce the estate to possession and protect it; but when once in his hands his personal duty to dispose and manage it begins, and this duty is not to be delegated* [emphasis added]. [Citations.] [Fns. omitted.]' "

In the instant case, there was either a complete abdication of the administration of decedent's estate by appellant, or she knowingly acquiesced in the failure to comply with the Probate Code (§§ 770, 772, 773). We cannot say that the trial court erred in its implied finding that appellant was aware of the need to secure court approval for the sale of the practice to Cuilty.

We have reviewed *all* of the records in an effort to reach the merits, to the fullest extent and find that appellant's contentions are without merit. With respect to the failure to secure court confirmation of the sale or to post notice and to open the sale up for bid, Evangelatos testified before Judge Koenig as follows:

"BY MR. HOBART: Is there anything by way of further clarification that you think would be necessary to show the state of mind between you and Mrs. Spirtos with respect to the necessity of the sale?

" * * *

"THE WITNESS: We had many conversations regarding the sale of the practice and negotiations with Dr. Cuilty, and the question of confirmation came up during our conversations and—

"Q BY MR. HOBART: Well, with respect to confirmation, since it was raised earlier, was there a purpose for not seeking—for, one, not filing or opening the bid, opening the sale up to publication in advance, and was there any reason for not filing for immediate confirmation at that time?

"A The purpose was the time element, that was the entire purpose of not bringing this to the Court's attention. We felt that if we filed a petition, the landlord would find out about it and we would be evicted out of there and probably lose the sale completely if they were to find out that we were negotiating, if we had sold the practice.

"Secondly, Dr. Cuilty wanted possession immediately: he said if he gave his $25,000 he wanted to take possession right now, so we let him take possession the following Saturday. He says, 'I have to have some time to familiarize myself with the practice, because I am going to be evicted out of there no doubt, and I need every day I can get.'

"And, like I say, Mrs. Spirtos and I had several conversations regarding this; in fact, we even discussed with her father and her father's attorney about this problem.

"Q Did Dr. Cuilty have any security or anything to your knowledge that you could take in order to protect the Estate any differently?

"A No. We asked him for that. He had none. I asked Mrs. Spirtos if she would please check with her banker about this person and see what she could find. I did the same. I went to the Bank of America and checked on Dr. Cuilty, my banker checked on him and said that he had a good rating; he had borrowed money at the bank and he had paid it back and they felt that he was a good—he had already—he had paid back his loans; that is as much as we could find out, because he said he had no security, he had nothing to give."

The record thus clearly reflects the fact that appellant was apprised of the need to inform the court of the sale; yet, in spite of this knowledge, appellant chose to rely upon her attorney's practical opinion of urgency and to bypass petitioning the court. Whether the record is devoid of any evidence purportedly excusing appellant from liability or whether the evidence taken before Judge Koenig is accepted on appeal the result is the same. Appellant, standing as a trustee with respect to the duty she owed to the estate, knowingly failed to execute the obligations she voluntarily assumed when she became the administratrix. Even though appellant may not have been negligent in the selection of her attorneys, it cannot be said that she was not negligent when she knowingly abdicated her duties to the estate.

* * *

Notes

1. The older cases frequently spoke of the liability for a wrongful delegation of trust responsibilities as being absolute. See e.g., In re Wood's Estate, 159 Cal. 466, 472, 114 P. 992, 994 (1911):

There is another rule * * * that * * * is well stated in the syllabus to McColister v. Bishop, 78 Minn. 228, 80 N.W. 1118, as follows: "If a trustee enters into any arrangement with reference to trust funds which surrenders or limits his control over them, he becomes a guarantor of the fund, irrespective of his motive or whether his surrender of control was the cause of the loss of the fund." In such a case, in the event of loss of the fund, the court will not enter upon an inquiry whether the loss is due to such abdication of control.

Although the court in the principal case adopts a stern approach, as it dismisses Mrs. Spirtos's arguments that she acted in good faith, its analysis does not rest on an absolute liability theory but rather depends on Mrs. Spirtos's negligence in disregarding the statutory requirement for a confirmation of a sale of estate assets. This is in line with the modern authority that tests the fiduciary's actions against a standard of due care in the selection of agents, attorneys, and advisers and in the continuous supervision of their activities. See Annot., Liability of Executor or Administrator, or His Bond, for Loss Caused to Estate by Act or Default of His Agent or Attorney, 28 A.L.R.3d 1191.

2. The prohibition against delegation serves useful objectives in safeguarding the trust from having to pay twice for the same services and in compelling the trustee to use care in selecting agents, but the rule has been criticized as unrealistic when it comes to putting together a modern trust portfolio. Langbein and Posner, Market Funds and Trust-Investment Law, 1976 A.B.F.Res.J. 1, 18–24; Cary and Bright, The Delegation of Investment Responsibility for Endowment Funds, 74 Colum.L.Rev. 207 (1974); see Note 1.(c) on p. 705, infra. See also Note, Trustee's Power to Delegate: A Comparative View, 50 Notre Dame L.Rev. 273 (1974). It is common practice today for fiduciaries, corporate as well as individual, to seek the assistance of outside advisers and market analysts in designing an investment strategy. The trustee may be required to pay the adviser's fee out of the trustee's commission. See Chase v. Pevear, 383 Mass. 350, 419 N.E.2d 1358, 1364 (1981) (payment to adviser approved where trustee was taking no separate trustee's fee). Employment of securities analysts and use of data from "various high quality 'Wall Street' research firms" has been accepted as evidence of the trustee having satisfied the standard of prudence and due care required of a corporate fiduciary. In re Estate of Niessen, 489 Pa. 135, 413 A.2d 1050 (1980). Corporate fiduciaries are reluctant to accept a trust when the testator directs that investment policy is to be set by an outside investment adviser. Heiss, Minimizing the Role of the Outside Investment Adviser, 121 Trusts & Estates 25 (Dec.1982).

4. Duty to Treat Beneficiaries Impartially

Restatement of the Law of Trusts 2d § 183.

Duty to Deal Impartially with Beneficiaries

When there are two or more beneficiaries of a trust, the trustee is under a duty to deal impartially with them.

Note

As is developed in the next two sections, a trustee may have difficulty balancing the competing claims of the income beneficiaries who want a maximum income return and the remaindermen who want the real value of the corpus preserved. Investment strategy may be the first concern, but it is not the only area of fiduciary responsibility that may give rise to conflicts.

The tax laws, federal and state, impose major responsibilities on fiduciaries during the administration of an estate. On the federal level, personal representatives must file income and gift tax returns that the decedent would have been required to file if living, an estate tax return within nine months of death to the extent that the gross estate exceeds the amount of the unified credit

($600,000 as of 1987) available to the estate, and fiduciary income tax returns for each year the administration is open. State laws duplicate many of these requirements. The details of the obligations imposed by the tax laws are beyond the scope of this book, but see generally Bittker, Federal Taxation of Income Estates and Gifts, Vol. 5, ch. 135 (1984).

Tax codes contain numerous provisions requiring executors, administrators, and trustees to make elections that affect such crucial issues as the identification of the beneficiaries, the size of deductions and the tax against which they are to be taken, the valuation of assets, the time when the tax is to be paid, etc. Fiduciaries have the duty to conserve the assets of the estate, which presumably includes minimizing its overall tax burden, to treat all beneficiaries impartially, and to refrain from self-dealing, but the exercise of any one of these elections almost invariably results in a benefit to one set of beneficiaries to the detriment of other beneficiaries. Thus, an election may put the fiduciary, particularly one who is also a beneficiary, in breach of basic fiduciary duties.

In such circumstances, is the fiduciary under a duty to effect an equitable adjustment among the beneficiaries to compensate for a disproportionate sharing of a tax burden resulting from an election by the fiduciary? This issue has received both judicial and legislative attention in the context of an election under IRC § 642(g) to deduct § 2053 claims and administration expenses and § 2054 casualty losses on the fiduciary income tax return rather than on the estate tax return. It may be that by this election the estate's total tax burden is reduced, but because administration expenses and casualty losses are ordinarily paid out of the estate's principal whereas the fiduciary income tax is paid from income, the election forces the beneficiaries of the principal to subsidize a windfall for the income beneficiaries. In a 1955 decision, the New York Surrogate's Court became the first court to rule that the principal account must be reimbursed by the amount of saving in estate tax that would have resulted had the deductions been taken on the estate tax return. In re Estate of Warms, 140 N.Y.S.2d 169 (Sur.Ct.N.Y.County 1955). See also In re Bixby's Estate, 140 Cal.App.2d 326, 295 P.2d 68 (1956); Rappaport's Estate, N.Y.L.J., Oct. 27, 1983, page 17 (Sur.Ct. Nassau County 1983) (in the reverse situation, the court directed the fiduciaries to deduct the administration expenses on the estate tax return, provided that the nonmarital beneficiaries make reimbursement of the tax savings that could have been realized by deducting the expenses on the fiduciary income tax return). Several statutes have followed the *Warms* lead. See N.Y.—McKinney's EPTL 11–1.2; Md.Code 1, Est. and Trusts, § 11–106; but see to the contrary, Mich.Comp. Laws Ann. § 700.829(1)(e)(2) that specifically authorizes this tax election and bars any equitable adjustments. Adjustments have been authorized in several other situations arising from tax elections, but uniform practices have not been developed either by fiduciaries or the courts. See Dobris, Equitable Adjustments in Postmortem Income Tax Planning: An Unremitting Diet of *Warms,* 65 Iowa L.Rev. 103 (1979) (analysis of cases requiring equitable adjustments); Dobris, Limits on the Doctrine of Equitable Adjustment in Sophisticated Postmortem Tax Planning, 66 Iowa L.Rev. 273 (1981) (analysis of cases not requiring equitable adjustments); Carrico and Bondurant, Equitable Adjustments: A Survey and Analysis of Precedents and Practices, 36 Tax Lawyer 545 (1983) (analysis of precedents and practices in twenty-two problem areas arising from tax elections). Because the number and variety of conflicts that may result from tax elections are practically limitless, prudent practice suggests that specific directions be included in the will or trust instrument, absolving the fiduciary from liability for breach of duty and making explicit the conditions, if any, under which an equitable adjustment is required.

D. INVESTMENT OF TRUST FUNDS

In the early part of this century trust administration was, by today's standards, simple.   A trustee's responsibility began and practically ended with the investment of the trust corpus in government bonds, first mortgages and occasionally high grade industrial bonds.   Because these traditional investments combined both security and high yield there was little call for a more diversified portfolio.   The depression of the thirties showed the previously accepted premises as to trust investments to be untenable.   Real estate mortgages did not stand up as the ultimate in security as defaults followed by foreclosures forced trustees to buy in practically valueless land.   Moreover, income from the standard investments fell off from a then handsome five to six percent or more, to nothing or one or two percent.   After World War II trustees were to face a new set of problems in the form of high personal income taxes on beneficiaries and an ever ascending inflationary trend, while prosperous business conditions and a constantly rising stock market seemed to offer new opportunities for trust investment.   Predictably, principles governing fiduciary investment changed to meet modern circumstances.

Two famous cases are often cited as the source of today's rules on trust investments.   The first is Harvard College v. Amory, 26 Mass. (9 Pick.) 446, 461 (1831), which states the following test:

> All that can be required of a trustee to invest, is, that he conduct himself faithfully and exercise a sound discretion.   He is to observe how men of prudence, discretion, and intelligence manage their own affairs, not in regard to speculation, but in regard to the permanent disposition of their funds, considering the probable income, as well as the probable safety of the capital to be invested.

The second is King v. Talbot, 40 N.Y. 76, 85–86 (1869), in which the court observed:

> My own judgment, after an examination of the subject, and bearing in mind the nature of the office, its importance, and the considerations, which alone induce men of suitable experience, capacity, and responsibility to accept its usually thankless burden, is, that the just and true rule is, that the trustee is bound to employ such diligence and such prudence in the care and management, as in general, prudent men of discretion and intelligence in such matters, employ in their own like affairs.

> This necessarily excludes all speculation, all investments for an uncertain and doubtful rise in the market, and of course everything that does not take into view the nature and object of the trust and the consequences of a mistake in the selection of the investment to be made.

Out of these similar statements emerged two different rules.   The first spawned the Massachusetts "prudent man rule", a rule which even today is often cast in the language of the court's opinion.   The New York case served as prologue to adoption of the statutory legal list of permissible investments. In terms of effect, the former allowed investment in "seasoned" common stock while the latter prohibited any equity representation (except where authorized by the will). The legal list approach, which seeks preservation of the principal at its initial dollar level, has been unsatisfactory in meeting inflation and, to the extent that it prohibited any investment in common stocks, has been abandoned almost entirely throughout the country in favor of the more flexible rule. For a number of years New York maintained a middle position and permitted fifty per cent of the portfolio to be in common stock with the balance being controlled by the legal list. In 1970, New York amended its law and enacted the prudent man rule. N.Y.—McKinney's EPTL 11–2.2.

Vestiges of the legal list approach remain in a number of statutes. Usually the list is permissive rather than mandatory, setting out safe havens (prudence is still wise policy) within which trustees may invest but not prohibiting them from purchasing nonlist investments if ordinary care and prudence are used. A number of states classify their lists as permissive but limit the percentage of investments in certain categories. Alabama does not have a mandatory legal list, but its constitution prohibits investment by fiduciaries in bonds or stocks of any private corporation. Commentators regularly call for the elimination of these restrictions. See e.g., Tralins, Contemporary Fiduciary Investments: Why Maryland Needs the Prudent Man Rule, 12 U. of Balt.L.Rev. 207 (1983); Weil, Common Stock: The Forbidden Trust Investment, 33 Ala.L.Rev. 407 (1982).

The original prudent man rule, as set out in Harvard College v. Amory, envisioned a man of prudence managing his own affairs, and this language appears in many of the statutes. See Restatement sections below. Influential modern formulations, however, have shifted the focus to a hypothetical individual managing other people's affairs. See UPC section below.

Restatement of the Law of Trusts 2d §§ 227, 228

Investments Which a Trustee Can Properly Make

In making investments of trust funds the trustee is under a duty to the beneficiary

(a) in the absence of provisions in the terms of the trust or of a statute otherwise providing, to make such investments and only such investments as a prudent man would make of his own property having in view the preservation of the estate and the amount and regularity of the income to be derived;

*   *   *

Distribution of Risk of Loss

Except as otherwise provided by the terms of the trust, the trustee is under a duty to the beneficiary to distribute the risk of loss by a reasonable diversification of investments, unless under the circumstances it is prudent not to do so.

UPC § 7–302. [Trustee's Standard of Care and Performance]

Except as otherwise provided by the terms of the trust, the trustee shall observe the standards in dealing with the trust assets that would be observed by a prudent man dealing with the property of another, and if the trustee has special skills or is named trustee on the basis of representations of special skills or expertise, he is under a duty to use those skills.

———

For a critique of codifications that take the UPC approach and a plea for a return to the more flexible, original language, see Fleming, Prudent Investments: The Varying Standards of Prudence, 12 Real Prop. Probate & Trust Law 243 (1977).

It is not to be assumed from the imprecision of the prudent man rule that the law does not impose substantial controls on trustees.   There are five basic principles that influence a trustee's investment strategy:

1. Prudent man rule

2. Diversification of trust portfolio

3. Accountability for each investment;   gains not to be balanced against losses

4. Duty to deal impartially with beneficiaries

5. Practice of treating cash receipts such as dividends, rents, and interest as income and capital gains and stock dividends as principal

As is developed infra, the above principles have influenced trustees to be cautious, featuring in their investment portfolios safe investments that preserve principal, oftentimes with insufficient concern for the growth of principal to reflect true value as opposed to original dollar value, while eschewing untried ventures and risky speculation of any type.   It is rare today to find a trust instrument that does not contain a discretionary investment clause establishing the scope of the trustee's investment powers.   The above principles remain, nonetheless, influential as they set the general standards against which investment clauses are construed and tested.   For an analysis of how the prudent man rule shapes investment policy and tends to discourage use of new investment concepts, see Current Investment Questions and the Prudent Person Rules, 13 Real Prop. Probate and Trust J. 650 (1978) (discussion of options, indexing, and investment in new small companies).

In 1974, the prudent man rule received a significant new assignment. The Employee Retirement Income Security Act of that year, requires pension funds to be administered "with the care, skill, prudence, and diligence under the circumstances then prevailing that a prudent man acting in a like capacity and familiar with such matters would use in the conduct of an enterprise of a like character and with like aims."   29 U.S. C.A. § 1104(a)(1)(B).   It is estimated that as of 1985 corporate and public pension plans have total assets of approximately $1.3 trillion dollars and own more than 25% of all publicly traded stock.   McCarroll, Socially

Responsible Investment of Public Pension Funds: The South Africa Issue and State Law, 10 N.Y.U.Rev. of Law and Social Change 407 (1980); see also Klein, Investments for Pension Funds, 42 N.Y.U.Inst. on Fed.Tax. § 23 (1984). The proceedings of the Section of Corporation, Banking and Business Law of the American Bar Association, analyzing in depth the fiduciary responsibilities under the Pension Reform Act, are reported in 31 The Business Lawyer, 1 (1975).

IN RE BANK OF NEW YORK

Court of Appeals of New York, 1974.
35 N.Y.2d 512, 364 N.Y.S.2d 164, 323 N.E.2d 700.

JONES, Judge. We hold that on the record in this case objections filed by the guardian ad litem to certain decisions of a bank acting as trustee of its own common trust fund were properly dismissed on a motion for summary judgment.

In 1952 Empire Trust Company established a discretionary common trust fund pursuant to section 100-c of the Banking Law, Consol.Laws, c. 2. In conformity with the provisions of that section The Bank of New York (into which Empire was merged in 1966) as continuing trustee of the common trust fund made a periodic accounting of the proceedings of the trustee for the four-year period ending September 30, 1968. In his report the guardian ad litem and attorney for principal questioned four investments made by the trustee. The trustee moved to dismiss these objections. In opposing the motion the guardian took the position that he had not been permitted to make copies of certain records of the trustee which he deemed relevant and that he sought opportunity to examine representatives of the trustee having knowledge concerning the questioned investments. The Surrogate, treating the motion to dismiss as in the nature of a motion for summary judgment, denied the motion without prejudice to its renewal after the guardian had examined the appropriate employees of the trustee as to the relevant facts with respect to each investment to which objection had been raised.

Thereafter the guardian examined the chairman of the bank's Trust Investment Committee and its chief investment officer, as well as three members of its research and investment analysis department. Information was developed from the records of the trustee and from the personal knowledge of these witnesses both as to the general practices of the trustee in the investment of the common trust fund and as to the particular history of each of the four challenged investments. It appears that the decision as to which witnesses were to be examined was that of the guardian and that all witnesses whose testimony was sought were produced.

On completion of these examinations the trustee renewed its motion for summary judgment dismissing the objections of the guardian. At the conclusion of oral argument on this motion, the guardian was prepared to submit the issues for determination on the record then available, without trial. That procedural proposal was unacceptable to the trustee,

Clark, Lusky, Murphy Grat.Tr. 3rd ACB—17

however, since it desired, failing success on its motion, the opportunity to present further evidence on trial. It had not undertaken to elicit affirmative testimony from its representatives on the occasions of their examinations by the guardian.

The Surrogate granted the trustee's motion for summary judgment as to the objections to two investments (Harcourt, Brace & World, Inc. and Mercantile Stores Company, Inc.) and denied it as to the objections with respect to the other two investments (The Boeing Company and Parke, Davis & Company). The majority at the Appellate Division modified by granting summary judgment for the trustee with respect to the objections which the Surrogate had reserved for trial. We now affirm the determination at the Appellate Division, thus dismissing all objections raised by the guardian.

We first note that in the circumstances presented in this record, disposition of the guardian's objections on a motion for summary judgment is not inappropriate. The guardian had completed the examination desired by him both of the trustee's records and of its personnel. He affirmatively indicated his readiness to dispose of the objections on the record before the court on the trustee's motion to dismiss. There is here no factual dispute between the parties as to what the trustee and its representatives did or omitted to do. The difference between them relates only to the legal conclusion to be drawn from conceded facts—the one contends that the trustee did not meet the duty imposed on it by law; the other, that such duty was discharged. Thus there is presented an issue of law for resolution by the court, including a court at the appellate level.

We take occasion to commend the guardian for the thoroughness of his investigation and, such investigation having been completed to his satisfaction, for his further readiness to adopt what appears to be a sensible procedural vehicle, at least in this case, for the disposition of the objections raised by him. The statutory requirement for accounting every four years with respect to common trust funds presents an occasion for the exercise of a particularly sagacious prudence. Primarily, we observe that most of the trust beneficiaries have so limited an economic interest in a common trust fund that it is unrealistic to place practical reliance on the disposition of any of them carefully to scrutinize a trustee's account. Thus the role of the guardian[6] takes on a special significance, for the trust beneficiaries must be assured that the trustee's accounts will receive careful and thorough review. At the same time if it is to serve the useful purpose for which it was designed, the common trust fund must be spared the adverse economic impact of the types of harassing litigation to which the mandatory four-year accounting requirement may expose it.

We turn then to the objections raised here. Initially we do not agree with what appears to have been in part the basis on which the majority

---

6. The guardians ad litem are appointed not only to protect the interests of infants, incompetents and unknowns, as in the usual case, but also to represent all others who do not appear in the proceeding (Banking Law, § 100–c, subd. 12).

at the Appellate Division reached its conclusion. The fact that this portfolio showed substantial overall increase in total value during the accounting period does not insulate the trustee from responsibility for imprudence with respect to individual investments for which it would otherwise be surcharged (cf. King v. Talbot, 40 N.Y. 76, 90–91; 3 Scott, Trusts [3d ed.], § 213.1, pp. 1712–1713). To hold to the contrary would in effect be to assure fiduciary immunity in an advancing market such as marked the history of the accounting period here involved. The record of any individual investment is not to be viewed exclusively, of course, as though it were in its own water-tight compartment, since to some extent individual investment decisions may properly be affected by considerations of the performance of the fund as an entity, as in the instance, for example, of individual security decisions based in part on considerations of diversification of the fund or of capital transactions to achieve sound tax planning for the fund as a whole. The focus of inquiry, however, is nonetheless on the individual security as such and factors relating to the entire portfolio are to be weighed only along with others in reviewing the prudence of the particular investment decisions.

The issue raised by the guardian with reference to the trustee's purchase and retention of the stock of Harcourt, Brace & World, Inc., is in a different category from that of the other three investments as to which he filed objections. When the guardian raised question as to this security, the Surrogate ruled that since this security was still on hand at the close of the accounting period, objections with respect to it must await its liquidation in a subsequent accounting period. This was error; the trustee acknowledged as much and the Surrogate himself recognized and corrected the error in a subsequent case (Matter of Marine Midland Bank-New York, 77 Misc.2d 543, 354 N.Y.S.2d 332). Confronted, however, with this ruling of the Surrogate as the law of this case, the guardian was left with no tenable position but to request that the trustee be directed to file a supplemental account through the date in 1969 when the holdings in Harcourt, Brace were sold. The Surrogate properly rejected this proposal, however, as violative of the integrity of the statutory pattern for quadrennial accounting proceedings (cf. Banking Law, § 100–c, subds, 14, 15; Matter of Roche, 259 N.Y. 458, 182 N.E. 82). On the record now before us, therefore, while it appears that the guardian would doubtless have objected had there been procedural opportunity to do so, no formal objection was ever filed with reference to the investment in Harcourt, Brace. All questions on this issue have now become moot, however, and no useful purpose would be served by remitting this case to permit the guardian now to file an objection as he should initially have been allowed to do, since it appears that a final decree has now been entered in the quadrennial accounting proceeding for the following four-year period, September, 1968 to September, 1972, in which no objection was raised as to the retention of the Harcourt, Brace stock here involved or as to the later acquisition of an additional 500 shares of the same stock, and the account of the trustee with respect thereto has been approved. In any event, for reasons similar to those discussed below with reference to the other three investments, we conclude that there was no sufficient predicate to surcharge the trustee with respect to this investment during the period of the present accounting.

The guardian objected to the trustee's purchase, retention and sale of the shares of Parke, Davis & Company, its sale of the holding in Mercantile Stores Company, Inc., and its purchase of shares of The Boeing Company. We conclude that there is no sufficient basis for surcharge as to any of such objections. The record discloses that with respect to each investment the trustee acted in good faith and cannot be said to have failed to exercise " 'such diligence and such prudence in the care and management [of the fund], as in general, prudent men of discretion and intelligence in such matters, employ in their own like affairs' " (Matter of Clark, 257 N.Y. 132, 136, 177 N.E. 397, 398; Costello v. Costello, 209 N.Y. 252, 261, 103 N.E. 148, 152; cf. EPTL, Consol.Laws, c. 17–b, 11–2.2). It was not shown in any instance that the losses to the trust fund resulted from imprudence or negligence. There was evidence of attention and consideration with reference to each decision made. Obviously it is not sufficient that hindsight might suggest that another course would have been more beneficial; nor does a mere error of investment judgment mandate a surcharge. Our courts do not demand investment infallibility, nor hold a trustee to prescience in investment decisions. (Matter of Hubbell, 302 N.Y. 246, 257, 97 N.E.2d 888, 893.)

Whether a trustee is to be surcharged in these instances, as in other cases, must necessarily depend on a balanced and perceptive analysis of its consideration and action in the light of the history of each individual investment, viewed at the time of its action or its omission to act. In our opinion no sufficiently useful purpose would be served by a detailed description of the analysis by which we reach the conclusion that there is no basis for surcharge with respect to any of the four investments here called into question. Procedures we now find acceptable with respect to these investments at the time of this accounting may not be satisfactory at another time in other circumstances. It suffices here to state that we do not find sufficient basis for surcharge in this case.

The order of the Appellate Division should accordingly be affirmed.

BREITEL, C. J., and JASEN, GABRIELLI, WACHTLER and SAMUEL RABIN, JJ., concur.

STEVENS, J., taking no part.

Order affirmed, with costs to all parties appearing separately and filing separate briefs payable out of the trust fund.

Notes

1. As the court holds, if trustees have acted with prudence in acquiring an investment, they will not be held liable because the investment later depreciates in value due to a depression in the economy. Wisdom born of hindsight will not set the standards against which a trustee's performance is to be judged. Continuous supervision is, however, required and the trustee may be held liable for losses if the economic decline was foreseeable. Typically, the trustee looks for stock in a company that has a solid capital structure, competency of management, and a long history of productive return. These and other factors to

be considered in establishing prudence are discussed in 3 Scott on Trusts § 227 (3d ed. 1967).

The Supreme Judicial Court of Massachusetts recently reviewed its experience in applying the prudent man rule, which it had originally authored, and noted that it had rejected numerous efforts to establish specific categories of investment that were violative of the rule. The court quoted an earlier statement made by it to the effect that the prudent man standard "avoids the inflexibility of definite classification of securities, it disregards the optimism of the promoter, and eschews the exuberance of the speculator. It holds fast to common sense and depends on practical experience." Chase v. Pevear, 383 Mass. 350, 419 N.E.2d 1358, 1365 (1981).

Other factors to be considered in putting together an investment portfolio include:

(a) Retention of Securities Originally Acquired by the Testator. If trustees retain stock coming to them from the testator, they can argue that the testator had particular confidence in the investment and that they are therefore justified in retaining it during a downward trend. In re Casani's Estate, 342 Pa. 468, 21 A.2d 59, 135 A.L.R. 1513 (1941); Moore, A Rationalization of Trust Surcharge Cases, 96 U. of Pa.L.Rev. 647, 653–656 (1948). There comes a point, however, when the prudent trustee must abandon a losing enterprise. The point is not easy to define. Estate of Knipp, 489 Pa. 509, 414 A.2d 1007 (1980) (not imprudent to hold Sears stock while it dropped from $117 to $88 per share in fifteen months; dissent found performance did not meet standards required of a corporate fiduciary). Trustees may justify their retention even after it has become an improper investment by proving that disposition of the stock is impossible because there is no market for it and that the absence of a market is not due to any negligence on the part of the trustee. Estate of Stetson, 463 Pa. 64, 345 A.2d 679 (1975).

(b) Diversification. Under the prudent man rule, it is accepted that a trustee has the duty to diversify the investments in order to minimize the risk of losses. The careful trustee should not therefore invest more than a reasonable portion of the portfolio in a single security or a single type of security. New England Trust Co. v. Paine, 320 Mass. 482, 70 N.E.2d 6 (1946). It has been held that, although diversity of investments is a desirable course for trust management, "a judicial decision declaring non-diversification to be presumptively imprudent would arbitrarily foreclose executors and trustees from opportunities to retain beneficial holdings." A case-by-case analysis of propriety is preferable. Estate of Knipp, supra, 414 A.2d at page 1009. Tradition in legal list states has not held so strongly to the principle. In re Mendleson's Will, 46 Misc.2d 960, 261 N.Y.S.2d 525 (1965).

(c) Investment in an Investment Company Mutual Fund. Early authority concluded that such an investment violated the duty not to delegate discretionary responsibilities, but an influential article, Shattuck, The Legal Propriety of Investment by American Fiduciaries in the Shares of Boston-Type Open-End Investment Trusts, 25 B.U.L.Rev. 1, (1945), and an Ohio decision, In re Rees' Estate, 53 Ohio Abs. 385, 85 N.E.2d 563 (1949), set a trend in the other direction. Many states authorize such investments by statute. 3 Scott on Trusts § 227.9A (3d ed. 1967). The line between

propriety and impropriety has been described as "nonsensical" in states
that permit investments in common stocks. "A trustee's purchase of shares
in a company entails his 'delegating' the management of the company to
its officers and directors." Langbein and Posner, Market Funds and Trust-
Investment Law, 1976 A.B.F.Res.J. 1, 21. The manager of relatively small
funds may find that mutual funds offer the only investment that provides
an adequate return, diversification and full employment of the funds. Directors of nonprofit corporations who "are chosen for a variety of reasons,
few of which have anything to do with expertise in portfolio management"
may also find it necessary to get outside help with the endowment. Cary
and Bright, The Delegation of Investment Responsibility for Endowment
Funds, 74 Colum.L.Rev. 207 (1974).

2. The court in the principal case recognized that the record of an individual
investment is not to be viewed exclusively "as though it were in its own water-
tight compartment" but then went on to do an item by item analysis of the
trustee's performance. Thus the court on the one hand gives a nod to modern
investment theory that stresses total portfolio performance, while on the other
it reaffirms the traditional rule that the trustee cannot balance gains against
losses. This rule compels the trustee to justify the propriety of each security
as a separate entity rather than to concentrate on the overall performance of
the portfolio which is the real concern of the beneficiaries. Modern commentators are practically unanimous in their condemnation of the rule. See e.g.,
Fleming, Prudent Investments: The Varying Standards of Prudence, 12 Real
Prop. Probate and Trust J. 243, 248–249 (1977) (description of how the rule
makes trustees overly conservative); Current Investment Questions and the
Prudent Person Rule, 13 Real Prop. Probate and Trust J. 650 (1978) (discussion
of how the rule, along with other factors, discourages use of new investment
strategies such as the purchase of stock options, indexing, and investment in
new small companies); Hirsch, Inflation and the Law of Trusts, 18 Real Prop.
Probate and Trust J. 601 (1983) (analysis of the rule as one factor that inhibits
the development of strategies to offset inflation).

The development of "indexing" as an investment strategy is the result of
"dissatisfaction with the performance of conventional investment funds, which
sacrifice diversification and incur heavy research and transaction costs in an
apparently vain effort to outperform the broad market indices such as the S &
P [Standard and Poor] 500." Langbein and Posner, Market Funds and Trust
Investment Law, 1976 A.B.F.Res.J. 1, 2. See also Langbein and Posner, The
Revolution in Trust Investment Law, 62 A.B.A.J. 764 (1976). The new strategy
is to "buy-the-market" and to invest in "index" or "market" funds. "These are
mutual or other investment funds that have abandoned the traditional attempt
to 'beat the market' by picking and choosing among securities—buying stocks
or bonds that they believe to be undervalued and selling those they believe to
be overvalued. Instead, they create and hold essentially unchanged a portfolio
of securities that is designed to approximate some index of market performance
such as the Standard & Poor's 500. The S&P 500 is a hypothetical portfolio
consisting of 500 major nonfinancial companies on the New York Stock Exchange weighted by the market value of each company's total outstanding shares."
Langbein and Posner, Market Funds and Trust Investment Law, 1976 A.B.F.
Res.J. 1. A trustee who buys the market will "inevitably be acquiring an
interest in some stocks that if individually selected would be characterized as
wrongful or speculative and hence as imprudent for trust investment." The

authors predict that this strategy will produce better performance at reduced cost and express the expectation that the courts will apply as the standard of review collective performance of the entire portfolio. Id. at p. 26.

3. Executors may have an obligation to invest estate funds during the period of administration. Because the period will be short, their obligations and objectives differ from those of a trustee and the prudent man rule must be adjusted accordingly. Estate of Beach, 15 Cal.3d 623, 125 Cal.Rptr. 570, 542 P.2d 994 (1975).

4. The Connecticut General Statutes include the following directions to the state's treasurer when investing state trust funds, which consist of such large deposits as the state and municipal employees' retirement funds, the teachers' pension fund, and similar funds for persons who have worked for governmental agencies:

§ 3–13d(a)   *   *   *   Among the factors to be considered by the treasurer with respect to all securities may be the social, economic and environmental implications of investments of trust funds in particular securities or types of securities. In the investment of the state's trust funds the treasurer shall consider the implications of any particular investment in relation to the foreign policy and national interests of the United States.

* * *

§ 3–13f (a) In carrying out his fiduciary responsibility, the State Treasurer shall, within a reasonable period of time, disinvest all state funds currently invested in any corporation doing business in South Africa and invest no new state funds in any such corporation unless such corporation satisfies all the following minimum requirements: (1) Such corporation has adopted the Sullivan Principles and has obtained a performance rating in the top two categories of the Sullivan Principles rating system prepared by Arthur D. Little, Inc., (2) such corporation does not supply strategic products or services for use by the government of South Africa or for use by the military or police in South Africa and (3) such corporation recognizes the right of all South African employees to organize and strike in support of economic or social objectives, free from the fear of dismissal or blacklisting. * * *

(b) In determining whether or not to invest state funds in any corporation, the state treasurer, in administering this section, may require a social audit of any corporation doing business in South Africa.

* * *

§ 3–13g The state treasurer shall review the major investment policies of the state for purposes of ensuring that state funds are not invested in any corporation engaged in any form of business in Iran which could be considered to be contrary to the foreign policy or national interests of the United States, particularly in respect to the release of all American hostages held in Iran.

Several other states and a number of municipalities, including New York, Philadelphia, Boston and the District of Columbia, have enacted similar divestment laws. For a review of many of these statutes and an analysis of their legality and affect, see McCarroll, Socially Responsible Investment of Pension Funds: The South Africa Issue and State Law, 10 N.Y.U.Rev. of Law and Social Change, 407 (1980). Many contracts between unions and industry contain provisions calling for social investment in activities to buttress local economies or particular industries, as well as prohibitions against investments in firms that do business in South Africa. Murrmann, Schaffer, and Wokutch, Social Investing by State Public Employee Pension Funds, 35 Lab.Law J. 360 (June 1984).

Is the trustee who accepts some reduction in return on investments in order to foster political, social, or other noneconomic objectives in violation of the prudent man rule? To the effect that social investments may be made in compliance with the rule, see Ravikoff and Curzan, Social Responsibility in Investment Policy and the Prudent Man Rule, 68 Cal.L.Rev. 518 (1980); for a contrary view to the effect that social investing violates fiduciary duties unless the beneficiaries of the fund are allowed to opt out of the socially-invested fund and into a fund that is managed solely to achieve economic return, see Langbein and Posner, Social Investing and the Law of Trusts, 79 Mich.L.Rev. 72 (1980). Judicial authority to date has not dealt directly with the issue. Compare Withers v. Teachers' Retirement System of the City of New York, 447 F.Supp. 1248 (S.D.N.Y.1978) (investment of $2.53 billion of municipal pension funds in low-rated, highly speculative city bonds to help stave off city's possible bankruptcy approved as prudent because city was major contributor to fund and ultimate guarantor of the benefits) with Blankenship v. Boyle, 329 F.Supp. 1089 (D.D.C. 1971) (failure to invest large sums of employees' welfare fund, which benefited the union and a bank controlled by it, violated trustees' duty of loyalty and was imprudent). The Internal Revenue Service has ruled that low-risk income-producing investments that serve social purposes do not jeopardize the tax exempt status under I.R.C. § 501(c)(17) of an unemployment benefit trust, even though a lower than market rate of return is expected. Rev.Rul. 70–536, 1970–2 C.B. 120. Might an argument be developed that a statute such as Connecticut's requires the state to intrude into the field of foreign affairs, which is reserved by the Constitution to the federal government, in violation of the principles set out in Zschernig v. Miller, supra p. 35, note 7? An opinion of the Wisconsin attorney general answers that question in the negative. 67 Wis. Op.Att'y.Gen. (Jan. 31, 1978).

Langbein and Posner suggest the variety of investments that may appear on a prohibited list, 79 Mich.L.Rev. at pps. 83–84:

It is not easy to specify the portfolio adjustments that an investor committed to social investing would have to make, because the social principles are poorly specified. There is no consensus about which social principles to pursue and about which investments are consistent or inconsistent with those principles. At a time when most of the social activism in investing was liberal or radical rather than conservative, there was some agreement among the activists as to the types of companies that should be avoided and the types that should be embraced. The ranks of the disapproved included companies lending to or having branches or subsidiaries in the Republic of South Africa, big defense contractors, nonunion companies, and prominent or recurrent violators of federal discrimination, pollution, safety, and antitrust laws. More recently, the nuclear power and herbicide industries have also fallen into disfavor. The ranks of the approved included companies that manufactured anti-pollution equipment, or used especially clean technologies, or invested in the inner cities. * * * With the rapid rise of right-wing social activism, we can expect social-investment advocates to appear who will urge investment managers not to invest in corporations that manufacture contraceptive devices, or publish textbooks that teach the theory of evolution, or do business with the Soviet Union. * * *

IN RE TRUSTEESHIP AGREEMENT WITH MAYO

Supreme Court of Minnesota, 1960.
259 Minn. 91, 105 N.W.2d 900.

DELL, Chief Justice. Appeals from orders of the district court denying the petitions of Esther Mayo Hartzell, as beneficiary, for orders authorizing the trustees of two separate trusts created by the late Dr. Charles H. Mayo on August 17, 1917, and March 28, 1919, to deviate from identical investment restrictions in the trust instruments or to construe the term "other forms of income bearing property" as used therein as authorizing investment of trust funds in corporate stock. The donor died May 26, 1939.

The petitions were opposed by the trustees. Roderick D. Peck was appointed guardian ad litem and appeared for all "unknown, unascertained, minor and incompetent beneficiaries" with respect to both trusts. Appearances were also made on behalf of the petitioner, William J. Mayo II, one of the beneficiaries, and the trustees. The present appeals are taken by the petitioner and by a number of other beneficiaries of the trusts.

With reference to investments the provisions of both trusts are in substance as follows:

"* * * The TRUSTEES shall hold said property as a trust fund and collect the interest, income and profits therefrom as the same accrue; *manage, care for and protect said fund all in accordance with their best judgment and discretion,* invest and re-invest the same in *real estate mortgages, municipal bonds or any other form of income bearing property (but not real estate nor corporate stock),* * * *." (Italics supplied.)

At the time of the hearing the value of the assets of the first trust was approximately $1,000,000, invested mostly in municipal bonds and in 1,944 shares of common stock of the Kahler Corporation, the latter coming into the trust at the time of its creation from the donor. The value of the assets of the second trust at the time of the hearing was approximately $186,000 invested mostly in municipal bonds. The first trust by its terms will continue until 21 years after the death of the petitioner, who was 51 years of age at the time of the hearing; while the second trust by its terms will partially terminate as each surviving child of petitioner attains the age of 30 years and will fully terminate when the last of such children attains such age; but in the event of certain alternatives it will not continue longer than 21 years after the death of all of donor's children.

In support of the petition, evidence was submitted that an inflationary period, which could not have been foreseen, had commenced shortly after the donor's death in 1939; that it had reduced the real value of the trust assets by more than 50 percent; that a further inflationary period or a permanent "creeping inflation," which the donor could not have foreseen, must be expected; that on December 30, 1940, when the trustees filed their first accounting, the value of the assets of the first trust was $957,711.60; that in October 1958, at the trustees' most recent accounting, the value of such assets was $968,893.08, which in terms of 1940 dollar values meant that in 1958 the assets of the first trust were worth only $456,139.67; that the same percentage of shrinkage was experienced in the second trust; that the provisions of the trust prohibiting investments in real estate and corporate stocks had caused such shrinkage; and that the market value of common stocks had almost doubled since 1939 while the actual value of bonds, in terms of purchasing power, had been cut almost in half since that time. Appellants state that even in the short period between March 1959 and November 1959 the Consumer Price Index of the Bureau of Labor Statistics has increased from 123.7 to 125.6, representing an increase of almost 2 percent in 8 months.

Petitioner urges that the donor's ultimate and dominant intention was to preserve the value of the trust corpus and that this will be circumvented unless the court authorizes the trustees to deviate from the investment provisions of the trust and invest part of the funds in corporate stocks; that it is common practice of trustees of large trusts which have no restrictive investment provisions (including the First National Bank of Minneapolis, one of the trustees in both trusts here) to invest substantial proportions of trust assets in corporate stocks to protect such trusts against inflation, and she asserts that if no deviation is permitted and the next 20 years parallel the last 20 years the ultimate beneficiaries of these trusts will be presented with assets having less than one-fourth of the value which they had at the time of the donor's death.

In opposition to the petition, the trustees refer to the donor's clear intention, as expressed in the trust instruments, that no part of the trust funds should be invested in real estate or corporate stocks, and urge that, since no emergency or change of circumstances which could not have been foreseen or experienced by the donor during his lifetime has been shown, no deviation from the donor's clearly expressed intention would be justified. They urge that the rule is well established that where prospective changes of conditions are substantially known to or anticipated by the settlor of a trust the courts will not grant a deviation from its provisions. They point out that the donor here had survived some 20 years after the creation of the trusts during a period in which there had been both a great inflation and a severe depression; that after creating such trusts he had observed the inflation of the post-World-War-I period, the stock market fever of the pre-1929 era, the market crash of 1929, and the subsequent depression and lowering of bond interest rates during the late 1930's; that despite these economic changes he had never altered the investment restrictions in these trusts; and that he was always aware of his right to amend the trust instruments and, in fact, had consented to minor departures from the provisions of one of the trusts in 1932 and had once amended another trust to permit acquisition of common stocks, but had never requested any change in the investment provisions of the trusts now under consideration and apparently was satisfied with them exactly as they had been drawn and executed.　Petitioner offered expert testimony favoring deviation and respondents' expert testimony was to the contrary.　The lower court found in favor of respondents and these appeals followed.

* * *

In our opinion the evidence here, together with economic and financial conditions which may properly be judicially noticed, compels us to hold that unless deviation is ordered the dominant intention of the donor to prevent a loss of the principal of the two trusts will be frustrated. When the trusts were created and for many years prior thereto, the dollar, based upon the gold standard, remained at a substantially fixed value. On March 9, 1933, the United States went off the gold standard and has since that time remained off from it domestically.　While some inflation shortly thereafter followed, it was not until after the death of the donor that inflation commenced to make itself really known and felt.　Since then it has gradually increased until at the time of the trial of this case the purchasing power of the dollar, measured by the Consumer Price Index of the U.S. Bureau of Labor Statistics, had depreciated to one-half of its 1940 value.　While the experts called by the respective parties disagreed as to when inflation, which they felt was then dormant, would start again and at what percentage it would proceed, there was no disagreement between them that further inflation "in the foreseeable future" could be expected.　There was testimony that there would possibly be none for the next year or two and that then it would "increase so that over the period of ten years, on the average, the trend line would be between one and a half and two per cent　*　*　*."　But from the date of trial to November 1959 there was an increase of almost 2 percent in the cost of living index.

At the time these trusts were created it was common practice for business men, in protecting their families through the creation of trusts, to authorize investments to be made by their trustees only in high-grade bonds or first mortgages on good real estate.　Many of the estates [sic] then had statutes preventing trustees from investing in corporate stocks or real estate.　Since that time many of the states, including Minnesota, have enacted statutes permitting trustees to invest in corporate stocks and real estate.　In recent years most trust companies have encouraged donors, when naming the companies as trustees, to permit investment in common stocks as well as bonds and mortgages.　And these trustees maintain competent and efficient employees, well acquainted with the various aspects of corporations having listed stocks, so as to enable them to make reasonably safe and proper corporate-stock purchases.

Throughout the trial considerable reference was made to the 1929 stock-market crash as a reason why deviation would not be granted.　There are many reasons, however, why the market action of that period is not a controlling factor today.　At that time, many of the corporations, including some of the very best, did not maintain sufficient current assets in relation to current liabilities. And several of them then carried a large funded indebtedness drawing high interest rates with comparatively early maturities. Many companies also, during that period, declared and paid higher dividends than should have been paid. As a result they did not retain and build up a sufficient surplus for future use in the business. When the crash came, many of them, because of such practices, had great difficulty for a long period of time in extricating themselves from their unfortunate financial positions. Dividends from many of such companies were stopped or greatly reduced. A few of them failed altogether. This caused the market value of stocks for a long period of time to greatly decline. But even so, almost all of the companies having corporate stock classified as "good, sound investment stocks" not only survived but have been paying regular and substantial dividends. Many of them are now considered outstanding, safe, investment stocks. Now almost all of these companies maintain a high ratio between their current assets and their current liabilities. They have also built up and retain large surpluses for use in their business. Many of them now have no funded debt at all; and those that do, in most instances, have fixed maturity dates well ahead in years with a satisfactory rate of interest.

Officers and directors of companies registered and listed on the New York and American Stock Exchanges, as well as beneficial owners of more than 10 percent of any of its securities, must now, under the Securities Exchange Act of 1934, 15 U.S.C.A. § 78a et seq., file a statement with the exchange where the stock is registered and listed, and a duplicate original thereof with the Securit[ies] Exchange Commission, indicating their ownership at the close of the calendar month and such changes in their ownership as have occurred during such calendar month. Such statements must be in the hands of the commission and the exchange before the 10th day of the month following that which they cover. The information thus made available is published for the benefit of the public. Large investment companies have been organized under the Investment Company Act of 1940, 15 U.S.C.A. § 80a–1 et seq. They now buy, sell, and own large amounts of corporate stocks in various companies. This assists in stabilizing the market in difficult financial times.

In 1929 there was no Securit[ies] Exchange Commission to regulate and control corporate stock purchases or sales. Many of the people of that era were not investing in stocks at all but were gambling in them. At that time the margin requirement was only 10 percent and brokers' loans reached an alltime high of approximately $8,500,000,000. Until recently margin requirements were, as fixed within the framework of the Securities Exchange Act, 90 percent. As a result there has been very little speculation and brokers' loans have been relatively small. In 1929 large speculators pooled their resources with a premeditated plan to buy and force certain stocks upward. This upward surge prompted uninformed people to purchase those stocks. When the stocks had reached a predetermined value, the pool operators sold out, the stocks declined, and the people took the losses. During that period promoters were dealing in public utilities stocks, merging companies together without proper relation one to the other geographically or otherwise. When the crash came those stocks suffered greatly. Some of the companies never recovered at all. And it took many of those that did recover several years to reestablish themselves again. Several of them were required to divest themselves of their complex and wide holdings under the Public Utility Holding Company Act of 1935, 15 U.S.C.A. § 79a et seq. These practices are no longer permissible under that act and the rules and regulations of the Securit[ies] Exchange Commission. Since 1932, because of heavy Federal expenditures, the national debt has grown from a high of approximately $25,400,000,000 at the end of World War I to approximately $258,600,000,000 at the end of World War II and to approximately $290,000,000,000 at the present time.* Inflation has been steadily increasing. None of this was foreseeable by an ordinary prudent investor at the time these trusts were created, nor at the time of the donor's death in 1939, since these inflationary practices did not become noticeably fixed and established until after his death.

It appears without substantial dispute that if deviation is not permitted the accomplishment of the purposes of the trusts will be substantially impaired because of changed conditions due to inflation since the trusts were created; that unless deviation is allowed the assets of the trusts, within the next 20 years, will, in all likelihood, be worth less than one-fourth of the value they had at the time of the donor's death. To avoid this we conclude that in equity the trustees should have the right and be authorized to deviate from the restrictive provisions of the trusts by permitting them, when and as they deem it advisable, to invest a reasonable amount of the trust assets in corporate stocks of good, sound investment issues. Through an investment in bonds and mortgages of the type designated by the donor, plus corporate stocks of good, sound investment issues, in our opinion, the trusts will, so far as possible, be fortified against inflation, recession, depression, or decline in prices. Corporate trustees of the kind here [sic] are regularly managing trusts consisting of corporate stocks, bonds, and mortgages, on a successful basis. There appears to be no sound reason why they cannot do the same thing here.

Reversed and remanded for further proceedings in conformity with this opinion.

THOMAS GALLAGHER, J., took no part in the consideration or decision of this case.

Note

The principal case represents a dramatic example of how changing economic conditions impact on investment strategy. Conditions are vastly different today than when the principal case was decided, leading some commentators to conclude that investment in common stocks is not a complete answer to inflation and that the traditional trust rules must be made more flexible to meet the

---

* In 1983 the national debt was $1,377,211,000,000 and rising. Eds.

demands of changing times. See e.g., Hirsch, Inflation and the Law of Trusts, 18 Real Prop. Probate and Trust J. 601 (1983).

Modern trustees, who must be even-handed in their treatment of income beneficiaries and remaindermen, face a dilemma. The income beneficiaries will urge a strategy that emphasizes investment in bonds, which return a much higher income than common stocks (government bonds, for example, were paying over 14% in 1981), but such fixed-dollar investments allow for no growth in principal to offset inflation. The remaindermen, on the other hand, will argue for investment in growth stocks to preserve the real, not just the nominal, value of the principal, but most "successful and expanding corporations distribute in current dividends a half of their earnings or less, plowing back the rest of their earnings into the business". 3 Scott on Trusts § 236.17, 1984 Supp. p. 80. These corporations may pay cash dividends which amount to only one or two per cent of the value of the shares, an amount that the income beneficiaries would find totally inadequate. They may also declare stock dividends, but these are treated as principal rather than income. Furthermore, the rule against balancing gains against losses makes it risky for the trustee to invest a portion of the portfolio in high-yield bonds and the balance in growth stocks. The difference in performance between a bond and stock portfolio is demonstrated in a chart appearing in note 2, p. 728, infra.

A sampling of decisions indicates that the courts try to hold trustees to a middle course. Demands by income beneficiaries that the trustee maximize the income return have not generally been successful. See e.g., Estate of Hamill, 487 Pa. 592, 410 A.2d 770 (1980) (bank's refusal to accept widow's instructions to invest in U.S. Treasury notes or high quality industrial bonds upheld; 6% income return reasonable); State of Delaware, ex rel. Gebelein v. Belin, 456 So.2d 1237 (Fla.App.1984) (3% return on $805 million charitable trust created by Alfred I. duPont constituted reasonable exercise of trustees' discretion); Estate of Stillman, supra p. 656 (modest return of income upheld as principal of two trusts increased from $2 million in 1944 to $8.5 million in 1977). A trustee has successfully defended against a surcharge action for investing in low-yield, tax-exempt government bonds by contending that such a portfolio better meets the needs of the high bracket income beneficiaries. Commercial Trust Co. v. Barnard, 27 N.J. 332, 142 A.2d 865 (1958). On the other hand, trustees will be held liable if they put the principal at risk in order to maximize income. Matter of Will of Newhoff, 107 Misc.2d 589, 435 N.Y.S.2d 632 (Sur. Ct., Nassau County 1980) (investment in real estate investment trusts, so-called REITS, without history of a productive return speculative and imprudent); but see Klein, Investments for Pension Funds, 42 N.Y.U. Inst. on Fed.Tax. § 23 (1984) (analysis of investment in real estate by pension funds). On the impact of the rules governing the allocation of cash and stock dividends, capital gains, and the like between income and principal, see note 2, pp. 726–729, infra.

E. VARIABLES AFFECTING THE IMPOSITION OF LIABILITY

1. *The Remedy Requested*

A question with regard to a fiduciary's conduct may come up in the following ways: (a) request by the fiduciary for instructions, (b) injunction against a threatened breach of trust, (c) request by the beneficiaries for specific performance of some obligation imposed by the trust, (d) action, usually on the accounts, to surcharge the fiduciary for damages occasioned by a breach, (e) removal of the fiduciary, (f) request for the appointment of a receiver, (g) action to reduce or dispense with the fiduciary's compensation. If there is an obligation to pay money or convey property to a beneficiary there may be an action for damages against the fiduciary as well. The court will view the trustee's conduct from a different perspective under each of these headings and, as a result, its judgment as to the propriety of that conduct will vary with the context.

Where loss is determined, another variable may be the rate of interest imposed. Fiduciaries need not be charged interest at all, or they may be charged at the rate earned by the average trust in the community. If their breach has been flagrant they can be assessed at the legal rate. See 2 Scott on Trusts §§ 199, 207 (3d ed. 1967).

2. *Identification of the Fiduciary*

(a) *Multiple Fiduciaries*—The stated rule with regard to several co-trustees of private trusts is that they must act with unanimity.* One cannot take a passive position leaving the active administration to others. Limited authority can be granted to one trustee if such action does not constitute a wrongful delegation of discretionary power. In actual operation this may work to give a dissenting trustee of three or more a veto power. In such an event the court can resolve the conflict. It is common, in trusts which are to be administered by more than two trustees, for the draftsman to provide that a majority will control. Because of the theory of unanimity, a trustee's liability need not be predicated on direct participation in the breach. If the trustees have been passive they may be held liable for not policing their colleagues or for wrongfully delegating their authority to them. Because of these independent responsibilities, a minority trustee may hire an attorney of his or her own choice and have the attorney compensated out of the trust. Belcher v. Conway, 179 Conn. 198, 425 A.2d 1254 (1979).

The unanimity rule does not apply to co-executors or co-administrators. Each of them is ordinarily competent to act for the estate. They

---

* In New York, majority rule prevails when there are three or more fiduciaries. No liability may be visited upon any dissenting trustee if such dissent is expressed promptly in writing, but " * * * liability for failure to join in administering the estate or trust or to prevent a breach of trust may not thus be avoided." N.Y.—McKinney's EPTL 11–1.1(b)(13).

In addition to providing for majority rule, N.Y.—McKinney's EPTL 11–1.1(b) gives fiduciaries many administrative powers which are exercisable along with those powers granted by the terms of the instrument or by law. These statutory powers include the power to: sell, lease, mortgage, or collect rents from real property; sell or lease personal property; compromise or settle claims; vote shares of stock; insure and repair property; foreclose mortgages; distribute property in kind; and cause stock or securities to be registered and held in the name of a nominee. Furthermore, fiduciaries may petition the court for authority to exercise any power not included in the statute when such power is necessary for the proper administration of the estate or trust. N.Y.—McKinney's EPTL 11–1.1(c). One effect of this detailed statutory grant of fiduciaries' powers will be to eliminate the need for most or all of the long "boilerplate" provisions customary in will and trust instruments. The statutory powers can be narrowed or eliminated by contrary provisions in the will or other instrument. The New York approach is representative of that taken in a large number of jurisdictions.

are therefore held less strictly accountable for each other's defaults, though they do have an obligation to seek redress for the estate against such defaults.   See Estate of Rothko, supra, p. 667.

(b) *Degree of Expertise*—The Restatement of Trusts § 174 and UPC § 7–302, supra p. 700, state that a trustee who has special skills or makes representations of special skills is under a duty to use those special skills. A statute setting out a similar standard has been enacted in New York. N.Y.—McKinney's EPTL 11–2.2(a), see discussion, supra, p. 642.   Under this principle, a corporate fiduciary is judged by a higher standard than is an individual who, although prudent, possesses no particular expertise or skills as a trustee.   See e.g., In re Mendenhall, 484 Pa. 77, 398 A.2d 951 (1979); In re Estate of Killey, 457 Pa. 474, 326 A.2d 372 (1974).

3.   *Consent of the Beneficiaries*

Knowledge and approval of the fiduciary's conduct by the beneficiaries may be held to constitute a ratification of that conduct which estops the beneficiaries from making a challenge.   It appears that the knowledge must be complete and that mere silence does not constitute acquiescence.   See Renz v. Beeman, supra p. 680.   Under the doctrine of virtual representation, ratification by adult beneficiaries may bind contingent beneficiaries, who are not yet ascertained or are minors, so long as the adults have no conflict of interest or other hostility toward those whom they represent.   See e.g., Matter of Estate of Lange, 75 N.J. 464, 383 A.2d 1130 (1978).

4.   *Advice of Counsel*

The fiduciaries who were under challenge in the Rothko and Spirtos cases, supra pp. 667, 691, put in as one ground of defense that they were acting on the advice of their counsel.   These defenses did not immunize the fiduciaries from the consequences of their defaults.   Because a main thrust of fiduciary laws holds that fiduciaries are the ones to act and that they are not to delegate their responsibilities, it is not surprising that courts give only limited effect to this defense.   Reliance on advice of counsel is a factor in determining good faith and due diligence, even though it does not give blanket immunity.   See e.g., In re Trust of Mintz, 444 Pa. 189, 282 A.2d 295 (1971); same, as regards the advice of an investment analyst, In re Estate of Poulsen, 54 Wis.2d 139, 194 N.W.2d 593 (1972).   Indeed, it may be imprudent for the trustee not to seek investment advice.   See discussion supra p. 696.

5.   *Exculpatory Clauses*

Frequently, a will or trust instrument will contain a paragraph that purports to immunize the fiduciaries from liability for breaches of their duties.   It is a contradiction in terms to suggest that fiduciaries may be rendered totally exempt from accountability; they would then own the property in fee simple.   Exculpatory clauses may, however, reduce the degree of care and prudence required of the fiduciary.   See e.g., In re Estate of Niessen, 489 Pa. 135, 413 A.2d 1050 (1980) (corporate trustee held to reduced standard set out by trust instrument). Exculpatory provisions should be distinguished from grants of discretionary power. As one commentator puts it: "This [an exculpatory clause] is not an enlargement of power, but a limitation of liability. As such it is more in the nature of an affirmative defense than a factor bearing on the standard of care," Moore, A Rationalization of Trust Surcharge Cases, 96 U.Pa. L.Rev. 647, 674–675 (1948). These provisions are generally strictly construed. The breach must be within the scope of the immunity, and to the extent that the clause attempts an absolute immunity it is held violative of public policy. N.Y.—McKinney's EPTL 11–1.7. And see Note, Directory Trusts and the Exculpatory Clause, 65 Colum.L.Rev. 138 (1965).

6. Court Approval

Fiduciaries need not act at their peril but are entitled to the instructions of a court as protection. 1 Scott on Trusts § 69 (3d ed. 1967). The New York Court of Appeals has applied this principle even in cases involving the most sacrosanct trust duty: " * * * the rule against self-dealing has not been applied, and does not apply, to interdict the purchase of trust property by a trustee where the court, after conducting a full adversary hearing at which all interested parties are represented, approves and authorizes the sale."

On the above topics, see Surcharge Litigation and How to Avoid It, 16 Real Prop. Probate and Trust J. 715–805 (1981).

F. INCOME AND PRINCIPAL

1. Successive Beneficiaries

The Revised Uniform Principal and Income Act (1962 Act), set forth in Volume 7A of the Uniform Laws Annotated, provides:

§ 4. [When Right to Income Arises; Apportionment of Income].

(a) An income beneficiary is entitled to income from the date specified in the trust instrument, or, if none is specified, from the date an asset becomes subject to the trust. In the case of an asset becoming subject to a trust by reason of a will, it becomes subject to the trust as of the date of the death of the testator even though there is an intervening period of administration of the testator's estate.

(b) In the administration of a decedent's estate or an asset becoming subject to a trust by reason of a will:

(a) receipts due but not paid at the date of death of the testator are principal;

(2) receipts in the form of periodic payments (other than corporate distributions to stockholders), including rent, interest, or annuities, not due at the date of the death of the testator shall be treated as accruing from day to day. That portion of the receipt accruing before the date of death is principal, and the balance is income.

(c) In all other cases, any receipt from an income producing asset is income even though the receipt was earned or accrued in whole or in part before the date when the asset became subject to the trust.

(d) On termination of an income interest, the income beneficiary whose interest is terminated, or his estate, is entitled to

    (1) income undistributed on the date of termination;

    (2) income due but not paid to the trustee on the date of termination;

    (3) income in the form of periodic payments (other than corporate distributions to stockholders), including rent, interest, or annuities, not due on the date of termination, accrued from day to day.

(e) Corporate distributions to stockholders shall be treated as due on the day fixed by the corporation for determination of stockholders of record entitled to distribution or, if no date is fixed, on the date of declaration of the distribution by the corporation.

§ 5. [Income Earned During Administration of a Decedent's Estate].

(a) Unless the will otherwise provides and subject to subsection (b), all expenses incurred in connection with the settlement of a decedent's estate, including debts, funeral expenses, estate taxes, interest and penalties concerning taxes, family allowances, fees of attorneys and personal representatives, and court costs shall be charged against the principal of the estate.

(b) Unless the will otherwise provides, income from the assets of a decedent's estate after the death of the testator and before distribution, including income from property used to discharge liabilities, shall be determined in accordance with the rules applicable to a trustee under this Act and distributed as follows:

    (1) to specific legatees and devisees, the income from the property bequeathed or devised to them respectively, less taxes, ordinary repairs, and other expenses of management and operation of the property, and an appropriate portion of interest accrued since the death of the testator and of taxes imposed on income (excluding taxes on capital gains) which accrue during the period of administration;

    (2) to all other legatees and devisees, except legatees of pecuniary bequests not in trust, the balance of the income, less the balance of taxes, ordinary repairs, and other expenses of management and operation of all property from which the estate is entitled to income, interest accrued since the death of the testator, and taxes imposed on income (excluding taxes on capital gains) which accrue during the period of administration, in proportion to their respective interests in the undistributed assets of the estate computed at times of distribution on the basis of inventory value.

(c) Income received by a trustee under subsection (b) shall be treated as income of the trust.

See Dole, A Technique for Making Distribution from Principal and Income to Residuary Beneficiaries during Administration of Estates— With Application to Trusts, 79 Harv.L.Rev. 765 (1966).

2. *Corporate Distributions*

BOWLES v. STILLEY'S EXECUTOR

Court of Appeals of Kentucky, 1954.
267 S.W.2d 707, 44 A.L.R.2d 1273.

DUNCAN, Justice. The determination of this appeal requires a reexamination of our rule relating to apportionment of stock dividends between the life tenant and remaindermen under a devise creating a life estate in corporate stock.

Solon L. Palmer, by his will and several codicils, probated on August 5, 1931, devised to Mary Liles, a household employee, a life estate in certain real estate and "during her natural life, all dividends accruing and payable on the fifty shares of capital stock I own in the Bank of Benton, Benton, Kentucky, as well as all dividends on my seventeen shares of capital stock in the Citizens Savings Bank, Paducah, Kentucky." Subsequent to testator's death, Mary Liles transferred her life estate to J. P. Stilley and G. A. Thompson.

G. A. Thompson died intestate on May 18, 1946, and the appellee, H. H. Lovett, qualified as his administrator. J. P. Stilley died on January 17, 1952, during the pendency of this action, and his daughter, the appellee, Sarah Elizabeth Simmons, qualified as executrix of his estate. Since the date of the transfer, Stilley and Thompson, or their personal representatives, have collected all of the cash dividends paid on the fifty shares of capital stock in the Bank of Benton and seventeen shares of stock in the Citizens Savings Bank. Mary Liles is still living and, consequently, there has been no termination of the life estate.

The Citizens Savings Bank, on September 13, 1941, August 23, 1944, and October 30, 1950, declared successive common stock dividends of 50%, 33⅓%, and 25%. The ownership of the twenty-five and one-half shares issued as a result of the several stock dividends is involved in this action. The Chancellor, following the rule announced in several opinions of this Court, adjudged title in the life tenants.

The question of law here involved is one on which there is a wide divergence of opinion among the various jurisdictions of this country, although practically all of the cases fall into one or the other of three well-defined groups. The three divergent views have been frequently designated as the Kentucky rule, the Massachusetts rule, and the Pennsylvania rule.

The Kentucky rule awards all extraordinary corporate dividends in their entirety to the life tenant without regard to whether it is a stock dividend or a cash dividend, or whether it represents earnings that accumulated wholly before or wholly after, or partly before or partly after, the commencement of the life estate. The rule was first announced in Hite's Devisees v. Hite's Ex'r, 93 Ky. 257, 20 S.W. 778, 19 L.R.A. 173. It has been consistently adhered to since that time although its inequity has been frequently recognized. Cox v. Gaulbert's Trustee, 148 Ky. 407, 147 S.W. 25; Goff v. Evans, 217 Ky. 664, 290 S.W. 490; Hubley's Guardian v. Wolfe, 259 Ky. 574, 82 S.W.2d 830, 101 A.L.R. 1359; Laurent v. Randolph, 306 Ky. 134, 206 S.W.2d 480. Our examination indicates that the Kentucky rule is not followed by the courts of any other state. At one time it was the rule in New York but was definitely abandoned in Re Osborne, 209 N.Y. 450, 103 N.E. 723, 823, 50 L.R.A.,N.S., 510.

The Massachusetts rule, which is followed by a majority of the states, awards to the corpus (remaindermen) the entire extraordinary dividend from earnings, if essentially a stock dividend, and to income (life estate) if essentially a cash dividend, without inquiry in either case as to the time covered by the accumulation of earnings which the dividend represents, and without undertaking to apportion the benefit in the event the earnings accrued partly before and partly after the stock became subject to the life interest. This rule is sometimes known as the rule in Minot's case and was first announced in Minot v. Paine, 99 Mass. 101, 96 Am.Dec. 705.

The Pennsylvania rule occupies a medium position between the extremes of the other two rules and inquires as to the time covered by the accumulation of earnings embraced by the extraordinary distribution. If earned before the commencement of the life estate, it goes to the corpus; if earned after that time, then to the life estate as income; if earned partly before and partly after the beginning of the life estate, it is apportioned on proper basis between the corpus and the income. The rule seems to have been first announced in The Case of Earp's Appeal, 28 Pa. 368.

Notwithstanding our previous adherence to the Kentucky rule, this Court, as presently constituted, is convinced that it is unsound. It fosters inequities, and usually ignores the intention of the testator where the life estate is created by will. The inequity of the rule is aptly illustrated by the facts of this case. The seventeen shares of stock in the Citizens Savings Bank at the time of testator's death were appraised at $200 per share, or a total of $3,400. The present value of the seventeen shares, by reason of the substantially smaller proportionate interest in the corporate assets which they represent, is $125 per share, or $2,125.

At one time the trend of the courts in the various jurisdictions seemed to be away from the Massachusetts rule. In fact, this trend continued until about 1930. However, during the last fifteen or twenty years the pendulum has swung in the opposite direction. The court of last resort of several jurisdictions in which the question of distribution of extraordinary dividends was squarely presented for the first time have decided, with no little emphasis, in favor of the Massachusetts rule, commending it for its directness, simplicity, and ease of application. In addition to those states which have made it the rule by judicial interpretation, several states have adopted it by legislative enactment through the passage of the Uniform Principal and Income Act.

The basic argument in favor of the Massachusetts rule is the fact that a stock dividend is not in any true sense a dividend at all, since it involves no division or severance from the corporate assets of the subject of the dividend. A stock dividend does not distribute property but simply dilutes the shares as they existed before. There is no more reason in principle and justice for giving the life beneficiary any part of the new shares represented by the stock dividends, although declared wholly or in part from earnings accumulated during the life interest, or in denying him benefits therefrom (other than cash dividends which may be declared thereon during the continuance of the life interest), than there is in the case of accumulation of earnings by the corporation during the life interest without the declaration of any dividends at all.

We favor the adoption of the Massachusetts rule, with the provision that all cash dividends declared during the continuance of the life interest on the stock issued as a result of a stock dividend shall be payable to the life beneficiary. Not only does this view conform to a majority of the states which have considered the question but it is in harmony with the view of stock dividends taken by the Supreme Court of the United States. Gibbons v. Mahon, 136 U.S. 549, 10 S.Ct. 1057, 34 L.Ed. 525. It is also consistent with the position taken by the Supreme Court in holding that stock dividends representing surplus profits transferred to capital account are not income within the meaning of the Federal Income Tax Law, 26 U.S.C.A. § 1 et seq.

In fairness to the trial court, it may be emphasized that the judgment follows our prior opinions. However, since it is not in harmony with the views of this Court as presently constituted, it is reversed with directions to enter one in conformity with this opinion.

Note

It is recognized that a change in the rule allocating principal and income may be retroactively applied to trusts in existence before the new law becomes official without violating constitutional principles. 3 Scott on Trusts § 236.3 (3d ed. 1967). The Pennsylvania Supreme Court at first held against retroactive application but later reversed itself. In re Catherwood's Trust, 405 Pa. 61, 173 A.2d 86 (1961); In re Estate of Tyler, 447 Pa. 40, 289 A.2d 441 (1972). Not all states have applied their statutes retroactively, and, as a consequence, the rule that apportions a stock dividend in accordance with its source still has some vitality. In re Estate of Talbot, 269 Cal.App.2d 526, 74 Cal.Rptr. 920 (1969). See generally Annot., Allocation: Stock Dividends and Splits, 81 A.L.R. 3d 876.

TAIT v. PECK

Supreme Judicial Court of Massachusetts, 1963.
346 Mass. 521, 194 N.E.2d 707, 98 A.L.R.2d 503.

CUTTER, J. Letitia M. Tait (the widow) seeks a declaratory decree with respect to an inter vivos trust (the trust) executed in 1935 by her late husband (the settlor). She asks the court to determine whether a certain distribution of capital gains to the trust, made by Broad Street Investing Corporation (Broad Street) in December, 1961, is to be treated as principal or income of the trust. The widow, life beneficiary of the trust, asserts that the capital gains distribution is income. The individual remaindermen and the trustees assert that it is a return of capital and hence should be added to principal. The parties filed an "Agreement as to the Evidence and All Material Facts," constituting a case stated. The probate judge reported the case, without decision, for the consideration of the full court. The facts as agreed are set forth below.

On December 9, 1935, the settlor transferred to the trustees, subject to the trust, 100 shares of Linden Associates (Linden) a Massachusetts trust. He "provided * * * that in the event of * * * liquidation of * * * Linden * * * during the [widow's] life * * *

the [t]rustees * * * shall receive from * * * Linden * * *
'the distributive share in the assets of * * * Linden * * * properly allocable to them' " in trust "to pay over the net income * * *
monthly to * * * [the widow] during her life, and upon her death to
pay over * * * [the] trust fund * * * to" others. The settlor
died on September 20, 1940. The holders of the vested remainder interests have been determined by an earlier court decree.

"Linden * * * was liquidated following the sale, as of July 12,
1961, of all its assets to Broad Street." The trust received 55,434 shares
of Broad Street in exchange for the shares of Linden then held by it. In
1961, subsequent to July 12, Broad Street paid to the trustees of the trust
two cash dividends from income and in addition, in December, 1961, Broad
Street delivered to the trustees 1,463 additional shares of Broad Street
as "distributions of gain," as distinguished from "dividend from income,"
on the shares then held by the trustees. The trustees paid to the widow
the 1961 dividends from income paid to them by Broad Street in 1961
(less expenses and taxes) "but refused and still refuse to transfer" to the
widow the 1,463 shares of Broad Street (less any expenses or taxes thereto
allocable). The trustees, in support of their position, state that under
Int.Rev.Code of 1954, § 852, the trustees must pay a Federal capital gains
tax * * * on these shares of Broad Street so received as "distributions of gain."

"In the past quarter of a century or so, there * * * [have] grown
up [see Wiesenberger, Investment Companies (1963 ed.) part 1] in our
investment economy so-called [m]utual [i]nvestment [t]rusts, wherein each
share of the [t]rust * * * held * * * represents a share in the
ownership of a number of [diversified] companies * * * [so that] the
investor has a broad spread of risk and the benefit of the general investment management of the [m]utual [t]rust. It derives its earning
from net income received in the form of dividends and interest paid on
securities * * * held by the [investment] company, and also from
net profits realized on the sale of [its] investments * * *. Broad
Street * * * is such a * * * [company], subject to the operation
of the Investment Company Act of 1940, as amended [see 15 U.S.C. §§ 80a–
1 to 80a–52 (1958), and Supp. IV, 1959–1962]. It is so classified for tax
purposes under the Internal Revenue Code" (Subchapter M—Regulated
Investment Companies, Int.Rev.Code of 1954, §§ 851–855).

In its statements to the public, Broad Street says that its investments
have two goals—(1) favorable current income, and (2) long term growth
in both income and capital value. Dividends payable out of net income
are paid quarterly, whereas distributions of gain realized on the sale of
investments are paid at the end of each year. Since 1945, except for
1949, Broad Street has paid dividends from income. It has also paid
distributions of capital gain to its shareholders either in stock, or in cash,
at the option of the shareholder, except for the years 1936, 1937, and 1944
when capital gain distributions were paid in cash. The 1,463 shares
were paid to the trustees in December, 1961, at their request. At their
option, they could have received the equivalent of these shares in cash.

1. No party contends that the inter vivos trust shows what the settlor's intent was with respect to capital gains dividends. There are no special provisions concerning the allocation of receipts as between principal and income. Cf. Dumaine v. Dumaine, 301 Mass. 214, 222–224, 16 N.E.2d 625, 118 A.L.R. 834. Because the original trust fund consisted of shares of Linden, there may be (wholly apart from the usual investment powers of a trustee in Massachusetts) special indication of the settlor's approval of investment trust shares as a trust investment. See Loring, Trustee's Handbook (Farr Rev.) § 81. The settlor included in the trust no discretionary power to expend principal for the widow, which would have been a natural provision for him to make if he had intended that she be given more than the normal benefits afforded to a life beneficiary. Beyond these slight indications of the settlor's views, interpretation of the trust instrument seems to us to be of no assistance. See Scott, Trusts (2d ed.) § 236.3, pp. 1819–1821.

2. The usual Massachusetts rule for the allocation of dividends was stated in Minot v. Paine, 99 Mass. 101, 108, "A trustee needs some plain principle to guide him; and the cestuis que trust ought not to be subjected to the expense of going behind the action of the directors, and investigating the concerns of the corporation, especially if it is out of our jurisdiction. A simple rule is, to regard cash dividends, however large, as income, and stock dividends, however made, as capital." See Lyman v. Pratt, 183 Mass. 58, 60, 66 N.E. 423. This simple rule, in practice, has come to be based in some degree, in certain instances, upon the substance, rather than the form alone, of the transaction as carried out by the entity declaring the dividend. * * * Dividends in cash in substance paid out of capital or in liquidation have been treated as belonging to principal. * * * The substance of a transaction has been examined to determine whether it was equivalent to a stock dividend. * * * Where the trustee, as shareholder, is given the option to receive a dividend in stock or in cash, the later cases, in effect, treat the dividend as a cash dividend and as income. * * * We look at the substance of the capital gain distribution made by Broad Street in December, 1961, against the background of these authorities. No prior Massachusetts case has presented the question whether such a distribution, received by a trustee, is to be treated as capital or income.

Decisions outside of Massachusetts have generally treated such capital gain dividends as income rather than principal.

* * *

Some commentators have felt that dividends from net capital gains from the sales of securities held in a mutual fund's portfolio are income from the ordinary conduct of the fund's business, that the portfolio holdings are bought and sold like inventory or other corporate property of a business corporation, and that distributions from such gains, at least where there is opportunity to receive the distribution in cash, should be treated as income. Weight is given by these commentators to the circumstance that investors in investment companies rely on both income and capital gains as a part of the expected yield. It is suggested by at least one author (Professor Bogert) [Trusts and Trustees (2d ed.) § 858] that to invest in mutual funds would be a breach of trust, about which the life beneficiary could complain, unless the investment produced a normal trust investment yield.   The contrary view is that the sale of a security in an investment company portfolio involves the sale of a capital item, so that, if the gain is distributed the capital is necessarily reduced. In some years such a company may experience net losses.   It is argued that if capital gain distributions of other years have been paid to the income beneficiary, the trust principal will inevitably suffer in years of losses, which must be expected even in an era generally inflationary, so that, in effect, the investment company shares may become a wasting investment.   It is also urged that a trustee's investment in an investment company is in substance nothing more than a fractional ownership in a diversified portfolio of securities, as to which the trustee should account as if he held the portfolio securities directly.   The special character of regulated investment companies and their specialized tax treatment under the Internal Revenue Code also have some tendency to give capital gains distributions the aspect of principal.

If the dividends and distributions of a regulated investment company should be regarded as inherently the same as those of an ordinary industrial company, then the rule of Smith v. Cotting, 231 Mass. 42, 48–49, 120 N.E. 77, should be applied to Broad Street's 1961 capital gain distribution, which the trustees, at their option, could have received either in cash or in shares.   It seems to us, however, that, when a fiduciary invests in investment company shares, he is entering into an arrangement more closely like participation in a common trust fund (see G.L. c. 203A) than like an investment in the shares of an industrial company.   His purpose generally will be to obtain for his trust beneficiaries (usually of a small trust) the same type of spread of investment risk which the trustee of a common trust fund can obtain for its participating trusts, or which the trustee of a large trust fund can obtain by a well conceived program of diversified direct investment.[7]

The arguments against the soundness of the analogy between investments in mutual funds and in a common trust fund (see e.g. Bogert, Trusts and Trustees [2d ed.] § 858, pp. 557–558, and The Revised Uniform Principal and Income Act, 38 Notre Dame Lawyer 50, 54–55) are to us unconvincing.   It may be a sound reason for a trustee to refrain from investing in investment company shares that the return from dividends paid from ordinary income of such companies is low, so that the life beneficiary will suffer unless he receives also the capital gain distributions.   It may be also that appropriate downward adjustment in the rate of trustee's fees should be made, if he invests substantially in in-

---

7.   Broad Street as of December 31, 1962, is reported by a standard manual to have had $249,079,948, invested in the common shares of 99 companies, in the preferred shares of seven companies, and in the bonds of twenty-four companies, plus some government bonds.   See Wiesenberger, Investment Companies (1963 ed.) part 5, p. 12.   Such an investment diversification could not possibly be directly achieved by any trustee unless the trust res was extraordinarily large.

vestment company shares (because he is not burdened with investment management), with the consequence that the income return to the life beneficiary will be improved pro tanto. See discussion in Scott, Trusts (2d ed.) § 227.9A; Bogert, Trusts and Trustees (2d ed.) § 679, pp. 311–313. These matters we need not determine. The possible meager return does not change the substance of the investment as a reasonable attempt at risk diversification similar to that of the common trust fund. To say that the realized gains of a common trust fund are not distributed to the participating trust, whereas those of an investment company are distributed (primarily for tax reasons) to fiduciaries who are shareholders, is merely to state the obvious fact that a common trust is administered by the trustee itself, whereas the regulated investment company is a separate entity from the trustee who invests in its shares. If a trustee elects to take shares of the investment company in payment of any distribution made to him of capital gains, he will be able to achieve the same substantive result as that achieved by the common trust fund.

The method of determining the purchase and sale prices of investment company shares, in relation to the net asset value of shares, is consistent with the concept that the trustee is obtaining diversification by an indirect participation in the investment company's portfolio. It is apparent that if a fiduciary were to redeem his shares at a profit just before a capital gain distribution, he would necessarily allocate any gain to principal. No practical reason requires treating the capital gain distribution, when made, in any different way, or prevents retaining it as a part of the principal of the trust.

One major virtue of our Massachusetts rule for allocation between principal and income has been its simplicity as a rule of convenience. See Minot v. Paine, 99 Mass. 101, 108; Third Natl. Bank & Trust Co. v. Campbell, 336 Mass. 352, 354–355, 145 N.E.2d 703. To treat capital gains distributions of regulated investment companies as principal will not impair the simplicity of our rule, for no inquiry need be made as to the source of the distribution. The source must be announced, as it was in respect of Broad Street's capital gain distribution in December, 1961.

Since no binding precedent controls our decision, we are guided by the substance of the situation. We adopt the rule that distributions by a regulated investment company, from capital gains (whether made in the form of cash or shares or an option to take or purchase new shares), are to be allocated to principal. This is essentially the view adopted by the Commissioners on Uniform State Laws in 1962 after full deliberation * * *. The Commissioners' action can be taken as reflecting a considered current view of what is in the public interest. In effect, we think that the regulated company, from the standpoint of a trustee investing in its shares, is merely a conduit of its realized gains to the trust fund and that, in the hands of the trustee, the gains should retain their character as principal.

3. A decree is to be entered in the Probate Court (a) that the distribution of capital gains by Broad Street in December, 1961, in the hands of the trustees of the settlor's trust is to be treated as principal and not

as income, and (b) that future similar distributions to the trustees of capital gains by Broad Street also are to be allocated to principal. Costs and expenses of this appeal are to be in the discretion of the Probate Court.

So ordered.

Notes

1. The Uniform Principal and Income Act (1962), 7A ULA 444–445, provides:

§ 6. *[Corporate Distributions]*.

(a) Corporate distributions of shares of the distributing corporation, including distributions in the form of a stock split or stock dividend, are principal. A right to subscribe to shares or other securities issued by the distributing corporation accruing to stockholders on account of their stock ownership and the proceeds of any sale of the right are principal.

(b) Except to the extent that the corporation indicates that some part of a corporate distribution is a settlement of preferred or guaranteed dividends accrued since the trustee became a stockholder or is in lieu of an ordinary cash dividend, a corporate distribution is principal if the distribution is pursuant to

(1) a call of shares;

(2) a merger, consolidation, reorganization, or other plan by which assets of the corporation are acquired by another corporation; or

(3) a total or partial liquidation of the corporation, including any distribution which the corporation indicates is a distribution in total or partial liquidation or any distribution of assets, other than cash, pursuant to a court decree or final administrative order by a government agency ordering distribution of the particular assets.

(c) Distributions made from ordinary income by a regulated investment company or by a trust qualifying and electing to be taxed under federal law as a real estate investment trust are income. All other distributions made by the company or trust, including distributions from capital gains, depreciation, or depletion, whether in the form of cash or an option to take new stock or cash or an option to purchase additional shares, are principal.

(d) Except as provided in subsections (a), (b), and (c), all corporate distributions are income, including cash dividends, distributions of or rights to subscribe to shares or securities or obligations of corporations other than the distributing corporation, and the proceeds of the rights or property distributions. Except as provided in subsections (b) and (c), if the distributing corporation gives a stockholder an option to receive a distribution either in cash or in its own shares, the distribution chosen is income.

(e) The trustee may rely upon any statement of the distributing corporation as to any fact relevant under any provision of this Act concerning the source or character of dividends or distributions of corporate assets.

2. In 1963, New York rejected the Massachusetts stock distributions rule in favor of what has come to be known as the "six per cent rule." Comment, Principal and Income Allocation of Stock Distributions—The Six Per Cent Rule, 64 Mich.L.Rev. 856 (1966). Pennsylvania, long a leader of the jurisdictions that required apportionment of stock dividends, now takes a similar approach.

Pa.Stat.Ann.tit. 20 § 8105. For an application of the statute, see Estate of Reynolds, 494 Pa. 616, 432 A.2d 158 (1981). A portion of the present New York statute, N.Y.—McKinney's EPTL 11–2.1(e) reads:

> (2) A distribution by a corporation or association made to a trustee in the shares of the distributing corporation or association held in such trust, whether in the form of a stock split or a stock dividend, at the rate of six per cent or less of the shares of such corporation or association upon which the distribution is made, is income. Any such distribution at a greater rate is principal.

As noted in the previous section pertaining to investments, commentators criticize the inflexible rules governing the allocation of receipts between principal and income and the courts' refusal to adopt a "total portfolio" approach in judging a trustee's performance as greatly complicating a trustee's obligation to treat impartially the income and remainder beneficiaries. See citations, supra, pp. 706–707. The Uniform Management of Institutional Funds Act grants trustees and boards, who are managing educational, religious, or charitable organizations, more flexible authority. They may adopt a "total return" investment policy and invest in securities that offer the potential of capital appreciation, while maintaining current income by treating some of the appreciation in endowment as income. §§ 2, 6, 7A ULA 415–416, 421; these provisions are discussed in Cary and Bright, The Law and the Lore of Endowment Funds 32–52 (Report to the Ford Foundation 1969).

Existing rules have been criticized as not being sufficiently mindful of the declining rate of cash dividends being paid on corporate stock. Robinson, Trust Allocation Doctrine and Corporate Stock: The Law Must Respond to Economics, 50 Texas L.Rev. 747 (1972). The author sets out a chart comparing a trust of $100,000 which is made up of typical common stocks appreciating at a 7 percent annual rate and paying 3 percent cash dividends with one which holds a $100,000 bond paying a fixed 7 percent interest. He assumes the Massachusetts rule whereby cash dividends are paid to the income beneficiary and stock appreciation goes to the remaindermen and a constant 4 percent inflation rate which is based on the history of the consumer price index since 1966. Robinson at pp. 762–63 (footnotes omitted):

> The income beneficiary of the stock trust must wait fourteen years before his annual income equals that of his bond trust counterpart, and he must wait a full twenty-four years to recover the accumulated income deficit. Thus the income beneficiary of a short-term common stock trust suffers a distinct disadvantage. His injury, however, is not limited merely to the amount by which bond interest payments in any given year exceed cash dividends. His real injury is the amount by which dividend payments fall short of a reasonable trust income, an amount based on a percentage of trust principal, which in Table 1 would be at least 6 percent * of the rapidly appreciating stock value in column 2. Since dividend payments are frozen at 3 percent, the income beneficiary's full injury is actually permanent, and each year it will equal that difference between the going

---

* The author states that: "[W]hen corporate stock is held in trust, trust income can currently be defined as a return of at least 6% of trust principal. This figure represents the sum of current cash dividend yields (3%) and stock appreciation in excess of the amount needed to ensure the remainderman a constant-value trust principal." 50 Texas L.Rev. at p. 758, n. 52.

trust income rate and the prevailing cash dividend rate (in the illustration, 6 percent minus 3 percent). Thus he can never recover the real income deficit. On the other hand, the remainderman's interest will quadruple in twenty-one years, although in terms of constant dollars it will only double. In light of the remainderman's traditional right merely to have the value of trust principal preserved, the full imbalance between income beneficiary and remainderman becomes clear: the remainderman, who is entitled only to a constant value trust principal, sees the real value of trust principal double, while the income beneficiary, who is entitled to a reasonable trust income, must permanently settle for an income only half that rate—and that only if the cash dividend rate holds firm at 3 percent.

TABLE 1

	COMMON STOCK TRUST			BOND TRUST	
Trust Year	Year End Principal	Annual Income From Dividends	Cumulative Income	Year End Principal [constant $s]	Cumulative Income
	7%	3%		(CCPI = 4%)	
1	2	3	4	5	6
0	100,000			[100,000]	
1	107,000	3,000	3,000	[96,154]	7,000
2	114,490	3,210	6,210	[92,456]	14,000
3	122,504	3,435	9,645	[88,900]	21,000
4	131,080	3,675	13,320	[85,480]	28,000
5	140,255	3,932	17,252	[82,193]	35,000
6	150,073	4,208	21,460	[79,031]	42,000
7	160,578	4,502	25,962	[75,992]	49,000
8	171,819	4,817	30,779	[73,069]	56,000
9	183,846	5,155	35,934	[70,259]	63,000
10	196,715	5,515	41,449	[67,556]	70,000
11	210,485	5,901	47,350	[64,958]	77,000
12	225,219	6,315	53,665	[62,460]	84,000
13	240,984	6,757	60,422	[60,057]	91,000
14	257,853	7,230	67,652	[57,747]	98,000
15	275,903	7,736	75,388	[55,526]	105,000
16	295,216	8,277	83,665	[53,391]	112,000
17	315,881	8,856	92,521	[51,337]	119,000
18	337,993	9,476	101,997	[49,363]	126,000
19	361,653	10,140	112,137	[47,464]	133,000
20	386,968	10,850	122,987	[45,639]	140,000
21	414,056	11,609	134,596	[43,883]	147,000
22	443,040	12,422	147,018	[42,196]	154,000
23	474,053	13,291	160,309	[40,573]	161,000
24	507,237	14,222	174,531	[39,012]	168,000

As illustrated in Table I, currently popular high-yield bonds offer a trustee no refuge from the quandary he faces with common stock. Bonds also create an imbalance between beneficiaries, but with bonds it is the remainderman who suffers, not the income beneficiary. Because bond principal is fixed at $100,000, its real value depreciates inversely to the rate of inflation. Given 4 percent inflation, the remainderman will see the real value of his interest drop to less than half in just eighteen years, as illustrated in column 5. Thus the bond trust income beneficiary gains an early advantage over his stock trust counterpart only at the expense of a greatly depreciated trust principal.

The author suggests as a solution, noting both its advantages and problems, "floating apportionment," an approach that establishes the value of the principal each year in terms of the consumer price index and assigns the excess in value from stock appreciation over the floating principal to the income beneficiary. Robinson at pp. 771–779.

If the trustee pursues a policy of maximizing income, concern has been expressed that the real value of the principal will be reduced. One solution is to allocate to principal from current income an amount sufficient to offset a rise in the consumer price index and thus to preserve the real value of the principal. Hirsch, Inflation and the Law of Trusts, 18 Real Prop. Probate and Trust J. 601, 648 (1983).

3. The competing claims to receipts from natural resources, wasting assets and unproductive property are resolved by apportionment. Uniform Principal and Income Act §§ 9–12, 7A ULA 449–454. Younger, Apportioning Receipts from Wasting and Unproductive Assets: A Comment on the New Principal and Income Act, 40 N.Y.U.L.Rev. 1118 (1965) (criticizing the New York legislation).

4. Under § 13 of the Uniform Principal and Income Act, 7A ULA 455–456, the liabilities for expenses, reasonable depreciation allowances, court costs, attorney's fees, compensation to the trustee, taxes, repairs, and other claims against a trust are allocated between income and principal beneficiaries. See also N.Y.—McKinney's EPTL 11–2.1(l).

G. ACCOUNTING

At the termination of a trust or completion of the administration of an estate, fiduciaries must file an account with the court before they can be discharged from office. The account is a summary of the conduct of their administration, describing items of property received, income earned, disbursements for taxes, claims, and administration expenses made, and the distribution of remaining property required by the governing instrument or law. Notice is given to all persons who have an interest in the estate or trust, and they may challenge the account. Specifically, fiduciaries may seek credit for a loss in the value of an item of estate property. Beneficiaries may request that the credit be denied and that the fiduciaries be surcharged with the loss because it was occasioned by their breach of duty. The issue is then heard and decided by the court. Upon settlement of the final account, distribution to the beneficiaries is made, and the fiduciaries are discharged. Trustees may file an interim account before the trust has run its full course in order to receive the court's approval of their administration up to the time of the accounting. (Approval of specific actions can of course be sought without an accounting.) Courts have regularly allowed a waiver of an accounting on the agreement of all interested parties. Comment, Waiver of Accounting in

Estate Administration—A Legislative Proposal, 6 Santa Clara Lawyer 59 (1965). Westfall, Nonjudicial Settlement of Trustees' Accounts, 71 Harv.L.Rev. 40 (1957). The work of the National Fiduciary Accounting Project attempting to bring greater uniformity to the fiduciary accounting field should be noted. A draft report of the Project with a model account appears in Thompson, Whitman, Phillips and Warren, Accounting and the Law 460, 466–472 (4th ed. 1978).

Subdivision 10 of Section 100–c of the N.Y. Banking Law requires a trust company which maintains one or more common trust funds to account to the court once every six years (changed from four years in 1975) for its administration of the fund or funds. The procedure is described and the standards against which the trustee's performance are to be judged are set out in In re Bank of New York, supra, p. 701. The magnitude of the undertaking and the task of the special guardian who is appointed to protect the interests of the beneficiaries is impressive. A typical special guardian's report filed in the New York County Surrogate's Court analyzes the performance of five common trust funds, which were increased to eight during the accounting period, totaling in excess of seventy million dollars, encompassing at various times between 99 and 134 different issues of securities and involving almost 300 transactions effecting substantial changes in investments.

The protections which result from an accounting have been described as follows (2 Scott on Trusts § 220 (3d ed. 1967)):

> In general the settlement of an account renders res judicata all matters in dispute and determined by the court in the settlement of the account, and all matters which were open to dispute although not actually disputed, and this although the account was an intermediate and not a final account. On the other hand, although an account is settled and approved, it may be reopened where the trustee was guilty of fraudulent concealment or misrepresentation in presenting his account or in obtaining the approval of the court.

Chapter Nine

FUTURE INTERESTS

SECTION ONE. INTRODUCTION

Future Interests is a subject which, if you mention it to a law school graduate of an earlier era, is almost certain to provoke some kind of reaction—usually somewhere between amused tolerance and apoplectic rage.   The reason for the reaction is partly the subject matter; Future Interests is one of the last strongholds of hypertechnicality in the law, full of anachronistic, intent-defeating rules.   In part, the reaction is due to the way in which Future Interests was frequently taught.   Building on the pretensions of the subject to mathematical precision, many law teachers, including some of the greats, used the course in Future Interests as a medium of instruction in precise legal reasoning.   Woe betide the student who could not tell the difference between a condition subsequent and condition precedent!   Whether the reality ever lived up to the ideal is an argument we will not enter.   It does seem to us that modern courts are apt to disregard insubstantial differences based on largely fortuitous differences in language.   If that is so, the course can no longer be justified as an exercise in structured reasoning but must be justified on the basis of its intrinsic importance.   The extent to which it can be useful in the real property curriculum, or as part of a legal history course, we leave to others.   We will limit our consideration to those aspects of the subject which concern gratuitous transfers—largely within a family by will or inter vivos disposition—most of which will be in trust.   Accordingly, our focus will be on the kinds of transactions usually involved today in family wealth transmission and on those aspects of the law of future interests most likely to affect such dispositions.   The center of our discussion will be the Rule against Perpetuities.

No doubt many will find the material in this chapter too much or too little; there is a respectable argument that one cannot teach "a little" future interests.   We believe that some learning about perpetuities is an essential part of the preparation of any lawyer in this field and that enough can be taught to enable him or her to handle most potential problems.   And, if it is any consolation to the traditionalist, we would point out that, even leaving out most of the absurdities of the ancient

731

law, there is still enough left to engage and challenge the minds of most students.

Why use future interests? Future interests serve an important function in family arrangements. Before 1977, under our federal tax laws, the estate of the owner of a life interest in property was not ordinarily taxed on that property when he died, so that the creation of a life estate in a testator's daughter, and a remainder in her children, enabled the property to skip a generation of estate tax. Though the Tax Reform Act of 1976 (see p. 887, infra) seriously limits the tax advantages of such transfers, substantial savings are still possible. And even where tax considerations are not important a testator may wish, for any number of reasons, that his children (or surviving spouse) receive only the income from property, with ultimate ownership in the next generation.

What are future interests? The first thing to note about future interests is that they are somewhat misleadingly named; they are, in fact, present rights to future possession (or enjoyment *) of property. By the time they take this course almost all students will have taken a basic course in property. They will have learned that one way of measuring ownership of property is along the plane of time. So measured, the ultimate in ownership is the fee simple or, as it is sometimes called, the fee simple absolute.** Ownership in fee simple may be something less than total; the right of the owner may be restricted by covenants, zoning laws, mortgages, etc.; it will certainly be subject to tax. But for our purposes, ownership in fee simple, because it is infinite in duration, is complete ownership.

A fee simple is a present—or "possessory"—interest; i.e., it is a right to present possession of the property. Since it is infinite in duration, when a person owns a fee simple there can be no future interests in that property. So, too, when the owner of a fee simple transfers to another his entire ownership, no future interest will be created. However, if he transfers anything less—whether by design or inadvertence—some future interest or interests will be created. And, of course, the owner of the fee simple may create future interests by transferring part of his interest to one person and the rest to someone else. One must always be able to account for infinity of ownership in temporal terms. Unless some person (or group of persons as, e.g., tenants in common) owns a fee simple, future interests will exist.

A second thing to note about future interests is that they may be substantial or very insubstantial. The right to future possession*** may

---

* If the future interest is an income interest in trust, the owner may be entitled to enjoyment but not possession.

** Prop.Rest. Ch. 3. We shall use the shorter term "fee simple" as the equivalent of "fee simple absolute," and, by the same token, as excluding other forms of fee simple such as the "fee simple determinable," the "fee simple subject to a condition subsequent," and the "fee simple subject to an executory limitation." For a brief description of the characteristics of these estates in "fee simple defeasible" see p. 800, infra. For a full description, see Prop.Rest., Ch. 4.

*** For these purposes the right to possession may be enjoyed personally, or vicariously through one's estate.

be certain to ripen in the near future, or it may be subject to the prior occurrence of one or more highly improbable and distant events. Whether substantial or insubstantial a future interest (as contrasted with a "mere expectancy" such as the interest of a potential taker under the will of a living person) has many of the attributes normally associated with "property." With rare exceptions, future interests may be transferred inter vivos or by will, may be inherited, may be taxed, and may be subjected to the claims of creditors.

SECTION TWO. CLASSIFICATION OF FUTURE INTERESTS

Theoretically, future interests could come in infinite variety. In practice they come in standard forms capable of classification by standard, if not universally accepted, criteria. It is in the area of classification that we will make our first major departure from the traditional Future Interests course. Future interests law—and particularly its terminology—is rooted in land law; but many of the interests common in land law of an earlier era occur only infrequently in wills and trusts (and even in real estate transactions) today. Accordingly we will not devote any time to discussion of the interests following defeasible fees (see footnote, p. 732, supra and Note, p. 800, infra). Instead we will concentrate on those interests following life estates, i.e., remainders, executory interests, and reversionary interests.

For purposes of the Rule against Perpetuities (our primary focus) the first important distinction is between interests created in third parties and those created in the transferor or his estate.* The latter—which we shall call, collectively, reversionary interests—are not subject to the Rule against Perpetuities. The explanation is historical rather than rational but there it is. Some interests in third parties are subject to the Rule, however, and it becomes necessary to distinguish among various types. Two broad classifications exist: remainders and executory interests. We will describe the difference between them below. For now let us concentrate on the differences among remainders. Here one has a choice of terminology. We have adopted, with one exception, the terminology of the Restatement of Property (§ 157) (which has also been adopted by the New York Estates, Powers and Trusts Law) and classify remainders as follows:

> Indefeasibly Vested Remainders;
>
> Remainders Vested Subject to Open;
>
> Remainders Vested Subject to Complete Defeasance;
>
> Contingent Remainders.

---

* It is assumed that the future interest is created by the same instrument as the preceding interest (the "particular estate"). If the interests are transferred by different instruments, a different classification may ensue. For example, if A transfers by one instrument to B for life, then to C, C gets a vested remainder; but if A transfers to B for life, and then A by a later instrument gives C the right to possession after B's life estate, the second instrument is an assignment by A to C of the reversion left in A after the first transfer.

The exception to the Restatement terminology is that we continue to use the term contingent remainder rather than the term "remainder subject to a condition precedent" of the Restatement. We do so partly because it is shorter, partly because the Restatement term has not achieved wide acceptance, but mostly because, unlike the sub-classification of vested remainders, the new term for the traditional "contingent remainder" does nothing to enhance understanding.

For most limitations, classification is fairly easy. Before turning to a discussion of particular types of remainders, a few general observations are in order. The word "vest" is, it has been said, a four letter word that has given rise to the use of many other four letter words. Whether an interest is "vested" can be of critical importance since, except for the remainder vested subject to open, the Rule against Perpetuities does not apply to vested interests. Unfortunately, the term does not have a fixed meaning and is used to describe a number of quite different things. Many cases which discuss the difference between vested and contingent remainders really turn on whether there is or is not a requirement of survival. In its normal connotation, "vest" probably connotes becoming possessory; but in future interests parlance, it usually means vest in "interest" rather than vest in possession. At the least, it ought to mean that the interest has become certain—no longer subject to contingency— but it clearly does not mean that, witness the "remainder vested subject to complete defeasance." The truth is that one can only define "vest" in terms of specific interests, which we shall attempt to do shortly.

A second general observation is that an interest cannot vest in an unborn or unascertained person. In the limitation A to B for life, remainder to the children of B, the remainder cannot vest until a child of B is born. So, too, in the limitation A to B for life, remainder to the last survivor of the children of B, none of B's children can have a vested remainder until we know which of them is the last survivor.

A third general observation is that ordinarily the courts will not infer a requirement of survival where none is stated—except that survival to the effective date of the instrument creating the interest will ordinarily be required. Thus, absent evidence of a contrary intent, in the limitation A to B for life, remainder to C, there is no requirement that C survive B in order to take "possession" of the property. Ordinarily, it does not matter that C's possession may be vicarious, i.e., through his estate.

Finally, it should be pointed out that the classification of a future interest is made with reference to a particular moment—usually the effective date of the creating instrument or the end of the permissible period of the Rule against Perpetuities. It is important to remember that the leopard can change its spots; e.g., a contingent interest can become vested, and an interest vested subject to defeasance can become indefeasibly vested.

With that background, let us look at the categories of remainder interests:

The indefeasibly vested remainder. The typical example of such a remainder is the limitation A to B for life, remainder to C. It is the type of interest most likely to be meant by the term, "vested remainder" (and is often simply so called). As the name implies this type of remainder vests an interest, to become possessory after the end of the life estate, which cannot be divested. Either C during his lifetime, if he outlives B (or if the life estate of B should terminate prematurely during C's life), or C's estate after his death, will be entitled to possession when the life estate ends.

N.Y.—McKinney's EPTL 6–4.7 defines a "future estate indefeasibly vested" as follows:

> A future estate indefeasibly vested is an estate created in favor of one or more ascertained persons in being which is certain when created* to become an estate in possession whenever and however the preceding estates end and which can in no way be defeated or abridged.

Ordinarily there should be no difficulty in identifying a remainder of this sort.

(B)   *The remainder vested subject to open.* The typical example of such a remainder is the limitation A to B for life, remainder to the children of B, where B has at least one living child. As the name implies, this type of remainder vests an interest in a member of a class, subject to the "opening" of the class to admit new members. Once the interest vests, the owner of the interest has an indefeasibly vested interest in *some* share of the property, but the precise share must await determination of the number of members of the class who share in the gift, e.g., in the limitation above, the number of children fathered or borne by B during his or her life.

N.Y.—McKinney's EPTL 6–4.8 defines a "future estate vested subject to open" as follows:

> A future estate vested subject to open is an estate created in favor of a class of persons, one or more of whom are ascertained and in being, which is certain when created to become an estate in possession whenever and however the preceding estates end, and is subject to diminution by reason of another person becoming entitled to share therein.

Here again the classification of the remainder should not be difficult. Provided that one member of the class is ascertained and in existence, the remainder is vested; if not, the entire remainder is contingent. As will be elaborated below, for our purposes the difference may not be very important since the remainder vested subject to open is subject to the Rule against Perpetuities.

(C)   *The remainder vested subject to complete defeasance, and the contingent remainder.* The serious problems of classification arise with these types of remainder. The difficulty lies in the fact that in both cases, whether the holder of the interest will ever be entitled to possession

---

* Although a literal reading of the words "when created" (see also §6–4.8) would seem to exclude an interest which does not become indefeasibly vested until sometime after its creation, (see p. 734 supra) there would not seem to be any reason for the legislature to have intended such a narrow meaning.

depends on the happening of a presently unpredictable contingency—usually the outliving of some other person or the survival to a particular age, although the contingency may be of any kind within the fertile invention of the legal mind.   The classification of these interests may be critical since if the remainder is called vested—even if subject to complete defeasance—it is not subject to the Rule against Perpetuities; if, on the other hand, the remainder is called contingent it is so subject.   Thus, at least in theory the classification of substantively indistinguishable interests will determine whether they are declared void.   These interests are defined in N.Y.—McKinney's EPTL:

> § 6–4.9   A future estate vested subject to complete defeasance is an estate created in favor of one or more ascertained persons in being, which would become an estate in possession upon the expiration of the preceding estates, but may end or may be terminated as provided by the creator at, before or after the expiration of such preceding estates.

> § 6–4.10   A future estate subject to a condition precedent [the Restatement and N.Y. EPTL term for "contingent remainder"] is an estate created in favor of one or more unborn or unascertained persons or in favor of one or more presently ascertainable persons upon the occurrence of an uncertain event.

As has been true of other efforts, these definitions are only partly successful.   The chief difficulty lies in the fact that an interest may be vested subject to defeasance even though it may be terminated *at* or *before* (as well as after) the expiration of the preceding estate.   If the "divestment" could occur only after the interest became possessory, there would be no difficulty; but since the vested interest can be divested before it ever becomes possessory, it is very hard to distinguish it from an interest limited to an ascertained person "on the happening of an uncertain event." In such a case, the statutory definitions are no more helpful than the distinction between "conditions subsequent" and "conditions precedent" on which scholars, lawyers, and judges have labored long and in vain. (See on this point Simes and Smith § 147).

It is here that a page of history is worth a volume of logic.

A number of efforts have been made to devise rules of thumb or formulas to make classification easy; all of them break down in the close cases but they are worth looking at.   The first explains the difference between vested and contingent interests as follows: *

Future interests in transferees are classified in terms of two ideas: (1) "gaps," by which is meant for this purpose an interval of time during which, by the terms of the transfer, no transferee would be entitled to possession; (2) "divestment," meaning the termination of a transferee's interest prior to its normal expiration.   A vested remainder is a future interest in a transferee that will not under any circumstances be preceded by a gap and that will not divest the interest of any other transferee.

---

* This explanation is derived from Gulliver, Cases and Materials on the Law of Future Interests 55–57 (1959).

Transfers from A to B for life, then to C give C a vested remainder. There is no possibility of a gap occurring because C (or his successor as owner of the remainder) will be entitled to possession whenever the life estate terminates, and there can thus be no interval of time between the end of the life estate and the commencement of possession under the remainder. And C's interest will not divest the life estate, since there is no language authorizing the holder of C's interest to take possession prior to the expiration of the life estate.

The classification in terms of the possibility of a "gap" in the right to possession between the end of the "particular" estate and the taking effect of the remainder serves satisfactorily to explain most contingent remainders. Where the remainder is subject to a requirement that the remainderman reach a particular age (a common requirement) and he has not done so when the interest is being classified, the interest is clearly contingent. E.g., A to B for life, remainder to C if he reaches the age of 25. At any time before C reaches 25 (if ever) B may die. If he does, there will be a gap between the end of the life estate and the taking effect of the remainder (assuming that C does live to age 25). So too, if the contingency is of the kind that requires a particular action, e.g., finishing medical school, or the happening of an event, e.g., the "incorporation of Gloversville," which action or event has not yet occurred, there is usually no trouble in classifying the remainder as contingent. Here again the gap theory is satisfactory. If the life estate ends before the conditioning event occurs or the required action is performed, there will be a gap between the end of the life estate and the taking effect of the remainder in possession or enjoyment.

Finally, where the contingency involves the coming into existence or identification of a person and he remains unborn or unascertained when the interest is classified, the gap theory works pretty well except where the death of the life tenant will resolve the contingency. For example, A to B for life, remainder to the oldest child of B living at B's death. The remainder would certainly be classified as contingent during B's life (since his oldest surviving child is unascertainable). On the other hand, since the termination of the life estate by B's death will also determine who his oldest surviving child will be, there is no possibility of a gap between B's death and the taking effect of the remainder. However, a life estate may terminate prematurely, e.g., by renunciation of the life estate. The gap theory only works if that possibility is taken into account.

But, let us postpone an inquiry into the phenomenon of premature termination and consider another attempt to provide a formula for classification, this one by Professor Richard R. B. Powell (Powell, ¶274):

> A somewhat mechanical test has such a high degree of utility that it is set forth herein. Suppose that one has before him the following series of limitations:
>
> (1) A to B for life, remainder to C.*

---

* For the sake of uniformity, the phrase "and his heirs" or similar language has been deleted from this quotation.

(2) A to B for life, remainder to the children of C, and C has two children D & E.

(3) A to B for life, remainder to C, subject however to any appointment made by will of B.

(4) A to B for life, remainder to the children of B who attain the age of twenty-one years. B's oldest child is ten years of age.

"Ask first, as to each limitation, this question: 'Is there *now* a person who in his own right, or as a part of his estate, will be certain to receive all this property *whenever and however* B's estate ends?' The answer is 'yes' as to the first limitation. That entitles one to say that under that first limitation C has an 'indefeasibly vested remainder.' The answer is 'no' as to each of the remaining three remainders. Ask, therefore, as to each of these three, this second question: 'Is there *now* a person who in his own right, or as part of his estate, would take all of this property if B's estate ended now?' The answer is 'no' only as to the fourth limitation. That entitles one to say that under the fourth limitation the remainder is 'subject to a condition precedent' [i.e., contingent]. As to the second and third limitations one is now entitled to say that both of those remainders are neither 'indefeasibly vested' nor 'subject to a condition precedent.' They are, therefore, both in one or the other of the two intermediate categories. The types of limitation found to create a remainder 'vested subject to open' are few. The form illustrated by the second limitation is the only common one. Thus this mechanical approach, by excluding successively remainders indefeasibly vested, remainders subject to a condition precedent and remainders vested subject to open, produces a residuum which are the remainders vested subject to complete defeasance.

"This method is not 100 percent perfect, but, in the author's experience, it brings one to the conclusion reached by the courts in a very high percentage of the cases to which it is applicable. A device having that degree of utility in a field such as this is not to be despised. It is presented to the profession (as it has been to several generations of law students) as a tool believed to be genuinely helpful.

Professor Powell concedes that his system is not foolproof and in fact it works about as well as the gap explanation. However, neither is of much help with the hard cases. Most, if not all, of the hard cases are those in which the precondition to permanent possession of the property is the survival of the life tenant. Take, for example, the limitation A to B for life, remainder to C, but if C predeceases B, to D. Classical analysis would almost certainly classify the remainder to C as vested subject to being divested if C should fail to outlive B. What then about the limitation A to B for life, remainder to C if C outlives B, otherwise to D. Here classical analysis would classify the remainder to C as contingent. What is the difference? The 'simple' answer is that in the first case C's remainder is subject to a condition *subsequent,* his failing to outlive B, whereas in the second case his interest is subject to the condition *precedent.** But you may ask, how do we know which is subsequent and which

---

* See, for example, Harvey v. Harvey, 215 Kan. 472, 478, 524 P.2d 1187, 1192 (1974): "Essentially the distinction is this: If the condition on which the estate depends is precedent, the estate is contingent; if subsequent, the estate is vested subject to defeasance."

precedent. The honest answer would probably be: "no way." But if the law of future interests was to have the mathematical certainty with which some invested it, uncertainty on such a point would be unthinkable. Under the "gap test" or Professor Powell's test, one would ask what would happen if the life estate were to terminate prematurely? * If, for example, B were to renounce his life estate, would the remainder to C be accelerated? If it would, there would be no gap, and there would be an identifiable person who would be ready to take "if the prior estate ended now"; hence the remainder is vested; if not, the remainder is contingent. But, you ask, how does one decide whether the remainder will accelerate? Alas, the answer seems to depend on whether the condition attached to taking is deemed (as a matter of interpretation of the instrument) to be subsequent or precedent. Since that is the question we started out with, this approach does not seem promising. (On the subject of acceleration, generally, see Simes & Smith, ch. 25.)

Probably the surest guide to the result is the form of the *language* used to create the interest. According to Professor Gray, "whether a remainder is vested or contingent depends upon the language employed. If the conditional element is incorporated into the description of, or into the gift to, the remainder-man, then the remainder is contingent; but if, after words giving a vested interest, a clause is added divesting it, the remainder is vested." (Gray, § 108). In the first limitation in the preceding paragraph, the language may be said to first give an unconditional remainder to C—if the limitation stopped after A to B for life, remainder to C, C would have an indefeasibly vested remainder; when the language goes on to attach a condition, i.e., that C outlive B, it operates to take away what previous language has given. On the other hand, or so it may be argued, in the second formulation the remainder is not given and then taken away. C is only to take the remainder if he outlives B—in Gray's words, "the conditional element is incorporated into the gift." This distinction based on slight differences in language has, of course, its counterpart in other areas of real property law. The classification of a fee interest as "fee simple determinable" or "fee simple subject to an executory interest" is said to depend on the particular words used. Whether courts do in fact give the weight to language advocated by the scholars seems doubtful. In the last analysis, the job is to give effect to the intention of the person creating the interest, and it seems hardly conceivable that most draftsmen would intend such small differences in language to be important. (Cf. the discussion in Berger, Land Ownership and Use (3d ed. 1983) 156–59).

Ⓓ *Remainders distinguished from executory interests.* A final distinction which may have importance—and certainly is an important part of your terminology—is that between remainders and executory interests.

---

* In a much earlier era, the major causes of premature termination were "forfeiture" for "tortious alienation" and merger of the life estate with another interest. (For a discussion of forfeiture and merger in the context of premature termination, see Gulliver, Future Interests 204–211 (1959).) Today the usual cause of premature termination is renunciation by the life tenant—typically under a statute providing for a right of election to take against a will by a surviving spouse.

Executory interests are defined—not very helpfully—as all interests in third persons, other than remainders. Historically, they are those interests the creation of which was made possible by the Statute of Uses (1535) and the Statute of Wills (1540). Those interests, known by such exotic names as "shifting" and "springing" "uses" and "devises," were extremely important in the development of the Rule against Perpetuities; however, their importance today—as a category of interest separate from the contingent remainder—is more doubtful.

An executory interest has been defined by Gulliver as follows:

An executory interest is a future interest in a transferee which will either (1) certainly be preceded by a gap, or (2) operate by divesting an interest of another transferee. An example of the first type of executory interest would be: A to B for life and one year after B's death to C. It is absolutely certain that a gap will precede C's possession, since no *transferee* would be entitled to possession during the one-year period. An example of the second type of executory interest would be: the interest of C in a transfer from A to B, but if C pay B $25,000 then to C. The executory interest is a divesting one because, if effective, it would terminate a fee simple prior to its normal infinite duration.

Executory interests having the characteristic that they will certainly be preceded by a gap are easy to identify. They are also rarely created. Where the interest is classified as executory because it divests a prior interest, identification may be more difficult. If the interest to be divested is a possessory interest, a life estate, or a defeasible fee, there should be little difficulty. In the limitation A to B for life, but if B remarries, then to C, the interest of C, if it ever becomes possessory, will cut short B's life estate. So, too, in the limitation A to B, but if B die without having had issue, to C, the interest of C is clearly divesting, and so executory. This kind of executory interest is not apt to be of great importance to us here. Defeasible fees are not often encountered in trusts and estates, although they may be important in real property law. Interests which divest life estates are found more often (probably most often in marital separation agreements) but the classification of such interests as executory—rather than as contingent remainders—would not seem to have any consequences.

Where, however, the interest divested is itself a future interest, the situation becomes fairly murky. Take, for example, the limitation set forth above: A to B for life, remainder to C, but if C predecease B, then to D. On traditional analysis the interest of C is vested subject to divestment by the executory interest in D. Let us suppose now the slightly different limitation: A to B for life, remainder to C if C outlives B, otherwise to D. Here, traditional analysis would classify C's and D's interests as contingent remainders—assuming of course that both B and C are alive. (See Simes and Smith § 149.) To the untrained eye it is hard to see how in one case the interest of D divests the interest of C, and hence is an executory interest, but in the second case there is no divestment. The practice of attaching significance to such slight differences in language is criticized in Halbach, Vested and Contingent Remainders: A Premature Requiem for Distinctions between Conditions Precedent and Subsequent, Essays for Austin Wakeman Scott (1964) 152.

The distinction between executory interests and contingent remainders, although once of importance, is rapidly disappearing if indeed it has not already completely disappeared. See Dukeminier, Contingent Remainders and Executory Interests: A Requiem for the Distinction, 43 Minn.L.Rev. 13 (1958). In New York, it is doubtful that the distinction has existed at all since 1830; see Doctor v. Hughes, 225 N.Y. 305, 312, 122 N.E. 221, 222 (1919), and, in any event, it has been obliterated under the Estates, Powers and Trusts Law which defines all future estates created in third persons as "remainders." N.Y.—McKinney's EPTL 6–4.3.

Two distinctions, the first of current interest and the second of historical interest mainly, should be noted. To satisfy the Rule against Perpetuities, discussed below, an interest must be certain either to vest or to disappear within the period of the Rule. For purposes of the Rule, vesting in interest is enough; vesting in possession is not required. However, classical doctrine says that a characteristic of executory interests, as distinguished from remainders, is that they cannot vest in interest until they vest in possession. Thus, for perpetuities purposes, an executory interest must be certain to vest in possession within the prescribed period whereas a contingent remainder need only be certain to vest in interest (or fail). In so far as the executory interest in question operates to divest a possessory interest, the classical doctrine is probably correct. But see Hunt v. Carroll, 157 S.W.2d 429 (Tex.Civ.App.1941), appeal dismissed 140 Tex 424, 168 S.W.2d 238 (Comm. of App.1943), discussed by Professor Dukeminier in the article referred to in the preceding paragraph. Where the interest to be divested is a remainder, the difference is probably meaningless. For example, in the limitation given above of A to B for life, remainder to C but if C dies before B, to D, while D's interest cannot ever become a vested executory interest, it will, on C's death before B, become a vested remainder.

The second distinction relates to the doctrine of the destructibility of contingent remainders. Until well into the 19th century in England a contingent remainder would be destroyed if there was in fact a gap between the end of the life estate and the taking effect of the remainder. The destruction would result whether the gap occurred because of a natural termination (the death of the life tenant before the happening of the contingency) or because of a premature termination by renunciation, merger or forfeiture. (See p. 739, supra and see Simes and Smith §§ 195–197).

Destructibility of contingent remainders was abolished by statute in England for the case of premature termination of the particular estate in 1845, and for natural termination in 1877. In the United States, statutes have abolished the doctrine entirely in twenty-one jurisdictions, and in five other jurisdictions for premature termination only. Simes (hb) 41; Simes and Smith, § 207; Am.L.Prop., § 4.63; Powell, ¶ 314; Prop.Rest. (1948 Supp.) 463. There is no conceivable justification for limiting its abolition to the case of premature termination of life estates. The enactment of such statutes has often been triggered by previous decisions applying the doctrine in the jurisdiction involved, and thus calling the problem to public attention.

Some of these statutes deal separately with premature and natural termination, and in this and other respects seem unnecessarily verbose. Compare N.Y.—McKinney's Real Property Law, §§ 57, 58 with the superseding legislation, N.Y.—McKinney's EPTL 6–5.10 and 6–5.11. All that is needed is a simple statement to the effect that no future interest shall fail or be defeated by the termination of any precedent estate prior to the happening of the contingency on which the future interest is limited to take effect. Cf. Ill.—Smith-Hurd Ann. ch. 30, ¶ 40.

The doctrine has also been abolished by judicial decision in several states, and even in jurisdictions where destructibility of contingent remainders has not been abolished by statute or case law, it has no application to equitable interests or to interests in personal property, and most future interests problems today arise out of trusts of personalty. The Property Restatement, § 240, which has engendered some controversy, would make it nonexistent. In about one-half of the American jurisdictions it is still at least potentially applicable to legal contingent remainders in land, not having been abolished by statute, the tendency so far having been to consider it adopted as a part of the common law and to follow it even in the absence of binding authority in the particular state. However, as noted above, decisions adopting it have often been followed by statutes abolishing it. It is thus obviously a dying doctrine, though one which provided a significant part of the background for the Rule against Perpetuities.

All in all it seems likely that the distinction between executory interests and remainders has little importance today. On the other hand, it seems unlikely that the term executory interest will entirely disappear. Even in New York where the term has in theory been abolished, interests in third persons following defeasible fees will probably be called executory interests* and, tradition being what it is, it may be some time before the interest following the remainder vested subject to complete defeasance is called a remainder.

Why do we care? Classification for its own sake may be of interest to collectors of stamps or butterflies but the classification of future interests is not of any use unless different legal consequences ensue. As has already been indicated, the classification of an interest may be critically important for purposes of the Rule against Perpetuities. Are there other purposes for which it is important?

"The characteristics as to which future interests typically and significantly differ are not very numerous. They consist chiefly in (a) the transferability of the interest by conveyance inter vivos, by descent on

---

* Interests in transferees following fees simple defeasible have traditionally been regarded as executory interests even though, in the case of the fee simple determinable (base fee), the classification is illogical, i.e., since the interest does not divest the prior interest, and is not necessarily preceded by a gap, it should be classified as a remainder. See Gulliver, Future Interests 60 (1959).

intestate death of the former owner thereof and by devise; (b) the subjection of the interest to the satisfaction of the claims of creditors; (c) the power of the owner to partition the affected thing or to procure a judicially ordered sale thereof or his liability to such procedures initiated by other persons; (d) the presence or absence of a necessity for making the owner of the interest a party in litigation affecting the ownership of the thing as to which the interest exists; (e) the degree of protection to which the owner of the interest is entitled as against conduct of the owner of a prior interest, or of a third person, injurious to the thing as to which the interest exists; (f) the mode in which the statute of limitations or the doctrine of prescription restricts or increases the protections of the interest; (g) the effect, upon such interest, of the failure of an anterior or subsequent interest; (h) the extent to which the interest can be subject to the burden of a tax enacted after the creation of the interest but before it becomes a present interest; and (i) the applicability thereto of the rule against perpetuities." Powell, Future Interests (1961) at 13–14.

Many of these differences are disappearing; many others, even if they persist, are of little importance in the context of trusts and today most future interests are created in trust. One question as to which "vestedness" may still be important is that of acceleration of remainders after premature termination of the life estate. However, although as noted earlier, traditional analysis would make the question of acceleration depend on the classification of the remainder, the cases seem to turn more on the intent of the person creating the interest (Simes and Smith §§ 796, 798) and in some cases on statutes. See Ill.Rev.Stat.1957, c. 3, ¶ 168a; N.Y.—McKinney's EPTL 2–1.11(d).

The classification of an interest as contingent or vested may still make a difference with respect to alienability, or subjection of an interest to the claims of creditors. Thus, for example, somewhat irrationally, a remainder vested subject to complete defeasance ordinarily will be subject to the claim of a creditor but a contingent remainder may not. Cf. In re McLoughlin, 507 F.2d 177 (5th Cir. 1975). On the subject of the voluntary and involuntary alienability of future interests, see Simes and Smith Ch. 53 and 56; Powell Ch. 21; Halbach, Vested and Contingent Remainders: A Premature Requiem for Distinctions between Conditions Precedent and Subsequent, Essays for Austin Wakeman Scott (1964) 152.

By way of transition between the foregoing Section Two, "Classification," and the next Section, "The Rule against Perpetuities," consider the following paragraph from Lynn, The Modern Rule Against Perpetuities (1966) 157:

Gray made the common-law Rule Against Perpetuities a rule against remoteness of vesting, and urged remorseless application of the Rule. Through a chance combination of factors—persistent insistence on reform, impatience of powerful groups with inappropriate rules of property, indifference of counsel and court—the Rule has been modernized since Gray wrote. Applying Gray's Rule presupposes classification of future interests in the dispositive instrument as a prerequisite to determining validity under the Rule, and indeed that is true irrespective of the form that the Rule takes. The rub is that meticulous characterization of future interests is not typical of modern perpetuities cases. Limitations are not standardized and readily recognizable as falling within a particular category in the future interests hierarchy. Ambiguities frequently abound and it is sometimes almost impossible to assimilate the half-articulated expressions of the grantor, settlor, or testator to the ideal types used in this book to illustrate application of the black-letter rule.

SECTION THREE. THE RULE AGAINST PERPETUITIES

A. THE OBJECTIVE OF THE RULE

The starting point for the consideration of the Rule against Perpetuities is the case of Pells v. Brown, King's Bench 1620, 79 Eng.Rep. 504, which held, among other things, that, unlike contingent remainders, executory interests were indestructible. As will be discussed below, the existence of any future interest, and especially a contingent future interest, is a clog on the alienability of property. Up to this time, the traditional way of eliminating future interests—and, hence, promoting alienability—was to hold them destructible. When executory interests were held indestructible, a new method was required, which ultimately turned out to be the Rule against Perpetuities. This holding was thus directly responsible for the initiation of the Rule against Perpetuities in the Duke of Norfolk's Case in 1682. 3 Ch.Cas. 1. If executory interests had been held destructible, it is entirely possible that the Rule against Perpetuities would never have been thought of, and the modern law of future interests might have been entirely different. The statement by Gray (§ 159) that "it is hard to overestimate the importance" of this holding in Pells v. Brown seems amply justified.

The "common law" Rule against Perpetuities*—so called to distinguish it from statutory rules enacted in some jurisdictions—was not fully formulated as a comprehensive rule all at once. After the first formulation of the general rule in the Duke of Norfolk's case, the English courts took more than two hundred years to work out the details; the *duration* of the period of the rule was not finally fixed in England until 1833 in Cadell v. Palmer, 1 C*l*. & F. 373. And it was not until 1890, in In re Hargreaves, infra p. 751, that the *objective* of the rule was settled.

The general idea of the rule is to invalidate *ab initio* certain future interests that might otherwise remain in existence for too long a time. The two chief policies underlying the rule were to curtail "dead hand"

---

* The common law Rule has been codified in some states, e.g., West's Ann.Cal.Civ.Code § 715.2:

No interest in real or personal property shall be good unless it must vest, if at all, not later than 21 years after some life in being at the creation of the interest and any period of gestation involved in the situation to which the limitation applies. The lives selected to govern the time of vesting must not be so numerous or so situated that evidence of their deaths is likely to be unreasonably difficult to obtain. *It is intended by the enactment of this section to make effective in this State the American common-law rule against perpetuities.* (Italics added.)

domination and ② to facilitate marketability of property. For reasons discussed below, the curtailment of "dead hand" control seems by far the most compelling today; however, the most frequently heard theoretical justification of the rule is in terms of promoting alienability, and a word should be said on that score.*

Any division of the ownership of property affects alienability. Take the simple transfer by A (holding property in fee simple) to B for life, remainder to C, where both B & C are *sui juris*. When A owned the property, the decision to sell or otherwise transfer it was his alone. Now that B & C collectively own the property, the decision whether to sell, and, if so, the terms, must be agreed on between them. In theory B can sell his life estate—or C his remainder—but the uncertainties of B's life expectancy make the purchase too chancy for most buyers and those who do buy are likely to insist on a price which reflects that uncertainty. B and C together can sell—there is no legal impediment to a sale—but they are apt to disagree about the wisdom of a sale and almost certain to disagree about how the purchase price is to be split. B will regard the life expectancy tables as much too conservative, and C may feel that they wildly overstate B's actual life expectancy.

If the division of ownership affects alienability in the simple situation where B has a life estate and C an indefeasibly vested remainder, how much worse is it apt to be where C's interest is vested subject to defeasance, or contingent. In the case of the limitation A to B for life, remainder to C if he survives B, or if he predeceases B, to D, B, C, and D can collectively convey a fee simple title to the property to anyone, but will they ever be able to agree on a sale or a price?

In the examples set out above, the effect on marketability is practical; in all cases there are people in existence who can collectively convey good fee simple title to the property. In other cases, the interference with marketability is not only practical but legal. In the limitation A to B for life, remainder to the first child of B to reach 21, where B has no children or no child who has reached 21, there is no combination of people who can collectively transfer good fee simple title. The ultimate taker may be a presently unborn child of B or, if no child of B ever reaches 21, A or A's successor in interest. In the discussion which follows we refer to this situation as a *suspension of the power of alienation;* ** the situation

---

* The Rule has also served as an important supplement to our estate tax laws by limiting the extent of "generation-skipping" tax free transfers. See I.R.C. § 2041(a)(3) infra, p. 924. This function of the Rule is less important now because of the new generation-skipping transfer tax. See p. 959, infra.

** This terminology has been used in some statutes, e.g., West's Ann.Cal.Civ.Code, § 716, as it read prior to 1959:

Every future interest is void in its creation which, by any possibility, *may suspend the absolute power of alienation* for a longer period than is prescribed in this chapter. *Such power of alienation is suspended* when there are no persons in being by whom an absolute interest in possession can be conveyed. The period of time during which an interest is destructible pursuant to the uncontrolled volition and for the exclusive personal benefit of the person having such a power of destruction is not to be included in determining the existence of a *suspension of the absolute power of alienation* or the permissible period for the vesting of an interest within the rule against perpetuities. (Italics added)

where alienability is practically but not legally inhibited we will call (as did the First Restatement of Property) a *fettering of alienability*.

An early question about the Rule was whether it applied only where there was a suspension of the power of alienation or also in instances where alienability was fettered. The argument that the Rule against Perpetuities should only operate where there is a suspension of the power of alienation proceeds on the theory that the Rule against Perpetuities is only violated by an interest that may remain legally inalienable for longer than the period of the Rule. Under this theory an interest, even if it may remain contingent beyond the period, will not violate the Rule if it is certain to be alienable before the period expires. An interest capable of being released is alienable for this purpose. Any future interest is releasable, even if not otherwise alienable, provided that its owner is in being and ascertained.* The rule against suspension of the power of alienation thus only invalidates transfers to people who may not be born or ascertained until after the period has expired. The assumption underlying this theory is that, if all interests are legally alienable, there is no legal impediment to the conversion of the various interests into fee simple ownership, and that the only objective that the Rule against Perpetuities needs to achieve is to make legally possible a return to fee simple ownership at or before the end of the period. The difficulty with this reasoning is that, as noted above, divided ownership will not necessarily be easily convertible into fee simple ownership merely because the interests are legally alienable; there may still be many practical obstacles to such conversion. And in the *Hargreaves* case, infra p. 751, it was decided for England (and essentially for the United States) that the Rule against Perpetuities applies where alienability is "fettered," as well as where the power of alienation is suspended.

Note, however, that the Rule does not apply to all instances of fettering (or, for that matter, of suspension of the power of alienation) but only where the fettering is caused by the existence for too long a period of unvested interests in transferees. For example the fact that an interest is vested in an infant, or an incompetent, and, so may be difficult to market does not matter. Gertman v. Burdick, 123 F.2d 924 (D.C.Cir. 1941), certiorari denied 315 U.S. 824, 62 S.Ct. 917, 86 L.Ed. 1220 (1942). In order to reconcile this proposition with the accepted notion that the Rule is designed to prevent undue fettering of alienability, one must embrace the partly fictional idea that *all unvested interests fetter property more tightly than does any vested interest.* It is easy to think of estates that are legally vested but highly unlikely to take effect in possession (e.g., the reversionary interest reserved by a will giving property to the testator's ten healthy children for life, remainder to testator's then living grandchildren). It is also easy to think of estates that are legally unvested although highly likely to take effect in possession (e.g., a convey-

---

* For these purposes the owner is "ascertained" if he is a member of a group of people all of whom are identified, for example, a child of C in the limitation, "to the last survivor of the children of C," where C is dead.

ance from A to B for life, remainder to C or his estate one year after B's death). To some considerable extent, the incidence of the Rule is therefore arbitrary. But if one is able to swallow the partly fictional proposition stated above, he will find the case law much easier to grasp.

Alienability and the Trustee's power to sell. In a modern trust (and most future interests are created in trust) a trustee ordinarily has the power to sell any of the trust assets and substitute others. The result is that as to any particular item of property, there is usually someone in existence with power to convey good title. Thus, as to each item of property, there is neither a suspension of the power of alienation nor a fettering of alienability. How does that affect the application of the Rule against Perpetuities?

According to the Restatement of Property, the possession of such a power will have no effect. As the First Restatement (§ 370, comment p) put it:

> *Immateriality of trustee's power to change the trust res.* When a limitation attempts to create a future interest under or after a trust, and such future interest is otherwise invalid under the rule [against perpetuities], such invalidity is not eliminated by the fact that the trustee under such limitation has an unqualified power to dispose of assets constituting the trust corpus and reinvest the funds so obtained. Such a power does eliminate the inalienability of the specific subject matter of the trust but does leave the quantum of wealth, which is the subject matter of the limitation, devoted to the accomplishment of specified purposes for the benefit of designated persons. This is a fettering of property of a type which is objectionable, under the rule against perpetuities, if it continues for "longer than the maximum period" * * * *

Not all courts agree. See, e.g., Pipkin v. Pipkin, 370 P.2d 826, 829 (Okl. 1961):

> The trust in this case provided that the trustee had the full power to sell, transfer, convey and dispose of the trust estate for such price as he deemed meet and proper. With such a provision we see no suspension of the power of alienation. We have not passed on this exact point but the Supreme Court of Missouri had this identical question before it in Trautz v. Lemp, 329 Mo. 580, 46 S.W.2d 135, and held that where testamentary trustees have unlimited power to sell trust property, there is no unlawful restraint on alienation. To us this is a sound rule and we adopt it.

The Wisconsin Statute (Wisc.Stat.Ann. 700.16 (2) & (31), specifically so provides.

If the only justification for the Rule were to promote marketability of particular pieces of property it would be hard to fault the reasoning of the quoted decision. But today most observers agree that the primary justification for the Rule is to set a limit on the duration of "dead-hand" control. See, for example, Simes and Smith, § 1117 (footnotes omitted):

---

* The Restatement, Second, although it does not use the term "fettering of alienability" is in accord. Restatement, Second, Property (Donative Transfers) Introductory note to part I, pp. 9 & 10.

However, if alienability for the purpose of productivity were the only reason for the rule against perpetuities, then it is doubtful whether such a rule would be justified today. This is true, first, because today most future interests are equitable interests in trusts; thus, the trustee generally has a power to sell an absolute interest, and is under a duty to make the trust estate productive. Second, the subject matter of most future interests is corporate shares or bonds or government bonds. In such situations the actual economic value is in the corporation or the governmental unit, and this is being put to productive use. Third, as will appear in a subsequent chapter, even though contingent future interests in specific land are created without the use of a trust, there are situations where the court will order a sale of the land in fee simple absolute. If, due to changed circumstances, it is necessary for the preservation of all interests in the land to have it sold, the court can order a sale in fee simple absolute and direct that the proceeds be held in trust, with the beneficial interests in the persons who had legal interests in the land.

It is believed, therefore, that, today, the principal reason for the rule against perpetuities is not to secure alienability for the purpose of productivity. Various other reasons for the rule have been suggested. Thus, it has been suggested that the rule exists to prevent "the power and grandeur of ancient families," or to prevent "the threat to the public welfare of great family dynasties built either on great landed estates or great capital wealth." It would seem, however, that succession and estate tax laws can more effectively cope with the problem, and, indeed, are now doing so. It has also been suggested that the rule is designed to permit a kind of economic survival of the fittest; that those who are less able to succeed in the economic struggle should not be protected by a tying up of property for their benefit. Yet it would seem that the whole trend of modern society is in the direction of protecting those who are incompetent.

The compelling reasons for the rule against perpetuities are believed to be these. First, it strikes a fair balance between the satisfaction of the wishes of members of the present generation to tie up their property and those of future generations to do the same. The desire of property owners to convey or devise what they have by the use of trusts and future interests is widespread, and the law gives some scope to that almost universal want. But if it were permitted without limit, then members of future generations would receive this property already tied up with future interests and trusts, and could not give effect to their desires for the disposition of the property. Thus, the law strikes a balance between these desires of the present generation and of future generations.*

A further reason is that, other things being equal, society is better off, if property is controlled by its living members than if controlled by the dead. Thus, one policy back of the rule against perpetuities is to prevent too much dead hand control of property.

See also Morris and Leach, The Rule Against Perpetuities 13–18 (2d Ed.

---

* In commenting on these sentiments, Professor Lynn observes: "Strictly speaking, the compromise is between those of the living willing to accede to the wishes of persons now dead, and those of the living unwilling to allow the wishes of the dead to affect the use of property." Lynn, The Modern Rule Against Perpetuities 10, note 21 (1966). Ed.

1962); Fetters, Perpetuities: The Wait-and-See Disaster—A Brief Reply to Professor Maudsley, with a Few Asides to Professors Leach, Simes, Wade, Dr. Morris, et al., 60 Corn.L.Rev. 380, 381–388 (1975). And, for a very different view of the reasons for the adoption of the Rule, see Haskins, Extending the Grasp of the Dead Hand: Reflections on the Origins of the Rule Against Perpetuities, 126 U. of Pa.L.Rev. 19 (1977) where the author concludes (at 46): "The rule meant that what had once been considered a perpetuity was one no longer. In this sense the new rule was a clear victory for the 'dead hand,' not for free alienability. The rule served the fathers, not the sons * * *."

While there is considerable disagreement about exactly what purpose—if any—the Rule serves today, it seems unlikely to be abolished. "Neither perfect in conception, nor clear in application, the Rule has withstood repeated assaults. * * * [I]t will be with us for a long long time." Lynn, The Modern Rule Against Perpetuities 10 (1966).

What interests are affected? The classic statement of the Rule is that of Professor John Chipman Gray, originally put forward in 1886: "No interest is good unless it must vest, if at all, not later than twenty-one years after some life in being at the creation of the interest." (Gray § 201). This formulation has been criticized by many, and was rejected by the First Restatement of Property for several reasons. A first reason was that stating the Rule as one against remote vesting did not make clear that the objective of the Rule was to promote alienability; a second was that the Rule did in fact apply to one type of vested interest—the remainder vested subject to open; a third reason was that the rule does not apply to certain unvested interests—namely contingent interests which are freely destructible. (Prop.Rest. § 370, Comment j; § 372, Comment e; § 373, Comment a; Powell, ¶ 762.) The Restatement formulation did not carry the day and, indeed, has been abandoned by the Restatement, Second; it has its own imperfections in any event. But, for whatever reason, the Rule is almost always stated in Gray's terms as one against remoteness of vesting rather than fettering of alienability. As a practical matter the approaches are indistinguishable: both operate by striking down indestructible interests in transferees which may remain contingent beyond the permissible period, and some remainders vested subject to open. Professor Barton Leach (about whom more will be said later) has suggested that the Gray formulation should be modified by adding the words "Generally speaking" at the beginning and putting the word vest in quotation marks. (Leach, Perpetuities in a Nutshell, 51 Harv.L.Rev. 638, 639 (1938)). With these modifications the Gray formulation will accommodate the Restatement, First, objections and it has the strong recommendation that it is the formulation ordinarily used by courts.

B. THE PERIOD OF THE RULE

The period of time within which an interest must be certain to vest, *if at all* (an important qualification to be discussed below), is (subject to the exception for destructible interests) measured from the creation of the interest, i.e., the date of death in the case of a will, or the date of trust declaration or delivery of the instrument of transfer in the case of an inter vivos transfer. There are three different units of "perpetuities time": lives in being; periods of gestation; and the 21-year period "in gross." Except for the ascertainment of which lives are usable as "measuring lives," the concept of lives in being should cause no difficulty; the lives must be human rather than animal or corporate, and any number may be used provided the number is not so large as to make ascertainment of death too difficult, as an administrative matter. For example, a gift to vest at the death of the survivor of all people now citizens of the United States would be void under the Rule, not because they are not lives in being, but because it would be administratively impossible to give effect to any such gift. Even assuming a multimillion dollar estate sufficient to finance the years of investigation that would be required, it would be impossible for the fiduciary to trace all such people through the years for the purpose of determining who the survivor was and whether he was dead. Subject to this administrative limitation, however, the rule assumes that the expectancy of a survivor of a group will not vary enough with the size of the group to warrant the inconveniences involved in limiting the permissible lives in being to a specific number.*

The so-called "period in gross" is a flat 21-year period which may either be used independently of any life in being (for example, a gift to "the issue of B living twenty-one years from today,") or added on to the end of lives in being. However, the 21-year period cannot precede measuring lives. Thus, a gift to vest on the death of the survivor of all issue of the testator born within 21 years after the testator's death would be void. The measuring lives must be "lives in being" at the effective date of the instrument, not 21 years thereafter. One of the functional justifications of the period in gross is to permit dispositions that tie up property during the lives of the children of the testator and the minorities of his grandchildren; no such justification can be made for allowing a reversal of the order of measuring lives and the period in gross.

Finally, the period may include such periods of gestation as actually exist. (Thus, a flat period of nine months cannot be added to the 21-year period in gross). What this amounts to is that, for purposes of the Rule (as in some other areas of the law) a person is regarded as having been in being from the moment of conception. The actual period of gestation may also be used to save a gift to a person whose attainment of the age of 21 is a stated condition precedent, if otherwise the contingency would not occur until more than 21 years after a life in being.

The use of periods of gestation is illustrated by the following hypothetical situation taken from Gray, § 222:

---

* The difficulties occasioned by limiting the number of lives to two (as was formerly done in New York and a few other jurisdictions) are described in detail in Powell and Whiteside, The Statutes of New York Concerning Perpetuities and Related Matters, a Report to the New York State Law Revision Commission, 1936 Reports to the Law Revision Commission 475. And see p. 782, infra.

Good Examples

Suppose a gift by will of principal to be divided per stirpes among such issue of the testator as shall be living when the testator's youngest grandchild reaches 21. This gift is valid, because there is no possibility of any interest vesting beyond the period of the Rule. This may be demonstrated by assuming that the time of vesting is extended to its utmost limit by a highly unlikely sequence of human events: At testator's death, he has no child as yet born, but his widow is pregnant and gives birth to son A after testator dies. The period of gestation is added here to make A a "life in being," he having been conceived before testator died. When A dies he has one son, M, already born, and A's wife is pregnant and gives birth after A's death to another son, N. N is testator's youngest grandchild and later reaches 21, thus causing the stipulated contingency to occur. N reaches 21 more than 21 years after the death of A, the life in being, but the period of gestation between A's death and N's birth may again be added. Before N reaches 21, M dies leaving his widow pregnant, and she, after N has reached 21, gives birth to a child, X. Under a per stirpes gift, X would be entitled to share since his father M was dead when the contingency occurred. But, to assume that X's share would vest in time, another period of gestation has to be added, since he was not actually born until after N reached 21.

IN RE HARGREAVES

Court of Appeal, 1890.
43 Ch.Div. 401.

Hannah Hargreaves, by will dated the 24th of November, 1838, devised to John Townsend and Henry King certain specified freeholds, "To have and to hold the same unto and to the use of them, the said John Townsend and Henry King, and the survivor of them, and the heirs and assigns of such survivor upon the trusts, nevertheless, and to and for the several uses, ends, intents, and purposes thereinafter mentioned, expressed, and contained of and concerning the same." The trusts were to receive the rents and pay the residue, after deducting expenses, to her sister Mary for life, for her separate use, as therein mentioned, and after her decease "upon further trust to pay the residue of such rents to her oldest child during his or her life, and after the decease of such oldest child to the next oldest child during his or her life, and so on in succession to the next oldest child during his or her life, till all the children of my said sister Mary shall depart this life, and from and after the decease of my said sister Mary and all her children upon further trusts to pay the residue of such rents, issues, and profits" to the testatrix's sister Eliza for life for her separate use as therein mentioned, and after her decease to pay the residue to her children successively in the same way as to Mary's children. "And from and after the decease of my said sisters Mary and Eliza and all their children, upon further trusts that they, my said trustees, or the survivors of them, or the heirs or assigns of such survivor do and shall stand seized of the said freehold hereditaments and premises, in trust for such person or persons, in such parts, shares, and proportions, and in such manner and form, and under and subject to such

powers, provisions, directions, limitations, and appointments as the longest liver of them, my said sisters Mary and Eliza and their children,
notwithstanding coverture, by any deed or deeds, instrument or instruments in writing, or by his or her last will and testament in writing, or
any codicil or codicils thereto to be respectively duly executed and attested, direct, limit, or appoint, give, or devise the same, and in default
of any such direction, limitation, or appointment, gift, or devise then upon
further trust of the same freehold hereditaments and premises for my
own heir-at-law absolutely."

The testatrix died in December, 1838. Her sister Mary died in 1864,
leaving two children surviving her, one of whom died in 1871; the other,
Hannah Tatley, lived till 1889, when she died, leaving a will, made in
1885, by which she appointed this property to a trustee in trust for her
children. The testatrix's sister Eliza had died childless in 1873.

The persons on whom the legal estate vested in the trustees of the
will of Hannah Hargreaves had devolved took out an originating summons
to have it decided whether the trust limitations, to take effect after the
deaths of the testatrix's sisters Mary and Eliza and all their children,
were valid, and who in the events which had happened was entitled to
the property. The Defendants were the trustee under the will of Hannah
Tatley and the person who claimed under the heir-at-law of the testatrix.

* * *

COTTON, L. J. * * * The question to whom the beneficial interest
in the property now belongs turns upon the point whether the power of
appointment given by the will of the testatrix is void for remoteness.
The limitation to the sisters for life and to their children for their lives
are perfectly good, but in my opinion the power to appoint is void for
remoteness. This power is given to the last survivor of the sisters and
their children. The children might not all be in being at the death of
the testatrix; the power, therefore, is not given to a person who must
necessarily be ascertained within the period allowed by the rule against
perpetuities. On the death of the last surviving child the equitable estate
devolved on the heir-at-law of the testatrix, not under the trusts declared
by her will, but as on a partial intestacy occasioned by the failure of the
ulterior trust.

I must say a few words as to Avern v. Lloyd [see Note 4, infra], which
is very like the present case. The Vice-Chancellor there says that as
there may be a limitation of valid life estates to the unborn children, why
may there not be this ultimate limitation after their determination? No
doubt there may, if it is limited to a person who is necessarily ascertainable within the prescribed period. It is very true that after the decease
of the tenants for life the children could have disposed of their interests,
vested and contingent, so that (apart from the question of the validity of
the limitations) the estate might have been disposed of as soon as the
tenants for life were dead, and it may be contended that as the alienation
of the estate is not prevented the case is not within the rule as to remoteness. But that is not the true way of looking at it. An executory
limitation to take effect on the happening of an event which may not take

place within a life in being and twenty-one years, is not made valid by the fact that the person in whose favour it is made can release it. [The concurring opinions of LINDLEY, L. J., and LOPES, L. J., are omitted.]

Notes

1. Note the statement that "The limitations to the sisters for life and to their children for their lives are perfectly good   *   *   *." Why would that be true? Why would it not be possible that the interest in the income trust of an afterborn child of Mary or Eliza might vest beyond the period of the rule?

2. The actual issue here is the validity of the power of appointment exercised by the testatrix's niece, Hannah Tatley, the surviving life tenant. But, for the purpose of the Rule against Perpetuities, a general power of appointment by deed or will, as in this case, is treated as the equivalent of ownership, since the holder of the power can appoint to himself at any time. See Leach, 51 Harv.L.R. 638, 653 (1938); Gray § 477. For the purpose of analyzing this case, therefore, the final limitation following the income trust can be treated as if it read: *"And from and after the decease of my said sisters Mary and Eliza and all their children, to the longest liver of them and his heirs"*—i.e., the equivalent of a remainder in fee simple to the surviving life tenant. The application of the Rule against Perpetuities to powers of appointment will be considered later. See p. 841 et seq., infra.

3. The Hargreaves case is taken as settling for English law the proposition that the Rule against Perpetuities is a rule against remoteness of vesting rather than a rule against suspension of the power of alienation.

This was a matter of ultimate clarification of the issue, not of orginating the idea. A previous decision proceeding on the remoteness of vesting theory was London & South-Western Railway Co. v. Gomm, 20 Ch.Div. 562 (1882). This is sometimes treated as the case that turned the tide, but the question was not raised quite as clearly as in the Hargreaves case and was somewhat obscured by various other issues discussed in the opinions.

4. In In re Hargreaves, why would the power of appointment (or the equivalent disposition italicized in note (2), supra)

(a) be void under a rule against remoteness of vesting?

(b) be valid under a rule against suspension of the power of alienation?

The phrase "tenants for life", in the second paragraph of the opinion, must refer to Mary and Eliza, the specifically named beneficiaries, and not to all of the life tenants.

Avern v. Lloyd, L.R. 5 Eq. 383 (1886), here overruled, involved limitations identical in effect with those in the Hargreaves case. The income from securities was given in a succession of life estates to the testator's two brothers and their children, with an ultimate gift of the principal to "the executors, administrators, and assigns of the survivor" of the life tenants. The latter clause was construed by the court as giving the absolute interest in the property to the surviving life tenant, and was held valid, the opinion reading in part: "The gift to the executors, administrators, and assigns of the surviving tenant for life attaches to the life estate, so as to give a contingent absolute interest to each tenant for life. * * * Each of the tenants for life in this case had as much right to alien his contingent right to the absolute interest as to alien his life estate * * *. It seems obvious that such a case is not within the principle on which the law against perpetuity rests, and that the limitation in question of the absolute interest does not fail as being too remote."

For a discussion of these and other cases and a clear delineation of the two theories, see Gray §§ 268–278.4.

THOMAS v. HARRISON

Probate Court of Ohio, Cuyahoga County, 1962.
191 N.E.2d 862.

MERRICK, Presiding Judge.

* * *

The will directs in Item IV (3) that half of the residuary estate is to be held in trust for the benefit of testatrix's son, Jean B. Harrison, his wife, and his issue. The trustees are given absolute discretion to expend so much of the income and/or principal of the trust as they deem necessary to alleviate the financial burdens of, or to provide education for, any or all of the designated beneficiaries and to accumulate in any year the income not so spent. The trust is to continue as long as any of the beneficiaries who are born within twenty years after testatrix's death remain alive. This Court is asked to determine whether the provisions of this trust violate the rule against perpetuities.

* * *

It has been said that the fundamental policy behind the rule is to preserve the freedom of alienation of property. Joseph Schonthal Co. v. Village of Sylvania, 60 Ohio App. 407, 21 N.E.2d 1008 (1938); Braun v. Central Trust Co., 104 N.E.2d 480 (Ohio Com.Pl.1951), aff'd 92 Ohio App. 110, 109 N.E.2d 476. But Professor Gray, in his famous treatise, states that the immediate purpose of the rule is to prevent the creation of interests which may vest too remotely. Gray, The Rule Against Perpetuities Secs. 1–4 (4th ed. 1942). Consequently, the rule applies only to the *vesting* of interests. It applies to equitable as well as legal interests. Rudolph v. Schmalstig, 4 Ohio Supp. 58, 25 Ohio L.Abs. 249 (Ohio Com. Pl.1937). Cf. Jones v. Webster, 133 Ohio St. 492, 14 N.E.2d 928 (1938); Cleveland Trust Co. v. McQuade, 106 Ohio App. 237, 142 N.E.2d 249 (1957). Let us first see then, whether the interests created under this trust are vested.

An interest is not vested if, in order for it to come into possession, the fulfillment of some condition precedent other than the determination of the preceding estate is necessary. 20 Ohio Jur.2d Estates Sec. 136 (1956); Gray, The Rule Against Perpetuities, supra Sec. 101; Restatement[,] Property Sec. 157 comment a. A remainder may be contingent because it is to take effect upon the happening of some event not certain to occur which is independent of the termination of the preceding estate. 20 Ohio Jur.2d Estates Sec. 137 (1956). It may also be contingent because the person to whom the remainder is limited is not yet ascertained or not yet in being. Smith v. Block, 29 Ohio St. 488 (1876); Barr v. Denny, 79 Ohio St. 358, 87 N.E. 267 (1909).

In a discretionary trust the beneficiary has no definitely ascertainable interest. He cannot compel the trustee to give him any portion of the income where the trust gives the trustee absolute discretion as to the amounts of income to distribute. See Scott on Trusts Sec. 128.3 (2d ed. 1956). The beneficiary cannot be certain that he will ever enjoy any of proceeds of the trust. Consequently, where the extent of the interest of the beneficiary is dependent upon the exercise of discretion by the trustee, that interest is contingent. Thomas v. Gregg, 76 Md. 169, 24 A. 418 (1892); Andrews v. Lincoln, 95 Me. 541, 50 A. 898, 56 L.R.A. 103 (1901); Moore v. Moore, 59 N.C. (6 Jones Eq.) 132 (1860); Angell v. Angell, 28 R.I. 592, 68 A. 583 (1908); Denny v. Hyland, 162 Wash. 68, 297 P. 1083 (1931)[.] English: In re Vaux (1939) Ch. 465; In re Bernard, (1916) 1 Ch. 552; In re Bleu (1906) 1 Ch. 624. Gray, Perpetuities, supra, Sec. 246; Restatement, Trusts 2d Sec. 62q. Such interest does not vest until the trustee exercises his discretion.

[handwritten margin notes: ?; but βof Fid Duty if doesn't exercise discretn]

Viewed in another way, the discretion in a trustee to distribute principal and income to any or all members of a designated class is tantamount to a special power of appointment. Simes and Smith, The Law of Future Interests 216 Sec. 1277 (2d ed. 1956); VI American Law of Property Sec. 24.30 (1952). The exercise of the power is a condition precedent to the vesting of any interest in a beneficiary of the trust. Simes & Smith, supra, Sec. 1274; Gray, Perpetuities, supra Sec. 515.

Thus it is obvious that the interests of Jean B. Harrison, his wife, and his issue, are contingent. Their interests in the income and principal of the trust are wholly dependent upon the trustee's discretion. The interests of all the beneficiaries are contingent because subject to a condition precedent. In addition, they are contingent because the beneficiaries are unascertained, in the sense that the trustee may select one or more of them to receive proceeds from the trusts, or unborn in the case of possible further issue of Jean.

Having determined that these interests are contingent, it still remains to be seen whether these interests must vest within the period of the rule. The Ohio statute, echoing the common law, says that interests must vest, if at all, not later than twenty-one years *after lives in being at the creation of the interest.* Ohio Rev.Code Sec. 2131.08. As the statute expressly states, and as the authorities unanimously proclaim, the twenty-one year period must *follow,* not precede, the lives in being by which the period of the rule is measured. Simes & Smith, supra, Sec. 1225; Restatement, Property Sec. 374, comment e, Illus. 6, comment o; VI American Law of Property, supra, Sec. 24.14. Furthermore the measuring lives must be lives *in being at the creation of the interest,* i.e. in the case of a testamentary trust, at the death of the testator. 42 Ohio Jur.2d Perpetuities Secs. 27–28 (1960).

A simple illustration will indicate that the interests created under the testamentary trust of Mrs. Harrison will not necessarily vest within the period of the rule. Mrs. Harrison was survived by her son, Jean, his wife and their three children. Since the death of Mrs. Harrison, four more children have been born to Jean. Let us suppose that tomorrow

Jean, his wife, and the three children who were alive at the death of Clara Harrison are all killed in a common accident. Let us suppose further that the inheritance of the four surviving children of Jean is adequate to take care of their needs for twenty-five years; therefore, the trustees of the Clara Harrison trust deem it unnecessary to distribute any income or principal to the children until that time. The interests of the children would not vest until twenty-five years from now. This would be more than twenty-one years after the expiration of lives in being at the death of Mrs. Harrison. Consequently, the rule against perpetuities would be violated.

It is no defense that the probabilities are greater that the interests under the trust will vest within the period of the rule. The statute says the interests *must* vest within the prescribed time. If there is any possibility that the interests will not vest within lives in being plus twenty-one years then the interests are void ab initio. Cleveland Trust Co. v. McQuade, 106 Ohio App. 237, 142 N.E.2d 249 (1957); Rudolph v. Schmalstig, 4 Ohio Supp. 58, 25 Ohio L.Abs. 249 (Ohio Com.Pl.1937).

There is no question of severability of interests here. That is, the contingent interests of Jean, his wife and his issue who were alive at the time of Mrs. Harrison's death, cannot be separated from the interests of later born issue. To eliminate the after born issue would warp the testamentary scheme. It would deprive the trustees of their full discretion by narrowing the class of beneficiaries. Therefore, the entire trust fails. Andrews v. Lincoln, 95 Me. 541, 50 A. 898, 56 L.R.A. 103 (1901); Thomas v. Gregg, 76 Md. 169, 24 A. 418 (1892). The Trustees hold upon a resulting trust for Mrs. Harrison's heirs at law. Andrews v. Lincoln, supra. See Bogert, Trusts and Trustees Sec. 468 n. 16 (2d ed. 1953).

*   *   *

[Judgment in accordance with opinion.]

IN RE VILLAR

Chancery, 1929.
[1929] 1 Ch. 243.

Appeal from a decision of Astbury, J.

By his will dated June 14, 1921, a testator appointed the Public Trustee and the testator's adult sons ordinarily resident in England his executors and trustees.

He defined the meaning of certain expressions used in his will as follows:—

" 'The period of restriction' shall mean the period ending at the expiration of 20 years from the day of the death of the last survivor of all the lineal descendants of Her Late Majesty Queen Victoria who shall be living at the time of my death."

" 'Participating issue' shall mean all my issue for the time being living who shall not have any ancestor (being issue of mine) living." A beneficiary forfeited his interest in income on bankruptcy or alienation.

After certain specific gifts he devised and bequeathed all his property to his trustees upon trust out of the income to pay expenses of management and insurance and to pay his wife an annuity of £1000 a year during widowhood and a life annuity of £500 a year on remarriage, each annuity being free of all deductions (including income tax).

Subject thereto and to the provisions thereinafter contained the trustees were during the period of restriction to pay and divide the income equally per stirpes among the testator's participating issue.

The testator then declared: First, that if any person who if living would be one of the participating issue died leaving children they should take their parent's share of income. Secondly, that if a son died he might by will appoint up to one-half of his income to his wife for her life or widowhood. Thirdly, he created a discretionary trust giving a protected life interest to any beneficiary who forfeited his original interest in income by bankruptcy or alienation.

The testator then declared that from and after the expiration of the period of restriction his trustees should hold his residuary trust estate on the trusts following—namely, if any share of income was then subject to the discretionary trust the trustees were to hold a proportionate share of corpus upon trust for such one or more of the participating issue then living (including the forfeiting beneficiary) and the children of the forfeiting beneficiary as the trustees should within six calendar months after the testator's death [sic. Probably should have read "after the expiration of the period of restriction". Ed.] nominate and in such shares as they should in like manner specify. And the trustees should hold the rest of the corpus upon trust for the participating issue living at the expiration of the period of restriction (other than and except any forfeiting beneficiary) in proportion to their previous shares of income.

By a codicil dated February 2, 1926, the testator gave his wife an additional annuity of £200 during widowhood and a £10 life annuity to Louisa Jane Langdon and confirmed his will.

The testator died on September 6, 1926, and his will was proved by the Public Trustee and a son Arthur, who was qualified to be an executor. He left a widow, three sons, a spinster daughter and a married daughter with two infant children.

There was great difficulty in ascertaining the descendants of Queen Victoria living on September 6, 1926. It appeared, however, from an affidavit of A. T. Butler, Portcullis Pursuivant of Arms, that in 1922 there were about 120 descendants who had then to be sought in England, Germany, Russia, Sweden, Denmark, Norway, Spain, Greece, Jugo-Slavia and Rumania, and many of whom had probably become scattered over the entire continent of Europe, and might even have gone much further afield. It was not certain whether any of the late Tsaritsa's children were living, and owing to the war many of the continental descendants might fall into penury and obscurity, rendering any future tracing extremely difficult, if not impossible. The expense of a strictly proved pedigree of the descendants living at the testator's death would be very heavy.

In these circumstances the Public Trustee issued this summons on October 10, 1927, to determine (inter alia) whether the trusts of the income during the period of restriction and the trusts of the corpus at the expiration of that period were void for uncertainty or on any other ground. The summons also asked that if the trusts were valid an inquiry might be directed to ascertain who were Queen Victoria's lineal descendants living at the testator's death and whether any and which of them had since died.

Astbury, J., said that although it would be extremely difficult and expensive to ascertain the period when the capital became distributable twenty years after the death of the survivor of the lineal descendants of Queen Victoria living on September 6, 1926, he could not say that it would be impracticable or beyond the scope of legal testimony. He must hold, therefore, that the trust was valid.

The testator's three sons and spinster daughter appealed.

* * *

LORD HANWORTH, M. R.   This is an appeal from Astbury, J., who had to determine whether or not in the main the will of the testator ought to be declared ineffective and that the proposed trust disposition of his residuary estate failed on the ground that it was void for uncertainty, or, in other words, that it was impracticable.   [His Lordship then stated the facts and continued:]   It is said that the terms of the residuary gift which are easy to carry out as regards the payment of income at the present time are to be treated as invalid, because of the period of restriction to the end of which distribution of the capital was postponed.   The argument is that as the ascertainment of the end of this period will create serious difficulty in time to come, the residuary gift ought to be set aside as invalid.   The period of restriction is defined as "the period ending at the expiration of 20 years from the day of the death of the last survivor of all the lineal descendants of Her Late Majesty Queen Victoria who shall be living at the time of my death."   We have the evidence of a member of the College of Arms, who says the descendants of Queen Victoria numbered not less than 120 in 1922, and that they might have increased in number by 1926.   On the other hand, I suppose they might have decreased in number, for I do not know whether the births of new descendants between 1922 and 1926 were sufficient to fill the vacancies among the descendants caused by death.   However it is quite clear that there were a large number of descendants of Queen Victoria in being on September 6, 1926, and obviously there may be great difficulty in ascertaining whether and when the last of these lineal descendants had passed away.   That is what has to be ascertained, and it depends on the existence of one single life out of many others.   I recognize that serious difficulty might well arise in the future in ascertaining the date when that life ceased.

* * *

* * * it is said that the Courts ought to take into consideration the difficulty that will arise in the future when, it may be 100 years hence, their successors will be faced with the problem of finding out who is the last survivor of this body of 120 or 130 persons and when he died. That is a difficulty which may arise by reason of the vicissitudes of life, but it may not. It is possible that 120 years hence the Court may find a number of problems relating to the births, marriages and deaths of various persons; but they appear to me to be matters which we ought not to take into account. The difficulties are not insurmountable, and they may in fact never arise. Therefore I return to the view that the only matter I have to consider is whether the residuary gift of the testator can be declared invalid on the ground that it has transgressed some rule of law at the present time. The answer must be that it has not so transgressed, and, if so, we cannot by reference to difficulties that may arise hereafter make a new will for the testator.

[handwritten margin note: lawfullness outweighs impracticality]

I regret the decision, as there is no reason for such a fanciful disposition; but testing it by the rules which have to be applied, I can find no breach of the existing law, and the will must therefore stand. The appellant has suggested that the whole residuary gift should be set aside, but at the present time there is no difficulty in dealing with the estate as directed by the testator. It seems impossible to set aside a gift which works well in the present but which may in the future cause difficulty. I think that the decision of Astbury J. was right, and that the appeal must be dismissed. *[handwritten: aff'd]*

[The concurring opinions of LAWRENCE, L. J., and RUSSELL, L. J., are omitted.]

Notes

1. The statement that "It was not certain whether any of the late Tsaritsa's children were living" presumably refers to the controversy as to whether the Grand Duchess Anastasia, daughter of the Tsar, survived the execution of the Russian imperial family at Ekaterinburg in 1918. Her mother, Empress Alexandra, was a granddaughter of Queen Victoria. The lady who claimed to be Anastasia has been rescued from obscurity by the dramatic arts. It was a cause celebre at the time of this decision. See von Rathlef-Keilman, Anastasia (1929); Botkin, The Woman Who Rose Again (1937). More recently, the claim has been made that the brother and the three sisters of Anastasia (Alexei, Olga, Glenda Tatiana and Maria) were also alive in 1926. See Richards, Imperial Agent (1966).

2. One of the arguments in favor of this trust that was made in the lower court was that it complied with a limitation sanctioned in a form book commonly employed by lawyers, and that many dispositions might be upset if the precedent set by the form book were not followed. In re Villar (1928) Ch. 471, at 474. This may have had some influence on the decision. See Gray, § 218; Simes (hb) 266; Leach, Cases on Future Interests (2d ed., 1940) 753.

The purpose of the provisions forfeiting the interest of a beneficiary who should become bankrupt or attempt to alienate his interest, and thereupon converting the trust for that beneficiary from a mandatory trust to a discretionary trust, was, of course, to prevent any creditor of a beneficiary from reaching that beneficiary's interest in advance of actual payment to the beneficiary by the trustee. How could this objective be accomplished more directly in most states of the United States? See Chapter Seven, Section Four, p. 477, supra.

3. What would be the reason for holding the specified "period of restriction" invalid?

4. In re Villar was followed in a later Chancery case, with obvious reluctance, on the basis that, since the testator in that case died in 1925, one year before the testator died in the Villar case, stare decisis required the result. In re Leverhulme, 169 L.T.R. 294 (1943). The court remarked (169 L.T.R. at 298): "I hope that no draftsman will think that because of my decision today he will necessarily be following a sound course if he adopts the well-known formula referring to the descendants living at the death of the testator of her late Majesty Queen Victoria. When that formula was first adopted there was, no doubt, little difficulty in ascertaining when the last of them died. * * * I do not at all encourage anyone to use the formula in the case of a testator who dies in the year 1943 or any later date."

How to identify persons whose lives may be used as "measuring lives." In the Villar case, the testator specified that the interests of the ultimate takers were to vest 20 years after the death of the last survivor of the descendants of Queen Victoria living at his death. In such a case there may be little difficulty in ascertaining who the measuring lives are (although there will be more difficulty in finding out when they end). Ordinarily, however, a testator is not interested in prolonging a trust for the maximum (or near-maximum) period of the Rule and will not designate measuring lives in this fashion. One of the most frequent questions of students first wrestling with the Rule is "How do I decide who are the measuring lives?" Usually the person who asks the question wants to know whether the life of a particular person or class of persons mentioned in the will or trust instrument may be used as a measuring life or lives. Almost always the question betrays a basic misunderstanding of the operation of the common law Rule against Perpetuities. The question to ask is not whether the life of a particular person *may* be the measuring life but whether there is anyone whose life may be used to demonstrate compliance with the Rule.*

Professor Gray (Gray, § 219.2, note 2) says:

"For the purpose of sustaining a limitation, reference may be made by the Court to the lives of any persons living at the testator's death, whose lives have a necessary relation to the event on which the limitation vests, whether or not those persons take any interest in the property * * * or are mentioned in the will."

A somewhat different formulation is given by Prof. Dukeminier (Dukeminier, Perpetuities Law in Action (1962) 7–8 (footnotes omitted)): "The answer [to the question who is a life in being] is that it can be any person alive (or in the womb) at the creation of the interest, so long as

---

* This aspect of the operation of the common law Rule has led Professor Waggoner to use the term "validating life" instead of "measuring life". Waggoner, Perpetuity Reform, 81 Mich. L. Rev. 1718, 1722 (1983). While "validating life" undoubtedly conveys better the message in the text, we have stayed with the traditional usage—which is, in any event, as Professor Waggoner points out, more apt in the context of wait-and-see. See p. 821, infra.

his death or some event which will necessarily happen or fail to happen within his life will *insure* vesting or failure of the interest within twenty-one years of his death. The lives in being 'may be any lives which play a part in the ultimate disposition of the property.' They need not be given any beneficial interest in the property nor be referred to in the instrument, but the causal connection which insures vesting must be express or implied."

The editors prefer a third way of putting it: Ask yourself, "Is there a living person or group of persons to whom you can point and say that within twenty-one years after his or their deaths the contingency as to the future interest's becoming or not becoming vested will *necessarily* be resolved?"

All of these formulations will lead to the same result. They are premised on the so-called "remote possibilities test," i.e., the proposition that under the common law Rule against Perpetuities we are not interested in what actually happens, but what might happen, even by the remotest possibility, according to circumstances as they exist at the effective date of the instrument. The remote possibilities test, while it contributes substantially to the more bizarre results under the common law Rule, has at least the virtue that it makes the identification of the measuring lives relatively easy (as we shall see when we look at the situation under so-called "wait and see" rules in jurisdictions which have abolished the remote possibilities test). Under the common law Rule, if the contingency is not *certain* to be resolved within the period, the interest is void. Any possibility, no matter how improbable, that the contingency will not be resolved is enough. The search for the measuring life or lives is simplified; if there is any life (or group of lives) which will certainly suffice, that is the measuring life (or lives). If there is not, the interest is void.

C. THE REMOTE POSSIBILITIES TEST IN OPERATION

One of the most famous (or infamous) of all perpetuities cases illustrates the operation of the remote possibilities test.

JEE v. AUDLEY
Chancery, 1787.
1 Cox 324, 29 Eng.Rep. 1186.

Edward Audley, by his will, bequeathed as follows, "Also my will is that £1000 shall be placed out at interest during the life of my wife, which interest I give her during her life, and at her death I give the said £1000 unto my niece Mary Hall and the issue of her body lawfully begotten, and to be begotten, and in default of such issue I give the said £1000 to be equally divided between the daughters *then* living of my kinsman John Jee and his wife, Elizabeth Jee."

It appeared that John Jee and Elizabeth Jee were living at the time of the death of the testator, had four daughters and no son, and were of a very advanced age. Mary Hall was unmarried and of the age of about 40; the wife was dead. The present bill was filed by the four daughters of John and Elizabeth Jee to have the £1000 secured for their benefit upon the event of the said Mary Hall dying without leaving children. And the question was, whether the limitation to the daughters of John and Elizabeth Jee was not void as being too remote; and to prove it so, it was said that this was to take effect on a general failure of issue of Mary Hall; and although it was to the daughters of John and Elizabeth Jee, yet it was not confined to the daughters living at the death of the testator, and consequently it might extend to after-born daughters in which case it would not be within the limit of a life or lives in being and 21 years afterwards, beyond which time an executory devise is void.

On the other side it was said, that though the late cases had decided that on a gift to children generally, such children as should be living at the time of the distribution of the fund should be let in, yet it would be very hard to adhere to such a rule of construction so rigidly, as to defeat the evident intention of the testator in this case, especially as there was no real possibility of John and Elizabeth Jee having children after the testator's death, they being then 70 years old; that if there were two ways of construing words, that should be adopted which would give effect to the disposition made by the testator; that the cases, which had decided that after-born children should take, proceeded on the implied intention of the testator, and never meant to give an effect to words which would totally defeat such intention.   *   *   *

MASTER OF THE ROLLS [Sir Lloyd Kenyon]. Several cases determined by Lord Northington, Lord Camden, and the present Chancellor, have settled that children born after the death of the testator shall take a share in these cases; the difference is, where there is an immediate devise, and where there is an interest in remainder: in the former case the children living at the testator's death only shall take: in the latter those who are living at the time the interest vests in possession; and this being now a settled principle, I shall not strain to serve an intention at the expense of removing the land marks of the law; it is of infinite importance to abide by decided cases, and perhaps more so on this subject than any other. The general principles which apply to this case are not disputed: the limitations of personal estate are void, unless they necessarily vest, if at all, within a life or lives in being and 21 years or 9 or 10 months afterwards. This has been sanctioned by the opinion of judges of all times, from the time of the Duke of Norfolk's case to the present, it is grown reverend by age, and is not now to be broken in upon; I am desired to do in this case something which I do not feel myself at liberty to do, namely to suppose it impossible for persons in so advanced an age as John and Elizabeth Jee to have children; but if this can be done in one case it may in another, and it is a very dangerous experiment, and introductive of the greatest inconvenience to give a latitude to such sort of conjecture. Another thing pressed upon me, is to decide on the events which have happened; but I cannot do this without overturning very many cases. The single question before me, is, not whether the limitation is good in the events which have happened, but whether it was good in its creation; and if it were not, I cannot make it so. Then must this limitation, if at all, *necessarily* take place within the limits prescribed by law? The words are "in default of such issue I give the said £1000 to be equally divided between the daughters *then* living of John Jee and Elizabeth his wife." It if had been to "daughters now living," or "who should be living at the time of my death," it would have been very good; but as it stands, this limitation may take in after-born daughters; this point is clearly settled by *Ellison v. Airey,* [1 Ves. 111] and the effect of law on such limitation cannot make any difference in construing such intention. If then this will extended to after-born daughters, is it within the rules of law? Most certainly not, because John and Elizabeth Jee might have children born ten years after the testator's death, and then <u>Mary Hall might die without issue</u> 50 years afterwards; in which case it would evidently transgress the rules prescribed. I am of opinion, therefore, though the testator might possibly mean to restrain the limitation to the children who should be living at the time of the death, I cannot, consistently with decided cases, construe it in such restrained sense, but must intend it to take in after-born children. This therefore not being within the rules of law, and as I cannot judge upon subsequent events, I think the limitation void. Therefore dismiss the bill, but without costs.

Notes

1. Everyone should read Leach's clear and entertaining analysis of this poorly argued and vaguely decided, but nevertheless extremely influential, case in 51 Harv.L.R. 1338–41 (1938).

Note that this was a bill filed by the Jee daughters "to have the £1000 secured for their benefit." We have here the unusual situation of an attempt to create legal future interests in personal property, without any trust. The Jee daughters are trying to compel a bond as security against dissipation of the principal. Such a bond will be required in certain circumstances. See Prop. Rest. §§ 201–203. But, of course, if as here held, the gift to the daughters is void, they have no interests to protect, and the bill will be dismissed.

2. There are at least three possible constructions of the phrase "die without issue", as in a grant from *A to B and his heirs, but if B die without issue, then to C and his heirs:* (1) An unusual but possible construction is that this means that the gift to C is to take effect if, but only if, B never has any issue born to him. If so, the gift to C would fail if B at any time had a child born alive, whether or not such child survived B. For example, B has a child, X, born; the gift to C immediately fails under this construction, because B has had issue born to him, and this would be true even if X died the day after he was born and B did not die for many years thereafter. (2) The *"definite failure of issue"* construction. Failure of issue means, of course, non-existence of issue. "Definite failure of issue" means nonexistence of issue at a definite time. A gift to C "if there are no issue of B living on May 1, 1985" or at any other stipulated time would specifically provide for a definite failure of issue as the condition precedent to C's gift. In the case stated above, however, no time is explicitly stated, and the definite failure of issue construction supplies it by interpreting "if B die without issue" as *"if B die without issue living at B's death"*, the death of B being assumed to be the definite time intended. Under this construction,

if B should die leaving a child X surviving him, C's gift would completely fail, regardless of later events.   This seems to be the most reasonable interpretation of the language, and is the one favored by modern American statutes.   (3) The *"indefinite failure of issue"* construction is that the gift to C is to become effective whenever B's issue become non-existent.   Under this, C's interest would not fail if B died leaving a child X surviving him;   even though X should have a long line of lineal descendants the last survivor of whom did not die until the expiration of several centuries after the date of the transfer, this construction would be that C or his successors in interest were intended to take whenever such survivor died.

   Although the indefinite failure of issue interpretation seems a warped construction and may today have intent-defeating consequences, it was the one preferred by the English common law, owing to a rule that was formulated by the law courts before the Statute of Uses.   This rule was that a grant from A to B and his heirs, but if B die without issue then to C and his heirs, gave B a fee tail with a vested remainder in C to become possessory on the indefinite failure of B's issue.   One explanation of this curious result may be that, during the period after the 1472 decision that a common recovery would bar the entail and before the Statute of Uses, it enabled the law courts to reach a compromise between the conflicting objectives of carrying out the grantor's intent and of avoiding indestructible future interests.   The most reasonable grammatical construction of such a grant would be that it gave B a fee simple subject to be divested by a gift to C on failure of B's issue.   But, before the Statute of Uses, such a construction would result in C's interest being void, because of the rule of the law courts invalidating transferee interests that would divest previous transferee interests.   If construed as a fee tail with a vested remainder in C, the gift to C would be valid.   On the other hand, such a remainder would create no problem in the form of an indestructible future interest, because B, having a fee tail, could destroy C's interest at any time by suffering a common recovery.   Another reason that has been suggested for the fee tail construction is that it was then customary to introduce remainders after a fee tail by such expressions as "if B die without issue", and that the language introducing the gift over was read back into the interpretation of the preceding gift.   On the origins of this rule, see Warren, Gifts Over on Death Without Issue, 39 Yale L.J. 342 (1930).

   To accord a gift on failure of issue its more natural construction, statutes have been enacted in more than half of the United States preferring a definite failure of issue construction.   For the general status of this unnecessarily complicated set of problems, see Simes (hb) 196–202.

   3. As noted by Leach in his discussion of this case (see note 1, supra) Mr. Audley intended to give Mary Hall a fee tail (see p. 800 infra).   Since her interest was in personal property rather than real property, the effect was to create a fee simple in Mary, subject to an executory interest in the daughters of John and Elizabeth Jee.

   4. It was here argued (second paragraph of statement of facts) and apparently assumed by the court that the gift to the Jee daughters was on a "general" (indefinite) failure of Mary's issue.   If the court had construed "in default of such issue" as meaning "if Mary Hall die without issue living at the time of her death" (definite failure), would the gift to the Jee daughters have been void?

   5. Assuming an indefinite failure construction, would the gift be valid under the rule against remoteness of vesting if made to

(a) "the daughters of John and Elizabeth Jee living at my death"?

(b) "the daughters of John and Elizabeth Jee living at my death who are also living at the time of failure of Mary's issue"?

Note the dictum of the court on this question.

6. The opinion states that the court was urged "to decide on the events which have happened", without specifying what they were. Perhaps, between the death of the testator and the time of this suit, Mary Hall had died without issue, or John or Elizabeth Jee had died without producing any more daughters.

Why would the occurrence of any of these events have insured that the interests of the Jee daughters would "in fact" vest within the period of the Rule?

This court is orthodox in stating that it cannot take into consideration events happening after the operative date of the instrument, even if they occurred before the suit was brought. By the standard case law rule, the interest is void if, at the time of its creation, there was any possibility that it might vest too remotely. This proposition, and the contrary "wait and see" philosophy of some recent legislation, will be considered later.

7. Counsel for the Jee daughters seems to have argued that the will in this case should be interpreted as if it had been phrased like the hypothetical gift in note 5(b), supra.

(a) Assuming that the will (the date of which is not stated in the report) was executed within a few years of the testator's death, how could it be argued that the testator intended to confine the beneficiaries to the four living daughters of John and Elizabeth Jee? See Wright's Estate, page 815, infra.

(b) Would the testator's use of "daughters", rather than "children", in describing the beneficiaries, be significant on this issue?

See Leach, 51 Harv.L.R. 1329, 1339 (1938); Simes (hb) 288; Prop.Rest., § 377, Comment c (approving construction of an instrument to avoid "a result which seems highly unreasonable"). The trend, however, has been to follow the precedent of Jee v. Audley in refusing to save gifts of this type by construing the intent of the transferor to be to restrict the beneficiaries to lives in being. Wright's Estate (infra p. 815) is an unusual holding.

8. Another point made by counsel for the Jee daughters was that, since John and Elizabeth Jee were 70 years old at the testator's death, "there was no real possibility" of any daughters being born to them thereafter. It is not clear from the report whether this was an independent argument or merely a part of that mentioned in note 7, supra. However, it could be stated separately in this form: Even if it is assumed that the testator intended to include after-born daughters as beneficiaries (suppose, e.g., that the will were executed 40 years before the testator's death), the court should hold that the birth of any such daughters had become a physiological impossibility when the will became operative at the testator's death. For the purpose of the Rule against Perpetuities, an instrument is always construed in the light of the human situation existing at the time it becomes effective. If Elizabeth Jee had predeceased the testator, the gift would have been valid, because all possible takers under it would then necessarily be lives in being. Why should not the court hold that Elizabeth, aged 70, was as good as dead for reproductive purposes?

This decision, refusing to inquire into such matters, established the conclusive presumption of fertility, or, in Leach's phrase, the "fertile octogenarian" doctrine, that any living person will be treated as capable of having children. The more unrealistic applications of this proposition have usually, as in this case, involved women of advanced age. But it could logically be extended to the other end of the scale so as to assume a one-year-old child capable of reproduction. See Leach's entertaining account of the "Case of the Precocious Toddler" in 65 Harv.L.R. 721, 732 (1952). This was Gaite's Will Trusts, [1949] 1 All Eng.R. 459, the gift in which would be void if it were assumed that, all in the space of five years, a 67-year-old widow could have a child and that child in turn could have a child who could take as a beneficiary. The court did not consider two such rapid-fire births a physical impossibility, but saved the gift on the theory that the hypothetical child would be too young to marry legally, and that the hypothetical grandchild would thus be illegitimate and incapable of taking under the gift. For certain other matters, evidence of impossibility of issue has sometimes been received. See Gray, § 215.1, note 4 and see infra, p. 932. But the conclusive presumption of fertility is settled doctrine for the purpose of the Rule against Perpetuities. "The possibility of childbirth is never extinct." Turner v. Turner, 260 S.C. 439, 445, 196 S.E.2d 498, 501 (1973). See Annots. 67 A.L.R. 546 (1930); 146 A.L.R. 798 (1943).

The origin of this proposition may well have been influenced by incomplete and inaccurate medical information about the process of conception, by lack of statistics about the ages of child-bearing, and by the literal acceptance of stated Biblical ages in such stories as the birth of Isaac to Sarah when she was ninety years old and Abraham was a hundred years old. Genesis, 17:17; 21:5. See Leach, 51 Harv.L.R. 638, 643 (1938); Prop.Rest., § 377, Comment a. But, now that we know more about the birds and the bees, what accounts for the retention of this proposition in modern perpetuities cases?

What objections would there be to

(a) A flat and irrebuttable rule based on judicial notice or legislation that a woman over a certain age (55? 60?) was physically incapable of having more children?

Statistics of the United States Department of Commerce for 20,389,873 births between 1923 and 1932 show no birth to any woman aged 55 or over. City Bank Farmers' Trust Co. v. United States, 74 F.2d 692, 693 (C.C.A.N.Y. 1935). However, in connection with this citation, Leach also quotes an article in the Boston American of May 24, 1934, reporting the birth of twins to Senora Llanas, aged 70, in Mexico. See Leach, Cases on Future Interests (2d ed., 1940) 757; Leach, 51 Harv.L.R. 638, 643 (1943). And see The [London] Observer, Dec. 18, 1966, p. 2 (daughter born to Mr. & Mrs. Zuleika Beridze of Tolisi, Georgia, U.S.S.R., aged 79 and 66 respectively).

With men, of course, it's different. Newsweek of May 23, 1955 reported that the 3,134th baby delivered by Dr. John D. Hullinger, of Clinton, Iowa, was a son born to his 34-year-old wife when the doctor was 94; the proud father is said to have remarked after this event: "I think that this one is possibly the end."

(b) Taking voluntary or compelled testimony on such questions as whether a woman has passed the menopause, whether an operation has terminated procreative capacity, what may be the reasons for a so far childless marriage, the taking of a vow of celibacy, etc.

In In re Dawson, 39 Ch.Div. 155, 161 (1888), the court remarked:

*   *   *   if medical testimony was admitted in this case for the purpose of shewing that the lady was past child-bearing, it would equally be admitted as a matter of law in the case of a woman of younger age, and it may be medical testimony could shew that she was incapable of bearing a child, and evidence of that class might, therefore, consistently with the supposed principle, be adduced in the case of a woman of thirty or even younger; and if the principle is pursued in this way, there could be no ground for rejecting evidence in the case of a man.

See Simes (hb) 288, Gray, § 215; Prop.Rest., § 377, Comment a.

9. England did not recognize adoption until 1926, so that that possibility did not enter into the English cases formulating the above rules. The American jurisdictions vary as to whether and, if so, under what circumstances, an adopted child may take under a gift to "children", "issue", etc. See Chapter Two, Section Six, p. 88, supra; and see Annots. 70 A.L.R. 621 (1931); 144 A.L.R. 670 (1943). Except under such statutes as N.Y.—McKinney's EPTL § 2–1.3, there is not much likelihood of the inclusion of a child adopted by another after the death of the testator, and therefore without the latter's knowledge. But any such possibility would support the desirability of the present rule, since inquiry into the physiological situation would be academic if an afterborn adopted child could qualify as a beneficiary.

10. Several statutes have been enacted to deal with the "fertile octogenarian" problem and other aspects of the remote possibilities test. The New York statute (N.Y.—McKinney's EPTL 9–1.3) reads as follows:

§ 9–1.3   Rules of Construction

(a) Unless a contrary intention appears, the rules of construction provided in this section govern with respect to any matter affecting the rule against perpetuities.

(b) It shall be presumed that the creator intended the estate to be valid.

(c) Where an estate would, except for this paragraph, be invalid because of the possibility that the person to whom it is given or limited may be a person not in being at the time of the creation of the estate, and such person is referred to in the instrument creating such estate as the spouse of another without other identification, it shall be presumed that such reference is to a person in being on the effective date of the instrument.

(d) Where the duration or vesting of an estate is contingent upon the probate of a will, the appointment of a fiduciary, the location of a distributee, the payment of debts, the sale of assets, the settlement of an estate, the determination of questions relating to an estate or transfer tax or the occurrence of any specified contingency, it shall be presumed that the creator of such estate intended such contingency to occur, if at all, within twenty-one years from the effective date of the instrument creating such estate.

(e)(1) Where the validity of a disposition depends upon the ability of a person to have a child at some future time, it shall be presumed, subject to subparagraph (2), that a male can have a child at fourteen years of age or over, but not under that age, and that a female can have a child at twelve years of age or over, but not under that age or over the age of fifty-five years.

(2) In the case of a living person, evidence may be given to establish whether he or she is able to have a child at the time in question.

(3) Where the validity of a disposition depends upon the ability of a person to have a child at some future time, the possibility that such person may have a child by adoption shall be disregarded.

(4) The provisions of subparagraphs (1), (2) and (3) shall not apply for any purpose other than that of determining the validity of a disposition under the rule against perpetuities where such validity depends on the ability of a person to have a child at some future time. A determination of validity or invalidity of a disposition under the rule against perpetuities by the application of subparagraph (1) or (2) or (3) shall not be affected by the later occurrence of facts in contradiction to the facts presumed or determined or the possibility of adoption disregarded under subparagraphs (1) or (2) or (3).

Similar statutes have been adopted in Florida (West's FLA.STAT.Ann. § 689.22(5) (1981)) and Illinois (Ill.—Smith-Hurd Ann. ch. 30, ¶ 194(c)).

11. The cases (unidentified) referred to in the first sentence of the opinion in Jee v. Audley and, presumably, in the third sentence from the end, involve an important aspect of class gifts—the time at which a class "closes"—discussed infra at p. 803 et. seq.

———

Jee v. Audley is the most famous example of one manifestation of the remote possibilities test. The next two cases involved two other remote possibilities—the case of the "slothful executor" and the case of the "unborn widow," the latter also named by Professor Leach and the former (so far as the editors know) by Professor Dukeminier, op. cit. supra p. 760, at 12.

IN RE CAMPBELL'S ESTATE

District Court of Appeal of California, Fourth District, 1938.
28 Cal.App.2d 102, 82 P.2d 22.

BARNARD, Presiding Justice. Wesley S. Campbell died on October 4, 1935, leaving a will containing the following clause:

"All the rest, residue, and remainder of my estate, of whatsoever kind and nature and wheresoever situated, I give, devise and bequeath to the four chair officers of San Diego Lodge No. 168 Benevolent and Protective Order of Elks, being the four chair officers in office at the time of distribution of my estate, designated as 'Exalted Ruler', 'Exalted Leading Knight', 'Lecturing Knight' and 'Loyal Knight'. Such officers shall take the same free of any trust, but it is my expectation that they will employ the same for charitable purposes conformable to the policies of such San Diego Lodge No. 168, and I earnestly request them to make such use thereof. I particularly commend to them my friend May Skinner, if she should survive me, with the purpose that her needs be provided for should her own resources be insufficient."

The will was admitted to probate and in due course a final account and petition for distribution, with objections thereto, came on for hearing, it being stipulated that "the four chair officers" of this lodge were elected annually, and that the individuals who occupied those positions at that time were not the same individuals who had occupied them at the date of decedent's death. The court found that the quoted clause of the will is invalid and void as in contravention of the provisions of sections 715 and 716 of the Civil Code, and that the said Campbell died intestate as to the residue of his estate, and ordered the same distributed to his heirs at law. The four individuals who at that time held the designated positions in this lodge have appealed from the decree of distribution.

The sole question presented is whether this provision of the will is invalid because of a possibility that distribution of the estate might not take place for more than twenty-five years after the death of the testator. If distribution should be thus delayed the provision in question would contravene the rule against perpetuities (sec. 9, art. 20, State Constitution), and also section 716 of the Civil Code, which reads in part: "Every future interest is void in its creation which, by any possibility, may suspend the absolute power of alienation for a longer period than is prescribed in this chapter." This includes the provision of section 715 of that code that such a power shall not be suspended for more than twenty-five years from the time of the creation of the suspension, which in this case would be the date of the decedent's death.

The appellant relies particularly on the case of Belfield v. Booth, 63 Conn. 299, 27 A. 585. That case involved a provision of a will which left certain property in trust, the trust to continue for fourteen years after the executor "has settled with the judge of probate". In considering this provision, under the common-law rule against perpetuities, it was held that the time set for the division of the trust estate was not so remote as to contravene that rule. In so holding the court interpreted the will as, in effect, providing that the fourteen-year trust period was to commence "at the expiration of such reasonable time after his decease as will suffice for the proper settlement of his estate", and stated that it was not to be presumed that such settlement would be delayed longer than that. To follow this reasoning in the instant case would be not only to read into the will something which is not there but to flatly disregard the provision of our statute which makes void any future interest which by any possibility may suspend the absolute power of alienation for a period longer than that prescribed.

In considering a problem similar to the one now before us the supreme court of Illinois in Johnson v. Preston, 226 Ill. 447, 80 N.E. 1001, 10 L.R.A.,N.S., 564, said (page 1004):

"It is clear, from the language of the will itself, that whatever interest the executor took under it could not vest in him until the probate of the will, and while this event would, in the ordinary and usual course of events, probably occur within a few months, or at most a few years, after the death of the testatrix, yet it cannot be said that it is a condition that must inevitably happen within 21 years from the death of the testatrix. Since a bare possibility that the condition upon which the estate is to vest may not happen within the prescribed limits is all that is necessary to bring the devise in conflict with the rule, we see no escape from the conclusion that the devise to the executor offends the rule against perpetuities, and is therefore void."

That decision quoted from the case of Husband v. Epling, 81 Ill. 172, 25 Am.Rep. 273, as follows:

" 'The event here is: "When the estate of Thomas Mason is settled up." Can it be said to have been morally certain, when the instrument was executed, that the estate ever would be settled up? The law requires estates to be settled, and fixes a period within which it shall be done; but it does not, of and by itself, settle them. The presumption is that the law in this regard, as in others, will be obeyed. But this presumption does not amount to absolute certainty. The enforcement of the law, depending on human agencies, is liable to be affected or controlled by many circumstances, and instances where it is not only not fully enforced, but is openly violated, are within the experience of all, so that it is impossible to predict with moral certainty that a thing will be done simply because it is the command of the law that it shall be.' "

Similar principles have been applied, although upon very different facts, in People v. Simonson, 126 N.Y. 299, 27 N.E. 380, and in Cruikshank v. Chase et al., 113 N.Y. 337, 21 N.E. 64, 4 L.R.A. 140.

In Estate of Troy, 214 Cal. 53, 3 P.2d 930, the court said (page 932):

"It has frequently been stated that the provisions of section 716 of the Civil Code do not permit us to wait and see what happens in order to determine the validity or invalidity of the limitation. It is the possibility of the event that will suspend unlawfully the power of alienation which serves to void the limitation at the time of its creation."

The question before us narrows down to whether or not it can be said that this estate must of necessity have been distributed within twenty-five years after the testator's death and that such distribution could not "by any possibility" have been longer delayed. One possibility, which cannot be overlooked, is that probate proceedings might not have been started for many years. Cases are not unknown where parties, through ignorance or neglect, have continued to occupy and use for a long period property left by a decedent before resorting to probate. Property in the form of bank deposits has remained unclaimed for years before probate proceedings were commenced. The closing of many estates has been delayed for years both through neglect and by intention, because of circumstances and conditions. A long delay by reason of protracted litigation is a very real possibility. All of these possibilities, not to mention others, might become realities in a particular case, causing a delay beyond the time limited. While it can be said that the reasonable probabilities were in favor of a distribution of this estate well within the time required, to hold that such a result, with the consequent vesting of interest, was certain to occur and would inevitably take place would be to disregard the statute by accepting a high degree of probability as a certainty.

While statutes of the kind here in question may at times seem unnecessarily harsh in a particular case, they are adopted with a definite aim and purpose in view. These particular statutes are a part of the expression of well-defined public policy. In so far as material here the language therein used is not ambiguous and to interpret the phrase "by any possibility" as in effect meaning "by any probability" would be to alter a plain provision of the statute. Such a change in statutory law should come, if at all, from the legislature and not from the court.

The judgment and decree is affirmed.

I concur: MARKS, J.

Notes

1. What would be the arguments for or against the validity of the following gifts by will?

(a) After the payment of my debts and funeral and administration expenses, I give the rest, residue, and remainder of my estate to B. See Collis v. Walker, 272 Mass. 46, 172 N.E. 228 (1930) (valid); 49 Mich.L.R. 281 (1950).

(b) I give $50,000 to such of B's issue as shall be living at the date of my death, per stirpes, to be paid to them at the time of distribution of my estate. Cf. Trautz v. Lemp, 329 Mo. 580, 46 S.W.2d 135 (1932) (residuary estate given to trustees on a trust "to commence immediately upon the termination of the administration of my estate"; valid).

(c) I give $50,000 to such of B's issue as shall be living at the date of distribution of my estate. Cf. In re Campbell's Estate, supra.

(d) I give $5,000 to my sister Susie, to be paid immediately after the probate of my will. My purpose in desiring that the payment of this legacy be accelerated is to provide greatly needed funds to my said sister, who has been an invalid for many years. Cf. Union Trust Co. of Springfield v. Nelen, 283 Mass. 144, 186 N.E. 66 (1933) (share of stock given in trust to "be assigned and transferred to said trustee as soon as expedient after the probate" of the will; valid).

(e) I give $5,000 to my sister Susie, to be paid immediately after the probate of my will, if my said sister is still alive at the time of such payment.

Provisions conditioning bequests on survival to the date of distribution (for example (c) and (e) above) are commonly used to avoid the cost and inconvenience of having property pass through the estate of a beneficiary who dies before he receives his share.

2. The most extensively discussed decision departing from orthodoxy in this context is Belfield v. Booth, 63 Conn. 299, 27 A. 585 (1893), referred to in the principal case. The author of that opinion was Simeon E. Baldwin, who, in addition to many other claims to fame, was an active member of the Yale Law School faculty for 51 years. On this gentleman's extraordinary career, see Hicks, Yale Law School, 1895–1915, Yale Law Library Publication, No. 7 (1938) 63–85; Yale Law School Catalogue 1958–9, page 14; Corbin, The First Half Century, 50 Yale L.J. 740 (1941). Judge Baldwin's decision was iconoclastic in two respects: (1) holding that 14 years after the settlement of the executor's final account would not exceed 21 years, since the time when the executor's accounts "are, or should be, settled in the due course of administration

* * * cannot be delayed so long as seven years" after the testator's death; (2) apparently holding that, even if the period were too long, the gift to a class to be ascertained at the end of the period would nevertheless be valid because he held that some members of the class had a vested interest at the testator's death; "the estate, having vested at his decease in a definite class, cannot be divested by any change in the membership of that class. It remains the same class, though composed, from time to time, of different individuals." The latter holding is, of course, the antithesis of the usual rule. This decision is deplored in Gray, §§ 205.3, 214.2–214.5. Leach likes the approach in the first holding. 51 Harv.L.R. at 638, 645 (1938); cf. Morris and Leach, The Rule Against Perpetuities 73 (1956).

See generally, on these issues, Simes (hb) 286; Gray, § 214.1; Simes and Smith, § 1228; Annots. 13 A.L.R. 1033 (1921); 110 A.L.R. 1450, 1452 (1937).

3. The New York statute (N.Y.—McKinney's EPTL 9–1.3(d)) dealing with this aspect of the remote possibilities test is set out at p. 767 supra. As originally enacted, the language "or the occurrence of any specified contingency" read "or the occurrence of any *like* contingency." The change was, presumably, to broaden the category of contingencies covered beyond the type of administrative contingencies specifically mentioned. See the Practice Commentary by Professor Patrick J. Rohan on N.Y.—McKinney's EPTL 9–1.3. Could the drafters have intended the statute to be read literally? If it is so read, what is left of the remote possibilities test—or the Rule against Perpetuities? What happens under this statute if the contingency is not in fact resolved within twenty-one years? Although not common, estates occasionally remain open for more than 21 years. E.g. Hostetter v. Hostetter's Estate, 75 Ill.App.3d 1020, 31 Ill. Dec. 161, 394 N.E.2d 77 (1979); Matter of Van Wezel, 84 Misc.2d 664, 379 N.Y.S.2d 905 (Sur.Ct.1973). See Glasser, Trusts, Perpetuities, Accumulations and Powers Under the Estates, Powers and Trusts Law, 33 Brook.L.Rev. 551 (1967).

PERKINS v. IGLEHART

Court of Appeals of Maryland, 1944.
183 Md. 520, 39 A.2d 672.

MARBURY, Chief Judge. This case arose through a trustee's petition filed in the Circuit Court for Baltimore County, asking for a construction of the will of Lucy James Dun. She died in 1921, a widow with one child, a son, William James Rucker. All parties thought by the trustee to have a possible interest in the estate were brought in by summons or order of publication, and those claiming interest appeared by counsel. Testimony was taken, numerous exhibits were filed, and from the decision of the chancellor four appeals were taken, all combined in one record, and all heard together in this Court.

Mrs. Dun had been twice married. Her first husband was Major William A. Rucker. William James Rucker was the son of this marriage. Major Rucker died in 1893, and in 1899 Mrs. Rucker married her second cousin, James Dun, who died in 1908. There were no children of this marriage. The estate which Mrs. Dun left was a valuable one, consisting very largely of an interest she had in the business of R. G. Dun and Co. See Douglass v. Safe Deposit & Trust Co., 159 Md. 81, 150 A. 37. This interest became part of her residuary estate, was subsequently disposed of by the trustee, and the proceeds invested in securities which now constitute the estate which is to be distributed in these proceedings.

Mrs. Dun, in her will, gave various specific and pecuniary bequests, and then by the fourteenth clause provided as follows:

"14. All the rest and residue of my property of every kind, I give, devise and bequeath to the Safe Deposit and Trust Company of Baltimore, in trust to hold the same, with full power to the said Trustee, both as to this trust and as to the trust created by the second clause of this my will, to make and change investments from time to time in its discretion and to sell the whole or any part of the trust estate for any purpose which, in its discretion, may be for the best interest of the same, without obligation on the part of any purchaser to see to the application of the purchase money, and to collect the income of the said trust estate and, after deducting taxes and expenses of administration, to pay over the net income thereof in monthly or quarterly installments, as it may deem best, to my son William James Rucker, during his life, into his own hands and not into the hands of another and without power of anticipation, or, if my said Trustee shall deem it to be for the best interest of my said son, to apply the said net income for his benefit and for the benefit of his family in its discretion, during his life; and from and after the death of my said son to set apart one-third of said trust estate and pay the net income thereof to his widow during her life or widowhood, and to hold the remaining two-thirds of said trust estate for the benefit of his child or children living at the time of his death and the descendants then living of his deceased children, per stirpes and not capita, and to pay over and transfer the same, free of any trust, to such of them as shall attain the age of twenty-one years, the original share of each therein to be paid when such age is attained, and any addition thereto, accruing by reason of the death under such age of any beneficiary, to be paid upon such event or as soon thereafter as the person hereby entitled to receive the same is of full age, and until each of them shall attain such age, to apply his or her share, original or accruing, of the net income of said trust estate to and for his or her benefit, maintenance and education, in its discretion; but, if my son shall die without children or descendants him surviving, or if all of them shall die before attaining the age of twenty-one years, then to divide, pay over and transfer the same, free of any trust, to and among the persons who may be the next of kin of my said son according to the laws of Maryland at the time of his death; and from and after the death or remarriage of the widow of my said son, to hold the one-third part of the trust estate, so as above set apart for her, for the benefit of the child or children of my said son then living and the descendants then living of his deceased children, per stirpes and not per capita, under the same limitations as are herein above set forth as to the two-thirds part of the trust estate; but if there shall be no such children or descendants then surviving, or if all of them shall die before attaining the age of twenty one years, to divide, pay over and transfer the same, free of any trust, to and among the persons who would be the next of kin of my said son according to the laws of Maryland if he were living at the time of the death or remarriage of his widow. I authorize and empower my said Trustee to invest fifty thousand ($50,000.00) dollars of the trust estate, or so much thereof as may be requisite, in the purchase for my said son and his family of a home such as he may desire and select, the house and land so purchased to continue however as a part of the trust estate."

The son, William J. Rucker, was twice married; both wives predeceased him. He was a resident of Virginia and died there December 19, 1941, testate, and without issue. W. Allen Perkins and George Pausch were made his executors. They are parties herein, and appellants in No. 4. The appellants in Nos. 5 and 6 are, respectively, a first cousin of William J. Rucker on his father's side, and the executor of a similar first cousin who has died since William J. Rucker's death. The appellants in No. 7 are the widow and administratrix and only child of another first cousin on the Rucker side, who, however, predeceased William J. Rucker. The appellees are three first cousins of William J. Rucker on his mother's side. They are nieces of the testatrix, Mrs. Dun. Other facts in the case will be mentioned and discussed when the parts of this opinion to which they are pertinent are reached.

All of the questions here involved concern that part of the residuary clause of Mrs. Dun's will which disposes of one-third of the residuary estate, after the death of the testatrix's son. There is no dispute that the two-thirds, after the death of the son without leaving any children or descendants, went to the next of kin of the son at the time of his death, and we are advised that it has already been so distributed. The remaining one-third, however, is set apart under separate provisions, and it is in respect to this one-third that the parties have conflicting theories.

It is contended by the Rucker executors that the two gifts over, each to take effect from and after the death or remarriage of the son's widow, violate the rule against perpetuities. This rule is stated by Gray on Perpetuities, Fourth Edition, page 191, paragraph 201 as follows: "No interest is good unless it must vest, if at all, not later than 21 years after some life in being at the creation of the interest." The decisions of this Court follow this rule. It is stated in Graham v. Whitridge, 99 Md. 248, 274, 275, 57 A. 609, 671, 58 A. 36, 66 L.R.A. 408: "The period fixed and prescribed by law for the future vesting of an estate or interest is a life or lives in being at the time of its commencement, and 21 years and a fraction of a year beyond, to cover the period of gestation; and, where property is rendered inalienable or its vesting is deferred for a longer period, the law denounces the devise, the bequest, or the grant as a perpetuity, and declares it void." This statement is quoted with approval in the case of Gambrill v. Gambrill, 122 Md. 563, 89 A. 1094, and the Court further said, 122 Md. at page 569, 89 A. at page 1095: "In determining this question of remoteness, there is an invariable principle that regard is to be had to possible, and not merely actual, events. It is not determined by looking back on events which have occurred and seeing whether the estate has extended beyond the prescribed limit, but by looking forward from the time the limitation was made and seeing whether, according to its terms, there was then a possibility that it might so extend. * * * The event upon the happening of which the remainder is to vest must be one that is certain to happen within the prescribed period, or the limitation will be bad." There is quite a full discussion of the origin and applicability of the rule in the late case of Safe Deposit & Trust Co. v. Sheehan, 169 Md. 93, 179 A. 536, 542, where it was said: "The rule is applicable to limitations of either legal or equitable estates in either real or personal property."

The contention of the Rucker executors is that the widow of the son of the testatrix might have been born after the death of the testatrix, and might have lived longer than 21 years and the period allowed for gestation after the death of the son. Therefore, the gift over to the children and descendants, and the gift over to the next of kin in the absence of children and descendants are both void, because both might fail to vest within the required period. This view, which was adopted by the chancellor, seems to be correct, if we read the residuary clause as it is written. It is, however, strenuously resisted for various reasons by other parties to the case. We will take up their contentions in the order which seems most logical. Before doing so, however, it may be well to restate the general rules of construction of wills, so that they may be borne in mind. The whole intention of the testatrix is to be ascertained from the entire will, as well as any specific intention shown in the particular clause under discussion. This intention is to be gathered not only from the will, but from pertinent circumstances surrounding the testatrix at the time of making the will. In cases where it is claimed that the rule against perpetuities is violated, the Court first decides what the will means, and then determines whether the will so interpreted violates the rule. There is a presumption against intestacy, especially where there is a residuary clause, indicating that the testatrix intended to dispose of her entire estate. If there are two constructions, either of which can be adopted without straining the words of the will, the court will adopt that one which disposes of the entire estate, rather than one which results in a total or partial intestacy. But the Court will not write a new will, nor attempt to surmise what the testatrix would have done had she thought of the contingency which has arisen. Nor will the Court substitute its own judgment for hers, as to what she should have done. It will interpret what she said, in the light of the circumstances which have arisen, and determine, from the will itself, what she meant.

The general intention of the residuary clause before us seems to be to provide for the son of the testatrix, his widow, his descendants and his next of kin. The entire clause revolves around the son. No question arises, or could arise, as to the estate given to the son's widow during her unmarried life. It vests within the required period. The question arises as to the two subsequent bequests of the one-third taking effect "from and after the death or remarriage of the widow." The first of these directs the one-third residuary estate to be held for the benefit of the child or children of the son "then living," and the descendants "then living," of his deceased children per stirpes and not per capita. It has been suggested in connection with this bequest that it comes within the rule that a contingent estate to a class vests immediately upon the birth of a member of that class, and becomes vested as to him, with the possibility of his being divested as to part by the subsequent birth of other members of the class.   The latest applications of this rule are found in the cases of Bishop v. Horney, 177 Md. 353, 9 A.2d 597;   Hans v. Safe Deposit & Trust Co., 178 Md. 52, 12 A.2d 208, and Safe Deposit & Trust Co. v. Bouse, 181 Md. 351, 29 A.2d 906.   The argument for its application to the present case is that any children of the son must have been in being at his death, or within the usual period of gestation thereafter, and therefore the gift must have taken effect within the period.   This view, however, does not take into account the fact that the bequest is not only to the children, but to descendants of deceased children and the further fact that the time of ascertainment of the beneficiaries is fixed at the death or remarriage of the widow.   Descendants of deceased children might be the only persons of the class in existence at the death or remarriage of the widow, and they might not have been born during the lifetime of William James Rucker or 21 years thereafter.   "If a gift is to a class in this technical sense, and the gift is good as to some members of the class, but is within the rule against perpetuities as to other members, the entire gift must fall.   The general rule is that if a gift is void as to any of a class, it is void as to all the class."   Miller on Construction of Wills, paragraph 328, page 932.   "Assuming then that the devise is not to vest until the remote period, the devise to the whole class is bad;   and it is immaterial that some persons are in esse who should they reach 25 would be entitled to share."   Gray on Perpetuities, 4th Edition, paragraph 373, page 394, and paragraph 537, page 522.   See also 48 Corpus Juris, Perpetuities, paragraph 44, page 964 and paragraph 46, page 965.   The principle that a contingent gift to a class vests on the birth of a member of the class cannot be applied to make a void estate valid, because it would then conflict with the rule that whether an estate is void as a perpetuity must be determined by what might happen, rather than by what has happened.

It is contended by the appellants in all four appeals that neither the bequest to the children and descendants, nor that to the next of kin are void because the word "widow" in the will does not mean widow in the usually accepted sense of a surviving wife, but means Sally Woods who was engaged to the son at the time the will was made on April 7, 1910, and who married him 21 days later.   She was in being at the death of the testatrix, dying on December 20, 1932.   The surrounding circumstances which we are asked to consider in connection with this contention are that the will was made at the time when Mrs. Dun had come to Baltimore to take part in the festivities in connection with her son's approaching marriage to Sally Woods;   that she undoubtedly had no other thought except that Sally Woods would ultimately become her son's wife, and might become his widow;   that she did not name Sally Woods because of a natural delicacy under the circumstances, but that she meant Sally Woods when she used the word "widow."   Maryland cases and cases from other jurisdictions are cited in support of this contention.   The Maryland case principally relied on is Lavender v. Rosenheim, 110 Md. 150, 72 A. 669, 132 Am.St.Rep. 420.   In that case a mother left her estate to a trustee to pay income to her son during his life, and upon his death to pay the principal to his children.   In the event no children survived, the principal of the trust estate was given absolutely to "the wife of my said son." The son, at the time the will was made, was married. His wife subsequently divorced him and married another man. The son died, leaving no children, and the Court held that his former wife was entitled to the estate. Other cases which hold that if at the time of the making of the will, there is a person who would fully answer the description of a widow should she survive her husband such person is meant by the word "widow" are Mercantile T. & D. Co. v. Brown, 71 Md. 166, 17 A. 937; In re Solm's Estate, 253 Pa. 293, 98 A. 596; Anshutz v. Miller, 81 Pa. 212; Van Brunt v. Van Brunt, 111 N.Y. 178, 19 N.E. 60; In re Friend's Estate, 168 Misc. 607, 6 N.Y.S.2d 205; Willis v. Hendry, 127 Conn. 653, 20 A.2d 375. It is, of course, well recognized that a beneficiary may be designated by description rather than by name, and that who is intended can be determined by who would answer that description had the contingency upon which the estate to such person is limited, happened at the time of making the will. That is all these cases hold. In each case the widow was the wife at the time of the making of the will. Had her husband's death occurred at that time, she would have been the widow. In the case before us we are asked to go much further. We are asked to hold that a person who is not married to the testatrix's son is the person she means by her son's widow. It so happened that this person did marry the son, that she died before he did, and that he then married another wife who also predeceased him, and that he died leaving no widow at all. If we should say that Mrs. Dun meant Sally Woods by the word "widow" she used, and if it should have happened that Sally Woods had not married the son at all, but that he had married someone else who survived him, it would necessarily follow that Sally Woods would get the bequest although she had never actually become connected with the testatrix by marriage to her son. The real widow would not take at all. This possible contingency illustrates the instability of the contention. What Mrs. Dun was interested in doing was to take care of her son and his relations. He was taken care of for his life, his widow was taken care of for her unmarried life, his children and descendants and finally his next of kin were attempted to be taken care of. All the residuary clause related to the son, and all the beneficiaries were to take by virtue of their relationship to the son. It was the relationship to the son, and not any particular friendship for Sally Woods which motivated the bequest. Mrs. Dun said she was providing for her son's widow. We must assume that was what she was doing, and not that she was trying to take care of a particular person, even though she thought that person might some day be the widow of her son.

* 　 * 　 *

* 　 * 　 * We, therefore, have here an absolute estate in the trustee for the duration of the life of the son and for the duration of the unmarried life of the widow, and then an indefeasibly vested reversion in the heir of the testatrix at the time of her death. That is the effect of an intestacy caused by a void bequest. In Heald v. Heald, 56 Md. 300 where a limitation over on the death of the children of Charles Heald leaving issue, to such issue, was held void, the Court said: "It follows, therefore, that when one of the children of Charles dies leaving issue surviving, the share of such child does not survive to the remaining brothers or sisters, nor does it go to the issue of such child; but vests at once in the persons and their heirs who were heirs-at-law of the testator at the time of his death." See also Mines v. Gambrill, 71 Md. 30, 18 A. 43. In Graham v. Whitridge, 99 Md. 248, at page 281, 57 A. 609, at page 614, 58 A. 36, 66 L.R.A. 408, the Court said: "Where an interest or estate is given by deed or will, with a limitation over on a specified contingency, such limitation, if it violates the rule against perpetuities, is for the purpose of determining the effect on the prior disposition of the property, to be considered as stricken out, leaving the prior disposition to operate as if a limitation over had never been made." This quotation was approved in the case of Turner v. Safe Deposit & Trust Co., 148 Md. 371, 129 A. 294. If it is applied to the present case in which the prior limitations were only for life, we have the same situation as if the estate were granted only to the trustee for the life of the son and for the unmarried life of the widow, leaving no granted estate beyond, but a reversion to the heir of the testatrix at the time of her death, who was her son. This, of course, goes to his personal representatives who are the executors of William J. Rucker.

Notes

1. The opinion (ninth paragraph) states: "No question arises, or could arise, as to the estate given to the son's widow during her unmarried life."

(a) What is the explanation of the next statement in the opinion: "It vests within the required period"?

(b) Would this provision have been valid if the will had read "pay such income as the trustee shall in its absolute and uncontrolled discretion determine to his widow during her life or widowhood", instead of "pay the net income thereof to his widow during her life or widowhood"?

2. On what grounds did the court hold invalid the provision to take effect on the death or remarriage of the son's widow for the benefit of

(a) The son's descendants?

(b) The son's next of kin?

3. What effect, if any, would the Rule against Perpetuities have on a testamentary trust to pay the net income to testator's son John for life, and after his death to pay the net income for her life to such person as should at the date of his death be his surviving widow, and after her death to transfer the principal to John's children?

4. What argument could have been made for the validity of the provisions referred to in note 2 if testatrix's son William had been married to Sally at the date when the will was executed?

To what extent might the force of such argument be affected by whether

(a) The will referred to the son's "wife", or to the son's "widow"?

(b) Sally were in fact William's surviving widow, or Sally should predecease William who should then remarry and leave Mary as his surviving widow?

Matter of Friend, 283 N.Y. 200, 28 N.E.2d 377 (1940) involved the effect of the New York rule limiting income trusts to two lives in being. The will divided the residuary estate into four shares, two of which were to be held in trust to pay the income from each respectively to testator's son Sol for life and to testator's son Ike for life. It was provided as to each share that, if the son should die without leaving issue him surviving, one-half of his share should be held in trust to pay the income to his "widow" for life or until she remarried. Both sons died without issue, leaving surviving widows to whom they were married at the date of execution of the will. The court held the income provision for the "widow" valid on the theory that the beneficiary was a life in being, and that the provision for her would thus not run the income trust for longer than two lives in being. Surrogate Foley's opinion below (168 Misc. 607, 610–12, 6 N.Y.S.2d 205, 209–11 (1938)), affirmed on this point, read in part:

> It has been generally held in this State that a gift to a "wife" of a legatee or beneficiary is a gift to one who occupies that relation at the making of the will, while a gift to the "widow" of a designated person is a gift to the lawful widow who may survive him. * * * There appears, however, to be no arbitrary rule that the word "widow" necessarily denotes a wife who shall survive a legatee or beneficiary, to the exclusion of a wife who was such at the time of the making of the will. * * *

>   * * *

> There is sufficient competent evidence in this proceeding to show generally an attitude on the part of the testator of solicitude for his daughters-in-law. When he wrote his will his sons had been married to them for a number of years. Sol was at that time forty-nine years of age; Ike was forty-five. Their wives were well known to the testator. To some extent they had been dependent upon him for support. The marriages of his sons having occurred late in life, it is extremely unlikely that the testator had in mind possible divorces of his sons, or their remarriages to other women. It is quite evident from a reading of the whole will that the testator was thinking of living persons when he referred to the "widows" of his sons. * * *

>   * * *

> An intention to use the word "widow" in a sense which would result in invalidity should not be attributed to the testator if a more reasonable indication which would sustain the validity of the provisions of the will may fairly be inferred. Certainly, the secondary life estates may be saved for the widows of Sol and Ike without in any way doing violence to the language used by the testator.

Cf. Matter of Chemical Bank, 90 Misc.2d 727, 395 N.Y.S.2d 917 (Sup.Ct.1977).

In Greenwich Trust Co. v. Shively, 110 Conn. 117, 147 A. 367 (1929), the will left $100,000 in trust to pay, during the life of testatrix's son Edmund, the net income (and, in the discretion of the trustee, principal) for the support of Edmund "and of his wife and child or children"; and, on Edmund's death, "if he leave a wife him surviving", to pay the income "unto the wife of my said son during her lifetime or until she remarry"; and, on her death or remarriage, to distribute the principal among Edmund's issue per stirpes. At the time of the execution of the will, Edmund was married to Judith, but, after the death of the testatrix, they were divorced, and both remarried. On Edmund's later death, his surviving widow was Estella, and two sons of his first marriage also survived him. (For more details about this family, see Cromwell v. Converse,

108 Conn. 412, 143 A. 416 (1928).)   The court held that (1) the income trust for Edmund's wife was valid, and (following the previous holding on the same will in Greenwich Trust Co. v. Converse, 100 Conn. 15, 122 A. 916 (1923)) the income was payable to Estella;   (2) the gift of the principal to Edmund's issue, construed by the court as postponing the ascertainment of the beneficiaries until Estella's death, was void under the Rule against Perpetuities.   What was there in either the language of the will or the situation before the court that might militate against the construction that Judith, rather than Estella, was the beneficiary of the second income trust?

See, generally, Leach, 51 Harv.L.R. 638, 644 (1938);   Leach, 65 Harv.L.R. 721, 731 (1952);   Simes (hb) 285;   Morris and Leach, The Rule against Perpetuities, 70 (1956) (English Cases);   Gray, § 214.

5. The New York statute dealing with the unborn widow problem (N.Y.—McKinney's EPTL 9–1.3(c)) is set out at p. 767, supra.   Would such a statute save the interests found invalid in Perkins v. Iglehart?   Suppose, in a case under such a statute, that the widow is in fact unborn at the time the interests are created—is the estate valid?   Compare West's Ann.Cal.Civ.Code, § 715.7.

6. For other extreme applications of the remote possibilities test, see Leach, 51 Harv.L.R. 638, 644–646 (1938);   Dukeminier, op. cit. supra p. 760, 9–14.

"Vest if at all."   One point of frequent confusion about the Rule stems from the requirement that the interest be certain to vest *if at all* within the permissible period.   The Rule does not require that the interest be certain to vest within the period but only that it be certain to vest *or* disappear within the period.   The vice aimed at is not the state of contingency but the possibility that an interest may remain contingent too long;   the Rule is satisfied either if the interest must become vested or if the life of the interest is so limited that it cannot remain contingent beyond the period.

An illustration of how the phrase "vest if at all" comes into play would be the hypothetical of note 5(b), p. 765.   Suppose the limitation in Jee v. Audley had been "to the daughters of John and Elizabeth Jee living at my death who are also living at the time of failure of Mary's issue"?   Assuming that the court would construe the gift to Mary as one on indefinite failure of issue, when would the gift to the daughters take effect?   Can we be sure that Mary's issue will fail within 21 years after some life in being?   Assuming that your answer is no (it should be), is the gift to the daughters void?   Why not?

D. MISCELLANEOUS ASPECTS OF THE RULE

1. The Effect of the Rule Against Perpetuities on Trust Duration

No limit is placed on the duration of either legal or equitable interests by any general case law rule.   The Rule against Perpetuities invalidates interests that may remain contingent (or, under the alternative theory, suspend the power of alienation) for longer than the period of the Rule;

it does not curtail the length of enjoyment of interest; if it did, the most obvious interest for it to cut down would be the longest in duration, a fee simple, which is the very type of ownership that the Rule seeks to promote.

There is no case law rule limiting the duration of either a private or a charitable trust as such,* as far as their original creation is concerned, as distinguished from the possibility of their being terminated later. See Scott, Trusts (3d ed., 1967) § 62.10 (private trusts); § 365 (charitable trusts). Charitable trusts may, and usually do, last indefinitely. It is, however, impossible to create a perpetual private trust, because income rights under such a trust will terminate with the death of the income beneficiary and because the Rule against Perpetuities will invalidate attempts to create subsequent rights to income that may vest too remotely.** As indicated above, a mandatory income trust for a living person and for that person's children would be valid, although it might last longer than the perpetuities period, but an attempt to continue the income trust for more remote generations would probably be void under the Rule against Perpetuities, thus eliminating anything in the nature of a private trust of indefinite duration.***

A notable exception to the statement that the Rule against Perpetuities does not affect the duration of interests is the law of New York. As originally adopted the New York statute on perpetuities was a rule against suspension of the power of alienation. Although, first by case law and now explicitly by statute (N.Y.—McKinney's EPTL 9–1.1(b)), the New York Rule against Perpetuities is also a rule against remoteness of vesting, the statutes still prohibit suspension of the power of alienation for longer than the period of the Rule (N.Y.—McKinney's EPTL 9–1.1(a)). The retention of the theory of suspension of the power of alienation would not ordinarily have significant consequences since interests which suspend the power of alienation too long will ordinarily vest too remotely. However, as discussed in Chapter 7, New York law made *all* trusts to receive the income from property spendthrift; and the New York courts held that the creation of a right to receive the income from a trust suspends the power of alienation of the income interest, and that an income trust to last longer than the perpetuities period is therefore void.

For trusts created prior to September 1, 1958 the effect of the application of the Rule to trusts in New York was greatly multiplied by the

---

 * In the very limited context of transfers with the misleading nickname of "honorary trusts," the courts have formulated a special rule restricting their duration to the period of the Rule against Perpetuities. Scott, Trusts §§ 124, 124.1 (3d ed., 1967). See Chapter Seven, Section Seven, Part D., supra, p. 578.

 ** This does not appear to be true in Wisconsin which has no rule against remoteness of vesting and where it is specifically provided by statute that a trust does not suspend the power of alienation if the trustee has power to sell the assets. (See p. 747, supra.)

 *** Although, in the absence of statute, there is general agreement that interests in a trust are not invalid because they may last beyond the permissible period—provided that they are certain to vest within the period—there is some uncertainty as to whether a non-charitable trust may be indestructible beyond the perpetuities period. The Restatement, Second, Property (Donative Transfers) § 2.1 takes the position that a trust may not be made forever indestructible "internally" (i.e., by the beneficiaries) beyond the period of the Rule. See p. 517 supra and see Simes and Smith, § 1393; Scott, Trusts, § 62.10 (3d ed. 1967).

limitation of the period of the Rule to two lives in being* (with no period in gross).   The origins of this strange provision and its effect are detailed in The Statutes of the State of New York Concerning Perpetuities and Related Matters, a Report to the New York Law Revision Commission by Professors Richard R. B. Powell and Horace E. Whiteside (1936 Reports of the Law Revision Commission 475).   At best, the limit of two lives in being was a trap for the unwary draftsman, who might easily assume, for example, that there could be no objection to an income trust to last for the lives of four surviving children of a testator.   The experienced lawyer could use several devices to escape the Rule and still give more than two beneficiaries the benefit of an income trust.   One would be to limit the duration of the trust to two specifically designated measuring lives in being, who need not be beneficiaries.   For example, a trust to pay the income to testator's four children could be restricted to the lives of two young and healthy grandchildren.   This, however, would be an unsatisfactory disposition, because both grandchildren might die before the income beneficiaries did.   Another drafting technique would be to set up separate trusts, rather than a single trust, and limit each separate trust to the statutory period.

In order to avoid the lethal aspects of the Rule, the New York courts tended to interpret language in such a way as to avoid its operation—for example, by construing an instrument as creating valid separate trusts rather than a void single trust.   The intricacies of this interpretive process are illustrated by Matter of Horner, 237 N.Y. 489, 143 N.E. 655 (1924).

The destructive effect of the New York Rule on trust duration was substantially mitigated by amendments to the New York statute in 1958 and 1960.   Effective September 1, 1958 the period of the Rule in New York was changed to "lives in being" plus an actual minority;   a further change, effective April 12, 1960 permitted the use of a twenty-one year period in gross and the period of the New York Rule finally coincided with that of the common law.   However, the Rule against Perpetuities in New York still limited trust duration;   a trust could not be created in New York to last longer than lives in being plus 21 years.   This remains true as to all trusts created before September 1, 1973, but may not be true in *all* cases of trusts created after that date because of the amendment to N.Y.—McKinney's EPTL 7–1.5 (see Ch. 7, supra) which permits the settlor of a trust to make the income interest alienable.   The effect of this provision, in the view of one observer, Professor Patrick J. Rohan, is that a trust in which the settlor provides that the income beneficiary has an unconditional right to alienate his interest, will not suspend the power of alienation for perpetuities purposes.   See N.Y.—McKinney's EPTL 9–1.1 Supplementary Practice Commentary by Patrick J. Rohan. Professor Rohan is probably correct as a matter of analysis and a predicter

---

* Not only did New York law limit the duration of trusts to two lives in being; until 1960 it also prohibited the creation of more than two successive *legal* life estates.   N.Y.—McKinney's Real Property Law § 43).   For an illustration of the operation of Real Property Law § 43, see In re Ball's Will, 57 Misc.2d 683, 293 N.Y.S.2d 561 (Sur.Ct.King's Cty.1968).

of court behavior but query, will the result be beneficial. One practical effect of the New York Rule has been to ensure in most cases that interests will vest in *possession* within the period of the Rule—a result which some scholars advocate as a requirement of the common law Rule itself. See, e.g., Schuyler, Should the Rule Against Perpetuities Discard Its Vest?, 56 Mich.L.Rev. 887 (1956); Dukeminier, Perpetuities Law in Action 77 (1962).

Notes

1. Are the interests of B, B's oldest surviving child, and C in the following limitation valid under the common law Rule against Perpetuities? In New York?

A by will transfers property to T, in trust to pay the income to B for B's life, on B's death to pay the income to the oldest child of B living at B's death for his life, remainder to C. A died on January 1, 1970, at which time B and C were both alive.

2. It was held in the famous Thellusson case (Thellusson v. Woodford, 4 Ves. 227, 31 Eng.Rep. 117, 11 Ves. 112, 32 Eng.Rep. 1030 (1805)) that a direction to accumulate income for the permissible period of the Rule against Perpetuities was valid. Although in many jurisdictions, including England, there have been statutory departures from that decision, it is the general rule today. See Simes and Smith, §§ 1461–1468; Powell, ¶¶ 828–838; Restatement, Second, Property (Donative Transfers) § 2.2.

2.   *The Effect of Invalidating Interests Under the Rule*

As indicated earlier, the effect of the Rule on an interest not certain to vest in time is to make the interest void *ab initio*. But what is the effect of the Rule on interests which precede or follow the void interest but are themselves valid under the Rule?

LOVERING v. WORTHINGTON

Supreme Judicial Court of Massachusetts, 1870.
106 Mass. 86.

MORTON, J. This is a bill in equity, brought by the trustees under the will of Joseph Lovering, to obtain the instructions of the court as to their duties under said will.

The thirteenth article of the will devises certain real estate to the trustees upon the following trusts: To pay the net rents and profits to Nancy Gay, a daughter of the testator, during her life, "and on this further trust, upon the decease of said Nancy Gay, to pay the net income of said two stores in State Street, and said house in Tremont Street, to her children, half yearly or oftener, if convenient to said trustees, during the lives of said children. And as the children of said Nancy shall successively decease, said stores in State Street, and said house in Tremont Street, are to be conveyed in fee, or in case the same be sold, the proceeds are to be paid and distributed, to and among the heirs at law of all the children of said Nancy, that is to say, that, as said Nancy's children shall succes-

[margin handwritten notes:] what %? / a/k class can't close until all of N's children die. (> 21 yrs after N)

sively decease, a proportion of said estates or the proceeds are to be conveyed or distributed to and among the respective heirs at law of each child so deceasing, said Nancy's grandchildren to take in right of representation of their deceased parents."

At the date of the will, and at the death of the testator, the said Nancy Gay was a widow having eight children, and she died in 1870 leaving the same eight children.

[margin: I]

The first question presented by the trustees is, whether the limitations of said trust estates are valid beyond the life estate limited to the said Nancy Gay, or are void as tending to create perpetuities.

The will presents a case of a devise to Nancy Gay for her life, with a limitation over of a life estate to her children, and a further limitation over of a fee in the heirs at law of such children. The rule as to perpetuities is fully established, and has been recognized and applied in numerous recent decisions of this court. * * * Applying the rule to this case, we see no ground upon which it can be held that the devise of life estates to the children of Mrs. Gay is invalid. If we assume that this devise includes children born after the death of the testator, and therefore that it is contingent and executory, yet it is not void for remoteness. The devise takes effect, and the life estate in each child necessarily becomes absolute, at the death of Mrs. Gay. If, as is claimed by the defendants, the gift over of the fee to the grandchildren is void, then at the death of Mrs. Gay the remainder in fee would vest either in the residuary devisees or in the heirs at law of the testator. In either event, there were persons in being who by joining with the tenants for life could convey the whole estate. In other words, if this devise is upheld, it does not render the estate incapable of alienation for a longer period than the life of Mrs. Gay, and therefore it is not within the rule against perpetuities.

If the limitation over of the fee to the heirs at law of the children of Mrs. Gay is void, it is clear that the effect of such invalidity is not to defeat the prior life estates. The general rule is, that, if a limitation over is void for remoteness, it places all prior gifts in the same situation as if the devise over had been wholly omitted. If the prior gift was in fee, the estate is vested in the first taker discharged of the limitation over; if for life, it takes effect as a life estate. Brattle Square Church v. Grant, 3 Gray, 142. Lewis on Perpetuities, 657. In 1 Jarman on Wills, 240, the rule is stated to be, that "if a testator devise his lands to his son A. for life, with remainder to the children of A. for life, with remainder to the children of such children in fee, the last limitation would certainly be void; but it is clear that the prior devises to the testator's son and his children would be valid, and the reversion in fee, subject to those devises, and that only, would descend to the testator's heir at law as real estate undisposed of. So, if the personal estate were bequeathed in a similar manner, the gifts to A. and his children successively for life would be good, and the ulterior interest only would devolve to the next of kin." The rule is based upon the paramount consideration in the construction of wills, that the intentions of the testator are to be carried into effect as far as they can be consistently with the rules of law.

[margin handwritten notes:] a/k b/c class can't close until death of kids (> 21 yrs)

We have considered the case as though the devises were directly to Mrs. Gay and her children. The fact that trustees are appointed by the will to hold the legal title does not affect the principle. The estate is not thereby made incapable of alienation. At any time after the death of Mrs. Gay, the persons beneficially interested may, with the consent of the trustees, terminate the trust and convey the estate. *Bowditch v. Andrew,* 90 Mass. (8 Allen) *339. Otis v. McLellan,* 95 Mass. (13 Allen) 339. * * *

We have not deemed it necessary to consider the other questions argued by the counsel. Our decision determines fully all the present duties of the trustees. The other questions may never be litigated, and if litigated may involve the rights of parties not now before the court. We, therefore, refrain from expressing an opinion upon them.

The result is, that the limitation of life estates to the children of Mrs. Gay is valid, and they are entitled to the net income of the trust estate during their lives.

Decree accordingly.

Notes

1. It is not unusual to find a mixture of remoteness of vesting and suspension of the power of alienation language in decisions at the time of this one.

2. On the issue of the validity of beneficial interests in trusts under the Rule against Perpetuities, it is the Massachusetts procedure not to pass on the validity of a gift of principal until the income trusts have expired. Durfee Trust Co. v. Taylor, 325 Mass. 201, 89 N.E.2d 777 (1950); Am.L.Prop., § 24.21; Leach, 65 Harv.L.R. 721, 729 (1952). This practice, which is also followed by the Pennsylvania courts, is criticized in Mechem, Further Thoughts on the Pennsylvania Perpetuities Legislation, 107 U.Pa.L.Rev. 965, 979–80 (1959).

3. Why would the gifts to Nancy's children be independently valid?

4. This court, in holding that, even if the gift to the heirs of Nancy's children were void, the invalidity of that gift would not affect the otherwise valid interests of Nancy's children, follows the usual rule. In other words, life estates, including income trusts, are held separable from following remainders in fee simple, or of the principal, and the former are therefore not invalidated simply because the latter are void. See Gray, § 249.1; Am.L.Prop. § 24.48; Annots. 28 A.L.R. 375 (1924); 75 A.L.R. 124 (1931); 168 A.L.R. 321 (1947).

5. Is there any reason, other than some general conception that a disposition should be salvaged as far as possible, for assuming that a transferor would prefer to have life estates or income trusts stand even if the ultimate gift is void?

6. Occasionally the courts find that the invalidation of an interest will so distort the estate plan as to require the voiding of other interests—even interests independent of the void future interest. In Richards v. Stone, 283 Mich. 485, 278 N.W. 657 (1938) a testator gave one third of his estate to his daughter, outright. The other two thirds were put in trust for his two sons and their issue in a manner which violated the Rule against Perpetuities (at that time the Michigan rule was similar to the pre-1960 New York Rule, see p. 781 supra.) The daughter and two sons were the sole heirs of the testator. The effect of

invalidating only the trusts would be a partial intestacy of two thirds of the estate in which event the daughter would receive five ninths and the sons two ninths each. The court, finding a general intention to treat the children equally, held the outright gift invalid so that all of the estate passed by intestacy, equally to the three children. Compare In re Estate of Davis, 449 Pa. 584, 297 A.2d 451 (1972) where the court refused to invalidate life estates preceding invalid remainders.

7. Subject to what is said in note 6 supra, valid interests which follow void interests are usually unaffected by the invalidity. (See Simes and Smith, § 1264; Powell, ¶ 311). In a common law jurisdiction, interests which follow remote interests are likely to vest too remotely; under the New York Rule, however, valid interests following invalid trusts are more likely to be encountered.

8. Where an interest in property is invalid under the Rule, the Restatement, Second, Property (Donative Transfers) § 1.5 would give the courts considerable freedom to dispose of the property "in the manner which most closely effectuates the transferor's manifested plan of distribution"—including the creation of new interests by implication and the invalidation of otherwise valid interests.

3. The Rule Against Perpetuities and Destructible Interests

RYAN v. WARD

Court of Appeals of Maryland, 1949.
192 Md. 342, 64 A.2d 258, 7 A.L.R.2d 1078.

Suit by the Baltimore National Bank, substituted trustee under deed of trust of John R. Ward, against James J. Ryan, guardian ad litem, etc., Ruth Eleanor Ward, and others, for construction of the deed of trust. From a decree construing the deed of trust, James J. Ryan, guardian ad litem, etc., appeals, and all other parties cross-appeal.

Before MARBURY, C. J., and DELAPLAINE, COLLINS, GRASON, HENDERSON, and MARKELL, JJ.

MARBURY, Chief Judge. On April 16, 1928, John R. Ward of Baltimore City executed and delivered a deed of trust to the Baltimore Trust Company conveying to the latter certain personal property consisting of stocks and bonds. The record does not show the value of this personal property at the date of the deed of trust, but it appears that the corpus of the estate, as of September 26, 1945, was approximately $32,500. John R. Ward died on October 27, 1928, and Frank R. Ward, who was given a life estate by the terms of the deed of trust, died on September 26, 1945, as of which date the estate was valued as above set out. In 1934 the Baltimore Trust Company was removed as trustee by an order of the Circuit Court No. 2 of Baltimore City, and the Baltimore National Bank was appointed substituted trustee. The latter filed its bill of complaint in the Circuit Court of Baltimore City in 1946, asking for a construction of the deed of trust, and naming as parties all the living parties who might possibly have an interest in the matter, as well as the administratrix d. b. n. c. t. a. of the estate of John R. Ward. By the will of John R. Ward, all of his estate and property was left to his son, Frank R. Ward, if the latter survived him, which was the case. Frank R. Ward, who was a resident of New Jersey, left a will by which all of his estate was left to his wife, Olive Maria Ward, provided she survived him, which was the case. He also left three children, Ruth E. Ward, David E. Ward, and John F. Ward. Olive M. Ward is the executrix of the estate of Frank R. Ward and also the administratrix d. b. n. c. t. a. of the estate of John F. Ward. James J. Ryan was appointed by the court as guardian ad litem for all persons not in being whose interests might be affected by the proceedings. Answers were filed by the guardian ad litem, and the parties in being, and testimony was taken, after which the chancellor filed his decree holding some of the future interests good and some void. From this decree the guardian ad litem appeals here, and cross appeals were filed by all other parties.

The deed of trust gives the trustee full and complete power to manage, sell, reinvest, and otherwise deal with the trust estate, and to collect the dividends and profits and to pay over the entire net income in monthly installments to the grantor, John R. Ward, during the term of his natural life. It is further provided that " * * * during the life of the Grantor he shall have the right by one or more instruments in writing, personally signed by him and delivered to the Trustee, to withdraw from the operation of this Deed of Trust such sum or sums as he may in his absolute discretion see fit, such withdrawals, however, shall not be in excess of the sum of Fifteen Hundred Dollars ($1500.00) per annum during his lifetime, and to the extent of any sum or sums so withdrawn, the principal of the trust hereby created shall be reduced accordingly, or expended entirely." It is further provided by the deed of trust:

"From and after the death of the Grantor, the Trustee shall pay over the net income derived therefrom in monthly instalments unto Frank R. Ward, son of the Grantor, during his lifetime, and upon the death of the Grantor's said son, Frank R. Ward, or from and after the Grantor's death in case his said son should predecease him, the Trustee shall pay the net income derived from the trust fund unto the lineal descendants, per stirpes, from time to time living, of the Grantor's said son until the death of the last surviving child of the Grantor's said son, who shall be living at the time of the Grantor's death, and upon the death of the last surviving child of the Grantor's said son, who shall be living at the time of the death of the Grantor, the trust hereby created shall terminate, and the corpus or principal thereof shall be by the Trustee conveyed, delivered and paid over absolutely free, clear and discharged of any further trust, in equal and even shares unto the then living children of the Grantor's said son, and unto the issue then living of each then deceased child of the Grantor's said son, so that each then living child of the Grantor's said son shall take and receive, absolutely, one equal share thereof, and the issue then living of each then deceased child of the Grantor's said son shall take and receive, per stirpes and not per capita, one equal share thereof absolutely."

There is a spendthrift provision for both principal and income, applicable after the death of the grantor, and it is also provided that the Trustee shall have authority to receive any other funds granted, devised, or bequeathed by the grantor or any other person for the uses of the trust created, with a proviso that during the life of the grantor, at his written request, the Trustee is directed to pay over to him the principal of any funds or property, or any part thereof, which may be received by the Trustee as an addition to the original principal of the trust. This right of withdrawal is limited to the additions to the trust fund.

The question before the court is whether any of the estates attempted to be created by this deed of trust are in violation of the rule against perpetuities. This rule requires that an interest or an estate, to be good, must vest not later than twenty-one years, plus the usual period of gestation, after some life in being at the time of its creation. In determining its applicability, the court looks forward from the time of the taking effect of the instrument in question to determine whether a possible interest is certain to vest within the prescribed period. Perkins v. Iglehart, 183 Md. 520, 39 A.2d 672. The rule was established by the courts to preserve the freedom of alienation, and to prevent restrictions on the circulation of property. Safe Deposit & Trust Co. v. Sheehan, 169 Md. 93, 179 A. 536.

Where an interest or an estate is created by will, the question is determined by looking forward from the date of the taking effect of the will which is, of course, the death of the testator, and not the date of the will. Gray's The Rule Against Perpetuities, 3rd Ed., Paragraph 231, p. 205; 4th Ed., Paragraph 231, p. 235. Where the interest or estate is created by deed, its effectiveness vel non is determined as of the time "when the deed became operative." Bowerman v. Taylor, 126 Md. 203 at page 212, 94 A. 652, 654; Goldberg v. Erich, 142 Md. 544, at page 548, 121 A. 365; Hawkins v. Ghent, 154 Md. 261, at page 265, 140 A. 212; Miller on Construction of Wills, Paragraph 323, p. 914.

The appellant Ryan suggests (without any citation of authority) that since there is an element of revocability in the deed, the effective date from which we must consider the succeeding estates is not the date of the execution and delivery of the deed, but the date of the death of the grantor. The element of revocability is the right of withdrawal of the original trust fund, not, however, to be "in excess of the sum of $1500.00 per annum during his lifetime" and the unlimited right of withdrawal of any funds or property, or any part thereof, which may have been added to the trust estate from time to time. The terms of the provision authorizing the withdrawal of the original principal do not clearly indicate whether this right is cumulative or not, that is, whether the right must be exercised each year, if at all, or whether the grantor could withdraw at any time, not only the $1500 allowed during that year, but also $1500 for each previous year in which he had not exercised the right. Since, however, the grantor attempted to put a limitation upon his own actions, and did not reserve to himself the right to withdraw any or all of the original principal at any time he saw fit, while reserving that right as to subsequent additions, we hold that the right should be construed as non-cumulative, and lost as to the amount authorized to be withdrawn in any year, if not exercised during that year. We are not advised what was his age at the time he created it. No matter what it was, we cannot assume, viewing it prospectively, that he would not live long enough to withdraw the entire principal. Until the grantor actually died, therefore, he had the possible right to destroy the trust estate by withdrawals, although this destruction could be only partial until the end of twenty-two years.

Professor Gray, in his work "The Rule Against Perpetuities" (3rd Ed., Paragraph 203, p. 175; 4th Ed., Paragraph 203, p. 193), states that "* * * a future interest, if destructible at the mere pleasure of the present owner of the property, is not regarded as an interest at all and the Rule does not concern itself with it." This statement is applied to revocable trusts in Paragraph 524.1 of the 4th Edition beginning on page 510. This paragraph is the work of Roland Gray, son of the original author, who died in 1915. The 4th Edition was prepared in 1942. In paragraph 524.1 a case is suggested where a conveyance is made to A for life, with a power of revocation, A being the settlor, and, in default of exercise, to A's children at 25. If the period of the rule against perpetuities runs from the date of the conveyance, the ultimate limitation is too remote, but the author states that it seems to be correct to take A's death as the critical date, because A is at liberty to destroy the future interest.* He cites the prevailing doctrine that the remoteness of limitations under a general power to appoint by deed is to be reckoned from the exercise of the power, as a reason why the same construction, by analogy, should be used in a revocable deed. In that connection he approves the reasoning of the Supreme Court of Hawaii in the case of Manufacturers' Life Insurance Company v. von Hamm-Young Company, 34 Hawaii 288. The case, decided in 1937, involves the application of the rule against perpetuities to a life insurance trust agreement. The settlor reserved the right to revoke the trust agreement or to change the beneficiary. If the trust became effective at the time of its execution, there was a possibility that the future interest might not vest within the required period after that date. On the other hand, if the future interest did not come into being until the death of the settlor, no transgression of the rule could occur. The court, on the authority of Gray and of other cases, determined that the effective date from which to view the future interest was the death of the settlor, on the ground that such interest was destructible at his pleasure up until that time.

In the case of Hillyard v. Miller, 10 Pa. 326, 334, the learned Chief Justice Gibson cited Lewis on Perpetuities, Chapter 12, as giving the nearest approach to a perfect definition of a perpetuity. See Graham v. Whitridge, 99 Md. 248, at page 274, 57 A. 609; 58 A. 36, 66 L.R.A. 408. This definition included a provision that the future limitation which would not necessarily vest within the prescribed period should not be destructible by the person for the time being entitled to the property, except with the concurrence of the person interested in the contingent event. The Chief Justice said: "It was the indestructibility * * * of future trusts which forced upon the judges the rule against perpetuities, in order to set the bounds to the remoteness of, not only legal, but equitable limi-

---

* For the application of the Rule against Perpetuities to powers of appointment, see Section Four B of this chapter, infra, p. 841.   Ed.

tations; and it acts upon perpetuities wherever they appear, except in conveyances in mortmain, or to charitable uses." That decision was used as a basis for holding that a deed of trust with a power to sell in the life tenant and use the proceeds was destructible, and therefore not subject to the rule against perpetuities. Mifflin's Appeal, 121 Pa. 205, 15 A. 525, 1 L.R.A. 453, 6 Am.St.Rep. 781. See also Cooper's Estate, 150 Pa. 576, 24 A. 1057, 30 Am.St.Rep. 829. The Supreme Court of the United States, in the case of Goesele v. Bimeler, 14 How. 589, 14 L.Ed. 554, decided that an agreement by members of a religious society called "Separatists," composed of Germans who had emigrated to the United States, by the terms of which the parties renounced all individual ownership of property, present and future, and transferred such property to three directors, was not a perpetuity because the majority of the members might require sale of the property at any time and therefore, even though the articles of association provided for its continuance for an indefinite period of time, nevertheless it was destructible at any time by the will of the majority. In the case of Pulitzer v. Livingston, 89 Me. 359, 36 A. 635, the court held that the rule against perpetuities did not apply to future interests which were destructible at the will and pleasure of the present owner. The deeds in question in that case contained express powers of revocation, and the court held that they were thereby removed from the operation of the rule against perpetuities. In the case of Equitable Trust Co. of New York v. Pratt, 117 Misc. 708, 193 N.Y.S. 152, the Supreme Court of New York had before it a trust agreement which provided that it was revocable at will. The New York statute, which took the place of the common law rule against perpetuities, provided that the absolute ownership of property should not be suspended for a longer period than two lives in being at the date of the instrument. In the case before it, there was a suspension for three lives on the face of the deed of trust, but the court held that as a result of the revocation clause, absolute ownership was not suspended at all during the life of the settlor, and therefore the New York statute did not commence to operate until after his death. In Lewis on Law of Perpetuity, Law Library Ed., Ch. XX, p. 483, it is stated that "the great aim of the laws against remoteness is secured in the immediate and unrestrained alienability of the property by means of a power of appointment." In an article in 45 Harvard Law Review, beginning at p. 896, the effect of the rule against perpetuities on insurance trusts is discussed, and the conclusion is reached that in calculating the period of perpetuity the courts have wisely excluded that period during which the property was subject to the absolute control of a single person. In another article in 51 Harvard Law Review by W. Barton Leach, entitled "Perpetuities in a Nutshell," at p. 638, it is stated: "So long as one person has the power at any time to make himself the sole owner (of the trust estate) there is no tying-up of the property and no violation of the policy of the rule against perpetuities." In 86 Univ. of Pa. Law Review 221, the decision of the Hawaii court above quoted is discussed and is stated to be the first decision on the question. The writer says that "unhampered by precedent, the Hawaiian court has enunciated a salutory [sic] rule which should be followed in this country."

A contrary view is taken by a member of the Ohio Bar in an article on "The Rule Against Perpetuities as Applied to Living Trusts and Living Life Insurance Trusts" found in 11 University of Cincinnati Law Review beginning at p. 327.

Restatement, Property, Section 373, states "The period of time during which an interest is destructible, pursuant to the uncontrolled volition, and for the exclusive personal benefit of the person having such a power of destruction is not included in determining whether the limitation is invalid under the rule against perpetuities." Comment d states that the required destructibility exists only when some person possesses a complete power of disposition over the subject matter of the future interests, and can exercise this power of disposition for his own exclusive benefit. The destructibility prerequisite for an application of the rule stated in Section 373 can exist when the power of disposition (or revocation) is not presently exercisable at the time of its creation, provided that the period, during which the exercise of such power is postponed, does not invalidate all interests created by the exercise of such power, and thus, in effect, invalidate the power itself.

These cases and statements from recognized authorities amply sustain the proposition that, where a settlor has power during his lifetime to revoke or destroy the trust estate, the question whether interests, or any of them, created by a deed of trust are void because in violation of the rule against perpetuities, is to be determined as of the date of the settlor's death, and not as of the date when the deed of trust takes effect. It will be observed, however, that the cases cited involve situations where the trust is revocable at will, or could be destroyed by a single act of the settlor such as a change of beneficiary in an insurance policy, or a sale of the trust property and the use of the proceeds. It is stated in the article in 51 Harvard Law Review, already referred to, at p. 663:

> "The situation is analogous to future interests after an estate tail, where the period of perpetuities is computed from the date of expiration of the estate tail; the power to disentail makes the tenant in tail the substantial owner and causes interests after the estate tail to be in substance gifts by the last tenant in tail at the time of expiration of his estate. The situation is also analogous to gifts in default of the exercise of a general power by deed or will, the period of perpetuities being computed from the expiration of the power—i.e., the death of the donee."

There is no case, so far as we have been able to find, which deals with a strictly limited power of withdrawal which can be exercised only over a period of years, and which cannot be used to destroy the entire estate until a number of years has elapsed. In the case before us, as we have shown, the estate could not be entirely destroyed during the first twenty-two years of its existence. There is some difference of opinion among the text writers whether the power to encroach upon the corpus is the same as the power to revoke. Professor Scott thinks it is. Trusts, Paragraph 330.11. Bogert thinks not. Vol. 4, Bogert on Trust and Trustees, Part 2, § 994. The cases we have cited indicate that it is not the method of destruction but the destructibility which is the controlling factor. That being so, we are unable to say that in a case such as the one before us, the trust estate is destructible, as that word is used in connection with the Rule against Perpetuities. There is a possibility of ultimate destruction, but the estate is not destructible at the time of its creation, or at any one time thereafter. Any destruction must be by a gradual diminishing of the corpus, until, at the last, there is left only a balance equal to the amount which can be withdrawn in any year. At that time, the grantor can destroy the trust, but his right to do so is contingent upon the previous withdrawals, and does not become absolute until he has completed all such withdrawals, over a period of years. What would be the situation if the settlor were given power to revoke after twenty-two years, or power to withdraw the entire trust estate at that time, need not be decided, because we have no such situation here. It is our conclusion, therefore, that the rule against perpetuities operates upon the estates created, as of the date of the execution and delivery of the deed of trust.

There is, of course, no question that the beneficial life estate of Frank R. Ward, son of the grantor, was valid. Thereafter, the net income is to be paid *unto the lineal descendants per stirpes from time to time living* of Frank R. Ward until the death of the last surviving child of said Frank R. Ward who shall be living at the time of the death of the grantor. At that time, the trust is to terminate, and the residuary estates are to commence. It is apparent that Frank R. Ward could have had a son born prior to the death of John R. Ward, who could have been living at the death of John R. Ward, and who could have lived more than twenty-one years after the death of Frank R. Ward. The death of such child, if he were the last survivor of the children of Frank R. Ward, would fix the date of the ending of the trust estate and the commencement of the estates in remainder created by the deed of trust. It was quite within the bounds of possibility, at the time of the creation of the trust, that this date might be beyond a life and lives then in being and twenty-one years thereafter, plus the usual period of gestation. Consequently, it is agreed by everyone, and the court so held, that the remainders, after the termination of the trust estate, were void.

The gift of the beneficial estates pur autre vie, after the death of Frank R. Ward which gift, as we have shown, is to the lineal descendants per stirpes, *from time to time living*, of the grantor's son, might vest in one of those lineal descendants who was born more than twenty-one years after the death of Frank R. Ward, but before the death of his last surviving child. This is a class gift. In such a case, it is well recognized that if it "is good as to some members of the class, but is within the rule against perpetuities as to other members, the entire gift must fail. The general rule is that if a gift is void as to any of a class, it is void as to all of the class." Miller, Construction of Wills, Paragraph 328. The reason for this rule is that the courts cannot split into portions the gift to the class, and make these gifts what they were never intended to be by the grantor. Goldsborough v. Martin, 41 Md. 488, at page 502; Albert v. Albert, 68 Md. 352, 12 A. 11; Bowerman v. Taylor, 126 Md. 203, 94 A. 652.

*   *   *

*   *   *   [W]e hold that the gifts pur autrie [sic] vie are void and the trust estate has now ended. As John R. Ward, by his will, left all his property to Frank R. Ward, who was his only child, the trust property belongs to the latter's estate. As we said in Perkins v. Iglehart, supra, there is no necessity for the property to be administered through the estate of John R. Ward, thereby multiplying the costs and expenses. Distribution can be made directly by the trustee to Olive M. Ward, Executrix of the estate of Frank R. Ward, and such distribution will relieve the trustee of further responsibilities. Decree reversed and case remanded for the passage of a decree in accordance with this opinion. Costs to be paid out of the trust estate.

Notes

1. If the court had held that the effective date of the trust was the date of death of the settlor, John R. Ward (Oct. 27, 1928), rather than that of the delivery of the trust deed (Apr. 16, 1928), would that holding have validated

(a) The income trust for the lineal descendants of Frank R. Ward?

(b) The gift of the principal to the issue of Frank R. Ward?

2. Assuming that the effective date of the trust was that of the delivery of the trust deed,

(a) Why was it "agreed by everyone" (page 792, supra) that the gift of the principal was void?

(b) Under the terms of the income trust for Frank's lineal descendants, what event or events would have to occur during the period specified for the income trust in order to give any such lineal descendant a "vested" right to the income?

3. Suppose that A, by an inter vivos trust, reserves to himself a life estate, and gives the remainder to his children at age 25. Is the remainder valid? Suppose that, in addition, he reserves to himself power to revoke the trust. Is the result the same? On the effect of a power of revocation on the Rule against Perpetuities, see 3 Simes & Smith, § 1252 (2d ed. 1956); 5 Powell ¶ 767A(5); Prop.Rest. § 373, comment c (1944); Equitable Trust Co. v. Pratt, 117 Misc. 708, 193 N.Y.S. 152 (1922), affirmed 206 App.Div. 689, 199 N.Y.S. 921 (1923); Cook v. Horn, 214 Ga. 289, 104 S.E.2d 461 (1958); Fitzpatrick v. Mercantile-Safe Deposit & Trust Co., 220 Md. 534, 155 A.2d 702 (1959), discussed in 21 U.Pitt.L.Rev. 748 (1960).

4. The opinion's discussion of the effect of the settlor's reservation of a power of revocation on the application of the Rule against Perpetuities to living trusts is so clear and complete in terms of both theory and authorities that it seems self-explanatory. Cases are collected in Annot. 7 A.L.R.2d 1089 (1949).

5. Assuming that the trust contained no power of revocation as such, what would be the effect of the settlor's reserving the power to withdraw any or all of the principal at any time? See Am.L.Prop., § 24.59.

The discussions by Scott and Bogert, referred to in the opinion, are in general terms, and not with reference to the Rule against Perpetuities.

6. The Pennsylvania Estates Act of 1947 (Purdon, Tit. 20, § 6104(c)) provides that the period of the Rule "shall be measured from the expiration of any

time during which one person while living has the unrestricted power to transfer to himself the entire legal and beneficial interest in the property." The Commission's Comment includes the following among the cases intended to be covered by this section: "For revocable trusts the period would begin as of the settlor's death."

E. THE APPLICATION OF THE RULE TO CHARITABLE GIFTS, OPTIONS AND CONTRACTS

1. *Charitable Gifts*

INSTITUTION FOR SAVINGS IN ROXBURY AND ITS VICINITY v. ROXBURY HOME FOR AGED WOMEN

Supreme Judicial Court of Massachusetts, 1923.
244 Mass. 583, 139 N.E. 301.

CARROLL, J. This is a petition to register title to land. Aaron D. Williams, who died December 8, 1863, was the owner of the property. On May 12, 1863, he wrote to Col. A. D. Hodges, president of the Institution for Savings in Roxbury and Its Vicinity (the petitioner), as follows:

"Dear Sir: The undersigned would be obliged if you would offer to the trustees of the above-named institution the free use of the banking rooms in the new building now being finished on Washington St. opposite the City Hotel in Roxbury, and also offer them a deed in trust of the whole property for their use as long as the present institution shall continue to exist on the following conditions, viz.: That the income of the building (except that part used by the Savings Institution) shall be applied to the payment of a debt of about eight thousand dollars contracted upon said building. (2) That when the institution shall cease to exist the trustees shall convey the whole estate to the then authorized managers of the Old Ladies' Home in Roxbury for the sole benefit of that worthy institution, or if said Old Ladies' Home shall not be in existence at the time then to be conveyed to the mayor and aldermen for the support of the aged poor within the limits of the territory now comprising the city of Roxbury. Should the trustees accept of the above proposition upon the conditions named, such papers shall be executed as are necessary to carry out the design. The rent of the said building exclusive of that part offered to the Savings Institution is estimated at about fifteen hundred dollars per year. The cost of the building, including the land, is about $22,000.

"Yours very respectfully,

"Aaron D. Williams."

In March, 1864, the Institution for Savings in Roxbury and Its Vicinity brought a petition in the probate court, setting out the above offer, that it had been accepted by the institution, and praying for its specific performance. A decree was entered in that court directing the administrator of Aaron D. Williams to convey the premises to the institution "comformably with the full intent and meaning of the agreement," and in 1867 the administrator conveyed to the institution all the title and interest of Williams in the land. The habendum in the deed was:

To the said institution, "its successors and assigns, forever, for the uses and upon the trusts, however expressed in a certain proposition signed by Aaron D. Williams, deceased, dated May 12, 1863, addressed to Col. A. D. Hodges, president of the Institution for Savings in Roxbury and Vicinity, a copy of which is hereto annexed."

The petitioner contends that the gift over to the Old Ladies' Home in Roxbury is void for remoteness and that the institution has an estate in fee simple which may be registered. The Old Ladies' Home is a corporation: its name was changed by the statute of 1874, chapter 199, and its identity with the "Roxbury Home for Aged Women and Others" is admitted. It contends that the gift to the petitioner is a gift upon a charitable trust and the gift over is not void for remoteness within the meaning of the rule against perpetuities; that even if the gift to the petitioner is not a charity within the meaning of the said rule, the gift over to the respondent is valid; and that the petitioner took only a qualified or determinable equitable fee.

The land court decided that the petitioner took a determinable or qualified fee, that the gift to the petitioner was not a gift to a public charity, and that the gift over was void for remoteness. That court also decided that as the petitioner's estate was not in fee simple as required by G.L. c. 185, § 26, its title could not be registered.

Such an estate in land as a qualified or determinable fee is recognized in this commonwealth. The question whether this form of estate was done away with by the statute quia emptores was considered in First Universalist Society v. Boland, 155 Mass. 171, 29 N.E. 524, 15 L.R.A. 231; and it was decided that a qualified or determinable fee may exist in this commonwealth.

The proposal to the petitioner by Mr. Williams was to convey the land—

"for their use as long as the present institution shall continue to exist on the following conditions: * * * (2) That when the institution shall cease to exist the trustees shall convey the whole estate to the then authorized managers of the Old Ladies' Home in Roxbury."

The conveyance by the order of the probate court was to conform with the meaning and intent of the donor and was for the uses and upon the trust expressed in his letter to the Institution for Savings. The institution was to continue to hold the estate "as long as the present institution shall continue to exist." These words create a qualified or determinable fee. They indicate that the grantee was to own the estate as long as it continued to exist and that its ownership was to cease on the happening of that event. The petitioner owned a fee, as the land court decided, because it might last forever; but as the estate would end when the circumstances mentioned occurred, the fee was not absolute but was qualified or determinable.

In First Universalist Society v. Boland, supra, the plaintiff was to hold the estate—

" 'so long as said real estate shall by said society or its assigns be devoted to the uses' * * * as specified. 'And when * * * diverted from the uses   *   *   *   then the title of said society   *   *   *   shall forever cease, and be forever vested in the following named persons.' "

And it was held that these words did not create an absolute fee, nor an estate on condition, but an estate to continue till the happening of a certain event and then to cease; that the grant was not upon a condition subsequent and a re-entry would be unnecessary; that the estate was terminated by its own limitations when it was no longer devoted to the specified uses. That case is decisive of the case at bar. The land court was right in deciding that the petitioner had a qualified or determinable fee. See Easterbrook v. Tillinghast, 5 Gray, 17.

The gift over in First Universalist Society v. Boland, supra, was decided to be void under the rule against perpetuities. The respondent, the Roxbury Home for Aged Women, is a public charity, and the gift over to the mayor and aldermen for the aged poor is a gift for a charitable use. Norris v. Loomis, 215 Mass. 344, 102 N.E. 410; Bowden v. Brown, 200 Mass. 269, 86 N.E. 351, 128 Am.St.Rep. 419.

If the gift in the first instance is not for the benefit of a charity and then over, upon a contingency which may never happen within the prescribed limit, to a charity, the gift to the charity is void. Odell v. Odell, 10 Allen, 1, 7. If the gift over is supported by a gift to a public charity, it is not invalid, even though the gift over will not vest until a period beyond that stated in the rule against perpetuities. Odell v. Odell, supra. Although savings banks under our laws are incorporated to encourage habits of thrift by the allowance of interest on small accounts and their funds and deposits are held for the exclusive benefit of depositors, and they do in fact approximate somewhat to the character of charitable institutions (Lewis v. Lynn Institution for Savings, 148 Mass. 235, 19 N.E. 365, 1 L.R.A. 785, 12 Am.St.Rep. 535; Gilson v. Cambridge Savings Bank, 180 Mass. 444, 446, 62 N.E. 728; Greenfield Savings Bank v. Abercrombie, 211 Mass. 252, 97 N.E. 897, 39 L.R.A. [N.S.] 173) they are not charities in the true sense of the term. They are private corporations. See Opinion of the Justices, 9 Cush. 604. Their purpose is not within the meaning of the statute of Elizabeth (St. 43 Eliz. c. 4), or its object as applied in this commonwealth. See Reed v. Home Savings Bank, 130 Mass. 443, 39 Am.Rep. 468; Commonwealth v. Reading Savings Bank, 133 Mass. 16, 19, 43 Am.Rep. 495.

As the gift to the Institution for Savings in Roxbury and Its Vicinity was not a charitable gift, the gift over to the respondent must fail, because it is void for remoteness. Odell v. Odell, supra; Gray, The Rule against Perpetuities (3d Ed.) §§ 592, 594.

The gift over is void, but it does not follow from this that the estate in the original grantee, the Institution for Savings in Roxbury and Its Vicinity, is unaffected by the limitation over. There is a possibility of reverter to the original donor or his heirs. First Universalist Society v. Boland, supra. On this ground the case at bar is to be distinguished from Proprietors of the Church in Brattle Square v. Grant, 3 Gray, 142, 63 Am.Dec. 725, and analogous cases, where the entire estate of the owner passed by the grant, and the conditional limitation imposed being void for remoteness the original estate in the grantor was unaffected by the limitation over and was in the same situation as if the devise over had been wholly omitted.

The decision of the land court was right. The petitioner took a qualified or determinable fee. The gift over on the termination of the precedent estate is void because it violates the rule against perpetuities, and as the petitioners did not have the entire title under G.L. c. 185, § 26, the title could not be registered.

Exceptions overruled. *(aff'd)*

Notes

1. Vague statements are sometimes encountered to the effect that the Rule against Perpetuities does not apply to gifts to charity. Such a statement may refer to the settled rule that (in contrast to so-called "honorary trusts" for dogs et al.) there is no limit on the duration of charitable trusts, which may, and usually do, last perpetually. As shown by the principal case, however, any such statement would be an erroneous over-generalization about the scope of the Rule against Perpetuities itself.

2. The following propositions seem well established:

(a) A future interest for a charitable purpose is exempt from the Rule against Perpetuities if preceded by a present interest for a charitable purpose.

See, e.g., Storrs Agricultural School v. Whitney, 54 Conn. 342, 8 A. 141 (1887), in which the court said (54 Conn. at 345, 8 A. at 143):

> The gift of property first to one charitable use and then to another upon the determination of the first trustee no longer to use, as was done in this case, does not offend the statute of perpetuities. The law favors charitable uses. It does so with knowledge that in most cases they are intended to be practically perpetual; and it is willing to permit what of evil results from the devotion to such length of use in consideration of the beneficent results flowing therefrom. As one charitable use may be perpetual, the gift to two in succession can be of no longer duration nor of greater evil. The property is taken out of commerce, but it instantly goes into perpetual servitude to charity.

(b) A future interest for a charitable purpose is subject to the Rule against Perpetuities if preceded by a present interest for a noncharitable purpose. See, e.g., the principal case, and In re Estate of Pearson, infra p. 830.

(c) A future interest for a noncharitable purpose is subject to the Rule against Perpetuities even if preceded by a present interest for a charitable purpose. See, e.g., Proprietors of Church in Brattle Square v. Grant, 69 Mass. (3 Gray) 142 (1855).

See Gray, §§ 589–603.8; Prop.Rest., §§ 396–8; Simes (hb) 296–97; Simes and Smith, §§ 1278–87; Simes, Public Policy and the Dead Hand, 110–140 (1955); Morris and Leach, The Rule against Perpetuities, 179–188 (1956); Annot. 30 A.L.R. 594 (1924).

3. What justifications of policy are there for the following results that would be reached under the above rules? In the cases where the transfer is valid, are there any elements in the situation that would reduce the force of the usual objections to dead hand control and unmarketability of title?

(a) Transfer of securities to the X Trust Company to expend the income perpetually for the benefit of B Church.   Valid.

(b) Transfer of securities to the X Trust Company to expend the income for the benefit of B Church, but if at any time the income should not be used for that purpose then to expend the income for the benefit of C Church.   Valid.

(c) Transfer of securities to the X Trust Company to expend the income for the benefit of B Church, but, if at any time the income should not be used for that purpose, then to the Y Trust Company to expend the income for the benefit of C Church.   Valid.

(d) Transfer of land to the B Church, but if said Church should cease to exist then to the C Church.   Valid.

(e) Transfer of land to B and his heirs, but if at any time B and all of B's issue should die then to the C Church.   Gift to C Church void.

(f) Transfer of land to the B Church, but if said Church should cease to exist then to C and his heirs.   Gift to C void.

4. What would be the effect of a transfer from A of $100,000 to Yale University on the condition, however, that, if Yale shall ever fail to pay annually the sum of $2,000 to such person as shall on December 31 of each year be A's then oldest living lineal descendant, then to Columbia University?

In re Tyler, [1891] 3 Ch. 252 involved a bequest of £42,000 to the London Missionary Society with the condition that if the Society should fail to keep the testator's family vault at Highgate Cemetery in good repair the money was to go to the Blue Coat School (Christ's Hospital).   The court, conceding that a gift "in trust" to keep a tomb in repair perpetually would be void, held the gift to the Blue Coat School valid, despite the contention of the Missionary Society that it should be held void as tending to divert some of the donated funds to non-charitable purposes.   The lower court opinion said that enough money to keep the vault in repair might be obtained "without in the least trenching on any funds devoted to charitable purposes" through the contributions of other supporters of the Society who would not wish to see it lose this large fund. Compare In re Chardon, [1928] 1 Ch. 464.

In re Lopes, [1931] 2 Ch. 130 held entirely valid a gift of the residuary estate (following an income trust for the testator's wife for life) to the Zoological Society of London with the condition that, if the Society should fail to keep certain graves in repair or to hang a portrait of the testator's mother bequeathed to the Society in the will in the Society's board room, the property should go to St. Bartholomew's Hospital.   The gift to the Hospital was held valid without discussion, the opinion being devoted to the proposition that the first use was charitable, for the reason, inter alia (at 136): "A ride on an elephant may be educational.   At any rate it brings the reality of the elephant and its uses to the child's mind, in lieu of leaving him to mere book learning.   It widens his mind, and in that broad sense is educational."

Should the type of contingency on which a donor may shift property from one charity to another charity be restricted, and, if so, how?   See Morris and Leach, The Rule against Perpetuities, 187 (1956);   Gray, § 603.8, note 1. Prop.Rest., § 397, Comment d. would validate such a gift "even when the retention of ownership by the first charity necessarily involves, in effect, a diversion of part of the subject matter of the gift to a non-charitable objective."

5. Another problem concerns the effect of an attempt to give property to charity at some future time not restricted to the period of the Rule, without any preceding gift of the property or its income.

In First Camden National Bank & Trust Co. v. Collins, 114 N.J.Eq. 59, 168 A. 275 (1933), reversing 110 N.J.Eq. 623, 160 A. 848 (1932), the court held void a disposition of the residuary estate (worth about $622,000) which (114 N.J.Eq. at 60) "cut off testator's widow and children with a pittance". The residue was given to the trustee of an inter vivos trust set up by the settlor with an initial $20,000, which had increased by his death to about $80,000; the terms of this trust were incorporated by reference into the will. Under them, the trustee was to reinvest and accumulate the income from the fund until the expiration of 21 years after the death of the survivor of six specifically named very young children, and then:

"Upon the termination of the trust as herein provided the trustees shall turn over the fund to a corporation to be organized under the laws of the State of New Jersey under such acts of the legislature as may be sufficient for the accomplishment of the purposes herein provided, the name of the corporation to be the 'John J. Albertson [the testator's name] Foundation'." "After the expiration of twenty-one years from the death of the survivor of the said persons, said trustee shall proceed to form the corporation * * * and shall then pay over the principal and accumulations of said trust fund to said corporation." The trust provided that the corporation should then purchase land, erect buildings, and establish and maintain "a school or schools for boys, girls, young men and young women, to be devoted to the upbuilding of the physical, moral, intellectual and religious growth of the youth of succeeding generations * * *." The trust concluded with the request that, if further accumulation were legally possible, the corporation should add income to principal until the fund reached $327,000,000.

The court said, in part (114 N.J.Eq. 61–63, 168 A. at 276):

We incline to agree that the intended ultimate disposition of the fund is a charitable one, and that the charity indicated is sufficiently definite to support the gift, and not so broad as to invalidate it. But we are unable to take the view that the title to the fund vests within the period limited by the rule against perpetuities. * * *

* * *

Whatever public policy there is in this case operates, as we think, against the validation of the trust under consideration. We construe it as requiring the fund to be held until after the lawful period has elapsed, and until some specially constituted corporation can and shall be organized to receive it * * *. The hiatus we deem fatal to the trust.

What might be the explanations of such a result in terms of (1) doctrine? (2) policy?

However, in the absence of factors that might arouse antagonism, and particularly if the commencement of the charitable use would, if the gift were sustained, almost certainly occur promptly, although not specifically required to do so within the period of the Rule, the general trend of the American decisions has been to validate the gift and thus carry out the very prevalent policy of favoring the dedication of private funds to charitable purposes. Some of the opinions are extremely vague in rationale, but give the impression that a desirable result has been accomplished, even though its justification in terms of either doctrine or semantics is far from clear. See, e.g., Kingdom v. Record, 58 Ohio O. 407, 72 O.L.A. 249, 133 N.E.2d 921 (1954); Gould v. Taylor Orphan Asylum, 46 Wis. 106, 50 N.W. 422 (1879). See also Simes and Smith, §§ 1284–5.

The careful draftsman will, of course, keep such problems from arising by requiring the use to commence within the period of the Rule: e.g., "such incorporation to be procured not later than 21 years after the death of the survivor of X, Y and Z".

Note on the Fee Tail and Fees Simple Defeasible

As pointed out at the beginning of Section 2 of this Chapter, defeasible fees, although important to the development of the Rule, are rarely encountered in family dispositions today.   Gifts to charity, like that involved in the *Roxbury* case, supra, may represent a type of gift in which defeasible fees are more frequently encountered.   In any event, this seems to us an appropriate occasion for a brief treatment of defeasible fees and an even briefer treatment of the fee tail.

Defeasible fees, as the fee tail before them, are, of course, devices for maintaining "dead-hand control," of the sort which the Rule against Perpetuities aims to limit.   For a variety of reasons the Rule has been largely ineffective in controlling these devices. The heyday of the fee tail was over long before the Rule was invented. The typical fee tail limitation, "A to B and the heirs of his body," (refinements such as "male heirs" or "female heirs" were common) created, in effect, a series of life estates in B and successive generations of his lineal descendants.   Upon failure of B's blood line the property would revert to A and his heirs or, if a remainder had been created, would pass to the remainderman.   As early as 1472, in Taltarum's case (Y.B. 12 Ed. IV 19 (1472)), it was held that the "tenant in tail" (i.e., the current holder of the "life estate") could, through an ingenious device called a "common recovery," transmute the fee tail into a fee simple absolute.   As a clog on alienability the fee tail was no longer important after that date.

Defeasible fees simple continue to be troublesome, although as noted earlier they are not often encountered in family transactions.   They are somewhat difficult to treat in summary fashion, partly because of inconsistent terminology, and partly because the classifications devised by scholars seem to have had relatively little influence on the courts.   The essence of the defeasible fee simple is that the owner of the fee has an estate potentially infinite but subject to termination or divestment on the happening of a contingency.   The *Roxbury* case is typical: the bank's interest is to last "as long as the present institution shall continue to exist."   Other typical examples of conditions attached to the fee are "continued use for church purposes"; "so long as alcoholic beverages are not used on the premises"; and "maintenance of a railroad line."   The present interest (the defeasible fee) may be followed by an executory interest in a third person, or by an interest in the grantor, either a "possibility of reverter" which is said to become effective automatically on the happening of the contingency, or a "power of termination" (also called a "right of entry") which is said to become effective only on the exercise of the power by its owner.

Since the typical contingency is one not related to the life of a particular person or group, an executory interest to take effect upon its occurrence is almost always void under the Rule. However, the interests reserved in the grantor are not ordinarily subject to the Rule and can be significant clogs on marketability. In a number of jurisdictions statutes have been enacted to subject these interests to the Rule or otherwise limit their duration.

Although many important "perpetuities" cases have involved defeasible fees the real point of interest in these cases is not the operation of the Rule (which is usually not disputed) but the nature of the present interest. For example, in the cases of First Universalist Church v. Boland, 155 Mass. 171, 29 N.E. 524 (1892) and Proprietors of the Church in Brattle Square v. Grant, 69 Mass. (3 Gray) 142 (1855) which are discussed in the *Roxbury* case, supra, the executory interests involved were clearly invalid under the Rule, and the interests in the grantor (if any) were equally clearly not affected by the Rule. The question was whether there was any reversionary interest and the answer to this question turned on the nature of the defeasible fee. If (as the court in the *First Universalist Church* case held) the present interest was a fee simple determinable (a/k/a "base" fee, "qualified fee," or "fee simple on a special limitation"), it ended automatically upon the happening of the contingency, and even though no interest was explicitly reserved in the grantor, a possibility of reverter would be implied. If, on the other hand, the fee interest was classified (as it was in the *Brattle Square Church* case) as an "estate on condition," which in modern terminology would be called a "fee simple on a condition subsequent" by some or a "fee simple subject to an executory limitation" by the Restatement * (Prop.Rest., § 46) then the voiding of the executory interest would promote the fee to a fee simple absolute. On these and related matters see Powell, ¶¶ 186–190, 271, 272; Prop. Rest., Ch. 4; Am.L.Prop. §§ 2.6–2.10 and Part 4; Simes and Smith, §§ 241–294. For an interesting discussion of the differences between the fee simple determinable and the fee simple subject to a condition subsequent, with particular reference to the supposed automaticity of termination of the former on breach of condition, see Dunham, Possibility of Reverter and Powers of Termination—Fraternal or Identical Twins?, 20 U.Chi.L.Rev. 215 (1952). For a breakdown of state statutes imposing restrictions on defeasible estates, see Berger, Land Ownership and Use (3d ed. 1983) 177–183.

2. *Options and Contracts*

The cases thus far considered posed perpetuities questions raised by testamentary or lifetime gratuitous transfers. The Rule against Per-

---

* The Restatement restricts the term "fee simple on condition subsequent" to a transfer in which the grantor reserves a power of termination—a position which is justified on the ground that a power of termination cannot be created in a third person. Prop.Rest. §§ 45, 24, comment d.

petuities has also been applied in cases of commercial transactions such as options to purchase and options to renew a lease. The Rule is also potentially applicable, although no cases have been found in which it has been applied, to stock options and conversion privileges in bonds. The question whether such commercial transactions should be subject to time limits and, if so, what limits are appropriate is beyond the scope of these materials. One thing does seem clear however, and that is that the Rule against Perpetuities is an inapt tool for controlling the duration of such commercial interests. Donative transfers are by and large generational in nature and a rule phrased in generational terms makes sense in the case of such transactions. Commercial transactions on the other hand are not generational in nature and there seems no good reason why a time limit, if one is desired, should be measured by lives in being.

Conversely, contracts are said not to be subject to the rule against perpetuities since they are not "property interests". Thus it has been held that interests created under a settlement option of a life insurance policy for the benefit of the insured's widow and descendants were not subject to the Rule. Holmes v. John Hancock Mutual Life Insurance Co., 288 N.Y. 106, 41 N.E.2d 909 (1942). On a functional level it is hard to distinguish such an arrangement from a trust for members of the family and, thus, hard to justify exempting one from, and subjecting another to, the Rule against Perpetuities.

F. CLASS GIFTS

1. Creation and Construction of Class Gifts

In modern future interests cases, gifts to classes are frequently encountered: for example, the typical gift of principal following an income trust is to a class rather than to named individuals. Gifts to classes present special problems under the Rule against Perpetuities. Before turning to those problems, however, we must have some preliminary understanding of class gifts.

Defined and illustrated. A gift to a class is a gift of an aggregate amount of property to a number of persons collectively described, the share of each member of the class depending on the total number of members of the class as finally ascertained; i.e., if there are ultimately five members entitled to share, each will take one-fifth, if six, each will take one-sixth, etc. It differs from a gift of individual interests to several persons, where the share of each is considered as fixed by the terms of the instrument. Suppose that a testator bequeaths $150,000 "to my brothers, B, C, and D", and gives his residuary estate to X; and that B predeceases the testator so that B's interest in the gift fails by lapse. This legacy, if construed as a gift of individual interests, would be a gift of a one-third interest in the fund ($50,000) to each beneficiary; and, under such a construction, C and D could not profit from the lapse of B's interest, but would merely take $50,000 apiece, B's share going to the residuary legatee X as a lapsed legacy. If the legacy were construed as a gift to a class, however, the share of each member of the class would be determined (in this case) at the testator's death, and C and D, the qualifying members of the class, would share the fund, each taking $75,000. (The effect in this situation of statutes preventing lapse is controversial. See Death of a legatee—Lapsed and void bequests, supra p. 360).

Dispositions describing a group of persons generally and collectively will usually be construed as a gift to a class. Typical examples would be gifts to "my issue", "B's children", "C's heirs", "D's brothers and sisters". If, however, the beneficiaries are designated solely by their particular names, as "to B, C, and D", the gift will be held one of individual interests rather than a gift to a class. On the borderline are dispositions like that mentioned above, where both a collective and an individual description are used ("to my brothers, B, C, and D"); in such situations, the cases are hard to reconcile.

It is useful to approach the subject of class gifts by asking a series of questions. The first question is whether a gift to a class was intended. *← ① Class gift intended?* As indicated above this question is seldom difficult to answer. The second question is, assuming that a class gift was intended, what is the primary meaning of the class term used. For example, suppose a gift to *② who's incl'd?* "the children of J." Would the class of J's children include an adopted child, an illegitimate child, or someone raised as his child by J but unrelated and never adopted? The answer will depend on the intention of the transferor and will be determined in the same manner as other problems of construction.*

In this connection (and for other aspects of this note) it is necessary to distinguish classes of "children," "issue," and the like from classes of "heirs," "next of kin," "distributees," or similarly described groups. In the case of gifts to "heirs," etc., the makeup of the class is, generally speaking, determined by reference to the applicable statute of intestate succession as it reads at the time of death of the person whose heirs make up the class; and the share of each taker is controlled by the statutory scheme, rather than by the rule of equality that applies to classes of relatives such as "children" or "brothers." ** See generally Casner, Construction of Gifts to Heirs and the Like, 53 Harv.L.Rev. 207 (1939).

The "closing" of the class. Assuming that a class gift was intended, and that the primary meaning of the class term has been identified, the *③ When does it close?* next question to be asked is how soon does a person have to be born in order to have a chance to share in the distribution. If A by will makes a gift to "my grandchildren," does he mean only those grandchildren alive when he made his will, only those grandchildren born before his death, or all grandchildren whenever born? This question is phrased variously. The Restatement of Property (Ch. 22, Topic 3) speaks of "the duration of

---

* An example of the kind of problem which can arise was involved in In re Estate of Conway, 74 Misc.2d 909, 346 N.Y.S.2d 682 (Sur.Ct.N.Y.Cty.1973) where a class gift was made to "the children then living," (i.e., living at the death of the testator) of X, Y and Z. The testator died on April 21, 1966; on January 1, 1967 X adopted a child who had been born on April 12, 1966 (before the testator's death). The court held that the child was not a member of the class.

** The members of classes of "issue" and "descendants" may also take unequally. See Simes and Smith, §§ 743–746; Prop.Rest. § 303.

the period within which a class may increase in membership." Others, and we shall join them, speak of the time when a class closes. Both mean the same thing. The statement that a class closes at a certain time means that nobody born after that time can share, except that here, as elsewhere, a child who is later born alive is considered as in being from the date of conception. It is important to realize that nothing else than this is meant by the statement that a class is closed. It does not mean that a person has to be alive when the class closes in order to take, since the estate of a person then dead may be entitled to a share; nor does it insure that those living at the time will take, since their interest may still be subject to some condition that has not been fulfilled.

The time for closing a class will be determined in one of three ways. It may be (and ought to be) fixed by the instrument creating a gift. For example, A may by will make a gift "to my grandchildren living at my death." Unfortunately, grantors or testators (and their lawyers) do not have a good track record on this score. A second way in which the time for closing may be fixed is physiologically. In the case of a gift to the children of B, the class is certain to close on the death of B, or (if B is a man) within a period of gestation thereafter. The third way used to determine the time of closing is by reference to a "rule of construction" which operates to close the class before it would close physiologically. This "rule" is sometimes justified as carrying out the presumed intent of a grantor, and sometimes as a "rule of convenience" to expedite the distribution and enjoyment of property at an earlier time than would otherwise be the case. One can also have the best of both worlds by assuming that the grantor would desire such early distribution and enjoyment. In fact the rule is not entirely consistent either with a theory of presumed intent or a theory of early distribution and enjoyment. It is, instead, somewhat arbitrary in operation.

under RvP, must be all

exceptn to RvP !

The general "rule of convenience" is that, if no contrary intent is expressed, *the class will close at the time when any member of the class is entitled to immediate possession and enjoyment of his share of principal.* This rule, in the case of personalty, permits immediate distribution of at least a minimum share to the member who first qualifies; and, in the case of realty, it tends to make the title more marketable by identifying the potential parties in interest and eliminating claims by people who might be born thereafter.

The following examples of a gift "to the children of B" will illustrate the operation of this rule, it being assumed in all cases that B is still alive, since, if he were dead, the class would have been physiologically closed at his death.

(1) In the case of an outright gift *"to the children of B"*, the beneficiaries will be entitled to enjoyment immediately on the operative date of the instrument (death of testator in case of a will; date of delivery in case of a deed), and the class will therefore close at that time. Suppose a legacy of $100,000 to the children of B, and that, at the death of the testator, B has two children, X and Y. Since the class is then closed, no children of B born thereafter will share, and immediate distribution of

$50,000 apiece will be made to X and Y. If the class were kept open until the death of B, it would be impossible to determine immediately even the minimum share of X and Y, since it would be impossible to predict how many more children B might have. This would make any distribution whatever to X and Y unsafe, without some such cumbersome and perhaps expensive procedure as the fiduciary's taking refunding bonds from them, and would prejudice X and Y by making it impossible for them to predict even the minimum amount of their interests. No careful fiduciary would take a chance on guessing that B would not have more than five children and thus distributing $20,000 apiece to X and Y, since, if the class were kept open, there might ultimately be ten children of B entitled to share, reducing each share to $10,000, and making it necessary for the fiduciary to try to get back from X and Y the excess of $10,000 apiece, which they might by then have dissipated. To avoid these difficulties, then, the courts have held that, in the absence of any manifestation of contrary intent, the class closes at the death of the testator or the date of deed delivery. In other words, the transferor's apparent intention to make an immediate and irrevocable gift is held to override his apparent (conflicting) intention that all children of B, whenever born, share in the gift. An exception to this general rule is made when, on the effective date of the instrument, there are no members of the class— e.g., if, in the example above, B has no children when the testator dies. In that case, the class will not close until B's death.

(2) In the case of a gift *"to X for life, and then to the children of B"*, the class will close at the death of X, since that is the time when the remaindermen will be entitled to possession and enjoyment of principal. (Here, too, if B has had no children the class will not close until his death.) As pointed out above, the statement that the class closes at the death of X merely means that no children of B born thereafter will share. It does not mean that all those who are alive at the end of the life estate will share. Whether the estate of a member of a class who died before the end of the life estate is entitled to share is not in any way controlled by the class-closing rule, but depends on whether the language of the gift made *survival* to the end of the life estate a condition. With the above language, for example, the estate of a child of B who was alive at the operative date of the instrument but who predeceased X would be entitled to a share, since there is nothing in the language to require survival. If, however, the gift had been "to X for life and then to the children of B then living", the interest of any child of B who predeceased X would be extinguished at that child's death.

(3) In the case of a gift *"to the children of B, payable at 21"*, the class will close as soon as any child of B, or the estate of any child of B, is entitled to possession. If B's oldest child reaches 21, the class will close at that time. If B's oldest child dies under 21, the first problem is to determine whether his interest is extinguished by his death. With the above language, it probably would not be, "payable at 21" being construed as merely specifying the time of payment, rather than requiring survival to the age; the estate of such child of B would therefore be entitled to a

share, and the class would close at the time when his estate was entitled to get possession. Under some circumstances the estate of the child would be entitled at the child's death (at the age of 18, for example); under others, the estate is not entitled until the 21st anniversary of the child's birth, and would have to wait for that additional time after his death. The class will close at whichever time is decided on, since the estate will then be entitled to possession of a share. If the disposition had read "to such children of B as reach the age of 21", the interest of any child who died under 21 would be extinguished by his death. In other words, the class would close on attainment of the age of 21 by the first child of B to reach that age. Again, the class-closing rule would merely mean that children of B born thereafter would not share; it would not mean that all children of B then alive would share; if, when the first child of B reached 21, there was another child aged 18 and that other child should die at 19, his interest would be lost when he died. The class-closing rule merely fixes the maximum, not the ultimate, number of the members of the class, and the minimum, not the ultimate, size of the share of the first member of the class to qualify. The object of the rule is not to permit immediate final and complete distribution (though this would be the effect of it in case 1, supra), but merely immediate distribution of the minimum present share to the first to qualify.

(4) In the case of a gift *"to X for life, and then to the children of B, payable at 21"*, the death of X and one of the conditions to immediate enjoyment described in case 3, supra, must occur before the class closes. For example, the class will not close when the oldest child of B reaches 21, if he does so before the end of the life estate, but will remain open until the life estate terminates, since not until then will any child of B be entitled to possession and enjoyment of principal.

Special problems are posed by limitations to children (or others) when "the youngest" reaches a particular age. Possible constructions are: (a) the youngest refers to the youngest alive on the effective date of the creating instrument; (b) the youngest means the last child in fact born, i.e., the class does not close until no other children can be born; (c) the youngest means the youngest alive when all those living at a particular time have reached the stated age. Generally speaking, the last is the favored construction and the class will close when all the children alive have reached the stated age. For the reasons underlying this choice, and the effect of the Rule against Perpetuities in sometimes dictating the choice of alternative (a), see Powell, Real Property, ¶ 364; Casner, Class Gifts to Others than to "Heirs" or "Next of Kin": Increase in the Class Membership, 51 Harv.L.Rev. 254 (1937).

It is important to understand that, as stated above in the definition of a gift to a class, such a gift is not merely one to a group collectively described, but also one of an *aggregate amount* of property to be divided among them. For example, a legacy of *"$10,000 apiece to each child of B, payable at 21"* is not a gift to a class for the purpose of the above rule, although it is possible to call it "a per capita gift to each member of the class" (Simes on Future Interests (Hornbook) 209). (Note, however, that such a gift is labeled a "class gift" by Restatement of Property, § 279, comment g.) In the case of such a disposition, the usual rule is that no child of B born after the testator's death can share, whether or not there are any children of B living at his death. The difference between this situation and the regular class gift is this: in the regular class gift, the problem is to determine the minimum distributable share of the first member of the class to qualify; here, however, it would be impossible to distribute *any part of the residuary estate* unless the potential beneficiaries of the legacy were limited to those living at the testator's death, because it would be impossible to determine how much of the total estate would have to be retained by the fiduciary to pay the legacy. If, for example, the entire distributable estate were $100,000, there would be no balance if ten children of B could share, but there would be a balance of $90,000 if only one could. This differs from a regular class gift of $50,000 to the children of B, payable at 21, where the amount given to the class can be earmarked and the balance of the estate immediately distributed.

See Simes (hb) 204–216; Simes and Smith, §§ 611–770; Am.L.Prop., §§ 22.1–22.63; Powell, ¶¶ 351–377; Kales, §§ 553–595.

2. Class Gifts and the Rule against Perpetuities

With this background, let us now turn to the subject of class gifts under the Rule against Perpetuities. Our starting point is another famous/infamous case of great age.

LEAKE v. ROBINSON

Chancery, 1817.
2 Mer. 363, 35 Eng.Rep. 979.

[Parts of the statement of facts and the opinion are omitted below. The former has a detailed account of the provision of the will of the testator, John Milward Rowe, that need not be reproduced in full. The relevant issue involved a trust in the will to use the income to support the testator's grandson, William Rowe Robinson, until he reached 25; to pay him the income thereafter during his life; and after his death to pay the income to his children until they reached 25 (or, if a daughter, previously married with the consent of her parent or guardian) and to pay the principal to "such children * * * who shall attain" 25 (or, if a daughter, shall be previously married with such consent). The will then proceeded with the alternative gift of the principal described in the next paragraph, which was the clause in issue. The plaintiffs were the trustees of this trust. Matter following this parenthesis is taken from the original report.]

The testator then directed as follows: that "in case the said William Rowe Robinson shall happen to die without leaving issue, living at the time of his decease, or leaving such, they shall all die before any of them shall attain twenty-five, if sons, and if daughters, before they shall attain such age, or be married as aforesaid;" then the plaintiffs should pay, apply, and transfer the said principal sums of stock, ground-rents, estates and mortgage moneys, "unto and amongst all and every the brothers and sisters of the said William Rowe Robinson, share and share alike, upon his, her, or their attaining twenty-five, if a brother or brothers, and if sister or sisters, at such age or marriage, with such consent as aforesaid." * * *

On the 17th of June, 1790, when the testator made this will, his grandson William Rowe Robinson, had one brother and three sisters living. Between the date of the will and the testator's death, he had another sister born.

On the 9th of February, 1792, the testator died. Between the death of the testator and the death of William Rowe Robinson, the said William Rowe Robinson had two other brothers born. On the 10th of October, 1800, William Rowe Robinson died; having attained twenty-five without issue, unmarried and intestate; and another sister was born after his death. * * *

Under these circumstances, the question for the decision of the court was, whether, in the event which happened, of the death of William Rowe Robinson without issue, the limitation to his Brothers and Sisters, to take effect on their attainment of the age of twenty-five, or marriage as aforesaid, was a good and effectual limitation, or was void, as being too remote. And this principally depended on the determination of two other questions, viz. first, what classes of persons were those intended by the Testator to take, in the event of William Rowe Robinson dying without issue, or without issue living to attain the age of twenty-five, under the description of "all and every the Brothers and Sisters of the said William Rowe Robinson;" because, if that limitation were held to extend to all the Brothers and Sisters who might be born, and (in the event which happened) actually were born, after the death of the Testator, and the period of vesting was postponed by the will till their attainment of the age of twenty-five, it is obvious that more than twenty-one years (the period beyond which a limitation by way of executory devise cannot take effect) might pass after the death of the Testator before the arrival of the limited time; and this, consequently, gave rise to the second question; which was, whether the attainment of twenty-five was in fact the period assigned for the vesting of the several shares, or was to be taken only as the time fixed for the payment of the several shares which had already vested at some antecedent period. * * *

THE MASTER OF THE ROLLS [Sir William Grant]. The first point to be determined in this case is, Who are included in the description of brothers and sisters of William Rowe Robinson, * * * whether those only who were in being at the time of the testator's death, or all who might come *in esse* during the lives of the respective tenants for life. Upon that point I do not see how a question can possibly be raised. Not only is the rule of construction completely settled, but in this case, I apprehend the actual intention of the testator to be perfectly clear. * * *

* * * According to the established rule of construction, and what I conceive to have been the actual intention of the testator, all who were

living at the time of William Rowe Robinson's death must be held to be comprehended in the description.

Having ascertained the persons intended to take, the next question is at what time the interests given to them were to vest.

There is no direct gift to any of these classes of persons. It is only through the medium of directions given to the trustees, that we can ascertain the benefits intended for them.   *   *   *

As to the capital, there being, as I have already said, no direct gift to the grandchildren, we are to see in what event it is that the trustees are to make it over to them. There is, with regard to this, some difference of expression in the different parts of the will. In some instances the testator directs the payment to be to such child or children as shall attain twenty-five. In others the payment is to be made upon attainment of the age of twenty-five.   *   *   * But I think the testator in each instance means precisely the same thing, and that none were to take vested interests before the specified period. The attainment of twenty-five is necessary to entitle any child to claim a transfer. It is not the enjoyment that is postponed; for there is no antecedent gift, as there was in the case of May v. Wood, 3 Bro.C.C. 471, of which the enjoyment could be postponed. The direction to pay is the gift, and that gift is only to attach to children that shall attain twenty-five.   *   *   *

It was supposed that the clauses in the will, where the word *such* is left out, might be construed differently from those in which it is inserted; and that, although the payment is to be to *such* child or children as shall attain twenty-five, nothing could vest in any not answering that description, yet where the payment is to be to children upon the attainment of twenty-five, or from and after their attaining twenty-five, the vesting is not postponed. If there were an antecedent gift, a direction to pay upon the attainment of twenty-five certainly would not postpone the vesting. But if I give to persons of any description *when* they attain twenty-five, or upon their attainment of twenty-five, or from and after their attaining twenty-five, is it not precisely the same thing as if I gave to *such* of those persons as should attain twenty-five? None but a person who can predicate of himself that he has attained twenty-five, can claim anything under such a gift.   *   *   *

Then, assuming that after-born grandchildren were to be let in, and that the vesting was not to take place till twenty-five, the consequence is, that it might not take place till more than twenty-one years after a life or lives in being at the death of the testator. It was not at all disputed that the bequests must for that reason be wholly void, unless the court can distinguish between the children born before, and those born after, the testator's death. Upon what ground can that distinction rest? Not upon the intention of the testator; for we have already ascertained that all are included in the description he has given the objects of his bounty. And all who are included in it were equally capable of taking. It is the period of vesting, and not the description of the legatees, that produces the incapacity. Now, how am I to ascertain in which part of the will it is that the testator has made the blunder which vitiates his bequests?

He supposed that he could do legally all that he has done;—that is, include after-born grandchildren, and also postpone the vesting till twenty-five. But, if he had been informed that he could not do both, can I say that the alteration he would have made would have been to leave out the after-born grandchildren, rather than abridge the period of vesting?   I should think quite the contrary.   It is very unlikely that he should have excluded one half of the family of his daughters, in order only that the other half might be kept four years longer out of the enjoyment of what he left them. It is much more probable that he would have said, "I do mean to include all my grandchildren, but as you tell me that I cannot do so, and at the same time postpone the vesting till twenty-five, I will postpone it only till twenty-one."   If I could at all alter the will, I should be inclined to alter it in the way in which it seems to me probable that the testator himself would have altered it.   That alteration would at least have an important object to justify it;   for it would give validity to all the bequests in the will.   The other alteration would only give them a partial effect; and that too by making a distinction, which the testator himself never intended to make, between those who were the equal objects of his bounty. In the latter case, I should be new-modelling a bequest which, standing by itself, is perfectly valid;   while I left unaltered that clause which alone impedes the execution of the testator's intention in favour of all his grandchildren.   Perhaps it might have been as well if the Courts had originally held an executory devise transgressing the allowed limits to be void only for the excess, where that excess could, as in this case it can, be clearly ascertained.   But the law is otherwise settled.   In the construction of the Act of Parliament passed after the *Thellusson* cause, I thought myself at liberty to hold that the trust of accumulation was void only for the excess beyond the period to which the act restrained it.   And the Lord Chancellor afterwards approved of my decision.   But there the Act introduced a restriction on a liberty antecedently enjoyed, and therefore it was only to the extent of the excess that the prohibition was transgressed. Whereas Executory Devise is itself an infringement on the rules of the common law, and is allowed only on condition of its not exceeding certain established limits.   If the condition be violated, the whole devise is held to be void.

To induce the court to hold the bequests in this will to be partially good, the case has been argued as if they had been made to some individuals who are, and to some who are not, capable of taking.   But the bequests in question are not made to individuals, but to classes;   and what I have to determine is, whether the class can take.   I must make a new will for the testator, if I split into portions his general bequest to the class, and say, that because the rule of law forbids his intention from operating in favor of the whole class, I will make his bequests, what he never intended them to be, viz. a series of particular legacies to particular individuals, or what he had as little in his contemplation, distinct bequests, in each instance, to two different classes, namely to grandchildren living at his death, and to grandchildren born after his death.

If the present case were an entirely new question, I should doubt very much whether this could be done.   But it is a question which appears to me to be perfectly settled by antecedent decisions, and in cases in which there were grounds for supporting the bequests that do not here exist. In Jee v. Audley, 1 Cox, 324, there were no after-born children—no distinction therefore to be made between persons capable and persons incapable—(all were capable)—no difficulty, consequently, in adjusting the proportions that the capable children were to take, or in determining the manner, or the period, of ascertaining those proportions. I am asked why the existence of incapable children should prevent capable children from taking. But in Jee v. Audley, the mere possibility that there might have been incapable children was sufficient to exclude those who were capable. It is said, the devise there was future. Certainly; but only in the same sense in which these bequests are future; that is, so conceived as to let in after-born children; which was the sole reason for its being held to be void. Unless my decision on the first point be erroneous, the bequests in this case do equally include after-born children of the testator's daughters, and are therefore equally void.

Notes

1. This is the leading case for the proposition that a class gift is inseparable for the purpose of the Rule against Perpetuities; it will not be split so as to uphold what would be the independently valid interests of some members of the class. In other words, if there is any possibility that the interest of any present or potential member of the class may vest too remotely, the entire class gift fails. Note this court's reliance on Jee v. Audley, supra, page 761. As the court says, the void interests that were assumed in that case to invalidate the whole gift were those for a group (after-born Jee daughters) whose existence, while legally possible, would physiologically be entirely hypothetical.

This proposition has been followed as an automatic rule since Leake v. Robinson in both England and America. It is assumed to be valid in decisions that do not discuss the question, and has been specifically adopted in others. Leach, who disapproved of any such automatic rule, was hopeful that the tide might turn in America by decisions to the contrary in the many states that had no explicit holding on the point, but there are no indications of such a shift. Everyone should read his attack on this doctrine in Leach, Perpetuities and Class Gifts, 51 Harv.L.R. 1329 (1938), which discusses Leake v. Robinson itself at 1343–45. See also Gray, §§ 373–74; Simes (hb) 289; Annots. 66 A.L.R. 1348 (1930); 155 A.L.R. 698 (1945).

2. Assuming that a gift includes some interests that would be independently valid and some interests that would be void under the Rule against Perpetuities, which of the following alternative solutions would be likely to approximate most closely the probable desires of the transferor?

(a) The present rule holding all the interests void.

(b) Upholding the independently valid interests despite the failure of the void interests.

(c) Making the decision turn on such factors as the comparative similarity to the gift as made of the two alternative solutions just mentioned. For example, should the court consider, if the class is B's children, whether holding it entirely void will give the property, either under a residuary clause or by intestacy, to (i) B's children or (ii) B himself or (iii) C? See Leach, 51 Harv. L.R. 1329, 1336–37 (1938).

What objections might there be to adopting the third solution?

3. Note the expression in this opinion of some personal inclination to validate the gift by a judicial alteration of the age to be attained from 25 to 21. "But the law is otherwise settled." That is, the courts will not rewrite a disposition in this way in order to validate a gift. As a result, a great many gifts are invalidated because the draftsman forgets about the Rule against Perpetuities, and simply accedes to the natural desire of his client to postpone receipt of principal until the beneficiaries are not merely legally adults but also mature enough to handle property carefully and intelligently. See Leach, 51 Harv. L.R. 1329, 1332 (1938).

For many years the only case law departure from this was in New Hampshire. Edgerly v. Barker, 66 N.H. 434, 31 A. 900 (1891). The will in that case, as construed by the court, gave the principal of the residuary estate (after trusts for the testator's daughter, son, daughter-in-law, and grandchildren) to such grandchildren of the testator as should be living, and the children then living of any grandchild then dead, when the testator's youngest grandchild should arrive at the age of 40. The court, in a lengthy and learned opinion of Chief Justice Charles Doe, reduced the age from 40 to 21 and held the gift valid. (Leach would place Judge Doe "well up in any list of the dozen most eminent American judges of all time." 65 Harv.L.R. 721, 735, note 28 (1952). He is, of course, not alone in this opinion. Mr. Wigmore's magnificent treatise on Evidence is dedicated to James Bradley Thayer and to "Charles Doe of New Hampshire, Judge and Reformer"). The basic idea of this opinion is predicated on the theory of cy pres or approximation, traditionally used for charitable gifts. The court concluded from all the provisions of the will, which were detailed and included such conditions as that his son should "become and remain temperate, sober, and correct in his habits" before receiving payments from the trustees, that the testator clearly desired his grandchildren to receive the principal in preference to his two children, who would take it by intestacy if the gift were void. Postponement of the interests of the grandchildren was held secondary to this major objective. Therefore, in the language of the cy pres doctrine, the specific intent to postpone their taking until the youngest reached 40 being void, the court carried out the general intent that they should have the property cy pres (as near as possible to the inoperative specific intent) by reducing 40 to 21, and thus validating the gift. The opinion admitted that the cy pres principle could not be applied as liberally in private gifts as in charitable ones, but felt it proper to utilize the same technique when the intent of the testator seemed clear. The opinion concluded as follows:

> * * * this will is competent and sufficient evidence that if he had been informed (when he gave instructions for drafting it) that his intent that his grandchildren should have the remainder could not stand with his intent that they should not have it till the youngest was 40 years old, and had been asked which of these intents should prevail, he would have given an answer that is comprehended in his intent on the subject of approximation. The law determines not what will he would have made if he had known that the last 19 of the 40 years were too remote, but what will he did make in ignorance of this flaw in his appointment of time. His intent that the grandchildren shall not have the remainder till the youngest ar-

rives at the age of 40 years is modified by his intent that they shall have it, and that the will shall take effect as far as possible. The 40 years are reduced to 21 by his general approximating purpose, which is a part of the will.

This deviation from the norm disturbed Gray. See Gray, §§ 857–893. The fact that other judges declined to follow Judge Doe disturbed Leach. See 65 Harv.L.R. 721, 734–6 (1952). In 1962 the rule of Edgerly v. Barker was approved and applied by the Supreme Court of Mississippi in a carefully reasoned opinion. Carter v. Berry, 243 Miss. 321, 140 So.2d 843, 95 A.L.R.2d 791 (1962). See also In re Foster's Estate, 190 Kan. 498, 376 P.2d 784, 98 A.L.R.2d 795 (1962), holding that an invalid age contingency should be excised from the will.

4. The English Law of Property Act of 1925, 15 Geo. 5, c. 20, § 163(1), provides that the age of 21 "shall be substituted" for any age in excess of 21 that would render any disposition ("gift, gift over, remainder, executory limitation, or trust") of either capital or income, in "a will, settlement, or other instrument", "void for remoteness".

Mass.L.1954, c. 641, Mass.Gen.Laws Ann. c. 184A § 2 provides:

> If an interest in real or personal property would violate the rule against perpetuities * * * because such interest is contingent upon any person attaining or failing to attain an age in excess of twenty-one the age contingency shall be reduced to twenty-one as to all persons subject to the same age contingency.

This section is discussed in Leach, Perpetuities Legislation, Massachusetts Style, 67 Harv.L.R. 1349, 1353–54, 1360–62 (1954).

The same section is in Conn.Gen.Stat.Ann. § 45–96 and 33 Me.Rev.Stat. § 102, both enacted in 1955. New York, Florida and Illinois have enacted similar statutes. See p. 767, supra. For § 1 of the Massachusetts statute, see p. 827, infra.

5. Other commentators favor legislative or judicial adoption for the Rule against Perpetuities of the cy pres philosophy somewhat wistfully dreamed of by the Master of the Rolls in Leake v. Robinson, and forcibly expounded by Judge Doe. See Simes, Public Policy and the Dead Hand, 74–79 (1955).

In dealing with class gifts under the Rule against Perpetuities, the first question to ask is: when will the class close? Unless the class is certain to close within the permissible period, the gift (assuming the all or nothing approach of Leake v. Robinson) is void. If the class is certain to close within the period *and* there are no conditions attached to an interest other than being born, then the gift is good. If, however, as in Leake v. Robinson, another condition is attached—e.g., reaching age 25— then it is not enough that the class will certainly close within the period; the contingency of a potential class member's satisfying the other condition, in the case given reaching age 25, must also be certain to be resolved within the period.

The rule of convenience (see p. 804 supra) can save gifts from invalidity by closing the class earlier than it would otherwise close.

PICKEN v. MATTHEWS

Chancery, 1878.
10 Ch.Div. 264.

FRANCIS HOOFF, by his will, gave his property, real and personal, to trustees on trust to pay certain legacies and annuities, and continued as follows: "Subject as aforesaid, I direct my trustees to stand possessed of my said trust estate, upon trust for such of the children of my daughter Helen by her first husband (but not her children by her present husband), and the children of my daughter Charlotte, who being sons shall live to attain the age of twenty-five years, or being daughters shall attain that age or previously marry, whichever shall first happen; and I expressly direct that all such grandchildren shall participate equally without regard to the number of each family." And the testator empowered his trustees to maintain the children out of their expectant shares until they should respectively acquire vested interests in the trust estate.

The testator died in December, 1865. The testator's daughter Helen had at the date of the testator's death three children by her first husband, of whom the Plaintiff had attained the age of twenty-five at the date of the testator's death. Charlotte had two children who were infants. * * *

MALINS, V. C.:—I have very carefully considered the cases which have been cited; and the conclusion to which I have come will have the advantage, that it will, I think, carry into effect the intention of the testator.

If the two daughters of the testator had had no children living at his death, the gift would have been void for remoteness; because it would not be certain that the property would vest within a life or lives in being and twenty-one years after. But this is a gift to living grandchildren. The testator evidently knew that his grandchildren were in existence, and I must attribute to him knowledge of their ages, knowledge therefore that before his death the Plaintiff had attained the age of twenty-five years. Now, the rules of law applicable to this case are, first, that a gift to a class not preceded by any life estate is a gift to such of the class as are living at the death of the testator. * * * It is a rule of convenience.

The second rule is, that where you have a gift for such of the children of A. as shall attain a specified age, only those who are *in esse* when the first of the class attains the specified age can take. All after-born children are excluded. This also is a rule of convenience.

* * *

Upon the authority of these cases I come to the conclusion that the persons who can take under this limitation are those who were living at the death of the testator. Viner v. Francis, 2 Bro.C.C. 658, a leading authority on the subject, shews that the same principle prevails whether the parent of the children who are to take be alive or dead at the date of the will. * * *

Here there is a gift to such of a class as shall attain twenty-five. The class was ascertained at the death of the testator because one of them had then attained twenty-five. The two infant children of Charlotte Heale who were alive at the death of the testator are entitled to take provided they attain the age of twenty-five years. * * *

Here I hold that there is a valid gift because one of the children of Helen (by her former husband) had attained twenty-five at the death of the testator; the maximum number to take was, therefore, then ascertained, and the gift in question is not void for remoteness.

Notes

1. A's will gives property to B for life, then to B's oldest son for life, then to such of C's children as reach the age of 25. B has no son born at the date of the testator's death. Would the gift to C's children be valid if, at the death of the testator,

(a) B were dead, and C were living, and one of C's children then living had reached 25?

(b) B were alive, and C were dead, and all of C's living children were under the age of 25?

(c) B and C were both alive, and one of C's children then living had reached 25?

See Gray, § 205.2; Am.L.Prop., § 24.25.

2. A's will gives property to B for life, remainder to B's grandchildren. Would the gift to B's grandchildren be valid if at the time of the gift,

(a) B were dead and no grandchildren had been born;

(b) B and one grandchild were alive;

(c) B were alive but no grandchild were living, although one had been born and died;

(d) B were alive but no grandchild had been born?

Cf. Turner v. Turner, 260 S.C. 439, 196 S.E.2d 498 (1973) where A's will gave property to B for life remainder to C's grandchildren. At A's death B and C were alive but no grandchild had been born.

3. A's will gave his wife a life estate, remainder to their children, but "if they had no children, to the children of my brothers and sisters who shall be living at the time of my wife's death or born at any time afterwards before any one of such children for the time being in existence attains a vested interest and who shall attain the age of 21." A was survived by his wife, his father, one brother, one sister and two nieces aged 22 and 24.

Are the remainder interests valid? See Ward v. Van Der Loeff, [1924] A.C. 653.

WRIGHT'S ESTATE

Supreme Court of Pennsylvania, 1925.
284 Pa. 334, 131 A. 188.

[The will of George W. Wright, who died February 21, 1921, left his residuary estate, valued at about $426,000, to trustees in trust for educational scholarships and loans, with the following additional provision, here contested by the testator's next of kin:

"I desire and so direct that the above named trustees may, from the income of the said trust, pay to my nieces and nephews, by blood or marriage, such sum or sums as in their discretion, after investigation, may be necessary."]

WALLING, J.   *   *   *

Of course, the rule against perpetuities does not apply to a charitable trust, but it is urged that the provision for nephews and nieces may tie up the fund for more than 21 years after the death of those in being during the life of testator. This is based on the contention that the provision includes afterborn nephews and nieces, but in our opinion it does not. The general rule is that a will speaks as of the date of testator's death, and, unless it provides otherwise, the beneficiaries are to be determined as of that time. In the language of Mr. Justice Potter, in Tatham's Estate, 250 Pa. 269, 276, 95 A. 520, 522:

"That the class described as testator's 'heirs,' to whom a remainder or executory interest is given by a will, are to be ascertained at the death of the testator, is admittedly the general rule. This is so well recognized that nothing but the expression of a clear intention to the contrary in the will can be allowed to alter the rule"—citing numerous cases.

In Murphey's Estate, 276 Pa. 498, 120 A. 455, the Chief Justice says:

"A devise or bequest to heirs at law of a testator, or to his next of kin, will be construed as referring to those who are such at the time of testator's decease, unless a different intent is plainly manifested by the will."

Schouler on Wills, etc. (6th Ed.) vol. 2, § 1016, states the general rule:

"Testator has a right to fix a time other than his death, when the members of a class are to be ascertained but where nothing appears to the contrary the members of the class will be ascertained as of the date of the death of the testator, and it is the universal rule that the class is determined as of the time of the death of the testator rather than of the execution of the will."

So, "persons born after the death of the testator cannot take under a legacy to a class, unless there is a fixed period for the distribution other than that of the testator's death." 28 R.C.L. p. 261.

Numerous other authorities of like import might be cited; it is uniformly true in gifts to a class unless a definite later date is fixed for distribution, and here there is none; as the period is indefinite, those only take who are in esse at the testator's death. Myers v. Myers, 2 McCord, Eq. 214, 16 Am.Dec. 648. See, also, 40 Cyc. 1481. There is nothing to take this case out of the general rule above stated, that the members of the class must be determined at testator's death, and only such individuals thereof, if any, as come or may come within the terms of the will can receive any benefit thereunder.

We concede the legal possibility of children being born to parents of any age (List v. Rodney, 83 Pa. 483), yet, as testator's two brothers, one 82 and the other 77 years of age, and a sister-in-law 75 years of age were the only persons whose after-born children would be testator's nephews and nieces, while not controlling, is a fact which lends strength to the conclusion that the testator had in mind merely the nephews and nieces then in being. So construing the will, there is no possibility of a violation of the rule against perpetuities; and, if reasonably possible, a will should always be so construed as to make its provisions legally effective. Anderson's Estate, 269 Pa. 535, 112 A. 766; McClellan's Estate, 221 Pa. 261, 70 A. 737.

The decree is affirmed, and appeal dismissed at the cost of appellant.

Notes

1. This case is introduced at this point for the purpose of illustrating that courts can, if they are so disposed, circumvent the Rule against Perpetuities by "construction." In theory courts are supposed to construe limitations without reckoning the consequences of the Rule (Gray, § 629). But intuition suggests and experience confirms that courts often peek at the consequences first and construe the limitation second. See Powell, ¶ 777.

The case also serves as a reminder of the problem of the application of the Rule against Perpetuities to income trusts. Compare Thomas v. Harrison, supra, p. 754. Note that this opinion assumes that the income trust would be void if afterborn nieces and nephews of the testator were included as beneficiaries.

The generalizations on this issue are stated as follows in Gray, § 246: "If the trust is discretionary, no interest will vest in a beneficiary until the trustee exercises his discretion and makes a payment. But, in the case of a mandatory trust, the right of the beneficiary to receive the income is regarded as 'a single entire interest'." See also Leach, 51 Harv.L.R. 638, 652 (1938).

In Re Vaux, [1938] 4 All Eng.R. 297, the court stated, with reference to a discretionary trust:

> * * * it creates beneficial interests in the persons named * * *, such interests not being absolute interests, but contingent, both as to exercise and as to extent, upon the exercise of the trustees' discretion. If, as a matter of construction, a discretion may be exercised more than 21 years after the termination of any life in being at the creation of the interest, no interest created under the discretion can fail to infringe the rule against perpetuities, since it cannot be predicated of the interest created by the testator's will (i.e., an interest contingent on the exercise of the trustees' discretion) that it must vest, if at all, not later than 21 years after some life in being at the creation of the interest, *scilicet,* at the death of the testator.

2. Note that the first paragraph of the opinion utilizes the class closing rule to limit the beneficiaries to nieces and nephews who are lives in being.

(a) Are the first two cases cited by the court relevant to the issue in this case?

(b) Is the court's statement that there is no "later date fixed for distribution" correct? Does this holding correspond with the purpose of the class closing rule? See page 804, supra; Casner, Class Gifts to Others than to "Heirs" or "Next of Kin": Increase in the Class Membership, 51 Harv.L.R. 254, 304–07 (1937); Am.L.Prop., § 22.46.

G. SALVAGE DOCTRINES *(ie to salvage part/all of T's intent)*

Lawyers, and courts, frequently give the impression that the Rule against Perpetuities is a malevolent force against which they are powerless.   In fact most potential violations of the Rule can be avoided in the creation by careful drafting.   Some of the precautions are obvious. In the case of Ryan v. Ward, supra, p. 786 the problem seems to have arisen because the draftsman used a form appropriate for a will instead of a form for an inter vivos trust.   At least it is hard to imagine why else a document which seems so carefully crafted to avoid the Rule could have failed as it did.   By the same token, many, perhaps most, class gift problems can be taken care of by specifying that the class is to close immediately, i.e. at the date of the testator's death or the effective date of an inter vivos trust.

Some booby traps are less obvious but can be avoided by the use of saving clauses.   One "catch-all" type of clause is suggested in Leach, Perpetuities: The Nutshell Revisited, 78 Harv.L.Rev. 973, 986 (1965):

> In any disposition in this instrument, or an instrument exercising a power of appointment created herein, I do not intend that there shall be any violation of the Rule Against Perpetuities or any related rule. If any such violation should inadvertently occur, it is my wish that the appropriate court shall reform the gift or appointment in such a way as to approximate most closely my intent or the intent of the appointor, within the limits permissible under such rule or related rule.

While the use of such a clause has considerable backing, it should not be thought of as a substitute for careful drafting.   It may save the will, but the disposition of the property by the court may not be what the testator would have wished if he had been properly advised; and, in any event, the construction proceeding will involve the estate in expense which might have been avoided.

A somewhat differently worded saving clause can be useful in dealing with what Professor Waggoner has called "technical" violations of the Rule against Perpetuities; i.e. violations in which the actual occurrence of the remote possibility is exceedingly unlikely—for example the possibility that a woman past childbearing age shall, nevertheless, have a child; that a man or a woman of mature age when an interest is created shall be survived by a widow or widower who is unborn at that time; that an executor shall fail to complete his administration of an estate in twenty-one years.

One type of such a saving clause (from Waggoner, Future Interests in a Nutshell 188 (1984) derived from one suggested in Simes & Smith § 1295) is as follows:

> The trust hereby created shall terminate in any event not later than twenty-one years after the death of the last survivor of all beneficiaries of this trust who are in being at the time this instrument becomes effective, and unless sooner terminated by the terms hereof, the trustee shall, at the termination of such period, make distribution to the persons then entitled to the income of this trust, and in the same shares and proportions as they are so entitled.

[handwritten: gen't + tech SC's]

[handwritten right margin: good point!]

Note, the difference in operation between such a clause and that suggested by Professor Leach. If the Leach clause had been used by the draftsman of the will in Perkins v. Iglehart supra, p. 772 the possibility that the life tenant might be survived by an "unborn widow" would seem to lead to the invocation of the saving clause empowering the court to provide an alternative plan of disposition. However, if the draftsman had used the other type of clause, which is designed so that it will never become effective unless the remote possibility occurs, there would have been no violation, and hence the clause would not come into play. As noted such a clause works best when the invalidating possibility is, indeed, remote. Where the possibility is less remote, saving clauses tailored to the specific case can be used. On the subject of drafting to avoid perpetuities problems, generally, see McGovern, Perpetuities Pitfalls and How Best to Avoid Them, 6 Real Prop.Prob. & Tr.J. 155 (1971).

Nor are the courts helpless. It is frequently possible to construe a limitation so as to avoid the violation. (See p. 817 supra). Sometimes construction enables the court to reach the result probably intended by the testator but inadequately expressed by counsel. See, for example Worcester County Trust Co. v. Marble, 316 Mass. 294, 55 N.E.2d 446 (1944) where the court construed a gift to the testator's nephews and nieces as meaning nephews living at his death and as not including any who might be born to his 82-year old, childless sister.

Sometimes, however, the construction yields a result that does not seem to correspond with the probable wishes of the testator. One example is the class of cases in which the court indulges in the "preference for early vesting." This preference, while it undoubtedly saves some interests from the Rule against Perpetuities, tends to result in the passage of property to dead persons' estates, and has other unfortunate consequences including unnecessary increase in estate taxes. In recent years, the preference has been the subject of much criticism. See Rabin, The Law Favors the Vesting of Estates. Why?, 65 Colum.L.Rev. 467 (1965); Schuyler, Drafting, Tax and Other Consequences of the Rule of Early Vesting, 46 Ill.L.Rev. 407 (1951); Powell, ¶ 318.

Occasionally the courts go even further, by ignorance or design, and avoid the Rule by brute force. One example is the decision in Mercantile Trust Co. v. Hammerstein, 380 S.W.2d 287 (Mo.1964) (see particularly the opinion on rehearing), carefully analyzed in Eckhardt, Rule Against Perpetuities in Missouri, 30 Mo.L.Rev. 27 (1965). Another is In re Allar's Will, 36 Misc.2d 405, 232 N.Y.S.2d 173 (Surr.Ct.N.Y.County, 1962). Others could easily be supplied. The New York courts, during the time when the period of the Rule was limited to two lives in being (see p. 781 supra), were most resourceful in finding ways to validate seemingly invalid limitations.

[handwritten left margin: "wait + see"]

One device available in some situations was the so-called alternative contingencies rule referred to in Merchants National Bank v. Curtis, infra p. 821. The idea is that if an interest is limited by the terms of the instrument to take effect on the happening of alternative contingencies one of which is certain to be resolved within the period of the Rule, but the other is not, the court should wait and see which one happens.   The classic example is the devise to the first son of X who shall become a clergyman but if X should have no such son, to Y.   But for the Rule against Perpetuities, the gift over to Y would take effect if either X had no sons at all, or X had sons but none became a clergyman.   The first contingency would certainly be resolved by X's death; the second could remain unresolved until all of X's sons died, a time which might be beyond the period of the Rule.   The approach of the courts has been to strike down the limitation *in toto* unless the alternative contingencies are *separately* stated in the creating document.   In other words, in the example given, if the will had provided "but if X shall have no son, or if he has no son who becomes a clergyman, to Y," the gift to Y would have been good if X had no son, but void if X had a son.   Since, however, the will simply provided (in substance) "if X shall have no son who becomes a clergyman," the requirement of separate statement of the contingencies was not met and the gift to Y violated the Rule. [It should be obvious that whether or not the contingencies are separately stated is a matter of chance—the draftsman would hardly state the invalid contingency if he was aware of the problem.] Thus the alternative contingencies approach cannot be justified as a rational application of the Rule; however, as a practical matter, it does permit the courts to save some gifts from invalidity.   See note 2, p. 825 infra.   See Simes and Smith, § 1257.

Another salvage device with specific application to class gifts is illustrated by the famous case of Cattlin v. Brown, 11 Hare 372, 68 Eng. Rep. 1218 (Ch.1853).   In that case a provision in A's will gave property to B for life, then to the children of B who survive B in equal shares during their lives, and on the death of any such child her share to her children. When A died B was alive and had five living children.   At common law the gift to B for life would clearly be good as would the gift to B's children for their lives since all would vest no later than the death of B.   What about the gift of the remainders to B's grandchildren?   If the class of grandchildren is regarded as a single class then, under the principles examined earlier, the gift will fail since the makeup of the class is not certain to be determined within the period of the Rule.   But suppose we do not regard it as a single class gift but as separate class gifts of shares to the children of each child of B to take effect upon that child's death. So viewed some of the class gifts will be perfectly fine, i.e. those to the children of children who are lives in being when A dies.   If, however B has more children after A's death, the gifts to *their* children will be void. Following the lead of Cattlin v. Brown, courts have not applied the "all or nothing rule" to cases in which they have found an intent to make separable gifts to "sub-classes."   See Simes & Smith, § 1267.

Despite the availability of these devices, considerable dissatisfaction with the Rule has persisted and in recent years a number of new approaches have been fashioned by legislatures and courts.   One primitive step is a simple enlargement of the period in gross. (See, e.g. West's Ann.Cal.Civ.Code, § 715.6: "No interest * * * which must vest, if at all, not later than 60 years after the creation of the interest violates [the Rule].") Such a provision, while it might be helpful in commercial transactions, would not seem to be of much use in family transfers. Another device is to reduce age contingencies to 21 as provided by Massachusetts, New York and several states (p. 813 supra), an approach which seems likely to save a large percentage of gifts which would otherwise violate the Rule. Another method is the creation of presumptions to avoid the more bizarre applications of the remote possibilities test. See, e.g., N.Y.—McKinney's EPTL 9–1.3, pp. 767–8, supra.

Two other major innovations remain to be discussed: the "wait and see" approach, and "cy pres."

Wait and see. The underlying idea of "wait and see" is quite simple. Instead of invalidating an interest which *might* under some hypothetical circumstances, vest too remotely, why not wait and see if, in fact it does. At first look, the wait and see approach may seem the least radical of departures from the common law Rule. It does not require the court to rewrite the will as is the case when age contingencies are reduced. It does not require the courts to indulge in sometimes fanciful presumptions. It does not require the court to distort the normal meaning of the language used. Nevertheless, it has been termed "by far the most revolutionary" of the proposed modifications (Simes (hb) 270).

MERCHANTS NATIONAL BANK v. CURTIS

Supreme Court of New Hampshire, 1953.
98 N.H. 225, 97 A.2d 207.

Petition, for partition of certain real estate situated at the corner of Elm and Manchester Streets in Manchester. The real estate was sold and a portion of the proceeds of the sale amounting to $32,975.11, together with accumulating interest, is in the hands of the clerk of the Superior Court for distribution in accordance with the ruling of the Supreme Court on certain stipulated facts agreed to by all the parties. On the basis of the stipulated facts, and the exhibits, the Court (Wheeler, C. J.) transferred without ruling the following question of law: "What individuals are entitled to participate in the distribution of the trust moneys deposited with the Clerk of Court, and in what proportions are they entitled to share"?

The petition was originally brought by the plaintiff in March 1914, claiming an undivided two-thirds interest in said real estate, the defendant Delana B. Curtis owning an undivided eleven fifty-fourths interest and the devisees under the will of Margaret A. Harrington a seven fifty-fourths interest. Margaret A. Harrington had previously died in 1902, leaving a will which was duly probated. At her death she owned the undivided seven fifty-fourths interest in this real estate. Under the provisions of her will her only children, a son, Edward Harrington, and a daughter, the abovementioned Delana B. Curtis, received a life estate in this real estate. By clause fourth the remainder was devised "to my granddaughter Margaret May Curtis and her heirs forever." The will further provided:

"Fifth: In the event of either of my children having other heirs of their body, surviving them such heir or heirs shall share equally with Margaret May Curtis, and in that event I give, bequeath and devise my estate to them, and their heirs, on the death of my children.

"Sixth: If my Grand Daughter Margaret May Curtis or other grand children shall survive both of my children and shall have and leave no heirs of her or their body, then and in that event, I give, bequeath and devise all my estate unto my brothers and sisters then living and to the representatives of those not living, and to my late husbands niece, Almeda S. Goyscan formerly Almeda S. Harrington, in equal shares * * *."

The said Almeda S. Goyscan predeceased the testatrix leaving no issue. The testatrix' son, the said Edward W. Harrington, survived the testatrix and died leaving no issue. The testatrix' daughter, the said Delana B. Curtis, also survived the testatrix and died leaving no children other than her said daughter, Margaret. Margaret was twice married and, at the time of her death without issue, on January 16, 1951, her name was Margaret May Curtis Reynolds Vreeland.

The testatrix, Margaret A. Harrington, had three sisters and three brothers, who were living or who had issue living at the time of her death, namely: Abigail Bond Chandler, Nancy Bond Corliss, Maria Bond Hill, James B. Bond, Jonathan Bond and John R. Bond. All of these brothers and sisters left representatives in interest in this case, with the exception of Nancy Bond Corliss, who died on July 1, 1910, leaving an only child, George W. Corliss, who died unmarried and without issue on September 6, 1922. Accordingly, the parties to this proceeding are the representatives in interest of five brothers and sisters of Margaret A. Harrington, who were living at the death of Margaret May Curtis Reynolds Vreeland on January 16, 1951. The representatives of these brothers and sisters have been stipulated by the parties.

* * *

KENISON, Chief Justice. The question transferred in effect asks us to decide who is entitled to how much of what trust moneys. This question depends in part on whether clause sixth of the will violates the rule against perpetuities. * * *

The Rule against Perpetuities, hereinafter called the rule, prevails in this state, Gale v. Gale, 85 N.H. 358, 159 A. 122, but it has never been "remorselessly applied" as advocated by Gray in "The Rule against Perpetuities" (4th ed.) § 629. The genesis of the modified rule in New Hampshire began in 1891 with Edgerly v. Barker, 66 N.H. 434, 31 A. 900, 28 L.R.A. 328, when a gift of a remainder interest to grandchildren reaching forty years of age, which offended the rule, was cut down to a gift to grandchildren reaching twenty-one years of age so as not to offend the rule. This decision was bitterly assailed by Gray in his treatise (appendix G) since he thought it was a dangerous thing to tamper with this ancient English rule "which is concatenated with almost mathematical precision." Gray, supra, § 871. Nevertheless, Edgerly v. Barker, supra, has been followed in subsequent decisions in this state and continues to remain in good standing here. Wentworth v. Wentworth, 77 N.H. 400, 92 A. 733; Flanders v. Parker, 80 N.H. 566, 120 A. 558; Gale v. Gale, supra; Amoskeag Trust Company v. Haskell, 96 N.H. 89, 91, 70 A.2d 210, 71 A.2d 408. See Quarles, The Cy Pres Doctrine; Its Application to Cases Involving the Rule against Perpetuities and Trusts for Accumulations, 21 N.Y.U.L.Q.Rev. 384 (1946). In England the same result has been achieved by legislation. Laws of Property Act, 1925, 39 & 40 Geo. V., c. 98, Sec. 163.

The rationale of the Barker case was that, wherever possible, a will should be construed to carry out the primary intent to accomplish a legal testamentary disposition even though the will may have inadvertently exposed a secondary intent to accomplish the testamentary disposition in an ineffective manner. That rationale has been applied in many recent will cases that have not involved the rule itself. "Traditionally, the courts of this jurisdiction have shown a signal regard for the intent of the testator * * * at times at the expense of other recognized principles deemed less cogent in their application. Cf. Edgerly v. Barker, 66 N.H. 434, 31 A. 900, 28 L.R.A. 328." Petition of Oliver Wolcott, 95 N.H. 23, 26, 56 A.2d 641, 643, 1 A.L.R.2d 1323. The same thought received expression in different language in Burtman v. Butman, 97 N.H. 254, 258, 85 A.2d 892, 895: "Probably no jurisdiction has stood more steadfastly for giving effect to the intention of the testator rather than to arbitrary rules of law than New Hampshire." The refusal of this court to apply in unmodified form common law principles which defeat normal and reasonable estate plans has not been limited to wills but applies to conveyances as well. Therrien v. Therrien, 94 N.H. 66, 46 A.2d 538, 166 A.L.R. 1023.

The rule is a technical one, difficult of application and is often enforced to frustrate testamentary intent although the policy of the rule may not require such enforcement in a particular case. It is not surprising, therefore, that there has been an increasing tendency to avoid the application of the rule by various judicial techniques. There is a constructional preference for considering interests vested rather than contingent. Upton v. White, 92 N.H. 221, 29 A.2d 126. "The public interest in keeping *the destructive force of the rule against perpetuities within reasonable limits* is a considerable present factor supporting the public interest in that construction which accomplishes the earlier vesting." 3 Restatement, Property, § 243 comment i. (Emphasis supplied). If a gift is made upon alternative contingencies, one of which might be remote, while the other is not, the gift is valid where the second contingency actually happens. This doctrine is used to prevent the application of the rule in many cases. Annotation 64 A.L.R. 1077. "Essentially this represents a revulsion against the rule requiring absolute certainty of vesting as viewed from the creation of the interest. * * * Courts have a strong tendency to 'wait and see' wherever possible." 6 American Law of Property (1952) § 24.54. These techniques have the salutary effect of avoiding the punitive and technical aspects of the rule but at the same time confirming the policy and purpose of the rule within limits. Wentworth & Co. v. Wentworth, 77 N.H. 400, 92 A. 733.

Clause sixth of the will is capable of at least two possible constructions. The first construction is that clause sixth created two contingencies upon which it would take effect: one to occur, if at all, on the death of Margaret May Curtis; the other to occur, if at all, on the death of unborn grandchildren. Since the first contingency actually occurred and is within the period of perpetuities, the gift may be considered valid. A closely parallel case is Springfield Safe Deposit & Trust Co. v. Ireland, 268 Mass. 62, 167 N.E. 261, 64 A.L.R. 1071. Under this construction the event occurs at the death of Margaret May Curtis, a life in being, and clause sixth would not be considered violative of the rule.

The second possible construction of this sixth clause is the one urged by the Bean-Quirin interests. They argue that the will gives the brothers and sisters an executory interest upon a single contingency which may occur at the death of as yet unborn grandchildren. While this is not the only construction that the clause is susceptible of, it is not a labored one. There is no doubt that, if there had been another grandchild who died after Margaret May Curtis without leaving heirs of his body, this event would have occurred beyond the period allowed by the rule against perpetuities.

Assuming this second construction to be permissible, we come to the crucial question whether we are justified in deciding the perpetuities issue on the facts which actually occurred rather than on facts that might have happened viewed as of the death of the testator. There is little case authority for deciding upon facts occurring after the testator's death in a case such as the one before us. However, recognized modern commentators present convincing arguments for doing so. Leach, Perpetuities in Perspective: Ending the Rule's Reign of Terror, 65 Harv.L.Rev. 721 (1952); 6 American Law of Property (1952) § 24.10; and a full study by a Pennsylvania law revision commission resulted in a statute that permits such events to be considered. Pa.Estates Act of 1947, § 4, Pa. Stat.Ann. (Purdon, 1947) tit. 20, § 301.4. There is no precedent in this state that compels us to close our eyes to facts occurring after the death of the testator.

In the present case we are called on to determine the validity of a clause of a will that did not in fact tie up property beyond the permissible limit of lives in being plus twenty-one years. There is no logical justification for deciding the problem as of the date of the death of the testator on facts that might have happened rather than the facts which actually happened. It is difficult to see how the public welfare is threatened by a vesting that might have been postponed beyond the period of perpetuities but actually was not. The recent decision in Sears v. Coolidge, 329 Mass. 340, 108 N.E.2d 563, allows the court to take a "second look" under powers of appointment. While this is not direct authority for doing the same thing with a devise or bequest, it is bottomed on the same proposition that the glacial force of the rule will be avoided where the interests actually vest within the period of perpetuities. 6 American Law of Property, § 24.35. When a decision is made at a time when the events have happened, the court should not be compelled to consider only what might have been and completely ignore what was. Analogy may be found in cases where the validity of a remainder interest is not considered until the facts existing on the death of the life tenant can be established. See Orr v. Moses, 94 N.H. 309, 52 A.2d 128; B. M. C. Durfee Trust Co. v. Taylor, 325 Mass. 201, 89 N.E.2d 777.

At the death of the survivor of the life tenants, Edward Harrington and Delana B. Curtis, both of whom were lives in being at testatrix' death, it became certain that no grandchildren of the testatrix would be born after her death. This in turn made it certain that the gift in clause sixth of the will would in fact vest at the death of Margaret May Curtis Reynolds Vreeland, also a life in being at testatrix' death. Consistent with the principles above stated, the facts existing at the death of the two life tenants are taken into consideration in applying the rule.

We therefore conclude that clause sixth does not violate the rule against perpetuities. The individuals who are entitled to participate in the distribution of the trust moneys and the extent of their interests are to be determined under this clause.

Since Almeda S. Goyscan predeceased the testatrix leaving no issue and since the testatrix' sister, Nancy Bond Corliss and her only child George died without issue before the death of Margaret, the division is to be made among the representatives in interest of five brothers and sisters of the testatrix as stated in In re Harrington's Estate, 97 N.H. 184, 187, 84 A.2d 173.

* * *

Notes

1. About one-half of the statement of facts in the original report is omitted above. There were various transfers of interests in this property, including those to the people referred to in the sixth paragraph of the opinion as "the Bean-Quirin interests". Pursuant to the original partition petition brought in 1914, the property was sold for a total price of $297,500. In the partition decree of October, 1914, $38,564.82 of this total price, representing the 7/54 interest in the land that had passed under the will of Margaret Harrington, was directed to be administered by a trustee appointed by the court until the death of Margaret May Curtis. The latter having died in 1951, the issue here was the distribution of that fund, which, according to the second sentence of the statement of facts, supra, apparently shrank in capital value to $32,975.11 by the time of this hearing.

The parts of the opinion dealing with the transfers of interests and with a holding that a previous decision construing the will was not res judicata are omitted.

2. The "first construction" suggested in the fifth paragraph of the opinion would require the court to deal with the alternative contingencies approach, p. 819, supra.

One anomaly of that approach is illustrated by Springfield Safe Deposit & Trust Co. v. Ireland, 268 Mass. 62, 167 N.E. 261, 64 A.L.R. 1071 (1929), cited by the court. The will of a testator who died in 1891 gave the principal of his estate (after income trusts for his widow, his daughter Jeannie, and the latter's issue) to such issue of his daughter Jeannie as should be living in January, 1922, if Jeannie were then dead, or in the first January following Jeannie's death if Jeannie should be alive after January, 1922. (This is the court's construction of the disposition, rather than the language verbatim.) Jeannie died in February, 1928, and her only child, a son who was living in January, 1929, was held entitled to the property. The court stated that, if Jeannie had died before January, 1922, her son would not have been entitled to the property, although he was then alive. How does he happen to get the property because the vesting was in fact delayed for a longer period?

See Gray, §§ 331–355; Leach, 51 Harv.L.R. 638, 654–55 (1938); Prop. Rest., § 376; Annot. 64 A.L.R. 1077 (1929).

The great interest in the Curtis case is due to its adoption under "the second possible construction" of the "wait and see" approach. Sears v. Coolidge, 329 Mass. 340, 108 N.E.2d 563 (1952), cited in this opinion, supports it in the special context of a gift in default of appointment, but, as will be seen later, that situation presents special considerations that would not necessarily apply in general. Story v. First National Bank & Trust Co., in Orlando, 115 Fla. 436, 439, 449, 450, 156 So. 101, 103, 107 (1934) has some statements favoring it ("In an old case * * * Public Policy was described as a very unruly horse, and when once you get astride it you never know where it will carry you. * * * The act of striking down a will is no trivial matter. * * * To strike the will down now because of the possibility of * * * contingencies arising would defeat every purpose of the testator * * *. It would be highly improper to strike a will down because of a contingency that may never arise * * *."), but the decision was not clearly based on that ground.

In the third paragraph from the end of the Curtis opinion, the court points out that it became certain at the death of the survivor of Edward and Delana that the gift to take effect if Margaret should die without issue would not violate the Rule against Perpetuities. Would this court have held the gift invalid under "the second possible construction" if Delana had left three surviving children in addition to Margaret, but the three other children all died without issue before Margaret died without issue? Whether the court would so hold would depend upon its answer to a major question raised by the wait and see approach, i.e., how long are we to wait; in essence this is the same as asking what lives we are to use as the measuring lives. Unlike the common law rule where the choice of the measuring lives is necessarily governed by the terms of the gift, under wait and see the ascertainment of those lives can be difficult. The problem is illustrated by the first statute to adopt the "wait and see" philosophy, the Pennsylvania Estates Act of 1947 (20 Pa.Stat. §§ 6010 et seq.). Section 6104 reads, in part:

> (a) General. No interest shall be void as a perpetuity except as herein provided.
>
> (b) Void interest—exceptions. Upon the expiration of the period allowed by the common law rule against perpetuities as measured by actual

rather than possible events any interest not then vested and any interest in members of a class the membership of which is then subject to increase shall be void. * * *

If this statute were literally applied, an interest would be good if, at the time of vesting, any person alive at the time of creation were still alive—or had died within the previous 21 years—a result which all agree could not have been intended. See Leach, Perpetuities Legislation: Hail, Pennsylvania, 108 U.Pa.L.Rev. 1124 (1960). And compare Mechem, A Brief Reply to Professor Leach, 108 U.Pa.L.Rev. 1155 (1960).

The problem of what lives can be used as measuring lives without destroying the utility of the Rule has been a major focus of attention in wait and see statutes.

One approach is exemplified by § 381.216 of the Kentucky Revised Statutes which provides that "the period shall not be measured by any lives whose continuance does not have a causal relation to the vesting or failure of the interest." Doubt that this provision is workable has been expressed by Professor Simes (Simes (hb) 273) who is "unable to see any question of causation as that term is properly used."

Another approach is represented by the Massachusetts statute (Mass. Gen.Laws Ann. c. 184A), copied in 1955 in Connecticut (L.1955, P.A. 233, C.G.S.A. §§ 45–95, 45–96, 45–97) and Maine (33 R.S.A. § 101):

> 1. In applying the rule against perpetuities to an interest in real or personal property limited to take effect at or after the termination of one or more life estates in, or lives of, persons in being when the period of said rule commences to run, the validity of the interest shall be determined on the basis of facts existing at the termination of such one or more life estates or lives. In this section an interest which must terminate not later than the death of one or more persons is a "life estate" even though it may terminate at an earlier time.

The Massachusetts type statute, by requiring the determination of invalidity to be made at the end of a life estate—or designated life—considerably eases the burden of identifying the measuring lives. On the other hand, it falls far short of exhausting the potential for validating interests of the wait and see approach.

Still a third approach is to prescribe who may be used as measuring lives by specifying necessary relationships to the interest or the beneficiaries. A very complicated example of such an effort is the statute adopted in Great Britain, after considerable debate, by the Perpetuities and Accumulations Act, 1964, 13 Eliz. 2, c. 55, § 3:

* * *

> (4) Where this section applies to a disposition and the duration of the perpetuity period is not determined by virtue of section 1 or 9(2) of this act, it shall be determined as follows:
>
> > (a) where any persons falling within subsection (5) below are individuals in being and ascertainable at the commencement of the perpetuity period the duration of the period shall be determined by reference to their lives and no others, but so that the lives of any description of persons falling within paragraph (b) or (c) of that subsection shall

be disregarded if the number of persons of that description is such as to render it impracticable to ascertain the date of death of the survivor;

(b) where there are no lives under paragraph (a) above the period shall be twenty-one years.

(5) The said persons are as follows:

(a) the person by whom the disposition was made;

(b) a person to whom or in whose favor the disposition was made, that is to say

(i) in the case of a disposition to a class of persons, any member or potential member of the class;

(ii) in the case of an individual disposition to a person taking only on certain conditions being satisfied, any person as to whom some of the conditions are satisfied and the remainder may in time be satisfied;

(iii) in the case of a special power of appointment exercisable in favour of members of a class, any member or potential member of the class;

(iv) in the case of a special power of appointment exercisable in favour of one person only, that person or, where the object of the power is ascertainable only on certain conditions being satisfied, any person as to whom some of the conditions are satisfied and the remainder may in time be satisfied;

(v) in the case of any power, option or other right, the person on whom the right is conferred;

(c) a person having a child or grandchild within subparagraphs (i) to (iv) of paragraph (b) above, or any of whose children or grandchildren, if subsequently born, would by virtue of his or her descent fall within those sub-paragraphs;

(d) any person on the failure or determination of whose prior interest the disposition is limited to take effect.

A less complicated effort to prescribe the measuring lives is that of the Restatement, 2d, Property (Donative Transfers) § 1.3(2) which provides:

(2) If no measuring life with respect to a donative transfer is produced under subsection (1) [see p. 829, infra] the measuring lives for purposes of the rule against perpetuities as applied to the non-vested interest in question are:

(a) The transferor if the period of the rule begins to run in the transferor's lifetime; and

(b) Those individuals alive when the period of the rule begins to run, if reasonable in number, who have beneficial interests vested or contingent in the property in which the non-vested interest in question exists and the parents and grandparents alive when the period of the rule begins to run of all beneficiaries of the property in which the nonvested interest exists; and

(c) The donee of a nonfiduciary power of appointment alive when the period of the rule begins to run if the exercise of such power could affect the non-vested interest in question.

A child in gestation when the period of the rule begins to run who is later born alive is treated as a life in being at the time the period of the rule begins and, hence, may be a measuring life.

A similar provision has been adopted in Iowa (Iowa Code Ann. § 558.68).

But apart from the mechanical problem of determining the measuring lives, there is a major substantive objection to wait and see—that it undermines a basic objective of the rule—alienability of property—by postponing the determination of ownership. Whereas the common law Rule permits an immediate test of the validity of contingent future interests, the determination (at least the determination of invalidity) cannot be made in a wait and see jurisdiction until a later—perhaps a much later—time. Until then no one can know whether the interest is valid or void. It is true that in a jurisdiction like Massachusetts where the practice has been not to decide the validity of remainders until after the life estate is ended, the drawback is less serious. Indeed, it is argued that in such jurisdictions wait and see has the positive advantage of permitting the court to avoid the embarrassment of declaring interests invalid on the basis of "possibilities" which are no longer in fact possible. On the other hand, even in those jurisdictions, the adoption of wait and see has been criticized as reinforcing an already bad practice. See Simes, "Is the Rule Against Perpetuities Doomed? The Wait and See Doctrine," 52 Mich.L.Rev. 179, 185 (1953); Mechem, "Further Thoughts on the Pennsylvania Perpetuities Legislation," 107 U.Pa.L.Rev. 965, 980 (1959).

A partial answer to this objection is given by the Restatement 2d § 1.3(1) which provides:

(1) If an examination of the situation with respect to a donative transfer as of the time the period of the rule against perpetuities begins to run reveals a life or lives in being within 21 years after whose deaths the non-vested interest in question will necessarily vest, if it ever vests, such life or lives are the measuring lives for purposes of the rule against perpetuities so far as such non-vested interest is concerned and such non-vested interest cannot fail under the rule. A provision that terminates a non-vested interest if it has not vested within 21 years after the death of the survivor of a reasonable number of persons named in the instrument of transfer and in being when the period of the rule begins to run is within this subsection.

Under such a rule, it should be possible to get an immediate determination of validity where an interest would be valid at common law. It does not, of course, meet the objection that the status of interests not clearly valid may not be determined for a long time.

What would be the effects of the various wait and see formulations discussed above on the future interests in the following dispositions that would be void under the orthodox Rule against Perpetuities?

(a) A to T in trust to pay the income to B for life, then to pay the income to B's children during their lives; and, on the death of the survivor of B's children, to transfer the principal per stirpes to B's issue then • living.

(b) A to T in trust to pay the income to B for life, then to pay the income to B's children during their lives; and, on the death of the survivor of B's children, to transfer the principal per capita to such of B's grandchildren as shall attain the age of 25 years.

(c) A by will to such person as shall, 100 years after A's death, be A's then oldest living lineal descendant.

IN RE ESTATE OF PEARSON

Supreme Court of Pennsylvania, 1971.
442 Pa. 172, 275 A.2d 336.

JONES, Justice. Robert Pearson [testator] died on July 27, 1967, leaving a holographic instrument dated January 7, 1958, and entitled "Will and Testimony" [will], which was admitted to probate and letters of administration c. t. a. were granted to Dauphine Deposit Trust Company [administrator]. Testator, a childless widower, was survived by six brothers and sisters, thirteen nephews and nieces and twenty-nine grandnephews and grandnieces.

The controversial portions of the will prompting these appeals are:

"[2] It is the hope and prayer, that my estate, be placed in trust for the benefit of the legal heirs, entitled to succeed to my estate.

"[3] It is the further instruction that the proceeds of my estate be placed in a Trust Fund, under the management of a reliable Agency or Banking Firm, and administered throughout the life and period of the Estate, as long as there are living legal heirs. The heirs or beneficiary to share the income from the Trust Fund.

"[4] The rate or partition shall be apportioned according to the number of living nephews and neices [sic], and thereafter equally proportioned to the surviving heirs. There shall be an exception provided in the afore-stated declaration, in the event of special hardships. The first apportionment of the income from the Trust Fund shall accrue to the benefit of the brothers and sisters, during their life.

* * *

"[7] When the Trust Fund has fulfilled its obligation to the heirs, and thereby spent its usefulness of the legal requirements, the estate shall be awarded to benevolent organizations, educational Institutions, and Charities [hereinafter collectively termed 'Charities']."

* * *

[The portion of the opinion dealing with enforceability of the trust and most of the discussion of the testator's intent are omitted.] In our view, a more accurate exposition of testator's scheme is achieved if the last sentence of paragraph four is placed first,[1] which would make the fourth paragraph read as follows:

"The first apportionment of the income from the Trust Fund shall accrue to the benefit of the brothers and sisters, during their life. The rate or partition shall [then] be apportioned according to the number of

---

1. For purposes of clarification, the original fourth paragraph reads as follows: "[4] The rate or partition shall be apportioned according to the number of living nephews and neices [sic], and thereafter equally proportioned to the surviving heirs. There shall be an exception provided in the aforestated declaration, in the event of special hardships. The first apportionment of the income from the Trust Fund shall accrue to the benefit of the brothers and sisters during their life."

living nephews and nieces, and thereafter equally proportioned to the surviving heirs. There shall be an exception provided in the aforesaid declaration, in the event of special hardships."

This rearrangement accords with our previous interpretation of testator's intent to be that *all* the brothers and sisters should share equally, or per capita, in the first life estates of income and that testator's "partition" language indicates an intent that the nieces and nephews, the recipients of the second life estates, should also share per capita as representatives of their parents. However, as testator has directed that income "shall accrue to the benefit of the brothers and sisters, during their life," we believe that *no* nephew or niece will take until the death of *the last surviving brother or sister* and not immediately upon the death of his or her parent. Lastly, we conclude from testator's language in paragraphs three ("Trust Fund * * * [to be] administered throughout the life and period of the Estate") and four ("thereafter *equally* apportioned to the surviving heirs") that testator intended class gifts of successive life estates, per capita, to his collateral descendants *ad infinitum*.[2] Thereafter, and only then, a gift over of the remainder was intended for the charities.

LEGALITY OF TESTATOR'S INTENT

At this stage we are squarely confronted, for the first time, with the controversial "wait and see" version of the Rule Against Perpetuities.[3] So much has been already written on the history and development of this subject that any further discussion would be unduly repetitious.[4] Nonetheless, the statute cannot be understood and applied without reference to the classic statement of the common law Rule Against Perpetuities as set forth in Gray, *The Rule Against Perpetuities*, § 201 (4th ed. 1942) (hereinafter "Gray"): "No interest is good unless it must vest, if at all, not later than twenty-one years after some life in being at the creation of the interest."[5] The relevant portions of the statute provide:

---

2. We cannot accept the contention advanced by the Commonwealth that the testator, by evidencing an intent to give to charity, did not want to postpone vesting indefinitely and that, therefore, testator did not intend to provide for his nephews and nieces and/or their issue. Besides ignoring one of the few unambiguous provisions of the will, this interpretation, in our opinion, would rewrite rather than construe decedent's will.

3. In previous opinions, the "wait and see" legislation was inapposite as (a) the instrument took effect before January 1, 1948, see, e.g., Taylor Estate, 384 Pa. 550, 121 A.2d 119 (1956), and Harrah Estate, 364 Pa. 451, 72 A.2d 587 (1950); or (b) a contractual provision was involved, Southeastern Pa. Trans. Auth. v. Phila. Trans. Co., 426 Pa. 377, 233 A.2d 15 (1967), cert. denied, 390 U.S. 1011, 88 S.Ct. 1259, 20 L.Ed.2d 161 (1968); or (c) as it involved an interest expressly made exempt by statute, see, e.g., Dreisbach Estate, 384 Pa. 535, 121 A.2d 74 (1956) (cemetery trust). Since this will took effect on July 27, 1967, the date of testator's death, the "wait and see" statute is applicable. Estates Act of 1947, Act of April 24, 1947, P.L. 100, § 21, 20 P.S. § 301.21.

4. See, Bregy, Intestate, Wills and Estates Acts of 1947, §§ 4, 5 (1949); Bregy, A Defense of Pennsylvania's Statutes on Perpetuities, 23 Temp.L.Q. 313 (1949); Leach, Perpetuities Legislation: Hail, Pennsylvania, 108 U.Pa.L.Rev. 1124 (1960).

5. To this statement may also be added periods of gestation. Gray, §§ 220–22; Bregy, Intestate, Wills and Estates Acts of 1947, § 4 at 5272 (1949). In this manner, one grand-nephew, born after testator's death but conceived before his death, may be considered a life in being. For purposes of brevity and simplicity, we will not refer in the text to this period of gestation although it is encompassed in the full statement of the Rule Against Perpetuities.

"Rule against perpetuities

(a) General.   No interest shall be void as a perpetuity except as herein provided.

(b) Void interest—exceptions.   Upon the expiration of the period allowed by the common law rule against perpetuities as measured by actual rather than possible events any interest not then vested and any interest to members of a class the membership of which is then subject to increase shall be void.   This subsection shall not apply to:

(1) Interest exempt at common law.   Interests which would not have been subject to the common law rule against perpetuities."

Estates Act of 1947, Act of April 24, 1947, P.L. 100, § 4, 20 P.S. § 301.4. As succinctly stated in the Commission's comments, to which we may refer, Martin Estate, 365 Pa. 280, 74 A.2d 120 (1950): "This subsection is intended to disturb the common law rule as little as possible, but to make actualities at the end of the period, rather than possibilities as of the creation of the interest, govern and to provide a more equitable disposition of void gifts."[6]

The court below, in derogation of both Quigley's Estate, 329 Pa. 281, 198 A. 85 (1938), and the "wait and see" statute, proceeded to a determination of the legality of all the future interests *upon testator's death.* The lower court's rationale was the necessity to pass on the eligibility of the charities to take under the will since the extent of their taking will affect the tax liability of the estate.   It may be true that cases such as Carter Estate, 435 Pa. 492, 257 A.2d 843 (1969), exemplify this Court's recognition of the necessity, occasioned by the federal estate and state inheritance tax laws, for a prompt determination of questions concerning future interests; however, owing to the ever-increasing extent of estate tax liability,[7] to recognize this principle in this context would emasculate the "wait and see" rule.   We cannot adopt the rationale of the court below in this respect.

In our analysis we deem it best to first consider the legality of the most remote interest—the remainder over to the charities.   Both at common law, Philadelphia v. Girard's Heirs, 45 Pa. 9, 26 (1863), and by later legislation, Act of May 9, 1889, P.L. 173,[8] it was provided that a charitable gift can be given in perpetuity.   Accordingly, it is sometimes said to be the general rule that a charitable bequest or devise is not subject to the

---

6.   The Commission further noted:

"By regarding actualities at the end of the period, the unrealistic results based on purely theoretical possibilities are avoided.   The possibility test seems peculiarly inappropriate in most Pennsylvania cases because by the time the courts do decide upon the validity of the remainders, possibilities have become actualities.   This results because (1) the modern tendency is to uphold valid life estates even though the ultimate remainder seems obviously void, and (2) the court refuses to decide on the validity of future estates until the termination of the valid life estates. See Quigley's Est., 198 A. 85, 329 Pa. 281, on both points."

7.   Particularly apropos is the famous aphorism attributed to Benjamin Franklin that nothing is as certain as death and taxes.

8.   This Act was repealed by the Estates Act of 1947, Act of April 24, 1947, P.L. 100, § 20, 20 P.S. § 301.20, but is now incorporated in 20 P.S. § 301.4(b)(1).   See Commission's comment to subsection (b)(1).

Rule Against Perpetuities. See, Scholler Trust, 403 Pa. 97, 105, 169 A.2d 554, 558 (1961); Gray, § 589. Thus, it would appear, at first glance, that the remainder to the charities is not subject to the "wait and see" rule since Section 4(b)(1) of the statute exempts all those interests not subject to the common law Rule Against Perpetuities. However, it was also settled at common law that if a remainder over to charity constituted a contingent interest and followed an interest violative of the Rule Against Perpetuities, the charitable bequest or devise was illegal. Compare Ledwith v. Hurst, 284 Pa. 94, 130 A. 315 (1925), and Penrose Estate, 257 Pa. 231, 101 A. 319 (1917), with Gageby's Estate, 293 Pa. 109, 141 A. 842 (1928). See, also, Bregy, Intestate, Wills and Estates Acts of 1947, § 4(b)(1) at 5304 (1949); Gray, § 594; Simes, Future Interests, 279 (1951); Najarian, Charitable Giving and the Rule Against Perpetuities, 70 Dick.L.Rev. 455, 465 (1966).[9] The remainder over to charity may or may not be valid depending upon (1) whether the interest is contingent; and (2) even if contingent, whether any of the preceding interests run afoul of the Rule Against Perpetuities. In accordance with both *Quigley's Estate* and the "wait and see" rule, we will not now determine the validity of the interest to charity. In the same manner, we will discuss, but not determine, the legality of the preceding estates.

The first complicating factor is the existence of successive class gifts in this appeal. At common law it was said: "Where the gift is to a class, the class must be such that all the members of it must necessarily be ascertained and take absolutely vested interests within the period. If the gift is to a class and it is void as to any one of the class, it is void as to all: [Citations omitted]." Lockhart's Estate, 306 Pa. 394, 401, 159 A. 874, 876 (1932). Specifically, we are confronted with "gifts to a class, the membership of which is still subject to increase at the expiration of the period," Commission's comments to subsection (b), which is explicitly covered by Section 4(b) of the statute: "any interest in members of a class the membership of which is then subject to increase shall be void." Accordingly, "[u]nder the statute, the class must actually close within the period, even though it might not have." Bregy, Intestate, Wills and Estates Acts of 1947, § 4(a) and (b) at 5278 (1949).

Although its underlying premise is incorrect, the opinion of the court below effectively mirroring the common law's emphasis on possibilities at the beginning of the period rather than actualities at the end of the period, provides us with an opportunity to contrast the common law and statutory Rule Against Perpetuities. As correctly noted by the lower court, the respective interests devised and bequeathed to testator's brothers and sisters and nephews and nieces must necessarily vest within the period provided by the Rule Against Perpetuities and are valid: (1) the

---

9. Our textual discussion is not meant to disturb the equally well-established principle that a gift over taking effect upon a remote contingency from one charity, not subject to the Rule Against Perpetuities, to another charity does not run afoul of the Rule Against Perpetuities. *See* Levan's Estate, 314 Pa. 274, 171 A. 617 (1934); Lennig's Estate, 154 Pa. 209, 25 A. 1049 (1893); Lehigh University v. Hower, 159 Pa.Super. 84, 46 A.2d 516 (1946); Restatement of Property, § 397(1) (1944).

brothers and sisters because the previous death of testator's parents ensures that testator can have no other brothers and sisters; and (2) the nephews and nieces because no other nephews and nieces can be born after the death of the last surviving brother and sister, and the interest of the nephews and nieces must vest, if not immediately, within the period enunciated by the Rule Against Perpetuities. The thought implicit in this rationale is that only the brothers and sisters could qualify as measuring lives since the prior demise of their parents precludes the possibility of a "fertile octogenarian" adding yet another member to the class of brothers and sisters. Leach, Perpetuities in a Nutshell, 51 Harv. L.Rev. 638, 643–44 (1938); see, Jee v. Audley, 1 Cox 324, 29 Eng.Rep. 690 (1787). However, under the common law rule, the nephews and nieces could not be measuring lives since there was a *possibility* of "fertile octogenarian" parents (brothers and sisters) giving birth to an additional nephew and/or niece after testator's death. Thus, any interest to follow the interest of the nephews and nieces, including the remainder over to the charities, if contingent, would fall victim to the Rule Against Perpetuities. It is toward the prevention of such results that the General Assembly enacted the "wait and see" version of the Rule Against Perpetuities. In our view, three possible situations could occur by waiting and seeing.

First, if no additional nephews and nieces are born, not only do the brothers and sisters qualify as measuring lives *but also* the six nephews and nieces. Thus, the interest given to the grandnephews and grandnieces must necessarily vest within twenty-one years following the death of the last surviving nephew or niece since membership in the class of grandnephews and grandnieces could not, thereafter, increase. The gift to the charities, if contingent, however, would be valid only if all the grandnephews and grandnieces should produce no offspring.

Secondly, if no additional nephews and nieces *and* grandnephews and grandnieces are born, not only do the brothers and sisters *and* nieces and nephews qualify as measuring lives *but also* the twenty-nine grandnephews and grandnieces. In this situation, the interest to great-grandnephews and great-grandnieces would be valid since that interest must necessarily vest within twenty-one years after the death of the last surviving grandnephew or grandniece. As before, the gift to charities, if contingent, would be invalidated if any of the great-grandnephews or great-grandnieces should produce offspring.

Thirdly, if any of the brothers and sisters should prove to be "fertile octogenarians," then the common law's stress on *possibilities* coincides with the statute's emphasis on *actualities* and our earlier discussion of the opinion of the court below controls.

Since which of the three situations will eventuate is unpredictable, it is necessary that the "wait and see" rule be applied. In failing to do so, the court below fell in error.

Occurrence of Invalid Interest

Finally, we reach the fourth level of discussion: if any interest be found violative of the Rule Against Perpetuities, what disposition will be made of the corpus? It was the theory of the lower court that the intended distribution of trust income after the extinction of testator's nephews and nieces, along with the gift over in remainder to the charities, violated the Rule Against Perpetuities and that, upon the death of the last surviving nephew or niece, the corpus would pass by intestacy. Again the court below ignored the Estates Act of 1947. Section 5(c) of that Act provides:

> "Other void interests. Any other void interest shall vest in the person or persons entitled to the income at the expiration of the period described in section 4(b) ('Wait and see')."

Act of April 24, 1947, P.L. 100, § 5(c), 20 P.S. § 3015(c). Moreover, if the charitable remainder is vested, that interest is valid and Section 5(a) would then control:

> "Valid interests following void interests. A valid interest following a void interest in income shall be accelerated to the termination date of the last preceding valid interest."

Act of April 24, 1947, P.L. 100, § 5(a), 20 P.S. § 301.5(a). Since we cannot now determine with certainty what interests do not violate the Rule Against Perpetuities, we cannot determine this issue except to note that the court below's conclusion was erroneous in this respect.

Decree vacated and the matter remanded to the court below with directions to proceed in accordance with the views expressed in this opinion. Estate pay costs.

COHEN, J., did not participate in the decision of this case.

ROBERTS, J., did not participate in the consideration or decision of this case.

Notes

1. The *Pearson* decision is discussed at some length in Waggoner, Perpetuity Reform, 81 Mich.L.Rev. 1718, 1762 et seq. (1983).

2. Subsection 5(c) (now § 6105(c)) of the Pennsylvania statute quoted in the *Pearson* opinion makes a radical change in the present law under which a void interest usually results in the property's either remaining in the transferor, or passing under the residuary clause of his will or by intestacy from him. The Commission's two arguments for it are that (1) it simplifies the identification of the owner and avoids the possibility of having to trace the ownership of reversionary interests through many devolutions; (2) it may in many cases more closely approximate the expressed intent frustrated by the Rule than giving the property to those not named as beneficiaries of any interest in it— "Void remainders are usually to the issue of a life tenant, so that the void gift will usually go to the parent of the disappointed remainderman".

In Mumma v. Hinkle, 138 Legal Intelligencer, No. 47, p. 1 (Pa.Common Pleas, 1958), the court held valid under the 1947 Act an agreement that "Ethel Mumma, her heirs, executors, administrators and assigns, shall at all times in the future have an option to purchase" for $30,000 a lot of land and a restaurant and cabin business on it entitled "This is It". The option was exercised by Ethel Mumma personally six years after it was acquired. Such options are subject to the Rule against Perpetuities in Pennsylvania. See Barton v. Thaw,

246 Pa. 348, 92 A.2d 312 (1914). The court rejected the argument that the Act was not intended to apply to commercial transactions. It held the option valid because it was in fact exercised during the life of the optionee, one of the parties to the contract, giving her at that time a vested right to a conveyance.

3. Would the interests created in *Pearson* (as found by the court) be valid under the Restatement or any of the statutory wait and see formulations discussed above?

4. For discussions of the Pennsylvania Act, see Phipps, The Pennsylvania Experiment in Perpetuities, 23 Temp.L.Q. 20 (1949); Bregy, A Defense of Pennsylvania's Statute on Perpetuities, 23 Temp.L.Q. 313 (1950); Cohan, The Pennsylvania Wait-And-See Perpetuity Doctrine—New Kernels From Old Nutshells, 28 Temp.L.Q. 321 (1955); Mechem, Further Thoughts on the Pennsylvania Perpetuities Legislation, 107 U.Pa.L.Rev. 965 (1959); 60 Harv.L.Rev. 1174 (1947); 97 U.Pa.L.Rev. 263 (1948); 23 N.Y.U.L.Rev. 511 (1948); 26 Temp. L.Q. 148 (1952); 48 Mich.L.Rev. 1158 (1950) (statutory changes in general); 38 Corn.L.Q. 543 (1953) (same).

The debate over "wait and see" has been long and sometimes heated. (See for example, Leach, supra p. 827), Mechem, supra pp. 827, 829 and Fetters, supra p. 749)* It reached a climax of sorts in the meeting of the American Law Institute in 1978 when Professor Richard R. B. Powell, the Reporter for the First Restatement of Property, led an attack on a proposal to adopt the wait and see approach in Restatement, 2nd. (Proceedings of the 55th Annual Meeting of the American Law Institute (1978) pp. 222–307.) An interesting aspect of the debate was that Professor Powell and his supporters were in favor of efforts like that in New York (see p. 767 supra) to ameliorate the harsher aspects of the remote possibilities test, but drew the line at wait and see. The adoption, in 1979, of wait and see by the Restatement 2nd may be a sign of things to come although to date there have been few additional converts.

Cy pres. The final "reform" to be considered is that which would permit the reformation of instruments to the extent necessary to avoid violations of the Rule. At last count sixteen states, most by statute but four without benefit of statute, permit courts to reform instruments that violate the Rule. Nine combine cy pres with wait and see and that approach was adopted by the Restatement, Second Property. This "unlimited cy pres" approach goes far beyond the reduction of age contingency employed in Edgerly v. Barker (supra p. 812, note 3) and mandated by several statutes (supra p. 813).

The Restatement, 2d provision is typical:

§ 1.5　Consequences of the Failure of an Interest Under the Rule Against Perpetuities in a Donative Transfer

---

* On the "wait and see" philosophy in general and discussion of other possible changes, see Leach, Perpetuities in Perspective: Ending the Rule's Reign of Terror, 65 Harv.L.Rev. 721 (1952), and Leach, Perpetuities: Staying the Slaughter of the Innocents, 68 L.Q.R. 35 (1952) (similar and in part identical articles); Simes, Is the Rule against Perpetuities Doomed? The "Wait and See" Doctrine, 52 Mich.L.Rev. 179 (1953); Tudor, Absolute Certainty of Vesting under the Rule against Perpetuities—A Self-Discredited Relic, 34 B.U.L.Rev. 129 (1954); Simes, The Policy Against Perpetuities, 103 U.Pa.L.Rev. 707 (1955); Simes, Public Policy and the Dead Hand, 32–82 (1955) (same material as in article just cited, with minor verbal changes); 92 Trusts and Estates 768 (1953) (panel discussion with Looker, Leach, Simes, and Newhall). Lynn, The Modern Rule Against Perpetuities (1965).

If under a donative transfer an interest in property fails because it does not vest or cannot vest within the period of the rule against perpetuities, the transferred property shall be disposed of in the manner which most closely effectuates the transferor's manifested plan of distribution and which is within the limits of the rule against perpetuities.

Like "wait and see" the cy pres provisions have been the subject of considerable debate. It was strongly praised by Leach and others, but the English Law Reform Commission and the drafters of the recent Illinois statute rejected it. At the least it would seem to create a risk of litigation and uncertainty that may not be worth the candle. For a discussion of some of the problems see Schuyler, The Statute Concerning Perpetuities, 65 Nw.L.Rev. 3, 22–25 (1970); Sparks, A Decade of Transition in Future Interests, 45 Va.L.Rev. 339, 495–498 (1959); Powell, How Far Should Freedom of Disposition Go, 26 Record of Ass'n of the Bar, City of N.Y. 8, 14–15 (1971).

In any event, cy pres should not be relied on by the lawyer who practices in the field, any more than a saving clause or the chance that a court may save an interest by artificial construction. Given the low level of competence on the subject frequently exhibited by lawyers and courts, the existence of salvage devices is no doubt reassuring. But litigation over the effect of a provision means that the draftsman has failed in one of his important objectives; and if litigation is to be avoided, the Rule must still be mastered.

The reforms have been responsive to a wave of criticism, mostly by scholars, and some of it undoubtedly over-exuberant. (Even Professor Leach conceded that his articles in 1952—"Ending the Rule's Reign of Terror" and "Staying the Slaughter of the Innocents" (cited supra p. 836) were in part the product of "hamming it up." 108 U.Pa.L.Rev. 1124, 1152. Whether the Rule was quite as destructive as depicted is a debated question. Except for the old New York rule which did seriously interfere with normal family arrangements, there does not seem to be much evidence of difficulty. Most of the reported violations seem to involve unwitting failure to take into account the more extreme applications of the remote possibilities test or the postponement of vesting beyond age twenty-one and many people believe reform should be limited (as in New York, see p. 767 supra) to curing these "technical" violations. Others feel (and the 2nd Restatement of Property is in accord) that reform should apply to all violations. In some respects the argument is between those who believe that testators who don't understand the Rule (or whose lawyers don't) should suffer the consequences and those who believe the law should provide to everyone the protection against the Rule that a sophisticated lawyer would ordinarily provide. On this question and other aspects of the debate over reform, see Waggoner, Perpetuity Reform, 81 Mich.L.Rev. 1718 (1983).

SECTION FOUR. POWERS OF APPOINTMENT

A. INTRODUCTION

A power of appointment may be generally defined as a power created by one person (the donor) in another (the donee), or reserved by the donor to himself, to determine the transferees of property (the appointees) or the shares of interests which the appointees are to take. Instruments creating such powers frequently make gifts in default of appointment to those who are to receive the property if the power is not effectively exercised (the takers in default).

Powers of appointment, which were little used in the United States at the turn of the century, are now among the most important of estate planning devices. While, for somewhat arbitrary reasons, they are not regarded as "future interests," they involve many of the same problems—notably the application of the Rule against Perpetuities. The perpetuities aspects of powers of appointment are dealt with in Subsection B; Subsection C deals with several non-perpetuities (and non-tax) aspects of the creation and exercise of powers; the Estate and Gift tax treatment of powers is discussed in Chapter Ten.

The treatment of powers of appointment for tax, perpetuities and other purposes depends upon a rather elaborate classification of powers of appointment which has developed over the years. A basic distinction has been that between general and special powers. A popular notion of a general power is that it is one that may be exercised in favor of anybody. A special power is one that may be exercised only in favor of a limited group, not including the donee or his estate, such as a power given to a life tenant to appoint among his children. These definitions work well enough for most practical purposes, although they are not all-inclusive. For example, under them, a power to appoint to anybody in the world except the donee or his estate or their creditors would not be either a general power, because of the exclusion of the donee or his estate, and their creditors, or a special power, because the appointees are otherwise unlimited. The drafters of the First Restatement of Property felt, and until recently it was probably true, that such powers were so rarely created as to make further sub-classification unnecessary. However, the Internal Revenue Code of 1954 (Sec. 2041) defines (with certain exceptions) a general power as "a power which is exercisable in favor of the decedent, his estate, his creditors, or the creditors of his estate * * *." The Code does not use the term "special power" although the term has been applied colloquially to all other powers (which have significant tax advantages over general powers). In 1965, New York adopted the Internal Revenue Code definition of general powers and, in addition, defined all other powers as special. N.Y.—McKinney's EPTL 10–3.2.

Given the importance of tax considerations in estate planning it is not surprising that today powers are frequently drafted to permit exercise in favor of anyone except the donee or his estate or the creditors of either. Presumably in response to the development of that practice the Restatement of Property 2nd (Donative Transfers) has adopted the Internal Revenue Code definition of a general power. (§ 11.4(1)) It has also abandoned the term special power of appointment in favor of "non-general" which includes all powers of appointment not exercisable in favor of the donee, his estate, his creditors or the creditors of the estate. (§ 11.4(2)) The new usage has the virtue of avoiding the gap in the First Restatement—a class of powers not satisfying either definition. It has the drawback of requiring, in the treatment of some aspects of special powers, a sub-classification of non-general powers exercisable only in favor of a "particularly defined limited class." It has, in our view, the further drawback of abandoning a traditional usage without much gain and, while the new usage may eventually carry the day, we shall continue to use the traditional term special power of appointment.

Another distinction with important legal consequences is that between powers "presently exercisable" and powers which, at the time in question, are not exercisable until the occurrence of some event, or the passage of some specified period of time. In theory, powers "not presently exercisable" could come in infinite variety; in practice, the characteristic which makes them "not presently exercisable" is almost always that they can only be exercised by the will of the donee. Accordingly, we shall use the term "testamentary" as the complement of "presently exercisable."

The basic common law theory of the effect of exercising a power of appointment was that the appointee took under the instrument creating the power, rather than under the instrument exercising it. This is often referred to as the "relation back" doctrine, the conception being expressed by saying that the exercise of the power relates back to its creation and operates as if it were incorporated in the instrument creating it. A somewhat less abstract explanation of the same theory is that the exercise of the power is regarded not as a dispositive act, but as the occurrence of a factual event specified in the instrument creating the power as a condition precedent to the appointee's receiving an interest under that instrument. Simes and Smith, Law of Future Interests § 913. This is, of course, not an essential conclusion, since it would be perfectly reasonable to consider the exercise of the power a legal disposition, and the common law theory has not been followed uniformly.

This common law theory was adopted with the first extensive employment of powers of appointment, which was in connection with the system of uses. A major reason for the popularity of that system was that it enabled landowners to achieve the effect of a will, despite the rule existing in England from the thirteenth century until the Statute of Wills of 1540 that real property could not be devised. The advantages of a will could be most closely approximated by the owner's reservation of a power of appointment that would leave him free to choose his successors in ownership at any time up to his death. For example, A could transfer land to B and his heirs to the use of such persons as A should by will appoint, and until or in default of such appointment to the use of A and his heirs. Before the enactment of the Statute of Uses in 1535, the Chancellor would enforce against B any appointment made by A. The appointees were considered as taking under the inter vivos transfer reserving the power rather than under the will exercising it, thus avoiding any verbal or doctrinal conflict with the rule against devising land. When, after the Statute of Uses and the Statute of Wills of 1540, the law courts acquired jurisdiction over many of the former equitable interests, they followed the same theory for powers of appointment. 7 Holds. 153–9; Simes and Smith, § 872; Am.L.Prop., § 23.2. The exercise of a power could be analogized to any other event the occurrence of which would shift the right to possession from one person to another. If A should transfer to the use of B and his heirs but if B die without issue living at his death then to the use of C and his heirs, and if B died without issue, C would be entitled under a shifting use. If A should transfer to the use of B and his heirs but if A should appoint then to the use of A's appointees, and if A later appointed to C and his heirs, C could also be deemed to take under a shifting use. In both cases it could be said that C took under A's original transfer, exercise of the power being considered as much of a factual contingency (as distinguished from a legal disposition) in the second case as death without issue would be in the first. Simes and Smith, § 912.

The general function of a power of appointment today is to make a disposition more flexible than it would be if it finally and irrevocably named all takers, either as individuals or as a class. The exigencies of the future cannot be foreseen. For example, a father might set up a trust to pay the income to his daughter for life and the principal on her death to her surviving issue per stirpes or in default of such issue to his son. But events may occur during the daughter's lifetime that would make this disposition of the principal inappropriate. General economic or legal conditions may change. The extent to which different children or grand-children of the daughter may ultimately need or deserve property or be capable of handling it may vary considerably. Any number of unpredictable eventualities may arise. Giving the daughter a power of appointment over the principal will enable her to adjust the disposition to the situation existing when the power is exercised. If the father wished to project his control to the extent of insuring that the principal would go to the daughter's surviving issue if she had any, and at the same time to give his daughter discretion to determine the shares, he could give her a special power to appoint among such issue, with a gift in default of appointment to such issue or in default of such issue to his son. Or, if the father wished to yield all control over the principal to his daughter if she chose to assert it, but wanted to prevent her from making any final disposition until her death, so that she could adjust the appointment to changing conditions during her lifetime, he could give her a general testamentary power of appointment, with like gifts in default. The combination of a trust and a power of appointment will thus enable the transferor to prescribe for those whose circumstances and characteristics are known to him and to indicate any general preferences for ultimate distribution, and at the same time to avoid irrevocable and perhaps unduly rigid restrictions for the unpredictable future.

Notes

1. The English law developed a threefold classification of powers of appointment based on the criterion of what other interest, if any, donees had in the property subject to the power. If the donee had no interest in the property other than the power of appointment (to B for life and after his death as C shall appoint), the power was said to be simply or purely collateral. If the donee had an interest in the property, but it would not be affected by the exercise of the power (to B for life and after his death as B shall by will appoint), the latter was called a power in gross. If the donee had an interest in the property which

would be affected by the exercise of the power (to such persons as B shall appoint and in default of appointment to B and his heirs), the donee was said to have a power appendant or appurtenant.

The idea of a power appendant is difficult to justify conceptually. For example, if a deed should give the same grantee both a fee simple and a power of appointment over the same land, it would seem reasonable to write off as nugatory surplusage the language purporting to create the power, since it would add nothing to the complete power of disposition which the grantee would have as fee simple owner. The concept did have an ad hoc utility in the early English law, for example as a means of avoiding certain restrictions on the devise of land held by knight's service, and as a means of avoiding dower. But there is very little American case law dealing with powers appendant, and they would seem to serve no justifiable modern purpose. Both the Property Restatement and modern commentators would eliminate the concept of a power appendant. Rest. 2d Prop. (Donative Transfers) § 12.3; Simes (hb) 125; Simes and Smith, § 914; Am.L.Prop., § 23.13.

2. A few American jurisdictions, following the lead of the New York legislation of 1828, have made statutory modifications of the law of powers of appointment. For references to these statutes, see Simes and Smith, § 1081; Am.L.Prop., § 23.2.

B. POWERS OF APPOINTMENT AND THE RULE AGAINST PERPETUITIES

For a variety of reasons, it seems preferable to deal with the application of the Rule to powers of appointment mainly through textual exposition rather than through cases. This long note attempts to classify the problems in orderly sequence stating and quoting from leading decisions, and suggesting some simple "rules" which should help your analysis of those problems. We are concerned with the common law Rule and the common law of powers of appointment.

The first step in understanding the application of the Rule to powers of appointment is to realize that there are two ways in which the Rule may invalidate a disposition: (1) the Rule may make the power itself void in the sense that no valid appointment can be made under it; or (2) even though the power is itself valid, it may be exercised in such a way as to make the attempted appointment void under the Rule.

For both questions—the validity of the power itself, and the validity of the appointed interests—it is necessary to distinguish between a general power "presently exercisable" * and *all* other powers of appointment,

---

* The term "presently exercisable" is somewhat awkward in analyzing the validity of a power of appointment under the Rule, where the question often is when the power will become exercisable. Nevertheless, for the sake of consistency we prefer "presently exercisable" to the more descriptive (in this context) term "exercisable by deed." For perpetuities purposes, the critical element is that the power will be exercisable in the lifetime of the donee, and not only by his will. In addition, since powers exercisable by deed only are thought to be extremely rare (See Third Report, New York Temporary Commission on Estates 622 (1964)) "presently exercisable" includes powers exercisable by deed or will. In at least two states, it is provided by statute that where a power is made exercisable by deed only, it is nevertheless exercisable by will unless such exercise is expressly excluded. McKinney's N.Y. EPTL 10–6.2; Minn.Stat.Ann. § 502.64. This seems to be the position of the Restatement. Restatement Second, Property (Donative Transfers) § 12.2, Comment b.

namely, general testamentary powers and special powers whether testamentary or presently exercisable. Since the donee of a general power presently exercisable can appoint to himself at any time, such a power is considered the equivalent of ownership of a fee simple for the purpose of the Rule. However, the great majority of American decisions have refused to apply the "equivalent of ownership" theory to a general testamentary power. The logic of the American rule depends on the associated rule that a contract to exercise a testamentary power in a particular way is unenforceable. See Section C–3, infra p. 858.

The following excerpts from Northern Trust Co. v. Porter, 368 Ill. 256, 13 N.E.2d 487 (1938) (368 Ill. at 261–63, 13 N.E.2d at 490) indicate the nature of this problem:

> Professor Gray asserted that the period of perpetuities begins to run from the date of the creation of a general testamentary power. On the other hand, Professor Kales argued that the date of the exercise of the power was the time from which the period should be computed. (26 Harvard Law Review 64, 26 H.L.R. 720–727.) Both Gray and Kales agreed that the test as to when the period of perpetuities should start to run depended upon whether the donee was "practically the owner" of the appointive fund. Gray contended, with forcefulness, that the donee of a testamentary power of appointment "is not practically the owner; he cannot appoint to himself; he is, indeed, the only person to whom he cannot possibly appoint, for he must die before the transfer of the property can take place." (Gray on Perpetuities, (3d Ed.) sec. 526(b).) Kales replied that the time for determining whether or not the donee was "practically the owner" was at the moment of exercising the power. It was his view that the donee of a general power to appoint by will is, at the moment when he may exercise the power, practically the owner. (Kales, Estates and Future Interests, (2d Ed.) sec. 695.) To this, Gray countered: "But a man cannot, in the eye of the law, be at the same time alive and dead. So long as he is alive, the condition necessary for the exercise of the power is not fulfilled, and after he is dead, he cannot be an appointee." (Gray on Perpetuities, sec. 952). * * *

> The most recent text-writer upon this subject is Professor Simes of Michigan. He sums up the law as follows: " * * * The weight of authority in the United States, and, it is believed, the better reason is in favor of the view that a general power to appoint by will should be treated as a special power in this respect, and that the period should be computed from the time of the creation of the power. * * * [F]rom a practical standpoint the position of the donee of a general power to appoint by will is very different from that of the donee of a power to appoint by deed. Wills are not, as a rule, commercial transactions. The fact that a man has an unrestricted power to appoint property by will does not mean that he is likely to put the property on the market and sell it. * * * "

> After a careful consideration, we prefer to adopt the views expressed by Professors Gray and Simes * * *.

For the rest of this note we follow the prevailing American practice and classify (for purposes of the Rule) general testamentary powers with special powers rather than with general powers presently exercisable.

1. Validity of the power

(a) *General powers presently exercisable.* A general power presently exercisable is valid if it is *certain to become exercisable* within the period of the rule. (The cases and scholars usually talk in terms of the interest being certain to *vest* within the period. As long as by *vest* they mean become exercisable there is little difficulty; but vest, as we know, is a word easily misunderstood, and in our view it is best avoided in this context.)

How would the Rule against Perpetuities affect the following powers?

(1) Testamentary trust to pay the income to B (who survived the testator) for life, and on B's death to pay the income in equal shares to B's surviving children for their lives, and on the death of any such child of B to pay a proportionate part of the principal equal to his share of the income to such person or persons as such child shall appoint. See Am. L.Prop., § 24.31; cf. Leach, 51 Harv.L.R. 638, 653 (1938).

(2) Testamentary trust to pay the income to B (who was living and unmarried at the testator's death) for life, and on B's death to pay the income in equal shares to B's surviving children for their lives, and on the death of any such child of B to pay a proportionate part of the principal equal to his share of the income to such person or persons as such child shall, if and after he attains the age of 25 years, appoint. See Prop.Rest., § 390, Comment e.

(3) Testamentary trust to pay the income to B (who survived the testator) for life, and on B's death to pay the income in equal shares to B's surviving children for their lives, and on the death of the last life tenant to pay all of the principal to such person or persons as the last surviving life tenant shall appoint. See In re Hargreaves, supra, p. 751.

(b) *General testamentary and special powers.*

A general testamentary power or a special power whether testamentary or presently exercisable is invalid if it *may be exercised* beyond the permissible period of the Rule.

For example, in Burlington County Trust Co. v. Di Castelcicala, 2 N.J. 214, 66 A.2d 164 (1949), a will gave the residuary estate in trust to pay the income to testatrix's husband for life, then to divide the income equally between her two daughters (her only children) during their lives; on the death of either daughter to pay her share of the income to her children during their lives, "with the power of disposal by will of the mother's share of the principal". The majority of the court held all the life estates valid, but the power void; they interpreted the quoted language as giving the testamentary power to dispose of one-half of the principal to the survivor of the children of each daughter. The majority opinion stated (2 N.J. at 224, 66 A.2d at 169):

> A power is subject to the rule against perpetuities and is, when created by will, void unless, by its authorizing language, it must be exercised within a life or lives in being and twenty-one years thereafter. * * * If a power can be exercised at a time beyond life or lives in being plus twenty-one years from its creation, it is bad. * * * If it be, as we have found,

that the gift of the life estates to grandchildren was not to living individuals but to a class which might be augmented at an undetermined date after the testatrix' death   *   *   *   it follows that the death of the survivor and therefore the exercise of the power of disposition might come at a period too remote to be effective; and that spells the invalidity of the power.

The dissent is this case construed the quoted language as giving each child of each daughter a power of appointment over that grandchild's share and held that such powers were valid as to any grandchild of the testatrix who was in being at the death of the testatrix (i.e., the opinion assumed that the powers would be separable for the purpose of the Rule against Perpetuities).   Since, at the time of the suit, both of the daughters were dead (although they survived the testatrix), and since in fact all of the grandchildren were born before the testatrix died, the dissent would have held the powers totally valid.

What is the theory on which such powers are held void ab initio if it is possible that they may be exercised after the expiration of the period of the Rule?   See Simes (hb) 293; Simes and Smith, § 1273.

It should be emphasized that the requirement for the initial validity of such a power is merely that it be certain that it will be exercised within the period of the Rule, and not that it also be certain that any appointment made under it will also comply with the Rule.   In other words, as indicated infra, *the validity of appointments under a power that must be exercised within the period of the Rule is determined by the appointments actually made, and not on the basis of the possibility existing at the time of the creation of the power that such appointments might be too remote.* In view of the prevalent tendency to invalidate a disposition if there is any possibility of its creating interests that may vest too remotely, why have not the courts invalidated powers ab initio if there is a chance that appointments made under them might violate the Rule?   See Gray, § 510.

What would be the effect of adopting the alternative just suggested on the following types of dispositions: B for life, then to such of B's issue and in such shares as B shall by deed appoint; B for life, then to such person or persons as B shall by will appoint?

2. *Validity of the appointed interests*

If the power of appointment is invalid, no valid appointment may be made by the donee.   Assuming that the power is valid, the next question is whether the appointed interests are valid.   Here again it is important to distinguish between general powers presently exercisable and all other powers.

(a) *General powers presently exercisable.*

In the case of general powers presently exercisable, the validity of the appointed interests is measured from the date of exercise, i.e., there is no difference under the Rule between interests created pursuant to such a power and interests created in property owned in fee simple.

A leading American case on this point is Mifflin's Appeal, 121 Pa. 205, 15 A. 525 (1888).   The actual dispositions in that case are too complicated to justify complete reproduction here; but, simplified, they would be the equivalent of the following: An inter vivos trust of land for Sarah Mifflin for life gave Sarah the power to transfer the land to any person or persons either during her lifetime or by will. Sarah later died leaving a will in which she exercised the power by appointing the property as follows: in trust to pay one-seventh of the income to each of Sarah's seven children during their lives and on the death of any such child a one-seventh interest in the land to his or her surviving issue (with various other alternative gifts over). The decision would support the validity of the gift to the issue of Sarah's children, whether or not such children were in being at the date of the inter vivos trust creating the power; one son of Sarah's was born several years after that trust was created. The court followed the orthodox view that the validity of an appointment by one holding a general power presently exercisable should be determined by running the period of the Rule from the date of the exercise of the power. Since the power was exercised at Sarah's death, this would of course make all Sarah's children lives in being, so that gifts vesting at the deaths of such children would be valid. If, on the other hand, the period of the Rule were to run from the date of the inter vivos trust creating the power, the gift to the issue of Sarah's children would be void at least as to the issue of such children as were not in being at the date of that trust.

The lower court opinion (affirmed on appeal) read in part (121 Pa. at 213):

> In whatever words an estate is conferred, and although it be only for life, it cannot * * * be a perpetuity, if the holder is clothed with power that will enable him to set aside the limitations imposed by the original grantor and confer an absolute interest on himself or on another person. Such a tenant is, so far as he himself is concerned, and in every essential particular, as much an owner as if he had the fee * * *. He can at any moment loose the bonds by which it is fettered and render it as available for the purposes of life and business as if there were no settlement. It is not therefore surprising that the English courts should have held that when property is settled on A. for life, with power to will and convey, he may make any disposition of it which would be valid if he were absolutely the owner; and, in determining whether the limitations which he creates contravene the rule against perpetuities, the computation will date from the period when the power is exercised, and not from the execution of the instruments by which the power was conferred.

The appellate court, speaking of Sarah Mifflin's power, said (121 Pa. at 224, 15 A. at 528):

> As a matter of course, if Mrs. Mifflin had actually executed the power of sale and caused the title to be conveyed to herself in fee simple, as she had the plain right to do, the limitations of her will would have to be determined upon their own merits, regarding her as the owner in fee and disregarding the previous state of the title. But so far as the application of the rule against perpetuities is concerned, the situation is precisely the same as if she had executed the power * * *. It was entirely within her power to become the owner in fee simple of the estates granted and to totally

defeat any ulterior limitations. It proves nothing to say she did not exercise her power [by this the court means that she did not exercise the power to transfer to herself during her lifetime, as distinguished from the appointment in fact made in her will] and that therefore the situation is the same as though she never had the power. For certain purposes and in certain cases that, of course, is true. But in considering merely the application of the rule against perpetuities, it is not true, because that rule requires that the estates in question should be indestructible, and an estate which can be destroyed by the person who holds it for the time being is not indestructible.

(b) *General testamentary powers and special powers.*

For all other powers, the normal rule is that the perpetuities period begins to run on the effective date of the creation of the power. However, in testing the validity of the appointed interests circumstances are ascertained as they actually exist at the time of exercise. This latter aspect—known as the second look doctrine—has some of the effect of a wait and see approach but it is not the same and must be carefully distinguished.

Treating the appointed interests as though they were created by the donor is, of course, entirely consistent with the relation back doctrine. For a justification of this approach in terms of doctrine and policy, see Gray, § 514; Leach, 51 Harv.L.R. 638, 653 (1938).

The exhaustive opinion in Minot v. Paine, 230 Mass. 514, 120 N.E. 167, 1 A.L.R. 365 (1918) reads in part (230 Mass. at 518–523, 120 N.E. at 169–171):

The nature of the power created by will and conferred upon a donee to appoint property by will has been considered by this court in several different aspects. * * *

This review of our decisions demonstrates that in all other respects where the question has arisen, the property appointed is regarded as the property of the donor and is treated as passing under his will, manifested by the words employed by the person upon whom he has conferred the power to express his testamentary design in specified particulars. It seems difficult to say, in view of the reasoning upon which these decisions rest, that, when the rule against perpetuities is to be applied, the ground is to be shifted and the property is to be regarded as that of the donee and disposed of by his will.

* * * As was said by Chief Justice Baldwin in Bartlett v. Sears, 81 Conn. 34, 44, 70 A. 33, 37 (1908): "One to whom a power of appointment is given by will stands to the testator substantially in the position of an agent toward his principal. An agent cannot do that which the principal cannot do." The essential nature of his act in exercising the power is that he is speaking for the original testator in directing the devolution of the property of the latter. * * *

The donee in exercising the power is in effect writing the will of the donor respecting the appointed property. The donee in doing this in reason is bound by the same limitations of the law as bound the original testator. The donee can take advantage of facts of which the donor was ignorant because they were not in existence when he made his will. But the donee cannot free himself from the rules of law which limited the power of the donor. The will of the donor and that of the donee so far as it exercises the power of appointment in a sense together constitute the complete testamentary design of the donor respecting the donor's estate. The words used by the donee in exercising the power are to be construed and interpreted as to their meaning in the light of the facts as they are at the time the power is exercised. The will of the donor is projected forward to the time of the exercise of the power so as to receive the benefit of the facts which have appeared since his decease. * * *

Both on principle and on authority our conclusion is that the remoteness of an appointment, made in the exercise of a power to appoint by will alone, so far as affected by the rule against perpetuities must be measured from the time of creation and not the exercise of the power.

As noted above, this treatment of general testamentary powers, although the prevailing American view, is not unanimous. See, e.g., Industrial National Bank of Rhode Island v. Barrett, 101 R.I. 89, 220 A.2d 517 (1968) where the court discusses the pros and cons of the argument and adopts the minority rule by which the validity of interests appointed under a general testamentary power is measured from the date of exercise.

In your view, which approach is more likely to achieve the objectives of the Rule? See the discussion of this question in Proceedings, American Law Institute, 56th Annual Meeting, 434–442. In the end, the Restatement, Second, Property (Donative Transfer) § 1.2, Comment d, adheres to the general American rule.

An even more radical view is espoused by the Delaware statute (25 Del.Code § 501) under which the validity of interests created by the exercise of powers, including special powers, is measured from the date of exercise rather than the date of creation. This statute has necessitated a special provision of the Federal Estate Tax law. See p. 924, infra.

It is sometimes said that appointed interests are "read back" into the will of the donor (or other creating instrument); this is a reasonably descriptive phrase for most purposes but it does not reflect the potential importance of the second look doctrine. The effect of that doctrine is described in In re Warren's Estate, 320 Pa. 112, 182 A. 396, 104 A.L.R. 1345 (1936):

> Suppose A bequeaths his estate to B for life, and after B's death to B's children for the life of the survivor with provision that upon the death of any of B's children so possessing a life estate, their children should take the deceased parent's share until the decease of the surviving child, with remainder over to the issue of all children. Obviously, the substitutionary provisions for the disposition of the income until the death of the surviving child would be void as too remote. It would be possible that one of B's children might die over 21 years after B's death, and then let in a new estate. Therefore, the whole provision as to the substitutionary gift of income would be void, as would the remainder. On the other hand, if A gives his estate to B for life with a general power of appointment, and B gives the estate to her children for life of the survivor (who are all living at the death of A) and under exactly the same provisions as above stated,

then the whole disposition is valid. The naming of these children, so living, is but "lighting another candle" which is burning during the lives of A and B. It is still necessary to look to the original will or deed, and to read into it the terms of the appointment. However, where it appears that the appointment in fact names persons in being in the lifetime of the donor, the disposition is valid and is not rendered void because it might have been possible to appoint otherwise.

In re Warren's Estate represents the prevailing American and English point of view.

What would be the doctrinal basis for determining this issue in the context only of such circumstances as existed at the time the power was created?

Is there any justification for distinguishing for this purpose between ordinary gifts and those made by exercising a power, so as to permit the court in the latter case to take into consideration circumstances existing at the time of the appointment? See Am.L.Prop., § 24.35; Gray, §§ 523–523.6.

The following appointments would be valid under the prevailing view. Why?

(a) A's will created a testamentary trust to pay the income to B for life, and to pay the principal on B's death to such persons as B should by will appoint. B later died, leaving a will appointing the property to a trustee in trust to pay the income to B's husband for life, and from his death until the death of the last surviving child of B to pay the income in equal shares per stirpes to B's living children and to the living issue of any deceased child of B; and on the death of B's last surviving child, to divide the principal per stirpes among the issue then living of B's deceased children. B had two children, X and Y, both of whom survived B and both of whom were born before the death of A.

(b) A's will created a testamentary trust to pay the income to B for life, and on B's death to hold the property in trust for such issue of B, and on such terms and in such shares, as B should by deed appoint. B later died, leaving a will appointing the property to the trustees of A's estate to pay the income in equal shares per stirpes to B's living children and to the living issue of any deceased child of B until B's youngest child should reach the age of 30 or die under that age; and when B's youngest child should reach the age of 30 or die under that age to divide the principal per stirpes among B's issue then living. B had three children, X, Y, and Z, all of whom were conceived and born after A's death, and all of whom survived B. At B's death, X was 29 years old, Y was 28, and Z was 25.

(c) A's will created a testamentary trust to pay the income to B for life, and to pay the principal on B's death to such persons as B should by will appoint. B's son, S, was conceived and born after A's death, but S predeceased B. B later died, leaving a will appointing the property in equal shares to "the children of my son, S". If B's appointment to S's children would give the latter the right to possession at B's death, would the appointment be valid if S survived B?

For additional discussion of the second look doctrine, see Simes (hb) 294; Simes and Smith, § 1274; Am.L.Prop., § 24.35; Prop.Rest., § 392. See also In re Estate of Bird, 37 Cal.Rptr. 288 (Dist.Ct.App.1964).

3. Validity of gifts in default of appointment

The final problem in this area is that of the *appropriate criteria for determining the validity under the Rule against Perpetuities of a gift in default of appointment, in the event that the power of appointment expires* (by, e.g., the death of the donee) *without having been exercised.*

(a) If the donee of a *general power presently exercisable* should die without exercising it, what would be the argument for judging the validity of the gift in default by running the period from, and considering the circumstances existing at, the time of the donee's death? This approach is favored by Prop.Rest., § 373, Comment c, and by Am.L.Prop., § 24.36. The latter authors, for example, would sustain the validity of the gift in default in a case like the following:

A's will created a testamentary trust to pay the income to B for life, and then to transfer the principal to such person or persons as B should by deed appoint, and in default of appointment to pay the principal to such of B's children as should reach the age of 30. B later died without making any appointment. B had two children, X and Y, both of whom were conceived and born after A's death. At the time of B's death, X was 5 years of age, and Y was 3.

What would be the argument in such a case for allowing X and Y to take the property if they reach thirty?

No case on this point has been found, perhaps because general powers presently exercisable are not frequently created. Cf., however, Ryan v. Ward, supra, p. 786.

(b) *If the donee of a general testamentary power* or of a *special power* should die without exercising it, the period of the Rule would presumably run for the purpose of determining the validity of a gift in default from the effective date of the instrument creating the power and making such gift in default, since this would be true if the power were exercised.

Would the circumstances determining whether such a gift in default was void be those at the time of the instrument making the gift in default also? Or would the court consider the circumstances existing at the time when the power expired by the donee's death?

In Sears v. Coolidge, 329 Mass. 340, 108 N.E.2d 563 (1952), an inter vivos trust created by the settlor's deed in 1913, following certain income trusts, gave the principal in equal shares to the settlor's issue who should be living (1) at the death of the survivor of the settlor's issue who should be living at the settlor's death or (2) when the settlor's youngest surviving grandchild who should be living at the settlor's death should attain the age of fifty. The trust deed then reserved to the settlor the power to change the trust in any manner "except such as will vest in myself the trust property or any beneficial interest therein", and to appoint the property to persons other than those specified in the deed; any such change or appointment to be made by deed of the settlor delivered to the trustee. The court treated this as the equivalent of "a special power to appoint by deed". 329 Mass. at 344, 108 N.E.2d at 566. The settlor died in 1920 without exercising the power, and the second of the two alternative conditions occurred in 1951, when the youngest grandchild living at the settlor's death attained the age of fifty.

At the time of the trust deed, the settlor was a widower aged 81, and two of his four children had died; his two living children were daughters aged 59 and 55 respectively; his ten living grandchildren ranged in age from 7 to 35; no more grandchildren were born after the trust deed, which is scarcely surprising. However, the opinion does not refer to any argument that the settlor would contemplate only his grandchildren existing at the time of the trust deed, so as to make the youngest grandchild to reach 50 a life in being and validate the gift on the second alternative contingency. See Simes and Smith, § 1230; Wright's Estate, p. 815, supra.

The court, however, validated the gift in default with the following reasoning; since the circumstances existing when a special power is exercised are taken into consideration in determining the validity of an appointment, it is reasonable to consider the circumstances at the time when such a power expires in determining the validity of a gift in default; operating on that theory, the gift in default was valid because it was known at the death of the settlor that any grandchild then living (whose attainment of 50 would cause the second alternative contingency to occur) would also have been living at the date of the trust deed (and was thus a life in being who would have to attain 50 within his own lifetime). The court specifically relied on the recommendation of such a result in Am. L.Prop., § 24.36 (Leach and Tudor). The opinion read in part (329 Mass. at 346, 108 N.E.2d at 567):

> In the case of the trust instrument under consideration until it became too late for the settlor to exercise the reserved power no one could tell what might be the ultimate disposition of the trust property. As long as there remained a right to change, alter, and make new appointments, no instruction to the trustees or declaratory decree would ordinarily have been given as to the validity of the settlor's limitations. * * * Upon his death it could be learned for the first time what definitely were to be the terms of the trust. * * * The appellees strongly urge that the doctrine of a "second look" has no place in reading the original limitations in default of appointment, which were capable of examination when created, and which should retain the same meaning throughout. They argue that its adoption would be a nullification of the rule "that executory limitations are void unless they take effect ex necessitate and in all possible contingencies" within the prescribed period. Hall v. Hall, 123 Mass. 120, 124. But this rule, while recognized, was assuaged as to the exercise of a power of appointment in Minot v. Paine, 230 Mass. 514, 522 [120 N.E. 167, 170]. It was there deemed wise not to apply unmodified a remorseless technical principle to a case which it did not fit. That principle seems equally inappropriate here.

Leach and Tudor, in the section cited above, raise the question as to whether there should be any difference in result in the following cases:

A's will leaves property in trust to pay the income to B for life, and on B's death to pay the principal as B shall by will appoint or in default of appointment to such of B's children as attain the age of 25. B has no children at A's death, but later has two children born, X and Y. At B's death, X is 20 and Y is 15. X and Y both later reach 25. Should their rights to the property be affected by whether

(1) B leaves a will appointing to "such of my children as attain the age of 25," or

(2) B leaves a will stating, "I make no appointment under the power given to me by A's will because I desire the property to go in default of appointment under A's will," or

(3) B leaves no will?

Sears v. Coolidge appears to be the only decision on this problem. It is discussed in Simes and Smith, §§ 1230, 1277; Morris and Leach, The Rule against Perpetuities, 129, 153 (1956).

For the relationship between the Rule against Perpetuities and powers of appointment in general, see Am.L.Prop., §§ 24.30–24.36; Simes (hb) 292–95; Simes and Smith, §§ 1271–7; Gray, §§ 473–561.7; Prop. Rest., §§ 390–2; Morris and Leach, The Rule against Perpetuities, 126–155 (1956); Leach, 51 Harv.L.R. 638, 651–6 (1938); Annots. 1 A.L.R. 374 (1919); 101 A.L.R. 1282 (1935); 104 A.L.R. 1352 (1936).

4. Discretionary trusts

A discretionary income trust is void, if, under its terms, the trustee is authorized to make payments of income after the expiration of the period of the Rule against Perpetuities. Thomas v. Harrison, supra, p. 754. For example, a trust to pay over to B's children until the death of the survivor of B's children such income as the trustee shall in its absolute and uncontrolled discretion determine would be void if B were alive at the effective date of the trust.

A justifiable explanation of that result is that such a trust gives the trustee a special power to appoint the income among a class, and that, since such power is not required to be exercised within the period of the Rule, it is void ab initio and no effective appointment can be made under it. In this connection it should be noted that, unlike the First Restatement, Restatement Second, Property treats the trustee's discretion as a power of appointment (§ 11.1, Comment d).

The opinion in Re Vaux, [1938] 4 All Eng.R. 297, gave this as the alternative reason:

> Secondly, if the cause be regarded as creating a power in the trustees for the time being of the will to appoint the fund among the testator's children, or the issue of any deceased child of his, the case is one of a power which, according to its terms, can be exercised beyond the limits of the rule against perpetuities, under which an appointment can be made which would be too remote. It is well settled that the fact that within the terms of the

power an appointment can be made which would be too remote does not render the power void if it is one which cannot be exercised beyond the limits of the rule against perpetuities, but it is equally well settled that a power cannot be held to be valid if, according to its terms, it can be exercised by persons not necessarily ascertainable within the limits of the rule against perpetuities. * * *

This explanation of the invalidity of such a trust is favored by Leach, 51 Harv.L.R. 638, 652 (1938); Am.L.Prop., § 24–32; Morris and Leach, The Rule against Perpetuities, 134 (1956); Simes and Smith, § 1277.

5. Administrative powers

It is, of course, common in modern trusts to give the trustee such administrative powers as those to sell, invest, reinvest, mortgage, or lease the trust assets. Charitable trusts may last indefinitely and private trusts may endure beyond the expiration of the period of the Rule if the beneficial interests vest within the period (e.g., mandatory income trust for B's children during their lives, if B is living when the trust is created).

May such administrative powers given the trustee of such a trust be held void under the Rule on the ground that they might be exercised after the period expired? The cases are scarce. Some English decisions cast doubt on the validity of such powers. While, of course, it can be argued that such powers make possible the creation of new interests in property after the period expires, it seems nonsense in terms of policy to hold such powers void under the Rule. As the court said in Melvin v. Hoffman, 290 Mo. 464, 235 S.W. 107 (1921) (290 Mo. at 499, 235 S.W. at 116): "The power to lease, sell and reinvest, instead of impeding, facilitates the transfer of property, and is the very purpose the rule against perpetuities seeks to promote." See Leach, Powers of Sale in Trustees and the Rule against Perpetuities, 47 Harv.L.R. 948 (1934); Am.L.Prop., § 24.63; Simes and Smith, § 1277. The Restatement Second, Property (Donative Transfers) (§ 11.1 Comment e) takes the position that the obligation imposed on a trustee to be fair to all beneficiaries prevents a power of sale and reinvestment in a trustee from being a power to designate beneficial interests and, hence, from being a power of appointment. Would the same rationale apply to powers, such as the power to allocate between principal and income, which can alter beneficial interests?

C. POWERS OF APPOINTMENT—MISCELLANEOUS ASPECTS

The estate and gift tax implications of powers of appointment are covered in the next chapter. The remainder of this chapter is devoted to various matters including the creation and exercise of powers, contracts to appoint, and claims of creditors.

1. Creation of Powers of Appointment

The general rule is that no particular language is required to create a power of appointment. Although occasionally a question arises whether a power was or was not created (see, e.g., Matter of Clark, 274 App.Div.

49, 80 N.Y.S.2d 1 (1st Dep't 1945)), problems of this kind are not often encountered. N.Y.—McKinney's EPTL 10–4.1 establishes the following modest "rules for creation of a power of appointment."

(a) The donor of a power of appointment:

(1) Must be a person capable of transferring the appointive property.

(2) Must have created or reserved the power by a written instrument executed by him in the manner required by law.

(3) Must manifest his intention to confer the power on a person capable of holding the appointive property. * * *

Notwithstanding the lack of formal requirements the instrument creating the power should leave no doubt about the extent of the power, the property subject to it, the identity of the donee or donees, the identity of the permissible appointees, the identity of the takers in default of exercise, and the manner of exercise. To prevent inadvertent exercise under statutes line that in New York (p. 857, infra), it is good practice to require a specific manner of exercise.

2. Exercise of Powers of Appointment

Where a particular manner of exercise is specified in the creating instrument, e.g. a requirement that exercise be by a will specifically referring to the creating instrument, the courts will ordinarily insist that the donor's direction be followed. (Powell, ¶ 398). Even the expression of an intention to exercise "all powers of appointment" will not suffice. E.g. Schede Estate, 426 Pa. 93, 231 A.2d 135 (1967). But cf., Cross v. Cross, 559 S.W.2d 196 (Mo.1977) and First Union National Bank v. Moss, 32 N.C.App. 499, 233 S.E.2d 88 (1977).

Except for those specified in the creating instrument, if any, no particular formality or mode of expression is ordinarily required to exercise a power, provided that the intent to exercise is manifested. Here again, it does not need emphasizing that the intention to exercise should be expressed in precise terms. Where the intention is not so expressed, it is to be "ascertained from all the facts and circumstances." See Illinois State Trust Co. v. Southern Illinois National Bank, 29 Ill.App.3d 1, 329 N.E.2d 805 (5th Dist.1975) (permitting extrinsic evidence of intent to exercise).

One question that frequently arises is whether the making of a will which makes no reference to the power is to be deemed an exercise.

IN RE PROESTLER'S WILL

Supreme Court of Iowa, 1942.
232 Iowa 640, 5 N.W.2d 922.

MILLER, Justice.

* * *

Henry T. Proestler died July 4, 1919, leaving his widow, Mathilde B. Proestler, but no children, surviving him. His will was admitted to probate September 11, 1919. It provided for the payment of his debts and funeral expenses, made a number of bequests, following which, Item 13 of the will provided as follows: "All the rest, residue and remainder of the property, real, personal or mixed, of which I die seized or possessed, or to which I may be entitled, I give, devise and bequeath to Matilda B. Proestler and William Heuer in trust for the following uses and purposes: I direct that the net income from this trust fund shall be paid to my wife, Matilda B. Proestler, during her lifetime. I direct that my wife, Matilda B. Proestler, shall have the right to dispose by will of Twenty Thousand ($20,000.00) Dollars of said trust fund. All the rest, residue and remainder of said trust fund, after the death of my wife, Matilda B. Proestler, I give, devise and bequeath as follows:" (Following are set forth a number of bequests for the disposition of said trust fund.)

On September 15, 1919, the widow filed an election to take under the will and, with William Heuer, qualified as executor. The executors' final report was approved and the executors discharged January 22, 1921. The trustees named in the will carried out the provisions of the trust. On October 26, 1935, the widow died testate. Her will was admitted to probate and provides as follows:

"I, Mathilde B. Proestler, of Davenport, Scott County, Iowa, being of sound and disposing mind and memory, do hereby make, publish and declare the following as and for my Last Will and Testament, hereby revoking all former Wills.

"I. It is my will that all my just debts be first paid out of my Estate.

"II. All the rest, residue and remainder of my Estate of whatever kind and wherever situated, I will, devise and bequeath to my nephew, Werner H. Grabbe, with the request, however, that the income derived therefrom be used for the benefit, during her lifetime, of my sister, Christiane Hensen.

"III. I nominate, constitute and appoint my said Nephew, Werner H. Grabbe, Executor of this my Last Will and Testament, and exempt him from giving any bond, and I hereby grant and delegate to him as Executor full power and authority to sell and convey, mortgage or otherwise encumber, any real or personal property, should he deem it advisable, and to do any and all things as freely and fully as I myself might do, were I living, without the necessity of first obtaining an Order of Court.

"In Testimony Whereof, I have hereunto set my hand at Davenport, Iowa, this 13th day of February, A.D.1933.

"(Signed) Mathilde B. Proestler."

On March 28, 1937, Paul A. Tornquist, trustee under the will of Henry T. Proestler, appointed to succeed William Heuer, deceased, made application for instructions as to the distribution of certain funds in the trust estate, asserting among other things as follows: "That this Trustee is unable to determine whether or not the said Mathilde B. Proestler by her will did dispose of Twenty Thousand ($20,000.00) Dollars of said trust fund. Consequently, this Trustee is unable to determine how the money should be distributed which he has on hand ready for distribution." Various petitions of intervention were filed. One of the interveners, Werner H. Grabbe, the sole legatee under the will of Mathilde B. Proestler, asserted "that said Mathilde B. Proestler intended by the terms of her said Will to devise and bequeath the said Twenty Thousand ($20,000.00) Dollars to this Intervenor and that by the terms of her said Will the said Twenty Thousand ($20,000.00) Dollars was so devised and bequeathed to him." Grabbe also moved to transfer the cause to equity. This motion was sustained * * *.

Pursuant to the foregoing, the trial has now been had, in the course of which, oral testimony was offered for the purpose of showing that Mathilde B. Proestler intended by the terms of her will to devise and bequeath to Werner H. Grabbe the $20,000 referred to in her husband's will. Timely objection was interposed to the competency of such testimony. At the close of the trial, the court made the following findings:

"That there is no ambiguity in the will of Mathilde B. Proestler; nor a word nor an expression of doubtful or uncertain meaning; and hence no evidence is necessary or admissible, to clear up any doubt, or to show any surrounding facts or circumstances, or to explain or make more certain any of the wording contained in her said will.

"That the power of appointment, the right of disposal of $20,000.00 of the trust fund given to her under the provisions of the will of Henry T. Proestler, deceased, is not, and was not exercised by the will of Mathilde B. Proestler, and there is nothing in the language of her will to show that she intended to exercise it."

Pursuant to the foregoing, the decree determined "that Paul A. Tornquist, Trustee under the Will of Henry T. Proestler, deceased, be and is hereby ordered and directed, as to all the moneys now on hand in said trust and all that may hereafter be on hand and ready for distribution, to distribute the same in strict accord with the terms and provisions of the will of said Henry T. Proestler, deceased, exactly in the manner the same should and would be distributed if there had been no provision in said will giving the widow of said testator the power of disposal of $20,000.00 of said trust estate." The intervener, Werner H. Grabbe, has appealed to this court.

* * *

Both parties concede, and our investigation confirms the fact, that there is no Iowa statute upon the precise question here presented for our decision. Such being the case, it is our duty to "recognize and enforce the rules and principles of the common law," unless "the principle sought to be applied is unsuitable to our own social or political conditions, or not in harmony with the policy and objects of our own peculiar institutions". Hastings v. Day, 151 Iowa 39, 41, 130 N.W. 134, 135, 34 L.R.A.,N.S., 1021, Ann.Cas.1913A, 214, and cases cited therein.

The general common law principle is set forth in paragraph 343 of the Restatement of the Law of Property (Vol. 3, page 1913) as follows: "When the donee by his will makes a gift of the residue of his estate or otherwise manifests an intent to pass all of his property, this of itself does not manifest an intent to exercise any power." This statement is in accord with repeated pronouncements of various text books and annotators to the effect that, in the absence of statute, it is generally held that a power of appointment is not executed by the residuary clause in a will unless an intent to exercise the power appears in addition thereto from the terms of the will. See 91 A.L.R. 442, 443; 32 A.L.R. 1395; 16 Ann. Cas. 203, 204; 21 R.C.L. 796; Ann.Cas.1914D, 586, 587. This principle of the common law has been repeatedly recognized and applied in at least a dozen of the several states. [Citations omitted.]

Many well established principles of the common law are recognized and applied in the application of the rule above referred to. One principle is applied herein, namely, that, where the will is unambiguous, its interpretation is for the court and oral testimony is not admissible as a basis for the interpretation of the will. Another principle is that the will is to be interpreted from the language used therein and the words used are to be understood to mean what they say, no less and no more. Where a power of appointment is vested in one who has become deceased, it is usually held that the will of the decedent will constitute an exercise of the power in three classes of cases, to-wit: (1) Where there is a reference to the power in the will, (2) where there is a reference to the property which is the subject on which it is to be executed, and (3) where the provisions of the will would otherwise be ineffectual. In the absence of any of these three requirements, it is usually held that the power of appointment does not constitute a part of the estate and therefore a general devise of "all the rest, residue and remainder" of the estate does not constitute an exercise of the power of appointment. Accordingly, the will relied upon by the appellant herein was insufficient to constitute an exercise of the power of appointment granted to Mrs. Proestler by the will of her deceased husband. Under the principles of common law, recognized and applied in the jurisdictions above referred to, the decree of the trial court was clearly right.

* * *

By reason of the foregoing, the decree of the trial court herein must be, and it is, affirmed.

Chief Justice and all Justices concur.

Notes

1. The overwhelming majority of American decisions hold that, in the absence of statute, a general clause in a will purporting to convey all the testator's property will not as such exercise a testamentary power of appointment. (Annot. 15 A.L.R.3d 346 (1967)). And the Restatement, Second, Property (Donative Transfers) § 17.3 is in accord.

More than half the states now have statutes dealing with the question. Of these, sixteen (at last count) are patterned on § 2–610 of the Uniform Probate Code which follows the common law rule:

A general residuary clause in a will, or a will making general disposition of all of the testator's property, does not exercise a power of appointment held by the testator unless specific reference is made to the power or there is some other indication of intention to include the property subject to the power.

On the other hand, there are a substantial number of jurisdictions which have adopted statutes creating the opposite presumption. For example, N.Y.—McKinney's EPTL § 10–6.1 provides:

(a) Subject to paragraph (b), an effective exercise of a power of appointment does not require an express reference to such power. A power is effectively exercised if the donee manifests his intention to exercise it. Such a manifestation exists when the donee:

(1) Declares in substance that he is exercising all the powers he has;

(2) Sufficiently identifying the appointive property or any part thereof, executes an instrument purporting to dispose of such property or part;

(3) Makes a disposition which, when read with reference to the property he owned and the circumstances existing at the time of its making, manifests his understanding that he was disposing of the appointive property; or

(4) *Leaves a will disposing of all of his property or all of his property of the kind covered by the power, unless the intention that the will is not to operate as an execution of the power appears expressly or by necessary implication.* (Italics added.)

(b) If the donor has expressly directed that no instrument shall be effective to exercise the power unless it contains a specific reference to the power, an instrument not containing such reference does not validly exercise the power.

For a discussion of the statutes and cases, see Statutory Note and Reporter's Note to § 17.3 Restatement, Second, Property (Donative Transfers).

2. The difference of opinion just described is only about the appropriate initial presumption of intent under a rule of construction; neither view will necessarily dictate the result in the particular case, since the presumption may be held rebutted.

What would be the arguments for and against the prima facie interpretation that intent to exercise a power of appointment is manifested by such a clause in a will as "I give all the rest, residue, and remainder of my estate to B"?

3. As noted above, (see p. 853) the *donor* of a power can specify a particular manner of exercise. Can she create a presumption of exercise? In Stewart v. United States, 512 F.2d 269 (5th Cir. 1975) the trust instrument creating the power contained the following provision:

It is the true intent and meaning of this Declaration of Trust that in the making of a will by either or both the said Mildred L. Stewart or William T. Lynam, Jr., it shall not be necessary for her or him to make reference to her or his share and interest in the Trust Estate herein established, but the said share and interest shall be held to vest in their respective legatees as fully and to all intents and purposes, in the same manner as any other portion of her or his estate then actually in her or his possession, any law, custom or usage to the contrary notwithstanding.

The will of the donee did not mention the power. Despite the fact that Florida (the donee's domicile at death) follows the general common law rule (see principal case and note 1 above) the court held that the power was exercised: "The positive terms of the trust instrument therefore support the conclusion that the decedent-donee intended to exercise the power when she executed her will." 512 F.2d at 273.

4. The donee of a general power of appointment exercisable in favor of himself or his estate can create any interests in the appointive property which he could create if the property were his own. Thus he may appoint it outright or in trust or may (subject to the Rule against Perpetuities) create a power, general or special, in another. Where the power is special, of course, the donee may appoint only to an object of the power. Moreover, some decisions have held that the donee of a special power cannot appoint the property in further trust or create a new power of appointment. The Restatement, Second, Property (Donative Transfers) § 19.4 provides that, in the absence of a contrary intent by the donor, the donee of a special power may appoint in trust and may create a new power, either general or special, although the objects of a special power so created are restricted to permissible objects of the original power. For a discussion of the subject generally, see Restatement, Second, Property (Donative Transfers) Ch. 19.

3. *Contracts to Appoint and Releases of Powers of Appointment*

a. *Contracts to Appoint.*

IN RE ESTATE OF BROWN
New York Court of Appeals, 1973.
33 N.Y.2d 211, 306 N.E.2d 781, 351 N.Y.S.2d 655.

JONES, Judge.

We hold that the proscription of EPTL 10–5.3 renders unenforceable the agreement made by this decedent to exercise two general testamentary powers of appointment in favor of his son.

The decedent was the donee of two separate powers of appointment—one over the assets of a trust under his mother's 1925 will, the other over the assets of an *inter vivos* trust he himself had created in 1927. Incident to the resolution of family differences, in 1944 he agreed to exercise his powers in part in favor of his son, James, respondent herein, and at the same time executed a will making appointments in accordance with that agreement. Some 20 years later, in 1964, the decedent executed a new will in which he appointed the assets of both trusts to his estate, with no benefits flowing to the son. On his death the 1964 will was admitted to probate. In the present proceeding the son seeks to enforce his father's 1944 agreement to exercise the powers in his favor.

Surrogate's Court, Queens County, held the agreement unenforceable as to the assets of both trusts under EPTL 10–5.3. The Appellate Division reversed in part, holding that the 1944 agreement was enforceable against the assets of the *inter vivos* trust, but agreeing that enforcement was barred as to the assets of the testamentary trust.

All of us agree that the agreement cannot be enforced as to the testamentary trust; a majority of us agree with the Surrogate that the agreement cannot be enforced as to the *inter vivos* trust either.

EPTL 10—5.3 provides: "Contract to appoint, power not presently exercisable. (a) The donee of a power of appointment which is not presently exercisable, or of a postponed power which has not become exercisable, cannot contract to make an appointment. Such a contract, if made, cannot be the basis of an action for specific performance or damages, but the promisee can obtain restitution of the value given by him for the promise unless the donee has exercised the power pursuant to the contract."

It is urged, however, that, notwithstanding that EPTL 10–2.2 specifically defines "donee" of a power of appointment to include a person "in whose favor a power is reserved"—obviously a grantor—EPTL 10–5.3 should not be applied where the donee of the power is also the grantor of the trust.

We recognize that the statute may have been addressed primarily to powers of appointment created by a testator or a grantor other than the donee as to property of such testator or grantor over which the donee is accorded a power of disposition only on death (e.g., Farmers' Loan & Trust Co. v. Mortimer, 219 N.Y. 290, 114 N.E. 389)—here the mother's testamentary trust. We would be disposed, however, notwithstanding the explicit terminology of the statute, to exclude from its operation *inter vivos* trusts of which the donee was also the grantor, if in addition, by provision of the trust instrument or by operation of law, the grantor had an unlimited power to revoke the trust and thus had retained substantial dominion over the trust assets. In such instance as a practical matter any proscription of EPTL 10–5.3 could readily be circumvented by a revocation or modification of the trust to assure precisely the disposition otherwise proscribed by statute. It surely could then be argued that the Legislature could scarely have intended to prohibit a grantor from exercising a limited power as to assets over which he otherwise had unlimited power. Further, to say that where the grantor had power to *revoke* and thus to recapture the trust assets, he nevertheless could not agree to *appoint* the same assets, would be to exalt form over substance.

That is not, however, this case. Here the decedent's rights as grantor over the assets of the 1927 *inter vivos* trust must be determined under pre-1951 law (L.1951, ch. 180). Under the terms of this trust instrument itself the grantor retained very limited and carefully circumscribed powers of invasion of principal, certainly no general power of revocation. Nor, in our view, could this grantor have effected a revocation under former section 23 of the Personal Property Law, applicable to this trust. In this trust instrument following the reservation of the general testamentary power of appointment, the first gift in default of its exercise was "to the issue of the 'Grantor' *per stirpes*". The following and final limitation was "unto the next of kin of the 'Grantor' in accordance with the laws of the State of New York, in the shares and proportions to which such next of kin would be entitled". While this latter limitation in default, standing alone, might be held to have created a reversion, the specific intervening gift to issue must be held to have created a remainder. (Richardson v. Richardson, 298 N.Y. 135, 81 N.E.2d 54; cf. Matter of

Burchell, 299 N.Y. 351, 87 N.E.2d 293.) Thus the consent of these contingent remaindermen would have been a prerequisite to any revocation or amendment of the trust by the grantor under section 23 of the Personal Property Law. (2 Scott, Trusts [3d ed.], § 127.1, pp. 986–987.) It cannot be said that by operation of law the grantor of this trust had a power of revocation. Without a power reserved in the instrument or implied in law this decedent did not have such power of dominion over the assets of the 1927 *inter vivos* trust as in our view would support an argument that it should be excepted from the operative scope of EPTL 10–5.3.

Nor, in view of the explicit and distinctive provisions of EPTL 10–5.3, do we conclude that that section does not apply to trusts in which grantor and donee are the same because under the provisions of another section, EPTL 10–7.4, the creditors of such grantor-donee might reach the trust assets. We consider the rights of creditors clearly distinguishable from those of the grantor-donee.

We accordingly hold that EPTL 10–5.3 is applicable to both testamentary and *inter vivos* trusts in this case and that this decedent's agreement to exercise his powers of appointment in the prescribed manner is unenforceable as to the assets of both trusts.

We further agree with the Surrogate that on the facts in this case respondent is not entitled to any restitution under the provisions of the last sentence of EPTL 10–5.3 (subd. [a]).

Accordingly the order of the Appellate Division is reversed, the decree of Surrogate's Court is reinstated and the case is remitted to the Surrogate's Court.

[The dissenting opinion of Judge Gabrielli is omitted.]

Notes

1. The New York Statute, N.Y.—McKinney's EPTL § 10–5.3 was amended in 1977 to make clear that the prohibition of contracts to appoint does *not* apply where the donor and donee are the same person. What justification is there for a contrary position?

2. The principal case is discussed in detail in Fetters, Future Interests, 1974 Survey of N.Y.Law, 26 Syr.L.Rev. 341 (1975). In Farmers' Loan & Trust Co. v. Mortimer (cited in the principal case) Judge Cardozo stated the rationale for not permitting contracts to appoint as follows:

> The exercise of the power was to represent the final judgment, the last will, of the donee. Up to the last moment of his life, he was to have the power to deal with the share as he thought best. * * * To permit him to bargain that right away would be to defeat the purpose of the donor. Her command was that her property should go to her son's issue unless at the end of his life it remained his will that it go elsewhere. It has not remained his will that it go elsewhere; and his earlier contract cannot nullify the expression of his final purpose. (219 N.Y., at 293, 294, 114 N.E. at 390).

3. The New York statute is in accord with the common law in denying specific enforcement. Whether, at common law, damages for breach of contract can be recovered is less clear.

In Northern Trust Co. v. Porter, 368 Ill. 256, 13 N.E.2d 487 (1938), the court, after holding that an ineffective appointment void under the rule against perpetuities would constitute a breach of the contract in that case to exercise a general testamentary power of appointment, held that the promisees could not recover damages from the donee's estate, saying in part (368 Ill. at 266, 13 N.E.2d at 492):

It is conceded that the contract is not specifically enforceable.

The donor, in giving a general power of appointment by will, only, intends that the donee shall retain his discretion as to who shall receive the property subject to appointment, until the time of his death. The purpose of giving such power is to allow the exercise of such power to represent the final judgment of the donee. To permit a contract to appoint in a certain way to be binding would be, in effect, to change the power from a general testamentary power to a power to appoint by deed or will. The intention of the donor must not be thus circumvented. * * *

Moreover, the knowledge that damages would be given in case she did not comply with the contract would make the donee reluctant to breach the contract and thus to exercise her freedom of choice up to the last moment of her life,—a thing which the donor intended. In other words, if damages are allowed against the estate of the donee, it has the effect of exerting coercion of a threatened judgment to compel voluntary performance of an act which could not be judicially enforced by specific performance. For this reason, damages may be recovered from neither the individual estate of the donee nor from the appointive fund.

There are a few other cases in accord with this one.

In In re Parkin, [1892] 3 Ch.Div. 510, the court denied specific performance but allowed damages for breach of a contract to exercise a testamentary power in a decision assuming, rather than justifying, the propriety of awarding damages, and not discussing the point made in Northern Trust Co. v. Porter, supra. There are dicta, without supporting argument, to the same effect in Vinton v. Pratt, 228 Mass. 468, 117 N.E. 919, 920 (1917).

The Restatement, Second, Property (Donative Transfers) § 16.2, would deny the promisee either damages or the specific appointive property under such circumstances, but would allow him restitution of any value he had given for the promise. The latter result would seem to follow from the general principles of restitution, since the contract, although unenforceable, should not be considered "illegal" for the purpose of invoking the clean hands doctrine. Simes and Smith, § 1015.

4. The objections that have been raised against the enforceability of a contract to exercise a testamentary power do not apply either to (a) a contract to exercise a power presently exercisable inter vivos (such a contract would be enforceable under the English law, under Restatement, Second, Property (Donative Transfers) § 16.1, and under several statutes including the New York statute discussed in the principal case); or (b) a contract to leave individually owned property by will.

What is the distinction between those situations and that involved in the principal case?

b.   Releases of Powers of Appointment.

The donee of a power of appointment may, if she acts in time, refuse to accept the power, i.e. "disclaim" or "renounce" it; even if she initially accepts the power, she may (in most circumstances) later give up her right to exercise it, i.e. "release" it.   Where the donor has designated persons to take in default of appointment, the effect of a release is to make a gift to those persons.   Some tax aspects of disclaimers are discussed at p. 927 infra.

Where the takers in default are the same people as the intended beneficiaries of a contract to appoint, it is often argued that the contract to appoint is really a release of the power.   In Wood v. American Security & Trust Co., 253 F.Supp. 592 (D.D.C.1966) the court sustained as a release of the power an agreement as to the ultimate disposition of property subject to a power among three life tenants where a testamentary power of appointment was given to the "surviving" life tenant.

The following case is probably the more usual result.

SEIDEL v. WERNER
New York Supreme Court, N.Y. County, 1975.
81 Misc. 220, 364 N.Y.S.2d 963.

[Steven Werner, the donee of a general testamentary power, agreed in a separation agreement to execute the power irrevocably in favor of his children Anna and Frank by his second wife Harriet.   Instead, he executed a will leaving all of his property, including property subject to the power, to his third wife Edith.   After his death his children sought to enforce the agreement, or, alternatively, a judgment that the separation agreement was a release of the power.]

SAMUEL J. SILVERMAN, J.

* * *

Under the terms of the trust instrument, if Steven fails to exercise his power of appointment, Anna and Frank (along with the children of Steven's first marriage) take the remainder, i.e., the property which is the subject of Steven's power of appointment.   Therefore, Harriet, Anna and Frank argue that at a minimum Steven's agreement should be construed as a release of his power of appointment, and that Anna and Frank should be permitted to take as on default of appointment.

There is respectable authority—by no means unanimous authority, and none binding on this Court—to the effect that a promise to appoint a given sum to persons who would take in default of appointment should, *to that extent,* be deemed a release of the power of appointment.   See Restatement of Property § 336 (1940); Simes and Smith, The Law of Future Interests § 1016 (1956).

This argument has the appeal that it seems to be consistent with the exception that the release statute (EPTL 10–5.3(b)) carves out of EPTL 10–5.3(a); and is also consistent with the intentions and reasonable expectations of the parties at the time they entered into the agreement to appoint, here in the separation agreement; and that therefore perhaps in these circumstances the difference between what the parties agreed to and a release of the power of appointment is merely one of form. Whatever may be the possible validity or applicability of this argument to other circumstances and situations, I think it is inapplicable to this situation because:

(a) It is clear that the parties did not intend a release of the power of appointment. Cf. Matter of Haskell, 59 Misc.2d 797, 300 N.Y.S.2d 711 (N.Y.Co.1969). Indeed, the agreement—unlike a release of a power of appointment—expressly contemplates that something will be done by the donee of the power in the future, and that that something will be an exercise of the power of appointment. Thus, the agreement, in the very language said to be a release of the power of appointment, says (Par. 10):

"The Husband *shall* make * * * a will in which he *shall exercise* his testamentary power of appointment * * *". (emphasis added)

(b) Nor is the substantial effect of the promised exercise of the power the same as would follow from release of, or failure to exercise the power.

(i) Under the separation agreement, the power is to be exercised so that the entire appointive property shall be for the benefit of Anna and Frank; under the trust instrument, on default of exercise of the power, the property goes to all of Steven's children (Anna, Frank and the two children of Steven's first marriage). Thus the agreement provides for appointment of a greater principal to Anna and Frank than they would get in default of appointment.

(ii) Under the trust instrument, on default of exercise of the power, the property goes to the four children absolutely and in fee. The separation agreement provides that Steven shall create a *trust,* with *income* payable to *Harriet as trustee,* for the support of Anna and Frank until they both reach the age of 21, at which time the principal shall be paid to them or the survivor; and if both fail to attain the age of 21, then the principal shall revert to Steven's estate. Thus, Anna and Frank's interest in the principal would be a defeasible interest if they did not live to be 21; and indeed at Steven's death they were both still under 21 so that their interest was defeasible.

(iii) Finally, under the separation agreement, as just noted, if Anna and Frank failed to qualify to take the principal, either because they both died before Steven or before reaching the age of twenty-one, then the principal would go to Steven's estate. Under the trust instrument, on the other hand, on default of appointment and an inability of Anna and Frank to take, Steven's share of the principal would not go to Steven's estate, but to his other children, if living, and if not, to the settlor's next of kin.

In these circumstances, I think it is too strained and tortuous to construe the separation agreement provision as the equivalent of a release of the power of appointment. If this is a release then the exception of EPTL 10–5.3(b) has swallowed and destroyed the principal rule of EPTL 10–5.3(a).

I note that in Wood v. American Security and Trust Co., 253 F.Supp. 592, 594 (D.D.C.1966), the principal case relied upon by Harriet, Anna and Frank on this point, the Court said:

"The Court finds that it is significant that the disposition resulting from the agreement is in accordance with the wishes of the testator in the event the power should not be exercised."

Furthermore, the language of the instrument in that case was much more consistent with the non-exercise of the power of appointment than in the case at bar.

Accordingly, I hold that the separation agreement is not the equivalent of a total or partial release of the power of appointment.

(4) Anna and Frank also seek restitution out of the trust fund of the value given by them in exchange for Steven's unfulfilled promise. EPTL 10–5.3(a) provides that although the contract to make an appointment cannot be the basis for an action for specific performance or damages, "the promisee can obtain restitution of the value given by him for the promise unless the donee has exercised the power pursuant to contract."

Anna and Frank's remedy is limited, however, to the claim for restitution that they have (and apparently have asserted) against Steven's estate. They may not seek restitution out of the trust fund, even if their allegation that the estate lacks sufficient assets to meet this claim were factually supported, because the trust fund was not the property of Steven, except to the extent of his life estate, so as to be subject to the equitable remedy of restitution, but was the property of the donor of the power of appointment until it vested in someone else. Farmers' Loan & Trust Co. v. Mortimer, 219 N.Y. 290, 295, 114 N.E. 389, 390 (1916); see Matter of Rosenthal, 283 App.Div. 316, 319, 127 N.Y.S.2d 778, 780 (1st Dept.1954); see also EPTL 10–7.1 and 10–7.4.

(5) Finally, Edith moves for summary judgment that she is entitled to receive Steven's share of the trust fund on the ground that Steven exercised his testamentary power in her favor in his will of March 20, 1964, in the provision quoted at the beginning of this decision.

Since there are no factual questions raised as to Steven's exercise of his testamentary power of appointment in Edith's favor in that will provision, and since each of the other defendants' conflicting claims to the share of trust principal has been dismissed, Edith's motion for summary judgment is granted.

(6) Accordingly, on the motions for summary judgment I direct judgment declaring that defendant Edith Fisch Werner is entitled to the one-half share of Steven C. Werner in the principal of the Abraham L. Werner trust; to the extent that the counterclaims and cross-claims asserted by Harriet, Anna and Frank seek relief other than a declaratory judgment, they are dismissed.

Notes

1. To the same effect, see O'Hara v. O'Hara, 185 Md. 321, 44 A.2d 813, 163 A.L.R. 1444 (1945). The O'Hara case also expressed doubt as to the propriety

of an automatic rule authorizing the release of any testamentary power, suggesting instead that a general testamentary power could only be released if there were "no frustration of the donor's intention". On this point, Maryland is not in accord with most jurisdictions.

There have not been very many American cases on releasability of powers of appointment, but the trend has been to hold all powers, whether general or special, testamentary or exercisable inter vivos, releasable, with the exception of "powers in trust." That is, essentially, the position taken by the Restatement, Second, Property (Donative Transfers) §§ 14.1 and 14.2. See Simes (hb) 173–79; Simes and Smith, §§ 1054–57; Am.L.Prop., §§ 23.26–23.28; Nossaman, Release of Powers of Appointment, 56 Harv.L.R. 757 (1943); Annot. 76 A.L.R. 1430 (1932). The principal case is discussed at length, and the doctrine permitting release of testamentary powers is criticized, in Fetters, Future Interests, 1975 Survey of N.Y.Law, 27 Syr.L.Rev. 365 (1976).

A great many American jurisdictions have enacted statutes authorizing the release of powers of appointment with some limited exceptions. For statutory references, see Restatement, Second, Property (Donative Transfers) statutory note to § 14.2. Examples are N.Y.—McKinney's EPTL 10–9.2 (all releasable except an imperative power); Conn.G.S.A. § 45–120 (all releasable "unless otherwise provided in the instrument creating the power"). The stimulus for these statutes arose from the provisions of the Internal Revenue Act of 1942 which, for the first time, brought within the Estate Tax the property subject to a power of appointment even if the power was not exercised, but excluded from such taxation powers created before the Act and released prior to a date that was later extended to 1951, and also exempted such releases from the gift tax. The Powers of Appointment Act of 1951 eliminated the tax incentive for releasing pre-1942 powers by providing that they should be taxable only if exercised; the holder of such a power, who would have had to release it under the 1942 Act to avoid taxation, could under the 1951 Act achieve the same result by simply refraining from exercising it. During the period from 1942 to 1951, however, many legislatures felt it desirable to provide for the general releasability of powers because of the tax advantages that would accrue to their constituents from such releases. See Eisenstein, Powers of Appointment and Estate Taxes, 52 Yale L.J. 494 (1943); Ball, Release of Powers of Appointment for Federal Estate Tax Purposes, 4 Ark.L.R. 66 (1949–50).

2. A transfers property to B for life, then to such persons as B shall by will appoint and in default of appointment to C.

(a) B contracts to appoint the property to X. Subject to the as yet somewhat uncertain question as to whether X could recover damages for breach of contract, the contract would probably be unenforceable.

(b) B executes a release of the power. The release would probably be effective, either by statute or, in the absence of statute, by case law. See, e.g., Lyon v. Alexander, 304 Pa. 288, 156 A. 84, 76 A.L.R. 1427 (1931) (general testamentary power released by life tenant-donee joining in deed to another; dictum that special power might not be releasable, at least if it were construed as a power in trust; no recognition of any distinction between testamentary powers and those exercisable inter vivos).

Can the results in (a) and (b) be reconciled in terms of the donor's intent or any other factor? See Gray, Release and Discharge of Powers, 24 Harv.L.R.

§§ 511, 531 (1911); Simes (hb) 175; Simes and Smith, § 1054; Am.L.Prop., § 23.28.

On contracts to exercise powers, see Simes (hb) 166–68; Simes and Smith, §§ 1011–16; Am.L.Prop., §§ 23.33–23.36; Annot. 163 A.L.R. 1449 (1946).

3. As noted above, a release of a power of appointment is to be distinguished from a "disclaimer" of the power. To disclaim the power is, in effect, to refuse to accept it and the disclaimer must be made within a reasonable time after the donee learns of the power. (For federal tax purposes the question of timing is governed by statute. See p. 927 infra). A release presupposes acceptance by the donee and has legal consequences, e.g., the making of a gift by the donee, not present in the case of disclaimer.

4. Most statutes specify methods by which a power of appointment may be released, including typically by delivery of a signed instrument to some person who could be adversely affected by an appointment—a taker in default, for example. See e.g. N.Y.—McKinney's EPTL § 10–9.2 Restatement; Second, Property (Donative Transfers) § 14.3.

5. A release (and a disclaimer) may be total or partial—as, for example, the release by the donee of a general power of the power to appoint to herself, her estate or the creditors of either, but retaining the power to appoint to anyone else. For a discussion of the consequences of such a partial release, see pp. 928–29.

4. *Characteristics of Special Powers of Appointment*

IN RE CARROLL'S WILL
Court of Appeals of New York, 1937.
274 N.Y. 288, 8 N.E.2d 864, 115 A.L.R. 923.

Proceeding in the matter of the petition of Harold A. Content, as one of the executors under the last will and testament of Elsa C. Milliken, deceased, for a construction of the last will and testament of William Carroll, deceased, with respect to a power of appointment therein given and attempted to be exercised by Elsa C. Milliken. From an order (247 App.Div. 11, 286 N.Y.S. 307) modifying a decree of the Surrogate's Court, New York County (153 Misc. 649, 275 N.Y.S. 911), determining that a bequest to Paul Allan Curtis by Elsa C. Milliken was entirely void, Ralph C. Carroll, individually, Grace Carroll and the Central Hanover Bank & Trust Company, as trustees under the will of William Carroll, Ralph C. Carroll, Jr., and others, by Benjamin F. Schreiber, special guardian, appeal.

The surrogate held that a bequest of $250,000 made to the respondent, Paul A. Curtis, by the terms of the will of Elsa C. Milliken, deceased, as a purported exercise of the said power of appointment, was void in its entirety as a fraud upon such power. The modification by the Appellate Division consisted of an adjudication that the bequest was valid to the extent of $150,000.

HUBBS, Judge. In 1910 William Carroll died leaving a will by the fourth paragraph of which he devised and bequeathed the residue of his estate to his executors in trust to pay the income to his wife during her life. By the fifth paragraph he directed that upon the death of the wife the residuary trust be divided into two equal shares, the proceeds of one to be for the use and benefit of his daughter, Elsa, during her life, and the proceeds of the other share for the use and benefit of his son, Ralph, during his life. In the fifth paragraph he gave his daughter power by her last will and testament to dispose of the property so set aside for her use "to and among her children or any other kindred who shall survive her and in such shares and manner as she shall think proper." A similar power of appointment was given to Ralph to dispose of his share "to and among his kindred or wife." With respect to the share set aside for the use of the daughter, Elsa, the will provided that, in the absence of any valid disposition of the corpus by her, it should pass "to her then surviving child or children, descendant or descendants" and, should there be no surviving child or descendant of the daughter, then the share on her decease should pass to the donor's "surviving heirs or next-of-kin, according to the nature of the estate."

Elsa died on June 26, 1933, without leaving any child or descendant her surviving. The mother, Grace Carroll, survived her and was living at the time of the trial, as was also the brother, Ralph. Elsa left a will by which she left $5,000 to her brother, and $250,000 to one Paul Curtis, a cousin, such bequest to go to his son if he predeceased her. The remainder of her share of the estate of her father she gave to her executors in trust.

When Elsa's will was drawn, the petitioning executor, Content, as her attorney, prepared the will and attended to its execution and also prepared a letter directed to Elsa by the legatee Paul Curtis, which letter read as follows: "I am informed that by your last will and testament you have given and bequeathed to me the sum of Two Hundred and Fifty Thousand Dollars ($250,000). In the event that you should predecease me and I should receive the bequest before mentioned, I hereby promise and agree, in consideration of the said bequest, that I will pay to your husband, Foster Milliken, Jr., the sum of One Hundred Thousand Dollars ($100,000) out of the said bequest which you have given to me by your said will."

It is not contended by any of the parties to this proceeding that Foster Milliken, Jr., husband of Elsa, was of her kindred, and, therefore, a proper object of the power granted to his wife in her father's will. The question here involved is as to the effect of the attempted provision for her husband upon the bequest to Paul Curtis.

Content testified that he had advised Elsa that she could not lawfully make her husband a beneficiary of any part of her father's estate; that she had drawn a previous will in which she had given the residue of the estate of her father to her brother, Ralph, with a request that he pay to her husband the sum of $10,000 per annum; that he advised her that that provision could not be enforced; that on October 6, 1931, she told him that she was not satisfied; that she was growing away from her brother and that she wanted to increase the bequest to her cousin Paul Curtis; that she had given Curtis $50,000 in a prior will; that she wanted to leave him $250,000 and that he prepared the will with the prior will before him and on October 13 she and Mrs. Elliott came to his office where she executed the will; that after the will was executed she told him: "Paul would like to do something for Foster. He would like to leave him some of this money I am leaving to him, and Paul is perfectly willing to put this in writing to show his good faith." He then talked with Paul, dictated the letter, and had it signed. He was not sure whether the letter was delivered to Elsa or whether he kept it for her. Curtis testified that several days before the will was executed Elsa told him she was going to make a new will; that she knew if her brother, Ralph, heard about it he would probably start a row with her mother; that she had previously left Curtis $50,000 and his son $50,000, and that she was going to leave him $150,000, and add to it $100,000 which she would like him to give to Mr. Milliken; that he told her if she wanted him to do so, he would sign a paper to that effect; that she said she did not know whether it would be necessary but if she wanted him to she would make a date for him to go down to Mr. Content's office; that she called him upon the day the will was executed and asked him to meet her there; that he was not present when the will was executed but that he went in afterwards and heard the letter dictated and signed it.

The surrogate determined that the promise made by Curtis so vitiated and permeated the bequest to him that the appointment constituted a fraud upon the power and made the bequest to him void.

The Appellate Division, two justices dissenting, decided that the only reasonable interpretation to be placed upon the transaction is that Elsa desired to appoint $150,000 to her cousin and an additional $100,000 to her husband; accordingly, that the lawful appointment of $150,000 to Curtis is separable from the unlawful appointment of $100,000 to him for the benefit of the husband.

It seems to us that the conclusion is inescapable that the testimony of Content, the attorney who drew the instruments, and of Curtis, who was the legatee, do not affect the true intent and purpose of the letter. Stress is laid upon the fact as testified to by Content that the testatrix, Elsa, did not tell him of the understanding with Curtis until after the will had been executed. Nevertheless, it appears from the testimony of Curtis that she had an understanding with him prior to the execution of the will and the writing constituted only a record of the actual prior agreement. The surrogate had the benefit of hearing the witnesses testify and of observing their conduct. He found nothing in their testimony to detract from the force of the letter signed by Curtis. Concededly, the attempted bequest for the benefit of the husband was not valid. Curtis alone testified that he was to receive $150,000 and the husband $100,000. Content testified that she told him she wanted to leave Curtis $250,000, and that he did not know until after the will was drawn of the understanding between Curtis and the testatrix. The letter says that the agreement to pay the husband $100,000 is in consideration of a bequest of $250,000. No one can say whether she would have left Curtis $100,000, $150,000, or a lesser or greater sum had it not been for the agreement to take care of her husband. Only by speculation can it be said that she would have left him $150,000 had it not been for that agreement. Had it not been for her continued possession either personally or by her attorney of the promise on the part of Curtis, no one can say but what she might have changed the will. Curtis was a party to the attempted fraud on the power. If the bequest to him be sustained to the extent of $150,000 on his own testimony, he suffers no penalty. It seems to us that on the facts, the conclusion of the surrogate was correct; that the entire bequest is involved in the intent to defeat the power and that it is impossible to separate and sustain the bequest to Curtis to the extent of $150,000.

Upon the general question the law of England is correctly stated in Halsbury's Laws of England (Vol. 23 [1st ed.], pp. 58–62):

"A person having a limited power must exercise it bona fide for the end designed; otherwise the execution is a fraud on the power and void. Fraud in this connection does not necessarily imply any moral turpitude, but is used to cover all cases where the purpose of the appointor is to effect some bye or sinister object, whether such purpose be selfish or, in the appointor's belief, a more beneficial mode of disposition of the property and more consonant with that which he believes would be the real wish of the creator of the power under the circumstances existing at the date of the appointment. In all cases of fraudulent execution, the fraud consists in the exercise of the power for purposes foreign to those for which it was created and the exercise of the power may be held fraudulent on any of the three following grounds:

"(1) If the execution was made for a corrupt purpose.

"(2) If it was made in pursuance of an antecedent agreement by the appointee to benefit persons not objects of the power, even although the agreement in itself is unobjectionable. An appointment to a child an object of the power, and a contemporaneous settlement by him of the appointed fund, is, however, valid unless it can be shown that the appointment was made in pursuance of a contract inducing the appointment.

"(3) If it was made for purposes foreign to the power, although such purposes are not communicated to the appointee before the appointment and although the appointor gets no personal benefit. * * * Appointments cannot be severed, so as to be good to the extent to which they are bona fide exercises of the power, but bad as to the remainder, unless (1) some consideration has been given which cannot be restored, or (2) the court can sever the intentions of the appointor and distinguish the good from the bad."

In a footnote on page 60 it is said: "The fact that the appointor knows that the object intends to dispose of the fund in favour of a stranger to the power does not necessarily vitiate the appointment, but it may have that effect if it can be shown that the appointment would not have been made but for the agreement. Pryor v. Pryor, 2 DeGex, J. & S. 205, C.A.; Daniel v. Arkwright, 2 Herm. & M. 95; Re Foote and Purdon's Estate (1910) 1 I.R. 365. The question in each case is the character in which the appointee takes the property; if it is for his absolute benefit the appointment is good, but if this is not the appointor's purpose it is bad. Langston v. Blackmore, Amb. 289; FitzRoy v. Richmond, Duke (No. 2),

27 Beav. 190; Birley v. Birley, 25 Beav. 299; Pryor v. Pryor, supra; Cooper v. Cooper, L.R. 8 Eq. 312; Roach v. Trood, 3 Ch.Div. 429, C.A.; In re Turner's Settled Estates, 28 Ch.Div. 205, C.A."

* * *

In the case at bar we have written evidence which is corroborative of a prior agreement. It seems to us that the surrogate was quite correct in concluding that it is impossible to separate the valid from the invalid disposition. To say that it clearly appears that the donee would have given $150,000 to Curtis had the bargain not been made is not justified. It clearly appears that an object of the appointment to Curtis was to secure a benefit to the husband of the donee who was excluded by the donor of the power from being an appointee or benefiting from the exercise of the power. The purpose of the donee was to accomplish by an agreement with Curtis an end entirely foreign to the intent of the donor of the power. Her act constituted a fraud on the power in which Curtis actively participated. There was a bargain between the donee and Curtis by which, in consideration of the appointment, he agreed to dispose of a part of the legacy in favor of a person who was not an object of the power. That bargain resulted in vitiating not only the provision for donee's husband but also the bequest to Curtis within the meaning of the authorities heretofore cited.

The wording of the letter which he signed was "in consideration of the said bequest" he would pay to donee's husband $100,000 "out of the said bequest" of $250,000. It is hard to see how those plain words can be construed otherwise than a bargain to share his bequest of $250,000 with another not an object of the power. Such a bargain under all the authorities makes the entire bequest void. Cf. 46 Yale Law Journal, 344; 49 C.J. 1298.

The appellant Ralph C. Carroll contends that, in permitting the donee to appoint to any of her kindred, the donor used the word "kindred" in a narrow sense and intended to limit the possible beneficiaries of the power to her next of kin. If correct in that contention, since the donee died without children, the result would be that she could appoint only to her brother, the appellant Ralph Carroll. There is no inconsistency or ambiguity in the will of William Carroll evidenced by the fact that he gave to his daughter a power of appointment to her children or any other of her kindred. Kindred has a well-established meaning, "blood relatives," as distinguished from that limited number of blood relatives embraced under the term "next of kin." William Carroll in his will used the words next of kin where it is apparent that it was his intention that the property was to pass as in the case of intestacy. The surrogate has determined that kindred was used in the generally accepted meaning of the word. That determination has been affirmed by the Appellate Division and there appears no reason for according to it a limited application.

A question is raised also as to whether the appointment of testatrix to the children of her brother, Ralph C. Carroll, of the residue of the property of which she had power of appointment did not violate the statute against perpetuities. Her direction is that the property shall be divided by her trustees; that out of the income they shall provide for the care, maintenance, and support of each of the children until the child becomes twenty-one years of age, when the principal of the fund shall be paid over. If there was a vesting of the shares in the children upon the death of Elsa with custody subject to termination of the primary life estates, that is, the life tenancy of Grace Carroll, mother of Elsa, and during the minority of the children, there is no violation of the statute, for the only life estates of the property involved under the will of William Carroll are the life estates of Grace Carroll and of Elsa. As determined in Matter of Hitchcock's Will, 222 N.Y. 57, 71, 118 N.E. 220, where it is clear that the testamentary intent is to confer absolute ownership within the statutory period, the withholding of custody and physical possession for an additional term, during which the power to administer is intrusted to a third party, does not create an unlawful perpetuity. Here the withholding of custody and control is only during the minority of the children when they could not act for themselves and it seems that there was no intent other than that the interests of the infants were to vest subject to such power of control.

The order of the Appellate Division should be modified in accordance with this opinion, and, as so modified, affirmed, without costs.

CRANE, C. J., and O'BRIEN, LOUGHRAN, FINCH, and RIPPEY, JJ., concur.

LEHMAN, J., dissents and votes to affirm.

Judgment accordingly.

Notes

1. There are various ways by which a donee of a special power may try to exercise it for the benefit of himself or some other person outside the class of appointees specified by the donor and thus not a permissible object of the power. This may be directly attempted by a specific exercise of the power in favor of a non-object, as where the donee of a special power to appoint among his children executes an instrument purporting to appoint all or part of the appointive property to his wife. Such an attempted appointment is void, and has been termed "excessive", meaning that it exceeds the scope of the power. Restatement, Property, Second (Donative Transfers) § 20.1.; Am.L.Prop. § 23.52.

Even if the appointment is confined on its face to proper objects of the power, it may be held wholly or partly void if other evidence shows the donee's purpose to benefit a non-object. Such furtive attempts to escape the limitations of the special power have been described as "frauds on the power" or "fraudulent appointments". This terminology is misleading, as indicated by the excerpt from Halsbury quoted in the principal case and by the following language in the opinion in Vatcher v. Paull, [1915] A.C. 372 at 378:

> The term fraud in connection with frauds on a power does not necessarily denote any conduct on the part of the appointor amounting to fraud in the common law meaning of the term or any conduct which could be properly termed dishonest or immoral. It merely means that the power has been exercised for a purpose, or with an intention, beyond the scope of or not justified by the instrument creating the power. Perhaps the most

common instance of this is where the exercise is due to some bargain between the appointor and appointee, whereby the appointor, or some other person not an object of the power, is to derive a benefit. But such a bargain is not essential. It is enough that the appointor's purpose and intention is to secure a benefit for himself, or some other person not an object of the power. In such a case the appointment is invalid, unless the Court can clearly distinguish between the quantum of the benefit bona fide intended to be conferred on the appointee and the quantum of the benefit intended to be derived by the appointor or to be conferred on a stranger. * * *

The principal case is clearly one of a "bargain between the appointor and appointee". In other situations, the donee's purpose to benefit a non-object is not nearly so obvious. For examples of fraudulent appointments, see Simes and Smith, § 981; Am.L.Prop., §§ 23.53–23.56; Annot. 115 A.L.R. 930 (1938).

2. If either a fraudulent or an excessive appointment purports to benefit permissible objects of the power as well as non-objects, the issue arises as to whether the appointment is entirely void or may be sustained pro tanto for the legitimate appointees. The solution of this problem should probably depend on whether the donee should be assumed to have desired the permissible objects to take even if the improper purpose were nullified.

In the principal case, what would be the reasons for concluding that, contrary to the holding of the Court of Appeals, Paul Curtis should be entitled to $150,000 even though the attempted provision of $100,000 for the donee's husband failed? See opinion of majority of Appellate Division in 247 App.Div. at 18, 286 N.Y.S. at 314.

3. The Restatement, Second, Property (Donative Transfers) Ch. 20 applies the prohibition on fraudulent or excessive appointment both to special powers (in the Restatement's terminology "non-general powers exercisable in favor of a defined limited class") and to other non-general powers, e.g., powers exercisable in favor of anyone except the donee, her estate or the creditors of either. Does the same rationale support the prohibition in both cases?

4. Where a special power is created, the question may also arise whether the power is "exclusive" (in which case the donee may exercise it in favor of one or more of the permissible objects to the exclusion of others) or "non-exclusive" (in which case he must appoint some of the property to each of the permissible objects). Where the power is held to be non-exclusive, the further question arises as to how large a share must be given to each in order to make the appointment not "illusory." As Simes and Smith point out (§ 982) "there would appear to be no valid reason for creating a non-exclusive power"; and the courts are likely to find an exclusive power absent a specific direction by the donor. The Restatement, Second, Property, (Donative Transfers) § 21.2 takes the position that powers are exclusive "unless the donor specifies the share of appointive assets from which an object may not be excluded" (a definition which eliminates the possibility of "illusory" appointments).

Several American jurisdictions have passed statutes on this subject, most with the objective of preferring the construction that a special power is exclusive. Restatements, Second, Property (Donative Transfers) Statutory note to § 21.1. The New York statute, N.Y.—McKinney's EPTL 10–6.5, takes care of the problem of illusory appointments by providing that, "[u]nless the donor expressly provides otherwise * * * [t]he donee of a non-exclusive power must appoint in favor of all of the appointees equally."

On the above issues, see Simes (hb) 159–60; Simes and Smith, § 982; Am. L.Prop., §§ 23.57–23.58; Howe, Exclusive and Non-exclusive Powers and the Illusory Appointment, 42 Mich.L.R. 649 (1944); 48 Harv.L.R. 1408 (1935); Annot. 100 A.L.R. 343 (1936).

Powers in Trust; Implied Gifts in Default of Appointment

The issue which arises under this heading may be illustrated by the following hypothetical situation: A's will leaves property in trust to pay the income to B for life and then the principal to such children of B as B shall appoint; and makes no express gift in default of appointment. B later dies without exercising the power. It may reasonably be inferred from the absence of any gift in default coupled with the specification of appointees in the creation of the special power that A intended to have B's children get the property and expected that B would of course exercise the power in their favor. It may be assumed that, if A had envisaged the possibility of B's not exercising the power, A would have made an express gift in default of appointment to B's children in equal shares. Operating on these premises, many decisions in England and America have awarded the property under these circumstances to B's children in equal shares.

There has been extensive discussion of this issue, chiefly in terms of the appropriate doctrinal explanation of what seems generally agreed to be a fair result. Since it is not likely to make any difference in most situations which explanation is adopted, it seems sufficient to call attention to this issue and to enumerate the three different theories that have been suggested, which are as follows:

(1) That the donee of such a special power holds the power "in trust" imposing a duty on him to execute it, and that, if he fails to do so, the court will remedy that breach of obligation by distributing the appointive property equally among the class of appointees. The same idea has been expressed by calling the power mandatory or imperative.

(2) That those who would otherwise take the property should be held constructive trustees for the objects of the power, since they would otherwise be unjustly enriched by retaining property that the donee was obligated to appoint to others.

(3) That there is an implied gift in default of appointment to the objects of the power, resulting from the assumed intent of the donee to have them receive it, even if the power is not exercised.

For discussions of these theories and collections of cases, see Simes (hb) 169–72; Simes and Smith, §§ 1032–34; Am.L.Prop., § 23.63; Restatement, Second, Property (Donative Transfers) § 24.2; Annot. 80 A.L.R. 503 (1932).

Note on Lapse

At common law, an appointment lapses if the appointee is not alive at the death of the donee. Prop.Rest., § 349. At least in the case of general powers, anti-lapse statutes have been held applicable to preserve the gift to the intended appointee, and any relationship required by the statute has been tested in terms of that between the appointee and the donee, rather than that between the appointee and the donor.   Thompson v. Pew, 214 Mass. 520, 102 N.E. 122 (1913) (statute applicable if predeceased legatee "child or other relation of the testator"; donee of general testamentary power created in will of donee's husband appointed to donee's brother who predeceased donee; statute held applicable to give property to appointee's children, since appointee "relation" of donee, though not of donor, a brother-in-law not being within the terms of the statute); Rowland's Estate, 17 D. & C. 477 (Pa.Orphans' Ct.1932) (donee of general testamentary power appointed to two people who predeceased donee; statute held applicable to appointee related to donee but not to donor, and inapplicable to appointee related to donor but not to donee); Prop. Rest., § 350; Simes (hb) 168; Simes and Smith, § 984; Am.L.Prop., § 23.47; Annot. 75 A.L.R. 1383 (1931).   How may this result be explained in view of the relation back theory?   Are these statutes designed as a pro tanto repudiation of the doctrine of lapse or as a legislative rule of construction?   See Am.L.Prop., § 23.47; Atkinson, Wills, 779 (2d ed., 1953).

There are very few cases dealing with the application of anti-lapse statutes to special powers of appointment.   In Daniel v. Brown, 156 Va. 563, 159 S.E. 209, 75 A.L.R. 1377 (1931), an anti-lapse statute covering the predecease of a devisee or legatee (i.e., without specifying a required relationship to the testator) was held inapplicable to a special testamentary power of appointment among the nieces and nephews of the donor, and the child of a nephew-appointee who predeceased the donee was held not entitled to the property.   Would the same result follow if the class named in the special power had been the descendants of the brothers and sisters of the donor?   See Simes on Future Interests (Hornbook) 168; Simes and Smith, § 984; Am.L.Prop., § 23.47.   The Restatement, Second, Property (Donative Transfers) § 18.6 would save the bequest in a case like Daniel v. Brown, supra.

5. Appointive Property as Assets of the Donee

In the case of special powers of appointment, the relation-back doctrine works pretty well.   Since the donee of a special power—by definition—cannot have a beneficial interest in the property subject to the power, the property can conveniently be regarded as belonging to the donor, with the donee merely exercising delegated authority.   In the case of general powers, however, it is more difficult to sustain the fiction that the property subject to the power is not an asset of the donee for at least some purposes.   One obvious case is tax liability—discussed in the next chapter.

Apart from tax considerations, if the donee does not exercise the power, and no claims of his creditors (or surviving spouse) are involved, treatment of the property as the donor's seems reasonable.   In such a case, if there is a provision for a gift in default of appointment, the property will go to the taker or takers in default; if there is no such provision, the property will go back to the donor's estate and pass by will or intestacy, or to the donor himself.

But what about the case where an ineffective attempt is made to exercise the power or where creditors of the donee are in the picture? The answers to these questions vary with the jurisdiction and in some cases with the manner of exercise.

The donee of a power may, in exercising it, treat the appointive assets separately from his owned assets: e.g., "I give any property over which I have a power of appointment to X. I give the rest of my property to Y." Or he may treat all the property—owned and appointive assets— as a single fund: e.g., "I give all my property, including property over which I have a power of appointment, as follows." The latter treatment, called "blending," may apply to all property or only to the residue after particular gifts. Blending may be specifically provided for or may result even by operation of law where the power is not mentioned, in a jurisdiction where the making of a will or the inclusion in a will of a residuary clause operates as an exercise of the power. The fact of blending, and the manner of blending, whether by the will as a whole or by the residuary clause, are frequently regarded as important by the courts.

a. Rights of Creditors of the Donee.

Except where the donee has himself created the power of appointment, the creditors of the donee—whether the power is presently exercisable or testamentary—cannot reach the property subject to the power unless it is exercised. If the power is exercised by will, about one half of the American decisions (the English rule is in accord) follow the so-called "equitable assets" doctrine and allow creditors of the donee of a general* power to reach the property subject to it, even though the appointment is not either to the creditors themselves or to the donee's estate. Some decisions permit the property to be reached only if appointive and owned property are "blended." Some decisions permit the property to be reached only if the exercise is in favor of the donee's estate or the creditors.

It should be noted that even in jurisdictions which permit the appointive property to be reached, the creditors ordinarily will have recourse against appointed property only in so far as the donee's owned property in his estate is insufficient to pay their claims. The draftsman of a will exercising a power of appointment should recognize the consequences of following this order of abatement or, contrariwise, excluding creditors under the view of such cases as St. Matthews Bank v. De Charette, 259 Ky. 802, 83 S.W.2d 471, 99 A.L.R. 1146 (1935), since either may result in unexpected distortion of an intended equal distribution. In Tuell v. Hurley, 206 Mass. 65, 91 N.E. 1013 (1910), the donee, having four daughters, devised all of the property owned by her to one daughter, and exercised a power of appointment chiefly in favor of the other three; and

---

* Unless the power is general, the creditors cannot reach the property whether or not the power is exercised.

the court held that the donee's individual property given to the first daughter would have to be exhausted to satisfy creditors before any of the appointed property was used for that purpose.

On these issues, see Restatement, Second, Property (Donative Transfers) Ch. 13; Simes (hb) 134–38; Simes and Smith, §§ 944–5; Am. L.Prop., §§ 23.16, 23.17; Annots. 59 A.L.R. 1510 (1929); 97 A.L.R. 1071 (1935); 121 A.L.R. 803 (1939); 27 Va.L.R. 1052 (1941); 84 U.Pa.L.R. 107 (1935).

Query, is the remedy given creditors by the equitable assets doctrine

(a) consistent with the relation back theory?

(b) consistent with denying relief if the power is not exercised?

(c) justifiable in terms of policy or general fairness?

There does not seem to be any American case law on the question of whether, and, if so, under what circumstances, creditors of the donee of a general power can reach the property if the power is exercised inter vivos rather than by will. For ordinary transfers, not involving any power of appointment, the rights of creditors differ in the two situations. Creditors of a testator have an automatic right to assets in his decedent estate that must be satisfied in priority to the claims of the beneficiaries of his will. This is not true of creditors of an inter vivos transferor. The Second Restatement of Property would allow creditors of the donee of a general power to reach property appointed inter vivos if, but only if, owned property transferred under the same circumstances could be subjected to their claims, i.e., by setting aside the transfer as a fraudulent conveyance, or, if the transferee is a creditor, avoiding it as a preference in bankruptcy. § 13.5. An English decision allowed creditors of the donee of a general power recourse against property appointed inter vivos under circumstances that would have made a regular transfer of owned property a fraudulent conveyance. Townshend v. Windham, 2 Ves.Sr. 1, 28 Eng. Rep. 1 (1750) (general power exercised by deed for benefit of donee's daughter held fraudulent as to donee's creditors existing at the time of the exercise of the power). See Simes (hb) 137; Simes and Smith, § 945; Am.L.Prop., § 23.16.

New York has rejected the equitable assets doctrine. The fact of exercise or non-exercise does not matter. If the power is testamentary, the assets *cannot* be reached (unless the power was created by the donee) (N.Y.—McKinney's EPTL 10–7.4); if the power is presently exercisable, they can be reached (N.Y.—McKinney's EPTL 10–7.2).* See In re Simon's Estate, 75 Misc.2d 361, 348 N.Y.S.2d (Surr.Court Nass.Cty.1973). A few other jurisdictions have passed statutes affecting the rights of creditors of the donee. For references to such statutes, see Am.L.Prop., § 23.17; Simes and Smith, § 1082; Restatement, Second, Property (Donative Transfers) § 13.6.

---

* This is apparently the result under the Federal Bankruptcy Code (11 U.S.C.A. § 541). See Restatement, Second, Property (Donative Transfers) § 13.6. Cf. Montague v. Silsbee, 218 Mass. 107, 105 N.E. 611 (1914).

In Kates' Estate, 282 Pa. 417, 128 A. 97 (1925), the donee of a general testamentary power of appointment given him by the will of his father died leaving a will providing, "I make this will to dispose of as well my own property as the property over which I have a power of appointment under the will of my father, Horace N. Kates, deceased, or of any other person", and divided the property thus described between his wife and other legatees. The donee's widow elected to take against the will, and claimed to be entitled to one-third of both the appointed property and that personally owned by the testator, under a statute giving the surviving spouse so electing "such interests in the real and personal estate of the deceased spouse as he or she would have been entitled to had the testator died intestate". The court held her entitled to a statutory share only in the property personally owned by her husband, and not in the appointed property. What would be the arguments for or against the widow's claim against the appointed property in such a case?

The rights of a surviving spouse in the property of a decedent are largely governed by statute. See Ch. 3 supra. In only one state (Delaware) is it clear that property subject to a power of appointment (other than a power created by the donee) can be reached by a spouse. The Restatement, Second, Property (Donative Transfers) § 13.7 takes the position that the spouse is entitled to treat appointive assets as owned assets "only to the extent provided by statute." The statutes and case law are summarized in the notes to § 13.7 of the Restatement. See also Simes (hb) 140, Simes and Smith § 947; Am.L.Prop. § 23.22.

b. "Capture" of Appointive Property.

Where the donee of a *general* power attempts to exercise the power but the exercise is ineffective because of such reasons as invalidation of interests under the Rule against Perpetuities, lapse of an interest because of the appointee's predeceasing the testator, failure of a trust for indefiniteness, or nullification by a purging statute of a testamentary gift to an attesting witness, some courts have held that the property subject to the power does not go to the takers in default—or back to the donor's estate—but is *captured* for the donee's estate.

The "capture" doctrine is well established in Massachusetts (see e.g. Talbot v. Riggs, 287 Mass. 144, 191 N.E. 360, 93 A.L.R. 964 (1934)) and has been endorsed by the Restatement (Restatement, Second, Property (Donative Transfers) § 23.2) but is of uncertain status elsewhere. See, e.g., In re Hellinger's Estate, 83 N.Y.S.2d 10 (1948).

One difficulty with the concept of "capture" is that it is said to turn on a manifestation of intent by the donee "to assume control of the appointive property for all purposes." Restatement, Second, Property (Donative Transfers) § 23.2. Unfortunately, a clear manifestation of such an intent is rarely encountered. One substitute for such a manifestation sometimes relied on is "blending," either expressly by the donee or by operation of law. Another is that the ineffectively appointed interests were in trust. How realistic is a distinction, for these purposes, between appointments in trust and outright appointments? See Old Colony Trust

Co. v. Allen, 307 Mass. 40, 29 N.E.2d 310 (1940). What criteria should control the disposition of the property in the case of an ineffective appointment? Should the donor's "intention" be material?

On all of the above issues, see Simes (hb) 149–51; Simes and Smith § 974; Am.L.Prop., § 23.61; Scott, Trusts §§ 426–27 (3d Ed. 1967); Stokey, Two Problems Arising From Powers of Appointment, 28 B.U.L.R. 335 (1948); Carleton, The Doctrine of Capture under a General Power of Appointment, 35 Mass. L.Q. 23 (1950); Annot. 93 A.L.R. 967 (1934); Restatement, Second, Property (Donative Transfers) § 23.2.

c. *"Allocation" ("Marshalling") of Owned and Appointive Property.*

The exercise of a power of appointment is frequently (almost always in the case of a will) by an instrument in which owned property of the donee is transferred. While for some purposes appointive property and owned property are treated as fungible, for other purposes different rules govern the effectiveness of the disposition. For example, as noted above, even where appointive assets are available to claims of creditors, it may be required that owned assets be exhausted first. The same is true of administrative expenses (Slayton v. Fitch Home, Inc., 293 Mass. 574, 200 N.E. 357, 104 A.L.R. 669 (1936)). Another example is the application of the Rule against Perpetuities. Because the period of the Rule runs from the date of the creation of a power of appointment (except a general power presently exercisable) a bequest of appointive property may be invalid under the Rule even though the same bequest would be valid if the property disposed of were owned by the transferor. In such a case it may be possible to save, in whole or part, the otherwise invalid disposition by substituting owned property for appointive property.

The question of how owned and appointive property will be allocated (or as some courts and commentators put it, "marshalled") among the provisions of a will (or other document) exercising a power of appointment cannot be analyzed in terms of black and white rules. The solution theoretically depends on the "intent" of the donee. But if that intent is clearly expressed by specific language, there will be no lawsuit on the issue. The dispositions that give rise to litigation in this context are, typically, wills which either make no reference to powers of appointment but are deemed to exercise them because of a statutory or case law presumption, or else contain a general blending clause purporting to dispose of owned and appointive property together. In such cases, speculation about what alternative the deceased donee would have preferred if confronted with the situation before the court is so uncertain that individual judges may well differ in their conclusions. And the bases for such conclusions involve such variables as differences in testamentary language, in the wording and interpretation of statutes creating a presumption that a will exercises a power, and in the circumstances surrounding the testator in the particular case. Allocation is, theoretically, available in any case in which a contrary intention is not manifested by the donee—whether the power is general or special. For a discussion of the doctrine, examples of its application and relevant cases, see Restatement, Second,

Property (Donative Transfers) Ch. 22; Simes (hb) 151–53; Simes and Smith, § 975; Am.L.Prop. §§ 23.59–23.60; Powell, ¶ 401.

It should be obvious by now that the drafter of the will should be alert to the problems which may arise where appointive assets are involved, and expressly provide for their treatment. The obvious first step is to ascertain whether the testator possesses any powers of appointment; the second step is to decide whether to exercise such powers. What should be done about undiscovered powers or after-acquired powers? Should they be "blindly" exercised? Expert views on this point are in conflict. See, Rabin, Blind Exercise of Powers of Appointment, 51 Corn.L.Q. 1 (1965) for a discussion of this question and citations to various points of view. If powers are to be exercised, the "natural" disposition would seem to be to treat owned and appointive assets alike for all purposes. However, care must be taken that the "natural" disposition does not create perpetuities or other problems.

DOLLAR SAVINGS & TRUST CO. v. FIRST NATIONAL BANK OF BOSTON

Court of Common Pleas of Ohio, 1972.
32 Ohio Misc. 81, 285 N.E.2d 768.

HENDERSON, Judge.   This is an action seeking a declaratory judgment and instructions brought by the Dollar Savings & Trust Company of Youngstown, testamentary trustee under the will of Grace Tod Arrel, deceased.

Grace Tod Arrel died testate on November 17, 1921, domiciled in Mahoning County Ohio.   Under paragraph third of Item XVI of her will she left one-fourth of her residuary estate to the plaintiff in trust for the benefit of her daughter, Frances Arrel Parson during her lifetime, and thereafter as follows:

"and after the decrease [sic] of my said daughter, the principal of said Trust Fund shall be distributed among her legal heirs in such manner as it would be distributable, had she at her death, been the absolute owner thereof, in her own right.   It is hereby provided however, that my said daughter shall have power to direct by her Will, the manner in which said Trust Fund shall be distributed and the persons to whom the same shall go."

Frances Arrel Parson died testate December 2, 1969, domiciled in Hancock County, Maine.   At the time of her death there was about $500,000, all personalty, in the Arrel trust fund and about $164,000 in her own probate estate.   Her will, which was executed September 7, 1967, contains no specific reference to the Arrel power of appointment, but Article Fifth thereof provides as follows:

"ARTICLE FIFTH: All the rest and residue of my property and estate of every kind and nature of which I shall die seized or possessed or to which I shall in any way be entitled or to which my estate may subsequently become entitled or over which I may have any power of appointment at the time of my death, I devise and bequeath to the then Trustee or Trustees under a certain Indenture of Trust heretofore executed by me on the 7th day of September, 1967, as the same may be from time to time amended, between myself, as Settlor, and the Old Colony Trust Company, of Boston, County of Suffolk, Commonwealth of Massachusetts and George Arrel Parson of said Boston, as Trustees, which is known as the 'Frances A. Parson Trust' to be added to the principal of the trust estate created under said Indenture and to be held, administered and distributed in all respects as an integral part thereof."

The indenture of trust of September 7, 1967, mentioned in her will, is a living trust executed on that date by Frances Arrel Parson and the corporate predecessor of the defendant The First National Bank of Boston, and the defendant George Arrel Parson as trustees. It was a revocable trust but it was not revoked by Mrs. Parson during her lifetime. The trust agreement contains provisions for the inalienability of principal and income by the beneficiaries and freedom from the claims of creditors. It also recites that the trust was created and is governed by, and is to be construed and administered according to the laws of Massachusetts. The assets in the trust, at the time of death of Mrs. Parson, amounted to about $3,100,000 in addition to her probate assets. The trustees of Mrs. Parson's trust are also the executors of her estate.

The trust indenture provides that after the settlor's death, certain payments are to be made to persons not the issue of the settlor, and that the remainder of the trust property is to be held for the benefit of the settlor's children for their lives. Each child is given a testamentary power of appointment "to or among" his own issue. In default of such appointment by any child, his share is to be retained in trust for the benefit of his issue, or the issue of the settlor, by representation, until each of such issue reaches the age of 21 years, at which time he is to receive his share of the principal, but in no event later than 21 years after the death of the last to die of the settlor and all her issue living at the date of the execution of the trust indenture.

Mrs. Parson is survived by three children, George A. Parson, Donald Parson, Jr., and Frances P. Hunt, all of whom were living at the death of Grace Tod Arrel, and eight grandchildren and seven great grandchildren, all of whom were born after the death of Mrs. Arrel. The children maintain that they are entitled to the Arrel Trust assets outright because Mrs. Parson, their mother, did not intend to exercise the Arrel power of appointment in favor of her living trust, and could not have done so legally even if she had so intended.

It is axiomatic that it is the duty of this court to determine, as nearly as possible, the intent of the decedent, and to see such intent is fulfilled if the law permits. This seems especially true in this case in which there are contingent beneficiaries, and the living trust created by the donee of the power of appointment, Frances A. Parson, is a spendthrift trust.

The question first presented is the nature of the power of appointment which Grace Tod Arrel gave to her daughter. The Parson children maintain that the power is a special power, that the objects of its exercise are limited to the "legal heirs" of her daughter, and that therefore she was unable to appoint the Arrel trust assets to her living trust because the beneficiaries of the latter include many persons who were not her legal heirs at her death.   They reason that by application of the doctrine of *ejusdem generis,* the sentence "(It) is hereby provided however, that my said daughter shall have power to direct by her will, the manner in which said trust fund shall be distributed and the persons to whom the same shall go" is limited by the preceding clause, "after the decease of my said daughter, the principal of said trust fund shall be distributed among her legal heirs in such manner as it would be distributable, had she at her death, been the absolute owner thereof, in her own right".

It appears to the court to be unnecessary for the purposes of this proceeding to determine whether the power of appointment is a special one or a general one.   For although the non-applicability of the doctrine of *ejusdem generis* to the facts of this case seems arguable, nevertheless Mrs. Parson acted within the scope of her power, in the court's opinion, even though the power be deemed a special one with the objects of its exercise limited to Mrs. Parson's heirs.   For the fact is that if Mrs. Parson exercised the power at all, she exercised it primarily for the benefit of her children who were her only "legal heirs".   It would seem that the power to direct "the manner in which said Trust Fund shall be distributed and the persons to whom the same shall go" is broad enough to permit Mrs. Parson to appoint to her "legal heirs" by way of an *inter vivos* trust, whose provisions limit the interests of her children to life estates, with testamentary powers of appointment in them for the benefit their issue, and remainders over to their issue in default of exercise.   Furthermore, such manner of distribution by Mrs. Parson, in limiting the interests of her children to life estates, is similar to that utilized by Mrs. Arrel herself. Mrs. Arrel's will recites that she did so "thru no lack of confidence either in Fanny (Mrs. Parson), or in her husband, but because I believe it wise to follow the precedent which is found in the will of my father insuring similar provision in respect to a portion of his estate left by him to my sister and myself, by thus placing a portion of Fanny's share beyond the ordinary hazards of business".   To conclude that Mrs. Arrel intended to limit her daughter's power to one authorizing her to appoint only absolute interests to her heirs in the technical sense, would confine her authority to a right of selection or rejection among her own children, which would appear to be not only strained and unnatural but also at variance with both the language of the power itself and the Arrel tradition.

But the Parson children maintain further that their mother's power of appointment is certainly not broad enough to permit her to appoint the assets of her trust fund to a living trust which authorizes the payment of their mother's debts and death taxes and benefits strangers.   This raises the question of the effect of the "pour-over" into the donee's *inter vivos* trust.   Article Fifth of Mrs. Parson's will, by which the power was exercised, if at all, purports to blend all her property and transmit it to the trustees "to be added to the principal of the trust estate created under said Indenture and to be held, administered and distributed in all respects as an integral part thereof".   Paragraph 15 of Article Eleventh of Mrs.

Parson's trust indenture empowers the trustees to receive additional property from the settlor "by will or otherwise, to be added to the trusts herein created and to be held, administered and accounted for as a part thereof". It appears to the court that because of this blending, the appointive assets can be utilized in the trust completely and exclusively for the benefit of the Parson children and their issue by the application of the principle of selective allocation or marshalling. Simes and Smith, The Law of Future Interests (2nd Ed.) § 975, p. 437; 3 Restatement of the Law, Property, Future Interests (1940) § 363, p. 2004, § 364, p. 2015; 46 Cornell Law Quarterly 416; Stone v. Forbes (1905) 189 Mass. 163, 75 N.E. 141. The foregoing authorities involve not living trusts but wills only which recite the intent to dispose of both owned and appointive property in fulfilling bequests, some of which prove to be invalid as to the appointive property though valid as to the owned property. Under these circumstances, courts have, as a rule of construction, or implied appointment, allocated the owned assets to the fulfillment of objects not authorized by the power, and the appointive assets to the valid objects of the power. There would seem to be no reason why this same principle should not be extended to the instant case, in which the donee blended her owned assets with her appointive assets, and poured them both into her *inter vivos* trust to be administered thereunder, along with her previously transferred assets, as one fund. The trustees of Mrs. Parson's *inter vivos* trust, then, would allocate sufficient of Mrs. Parson's own assets for the payment of her expenses of administration, taxes, debts and to the fulfillment of bequests to persons not her issue; and they would allocate the appointive assets to the trusts for Mrs. Parson's children and their issue. Hence Mrs. Parson could have exercised the Arrel power in favor of her trust even though the power be considered limited or special.

The next question, then, is whether Mrs. Parson did exercise the Arrel power of appointment. Article Fifth of the Parson will is basically a general residuary clause. It has been the law in Ohio that a general bequest or residuary clause in and of itself does not exercise a testamentary power of appointment. Kiplinger v. Armstrong (C.A., Summit, 1930) 34 Ohio App. 348, 8 Ohio Abst. 286, 171 N.E. 245; Bishop v. Remple (1860) 11 Ohio St. 277; Arthur v. Odd Follows (1876) 29 Ohio St. 557. But since the submission of this case, the Court of Appeals of this county has furnished this court with an opinion, as yet unpublished, in the case of Dollar Savings & Trust Company v. Kirkham, Case No. 4993 in which the appellate court has reversed the judgment of this court as reported in 21 Ohio Misc. 163, 50 O.O.2d 318, 255 N.E.2d 892 (1969). In so doing, the court held that the testamentary power of appointment in that case was an estate, right or interest in property within the meaning of O.R.C. § 2107.50, and that such power, therefore, was exercised, under the statute, by the general residuary clause of the donee's will, there being no different intention manifested. O.R.C. § 2107.50 provides as follows:

> "Property acquired subsequent to will. Any estate, right, or interest in any property of which a decedent was possessed at his decease shall pass under his will unless such will manifests a different intention".

The decision of the Court of Appeals in the *Kirkham* case, if applicable to this case, as it appears to be, would mean that Frances A. Parson exercised her power of appointment by the residuary clause of her will alone, there being no evidence of any different intention manifested by her will. However, it is believed that the same conclusion must be reached irrespective of the effect of the *Kirkham* decision. For Article Fifth, of the Parson will, is more than a mere residuary clause. It contains, also, a bequest of all "my property" "over which I may have any power of appointment at the time of my death". The Parson children maintain that this could not have been intended to exercise the power because a power of appointment is not the property of the donee of the power, and the Parson will expressly limits the powers of appointment mentioned to those over the donee's own property. See Tax Commission v. Oswald (1923) 109 Ohio St. 36, at p. 51, 141 N.E. 678; Cleveland Trust Co. v. McQuade (C.A., Cuyahoga, 1957) 106 Ohio App. 237, at p. 250, 6 O.O.2d 493, 142 N.E.2d 249; Moore v. Emery (1941) 137 Me. 259, 18 A.2d 781. The case cited by counsel which appears to be most nearly in point is that of Matteson v. Goddard (1891) 17 R.I. 299, 21 A. 914. In that case the will language was as follows:

> "All the rest and residue of my property, real, personal and mixed, wherever situated and of whatever kind, of which I may be possessed at the time of my death, or over which I at the time of my death may have the power of testamentary disposition, I give, devise, and bequeath to my wife, Elizabeth Cass Goddard".

However, in that case, the power of appointment involved was one created by the donor in an *inter vivos* trust instrument executed six years after the making of his will. The Rhode Island Supreme Court bases its decision upon this circumstance, distinguishes several English cases upholding the exercise by similar language of powers previously created, and adds the following significant language: "We think it doubtful if it would have occurred to any person to read the clause in any other way (i.e. that it was intended to exercise the power) if the trust-deeds had not been subsequently executed;—" (p. 915). The Rhode Island court also observes that one ground for the English decisions was "that the language having reference to power was strange and purposeless if the testator intended to dispose of his own property, whereas it was what might be expected, if he likewise intended to dispose of the property over which he had simply an appointing power". (p. 914). See Bailey v. Lloyd (1829) 38 Eng.Rep. 1051, 5 Russ. 330.

Technically, with respect to Mrs. Parson's will, the appointive assets were to a degree her property in that she had a life estate in them, thus justifying her use of the possessive pronoun "my". Furthermore, although the grammar of Article Fifth is not strictly correct insofar as the antecedent of the power of appointment is concerned, it is equally incorrect or inappropriate as to other clauses of the article, to-wit: "my property"—"to which I shall in any way be entitled or to which my estate may subsequently become entitled". Consequently, the use of "my property" would not seem to impart any special limitation to the language exercising powers.

While some writers advise against the use of "blind" or "blanket" testamentary exercises of powers of appointment, the following somewhat similar language is said to have been in common usage for many years: "all the rest and residue of my property of whatever kind and wherever situated, including any property over which I may have any power of appointment, I devise, bequeath and appoint as follows". 64 Harvard Law Rev. 185, at p. 202; 51 Cornell Law Quarterly 1; Prentice-Hall, Inc., "Wills-Trusts—Estate Planning Forms" Par. 59,201; Simes and Smith, The Law of Future Interests, 2d § 988, p. 484.

Generally, the answer to the question whether a provision in a will is in execution of a power depends upon the intention of the donee of the power. Earlier cases hold that to sustain the exercise of a power, the language of the will must not be fairly susceptible to any other interpretation, and the intent must be so clear that no other reasonable intent can be imputed to the will. Arthur v. Odd Fellows (1876), 29 Ohio St. 557, at p. 561; Kiplinger v. Armstrong (C.A., Summit, 1930), 34 Ohio App. 348, 8 Ohio Abst. 286, 171 N.E. 245. According to the latter case, the modern tendency seems to be to relax the rule to hold that if it can be fairly determined from all the competent evidence available that it was the intention of the testator to execute the power, such intention will be given effect (p. 352, 80 Ohio Abst. 286, 171 N.E. 245). Under either the earlier, strict rule, or under the more modern, relaxed rule, the court concludes that Mrs. Parson, by the language of Article Fifth of her will must be deemed to have exercised the testamentary power given her by the will of Grace Tod Arrel. Her intent, as evidenced by the blanket appointment included in the residuary article, was to blend together her appointive property and her own property, and to distribute the whole to her existing, living trust.

[The court's discussion of the argument that the assets of the Ohio Trust could not be appointed to Massachusetts trustees not qualified in Ohio is omitted.]

It is maintained, finally, that the appointment of the corpus of the Arrel trust into the donee's living trust violates the Ohio rule against perpetuities.

On the perpetuities question, the law of Ohio, the donor's domicil, rather than the law of Maine, the donee's domicil, is held to be applicable. V Scott on Trusts (3rd ed., 1967) § 635, p. 4038. In Ohio, the common law rule, in modified form, has been codified by O.R.C. § 2131.08, providing, in pertinent part, as follows:

"(A) No interest in real or personal property shall be good unless it must vest, if at all, not later than twenty-one years after a life or lives in being at the creation of the interest. * * * It is the intention by the adoption of this section to make effective in Ohio what is generally known as the common law rule against perpetuities, except as set forth in paragraphs (B) and (C) of this section.

"(B) For the purpose of this section, the time of the creation of an interest in real or personal property subject to a power reserved by the grantor to revoke or terminate such interest shall be the time at which such reserved power expires, either by reason of the death of the grantor or by release of the power or otherwise.

"(C) Any interest in real or personal property which would violate the rule against perpetuities, under paragraph (A) hereof, shall be reformed, within the limits of the rule, to approximate most closely the intention of the creator of the interest. In determining whether an interest would violate the rule and in reforming an interest the period of perpetuities shall be measured by actual rather than possible events."

[The Court's discussion of the applicability of Paragraph C to interests created prior to December 31, 1967 is omitted. The court concluded that Paragraph C was applicable to the powers of appointment created by the will of Grace Arrel.]

In the instant case, as stated above, Grace Tod Arrel left the trust to her daughter Frances A. Parson for life, with a power to appoint by will. Mrs. Parson appointed the trust into her own *inter vivos* trust which provided for life estates for her children, as a class, each child to have a power to appoint the remainder of his share by will to or among his issue, with remainders to issue of the children in default of appointment. Under the common law and, in the opinion of the court, under the statute, the period of the perpetuities would run from the death of Mrs. Arrel. Under the common law, the life in being, or the measuring life, would have to have been that of Mrs. Parson, because at the time of Mrs. Arrel's death it could not be said that her daughter would not have more children. Bogert, Trusts and Trustees (2d Ed. 1965) § 213, p. 486. But even under the pre-1967 Ohio rule the life estates in Mrs. Parson's three children vested at the death of their mother, and hence do not violate the rule. Cleveland Trust Co. v. McQuade, supra. The powers of appointment of the remainders given to the children, and the remainders over in default of exercise may not result in vesting within twenty-one years after Mrs. Parson's death, and hence would violate the rule under the common law. These interests, however, under paragraph (C) of O.R.C. 2131.08, would not fail, but would, if necessary, be reformed within the limits of the perpetuities rule, presumably by the Massachusetts courts. In determining whether reformation were necessary under this paragraph, which constitutes the *"cy pres"* and "wait and see" provisions of the Ohio statute, the court of jurisdiction would measure the period of perpetuities by events actually transpired, rather than by events as they might possibly have been from the viewpoint of the original donor at the time of her death. Thus the lives in being, or measuring lives, would be the children themselves, since all of them were actually in being at Mrs. Arrel's death and their powers of appointment would have to be exercised so that the interests subject to their powers would vest within twenty-one years thereafter. In case of the failure of exercise of any power, the remainders over, to the extent that they would actually violate the rule, would be reformed. Mrs. Parson's trust indenture contains a saving clause requiring the vesting of the remainders not later than twenty-one years after the last to die of her issue living at the date of the execution of the indenture, but this, of course, would be reformed, if necessary, with respect to the Arrel assets, to designate the date of death of the last to die of Mrs. Parson's own children as the measuring event.

In conclusion, this court holds that the power of appointment contained in paragraph Third of Item XVI of the will of Grace Tod Arrel is broad enough to permit the donee Frances A. Parson to give her children life estates with powers of appointment for the benefit of, and with remainders over in default of exercise to their issue; that Mrs. Parson did exercise that power by blending her appointive assets with her own into her *inter vivos* trust; that there is no applicable law or policy to prohibit her so doing; that any violations of the rule againt perpetuities resulting therefrom will be reformed; and that, consequently, Mrs. Arrel's testamentary trustee must transmit the balance of the trust assets to Mrs. Parson's trustees.

Note

1. Generally it is held that the validity of the exercise of a power of appointment is governed by the law of the place of creation. Thus the exercise in England of a power created in New York—which would have been valid under the English Rule against Perpetuities—was invalid under the New York Rule, even though the donor and the donee were the same. Matter of Bauer, 14 N.Y.2d 272, 251 N.Y.S.2d 23, 200 N.E.2d 207 (1964). But cf. Matter of Acheson, 28 N.Y.2d 155, 320 N.Y.S.2d 905, 269 N.E.2d 571 (1971) where the New York court gave full faith and credit to a California judgment applying the California cy pres provision (West's Ann.Cal.Civ.Code, § 715.5) to save the testamentary exercise by a California domiciliary of a New York created power, where the exercise would have been invalid under New York law.

2. Was the resort of the court in the principal case to cy pres necessary? Since, in fact, all of Mrs. Parson's children were alive at her mother's death, would not their powers of appointment be valid in a common law jurisdiction under the second look doctrine?

3. On the question whether the donee of a special power can appoint the property in trust, see note 4, p. 858, supra.

Chapter Ten

ESTATE AND GIFT TAXATION

SECTION ONE. INTRODUCTION

A. SCOPE OF CHAPTER

The present chapter is devoted to an introduction to estate and gift taxation and a very brief summary of the more important aspects of the income taxation of trusts.   The subject of taxes is of great significance in the field of decedents' estates.   All substantial gratuitous transfers of property have tax consequences that no practitioner can afford to disregard.   Moreover, as noted earlier, estate taxes represent a substantial interference with the generally free transferability of property by will, and the status of freedom of testation under our law cannot be appreciated without some understanding of those taxes.

This introductory course cannot cover the field of gift and death taxation with any degree of completeness, and the present chapter is by no means a substitute for a tax course.   On the other hand, use of the materials contained in prior chapters requires familiarity with the basic structure of the federal gift and estate taxes, and knowledge of certain widely used tax avoidance possibilities (as well as awareness of the *un*-availability of other superficially plausible tax avoidance measures).

Selection of the materials for the present chapter reflects an effort to set forth the subject matters that a general practitioner would need to know about, for the planning of an estate of modest size—up to about $1,000,000—which is large enough to present substantial tax saving possibilities, and yet not so large as to call for provisions reaching beyond the grandchildren of the testator.   For larger estates, general practitioners will probably wish to consult a specialist in estate planning;   the following materials will not equip them to plan such an estate on their own.

B. RECENT HISTORY OF ESTATE AND GIFT TAXATION

Between 1948—when the marital deduction was adopted—and 1976, the estate and gift tax structure was essentially unchanged.   In 1976 major changes were made by the Tax Reform Act of 1976 and very shortly (as such things are measured) thereafter the Economic Recovery Tax Act of 1981 (ERTA) made further significant changes.

In this brief chapter we, perforce, concentrate on the law as it is, but before doing so we summarize the basic changes made by the recent legislation in the previous law.

Unification of rates.   Under prior law, i.e., before the 1976 changes, the estate tax—which is imposed on transfers at death—and the gift tax— which is imposed on transfers during life—had separate rate schedules and separate exemptions.   The gift tax was a cumulative tax imposed on all taxable gifts made by a person during his life after an initial exemption of $30,000.   The rate was progressive, ranging from 2¼% on the first $5,000 of gifts to a maximum of 57¾% on gifts over $10 million. The estate tax—also progressive—was imposed, after an initial exemption of $60,000, at rates ranging from 3% on the first $5,000 to 77% of the estate over $10 million.   The new statute provided for a single unified rate applicable to all transfers—during life or at death—after an initial "exemption."   The rates adopted in 1976 ranged from 18% to 70%, and, in 1981, a maximum rate of 50% was provided.   As originally enacted that maximum rate was to be phased in and to become fully effective in 1985, but, in 1984, the phase-in of the maximum rate was extended to 1988.

To illustrate the difference between the old and the new structures, let us suppose a person owning property worth $500,000.   Under the old system, he could give away $30,000 in otherwise taxable transactions* without incurring any gift tax.   If during his life he continued to make taxable gifts they would be taxed at increasing rates until the last gift was made.   He could, on the other hand, stop making gifts after the initial $30,000 and never pay a gift tax.   In either event, at his death he would no longer be subject to gift tax, but his remaining property would be subject to estate tax.   However, his estate would be entitled to another exemption of $60,000, i.e., there would be no tax payable on the first $60,000 of property transferred by him at death.   Any property over $60,000 (after allowable deductions, e.g., for debts and expenses) would be taxed at estate tax rates.   Under the new law the property owned during one's life is treated as a single fund and transfers are taxed according to a single rate schedule.   The initial "exemption"—as explained below, the new law uses a "credit" rather than an exemption—was raised in 1976 to $176,625 and in 1981 to $600,000 (when fully effective in 1987).

For a variety of reasons, explained below, there were many advantages to making lifetime transfers under the old law.   The new law eliminated many of the advantages, but not all.   Indeed, in the view of some observers, most of the major tax avoidance techniques of the sophisticated estate planner were not affected.

Generation-skipping transfers.   The new law provided for the first time a tax on generation-skipping transfers.   Formerly, a transfer by A

---

* As discussed below, gifts up to $3,000 per year (now $10,000) to any person were not subject to tax.

to B for life, remainder to C, would be taxed in A's estate but no tax would be payable on account of the transfer of possession from B to C. Under the new law—in some cases—a tax will be assessed on that transfer.

Unlimited marital deduction. Prior to 1976 the marital deduction, i.e. the deduction permitted for certain property passing to a spouse, was limited to one half of the estate of the decedent (or one half of the value of a gift). In 1981 (after a tentative step in 1976) the limitation on the marital deduction was removed to provide for essentially tax free interspousal transfers during life or at death.

Basis of property received from a decedent. Under pre-1976 law, and again today, the "basis", for capital gains tax purposes, of property received from a decedent is its estate tax value. The effect of this "stepped up" basis is that any appreciation in value in the hands of the decedent escapes capital gains tax. A major objective of the 1976 statute was to change that situation by providing, with many exceptions, that the basis of the property in the hands of the decedent (e.g., his cost of acquisition) would "carry over" to the transferee. The carryover basis provision was widely criticized and, after its effective date was extended several times, it was repealed.

Whether the unification of rates and the generation skipping transfer taxes will achieve their objective of making the estate and gift taxes more effective is far from clear. What is clear is that subject to future inflation the tax will affect very many fewer people than it once did and that it will be an even less important source of revenue than it has traditionally been. (See Chapter One, supra).

SECTION TWO. THE GIFT TAX

A. INTRODUCTION

Despite the unification of rates effected in 1976, the gift and estate taxes are separate taxes, separately administered.

The gift tax is levied annually on all taxable gifts made by the donor during the preceding tax year.

I.R.C. (26 U.S.C.A.) § 2501 provides, in part: "A tax, computed as provided in § 2502, is hereby imposed for each calendar year on the transfer of property by gift during such calendar year by any individual * * *."

The tax applies "whether the transfer is in trust or otherwise, whether the gift is direct or indirect, and whether the property is real or personal, tangible or intangible * * *" (I.R.C. § 2511).*

"The code does not specifically define the term 'taxable gift.' The Treasury and the courts have been forced to construct their own definitions by reasoning from general principles with the assistance of certain

---

*Sections 2501 and 2511 exempt certain transfers by non-residents who are not United States citizens.

oblique references in the statute. Without going into the supporting data at this point, a taxable gift may be defined as a voluntary and complete transfer of property by an individual, for less than an adequate and full consideration in money or money's worth, which is not a bona fide transfer at arm's length lacking donative intent." Lowndes, Kramer & McCord, Federal Estate and Gift Taxes (3d ed. 1974) § 24.1 (hereinafter cited as Lowndes, Kramer & McCord). [The authors' definition of a "taxable gift" does not take account of the "annual exclusion" discussed in Section 2B, infra.

Property is not specifically defined *, but the regulations indicate the breadth of the concept:

> Reg. § 25.2511–1 Transfers in general. (a) The gift tax applies to a transfer by way of gift whether the transfer is in trust or otherwise, whether the gift is direct or indirect, and whether the property is real or personal, tangible or intangible. For example, a taxable transfer may be effected by the creation of a trust, the forgiving of a debt, the assignment of a judgment, the assignment of the benefits of an insurance policy, or the transfer of cash, certificates of deposit, or Federal, State or municipal bonds. Statutory provisions which exempt bonds, notes, bills and certificates of indebtedness of the Federal Government or its agencies and the interest thereon from taxation are not applicable to the gift tax, since the gift tax is an excise tax on the transfer, and is not a tax on the subject of the gift.

The breadth of the concepts of "gift" and "property" has recently been reaffirmed by the United States Supreme Court in Dickman v. C.I.R. —— U.S. —— , 104 S.Ct. 1086, 79 L.Ed.2d 343 (1984) where the Court held that intra-family interest-free demand loans were "gifts" under the gift tax statute.

B. THE ANNUAL EXCLUSION AND "GIFT-SPLITTING"

Despite the generality of Sections 2501 and 2511, not all gifts are taxable.

Section 2503 provides:

> (a) General Definition.—The term "taxable gifts" means the total amount of gifts made during the calendar year, less the deductions provided in subchapter C (section 2522 and following).**

> (b) Exclusions From Gifts.—In the case of gifts (other than gifts of future interests in property) made to any person by the donor during the calendar year, the first $10,000 of such gifts to such person shall not, for purposes of subsection (a), be included in the total amount of gifts made

---

* Suppose that legatees under a will, or persons entitled to an estate by intestate succession, relinquish their interests. Have they made a gift to the person who takes the property? Suppose a fiduciary (a trustee or executor) waives the right to statutory commissions, has he made a gift to the beneficiaries? See Hardenburgh v. Com'r, 198 F.2d 63 (8th Cir. 1952): Revenue Ruling 66–167, 66–1 C.B. 20. On the effect of state law on the definition of "gift," see Lowndes, Kramer & McCord § 24.6.

** These deductions—for charitable and similar gifts (§ 2522) and for inter-spousal gifts (§ 2523) are discussed in the section on estate taxes, infra pp. 930–948.

during such year. Where there has been a transfer to any person of a present interest in property, the possibility that such interest may be diminished by the exercise of a power shall be disregarded in applying this subsection, if no part of such interest will at any time pass to any other person.

(c) Transfer for the Benefit of Minor.—No part of a gift to an individual who has not attained the age of 21 years on the date of such transfer shall be considered a gift of a future interest in property for purposes of subsection (b) if the property and the income therefrom—

(1) may be expended by, or for the benefit of, the donee before his attaining the age of 21 years, and

(2) will to the extent not so expended—

(A) pass to the donee on his attaining the age of 21 years, and

(B) in the event the donee dies before attaining the age of 21 years, be payable to the estate of the donee or as he may appoint under a general power of appointment as defined in section 2514(c).

(e) * Exclusion for Certain Transfers for Educational Expenses or Medical Expenses.—

(1) In general.—Any qualified transfer shall not be treated as a transfer of property by gift for purposes of this chapter.

(2) Qualified transfer.—For purposes of this subsection, the term "qualified transfer" means any amount paid on behalf of an individual—

(A) as tuition to an educational organization described in section 170(b)(1)(A)(ii) for the education or training of such individual, or

(B) to any person who provides medical care (as defined in section 213(e)) with respect to such individual as payment for such medical care.

For a married person, the utility of the annual exclusion may be doubled by the "split-gift" provisions of § 2513 which provide in part:

(1) In General.—A gift made by one spouse to any person other than his spouse shall, for the purposes of this chapter, be considered as made one-half by him and one-half by his spouse * * *.

(2) Consent Of Both Spouses.—Paragraph (1) shall apply only if both spouses have signified (under the regulations provided for in subsection (b)) their consent to the application of paragraph (1) in the case of all such gifts made during the calendar year by either while married to the other.

---

* Subsection (d) providing that payments to an Individual Retirement Account for a spouse were not gifts of "future interests" was repealed as to transfers after December 31, 1981 (the advent of the unlimited marital deduction.)

What was modestly conceived as an exemption to cover Christmas and wedding gifts (somewhat immodest gifts, to be sure) has been transmuted over time to an important tool in estate planning. An unmarried taxpayer may make non-taxable gifts of up to $10,000 (except gifts of future interests) to any number of individuals in any year, and there will be no tax consequences—not even a gift tax return. With the consent of her spouse a married taxpayer may make non-taxable gifts of $20,000 to each person. If a married couple has a number of children, or grandchildren, and they start a program of "annual giving" early enough, a substantial amount of property can be transferred with no tax consequences except the filing of a gift tax return, which contains the spousal consent.

So long as the objective of the exemption provision was viewed as permitting "Christmas and wedding gifts," the denial of exemption to gifts of future interests was not too troublesome. From the viewpoint of estate planning, however, the denial was quite serious. In the typical situation the tax objective is to pass the property to the younger generation tax-free, and if the donees are minors, there is the problem of making the gift "present" but keeping it out of the minor's control. Until the enactment of § 2503(c), supra, the favorite device for making such gifts— the trust—was unsatisfactory. See Stifel v. Commissioner, 197 F.2d 107 (2d Cir. 1952).

Perhaps an even more remarkable tribute to the importance of "estate planning" than the enactment of § 2503(c) was the invention of a new property arrangement: the holding of property by a custodian under the Uniform Gifts to Minors Acts. See p. 406, supra. Some form of this Act, first proposed in 1956, has now been enacted in every state. See Cary, Reflections upon the American Law Institute Tax Project and the Internal Revenue Code: A Plea for a Moratorium and Reappraisal, 60 Colum.L.Rev. 259, 263–64 (1960).

It should be noted that the importance of the "split gift" provisions of § 2513 is not limited to the annual exclusion. They also permit one spouse to take advantage of the credit and lower brackets of the other.* Where both spouses have considerable property, this aspect of § 2513 is probably not too important, but where only one spouse has property it permits him or her to give away twice as much before any tax is due.

Notes

1. If a donor has made birthday or similar presents to the donee, can she safely make another gift of $10,000 in the same year? Does the nature of the

---

* Under § 2001 (infra p. 958), where the split gift provision is used and the property subject to the gift is later included in the gross estate of the donor, the gift tax paid by the spouse can be offset against the estate tax due. The effect is to reverse the consequences of having treated the surviving spouse as the donor of one half of such a gift. The reversal is not complete, however, since there is no restoration of any portion of a surviving spouse's unified credit which may have been used up by a transaction later included in the gross estate of the donor.

first gift matter—a check or a sweater? The practice of many estate planners seems to be to ignore such gifts, but the statute seems clearly to the contrary.

2. For gift tax purposes the term "future interests" includes not only reversions, remainders and such interests but any interest "limited to commence in use, possession or enjoyment at some future date or time," regardless of its characterization under property law. 26 C.F.R. § 25.2503–3a. The Internal Revenue Service has taken the position that an outright gift to an infant is a present interest even though, in fact, he is incapable of possessing or enjoying the property. Revenue Ruling 54–400, 1934 C.B. 319. And in Crummey v. Commissioner, 397 F.2d 82 (9th Cir. 1968) it was held that where an infant or a guardian may demand a distribution from a trust, the interest subject to the power is a present interest even though no guardian has been appointed. This case has spawned a sub-specialty of estate planning, the "Crummey trust."

C. COMPUTATION OF THE GIFT TAX

Although simple in concept, the application of the gift tax is complicated by the fact that it is levied annually at rates based on the aggregate amount of taxable gifts made during the taxpayer's life, and by the system of credits against tax established in 1976.

I.R.C. § 2502 provides, in part:

(a) Computation of Tax—The tax imposed by section 2501 for each calendar year shall be an amount equal to the excess of—

(1) a tentative tax, computed in accordance with the rate schedule set forth in section 2001(c), on the aggregate sum of the taxable gifts for such calendar year and for each of the preceding calendar periods, over

(2) a tentative tax, computed in accordance with such rate schedule, on the aggregate sum of the taxable gifts for each of the preceding calendar periods.

The rates for both gift and estate taxes are established by § 2001(c):

(c) Rate Schedule.—

(1) In General

If the amount with respect to which the tentative tax to be computed is:	The tentative tax is:
Not over $10,000	18 percent of such amount.
Over $10,000 but not over $20,000	$1,800, plus 20 percent of the excess of such amount over $10,000.
Over $20,000 but not over $40,000	$3,800, plus 22 percent of the excess of such amount over $20,000.
Over $40,000 but not over $60,000	$8,200, plus 24 percent of the excess of such amount over $40,000.
Over $60,000 but not over $80,000	$13,000, plus 26 percent of the excess of such amount over $60,000.

Over $80,000 but not over $100,000	$18,200, plus 28 percent of the excess of such amount over $80,000.
Over $100,000 but not over $150,000	$23,800, plus 30 percent of the excess of such amount over $100,000.
Over $150,000 but not over $250,000	$38,800, plus 32 percent of the excess of such amount over $150,000.
Over $250,000 but not over $500,000	$70,800, plus 34 percent of the excess of such amount over $250,000.
Over $500,000 but not over $750,000	$155,800, plus 37 percent of the excess of such amount over $500,000.
Over $750,000 but not over $1,000,000	$248,300, plus 39 percent of the excess of such amount over $750,000.
Over $1,000,000 but not over $1,250,000	$345,800, plus 41 percent of the excess of such amount over $1,000,000.
Over $1,250,000 but not over $1,500,000	$448,300, plus 43 percent of the excess of such amount over $1,250,000.
Over $1,500,000 but not over $2,000,000	$555,800, plus 45 percent of the excess of such amount over $1,500,000.
Over $2,000,000 but not over $2,500,000	$780,800, plus 49 percent of the excess of such amount over $2,000,000
Over $2,500,000	$1,025,800, plus 50 percent of the excess of such amount over $2,500,000.

(2) Phase-in of 50 percent maximum rate.—

(A) In general.—In the case of decedents dying, and gifts made, before 1988, there shall be substituted for the last item in the schedule contained in paragraph (1) the items determined under this paragraph.

(B) For 1982.—In the case of decedents dying, and gifts made, in 1982, the substitution under this paragraph shall be as follows:

If the amount with respect to which the tentative tax to be computed is:	The tentative tax is:
Over $2,500,000 but not over $3,000,000	$1,025,800, plus 53% of the excess over $2,500,000.
Over $3,000,000 but not over $3,500,000	$1,290,800, plus 57% of the excess over $3,000,000.
Over $3,500,000 but not over $4,000,000	$1,575,800, plus 61% of the excess over $3,500,000.
Over $4,000,000	$1,880,800, plus 65% of the excess over $4,000,000.

(C) For 1983.—In the case of decedents dying, and gifts made, in 1983, the substitution under this paragraph shall be as follows:

If the amount with respect to which the tentative tax to be computed is:	The tentative tax is:
Over $2,500,000 but not over $3,000,000....................	$1,025,800, plus 53% of the excess over $2,500,000.
Over $3,000,000 but not over $3,500,000....................	$1,290,800, plus 57% of the excess over $3,000,000.
Over $3,500,000	$1,575,800, plus 60% of the excess over $3,500,000.

(D) For 1984, 1985, 1986, or 1987.—In the case of decedents dying, and gifts made, in 1984, 1985, 1986, or 1987, the substitution under this paragraph shall be as follows:

If the amount with respect to which the tentative tax to be computed is:	The tentative tax is:
Over $2,500,000 but not over $3,000,000	$1,025,800, plus 53% of the excess over $2,500,000.
Over $3,000,000	$1,290,800, plus 55% of the excess over $3,000,000.

The final piece in the puzzle is supplied by § 2505 which provides:

(a) General Rule.—In the case of a citizen or resident of the United States, there shall be allowed as a credit against the tax imposed by section 2501 for each calendar year an amount equal to—

(1) $192,800, reduced by

(2) the sum of the amounts allowable as a credit to the individual under this section for all preceding calendar periods.

(b) Phase-in of Credit.—

In the case of gifts made in:	Subsection (a)(1) shall be applied by substituting for "$192,800" the following amount:
1982..	$ 62,800
1983..	79,300
1984..	96,300
1985..	121,800
1986..	155,800

(c) Adjustment to Credit for Certain Gifts Made Before 1977.—The amount allowable under subsection (a) shall be reduced by an amount equal to 20 percent of the aggregate amount allowed as a specific exemption under section 2521 (as in effect before its repeal by the Tax Reform Act of 1976) with respect to gifts made by the individual after September 8, 1976.

(d) Limitation Based on Amount of Tax.—The amount of the credit allowed under subsection (a) for any calendar year shall not exceed the amount of the tax imposed by section 2501 for such calendar year.

Experience teaches that, on first encounter, these provisions can be more than a little confusing. It is hoped that the following illustration will help.

Suppose that A, a widow, who has not made any taxable gifts previously, makes the following gifts to her grandchildren: In 1985 to B, $10,000; to C, $10,000; to D, $50,000. In 1986, $50,000 to each. In 1987, $100,000 to each. In 1988, $100,000 to each. (Some people have the nicest grandmothers).

A's gift tax situation would be as follows: In 1985, the gifts to B and C would not exceed the annual exclusion and, therefore, would have no tax consequences. (They would not even have to be reported.) However, A would have made a taxable gift of $40,000 to D ($50,000 minus the $10,000 annual exclusion). Since this is A's first taxable gift, her tax, under § 2502 is the tax on the aggregate sum of the taxable gifts made in 1985. Under § 2001(c) the tax on $40,000 is $8,200. However, no tax is *payable* because of the credit to which she is entitled under § 2505. (Note that the use of the credit is mandatory, the taxpayer cannot pay the tax and preserve the credit for a later day.)

In 1986, A would have made taxable gifts of $120,000. Under § 2502, her tax would be *the excess* of a tentative tax on the aggregate sum of the taxable gifts made in 1986 plus the taxable gifts made in 1985 ($120,000 plus $40,000) *over a* tentative tax on the gifts made in 1985 ($40,000). Under § 2001(c) the tax on $160,000 is $42,000; the tax on $40,000 is $8,200 and the tax on account of the 1986 gifts is $33,800 (the excess of $42,000 over $8,200). Again, however, no tax would be payable because of the credit under § 2505.

In 1987, A would have made taxable gifts of $270,000. Her gift tax for that year would be $90,000 (the excess of a tentative tax on total gifts to date of $430,000 ($132,000) over a tentative tax on the $160,000 of gifts made in prior years ($42,000). Once again, no tax would be payable because of the credit under § 2505. Note however, that A would now have used up $132,000 of her lifetime credit.

In 1988, A again makes taxable gifts of $270,000. Her gift tax for 1988 is $97,800 against which she would have a credit of $60,800 (what is left of her lifetime credit of $192,800) and she would have to pay $37,000. Since her credit is now exhausted, any additional taxable gifts would require payment of tax.

The system of credits may seem (and be) unnecessarily cumbersome but the "bottom line" should be clear. Under existing law—when the credit is fully operative in 1987—an individual may make taxable gifts totalling $600,000 in her lifetime without paying any gift tax. However, any additional gifts will be taxed at progressive rates beginning at 37%. And, of course, there will be no credit left to offset against estate taxes.

SECTION THREE.　THE ESTATE TAX

A.　THE GROSS ESTATE

The estate tax is based upon the amount of property considered to "pass" from the decedent at death—in this respect it differs from inheritance taxes, discussed briefly at p. 36, supra, which are based on the amount of property received by each beneficiary. The taxable estate includes not only property of the kind normally thought of as part of the probate estate, but property such as annuities, joint interests, powers of appointment, and life insurance, which are usually not subject to probate but are essentially testamentary in nature. In addition the tax reaches property no longer owned by the decedent but as to which the decedent has retained certain strings such as enjoyment of the income during life, or the power to revoke the transfer.

In this section we will examine in some detail the nature of the inclusions in the gross estate. In succeeding sections we will treat the allowable deductions—most importantly, the marital deduction—the allocation of estate tax, the relationship between the estate and gift tax, and the provisions on generation-skipping transfers.

1.　*Property Owned at Death*

Internal Revenue Code (26 U.S.C.A.) § 2033:

The value of the gross estate shall include the value of all property to the extent of the interest therein of the decedent at the time of his death.

Treasury Regulations § 20.2033–1:

Property in which the decedent has an interest—(a) *In general.* The gross estate of a decedent who was a citizen or resident of the United States at the time of his death includes under section 2033 the value of all property, whether real or personal, tangible or intangible, and wherever situated, beneficially owned by the decedent at the time of his death * * *. Real property is included whether it came into the possession and control of the executor or administrator or passed directly to heirs or devisees. Various statutory provisions which exempt bonds, notes, bills, and certificates of indebtedness of the Federal Government or its agencies and the interest thereon from taxation are generally not applicable to the estate tax, since such tax is an excise tax on the transfer of property at death and is not a tax on the property transferred.

(b) *Miscellaneous examples.* A cemetery lot owned by the decedent is part of his gross estate, but its value is limited to the salable value of that part of the lot which is not designed for the interment of the decedent and the members of his family. Property subject to homestead or other exemptions under local law is included in the gross estate. Notes or other claims held by the decedent are likewise included even though they are cancelled by the decedent's will. Interest and rents accrued at the date of the decedent's death constitute a part of the gross estate. Similarly, dividends which are payable to the decedent or his estate by reason of the fact that on or before the date of the decedent's death he was a stockholder of record (but which have not been collected at death) constitute a part of the gross estate.

Notes

1. As the Regulation indicates, the section is designed to bring within the gross estate property of all kinds. Its reach is only to property interests which survive the death of the decedent. Thus, a life estate for the life of the decedent is not part of his gross estate, nor is a contingent remainder defeated by his death.

2. Had § 2033 been given a broad construction—as the concept of income has, under the income tax provisions—many of the other sections of the Code would probably have been unnecessary. On the relationship of § 2033 to the other sections, see Lowndes, Kramer & McCord, §§ 4.4 and 4.5.

2. Transfers Within Three Years of Death

Prior to the Tax Reform Act of 1976, § 2035 provided for inclusion in the gross estate of "transfers in contemplation of death." * The statute expressly provided that no transfer made more than three years prior to death was to be treated as in contemplation of death. For transfers made within three years prior to death, the statute created a *rebuttable* presumption that the gift was in contemplation of death. Rebuttal required a showing that the gift was not motivated by considerations of the sort that lead to testamentary disposition. United States v. Wells, 283 U.S. 102, 51 S.Ct. 446, 75 L.Ed. 867 (1931).

Since the question turned on the subjective state of mind of the decedent, a difficult factual determination was required in each case. For the lawyer whose elderly client was about to make inter vivos gifts it was important to create a record of a "life purpose." See, e.g., Kniskern v. United States, 232 F.Supp. 7 (S.D.Fla.1964), where gifts by a 99 year old man one year before his death were held *not* to be in contemplation of death.

But even where there was thought to be little chance that a gift would escape tax under § 2035, there were advantages in making the gift and paying the gift tax. As pointed out by the House Ways and Means Committee: "Since the gift tax paid on a lifetime transfer which is included in a decedent's gross estate is taken into account both as a credit against the estate tax and also as a reduction in the estate tax base, substantial tax savings can be derived under present law by making so-called "deathbed gifts" even though the transfer is subject to both taxes." H.R. 94–1380 at 12.

The 1976 statute removed the uncertainty about whether a gift was "life motivated" or "death motivated" by including within the gross estate all transfers made within three years before death. In addition, to elim-

---

* The concept of "contemplation of death" under § 2035 was very different from "causa mortis" discussed at pp. 373 et seq. supra.

inate any tax incentive for "deathbed" transfers, the 1976 statute "grossed up" the amount of the gift tax paid, i.e., it included that amount in the gross estate.

As noted earlier, the adoption of the unified rate structure made the distinction between lifetime and death transfers considerably less important, so that the chief adverse consequence for taxpayers of the change from a rebuttable to a conclusive presumption was that it subjected to tax any appreciation in value of property transferred between the time of transfer and the transferor's death. In 1981, § 2035 was amended to eliminate, in estates of decedents dying after December 31, 1981, the tax on post-gift appreciation on most transfers. However, the gross-up provisions remain in effect.

Section 2035 now provides (with respect to estates of decedents dying after December 31, 1981):

(a) Inclusion of Gifts Made by Decedent.—Except as provided in subsection (b), the value of the gross estate shall include the value of all property to the extent of any interest therein of which the decedent has at any time made a transfer, by trust or otherwise, during the 3-year period ending on the date of the decedent's death.

(b) Exceptions.—Subsection (a) shall not apply

(1) to any bona fide sale for an adequate and full consideration in money or money's worth, and

(2) to any gift to a donee made during a calendar year if the decedent was not required by section 6019 (other than by reason of section 6019(2)) to file any gift tax return for such year with respect to gifts to such donee. Paragraph (2) shall not apply to any transfer with respect to a life insurance policy.

(c) Inclusion of Gift Tax on Certain Gifts Made During 3 Years Before Decedent's Death.—The amount of the gross estate (determined without regard to this subsection) shall be increased by the amount of any tax paid under chapter 12 by the decedent or his estate on any gift made by the decedent or his spouse after December 31, 1976, and during the 3-year period ending on the date of the decedent's death.

(d) Decedents Dying After 1981.—

(1) In general.—Except as otherwise provided in this subsection, subsection (a) shall not apply to the estate of a decedent dying after December 31, 1981.

(2) Exceptions for certain transfers.—Paragraph (1) of this subsection and paragraph 2 of subsection (b) shall not apply to a transfer of an interest in property which is included in the value of the gross estate under section 2036, 2037, 2038, or 2042 or would have been included under any of such sections if such interest had been retained by the decedent.

(3) 3-year rule retained for certain purposes.—Paragraph (1) shall not apply for purposes of—

(A) section 303(b) (relating to distributions in redemption of stock to pay death taxes),

(B) section 2032A (relating to special valuation of certain farm, etc., real property), and

(C) subchapter C of chapter 64 (relating to lien for taxes).

* * *

Notes

1. Subsection d(2) is aimed at "two-step" transactions—where the transferor transfers property but retains a string sufficient to subject the property to estate taxation, and, later, gives away the retained string within three years of death. (See p. 906, infra.)

2. Section 2035(d)(3) prevents the use of last-minute gifts to remove property from the estate in order to qualify the estate for statutory allowances where availability depends on the size and composition of the gross estate, and makes property transferred within three years of death liable for certain tax liens.

3. Gifts included in the estate under Sections 2035–2038 are valued for estate tax purposes not at the time of transfer but at the time of the transferor's death. Where the transferee has retained the property intact there should be few problems, but suppose the property has been sold and the proceeds invested. See Lowndes, Kramer & McCord § 18.7.

3. Incomplete Transfers

As in the case of gifts in contemplation of death, it was recognized from the beginning that if wholesale avoidance was to be prevented, some provision had to be made for taxing lifetime transfers in which the transferor retained some string on the property. Accordingly the first estate tax statute in 1916 taxed transfers by "trust or otherwise * * * intended to take effect in possession or enjoyment at or after his death." Revenue Act of 1916, ch. 463, § 202(b), 39 Stat. 777.

Had that provision been given full effect in light of the policy of the statute, much of the controversy which has surrounded the subject of incomplete transfers might have been avoided; in fact the provisions have had an extraordinarily complicated history and have produced a large volume of litigation. As necessary as a grasp of that history may be for a complete understanding of the subject, the time available here must be spent on the law in its present form. There are three provisions of the Code dealing with incomplete transfers: Section 2036 deals with transfers as to which the decedent has retained the income, or the right to designate who will receive the income. Section 2037 deals with transfers as to which the decedent has retained a reversionary interest and where enjoyment of the property transferred can be obtained only by surviving the decedent. Section 2038 deals with transfers as to which the decedent has reserved a power of revocation or any other of various powers over the property or income therefrom. A particular transfer may of course be includible under more than one section, for example where a decedent has retained both a power to revoke, and the income for life. It is important to realize that the entire value of the interest as to which the "string" is retained—valued as of the death of the transferor—is taxable, and not just the value of the string itself.

Because of the complex overlap of judicial decisions and Congressional responses which make up the history of §§ 2036–2038, the precise date of any transfer may be of great importance. For example, a retained life estate does not cause inclusion in the gross estate if the life estate was created prior to March 4, 1931.

1976 and 1981 statutes did not make major changes in the provisions on incomplete transfers. Assuming that the unification of rates achieves the objective of lessening the importance of the distinction between life and death transfers, those provisions will be less important than they were. Their major effect will be to bring the property transferred back into the estate at date of death values. There will still be an overlap of the gift and estate taxes (see Section D, infra). And, unlike transfers within three years of death, incomplete transfers will not be "grossed up" in the estate; i.e., the amount of any gift tax on the transfer will not be included in the estate.

a. Transfers With Retained Life Interest.

Internal Revenue Code (26 U.S.C.A.) § 2036:

(a) General Rule.—The value of the gross estate shall include the value of the property to the extent of any interest therein of which the decedent has at any time made a transfer (except in case of a bona fide sale for an adequate and full consideration in money or money's worth), by trust or otherwise, under which he has retained for his life or for any period not ascertainable without reference to his death or for any period which does not in fact end before his death—

(1) the possession or enjoyment of, or the right to the income from, the property, or

(2) the right, either alone or in conjunction with any person, to designate the persons who shall possess or enjoy the property or the income therefrom.

(b) Voting Rights.—

(1) In general.—For purposes of subsection (a)(1), the retention of the right to vote (directly or indirectly) shares of stock of a controlled corporation shall be considered to be a retention of the enjoyment of transferred property.

(2) Controlled corporation.—For purposes of paragraph (1), a corporation shall be treated as a controlled corporation if, at any time after the transfer of the property and during the 3-year period ending on the date of the decedent's death, the decedent owned (with the application of section 318), or had the right (either alone or in conjunction with any person) to vote stock possessing at least 20 percent of the total combined voting power of all classes of stock.

(3) Coordination with section 2035.—For purposes of applying section 2035 with respect to paragraph (1), the relinquishment or cessation of voting rights shall be treated as a transfer of property made by the decedent.

(c) Limitation on Application of General Rule.—This section shall not apply to a transfer made before March 4, 1931; nor to a transfer made after March 3, 1931, and before June 7, 1932, unless the property transferred would have been includible in the decedent's gross estate by reason of the amendatory language of the joint resolution of March 3, 1931 (46 Stat. 1516).

Treasury Regulations § 20.2036–1 (in part):

(b) * * * (2) The "use, possession, right to the income, or other enjoyment of the transferred property" is considered as having been retained by or reserved to the decedent to the extent that the use, possession, right to the income, or other enjoyment is to be applied toward the discharge of a legal obligation of the decedent, or otherwise for his pecuniary benefit. The term "legal obligation" includes a legal obligation to support a dependent during the decedent's lifetime.

(3) The phrase "right * * * to designate the person or persons who shall possess or enjoy the transferred property or the income therefrom" includes a reserved power to designate the person or persons to receive the income from the transferred property, or to possess or enjoy nonincome-producing property, during the decedent's life or during any other period described in paragraph (a) of this section. With respect to such a power, it is immaterial (i) whether the power was exercisable alone or only in conjunction with another person or persons, whether or not having an adverse interest; (ii) in what capacity the power was exercisable by the decedent or by another person or persons in conjunction with the decedent; and (iii) whether the exercise of the power was subject to a contingency beyond the decedent's control which did not occur before his death (e.g., the death of another person during the decedent's lifetime). The phrase, however, does not include a power over the transferred property itself which does not affect the enjoyment of the income received or earned during the decedent's life. (See, however, section 2038 for the inclusion of property in the gross estate on account of such a power.) Nor does the phrase apply to a power held solely by a person other than the decedent. But, for example, if the decedent reserved the unrestricted power to remove or discharge a trustee at any time and appoint himself as trustee, the decedent is considered as having the powers of the trustee.

ESTATE OF RAPELJE v. COMMISSIONER
73 T.C. 82 (1979).

[On August 11, 1969, the decedent (who died in 1973) transferred his personal residence in Saratoga Springs, New York, to his two daughters, Mrs. Wright and Mrs. Mulligan. Except for a vacation in Florida from November, 1969, to May, 1970, he continued to live in the house until he died.]

Dawson, Judge:

The issue presented here is whether the value of decedent's residence must be included in his gross estate pursuant to section 2036. * * *

This section requires property to be included in the decedent's estate if he retained the actual possession or enjoyment thereof, even though he may have had no enforceable right to do so. Estate of Honigman v. Commissioner, 66 T.C. 1080, 1082 (1976); Estate of Linderme v. Commissioner, 52 T.C. 305, 308 (1969). Possession or enjoyment of gifted property is retained when there is an express or implied understanding to that effect among the parties at the time of transfer. Guynn v. United States, 437 F.2d 1148, 1150 (4th Cir. 1971); Estate of Honigman v. Commissioner, supra at 1082; Estate of Hendry v. Commissioner, 62 T.C. 861, 872 (1974); Estate of Barlow v. Commissioner, 55 T.C. 666, 670 (1971).[1] The burden is on the petitioner to disprove the existence of any implied agreement or understanding, and that burden is particularly onerous when intrafamily arrangements are involved. Skinner's Estate v. United States, 316 F.2d 517, 520 (3rd Cir. 1963); Estate of Hendry v. Commissioner, supra at 872; Estate of Kerdolff v. Commissioner, 57 T.C. 643, 648 (1972).

In the present case, there was no express agreement allowing decedent to retain possession and enjoyment of the home. Respondent, however, contends that the facts support an inference of an implied understanding between the decedent and his daughters whereby decedent was allowed to live in the house until he was able to locate a new home. Petitioners maintain that although such an understanding may have arisen after decedent suffered his stroke, there was no such agreement in existence at the time of the gift. [In July 1970, decedent suffered a stroke that left him paralyzed on his right side and unable to speak.] Based on our review of the record before us, we conclude that petitioners have failed to meet their burden of proving that a tacit agreement did not arise contemporaneously with the transfer.

In determining whether there was an implied understanding between the parties, all facts and circumstances surrounding the transfer and subsequent use of the property must be considered. The continued exclusive possession by the donor and the withholding of possession from the donee are particularly significant factors. Guynn v. United States, supra at 1150; compare Estate of Linderme v. Commissioner, supra at 309, with Estate of Gutchess v. Commissioner, 46 T.C. 554, 557 (1966). In the present case, the donor maintained almost exclusive occupancy of the residence until his death in 1973. The transfer took place in August 1969. Decedent continued to live there alone until September 1969. Sometime in September, Mrs. Mulligan's niece moved in with her husband and they stayed until January 1970. In November 1969, the decedent went to Florida and did not return until May 1970. From May 1970

---

1. We note here that under sec. 2036 it is irrelevant whether the parties *intended* at the time of transfer that the decedent would retain possession and enjoyment *for his life*. The statute requires only that the decedent retain possession or enjoyment "for any period which does not *in fact* end before his death." See Estate of Honigman v. Commissioner, 66 T.C. 1080 (1976). Thus, even if the donees in the present case understood at the time of transfer that decedent would remain in the house only until he found a new home, there would still be inclusion under sec. 2036 because he retained possession or enjoyment of the property up to the time of his death.

until September 1971, the decedent lived alone at the residence.   In September 1971, Mrs. Mulligan's daughter moved in and stayed for several months.   Thereafter, the decedent was the sole occupant of the residence.

A plausible argument could be made that the donees were making indirect use of the property by allowing their relatives to stay there, particularly if they did so over the decedent's objection.   There is nothing in the record, however, to support that proposition.   Decedent may have been wholly indifferent to their use of the property, or he may even have invited them himself.   Even if he had violently opposed the presence of the guests, that would only tend to show an intent by the donees to exercise dominion and control over the property, which is only one factor to be considered in deciding whether decedent retained possession pursuant to an implied agreement.

In spite of the donees' continued residence in their original houses after the gift, petitioners argue that the conduct of the parties subsequent to the transfer negates the existence of any implied agreement.   For example, they contend that the primary purpose of decedent's 6-month sojourn in Florida soon after the transfer was to purchase a new house. We disagree.   Although decedent did look at one house for sale in Fort Lauderdale, the record does not reveal any extensive house hunting activity.   Moreover, the decedent had made identical winter trips to Florida every year for the past 10 years.   Thus, we are not convinced that the decedent felt any compelling need to locate a new home on this particular visit.

Petitioners also maintain that Mrs. Mulligan intended to move into the residence in 1971 when her husband was due to retire.   In anticipation of this event, the couple visited the home frequently on weekends and vacations and made some repairs.   Mrs. Mulligan also notified her employer in Buffalo that she would be leaving in 1971.   This planned move was abandoned, of course, when the decedent suffered his stroke. We think that Mrs. Mulligan did intend to move into the residence eventually, but the facts suggest to us that the move was implicitly conditioned on the successful conclusion of the decedent's search for a new home.

There are other facts which support an inference of an implied understanding between the parties.   The decedent paid no rent to his daughters for the continued use of the property.   Although Mrs. Wright did pay some utility bills relating to the property, the decedent continued to pay the real estate taxes.   Neither daughter made any attempt to sell her own house.   Nor did they ever attempt to sell or rent the residence prior to the decedent's death.   The plain fact of the matter is that with the exception of the change in record title, the gift of the property did not effect any substantial changes in the relationship of the parties to the residence.   Thus, we find that there was an implied understanding between the parties arising contemporaneously with the transfer whereby the decedent was allowed to retain possession or enjoyment of the residence for a period which did not in fact end before his death.

Accordingly, we hold that under section 2036 the value of the residence must be included in decedent's gross estate.

Notes

1. Compare Estate of Sylvia H. Roemer, T.C. Memo. (P-H) para. 83,509, where the decedent and her daughter jointly occupied a residence owned by the decedent for several years before the decedent transferred the residence to the daughter and continued to occupy the residence jointly thereafter. The Tax Court held the property transferred was not includible in the gross estate under § 2036.

2. The introduction (in 1932) of the language "or for any period not ascertainable without reference to his death or for any period which does not in fact end before his death" is illustrative of the continuing battle between the tax laws and the ingenuity of taxpayers. Suppose, for example, the testator transferred property reserving to himself the income payable semi-annually but providing that no income between the last semi-annual payment and death would be paid to him or his estate. Would that be a transfer with income retained "for life"? See H.R.Rep.No. 708, 72d Cong., 1st Sess. 47 (1933). Or suppose a 70 year old person transfers property reserving to himself the income for ten years, and dies five years later. Has he made a transfer retaining a life interest? Ibid., and see Reg. § 20.2036–1(b)(i).

3. In the case of income producing property, the "right to income" is the "possession or enjoyment" thereof. The "possession or enjoyment" language allows the inclusion in the gross estate of "property that does not produce income in the conventional sense, such as a work of art given to a donee subject to the donor's right to retain it in his home for life or for either of the two other periods specified by section 2036(a)(1)." Bittker, Transfers Subject to Retained Right To Receive The Income or Designate The Income Beneficiary, 34 Rutgers L.Rev. 668, 669 (1982).

4. The settlor of a trust who would declare himself trustee must be careful not to retain any power to affect beneficial interests. An independent trustee can, of course, safely be given such powers. If the independent trustee is given such powers, can the settlor retain the power to change trustees? In Rev.Rul. 79–353, the IRS took the position that "reservation by the settlor of the power to remove a corporate trustee at will and appoint another corporate trustee is equivalent to reservation of the trustee's powers." The value of the trust property was included in the gross estate under 2036(a)(2) and 2038(a)(i). See p. 920, infra, for a discussion of the relationship of § 2036(a)(2) and § 2038.

5. Regulations § 20.2036–1(b) supra defines "use, possession" etc. to include the discharge of a legal obligation of the grantor, including a legal obligation to support a dependent. The application of this provision is discussed in Lowndes, Kramer & McCord § 9.14:

> The most litigated problems in connection with taxing trusts to discharge a legal obligation of the transferor under Section 2036(a) have arisen in connection with trusts for the benefit of someone whom the grantor of the trust was under a legal obligation to support. If the income from the trust is to be used to discharge the grantor's liability, and the grantor can compel its devotion to this purpose, then the trust property is taxable to his estate under Section 2036(a). If, however, the trustees have discretion about applying the income from the trust for the support of the dependent,

the trust property will not be taxed to the grantor of the trust, if he is not a trustee and cannot direct the use of the trust income for this purpose. However, if the grantor is one of the trustees who has the power to direct the use of the trust income to support his dependents, the trust property will be taxable to his estate irrespective of whether the trust income is actually so employed. The fact that the trust specifies that the trust income is to be used for this purpose does not justify the taxation of the trust property to the grantor's estate if the beneficiaries are entitled to the trust income without any restriction and the grantor cannot compel its use for their support unless under local law the receipt of the trust income operates to discharge either in part or in full the obligations of support. If the trust was for the support of a child who reached 21 before the settlor's death it cannot be taxed to his estate in any event, since the obligation to support the child ceased before the transferor's death.

6. The provision dealing with the retention of the right to vote stock, now appearing as 2036(b) was added by the Tax Reform Act of 1976, to overrule the Supreme Court decision in United States v. Byrum, 408 U.S. 125, 92 S.Ct. 2382, 33 L.Ed.2d 238 (1972), where the Supreme Court held that the stock of a closely held corporation was not includible in the decedent's gross estate where the decedent had irrevocably transferred the stock in trust reserving the power to (1) remove the trustee and appoint another corporate trustee, (2) vote the closely held stock, (3) veto the sale or other transfer of the trust property, and (4) veto any change in investments. The Court found that the reserved rights did not constitute retained enjoyment of the stock or the right to designate the person or persons who would enjoy the stock or the income from the stock. Section 2036(b) applies to transfers made after June 22, 1976.

UNITED STATES v. ALLEN

United States Court of Appeals, Tenth Circuit, 1961.
293 F.2d 916, certiorari denied, 368 U.S. 944, 82 S.Ct. 378, 7 L.Ed.2d 340 (1961).

Before MURRAH, Chief Judge, and BRATTON and BREITENSTEIN, Circuit Judges.

MURRAH, Chief Judge. This is an appeal from a judgment of the trial court awarding plaintiff-executors a refund for estate taxes previously paid.

The pertinent facts are that the decedent, Maria McKean Allen, created an irrevocable trust in which she reserved ⅗ths of the income for life, the remainder to pass to her two children, who are the beneficiaries of the other ⅖ths interest in the income. When she was approximately seventy-eight years old, the trustor-decedent was advised that her retention of the life estate would result in her attributable share of the corpus being included in her gross estate, for estate tax purposes. With her sanction, counsel began searching for a competent means of divesture, and learned that decedent's son, Wharton Allen, would consider purchasing his mother's interest in the trust. At that time, the actuarial value of the retained life estate based upon decedent's life expectancy, was approximately $135,000 and her attributable share of the corpus, i.e., ⅗ths was valued at some $900,000. Upon consultation with his business advisers, Allen agreed to pay $140,000 for the interest, believing that decedent's actual life span would be sufficient to return a profit to him on the investment.   For all intents and purposes, he was a bona fide third party purchaser—not being in a position to benefit by any reduction in his mother's estate taxes.   The sale was consummated and, upon paying the purchase price, Allen began receiving the income from the trust.

At the time of the transfer, decedent enjoyed relatively good health and was expected to live her normal life span.   A short time thereafter, however, it was discovered that she had an incurable disease, which soon resulted in her untimely death.   As a result of the death, Allen ceased receiving any trust income and suffered a considerable loss on his investment.

The Internal Revenue Commissioner determined that ⅗ths of the corpus, less the $140,000 purchase money, should be included in decedent's gross estate because (1) the transfer was invalid because made in contemplation of death, and (2) the sale was not for an adequate and full consideration.

Plaintiff-executors paid the taxes in accord with the Commissioner's valuation of the estate, and brought this action for refund, alleging that the sale of the life interest was for an adequate consideration; and that, therefore, no part of the trust corpus was properly includible in the gross estate.

The trial court held for plaintiffs, finding that the transfer was in contemplation of death, but regardless of that fact, the consideration paid for the life estate was adequate and full, thereby serving to divest decedent of any interest in the trust, with the result that no part of the corpus is subject to estate taxes.

Our narrow question is thus whether the corpus of a reserved life estate is removed, for federal estate tax purposes, from a decedent's gross estate by a transfer at the value of such reserved life estate.   In other words, must the consideration be paid for the interest transferred, or for the interest which would otherwise be included in the gross estate?

In one sense, the answer comes quite simply—decedent owned no more than a life estate, could not transfer any part of the corpus, and Allen received no more than the interest transferred.   And, a taxpayer is, of course, entitled to use all proper means to reduce his tax liability. See Cravens v. C.I.R., 10 Cir., 272 F.2d 895, 898.   It would thus seem to follow that the consideration was adequate, for it was in fact more than the value of the life estate.   And, as a practical matter, it would have been virtually impossible to sell the life estate for an amount equal to her share in the corpus.   Cf. Sullivan's Estate, v. C.I.R., 9 Cir., 175 F.2d 657.

It does not seem plausible, however, that Congress intended to allow such an easy avoidance of the taxable incidence befalling reserved life estates.   This result would allow a taxpayer to reap the benefits of property for his lifetime and, in contemplation of death, sell only the interest entitling him to the income, thereby removing all of the property which he has enjoyed from his gross estate.   Giving the statute a reasonable interpretation, we cannot believe this to be its intendment. It seems certain that in a situation like this, Congress meant the estate to include the corpus of the trust or, in its stead, an amount equal in value. I.e., [sic], see Helvering v. Hallock, 309 U.S. 106, 60 S.Ct. 444, 84 L.Ed. 604; C.I.R. v. Wemyss, 324 U.S. 303, 65 S.Ct. 652, 89 L.Ed. 958; C.I.R. v. Estate of Church, 335 U.S. 632, 69 S.Ct. 322, 93 L.Ed. 288.

The judgment of the trial court is therefore reversed and the case is remanded for further proceedings in conformity with the opinion filed herein.

BREITENSTEIN, Circuit Judge (concurring in result).

Section 811 of the 1939 Internal Revenue Code provides for the determination of the value of the gross estate of a decedent for federal estate tax purposes. Among other things, it requires the inclusion of property "(1) to the extent of any interest therein of which the decedent has at any time made a transfer (except in case of a bona fide sale for an adequate and full consideration in money or money's worth), by trust * * * (B) under which he has retained for his life or for any period not ascertainable without reference to his death (i) * * * the right to income from, the property * * *."

Trustor-decedent in 1932 created an irrevocable trust and received no consideration therefor. She retained for life the right to income from ⅗ths of the property which she placed in the trust. By the plain language of the statute that portion of the property held in the trust and devoted to the payment to her of income for life is includible within her gross estate. Such property is an "interest" of which she made a transfer with the retention of income for life.

The fact that the transfer of the life estate left her without any retained right to income from the trust property does not alter the result. As I read the statute the tax liability arises at the time of the inter vivos transfer under which there was a retention of the right to income for life. The disposition thereafter of that retained right does not eliminate the tax liability. The fact that full and adequate consideration was paid for the transfer of the retained life estate is immaterial. To remove the trust property from inclusion in decedent's estate there must be full and adequate consideration paid for the interest which would be taxed. That interest is not the right to income for life but the right to the property which was placed in trust and from which the income is produced.

As the 1932 trust was irrevocable, trustor-decedent could thereafter make no unilateral transfer of the trust property. Granting that she could sell her life estate as that was a capital asset owned by her, such sale has no effect on the includibility in her gross estate of the interest which she transferred in 1932 with the retention of the right to income for life.

For the reasons stated I would reverse the judgment with directions to dismiss the case.

Notes

1. Would Judge Breitenstein, who wrote the concurring opinion, have reached the same result even if the decedent had lived for more than three years after the sale of the life estate?

2. The result in the Allen case seems sensible but is hard to justify as a matter of the language of the statute. Nevertheless, Congress has ratified the result in the 1981 amendments to § 2035. (See p. 899 supra). Given the unification of gift and estate tax rates what is the need for the *Allen* rule, or the rest of § 2035(d)(2)?

3. Assuming that the decedent lives more than three years after relinquishing the string, does it matter whether the relinquishment was by gift or (as in Allen) by sale?

b. Transfers to Take Effect at Death.

Section 2037 is the direct descendant of the provision in the first 1916 Act taxing "transfers intended to take effect   *   *   *   at or after death." The statutory language remained substantially unchanged until 1949 when it was completely revised. Further revisions were made in 1954, but no significant changes have been made since.

Internal Revenue Code (26 U.S.C.A.) § 2037:

(a) *General Rule.*—The value of the gross estate shall include the value of all property to the extent of any interest therein of which the decedent has at any time after September 7, 1916, made a transfer (except in case of a bona fide sale for an adequate and full consideration in money or money's worth), by trust or otherwise, if—

   (1) possession or enjoyment of the property can, through ownership of such interest, be obtained only by surviving the decedent, and

   (2) the decedent has retained a reversionary interest in the property (but in the case of a transfer made before October 8, 1949, only if such reversionary interest arose by the express terms of the instrument of transfer), and the value of such reversionary interest immediately before the death of the decedent exceeds 5 percent of the value of such property.

(b) *Special Rules.*—For purposes of this section, the term 'reversionary interest' includes a possibility that property transferred by the decedent—

   (1) may return to him or his estate, or

   (2) may be subject to a power of disposition by him,

but such term does not include a possibility that the income alone from such property may return to him or become subject to a power of disposition by him. The value of a reversionary interest immediately before the death of the decedent shall be determined (without regard to the fact of the decedent's death) by usual methods of valuation, including the use of tables of mortality and actuarial principles, under regulations prescribed by the Secretary. In determining the value of a possibility that property may be subject to a power of disposition by the decedent, such possibility shall be valued as if it were a possibility that such property may return to the decedent or his estate. Notwithstanding the foregoing, an interest so transferred shall not be included in the decedent's gross estate under this section if possession or enjoyment of the property could have been obtained by any beneficiary during the decedent's life through the exercise of a general power of appointment (as defined in section 2041) which in fact was exercisable immediately before the decedent's death.

Treasury Regulations § 20.2037–1 (in part):

Transfers taking effect at death—(a) *In general.* A decedent's gross estate includes under section 2037 the value of any interest in property transferred by the decedent after September 7, 1916, whether in trust or otherwise, except to the extent that the transfer was for an adequate and full consideration in money or money's worth (see § 20.2043–1), if—

(1) Possession or enjoyment of the property could, through ownership of the interest, have been obtained only by surviving the decedent,

(2) The decedent had retained a possibility (hereinafter referred to as a "reversionary interest") that the property, other than the income alone, would return to the decedent or his estate or would be subject to a power of disposition by him, and

(3) The value of the reversionary interest immediately before the decedent's death exceeded 5 percent of the value of the entire property.

However, if the transfer was made before October 8, 1949, section 2037 is applicable only if the reversionary interest arose by the express terms of the instrument of transfer and not by operation of law (see paragraph (f) of this section). See also paragraph (g) of this section with respect to transfers made between November 11, 1935, and January 29, 1940. The provisions of section 2037 do not apply to transfers made before September 8, 1916.

* * *

(c) *Retention of reversionary interest.* (1) As indicated in paragraph (a) of this section, the value of an interest in transferred property is not included in a decedent's gross estate under section 2037 unless the decedent had retained a reversionary interest in the property, and the value of the reversionary interest immediately before the death of the decedent exceeded 5 percent of the value of the property.

(2) For purposes of section 2037, the term "reversionary interest" includes a possibility that property transferred by the decedent may return to him or his estate and a possibility that property transferred by the decedent may become subject to a power of disposition by him. The term is not used in a technical sense, but has reference to any reserved right under which the transferred property shall or may be returned to the grantor. Thus, it encompasses an interest arising either by the express terms of the instrument of transfer or by operation of law. (See,

however, paragraph (f) of this section, with respect to transfers made before October 8, 1949.) The term "reversionary interest" does not include rights to income only, such as the right to receive the income from a trust after the death of another person. (However, see section 2036 for the inclusion of property in the gross estate on account of such rights.) Nor does the term "reversionary interest" include the possibility that the decedent during his lifetime might have received back an interest in transferred property by inheritance through the estate of another person. Similarly, a statutory right of a spouse to receive a portion of whatever estate a decedent may leave at the time of his death is not a "reversionary interest".

(3) For purposes of this section, the value of the decedent's reversionary interest is computed as of the moment immediately before his death, without regard to whether or not the executor elects the alternate valuation method under section 2032 and without regard to the fact of the decedent's death. The value is ascertained in accordance with recognized valuation principles for determining the value for estate tax purposes of future or conditional interests in property. (See §§ 20.2031–1, 20.2031–7, and 20. 2031–9.) For example, if the decedent's reversionary interest was subject to an outstanding life estate in his wife, his interest is valued according to the actuarial rules set forth in § 20.2031–7. On the other hand, if the decedent's reversionary interest was contingent on the death of his wife without issue surviving and if it cannot be shown that his wife is incapable of having issue (so that his interest is not subject to valuation according to the actuarial rules in § 20.2031–7), his interest is valued according to the general rules set forth in § 20.2031–1. A possibility that the decedent may be able to dispose of property under certain conditions is considered to have the same value as a right of the decedent to the return of the property under those same conditions. * * *

The kind of transfer with which I.R.C. (26 U.S.C.A.) § 2037 is concerned is illustrated by the famous case of Helvering v. Hallock, 309 U.S. 106, 60 S.Ct. 444, 84 L.Ed. 604 (1940). There, a husband established a trust with income to his wife for life, and principal to himself if he survived her, but if not to his children. To one unversed in the law of future interests, it would seem reasonably clear that the transfer to the children is one to take effect "at or after the death of" the transferor. By some lawyers, and for a time by the United States Supreme Court, it was thought to matter whether a husband's interest was, under state law, regarded as being subject to the "condition precedent" of surviving his wife, or to the "condition subsequent" of failing to survive his wife. Helvering v. Hallock established that such transfers were indeed transfers to take effect at death, however the "unwitty diversities" of state law might characterize them. The effect of the decision is described in Bittker, The Church and Spiegel Cases: Section 811(c) Gets a New Lease on Life, 58 Yale L.J. 825, 828 (1949):

The *Hallock* opinion had started the "possession or enjoyment" clause back on the road from rags to riches. But it left unanswered a number of questions, among them the following:

(1) Is the transfer taxable if the settlor's reversionary interest is not expressly reserved, as in the *Hallock* case, but arises "by operation of law"? This occurs, for example, when the settlor provides that the remaindermen must be living at his death to receive the corpus, but neglects to name an alternate taker. Consequently, a "resulting trust" (a reversionary interest) may arise in favor of the settlor.

(2) Is the transfer taxable no matter how slim the settlor's chance to reacquire the property? In the *Hallock* case, the corpus would revert to him if he survived his wife. But what if the return of the corpus to the settlor depends upon an unlikely contingency, such as his survivorship of children and grandchildren?

(3) In what sense must the transfer have been "intended" to take effect in possession or enjoyment at or after death? Suppose, for example, the reversionary interest, especially if remote, exists only because the draughtsman of the trust instrument (without the settlor's knowledge) had either overlooked a contingency which would create a resulting trust or, out of an excess of caution, provided for return of the corpus upon some contingency?

In 1949, in Spiegel's Estate v. Commissioner, 335 U.S. 701, 69 S.Ct. 301, 93 L.Ed. 330, rehearing denied 336 U.S. 915, 69 S.Ct. 599, 93 L.Ed. 1079 (1949), the Supreme Court held that property was includible in the gross estate regardless of intent, whether the reversionary interest was expressly reserved or arose by operation of law, and no matter how remote were the chances of the decedent's getting the property. Indeed in Spiegel, at the moment before his death the decedent had 16 chances out of 100,000 of getting the property and the value of his reversionary interest was $85. The cost of his retaining that tiny interest was $450,000 in increased taxes.

In 1949, Congress amended the statute to eliminate the language taxing transfers "to take effect at death," and to substitute the tests which (as modified in 1954) are set out above.

Notes

1. What would the result be in the following cases, if the transfer was made *before* October 8, 1949? After?

(a) The decedent transferred property in trust with the income payable to his wife for life and at her death, remainder to the decedent's then surviving children, or if none, to the decedent or his estate.

(b) The decedent transferred property in trust with the income to be accumulated for the decedent's life, and at his death, principal and accumulated income to be paid to the decedent's then surviving issue, or if none, to A or A's estate.

(c) The decedent transferred property in trust with the income payable to his wife for life and with the remainder payable to the decedent or, if he should not be living at his wife's death, to his daughter or her estate. Assume that the decedent was survived by his wife and his daughter. (Compare your answer with that given in Reg. § 20.2037–1(e), Example 3.)

(d) The decedent transferred property in trust with the income payable to his wife for life and with the remainder payable to his son or, if the son should not be living at the wife's death, to the decedent or, if the decedent should not then be living, to X or X's estate. Assume that the decedent was survived by his wife, his son, and X.

2. For purposes of § 2037, the value of the reversionary interest is measured immediately *before* death. For purposes of § 2033, it is valued *at* death. Thus, for purposes of § 2037 it has value even though the decedent's death extinguishes it.

3. In valuing annuities, life estates, remainders, etc. the Service takes the position that actuarial tables are controlling unless the individual whose life expectancy is in issue "is known to have been afflicted, at the time of transfer, with an incurable physical condition that is in such an advanced stage that death is clearly imminent." Rev.Rul. 80-80, 1980-1 C.B. 194, citing with approval Estate of Roy v. Commissioner, 54 T.C. 1317 (1970) and Estate of Allen v. United States, 214 Ct.Cl. 630, F.2d 14 (1977). Even that limited exception—imminent death—is not applied where the life expectancy at issue is the decedent's own under § 2037 (and § 2042(2)).

c. *Revocable Transfers.*

A transfer subject to recall by the transferor until his death is, of course, essentially testamentary in nature, and although in other contexts the testamentary nature of the transaction is sometimes disregarded, such a transfer has, from an early date, been regarded as taxable. What about other powers such as the power to alter or amend or terminate? And suppose the power is exercisable only in conjunction with some other person—say the life tenant or remainderman—or the exercise of the power is subject to some condition?

Internal Revenue Code (26 U.S.C.A.) § 2038:

(a) In General.—The value of the gross estate shall include the value of all property—

(1) Transfers After June 22, 1936.—To the extent of any interest therein of which the decedent has at any time made a transfer (except in case of a bona fide sale for an adequate and full consideration in money or money's worth), by trust or otherwise, where the enjoyment thereof was subject at the date of his death to any change through the exercise of a power (in whatever capacity exercisable) by the decedent alone or by the decedent in conjunction with any other person (without regard to when or from what source the decedent acquired such power), to alter, amend, revoke, or terminate, or where any such power is relinquished in contemplation of decedent's death.

(2) Transfers On Or Before June 22, 1936.—To the extent of any interest therein of which the decedent has at any time made a transfer (except in case of a bona fide sale for an adequate and full consideration in money or money's worth), by trust or otherwise, where the enjoyment thereof was subject at the date of his death to any change through the exercise of a power, either by the decedent alone or in

conjunction with any person, to alter, amend, or revoke, or where the decedent relinquished any such power in contemplation of his death. Except in the case of transfers made after June 22, 1936, no interest of the decedent of which he has made a transfer shall be included in the gross estate under paragraph (1) unless it is includible under this paragraph.

(b) Date of Existence of Power.—For purposes of this section, the power to alter, amend, revoke, or terminate shall be considered to exist on the date of the decedent's death even though the exercise of the power is subject to a precedent giving of notice or even though the alteration, amendment, revocation, or termination takes effect only on the expiration of a stated period after the exercise of the power, whether or not on or before the date of the decedent's death notice has been given or the power has been exercised.   In such cases proper adjustment shall be made representing the interests which would have been excluded from the power if the decedent had lived, and for such purpose, if the notice has not been given or the power has not been exercised on or before the date of his death, such notice shall be considered to have been given, or the power exercised, on the date of his death.

(c) Effect of Disability in Certain Cases.—For purposes of this section, in the case of a decedent who was (for a continuous period beginning not less than 3 months before December 31, 1947, and ending with his death) under a mental disability to relinquish a power, the term "power" shall not include a power the relinquishment of which on or after January 1, 1940, and on or before December 31, 1947, would, by reason of section 1000(e) of the Internal Revenue Code of 1939, be deemed not to be a transfer of property for purposes of chapter 4 of the Internal Revenue Code of 1939.

Treasury Regulations § 20.2038–1 (in part):

Revocable transfers—(a) *In general.* A decedent's gross estate includes under section 2038 the value of any interest in property transferred by the decedent, whether in trust or otherwise, if the enjoyment of the interest was subject at the date of the decedent's death to any change through the exercise of a power by the decedent to alter, amend, revoke, or terminate, or if the decedent relinquished such a power in contemplation of death.   However, section 2038 does not apply—

(1) To the extent that the transfer was for an adequate and full consideration in money or money's worth (see § 20.2043–1);

(2) If the decedent's power could be exercised only with the consent of all parties having an interest (vested or contingent) in the transferred property, and if the power adds nothing to the rights of the parties under local law; or

(3) To a power held solely by a person other than the decedent. But, for example, if the decedent had the unrestricted power to remove or discharge a trustee at any time and appoint himself trustee, the decedent is considered as having the powers of the trustee.   However, this result would not follow if he only had the power to appoint himself

trustee under limited conditions which did not exist at the time of his death. (See last two sentences of paragraph (b) of this section.)

Except as provided above, it is immaterial (i) in what capacity the power was exercisable by the decedent or by another person or persons in conjunction with the decedent; (ii) whether the power was exercisable alone or only in conjunction with another person or persons, whether or not having an adverse interest (unless the transfer was made before June 2, 1924; see paragraph (d) of this section); and (iii) at what time or from what source the decedent acquired his power (unless the transfer was made before June 23, 1936; see paragraph (c) of this section). Section 2038 is applicable to any power affecting the time or manner of enjoyment of property or its income, even though the identity of the beneficiary is not affected. For example, section 2038 is applicable to a power reserved by the grantor of a trust to accumulate income or distribute it to A, and to distribute corpus to A, even though the remainder is vested in A or his estate, and no other person has any beneficial interest in the trust. However, only the value of an interest in property subject to a power to which section 2038 applies is included in the decedent's gross estate under section 2038.

(b) *Date of existence of power.* A power to alter, amend, revoke, or terminate will be considered to have existed at the date of the decedent's death even though the exercise of the power was subject to a precedent giving of notice or even though the alteration, amendment, revocation, or termination would have taken effect only on the expiration of a stated period after the exercise of the power, whether or not on or before the date of the decedent's death notice had been given or the power had been exercised. In determining the value of the gross estate in such cases, the full value of the property transferred subject to the power is discounted for the period required to elapse between the date of the decedent's death and the date upon which the alteration, amendment, revocation, or termination could take effect. In this connection, see especially § 20.2031–7. However, section 2038 is not applicable to a power the exercise of which was subject to a contingency beyond the decedent's control which did not occur before his death (e.g., the death of another person during the decedent's life). See, however, section 2036(a)(2) for the inclusion of property in the decedent's gross estate on account of such a power.

OLD COLONY TRUST CO. v. UNITED STATES

United States Court of Appeals for the First Circuit, 1970.
423 F.2d 601.

ALDRICH, Chief Judge.

The sole question in this case is whether the estate of a settlor[2] of an intervivos trust, who was a trustee until the date of his death, is to be

---

2. Actually, the decedent was a donor to three trusts, similar in form, previously established by his wife—differences which we ignore as inconsequential.

charged with the value of the principal he contributed by virtue of reserved powers in the trust. The executor paid the tax and sued for its recovery in the district court. All facts were stipulated. The court ruled for the government, 300 F.Supp. 1032, and the executor appeals.

The initial life beneficiary of the trust was the settlor's adult son. Eighty per cent of the income was normally to be payable to him, and the balance added to principal. Subsequent beneficiaries were the son's widow and his issue. The powers upon which the government relies to cause the corpus to be includible in the settlor-trustee's estate are contained in two articles. A third article, purporting to limit the personal liability of the trustees for acts of mismanagement, although relied on by the government, has no bearing on the questions in this case because it does not affect the meaning, extent or nature of the trustee's duties and powers. Briggs v. Crowley, 1967, 352 Mass. 194, 224 N.E.2d 417. We will not consider it further.

Article 4 permitted the trustees to increase the percentage of income payable to the son beyond the eighty per cent,

"in their absolute discretion * * * when in their opinion such increase is needed in case of sickness, or desirable in view of changed circumstances."

In addition, under Article 4 the trustees were given the discretion to cease paying income to the son, and add it all to principal,

"during such period as the Trustees may decide that the stoppage of such payments is for his best interests."

Article 7 gave broad administrative or management powers to the trustees with discretion to acquire investments not normally held by trustees, and the right to determine, what was to be charged or credited to income or principal including stock dividends or deductions for amortization. It further provided that all divisions and decisions made by the trustees in good faith should be conclusive on all parties, and in summary, stated that the trustees were empowered, "generally to do all things in relation to the Trust Fund which the Donor could do if living and this Trust had not been executed."

The government claims that each of these two articles meant that the settlor-trustee had "the right * * * to designate the persons who shall possess or enjoy the [trust] property or the income therefrom" within the meaning of section 2036(a)(2) of the Internal Revenue Code of 1954, 26 U.S.C. § 2036(a)(2), and that the settlor-trustee at the date of his death possessed a power "to alter, amend, revoke, or terminate" within the meaning of section 2038(a)(1) (26 U.S.C. § 2038(a)(1)).

If State Street Trust Co. v. United States, 1 Cir., 1959, 263 F.2d 635, was correctly decided in this aspect, the government must prevail because of the Article 7 powers. There this court, Chief Judge Magruder dissenting, held against the taxpayer because broad powers similar to those in Article 7 meant that the trustees "could very substantially shift the economic benefits of the trusts between the life tenants and the remaindermen," so that the settlor "as long as he lived, in substance and effect and in a very real sense * * * 'retained for his life * * * the right * * * to designate the persons who shall possess or enjoy the property or the income therefrom; * * *.' " 263 F.2d at 639–640, quoting 26 U.S.C. § 2036(a)(2). We accept the taxpayer's invitation to reconsider this ruling.

It is common ground that a settlor will not find the corpus of the trust included in his estate merely because he named himself a trustee. Jennings v. Smith, 2 Cir., 1947, 161 F.2d 74. He must have reserved a power to himself[3] that is inconsistent with the full termination of ownership. The government's brief defines this as "sufficient dominion and control until his death." Trustee powers given for the administration or management of the trust must be equitably exercised, however, for the benefit of the trust as a whole. Blodget v. Delaney, 1 Cir., 1953, 201 F.2d 589; United States v. Powell, 10 Cir., 1962, 307 F.2d 821; Scott, Trusts §§ 183, 232 (3d ed.1967); Rest.2d, Trusts §§ 183, 232. The court in *State Street* conceded that the powers at issue were all such powers, but reached the conclusion that, cumulatively, they gave the settlor dominion sufficiently unfettered to be in the nature of ownership. With all respect to the majority of the then court, we find it difficult to see how a power can be subject to control by the probate court, and exercisable only in what the trustee fairly concludes is in the interests of the trust and its beneficiaries as a whole, and at the same time be an ownership power.

The government's position, to be sound, must be that the trustee's powers are beyond the court's control. Under Massachusetts law, however, no amount of administrative discretion prevents judicial supervision of the trustee. Thus in Appeal of Davis, 1903, 183 Mass. 499, 67 N.E. 604, a trustee was given "full power to make purchases, investments and exchanges * * * in such manner as to them shall seem expedient; it being my intention to give my trustees * * * the same dominion and control over said trust property as I now have." In spite of this language, and in spite of their good faith, the court charged the trustees for failing sufficiently to diversify their investment portfolio.

The Massachusetts court has never varied from this broad rule of accountability,[4] and has twice criticized *State Street* for its seeming departure. Boston Safe Deposit & Trust Co. v. Stone, 1965, 348 Mass. 345, 351, n. 8, 203 N.E.2d 547; Old Colony Trust Co. v. Silliman, 1967, 352 Mass. 6, 8–9, 223 N.E.2d 504. See also, Estate of McGillicuddy, 54 T.C. No. 27, 2/17/70, CCH Tax Ct.Rep. Dec. 29, 1965. We make a further observation, which the court in *State Street* failed to note, that the provision in that trust (as in the case at bar) that the trustees could "do all things in relation to the Trust Fund which I, the Donor, could do if * * * the Trust had not been executed," is almost precisely the provision which did not protect the trustees from accountability in Appeal of Davis, supra.

---

3. The number of other trustees who must join in the exercise of that power, unless the others have antagonistic interests of a substantial nature is, of course, immaterial. Treas.Reg. § 20.2036–1(a)(ii), (b)(3)(i) (1958); § 20.2038–1(a) (1958).

4. Cf. Briggs v. Crowley, supra: Copp v. Worcester County Nat'l Bank, 1964, 347 Mass. 548, 551, 199 N.E.2d 200; Corkery v. Dorsey, 1916, 223 Mass. 97, 101, 111 N.E. 795.

We do not believe that trustee powers are to be more broadly construed for tax purposes than the probate court would construe them for administrative purposes.　More basically, we agree with Judge Magruder's observation that nothing is "gained by lumping them together." State Street Trust Co. v. United States, supra, 263 F.2d at 642.　We hold that no aggregation of purely administrative powers can meet the government's amorphous test of "sufficient dominion and control" so as to be equated with ownership.

This does not resolve taxpayer's difficulties under Article 4.　Quite different considerations apply to distribution powers.　Under them the trustee can, expressly, prefer one beneficiary over another.　Furthermore, his freedom of choice may vary greatly, depending upon the terms of the individual trust.　If there is an ascertainable standard, the trustee can be compelled to follow it.[5]　If there is not, even though he is a fiduciary, it is not unreasonable to say that his retention of an unmeasurable freedom of choice is equivalent to retaining some of the incidents of ownership.　Hence, under the cases, if there is an ascertainable standard the settlor-trustee's estate is not taxed.　United States v. Powell, supra; Jennings v. Smith, supra;　Estate of Budd, 1968, 49 T.C. 468;　Estate of Pardee, 1967, 49 T.C. 140, but if there is not, it is taxed.　Henslee v. Union Planters Nat'l Bank & Trust Co., 1949, 335 U.S. 595, 69 S.Ct. 290, 93 L.Ed. 259;　Hurd v. Com'r, 1 Cir., 1947, 160 F.2d 610;　Michigan Trust Co. v. Kavanagh, 6 Cir., 1960, 284 F.2d 502.

The trust provision which is uniformly held to provide an ascertainable standard is one which, though variously expressed, authorizes such distributions as may be needed to continue the beneficiary's accustomed way of life.[6]　Ithaca Trust Co. v. United States, 1929, 279 U.S. 151, 49 S.Ct. 291, 73 L.Ed. 647;　cf. United States v. Commercial Nat'l Bank, 10 Cir., 1968, 404 F.2d 927, cert. denied 393 U.S. 1000, 89 S.Ct. 487, 21 L.Ed.2d 465;　Blodget v. Delaney, 1 Cir., 1953, supra.　On the other hand, if the trustee may go further, and has power to provide for the beneficiary's "happiness," Merchants Nat'l Bank v. Com'r of Internal Revenue, 1943, 320 U.S. 256, 64 S.Ct. 108, 88 L.Ed. 35, or "pleasure," Industrial Trust Co. v. Com'r of Internal Revenue, 1 Cir., 1945, 151 F.2d 592, cert. denied 327 U.S. 788, 66 S.Ct. 807, 90 L.Ed. 1014, or "use and benefit," Newton Trust Co. v. Com'r of Internal Revenue, 1 Cir., 1947, 160 F.2d 175, or "reasonable requirement[s]," State Street Bank & Trust Co. v. United States, 1 Cir., 1963, 313 F.2d 29, the standard is so loose that the trustee is in effect uncontrolled.

5.　See, e.g., Old Colony Trust Co. v. Rodd, 1970 Mass.A.S. 25, 254 N.E.2d 886, trustee of trust to provide "comfortable support and maintenance," rebuked for "parsimonious" exercise of judgment.

6.　Many of the cases we are about to cite consider whether there is an ascertainable standard with a different object in view, viz., whether the amount of uninvaded corpus there provided to go ultimately to charity could be reliably predicted, so as to permit an estate tax deduction under 26 U.S.C. § 2055(a)(2).　While the purpose of inquiry is different, we believe the existence and measurability of a standard to be the same.　Cf. Treas.Reg. § 20.2055–2(a) (1958);　4 Mertens, Law of Fed. Gift & Estate Tax § 28.38.

In the case at bar the trustees could increase the life tenant's income "in case of sickness, or [if] desirable in view of changed circumstances." Alternatively, they could reduce it "for his best interests." "Sickness" presents no problem. Conceivably, providing for "changed circumstances" is roughly equivalent to maintaining the son's present standard of living. But see Hurd v. Com'r of Internal Revenue, supra. The unavoidable stumbling block is the trustees' right to accumulate income and add it to capital (which the son would never receive) when it is to the "best interests" of the son to do so. Additional payments to a beneficiary whenever in his "best interests" might seem to be too broad a standard in any event. In addition to the previous cases see Estate of Yawkey, 1949, 12 T.C. 1164, where the court said, at p. 1170,

> "We cannot regard the language involved ['best interest'] as limiting the usual scope of a trustee's discretion. It must always be anticipated that trustees will act for the best interests of a trust beneficiary, and an exhortation to act 'in the interests and for the welfare' of the beneficiary does not establish an external standard."

Power, however, to decrease or cut off a beneficiary's income when in his "best interests," is even more troublesome. When the beneficiary is the son, and the trustee the father, a particular purpose comes to mind, parental control through holding the purse strings. The father decides what conduct is to the "best interests" of the son, and if the son does not agree, he loses his allowance. Such a power has the plain indicia of ownership control. The alternative, that the son, because of other means, might not need this income, and would prefer to have it accumulate for his widow and children after his death, is no better. If the trustee has power to confer "happiness" on the son by generosity to someone else, this seems clearly an unascertainable standard. *Cf.* Merchants Nat'l Bank v. Com'r of Internal Revenue, supra, 320 U.S. at 261–263, 64 S.Ct. 108.

The case of Hays' Estate v. Com'r of Internal Revenue, 5 Cir., 1950, 181 F.2d 169, is contrary to our decision. The opinion is unsupported by either reasoning or authority and we will not follow it. With the present settlor-trustee free to determine the standard himself, a finding of ownership control was warranted. To put it another way, the cost of holding onto the strings may prove to be a rope burn. State Street Bank & Trust Co. v. United States, supra.

Affirmed.

Notes

1. The principal case was cited with approval in United States v. Byrum, 408 U.S. 125, 127 N. 6 (1972) (see p. 906, note 6, supra). Nevertheless, in Lowndes, Kramer & McCord, the authors conclude that "the principal lesson taught by State Street Trust is of continuing validity: for planning purposes, the most desirable course is to steer as far from the demarcation line of estate tax inclusion as possible because, at the date of the settlor's death, the line may have moved." § 8.9.

2. The Treasury interpretation of § 2038 to include among powers "to alter or amend" powers not making a shift of benefits from one beneficiary to another,

e.g., a power to accelerate or postpone the beneficiary's receipt of the benefits has been upheld by the Supreme Court. Lober v. United States, 346 U.S. 335, 74 S.Ct. 98, 98 L.Ed. 15 (1953). On the subject of grantor powers generally, see Pedrick, Grantor Powers and Estate Taxation: The Ties that Bind, 54 Nw.U. L.Rev. 527 (1959).

3. Suppose that a parent makes gifts to his children under the Uniform Gift to Minors Act and designates himself as custodian. If he dies during the child's minority are the gifts includible in his estate? See Revenue Ruling 57–366, 1957–2 C.B. 618 and Revenue Ruling 59–357, 1959–2 C.B. 212. Cf. Estate of Chrysler v. C.I.R., 361 F.2d 508 (2d Cir. 1966).

4. As to the relationship between § 2038 and the gift tax, see Section Three, Part D, p. 950, infra. On the relationship of §§ 2038 and 2036, see Lowndes, Kramer & McCord § 9.22 (footnotes omitted):

There is an intimate and interesting relation between Section 2036(a)(2) and Section 2038, since the same power is frequently taxable under both sections. Most of the transfers which are taxable under Section 2036(a)(2), upon the theory that the decedent retained power to designate possession of, or the income from, property, which he transferred during his life, are also taxable under Section 2038, upon the theory that the decedent possessed a power to alter the enjoyment of the transferred property at his death. There are certain powers, however, which are taxed under one section but not the other. Moreover, the amount which is taxed may differ according to the section under which the tax is imposed. These differences, as well as the similarities between Section 2036(a)(2) and Section 2038, make it desirable to explore the relation between the two sections in some detail.

Ordinarily, a power to designate income from, or possession of, property transferred by a decedent during his life will also be a power to alter the enjoyment of the transferred property. Consequently, the same power will usually be taxable under Section 2036(a)(2) and Section 2038. Thus, for example, if A transfers property to T in trust for C for life, remainder to D, and retains power to revoke the trust, or to alter the beneficiaries under the trust, the trust property will be taxable to his estate under both Section 2036(a)(2) and Section 2038.

There are, however, several situations where a transfer which is taxable under Section 2038 is not taxable under Section 2036(a)(2) and, at least one situation where a power which is taxable under Section 2036(a)(2) is not taxable under Section 2038.

The tax under Section 2036(a)(2) is limited to a power which the decedent retained in connection with the transfer of property during his life. It does not extend to a power acquired from some other source as the tax under Section 2038 does in the case of transfers after June 22, 1936.

* * *

According to the Regulations, a power to designate the possession of, or income from, property is not taxable under Section 2036(a)(2) unless the power relates to the possession of the property during the decedent's life, or an equivalent statutory period, or to the income from the property realized during the decedent's life, or an equivalent statutory period. * * *

There is at least one situation where, according to the Regulations, a power is taxable under Section 2036(a)(2), which is not taxable under Section 2038. According to the Regulations, a contingent power, which depends upon an event beyond the decedent's control which has not happened before the decedent's death, is not taxable under Section 2038, although such a power may be taxable under Section 2036(a)(2). * * *

Although the same transfer may be taxed under both Section 2036(a)(2) and Section 2038, a different amount may be taxed when the tax is imposed under one section rather than the other. Section 2036(a)(2) taxes the full amount of property transferred by the decedent during his life, whose income or possession he retains power to designate, with the exception of any interest antecedent to the income or possession which the decedent may designate. Under Section 2038, however, only the value of the interest subject to the taxable power is taxed.

d. Notes on Sections 2039 and 2040.

1. Under the somewhat misleading title "annuities," Section 2039 taxes various forms of employee death benefits other than annuities, as well as survivor annuities unconnected with employee benefit plans.

Section 2039 was added to the Internal Revenue Code in 1954. Before 1954, the interests governed by § 2039 were taxed, if at all, only if they could be fitted into some other provision of the estate tax law. In enacting § 2039, Congress exempted from estate tax benefits paid to a beneficiary under "qualified" (i.e. meeting certain requirements as to vesting of benefits and other criteria) retirement plans or similar arrangements (§ 2039(c)). In later years the exemption was extended to several categories of employee benefit plans not originally covered and, in 1976, to individual retirement accounts (IRA's). The loss of revenue on account of the exemption was substantial and in 1982 a $100,000 ceiling was placed on the aggregate amount of benefits under any qualified plan to be excluded. In 1984, the exemption was repealed as to decedents dying after December 31, 1984. The history of the taxation of annuities generally and employee death benefits prior to the adoption of § 2039 in 1954 as well as the scope of the section are summarized in Kramer, Employee Benefits and Federal Estate and Gift Taxes, 1959 Duke L.J. 341. See, also, Solomon, Estate Taxes and the Employee Benefit Plan, 38 N.Y.U.Inst. on Fed.Tax § 37 (1980).

2. One of the most popular ways of holding property within families is, undoubtedly, in joint tenancy with right of survivorship or tenancy by the entirety (hereinafter referred to collectively as joint tenancy). It seems likely that in a high percentage of the cases the property held by the joint tenants originally belonged to one of them, e.g., a parent or a spouse, and that the other has made no financial contribution to the acquisition. Indeed, although there is little empirical basis for so concluding, it seems probable that the chief reason for so holding property is that it will pass to the surviving tenant upon death without the need for probate. While the avoidance of probate is an undoubted advantage, a person creating a joint estate should be aware of the booby traps—both tax and non-tax. As to the latter, experience suggests that very few

people who set up these estates realize that they may be creating an immediate interest in the property for the other tenant. It is an all too common occurrence for a person using a joint estate as a will substitute to provide for a beloved relative after his death to discover that the formerly loved one has taken half the property during his lifetime.

With respect to estate taxes, Section 2040 governs the inclusion in the gross estate of joint interests. Where the joint tenants are *not* husband and wife, Section 2040 provides for the inclusion of the whole of the property in the estate of the first to die, except for that portion which "*may be shown* to have originally belonged to" the other. The burden of proof on the estate is frequently difficult to sustain. An exception to the general rule provides that where joint tenants acquired the property by "gift, bequest, devise or inheritance" an amount proportionate to the number of tenants is includible in the estate.

Here again, there is a distinct possibility of encountering unforeseen problems. The presumption that the property all "belonged" to the first to die probably works out all right in the typical case—the parent predeceasing the child. But if the first to die is not the person to whom the property originally belonged, the survivor may have to pay tax on reacquisition of his own property unless he has kept adequate records—which is frequently not the case.

The gift tax aspects of joint interests were described by the Ways and Means Committee as follows (H.R.Rep. 94–1380 at 18–19.):

> For gift tax purposes, a completed transfer is a prerequisite to the imposition of the tax. If a joint tenant, who has furnished all the consideration for the creation of the joint tenancy, is permitted to draw back to himself the entire joint property (as in a typical joint bank account), the transfer is not complete and there is no gift at that time. If the creation of a joint tenancy has resulted in a completed transfer, the value of the gift will depend upon whether, under applicable local law, the right of survivorship may be defeated by either owner unilaterally. If either joint tenant, acting alone, can bring about a severance of his interest, the value of the gift will be one-half the value of the jointly held property. If the right of survivorship is not destructible except by mutual consent, then the value of the gift requires a calculation which takes into account the ages of the donor and the other concurrent owner. This calculation is necessary because the younger of the tenants, who has a greater probability of surviving and taking all the property, has a more valuable interest.

The Tax Reform Act of 1976 made a major change in the treatment of joint interests (and tenancies by the entirety) where the joint tenants are husband and wife, by providing that, in some circumstances, one half of the value of the jointly held property would be included in the estate of the first to die. In 1981, Congress went all the way and adopted the flat rule that one half of any interest held exclusively by a decedent and his or her spouse is includible in the gross estate, regardless of which spouse furnished the consideration and whenever the property was acquired.

Given the simultaneous adoption of the unlimited marital deduction (see p. 934, infra) the change in treatment of husband-wife joint interests under 2040 has little or no significance except for determining the basis of property to the survivor under I.R.C. § 1014.

4. Powers of Appointment

Sections 2035 through 2038 are concerned with the taxability of transferred property in the estate of the transferor. Section 2041, on the other hand, is concerned with the taxability of property subject to a power of appointment in the estate of the transferee (donee) of the power. The creation of the power may or may not have resulted in estate tax, depending on its circumstances, but the tax consequences to the transferor (donor) of the power are irrelevant to Section 2041.

In order to appreciate the importance of powers of appointment to estate taxation one must remember that, prior to the Tax Reform Act of 1976, the change in beneficial interest from a life tenant to a remainderman on the expiration of the life estate was not (except for situations covered by § 2036) a taxable event. Thus, if A bequeathed property outright to his son B and B in turn bequeathed it to his son C, the property would (and still will) be taxable in both A's and B's estate. If, however, A gave the property to B for life, with remainder to C, one generation of estate taxes would be avoided. The obvious non-tax drawbacks to such a disposition could be eliminated if B was given a life estate plus a testamentary power to appoint the property among members of the next generation. Could he be given such a power without losing the tax advantages? The answer turned on whether for tax purposes the donee of a power was regarded as the "owner" of the property subject to the power or merely as the agent of the donor.

From an early date, the federal estate tax has departed to some extent from the agency theory by taxing the *exercise* of a general power, including one exercisable only by will. For a long time, however, the agency theory prevailed to the extent that mere *possession* at death of a general testamentary power was not taxable. Today, except as to powers created on or before October 21, 1942, there is no longer any distinction drawn between the possession and exercise of a power, and the estate of a decedent who dies possessing a general power of appointment, whether or not exercised, is taxable on all property subject to the power.

On the other hand, non-general powers (all powers not exercisable in favor of the decedent, his estate, his creditors or the creditors of his estate) are not taxed (except in special circumstances) even if exercised. As to them, the agency theory persists.

Internal Revenue Code (26 U.S.C.A.) § 2041:

(a) In General.—The value of the gross estate shall include the value of all property—

(1) Powers of Appointment Created on or before October 21, 1942. To the extent of any property with respect to which a general power

of appointment created on or before October 21, 1942, is exercised by the decedent—

    (A) by will, or

    (B) by a disposition which is of such nature that if it were a transfer of property owned by the decedent, such property would be includible in the decedent's gross estate under sections 2035 to 2038, inclusive;

but the failure to exercise such a power or the complete release of such a power shall not be deemed an exercise thereof. If a general power of appointment created on or before October 21, 1942, has been partially released so that it is no longer a general power of appointment, the exercise of such power shall not be deemed to be the exercise of a general power of appointment if—

    (i) such partial release occurred before November 1, 1951, or

    (ii) the donee of such power was under a legal disability to release such power on October 21, 1942, and such partial release occurred not later than 6 months after the termination of such legal disability.

    (2) Powers Created After October 21, 1942.—To the extent of any property with respect to which the decedent has at the time of his death a general power of appointment created after October 21, 1942, or with respect to which the decedent has at any time exercised or released such a power of appointment by a disposition which is of such nature that if it were a transfer of property owned by the decedent, such property would be includible in the decedent's gross estate under sections 2035 to 2038, inclusive. For purposes of this paragraph (2), the power of appointment shall be considered to exist on the date of the decedent's death even though the exercise of the power is subject to a precedent giving of notice or even though the exercise of the power takes effect only on the expiration of a stated period after its exercise, whether or not on or before the date of the decedent's death notice has been given or the power has been exercised.

    (3) Creation of Another Power in Certain Cases.—To the extent of any property with respect to which the decedent—

    (A) by will, or

    (B) by a disposition which is of such nature that if it were a transfer of property owned by the decedent such property would be includible in the decedent's gross estate under section 2035, 2036, or 2037,

exercises a power of appointment created after October 21, 1942, by creating another power of appointment which under the applicable local law can be validly exercised so as to postpone the vesting of any estate or interest in such property, or suspend the absolute ownership or power of alienation of such property, for a period ascertainable without regard to the date of the creation of the first power.

(b) Definitions.—For purposes of subsection (a)—

(1) General Power of Appointment.—The term "general power of appointment" means a power which is exercisable in favor of the decedent, his estate, his creditors, or the creditors of his estate; except that—

(A) A power to consume, invade, or appropriate property for the benefit of the decedent which is limited by an ascertainable standard relating to the health, education, support, or maintenance of the decedent shall not be deemed a general power of appointment.

(B) A power of appointment created on or before October 21, 1942, which is exercisable by the decedent only in conjunction with another person shall not be deemed a general power of appointment.

(C) In the case of a power of appointment created after October 21, 1942, which is exercisable by the decedent only in conjunction with another person—

(i) If the power is not exercisable by the decedent except in conjunction with the creator of the power—such power shall not be deemed a general power of appointment.

(ii) If the power is not exercisable by the decedent except in conjunction with a person having a substantial interest in the property, subject to the power, which is adverse to exercise of the power in favor of the decedent—such power shall not be deemed a general power of appointment. For the purposes of this clause a person who, after the death of the decedent, may be possessed of a power of appointment (with respect to the property subject to the decedent's power) which he may exercise in his own favor shall be deemed as having an interest in the property and such interest shall be deemed adverse to such exercise of the decedent's power.

(iii) If (after the application of clauses (i) and (ii)) the power is a general power of appointment and is exercisable in favor of such other person—such power shall be deemed a general power of appointment only in respect of a fractional part of the property subject to such power, such part to be determined by dividing the value of such property by the number of such persons (including the decedent) in favor of whom such power is exercisable.

For purposes of clauses (ii) and (iii), a power shall be deemed to be exercisable in favor of a person if it is exercisable in favor of such person, his estate, his creditors, or the creditors of his estate.

(2) Lapse of Power.—The lapse of a power of appointment created after October 21, 1942, during the life of the individual possessing the power shall be considered a release of such power. The preceding sentence shall apply with respect to the lapse of powers during any calendar year only to the extent that the property, which could have

been appointed by exercise of such lapsed powers, exceeded in value, at the time of such lapse, the greater of the following amounts:

(A) $5,000, or

(B) 5 percent of the aggregate value, at the time of such lapse, of the assets out of which, or the proceeds of which, the exercise of the lapsed powers could have been satisfied.

Treasury Regulations § 20.2041–1 (in part):

(b) *Definition of "power of appointment"*—(1) *In general.* The term "power of appointment" includes all powers which are in substance and effect powers of appointment regardless of the nomenclature used in creating the power and regardless of local property law connotations. For example, if a trust instrument provides that the beneficiary may appropriate or consume the principal of the trust, the power to consume or appropriate is a power of appointment. Similarly, a power given to a decedent to affect the beneficial enjoyment of trust property or its income by altering, amending, or revoking the trust instrument or terminating the trust is a power of appointment. If the community property laws of a State confer upon the wife a power of testamentary disposition over property in which she does not have a vested interest she is considered as having a power of appointment. A power in a donee to remove or discharge a trustee and appoint himself may be a power of appointment. For example, if under the terms of a trust instrument, the trustee or his successor has the power to appoint the principal of the trust for the benefit of individuals including himself, and the decedent has the unrestricted power to remove or discharge the trustee at any time and appoint any other person including himself, the decedent is considered as having a power of appointment. However, the decedent is not considered to have a power of appointment if he only had the power to appoint a successor, including himself, under limited conditions which did not exist at the time of his death, without an accompanying unrestricted power of removal. Similarly, a power to amend only the administrative provisions of a trust instrument, which cannot substantially affect the beneficial enjoyment of the trust property or income, is not a power of appointment. The mere power of management, investment, custody of assets, or the power to allocate receipts and disbursements as between income and principal, exercisable in a fiduciary capacity, whereby the holder has no power to enlarge or shift any of the beneficial interests therein except as an incidental consequence of the discharge of such fiduciary duties is not a power of appointment. Further, the right in a beneficiary of a trust to assent to a periodic accounting, thereby relieving the trustee from further accountability, is not a power of appointment if the right of assent does not consist of any power or right to enlarge or shift the beneficial interest of any beneficiary therein.

* * *

(2) *Powers limited by an ascertainable standard.* A power to consume, invade, or appropriate income or corpus, or both, for the benefit of the decedent which is limited by an ascertainable standard relating to

the health, education, support, or maintenance of the decedent is, by reason of section 2041(b)(1)(A), not a general power of appointment. A power is limited by such a standard if the extent of the holder's duty to exercise and not to exercise the power is reasonably measurable in terms of his needs for health, education, or support (or any combination of them). As used in this subparagraph, the words "support" and "maintenance" are synonymous and their meaning is not limited to the bare necessities of life. A power to use property for the comfort, welfare, or happiness of the holder of the power is not limited by the requisite standard. Examples of powers which are limited by the requisite standard are powers exercisable for the holder's "support," "support in reasonable comfort," "maintenance in health and reasonable comfort," "support in his accustomed manner of living," "education, including college and professional education," "health," and "medical, dental, hospital and nursing expenses and expenses of invalidism." In determining whether a power is limited by an ascertainable standard, it is immaterial whether the beneficiary is required to exhaust his other income before the power can be exercised.

Disclaiming a Power

As noted in Chapter Nine (see p. 862, supra) the donee of a power can refuse to accept it. If he does so in timely and effective fashion he is treated as though he never possessed the power and there will be no gift or estate tax consequences attached to the disclaimer.

The question of what constitutes an effective disclaimer arises not only with respect to powers of appointment but under several other sections of the estate and gift tax law. The answer has not always been the same. To provide uniform treatment the Tax Reform Act of 1976 provided definitive rules relating to disclaimers under the estate, gift and generation-skipping taxes, which rules displace local law on the subject.

Section 2518 reads as follows:

(a) General Rule.—For purposes of this subtitle, if a person makes a qualified disclaimer with respect to any interest in property, this subtitle shall apply with respect to such interest as if the interest had never been transferred to such person.

(b) Qualified Disclaimer Defined.—For purposes of subsection (a), the term "qualified disclaimer" means an irrevocable and unqualified refusal by a person to accept an interest in property but only if—

(1) such refusal is in writing,

(2) such writing is received by the transferor of the interest, his legal representative, or the holder of the legal title to the property to which the interest relates not later than the date which is 9 months after the later of—

(A) the day on which the transfer creating the interest in such person is made, or

(B) the day on which such person attains age 21,

(3) such person has not accepted the interest or any of its benefits; and

(4) as a result of such refusal, the interest passes to a person other than the person making the disclaimer (without any direction on the part of the person making the disclaimer).

(c) Other Rules.—For purposes of subsection (a)—

(1) Disclaimer of Undivided Portion of Interest.—A disclaimer with respect to an undivided portion of an interest which meets the requirements of the preceding sentence shall be treated as a qualified disclaimer of such portion of the interest.

(2) Powers.—A power with respect to property shall be treated as an interest in such property.

Section (§ 2046) applies the same rules to the estate tax.

Exercise, Release and Lapse of a Power

Assuming that there has not been an effective disclaimer the donee of the power can exercise it, release it, or allow it to lapse (typically by dying without exercising the power). In the case of a post-October 21, 1942 general power any of those courses may be the occasion for gift or estate tax, or both. If during his lifetime the donee exercises the power in favor of anyone other than himself, or releases it, he will have made a gift. I.R.C. Section 2514 applies the gift tax to powers of appointment in a manner consistent with Section 2041. The donee may also remain subject to estate tax (under § 2041(a)(1)(b)) if the disposition is "of such a nature that if it were a transfer of property owned by the decedent, such property would be includible in the decedent's gross estate under sections 2035–2038." (For example, if the donee of a general power over trust property, who was also the life income beneficiary of the trust, released the power but retained the life estate until his death, the transfer would be subject to both taxes.) Finally, if the donee retains the power until he dies, the property subject to the power is includible in his gross estate whether he exercises it or not.

Treasury Regulations § 20.2041–3 (in part):

(d) *Releases, lapses, and disclaimers of general powers of appointment.* (1) Property subject to a general power of appointment created after October 21, 1942, is includible in the gross estate of a decedent under section 2041(a) (2) even though he does not have the power at the date of his death, if during his life he exercised or released the power under circumstances such that, if the property subject to the power had been owned and transferred by the decedent, the property would be includible in the decedent's gross estate under section 2035, 2036, 2037, or 2038. Further, section 2041(b)(2) provides that the lapse of a power of appointment is considered to be a release of the power to the extent set forth in subparagraph (3) of this paragraph. A release of a power of appointment need not be formal or express in character. The principles set forth in § 20.2041–2 for determining the application of the pertinent provisions of sections 2035 through 2038 to a particular exercise of a power of appointment are applicable for purposes of determining whether or not an exercise or release of a power of appointment created after October 21, 1942, causes the property to be included in a decedent's gross estate under section 2041(a)(2). If a general power of appointment created after October 21, 1942, is partially released, a subsequent exercise or release of the power under circumstances described in the first sentence of this subparagraph, or its possession at death, will nevertheless cause the property subject to the power to be included in the gross estate of the holder of the power.

———

The provisions of Section 2041(b)(2) ("Lapse of Power") come into play only where the life of the power is shorter than the life of the donee, e.g., a power exercisable until age 50 but not thereafter. If the power lapses during the life of the donee, the lapse is considered a release of the power but only to the extent that in any calendar year, the property subject to the power does not exceed the greater of $5,000 or 5% of the corpus. A trust can, thus, be created in which the beneficiary is given a non-cumulative power to appoint to himself the greater of $5,000 or 5% of the trust corpus in any year, without tax cost to the donee except in the year of death. See Covey, The Estate Planning Benefits Available Via a "$5,000 and 5%" Withdrawal Power 34 J.Tax 98 (1971).

Notes

1. At the present time the only cases coming within § 2041(a)(3) are those governed by the Delaware statute (25 Del.Code § 501) under which the validity of interests created by the exercise of powers, *including special powers*, is measured from the date of exercise rather than the date of creation. Wisconsin's Rule against Perpetuities, like the common law rule, measures the validity of interests created by the exercise of a special power from the date of creation. However, because Wisconsin's Rule does not apply to interests in trust where the trustee has power to sell assets and reinvest the proceeds, (see p. 747 supra) successive special powers can apparently be used to avoid estate tax indefinitely. Nevertheless, the Tax Court refused to apply Section 2041(a)(3) to the exercise of a special power governed by Wisconsin law. Murphy's Estate v. Commissioner, 71 T.C. 671 (1979).

2. A good exercise for the student at this point would be to try to draft a power of appointment giving maximum freedom to the donee without making the property subject to the power includible in his estate. If the donee of a power can be given so much control over property without tax consequences, under what circumstances would anyone create a general power?

3. The availability of powers through which the donee has virtual ownership of the property but is not subject to estate tax was an important factor in the decision to adopt the generation-skipping transfer provisions of the Tax Reform Act of 1976, discussed infra, at p. 959.

Note on Section 2042

Section 2042 governs the inclusion in the gross estate of proceeds of life insurance. In view of the nature of life insurance, one might expect that the proceeds of any insurance on a decedent's life would be includible in his gross estate; and, where the insurance is payable to the estate, *INCl in gross estate* that is the case. If, however, (as would be normal) the insurance is payable to some other beneficiary, the proceeds are includible only if the decedent retained some "incident of ownership" such as the right to designate the beneficiary, or a reversionary interest (at least 5%) in the proceeds. Prior to 1954 insurance proceeds were includible in the decedent's gross estate if he paid the premiums, even if he had divested himself of all incidents of ownership. The abandonment of the "premium payment test" in 1954 made insurance a major device for estate tax avoidance. An insured can transfer to another person all incidents of ownership but continue to pay premiums and escape taxation in his estate. Moreover, if the gift of the policy is outright rather than in trust, that gift and subsequent payments of premiums will qualify for the annual exclusion. Regs. 25.2503–3(a); Rev.Rul. 55–408, 1955–1 C.B. 113.

If payable to benef, not incl'd in gross estate.

B. DEDUCTIONS FROM THE GROSS ESTATE AND CREDITS

1. Introduction

The federal estate tax is computed upon the net or taxable estate, i.e., the gross estate minus the deductions for: (1) expenses, indebtedness, and taxes; (2) losses; (3) transfers for public, charitable, and religious uses; and (4) the marital deduction. Expenses include funeral expenses, administration expenses, claims against the estate, unpaid mortgages on, or any indebtedness in respect of, property included in the gross estate, and "other administration expenses" incurred in administering property not subject to claims which is included in the gross estate (I.R.C. § 2053). After the estate tax has been determined, a number of credits may be deducted from the tax. These credits include the "unified credit" (§ 2010), the credit for state death taxes (§ 2011), the credit for death taxes paid to a foreign country (§ 2014), and the credit for federal estate tax paid by another decedent on property transferred to the current decedent (§ 2013).

2. Transfers for Public, Charitable and Religious Uses

Internal Revenue Code (26 U.S.C.A.) § 2055:

(a) In General. For purposes of the tax imposed by section 2001, the value of the taxable estate shall be determined by deducting from the value of the gross estate the amount of all bequests, legacies, devises, or transfers—

(1) to or for the use of the United States, any State, any political subdivision thereof, or the District of Columbia, for exclusively public purposes;

(2) to or for the use of any corporation organized and operated exclusively for religious, charitable, scientific, literary, or educa-

tional purposes, including the encouragement of art, or to foster national or international amateur sports competition (but only if no part of its activities involve the provision of athletic facilities or equipment), and the prevention of cruelty to children or animals, no part of the net earnings of which inures to the benefit of any private stockholder or individual, which is not disqualified for tax exemption under section 501(c)(3) by reason of attempting to influence legislation, and which does not participate in, or intervene in (including the publishing or distributing of statements), any political campaign on behalf of any candidate for public office;

(3) to a trustee or trustees, or a fraternal society, order, or association operating under the lodge system, but only if such contributions or gifts are to be used by such trustee or trustees, or by such fraternal society, order, or association, exclusively for religious, charitable, scientific, literary, or educational purposes, or for the prevention of cruelty to children or animals, such trust, fraternal society, order, or association would not be disqualified for tax exemption under section 501(c)(3) by reason of attempting to influence legislation, and such trustee or trustees, or such fraternal society, order, or association, does not participate in, or intervene in (including the publishing or distributing of statements), any political campaign on behalf of any candidate for public office; or

(4) to or for the use of any veterans' organization incorporated by Act of Congress, or of its departments or local chapters or posts, no part of the net earnings of which inures to the benefit of any private shareholder or individual.

For purposes of this subsection, the complete termination before the date prescribed for the filing of the estate tax return of a power to consume, invade, or appropriate property for the benefit of an individual before such power has been exercised by reason of the death of such individual or for any other reason shall be considered and deemed to be a qualified disclaimer with the same full force and effect as though he had filed such qualified disclaimer.   Rules similar to the rules of section 501(j) shall apply for purposes of paragraph (2).

If the organization or purpose for which a "charitable" contribution is made satisfies the criteria of the Code, there is no limit on the amount which may be given.   Where the gifts are outright, few problems are encountered.   Where, however, the donor tries to combine a private with a public purpose, a number of problems arise.

Over the years one of the most troublesome areas was that of gifts of charitable remainders.   Where the remainder was unconditional, e.g., to my wife B for life, remainder to the Z charity, the remainder was clearly deductible.   The value of the remainder would be computed on the basis of life expectancy tables although in some circumstances the physical condition of the life tenant might be taken into consideration (see p. 913

supra).   Conditional remainders whether vested or contingent were not deductible unless the chance that the charity might not receive the property was so remote as to be negligible.   It was not enough that the charity's interest could be valued actuarially.   See, e.g., Commissioner v. Sternberger's Estate, 348 U.S. 187, 75 S.Ct. 229, 99 L.Ed. 246 (1955) where the court denied a deduction for a remainder contingent upon the death without issue of testator's 27-year-old unmarried and childless (albeit divorced) daughter.   Here again, however, unlike the case of the Rule against Perpetuities, the remoteness of the possibility is open to proof; female octogenarians are not considered fertile.   Prop.Rest. § 274; City Bank Farmers Trust Co. v. United States, 74 F.2d 692 (2d Cir. 1935). In Hamilton National Bank of Chattanooga v. United States, 236 F.Supp. 1005 (D.Tenn.1965), affirmed 367 F.2d 554 (6th Cir. 1966) the Court said:

> Upon the death of his father, W. R. Long, Jr., was a 54 year old bachelor, living alone in a trailer in El Paso, Texas.   He had been married in 1928 but shortly thereafter was divorced and had never remarried.   He had never had children and was unknown to have had any association of any kind with the opposite sex since 1928.   He was described as being very dirty, unkempt, and offensive in his personal habits, and was described as an "odd character" and as a "hobo."   His only occupation appears to have been the collecting of junked automobile batteries.   His medical history reflected that he was a heavy cigarette smoker, had a persistent cough and was obese with very poor dietary habits.   Between 1956 and 1959 he had received medical treatment for a congenital back condition described as spina bifida, a stomach ulcer which had resulted in internal bleeding, and had been examined for blood in his urine from a cause then unknown.   He was described as a very uncooperative patient and given to self-medication and home remedies, including the use of creosote for his cough and lung condition.   The Court is of the opinion that upon this state of the record the evidence was sufficient to present a jury issue as to the negligible possibility of W. R. Long, Jr., having issue.

The Tax Reform Act of 1969 completely revamped the law governing deductions in the case of "split interest" gifts.   In the case of a charitable remainder the statute provides that *no* deduction will be allowed (except in the case of a personal residence or farm) unless it is in a "charitable remainder annuity trust" (I.R.C. § 664(d)(1)), a "charitable remainder unitrust" (I.R.C. § 664(d)(2)), or a "pooled income fund" (I.R.C. § 642(c)(5)). The statutory provisions and regulations are very detailed and must be strictly observed.   The essential characteristics of a charitable remainder trust are summarized in 3 Bittker, Federal Taxation of Income, Estates and Gifts ¶ 82.1.2 (1981) at pages 82–5, 82–7 [footnotes omitted]:

> A charitable remainder trust, whether of the annuity trust or the unitrust variety, is a trust providing for annual or more frequent distributions for life or a term of years [not to exceed 20 years] to one or more beneficiaries, at least one of whom is not a charity, followed by an irrevocable remainder interest to be held for the benefit of, or paid over to, a charitable organization described in IRC § 170(c).   The periodic distribution must be (a) in the case of a charitable remainder annuity trust, a sum certain that is not less than 5 percent of the initial net fair market value of all property placed in

trust, or (b) in the case of a charitable remainder unitrust, a fixed percentage, not less than 5 percent, of the net fair market value of the trust assets, valued annually.   These elements cannot be combined in a single trust (e.g., by providing for a distribution equal to the greater of 5 percent of original corpus or 5 percent of current value); to qualify under IRC § 664, a trust must be either an annuity trust or a unitrust.   * * *

* * *

The requirement of IRC §§ 664(d)(1) and 664(d)(2) that charitable remainder trusts pay out 5 percent or more of the relevant base applies to the *aggregate* amount payable; it can be divided among two or more beneficiaries either in a ratio prescribed by the instrument or by the trustee in the exercise of a discretionary power.   If the aggregate amount is to be reduced on the death of a beneficiary or the expiration of a term of years, the 5 percent requirement will continue to be satisfied if the instrument requires the distribution of an appropriate fraction of the corpus to the charitable remainderman; and the adequacy of the annuity or unitrust amount thereafter will be measured against the remaining corpus.

Because the payout of a charitable remainder annuity trust is fixed when the trust is created, it is easier to administer than a unitrust, which requires an annual valuation—especially if the corpus consists of real estate, stock of closely held corporations, or other unique assets.   But this advantage in favor of annuity trusts may be offset, from a planning point of view, by the fact that the variable payouts to unitrust beneficiaries enable them to participate in increases and decreases in the value of the underlying assets.   A related distinction between the two species is that additions can be made to a unitrust but not to an annuity trust.   * * *

A pooled income fund is a trust or other fund maintained by a charitable organization as a vehicle for contributions of remainder interests following life estates of the donor or other beneficiary.   The transfer to the charity must be an irrevocable remainder interest; the property transferred by each donor must be commingled with property of others making similar transfers; the trust cannot have investments in tax-exempt securities; and an income beneficiary must receive an amount determined by the trust's rate of return for each year.

Split interest gifts can also take the form of "charitable lead" trusts where the gift to charity precedes the gift to the private person or persons. The same basic requirements apply to such trusts as to split interests of the more conventional sort.

The split interest provisions apply, with some limited exceptions, to the estates of all decedents dying after December 31, 1969.   For more on these provisions, see Lowndes, Kramer & McCord § 16.9; Burke, Charitable Giving and Estate Planning, 28 The Tax Lawyer 289 (1975); H. Harris, Handling Federal Estate and Gift Taxes (4th ed. Rasch) §§ 6.88 et seq.

3.   The Marital Deduction

The estate tax marital deduction was introduced into the Code in 1948, along with the split income provision of the income tax law and companion changes in the gift tax law, for the purpose of equalizing the tax treatment of married people in non-community property states with that in community property states. It accomplished its purpose by providing that certain transfers to a spouse up to a limit of one-half the "adjusted gross estate" would be tax free. ("Adjusted gross estate" is defined as the gross estate less expenses, etc., deductible under § 2053, and losses deductible under § 2054.)

In the Tax Reform Act of 1976 Congress took a first step toward tax-free interspousal transfers by providing that the maximum deduction should be the *greater* of $250,000 or one half the adjusted gross estate. In 1981, Congress went all the way and provided an unlimited marital deduction for both gift and estate taxes. The new law also effected a major relaxation of the previously existing limitations on the eligibility of life estates for the marital deduction.

Internal Revenue Code (26 U.S.C.A.) § 2056 (in part):

(a) Allowance of Marital Deduction. For purposes of the tax imposed by section 2001, the value of the taxable estate shall, except as limited by subsection (b), be determined by deducting from the value of the gross estate an amount equal to the value of any interest in property which passes or has passed from the decedent to his surviving spouse, but only to the extent that such interest is included in determining the value of the gross estate.

(b) Limitation in the Case of Life Estate or Other Terminable Interest.

(1) General rule. Where, on the lapse of time, on the occurrence of an event or contingency, or on the failure of an event or contingency to occur, an interest passing to the surviving spouse will terminate or fail, no deduction shall be allowed under this section with respect to such interest—

(A) if an interest in such property passes or has passed (for less than an adequate and full consideration in money or money's worth) from the decedent to any person other than such surviving spouse (or the estate of such spouse); and

(B) if by reason of such passing such person (or his heirs or assigns) may possess or enjoy any part of such property after such termination or failure of the interest so passing to the surviving spouse;

and no deduction shall be allowed with respect to such interest (even if such deduction is not disallowed under subparagraphs (A) and (B))—

(C) if such interest is to be acquired for the surviving spouse, pursuant to directions of the decedent, by his executor or by the trustee of a trust.

For purposes of this paragraph, an interest shall not be considered as an interest which will terminate or fail merely because it is the ownership of a bond, note, or similar contractual obligation, the discharge of which would not have the effect of an annuity for life or for a term.

(2) Interest in unidentified assets. Where the assets (included in the decedent's gross estate) out of which, or the proceeds of which, an interest passing to the surviving spouse may be satisfied include a particular asset or assets with respect to which no deduction would be allowed if such asset or assets passed from the decedent to such spouse, then the value of such interest passing to such spouse shall, for purposes of subsection (a), be reduced by the aggregate value of such particular assets.

(3) Interest of spouse conditional on survival for limited period. For purposes of this subsection, an interest passing to the surviving spouse shall not be considered as an interest which will terminate or fail on the death of such spouse if—

(A) such death will cause a termination or failure of such interest only if it occurs within a period not exceeding 6 months after the decedent's death, or only if it occurs as a result of a common disaster resulting in the death of the decedent and the surviving spouse, or only if it occurs in the case of either such event; and

(B) such termination or failure does not in fact occur.

(4) Valuation of interest passing to surviving spouse. In determining for purposes of subsection (a) the value of any interest in property passing to the surviving spouse for which a deduction is allowed by the section—

(A) there shall be taken into account the effect which the tax imposed by section 2001, or any estate, succession, legacy, or inheritance tax, has on the net value to the surviving spouse of such interest; and

(B) where such interest or property is encumbered in any manner, or where the surviving spouse incurs any obligation imposed by the decedent with respect to the passing of such interest, such encumbrance or obligation shall be taken into account in the same manner as if the amount of a gift to such spouse of such interest were being determined.

(5) Life estate with power of appointment in surviving spouse. In the case of an interest in property passing from the decedent, if his surviving spouse is entitled for life to all the income from the entire interest, or all the income from a specific portion thereof, payable annually or at more frequent intervals, with power in the surviving spouse to appoint the entire interest, or such specific portion (exercisable in favor of such surviving spouse, or of the estate of such surviving spouse, or in favor of either, whether or not in each case the power is exercisable in favor of others), and with no power in any other person to appoint any part of the interest, or such specific portion, to any person other than the surviving spouse—

(A) the interest or such portion thereof so passing shall, for purposes of subsection (a), be considered as passing to the surviving spouse, and

(B) no part of the interest so passing shall, for purposes of paragraph (1)(A), be considered as passing to any person other than the surviving spouse.

This paragraph shall apply only if such power in the surviving spouse to appoint the entire interest, or such specific portion thereof, whether exercisable by will or during life, is exercisable by such spouse alone and in all events.

*   *   *

(7) Election with respect to life estate for surviving spouse—

(A) In general.—In the case of qualified terminable interest property—

(i) for purposes of subsection (a), such property shall be treated as passing to the surviving spouse, and

(ii) for purposes of paragraph (1)(A), no part of such property shall be treated as passing to any person other than the surviving spouse.

(B) Qualified terminable interest property defined.—For purposes of this paragraph—

(i) In general.—The term "qualified terminable interest property" means property—

(I) which passes from the decedent,

(II) in which the surviving spouse has a qualifying income interest for life, and

(III) to which an election under this paragraph applies.

(ii) Qualifying income interest for life.—The surviving spouse has a qualifying income interest for life if—

(I) the surviving spouse is entitled to all the income from the property, payable annually or at more frequent intervals, or has a usufruct interest for life in the property, and

(II) no person has a power to appoint any part of the property to any person other than the surviving spouse.

Subclause (II) shall not apply to a power exercisable only at or after the death of the surviving spouse. To the extent provided in regulations, an annuity shall be treated in a manner similar to an income interest in property (regardless of whether the property from which the annuity is payable can be separately identified).

(iii) Property includes interest therein.—The term "property" includes an interest in property.

(iv) Specific portion treated as separate property.—A specific portion of property shall be treated as separate property.

(v) Election.—An election under this paragraph with respect to any property shall be made by the executor on the return of tax imposed by section 2001. Such an election, once made, shall be irrevocable.

*   *   *

(c) Definition. For purposes of this section, an interest in property shall be considered as passing from the decedent to any person if and only if—

(1) such interest is bequeathed or devised to such person by the decedent;

(2) such interest is inherited by such person from the decedent;

(3) such interest is the dower or curtesy interest (or statutory interest in lieu thereof) of such person as surviving spouse of the decedent;

(4) such interest has been transferred to such person by the decedent at any time;

(5) such interest was, at the time of the decedent's death, held by such person and the decedent (or by them and any other person) in joint ownership with right of survivorship;

(6) the decedent had a power (either alone or in conjunction with any person) to appoint such interest and if he appoints or has appointed such interest to such person, or if such person takes such interest in default on the release or nonexercise of such power; or

(7) such interest consists of proceeds of insurance on the life of the decedent receivable by such person.

Except as provided in paragraph (5) or (6) of subsection (b), where at the time of the decedent's death it is not possible to ascertain the particular person or persons to whom an interest in property may pass from the decedent, such interest shall, for purposes of subparagraphs (A) and (B) of subsection (b)(1), be considered as passing from the decedent to a person other than the surviving spouse.

In their short history the marital deduction provisions have given rise to a large amount of litigation. Most of the litigation has concerned the provision that no deduction shall be allowed on account of life estates or other "terminable interests" passing to the spouse.

WARREN AND SURREY, FEDERAL ESTATE & GIFT TAXATION
759–763 (1961 ed.).

The terminable interest rule and its various exceptions are, for the draftsman, probably the most important portion of the marital deduction provisions of the Code. Its requirements must be adhered to precisely if a gift or bequest is to qualify for the deduction. Almost all of the litigation with respect to the marital deduction has arisen in connection with these requirements.

* * * [O]ne of the basic policies underlying the marital deduction provisions was that property qualifying for the deduction be includible in the surviving spouse's gross estate. No marital deduction was to be allowed where an interest in the property bequeathed to the spouse could pass to other persons, after the termination of her interest, without the inclusion of such interest in the wife's gross estate. Such terminable interests have their own built-in estate tax avoidance, because the interests passing to third parties, stemming as they do from the decedent, automatically escape tax in the estate of the first legatee enjoying the property. * * *

It was also intended to require property qualifying for the marital deduction to be substantially the same type of interest which would have passed to the surviving spouse under the community property system. Under that system, the surviving spouse receives outright ownership of half the community property and only half of the decedent's property is included in his gross estate. If the wife then dies still owning half of the community property it will be included in her gross estate and all the family's community property will have been subject to estate tax at least once. Thus, only where the surviving spouse receives outright ownership or its practical equivalent should the property qualify for the marital deduction.

The terminable interest rule found in section 2056(b) attempts to incorporate the foregoing two policies in specific statutory language. By its operation, property which is not included in the decedent's estate because it qualifies for the marital deduction will if still in existence be subject to tax in his spouse's estate. Thus, all the family's property will have been subjected to the estate tax once, and a treatment equivalent to that accorded the community property spouse will have been achieved. But as will be seen * * * the equivalence is a rough one.

The general rule (section 2056(b)(1)) prevents an interest in property from qualifying for the deduction where all of the following conditions exist: (1) The interest passing to the spouse will fail or terminate upon the lapse of time or the occurrence or nonoccurrence of an event. (2) An interest in such property passes or has passed for less than an adequate consideration in money's worth from the decedent to a third person. (3) Such third person may, upon such termination or failure, possess or enjoy any part of such property. Moreover, even though otherwise allowable, the deduction is not allowed for a terminable interest which "is to be acquired for the surviving spouse, pursuant to directions of the decedent, by his executor or by the trustee of a trust". Section 2056(b)(1). Expressly excepted from this rule are bonds, notes or "similar contractual obligations, the discharge of which would not have the effect of an annuity for life or for a term."

Under this general rule, the following types of interest would be disqualified: "to my wife for life" or for "10 years"; "to my wife until she remarries"; or "to my wife, but if she fails to survive my brother, then over."

It will be noted that the mere termination of the spouse's interest, or the mere passing of an interest to a third party will not, by itself, disqualify the bequest. For example, a remainder interest to a wife will qualify even though an interest has passed to the life beneficiary because the interest passing to the third party does not take effect after the surviving spouse's interest. Moreover, a joint and survivor annuity payable to the surviving spouse for life and included in the decedent's gross estate under section 2039, will qualify for the marital deduction because no interest has passed to a third party. Reg.sec. 20.2056(b)–(1)(g) (example 3).

The "terminable" interest rule is expressly rendered inapplicable in three situations where it would otherwise be applicable but for special statutory provisions which have the effect of treating the entire interest in the property as passing to the surviving spouse and not to any other person.

(a) First, if the only condition under which the surviving spouse's interest can terminate is her death in a common disaster or within six months of the decedent's death and her death does not so occur, such interest is not disqualified. Section 2056(b)(3). This provision is necessary to permit the use of common disaster and early death clauses typically employed in wills and insurance policies.

(b) Second, under section 2056(b)(5), if the surviving spouse is entitled for life to all the income from an interest in property, or to the income from a specific portion of that interest and if she has a general power of appointment with respect to the interest in property or that specific portion thereof, the interest is not disqualified for the deduction. The property subject to the wife's income interest and power of appointment may or may not be held in trust. The surviving spouse's power may be exercisable only during life or only by will, but in either case it must be exercisable alone and in all events. The typical situation in which section 2056(b)(5) will apply to qualify for the deduction an interest which would otherwise be considered "terminable" is that in which the testator leaves property in trust "to pay income to my wife Jane for life, and at her death, to pay the corpus to such persons, including her estate, as she may appoint by will, but, in default of such appointment, to pay the corpus to my issue then living." The deduction is allowed in these cases because the wife's rights with respect to the property constitute the practical equivalent of outright ownership and the property would be included in her gross estate by virtue of her general power of appointment. Section 2041. A number of important liberalizing amendments were made in section 2056(b)(5) by the 1954 Code.   *   *   *

(c) Third, under section 2056(b)(6), an interest passing to the surviving spouse will qualify for the deduction if it consists of the proceeds of a life insurance, endowment, or annuity contract payable in installments or held by an insurance company under an agreement to pay interest thereon and the surviving spouse has rights under the contract analogous to those which she is required to receive in the case of an interest qualifying for the deduction under section 2056(b)(5).

The annuity referred to in this section, of course, presupposes a survivorship feature whereby an interest in corpus or a survivorship annuity will pass to a third person on the termination of the spouse's interest, in the absence of her appointment. Otherwise, it would qualify despite the termination because no interest would have passed to a third person. The reasons for the exception to the terminable interest rule provided in section 2056(b)(6) are the same as those underlying the exception made by section 2056(b)(5). Section 2056(b)(6) was also liberalized by the 1954 Code. * * *

Lastly, it should be noted that the terminable interest need not be specifically bequeathed to the surviving spouse, or even actually allocated to her in administration, to reduce the amount of the marital deduction. Section 2056(b)(2) provides that if the assets which may be included in the surviving wife's bequest or trust include any which would be considered "terminable" if they did pass to the surviving spouse, then the amount of the allowable marital deduction is to be reduced by the value of such interests. For this reason it has become fairly regular procedure to utilize provisions of the following type in providing for marital deduction trusts or bequests:

> "I further direct that in establishing this trust there shall not be allocated thereto any property or the proceeds of any property which would not qualify for the marital deduction allowable to my estate."

If the estate is fairly small and the testator wants his wife to have the entire amount provided for in the marital deduction trust even if the entire amount does not benefit from the deduction, the language above can be prefaced with "To the extent possible without reducing the amount of the bequest."

ESTATE OF McMILLAN v. COMMISSIONER
76 T.C. 170 (1981).

IRWIN, Judge: Respondent determined a deficiency of $359,300.35 in the estate tax of the Estate of Jesse E. McMillan. Due to a concession, the sole issue is whether under section 2056 the estate is entitled to a marital deduction in excess of $42,136.

* * *

Jesse E. McMillan died on July 14, 1975, in Gurdon, Ark. Mary E. McMillan, the decedent's surviving spouse and duly qualified executrix of the Estate of Jesse E. McMillan, was granted letters testamentary by the Probate Court of Clark County, Ark., on September 11, 1975.

* * *

The decedent was survived by his wife, two sisters, five nephews, and five nieces. His last will and testament, executed on or about March 18, 1955, provided as follows:

I, J. E. McMillan, residing in Gurdon, Ark. in the County of Clark being of sound mind and disposing memory do make, ordain, publish, and declare this to be my Last Will and Testament hereby revoking all former Wills and Codicils by me made.

I, J. E. McMillan here by Will everything that I have to my wife, Mary Ethel (Conn) McMillan for so long as she may live.

I wish to request that all property, money, money from life insurance, Stocks and Bonds or anything of value be used by her to the best of her ability for as long as she may live.

I wish to request that any financial favors that she may extend to any member of her family that like amount be extended to some member of my family that may need it most.

I wish to request that at her death the cashier of the Clark County Bank, Gurdon, Ark. and Charlie McMillan be appointed as Executors of the balance of the Estate which was left to my wife by me, J. E. McMillan.

I wish to request that the balance of the estate be sold for cash within a period not to exceed twenty four months and the following division be made at that time. Divide the total proceeds into six equal parts: One part to Hazel Conn Ewing; one part to Jewel Edward Conn; one part to Charlie C. McMillan; one part to Hattie McMillan Taylor; one part of [sic] Mecie McMillan Taylor; one part to Rosie McMillan Pruitt. In event that Rose McMillan Pruitt is not living at that time the proceeds is to be divided into five equal parts and given to the above mentioned five heirs. In event either of the above mentioned five heirs are not living at that time their part is to be divided equally to their living children.

I wish to request that any money or anything or anything of value that any member of my family or any member of my wife's family may have received from my wife during her life time after my death be deducted from their part of the estate and be equally divided among all the heirs. I wish to request that my wife Mary Ethel McMillan keep a record of all donations or loans to any member of my family or to her family and same be filed with this will the first of each and every year during her life time.

Lastly, I make constitute and appoint my wife Mary Ethel McMillan to be the Administratrix of this Last Will and Testament, and serve without bond.

IN WITNESS, WHEREOF, I have hereunto subscribed my name and affixed my seal the eighteenth of March, in the year of Our Lord, One Thousand Nine Hundred and Fifty five.

The estate tax return filed by Mrs. McMillan (hereinafter sometimes petitioner) reflected a gross estate of $1,870,991 and an adjusted gross estate of $1,798,526. Stocks and bonds in the estate were valued at $1,822,605 as of the date of death. Bonds owned by the estate were producing almost $80,000 of annual income, some of which was exempt from income tax under section 103. Stock owned by the estate consisted mainly of utility issues and other established corporations. Property held jointly by the decedent and his wife, amounting to $15,785, and insurance proceeds of $26,351, passing directly to the surviving spouse, were included in the gross estate. Taking the position that all of the decedent's property passed to the surviving spouse, the estate claimed one-half of the adjusted gross estate as a marital deduction. Thus, the claimed marital deduction amounted to $899,263.

In his notice of deficiency respondent determined that the estate is entitled to a marital deduction of $42,136.

* * *

Respondent maintains that under the Will of Jesse E. McMillan, Mary E. McMillan, decedent's surviving spouse, received a mere life estate with no power over the principal, thus constituting a nondeductible terminable interest. Alternatively, respondent argues that the surviving spouse was granted a life estate with a power, but not a general power of appointment as described in section 2056(b)(5).

Petitioner contends that decedent bequeathed to his surviving spouse a life estate with an unqualified and unrestricted power of disposition. It is argued that this power is tantamount to a general power of appointment, and therefore, the interest passing to the surviving spouse meets the requirements of section 2056(b)(5) and is thus deductible.

The dispute in this case centers on the proper construction of the last will and testament of Jesse E. McMillan. Principles of Arkansas law must guide us in our quest to define the legal interests which were created under the will, and the Federal taxing statute will then determine the tax consequences of the interests so created. Helvering v. Stuart, 317 U.S. 154, 162 (1942); Morgan v. Commissioner, 309 U.S. 78, 80 (1940).

* * *

Since the parties agree that the surviving spouse was granted a life estate in the decedent's property, the dispute more narrowly focuses on whether the life estate so granted was coupled with a power of appointment, and if so, whether such power was a general power of appointment.

The parties are also in agreement that nowhere in the will did Jesse E. McMillan expressly grant an unlimited power of disposition over corpus to the life tenant. Petitioner contends that such a power is to be implied from the will and that a power so implied is as effective as a power specifically expressed. While we most assuredly agree that express and implied powers are on equal footing (Johnson v. Lehr, 192 Ark. 1004, 96 S.W.2d 20 (1936)), we do not believe that any power of invasion or disposition over the principal of the estate was implied in the instant case.

After clause 2 of the will of Jesse E. McMillan grants Mary a life estate in the decedent's property, clauses 3, 5, and 6 provide in pertinent part:

> I wish to request that all property, money, money from life insurance, Stocks and Bonds or anything of value be used by her [i.e., Mary] to the best of her ability for as long as she may live.

> I wish to request that at her death the cashier of the Clark County Bank, Gurdon, Ark. and Charlie McMillan be appointed Executors of the balance of the Estate which was left to my wife by me, J. E. McMillan.

> I wish to request that the balance of the estate be sold for cash within a period of twenty four months. * * *

Petitioner impliedly suggests that the words "I wish to request" are merely precatory, thus evincing an intent that Mary have outright control of the corpus, and emphasizes that the word "balance" (clauses 5 and 6), coupled with the phrase "be used by her to the best of her ability" (clause 3), implies a power of disposition in the surviving spouse.

Whether words are merely precatory or impose an imperative obligation must be determined by the language actually used, the context, and the consideration of the will as a whole. [Citations omitted.] Directions are held to be mandatory when such words direct, command, or require something to be done, and are considered precatory when such words merely express a hope or wish of the testator, leaving it to the discretion of another whether or not to carry out the wish. [Citations omitted.] We hold that the expression "I wish to request" used in the will in the instant case is testamentary and not a naked expression of hope. Decedent's will consisted of eight clauses. Clauses 3 through 7 all begin with "I wish to request." We are hard pressed to find that after disposing of property in clause 2, the dispositive scheme of the testator had thus ended only to be followed by five expressions of hope which constituted the overwhelming majority of the instrument. To so hold seems plainly illogical.

Similarly, we do not think it reasonable to infer a power of invasion over principal from the testator's use of the word "balance" in clauses 5 and 6. * * *

The will of Jesse E. McMillan does not specifically address the needs or best interests of Mary, but rather mandates that property be used by Mary "to the best of her ability." We think this latter phrase more reasonably connotes a skill, i.e., the management of funds, than it does an unfettered right to dispose or consume the property in any manner that Mary pleases.

* * *

Petitioner, in asserting that the phrase "balance of the estate," as used in clause 6 of the will, implies a power of disposition over principal, relies on Johnson v. Lehr, supra, and Weeks v. Weeks, 211 Ark. 132, 199 S.W.2d 955 (1947). In *Johnson,* the following language was held to create an implied power of sale in the primary legatee:

> I give, devise, and bequeath unto my beloved wife   * * *   all of my property   * * *   for her own personal use as long as she may live and at her death *should there be any property or moneys left* after the payment of her funeral expenses and debts are paid it is my desire that the residue be divided equally   * * *   [96 S.W.2d at 20; emphasis supplied.]

In *Weeks,* the following will provision was viewed as bestowing upon the life tenant an absolute power of sale and disposition:

> I give and bequeath unto my beloved wife,   * * *   all the rest, residue and remainder of my estate   * * *   for her own personal use so long as she shall live, and at her death I direct that *whatever remains* of said bequest be divided   * * *   [199 S.W.2d at 956; emphasis supplied.]

Both *Johnson* and *Weeks* are distinguishable from the case at bar. The phrases "should there be any moneys or property left" and "whatever remains" clearly imply that the rights of remaindermen are contingent upon the life tenant's death prior to the depletion of the estate principal by the life tenant through use, sale, or otherwise. It is within the context of a remainderman's contingent interest that Arkansas cases have stated that a conveyance by a life tenant to a third party might actually defeat the rights of a remainderman. [Citations omitted.] However, where a testator uses the term "balance" connoting that something will indeed be left over, and then proceeds to mandate a detailed accounting system wherein advancements to remaindermen are taken into consideration (see will clause 7), we think it unreasonable to assume that an absolute power of disposition is implied.

Considering the above discussion, we believe that the power to extend financial favors to family members granted to Mary by clause 4 of the will relates to moneys derived from income of the estate principal. We derive support for this conclusion from the fact that the income earned on bonds owned by decedent was to be almost $80,000 per year, much of which would be exempt from tax under section 103. Additionally, decedent owned a significant number of shares of stock in utility companies and other established corporations which would in all likelihood result in Mary's receipt of significant dividend income. However, even assuming arguendo, that such a power to grant favors related to the principal of the estate, the marital deduction would likewise be unavailable to the estate for the reason that such a power is expressly limited so as to benefit only family members, and therefore, the interest passing would still not satisfy the mandate of section 2056(b)(5).

In summary, we hold that Mary E. McMillan received a life estate in the property of the decedent, Jesse E. McMillan, with no power over the disposition of the principal of the estate. The interest thus passing to Mary therefore does not qualify for the marital deduction. * * *

Notes

1. As discussed in Chapter 5, supra, the making of a joint will or mutual wills may create a contractual obligation on the part of the survivor to dispose of property in a particular way, which becomes irrevocable on the death of the first to die. In the case of a husband and wife such a contract, if enforceable under local law, will make the bequest to the spouse a terminable interest and lose the marital deduction. See e.g., Opal's Estate v. Commissioner, 450 F.2d 1085 (2d Cir.1971). In Estate of Emily McCune, T.C. Memo 1984–580 para. 14285.5, the Tax Court allowed the marital deduction for property passing to a husband under a will which read, in part: "All the rest, residue and remainder of my Estate, whatsoever and wheresoever situate, I give, devise and bequeath to my husband, with the understanding that should he re-marry, whatever monies he has received from me shall be equally bestowed upon my daughter * * * and my four granddaughters * * *."

2. In order to satisfy the requirement of § 2056(b)(5) that the spouse "be entitled for life to all the income," care must be taken to avoid giving the trustee any discretion to accumulate; indeed, any authority in the trustee over the

payment of the income may be dangerous. Tying the spouse's right to income to his or her needs for "support" or "maintenance" may also invite disallowance of the marital deduction. See, e.g., Estate of Mittelman, 522 F.2d 132 (D.C. Cir. 1975) where the Court of Appeals allowed a marital deduction where the trust was established "to provide for the proper support, maintenance, welfare and comfort of my beloved wife" over the objection of the Commissioner. The *Mittelman* case, particularly the arguments of the Commissioner and the opinion of the Tax Court denying a deduction, illustrates the technicality which has characterized interpretation of the terminable interest rule.

3. Despite the provisions of § 2056(b)(5), if a surviving spouse is given an "estate trust," i.e., a trust providing that corpus and accumulated income are payable at the spouse's death to his or her estate, the trust may qualify for the marital deduction even though the trustee has, among other powers, power to accumulate income. Can you justify the difference in treatment on the basis of the language of the statute?

———

The Qualified Terminable Interest (QTIP) Exception

As noted above, the general scheme of the marital deduction is to allow a deduction for property passing to a spouse where that property—if retained by the spouse until his or her death—will be taxable in the spouse's estate. Until 1981, this meant that to qualify property for the marital deduction a spouse had to be given at least complete freedom of testamentary disposition. This requirement was not too great a burden where the spouses were in general agreement about how the family property should be passed on to the next generation. However, even in first marriages, that is not always the case and, in the case of second marriages, particularly where one or both of the parties have grown children, there is a potential conflict of interest between the new and old families. Not infrequently, a spouse may wish to give the other a life income in his property but to have the principal—after the death of the survivor—go to his children. Prior to 1981, if the arithmetic of the two estates made use of the marital deduction advisable taxwise, there was a delicate problem. How could one take full advantage of the marital deduction and still assure that the survivor did not divert the property to his family— or friends—instead of the decedent's? The answer was that there was no way to be certain of accomplishing both objectives. Unless the survivor was given full control—at least by will—to dispose of property as he saw fit, the property would not qualify for the marital deduction. If the survivor wanted to divert the property to his own family—or a later spouse—and he had sufficient power over the property to qualify it for the marital deduction, there was no way to stop him.

In 1981 Congress removed the necessity of making the delicate choice between getting the marital deduction and losing control over the ultimate disposition of the property by enacting § 2056(b)(7) (see p. 936 supra) under which transfers of "qualified terminable interest property" (quickly dubbed QTIP transfers) qualify for the marital deduction. Essentially what the QTIP provisions accomplish is to permit a decedent to give his spouse a life estate *without* a general testamentary power of appointment and still take advantage of the marital deduction. The general scheme of the marital deduction mentioned above—that property which escapes tax in the first estate will be taxed in the second—is preserved by subjecting the property in which the survivor has a life estate to tax in his or her estate (I.R.C. § 2044) or to gift tax if the spouse disposes of the life interest during his or her life (§ 2519).

Another attractive feature—for estate planners—of the QTIP provisions is that the election to take the marital deduction—with its consequences—does not have to be made until the estate tax return of the transferor is filed. That election is made by the executor and the decision to elect (or not) is irrevocable.

Notes

1. A life estate, to satisfy the QTIP requirements, must meet the standards as to the frequency and certainty of payment of income discussed above at pp. 939–40. It would appear that, under current law, the life estate given to the wife in Estate of McMillan, supra p. 940, could be qualified for the marital deduction.

2. § 2056(c) provides, inter alia, that property passing to a surviving spouse because of a right to dower or curtesy or spouse's non-barrable share (see Chapter 3, supra) can qualify for the marital deduction (assuming it meets other criteria imposed by § 2056). In most states, for example those which have adopted the UPC, a surviving spouse is entitled to a share of the property outright and a QTIP interest will not satisfy that requirement. In New York, however (see pp. 166–173, supra) the spouse's non-barrable share above $10,000 can be satisfied by a life estate.

Marital Deduction Arithmetic

Taking advantage of the marital deduction will not always make sense tax-wise. The advisability of using it will depend on the arithmetic of the particular case. Where both spouses have substantial property they must take care that the tax saving in the first estate does not lead to a higher tax in the combined estates. For an illustration of how this could happen before the Tax Reform Act of 1976, see Kohn, The Marital Deduction: When and How to Use It, 16 Western Res.L.Rev. 237, 239–41 (1965). The sharp reduction in the maximum tax rate (from 77% in 1975 to 50% when the currently mandated phase-in is complete in 1988) effected in recent years makes the penalty for faulty arithmetic less severe. And, of course, other considerations than pure arithmetic will affect the decision. The surviving spouse, if she lives long enough, can reduce her estate by using up the property or giving it away in gifts that qualify for the annual exclusion. And, of course, the needs of the surviving spouse—for income and principal—may override other considerations. Still, the message that both estates must be considered remains valid.

Prior to 1981 the effort to fine tune the overall impact of the estate tax frequently took the form of giving the surviving spouse the maximum amount of property qualifying for the marital deduction, but *no more*. Since it is impossible to know what property a person will own at death, or what its value will be, that effort necessitated the use of a formula clause phrased in terms of a fraction of the estate as valued for estate tax purposes.

The enactment of the unlimited marital deduction made many pre-1981 formula clauses obsolete. However, the need for a new kind of formula clause remains, unless one wants to take the marital deduction for all of his or her property. Ordinarily, in an estate of substantial size, that will not be a good idea because it may "waste" the unified credit of one of the spouses. For example, take the case of a husband with a taxable estate of $1,200,000 and a wife with no assets. At his death, the husband, who has made no taxable gifts during his lifetime, leaves all of his property to his wife outright so that it all qualifies for the marital deduction. There will be no federal estate tax in his estate. However, when his wife dies, assuming she still owns all the property received from her husband and has not remarried, her estate will pay a tax on all property in excess of $600,000—at current rates a tax of $235,000. If, on the other hand the husband had left half of his property to his wife for life with a special testamentary power of appointment, his estate would have paid no tax ($600,000 unified credit and $600,000 marital deduction) and neither would his wife who would die with a taxable estate of $600,000, the equivalent of her lifetime credit of $192,800.

One popular device to ensure that the unified credit is used is the establishment of a "credit shelter trust" to use up any previously unused lifetime credit. For the same reasons noted above with respect to fine tuning the marital deduction before 1981, the optimal use of the credit shelter trust requires the use of a formula clause.

The following is an example of one such clause:

If my wife shall survive me, I give and bequeath to my Trustee, hereinafter named, an amount equal to the maximum amount that can pass free of Federal estate tax under this Clause by reason of the unified credit against Federal estate tax and any credit for State death taxes (to the extent that taking such credit into account does not cause the imposition or increase of any State death taxes) allowable to my estate after taking into account the value of all property includible in my gross estate for Federal estate tax purposes which shall pass under the preceding provisions of this Will, or shall pass or shall have passed outside the provisions of this Will, either at my death or at any time during my life, with respect to which neither a marital deduction nor a charitable deduction is allowed to my estate. Property (or the proceeds thereof) includible in my gross estate which would not qualify for the Federal estate tax marital deduction shall to the extent possible be used to satisfy this bequest. In computing the amount of this pecuniary bequest, the values used in finally determining the Federal estate tax on my estate shall control. If my Executor shall satisfy this pecuniary bequest in kind, the assets selected by my Executor for that purpose shall be valued at their respective values on the dates of their distribution.

The clause set forth above is an example of a "pecuniary" clause, so-called because it is designed to produce for the surviving spouse a specific dollar amount—once estate tax values are established. The other general type of clause in a common use is a "fractional" clause designed to give the surviving spouse a fractional share of the residue rather than a specific amount. See Bittker & Clark, Federal Estate and Gift Taxation (5th ed. 1984) 494–96. For other examples of formula clauses and a good discussion of the interplay of the unified credit and the marital deduction, see Kurtz, Marital Deduction Estate Planning Under the Economic Recovery Tax Act of 1981: Opportunities Exist But Watch the Pitfalls, 34 Rutgers L.Rev. 591 (1982); see also Blattmachr & Lustgarten, The New Estate Tax Marital Deduction: Many Questions And Some Answers, 121 Trusts and Estates (January, 1982) 18.

Note

After the estate tax has been determined, certain credits are computed and deducted from the tax. These credits include the "unified credit" (§ 2010) and credits for state death taxes paid with respect to property included in the gross estate (§ 2011), death taxes paid to a foreign country in respect of property situated in that country and included in the gross estate (§ 2014), and federal estate taxes paid by another decedent with respect to property transferred by him or her to the current decedent, subject to limitations that depend on the length of time that has elapsed between the original transfer and the current decedent's death (§ 2013).

C. ESTATE TAX APPORTIONMENT

Death Tax Clauses In Wills And Trusts: Discussion and Sample Clauses, 19 Real Property, Probate and Trust Journal 495, 500–505 (1984) (footnotes omitted):

II. ALLOCATION OF TAX BURDEN

In determining where the tax burden should fall, the attorney should be aware of all nonprobate assets or powers that will generate tax liability, so that he can assure himself that the client has made an informed determination of which of the beneficiaries of probate and nonprobate assets shall contribute to the death tax liability. The attorney will then probably want to draft a provision tailored to the client's situation—most "boiler plate" tax clauses place the burden of the estate tax on the residuary estate, which may produce a result that is inequitable to the estate beneficiaries and produce unnecessary tax liability by reducing the marital deduction or a charitable deduction.

The client and his attorney have the opportunity to determine where the tax burden, state and federal will fall. If the client does not specify where he wants the tax burden to fall through a specific administrative provision, both state and federal law will allocate the tax burden.

More than half the states have adopted apportionment statutes that allocate the tax burden between probate and nonprobate assets. In those states that have not adopted apportionment statutes, the general rule is that the burden of the entire tax, both that attributable to probate property and that attributable to nonprobate property, will fall on the residuary estate. There are potential problems with respect to which state law applies when the client has properties with a situs in more than one state.

* * *

A. State Laws

Congress intended that state law should determine the ultimate burden of the estate tax and, with certain exceptions discussed herein, has enacted no provisions concerning where that burden should fall. Examination of the chart following this article * * * will show that there is no uniformity among the states with respect to the ultimate burden of the estate tax.

* * *

There are different types of apportionment statutes. One type may provide that each beneficiary, whether of assets passing through the probate estate or of nonprobate assets, should bear a pro rata part of the tax liability. Another type may provide that the probate estate will bear the burden of the tax liability attributable to assets passing through the probate estate with the tax being paid out of residue, and that the recipients of nonprobate assets will each bear a share of the tax liability attributable to nonprobate assets. Although some statutes require a provision in the will and others do not, this article attempts to demonstrate that it is preferable to provide a tax clause in any event.

* * *

Thus, in deciding who should be responsible for the payment of death taxes, the client and his attorney must decide whether the applicable state law (statutory or judicial) places the death tax burden where the client wants it to fall. If it does, the client may simply let the law take its course (accepting the risk that the law may change before his death or that he may change his domicile to a state with a different law and fail to change his estate plan), or the client may choose to specify in his estate plan exactly where he wants the death tax burden to fall. The latter will generally prove to be the better course, particularly having in mind the mobility of clients and the possible problems of the interaction of state and federal law.

B. Federal Law

* * *

The executor is personally liable for the taxes due from the decedent's estate, if he makes distribution of assets and the taxes are not paid. As mentioned above, there are three Internal Revenue Code sections permitting the executor to seek reimbursement for taxes paid from beneficiaries of assets passing outside the probate estate. Section 2206 gives the executor a right of reimbursement from life insurance beneficiaries, and section 2207 provides the same right with regard to recipients of property over which the decedent had a general power of appointment at the time of his death. The Economic Recovery Tax Act of 1981 added a third provision under which additional estate taxes attributable to the taxation of a QTIP trust in the estate of the surviving spouse may be borne by such property.

All of the three sections cited above are enforceable "unless the decedent directs otherwise in his will." The Internal Revenue Code gives the executor the authority to seek a pro rata reimbursement of estate taxes from certain specified properties not included in the probate estate. There may be a conflict between federal law and state law in the case of at least one state, Alabama, which provides that all taxes are to be paid out of the residue. Short of trying to get the state law changed, this conflict emphasizes the need for the attorney to specify how the tax should be apportioned in the instruments. As noted, however, the federal provisions apply only to life insurance, appointive property and taxes resulting from the includibility of a QTIP trust; thus, they do not include such items as jointly-held property with the right of survivorship, inter vivos trust property, pension benefits or inter vivos gifts made within three years of death and other nonprobate assets that may be included in the client's taxable estate.

For two approaches to the problem of apportionment in the absence of a controlling provision in the will, see McKinney's N.Y. EPTL 2–1.8 and Uniform Probate Code § 3–916. For an example of the trouble which can be caused by failing to provide for apportionment, see Greene v. United States, 476 F.2d 116 (7th Cir. 1973).

D. OVERLAP BETWEEN THE GIFT AND ESTATE TAX

SMITH v. SHAUGHNESSY

Supreme Court of the United States, 1943.
318 U.S. 176, 63 S.Ct. 545, 87 L.Ed. 690.

Mr. Justice BLACK delivered the opinion of the Court.

The question here is the extent of the petitioner's liability for a tax under §§ 501, 506 of the Revenue Act of 1932, 47 Stat. 169, 26 U.S.C.A. Int.Rev.Acts, pages 580, 588, which imposes a tax upon every transfer of property by gift, "whether the transfer is in trust or otherwise, whether the gift is direct or indirect, and whether the property is real or personal, tangible or intangible; * * *."

The petitioner, age 72, made an irrevocable transfer in trust of 3,000 shares of stock worth $571,000. The trust income was payable to his wife, age 44, for life; upon her death, the stock was to be returned to the petitioner, if he was living; if he was not living, it was to go to such persons as his wife might designate by will, or in default of a will by her, to her intestate successors under applicable New York law. The petitioner, under protest, paid a gift tax of $71,674.22, assessed on the total value of the trust principal, and brought suit for refund in the district court. Holding that the petitioner had, within the meaning of the Act, executed a completed gift of a life estate to his wife, the court sustained the Commissioner's assessment on $322,423, the determined value of her life interest; but the remainder was held not to be completely transferred and hence not subject to the gift tax. 40 F.Supp. 19. The government appealed and the Circuit Court of Appeals reversed, ordering dismissal of the petitioner's complaint on the authority of its previous decision in Herzog v. Commissioner, 116 F.2d 591. We granted certiorari because of alleged conflict with our decisions in Helvering v. Hallock, 309 U.S. 106, 60 S.Ct. 444, 84 L.Ed. 604, 125 A.L.R. 1368, and Estate of Sanford

v. Commissioner, 308 U.S. 39, 60 S.Ct. 51, 84 L.Ed. 20. In these decisions, and in Burnet v. Guggenheim, 288 U.S. 280, 53 S.Ct. 369, 77 L.Ed. 748, we have considered the problems raised here in some detail, and it will therefore be unnecessary to make any elaborate re-survey of the law.

Three interests are involved here: the life estate, the remainder, and the reversion. The taxpayer concedes that the life estate is subject to the gift tax. The government concedes that the right of reversion to the donor in case he outlives his wife is an interest having value which can be calculated by an actuarial device, and that it is immune from the gift tax. The controversy, then, reduces itself to the question of the taxability of the remainder.

The taxpayer's principal argument here is that under our decision in the Hallock case, the value of the remainder will be included in the grantor's gross estate for estate tax purposes; and that in the Sanford case we intimated a general policy against allowing the same property to be taxed both as an estate and as a gift.

This view, we think, misunderstands our position in the Sanford case. As we said there, the gift and estate tax laws are closely related and the gift tax serves to supplement the estate tax.[7] We said that the taxes are not "always mutually exclusive", and called attention to § 322 of the 1924 Act, 26 U.S.C.A. Int.Rev.Acts, page 82, there involved (re-enacted with amendments in § 801 of the 1932 Act, 26 U.S.C.A. Int.Rev.Acts, page 640) which charts the course for granting credits on estate taxes by reason of previous payment of gift taxes on the same property. The scope of that provision we need not now determine. It is sufficient to note here that Congress plainly pointed out that "some" of the "total gifts subject to gift taxes * * * may be included for estate tax purposes and some not." House Report No. 708, 72d Cong., 1st Sess., p. 45. Under the statute the gift tax amounts in some instances to a security, a form of down-payment on the estate tax which secures the eventual payment of the latter; it is in no sense double taxation as the taxpayer suggests.

We conclude that under the present statute, Congress has provided as its plan for integrating the estate and gift taxes this system of secured payment on gifts which will later be subject to the estate tax.[8]

Unencumbered by any notion of policy against subjecting this transaction to both estate and gift taxes, we turn to the basic question of whether there was a gift of the remainder. The government argues that

---

7. The gift tax was passed not only to prevent estate tax avoidance, but also to prevent income tax avoidance through reducing yearly income and thereby escaping the effect of progressive surtax rates. House Report No. 708, 72d Cong., 1st Sess., p. 28; Brandeis, J., dissenting in Untermyer v. Anderson, 276 U.S. 440, 450, 48 S.Ct. 353, 356, 72 L.Ed. 645; Stone, J., dissenting in Heiner v. Donnan, 285 U.S. 312, 333, 52 S.Ct. 358, 363, 76 L.Ed. 772.

8. It has been suggested that the congressional plan relating the estate and gift taxes may still be incomplete. See e.g., Griswold, A Plan for the Coordination of the Income, Estate, and Gift Tax Provisions etc., 56 Harv.L.Rev. 337; Magill, The Federal Gift Tax, 40 Col.L.Rev. 773, 792; Kauper, The Revenue Act of 1942: Estate and Gift Tax Amendments, 41 Mich.L.Rev. 369, 388; and see Commissioner v. Prouty, 1 Cir., 115 F.2d 331, 337, 133 A.L.R. 977; Higgins v. Commissioner, 1 Cir., 129 F.2d 237, 239.

for gift tax purposes the taxpayer has abandoned control of the remainder and that it is therefore taxable, while the taxpayer contends that no realistic value can be placed on the contingent remainder and that it therefore should not be classed as a gift.

We cannot accept any suggestion that the complexity of a property interest created by a trust can serve to defeat a tax. For many years Congress has sought vigorously to close tax loopholes against ingenious trust instruments. Even though these concepts of property and value may be slippery and elusive they cannot escape taxation so long as they are used in the world of business. The language of the gift tax statute, "property * * * real or personal, tangible or intangible", is broad enough to include property, however conceptual or contingent. And lest there be any doubt as to the amplitude of their purpose, the Senate and House Committees, reporting the bill, spelled out their meaning as follows:

> "The terms 'property,' 'transfer,' 'gift,' and 'indirectly' [§ 501] are used in the broadest sense; the term 'property' reaching every species of right or interest protected by the laws and having an exchangeable value."

The Treasury regulations, which we think carry out the Act's purpose, made specific provisions for application of the tax to, and determination of the value of, "a remainder * * * subject to an outstanding life estate."

The essence of a gift by trust is the abandonment of control over the property put in trust. The separable interests transferred are not gifts to the extent that power remains to revoke the trust or recapture the property represented by any of them, Burnet v. Guggenheim, supra, or to modify the terms of the arrangement so as to make other disposition of the property, Sanford v. Commissioner, supra. In the Sanford case the grantor could, by modification of the trust, extinguish the donee's interest at any instant he chose. In cases such as this, where the grantor has neither the form nor substance of control and never will have unless he outlives his wife, we must conclude that he has lost all "economic control" and that the gift is complete except for the value of his reversionary interest.

The judgment of the Circuit Court of Appeals is affirmed with leave to the petitioner to apply for modification of its mandate in order that the value of the petitioner's reversionary interest may be determined and excluded.

It is so ordered.

Affirmed.

Mr. Justice ROBERTS.

I dissent. I am of opinion that, except for the life estate in the wife, the gift qua the donor was incomplete and not within the sweep of §§ 501 and 506, 26 U.S.C.A. Int.Rev.Acts, pages 580, 588. A contrary conclusion might well be reached were it not for Helvering v. Hallock, 309 U.S. 106, 60 S.Ct. 444, 84 L.Ed. 604, 125 A.L.R. 1368. But the decisions in Burnet v. Guggenheim, 288 U.S. 280, 53 S.Ct. 369, 77 L.Ed. 748, and Sanford v.

Commissioner, 308 U.S. 39, 60 S.Ct. 51, 84 L.Ed. 20, to which the court adheres, require a reversal in view of the ruling in the Hallock case.

The first of the two cases ruled that a transfer in trust, whereby the grantor reserved a power of revocation, was not subject to a gift tax, but became so upon the renunciation of the power. The second held that where the grantor reserved a power to change the beneficiaries, but none to revoke or to make himself a beneficiary, the transfer was incomplete and not subject to gift tax. At the same term, in Porter v. Commissioner, 288 U.S. 436, 53 S.Ct. 451, 77 L.Ed. 880, the court held that where a decedent had given property inter vivos in trust, reserving a power to change the beneficiaries but no power to revoke or revest the property in himself, the transfer was incomplete until the termination of the reserved power by the donor's death and hence the corpus was subject to the estate tax.

When these cases were decided, the law, as announced by this court, was that where, in a complete and final transfer inter vivos, a grantor provided that, in a specified contingency, the corpus should pass to him, if living, but, if he should be dead, then to others, the gift was complete when made, he retained nothing which passed from him at his death, prior to the happening of the contingency, and that no part of the property given was includible in his gross estate tax. McCormick v. Burnet, 283 U.S. 784, 51 S.Ct. 343, 75 L.Ed. 1413; Helvering v. St. Louis Union Trust Co., 296 U.S. 39, 56 S.Ct. 74, 80 L.Ed. 29, 100 A.L.R. 1239; Becker v. St. Louis Union Trust Co., 296 U.S. 48, 56 S.Ct. 78, 80 L.Ed. 35. So long as this was the law the transfer might properly be the subject of a gift tax for the gift was, as respects the donor, complete when made.

In 1940 these decisions were overruled and it was held that such a transfer was so incomplete when made, and the grantor retained such an interest, that the cessation of that interest at death furnished the occasion for imposing an estate tax. Thus the situation here presented was placed in the same category as those where the grantor had reserved a power to revoke or a power to change beneficiaries. By analogy to the Guggenheim and Sanford cases, I suppose the gift would have become complete if the donor had, in his life, relinquished or conveyed the contingent estate reserved to him.

In the light of this history, the Sanford case requires a holding that the gifts in remainder, after the life estate, create no gift tax liability. The reasoning of that decision, the authorities, and the legislative history relied upon, are all at war with the result in this case. There is no need to quote what was there said. A reading of the decision will demonstrate that, if the principles there announced are here observed, the gifts in question are incomplete and cannot be the subject of the gift tax.

It will not square with logic to say that where the donor reserves the right to change beneficiaries, and so delays completion of the gift until his death or prior relinquishment of the right, the gift is incomplete, but where he reserves a contingent interest to himself the reverse is true—particularly so, if the criterion of estate tax liability is important to the decision of the question, as the Sanford case affirms.

The question is not whether a gift which includes vested and contingent future interests in others than the donor is taxable as an entirety when made, but whether a reservation of such an interest in the donor negatives a completion of the gift until such time as that interest is relinquished.

All that is said in the Sanford case about the difficulties of administration and probable inequities of a contrary decision there, applies here with greater force.   Indeed a system of taxation which requires valuation of the donor's retained interest, in the light of the contingencies involved, and calculation of the value of the subsequent remainders by resort to higher mathematics beyond the ken of the taxpayer, exhibits the artificiality of the Government's application of the Act.   This is well illustrated in the companion cases of Robinette and Paumgarten, 318 U.S. 184, 63 S.Ct. 540, 87 L.Ed. 700.   Such results argue strongly against the construction which the court adopts.

LOWNDES, KRAMER & McCORD, FEDERAL ESTATE AND GIFT TAXES

§ 28.2 (3d ed. 1974) (footnotes omitted).

THE RELATION BETWEEN THE GIFT TAX AND THE ESTATE AND INCOME TAXES

Although it is settled that an incomplete transfer is not taxable as a gift, there is some uncertainty about when a transfer is complete and when it is incomplete under the gift tax.   This can be best resolved by an examination of various types of transfers.   Before embarking upon a detailed discussion, however, it will be helpful to get the general problem clearly in mind.   There are two possible approaches to the question of what constitutes a complete transfer under the gift tax.   The gift tax was designed as an addendum or supplement to the estate and income taxes.   Consequently, the definition of a complete transfer under the gift tax might be sought in the estate or income taxes.   On the other hand, the gift tax might reject estate and income tax analogies in favor of some independent test of what constitutes a complete transfer.   In a concrete case the question of whether a transfer is complete or not frequently turns upon whether the gift tax must be construed to reconcile it with the estate tax or the income tax.   It is important, therefore, to be clear about just what this involves.

Under the estate tax certain types of inter vivos transfers are treated as complete and final dispositions which are not subject to the tax and remove the transferred property from the transferor's estate.   Other types of inter vivos transfers, however, are treated as incomplete dispositions which are taxable under the estate tax and do not eliminate the transferred property from the estate of the transferor.   Since one of the principal purposes of the gift tax was to reach transfers by which a man might deplete his estate during his life and defeat the estate tax, it can be argued that the gift tax should be confined to the transfers which are treated by the estate tax as complete transfers, which are not subject to the estate tax. Without entering into the merits of the argument at this point, it should be noted that the correlation of the gift tax with the estate tax has a dual aspect. The two taxes might be correlated to the extent of holding that they are *all inclusive,* that is, of holding that a transfer which is treated as complete and free from tax under the estate tax must be treated as complete, and consequently taxable, under the gift tax, since one of the purposes of the gift tax was to reach any transfers which escaped the estate tax. Correlation between the two taxes seems to go this far. However, generally speaking, it is not pressed beyond this point to hold that the two taxes are *mutually exclusive* and that a transfer which is treated as incomplete and taxable under the estate tax will necessarily be treated as incomplete and free from tax under the gift tax.

* * *

It is perhaps worth noting that perfect correlation of the gift tax with both the income and estate taxes is impossible, because in some situations the estate and income taxes have different definitions of what constitutes a complete transfer. For example, under the estate tax a trust which can be revoked by the settlor with the concurrence of a person possessing a substantial adverse interest in the trust is treated as an incomplete transfer which is subject to the estate tax. Under the income tax, however, the creation of such a trust is treated as a complete transfer which relieves the transferor from any liability for a tax upon the income from the trust. It is obvious that in the case of this type of trust the gift tax cannot follow both the estate and the income tax conceptions of a complete transfer because they proceed in different directions. * * *

Although the 1976 statute adopted a unified rate schedule for gift and estate taxes, it did not eliminate the overlap between the taxes, e.g. where the gift, although complete for gift tax purposes, is subject to a string which results in taxation under §§ 2036, 2037 or 2038. Under prior law, where a transfer was subject to both gift and estate taxes, the estate was entitled to a credit for the gift tax paid. Although the system of credits generally achieved the objective of avoiding payment of a larger tax than would have been paid if no lifetime transfer had been made, the system was not entirely foolproof and there were circumstances in which the entire credit was not realized.

The 1976 statute abolished the credit and provided that the gift tax paid shall be offset against estate tax liability. To illustrate, let us assume that A, an unmarried widow, has made taxable gifts during her lifetime in the amount of $250,000, $100,000 of which was the value of a trust under which A retained power to designate how the income was to be spread among her children and grandchildren. As discussed earlier, retention of this power will result in inclusion of the trust corpus in her estate, under § 2036. Let us further assume that her taxable estate equals $1 million of which $250,000 is the appreciated estate tax value of the $100,000 trust previously established. Under § 2001 (infra p. 958) the tentative tax on her estate would be computed on the basis of her $1 million taxable estate plus her lifetime gifts, but *excluding* the $100,000 initial value of the trust.   The tentative tax would then be reduced by the amount of all gift tax including any tax paid on account of the trust.

The advantages of lifetime gifts.   Any comparison of the expense to an individual of inter vivos gifts and testamentary gifts must take into account the fact that gift taxes are payable at the time of giving whereas estate taxes are not due until after death.   Thus, the taxpayer loses the benefit of any income he might have received on the amount of the tax between the date of the gift and the date of death.   Additional complications in the arithmetic are caused by the possibilities of fluctuation in value, and of inflation or deflation.   Also important is the fact that, in the case of appreciated property, the income tax basis of the property in the hands of the recipient will be stepped up to its fair market value if the transfer is testamentary, while the donor's low basis will be taken by the donee if the transfer is inter vivos.   See, on this subject, Lowndes, Tax Planning for Estates, 27 N.C.L.Rev. 2 (1948).

Putting such factors aside, however, there are obvious tax savings to be had by inter vivos gifts which do not incur either the estate or gift tax, as will be the case as to gifts which qualify for the annual exclusion. In addition, before unification, there were several other advantages to lifetime gifts:

"Under present law, there is a substantial disparity of treatment between the taxation of transfers during life and transfers at death.   In general, there are three factors which provide a decided preference for lifetime transfers.   First, the gift tax rates are set at three-fourths of the estate tax rates at each corresponding rate bracket.   Second, lifetime transfers are not taken into account for estate tax purposes and the estate remaining at death is subject to tax under a separate rate schedule starting at the lowest rates.   Thus, even if the rates were identical, separate rate schedules would provide a preference for making both lifetime and deathtime transfers rather than having the total transfer subject to one tax.   Third, the gift taxes paid are not generally taken into account for either transfer tax base.   In the case of a gift, the tax base does not include the gift tax but the payment of the tax results in a decrease in the value of the estate retained by the donor.   However, if the property were retained until death, the tax base includes the full value of the property, even though a portion is likely to be required to satisfy estate taxes.   Thus, even if the applicable transfer tax rates were the same, the net amount transferred to a beneficiary from a given pre-tax amount of property would be greater for a lifetime transfer solely because of the difference in the tax bases."   (H.R.Rep. 94–1380 at 11)

A major objective of unification was to take away the advantages of lifetime gifts over transfers at death:

"As a matter of equity, your committee believes the tax burden imposed on transfers of the same amount of wealth should be substantially the same whether the transfers are made both during life and at death or made only upon death.   As a practical matter, the preferences for lifetime transfers are available only for wealthier individuals who are able to afford lifetime transfers.* The preferences for lifetime transfers are not generally available for those of small and moderate wealth since they generally want to retain their property until death to assure financial security during lifetime. Therefore, your committee believes that the preferences for lifetime transfers principally benefit the wealthy and result in eroding the transfer tax base." (H.R.Rep. 94–1380 at 11–12)

The 1976 statute did not go all the way, however, except in the case of gifts made within three years of death, and, in 1981, Congress all but abolished § 2035 for estates of decedents dying after 1981. (See p. 899, supra). However, it did retain the "gross up" provision of the 1976 statute under which any gift tax paid on transfers within three years of death is included in the gross estate for purposes of computing the estate tax. Despite its avowed intention to eliminate the advantages of lifetime gifts, Congress has not applied the gross-up principle to transfers includible in the estate under §§ 2036, 2037, 2038, and, of course it has not only preserved but materially enlarged the annual exclusion which permits tax free transfers of amounts which can be substantial if the practice of annual giving is begun early.

Notes

1. At least one observer has expressed serious doubts that the kind of reform effectuated by the 1976 statute is responsive to the real problems and, indeed, has suggested that it may simply drive taxpayers to resort to more sophisticated estate planning. Cooper, A Voluntary Tax? New Perspectives on Sophisticated Estate Tax Avoidance, 77 Colum.L.Rev. 161 (1977). Professor Cooper describes in detail the operation of a number of techniques available to the estate planner which are not touched by the 1976 law. The techniques discussed in the report include the diversion of future growth to subsequent generations (while retaining control) through the use of preferred stock, installment sales, family corporations, and the creation of "tax exempt wealth" such as insurance, annuities and survivorship benefit plans.

2. It is important that the arithmetic of estate planning not blind lawyers and clients to the real needs of the situation. Ordinarily, in order for a gift to be successful as an estate planning device, the property must not be subject to recall. This means that the tax advantages of lifetime gifts can usually be achieved only at the risk that changing circumstances will bring about a need for additional assets. So, too, the desire to qualify interests to children as "present interests" for gift tax purposes may result in making property available outright which would be better placed in trust.

3. Proposals for radical reform are not lacking, including the enactment of a "wealth tax" modeled on a form of tax used in many European countries. See Cooper, Taking Wealth Taxation Seriously, 34 Rec.A.B.City N.Y. 24 (1979).

---

    * Despite the marked tax benefits of making lifetime gifts, the available data indicate that (except perhaps for gifts subject to the annual exclusion, as to which data are unavailable), apparently very few people—even the wealthy—took advantage of the opportunity. See the discussion of several Treasury Department studies in Shoup, Federal Estate and Gift Taxation, 17–25 (1965). Ed.

For a general discussion of reform proposals see the Introduction to Bittker & Clark, Federal Estate and Gift Taxation (1984). As the authors point out, a major deterrent to change in the near future is the unpopularity with the American people of taxes on bequests.

Computation of the Estate Tax

I.R.C. Section 2001 provides: (subsection (c) is set forth at p. 893, supra):

(a) Imposition.—A tax is hereby imposed on the transfer of the taxable estate of every decedent who is a citizen or resident of the United States.

(b) Computation of Tax.—The tax imposed by this section shall be the amount equal to the excess (if any) of—

(1) a tentative tax computed in accordance with the rate schedule set forth in subsection (c) on the sum of—

(A) the amount of the taxable estate, and

(B) the amount of the adjusted taxable gifts, over

(2) the aggregate amount of tax payable under chapter 12 with respect to gifts made by the decedent after December 31, 1976, if the rate schedule set forth in subsection (c) (as in effect at the decedent's death) had been applicable at the time of such gifts.

For purposes of paragraph (1)(B), the term "adjusted taxable gifts" means the total amount of the taxable gifts (within the meaning of section 2503) made by the decedent after December 31, 1976, other than gifts which are includible in the gross estate of the decedent.

* * *

(d) Adjustment for Gift Tax Paid by Spouse.—For purposes of subsection (b)(2), if—

(1) the decedent was the donor of any gift one-half of which was considered under section 2513 as made by the decedent's spouse, and

(2) the amount of such gift is includible in the gross estate of the decedent, any tax payable by the spouse under chapter 12 on such gift (as determined under section 2012(d)) shall be treated as a tax payable with respect to a gift made by the decedent.

(e) Coordination of Sections 2513 and 2035.—If—

(1) the decedent's spouse was the donor of any gift one-half of which was considered under section 2513 as made by the decedent, and

(2) the amount of such gift is includible in the gross estate of the decedent's spouse by reason of section 2035.

such gift shall not be included in the adjusted taxable gifts of the decedent for purposes of subsection (b)(1)(B), and the aggregate amount determined under subsection (b)(2) shall be reduced by the amount (if any) determined under subsection (d) which was treated as a tax payable by the decedent's spouse with respect to such gift.

Essentially what § 2001 requires is the calculation of a tentative tax on the aggregate of all property passing at death plus all taxable transfers during life except transfers brought back into the estate, e.g., under

§§ 2036–2038.   This somewhat cumbersome retracing of the past is necessary in order to avoid a double use of the unified credit—against gift taxes during life and estate taxes after death—and to ensure that tax is imposed at the proper rate.

SECTION FOUR.   GENERATION-SKIPPING TRANSFERS

As noted earlier, historically the simple transfer of possession from a life tenant to a remainderman has not been regarded as a taxable event. As a result it has been possible to escape one or more generations of estate tax by giving a life interest to one generation, e.g., one's children, and a remainder to the next, e.g., one's grandchildren.   The only limit on the extent of generation-skipping has been the Rule against Perpetuities, and within the Rule a careful draftsman could ordinarily immunize property from tax for at least 80 to 100 years.   Moreover, the immunity existed even though the life tenant was given not only the income but substantial beneficial control over the principal.   (See p. 929 supra).   Although the number of people who have taken advantage of the opportunity is thought to be small, a tax on generation-skipping transfers has long been an important goal of those who would "reform" the estate tax.   That goal was achieved in the Tax Reform Act of 1976 which added a new chapter, Chapter 13, to the Estate and Gift tax provisions.   As with most recent tax legislation the new provisions are deplorably complex.   It is undoubtedly true that the problem is far from simple, (see, e.g., Kurtz and Surrey, Reform of Death and Gift Taxes: The 1969 Treasury Proposals, the Criticisms and a Rebuttal, 70 Colum.L.Rev. 1365, 1386–89 (1970)) but it is hard to believe that the solution requires language as turgid, prolix, and opaque as that used.

The general objective of the new provisions has been stated as follows: (H.R.Rep. 94–1380 at 47–48):

> The tax is to be substantially equivalent to the estate tax which would have been imposed if the property had been actually transferred outright to each successive generation.   For example, where a trust is created for the benefit of the grantor's grandchild, with remainder to the great-grandchild, then, upon the death of the grandchild, the tax is to be computed by adding the grandchild's portion of the trust assets to the grandchild's estate, and computing the tax at the grandchild's marginal transfer tax rate.   In other words, for purposes of determining the amount of the tax, the grandchild would be treated under the bill as a "deemed transferor" of the trust property.

> The grandchild's marginal estate tax rate would be used as a measuring rod for purposes of determining the tax imposed on the generation-skipping transfer, but the grandchild's estate would not be liable for the payment of the tax.   Instead, the tax would generally be paid out of the proceeds of the trust property.   However, the trust would be entitled to any unused portion of the grandchild's unified transfer tax credit, the credit for tax on prior transfers, the charitable deduction (if part of the trust property were left to charity), the credit for State inheritance taxes and a deduction for certain administrative expenses.

Transactions of the kind which will be affected by the generation-skipping provisions will ordinarily be beyond the scope of this brief treatment of estate and gift taxes. Nevertheless it seems appropriate to describe the major features of the tax and its current, somewhat shaky, status.

To begin with, it should be noted that the tax does not come into play in the case of every life estate (or equivalent device), but only where the life estate is given to a member or members of a generation later than the grantor's and the remainder is given to a still later generation. Thus if the grantor creates a life estate for his wife or sister or brother with remainder to his children or grandchildren or his nieces or grandnieces, there will be no generation-skipping tax at the end of the life estate. So too, if the life estate is given to one child of the grantor with remainder to his other children, the new provisions do not come into play. The provisions do apply if a life estate is given to a son, with remainder to grandchildren, or a later generation. On the other hand, there must be a division of interests between the generations. A trust for the benefit of great grandchildren where neither children nor grandchildren had an interest would not be a generation-skipping transfer.

The statute contains a special provision governing gifts to grandchildren. Essentially, this provision excludes transfers to grandchildren from the generation-skipping tax up to $250,000 per *child* (note, not per *grandchild*). Thus, if A had two children B and C to whom he gave life estates, with remainder to his grandchildren, up to $500,000 would escape the generation-skipping tax. (The House Bill would have permitted $1,000,000 per child to escape tax.)

When applied to lineal descendants the provisions are reasonably straightforward (at this point the proper rejoinder is probably, "Compared to what?"). But when the transfer is for the benefit of persons outside the family, the question "What is a generation?" can become troublesome. Another source of complexity is that although the tax is payable out of the corpus of the trust or other property transferred, the rate of tax depends on the size of the estate of the member of the intermediate generation (typically the life tenant) who is the "deemed transferor," i.e., the generation-skipping transfer is taxed at the marginal rate of the deemed transferor.

Like the carryover basis provisions of the 1976 statute, (see p. 889, supra), the generation-skipping transfer tax has been the subject of intense criticism since its enactment. Unlike carryover basis, however, it has survived and seems likely to be a permanent part of the estate tax, albeit not in its original form. Even those who defend the tax in principle, concede that it should be simplified. The direction of future changes may be indicated by a Treasury Department proposal submitted to Congress on April 29, 1983. The proposal would make three fundamental changes in the tax: (1) It would provide an exclusion of $1,000,000 per grantor ($2,000,000 per married couple) and thereby substantially reduce the incidence of the tax. (2) The rate of tax would be a flat rate equal to 80% of the highest estate tax rate in effect at the time of the transfer, thereby greatly simplifying the computation of the tax and getting rid of the concept of deemed transferor. (3) It would tax all generation-skipping transfers not covered by the $1,000,000 exemption, and not only transfers involving an intermediate generation. Thus an outright transfer to grandchildren would be taxable as a generation-skipping transfer.

Note on Income Taxation of Trusts and Estates

A trust is a separate tax entity for income tax purposes. So is an estate. With some exceptions, the rules governing the computation of taxable income are the same for trusts and estates as for individuals, so that the significant problems of income taxation are those concerned with the location of the incidence of the tax as between the grantor, the beneficiaries, the fiduciary, and, occasionally, some other person.

The provisions governing the location of tax are extremely complex and not susceptible of cursory treatment. There are, however, a few general concepts of which the student should be aware.

BITTKER, STONE, & KLEIN, FEDERAL INCOME TAXATION
738–40 (6th ed.1984).

In the ordinary case, where the trust is irrevocable and the grantor reserves little or no control over it, the trust income will be taxed either to the trust or to the beneficiaries. Trusts of this character, ordinary trusts, are governed by §§ 641 through 668 of the Code. However, a grantor who retains power over the economic benefits of the trust property may be taxed as the "substantial owner" thereof. These trusts, sometimes called grantor trusts, are governed by §§ 671 through 677 of the Code. Finally, a third person who has the right to get the income or corpus of the trust upon demand may be taxed as the substantial owner of the income under § 678.

The statutory provisions governing ordinary trusts are exceedingly complex. In an effort to make the statutory scheme less formidable, the Code distinguishes between *simple trusts* (those that are required to distribute all income currently, that have made no distributions of corpus, and that claim no charitable deduction in the taxable year) and *complex trusts* (all others). The statutory provisions applicable to simple trusts are found in Subpart B of Subchapter J, §§ 651–652; those applicable to complex trusts in Subparts C and D of Subchapter J, §§ 661–668.

Trusts are subject to taxation on their income. In computing its income, however, a simple trust deducts all the income that is required to be distributed currently (§ 651), and the beneficiary is taxed on that income (§§ 61(a)(15), 652(a)). The trust is sometimes described as a mere conduit. (A simple trust may be taxed on capital gain that is not treated as income for trust purposes and is retained by the trust.) With complex trusts, roughly speaking the objective still is to treat the trust as a conduit and impose the tax on the beneficiaries, so that the trust may not be used to gain an extra start at the bottom of the rate schedule. As with simple trusts, amounts of income distributed currently to beneficiaries by a complex trust are deducted by the trust and taxed to the beneficiary. §§ 661(a), 662(a). In some instances, however, income may be withheld for future distribution. That income is not available to the beneficiary. In fact, the identity of the person to whom the income will ultimately be distributed may be unknown—for example, where the trustee has the power to distribute accumulated income among a class of beneficiaries according to their needs. The Code provides that where a complex trust accumulates income, it is taxable on that income. Later, however, when the accumulated income is distributed it is subject to the "throwback" rules. §§ 665–668. [See note 1, infra. Ed.]

The conduit principle is applied in other ways. See, e.g., §§ 652(b) and 662(b), which provide that distributed income shall have the same character in the hands of the beneficiary as in the hands of the trust. Thus, tax-exempt interest and capital gains preserve their special character when distributed to the beneficiary. If there is more than one beneficiary, each receives an appropriate share of these items, unless they are allocated differently by local law or the trust instrument. See Regs. § 1.652(b)–1 and 2; similar but more intricate rules are applicable under § 662(b).

Note

1. Because prior to 1954, as a general rule, income taxed to the trust was not taxed again on distribution to the beneficiary, it was possible within limits for the trustee to accumulate income, pay tax in the trust, and pay out the income to the beneficiary tax-free in a subsequent year. Assuming that the trust tax bracket was below that of the beneficiary, the opportunities for tax avoidance are obvious. Moreover, by the use of separate trusts the benefits to a beneficiary could be multiplied. A partial response to the situation came in 1954 with the adoption of the so-called "throwback" rules which provided, with exceptions of major planning importance, for taxing to the beneficiary trust income distributed within five years of the accumulation. In 1969 Congress provided, prospectively, for unlimited "throwback," i.e., for taxation to the beneficiary of income distributions whenever made. The 1969 amendments would seem to have largely closed the loophole made possible by adroit timing of trust distributions and, although they were not directly dealt with, largely made academic the problem of multiple trusts for the same beneficiary. See Bittker Stone & Klein, supra, at 743; A. Michaelson, Income Taxation of Estates and Trusts (Rev.Ed.1974) 24–35, 67–68. Although Congress, in the Tax Reform Act of 1976, excepted from the throwback provisions income accumulated for a beneficiary "before the birth of such beneficiary or before such beneficiary attains the age of 21," (I.R.C. § 665(b)) the exception does not apply to distributions from more than two trusts; moreover, at that time, Congress added a new provision (§ 667(c)) which further discourages the use of multiple trusts.

2. An estate—which is not ordinarily required to distribute income currently—is treated as a complex trust subject to I.R.C. §§ 661–663. However, estates are not subject to the throwback rules and therefore, can be used to avoid taxes by accumulating income, having the estate pay tax on the income,

and distributing it to the beneficiaries.   To limit the use of the estate for tax avoidance the Regulations (§ 1.641(b)–3(a)) provide that an estate's existence for federal tax purposes terminates after a reasonable time.   See Bittker, Federal Taxation of Income, Estates and Gifts (1981) ¶ 81.8.

*

Index

References are to Pages

†